CASES AND MATERIALS
IN THE LAW MERCHANT

LONDON : HUMPHREY MILFORD
OXFORD UNIVERSITY PRESS

CASES AND MATERIALS
IN THE
LAW MERCHANT

BY

PHILIP WARREN THAYER

Research Associate in Comparative Law, Harvard University; Professor of International Commercial Law, Fletcher School of Law and Diplomacy

WITH AN INTRODUCTION BY

THE RIGHT HON. ROBERT ALDERSON, BARON WRIGHT

Lord of Appeal in Ordinary, Chairman of the Royal Commission on Historical Documents, and Chairman of the Law Revision Committee

CAMBRIDGE
HARVARD UNIVERSITY PRESS
1939

PRINTED AT THE HARVARD UNIVERSITY PRESS
CAMBRIDGE, MASSACHUSETTS, U.S.A.

FOREWORD

IT IS ASSUMED that the material assembled in this book will be used by students who already have some background in the law of contracts; a background in which they will have had occasion to survey the development of contractual theory as manifested in the attitude of the law toward consensual human relationships, in which they will have had opportunity to explore the effects of this attitude on immediate parties and on third persons, and in which they cannot fail to have noted on the horizon a glimmering of the idea of negotiability. In short, students are expected to have some familiarity in this regard with the impact of the law on individual conduct.

The contents of the present volume are concerned more with the impact of individual conduct on the law, for the history of the particular relationships commonly associated with the law merchant has been in effect a history of the influence on the law of the usages of trade. Merchants from time immemorial have builded of these usages their own law, a compounding of existing law and custom with sometimes curious results. The purpose of the material here presented however is to sweep no dusty trail to the remote past, but to depict a living process: to point in one direction to the technique of merchants in their dealings with one another, and in the other to the way in which the usages born of these associations, crystallizing into custom, become transmuted into law.

The term "law merchant" always has carried with it a notion of universality. Legal backgrounds may change with the differing needs and phenomena of purely national developments; so that codes and statutes and the precedents of decided cases form a constantly increasing and not always consistent body of law into which new ideas must be fitted in order to obtain the sanction of jurisprudence. Despite such obstacles, at once confusing and impeding, the usages of merchants have had a way of seeking simultaneous and common expression. There is about them an international character that cannot be denied: such typical devices of merchants as bills of exchange and of lading, c.i.f. contracts, irrevocable letters of credit, and marine insurance certificates, possess far more than merely local significance. To deal with topics of the kind entirely in national terms is thus to take the risk of dealing with them inadequately. Although stressing American and English treatment of the matters here considered, the possible value of comparative survey accordingly has not been ignored. Opportunity has been afforded for reference to pertinent provisions of French and German law, either through translations from the Codes or by citation of appropriate texts. Translations of foreign cases also have been included in a few instances where they might be not only of practical interest but helpful in contributing to a more appreciative understanding of the points under discussion.

In covering the field of study with any pretence to thoroughness and yet within the reasonable compass of a single volume, complete reproduction of the cases chosen would be impossible. Arguments and names of counsel, multiple case citations, and matter either repetitious or irrelevant, have been omitted as a matter of course. In order to aid in the development and discussion of situations incidental to the principal cases, many additional cases have been introduced in abstracted form, taking the place of footnotes ordinarily used to cite such cases and at the same time providing a convenient way of posing concrete problems for consideration. In the arrangement of cases an attempt has been made to marshal topics with an eye to mercantile sequence, and in general to emphasize commercial procedure, for the study of the law merchant is concerned in the long run more with what business does to the law than with what the law does to business. A topical bibliography follows the table of contents. Statutory and Code material, together with forms of instruments in common use, are contained in an appendix.

For the actual cases selected the compiler must take full responsibility. The problem has been one of omission rather than of inclusion. Many cases have become so closely associated with particular developments of the law merchant that to mention the one is to evoke the other. Still others have value for the present by pointing from the past. On the other hand, the law merchant is a living institution. The usages of yesterday are not necessarily the usages of to-day, and even less can they be employed always to forecast those of to-morrow. Codification in this country and in England of large segments of the law merchant also has had its effects; prominent among them has been a marked tendency in recent years on the part of courts in both countries to deprecate the citation of cases prior to the codes. As a result of these considerations, although many old friends will be noted, most of the cases chosen are from the present century and the majority have arisen since the war.

For whatever of value may abide in the result thanks are due to Professor George K. Gardner, of the Harvard Law School, without whose friendly aid and counsel the book could not have been; to Phillippa Patey, who undertook the preparation of the manuscript; to the Harvard University Press, for patience and understanding, as well as for skill in production; to Alfred H. Lovell, Jr., for material assistance in completing bibliography and index and in other particulars; and to many others who have been kind.

PHILIP W. THAYER

Cambridge, Massachusetts
September 1, 1939

CONTENTS

PART THREE

THE FINANCING OF THE CONTRACT: THE AUXILIARY INSTRUMENTS OF THE LAW MERCHANT

PART FOUR

THE EXECUTION OF THE CONTRACT: TRANSFER OF TITLE

PART FIVE

THE FAILURE OF THE CONTRACT: RIGHTS AND REMEDIES OF THE PARTIES

APPENDIX

INTRODUCTION

Sir Frederick Pollock in his *Essays on the Law* (at p. 55) has described the Law Merchant as a species of the Law of Nature, or Natural Law, and as having a Cosmopolitan character. The Law Merchant, he said, was always understood to be founded on general reason and convenience evidenced by the usages of merchants. He quoted Sir John Davis as saying in 1656 that "the Law Merchant as it is a part of the Law of Nations and Nature, is universal and one and the same for all countries of the World." These two aspects though related are in truth different. The Law Merchant was always concerned largely with dealings between different nations, as contrasted with the local or internal matters which afforded its principal scope for the Common Law. The same is true even today. A vast mass of business transactions are in the way of international trade. The need of uniformity between the laws of different countries is realized at least as much today as in earlier times in the sphere of mercantile law. Such uniformity prevails to a great extent, as will be seen indicated by the references to foreign law decisions contained in this work. International Conferences are held in order to unify certain branches of Commercial Law and some progress has been made to this desirable end. But even unified codes do not completely effect uniform law. Even if the language of the codes is identical, each Court will have its own methods of interpretation and these may lead in many cases to difference in practical results, more usually, however, in detail than in substance. Thus an important matter in Commercial Law questions is often to determine what is the proper law of the contract, that is, by the law of what country the transaction should be held to be governed. But all the same, international unformity, so far as it goes, is an important aspect of Commercial Law, and the student will be helped in mastering the law of his own country by looking into the corresponding rules adopted in another country.

The other aspect referred to by Sir Frederick Pollock was that the Law Merchant was a species of natural law. This may appear to be a hard saying when regard is had to the distinctions and complications and refinements which have grown up in the decisions of the Courts on Commercial Law. They seem to be remote from the law of Nature. Many indeed seem arbitrary and artificial. But what I think was meant was that Commercial Law in its early stages was not a product imposed by an outside authority, either Parliament or Judge. It naturally grew up among the merchants in their attempts to find rules which would regulate their dealings and help to settle their disputes. It was evolved empirically in order to meet the practical exigencies which emerged in the actual day-today conduct of business. It was in this sense extra-legal. Its rules were originally ascertained and administered by the merchants among themselves, in many cases at the Courts held actually at the mediaeval fairs at which so much of the international commerce was carried on. Thus it was more correctly called usage. It was not strictly law, until the usages were recognized and enforced by the Courts and thus acquired the character and name of Law. This reception of the Law Merchant by the King's Courts in England was comparatively late, dating from a time not much earlier than Holt. Under Mansfield a system of Commercial Law may be said to have grown up in the English Law. Its evolution went on all through the nineteenth century and, as the cases in the volume show, is still proceeding today. There may still be a new usage of merchants, which the Courts may recognize, thereby giving it the force of law. New conditions may still give rise to new usages in the Law Merchant. Thus mercantile usage may add a new instrument to the category of negotiable instruments, and the Courts may give the new usage the effect of law. In the main it is perhaps true to say that the modern development of the Law Merchant (a term which I now use interchangeably with the term Commercial Law) is to be found in the decisions of the Courts; but it is still necessary for the Courts to keep in close touch with the methods, purposes, and ideas of merchants. The origin and early development of commercial law were the spontaneous product growing naturally (as it were) out of the experiences and needs of merchants. Hence even today it has a character of its own, in many respects different in substance and in detail from the ordinary Common Law. Its method of approach to its problems is different both historically and in modern practice from that of the Common Law. Compare for instance the evolution of the land law or the law of family succession and relations from that of the Commercial Law. Not only is the content of the law different, but so is the method of approach. The lawyer must seek to approach Commercial Law, so far as he can, with the eyes of a business man and ask what is the viewpoint of the business man in the matter in hand and how does the business man seek to give effect to it. Lord Mansfield, the real founder of British Commercial Law as we know it, one of the greatest of the English Judges, used to try the Commercial Cases with a jury of merchants of the City of London, hear evidence as to the business usage, obtain the opinion of his jurors and then declare the law on the point in an exact and logical form so as to harmonize with legal rules. The modern lawyer, who has to deal with a question of commercial law, has not the advantage of the help of an expert jury, though he has the advantage of the reported decisions on or near the point. He still has to get himself into the business frame of mind. A family lawyer or a real property lawyer, faced with a commercial question, may study the cases and books, but he may find it difficult to live up to that common-sense practicality which is the vivifying spirit of commercial law. Hence it is generally thought that judges who try commercial causes should have practised at the Bar in that branch of law and thus acquired familiarity with business methods by associating in their practice with commercial clients. I do not indeed say that this is essential to the judge, but it is certainly desirable. Commercial questions need to be dealt with as far as possible on untechnical lines, and with greater regard to substance than to form. That, however, is not the whole truth. For instance, a large part, perhaps the much largest part, of Commercial Law is concerned with Contracts. The Common Law, in receiving into itself the Law Merchant, in many respects moulded it to fit its own ideas of contract. Thus the rules of Consideration are applied in Commercial Contracts, with some modifications, as for example, in regard to negotiable instruments. Again the Statute of Frauds has to be complied with in the cases in which it is relevant. On the other hand, the Common Law had to jettison some of its favorite doctrines, such as that the benefit of a contract could not be assigned so as to give the assignee a legal cause of action in his own name, or that no one could give a better title to goods (with unimportant exceptions) than he possessed. These sacrifices of principle were necessary if negotiable instruments were to be brought into the Common Law. Again the necessity in Commercial Law to recognize that seaborne goods could be transferred by the transfer of the bill of lading led to the special exception in such cases from the general rule that a transfer of goods in the possession of a bailee could not be effected unless the bailee attorned to the transferee. Again the old Common Law rule of *caveat emptor* has become so attenuated by exceptions implied by the Court on grounds of commercial equity that it has been said that it should now run *caveat venditor*. It is easy to multiply similar illustrations.

Although mainly and primarily occupied with commercial contracts, Commercial Law nevertheless has inevitably to handle general legal principles, such as certain rules which prohibit trading with the enemy, or other rules of the law of illegality, or the general principles of mistake or fraud, especially in their impact on commercial contracts. On the other hand questions of family law, libel, real property, personal injuries, tort in general, would naturally be regarded as lying outside the special limits of Commercial Law. Even in the realm of contract law, commercial contracts can be, more or less precisely, treated as forming a class by themselves. A promise to marry is a contract, but one would not classify it as a commercial contract, even if the promisor was a commercial traveller. Quite apart from subject matter, however, there is one important characteristic of common occurrence in a great mass of commercial contracts. That is, that the Courts have very often to write into commercial contracts stipulations which business men do not express. Business men in very many cases and types of cases do not write out their contracts in full, but take a great deal for granted, sometimes because it seems to them that the unexpressed term is so obvious as not to need to be expressed, in other cases because they rely on the settled law to fill in the defects, and perhaps for other reasons. Whatever the reason, it is clear that this habit affords scope for disputes beyond the ordinary questions of construction which may arise in any contract. Let me take as an illustration that most important contract, the contract contained in a bill of exchange. Nothing could be simpler in appearance than a bill of exchange; but as we all know that simplicity is delusive. The incidents and effects of the contract have required a mass of rules, evolved in the practice of merchants and by the decisions of the Courts, and now embodied in various Statutes. Again, the plain man reading a policy of marine insurance would have no idea of all that it imported. I do not mean merely that he would have to consult authorities on questions of disputed construction of the words, but many matters, such as the rules relating to deviation, unseaworthiness, general average, and many other things will not generally be expressed. Similarly in the case of a bill of lading, though the incorporation of the Hague Rules by way of contract or sometimes by positive law where the Sea Carriage of Goods Act is in operation, goes far to render the contract complete at least by reference. Again take a contract of sale c.i.f. These mystic initials without more conjure up to the business man a mass of complex rules as to passing of property and risk, transfer of documents, appropriate character of documents, implied warranties, and so forth. But it must not be forgotten that we are still in the realm of agreement. Hence with certain exceptions the rules of the law merchant as to the incidents and effects of the contract are not rules of obligatory law but are liable to be modified or excluded by the express terms of the particular contract. The governing object is still to give effect to the intention of the parties, either actual or presumed if it appears from the words or circumstances that they had any relevant intention. In general, then, the rules as to the effect of commercial contracts are not imperative or exclusive. There are, however, certain exceptions, as I have pointed out. Thus from the very nature of the thing, a bill of exchange cannot be a negotiable instrument unless it fulfills certain conditions, e.g., that it is an unconditional order, in writing, for money, payable at a time certain, to a certain person, or to bearer, and addressed to a named payer. It is clear that unless these conditions are fulfilled, the quality of negotiability will not work, and hence they are imperative. Then there are certain rules which public policy imposes, such as the law against gaming and wagering contracts, or the Stamp Acts in so far as they render unstamped documents void. And as I have already observed, the rules of consideration and of the Statute of Frauds must be complied with. But with exceptions of this nature parties, so far as they do not infringe the law, may make their own contracts, and the business of the Court is to adapt the contract otherwise implied under the Law Merchant to the express words of the parties. This has led to a great mass of litigation. It may perhaps be said with truth that the exposition of the general rules applicable to the special types of contract has involved fewer decisions than the determination of the effect in particular transactions of the special contractual provisions which express a departure from, or variation of, the general rules. There is also another large class of authorities, the object of which has been to solve the problems which have arisen in particular cases, consequent on the failure of the parties to provide for the contingencies which have actually arisen under the contract. This leads to a dispute as to what are the rights and liabilities when the event for which there is no provision occurs. The process which the court employs then is generally described as "implying a term" because it is said that the Court cannot make a contract, or a term in a contract, for the parties. This process is not peculiar to commercial contracts, but it is, I imagine, more frequently invoked in Commercial contracts than in any other class of contracts. As the term is "implied" because the parties have not provided for the event, since they did not anticipate it, the implication must be a fiction. The process has been described as due to the desire of the Court to reconcile the demands of justice with the absolute terms of the contract. This it does by determining what is the just way of dealing with the matter, assuming that the parties would have so dealt with it if they had thought of it, and giving effect to the contract in this way. This course is obviously only possible if there is nothing in the contract to tie the hands of the Court which cannot imply a term which contradicts the contract as expressed. As I have said, this very valuable remedial jurisdiction is especially important in commercial contracts, and is particularly illustrated by the many contracts which deal with the frustration of contracts by supervening impossibility. This in commerce does not mean final or irretrievable or absolute impossibility, but impossibility for such period or in such conditions as would be inconsistent with the commercial adventure, just as in marine insurance a ship is treated as totally lost if it is a "constructive" or "commercial" total loss, that is (*inter alia*) if the cost of recovering it or repairing it would exceed its value when repaired, or, in the case of an insurance on goods to a destination, if the insured peril makes its impossible for the goods to arrive within any time consistent with the adventure. These are cases of loss in a business sense and are illustrations of the way in which the Law Merchant, or the Courts developing the Law Merchant, have dealt with particular situations. In regard to the sale of goods, corresponding instances are afforded by such cases as those in which, unknown to the parties, specific goods have perished, at the time of the contract, or afterwards perish without fault on the seller's part before the time for the passing of the risk. A further illustration is afforded by the case of unascertained goods which are to be shipped by a particular date, if such shipment is prevented by unavoidable circumstances which the parties did not anticipate and did not provide for. The rules also as to the measure of damages are generally in commercial contracts left to be supplied by law. Hence, for example the general rule that in the absence of terms express or implied to another effect, the measure of damages for non-delivery of goods for which there is a market is the difference between the market price and the contract price at the time of breach. The buyer is assumed to be able to go into the market and supply himself with goods in substitution for those which the seller should have delivered. For convenience, no regard in general in such cases is paid to special circumstances peculiar to the particular buyer. Again the Courts have held that even without the special notice required by the rule generally described as that in *Hadley v. Baxendale*, a buyer may claim special damages based on the knowledge which the parties are assumed in the ordinary course to possess of the consequences which would result to the buyer in the normal course from the breach. In all these and many other such cases the rules have been evolved by the Courts in their work of carrying on the development of the Law Merchant and creating as law what the Merchants might or would have established by their usages, in order to give effect to the commercial equities of the situation.

There are many separate branches of Commercial Law, such as Sale of Goods, Insurance, Marine, Life, Accident, Third-party liability and others, Banking, Carriage of Goods by Land and by Sea, Principal and Surety and Agency. The cases collected in this book center round the Sale of Goods, and the matters ancillary to it so far as directly relevant. Thus shipping and insurance documents have to be considered and to a certain extent shipping and insurance law. But a complete examination of the detailed provisions of these branches of law is not directly material. It is enough for the purpose of this work to ascertain what are the documents which are required to implement the contract of sale, with some reference to usual clauses which may affect a buyer. Bills of Exchange call no doubt for somewhat fuller treatment. But the contract of sale itself, its form, its clauses, the financing of it, its performance and the various questions which arise if it is broken, require and receive more detailed illustration from the decisions which are collected. It would not be profitable here to attempt a specific examination of these decisions, a great many of which deal not so much with the general principles of the law, but with their modification and adaptation to suit particular circumstances or particular variations from the standard or normal contract. It is with such questions that the practitioner or judge has mostly to deal in actual disputes or opinions. Thus the cases are valuable as illustrating the principles not merely in the abstract or general enunciation but in their varied applications, and they will also help the lawyer in his actual practice because what has happened in the past or something very like it is likely to happen again. Thus the past throws light on the present and future. Each case therefore calls for detailed study.

It has seemed to me that I could best occupy the space at my disposal and also show the practical efficiency and also the simplicity with which the Law Merchant solves its problems, by one example, namely by stating the broad outlines of perhaps the most important commercial contract, that type of sale which is called a contract for the sale of goods c.i.f. C.I.F. means that the price includes the cost (or price) of the goods, the insurance on them and the freight for their carriage to the agreed destination. It is a contract which contemplates the sale of goods which are in one place but are to be delivered under the contract in another place. If seller and buyer are also in different places, the contract will generally be made by correspondence, by letter or cable, the offer speaking when it reaches the offeree, and the acceptance being complete when it is put into the contemplated medium of transmission, post or cable or so forth. This class of contract is used almost universally in international or interstate trade and in England, at least, is mostly thought of in connection with ocean transport. The goods are almost always what are called unascertained or future goods, such as bulk quantities of natural products, food or raw material, grown or to be grown, or minerals extracted or to be extracted, or consignments of goods manufactured or to be manufactured. It is obvious that such transactions raise very different problems from those of the simple sales of specific goods in the shop. Thus what may be called the law of the shopkeeper and his customer is of necessity largely different from the law of the exporter and importer. The goods in a c.i.f. contract, it is scarcely necessary to say, must be described. Bulk products may be described by some general description such as Manitoba winter wheat, coupled sometimes with reference to a certificate of some government or official grade. If the contract deals with manufactured goods of a general class, the patent or trade name or some ordinary description may suffice, but if with special goods, a detailed specification will be necessary. In any case the description is necessarily an essential part of the contract. If it is not complied with, the buyer has the right to reject the delivery if he duly exercises his right to do so. A part of the description commonly employed, at least in regard to bulk products, is the date of shipment, which again must be complied with strictly. Thus if a March shipment is stipulated, a shipment on the 1st April will be a bad tender, even if the difference in date makes no difference in market price or value. The reason is that the buyer is not in general buying for his own use, e.g., if it is wheat or beef, but is buying for resale (perhaps there may be a chain of buyers), and the Law Merchant has established the rule that in this, as generally in mercantile contracts, time is of the essence of the contract. The contract will generally state the price. If no price is stated either specifically or by reference the law does not treat the transaction as void, but implies an obligation of the buyer to pay a reasonable price.

I now turn to the more characteristic features of a c.i.f. contract. A mass of case law has gathered round these initials, but it is now possible to state the salient features in outline, briefly but I hope with sufficient accuracy, though I do not attempt even to indicate all the possible complications or refinements. The contract contemplates generally a sea transit at least in English usage but what I say applies *mutatis mutandis* to a land transit. The essential feature of a c.i.f. contract is that the seller must provide and ship goods which correspond to the contract description, in respect of quality, time &c. but he does not undertake that they will not be lost or damaged on the voyage. He satisfies that latter part of his obligation, which is embodied in the description of the agreed destination, by providing a freight contract for the voyage and an insurance on the goods to destination, and by transferring the appropriate documents to the buyer. Thus he appropriates the unascertained goods to the contract according to the usage of trade by shipping them in accordance with the terms of the contract or at least when he transfers the bill of lading. The assent of the buyer is presumed to the appropriation. He fulfills the remainder of his obligation by tendering the required documents in the usual and proper form. These are the insurance policy and the bill of lading. If all this is correctly done, the seller has fulfilled his obligation, even though the goods never arrive at their destination or come to the buyer.

By the transfer or the documents the buyer obtains the property in the goods and also the responsibility of the shipowner or carrier under the bill of lading and the responsibility of the insurer under the policy. In other words the risk of the transit is shifted off the shoulders of the seller. The usual course is for the seller to transmit the bill of lading and policy to the buyer, along with an invoice in which the freight is deducted, because as it is usually payable on arrival, it is convenient that it should be paid by the buyer when the ship delivers the goods. The transfer of the bill of lading is by the law merchant a transfer of the property in the goods, which takes place under a c.i.f. contract as under other contracts when the transfer is intended to take place, and it also by Statute constitutes a transfer of the contract contained in the bill of lading, just as the transfer of the policy in such a case transfers the rights under it. Thus in one sense the sale is completed by a transfer of documents. The buyer is vested with the property in the goods and all the rights of action which will indemnify him against misadventure until they reach him. It is accordingly sometimes said that a c.i.f. contract is not a sale of goods but a sale of documents. That, however, is inaccurate. It is a sale of goods all through, though it is generally completed by the transfer of the documents. This is clear from the right of the buyer to reject the goods on arrival if they do not conform to the contract description, even though the documents were in order and had been accepted by him in due course. There are other respects in which it is seen that the contract is for the sale of goods, not of documents; for instance, the seller may not have had a good title to the goods. He is bound to make a good shipment of the goods. There may also be other complications from circumstances of public policy or illegality for instance if war were to break out between the sellers nation and that of the buyer. But all the same, in ordinary course the contract is completed by the transfer of the documents. So far, however, I have neglected one important aspect, that of payment. The contract is dealing with goods which have to be carried over (say) an ocean voyage, and there will be a lapse of time between shipment by the seller and receipt by the buyer. Prima facie in this as in other contracts of sale payment and delivery are concurrent conditions. On this basis if the documents were transferred on shipment, payment would properly be against their delivery, or if they were transferred at a later period of the voyage, or on arrival, payment would be then. But either course would mean that one party or the other for a definite time is to be without either his money or his goods as the case may be. Hence come the questions connected with financing the shipment, which aim at bridging the gap between shipment and delivery by putting the seller in funds at an early stage without involving actual cash payment by the buyer, who is for the time financed by his bank. Another object is the division of the risk of credit just as the insurance policy relieves the merchants from the risk of sea perils in return for a premium. Banks and financial houses similarly relieve the merchant (exporter or importer) of the risks of credit. The legal machinery to deal with the problem is simple and is effective, save in comparatively rare and anomalous cases. The method adopted is that even if the goods are appropriated on shipment the property does not then pass provided that the seller reserves the *jus disponendi* to himself by taking the bill of lading in his own name or retaining it if to order. While that is the position no one else can deal with the property. If the contract is cash against Documents, the risk of finance is taken by the buyer. If it is cash against buyer's acceptance, the seller takes the risk of the buyer meeting his acceptance in due course. The risk of finance is thus taken by the seller, who has parted in such a case not only with the property in the goods but also their possession and the unpaid seller's lien, because the shipowner in that case holds for the buyer; the seller has no security save the limited right of stoppage in transitu which is only exercisable if the buyer is insolvent and is no more, at least in the first instance, than a right of retention. It is also liable to be defeated. The seller in fact bears the risk even if he gets cash by discounting the buyer's acceptance because he is liable on the bill. To meet these difficulties the services of the Banks are called in. It is their function to take risks of credit for a small premium. In this way the seller is promptly paid and the buyer has not to part with cash while the goods are on the voyage. Thus the dead period is bridged. The usual method of receiving this result is by the use of letters of credit. By the letter of credit the Bank or other financial house undertakes to honour the seller's draft for the price of the goods, though perhaps with some definitions and qualifications. This credit is in favour of the seller, but it is generally arranged and paid for by the buyer. These letters of credit, generally irrevocable or confirmed, present certain anomalies in principle and have raised certain problems in practice. These are well illustrated and explained in the Cases and cannot be discussed here.

I think the whole theory of the c.i.f. contract is one of the most elegant to be found in the Law. No doubt difficult questions have arisen from time to time in special cases, but these are due not to any defect in the general theory but to eccentric or accidental circumstances in particular cases, or variations from the standard form of documents which require the Court to make readjustments, and these are not always easy to make. These special difficulties do not impair the essential efficiency of the system.

The system depends for its operations on the assignability of the bill of lading and of the insurance policy, and almost universally on the negotiability of the bill of exchange. As to the latter, its function is to solve the double problem, that of paying money in a place other than the payer's residence, because the payer, that is the buyer, will often, perhaps generally, be at the place of destination, and not at the place of shipment, and that of providing an instrument of credit by the instrumentality of the acceptance. Both these aspects were understood by the Italian bankers in the middle ages, for instance by the Lombards who gave their name to the street in the City of London which is still called Lombard Street and is still at the heart of the financial and business operations of the City.

The bill of lading and the bill of exchange have the common feature that by their transfer not only is the piece of paper, the chattel, transferred, but normally also the benefit of the contract. Furthermore, in the case of bills of lading the property in the goods is also transferred. But there is a marked difference. Bills of Exchange are negotiable, that is, the right of the transferee depends on what he does or is, not on the rights of his transferor which do not affect the rights of a bona fide transferee for value. In the case of bills of lading, the old common-law rule applies that no one can give a better title than he possesses. Hence bills of exchange are negotiable, bills of lading only assignable, that is if these terms are used in their strict meaning. It may be that the distinction arose from the fact that bills of exchange were meant to approximate to currency, while bills of lading were a mode of transferring goods. But perhaps the obvious business exigencies required the same distinction.

There is a further distinction at least in the old law between the two types of documents. The transfer of the bill of exchange involved the transfer of the chose in action, the promise to pay. The transfer of the bill of lading constituted the transfer of the property in the goods which it represented. In each case the effect was outside the ordinary common-law rules, as I have indicated. But it is clear that the c.i.f. contract could not work on the lines which I have explained unless the bill of lading also transferred the rights of suit on the contract which it contained. The bill of lading, at least in modern times, is not only a document of title but is or may be a contract of carriage by sea. If the ship is a chartered ship, the bill of lading issued to the charterer is a receipt, but when it is transferred with the intention of transferring the property in the goods or is issued to a third party, it becomes a contract of carriage of the goods, perhaps quite different from the charterparty contract. By the law merchant, the transfer of the bill of lading was indeed effective to transfer the property in the goods, as I have pointed out above, but a legislative measure was necessary to make it also effective to transfer the contract of carriage, and thus prevent the whole theory of the c.i.f. contract from breaking down. I need not repeat that the bill of lading is only assignable, not negotiable, whereas the bill of exchange is negotiable and thus stands on a different footing. I do not intend to attempt here to summarize the rules which the Law Merchant evolved to give effect to the idea of negotiability. It is obviously necessary that these should be precise and as simple as possible. I shall leave the reader of the Cases to see how these rules have been devised to meet the different practical incidents and exigencies in business dealings of a bill of exchange.

I have so far not referred to the other main class of mercantile contract of sale used in connection with goods which are to be carried either by sea or by land. That is the f.o.b. contract, analogues of which in land transit are sometimes described by such initials as f.o.r. (free on rail) or f.o.t. (free on truck); whereas f.o.b. signifies "free on board." The contract price in such cases includes the cost (or price) of the goods and the cost of delivering them on board a ship; for the provision of the ship or space in it the buyer, not the seller, is responsible. The seller may reserve the *jus disponendi* in a manner similar to that in c.i.f. by taking the bill of lading to himself or to order. If so the property will not pass until the transfer of the bill of lading. Similar problems of financing to those in c.i.f. contract may also have to be dealt with, though the details necessarily differ.

I have so far only dealt with the main features of these most important mercantile contracts. But there are a great many questions in connection with contracts for the sale of goods in general, which are of very great importance in commercial law. I have already referred in general terms to the "implied" conditions. There are many common types of contract such as those which are called Hire Purchase agreements, for which clear and practical rules have been laid down by the Courts. To these I do not here refer, any more than I refer to the many special varieties of contract, as, for example, Conditional Contracts. The correct measure of damages for breach of a contract of sale has raised many difficult questions and led to many decisions, and in some cases it may be said that the law is not finally settled. I may instance the problems which have arisen in regard to instalment contracts, and in regard to what has been called the anticipatory breach.

But these, and a host of other questions of interest and importance, must be left for the student to grapple with, and perhaps to solve in his detailed study of the Cases. As always in the Common Law System, the study of general rules and principles must go hand in hand with the study of their special applications and of the complications which supervene on their simplicity. All that I have sought to do in these brief introductory observations has been to convey some preliminary idea of the methods and the spirit of Commercial Law, illustrated by the special instance of the c.i.f. contract. The student must not lose sight of the wood for the trees. He must not forget the general in the particulars. Above all, he must never forget the essential spirit of Commercial Law, which, though not deficient in ingenuity, above all things never aims at ingenuity for its own sake. Its aim is to appreciate the practical needs of the position and to meet these needs by a solution which itself is practical.

WRIGHT.

COLLATERAL READINGS

GENERAL

Origins of Commercial Law.
MacKinnon, 52 L. Q. Rev. 30 (1936).
Comparative Law and the Law Merchant.
Thayer, 6 Brooklyn L. Rev. 139 (1936).
Contract and Commercial Law.
Gutteridge, 51 L. Q. Rev. 91 (1935).
The Origins of the Law of Sales.
Stone, 29 L. Q. Rev. 442; 31:50 (1913, 1915).
Across Sales on Horseback.
Llewellyn, 52 Harv. L. Rev. 725 (1939).
The First Struggle to Unhorse Sales.
Llewellyn, 52 Harv. L. Rev. 873 (1939).
Some Differences between the English and American Law of Sale of Goods.
McCurdy, 9 Jour. Comp. Leg. (3d ser.) 15 (1927).
Sales under C.O.D., F.O.B., and C.I.F. Terms.
Vold, 2 Dak. L. Rev. 415 (1929).
C.I.F. Contracts in American Law.
Llewellyn, 32 Yale L. J. 711 (1923).

PART ONE: THE CONTRACT OF SALE AND ITS ELEMENTS

Sales Distinguished from Other Transactions.
Vold, 3 Dak. L. Rev. 3 (1930).
Are Sales of Corporate Stock Subject to the Sales Act?
Kaufman, 10 N. Y. U. L. Q. Rev. 157 (1933).
Corporate Stock and the Uniform Sales Act.
J. P. McKeehan, 40 Dick. L. Rev. 104 (1936).
Some Aspects of the Law Relating to Foreign Exchange.
Fraenkel, 20 Col. L. Rev. 832 (1920).
Border Line Topics on what Goods can be Sold.
Vold, 17 Va. L. Rev. 23 (1930).
Open Price in Contracts for the Sale of Goods.
Wm. L. Prosser, 16 Minn. L. Rev. 733 (1932).
Section 17 of the Statute of Frauds.
Stephen and Pollock, 1 L. Q. Rev. 1 (1885).
The Statute of Frauds, a Legal Anachronism.
Willis, 3 Ind. L. J. 427, 528 (1928).
Sales of Goods and the Statute of Frauds.
J. P. McKeehan, 28 Dick. L. Rev. 177 (1924).
A Statute for Promoting Fraud.
F. M. Burdick, 16 Col. L. Rev. 273 (1916).
The Application of the Statute of Frauds under the Uniform S. A.
Vold, 15 Minn. L. Rev. 391 (1931).
The Function of Earnest Money in the Civil Law of Sales.
Hebert, 11 Loyola L. J. 121 (1930).
Statute of Frauds and Part Performance.
Moreland, 78 U. of Pa. L. Rev. 51 (1929).

PART TWO: THE MAKING OF THE CONTRACT

Delivery as a Requisite in the Sale of Chattel Property.
Williston, 35 HARV. L. REV. 797 (1922).
Performance by Delivery.
Menzies, 64 L. J. 130 (1927).
Intervening Impossibility of Performance as Affecting the Obligations of Contracts.
Conlen, 66 U. OF PA. L. REV. 28 (1917).
The Doctrine of Frustration as Applied to Contracts.
Conlen, 70 U. OF PA. L. REV. 87 (1922).
The Operation of Description in a Contract of Sale of Goods.
Montrose, 15 CAN. BAR REV. 760 (1937).
Requirement and Output Contracts.
Havighurst and Berman, 27 ILL. L. REV. 1 (1932).
Installment Selling — a Symposium.
Issacs, Berger, Ecker, W. T. & L. R. Foster, 2 LAW & CONTEMP. PROB. 141 (1935).
Warranty in the English Law of Sale.
Brown, 15 JURID. REV. 50; 16:406 (1903, 1904).
Conditions and Warranties in the Sale of Goods.
Burdick, 1 COL. L. REV. 71 (1901).
Business Practice Regarding Warranties in the Sale of Goods.
Bogart and Fink, 25 ILL. L. REV. 400 (1930).
On Warranty of Quality, and Society.
Llewellyn, 36 COL. L. REV. 699; 37:341 (1936, 1937).
Retail Responsibility and Judicial Lawmaking.
Waite, 34 MICH. L. REV. 494 (1936).
Opposition to the Law of Business Usages.
Wright, 26 COL. L. REV. 917 (1926).
The Economic Advantages and Disadvantages of the Various Methods of Selling Goods on Credit.
Isaacs, 8 CORN. L. Q. 199 (1923).
Legal Advantages and Disadvantages of the Various Methods of Selling Goods on Credit.
Magill, 8 CORN. L. Q. 210 (1923).

PART THREE: THE FINANCING OF THE CONTRACT

Commercial Letters of Credit.
McCurdy, 35 HARV. L. REV. 539, 715 (1922).
The Right of a Beneficiary under a Commercial Letter of Credit.
McCurdy, 37 HARV. L. REV. 323 (1924).
Irrevocable Credits in International Commerce.
Thayer, 36 COL. L. REV. 1031; 37:1326 (1936, 1937).
The Development of Negotiable Instruments in Early English Law.
Beutel, 51 HARV. L. REV. 813 (1938).
The Negotiable Instruments Law.
Ames, 14 HARV. L. REV. 241, 442 (1901).
The Negotiable Instruments Law; a Rejoinder to Dean Ames.
Brewster, 15 HARV. L. REV. 26 (1902).

Some Necessary Amendments in the Negotiable Instruments Law.
Brannan, 26 HARV. L. REV. 493, 588 (1913).
The Uniform Negotiable Instruments Law, Is It Producing Uniformity and Certainty in the Law Merchant?
Henning, 59 U. OF PA. L. REV. 471, 532 (1910).
The British Conception of Negotiable Instruments against the French.
Mitchell, 10 JOUR. COMP. LEG. (3d ser.) 237 (1928).
The International Unification of Laws concerning Bills of Exchange.
Hudson and Feller, 44 HARV. L. REV. 333 (1931).
The Basis of the Negotiability of Commercial Paper.
(Note) 24 COL. L. REV. 757 (1924).
The Concept of "Negotiability" as used in Sec. 47 of the N. I. L.
Smith, 7 TEX. L. REV. 520 (1929).
The Payee as Holder in Due Course.
Britton, 1 U. OF CHI. L. REV. 728 (1934).
Some Aspects of Payment by Negotiable Instrument; a Comparative Study.
Kessler, Levi, and Ferguson, 45 YALE L. J. 1373 (1936).
Trust Receipts.
Hanna, 29 COL. L. REV. 545 (1929).
The Trust Receipt as Security.
Frederick, 22 COL. L. REV. 395, 546 (1922).
Trust Receipt Security in the Financing of Sales.
Vold, 15 CORN. L. Q. 543 (1930).
The Effect of the Trust Receipts Act.
Bogert, 3 U. OF CHI. L. REV. 26 (1935).
Documents of Title as Security Devices in Sales.
Vold, 11 BOSTON U. L. REV. 195 (1931).
The Evolution of the Ocean Bill of Lading.
McLaughlin, 35 YALE L. J. 548 (1926).
The Negotiability of Bills of Lading.
Negus, 37 L. Q. REV. 442 (1921).
Marine Insurance Certificates.
Thayer, 49 HARV. L. REV. 239 (1936).

PART FOUR: THE EXECUTION OF THE CONTRACT

The Intent to Pass Title in Sales of Goods.
Vold, 6 NEB. L. BULL. 257; 7:161, 257 (1928, 1929).
Transfer of Property and Title at Common Law and under the Uniform Sales Act.
(Note) 24 GEO. L. J. 165 (1935).
Ownership of Goods Shipped under a Bill of Lading to Seller's Order.
Williston, 82 U. OF PA. L. REV. 1 (1933).
Significance of the Concept "Title" where Seller Retains Bill of Lading.
(Note) 29 COL. L. REV. 1100 (1929).
Cash Sales.
Vold, 14 ST. LOUIS L. REV. 1 (1928).
"Sale or Return" and "Delivery on Approval."
Vold, 2 DAK. L. REV. 280 (1928).
The Evolution of Conditional Sales Law in New York.
Bogert, 8 CORN. L. Q. 303 (1923).
Codifying the Law of Conditional Sales.
Burdick, 18 COL. L. REV. 103 (1918).

The Validity of the Conditional Sale in Civil Law.
Cruz, 4 TULANE L. REV. 531 (1930).
Recent Developments in the Law of Conditional Sales.
Wilson, 66 U. S. L. REV. 421 (1932).
Fraud on the Seller.
Vold, 3 DAK. L. REV. 299 (1931).
The Sales Contract as a Limitation on the Privilege of Inspection.
(Note) 35 COL. L. REV. 64 (1935).

PART FIVE: THE FAILURE OF THE CONTRACT

Seller's Remedies, Refusal of Buyer to Accept Goods, etc.
(Note) 21 MINN. L. REV. 716 (1937).
The Res in Transitu and Similar Problems in the Conflict of Laws.
Hellendall, 17 CAN. BAR REV. 7, 105 (1939).
Resale by Unpaid Seller of Goods.
Russell, 7 CAN. BAR REV. 294 (1929).
The Right of a Seller of Goods to Recover the Price.
Williston, 20 HARV. L. REV. 363 (1907).
The Seller's Action for the Price.
Waite, 17 MICH. L. REV. 283 (1919).
Rescission for Breach of Warranty.
Williston, 16 HARV. L. REV. 465 (1903).
4 COL. L. REV. 195 (1904).
Rescission for Breach of Warranty.
Burdick, 4 COL. L. REV. 1 (1904).
Some Limitations on the Remedies of the Vendor in Conditional Sales Contracts.
Baker, 13 CHI-KENT REV. 1 (1934).

PART ONE

INTRODUCTORY: THE CONTRACT OF SALE AND ITS ELEMENTS

COMMENT

THE BASIC relationship of the law merchant, around which others revolve and on which they focus, is the transaction of sale. Without a sale there would be no operation to be financed and no goods to be carried or insured. There would be small use for letters of credit and bills of exchange, for bills of lading and warehouse and trust receipts; for all these customary instruments of the merchant are incidental in one way or another to the transfer under modern conditions of the property in goods for a price. Any study of the law merchant therefore is primarily a study of the contract of sale and of its incidents.

Certain indispensable elements of the transaction spring to mind readily enough. There must be of course a buyer and a seller; there must be equally goods to be sold, and a price for such goods. In regard to these essentials, as well as with reference to the nature and form of the contract which results from the bargain, the law lays down definite requirements. Consideration of these requirements is a necessary prelude to further exploration, for they constitute the bare framework on which merchants must build for their peculiar needs, and to which the drape of usage must be fitted. In the course of this consideration questions may arise that look beyond the framework, that hint at other aspects of the transaction where the touch of the mercantile hand is plainly discernible. In the present connection, however, such questions merely suggest possibilities for later scrutiny; the immediate task is to lay the foundation which is the prerequisite of further construction.

CHAPTER I

The Nature of the Transaction: Sales and Contracts or Agreements to Sell

CHRISTOU *v.* BARRIOS

California District Court of Appeal, 1923

[61 *California Appellate Reports*, 140]

Nourse, J. Defendant's demurrer to plaintiff's third amended complaint was sustained. Plaintiff declined to amend and judgment was thereupon entered in favor of defendant.

The amended complaint alleges that on the seventeenth day of May, 1920, plaintiff's assignors, Harry Kockos and Andrew Kockos copartners doing business as Kockos Bros., entered into a contract to purchase 300 tons of Java 24 table sugar for $20 per 100 pounds net c. i. f. San Francisco, California, in bond from A. B. Moulder & Co. Ltd., of Hongkong, China. The seller's confirmation of the sale, which is set forth in the complaint *in haec verba*, requires: "Irrevocable letter of credit at 60 days sight, without interest, to be cabled immediately to Hongkong, China. This credit to be established today, May 17th, 1920." The complaint then alleges that on the same day plaintiff's assignors, having said confirmed right to purchase said sugar, entered into the following agreement with defendant "to transfer to said defendant their confirmed right to purchase said sugar":

San Francisco, U. S. A., May 17, 1920.

Messrs. Barrios & Co.,
San Francisco, Cal.
Gentlemen:

We beg to confirm sale to you of 300 tons — 2000# each Java 24 sugar at $20.00 per hundred pounds, net c. i. f. San Francisco in bond — Hongkong Chamber of Commerce Certificate or any other certificate final as to quality and weight —May/June shipment from Orient to San Francisco — double mats 100# net.

It is understood that this sale has been confirmed by A. B. Moulder & Co., Ltd., Hongkong, to us through Bernhardt Fest & Co.

Terms:

It is understood and agreed that Barrios & Co. will immediately today open letter of credit at 60 days sight covering above merchandise in favor of Moulder & Co. and we will notify Moulder & Co. through Bernhardt Fest & Co. that we have transferred above merchandise to Barrios & Co. and credit will be established by Barrios & Co.

Furthermore, in consideration of the transfer of this purchase to you, you will pay us $6000 U. S. money on arrival of goods from the Orient with understanding that if we want you to give us bank guarantee you will furnish same without delay.

Furthermore, it is understood that if seller will fail to deliver above merchandise Kockos Bros. will not be responsible for any loss you may suffer in this transaction under any consideration.

It is furthermore understood that brokerage, if any, will be paid by Barrios & Co.

If the above is in order kindly sign the enclosed copy.

Yours respectfully,
KOCKOS BROS.
ANDREW KOCKOS.

Approved and accepted

BARRIOS & CO.
O. BARRIOS.

Witness
GILBERT A. ELLIS.

That Kockos Bros. notified A. B. Moulder & Co. of the transfer to defendant Barrios & Co. and that the latter would immediately establish the letter of credit; that plaintiff's assignors had performed each and every condition on their part to be performed; that defendant "did fail and refuse to open said letter of credit . . . at 60 days sight in favor of A. B. Moulder & Co." and failed and refused to carry out the terms of his contract; "that by reason thereof there became due and immediately payable to said Harry Kockos and Andrew Kockos, copartners doing business as Kockos Bros., the sum of six thousand ($6000) dollars." Then follows an allegation of demand for the payment of the sum of $6000 and defendant's refusal to pay the same, with a prayer for the recovery of this amount. The demurrer is both general and special.

Appellant concedes that the complaint fails to state a cause of action if the contract above set forth between his assignors and respondent was one for the sale of sugar and not, as claimed by him, merely a transfer by Kockos Bros. of their rights under their agreement with Moulder & Co. . . .

On the question of the construction of the contract, appellant argues that the opening recital, "We beg to confirm sale to you of 300 tons—2000# each Java 24 sugar at $20.00 per hundred pounds," is controlled by the recital: "In consideration of the transfer of this purchase to you, you will pay us $6000." Also that if the agreement was intended to be a sale there would be one recital of a consideration instead of $20 per hundred pounds to A. B. Moulder & Co. and $6000 to Kockos Bros., the letter of credit to be opened by respondent would have been payable to Kockos Bros., no mention would have been made of A. B. Moulder & Co., and they would not have been referred to as the seller; there would have been a direct obligation upon the part of Kockos Bros. to tender delivery of the sugar instead of the covenant releasing them from responsibility in the event of the seller's failure to deliver.

The opening recital must be read in connection with the other provisions of the contract. Standing alone, it quite clearly provides for a sale of sugar at $20 per hundred pounds. But it is apparent from the entire contract that the parties did not understand or intend that Kockos Bros. were contracting to sell the sugar to respondent at that price. The full payment required under respondent's contract was equivalent to 300 tons of sugar at the rate of $21 per hundred pounds; $20 was the price Kockos Bros. were to pay for it. It is obvious that the agreement between Kockos Bros. and respondent was made with reference to the former's agreement with Moulder & Co. covering the identical merchandise. Also that it is the Moulder & Co. sale which is embodied in the first paragraph of defendant's agreement. It sets forth a description of these goods, with the price, time of shipment, manner of packing, etc., as contained in their confirmation of sale. The following paragraph states that "this sale" has been confirmed to Kockos Bros. by Moulder & Co. The words "We confirm sale to you" have a well-defined and unambiguous meaning, the same as understood both in their ordinary and popular sense and according to their strict legal sense — a sale is contemplated. They are not the words ordinarily or technically used to express an assignment of a right under an executory contract. So that unless these words are disregarded as being entirely meaningless here, the only intent which can logically be deduced from them is to confirm a sale to defendant of the goods embraced in the Moulder & Co. contract — a resale. Under the heading "Terms" provision is made for payment of the full amount called for by the contract. First, it provides for the immediate establishment of a letter of credit "covering above merchandise" in favor of Moulder & Co.; second, for the payment of $6000 to Kockos Bros. on arrival of the goods from the Orient. The amount of the letter of credit required of respondent, as determined from the paragraph describing the merchandise, is based upon the sale price to Kockos Bros. and is similar in all respects to the letter of credit required of Kockos Bros. by their agreement with Moulder & Co. No significance inconsistent with a sale attaches to this fact or to the fact that defendant's letter of credit was made payable to Moulder & Co. instead of Kockos Bros. The seller may have the purchase price, or a portion thereof, made payable to a third person. Pointing toward a sale is the statement: "We will notify Moulder & Co. . . . that we have transferred above merchandise to Barrios & Co." A transfer of merchandise is quite distinct from an assignment or transfer of a right under an executory contract to purchase. The next provision appellant contends is controlling and determines the nature of the contract to be, not a sale, but a transfer of a right. It is: "Furthermore, in consideration of the transfer of this purchase to you, you will pay us $6000 . . . on arrival of goods from the Orient." Respondent insists this is simply a $6000 balance of the purchase price. Alone, this provision more nearly indicates an assignment than a sale. It is not in the usual form for either, and is perhaps not sufficient to outweigh the effect of other provisions indicating that a sale was intended. In addition to those mentioned is the provision relieving Kockos Bros. from responsibility for any loss suffered by respondent for failure to deliver. This was entirely superfluous if the instrument was regarded merely as an assignment. As assignor he would not have been liable for the seller's breach in any event.

But in the absence of such a provision Kockos Bros. would have been liable for failure to deliver under a contract of sale. The Moulder & Co. agreement excused them from responsibility for delays in delivery beyond their control, and Kockos Bros. were undoubtedly providing against this contingency.

Looking at the instrument as a whole, we think it must be construed as a contract of sale and that the demurrer was properly sustained.

Judgment affirmed.

LANGDON, P. J., and STURTEVANT, J., concurred.

THE KRONPRINZESSIN CECILIE

ADMIRALTY DIVISION, 1915

[32 *Times Law Reports*, 139]

The PRESIDENT, in giving judgment, said: — The subject-matter of the dispute in these proceedings is a consignment of 350 tons of pig lead laden in the steamship Kronprinzessin Cecilie, of the Hamburg-Amerika Line, bound from New York to Hamburg. The consignors were the American Smelting and Refining Company, a corporation of the State of New Jersey, U. S. A., who are the claimants. The consignment was shipped under bills of lading to the order of the shippers at Hamburg. The bills of lading were indorsed by the American Smelting and Refining Company, to the "Metall Gesellschaft, or order," and were sent forward to the Metall Gesellschaft at their head office at Frankfurt. The shipment took place at the end of July, 1914, and the goods were seized at Falmouth on August 5, 1914.

The question which falls to be decided is whether at the date of seizure the goods were the property of the American Smelting and Refining Company or of the Metall Gesellschaft.

The Metall Gesellschaft is a German company, well known as one of the largest metal merchants or dealers in the world before the present war. The claimants' contention is that this enemy company acted merely as selling agents for them in this transaction, and that they had no property in the goods. The business connexion between the American and the German companies requires to be stated.

In 1909 an arrangement, briefly described as the "Pig Lead Convention," was made between certain lead-producing concerns of Spain, France, the United States of America, Belgium, and Germany. It dealt with the sale in Europe of lead produced in the various countries named. It was what is sometimes called a "syndicate" or "combine." Six separate concerns in the producing countries, and three others, represented by the Metall Gesellschaft, entered into the arrangement and were described as the "producers," and the Metall Gesellschaft and Messrs. Henry R. Merton and Co., Ltd., of London, were described as "selling agents."

It was governed by an agreement dated March 19, 1909. This was produced, and can be referred to for its terms. Among the "producers" were the American Smelting and Refining Company, of New York, the present claimants. Later on — in 1913 — the claimants withdrew from the Convention, in view of certain legislation by the Congress of the United States, and of the attitude of public officials of the United States towards commercial dealings of a certain type. Their withdrawal, however, was more illusory than real, for they at once, according to their own showing, entered into an arrangement with the Metall Gesellschaft, which secured for them the substantial benefits of the old agreement, with what they appeared to deem an immunity from the possible results of the anticipated "legislation by the Congress of the United States," and "the attitude of the public officials of the United States toward commercial dealings of a certain type."

The proof of this is that in the present proceedings the claimants harked back to the agreement of 1909, in order to found and support their claim. The new agreement was the result of correspondence between May 29, 1913, and August 21, 1913. The facts with regard to the particular consignments with which the Court has to deal are as follows: —

Instructions for the shipment of the goods were sent by the Metall Gesellschaft to the American claimants on June 21, 1914, for shipment in July to order c. i. f. Hamburg. Towards the end of July the goods were shipped by the American Smelting and Refining Company on the Kronprinzessin Cecilie. On July 27 an invoice was sent to the Metall Gesellschaft for the goods at a provisional price of £6,241 *3s. 3d.* (in terms of the arrangement), with a statement that the American Smelting and Refining Company had drawn on Messrs. Henry R. Merton and Co., Ltd., for the amount.

The bills of lading, together with the insurance certificates, were also sent to the Metall Gesellschaft indorsed to their order. On the same day the American Smelting and Refining Company, through their bankers, sent to Messrs. Henry R. Merton and Co., Ltd., a copy of the invoice with a draft on demand for the amount, included with other amounts for shipments made to Messrs. Henry R. Merton and Co., Ltd., direct. Messrs. Henry R. Merton and Co., Ltd., refused to pay the £6,241 *3s. 3d.* on presentation of the draft on or about August 8 — a date subsequent to the seizure.

[Eight paragraphs of the opinion are here omitted.]

In order to avoid stating burdensome details, I will summarize the elements which appear to bear upon the question in discussion, *viz.*, whether the transactions were sales to the German company or not. Some time beforehand the various producers had to inform the Metall Gesellschaft of the quantities they estimated to produce and to supply in a particular month. The sales for that particular month were then allocated by the Metall Gesellschaft between the producers in agreed proportions. Shipping instructions were then sent by the Metall Gesellschaft to the claimant company. They shipped goods accordingly.

The invoices sent by the shippers were provisional and were made out at certain regulated prices. The bills of lading, invoices, and shipping documents were sent indorsed to the Metall Gesellschaft. Copies of the invoices with drafts on demand were sent to Messrs. Henry R. Merton and Co., Ltd., for the amount provisionally fixed. After the shipment the claimant company had nothing to do with the goods. They did not know what the Metall Gesellschaft did with them. They never knew a single purchaser who bought the goods. To use the words of Mr. Brush, the official of the claimants: —

"Through none of the statements furnished by the Metall Gesellschaft or otherwise is the claimant company ever advised as to the identity of individual purchasers from the Metall Gesellschaft, or as to the localities in Germany or elsewhere to which the lead is shipped after sale; any consignment by the American Smelting and Refining Company to Hamburg, as, for example, the consignment on the Kronprinzessin Cecilie, may have been intended for transshipment and forwarding to purchasers in Russia or Scandinavia."

The price to be paid to the claimants for the goods, again, appears to be important. If the Metall Gesellschaft were mere agents, it would follow that they would have to account to their principals for the exact sum for which the goods were sold, less, of course, their commission or other proper deductions. But the sum accounted for was not, in fact, that for which the goods had been sold, but a sum which was fixed by the computation of sales of pig lead supplied by other producers (including the Metall Gesellschaft themselves) and at other times. The description of the price payable in the letter of July 11, 1913, is as follows: —

"The price paid to us shall be the same as that paid by you to your other customers for similar shipment and similar delivery."

That may or may not be a precise description of what was done in the course of dealing, but it shows clearly that the Metall Gesellschaft were not accountable to the American Smelting and Refining Company as principals for the sums actually received by them as agents from the purchasers to whom they sold the goods. The words "price to be paid" are apt words to denote a sale, and not an accountability by agents for "sums received." One sum might be greater or less than the other.

Certain accounts were produced relating to declarations in February, 1914, and sales in April. The sales were accounted for by applying prices obtained for goods of a dozen companies sold at some time which has not been proved. An example of the working out of the system may be extracted from these accounts. The whole of the declarations made in February for sale on the Continent were 20,210 tons. Of this total a quantity of 2,176 tons was allotted to the claimant company. Instructions were given for shipment in April. Shipments amounting to 2,176 tons were accordingly made by the claimant company between April 6 and 17.

The price credited by the Metall Gesellschaft to the American Smelting and Refining Company was at £18 5*s.* 7*d.* per ton. No information was given as to any price of, or any sum realized by, the claimants' own goods. The £18 5*s.* 7*d.* was an average price allowed for the 20,210 tons declared in February and sold, according to Mr. Leslie Scott, at some other time.

I have taken two prices at which different lots were sold according to Exhibit F.1, one low and one high — £17 9*s.* 4*d.* and £19 7*s.* 7*d.* If the claimants' pig lead had been sold at either of these prices in April they were credited by the Metall Gesellschaft with £1,768 more than the goods would have realized in the one case, and £2,393 *12s.* less in the other case. The above appears to me to be consistent only with a sale of the goods by the claimant company to the German company.

It was contended that the circumstance that the Metall Gesellschaft were described as selling agents, and were paid by a commission, was to a great extent, if not absolutely, decisive of the question. That contention, in my opinion, is unsound. The commission they received — be it remembered not upon the sum realized for the claimants' goods, but upon all the lead they sold in Europe in a certain previous period of time — was a means of ascertaining the profit which they were content to have upon the lead that they distributed, with the great additional advantage accruing to them of obtaining the control of the market in that metal.

In my opinion it was never intended by the claimants to reserve any right of disposal of the goods after they were shipped to the Metall Gesellschaft under bills of lading indorsed to them. On the contrary, the whole control over and the property in the goods were intended thereupon to pass to the German company. It would not be extravagant to surmise that no one would be more surprised than the Metall Gesellschaft to hear it suggested that the goods were not their property — not even the claimant company itself. . . .

In my opinion, in any view of the case it is reasonably certain that both the claimant company and the Metall Gesellschaft intended the property in the lead to pass, and regarded it as having passed, to the latter company.

The decision of the Court is that at the time of the seizure of the lead at Falmouth it was the property of the enemy company.

AMERICAN EXPRESS COMPANY *v.* COSMOPOLITAN TRUST COMPANY

MASSACHUSETTS SUPREME JUDICIAL COURT, 1921

[239 *Massachusetts Reports*, 249]

PIERCE, J. This is an action of contract. The declaration is in two counts. The first count is for money had and received to recover $92,500, with interest at six per cent per annum from September 2, 1920, the date of the payment by the plaintiff to the defendant of said sum. The second count is for damages for the failure of the defendant to pay or cause to be paid to the plaintiff on presentment at Genoa, Italy, a check or draft which reads as follows:

2514
Boston, Mass., U. S. A.
Lit. 2,000,000
August Thirty First 1920
Against our balance
Pay to the order of American Express Company
Duplicate being unpaid
The sum of two million lire
To Credito Italiano, Cosmopolitan Trust Company.
Genoa,
Italy. (sgd.) W. W. Henderson
Assistant Manager
No. 25846 Foreign Department

The defendant denied each and every allegation of the first count, and admitted all the allegations of the second count except such as related to the measure of the plaintiff's damages. The case came on to be heard before a judge of the Superior Court on an agreed statement of facts, and is before this court on a report of that judge, without decision, on the facts agreed. G. L. c. 231, § 111.

The agreed facts in substance show that on September 2, 1920, the plaintiff paid the defendant $92,500 and received for such payment a check or draft, a copy of which is as above set forth. The plaintiff immediately forwarded the instrument to its agent in Genoa, Italy. On September 28, 1920, its agent in Genoa duly presented the instrument to said Credito Italiano and duly demanded delivery of 2,000,000 lire. Credito Italiano thereupon refused to deliver said 2,000,000 lire or any part thereof because it had been ordered by the defendant and by Joseph C. Allen, commissioner of banks of Massachusetts, acting in his official capacity and for and in behalf of the defendant, not to deliver the same. The instrument was duly protested and the protest thereof certified by a notary public, and the plaintiff caused the defendant and the commissioner of banks to be properly notified of the said refusal.

The commissioner of banks of Massachusetts took possession of the property and business of the defendant, by virtue of the authority vested in him by St. 1910, c. 399, on September 25, 1920, and since that time has been in charge of the property and business of the defendant. In accordance with St. 1910, c. 399, § 8, G. L. c. 167, § 28, the commissioner caused to be published a notice calling on all persons having claims against the defendant to present the same and make legal proof thereof not later than March 15, 1921. On January 27, 1921, the plaintiff tendered the defendant the said check or draft, and in compliance with the terms of the notice presented and made legal proof of a claim for $92,500, that being the amount paid by the plaintiff to the defendant on September 2, 1920, with interest thereon. The commissioner refused to accept the said tender and rejected the claim, giving notice of said rejection to the plaintiff by letter dated January 27, 1921. This action was brought on January 29, 1921.

On September 2, 1920, the rate of exchange was such that 2,000,000 lire were worth $92,500. On September 25, 1920, and on September 28, 1920, 2,000,000 lire were worth $83,717, and on January 27, 1921, 2,000,000 lire were worth $74,500. On the foregoing facts the "plaintiff claims that as a matter of law it is entitled to recover upon the first count of its declaration, and it is agreed by the parties that, if the plaintiff is so entitled to recover, judgment shall be entered for the plaintiff in the sum of $92,500 with such interest thereon as is legally due upon the facts herein agreed to. The defendant contends that the plaintiff as a matter of law is not entitled to recover upon said first count but the defendant admits that if the plaintiff as a matter of law is not entitled to recover upon said first count then the plaintiff is entitled to recover upon the second count of its declaration, and it is agreed that in this event judgment shall be entered for the plaintiff for a sum in dollars equivalent to two million (2,000,000) lire at such rate of exchange as ought legally to be used upon the facts herein agreed to with such interest thereon and such damages, if any, as are legally due upon the facts herein agreed to."

Upon the agreed facts the defendant bank sold and the plaintiff purchased credit in the form of a draft drawn against funds which the defendant had standing to its credit with a banking institution in Genoa, Italy, called Credito Italiano. The draft sold is a direction to the foreign correspondent bank to pay to the holder of the draft on demand the sum of money named therein as directed. The transaction was one of purchase and sale. It was not executory, it did not establish a trust or an agency, and it was completed with the delivery of the draft. *Beecher* v. *Cosmopolitan Trust Co., ante,* 48. *Cosmopolitan Trust Co.* v. *Ciarla, ante,* 32. *Kuehne* v. *Union Trust Co.* 133 Mich. 602. The thing sold was the credit; the draft was but a means of establishing or transmitting the credit; it was the evidence of a completed transaction. *Legniti* v. *Mechanics & Metals National Bank of New York,* 230 N. Y. 415. Should the draft in these circumstances be dishonored the plaintiff must seek his remedy in an action for damages for breach of the obligation which the law attached to the transaction; he cannot have the money paid restored in an action for money had and received because the consideration for the money so paid has not failed nor substantially failed. *Suse* v. *Pompe*, 8 C. B. (N. S.) 538, 565. It results that the plaintiff cannot recover on his first count.

[The last page of the opinion, giving judgment for the plaintiff on the second count, is here omitted.]

LEGNITI *v.* MECHANICS & METALS NATIONAL BANK

NEW YORK COURT OF APPEALS, 1921

[230 *New York Reports*, 415]

CRANE, J. It has long been an established custom among banks and financial institutions to sell credit usually represented by draft or check. Thus a bank having a credit with a correspondent in a foreign country will sell its draft or check, drawn upon such correspondent, to a purchaser who desires to make a foreign payment. The draft is not the credit but represents the credit, or in other words, it is a notification to the correspondent or foreign representative to pay the money as directed. The draft is a direction to pay. It is not, itself, money or credit. It is simply used as such. The money paid the bank by the purchaser of the draft becomes the bank's money. The transaction is that of purchase and sale. No trust relationship is established. (*Taussig* v. *Carnegie Trust Company*, 213 N. Y. 627.)

This practice of selling credit by means of drafts or checks grew up among merchants and bankers with the expansion of trade and the necessities of commerce. With the increase of foreign trade and the development of international relationships, communication by cable and wireless met the insistent demands for haste and dispatch. Thus the custom has developed of selling credit to be established by cable or wireless. A purchaser does not receive a draft or check which is to be transmitted by mail, but pays for a credit, which will be given him in the foreign country by an immediate cable or wireless from the seller to his correspondent at the foreign point. The thing sold is the same in the case of the cable or wireless transaction as in the case of the draft or check. It is the credit of the bank or seller. The means of establishing or transmitting the credit is simply an incident of the transaction. In the one case, it is a formal paper drawn up and signed by the seller directing his foreign correspondent to make payment of the amount and to the person therein stated. In the other case, it is a similar direction transmitted by cable or wireless. Cable transfers, therefore, mean a method of transmitting money by cable wherein the seller engages that he has the balance at the point on which the payment is ordered and that on receipt of the cable directing the transfer his correspondent at such point will make payment to the beneficiary described in the cable. All these transactions are matters of purchase and sale and create no trust relationships. (*Stroh-*

meyer & Arpe Co. v. *Guaranty Trust Co.*, 172 App. Div. 16; *Katcher* v. *American Express Company*, 109 Atl. Rep. 741; A. C. Whitaker on Foreign Exchange, section 26, p. 89.)

. In some of the cases this purchase of a cable transfer is referred to as a contract. (*Bank of British North America* v. *Cooper*, 137 U. S. 473; *Bank of China, Japan, and the Straits, Limited* v. *American Trading Company*, Law Reports A. C. 1894, page 266; *Atlantic Communication Co.* v. *Zimmermann*, 182 App. Div. 862.) The terms of the contract are in such a case that the banker agrees to send a cablegram establishing a credit with his foreign correspondent. The contract, it is said, is executory until the credit has been established and that upon failure to send the message the customer may rescind the contract and sue to get back his money or else sue for breach of contract. Whether the transaction be considered a purchase or an executory contract, we need not now determine. So far as this case is concerned, it is a mere matter of nomenclature. In either case, the money paid by the customer to the banker becomes the latter's property and does not establish a trust relationship; the banker does not hold the money as agent or trustee until the foreign credit is established.

There is a marked distinction between these transactions which I have just described and a direction to a bank or other person to transmit a certain specific sum of money to a person abroad. In such cases the bank or transmitter is the agent of the person paying the money, and until the money is sent holds it as agent or trustee for the owner. Such were the cases of *Musco* v. *United Surety Company* (132 App. Div. 300) and *People ex rel. Zotti* v. *Flynn* (135 App. Div. 276). In these latter transactions the intention of the payer is that the money he gives to his agent shall be sent abroad. It is the amount which he gives that is to be transmitted. How it is sent may be immaterial to him. If there be time, currency might be purchased and sent. If not, it may be transmitted in any form recognized in financial circles. It is not at all necessary that the sender or agent have credit in the place to which the money is to be sent. On the other hand, in the contract for credit it is not a specific sum which is to be sent but rather a specific credit which is to be purchased. The amount paid varies with the market. The actual thing that is done by the sender in both of these cases may or may not be the same, but the practice of the merchants and banks has recognized a difference; so have the courts. In the case now before us was the transaction between Angelo Legniti and A. Bolognesi & Co. a purchase of credit or the direction to transmit, as the plaintiff's agent, a specific sum of money? It is frankly conceded by the attorney for the respondent that if it be the former, the plaintiff has no right of recovery. The facts, therefore, must be briefly stated to determine this question.

In February of 1914 Alessandro Bolognesi and Aldo Bolognesi were copartners doing business in the city of New York under the firm name of A. Bolognesi & Co. The plaintiff was a banker at 64 Mulberry street in the city of New York who was in arrears in Naples on account of the failure of one Caesari Conti, and needed to transfer some money to that place at once. He applied to several banking houses in New York to obtain the best rate for the transfer of 18,000 lire to Naples, Italy. On the afternoon of February 10th, 1914, he made his arrangements for this purpose with A. Bolognesi & Co. He said to their representatives: "I give you the order to cable this money for me to Italy, on condition that you send the cable immediately, tonight because as you know, on account of the failure of Caesari Conti, I am overdrawn. I need this money to reach Naples tomorrow." A few minutes before six o'clock on that day a boy from Bolognesi & Co. brought to the plaintiff's office a bill which reads as follows:

NEW YORK, February 10, 1914.

MR. ANGELO LEGNITI,
Bought of A. BOLOGNESI & Co.,
52 Wall Street.

Cable Transfer to Italy to pay by cable to Banca Commerciale Italiana, Napoli, advice to be forwarded by Cable from New York.

Lire 18,000 at 5:19 7–8	$3,462.37
Cabling	1.24
Paid ck 3450	
(cash 13.61)	$3,463.61
Bolognesi & Co.	
Maselli	

Payments required in cash or certified cheques, otherwise order if accepted, will be executed after collection of cheque.

It is fully understood and agreed that no liability shall attach to us nor to our correspondent for any loss or damage in consequence of any delay or mistake in transmitting this message or for any other cause beyond our control.

Thereupon the plaintiff delivered to the messenger a certified check for $3,450 indorsed to A. Bolognesi & Co. and $13.61 in cash. This check was deposited the next day by A. Bolognesi & Co. in its account in the Mechanics and Metals National Bank of New York, collected and credited to the account of the depositor. The cable credit was never transmitted, as on the 11th day of February A. Bolognesi & Co. made a general assignment for the benefit of creditors. Later, in March of 1914, a petition in bankruptcy was filed against them, resulting in the election on the 14th day of August, 1915, of the trustees, parties to this litigation. On the 10th day of February, 1914, the firm of A. Bolognesi & Co. was indebted to the defendant, the Mechanics and Metals National Bank of New York, in the sum of $51,329.90 for moneys advanced, secured by discounts, acceptances and notes. There was a balance on deposit with the defendant, the Mechanics and Metals National Bank of New York, to the credit of A. Bolognesi & Co. of $18,985.05 which was increased by the deposit of the check delivered by the plaintiff to A. Bolognesi & Co. and $6,241.65 in addition thereto. This amount was reduced by three checks aggregating $732.94. As against this balance due to its depositor, the defendant bank claims the right to offset under the Bankruptcy Law the indebtedness of A. Bolognesi & Co. as above stated.

This action has been brought by Angelo Legniti upon the theory that A. Bolognesi & Co. became his agents for the sending of 18,000 lire to Naples, Italy, and that as the money was not sent, he may recover it from the bank into whose possession it can be traced. The bank, he claims, holds it, charged with a trust to pay it to him; it is his money, he says, as he never lost title to it. We do not think there is evidence here of any trust. It was stated by Alessandro Bolognesi in his examination as follows: "Q. As I understand it, you sold for a given number of American dollars a certain number of lire to be delivered in Italy to somebody else? A. To be transferred from my account. Q. That was the transaction in this particular matter? A. That was the regular transaction. Q. What is the difference between that and the sale of a draft for so many lire credit in Italy? A. Only that the draft is advised by mail and this is advised by cable."

It will be noted that the bill presented to the plaintiff late in the afternoon of February 10th, above quoted, upon which the plaintiff parted with his money, stated that he, Mr. Angelo Legniti, *bought* of A. Bolognesi & Co. cable transfer to Italy — to pay by cable to Banca Commerciale Italiana. This was not the case of a specific sum of American money being sent to Naples after being exchanged for lire. It was a case of 18,000 lire being needed in Naples and the purchase of A. Bolognesi & Company's credit with the Banca Commerciale Italiana for this amount which credit was to be used by and for the benefit of Legniti. The money was not to be sent to the Banca Commerciale Italiana for Legniti. It was A. Bolognesi & Co. who on February 10, 1914, had either money or credit at the Banca Commerciale Italiana of Naples, the use of which for compensation was sold and transferred to the plaintiff.

We are naturally impressed, as any one must be, with the fact that the plaintiff gave his money to establish a relative value or worth in Naples and that the receiver kept the money and did not deliver the value, and that this money the bank now holds. Why should not the plaintiff get it back? Upon the failure of A. Bolognesi & Co. many claims sprang into existence beside this of the plaintiff and it is the duty of the courts as far as possible to adjust these relationships according to well-established principles, usages and customs.

The Mechanics and Metals National Bank of New York also had given money or money value to A. Bolognesi & Co. and has a claim for $51,329.90. There were also many other claimants to the assets. To establish a rule that in a case like this the plaintiff becomes a preferred creditor; that the transaction is in the nature of a trust, and that checks deposited with banks upon the purchase of credit are trust funds held for certain and specified purposes, is apt to lead to much confusion, especially when those who have developed this method of doing business into a well-established custom have never treated them as such.

The judgment of the Appellate Division must, therefore, be reversed and that of the trial court affirmed, with costs in this court and in the Appellate Division.

HISCOCK, Ch. J., HOGAN, CARDOZO, POUND, McLAUGHLIN and ANDREWS, JJ., concur.

Judgment accordingly.

In EQUITABLE TRUST CO. *v.* KEENE, 232 N. Y. 290 (Court of Appeals, 1921), it was held that a similar transaction was a contract to create credit in the future rather than a sale of an existing credit, Hiscock, J., saying for the Court: "It seems to be clear that the agreement was not a sale of any existing right or credit but was an agreement to place a certain amount of foreign money to the credit of the defendant, which necessarily related to the future whether measured by the celerity of a cable dispatch or by the delay of a communication by mail. The complaint which was made is to the effect that under the term 'cable transfer of exchange,' 'the *person* contracting to deliver such exchange' contracts 'that he *will make available* by cable to the person contracting to take such exchange a credit of the amount specified at the point specified and at the time specified.' In such an agreement there is no guaranty or necessary implication that the contractor has any credit which he is selling or agreeing to sell or that he will place the credit through a third party as correspondent. He can fulfill the terms of such an agreement through his branch office and he can after making the agreement create for himself the credit which will enable him to place to the credit of the other party to the agreement the funds in question. We are unable to see how such an agreement is other than a contract for future action, no matter how speedily accomplished, or how it can be a sale of an existing right. The principles involved are not different than those which would be applicable to a contract dealing with ordinary articles of personal property. An agreement transferring to another an existing stock of goods would be a sale; an agreement specially to manufacture or create for another certain articles would be a contract looking to the future."

LEE *v.* GRIFFIN

QUEEN'S BENCH, 1861

[30 *Law Journal* (*New Series*), *Queen's Bench*, 252]

Declaration against the defendant as executor of Frances Penson for goods bargained and sold and delivered, and for work and labour done and materials provided by the plaintiff as a surgeon-dentist for the testatrix.

Plea — that the testatrix never was indebted.

At the trial, before Crompton, J., at the Sittings in Middlesex, in Michaelmas Term, 1860, it appeared that the action was brought to recover 21*l.*, the price of two sets of teeth made for the late Frances Penson, of whom the defendant was executor. According to the plaintiff's statement the deceased had ordered the teeth, but had left London for Folkestone, where she soon after died, before they could be fitted to her mouth. The plaintiff produced a letter from the testatrix, in answer to an application by him for a sitting a few days before she left London, in which "she regretted that her health would not permit her taking advantage of the plaintiff's kind efforts to oblige her, and feared it might be some days before she could see him." Upon this evidence the defendant's counsel claimed a nonsuit, as the 17th section of the Statute of Frauds (29 Car. 2. c. 3.) prevented the plaintiff from recovering for goods sold and delivered. The learned Judge was inclined to nonsuit, but it was suggested by the plaintiff's counsel that the count for work, labour and materials might be sustained, citing *Clay* v. *Yates* (1 Hurl. & N. 73; s. c. 25 Law J. Rep. (N.S.) Exch. 237); and a verdict was entered for the plaintiff, with leave to the defendant to move to enter a nonsuit or verdict, the Court to deal with any question of fact, if any should have been left to the jury.

A rule *nisi* having been obtained accordingly —

Patchett shewed cause. — The materials were only ancillary to the work and labour. The skill of the dentist was the thing really contracted for; therefore the count for work and labour can be maintained — *Clay* v. *Yates*.

[HILL, J. — That is a case *sui generis*. The printer, the plaintiff there, in effect, does work chiefly on the materials which the defendant supplied, although, to a certain extent, the plaintiff may be said to supply materials; moreover the printer could not sell the book to any one else. *Towers* v. *Osborne* (1 Strange, 506) is more in point.]

The test is whether the skill is the chief part of what is supplied. In *Clay* v. *Yates* (see 1 Hurl. & N. at p. 76) Martin, B. says, "Suppose an artist paints a portrait for 300 guineas, and supplies the canvas for it, worth 10*s*., surely he might recover on a count for work and labour," and Pollock, C.B. makes observations to the same effect.

[CROMPTON, J. — Assuming that to be the test, there can hardly be said to be more skill in fitting teeth than in fitting a pair of breeches. BLACKBURN, J. — *Atkinson* v. *Bell* (8 B. & C. 277; see pp. 283–4) shews that this count cannot be maintained; though what Bayley, J. there said, that in order to maintain a count for work and labour, the work must be on the employer's materials, cannot be held to be universally true; and this proposition has already been qualified in *Grafton* v. *Armitage* (2 Com. B. Rep. 336; s. c. 15 Law J. Rep. (N.S.) C.P. 20), as is pointed out by the Court in *Clay* v. *Yates*.]

[The opinions of Crompton and Hill, JJ. are here omitted.]

BLACKBURN, J. — I am of the same opinion. It is clear that there was no sufficient memorandum of the contract within the Statute of Frauds. The other question is, whether the present was a contract for the sale of goods, or for work and labour. In order to ascertain this you must of course, in each case, look at the contract itself. If the contract be such that it will result in the sale of a chattel, the proper form of action, if the employer refuses to accept the article when made, would be for not accepting. But if the work and labour be bestowed in such a manner as that the result would not be anything which could properly be said to be the subject of sale, then an action for work and labour is the proper remedy. An attorney employed to draw a deed is a familiar instance of the latter proposition; and it would be an abuse of language to say that the paper or parchment of the deed were goods sold and delivered. In *Clay* v. *Yates* the circumstances were peculiar, but had the contract been completed, it could scarcely perhaps have been said that the result was the sale of a chattel. In *Atkinson* v. *Bell*, had the contract been carried out, it would have resulted in the sale of the machine; and in *Grafton* v. *Armitage*, Tindal, C.J. observes of that case, "The substance of the contract was, goods to be sold and delivered by the one party to the other." Taking that as the true criterion, *Atkinson* v. *Bell*, *Grafton* v. *Armitage* and *Clay* v. *Yates* are not inconsistent; but the last case comes very near the line. Here, if the teeth had been delivered and accepted, the contract for the sale of a chattel would have been complete. I do not think that the relative value of the labour and of the materials on which it is bestowed can in any case be the test of what is the cause of action; and that if Benvenuto Cellini had contracted to execute a work of art for another, much as the value of the skill might exceed that of the materials, the contract would have been the less for the sale of a chattel.

Rule absolute.

Compare with ROBINSON *v.* GRAVES, (1935) 1 K. B. 579 (Court of Appeal), where it was held that a contract for the painting of a lady's portrait was a contract for work and labor, since it appeared on the facts of the case that "the material, the paint, and the canvas, were merely ancillary to the actual technical work of producing the work of art."

RACKLIN–FAGIN CONST. CORPORATION *v.* VILLAR

NEW YORK SUPREME COURT, APPELLATE TERM, FIRST DEPARTMENT, 1935

[281 *New York Supplement*, 426]

Appeal from Municipal Court, Borough of Bronx, Second District.

Action by Racklin-Fagin Construction Corporation, landlord, against Louis C. Villar, tenant, wherein defendant filed a counterclaim. From a final order and judgment of the Municipal Court, Borough of Bronx, Second District, in favor of tenant, plaintiff appeals. . . .

Per curiam. A contract to paint two pictures of a particular size for hanging in the lobby of plaintiff's apartment house is a contract for work, labor, and services, and is not within the purview of the Sales Act (Personal Property Law, § 82 *et seq.*). Since the paintings have been completed and are held by the tenant at the disposal of the plaintiff landlord, the former is entitled in accordance with the contract to be paid the full price by crediting him with the payment of ten months' rent as it comes due from October 1, 1934, through July 31, 1935. The rent for the last ten months was not due at the time of the commencement of this action, and affirmative judgment for the tenant should not have been granted.

Final order and judgment modified by striking out the award on the counterclaim and by dismissing the same without prejudice, and, as modified, affirmed.

GINSBERG *v.* KUGLER

NEW YORK SUPREME COURT, APPELLATE TERM, FIRST DEPARTMENT, 1919
[174 *New York Supplement*, 143]

Appeal from Municipal Court, Borough of Manhattan, Fourth District.

Action by Harry Ginsberg against Harry Kugler. From a judgment of the Municipal Court for plaintiff, after trial by judge without jury, the defendant appeals. . . .

BIJUR, J. Plaintiff delivered certain silk to defendant for manufacture into waists. While the silk was in defendant's possession, his premises were burglarized and the silk stolen. This action was brought to recover its value.

The sole question presented is whether the arrangement under which the silk was delivered constituted a bailment or a sale. It is conceded that, if the contract was of bailment, defendant is not liable, but that, if it was a sale, the judgment was right, and should be affirmed.

I think that upon plaintiff's own testimony the contract was one of bailment. He testified that he brought the defendant some waists and asked "if he [defendant] could manufacture some waists for me"; that the price fixed was $39 a dozen waists; that he "was supposed to sell" defendant the silk at $1.25 a yard; and that the price of the silk was to be credited against the contract price of the waists. The goods were sent to defendant with a memorandum, upon which appeared the words: "Sent to Alco Waist & Dress Co. for my use only. H. Kugler." And plaintiff further testified that the waists were to be manufactured for his use only, and delivered in two weeks.

From these facts it is quite clear that the defendant was bound under his contract to use the particular material delivered to him by the plaintiff for the latter's exclusive use, and to return it in the form of finished silk waists. The arrangement between the parties presents the familiar situation of a delivery of specific goods or property by one party to another for the performance of work thereon, with the obligation to return it in changed or improved form, which has always been held to constitute the party receiving it a bailee, as distinguished from a purchaser. The essential nature of the relation between the parties were not changed by the fact that the goods, as a matter of bookkeeping, were formally charged to defendant.

It follows, therefore, that the judgment should be reversed, and a new trial ordered, with $30 costs to appellant to abide the event. All concur.

COMMISSIONER OF INTERNAL REVENUE *v.* SAN CARLOS MILLING CO.

CIRCUIT COURT OF APPEALS, NINTH CIRCUIT, 1933

[63 *Federal Reporter* (*2d Series*), 153]

Petition to Review an Order of the United States Board of Tax Appeals.

SAWTELLE, Circuit Judge. The taxpayer is a domestic corporation organized under the laws of the territory of Hawaii, with its principal office at Honolulu, T. H. Its principal place of business is in the municipality of San Carlos, province of Negroes Occidental, Philippine Islands, where it operates a sugar mill for the manufacture of raw rugar from sugar cane, under a contract or contracts with certain planters who supply the sugar cane. These contracts will be discussed fully hereinafter. By the terms of the contracts, the taxpayer received as compensation for its milling services in the manufacture of the sugar 40 per cent. of the raw sugar manufactured from the cane supplied by the planters. The Commissioner of Internal Revenue determined that the sugar so received by the taxpayer under these contracts was income, because the contracts with the planters constituted a sale of the sugar to the taxpayer and therefore the taxpayer was not entitled to the benefits of section 262 (a) of the Revenue Act of 1921 (42 Stat. 271) in computing its tax for the year 1923. This determination was reversed by the Board of Tax Appeals (24 B. T. A. 1132), which held that the taxpayer was entitled to the benefits of section 262 (a) because the contracts constituted merely a bailment of the sugar and not a sale thereof. From this decision, the Commissioner has appealed.

[The text of the Statutes is here omitted.]

The sole question for our consideration, therefore, is whether the intention of the taxpayer and the planters, as disclosed by the contract for the transfer of the sugar cane to the taxpayer to be manufactured into sugar, was to constitute the transaction a sale of the sugar to the taxpayer or merely a bailment thereof.

[Two paragraphs quoted from Corpus Juris, on bailment, are here omitted.]

In 1911, Alfred D. Cooper, the taxpayer's agent in the Philippine Islands, entered into a contract with a number of planters in the Philippines to construct a sugar mill and maintain it for a period of thirty years, provided that the planters agreed to furnish the mill with a certain amount of sugar cane for a like period. This contract was later assigned to the taxpayer. Under the terms of the contract, the taxpayer agreed to construct and operate a railroad for use in transporting sugar cane, sugar, and fertilizer to the plantations of the growers free of charge to the planters. It also agreed to take delivery of all cane grown by the planters, properly loaded on cars at points along its railway, and to haul the cane free of charge to the mill. It agreed to supply the most approved modern means of weighing the sugar cane, and to have it accurately weighed, and issue to the owners of the cane weight certificates in due form. It agreed to crush, grind, and mill the sugar cane and manufacture the available sucrose contents of the sugar cane into merchantable sugar of certain grades. It agreed to furnish free of cost to the planters containers for the sugar. It agreed to deliver to each planter 60 per cent. of the sugar so made as computed from the weight and analysis of the sugar cane, or store the same at the planters' risk ninety days free of charge, making a reasonable charge for all sugar remaining in the warehouse for a longer period. The ownership of all sugar was to be represented by official warehouse receipts showing the number of bags of sugar and signed by a representative of the mill and the planter. It further agreed to deliver each week a statement for each plantation of the cane received and milled during the preceding week and a computation of the amount of sugar due each plantation. It was agreed that the mill would be operated regularly during the grinding season and maintained in good condition. The taxpayer further agreed that it would admit no planter to the milling contract at any future time on more favorable terms than those given at the time of signing the original agreement. It was agreed that "the mill will charge and accept as full compensation for the services rendered and agreed to be rendered hereunder forty per cent of the sugar and waste molasses manufactured as aforesaid, or, at the option of the mill, forty per cent of the net proceeds of sale of sugar manufactured, and of the waste molasses."

On the part of the planters, it was agreed that each planter would for a period of thirty years deliver to the mill all cane grown by him on lands which were generally designated and described in the contract. Delivery was to be made on cars of the mill's railroad. They agreed to furnish to the mill such a technical description of the plantation of each planter as would be sufficient for inscription in the registry of deeds, which description was to be attached to the agreement and to become a part thereof. It was further agreed that, if at any time during the term of the agreement the planter should fail to plant three-fourths of his land or cultivate, harvest, or deliver his cane, the mill should at its option have the right to plant and cultivate or harvest the crop. The planter also agreed that the mill should have the right to enter its land and examine the crops during the term of the contract.

In accordance with their agreement, the planters devoted certain lands to the production of sugar cane, which was loaded on cars in the field. The loaded cars were then hauled by the planters to the railroad tracks of the taxpayer, where the taxpayer took delivery of the cars and had them hauled to its mill. The cane was weighed at the can track of the mill before unloading and a weight certificate issued for each planter's cane. The cane was then placed on the cane carrier and transported to the mill, where it was crushed, and a sample of the juice from each planter's cane was analyzed to determine the sucrose content or value, of which a separate record was made. Thereafter the juices were mixed in the further processes of manufacturing the sugar. It would not be commercially practicable to extract the sugar from each planter's cane separately.

The sugar was then weighed, bagged, and stored in the taxpayer's warehouse. Once each week the taxpayer computed the amount of sugar manufactured from each planter's cane from the weight of the cane, its sucrose content, and the efficiency of the mill, deducting the amount of sugar to which it was entitled as compensation for its milling services, and issued to the planter a warehouse receipt for his share of the sugar.

The taxpayer always had on hand in its warehouse at San Carlos sufficient sugar manufactured at its mill to cover outstanding warehouse receipts. The taxpayer never paid any planter cash instead of returning to him his portion of the sugar; nor did it claim the right to sell for its own account all of the sugar produced under any of its milling contracts. The taxpayer has acted as selling agent for some planters, for which services it received a commission.

We cannot say that this agreement is inconsistent with the notion of a bailment. We believe that there is clearly manifested an intention on the part of the contracting parties that the transfer of the sugar cane to the mill should be governed by the legal relationship of bailor and bailee, and that their agreement cannot be construed to have the legal effect of a sale of the cane to the mill, nor was it so intended.

[The remainder of the opinion is here omitted.]

Affirmed.

TEMPLE *v.* KEELER

NEW YORK COURT OF APPEALS, 1924

[238 *New York Reports*, 344]

Appeal from Supreme Court, Appellate Division, Third Department.

Action by Jessie M. Temple against William H. Keeler. From judgment of Appellate Division (207 App. Div. 880, 201 N. Y. Supp. 951), unanimously affirming judgment for plaintiff on verdict, defendant appeals by permission. Affirmed.

The action was brought to recover for loss and damage alleged to have been caused plaintiff by sickness resulting, as alleged, from her eating fish in defendant's restaurant, which was unwholesome and unfit for human food, whereby she became ill from ptomaine poisoning.

[The arguments of counsel are here omitted.]

ANDREWS, J. We hold that, where a customer enters a restaurant, receives, eats, and pays for food, delivered to him on his order, the transaction is the purchase of goods. We hold also that under such circumstances the buyer does by implication make known to the vendor the particular purpose for which the article is required, and, where the buyer may assume that the vendor has had an opportunity to examine the article sold, it appears conclusively that he relies upon the latter's skill or judgment. *Rinaldi* v. *Mohican Co.*, 225 N. Y. 70, 121 N. E. 471. Consequently there is an implied warranty that the food is reasonably fit for consumption.

We have not before held that the owner of a restaurant sells the food which he provides for his guests. Indeed, in *Race* v. *Krum*, 222 N. Y. 410, 118 N. E. 853, L. R. A. 1918F, 1172, we refused to pass upon the precise question as not then before us. Yet we cannot logically differentiate the facts there involved from those in the case at bar. Miss Temple enters a restaurant, orders a portion of fish which the jury might find was unwholesome, receives it, eats it, pays for it, and later becomes ill, it may be inferred, as the result. Mr. Race enters a drug store, orders a portion of ice cream which was unwholesome, receives it, eats it, pays for it, and later becomes ill as a result. This, we said, was a sale. The names of the plaintiffs differ; one defendant owns a restaurant and the other a drug store. But these variances are not sufficient to lead us to distinguish the two cases. It has been said that a restaurant owner does not sell food but renders a service — that a seat is furnished, the services of a waiter and cook, the use of plates and silver. There are seats before an ice cream counter. A clerk takes the order and delivers the food. Mr. Krum made or prepared the ice cream. It is eaten from a plate or glass with a fork or spoon belonging to the proprietor. It has also been said that in a restaurant, while the customer may consume such portion of his order as he desires, he may not carry away with him the remainder. If this be so, the same rule must apply to ice cream bought to be eaten in a drug store. In any event, the consequences sought to be drawn from this proposition do not follow. Even if true, the transaction may still be a qualified sale — a sale of what is actually used. We suppose a merchant might sell for a fixed price all of a pile of potatoes a customer might wish or be able to carry away.

Apart, however, from *Race* v. *Krum*, we would still be compelled to reach the same result by an authoritative decision. Even in construing a criminal statute we have held that a hotel keeper who places before his guests at dinner partridges sells the birds, although the guests paid a total sum for board and lodging. *People* v. *Clair*, 221 N. Y. 108, 116 N. E. 868, L. R. A. 1917F, 766. Elsewhere, also, the same rule has been applied. *Friend* v. *Childs Dining Hall Co.*, 231 Mass. 65, 120 N. E. 407, 5 A. L. R. 1100.

Other questions have been argued before us. We have examined them and find no error. The judgment appealed from should be affirmed with costs.

HISCOCK, C .J., and CARDOZO, POUND, MCLAUGHLIN, CRANE, and LEHMAN, JJ., concur.

Judgments affirmed.

Compare with NISKY *v.* CHILDS CO., 103 N. J. L. 464 (Court of Errors and Appeals, 1926), where the plaintiff became seriously ill after eating fried oysters in the defendant's restaurant, and where the question was whether the oysters had been sold to the plaintiff. In affirming a non-suit, the Court through Lloyd, J., said on that point: "From the earliest times, however, a distinction has been drawn between a sale of an article and the furnishing of food at an eating house, hotel or restaurant; the latter partaking rather of the character of service, in which case the standard of liability is the failure to use that reasonable care which the circumstances require. As was said many years ago in *Parker* v. *Flint*, reported in 12 Mod. 254, 'an innkeeper . . . does not sell but utters his provisions,' and by Professor Beale, in his *Treatise on Innkeepers*, section 169: 'As an innkeeper does not lease his room, he does not sell the food he supplies to his guests. It is his duty to supply such food as the guest needs, and the corresponding right of the guest to consume the food he needs and to take no more. Having finished his meal he has no right to take food from the table, even the uneaten portion of the food supplied him. Nor can he claim a certain portion of the food as his own to be handed over to another in case he chooses not to consume it himself.'

"The authorities distinguishing the transaction from a sale recognize that while the food served constitutes, of course, an essential part, yet, serving it cannot be regarded as a sale of goods, and this we think the common understanding. A customer at an eating place seeks not to make a purchase, but to be served with food to such reasonable extent as his present needs require. With the service go a place, more or less attractive, in which to eat it, a table, dishes, linen, silver, waiters and sometimes music as an accompaniment — all tending to render more agreeable and palatable that which he eats. The food he obtains is then and there consumed; he does not eat the portion he can comfortably devour and place the remainder in his pockets or other receptacle, to be stored away for future needs. So, one who purchases a steamship ticket, or one who registers at a hotel, does not conceive the transaction as a sale of goods when, as part of his passage in the one case, and as a guest in the other, he is supplied with meals; nor does one who enters a restaurant to be supplied with a meal or any portion thereof so regard the supplying of his food. This attitude of the public mind is indicated by the familiar signs, 'Meals Served Here,' 'Dinners Served Here,' and the like.

"We think enough has been said to indicate that the service of food at eating houses has never been and cannot be regarded as a sale at common law, but this view is fortified by the absence of litigation (until quite recent years), based upon a claim of warranty, which would necessarily follow if the transaction constituted a sale. In no case in this state has such a contention ever been made, and even in the States of Massachusetts and New York from which cases so strongly relied upon by the appellant come, it remained for the modern Sale of Goods act to invite litigation along such lines."

CHAPTER II

The Essential Requirements of the Contract and its Form

1. THE PARTIES

PEER *v.* HUMPHREY

King's Bench, 1835

[2 *Adolphus & Ellis's Reports*, 495]

Trover for three oxen. On the trial before Littledale J., at the Northampton Spring assizes, 1834, a verdict was found for the plaintiff, subject to the opinion of this Court on the following case.

On the 24th of August 1832, three oxen, the property of the plaintiff, were by his direction delivered to Roundthwaite, his servant to drive to Northampton market. Roundthwaite, instead of taking them to Northampton, sold them to the defendant on the high road, but not in market overt, the same day, and absconded with the money. The defendant purchased bona fide. On the 26th day of August 1832, the plaintiff discovered that the cattle were in the defendant's possession, and on the same day he gave the defendant notice that they belonged to him, the plaintiff, and had been feloniously stolen from him by Roundthwaite, as above mentioned. He at the same time demanded possession of the cattle, which was refused. The oxen remained in the defendant's possession till the 26th of November 1832, when he sold them in market overt, received the price, and appropriated it to his own use. Roundthwaite was convicted of feloniously stealing the cattle, on the prosecution of the plaintiff, at the Northampton assizes in July 1833, and received judgment of transportation for life.

If the Court should be of opinion that the plaintiff was entitled to recover the value of the oxen, the verdict was to stand; otherwise a nonsuit to be entered.

[The arguments of counsel are here omitted.]

Lord Denman C. J. In *Davis* v. *The Bank of England* (2 Bing. 393) it was held that no property in stock passed by a transfer made under a forged power of attorney; and that the original owner, though he had not prosecuted, was entitled to recover his dividends from the Bank. Here the plaintiff has actually prosecuted the felon to conviction. It is quite clear that no property ever passed to the defendant, or from the plaintiff. One difficulty, indeed, arises from Lord Kenyon's expression in *Horwood* v. *Smith* (2 T. R. 755), that "the property remains *in dubio*." I think that either the expression was a hasty one, or it has been reported by mistake. A sale in market overt clearly gives a *prima facie* title to the purchaser. Another difficulty arises from the case of *Parker* v. *Patrick* (5 T. R. 175). There, indeed, the Court distinguished between fraud and felony: but in the argument for the present defendant it is denied that such distinction can be taken; if so, the decision in that case was incorrect. And if the question of goods fraudulently obtained were before us, I cannot help thinking that the case of *Parker* v. *Patrick* would not bear examination. The *Earl of Bristol* v. *Wilsmore* (1 B. & C. 514) seems to me to be quite inconsistent with it.

LITTLEDALE J. I also am clearly of opinion that the plaintiff must recover. The seller had no power to sell: the *prima facie* right is therefore in the plaintiff. But the law is, that no action shall be brought, under particular circumstances, until the owner has done his duty by prosecuting. Even that has been done here. In *Gimson* v. *Woodfall* (2 C. & P. 41) the property must have been changed by a sale in market overt: besides, in that case, the party robbed had done nothing towards bringing the thief to justice; here he has actually prosecuted him to conviction.

WILLIAMS J. That a party obtains a right to property by purchasing it in market overt, is a rule as old as the law itself. The property had so passed in *Horwood* v. *Smith* (2 T. R. 750), and it could not be in two parties at the same time. It had been parted with a second time before the conviction took place, which conviction was the only means of divesting it. Here there was no legal sale at all; the property, therefore, was still in the plaintiff; and any argument drawn from considerations of public justice is met by the fact that the prosecution has actually taken place.

Judgment for the plaintiff.

THE CASE OF MARKET OVERT

COMMON PLEAS, 1596

[3 *Coke's Reports, Part 5,* 83b]

At the sessions of Newgate now last past, it was resolved by Popham, Chief Justice of England, Anderson, Ch. Justice of the Common Pleas, Sir Thomas Egerton, Master of the Rolls, the Attorney-General, and the court, that if plate be stolen and sold openly in a scrivener's shop on the market-day (as every day is a market-day in London except Sunday) that this sale should not change the property, but the party should have restitution; for a scrivener's shop is not a market-overt for plate; for none would search there for such a thing; *& sic de similibus, &c.* But if the sale had been openly in a goldsmith's shop in London, so that any one who stood or passed by the shop might see it, there it would change the property. But if the sale be in the shop of a goldsmith, either behind a hanging, or behind a cupboard upon which his plate stands, so that one that stood or passed by the shop could not see it, it would not change the property: so if the sale be not in the shop, but in the warehouse, or other place of the house, it would not change the property, for that is not in market-overt, and none would search there for his goods. So every shop in London is a market-overt for such things only which by the trade of the owner are put there to sale; and when I was Recorder of London, I certified the custom of London accordingly. Note, reader, the reason of this case extends to all markets-overt in England.

JEBARA *v.* OTTOMAN BANK

COURT OF APPEAL, 1927

[*Law Reports,* [1927] 2 *King's Bench,* 254]

Appeal from a decision of Rowlatt, J.

[Eleven pages, containing statement of facts, arguments and the judgment of Bankes, L.J., are omitted.]

SCRUTTON L.J. This appeal raises questions of some difficulty as to the effects of war on a valid pre-war contract, questions not made easier by the scarcity of information on some questions of fact.

Mr. Jebara, a British subject resident in Manchester, was in the habit of procuring, to use a neutral word, Manchester goods for certain Turkish firms residing in Beyrout, then part of the Turkish Empire. There is no evidence to show whether he bought the goods so that the property passed to him, or whether the property passed at once to the Turkish firms. He certainly paid for the goods to the Manchester merchants; drew at sight for the price on the Turkish merchants; attached to the bill the bills of lading for the goods, as to which we are not told who were described as shippers, or what indorsements were on them; and financed himself by obtaining an advance on the documentary bill from the Ottoman Bank, whose headquarters were in Turkey, through its branch in Manchester. The Manchester branch would then forward the bill to their Beyrout branch, who would surrender the documents against payment by the Beyrout merchants. It is not clear whether Jebara bought so that the property passed to him, and passed the property to the Beyrout merchants against payment, or whether he secured himself for his commission and advances by exercising a lien on the documents and goods they represented for his advances. The bank certainly had a lien on the documents and goods for their advances.

The action is by Jebara against the Ottoman Bank, amongst other things, for wrongful dealing after the war broke out between England and Turkey on November 5, 1914, with goods and bills they received before the war.

[One and one-half pages dealing with the obligation of the bank on the bill of exchange are omitted.]

The original contract before the war being between an English subject resident in England and a Turkish subject resident in Turkey, involving the transfer of goods to the Turkish subject and the payment of money to the English subject, was at the outbreak of war between England

and Turkey still executory, neither goods nor money had passed. In my view, in the language of Willes J. in *Esposito* v. *Bowden* ([1857] 7 E. & B. 763, 783), the effect of the outbreak of war "is to dissolve the contract, and to absolve both parties from further performance of it," both by English and Turkish law. . . .

The Englishman could not deliver goods to the enemy of England, nor could the Turk pay money to the enemy of Turkey. There could be no commercial intercourse between them. And with the contract of sale went the subsidiary contract of agency. The Ottoman Bank, a Turkish subject, could not remain in contractual relations with a British subject in carrying out a void contract of sale. It was illegal for it to benefit the Turk, or to remit to the Englishman. The Proclamation of January 7, 1915, superseding an earlier proclamation, and the licence to the Ottoman Bank of November 30, 1914, fully support this view. The latter runs: "I hereby permit the Imperial Ottoman Bank to carry on banking business at all their establishments situated within the United Kingdom, subject to the following limitations, conditions and supervision: (1.) No transactions shall take place, directly or indirectly, with the establishments of the said banks situated in enemy territory, or with any persons resident in enemy territory." The result in my view was, that on November 4, 1914, the contract of Jebara with the Turkish consignees, and his contract with the Ottoman Bank as to action by them in Syria became null and void as involving intercourse with the enemy. The bank, however, did not take this view, and for some years after the outbreak of war continued to hand the goods to the consignees, and receive payment in piastres which they could not remit to England. I do not understand how, after two or three years' delay, the consignees were entitled to claim the goods. But, at any rate, I am satisfied that so far as the original contract of sale and employment were concerned, they were made invalid by the outbreak of war, and the bank could not rely on them as justification for their action. Unless, therefore, they could justify handing over the goods in some other way, they were liable for such handing over as a conversion.

It was argued that if the original contracts were void on the outbreak of war, the bank became agents of necessity and could justify their action in that way. I am not sure that it is not an answer to say that they never thought of themselves in that light, or considered whether it was necessary to act; they thought they were carrying out their contracts. But considerable difficulties arise on the question of agent of necessity in English law. Until recently it was treated as limited to certain classes of agents of whom masters of ships were the most prominent. High authorities had doubted whether it could be extended. I refer to the observations of Lord Esher M.R. in *Gwilliam* v. *Twist* ([1895] 2 Q. B. 84); to the judgment of Parke B. in *Hawtayne* v. *Bourne* ([1841] 7 M. & W. 595, 599), but especially to the careful judgment of Eyre C.J. in *Nicholson* v. *Chapman* (2 H. Bl. 254, 257). Many of the authorities are collected in a recent judgment of McCardie J. in *Prager's* case ([1924] 1 K. B. 566). He there finds the facts so as not to raise any question of action by an agent of necessity, but discusses what the law would be, if he had found the facts differently. He takes the view that judges should expand the common law to meet the needs of expanding society, and proceeds to expand the doctrine of agent of necessity without clearly defining the limits, if any, of its expansion. The difficulty may be seen by considering the case of the finder of perishable goods or chattels which need expenditure to preserve them. If the finder incurs such expenditure, can he recover it from the true owner when he finds him, as his "agent of necessity"? Eyre C.J. raises this difficulty in the case above cited, and cites *Binstead* v. *Buck* ([1777] 2 W. Bl. 1117), the case of the pointer dog. The pointer dog was lost, and his finder fed him for twenty weeks, and claimed the cost from his owner when he appeared, but the claim was treated as unarguable. The expansion desired by McCardie J. becomes less difficult when the agent of necessity develops from an original and subsisting agency, and only applies itself to unforeseen events not provided for in the original contract, which is usually the case where a shipmaster is agent of necessity. But the position seems quite different when there is no pre-existing agency, as in the case of a finder of perishable chattels or animals, and still more difficult when there is a pre-existing agency, but it has become illegal and void by reason of war, and the same reason will apply to invalidate any implied agency of necessity. How can one imply a duty in an enemy to protect the property of his enemy? Will he not be violating his duty to his own country if he takes active steps to preserve an enemy's property? I do not feel strong enough to expand the common law to this extent, and I do not see that McCardie J. has considered the effect of illegality and invalidity by reason of war in his doctrine. The principal in *Prager's* case ([1924] 1 K. B. 566) was a Roumanian, and Roumania was an ally of England, though it may be that the principal was in a part of Roumania occupied by the Germans, and was therefore to be treated as an enemy. Compare *Société Anonyme Belge des Mines d'Aljustrel (Portugal)* v. *Anglo-Belgian Agency* ([1915] 2 Ch. 409). The decision of Greer J. in *Ananiadi* v. *Ottoman Bank* (unreported; decided March 12, 1923), to which we were referred, gives more trouble. It is not very clear how the goods in question in that case got to Turkey, but apparently before the war they had got into the hands of the Ottoman Bank at Constantinople as bankers for reward, though the bank there did not know for whom they were acting, and the question who put the goods in bailment with the Ottoman Bank is left in doubt. Then came the war, and the first part of the judgment of Greer J., with which I agree, is that the war invalidated all obligations of the Turkish bank to the English enemy. The bank had not advanced any money on the security of the documents or goods. But having held that the bank were under no obligation as to the goods the learned judge says: "Now they (the bank) were in a position in which they were bound to do something, otherwise the goods would be entirely lost . . . and therefore they were in a position of agents of necessity." I do not follow the reasoning; if all prior obligations were invalidated by the outbreak of war, how could an implied obligation arise between enemies? How could the bank be "bound" to an enemy to do anything? How is an enemy bound to take steps to preserve the property of his enemy? So far as I understand the facts in this case, I doubt whether the latter part of the judgment of Greer J. can be supported.

[A paragraph dealing with the Treaty of Lausanne is omitted.]

Rowlatt J. gave judgment for the sterling amount of the bills on considerations of contract, and did not apparently deal with the effects of war, or the construction of the Treaty. In my view the true legal effect of what has happened is that the bank during the war converted the goods of the plaintiff, and, when the plaintiff sues after the war, must pay damages for conversion, to be ascertained by an inquiry unless the parties agree. The measure of damages was not argued before us, and I express no opinion on it.

The judgment of Rowlatt J. in favor of the plaintiff should be varied in the way indicated, but as the defendants have substantially failed they must pay the costs of the appeal. The costs of the inquiry should be in the discretion of the tribunal taking the inquiry.

ATKIN L.J. concurred.

Judgment varied.

Compare with PRAGER *v.* BLATSPIEL, STAMP & HEACOCK, LTD., (1924) 1 K. B. 566, where a London fur dealer, still in possession of furs sold to the plaintiff during the war and substantially paid for, resold the furs to others because of inability either to send the furs to the original purchaser or to communicate with him. On the facts of the case, it was held that there was no necessity for the resale; but McCardie, J., expressed the view that the doctrine of agency of necessity should not be restricted to carriers.

COMMONWEALTH TRUST LTD. *v.* AKOTEY

PRIVY COUNCIL, 1925

[*Law Reports*, [1926] *Appeal Cases*, 72]

Appeal (No. 131 of 1924) from a judgment of the Full Court of the Gold Coast Colony (November 12, 1923) reversing a judgment of Beatty J.

[One and one-half pages containing statement of facts and arguments of counsel are here omitted.]

The judgment of their Lordships was delivered by LORD SHAW. This is an appeal from a judgment of the Full Court of the Gold Coast Colony, reversing the judgment of the judge of first instance.

The action was brought by the respondent against the appellants and a co-defendant, named Laing, for damages for the conversion of 1050 bags of cocoa. This cocoa was consigned by respondent to Laing: the consignment notes were duly forwarded; Laing transferred these to the appellants, who, in entire good faith, took delivery of and paid Laing for the cocoa. The Full Court entered judgment for the respondent for the sum of

6375*l.* and costs. If the respondent is entitled to recover, this figure is not disputed. This means that the appellants are to pay a second time for the same cocoa on the alleged ground that the respondent cannot be charged with any responsibility for the sale by Laing, his consignee, and the receipt of payment by Laing.

The respondent is a grower of cocoa, and the appellants are a limited company carrying on business at Accra, including a business of general export and import. The co-defendant Laing is dead, but it is in evidence that he had on previous occasions in the year 1920 purchased cocoa on credit from the respondent, or the respondent's factor.

A question raised in the appeal is whether the cocoa about which the dispute has arisen had become the property of Laing, so as to place him in a position to transfer it with a good title to the appellants. The judge of first instance held that the property in the cocoa had passed from the respondent to Laing, and if it had so passed the appellants would be entitled to judgment. The Full Court held that the sale of the cocoa had not been completed between Laing and the respondent.

A material question in the case is whether a certain letter of April 30, 1920, is genuine. The judge of first instance was not satisfied as to the genuineness of this letter, but the Full Court held that without deciding whether it was genuine, or not, the case could be decided apart from that. The Board is of opinion that the alleged letter cannot be relied upon as a genuine letter.

The other correspondence is as follows: the first letter of April 28 states that the respondent has that day "consigned 492 bags, viz.: 242 in waggon No. 1274, and 250 bags in waggon No. 1213," and the letter adds this important sentence, "And consignment note of it I have attached to this letter and I am sure you will get it safely." This letter covers part of the cocoa in question in this case. The letter ends: "Expect me on the coming Monday, and I will come and see you."

A second letter was written on April 29 stating that a further consignment had been made, and adding: "Consignment note of it enclosed with my best compliments." The cocoa referred to in these two letters covers 756 bags out of the 1050 bags included in the writ of summons. A further letter was written on April 29 stating that the respondent had shipped 250 bags of cocoa, but these bags are not part of the cocoa in question. It includes, however, the sentence, "Find more money (cash) and I will come on Monday, May 3, 1920, to receive it."

Laing sold the cocoa to Lawson, the transport manager of the appellants, and handed him the consignment notes. Lawson took delivery by reconsigning the bags in which the cocoa was packed to the railway sidings of the appellants. It is not disputed that the actings of the appellants were in good faith, nor that the purchase was made in ordinary course of business and for full value.

It turns out that although Laing had the goods consigned to him, he and the respondent had a difference as to price, the respondent wishing Laing to increase the figure of 50*s*. a ton which Laing had named.

On May 1 the respondent came down to Accra and saw Laing, who stated that he was prepared to pay the respondent 50*s*. a load, but this the respondent refused to accept. Their Lordships inclined to agree with the decision of the Full Court that the price of 50*s*. had not been accepted by the respondent when he forwarded the consignment note to Laing, and that consequently no contract of sale had been completed at the material date.

It was further argued before their Lordships that although the property in the cocoa had not passed from the respondent, yet that the respondent had so acted as to estop him from setting up his title in answer to the claim of the appellants. Reliance was placed on the well-known statement of Ashhurst J. in *Lickbarrow* v. *Mason* (2 T. R. 63, 70), "that wherever one of two innocent persons must suffer by the acts of a third, he who has enabled such third person to occasion the loss must sustain it." Their Lordships are clearly of opinion that the present is a plain case for the application of that principle. There is no kind of specialty in this case such as occurred in *Farquharson Bros. & Co.* v. *King & Co.* ([1902] A. C. 325), the parallel to which would be that the goods were delivered to Laing by the fraudulent act of respondent's agent: the goods were in fact delivered over to Laing by the direct act of the respondent himself.

To permit goods to go into the possession of another, with all the insignia of possession thereof and of apparent title, and to leave it open to go behind that possession so given and accompanied, and upset a purchase of the goods made for full value and in good faith, would bring confusion into mercantile transactions, and would be inconsistent with law and with the principles so frequently affirmed, following *Lickbarrow* v. *Mason* (2 T. R. 63, 70).

Their Lordships will humbly advise His Majesty that the appeal should be allowed, the judgment of the Full Court set aside with costs, and the judgment of Beatty J. restored. The respondent will pay the costs of the appeal.

MOORE, NETTLEFOLD & CO. *v.* THE SINGER MANUFACTURING CO.

COURT OF APPEAL, 1904

[*Law Reports*, [1904] 1 *King's Bench*, 820]

Appeal from the judgment of a Divisional Court, reported [1903] 2 K. B. 168, upon an appeal from a decision of the judge of the Shoreditch County Court.

The action was brought to recover a sewing machine which the plaintiffs claimed as their property.

[The statement of facts and the proceedings on the hearing and argument of the appeal, totalling over four pages, are here omitted.]

COLLINS M.R. This is an appeal from a decision of a Divisional Court, and the question arises out of a distress for rent put in by the plaintiffs as landlords. Among the goods seized was a sewing machine which had been hired by the tenant from the defendants upon a hire-purchase agreement. Under the distress that was put in this machine was sold by public auction, and an agent employed by the landlords bought it apparently at a fair price, and they relet it on the hire-purchase system to the tenant. Thereupon the defendants, who had originally owned the machine and let it to the tenant seized it for default of payment of instalments under their agreement. The landlords thereupon brought this action, and the question is whether the landlords had on the sale by auction acquired a property in the machine. The case appears to me to be on all fours with *King* v. *England* (4 B. & S. 782), the only difference being that in that case an appraisement was necessary, and the landlord, who was the person authorized by s. 2 of 2 Will. & M. Sess. 1, c. 5, to sell the goods, took over the goods of a third person which had been distrained at the appraised value and with the consent of the tenant, and thus stood in the position both of buyer and seller. He then gave them to the plaintiff, and thereupon the true owner followed and seized them. The action was brought to recover the goods, and the question arose which is the same as that in the case before us. It was there held that the transaction with respect to the goods did not vest the property in them in the landlord. The difference between the cases is that here there was the formality of a sale by auction; but the substance of the cases is the same, namely, a sale by a landlord to himself. It is true, as has been suggested, that the auctioneer may be for some purposes the agent of both parties; but in selling he is the agent of the landlord who sold, though later on he might become for some purposes the agent of the buyer. It appears then that the same mischief arises in such a case as the present as would arise in a case like *King* v. *England* (4 B. & S. 782) by the landlord being himself both buyer and seller. As was pointed out by Blackburn J. in that case and by Wills J. in the present one, to hold that a landlord might sell to himself would open the door to abuses. It seems to me, both on principle and authority, that the judgment of the Court below was right. The appeal must therefore be dismissed.

[The brief concurring opinion of Mathew, L.J., is here omitted.]

Compare with GRAFF *v.* EVANS, 8 Q. B. D. 373 (1882), where the manager of a club was prosecuted under the Licensing Act on the charge that he did "unlawfully sell and expose for sale by retail certain intoxicating liquor." Foster, a member of the club, had purchased at the bar of the club a bottle of whisky and a bottle of pale ale, which were wrapped for him and taken from the premises by him. The rules of the club provided that all property acquired by the club should be vested in trustees elected by the members. Field, J., said, *inter alia*: "The question here is, did Graff, the manager, who supplied the liquors to Foster, effect a 'sale' by retail? I think not. I think Foster was an owner of the property together with all the other members of the club. Any member was entitled to obtain the goods on payment of the price. A sale involves the element of a bargain. There was no bargain here, nor any contract with Graff with respect to the goods. Foster was acting upon his rights as a member of the club, not by reason of any new contract, but under his old contract of association by which he subscribed a sum to the funds of the club, and became entitled to have ale and whisky supplied to him as a member at a certain price. I cannot conceive it possible that Graff could have sued him for the price as the price of goods sold and delivered. There was no contract between two persons, because Foster was vendor as well as buyer. Taking the transaction to be a purchase by Foster of all the other members' shares in the goods, Foster was as much a co-owner as the vendor. I think it was a transfer of a special property in the goods to Foster, which was not a sale within the meaning of the section. I am of opinion that the conviction should be reversed."

ARMSTRONG *v.* JACKSON

KING'S BENCH, 1917

[*Law Reports,* [1917] 2 *King's Bench,* 822]

Trial of action before McCardie J. without a jury.

The following statement of the facts is taken from the written judgment of the learned judge: —

The plaintiff is a medical man without business experience. The defendant is a stockbroker and a member of the London Stock Exchange. Prior to April, 1910, the defendant had acted as stockbroker for the plaintiff and had carried through several transactions for him. On April 12, 1910, the plaintiff by telegram instructed the defendant to buy for him 600 shares in a company known as the Champion Gold Reefs of West Africa, Limited. The capital of the company was 50,000*l.* in 200,000 shares of 5*s.* each. On the evening of April 12 the defendant wrote to the plaintiff informing him that his order had been executed, and sent with the letter a contract note in the ordinary form, purporting to show that the 600 shares had been purchased at the price of $2^{29}/_{32}$*l.* per share. The total amount debited against the plaintiff was the sum of 1758*l.* 16*s.* This sum included a charge of 15*l.* for the services of the defendant as broker. The plaintiff did not immediately take up the shares. The defendant purported to carry them over from account to account on the plaintiff's behalf. He charged a contango rate varying from 7 per cent. to 8 per cent. The continuation notes stated that this rate included remuneration to the defendant for his services as broker in effecting the continuations. The shares gradually fell. The plaintiff paid the resultant differences. He became anxious. He asked the defendant for his views. The defendant advised him to take up the shares. In pursuance of that advice the plaintiff took a transfer of the shares in December, 1910, and paid the price to the defendant. The plaintiff continued to hold the shares as the duly registered proprietor thereof. The years passed on. In the summer of 1915 the plaintiff heard rumors which awakened his suspicions. His solicitor wrote to the defendant for the name of the jobber from whom he had bought the 600 shares on the plaintiff's behalf. No satisfactory answer was given, and thereupon this action was commenced. Discovery of documents was obtained and interrogatories were administered. As a result of these proceedings it has been established that the defendant had never purchased any of the shares for the plaintiff. The contract note of April, 1910, was wholly fictitious. It was a mere sham. The defendant had not carried over any of the shares on behalf of the plaintiff. The contango notes were fictitious. It is equally clear that the shares which were transferred to the plantiff in December, 1910, were not the shares of a third party, but were the defendant's own shares. The defendant had been a promoter of the Champion Gold Reefs of West Africa. He had received by allotment a large block of shares on the formation of the company, including the shares transferred to the plantiff in December, 1910. From first to last the defendant made no disclosure whatever to the plaintiff of the true facts. He purported to act as a broker, whereas in fact he was really acting as a principal. The plaintiff was deceived throughout. Hence the plaintiff claims (*a*) that the whole transaction be set aside, or (*b*) alternatively that the defendant be ordered to pay compensation for breach of duty. It should be added that the value of Champion Gold Reef shares at the date of the writ was about 5*s.* per share. . . .

McCardie J. read a judgment which, after the statement of the facts set out above, proceeded as follows: — First as to the claim to avoid the transaction. It is obvious that the defendant gravely failed in his duty to the plaintiff. He was instructed to buy shares. But he never carried out his mandate. A broker who is employed to buy shares cannot sell his own shares unless he make a full and accurate disclosure of the fact to his principal, and the principal, with a full knowledge, gives his assent to the changed position of the broker. The rule is one not merely of law but of obvious morality. As was said by Lord Cairns in *Parker* v. *McKenna* ((1874) L. R. 10 Ch. 96, 118), "No man can in this Court, acting as an agent, be allowed to put himself into a position in which his interest and his duty will be in conflict." Now a broker who secretly sells his own shares is in a wholly false position. As vendor it is to his interest to sell his shares at the highest price. As broker it is his clear duty to the principal to buy at the lowest price and to give unbiassed and independent advice (if such be asked) as to the time when and the price at which shares shall be bought, or whether they shall be bought at all. The law has ever required a high measure of good faith from an agent. He departs from good faith when he secretly sells his own property to the principal. The rule has long been the same, both at law and equity: see Story on Agency, s. 210. It matters not that the broker sells at the market price, or that he acts without intent to defraud: see *Bentley* v. *Craven* ((1853) 18 Beav. 75). The prohibition of the law is absolute. It will not allow an agent to place himself in a situation which, under ordinary circumstances, would tempt a man to do that which is not the best for his principal: see per Romilly M.R. in *Bentley* v. *Craven* ((1853) 18 Beav. 75). The Court will not enter into discussion as to the propriety of the price charged by the broker, nor is it material to inquire whether the principal has or has not suffered a loss. If the breach of duty by the broker be shown, the Court will set aside the transaction: see *Gillett* v. *Peppercorne* ((1840) 3 Beav. 78). The rule was strikingly illustrated in the case of *Rothschild* v. *Brookman* ((1831) 5 Bli. (N.S.) 165, 197). The facts in that case were not dissimilar to the facts in the present action. The House of Lords (affirming the Court below) set aside transactions in which the agent had secretly acted as principal. In giving his opinion Lord Wynford (formerly Best C.J.) used these words: "If any man who is to be trusted places himself in a condition in which he has an opportunity of taking advantage of his employer, by placing himself in such a situation, whether acting fairly or not, he must suffer the consequence of his situation. Such is the jealousy which the law of England entertains against any such transactions."

It follows that in the present case the plaintiff is *prima facie* entitled to a decree setting aside the transaction in question.

[The remaining six and one-half pages of the opinion, holding the execution of this contract and change of circumstances to be immaterial, are omitted.]

Judgment for plaintiff.

Compare with HOCKER *v.* WALLER, 29 Com. Cas. 296 (K. B., 1924), where the plaintiff employed the defendant to sell certain furniture for £3,000. Being unable to find a purchaser, defendant agreed with plaintiff to buy the furniture himself, but claimed the right to retain £125 of the price as commission. In an action to recover this amount, Talbot, J., said in part: "There is one reported case, *Saloman* v. *Pender* ([1865] 3 H. & C. 639), which has been cited, in which an agent employed to sell property for his principal sold it to himself or to a company of which he was a director and shareholder, without disclosing to his principal what he was doing. Of course such a transaction as that could not stand at all. But there is nothing of that kind here. The plaintiff knew what Mr. Waller was doing, and he was perfectly above-board in his dealings with her. Among other questions that had to be decided between them was how much he should pay her for the furniture. There was apparently no dispute as to the lease; he was to take an underlease and pay £600 a year. As to the furniture, he thought something under £2,000 was quite enough. She thought the figure should be nearly £4,000; and ultimately he agreed to give and she agreed to accept £3,000.

"I think it a very important point in the case that (and there is no dispute as to the fact) down to February 24 there was no suggestion by the defendant that when he said he would give £3,000 for this furniture he meant £3,000 less his commission; and although, as I have said, there was no concealment or malpractice of any kind to be attributed to the defendant, I do think that if an agent turns himself into a principal in a transaction for the purchase of property and intends to charge his principal the commission which he would have charged if he had sold the property to a third party, he is bound to make that quite clear to his principal. I do not think that any person selling property would understand that if he sold it to a person who had previously acted as his agent he would have to allow a commission to that person, any more than he would have to allow a commission to any other purchaser. It is said against that — and one quite sees its force as an argument of equity or business — 'If you were prepared to take £3,000 from an outside purchaser on which you would have had to allow me commission you can afford to let me personally have the property for £3,000 less the commission.' That may be; but if an arrangement of that kind is to be made it should be made expressly; and I think that as a matter of law there can be no question that this commission was not payable unless an agreement to pay it can be proved."

2. THE GOODS

A. Existing and Future Goods

BRYAN *v.* LEWIS

King's Bench, 1826

[*Ryan & Moody's Reports*, 386]

This was an action against a broker for negligence in the sale of a certain quantity of nutmegs.

In February 1823, the defendant sold the nutmegs to one Dawson, to be delivered on the 6th of May following.

The warrants for the nutmegs were tendered to the purchaser on the 6th of May, but he was unable to pay for them. It also appeared that Dawson was a minor, and a person of no property or expectations.

It was proved that the plaintiff was not the owner of the nutmegs at the time of making the contract, and that he had bought them on the following 9th of March.

A question was likewise made whether the defendant had been employed by the plaintiff to sell the nutmegs, or by a person of the name of Sentence.

Abbott Ld. C. J. I am clearly of opinion that this action cannot be maintained; I have always thought, and shall continue to think, until I am told by the House of Lords that I am wrong, that if a man sells goods to be delivered on a future day, and neither has the goods at the time, nor has entered into any prior contract to buy them, nor has any reasonable expectation of receiving them by consignment, but means to go into the market and to buy the goods which he has contracted to deliver, he cannot maintain an action upon such a contract. Such a contract amounts, on the part of the vendor, to a wager on the price of the commodity, and is attended with the most mischievous consequences.

Campbell, for the plaintiff, observed, that however beneficial such a law might be, it would at first introduce a most material change in the proceedings of the Royal Exchange.

Abbott Ld. C. J. The law is not new, and if it had been acted upon during the last twelve months, much of that distress which now presses upon the community would have been avoided. I am anxious my opinion should be known, that if wrong it may be corrected, and if right that it may be acted upon. However, to give the plaintiff an opportunity of having my opinion reviewed, I shall put it to the jury to say whether the defendant was employed by the plaintiff to sell the nutmegs.

The jury found that the defendant was not employed by the plaintiff to sell the nutmegs, upon which the plaintiff was nonsuited.

Nonsuit.

Compare with MORTIMER *v.* M'CALLAN, 6 M. & W. 58 (Exchequer, 1840), where a contract for the sale of stock not at the time owned by the seller was held to be enforceable, Lord Abinger, C. B., saying: "The next point is, that the stock was not the stock of the plaintiff, but was Ward's stock; and it is said that the plaintiff could not enforce his contract for the sale of this stock, because he had none at the time of the contract. That general proposition certainly is not true; how many merchants are there who make contracts to sell things which they are not in possession of? Can it be doubted, that a man who has made a contract to sell that which he is not then possessed of, if he obtain means to perform that contract, and to deliver the thing sold, by his own hands or by the agency of another, is entitled to recover the price of it?"

Note also AJELLO *v.* WORSLEY, [1898] 1 Ch. 274, where the defendant advertised for sale a new piano of a certain make and description, although he had none of the kind in stock, and where Stirling, J., said: "I further think that as a general rule any person may sell or offer for sale at any price whatsoever goods of which he is not the owner, but which he expects or hopes to acquire."

GRANTHAM *v.* HAWLEY

COURT OF COMMON PLEAS, 1615

[*Hobart's Reports*, 132]

Robert Grantham brought an action of debt upon an obligation of forty pounds against Edward Hawley, the condition whereof was, that if a certain crop of corn growing upon a certain piece of ground, late in the occupation of Richard Sankee, did of right belong to the plaintiff, then the defendant should pay him for it twenty pounds. Now the case upon the pleading and demurrer fell out thus; that one Sutton was seised of the land, and 30 Eliz. in April, made a lease of it to Richard Sankee for twenty-one years by indenture, and did thereby covenant, grant to and with Sankee, his executors and assigns, that it shall be lawful for him to take and carry away, to his own use, such corn as should be growing upon the ground at the end of the term. Then Sutton conveyed the reversion to the plaintiff; and John Sankee, executor to Richard, having sowed the corn, and that being growing upon the ground at the end of the term, sold it to the defendant. And it was argued by Hutton for the plaintiff, that it was merely contingent whether there should be corn growing upon the ground at the end of the term, or not. Also, the lessor never had property in the corn; and therefore could not give nor grant it, but it sounded properly in covenant; for the right of the corn standing in the end of the term being certain, accrues with the land to the lessor; and it was said to be adjudged. And it was agreed by the court that if A., seised of land, sow it with corn, and then convey it away to B. for life, remainder to C. for life, and then B. die before the corn reapt; now

C. shall have it, and not the executors of B., though his estate was uncertain. Note, the reason of industry and charge in B. fails; yet judgment in this case was given against the plaintiff, that is, that the property and very right of the corn, when it happened, was past away; for it was both a covenant and a grant. And therefore if it had been of natural fruits, as of grass or hay, which run merely with the land, the like grant would have carried them in property after the term. Now though corn be *fructus industrialis*, so that he that sows it may seem to have a kind of property, *ipso facto*, in it, divided from the land; and therefore the executor shall have it, and not the heirs; yet in this case, all the colour that the plaintiff hath to it, is by the land which he claims from the lessor which gave the corn. And though the lessor had it not actually in him, nor certain, yet he had it potentially; for the land is the mother and root of all fruits. Therefore he that hath it may grant all fruits that may arise upon it after, and the property shall pass as soon as the fruits are extant, as 21 H. 6. A parson may grant all the tithe wool that he shall have in such a year; yet perhaps he shall have none; but a man cannot grant all the wool that shall grow upon his sheep that he shall buy hereafter; for there he hath it neither actually nor potentially. And though the words are here not by words of gift of the corn, but that it shall be lawful for him to take it to his own use, it is as good to transfer the property; for the intent and common use of such words, as a lease without impeachment of waste, for the like reason, and not *ex vi termini*, gives the trees.

LOW *v.* PEW

MASSACHUSETTS SUPREME JUDICIAL COURT, 1871

[108 *Massachusetts Reports*, 347]

Replevin by the firm of Alfred Low & Company of a lot of flitched halibut from the assignees in bankruptcy of the firm of John Low & Son, all of Gloucester. Writ dated August 24, 1869. The parties stated the following case for the judgment of the court:

On April 17, 1869, as the schooner Florence Reed, owned by John Low & Son, was about to sail from Gloucester on a fishing voyage, that firm received $1500 from the plaintiffs, and signed and gave the plaintiffs the following writing:

We, John Low & Son, hereby sell, assign and set over unto Alfred Low & Company all the halibut that may be caught by the master and crew of the schooner Florence Reed, on the voyage upon which she is about to proceed from the port of Gloucester to the Grand Banks, at the rate of five cents and a quarter per pound for flitched halibut, to be delivered to said Alfred Low & Company as soon as said schooner arrives at said port of Gloucester at their wharf. And we, the said John Low & Son, hereby acknowledge the receipt of $1500 in part payment for the halibut that may be caught by the master and crew of said schooner on said voyage.

In July 1869 proceedings in bankruptcy were begun against John Low & Son in the district court of the United States for this district, in which they were adjudged bankrupts on August 6, and on August 20 these defendants were appointed the assignees in bankruptcy, and the deed of assignment was executed to them. On Saturday, August 14, the Florence Reed arrived at the port of Gloucester on her home voyage, and was hauled to the plaintiffs' wharf; and on the morning of Monday, August 16, the United States marshal took possession of the vessel and cargo under a warrant issued to him on August 6 in the proceedings in bankruptcy, and transferred his possession to the defendants upon their appointment.

The catch of the schooner consisted of about 40,000 pounds of halibut, and of some codfish. The plaintiffs demanded the halibut of the defendants, and offered at the same time to pay the price of it at the rate of five and a quarter cents per pound, less the $1500 already paid. The defendants refused the demand; and the plaintiffs then replevied such a quantity of the halibut as represented the amount of $1500 at that rate per pound, and offered to receive the rest of the halibut and pay for it at the same rate, but the defendants refused to acknowledge any right whatever of the plaintiffs in or to the fish.

If on these facts the plaintiffs were entitled to recover, they were to have judgment for nominal damages; but if otherwise, the defendants were to have judgment for a return, with damages equal to interest at the annual rate of six per cent. on the appraised value of the fish replevied.

MORTON, J. By the decree adjudging John Low & Son bankrupts, all their property, except such as is exempted by the bankrupt law, was brought within the custody of the law, and by the subsequent assignment passed to their assignees. *Williams* v. *Merritt*, 103 Mass. 184. The firm could not by a subsequent sale and delivery transfer any of such property to the plaintiffs. The schooner which contained the halibut in suit arrived in Gloucester August 14, 1869, which was after the decree of bankruptcy. If there had been then a sale and delivery to the plaintiffs of the property replevied, it would have been invalid. The plaintiffs therefore show no title to the halibut replevied, unless the effect of the contract of April 17, 1869, was to vest in them the property in the halibut before the bankruptcy. It seems to us clear, as claimed by both parties, that this was a contract of sale, and not a mere executory agreement to sell at some future day. The plaintiffs cannot maintain their suit upon any other construction, because, if it is an executory agreement to sell, the property in the halibut remained in the bankrupts, and, there being no delivery before the bankruptcy, passed to the assignees. The question in the case therefore is, whether a sale of halibut afterwards to be caught is valid, so as to pass to the purchaser the property in them when caught.

It is an elementary principle of the law of sales, that a man cannot grant personal property in which he has no interest or title. To be able to sell property, he must have a vested right in it at the time of the sale. Thus it has been held that a mortgage of goods which the mortgagor does not own at the time the mortgage is made, though he afterwards acquires them, is void. *Jones* v. *Richardson*, 10 Met. 481. The same principle is applicable to all sales of personal property.

It is equally well settled that it is sufficient if the seller has a potential interest in the thing sold. But a mere possibility or expectancy of acquiring property, not coupled with any interest, does not constitute a potential interest in it, within the meaning of this rule. The seller must have a present interest in the property, of which the thing sold is the product, growth or increase. Having such interest, the right to the thing sold, when it shall come into existence, is a present vested right, and the sale of it is valid. Thus a man may sell the wool to grow upon his own sheep, but not upon the sheep of another; or the crops to grow upon his own land, but not upon land in which he has no interest.

The same principles have been applied by this court to the assignment of future wages or earnings. In *Mulhall* v. *Quinn*, 1 Gray, 105, an assignment of future wages, there being no contract of service, was held invalid. In *Hartley* v. *Tapley*, 2 Gray, 565, it was held that, if a person is under a contract of service, he may assign his future earnings growing out of such contract. The distinction between the cases is, that in the former the future earnings are a mere possibility, coupled with no interest, while in the latter the possibility of future earnings is coupled with an interest, and the right to them, though contingent and liable to be defeated, is a vested right.

In the case at bar, the sellers, at the time of the sale, had no interest in the thing sold. There was a possibility that they might catch halibut; but it was a mere possibility and expectancy, coupled with no interest. We are of opinion that they had no actual or potential possession of, or interest in, the fish; and that the sale to the plaintiffs was void.

The plaintiffs rely upon *Gardner* v. *Hoeg*, 18 Pick. 168, and *Tripp* v. *Brownell*, 12 Cush. 376. In both of these cases it was held that the lay or share in the profits, which a seaman in a whaling voyage agreed to receive in lieu of wages, was assignable. The assignment in each case was, not of any part of the oil to be made, but of the debt which under the shipping articles would become due to the seaman from the owners at the end of the voyage. The court treated them as cases of assignments of choses in action. The question upon which the case at bar turns did not arise, and was not considered.

Judgment for the defendants.

GILE & CO. *v.* LASSELLE

OREGON SUPREME COURT, 1918

[89 *Oregon Reports*, 107]

This is an action of replevin in which the plaintiffs seek to recover "about 794 bags of Oregon prunes," containing "about 70,000 pounds" of the value of $4,500. They allege that the property was in possession of one Percival I. Rust, on storage by them, subject to their order and shipping directions, and that the defendant wrongfully took the prunes from the possession of Rust, caused them to be loaded into a railway car and shipped to Albany where the defendant detains them unlawfully to the plaintiffs' damage in the sum of $350. They demand judgment for the recovery of possession of the property, or for $4,500 as its value alternatively, together with $350 damages.

The answer denies the whole complaint and avers that a partnership by the name of John H. Leslie & Company of Chicago, Illinois, employed the defendant, as its agent, to purchase, treat and pack prunes, in pursuance of which he purchased from Rust 74,661 pounds of prunes of the reasonable value of $5,200, the same being contained in the 794 bags and being the identical prunes described in the plaintiffs' complaint. He says, also, that for his services so rendered, he was to receive a commission of one cent per pound, and that after the fruit had been properly treated and packed he was required to ship it immediately to Leslie & Company. He avers that he bought the prunes in question with the money of his principal, took it into his own custody and, while he was engaged in treating and packing it, the plaintiffs took the same by virtue of a writ of replevin issued in the present case. He states that at the time alleged in the complaint he was, and at all times since then, has been and still is entitled to the immediate possession of the prunes and the whole thereof; that Leslie & Company are the absolute owners of said property and that this defendant as their agent is entitled to the immediate possession thereof.

Further answering, the defendant sets up a contract entered into on June 27, 1916, between the plaintiffs and Rust, of which the following is a copy:

[The complete contract is omitted. Material portions were: "In consideration of the prices per pound herein specified, Percival I. Rust, the seller, has sold, and H. S. Gile Company, the buyer, has bought the hereinbefore mentioned 1916 crop of prunes produced during the current year, upon the following described property, the output of his dryer at Cottage Grove, guaranteed to not be less than one minimum carload, which crop said seller agrees to properly dry, cure and deliver in its entirety, unless otherwise agreed to in writing by buyer, and hereby guarantees to be the sole and absolute property of seller, and free from all incumbrances. . . . This contract is understood by both parties to constitute an absolute sale, but until delivery has been completed seller agrees to and does assume all risk of loss or damage."]

He states that at the time this agreement was made, Rust was not the owner of any prunes of any kind or nature, nor of any orchard or trees upon which such fruit would grow, nor was he the owner of any contracts for prunes, all of which was known and understood by both him and plaintiffs. The defendant claims that he bought the property in question from Rust about November 23, 1916, in good faith, believing that Rust was the owner thereof.

For another answer the defendant pleads what he claims is an estoppel operating against the plaintiffs and denying them the right to claim property in the fruit in question on the ground that they permitted Rust to retain the possession of it, to employ labor in and about it and to exercise acts of ownership over it; that finding Rust in possession of the property under such circumstances and being without any knowledge or intimation that plaintiff had any right to it, the defendant bought the same for his principal, paid Rust the price thereof and took it into his own possession.

The reply challenges the new matter in the answer in material particulars, avows the making of the contract quoted in the defendant's pleading and states that in pursuance thereof Rust did afterwards produce, procure and have ready for delivery the prunes here involved and notified the plaintiffs that the same were ready for delivery; that they thereupon shipped to him the necessary sacks to contain them, having thereon the firm name of the plaintiffs, into which defendant Rust put the prunes for the purpose of fulfilling the contract; that the fruit was in those bags at the time the defendant took it, which he did with knowledge that it was the property of the plaintiffs. The jury rendered a verdict to the effect that defendant is entitled to a return of the property described as 74,661 pounds of prunes of the value of $5,000, together with damages in the sum of $500. Judgment was rendered upon this verdict in favor of the defendant for the return of the property with $500 damages, or, in case the property could not be returned, that the defendant have and recover from the plaintiffs $5,000, together with $500 damages and costs and disbursements. The plaintiffs appeal. Affirmed. . . .

Burnett, J. Both parties attempt to deraign title to the property from Rust. This is an action at law and not a suit in equity and the matter must be adjudicated by legal rules as distinguished from equitable maxims.

[A page of the opinion dealing with certain immaterial rulings of the court below is omitted.]

The theory of the plaintiffs is that the legal effect of the agreement in question was to transfer the title to the property from Rust to them, if not at its date, at least at the moment when he had in his possession as the output of his drier, dried prunes which were suitable for filling the contract. The defendant maintains that at best it was an executory agreement which conveyed to the plaintiffs no present title or right of immediate possession without which they cannot maintain replevin. Putting ourselves in the position of the parties on June 27, 1916, when the contract was made, as we are required to do by Section 717, L. O. L., we must know by the laws of nature and the fruit season in this country that there was then no present crop of prunes of the season of 1916, dried and ready for shipment, even if the seller had an orchard upon which potential property in such fruit could be predicated. The testimony shows without dispute that at that time Rust had no prunes of any kind and no orchard or contract by means of which he could expect to acquire them. It is common sense that a man cannot presently convey title to property which is not in existence. It is true that he may make a contract for future delivery, although he has no property of the kind on hand when the stipulation is made. The authorities, however, are practically unanimous that such a covenant is executory in its nature, notwithstanding it contains present words of selling and buying.

In the present instance the writing begins with the recital that the seller "has sold" and the buyer "has bought" the 1916 crop of prunes, the output of Rust's drier. It is also said in the body of the instrument: "This contract is understood by both parties to constitute an absolute sale, but until the delivery has been completed the seller agrees to and does assume all risk of loss or damage." This language is no stronger than that above mentioned and adds nothing to its force. It does not amount, in effect, to any more than saying that when the terms of the writing have all been fulfilled, the result will be an absolute sale. When we consider the whole instrument together we find that in it there are dependent covenants, the performance of which must be synchronous and that neither party can put the other in default until he has himself fully performed or tendered performance of what he is to do on his part. This doctrine is illustrated in such cases as *Lewis* v. *Craft,* 39 Or. 305 (64 Pac. 809); *Longfellow* v. *Huffman,* 49 Or. 486, 490 (90 Pac. 907). The principle that at law the seller cannot presently pass title to property which is not in existence, either actually or potentially, or which he must hereafter acquire, is enunciated in the cases of *Fonville* v. *Casey,* 5 N. C. 389 (4 Am. Dec. 559); *Moody* v. *Wright,* 13 Met. (54 Mass.) 17 (46 Am. Dec. 706); and *Dickey* v. *Waldo,* 97 Mich. 255 (56 N. W. 608, 23 L. R. A. 449, and notes). It is argued by the plaintiffs that although title did not pass at the date of the contract on account of the property not being then in existence, yet afterward when the seller did acquire the fruit of the kind and quality prescribed by the agreement, the ownership then automatically passed to the plaintiffs in manner and form sufficient to support replevin. The rule supported by the authorities quoted, as well as by most other precedents, however, is that in order really to pass the title, as distinguished from rights under an executory contract, when the property has actually come into existence and possession of the seller, there must be some further act of the parties amounting to a performance in that feature of the covenant which hitherto has been executory. The plaintiffs and Rust entered into an agreement the working out of which was designed to pass the title to personal property from the latter to the former. The terms of that process are described in their writing. They expressly say that the "buyer agrees to pay for said crop at the price named when delivery is completed." Without respect to the general property in the prunes, in whomsoever that may be, as against the action for mere possession of them Rust would be entitled to hold the property under this contract until plaintiffs had performed their concurrent covenant of paying at the time of delivery. This court has several times held that a claim under an executory contract will not support replevin by the buyer from the seller.

[The next three and one-half pages of the opinion, dealing largely with the question of damages, are here omitted.]

The most that the plaintiffs have shown is an executory contract on the part of Rust to sell and deliver prunes. For the default of Rust in failing to comply with his contract, if there was such a failure, the only remedy the plaintiffs have, if any, is by an action for damages for the breach of the executory contract so far as this record discloses.

These considerations lead to an affirmance of the judgment.

Affirmed.

McBride, C. J., Benson and Harris, JJ., concur.

HOGUE–KELLOGG CO. *v.* BAKER

California District Court of Appeal, 1920

[47 *California Appellate Reports*, 247]

James, J. Appeal from a judgment entered in favor of the plaintiff upon an alleged cause of action for damages arising because of defendant's failure to perform the obligations imposed by written contract.

The case went to judgment after answer and trial. The only contention made by appellant, however, is that the court erred in overruling his demurrer, which was interposed to the complaint of plaintiff. It is insisted that the complaint failed to state facts sufficient to constitute a cause of action. The contract for the breach of which plaintiff sought damages is set out in the complaint and is as follows:

J. S. Baker of Norwalk, California, does hereby agree to grow for The Hogue-Kellogg Company, of Ventura, California, 20 acres of Henderson Bush beans, to be grown during the farming season of 1917, on land situated near Norwalk, Calif., known as Baker ranch, and to deliver the entire crop product thereof. The beans are to be delivered as soon as possible after threshing, properly recleaned, free from damage of any kind, in first-class shipping condition, sacked in new bean bags to be even weighted and so stenciled, f. o. b. cars at Buena Park, Calif.

The Hogue-Kellogg Company agrees to pay for said beans on net weight at $4.25 dollars, per hundred pounds, delivered f. o. b. cars at Buena Park, Calif., on or before December 1st, 1917. And in case delivery is not made within the final time limit, it is optional with the Hogue-Kellogg Company to consider this contract in force or to cancel same.

In case it rains, damaging the beans, said beans shall be handpicked and put in the condition as above stated.

It is mutually agreed that The Hogue-Kellogg Company will sell seed beans for planting the above acreage at the rate of $4.25 dollars per hundred pounds, f. o. b. Ventura, Calif., payment to be made when the crop is delivered.

This contract is understood by both parties to pass title and constitute absolute sale, but until delivery has been completed grower agrees to and does assume all risk of loss or damage. Time is the essence of this contract and any controversy arising under this contract is to be settled by arbitration; each party hereto to select one arbitrator and the two jointly to select a third, the decision of a majority of said arbitrators to be final and binding on both parties.

Appellant insists that the contract was invalid because it contemplated a completed sale of property not in existence, and that it is void for want of mutuality. The third point made has to do with the sufficiency of the allegations in the complaint affecting plaintiff's alleged damages. It is well-settled law that a valid contract may be made for the sale of a crop to be grown in the future by the vendor where such vendor possesses the land upon which the crop is to be grown, for in such case it appears that the needful thing out of which the crop is to be produced is in existence, and hence the crop has legal potentiality. (*Arques* v. *Wasson*, 51 Cal. 620, [21 Am. Rep. 718]; *Cutting Packing Co.* v. *Packers' Exchange*, 86 Cal. 574, [21 Am. St. Rep. 63, 10 L. R. A. 369, 25 Pac. 52]; Benjamin on Sales, 7th ed., sec. 311.) It was alleged in the complaint that at the time of the making of the contract and subsequent thereto defendant was the owner and in possession of the twenty acres of land referred to in the written contract. We construe the contract to be executory. The mere fact that the writing provided that the contract should pass title and constitute an absolute sale, with a risk on the grower for loss or damage until delivery, should be held to mean only that title should be deemed to pass whenever the produce became a growing crop. It was competent for the parties to so contract. (*Farmer* v. *Leaf*, 46 Cal. App. 542, [189 Pac. 735].) But were we to assume that that particular term of the contract was void, it would not vitiate the main contractual obligation imposed upon the defendant, which was to grow and deliver the crop. In that case section 1141 of the Civil Code would apply, which declares that title is transferred by an executory agreement for the sale of personal property when the buyer has accepted the thing, or when the seller has completed it, prepared it for delivery, and offered it to the buyer, with intent to transfer title thereto. There was no lack of mutuality in the obligations imposed by the contract. Plainly its terms were sufficient to have enabled the defendant, had he produced a crop and offered it to the plaintiff and had the latter refused to accept it, to enforce that term which provides for the payment of the price agreed upon. That term is definitely stated, to wit: "The Hogue-Kellogg Company agrees to pay for said beans on net weight at $4.25 dollars, per hundred pounds, delivered f. o. b. cars at Buena Park, Calif., on or before December 1st, 1917." The condition immediately following, that in the event there was a failure to deliver it would be optional with the vendee to cancel the contract or continue it in force, was a mere statement of the legal right of the vendee upon default being made by the vendor.

[The last page of the opinion on the question of damage is here omitted.]

For the reasons stated, the judgment is affirmed.

Conrey, P. J., and Shaw, J., concurred.

IN RE WAIT

Court of Appeal, 1927

[*Law Reports*, [1927] 1 *Chancery Division*, 606]

Appeal from the Divisional Court in Bankruptcy ([1926] Ch. 962) in the following circumstances: —

By a c.i.f. contract of November 20, 1925, Wait (trading as Wait & James, Bristol) bought from Balfour Williamson & Co., London, 1000 tons of Western White wheat ex motor vessel *Challenger*, expected to load between December 16 and 31, 1925, from Oregon or Washington. The price was 57*s*. per 480 lbs.

By a c.i.f. contract of November 21, 1925, Wait sold 500 tons of this parcel by the same description and at the same price to Humphries & Bobbett, Bristol (hereinafter called "the sub-purchasers"), adding: "The wheat sold is part of a parcel bought from Balfour Williamson & Co. under contract dated November 20, and in the event of their not duly fulfilling same, it is understood that Messrs. Wait & James are not to be held liable to buyers."

The wheat was shipped in bulk on the *Challenger* by Balfour Williamson & Co.'s agent at Oregon on December 21, 1925, and a bill of lading of that date for the 1000 tons was issued. The freight was 1500*l*. This bill of lading was received by Wait on January 4, 1926, and the purchase price was payable on February 6 — i.e., thirty-three days after sight.

On January 5, 1926, Wait delivered to the sub-purchasers a provisional invoice for their 500 tons, the price of which, less 750*l*. half freight payable at destination, was 5933*l*., due February 6. On February 2 he delivered a confirmatory invoice, and on February 5 the sub-purchasers gave him a cheque for the 5933*l*.

On February 6 Wait paid this cheque of 5933*l*. with other cheques totaling 12,168*l*. into his bank. At the same time he hypothecated the above bill of lading and two bills of lading relating to two other shipments to the bank to secure his overdraft. He then had only one general account.

On February 9 — i.e., three days later — the bank on its own initiative and without any request from Wait opened three loan accounts relating to the three shipments. Account No. 1, which related to the 1000 tons transaction, commenced with a credit of the 5933*l*. cheque and a debit of 11,797*l*. transferred from the general account, against which debit the 1000 tons bill of lading was held.

On February 17, 1926, Wait gave notice of suspension of payment, and on February 24 he was adjudicated bankrupt on his own petition, and Collins was appointed special manager by the official receiver.

On February 26 the sub-purchasers sent Collins a cheque for 750*l*., the half freight, but he returned it by the official receiver's instructions.

On February 27, 1926, Collins, as special manager, discharged the 11,797*l*. debit, and received the 1000 tons bill of lading, leaving No. 1 account in credit 5933*l*.

On February 28 the *Challenger* arrived at Avonmouth with the 1000 tons in bulk. The sub-purchasers' 500 tons had never been appropriated.

On March 3 the sub-purchasers issued a notice of motion in the Bristol County Court asking that the trustee (then the official receiver) should specifically perform the contract of November 21, 1925, by delivering 500 tons out of the 1000 tons of wheat on the *Challenger* to the sub-purchasers on payment of the 750*l*. half freight. Alternatively they asked for an order for repayment of the 5933*l*. purchase money or alternatively for a declaration that they had a beneficial interest in the parcel of wheat to the extent of 500 tons, and a charge upon the wheat and the bill of lading for the 5933*l.* purchase money.

On March 5 Collins was appointed trustee. He was subsequently made a respondent. At the date of the motion some of the wheat had been disposed of, but 530 tons were left, the 500 being still unappropriated.

On March 13, 1926, the county court judge held that the 500 tons were not "specific" or "ascertained" goods within the authorities, and he could not order specific performance, but holding that the 5933*l.* purchase money was in the nature of a trust fund earmarked for a specific purpose, and that in any case it was unconscionable of the trustee, as an officer of the Court, to keep both the goods and the purchase money, he ordered the trustee to repay that amount.

On March 31 the trustee gave notice of appeal, and on April 1 the sub-purchasers gave a cross notice asking for specific performance if it were held that the county court judge's order for repayment could not stand.

The Divisional Court in Bankruptcy (Astbury and Lawrence JJ.) were of opinion that although, for want of appropriation, the property in the 500 tons had not passed to the sub-purchasers, those 500 tons were specific goods within s. 52 of the Sale of Goods Act, 1893, as defined by s. 62, and that the Court had jurisdiction to order specific performance of the contract; and the Court made a declaration that the sub-purchasers were entitled to specific performance on payment of the 750*l.* half freight, which had been tendered and refused.

The trustee in bankruptcy appealed.

[The Court of Appeal, Sargant, L. J., dissenting, allowed the appeal. Atkin, L. J., said in the course of his opinion]:

I now proceed to discuss the suggestion that apart from the right to specific performance under s. 52 of the Code, there was in this case an equitable assignment to the claimants of 500 tons of flour which entitled them to claim from the trustee delivery of 500 tons out of the 530 tons remaining in his possession. . . . Without deciding the point, I think that much may be said for the proposition that an agreement for the sale of goods does not import any agreement to transfer property other than in accordance with the terms of the Code, that is, the intention of the parties to be derived from the terms of the contract, the conduct of the parties and the circumstances of the case, and, unless a different intention appears, from the rules set out in s. 18. . . . A seller or a purchaser may, of course, create any equity he pleases by way of charge, equitable assignment or any other dealing with or disposition of goods, the subject-matter of sale; and he may, of course, create such an equity as one of the terms expressed in the contract of sale. But the mere sale or agreement to sell or the acts in pursuance of such a contract mentioned in the Code will only produce the legal effects which the Code states.

But without deciding this point, we have to apply the words of Lord Westbury in *Holroyd v. Marshall* (10 H. L. C. 191, 209): "In equity it is not necessary for the alienation of property that there should be a formal deed of conveyance. A contract for valuable consideration, by which it is agreed to make a present transfer of property, passes at once the beneficial interest, provided the contract is one of which a Court of equity will decree specific performance. In the language of Lord Hardwicke, the vendor becomes a trustee for the vendee; subject, of course, to the contract being one to be specifically performed. And this is true, not only of contracts relating to real estate, but also of contracts relating to personal property, provided that the latter are such as a Court of equity would direct to be specifically performed." It must be remembered that while Lord Westbury's proposition that a contract for valuable consideration, by which it is agreed to make a present transfer of property, passes at once the beneficial interest, provided the contract is one of which a Court of equity will decree specific performance, may be beyond dispute, the converse that when there is a contract of which the Court of equity will decree specific performance the beneficial interest has passed is not logically true, and is not the law. Nor is it true that in equity when a man agrees in a contract for the sale of goods to sell part of a specified whole, he agrees to make a transfer of property either present or when the property is in fact acquired. Agreements by a farmer to sell a lamb out of his flock, a ton of potatoes out of his crop grown on his farm, a bushel of apples from his orchard, a gallon of milk from this morning's milking, an egg out of the eggs collected yesterday, seem to me not to amount to an equitable assignment of any of the matters sold, or to give an equitable charge or lien over the whole subject-matter to secure the delivery of the part. The doctrine asserted seems to produce the result that in every case of the sale of future goods, as soon as the goods have become identifiable, the beneficial interest in them passes to the buyer, notwithstanding the provision in the Code that, in the absence of express intention, the property only passes when goods of that description and in a deliverable state are appropriated to the contract, either by the seller with the assent of the buyer, or by the buyer with the assent of the seller, and apparently notwithstanding an express agreement that the property shall not pass except on payment. So to hold would be to defeat the intention of the parties, either express or to be implied from their contract being bound by the terms of the Code, and it appears to me not to accord with the principles of equity to impose upon the parties rights which are contrary to their manifest intention. . . .

It is, however, said, "does not common honesty demand that such a beneficial interest should be created?" The answer is, I think, that the test of honesty is inadequate, it is too narrow or too wide. The sphere of honesty is not confined to dealings with beneficial interests in property. Many would think that deliberately to break a contract for the sale of future goods, where no question of property at law or in equity could arise, would be dishonest; but the law gives only a remedy in damages. In the simple cases suggested, which I hesitate to repeat, the farmer might be acting dishonestly in parting with the whole of his flock, his apples, his potatoes or his eggs to a different purchaser; but I venture to think that if he does the purchaser even with notice acquires a complete title to the property bought.

This brings me to the last subject of this too lengthy judgment. If the contentions put before the Court for the claimants be correct and beneficial interests in property are created as suggested, the whole course of business transactions will be fundamentally affected. Many large business transactions such as this, indeed nearly all import transactions, are financed by banks or financial houses, as this was. It is quite common for the banker to be given information of sub-sales, indeed he often asks for it, or it is proffered voluntarily as some guarantee of the stability of the bank's customer. Such notice was given here. If notice of the sub-sale under a contract which becomes specific when delivery is made, is notice of equitable interests in the sub-purchasers, the bank would be affected even though by taking the bills of lading, or other documents, they acquired the legal title. They would have to satisfy themselves on being paid off that the equitable interests were not being defeated, and their own powers of disposition if their customer made default would be enormously restricted. Presumably they would have to communicate with each sub-purchaser. The effect of the decision below when once appreciated would throw the business world into confusion, for credit would be seriously restricted.

The net result of this decision is that the buyer of goods in these circumstances is in no better position in bankruptcy than a seller. If a seller of goods delivers them to the buyer before payment, trusting to receive payment in due course, and the buyer becomes bankrupt, the seller is restricted to a proof, and can assert no beneficial interest in the goods. There seems no particular reason why a different principle should prevail where a buyer hands the price to the seller before delivery of the goods trusting to receive delivery in due course. In both cases credit is given to the debtor, and the buyer and the seller respectively take the well known risk of the insolvency of their customer.

B. Undivided Shares

KIMBERLY *v.* PATCHIN

New York Court of Appeals, 1859

[19 *New York Reports*, 330]

Appeal from the Supreme Court. Action to recover the value of six thousand bushels of wheat, alleged to have been the property of the plaintiffs, and to have been converted by the defendant. Upon the trial before Mr. Justice Greene, at the Erie Circuit, it was proved that, one Dickinson had in warehouse, at Littlefort, in Wisconsin, two piles of wheat, amounting to six thousand two hundred and forty-nine bushels. John Shuttleworth proposed to purchase six thousand bushels of wheat. Upon being shown the piles, he expressed a doubt whether they contained that quantity. Dickinson declared his opinion that they did, and agreed to make up the quantity if they fell short. A sale was then made at seventy cents per bushel, Dickinson signing and delivering to Shuttleworth a memorandum, as follows:

LITTLEFORT, February 17, 1848.

JOHN SHUTTLEWORTH,
Bought of D. O. DICKINSON,
6,000 bushels of wheat, delivered on board, 70 cents, $4,200.

Received his draft upon John Shuttleworth, of Buffalo, for	$2,100	
To remit me	1,600	
Five drafts of $100 each,	500	
		4,200.

D. O. DICKINSON.

He also signed and delivered to Shuttleworth, this paper, *viz*:

LITTLEFORT, February 18, 1848.

6,000 bushels wheat.

Received in store 6,000 bushels of wheat, subject to the order of John Shuttleworth, free of all charges on board.

D. O. DICKINSON.

The wheat was left undisturbed in the warehouse. Shuttleworth sold the wheat to the defendant, assigning to him the bill of sale and warehouse receipt. Dickinson, shortly afterwards, sold the whole quantity of wheat in the two piles, to a person under whom the plaintiffs derived title. The defendant having obtained the possession of the wheat, this action was brought. The judge, under exception by the defendant, directed a verdict for the plaintiffs, which was rendered, and the judgment thereon having been affirmed at general term, in the eighth district, the defendant appealed to this court.

COMSTOCK, J. Both parties trace their title to the wheat in controversy to D. O. Dickinson, who was the former owner, and held it in store at Littlefort, Wisconsin. The defendant claims through a sale made by Dickinson to one Shuttleworth on the 18th of February, 1848. If that sale was effectual to pass the title, it is not now pretended that there is any ground on which the plaintiffs can recover in this suit. The sale to the person under whom they claim, was about two and a half months junior in point of time.

The sale to Shuttleworth was by a writing in the form of a present transfer of six thousand bushels of wheat, at seventy cents per bushel. No manual delivery was then made, but instead thereof the vendor executed and delivered to the vendee another instrument, declaring that he had received in store the six thousand bushels subject to the vendee's order; of the price $2,600 was paid down, and the residue $1,600 which was to be paid at a future day, the purchaser afterwards offered to pay, according to the agreement. So far the contract had all the requisites of a perfect sale. The sum to be paid by the purchaser was ascertained, because the number of bushels and the price per bushel were specified in the contract. Although the article was not delivered into the actual possession of the purchaser, yet the seller, by the plain terms of his agreement, constituted himself the bailee, and henceforth stood in that relation to the purchaser and to the property. That was equal in its results to the most formal delivery, and no argument is required to show that the title was completely divested, unless a difficulty exists yet to be considered.

The quantity of wheat in store to which the contract related, was estimated by the parties at about six thousand bushels. But subsequently, after Dickinson made another sale of the same wheat to the party under whom the plaintiffs claim, it appeared on measurement that the number of bushels was six thousand two hundred and forty-nine, being an excess of two hundred and forty-nine bushels. When Shuttleworth bought the six thousand bushels, that quantity was mixed in the storehouse with the excess, and no measurement or separation was made. The sale was not in bulk, but precisely of the six thousand bushels. On this ground it is claimed, on the part of the plaintiffs, that in legal effect the contract was executory, in other words a mere agreement to sell and deliver the specified quantity, so that no title passed by the transaction. It is not denied, however, nor does it admit of denial, that the parties intended a transfer of the title. The argument is, and it is the only one which is even plausible, that the law overrules that intention, although expressed in plan written language, entirely appropriate to the purpose.

It is a rule asserted in many legal authorities, but which may be quite as fitly called a rule of reason and logic as of law, that in order to an executed sale, so as to transfer a title from one party to another, the thing sold must be ascertained. This is a self-evident truth, when applied to those subjects of property which are distinguishable by their physical attributes from all other things, and, therefore, are capable of exact identification. No person can be said to own a horse or a picture, unless he is able to identify the chattel or specify what horse or what picture it is that belongs to him. It is not only legally, but logically, impossible to hold property in such things, unless they are ascertained and distinguished from all other things; and this I apprehend is the foundation of the rule that, on a sale of chattels, in order to pass the title, the articles must, if not delivered, be designated, so that possession can be taken by the purchaser without any further act on the part of the seller.

But property can be acquired and held in many things which are incapable of such an identification. Articles of this nature are sold, not by a description which refers to and distinguishes the particular thing, but in quantities, which are ascertained by weight, measure or count; the constituent parts which make up the mass being undistinguishable from each other by any physical difference in size, shape, texture or quality. Of this nature are wine, oil, wheat and the other cereal grains, and the flour manufactured from them. These can be identified only in masses or quantities, and in that mode, therefore, they are viewed in the contracts and dealings of men. In respect to such things, the rule above mentioned must be applied according to the nature of the subject. In an executed and perfect sale the things sold, it is true, must be ascertained. But as it is not possible in reason and philosophy to identify each constituent particle composing a quantity, so the law does not require such an identification. Where the quantity and the general mass from which it is to be taken are specified, the subject of the contract is thus ascertained, and it becomes a possible result for the title to pass, if the sale is complete in all its other circumstances. An actual delivery indeed cannot be made unless the whole is transferred to the possession of the purchaser, or unless the particular quantity sold is separated from the residue. But actual delivery is not indispensable in any case in order to pass a title, if the thing to be delivered is ascertained, if the price is paid or a credit given, and if nothing further remains to be done in regard to it.

It appears to me that a very simple and elementary inquiry lies at the foundation of the present case. A quantity of wheat being in store, is it possible in reason and in law for one man to own a given portion of it and for another man to own the residue without a separation of the parts? To bring the inquiry to the facts of the case: in the storehouse of Dickinson there was a quantity not precisely known. In any conceivable circumstances could Shuttleworth become owner of six thousand bushels, and Dickinson of the residue, which turned out to be two hundred and forty-nine bushels, without the portion of either being divided from the other? The answer to this inquiry is plain. Suppose a third person, being the prior owner of the whole, had given to S. a bill of sale of six thousand bushels, and then one to D. for the residue more or less, intending to pass to each the title, and expressing that intention in plain words, what would have been the result? The former owner most certainly would have parted with all his title. If, then, the two purchasers did not acquire it no one could own the wheat, and the title would be lost. This would be an absurdity. But if the parties thus purchasing could and would be the owners, how would they hold it? Plainly according to their contracts. One would be entitled to six thousand bushels, and the other to what remained after that quantity was subtracted.

Again suppose, Dickinson having in store and owning two hundred and forty-nine bushels, Shuttleworth had deposited with him six thousand bushels for storage merely, both parties agreeing that the quantities might be mixed. This would be a case of confusion of property where neither would lose his title. In the law of bailments it is entirely settled that S., being the bailor of the six thousand bushels, would lose nothing by the mixture, and, it being done by consent, it is also clear that the bailee would lose nothing. (Story on Bailments, § 40; 2 Bl. Com., 405.)

These and other illustrations which might be suggested, demonstrate the possibility of a divided ownership in the six thousand two hundred and forty-nine bushels of wheat. If, then, the law admits that the property, while in mass, could exist under that condition, it was plainly competent for the parties to the sale in question, so to deal with each other as to effectuate that result. One of them being the owner of the whole, he could stipulate and agree, that the other should thenceforth own six thousand bushels without a separation from the residue. And this, I think, is precisely what was done. The six thousand bushels might have been measured and delivered to the purchaser, and then the same wheat might have been redelivered to the seller under a contract of bailment. In that case the seller would have given his storehouse receipt in the very terms of the one which he actually gave; and he might, moreover, have mixed the wheat thus redelivered with his own, thereby reducing the quantity sold and the quantity unsold again to one common mass. Now the contract of sale and of bailment, both made at the same time, produced this very result. The formalities of measurement and delivery pursuant to the sale, and of redelivery according to the bailment — resulting in the same mixture as before — most assuredly were not necessary in order to pass the title, because these formalities would leave the property in the very same condition under which it was in fact left; that is to say, in the actual custody of the vendor, and blended together in a common mass. Those formal and ceremonial acts were dispensed with by the contract of the parties. They went directly to the result without the performance of any useless ceremonies, and it would be strange, indeed, if the law denied their power to do so.

[Five pages in which other cases are discussed are here omitted.]

We are of opinion, therefore, both upon authority and clearly upon the principle and reason of the thing, that the defendant, under the sale to Shuttleworth, acquired a perfect title to the six thousand bushels of wheat. Of that quantity he took possession at Buffalo, by a writ of replevin against the master of the vessel in which the whole had been transported to that place. For that taking the suit was brought, and it results that the plaintiff cannot recover. It is unnecessary to decide whether the parties to the original sale became tenants in common. If a tenancy in common arises in such cases, it must be with some peculiar incidents not usually belonging to that species of ownership. I think each party would have the right of severing the tenancy by his own act: that is, the right of taking the portion of the mass which belonged to him, being accountable only if he invaded the quantity which belonged to the other. But assuming that the case is one of strict tenancy in common, the defendant became the owner of six thousand and the plaintiffs of two hundred and forty-nine parts of the whole. As neither could maintain an action against the other, for taking possession merely of the whole, more clearly he cannot if the other takes only the quantity which belongs to him.

The judgment must be reversed and a new trial granted.

Gray and Grover, Js., dissented; Strong, J., expressed himself as inclined to concur, if necessary to a decision, but it being unnecessary, he reserved his judgment.

Judgment reversed and new trial ordered.

Compare with Commercial National Bank *v.* Gillette, 90 Ind. 268 (1883), where there was a sale of 510 car wheels out of a mass of 1100. After the making of the contract the entire lot of wheels was seized upon executions against the seller, and in an action by the buyer for the possession of those sold the court said: "The contention of appellee is that appellant acquired no title, because the articles sold were not designated or separated from the common lot of which they formed a part, and this contention prevailed in the court below.

"There is much strife in the American cases upon this question, but none in the English. The weight of the former is, perhaps, with the theory of appellant, but the text-writers are, so far as we have examined, all with the English decisions. Our own cases are in harmony with the long established rule of the common law. . . .

"The civil law rule is the same as that of the common law, and our great lawyers have given it unhesitating approval. 2 Kent Com. 639; Story Sales, section 296.

"The American cases which have departed from the long settled rule, are built on the cases of *Kimberly* v. *Patchin*, 19 N. Y. 330, and *Pleasants* v. *Pendleton*, 6 Rand. 473, and these cases proceed upon the theory that commercial interests demand a modification of the rule. In our judgment, commercial interests are best promoted by a rigid adherence to the rule which the sages of the law have so long and so strongly approved. The rule secures real transactions and actual sales, and thus checks the wild spirit of speculation. It prevents, in no small measure, the making of mere wagering contracts; it puts business on a stable basis, and makes it essential that there should be real, and not sham, transfers of property; it makes titles secure, protects creditors and purchasers and represses fraud. If it were granted that the rule does somewhat interfere with the freedom of business transfers, still the good it produces far outweighs this inconvenience. But we do not believe it does interfere with actual business transfers, for common experience informs us that real sales are seldom, if ever, made without a specific designation of the thing bought. The rule may interfere with dealers in 'margins,' makers of 'corners,' and framers of 'options,' and to affirm that it does do this is to give it no faint praise. In principle the rule is sound, and in practical operation salutary.

"The efforts made by the courts that have departed from it to make exceptions, to manufacture distinctions and point out differences in order to escape disastrous consequences, affords strong evidence of the wisdom of the rule. The line of decisions in some of the States, where a departure has been taken, is a devious and tortuous one, and this is to be expected when once sound principle is turned from and new rules sought and adopted which have no support in fundamental principles.

"We have no disposition to depart from the rule which has so long prevailed in this State and elsewhere.

"Judgment affirmed.

"Petition for a rehearing overruled."

In LAURIE AND MOREWOOD *v.* DUDIN AND SONS, [1926] 1 K. B. 223, where there was a sale of 200 quarters of maize out of 618 quarters lying at a warehouse, a delivery order being given to the buyer for the amount, Scrutton, L. J., said: "The first contention, that upon a sale of goods forming a portion of a larger quantity the mere giving of a delivery order is sufficient to pass the property before severance from the bulk, was rested on the authority of *Whitehouse* v. *Frost* (12 East, 614). I personally have not understood why these old cases have been discussed, because it seems to me that the Sale of Goods Act has settled the question, whatever *Whitehouse* v. *Frost* (12 East, 614) may have said. Sect. 16 of that Act (56 & 57 Vict. c. 71) says: 'Where there is a contract for the sale of unascertained goods, no property in the goods is transferred to the buyer unless and until the goods are ascertained.' There is no doubt here that the goods were not ascertained. They were 200 quarters of maize, part of 618 then lying in the defendants' warehouse, but which had never been separated. It seems to me that there is no use in going into the old authorities where the question in dispute is settled by a later statute."

Contrast this with Cassinelli *v.* Humphrey Supply Co., 43 Nevada 208 (Supreme Court of Nevada, 1919), where there was a purported sale from two stacks of "all of my hay . . . except about thirty tons," and where the court said: "Counsel for respondent contend that the hay was not 'specific or ascertained goods,' but we are of the opinion that it was. It was in a specified mass of two stacks of hay which had been examined by Mr. Small on November 30, and it does not appear from the agreement or circumstances attending it that any selection as to quality or other character was to be made. From the written agreement it appears that all of the hay was included in the arrangement, except about thirty tons reserved by appellant, and its terms exclude any legitimate inference that it was the intention of the parties that either allotment was to come from any portion or section of the stacks. We need not determine whether the hay in the stacks was fungible goods or not, within the meaning of that section of the act which defines fungible goods to be 'goods of which any unit is from its nature or by mercantile usage treated as the equivalent of any other unit.' It is sufficient that the parties in their agreement treated the hay as fungible goods by making no reservation for selection from any part of the mass. Conceding for the purposes of this decision that the hay was fungible goods, it was still specific and ascertained goods, for it was all in a specified mass, and considered the same in quality and value. If appellant had sold an undivided share of it to respondent, segregation would be necessary to give each his property in severalty; but before such severance the property of each in a proportionate share of the entire mass would be no less definite and ascertained."

LOGAN *v.* CROSS

Oregon Supreme Court, 1921

[101 *Oregon Reports*, 85]

The plaintiffs are brothers and engaged in the stock business in Crook County. The defendant is the owner of a hay ranch near Prineville. In June, 1919, the plaintiffs entered into a written contract with the defendant for the purchase from him of 200 tons of hay in the stack at the agreed price of $20 per ton and at the time paid $500. In consideration thereof plaintiffs were to have certain pasture and feeding privileges on defendant's lands. At the time the contract was made the hay was growing in the field. A large portion of it was alfalfa, the third crop of which was cut some time in September and it was all to be stacked and fed on defendant's premises. The hay was put up in five different stacks at convenient places for feeding and stacks 1, 2, 3 and 4 were more or less mixed hay and stack 5 was all alfalfa. There was a driveway between stacks 4 and 5 and both were in the same inclosure. By the terms of the contract the hay was to be delivered and paid for November 1st. Desiring to obtain his money, the defendant asked the plaintiffs if they would be willing to have the hay measured and pay for it in September, to which they agreed and during that month stacks 1, 2, 3 and 4 were measured and the balance of $4,000 was then paid. In checking up the measurements, it was found that there were not 200 tons of hay in the four stacks but the parties could not and never did agree upon the amount of the shortage. The original measurement of the stacks was made by the defendant and one of the plaintiffs, and by mutual agreement the figures were submitted to Baldwin, a Prineville banker, for computation as to the number of tons and it seems that he made an error and rendered different statements of the amount. It was agreed that there was an actual shortage, the plaintiffs claiming it was about seven tons and the defendant about four. Plaintiffs claim that this resulted in an agreement that they should have a sufficient amount of hay out of stack 5 to make good the 200 tons. . . . In the course of time the plaintiffs became suspicious that the defendant had committed a fraud upon them and other measurements were made, from which it appeared there was an actual shortage of 21.4 tons. Claiming that they own and should have that amount of hay in stack 5 and its possession, plaintiffs commenced this action, in which they allege that on November 1, 1919, they were and are now the owners of and entitled to the possession of 21.4 tons of alfalfa hay in the stack on the defendant's place, commonly known as the Hoffman ranch in Crook County, State of Oregon; that the defendant wrongfully took and now withholds possession of the hay in Crook County to plaintiffs' damage in the sum of $535; that demand has been made and possession refused. For answer the defendant denies every allegation of the complaint. . . . After the testimony was taken, defendant moved for a nonsuit which was denied and the jury returned the following verdict:

"We, the jury impaneled and sworn to try the above-entitled cause find for the plaintiffs, and that the plaintiffs are the owners of and entitled to the possession of 21.4 tons of alfalfa hay as described in the complaint, and in case the delivery of the said hay cannot be had, then that plaintiffs have judgment against the defendant for the sum of five hundred thirty-five ($535) dollars."

On March 18th judgment was entered on the verdict and on March 31st the defendant filed a motion to set it aside and for a new trial. . . .

JOHNS, J. The June contract for the sale and purchase of the 200 tons of hay was executory but when the plaintiffs paid the defendant the full amount of the purchase price in September, the defendant then sold and plaintiffs bought and paid for 200 tons of hay and it then became an executed contract and was an actual sale and purchase. The defendant admits that there was an actual sale and delivery of all the hay in stacks 1, 2, 3 and 4, and that there were not 200 tons in those four stacks. The testimony is conclusive that the parties never did agree upon the amount of the shortage and for that reason they could not agree upon a final settlement. The plaintiffs claim and the defendant admits that they bought and paid for 200 tons of hay. The defendant also admits that the full amount of 200 tons of hay was not in the four stacks at the time the final payment was made in September. The plaintiffs contend that they wanted and insisted upon the full amount of the hay, that it was then agreed that they should have the amount of the shortage out of stack 5 and that through the agreement they became the owners of enough hay in stack 5 to make good the shortage; in other words, that the defendant not only sold and delivered to them the amount of hay in the four stacks but that he also then sold and delivered to them a sufficient amount of hay in and out of stack 5 to make the full 200 tons. The defendant denies this and upon that point there is a sharp conflict in the evidence but the fact remains and the defendant admits that the plaintiffs did buy and pay for 200 tons of hay and that there was a shortage. If only the four stacks were delivered the plaintiffs did not get the amount of hay they bought and for which they paid. Under the terms of the contract the hay was to be fed on the premises where it was stacked and the plaintiffs were to have the use of the meadow and a large number of their cattle were in the pasture. It is significant that the hay in stack 5 which was the last and third cutting of the alfalfa was stacked within twenty feet of stack 4 which the defendant admits was sold and delivered to the plaintiffs, and there was a driveway between the two stacks. The jury found and the testimony tends to show that there was fraud in the original measurements and that the four stacks were short in both breadth and length and that it was the defendant who made the errors or committed the fraud. There is ample evidence in the record from which a jury could find that the defendant sold and made a symbolical delivery to the plaintiffs of enough hay from and out of stack 5 to make good the shortage in the four stacks and complete the full amount of the purchase.

[Four pages of the opinion are here omitted.]

Judgment is affirmed.

ANDERSON *v.* CRISP

WASHINGTON SUPREME COURT, 1892

[5 *Washington Reports*, 178]

Appeal from Superior Court, Chehalis County.

The opinion of the court was delivered by

DUNBAR, J. It is contended by the appellants that the determining question in this case is, whether a sale of personal property constituting part of a large mass of like property passes title to the purchaser until it is separated from the mass, or in some other way designated or distinguished. And appellants' brief on this proposition is elaborate and painstaking, and would greatly aid the court in investigating this question, did we deem its determination necessary in this cause. The question presented by appellants is a new question in this state, and is an exceedingly important one, and in consideration of its importance, and in consideration of the fact that the authorities are so conflicting, we deem it advisable not to decide it until such decision is necessary to the determination of the cause at issue. We say this because, conceding the force of appellants' argument, this cause, we think, must be distinguished from the cases cited which sustain the rule contended for by appellants that it is not necessary to separate or distinguish a portion of personal property from the mass which includes it, to pass title to the portion sold. All those cases are based on the supposition that all the different portions of the mass are of equal value and of uniform quality, so that there is nothing left to be done by either party but to weigh, measure or count, which acts involve no discretion; that the intention of the parties to the contract is the only thing to be considered, and that when it can be definitely determined from the terms of the contract that the intention of the parties was to pass the title, the title is held to pass; or, in other words, we presume they mean to say that while the separation from the common mass is a circumstance going to show the intention of the parties to pass the title, it is not an essential circumstance.

Kimberly v. *Patchin*, 19 N. Y. 330, is the leading case supporting this rule, and has received much criticism, both favorable and adverse, by courts and text writers. There it was held, upon a sale of a specific quantity of grain, that its separation from a mass, indistinguishable in quality or value, in which it is included, is not necessary to pass the title when the intention to do so is otherwise clearly manifested. In that case it will be noticed that the goods were indistinguishable in quality or value, and it was upon that particular state of facts that the argument of the court was based. "It is," said the court, "a rule asserted in many legal authorities, but which may be quite as fitly called a rule of reason and logic as of law, that in order to an executed sale, so as to transfer a title from one party to the other, the thing sold must be ascertained. This is a self-evident truth, when applied to those subjects of property which are distinguishable by their physical attributes from all other things, and, therefore, are capable of exact identification."

But the court with great force proceeds to argue that other characters of property, such as grains, wines, oils, etc., which are not susceptible of definite description, are not subject to this rule, but that the title to such property can be held to pass by contract without separation or manual delivery if nothing further remains to be done in regard to it. But it must be admitted that if all the property in the mass is not of equal value something more does remain to be done. Thus, in the case at bar, another element is injected into the contract, and there is a question of relative values to be yet determined. The appellants did not buy a portion of an indistinguishable mass where all the component parts were of equal value; but their contract called for 162,000 merchantable brick, and the evidence was that the brick that were deemed unmerchantable were thrown aside and not counted in when they came to haul them, so that it is impossible to determine, before the segregation of the brick, not only what particular brick were sold, but what relative portions of the kiln were sold; and while, as we have said before, it may be conceded that the intention of the parties will be carried into effect if it can be ascertained, yet under this contract it is impossible to ascertain not only the particular brick sold, but the actual relative number of brick sold by reason of the unsettled question of what brick were and what were not merchantable, creating an element of uncertainty in the contract which does not exist in those cases where the vendor sells a certain number of bushels of grain or a certain number of gallons of oil, or tons of hay, in an undivided mass, where all the different portions are of equal value. We think to hold that the title passed in this case would be carrying the principles of liberal construction beyond the rule laid down in any of the cases cited by appellant. It is true that some of them were brick cases, similar in most respects to the case at bar; but in none of them did it appear that the brick in the kiln were not of uniform and equal value, and all the American cases were decided on the strength of *Kimberly* v. *Patchin*, *supra*, and the principles upon which that case was based are thus stated by Mr. Ralston, who is an earnest advocate of what he terms "the new rule":

"When the constituent parts which make up a mass are indistinguishable from each other by any physical difference in size, shape, texture or quality, and the quantity and general mass from which it is to be taken are specified, the subject of the contract is sufficiently ascertained, and the title will pass if the sale is complete in all its other circumstances."

Plainly the case at bar does not fall within those principles.

This being our view of the law covering this particular case, and there being no conflict in the testimony concerning the fact that it was only merchantable brick that were sold, the appellants could not have been injured by the instruction complained of, for they would not have been entitled to a verdict in any event. Reaching this conclusion renders unnecessary the investigation of the other questions raised.

The judgment is affirmed.

ANDERS, C. J., and HOYT, STILES and SCOTT, JJ., concur.

WAIT AND JAMES *v.* MIDLAND BANK

KING'S BENCH DIVISION, 1926

[31 *Commercial Cases*, 172]

Interpleader issue tried before Roche J.

The claimants in the issue, Messrs. Wait and James, were corn merchants carrying on business at Bristol, Gloucester, and Birmingham. They were the owners of a cargo of wheat amounting to about 136,000 bushels, which arrived at Avonmouth docks on the steamship *Thistleros* on August 19, 1925. Discharge of the cargo was completed on August 27, and except for a small quantity sold direct ex ship the whole of the wheat was stored in a warehouse of the Bristol Dock Authority at Avonmouth. On September 25 the claimants sold to a firm, Redlers and Co., of Sharpness, 250 quarters of the wheat, and gave Redlers a delivery order for that quantity. Redlers took delivery of 150 quarters and left the remaining 100 quarters in the warehouse at Avonmouth. On October 1 the claimants sold a further 750 quarters to Redlers, of which Redlers took delivery of 250 quarters, leaving 500 quarters in the warehouse; and on October 13 the claimants sold a further 250 quarters to Redlers, who left the whole amount in the warehouse. Thus, of the total quantity of 1,250 quarters sold to Redlers, 850 remained in the warehouse, and nothing was done to appropriate to Redlers' contracts any particular 850 quarters out of the bulk of the claimants' wheat lying there.

The sales to Redlers were made upon credit, bills being given in payment. The first 250 quarters were paid for in due course, but the bills for the remaining 1,000 quarters were dishonoured at maturity, and on November 27 the claimants instructed the Dock Authority not to deliver any of the remaining 850 quarters to Redlers. Meanwhile, the claimants had been disposing of the remainder of the cargo to other purchasers, and by November 16 there was none of the cargo of wheat left in the warehouse except the 850 quarters which had been sold to Redlers. On December 7 Redlers went into voluntary liquidation, having pledged the 850 quarters to the Midland Bank as security for an overdraft. The bank claimed delivery of the 850 quarters as pledgees, and the claimants contended that they had a right to the 850 quarters as unpaid vendors, and on the application of the Dock Authority an interpleader issue was ordered to determine the rights of the parties. . . .

ROCHE, J. — [Two and one-half pages of the opinion are here omitted.]

Now what happened was this. The 6,800 (850 quarters) bushels which we are now inquiring about were, as I say, part of a much larger quantity. Without going into precise figures, it is sufficient to say that the Dock Committee received ex the *Thistleros*, all for account of Messrs. Wait and James, some 43,642 bushels of this Australian wheat, that they issued to Messrs. Wait and James dock warrants, and that those dock warrants were returned by Messrs. Wait and James to the Dock Committee as they,

Messrs. Wait and James, issued corresponding delivery orders to their buyers which exhausted the dock warrant in question. The goods were weighed out so as to separate the parcels from the bulk as they were delivered to buyers, and it is not contended that until there was separation from the bulk the property in the goods could pass under such a contract and in such circumstances to any buyer. The matter is regulated by section 16 of the Sale or Goods Act, 1893, which is in the following terms: "Where there is a contract for the sale of unascertained goods, no property in the goods is transferred to the buyer unless and until the goods are ascertained." What is made the basis of the claim of the bank is the fact which they allege — I will say what I find the fact to be in a moment — that by November 16 these goods were ascertained, that these 6,800 bushels of wheat were ascertained. The method of the ascertainment relied upon is this. It is said that by November 16, 1925, all the rest of the cargo had been delivered to all the other buyers from Messrs. Wait and James, and that all that was left was the quantity sold to Messrs. Redlers, Limited, and by Messrs. Redlers, Limited, transferred to the bank; except, of course that part of the quantity which Messrs. Redlers, Limited, themselves had got possession of. I find as a fact, having heard the evidence, that there are left in the warehouses of the Corporation no more than 6,800 bushels of wheat ex the *Thistleros*. It is quite true that that quantity now left has never been weighed — in this sense, that it has never been weighed since it came into the warehouses. What happened was that the wheat was weighed in and that all that has been delivered has been weighed out, and I have no reason to doubt that the weighing was done accurately; and if that weighing was done accurately then there are no more than 6,800 bushels left. I am also satisfied that, having regard to the condition of the cargo, and having regard to the length of time which has expired, and the treatment by turning which this cargo has received, the weight is less rather than more than the 6,800 bushels, each of 62 lbs. I am also satisfied of that fact upon the collateral check which has been imposed by the estimation of a skilled gentleman, skilled in estimating weight by bulk. Under those circumstances I hold, subject, of course, to certain considerations of law with which I am going to deal, that the property in the quarters or bushels of wheat, which by the contracts between them it was agreed should be transferred to the bank, passed on November 16, when the quantity of goods covered by those contracts were the only goods left in the warehouses of the Bristol Corporation of that class and description. . . .

The next point which is interposed against the claim of the bank is an objection that this method of ascertainment by exhaustion, as it was usefully expressed by Mr. Rayner Goddard, is not a method of ascertainment which does ascertain, but that the only effective way of ascertaining the goods which are in bulk, such as these, and which are sold by weight, is by weighing; and I agree that the most usual and most natural way is to weigh. But I am not prepared to hold that that is the only way of ascertaining the goods dealt with, and that without such weighing there could be no ascertainment. . . . It seems to me that ascertainment might take place by any method which is satisfactory to the parties concerned. If the Dock Committee and the bank or Messrs. Redlers, Limited, chose to deal with this matter by measurement instead of by weight, there would be nothing to prevent them. In my judgment, the matter has been dealt with automatically by the facts, and the facts have provided the method of ascertainment in the manner I have already described through the delivery of the rest of the goods to other purchasers. I therefore hold that what remains in the warehouse has been ascertained to be the quantity of goods agreed to be sold by Messrs. Wait and James to Messrs. Redlers, Limited, and to be the goods transferred by Messrs. Redlers, Limited, to the Midland Bank.

[Two and one-half pages of the opinion are here omitted.]

Judgment for the defendants.

C. Specific Goods which already have Perished

HASTIE *v.* COUTURIER

Exchequer Chamber, 1853

[9 *Exchequer Reports*, 102]

[The introductory statement and arguments of counsel are here omitted.]

Coleridge, J. (After stating the pleadings and evidence his Lordship proceeded:) — The case was originally tried before Martin, B., who, in directing the jury, ruled that the contract imported that, at the time of the sale, the corn was in existence as such, and capable of delivery, and a verdict was found for the defendants, the plaintiffs having leave to move to enter a verdict in their favour on all the issues except those on the fifth and sixth pleas, and on those pleas for judgment *non obstante veredicto*. The case was argued before the Lord Chief Baron and Barons Parke and Alderson. The Lord Chief Baron agreed in the opinion expressed by Martin, B., at *Nisi Prius*; but the other learned Barons differed from him, and made the rule absolute; whereupon it was agreed that the question should be brought before this Court on a bill of exceptions, as if the Lord Chief Baron had directed the jury in conformity with the opinion of Barons Parke and Alderson. The case therefore comes before us without any great preponderance of authority in favour of the defendants in error. Nor do we find in the arguments of counsel, or in the judgment of the Court below, any case referred to upon which that judgment was founded. It turned entirely on the meaning of the contract made between the parties, which was in these terms: "Bought of Hastie & Hutchinson a cargo of about 1180 quarters of Salonica Indian corn of fair average quality when shipped per the 'Kezia Page,' Captain Page, from Salonica, bill of lading dated the 22nd of February, at 27*s.* per quarter, free on board, and including freight and insurance to a safe port in the United Kingdom, the vessel calling at Cork or Falmouth for orders, measure to be calculated as customary, payment at two months from this date, or in cash, less discount at the rate of 5*l.* per cent. per annum for the unexpired time upon handing shipping documents." An attempt was made to explain this document by evidence, but failed. There is, indeed, an expression in the bill of exceptions, "that the meaning of free on board is, that the goods are on board," which, taken literally, may import that they are on board at the time when the words are used; but it was not contended for the plaintiffs in error that such is the true meaning. The case, therefore, is not affected by that statement, and the question depends upon the words of the contract, unexplained by any evidence.

For the plaintiffs in error it was contended, that the parties plainly contracted for the sale and purchase of goods, that the price to be paid was for goods, and that for the price the purchaser was to have the benefit of a contract to carry them and a policy of insurance; that a vendor of goods undertakes that they exist, and that they are capable of being transferred, although he may not stipulate for their condition; and that as the goods in question had been sold and delivered to other parties before the contract in question was made, there was nothing on which it could operate; and *Barr* v. *Gibson* (3 M. & W. 390) and *Strickland* v. *Turner* (7 Exch. 208) were cited.

On the other hand it was argued, that this was not a mere contract for the sale of an ascertained cargo, but that the purchaser bought the adventure, and took upon himself all risks from the shipment of the cargo. It was said that the mention of the condition of the cargo at the time of shipment was a proof of the intention of the parties that the buyer should take all risks from that time; that its condition at the time of sale, or the fact of its existence, could not then be ascertained, and therefore the purchaser must be supposed to have taken the risks; that if it had existed, however much deteriorated, the purchaser must have taken it, although the loss had been all but total, and therefore there was no reason for excluding total loss from the risks that he was to bear; that if it had ceased to exist the consideration would not fail, for the purchaser would have the shipping documents. It was further argued that the stipulation for payment, which would probably have to be made before the arrival of the cargo, indicated an intention that the purchaser was in all events to pay for it, on account of the inconvenience that would ensue if he might have to reclaim the money back. It was not disputed that the cases of *Barr* v. *Gibson* (3 M. & W. 390) and *Strickland* v. *Turner* (7 Exch. 208) were well decided.

It appears to us that the contract in question was for the sale of a cargo supposed to exist, and to be capable of transfer, and that, inasmuch as it had been sold and delivered to others by the captain before the contract in question was made, the plaintiffs cannot recover in this action. With regard to the description of the cargo as "of fair average quality when shipped," we think that, if those words had not been introduced, it must have been held that the purchaser of a cargo on a voyage would take upon himself the chance of what its condition at the time of purchase might be, and that this clause was introduced for his benefit, by enabling him to object, if the fact were so, that the cargo was bad when shipped. If, in *Barr* v. *Gibson*, there had been a stipulation that the ship, when she sailed on the voyage during which she was sold, was seaworthy, that would not have made the purchaser liable, if a total loss had occurred before the contract was entered into. It has been said, that if the loss had been all but total, if the cargo had become all but worthless, yet, if it existed in specie, the purchaser must unquestionably have been bound, and therefore there is no reason for holding that he was not also to take the risk of a total loss. The same argument would have applied in *Strickland* v. *Turner*. If the annuitant, at the time of the sale of the annuity, had been *in extremis*, and had died the next hour, the purchaser would have been bound and could not have recovered the purchase-money, but was held to be so entitled, the annuitant having died before the sale. Again, it has been supposed that there is an inconsistency in saying that, if the cargo had sustained sea-damage, constituting an average loss covered by the policy, it would pass to the purchaser so as to secure to him an indemnity, but would not pass in the event of a total loss. This seems to depend upon the same point, and not to be attended with any real difficulty.

If the contract for sale of the cargo was valid, the shipping documents would pass as accessories to it; but if, in consequence of the previous sale of the cargo, the contract failed as to the principal subject-matter of it, the shipping documents would not pass. Although we cannot find any decision in point, there is a case of *Sutherland* v. *Pratt* (11 M. & W. 296), where this subject was mentioned. In that case, the plaintiff had bought goods on a voyage, and effected an insurance, lost or not lost. They had sustained sea damage before the sale, and the purchaser sued on the policy. The underwriters pleaded that the goods were damaged before the plaintiff had acquired any interest in them. On demurrer, it was held that the plea was bad; but the very learned counsel who argued for the plaintiff admitted, in answer to a question put by Parke, B., that, if the goods had been totally lost before his contract of purchase was made, there would not have been an insurable interest, as a person cannot buy a thing that has been totally lost.

For these reasons, it appears to us that the basis of the contract in this case was the sale and purchase of goods, and that all the other terms in the bought note were dependent upon that, and that we cannot give to it the effect of a contract for goods lost or not lost. The consequence is, that the judgment of the Court below must be reversed, and entered for the plaintiffs in error according to arrangement between the parties.

Judgment reversed.

BRASSERIE DE LA NOUVELLE GALLIA *c.* HAMBACH

COMMERCIAL COURT OF HAVRE, 1920

[1920 *Havre* 1.17]

(*Translation*)

BY THE COURT:

Considering that, by a registered contract of July 22, 1918, the Brasserie de la Nouvelle Gallia bought from Henri Hambach 50 tons of tapioca at a price of 240 francs per 100 kilos c.i.f. Marseille or Bordeaux;

That, subsequently to July 30, when it paid for these 50 tons, it learned that the goods had been requisitioned since July 13, a date prior to the contract;

Considering that, under these circumstances, it has summoned Henri Hambach, claiming that by application of Art. 1599 of the Civil Code the contract of July 22 was void, and that in consequence he should be compelled to reimburse the price paid . . . and to pay in addition the sum of 40,000 francs by way of damages;

Considering that Henri Hambach has sued his vendors, Henry Lefievre & Co.; that they, in their turn, have availed themselves of a recourse in guaranty against Bruce, from whom they had bought the 50 tons; and that finally Bruce himself has sued his vendor, A. Doy;

Considering that Henri Hambach and Henry Lefievre & Co. declare that having bought and resold on the same day, July 22, they were unaware of the requisition of the goods and pass the responsibility to their respective buyers and sellers;

Considering that Bruce contends that since in the case of a c.i.f. sale title to the thing sold passes on shipment, all the risks of the voyage are thrown retroactively on the buyer from the day of the sale; that furthermore it should be noted that he sold in good faith in ignorance of the requisition, the date of which moreover is not wholly clear; and that in any event he claims the responsibility is that of his vendor, A. Doy;

Considering that the latter, whose contract with Bruce was made February 23, 1918 and who appropriated the goods on June 3 by the S. S. Baytigern, that is to say on a date most certainly prior to the requisition, claims that his contract has been completely executed, and that in no way could he be held to guarantee Bruce on account of a resale effected by him on July 22;

Considering that, in a c.i.f. sale the transfer of title to the thing sold is effected by shipment at the port of embarkation, whence it follows, in the event of a sale subsequent to shipment, that the title is transferred and the risks pass retroactively to the buyer as from the date of shipment;

Considering that the goods, appropriated by loading and represented by the bill of lading, will not have ceased, even though they may have perished before the sale, to be part of the estate of the seller, who accordingly can pass title to them retroactively and who can effect delivery at the time fixed by surrendering to the buyer the bill of lading and the insurance policy;

Considering further that the requisition affects the owner of the goods, and that it is thus for the risk of the c.i.f. buyer when it takes place subsequent to shipment;

Considering that the application of these principles naturally presupposes that the parties have acted in good faith and without knowledge of the requisition. . . .

Considering that the provisions of Art. 1599 of the Civil Code . . . thus have no application in the present case and that it is fitting to conclude that the Brasserie de la Nouvelle Gallia, which was the owner of the goods at the time of the requisition, should suffer the consequences;

For these reasons,

The Court

Declares the Brasserie de la Nouvelle Gallia ill founded in its action against Henri Hambach, and dismisses the action;

Dismisses the action in guaranty of Henri Hambach against Henry Lefievre & Co.;

Dismisses the action in guaranty of Henry Lefievre & Co. against Bruce;

Dismisses the action in guaranty of Bruce against A. Doy;

Condemns the Brasserie de la Nouvelle Gallia to pay all costs.

Note also the *Eurana*, 19 Revue de Droit Maritime Comparé 388 (Italian Court of Cassation, 1929). In reaching a similar result on substantially similar facts the Court said: "One would seek in vain to object on the ground of the absurdity of a juridical act purporting to deal with non-existent things; for in a c.i.f. sale the object exists in substance, even though the goods be lost, in the substituted form of an indemnity, in that the buyer, acquiring an immediate right to the goods by indorsement of the bill of lading, is subrogated to whatever legal relationship has been established by the operations of shipment and insurance and becomes entitled *ex tunc*, that is to say with retroactive effect to that moment, to any rights inherent in the document."

BARROW, LANE AND BALLARD, LTD. *v.* PHILLIP PHILLIPS AND COMPANY, LTD.

King's Bench, 1929

[*Law Reports,* [1929] 1 *King's Bench,* 574]

[Detailed statement of facts and arguments of counsel are here omitted.]

Wright, J. — . . . As between the plaintiffs and the defendants the matter arises in this way. The plaintiffs had purchased under a contract in writing dated October 7, 1927: "E. C. P. Lot 7. 700 bags (about 25 tons) Chinese ground nuts in shell (about equal to sample) at 26*l.* 5*s.* . . . per ton, ex Store London. Lying at National Wharves. Gross landing weights. . . . Prompt 4th Nov. 1927. . . . Net cash against delivery order." On October 11, in the same year, the plaintiffs entered into an oral contract with the defendants, by which they sold to the defendants "700 bags marked E. C. P. and known as Lot 7 of Chinese ground nuts in shell then lying at the National Wharves in London at the price of *28l.* per ton to be computed by reference to the gross landing weights previously ascertained when the said goods were landed and placed in store at the said wharves." The price was computed on the gross landing weights and amounted to *727l. 18s. 3d.*, and about that there is no dispute. In respect of that price and a further sum, which is not very material to this case, of *78l. 4s.* for other goods sold by the plaintiffs to them, the defendants accepted two bills of exchange, one for *500l.* and the other for *306l. 2s. 3d.* each dated October 11, 1927, payable to the order of the plaintiffs. These bills of exchange were handed over to the plaintiffs on October 12, 1927, in return for a delivery order.

At the last mentioned date, in my judgment, it was intended that the property in the 700 bags should pass from the plaintiffs to the defendants. I regard this parcel as an indivisible parcel of goods within the description given by Bailhache J. in the case of *Behrend & Co.* v. *Produce Brokers' Co.* ([1920] 3 K. B. 530; 25 Com. Cas. 286). In that case the parcel was a parcel of 200 tons of Egyptian cotton-seed and the learned judge there held, and I think rightly, that in commerce that was an indivisible parcel of goods. The same is certainly true, in my judgment, *a fortiori* of this specific parcel of 700 bags, the location of which was expressly defined in the contract. The defendants on October 12, 1927, presented their delivery order to the wharf, and as no question was there raised they thereupon assumed that the matter was in order. [His Lordship stated the facts and the effect of the evidence relating to the inspection and sampling of the goods, the delivery to the defendants of 150 bags on December 6 or 7, 1927, and the return to the defendants of the delivery orders of December 12 and 13, 1927, and continued:] It has now been ascertained and agreed that at the date of the contract on October 11, 1927, there were not 700 bags in the parcel but only 591 bags, 109 having by that time been fraudulently abstracted or irregularly delivered. In the interval between October 11 and December 6 or 7 other bags had been taken, so that on December 12, after the 150 bags had been delivered to the defendants, none were left at all.

If the whole 700 bags had remained in the wharf on October 11, 1927, the fraudulent abstraction being subsequent to that date, and the parcel intact on that date, there could be no question, I think, that the property must have passed on October 12 from the plaintiffs to the defendants. But that in fact was not so. When the contract of October 11 was made, there was not in existence any parcel such as is described in the contract. There was a parcel of 591 bags, but there was not a parcel of 700 bags.

If, on the other hand, the whole 700 bags had been stolen on October 11, 1927, without the knowledge of either party, or if it had been destroyed by fire — if for any such reason it did not exist as a parcel at all on October 11, there can be no doubt that s. 6 of the Sale of Goods Act, 1893, would have applied. [His Lordship read that section.] The section says that as the contract has reference to specific goods and as those goods, without the knowledge of the seller, are not in existence at the date of the contract, there is nothing on which the contract can operate and it is void. In other words, because the parties are contracting about something which, unknown to them, has no existence in fact, the intention of both of them is completely frustrated and there is no contract between them. The rule has been established for many years that, where a contract relates to specific goods which do not then exist, the case is not to be treated as one in which the seller warrants the existence of those specific goods, but as one in which there has been a failure of consideration and mistake.

This case raises a further problem, which, so far as I know, and so far as learned counsel have been able to ascertain, has never hitherto come before the Court. The problem is this: Where there is a contract for the sale of specific goods, such as the parcel of goods in this case, and some, but not all, of the goods have then ceased to exist for all purposes relevant to the contract because they have been stolen and taken away and cannot be followed or discovered anywhere, what then is the position? Does the case come within s. 6 of the Sale of Goods Act, so that it would be the same as if the whole parcel had ceased to exist? In my judgment it does. The contract here was for a parcel of 700 bags, and at the time when it was made there were only 591 bags. A contract for a parcel of 700 bags is something different from a contract for 591 bags, and the position appears to me to be in no way different from what it would have been if the whole 700 bags had ceased to exist. The result is that the parties were contracting about something which, at the date of the contract, without the knowledge or fault of either party, did not exist. To compel the buyer in those circumstances to take 591 bags would be to compel him to take something which he had not contracted to take, and would in my judgment be unjust.

There is, as I have said, no authority so far on the point. There are, however, certain expressions of weight which have been referred to during the argument. In particular in Sir Mackenzie Chalmers' book on the Sale of Goods Act, 1893, 10th ed., p. 31, in a note to s. 6 of the Act there is this passage: "But if a man contracts to sell five dozen of a particular brand of champagne, it would be immaterial if unknown to him his whole stock of wine had been destroyed by fire. He must procure five dozen of that champagne elsewhere or pay damages. A mixed case might arise which is not covered by the section. Suppose a man contracts to sell to B. 'five dozen of the '74 champagne now in my cellar,' not knowing that all but three dozen had been destroyed by fire. The question has not been decided, but probably the contract would be void." I agree with that expression of opinion and adopt it in my judgment, although, in my opinion, the case put by the learned author is not so strong as the present case, because the contract here was for a parcel of goods which was indivisible and described in every particular. I have also been referred to certain passages in Benjamin on Sale, which I am quoting from the 6th edition of that work published in 1920. At p. 161 the author is dealing with a well known case to which I need not refer, where the contract relates to a specific chattel which at the date of the contract did not exist without either party knowing of that fact, and, after stating the rule, he says: "Pothier says: 'There must be a thing sold, which forms the subject of the contract. If then, ignorant of the death of my horse, I sell it, there is no sale for want of a thing sold. For the same reason, if when we are together in Paris, I sell you my house at Orleans, both being ignorant that it has been wholly, or in great part, burnt down, the contract is null, because the house, which was the subject of it, did not exist: the site and what is left of the house are not the subject of our bargain, but only the remainder of it.'" I think that in principle, though the facts are different, it is equally true in this case, that what was left of the parcel at the date of the contract, namely 591 bags, was not the subject of the bargain. The subject of the bargain was the entire parcel of 700 bags. On the following page the learned author deals with the perishing of part of the thing sold, and says: "Where two or more things are sold for an entire price, or otherwise under an entire contract, and one or more of them have perished at the date of the contract, it is conceived that the contract is also void as to the remainder." That in my judgment, for the reasons I have given, is an accurate statement. Then the author continues: "This was, at least, the rule of the civil law, which says: '*Si duos quis servos emerit pariter uno pretio, quorum alter ante venditionem mortuus est, neque in uno constat emptio*' (D. 18, 1, *de cont. empt.* 44); and is in accordance with principle." It may be said that here there was an entire price, because there was a lump sum ascertained in accordance with the contract and represented by the bills of exchange; but in any case the contract, in my judgment, was an entire contract. The general principle is also discussed in the work of Sir Frederick Pollock on Contracts, 9th ed., pp. 530 and 531.

[A page of the opinion is here omitted.]

The result is that in my judgment the plaintiffs fail in their claim on the bills of exchange. There has been a payment into Court of 258*l.* 4*s.* arrived at in this way. There is owing from the defendants to the plaintiffs 78*l.* 4*s.*, the balance of an account, and they have tendered before action brought, as I gather, the sum of 180*l.* as representing the price of the 150 bags which they actually received. The plaintiffs therefore are entitled admittedly to the sum of 258*l.* 4*s.* which has been brought into Court, and an order will be made for that sum to be paid to them. On the actual claim, however, there will be judgment for the defendants.

Judgment accordingly.

NAVARETTE *v.* TRAVIS-ZIEGLER CO.

MUNICIPAL COURT OF THE CITY OF NEW YORK, 1922

[194 *New York Supplement*, 832]

SPIEGELBERG, J. This action is brought to recover damages suffered by plaintiff through the defendant's rejection of 47 kegs of Almeria grapes, which it bid in at auction on December 22, 1919. It has been for many years the custom of Spanish grape growers to send their product in huge quantities to the Fruit Auction Company of this city, for sale at auction. The grapes, which are contained in sealed kegs, come from Spain by the shipload, and upon arrival of the steamer are allotted in large lots under the name of the owner. A few kegs of each lot are taken at random from the pier and exhibited in the auction room at the time of sale. The defendant rejected its purchase of the 47 kegs upon the ground that upon examination of 5 kegs it was found that 25 per cent. of the grapes were decayed. It returned the grapes to the Fruit Auction Company, with the request that the same be sold for account of whom it may concern. Due notice of the sale having been given to the defendant, the grapes were resold for its account. The plaintiff now sues for the loss occasioned upon the second sale, together with the expenses of the sale.

[One and one-half pages of the opinion are here omitted.]

The defendant also maintains that, even though the sale was not by sample, it may avail itself of section 88 of the Personal Property Law (Consol. Laws, c. 41). Its pertinent parts read:

> 1. Where the parties purport to sell specific goods and the goods without the knowledge of the seller have wholly perished at the time when the agreement is made, the agreement is void.
>
> 2. Where the parties purport to sell specific goods, and the goods without the knowledge of the seller have perished in part or have wholly or in a material part so deteriorated in quality as to be substantially changed in character, the buyer may at his option treat the sale —
>
> (a) As avoided. * * *

As stated by the Commissioners on Uniform State Laws in American Uniform Commercial Acts, p. 75:

> Subsection 1 corresponds to section 6 of the English act. The English section does not seem to cover the contingency of the deterioration or partial destruction, and subsection 2 has been added for that purpose. The section is believed to express the existing law.

There have been very few adjudications, prior to the enactment of the Uniform Sales Act, where the situation contemplated by the statute has arisen. This action deals with the sale of goods, and the analogous section 89 with contracts to sell goods. Both these sections have been cited in only two cases. *Automatic Time-Table Advertising Co.* v. *Automatic Time Table Co.*, 208 Mass. 252, 94 N. E. 462; *Kirsch & Co.* v. *Benyunes*, 105 Misc. Rep. 648, 174 N. Y. Supp. 794. Neither of these cases is of much aid in the disposition of this case. In the Massachusetts case it was held that the corresponding section of the Massachusetts Sales Act (St. 1908, c. 237) does not apply, where a part of the goods were damaged by fire, but not destroyed, nor so greatly deteriorated as to be substantially changed in character. The New York case, although the defendant intended to bring the case within sections 88 and 89, was decided without regard thereto. In my opinion, the statute cannot be invoked where there is a warranty of quality, nor where there is a specific refusal of a warranty, either express or implied. I think it is clear that the statute is applicable only where both parties mistakenly believed that they were selling and buying specific goods of a specific quality. In *Allen* v. *Hammond*, 11 Pet. 63, 71 (9 L. Ed. 633), the court says:

If a horse be sold which is dead, though believed to be living by both parties, can the purchaser be compelled to pay the consideration? These are cases in which the parties enter into the contract under a material mistake as to the subject-matter of it.

These significant words, in my opinion, sum up the situation. There was no mistake in this case as to the subject-matter of the sale. The grapes were sold "as are." The seller so stated. He said in substance to the buyer:

The grapes which I am about to sell may be better or worse than those on exhibition. You have to take your chances. What I guaranty is that the samples have been honestly selected.

The Sales Act (Personal Property Law, art. 5) provides for every conceivable situation arising between the buyer and seller. If the defendant's contention were upheld, it would mean that section 88 is applicable, no matter what the contract between the parties was, so long as the subject-matter of sale either perished or became materially deteriorated. The drafter of the Uniform Sales Act, discussing the leading case of *Barr* v. *Gibson*, 3 M. & W. 390, where it was held that a ship, though stranded and abandoned by the crew, still answered the description of a ship and bore the character thereof, sums up his views as follows:

It seems also clear that the fact that the ship was aground at the time of the bargain was so material that the buyer could have rescinded the transaction on account of mistake. [Williston on Sales, § 162, note 98.]

And the same learned author, at page 194, in commenting on the section of the Sales Act under consideration, says:

If the parties justifiably suppose that they are dealing with goods in ordinary merchantable condition, and the goods are not in such condition, there is a mutual mistake of a material fact, which should justify the buyer in rescinding the transaction.

Is section 88 to be construed as abolishing by implication the common law rule of *caveat emptor*? I find no warrant therefor. To my mind it is quite clear that its scope is limited to those cases where the parties at the time of the sale were laboring under a mistake as to the condition of the property sold.

In the view that I take of this case, that there was no sale by sample, and no mutual mistake as to the condition of the grapes, there must be judgment for the plaintiff, as demanded in the complaint.

RENDELL *v.* TURNBULL & CO.

Supreme Court of New Zealand, 1908

[27 *New Zealand Law Reports,* 1067]

Cooper, J. This is an action brought by the plaintiff to recover the sum of £212 1*s.*, being the balance claimed to be due by the defendants to the plaintiff upon 600 sacks of potatoes sold and delivered by the plaintiff to the defendants. The plaintiff also claims the further sum of £49 12*s.* as damages consequent upon the refusal of the defendants to take delivery of 16 tons of potatoes which the plaintiff alleges were part of the total quantity agreed to be purchased by the defendants from the plaintiff. The agreement upon which the potatoes were sold or agreed to be sold to the defendants was in writing, and expressed to be a sale to and purchase by the defendants of all the table-potatoes in the plaintiff's paddock at Kaikokopu for £3 15*s.* per ton on trucks at Aramoho, sacks 4*d.* each, to be delivered on or before the 16th of November, or, if weather prevented such delivery, the time to be extended to the 30th of November. The potatoes to be weighed on the railway-bridge at Wellington. The time for delivery was subject to weather permitting and labour obtainable, and the estimated quantity of potatoes was 75 tons. Six hundred sacks of the potatoes were delivered to the defendants, the weight being 54 tons 14 cwt. 1 qr. No part of the purchase-money has been paid by the defendants. On the 27th of November the defendants gave notice to the plaintiff not to deliver to them any more potatoes. At this time forty-nine sacks of potatoes were ready for delivery, and there were about 16 tons still in the ground. The plaintiff sold the forty-nine sacks by auction, and they realised a net amount of £4 17*s.* 4*d.* He claims to recover from the defendants in respect of the 600 sacks actually delivered and the forty-nine sacks ready for delivery, together with the sacks and certain freight paid by him, the net sum of £212 1*s.*, being the sum of £225 5*s.* less the £4 17*s.* 4*d.* and £8 6*s.* 8*d.*, the price of certain sacks supplied by the defendants to him, and he claims the sum of £49 12*s.* as damages in respect of the defendants' refusal to take the 16 tons.

[Nearly four pages of the opinion are omitted here.]

Now, section 8 of "The Sale of Goods Act, 1895," provides that where there is a contract for the sale of specific goods, and the goods without the knowledge of the seller have perished at the time the contract is made, the contract is void. This section is specially pleaded by the defendants as an answer to the action, and, in my opinion, they are entitled to succeed upon this ground. The fact that the potatoes existed *in specie* does not prevent the section applying. They were sold as "table-potatoes," and both parties believed them to be table-potatoes, and I am satisfied that, although to outward appearances they were "table-potatoes," they had, because of the second growth, which I am satisfied had fully developed, ceased to be "table-potatoes." Through this condition of second growth they had as "table-potatoes" perished, and neither party was aware of the fact. . . .

It is clear that the plaintiff would, if he had discovered after the contract that the potatoes, though existing in form, were perished in condition, have been excused from delivering them, and I see no reason why this defence should not be open to the defendants. They are sued for the contract price, and they are equally with the vendor entitled to show that the contract was void. As, therefore, it is clear that the defendants have received no benefit whatever from the delivery to them of any of the potatoes, they are entitled to judgment in the action.

[The balance of the opinion is omitted.]

RICHARDSON LUMBER CO. *v.* HOEY

MICHIGAN SUPREME COURT, 1922

[219 *Michigan Reports*, 643]

Assumpsit by the Richardson Lumber Company against William T. Hoey and another, doing business as the Western Cedar & Lumber Company, for the price of certain ties. Judgment for plaintiff. Defendants bring error. Reversed.

MCDONALD, J. On the 16th day of September, 1916, the parties hereto made the following contract for the sale and purchase of a quantity of ties:

Alpena, Michigan, September 16, 1916.

WESTERN CEDAR & LUMBER COMPANY,
City.

Gentlemen: We will sell you the cedar ties we now have on the Boyce property, Essexville, estimated to be 11,500 at 42c on the ground as they are. This to be for all — there are to be no rejects. You are to pay us in cash as soon as the ties have been counted. We have made this in duplicate and if you wish to purchase the same kindly sign your acceptance to one copy and return it to us, when we will notify Mr. MacDonald that you have purchased the same.

Yours very truly,
RICHARDSON LUMBER COMPANY,
By R. S. RICHARDSON.

Accepted this ——— day of Sept., 1916.
By WESTERN CEDAR & LUMBER COMPANY,
By W. T. HOEY.

It is the claim of the defendants that when the acceptance was signed Mr. Richardson said to Mr. Hoey: "You give me check for 11,500 ties and you can load the ties any time you want to." To which Mr. Hoey replied that he did not buy ties that way, but that he would make arrangements with plaintiff's Bay City office to count the ties and pay for them at Bay City; that Mr. Richardson then said: "The ties are ours until you pay for them"; and that to this Mr. Hoey replied; "All right, I will take care of that. I wouldn't touch the ties until I counted them and paid for them."

On the 19th of September, defendants began to load and move the ties.

They had taken out 1,721 when the remainder, not yet counted, were destroyed by fire. The defendant tendered plaintiff payment for 1,721 ties at 42c in full settlement of their obligations under the contract. The tender was refused and this suit brought to recover for the entire quantity of ties named in the contract. Plaintiff had judgment for the full amount of its claim.

Defendants insist on three defenses to the action:

[Statement of the first two defenses is omitted.]

Third. That there was a mutual mistake of fact in regard to the dangerous location and the liability of the ties being destroyed by fire, or that there was a mistake of fact on the part of the defendants while the plaintiff had full knowledge of it.

[Three pages of the opinion are omitted here.]

A more serious question is presented by the refusal of the circuit judge to submit to the jury defendants' claim of mutual mistake as to the danger from fire. The defendants claimed, and there was some testimony tending to support their claim, that, at the time the contract was made, fires were burning under the ground close to the place where the ties were piled, and shortly thereafter consumed them; that if this fact were unknown to the parties, that if they both believed that they were contracting for ties that were safe from fire and could be delivered, it was such a mutual mistake of fact as would avoid the contract. The circuit judge was of the opinion that the mistake was not as to the identity or existence of the subject-matter of the contract, and, therefore, should not be submitted to the jury as a defense to the action. In this, I think, the court erred.

This is not a case of accident or something happening after the contract which destroyed the thing contracted for. If the defendants' claim be true, at the very time the contract was made, the fire was near the ties under ground, about to destroy them, thus making delivery within a reasonable time impossible. It was a present imminent danger which did, in fact, wipe out the subject-matter of the contract. If the fire were not present at the time but originated afterwards, of course, it would have nothing to do with the contract, and would not affect defendants' liability. But that is not the claim here. It was an existing fact which continued until the property was destroyed. That the ties were in a safe place and could be delivered was a material element of the contract; it was one of the inducements which led to it. They would not have made it if they had known of the danger. They were mutually mistaken, and if defendants' claim as to the facts be true, it was a mistake that went to the entire consideration of the contract. If there was any evidence to support this theory, and I think there was some, the defendants were entitled to have it submitted to the jury.

I think it must be held that if the ties were contracted to be sold in the belief and with the understanding, by both parties, that there was no imminent danger from fire, and if there was in fact imminent danger, and they were liable to be destroyed before the defendants could, by reasonable diligence, move them, the defendants would have a right to rescind the contract; and that if, after knowledge of the facts, the defendants had no time or opportunity to rescind before the ties were destroyed by the fire which threatened them at the time the contract was made, defendants would not be liable except for the ties actually delivered. . . .

The judgment of the circuit court will be reversed and a new trial granted, with costs to the defendants.

Fellows, C. J., and Wiest, Clark, Bird, Sharpe, Moore, and Steere, JJ., concurred.

D. Specific Goods which Perish while the Contract is Executory

DEXTER *v.* NORTON

New York Court of Appeals, 1871

[47 *New York Reports*, 62]

Appeal from a judgment entered upon an order of the General Term of the Supreme Court in the first judicial district, overruling plaintiff's exceptions, and directing judgment dismissing the complaint, in accordance with ruling of the court at circuit.

This action is brought to recover damages for a breach of a contract to sell and deliver cotton. Defendants, on the 5th day of October, 1865, at the city of New York, agreed to sell and deliver to the plaintiff 607 bales of cotton, bearing certain marks and numbers, specified in the contract, at the price of forty-nine cents per pound, and fourteen bales, bearing marks and numbers, specified in the written contract, at the price of forty-three cents per pound, the cotton to be paid for on delivery. Defendants delivered to the plaintiff 460 bales of the said cotton, the remaining 161 bales were accidentally destroyed by fire without fault or negligence of the defendants. Cotton rose in value after the sale, and plaintiff claimed to recover the increase on the 161 bales. The court dismissed the complaint, upon the ground that a fulfillment of the contract by the sellers had become impossible by the destruction, without their fault, of the subject-matter of the sale, and they were, therefore, excused from the obligation to perform their agreement. Plaintiff excepted.

Church, Ch. J. The contract was for the sale and delivery of specific articles of personal property. Each bale sold was designated by a particular mark, and there is nothing in the case, to show that these marks were used merely to distinguish the general kind or quality of the article, but they seem to have been used to describe the particular bales of cotton then in possession of the defendant. Nor does it appear that there were other bales of cotton in the market of the same kind, and marked in the same way. The plaintiff would not have been obliged to accept any other cotton than the bales specified in the bought note.

The contract was executory, and various things remained to be done to the 161 bales in question by the sellers before delivery. The title, therefore, did not pass to the vendee, but remained in the vendor. (*Joice* v. *Adams*, 8 N. Y., 291.)

This action was brought by the purchaser against the vendor to recover damages for the non-delivery of the cotton, and the important and only question in the case is, whether upon an agreement for the sale and delivery of specific articles of personal property, under circumstances where the title to the property does not vest in the vendee, and the property is destroyed by an accidental fire before delivery without the fault of the seller, the latter is liable upon the contract for damages sustained by the purchaser.

The general rule on this subject is well established, that where the performance of a duty or charge created by law is prevented by inevitable accident without the fault of the party he will be excused, but where a person absolutely contracts to do a certain thing not impossible or unlawful at the time, he will not be excused from the obligations of the contract unless the performance is made unlawful, or is prevented by the other party.

Neither inevitable accident, nor even those events denominated acts of God will excuse him, and the reason given is that he might have provided against them by his contract. (*Paradine* v. *Jane*, Aleyn, 27; *Harmony* v. *Bingham*, 12 N. Y., 99; *Tompkins* v. *Dudley*, 25 N. Y., 272.)

But there are a variety of cases where the courts have implied a condition in the contract itself, the effect of which was to relieve the party when the performance had, without his fault, become impossible; and the apparent confusion in the authorities, has grown out of the difficulty in determining in a given case whether the implication of a condition should be applied or not, and also in some cases in placing the decision upon a wrong basis. The relief afforded to the party in the cases referred to, is not based upon exceptions to the general rule, but upon the construction of the contract.

For instance, in the case of an absolute promise to marry, the death of either party discharges the contract, because it is inferred or presumed that the contract was made upon the condition that both parties should live.

So of a contract made by a painter to paint a picture, or an author to compose a work, or an apprentice to serve his master a specified number of years, or in any contract for personal services dependent upon the life of the individual making it, the contract is discharged upon the death of the party, in accordance with the condition of continued existence, raised by implication. (2 Smith's Leading Cases, 50.)

The same rule has been laid down as to property: "As if A agrees to sell and deliver his horse Eclipse to B on a fixed future day, and the horse die in the interval, the obligation is at an end." (Benjamin on Sales, 424.) In replevin for a horse, and judgment of *retorno habendo*, the death of the horse was held a good plea in an action upon the bond. (12 Wend., 589.) In *Taylor* v. *Caldwell* (113 E. C. R., 824), A agreed with B to give him the use of a music hall on specified days, for the purpose of holding concerts, and before the time arrived the building was accidentally burned;

held, that both parties were discharged from the contract. BLACKBURN, J., at the close of his opinion, lays down the rule as follows: "The principle seems to us to be, that in contracts in which the performance depends on the continued existence of a given person or thing, a condition is implied that the impossibility of performance, arising from the perishing of the person or thing, shall excuse the performance." And the reason given for the rule is, "because from the nature of the contract, it is apparent that the parties contracted on the basis of the continued existence of the particular person or thing."

In *School District, No. 1* v. *Dauchy* (25 Conn., 530), the defendant had agreed to build a school-house by the first of May, and had it nearly completed on the twenty-seventh of April, when it was struck by lightning and burned; and it was held, that he was liable in damages for the non-performance of the contract. But the court, while enforcing that general rule in a case of evident hardship, recognizes the rule of an implied condition in case of the destruction of the specific subject-matter of the contract; and this is the rule of the civil law.

(Pothier on Contracts and Sale, art. 4, § 1, p. 31.) We were referred to no authority against this rule. But the learned counsel for the appellant, in his very able and forcible argument, insisted that the general rule should be applied in this case. While it is difficult to trace a clear distinction between this case and those where no condition has been implied, the tendency of the authorities, so far as they go, recognize such a distinction, and it is based upon the presumption that the parties contemplated the continued existence of the subject-matter of the contract.

The circumstances of this case are favorable to the plaintiff. The property was merchandise sold in the market. The defendant could, and from the usual course of business, we may infer, did protect himself by insurance; but in establishing rules of liability in commercial transactions, it is far more important that they should be uniform and certain than it is to work out equity in a given case. There is no hardship in placing the parties (especially the buyer) in the position they were in before the contract was made. The buyer can only lose the profits of the purchase; the seller may lose the whole contract price, and if his liability for non-delivery should be established, the enhanced value of the property. After considerable reflection, I am of the opinion that the rule here indicated of an implied condition in case of the destruction of the property, bargained without fault of the party, will operate to carry out the intention of the parties under most circumstances, and will be more just than the contrary rule. The buyer can of course always protect himself against the effect of the implied condition, by a provision in the contract that the property shall be at the risk of the seller.

Upon the grounds upon which this rule is based of an implied condition, it can make no difference whether the property was destroyed by an inevitable accident, or by an act of God, the condition being that the property shall continue to exist. If we were creating an exception to the general rule of liability, there would be force in the considerations urged upon the argument, to limit the exception, to cases where the property was destroyed by the act of God, upon grounds of public policy, but they are not material in adopting a rule for the construction of the contract so as to imply a condition that the property was to continue in existence. It can make no difference how it was destroyed, so long as the party was not in any degree in fault. The minds of the parties are presumed to have contemplated the possible destruction of the property, and not the manner of its destruction; and the supposed temptation and facility of the seller to destroy the property himself, cannot legitimately operate to affect the principle involved.

The judgment must be affirmed.

ALLEN, GROVER and RAPALLO, JJ., concur; PECKHAM and FOLGER, JJ., dissent.

Judgment affirmed.

IN RE SHIPTON, ANDERSON & CO. AND HARRISON BROTHERS & CO.

KING'S BENCH DIVISION, 1915

[*Law Reports*, [1915] 3 *King's Bench*, 676]

Case stated by arbitrators for the opinion of the Court, under s. 19 of the Arbitration Act, 1889.

On September 2, 1914, Shipton, Anderson & Co. by a contract in writing sold to Harrison Brothers & Co., on the terms of the Rules of the Liverpool Corn Trade Association, "about 42,800 centals winter wheat ex *Dalecrest* ex grain storage; payment cash within seven days against transfer order." The sellers were then the owners of wheat of that quantity and description discharged from the *Dalecrest* and lying at a warehouse in Liverpool. The wheat was then subject to a lien for freight and charges and not standing in the names of the sellers in the books of the warehousemen. On September 4, the lien having been satisfied, the wheat was transferred into the names of the sellers and they obtained a delivery order. On the same day the sellers were verbally informed that the wheat was requisitioned by His Majesty's Government. On September 8 the sellers received a written requisition requiring them to deliver the wheat to the agent of His Majesty's Government, and at once informed the buyers. On September 11 the agent for His Majesty's Government applied to the sellers for delivery of the wheat and obtained from them a delivery order therefor. No delivery order or transfer order was at any time given by the sellers to the buyers under the contract of sale.

The buyers claimed damages from the sellers for non-delivery of the wheat. The matter was referred to arbitration pursuant to the Rules of the Liverpool Corn Trade Association, and an award was made that the sellers were not relieved from their responsibility to the buyers under the contract. The sellers appealed to the appeal committee of the association, and contended that the property in the wheat had passed to the buyers before it was requisitioned, and that they were excused from carrying out the contract by reason of the wheat having been requisitioned.

The questions stated for the opinion of the Court were: (1.) When did the property in the wheat pass to the buyers under the contract? (2.) Were the sellers, owing to the action of the British Government, excused from carrying out their contract?

[Arguments of counsel and the first page of Lord Reading's opinion — concluding that title had not passed — are omitted here. His Lordship continued]:

Having come to that conclusion it becomes necessary to determine the second question, which is whether the sellers were excused from performance of the contract owing to the action of the Government in requisitioning the wheat. A question of law of considerable importance is raised because it is contended on the one hand by the buyers that this is an absolute contract, and that, consequently, if the sellers are unable to perform their contract by delivering the wheat, they are not excused by reason of the Government's requisition; and it is urged by the buyers that notwithstanding that this is a sale of specific goods, and that those goods had passed altogether out of the dominion of the sellers by virtue of the Government's requisition, nevertheless they were liable in damages to the buyers for failure to deliver the goods. It is conceded by the sellers that this in one sense no doubt is an absolute contract, for no act or default of the sellers could excuse them from the performance of the contract; but it is urged that where, as in this case, the performance of the contract had been rendered impossible, not by reason of any act or default of the sellers, but by the lawful act of the Executive, that is an excuse from the performance, because the contract must be taken as having been made subject to a possibility of requisition by the Government, and if so the sellers could not perform the contract and would be asked to do that which it was an impossibility for them to do. No doubt there are cases on either side of the line, and the application of the principles of law is a matter of some nicety and difficulty, but I have come to the conclusion that in this case the sellers are excused from the performance of the contract, and that the contract must be taken as an undertaking by the sellers to deliver the goods subject always to this condition, that if the Government requisition the goods and render it impossible by their act for the sellers to perform their contract they should be excused from performance. That conclusion is, I think, supported both by *Nickoll* v. *Ashton* ([1901] 2 K. B. 126) and the decision in *Baily* v. *De Crespigny* (L. R. 4 Q. B. 180). The particular passage in *Nickoll* v. *Ashton* ([1901] 2 K. B. at p. 132) upon which reliance has been placed on behalf of the sellers is that in which the Court in dealing with the principle of such cases as *Taylor* v. *Caldwell* (3 B. & S. 826) and *Howell* v. *Coupland* (1 Q. B. D. 258) cited the rule stated in *Taylor* v. *Caldwell* (3 B. & S. 826) to this effect: "Where from the nature of the contract it appears that the parties must from the beginning have known that it could not be fulfilled unless, when the time for the fulfilment of the contract arrived, some particular specified thing continued to exist, so that, when entering into the contract, they must have contemplated such continuing existence as the foundation of what was to be done, there, in the absence of any express or implied warranty that the thing shall exist, the contract is not to be construed as a positive contract, but as subject to an implied condition that the parties shall be excused in case before breach performance becomes impossible from the perishing of the thing without default of the contractor." It is to be observed that in that rule stress is laid upon the perishing before breach of the thing which was the foundation of the contract. The principle of the case seems to me equally applicable to that now under consideration, where by reason of the lawful act of the Executive the thing, in a sense, has perished. Certainly it is no longer in the power of the sellers to perform their contract. In my judgment, in the words of A. L. Smith M.R. in *Nickoll* v. *Ashton* ([1901] 2 K. B. 126, 132), "The true construction of the contract is that it is not a positive and absolute contract as contended for by the plaintiffs, but is a contract subject to the condition that the parties shall be excused if, before breach, performance becomes impossible by reason of the particular specified thing ceasing to exist without the defendants' default." In the case of *Baily* v. *De Crespigny* (L. R. 4 Q. B. 180, 186) the principles of law were considered by the Court of Queen's Bench consisting of Cockburn C.J. and Lush, Hannen, and Hayes JJ., and in the judgment of the Court, delivered by Hannen J., it is said, after reference to certain cases, "It is on this principle that it has been held that an impossibility, arising from an act of the Legislature subsequent to the contract, discharges the contractor from liability. . . . This is the principle of that which was laid down in *Brewster* v. *Kitchell* ((1697) 1 Salk. 198): 'Where H. covenants not to do an act or thing which was lawful to do, and an Act of Parliament comes after and compels him to do it, the statute repeals the covenant. So if H. covenants to do a thing which is lawful, and an Act of Parliament comes in and hinders him from doing it, the covenant is repealed.' " The principle of that case is, I think, applicable to the present case. It is true that the act to be performed was not rendered unlawful by an act of the Legislature passed since the entering into of the contract, but it was a lawful act of State which equally rendered the delivery of these specific goods impossible. Applying the principle of those cases, and bearing in mind also the principles laid down in *Krell* v. *Henry* ([1903] 2 K. B. 740), it seems to me that in this case the sellers were excused. It must be clearly understood, of course, that we are not in any way deciding that if the sale had not been of specific goods there would have been excuse; but it is because the sale is of specific goods, and is therefore rendered impossible of performance when the goods have been lawfully requisitioned, that I come to the conclusion that the sellers are excused. In my judgment, therefore, the answer to the second question is in the affirmative, that is, that the sellers were excused from carrying out their contract owing to the action of the British Government in requisitioning the wheat.

[Concurring opinions of Darling, J., and Lush, J., are omitted.]

J. A. KIRSCH & CO., INC. *v.* BENYUNES

NEW YORK SUPREME COURT, 1919

[105 *New York Miscellaneous Reports*, 648]

LEHMAN, J. The complaint herein alleges that the plaintiff and the defendant on the 27th day of November, 1916, entered into a written contract, a copy of which is annexed to the complaint.

The material parts of the said contract are as follows: "Sold to Messrs. J. A. Kirsch & Co., Inc., New York. For account of Mr. J. D. A. Benyunes, New York. Quantity (about) Twenty-eight hundred (2,800) baskets of about 110 net each, crop 1916, good quality Spanish chestnuts at seven cents (7c) per pound net, ex dock New York. Shipment. Reported by cable to be afloat per SS. 'Elef K. Venezelos,' scheduled to be due here to-day."

The complaint further alleges that the said 2,800 baskets of chestnuts duly arrived on the *Elef K. Venezelos* in the city of New York on the 28th day of November, 1916, but the defendant repeatedly neglected and refused to deliver the said 2,800 baskets of Spanish chestnuts purchased by the plaintiff from him, and still fails and refuses to deliver the same. The defendant claims that the steamer *Venezelos* sailed from the port of Lisbon, Portugal, on or about November 12, 1916, and did not arrive at the port of New York until December 2, 1916; that the chestnuts covered by the agreement of November twenty-seventh between the parties arrived in a mouldy condition, and that the department of agriculture directed that the entire shipment should be destroyed except approximately 228 baskets of the said chestnuts which had not deteriorated, and which were found to have passed the standards of the United States Government. The defendant has pleaded this claim, in various forms, in five separate affirmative defenses, and the plaintiff has demurred to the sufficiency thereof. Upon this motion the court must first consider whether the facts claimed by the defendant could constitute a defense to an action for non-delivery of the chestnuts, and second, if they could constitute a defense, whether they are sufficiently pleaded in any or all of the separate defenses contained in the answer.

The first affirmative defense alleges in effect that the contract of sale was for a specific shipment or consignment of 2,800 baskets of Spanish chestnuts at that time aboard the steamer *Venezelos*, on its way to the port of New York. That subsequent to the making of the aforementioned contract of sale of the said consignment of chestnuts, and before their arrival at a dock in the port of New York, without any fault on the part of the defendant, part of the consignment of chestnuts perished, or the whole or a material part of said consignment of chestnuts so deteriorated in quality as to be substantially changed in character.

The second defense contains the same allegation except that it states that subsequent to the making of the aforementioned contract the said consignment of chestnuts wholly rotted and perished.

The third affirmative defense alleges that at the time the agreement of sale was made the consignment of chestnuts had, without the knowledge of this defendant, perished in part or had wholly or in a material part so deteriorated in quality as to be substantially changed in character.

The fourth affirmative defense states that at the time when the said sale was made the consignment of chestnuts had, without the knowledge of this defendant, wholly rotted or perished.

It is quite evident that the defendant in pleading these defenses intended to allege facts which would bring this case within the rule announced in sections 88 and 89 of the Personal Property Law. The plaintiff, however, urges that sections 88 and 89 have no application, because (1) under the agreement between the parties the defendant did not sell specific goods on the steamship *Venezelos*, but merely agreed to deliver 2,800 baskets of chestnuts, complying with a certain description or warranty, and was absolutely bound to ship and deliver such goods, and that (2) if the contract was for the sale of specific goods it contained an express warranty that the goods were of good quality and that the rule announced in the statute has no application to a sale where there is an express warranty of quality. It seems to me quite clear under the terms of the written contract that the defendant agreed to sell and deliver certain goods described in the contract and that the contract was conditional upon the arrival of the steamship with the goods described in the contract upon it. In the case of *Shields* v. *Pettie*, 4 N. Y. 122, a broker negotiated a contract in these words: "Sold for Messrs. Geo. W. Shields & Co., to Messrs. Pettie & Mann, 150 tons Gartshemi pig iron, No. 1, at $29 per ton, one-half at 6 mos., one-half cash, less 4 pr. ct., on board Siddons." It was understood by both parties that the ship *Siddons* was at sea when the contract was made, and she arrived at the port of New York about ten days afterwards with the quantity of iron contracted for, but which turned out not to be the quality denominated No. 1. The court there held "There was no warranty, express or implied, either that any iron should arrive, or that arriving, it should be of a particular quality. One hundred and fifty tons of Gartshemi pig iron of the quality denominated No. 1, was expected to arrive by the *Siddons*, and the contract was to the effect, that if that quantity and quality of iron did so arrive one party should sell and the other should receive it at a certain price per ton. The iron called for by the contract did not arrive, but iron of a different quality, and I think the contract was at an end." It seems to me that the same rule of law applies to the facts in the present case as pleaded by the defendant. The defendant agreed under that contract to sell to the plaintiff certain specific goods described therein, which both parties evidently believed to be upon the steamship *Venezelos*. The defendant did not agree to deliver and the plaintiff did not agree to accept any goods of similar kind which might arrive upon another steamship. No goods of that description arrived on the steamship *Venezelos*, and the contract to sell was therefore at an end.

[Two pages of the opinion are here omitted.]

If these views are correct, then the fact that 2,800 baskets of good quality chestnuts did not arrive on the steamship as contemplated by the parties would in itself and without regard to sections 88 and 89 of the Personal Property Law put an end to the contract and release the defendant from any obligation thereunder, for the defendant's promise to sell and deliver such goods was based upon a condition which was never fulfilled. On the other hand, if the contract be regarded as a contract to sell specific goods which actually arrived in New York upon that steamer, and the description was inserted merely for the purpose of identifying the goods, then sections 88 and 89 of the Personal Property Law apply, and if the goods had perished at the time when the agreement was made, or the goods without the knowledge of the seller had deteriorated in quality so as to be substantially changed, or if after the contract was made the goods perished or so deteriorated in quality, the defendant could not be held liable for the loss which occurred without his fault. In other words, the defendant is clearly not bound under this contract to deliver the 2,800 baskets of Spanish chestnuts of good quality and in good condition unless he has expressly and unconditionally agreed to sell and deliver such chestnuts, and I think that, if the allegations of the answer are true, the defendant has not made such a promise.

[The remaining two pages of the opinion are omitted.]

Ordered accordingly.

Note AUTOMATIC TIME TABLE ADVERTISING CO. *v.* AUTOMATIC TIME TABLE CO., 208 Mass. 252 (1911), where an allegation in a bill of exceptions that certain machines under contract of sale had been "greatly damaged" was held insufficient to bring the case within Section 8 of the Act.

BAKER *v.* THE BROWN AND THOMAS AUTO COMPANY

CONNECTICUT SUPREME COURT OF ERRORS, 1924

[101 *Connecticut Reports*, 575]

Action to recover instalments paid by the plaintiff upon the purchase price of an automobile, sold to him by the defendant under a conditional bill of sale and alleged to have been destroyed by fire while in the defendant's possession and before delivery to the plaintiff, brought to the Court of Common Pleas in New Haven County and tried to the jury before Simpson, J.; verdict for the plaintiff which, upon motion of the defendant, the trial court set aside, and from this decision the plaintiff appealed. Error; judgment directed in conformity with verdict.

The jury might have reasonably found the following facts: Plaintiff and defendant entered into a contract which recited that defendant placed in the hands of plaintiff an automobile under an agreement of plaintiff to pay $1,675, payable $50 in cash, and $750 on a touring car for which credit on the purchase price was given to the defendant, and the balance, $875, payable in nine notes at varying times, in consideration of the agreement of defendant that when the balance of $875 had been fully paid the automobile should become the property of plaintiff, and until this balance was fully paid the title to the automobile should remain in defendant and that upon default of plaintiff in any payment defendant should have the right to take possession of it and all payments previously made and all rights of plaintiff in it should thereupon be forfeited. Defendant never made delivery of the automobile to plaintiff, but at all times retained it in its possession and control. At the time of the execution of this written agreement, defendant orally informed plaintiff that the automobile would not be delivered to him until the note which became due April 28th, 1923, was paid, and plaintiff consented to this and it thereupon became a part of the agreement of sale between the parties in reference to the automobile. On or about February 18th, 1923, the automobile while in the possession of defendant was destroyed by fire.

Defendant had this car insured and sold the remains of the automobile as junk. Defendant notified the plaintiff after the fire that it could not make delivery of the automobile as agreed and that plaintiff need not make any further payments on the remaining unpaid notes given in consideration of the purchase price. The parties further agreed that plaintiff should pay storage of $5 a month on the car and he had paid two months storage prior to the fire. On two occasions, he had done some slight work on this car and once he had used it with defendant's permission. The keys to the defendant's garage and for this automobile remained continuously in the possession and control of defendant.

Wheeler, C. J. — . . . Where there is no absolute sale and neither title in the automobile nor possession has passed, but there is merely an agreement to sell and to deliver at some future time, it is merely an executory agreement of sale, conditioned upon performance of named conditions. The destruction of the automobile rendered the performance of defendant's agreement to deliver in the future an impossibility and even though the loss was without its fault, it can neither compel performance by the buyer nor defend against reimbursement for payments made by the buyer on account of the purchase price, since the risk remained on the seller until delivery.

[The remaining page of the opinion is omitted.]

There is error, the judgment is set aside and the Court of Common Pleas is directed to render judgment upon the verdict.

In this opinion the other judges concurred.

RYLANCE *v.* THE JAMES WALKER CO.

Maryland Court of Appeals, 1916

[129 *Maryland Reports*, 475]

Thomas, J., delivered the opinion of the Court.

In December, 1911, the appellee, The James Walker Company, of Baltimore, sent to the appellant, James A. Rylance, of London, England, an order for forty-seven coils of Hoth's Russian Bolt Rope at $13.50 per hundred pounds. In September, 1912, the appellant shipped to the appellee a different kind of rope and drew a draft on the appellee for the price, which the appellee paid in advance of the arrival of the rope. When the rope shipped arrived in Baltimore the appellee discovered that it was not the rope ordered, and immediately wrote the appellant accordingly, and stated that as the appellee had paid the draft in advance of the arrival of the rope, it would charge the amount of the draft against him, and hold the rope subject to his order pending receipt of shipping orders from him. The appellant in reply requested the appellee to dispose of the rope for him, and after further correspondence, the appellee wrote the appellant in April, 1913, that it had not been able to dispose of the rope for him, and that while it did not mind holding the rope for him until he, the appellant, could dispose of it, the appellee would like to have a check for the amount of the draft paid by it.

On September 2nd, 1913, the appellee sent the appellant another order for seventy coils of Bolt Rope, to be shipped as soon as possible, "and in the usual way." At the same time the appellee again requested shipping instructions for the rope shipped to it in the fall of 1912, and which the appellee was holding for the appellant. The rope specified in the order of September 2nd, 1913, was shipped by the appellant to the appellee about the 5th of November, 1913, via steamship *Potomac*, and arrived in Baltimore about the 23rd of December following. The appellant had the bill of lading made out to his "order," and sent the same, properly endorsed by him, with a draft for the price of the rope attached, to Hambleton & Company, Baltimore bankers, with directions "to turn over the bill of lading" to the appellee upon payment of the draft. When the draft arrived, Hambleton & Company presented the same, with the bill of lading attached, to the appellee and requested it to pay the draft and take delivery of the rope. The appellee refused to pay the draft unless the appellant would allow it to deduct therefrom the amount of the draft which the appellee had paid for the shipment made in 1912. The appellant declined to allow the deduction and refused to deliver the bill of lading. When the rope arrived in Baltimore, the appellee was notified, and the rope was unloaded and after remaining on the dock for a few days, was stored by the dock authorities, without any order from either the appellant or appellee, "in a U. S. Bonded Warehouse" where it was subsequently, about February 13th, 1914, destroyed by a fire. The agreed statement of facts states: "Neither plaintiff nor defendant exercised any acts of ownership over the rope after its arrival in Baltimore."

In April, 1915, the appellant brought suit in the Superior Court of Baltimore City to recover the contract price of the rope, etc. The *narr.* contains the common counts and two special counts. The first of the special counts alleges the sale and shipment of the rope in compliance with the defendant's order, and that it arrived in Baltimore "and was delivered to the defendant, or, but for the defendant's delay and neglect to accept delivery after a request from the plaintiff so to do would have been delivered to the defendant, but the defendant in breach of its contract, neglected and refused to pay for said rope or any part thereof, though payment has often been demanded." The last count alleges the order for the rope, the acceptance of the order and the shipping of the rope in consideration of the promise of the defendant to pay therefor upon its arrival in Baltimore, and that the defendant, although it had due notice of the arrival of the rope, and was requested to accept delivery of the same, "in breach of its contract delayed and neglected to accept such delivery and to pay for the rope or any part thereof, by reason of which neglect and delay, and without any order or request from the plaintiff, the rope aforesaid was stored in a warehouse in Baltimore, Maryland, and while stored was entirely destroyed by fire."

The defendant pleaded "never promised" and "never indebted" and a set-off. The case was tried before the Court without a jury, upon issues joined on the first two pleas and on the replications of never promised, etc., to the defendant's plea of set-off. This appeal is from a judgment in favor of the defendant for the amount of the draft paid by it in the fall of 1912 produced in evidence.

[Two pages of the opinion repeating the plaintiff's prayers are here omitted.]

The real question in the case is, who is to stand the loss caused by the destruction of the rope by fire?

[Four pages of the opinion are here omitted.]

We are not required in this case to determine whether the appellee was justified in refusing to pay for the goods for the reason assigned by him. Assuming that the offer of the appellant to deliver the bill of lading in question was under the circumstances an offer to deliver the goods, and that the conduct of the appellee was in legal effect a refusal to accept the same and a breach of his contract with the appellant, the established rule in this State is that where a vendee declines to take the property and pay for it the vendor has the choice of three remedies: (1) He may store or retain the property for the vendee, and sue for the contract price. (2) He may keep the goods as his own, and recover the excess of the contract price over and above the market price of the goods at the time and place of delivery; or (3) he may sell them at the vendee's risk, and sue the vendee for the difference between the contract price and the price obtained at said sale. . . .

In the case at bar the vendor of the goods in question did not resort to any of the remedies open to him, but while reserving the property in, and the right to the possession of the goods, and refusing to deliver them to the vendee, except upon payment of the contract price, left them on the dock without making any effort to provide for their care or safety. The appellee could not take charge of the goods, and if the appellant had stored them for the appellee they might not have been destroyed by fire. The appellee should not therefore be required to suffer the loss of which his breach of the contract was not the proximate cause. . . .

Judgment affirmed, with costs.

3. THE PRICE

S. F. BOWSER & COMPANY *v.* MARKS

ARKANSAS SUPREME COURT, 1910

[96 *Arkansas Reports,* 113]

FRAUENTHAL, J. This was an action instituted by the appellant to recover the purchase price of an oil tank and pump which it alleged it sold to the appellees. The appellant was located at Fort Wayne, Indiana, and was engaged in the manufacture and sale of oil tanks and pumps and other wares; and the appellees were merchants located at Sheridan, Arkansas. On September 15, 1908, appellees made a written offer to purchase from appellant an oil tank and pump by the following letter:

Sheridan, Ark., September 15, 1908.

S. F. Bowser & Co.,
Fort Wayne, Ind.

Gentlemen: Please ship me at once one sixty-five gal. oil tank and pump. I bought one of these tanks of you in 1906. Now I would like to have another one.

Yours truly,
F. K. Marks & Co.

Upon receipt of said letter on September 17, 1908, appellant wrote to appellees, accepting the order and stating that it would make immediate shipment. Thereafter appellant promptly shipped the oil tank and pump by delivering same to a common carrier properly addressed to appellees, and also sent them bill of lading therefor and a statement showing that the price thereof was $55. Thereupon appellees wrote to appellant that they had paid $45 for the tank and pump of the same kind bought from it in 1906, and that they refused to pay $55 for this last tank and pump. Some further correspondence passed between the parties relating to the price of the tank and pump, and the appellant refused to reduce the price from $55. In the meanwhile the article had arrived at Sheridan, Arkansas, and remained with the common carrier during the correspondence. On November 21, 1908, appellees reshipped it to appellant, and notified it of that action. The appellant refused to accept the return of the property, and so notified appellees, and thereupon brought this suit for said $55.

The appellant introduced testimony tending to prove that the cost of the material of which the tank and pump was manufactured in 1906 had advanced, and that $55 was the current price at which it was sold in September, 1908. The case was tried by the court sitting as a jury, who, among others, made the following declarations of law:

"4. Where the minds of both parties have not met as to price and terms, then there is no sale, and the plaintiffs cannot recover."

"5. The oil pump and tank being shipped to the defendants by the plaintiffs without any agreement as to price, and the price being increased since the defendants previously ordered the same kind of goods from the plaintiffs, and the defendants returned the goods to the plaintiffs within a reasonable time, refusing to accept them at the advanced price, then the plaintiffs cannot recover."

The court thereupon made a finding in favor of appellees, and rendered judgment in their favor.

The question involved in this case is whether or not the parties had entered into a contract for the bargain and sale of the pump and tank. The appellees contend that the contract was not entered into because the price of the article had not been agreed upon, and that on this account there was no mutual assent to one of the essential terms of the alleged contract. The price is one of the essential elements involved in the agreement to make a contract of sale, and there must be an agreement of the parties to the price, either express or implied, before there can be a completion of a sale. But it is not necessary that the price be expressly stipulated by the parties. If the parties have agreed to all the other elements of the sale and have made no reference to the price, then the law will by implication fix the price, which will be what the article is then reasonably worth.

A contract not only includes the things said or written, but also terms and matters which, though not actually expressed, are implied by law, and these are as binding as those actually written or spoken. . . .

By their letter of September 15, 1908, the appellees made an unconditional offer to purchase the oil tank and pump, and this offer was accepted by appellant. No price was fixed or mentioned, and the law read the price into the offer. The agreement then became mutual, and the contract of sale completed. And when, in pursuance of such contract, the appellant delivered the tank and pump to a common carrier in the usual course of business, properly addressed to appellees, the title to the property passed to them, and they became liable for the reasonable value thereof at the time of the acceptance of the offer to purchase.

It is urged by counsel for appellees that there was a mistake in the price made by the parties, and that on this account the contract was not assented to by both, and therefore was not effective. It is contended that the appellees understood the price to be $45, and that appellant understood it to be $55. It is true that the appellees may have entertained an unexpressed intention to pay only $45 for the tank and pump. But an agreement is established by the words used, and the law imputes to the parties a meaning corresponding to those words. An unexpressed state of mind of one of the parties cannot affect the agreement as established by the words that are employed. In this case there was no dispute or disagreement about the price and no misunderstanding by either party thereto. There was simply no reference made to the price. It cannot be said therefore that there was any mistake made as to the price. The fact that appellees had purchased the same kind of article at a certain price in 1906 could not determine the price thereof in 1908. If they had intended to make the offer of purchase at the price paid in 1906, they should have made an express stipulation in their offer to that effect. Failing to name any price, the law implies that they intended to pay for the oil tank and pump the price that it was reasonably worth; and as to such an article as this that would be the current selling price thereof at the time the offer to purchase it was accepted.

The court therefore erred in its declarations of law.

The judgment is reversed, and the cause remanded for a new trial.

Note that in ACEBAL *v.* LEVY, 10 Bing. 376 (Court of Common Pleas, 1834) Tindal, C. J. said at page 382: "Whether in all cases of an executory contract of purchase and sale, where the parties are altogether silent as to the price, the law will supply the want of any agreement as to price, by inferring that the parties must have intended to sell and to buy at a reasonable price, may be a question of some difficulty. Undoubtedly the law makes that inference where the contract is *executed* by the acceptance of the goods by the Defendants, in order to prevent the injustice of the Defendant taking the goods without paying for them. (See note 2 of Mr. Serjt. Williams to *Webber* v. *Tivill*, 2 Saund. 121.) But it may be questionable whether the same reason applies to a case where the contract is *executory* only, and where the goods are still in the possession, or under the control, of the seller."

Contrast GREAT WESTERN DISTILLERY PRODUCTS *v.* JOHN A. WATHEN DISTILLERY CO., 66 P. (2nd) 717 (California District Court of Appeal, 1937), where the court said that "the rule is that when no price is specified in a contract for the sale of goods, whether executory or executed, the price is supplied by the implication that a reasonable price is intended."

HEYMAN COHEN & SONS, INC. *v.* M. LURIE WOOLEN COMPANY, INC.

NEW YORK COURT OF APPEALS, 1921

[232 *New York Reports*, 112]

Appeal from a judgment, entered July 8, 1921, upon an order of the Appellate Division of the Supreme Court in the first judicial department, which reversed an order of Special Term denying a motion by defendant for judgment on the pleadings and granted said motion.

CARDOZO, J. The pleadings show a written contract, dated April 10, 1919, by which the plaintiff agrees to buy and the defendant to sell two hundred pieces of tricotine at $3.02½ per yard, delivery to be completed by June 1, 1919. The plaintiff is given the "privilege . . . to confirm more of the above if M. Lurie Woolen Company [the defendant] can get more." The two hundred pieces were delivered and paid for. The plaintiff, exercising its option, demanded as much more of the cloth as defendant could procure. The defendant confirmed the exercise of the option, and delivered sixteen additional pieces with the statement that it could procure no more. In fact, it had procured five hundred pieces, which it withheld. The plaintiff suffered damage for which judgment is demanded.

We find no lack of consideration for the concession of an option. The privilege to order more is coupled with the promise and obligation to accept a stated minimum (1 Williston on Contracts, secs. 44, 140). *Schlegel Mfg. Co.* v. *Cooper's Glue Factory* (231 N. Y. 459) is not adverse to our conclusion. There the option stood alone; it was voluntary and revocable. Here the option is supported by the consideration of the sale.

The defendant, then, is bound, unless its promise is to be ignored as meaningless. Rejection on that ground is at best a last resort (*Matter of Buechner,* 226 N. Y. 440, 443; *Ellis* v. *Miller,* 164 N. Y. 434, 438; 1 Williston on Contracts, secs. 37, 137). Indefiniteness must reach the point where construction becomes futile. Uncertainties, thought to be impenetrable, are suggested in respect of subject-matter, time and price. They will be found to be unreal. It is said that we cannot tell whether the buyer, in exercising the option, must make demand for all that the seller can supply, or is free to call for less. We think the implication plain that the buyer is to fix the quantity, subject only to the proviso that quantity shall be limited by ability to supply. It is said the option does not state the time within which election is to be announced. We think a reasonable time is a term implied by law (*Pope* v. *Terre Haute Car & Mfg. Co.,* 107 N. Y. 61, 63). It is said the option does not embody a statement of the price. We think a "privilege to confirm more" imports a privilege to confirm at the price of the initial quantity. This option was drawn by merchants. We are persuaded that merchants reading it would not be doubtful of its meaning. It was meant to accomplish something. We find no such elements of vagueness as to justify the conclusion that in reality it accomplished nothing. . . .

The order of the Appellate Division should be reversed, and that of the Special Term affirmed, with costs in the Appellate Division and in this court.

HISCOCK, Ch. J., HOGAN, POUND, MCLAUGHLIN and ANDREWS, JJ., concur; CRANE, J., dissents.

Ordered accordingly.

ST. REGIS PAPER COMPANY *v.* HUBBS & HASTINGS PAPER COMPANY

NEW YORK COURT OF APPEALS, 1923

[235 *New York Reports,* 30]

Appeal from a judgment, entered June 19, 1922, upon an order of the Appellate Division of the Supreme Court in the fourth judicial department, which reversed an order of the court at a Trial Term setting aside a verdict in favor of plaintiff and granting a new trial and directed reinstatement of said verdict.

POUND, J. Plaintiff sues for an unpaid balance on the sale of paper. Defendant, not denying the allegations of the complaint, sets up a counterclaim, alleging that plaintiff is a manufacturer of print paper, such as newspapers are printed on, and the defendant is a broker in the sale of such paper; that defendant as such broker secured contracts for plaintiff from three newspaper publishers for their supply of paper for given periods; that the understanding was that defendant should guarantee the accounts and that the paper so shipped should in the first instance be charged to defendant and not to the newspaper publishers; that plaintiff, after furnishing the publishers paper under such contracts for some time, repudiated its agreement, delivered no more paper and refused to pay defendant the commissions to which it would have been entitled, to its damage.

On the trial it appeared that the transactions between the parties took the following form of written contracts, one set of which was in substance as follows:

Defendant as buyer (for Rochester Printing Company), and plaintiff as seller entered into a contract of sale of paper, 4,500 tons a year for two years from January 1, 1919, price for the first three months ending March 31, 1919, $3.77 per hundred pounds, "price for the balance of the year to be fixed by mutual consent. In the event that the parties to this agreement shall fail to arrange a price for any quarter before the expiration of the preceding three months, this contract, in so far as it pertains to delivery over the unexpired period shall terminate." "If at any time during the life of this contract, both parties can agree on a fixed price for the balance of the contract, that agreement shall take the place of the three months price agreement." The contract under the caption "Remarks" contains the usual provisions relieving either party from liability for failure to take or supply such paper in consequence of strikes and other causes beyond their control. It also provides that the provisions last referred to shall run through to "an original contract" between defendant and the Rochester Printing Company for whose use the contract is placed, and that the publisher and plaintiff are the contracting parties as "to said conditions," i.e., as to strikes, etc.

On the same date Rochester Printing Company as buyer and defendant as seller entered into a contract of sale in the same terms as the foregoing, excepting only that the price was fixed at $4.10 per hundred pounds.

The other two sets of contracts differ only as to name of publisher, price, amount of paper and period covered. In the last quarter of 1919 plaintiff refused to agree with defendant on a price for the first quarter of 1920, and finally quoted a price so high that the publishers could not agree on it with defendant. In so doing it acted arbitrarily without making an attempt to agree and for the purpose of terminating the contract, depriving defendant of its prospective profits on the transaction and placing the business in the hands of others.

Defendant contends that this transaction was a sale by the plaintiff to the publisher, the defendant acting as a broker and receiving a commission of two per cent on the contract price. Plaintiff's contention is that the transaction as evidenced by the formal written instruments was a sale to defendant and a resale by it to the publisher. The contract price for the first three months in each transaction was to net defendant two per cent, and this amount was referred to by the parties in their correspondence as a commission.

The trial court submitted to the jury the question whether the defendant was a broker in the transaction and whether plaintiff acted in good faith in trying to fix the price of paper. The jury found for the defendant. The trial justice set the verdict aside and granted a new trial, saying that, assuming defendant acted as broker, its commissions must be limited to two per cent on the paper to be delivered during the first three months of the contract, as the only enforcible contract between the parties was for the first three months' delivery and beyond that nothing but a possibility of future agreement remained.

The Appellate Division held that the contract was between broker and principal and that it implied good faith and required the exercise of an honest attempt to agree on the price of future deliveries; that the case was properly submitted to the jury and that the verdict should be reinstated.

Doubtless a broker's authority cannot be terminated in bad faith so as to permit the principal to take advantage of the broker's efforts in his behalf and at the same time escape the payment of his commissions (*Sibbald* v. *Bethlehem Iron Co.*, 83 N. Y. 378), but good faith does not require the contracting parties to do more than they are expressly or impliedly bound by their contract to do, and the question arises as to the real contract of the parties evidenced by their solemnly executed writings.

The written agreements, except as to price fixing, are complete, certain, explicit and free from ambiguity. They are unmistakably contracts, not of brokerage, but of purchase and sale. The parties have put their bargain into the form they chose. The court has no power to alter or vary the terms which they have deliberately used to express their intention. The real agreement of the parties as thus expressed is that plaintiff will sell and defendant will buy and that defendant will sell and the publisher will buy the paper on the conditions indicated. "When a legal act is reduced into a single memorial, all other utterances of the parties on the topic are legally immaterial for the purpose of determining what are the terms of their act." (Wigmore on Evidence, § 2425.) The evidence in the case all tends to establish that the written contracts are the full expression of the terms of the parties' agreement. When the question is one of the interpretation of a contract, entire in itself in all particulars, it is only when different inferences may fairly be drawn as to the meaning and effect of the written language used, that the relation of the parties and the surrounding circumstances are to be considered by the jury in arriving at their intention. (*Lamb* v. *Norcross Bros. Co.*, 208 N. Y. 427, 431.) Evidence of a parol brokerage agreement was, therefore, incompetent to show that the formal writings were not the final repository of the agreements before us. "You can no more add to or contradict its legal effect by parol stipulations preceding or accompanying its execution than you can alter it through the same means in any other respect." (*Thomas* v. *Scutt*, 127 N. Y. 133, 140.)

But one element of the contracts was left open to future negotiations. Prices were to be fixed by mutual agreement and if the parties did not agree, the contracts were to terminate. These terms are so indefinite as to have no legal significance; they amount to nothing more than an agreement to make a future agreement; an agreement to agree is not enforcible. Plaintiff exercised its legal right in refusing to be bound thereby. (*United Press* v. *N. Y. Press Co., Ltd.*, 164 N. Y. 406, 413; *Varney* v. *Ditmars*, 217 N. Y. 223.) Defendant's counterclaim should have been dismissed. . . .

The judgment should be reversed and judgment granted in favor of plaintiff against defendant for $44,426.03, with interest from January 15, 1920, with costs in all courts.

HISCOCK, Ch. J., HOGAN, CARDOZO, MCLAUGHLIN, CRANE and ANDREWS, JJ., concur.

Judgment reversed, etc.

SUN PRINTING & PUBLISHING ASSOCIATION *v.* REMINGTON PAPER & POWER COMPANY, INC.

NEW YORK COURT OF APPEALS, 1923

[235 *New York Reports*, 338]

Appeal, by permission, from an order of the Appellate Division of the Supreme Court in the first judicial department, entered April 24, 1922, which reversed an order of Special Term denying a motion by plaintiff for judgment on the pleadings and granted said motion.

The following question was certified: "Does the complaint state facts sufficient to constitute a cause of action?"

CARDOZO, J. Plaintiff agreed to buy and defendant to sell 1,000 tons of paper per month during the months of September, 1919, to December, 1920, inclusive, 16,000 tons in all. Sizes and quality were adequately described. Payment was to be made on the 20th of each month for all paper shipped the previous month. The price for shipments in September, 1919, was to be $3.73¾ per 100 pounds, and for shipments in October, November and December, 1919, $4 per 100 pounds. "For the balance of the period of this agreement the price of the paper and length of terms for which such price shall apply shall be agreed upon by and between the parties hereto fifteen days prior to the expiration of each period for which the price and length of term thereof have been previously agreed upon, said price in no event to be higher than the contract price for newsprint charged by the Canadian Export Paper Company to the large consumers, the seller to receive the benefit of any differentials in freight rates."

Between September, 1919, and December of that year, inclusive, shipments were made and paid for as required by the contract. The time then arrived when there was to be an agreement upon a new price and upon the term of its duration. The defendant in advance of that time gave notice that the contract was imperfect, and disclaimed for the future an obligation to deliver. Upon this, the plaintiff took the ground that the price was to be ascertained by resort to an established standard. It made demand that during each month of 1920 the defendant deliver 1,000 tons of paper at the contract price for newsprint charged by the Canadian Export Paper Company to the large consumers, the defendant to receive the benefit of any differentials in freight rates. The demand was renewed month by month till the expiration of the year. This action has been brought to recover the ensuing damage.

Seller and buyer left two subjects to be settled in the middle of December and at unstated intervals thereafter. One was the price to be paid. The other was the length of time during which such price was to govern. Agreement as to the one was insufficient without agreement as to the other. If price and nothing more had been left open for adjustment, there might be force in the contention that the buyer would be viewed, in the light of later provisions, as the holder of an option (*Cohen & Sons* v. *Lurie Woolen Co.*, 232 N. Y. 112). This would mean that in default of an agreement for a lower price, the plaintiff would have the privilege of calling for delivery in accordance with a price established as a maximum. The price to be agreed upon might be less, but could not be more than "the contract price for newsprint charged by the Canadian Export Paper Company to the large consumers." The difficulty is, however, that ascertainment of this price does not dispense with the necessity for agreement in respect of the term during which the price is to apply. Agreement upon a maximum payable this month or to-day is not the same as an agreement that it shall continue to be payable next month or to-morrow. Seller and buyer understood that the price to be fixed in December for a term to be agreed upon, would not be more than the price then charged by the Canadian Export Paper Company to the large consumers. They did not understand that if during the term so established the price charged by the Canadian Export Paper Company was changed, the price payable to the seller would fluctuate accordingly. This was conceded by plaintiff's counsel on the argument before us. The seller was to receive no more during the running of the prescribed term, though the Canadian maximum was raised. The buyer was to pay no less during that term, though the maximum was lowered. In brief, the standard was to be applied at the beginning of the successive terms, but once applied was to be maintained until the term should have expired. While the term was unknown, the contract was inchoate.

The argument is made that there was no need of an agreement as to time unless the price to be paid was lower than the maximum. We find no evidence of this intention in the language of the contract. The result would then be that the defendant would never know where it stood. The plaintiff was under no duty to accept the Canadian standard. It does not assert that it was. What it asserts is that the contract amounted to the concession of an option. Without an agreement as to time, however, there would be not one option, but a dozen. The Canadian price to-day might be less than the Canadian price to-morrow. Election by the buyer to proceed with performance at the price prevailing in one month would not bind it to proceed at the price prevailing in another. Successive options to be exercised every month would thus be read into the contract. Nothing in the wording discloses the intention of the seller to place itself to that extent at the mercy of the buyer. Even if, however, we were to interpolate the restriction that the option, if exercised at all, must be exercised only once, and for the entire quantity permitted, the difficulty would not be ended. Market prices in 1920 happened to rise. The importance of the time element becomes apparent when we ask ourselves what the seller's position would be if they had happened to fall. Without an agreement as to time, the maximum would be lowered from one shipment to another with every reduction of the standard. With such an agreement, on the other hand, there would be stability and certainty. The parties attempted to guard against the contingency of failing to come together as to price. They did not guard against the contingency of failing to come together as to time. Very likely they thought the latter contingency so remote that it could safely be disregarded. In any event, whether through design or through inadvertence, they left the gap unfilled. The result was nothing more than "an agreement to agree" (*St. Regis Paper Co.* v. *Hubbs & Hastings Paper Co.*, 235 N. Y. 30, 36). Defendant "exercised its legal right" when it insisted that there was need of something more (*St. Regis Paper Co.* v. *Hubbs & Hastings Paper Co.*, *supra*; 1 Williston Contracts, § 45). The right is not affected by our appraisal of the motive (*Mayer* v. *McCreery*, 119 N. Y. 434, 440).

We are told that the defendant was under a duty, in default of an agreement, to accept a term that would be reasonable in view of the nature of the transaction and the practice of the business. To hold it to such a standard is to make the contract over. The defendant reserved the privilege of doing its business in its own way, and did not undertake to conform to the practice and beliefs of others (*United Press* v. *N. Y. Press Co.*, 164 N. Y. 406, 413). We are told again that there was a duty, in default of other agreement, to act as if the successive terms were to expire every month. The contract says they are to expire at such intervals as the agreement may prescribe. There is need, it is true, of no high degree of ingenuity to show how the parties, with little change of language, could have framed a form of contract to which obligation would attach. The difficulty is that they framed another. We are not at liberty to revise while professing to construe.

We do not ignore the allegation of the complaint that the contract price charged by the Canadian Export Paper Company to the large consumers "constituted a definite and well defined standard of price that was readily ascertainable." The suggestion as made by members of the court that the price so charged may have been known to be one established for the year, so that fluctuation would be impossible. If that was its character, the complaint should so allege. The writing signed by the parties calls for an agreement as to time. The complaint concedes that no such agreement has been made. The result, *prima facie*, is the failure of the contract. In that situation, the pleader has the burden of setting forth the extrinsic circumstances, if there are any, that make agreement unimportant. There is significance, moreover, in the attitude of counsel. No point is made in brief or in argument that the Canadian price, when once established, is constant through the year. On the contrary, there is at least a tacit assumption that it varies with the market. The buyer acted on the same assumption when it renewed the demand from month to month, making tender of performance at the prices then prevailing. If we misconceive the course of dealing, the plaintiff by amendment of its pleading can correct our misconception. The complaint as it comes before us leaves no escape from the conclusion that agreement in respect of time is as essential to a completed contract as agreement in respect of price. The agreement was not reached, and the defendant is not bound. . . .

CRANE, J. (dissenting).

[One and one-half pages of the opinion are here omitted.]

Surely these parties must have had in mind that some binding agreement was made for the sale and delivery of 16,000 tons rolls of paper, and that the instrument contained all the elements necessary to make a binding contract. It is a strain upon reason to imagine the paper house, the Remington Paper and Power Company, Incorporated, and the Sun Printing and Publishing Association, formally executing a contract drawn up upon the defendant's prepared form which was useless and amounted to nothing. We must, at least, start the examination of this agreement by believing that these intelligent parties intended to make a binding contract. If this be so, the court should spell out a binding contract, if it be possible.

I not only think it possible, but think the paper itself clearly states a contract recognized under all the rules at law. It is said that the one essential element of price is lacking; that the provision above quoted is an agreement to agree to a price, and that the defendant had the privilege of agreeing or not, as it pleased; that if it failed to agree to a price there was no standard by which to measure the amount the plaintiff would have to pay. The contract does state, however, just this very thing. Fifteen days before the first of January, 1920, the parties were to agree upon the price of the paper to be delivered thereafter, and the length of the period for which such price should apply. However, the price to be fixed was not "to be higher than the contract price for newsprint charged by the Canadian Export Paper Company to large consumers." Here surely was something definite. The 15th day of December arrived. The defendant refused to deliver. At that time there was a price for newsprint charged by the Canadian Export Paper Company. If the plaintiff offered to pay this price, which was the highest price the defendant could demand, the defendant was bound to deliver. This seems to be very clear.

But while all agree that the price on the 15th day of December could be fixed, the further objection is made that the period during which that price should continue was not agreed upon. There are many answers to this.

We have reason to believe that the parties supposed they were making a binding contract; that they had fixed the terms by which one was required to take and the other to deliver; that the Canadian Export Paper Company price was to be the highest that could be charged in any event. These things being so, the court should be very reluctant to permit a defendant to avoid its contract. (*Wakeman* v. *Wheeler & Wilson Mfg. Co.*, 101 N. Y. 205.)

On the 15th of the fourth month, the time when the price was to be fixed for subsequent deliveries, there was a price charged by the Canadian

Export Paper Company to large consumers. As the defendant failed to agree upon a price, made no attempt to agree upon a price and deliberately broke its contract, it could readily be held to deliver the rest of the paper, a thousand rolls a month, at this Canadian price. There is nothing in the complaint which indicates that this is a fluctuating price, or that the price of paper as it was on December 15th was not the same for the remaining twelve months.

Or we can deal with this contract, month by month. The deliveries were to be made 1,000 tons per month. On December 15th 1,000 tons could have been demanded. The price charged by the Canadian Export Paper Company on the 15th of each month on and after December 15th, 1919, would be the price for the thousand ton delivery for that month.

Or again, the word as used in the miscellaneous provision quoted is not "price," but "contract price" — "in no event to be higher than the contract price." Contract implies a term or period and if the evidence should show that the Canadian contract price was for a certain period of weeks or months, then this period could be applied to the contract in question.

Failing any other alternative, the law should do here what it has done in so many other cases, apply the rule of reason and compel parties to contract in the light of fair dealing. It could hold this defendant to deliver its paper as it agreed to do, and take for a price the Canadian Export Paper Company contract price for a period which is reasonable under all the circumstances and conditions as applied in the paper trade.

To let this defendant escape from its formal obligations when any one of these rulings as applied to this contract would give a practical and just result is to give the sanction of law to a deliberate breach. (*Wood* v. *Duff-Gordon*, 222 N. Y. 88; *Moran* v. *Standard Oil Co.*, 211 N. Y. 187; *United States Rubber Co.* v. *Silverstein*, 229 N. Y. 168.)

For these reasons I am for the affirmance of the courts below.

HISCOCK, Ch. J., POUND, MCLAUGHLIN and ANDREWS, JJ., concur with CARDOZO, J.; CRANE, J., reads dissenting opinion with which HOGAN, J., concurs.

Order reversed, etc.

WESTON PAPER MFG. CO. *v.* DOWNING BOX CO.

UNITED STATES CIRCUIT COURT OF APPEALS, 7TH CIRCUIT, 1923
[293 *Federal Reporter*, 725]

EVAN A. EVANS, Circuit Judge. Defendant's demurrer to the plaintiff's declaration was sustained and the action was dismissed by the District Court. To review the judgment thus entered, the present writ of error was issued. The controversy arises out of a sales agreement, the material portions of which are set forth below.[1]

[1] "The buyer hereby purchases from the seller, and the seller hereby sells to the buyer, nine hundred (900) tons of standard corrugating strawboard, containing not

Defendant's refusal to accept the strawboard was occasioned by its belief that the agreement was not binding, due to the price provision, which read:

> Which price shall be the seller's market price then existing under this the seller's standard form of quarterly price fixing contract.

Plaintiff set forth its cause of action in three counts, and sought to strengthen its position under the contract by alleging:

". . . That at the time of entering into said agreement, and for more than a year prior thereto, the said defendant was engaged in the manufacture and sale of paper boxes and other paper products; that for such purpose said defendant purchased large quantities of strawboard for corrugating; that during all of said time this plaintiff was engaged extensively in the manufacture and sale of such corrugating strawboard; that this plaintiff had a large and extensive trade in the sale of such strawboard, and it sold to dealers and manufacturers in various parts of the United States, and had a very large number of customers; that, at the time said agreement was entered into, said defendant had knowledge of and knew the above facts, and further knew that this plaintiff had, from time to time, been making sales, and had been entering into contracts for the sale of corrugating strawboard, such as was being purchased by the said defendant; the said defendant did further know that, in the operation of its said business, this plaintiff would thereafter and from time to time be making sales to various persons and corporations desiring to purchase strawboard for corrugating of the kind which defendant agreed to purchase, and that in the making of such sales current conditions must of necessity influence and determine the price to be paid therefor; and that such sales price must necessarily be reasonable and determined by the demand and supply of the

---

to exceed ten per cent. (10%) of moisture, quality and finish same as heretofore furnished.

"Price: Shall be fixed by the seller on or before December 15, 1920, for the first three months' shipments, beginning January 1, 1921. Seller shall give the buyer notice, in writing, on or before the fifteenth (15th) day of third month thereafter, of the price for the tons to be shipped the ensuing three months' period, which price shall be the seller's market price then existing under this the seller's standard form of quarterly price fixing contract.

"Shipments shall be made as follows: Seventy-five (75) tons per month from January 1, 1921, to December 31, 1921, both inclusive.

"Terms: Cash in ten (10) days from date of invoice, less two per cent. (2%).

"Specifications: The buyer shall furnish to the seller, on or before the 15th of each month, specifications for the following month's requirements. If the buyer fails to furnish specifications for any month or months within the time provided above, the specifications last furnished by the buyer may be considered by the seller as specifications for future shipments until superseded by new specifications furnished by the buyer. The seller may at its option, however, cancel any tonnage not specified by the buyer within the time above provided.

"Sizes: Shall be such as will cut to advantage on machines which trim seventy-two and one half (72½), eighty (80), and one hundred and ten (110) inches of Terre Haute, Ind. mill, eighty-five (85) inches on Rockford, Ill., mill. Each month's requirements shall be considered as a separate contract, but, upon default of the buyer in payment, the seller may suspend or cancel this contract at seller's option."

product at the time such sales were being made, all of which facts defendant knew, and contracted with reference thereto."

In two separate counts, plaintiff sought to hold defendant because of acceptance or part performance of the contract. It will be necessary to separately consider whether these counts each set forth a cause of action, and the necessary fact statement will be made when reached.

Plaintiff asserts, and the defendant denies, the validity of a sales agreement where the "market price" is determined, as here, by the seller. In fact it is urged that such a provision is not a "market price" in any proper sense of the term, but is the seller's price, and brings the case squarely within the rule, announced in many cases, to the effect that an agreement which leaves the price to be fixed by the seller is too indefinite to be enforced and is void.

Plaintiff, contending that the contract should be construed, if possible, so as to uphold it, insists that it is neither unilateral nor uncertain, but governed by the maxim, *Id certum est quod certum reddi potest.* While so recognizing the rule for which plaintiff contends, we are unable to apply it to the facts in this case. We see nothing in this contract which takes from the seller the absolute right to fix the price in the future. Certainly defendant had no voice in fixing this price. Nor did any third party have any immediate influence upon plaintiff in determining the price. True, plaintiff may, in acting, have been governed by a desire to hold future business, or have been prompted by other laudable motives. But plaintiff could have arbitrarily changed the price each quarter, and from such arbitrary fixation defendant had no appeal. Upon the ground of uncertainty, and also for want of consideration, we conclude the agreement as drawn was unenforceable.

Plaintiff contends, however, that at least two of the counts are good as against attack by demurrer. As a basis for its position, it points to the allegation in count 1 of the declaration, which reads:

"That in accordance with said written agreement, Exhibit A, plaintiff did on December 15, 1920, give notice in writing to defendant and fix the price of the strawboard so agreed to be sold and purchased for the succeeding three months, to wit, January, February, and March, 1921, at the sum of one hundred ($100) dollars per ton; that said price so fixed was the seller's then existing market price, was fair and reasonable, and was determinable by sales which had been made; that thereupon said defendant acknowledged receipt of said written notice so fixing said price; that said defendant made no objection whatever to the price as so fixed by this plaintiff, but acquiesced therein, and did give specifications and order out part of the tonnage for said three months, and requested delay of shipping for the balance; that the said defendant did accept the said price so fixed by plaintiff as the price to be paid for the strawboard tonnage so to be manufactured and sold to said defendant during said three months; that this plaintiff did thereupon manufacture and offer to deliver during said three months two hundred twenty-five (225) tons of said strawboard so agreed to be sold and purchased, and this plaintiff has duly performed, fulfilled, and carried out all of the terms and provisions of said agreement on its part to be performed, and has been and still is ready and willing to perform said agreement," etc.

Under the authorities there can be no question but that goods shipped under contracts void because of uncertainty as to price, yet accepted by the purchaser when delivered, must be paid for, and at the price determined by the standard named in the contract. Such part performance, however, does not validate the entire agreement.

In the present case, we are dealing with a slightly different question, considering the sufficiency of a declaration, not passing upon the merits of the case. The question narrows itself down to the effect of the allegation that defendant — "acknowledged receipt of the said written notice so fixing said price . . . made no objection whatever to the prices as so fixed . . . and did give specifications and ordered out part of the tonnage for said three months and requested delay of shipment for the balance; that the said defendant did accept the said price so fixed by said plaintiff as the price to be paid for the strawboard tonnage so to be manufactured," etc.

Does this allegation charge defendant with liability under a contract which, though void at its inception, became valid and binding through accepted modifications that overcome the uncertainty? In other words, we have a situation where the parties entered into an agreement which as drawn was nonenforceable because of uncertainty as to price. Under these circumstances, had the vendor written to the defendant, and said: "The contract which we have entered into is indefinite and uncertain, and therefore invalid. I now propose to make it definite and certain, by making you the same proposal as found in the written agreement, excepting only the price provision, which was heretofore indefinite and uncertain, I now fix at $90 per ton. Will you accept?" — and had the purchaser replied, "I accept," could the validity of such a contract have been questioned? Obviously not. Nor can we escape the conclusion that such is the construction we must give to the foregoing allegation in the declaration, challenged only by demurrer.

The second count in the declaration, covering the second quarter of the year, differs materially from the first count, and fails to set forth the allegations of fact necessary to hold defendant under any modified contract. It is true the word "accept" is here used. But, as descriptive of defendant's action, it is limited and restricted by the words preceding it in the same sentence, which words are not sufficient to spell out a valid contract, without which defendant's liability cannot be established. It follows, therefore, that while the demurrer was properly sustained as to the second and third counts, it should have been overruled as to the first count of the declaration.

The judgment is reversed, with costs, with directions to proceed in a manner consistent with the views here set forth.

Compare KINGS COUNTY PACKING CO. *v.* SUNLAND SALES COOPERATIVE ASSOCIATION, 100 Calif. App. 126 (District Court of Appeal, 1929), where a contract for the sale of raisins contained the clause: "Buyer shall pay hereunder for 2-crown Loose Muscats per pound the price quoted by Seller on 15-ounce seeded cartons." It was held that the expression "price quoted by Seller" meant the price quoted in the general market to the general trade.

MEMPHIS FURNITURE MFG. CO. *v.* WEMYSS FURNITURE CO.

UNITED STATES CIRCUIT COURT OF APPEALS, SIXTH CIRCUIT, 1924

[2 *Federal Reporter (2d Series)*, 428]

Action at law by the Wemyss Furniture Company against the Memphis Furniture Manufacturing Company. Judgment for plaintiff, and defendant brings error. Affirmed.

The Wemyss Furniture Company, hereafter called the plaintiff, recovered a judgment against the Memphis Furniture Manufacturing Company, hereafter called the defendant, for breach of contract. Reversal of such judgment is sought.

About November 1, 1919, Janes, president of defendant, and Miller and Couch, of furniture companies located in Oklahoma and Little Rock, Ark., respectively, visited plaintiff's plant at Evansville, Ind., to buy furniture. Throughout that year the furniture market was very active. Jobbers, to meet the demands of trade, purchased extensively, and prices advanced about every 30 days. The cost of wages and raw material likewise advanced, and difficulty was experienced by manufacturers in obtaining and keeping labor and procuring needed material. Producing companies, on account of labor conditions, were not in a position to produce their normal output. Labor took advantage of the market situation, and jobbers bought to an extent which might be deemed speculative, and, as it sometimes proved, overloaded themselves. The continuing changes in the cost of production necessitated corresponding increases in the selling price of goods, and manufacturers, therefore, including plaintiff, began to accept orders subject to prices in effect on date of shipment at their factories and their ability to ship. The plaintiff and furniture manufacturers generally had oversold, and were not in a position to fill orders promptly, which fact was communicated to Janes and Miller. They were, however, willing to buy, notwithstanding the necessary delay in shipment. Prices were the highest ever known by any of the parties to this litigation, and were still advancing, and were expected to continue to do so, although Janes knew a decline was coming, but did not know when. . . .

The furniture purchased was of a special pattern or design of the Louis XV period, and was made for a New York jobber, H. Herman Manufacturing Company, but in reality for the Hudson Metal Bed Company. A pencil memorandum of the precise quantity of goods desired was made by Miller, who also placed an order for the same styles of furniture, on which memorandum was stamped: "Prices prevailing at time of shipment and subject to our ability to ship. Contingent on whether or not we can get H. Herman Mfg. Co.'s consent to use designs; if not, selection to be made from regular line." On November 26, plaintiff wrote defendant that it would be in position to take care of defendant on the pattern selected, and, having procured the eastern jobber's consent to the use of the special designs, mailed, on January 8, 1921, to defendant an acceptance of its order, which acceptance, after enumerating the items and styles of articles sold, provided as follows: "Due to the uncertainty of manufacturing, this order is accepted subject to prices in effect on shipping date, and our ability to ship. Your valued order received and entered as above." Thereafter the plaintiff began the fabrication of the goods sold.

On March 22, defendant, on account of the overcrowded condition of its warehouse, requested plaintiff to make no further shipments on the unfilled order for at least 60 to 90 days. Its purpose was to secure a postponement of shipments on both its November order and its order given in the preceding June for goods of the value of about $22,000, which, on account of the excessive number of its orders, the plaintiff had been unable entirely to fill. The plaintiff so understood, and notified defendant that the goods purchased by it were in process of manufacture, and that work on them would be put aside and their shipment delayed, as requested. In response the defendant wrote on March 26 that it was impossible for it to take care of further shipments inside of 60 to 90 days, and again requested no earlier shipments be made. At that time the plaintiff had purchased all the materials (which were then at the highest price) necessary to filling the order and had expended a considerable sum in manufacturing the goods, and, on account of the unusual conditions in the furniture business, had endeavored to complete its work on them as soon as practicable, and could have done so within 40 days. At no time after March 22 did the defendant request the shipment of goods, nor did it at any time complain of want of promptness on plaintiff's part in making and shipping them, or suggest that they were to have been shipped in 60 days from the date of the order, as claimed on the trial.

On May 3, plaintiff's factory was closed by a strike for a period of more than two months, excepting as to some of the shop foremen. At the end of that period manufacturing was resumed with such men as plaintiff was able to get and acquaint with its work, but the number did not exceed more than 60 per cent. of its usual force, until the day following Labor Day, when the strike ended. On July 8, defendant requested a cancellation of all unfilled orders. The request was granted as to the partially unfilled order of June, 1919, but refused as to the November order. On July 26, defendant wrote plaintiff not to ship further merchandise under any circumstances without order, as it would be unable to take and use further goods. On August 2, plaintiff notified defendant: "If the goods you had ordered had been our regular line, we would not object in the least to either canceling your order or postponing shipment to whatever date would suit your convenience. However, I believe you will agree with me that, when special suites are ordered, and they are cut and made up especially for a merchant or jobber, it is up to such merchant or jobber to take them when ready for shipment. * * * I think Mr. Kerr has explained to you the goods are not entirely ready as yet for shipment, but probably will be in the next three to six weeks." The evidence of both Wemyss and Kerr is that the goods had been manufactured by the last-named date, but had not been wrapped or crated for shipment. On August 3, the defendant wrote: "We are badly overstocked with goods, trade is at a standstill, and to take in further merchandise under these conditions is suicidal and out of the question." It again asked for a cancellation of its orders, notwithstanding the inconvenience and embarrassment which might arise to plaintiff.

On October 8, plaintiff informed defendant that, if it did not accept delivery, the plaintiff would be compelled to hold it responsible for any shrinkage in value between the then prices and what it might realize, if compelled to dispose of the goods in the open market, and suggested that it was willing to meet the defendant half way on any proposition it might care to make that would be fair to the plaintiff. As defendant did not take the furniture which, at plaintiff's price at its factory, after allowing discounts, was of the value of $12,220.42, it was sold by plaintiff, after diligent effort, on December 23, for $5,699. Suit was brought for the difference of $6,521.42, with interest. . . .

The price of furniture advanced until about March, 1920, following which the market became dull and prices stationary, or substantially so, until in July or August (the evidence being conflicting as to the precise date), when prices declined. The plaintiff issued a price list on or about March 1, 1920, at which time prices were at their peak. This price list, which did not designate the price of goods of the special pattern purchased by defendant, was continued throughout the year. Prices of furniture of the same grade and quality were substantially the same in the various furniture markets, the variation probably not exceeding 5 per cent. (excepting freight charges), but the cost of production in different factories differed on account of the variation in skill and economies in manufacturing. The plaintiff throughout the year maintained the prices fixed by it on March 1, and effected many sales and shipments at those prices; evidence being offered in its behalf that no decline in the prices of furniture of the special design purchased by defendant had occurred down to October 25. Janes fixed the period of greatest depression in August, September, and October, and stated that his company offered goods at 50 per cent. less than March prices, but that after November 1 there was some advancement in prices. Miller testified that during those months goods could be bought at the reduced price just mentioned.

McLure, Rhodes, and Kahn were dealers in furniture in Memphis. The evidence of McLure is that by September 15, the price had gone off a third, and by October 15 a half; that of Rhodes, that the depreciation was, down to October 25, from 15 per cent. to 50 per cent., and for the higher grades of goods from 25 to 40 or 50 per cent.; that of Kahn, that the decline down to the last-named date was from 25 to 50 per cent., and that much furniture could be bought at from 30, 35, and even 50 per cent. less than list prices. He bought furniture on September 10 at a price which was 27½ per cent. off the price list, and on October 25 at about 28 and 28½ per cent.

below such price. During the period of depression some manufacturers sold below their listed prices and some did not.

Before DONAHUE and MACK, Circuit Judges, and SATER, District Judge.

SATER, District Judge (after stating the facts as above). The defendant insists (1) that the arrangement between the parties under which the goods were to be manufactured and shipped was such as not to constitute a binding contract on the plaintiff, for want of consideration and mutuality — that is to say, the arrangement was such that the plaintiff was at liberty to carry it out or not, as it might elect, and, as it was not binding on both parties, it was not binding on either; and (2) that, if there was a contract, the price was not fixed, but stated to be "subject to prices in effect on shipping date," or "prices prevailing at the time of shipment," which necessarily meant the market price, and not the price which the manufacturer might fix at the time of shipment.

[A paragraph of the opinion is here omitted.]

In the instant case, an order was given for a specified quantity of goods. The plaintiff accepted that order, designating the price to be paid and the rate of discount for prompt payment. Both parties knew the fabrication and shipment of the goods would be delayed on account of the plaintiff's duty to fulfill prior contracts. The time of performance was not fixed. The law, therefore, fixed a reasonable time in which it was to be performed, and what was a reasonable time is a question to be determined in view of all the circumstances which may have been supposed reasonably to have been in contemplation of the parties.

[A paragraph of the opinion is here omitted.]

The contract did not specifically state the price to be paid for the goods on delivery. To constitute a sale the price need not be definitely fixed at the time the sale is effected, if the agreement contains express or implied provisions by which it may be rendered certain. Whether the price to be paid was the market price at the time of delivery, as claimed by defendant, or the price fixed by the plaintiff at its factory, as plaintiff asserts, the data for determining the price was present and easily ascertainable. Which of the contentions made is correct is immaterial, in view of the verdict (hereafter to be considered) returned by the jury and the failure of the plaintiff to assail its action.

The defendant, at all times down to the commencement of this suit, treated the contract as valid. Its request for delay carried with it the implication of willingness to perform at a later date. Its direction to cancel was also a recognition of the contract's binding force. With full knowledge that the plaintiff had undertaken its fulfillment, and had incurred expense in that behalf, and contemplated full performance, it suggested no infirmity in it, or intention to escape liability if damages were sought for its breach. The situation was such as to give full force to the rules of construction tersely stated in *American Sugar Refining Co.* v. *Newnan Grocery Co.*, 284 F. 835, 836 (C. C. A. 5), as follows:

"A contract will be given that construction which will make it valid and binding, instead of a construction which would make it void or unenforceable. *Hobbs* v. *McLean*, 117 U. S. 567, 6 S. Ct. 870, 29 L. Ed. 940. Likewise a contract should be construed in favor of mutuality. 13 C. J. 539; *Minn. Lumber Co.* v. *Whitebreast Coal Co.*, 160 Ill. 85, 43 N. E. 774, 31 L. R. A. 529. A construction which makes confused verbiage intelligible will be adopted. *Senter* v. *Senter*, 87 Ohio St. 377, 101 N. E. 272."

See, also, *La Grange Grocery Co.* v. *Lamborn & Co.*, 283 F. 869, 872 (C. C. A. 5).

Error is predicated upon the fact that in the court's general charge the jury was told that under the contract the price to be charged was, in conformity to defendant's contention, the market price at the time of shipment, which instruction was not at any time withdrawn, and that at the conclusion of such charge, and after inquiring if counsel had anything to suggest, the court thrice instructed the jury, with some variation in phraseology, that the contract price was the plaintiff's price in effect at its factory at the time when the goods were ready for delivery. Inconsistent and contradictory instructions, such as were given, tend to confusion and misapprehension, and, generally speaking, are ground for reversal, if given on a material point. 13 Standard Ency. Proc. 800, 802; *Deserant* v. *Cerillos Coal R. R. Co.*, 178 U. S. 420, 20 S. Ct. 967, 44 L. Ed. 1127. Had the jury allowed the price for the goods as fixed at the plaintiff's factory at the time the furniture was ready for shipment, its verdict would have been for $6,521.42, and, if interest had been computed on that sum, for more than $7,100. Its verdict, however, for $3,756, was manifestly based on the market price at that date, as that price was determined by the jury, to which fact plaintiff has entered no objection. If the verdict returned included interest as prayed for, and which the court said the jury might allow or not, as it deemed proper, if it found for the plaintiff, the plaintiff's factory price was reduced by the jury by just about 25 per cent. If interest was not included in the verdict, the reduction was a trifle less than 23 per cent. The divergence in the evidence as to the extent the market prices were below the list prices was great, being from 15 per cent. to 50 per cent. The jury having determined to base its verdict upon the difference between the market price and the sum realized by plaintiff on the sale of the goods, it was for it to say what the market price was, and how much the decline had been from the plaintiff's price as fixed at the factory. If the decline was fixed at the rate of 23 or 25 per cent., there is evidence to justify its action. Inasmuch as it adopted the rule as to the controlling price at the time of delivery for which the defendant has at all times contended, and of which the plaintiff does not complain, no benefit can accrue to defendant by the granting of a new trial, notwithstanding the contradictory nature of the charge.

We find no prejudicial error, and the judgment of the trial court is therefore affirmed.

Note FORD *v.* NORTON, 32 New Mexico 518 (Supreme Court, 1927), as to the meaning of the term "market price" and the time to which it attaches. Here in connection with the lease of a filling station there was a contract for the sale of gasoline during the life of the lease at "current market prices." A rival dealer in the course of a "gas war" put equivalent gasoline on the market at a price which the seller refused to meet, and the buyer thereupon purchased from the rival. The seller claimed that under such conditions the price set by the rival could not be deemed a "market price," and that in any event the term "market price" in the contract meant the highest market price and not the lowest. In upholding the denial of an application by the seller to enjoin the buyer from purchasing from the rival supplier, the court said: "We are to decide from the language used what was the reasonable intention of parties who contemplated a course of dealing involving daily purchases and sales extending over a term of years.

"The contract did not specify that appellees were to pay the 'highest' market price. It is safe to say that, if a contract containing such a provision had been tendered for appellee's signature, it would not have been signed. The word 'highest' would have suggested endless disagreement between the parties and the danger of being undersold by competitors who might be foresighted enough to supply themselves at the 'lowest' market price. It is much more reasonable to suppose that the contracting parties intended to sell and buy, respectively, at the 'lowest' market price. Appellees, bound for ten years, and themselves compelled to compete in the retail market, must, if their business was to prosper and survive, be able to buy as cheaply as competitors could. Of course, section 10 was for their benefit and should be so construed as to give them such advantage as may reasonably have been intended. So, if the expressions used were deemed ambiguous, calling for consideration of the conditions existing and the situation of the contracting parties and the bringing in of a qualifying adjective, we should prefer 'lowest' to 'highest.'

"We do not think, however, that there is ambiguity. 'Current market price' in a case of this kind, means that the contract shall run or flow with the market, following its fluctuations. The market price of a commodity is the exchange value. It is determined by the demand for it in relation to the supply, and is proved, when possible, by actual sales. Appellant argues that market price is to be determined by certain imaginary normal conditions of trade. This is unsound. Low markets are usually the result of being glutted by the anxiety or necessity of some owners to dispose of their goods, even at a loss. The costs of production and of doing business, of course, have their influence in establishing price. But it is only in the long run. Immediately, market price is fixed by supply and demand. The Clayton Coal & Oil Company, in order to move gasoline, put it on the market at 17 cents. So long as that supply lasted, the market price was 17 cents. We cannot see that it matters whether its motive was to destroy competition or quickly to raise money to meet pressing obligations, or whether it lost or profited by its transactions. When that supply was exhausted, the relation between supply and demand changed. Gasoline was then unobtainable in Springer at less than 18½ cents. So that became the market price."

Compare H. T. COTTAM & Co. *v.* MOISES, 149 Louisiana 306 (Supreme Court, 1921), where it was held that an unpriced order received at New Orleans for goods to be shipped to Honduras was correctly filled by charging prices based on "market values at the time of shipment."

Note also CORBETT *v.* WINSTON ELKHORN COAL CO., 296 Fed. 577 (Circuit Court of Appeals, 6th Circuit, 1924), in which there was a contract for the sale of the output of a coal mine during a period of five years "at market price at time of shipment . . . less 10 per cent commission." The conduct of both parties under the contract was more consistent with the view that their intention was for the seller to receive the price current on the days when orders were given, less 10 per cent. In an action by the seller to recover amounts claimed to be owed on the basis of the contract as written, the buyer in a cross-petition prayed for specific performance and an accounting. The court said on the question of price:

"A contract requiring a selling agent to pay the market price on day of shipment would be practically impossible of performance by the agent on a rising market, and especially so if the principal is permitted to delay shipment through necessity or whim until the market price on day of shipment is largely in excess of the price at which the agent had sold the coal. On the other hand, in case of a falling market, such a provision would be wholly inconsistent with the further provision in this contract that the principal is to receive the whole of the selling price, less 10 per cent. commission; that is to say, if coal were sold to-day for $3, and at date of shipment the market price were but $2, the principal under one provision of this contract would be entitled to all the money received by the agent, less 10 per cent., and under the other provision to but $2, less 10 per cent. although the agent, received $3 for his principal's coal. It must be remembered that this contract was to continue for practically five years, and it necessarily must have been within the contemplation of the parties that in that length of time there would be both a rising and falling market. Nor is it conceivable that a selling agent would be sent out by his principal to sell coal at the market price, or best price obtainable, upon day of shipment. If the agent were able to find any customers willing to buy upon these conditions, such customers would certainly demand, not only a further agreement as to prompt delivery, but also a definite date when such delivery would be made, and there is nothing in this contract that would authorize the agent to bind his undisclosed principal to a definite date of delivery."

OUTLET EMBROIDERY COMPANY, INC. *v.* DERWENT MILLS, LTD.

New York Court of Appeals, 1930

[254 *New York Reports*, 179]

Appeal, by permission, from an order of the Appellate Division of the Supreme Court in the first judicial department, entered January 31, 1930, which affirmed an order of Special Term denying a motion for a dismissal of the complaint.

The following question was certified:

"Does the amended complaint herein state facts sufficient to constitute a cause of action?"

Cardozo, Ch. J. The question to be determined is whether a complaint is sufficient, and this depends upon the question whether documents made part of it contain the essentials of a contract.

The defendant, by Brucks & Peyser, its agents, wrote the plaintiff as follows:

June 15, 1929.

Outlet Embroidery Co.,
412 6th Avenue,
New York City.

Gentlemen: Enclosed please find copy of your order placed with us today, terms on same 3/10 days, delivery as soon as possible.

We have cabled this order today to England as these goods will be made up special for you.

Please send us your confirmation of same by return mail.

Also note that the price of $3.10 per box on your Fil D'Angora brand which we are to ship to you is subject to change pending tariff revision.

Yours very truly
BRUCKS & PEYSER
Morell Peyser.

All Prices Subject to Change Pending Tariff Revision.

Accompanying this letter was an order specifying quantities and colors, and repeating the statement that the price was to be $3.10 per box. The plaintiff, on receipt of the letter and its inclosure, made answer as follows:

June 17, 1929.

Brucks & Peyser,
100 Fifth Avenue,
New York, N. Y.

Gentlemen: Received your letter dated June 15, 1929, enclosing copy of my order.

We confirm the same as requested.

We hope you will deliver the merchandise as soon as possible and avoid last seasons delays.

Very truly yours,
OUTLET EMBY. SUPPLY CO., INC.
per: A. Dratler.

Three days later (June 20, 1929)the defendant canceled its acceptance, and notified the plaintiff that it would refuse to make delivery.

The plaintiff sues for the damages resulting from the refusal. The defendant insists that since the price was subject to change pending revision of the tariff, the agreement, though in other respects complete, was inchoate and abortive (*United Press* v. *New York Press Co.*, 164 N. Y. 406; *Sun P. & P. Assn.* v. *Remington P. & P. Co.*, 235 N. Y. 338).

The letters between plaintiff and defendant were from one merchant to another. They are to be read as business men would read them, and only as a last resort are to be thrown out altogether as meaningless futilities (*Cohen & Sons, Inc.*, v. *Lurie Woolen Co.*, 232 N. Y. 112, 114; *Solter* v. *Leedom & Worrell Co.*, 252 Fed. Rep. 133). Read the privilege of change with inflexible adherence to its form, and one turns it into nonsense. If the change of price, to be valid, must be declared while revision is still pending, no change may be permitted after the revision is accomplished, which is the very time of all when a change will be essential. To read the reservation thus is to rob it of its efficacy as an implement to be used in furtherance of a business purpose. In the transactions of business life, sanity of end and aim is at least a presumption, albeit subject to be rebutted. The defendant like the plaintiff supposed that in signing these documents it was doing something understood to be significant and serious. It not only accepted the plaintiff's order, but it asked the plaintiff to confirm the terms of the acceptance, and followed this with a cable of the order to its manufacturer abroad. Was it all sound and fury, signifying nothing?

If literalness is sheer absurdity, we are to seek some other meaning whereby reason will be instilled and absurdity avoided. In June, 1929, Congress was debating a new tariff, and the debate continued for a year. Of this we take judicial notice. During the period of suspense, an importer could not be sure whether goods previously ordered from abroad would arrive in the United States before the change or after. If they did not arrive till after, the prices would be inadequate to the extent of the new duties. In the setting of these notorious facts the reservation now in question was written and accepted.

"All prices subject to change pending tariff revision." We think there is mere fatuity in a construction of the writing that would turn this reservation into a privilege of arbitrary change, at any time or for any reason, with change of tariff or without. No seller, drafting such a writing, would expect the customer receiving it to understand it in that way (*Moran* v. *Standard Oil Co.*, 211 N. Y. 187, 196; American Law Institute, Restatement of Law of Contracts, §§ 223, 232). No buyer would so read it. He would paraphrase the writing thus: "A change of price there may have to be if the tariff is revised. 'Pending such revision,' the buyer will have to take the risk that the price may be increased by the measure of the duty added." In the setting of the occasion, no other interpretation was possible for any reasonable mind. This being so, the court may fix the meaning as if the inference were one of law (Williston, Contracts, vol. 2, § 616, p. 1194).

We find it needless to determine whether the buyer would have been at liberty, if a revision of the tariff had been followed by a change of price, to declare the bargain off, or would be deemed to have assented by implication to the payment of another price, the one theretofore named but augmented by the duty. If the second be the true construction, a known and established standard has fixed the price payable in every possible contingency (*Franklin Sugar Refining Co.* v. *Lipowicz*, 247 N. Y. 465). If the first construction be preferred, there is still no failure of a contract, for revision did not follow until long after the time when performance became due. In that view of the meaning, there was a valid and perfected contract, though subject to a privilege of cancellation in a specified contingency (*Cohen & Sons, Inc.*, v. *Lurie Woolen Co.*, 232 N. Y. 112; Williston, Sales, vol. 1, § 8). No doubt there would be a risk in closing on such terms, yet a risk, after all, not inordinate or incredible. Buyer and seller may have had faith in their ability to come together as to terms if the seller was insistent that because of tariff changes the price should be increased. The increase would not be possible unless the change was an accomplished fact. Whatever loophole was left, whatever chance that the buyer might use the privilege of cancellation harshly, was of the seller's own creation, since the form of the agreement had been drafted by its agents. Theirs, and not the buyer's, is the blame, if there was improvidence or folly.

The complaint might better have stated more precisely the pleader's construction of writings so confusing. Even if this be granted, the construction urged by the defendant is so plainly unreasonable as to justify us in holding that it is to be rejected altogether. Alternative shades of meaning may remain. There is still a true contract, whichever shade shall be accepted.

The order should be affirmed with costs, and the question certified answered "yes."

POUND, CRANE, LEHMAN, KELLOGG, O'BRIEN and HUBBS, JJ., concur.

Order affirmed, etc.

BARNSDALL REFINERIES, INC. *v.* BIRNAMWOOD OIL CO.

UNITED STATES CIRCUIT COURT OF APPEALS, SEVENTH CIRCUIT, 1936

[81 *Federal Reporter* (*2d Series*), 569]

Appeal from the District Court of the United States for the Eastern District of Wisconsin; Ferdinand A. Geiger, Judge.

Suit by the Birnamwood Oil Company against Barnsdall Refineries, Inc. From a judgment for plaintiff, defendant appeals.

Reversed.

Before EVANS, Circuit Judge, and LINDLEY and BRIGGLE, District Judges.

LINDLEY, District Judge. Appellee, a wholesale dealer in gasoline and other petroleum products, brought suit in the District Court against appellant, a refiner of such commodities, upon a contract between the two, dated June 20, 1931, to recover the stipulated amount paid upon an alleged overcharge for "Be Square" gasoline purchased during the life of the contract. At the conclusion of the trial, the court directed a verdict for appellee and entered judgment for the stipulated amount.

The contract provided that appellee should buy and appellant should sell all gasoline and oils which appellee might require in its business, estimated at follows: Be Square gasoline minimum 65 tank cars; maximum 75 tank cars per year. Super-Gas Ethyl gasoline, minimum 3 tank cars, maximum 5 tank cars per year. It included certain other products. "Be Square" gasoline was defined as follows:

> This product shall be of similar quality to the regular "Be Square Gasoline" distributed by the Seller throughout its marketing territory and shall conform substantially to the current specifications of 58-60 U. S. Motor Gasoline, except as same may be improved upon by the Seller.

The price to be paid for the same was fixed as follows:

> Price Be Square Gasoline. The Buyer shall pay to the Seller for "Be Square Gasoline" in tank car lots, F. O. B. Group Three, Okla., the "Spot Market" Price for 58-60 U. S. Motor Gasoline on date same is ordered shipped by the Buyer, arrived at in the following manner:
>
> By taking the high and low price in the Chicago Journal of Commerce and dividing by two.

From the time the contract was entered into until September 30, 1931, the Chicago Journal of Commerce carried but one quotation, namely, "58–60, 437 end point, U. S. Motor." Beginning October 1, 1931, and thereafter, until the time the suit was instituted, instead of one quotation, the Journal of Commerce carried three, substantially as follows: (1) 58–60, U. S. Motor, below 57 octane, (2) 58–60, 57–64 octane, and (3) 58–60, 65 and above octane. For a short period the quotation included also the designation "437 end point," and at certain times, the words "U. S. Motor" were omitted from the quotations because, as the editor stated, of space consideration; but they were implied in the quotations at all times and the trade apparently so understood. During the latter part of the period the designation "58–60" was omitted. These figures had to do with specific gravity measurements. "437 end point" had to do with temperatures at which, under a certain method of distillation, the last traces of material capable of volatization will heat the thermometer bulb. Octanes are units of measurement, under which is calculated the tendency of gasoline to knock, the higher the octane number, the higher the anti-knock value. The specifications of U. S. Motor gasoline are not definite but prescribe minimum limits. Prior to October 1, 1931, trade journals in their quotations and the market generally took into consideration only gravity and end point requirements, but the industry had, preceding said date, already become interested in the octane rating rather than specific gravity rating or end point requirements.

It is undisputed that in the spring of 1931 a third grade gasoline came on the market, third because it was below the regular house brand product of each refiner, and, consequently, far below Ethyl gasoline. Prior to execution of the contract, appellant was already considering measuring its house brand gasoline, i. e., "Be Square" and its Ethyl or premium gasoline by octanes. The trade quite generally in October 1st reached a new basis for description of its product, namely, that of octane rating. About that time appellant determined the octane rating of each of its products and found that the house brand or regular gasoline, namely, its "Be Square" gasoline, fell in the rating of 57–64 octane; that the third grade gasoline fell below 57 octane; and that the premium or Ethyl gasoline fell in the high rating, 65 plus octane. The proof is clear that from time to time, after the changes in quotations, appellee ordered Be Square, Ethyl or premium gasoline, and third grade gasoline. The greater part of the demands of its customers was for Be Square gasoline, and most of its orders were for that product.

As a result of this situation in ordering Be Square gasoline, prior to the change in practice in the industry in adopting the new designations of these three brands and prior to the change in quotations in the Chicago Journal of Commerce, consistent with the change in practice, appellee encountered no difficulty in determining the price it should be charged. Appellee ordered "Be Square" gasoline. This was the regular or house brand product of appellant, and, as aforesaid, constituted the bulk of the refinery production. It came in direct competition with the regular house brands of other refiners, such as Red Crown, of Standard Oil of Indiana, and fell clearly within the quotation of the Chicago Journal of Commerce designated in the contract as the basis for the fixing of the price.

On October 1st, however, as we have seen, the quotation of the Journal of Commerce, mentioned in the contract as the measuring stick by which the price should be fixed, instead of one in number, became three in number, the difference in the three grades being measured by octanes. Then arose the question which is now presented, *viz.*, According to the quotations of which grade was the price of Be Square gasoline to be fixed? Whereas 58–60 U. S. Motor gasoline had been quoted in one quotation it was now quoted in three. Should appellee pay for its purchases of Be Square gasoline the low, medium, or high quotation?

The contract is clear to the effect that appellee was buying Be Square gasoline. Its orders clearly designated Be Square gasoline. Such gasoline conformed substantially "to the current specifications of 58–60 U. S. Motor gasoline" at the time the contract was executed. For this, under the contract, it was to pay the quotation upon the latter mentioned product in the Journal of Commerce. After the change in the additional quotations was made, the paper contained quotations of three grades of 58–60 U. S. Motor gasoline. The contract was still effective between the parties, but it became material, in order to carry out the intention thereof, to know which quotation covered the product specified in the purchase orders, namely, Be Square gasoline. Upon analysis, appellant found that its regular or house brand gasoline fell in the second bracket of quotations. It was between 57–64 octane. No other quotation included gasoline of the quality of Be Square gasoline. It promptly notified appellee to that effect, but the latter claims not to have observed the notice. The commodity purchased was the regular house brand product, Be Square gasoline, which was included within the single quotation prior to September 1st, but which was the second of the three grades quoted after October 1st. Appellee recognized this fact by ordering some smaller quantities of third grade and still smaller quantities of premium gasoline. When it ordered Be Square gasoline, it contemplated, as provided by its contract, that it would receive the regular house brand Be Square gasoline. This was in fact a 57–64 octane. Consequently, appellee received what it bargained for. There was delivered to it what it ordered, and it was charged for the same in accordance with the intent and meaning of the contract.

In this situation, the court erred, as a matter of law, in finding that the gasoline purchased fell within the lowest bracket. There was no proper evidence to support such finding, and the court should have directed a verdict for the appellant. . . .

The judgment will be reversed with costs.

Note also MICHLOVITZ & COMPANY *v.* EASTERN ROLLING MILL COMPANY, 158 Maryland 486 (Court of Appeals, 1929), where the buyer contracted to buy from the seller for five years its entire accumulation of "regular bundled steel scrap" at "the market price as quoted in the 'Iron Age' covering the Philadelphia market for bundled sheets." At the time the contract was made this was the only quotation for the Philadelphia market contained in the Iron Age, but quotations subsequently were added for hydraulically compressed sheets new and old. Since the seller's sheets were in fact hydraulically compressed, the seller claimed the benefit of these new quotations. It was held however that the quotation for bundled sheets still controlled; for "the thing concerning which the parties to this suit contracted at the time they entered into the agreement, and the method or basis adopted for the ascertainment of the price from time to time, are the controlling factors, and the construction will be as of the time the contract was made and not according to some factors which may be imported into it by the acts of outside parties."

NATIONAL IMPORTING & TRADING CO., INC. *v.* CLARK

UNITED STATES CIRCUIT COURT OF APPEALS, SECOND CIRCUIT, 1920

[270 *Federal Reporter*, 54]

In Error to the District Court of the United States for the Southern District of New York.

Action at law by Andrew Clark, doing business as L. D. Clark & Son, against the National Importing & Trading Company, Incorporated. Judgment for plaintiff, and defendant brings error. Reversed.

MANTON, Circuit Judge. Plaintiff below was engaged in the business of canning sardines, with a factory at Eastport, Me., and entered into a contract on the 11th of April, 1918, with the defendant below, a New York manufacturer, engaged in the import and export business. The contract provided for the sale of ten carloads of canned goods, one-fourth oil, Keyless sardines, in cotton seed oil. The contract provided:

> Price to be fixed by the government, f. o. b. Eastport, Maine. Shipment to go forward during the packing season, 1918, quantity to be named by the owners, not exceeding two cars for any one shipping month. Shipments on this contract will be made subject to packing.

Under the heading of "Remarks" it is provided:

> It is understood and agreed that whatever price the government deems proper to fix shall be acceptable to the buyer.

This contract was accepted by both litigants. The terms of the contract were, therefore, measured by the packing season of 1918; it was, however, subsequently extended to March 1, 1919. Subsequently the Food Administrator declared that a price above $6.50 would be considered unreasonable. Thereafter, and on May 28th, a conference was held of the sardine packers, where a maximum price of $6.50 was agreed upon by the packers. On the 28th day of May, the United States Food Administrator declared, after this conference with the sardine packers, that any price higher than $6.50 would be considered unreasonable. This price was recommended by 90 per cent. of the sardine packers. Under the contract, a carload was shipped to the plaintiff below about June 7, 1918, was invoiced and paid for at $6 a case. On July 8th, the plaintiff below wrote the defendant below, asking for shipping instructions for five carloads at a price of $6 at Eastport for the 1918 packed sardines. It was there stated:

> This is the price of reliable packers for new packed goods, and we do not have any 1917 packed goods to offer at all.

On July 18, 1918, a second carload was shipped and paid for at $6 a case, and on September 30, 1918, the plaintiff below wrote to the defendant below that it was holding eight carloads for the defendant below "as per contract for ten cars, two of which you have already taken," and, further, "the price is $6.50 Eastport for Keyless one-fourth oils." It will be noted that in this correspondence no reference is made to the government price as fixed, for the fact is that the government never fixed a price and no official action was taken for fixing a price, other than above referred to as the act of the Food Administrator.

On October 2d, the defendant below replied to the plaintiff's letter of September 30th. No price is mentioned therein, but it is stated that the defendant below is overstocked, and contended that, under the contract, it had the privilege of ordering cars up to and including February, 1919. The canning season under the Maine law extended from April 15th to December 1st. On October 5th, the plaintiff below again wrote, making no mention of price, but contending that the packing season ended December 1st, and that the defendant below must take the remaining eight cars in October and November. On October 11th, in a letter by the defendant below to the plaintiff below requesting the shipment of two cars in October, it was stated:

It seems to us that you should or could invoice the same somewhat below $6.50. Sardines are being offered in the local market at prices ranging from $6 to $6.25.

On October 14th the plaintiff below wrote the defendant below:

Your contract with us called for ten carloads of sardines at the government price. . . . We inclose you clipping from the New York Journal of Commerce which states the government price of sardines. . . . For your information, will say the packers have applied to the government to increase the price of sardines to $7 Eastport basis. . . . Our price is $6.50 Eastport, and we have been shipping at this price right along.

Subsequently, about October 31 and November 16, 1918, two cars were delivered to the defendant below. They were invoiced at $6.50 a case, and after some correspondence were paid for at the rate of $6 a case. Although the time of delivery for the remaining six cars was extended to March 1, 1919, no other cars were delivered by the plaintiff below to the defendant below or accepted. On February 26, 1919, the defendant below informed the plaintiff below that the contract was void. On January 10, 1919, the government terminated its control over canned sardines.

It thus appears that the plaintiff below and defendant below agreed upon the purchase and sale of the sardines, but at a price to be fixed by the government at a future time. No price was fixed by the government. At best, the Food Administrator by an order approved the price fixed by the sardine packers, who fixed a maximum price of $6.50. Before the maximum price was withdrawn, four carloads had been delivered. The first two were paid for at the price of $6 per case, and although the last two were invoiced at $6.50 per case, they were paid for by the acceptance by the seller of $6. The court may not enforce the terms of a contract, where the minds of the parties have not met. Nor can the court read into the contract a fixed price, when no price has been fixed by a third party, whom it has been agreed upon should fix the price. *Lobenstein* v. *U. S.*, 91 U. S., 324, 23 L. Ed. 410. The rights and obligations of the parties to the contract must be found within the terms of the contract, and, when legal responsibility is sought to be imposed, the measure of liability must be that contained in the contract. At best, the government here agreed upon the maximum price which was fixed by the sardine packers, and then issued an order, which was a warning to men engaged in this line of business, that a price above $6.50 per case would be considered unreasonable. With the most liberal construction given to the phrase of the contract, "It is understood and agreed that whatever price the government deems proper to fix shall be acceptable to the buyer," the seller could not impose upon the buyer the approved maximum price. The terms of the contract indicate a future act, a contemplated act, upon the part of the government, for it uses the phrase "to be fixed." The Food Administrator's intention was to enforce the provisions of the Lever Act of August 10, 1917. The phrase above quoted must be reconciled, if possible, with the price as stated in the contract, "to be fixed by the government."

When on January 10, 1919, the government terminated its control over food, the plaintiff below was no longer obligated to the maximum price, even if he were theretofore, for the restrictions placed upon the parties by reason of the maximum price approved by the Food Administrator did not prevail. Thereafter the market price prevailed. It is reasonable to suppose that the parties contemplated the contingency that the government might terminate its control over price fixing, but the court cannot read into the contract "maximum price," where the word "price" is used by the parties. The buyer had six weeks longer in which to buy when the government terminated its control. The original contract contemplated delivery of not more than two cars a month during the season, but since there was an extension to the 1st of March to take the remaining cars, which extension omitted the amount of deliveries per month, the buyer still had this time in which to call for deliveries.

We think the court should have directed a verdict for the defendant.

Judgment reversed.

Compare ARCOS, LTD. *v.* ARONSON, 36 Ll. L. L. R. 108 (King's Bench Division, 1930). In that case, in the course of negotiations attendant on completing a contract for the sale of timber to be shipped from Norway c. i. f. the East Coast of England, the timber was shipped and arrived duly at destination while the question of price remained unsettled. At the same time documents covering the shipment were sent forward through a financing bank to be surrendered to the buyer on payment of the invoice amount. With matters in this situation the buyer wrote to the seller: "With regard to the price invoiced for the goods by you, I understand you desire to leave these matters in abeyance for the time being, and would prefer arbitration on the matter. I accept your proposition, and under these circumstances I am prepared to take up the shipping documents against payment of your invoice figure." As a preliminary point in an action by the buyer against the seller for breach of contract by selling the timber elsewhere, the seller claimed a declaration that there was not and had not at any time been any contract between the parties relating to the sale and purchase of the timber. Denied. WRIGHT, J., held that the price was not uncertain, but was left to the decision of a third person in that the parties agreed to submit the point to arbitration, which would constitute a perfectly good bargain within the Sale of Goods Act.

4. THE STATUTE OF FRAUDS

A. Subject Matter

GODDARD *v.* BINNEY

Massachusetts Supreme Court, 1874
[115 *Massachusetts Reports*, 450]

Contract to recover the price of a buggy built by the plaintiff for the defendant.

Trial in the Superior Court before *Dewey*, J., who reported the case for the consideration of this court in substance as follows:

The plaintiff, a carriage manufacturer in Boston, testified that the defendant came to his place of business in April, 1872, and directed the plaintiff to make for him a buggy, and the plaintiff entered the order in his order-book; the defendant gave directions that the color of the lining should be drab, and the outside seat of cane, and as to the painting, and also that the buggy was to have on it his monogram and initials. The sum of $675 was agreed as the price. It was to be done in or about four months. The plaintiff immediately began work upon the buggy and made every part, it being painted, lined, and with the initials, as ordered.

The last of August, when the buggy was nearly completed, wanting only the last coat of varnish, and the hanging of it on the wheels, the defendant came to the plaintiff's place of business and asked when it would be done. The plaintiff replied in about ten days, and asked the defendant if he might sell the buggy, or if he wished it, as he, the plaintiff, had opportunities of selling it to others. The defendant then inquired if the plaintiff could furnish him another if he sold that, to which he replied, he could not, as he was going to give up the business of manufacturing, and that unless he took this he could not have any. The defendant then said he would keep this one.

The defendant did not at this, nor at any other time, see the buggy. The buggy was finished September 15, in accordance with the original order. It is usual to keep carriages some time after they are finished to let the paint and varnish harden.

October 14, 1872, the plaintiff sent to the defendant the following bill: "Boston, October 14, 1872. Mr. H. P. Binney. Bo't of Thos. Goddard, one new cane seat buggy, $675. Rec'd Pay't. (Buggy was finished Sept. 15.)"

The bill was presented by a clerk of the plaintiff. The defendant after looking at it, said he would see the plaintiff soon. The bill was in the plaintiff's handwriting and was kept by the defendant. The same clerk called again soon after and asked the defendant for a check, to which he replied that he would pay it soon, and would see the plaintiff. Calling a third time, before the fire of November 9th, the defendant said, "Tell Mr. Goddard I will come and see him right away." By the fire of November 9, 1872, this buggy and all the property on the plaintiff's premises were destroyed. After the fire the plaintiff again called on the defendant for payment. He wanted to know if it was insured, and said he would see the plaintiff about it.

After the buggy was finished, it was kept with the completed work on the plaintiff's premises; and it was at all times after it was finished till burned worth and could have been sold by the plaintiff for upwards of $700, the value of buggies of the plaintiff's manufacture having advanced after the contract was made in April.

The defendant put in no evidence, and contended that this action could not be maintained, that it came within the provisions of the Gen. Sts. *c.* 105, § 5, and that there had never been any delivery of the said buggy to the defendant, nor any acceptance thereof by him, and that the property belonged to and was at the sole risk of the plaintiff at the time of the fire, and that if any cause of action arose against the defendant for not taking away the said buggy, it arose prior to the fire, and no damage was caused to the plaintiff thereupon. The plaintiff contended that the contract did not come within the provision of the statute referred to, and that it was the duty of the defendant, upon being notified that the buggy was completed, to take the same away within a reasonable time, and that not having done so the buggy was at the risk of the defendant when burned.

The plaintiff further contended that upon the evidence the jury would be authorized to find that there had been a delivery of the buggy to the defendant, and an acceptance by him, and without submitting that question to the jury it was agreed by the parties, that if there was any evidence which could have properly been submitted to the jury as showing a delivery, and an acceptance of the buggy by the defendant, then it shall be taken that the jury would have found said delivery and acceptance.

Upon the evidence hereinbefore stated, the presiding judge directed a verdict for the defendant; and it was agreed that if the jury would have been authorized to find a delivery and an acceptance by the defendant, or if upon the facts above stated the court is of opinion that at the time of the fire the said buggy was on the premises of the plaintiff, at the risk of the defendant, the verdict is to be set aside, and judgment entered for $675 and interest, from October 15, 1872; otherwise, judgment on the verdict.

Ames, J. Whether an agreement like that described in this report should be considered as a contract for the sale of goods, within the meaning of the statute of frauds, or a contract for labor, services and materials, and therefore not within that statute, is a question upon which there is a conflict of authority. According to a long course of decisions in New York, and in some other states of the Union, an agreement for the sale of any commodity not in existence at the time, but which the vendor is to manufacture or put in a condition to be delivered, (such as flour from wheat not yet ground, or nails to be made from iron in the vendor's hands), is not a contract of sale within the meaning of the statute. *Crookshank* v. *Burrell*, 18 Johns. 58. *Sewall* v. *Fitch*, 8 Cow. 215. *Robertson* v. *Vaughn*, 5 Sandf. 1. *Downs* v. *Ross*, 23 Wend. 270. *Eichelberger* v. *M'Cauley*, 5 Har. & J. 213. In England, on the other hand, the tendency of the recent decisions is to treat all contracts of such a kind intended to result in a sale, as substantially contracts for the sale of chattels; and the decision in *Lee* v. *Griffin*, 1 B. & S. 272, goes so far as to hold that a contract to make and fit a set of artificial teeth for a patient is essentially a contract for the sale of goods, and therefore is subject to the provisions of the statute. See *Maberley* v. *Sheppard*, 10 Bing. 99; *Howe* v. *Palmer*, 3 B. & Ald. 321; *Baldey* v. *Parker*, 2 B. & C. 37; *Atkinson* v. *Bell*, 8 B. & C. 277.

In this Commonwealth, a rule avoiding both of these extremes was established in *Mixer* v. *Howarth*, 21 Pick. 205, and has been recognized and affirmed in repeated decisions of more recent date. The effect of these decisions we understand to be this, namely, that a contract for the sale of articles then existing, or such as the vendor in the ordinary course of his business manufactures or procures for the general market, whether on hand at the time or not, is a contract for the sale of goods, to which the statute applies. But on the other hand, if the goods are to be manufactured especially for the purchaser, and upon his special order, and not for the general market, the case is not within the statute. *Spencer* v. *Cone*, 1 Met. 283. "The distinction," says Chief Justice Shaw, in *Lamb* v. *Crafts*, 12 Met. 353, "we believe is now well understood. When a person stipulates for the future sale of articles, which he is habitually making, and which, at the time, are not made or finished, it is essentially a contract of sale, and not a contract for labor; otherwise, when the article is made pursuant to the agreement." In *Gardner* v. *Joy*, 9 Met. 177, a contract to buy a certain number of boxes of candles at a fixed rate per pound, which the vendor said he would manufacture and deliver in about three months, was held to be a contract of sale and within the statute. To the same general effect are *Waterman* v. *Meigs*, 4 Cush. 497, and *Clark* v. *Nichols*, 107 Mass. 547. It is true that in "the infinitely various shades of different contracts," there is some practical difficulty in disposing of the questions that arise under that section of the statute. Gen. Sts. *c.* 105, § 5. But we see no ground for holding that there is any uncertainty in the rule itself. On the contrary, its correctness and justice are clearly implied or expressly affirmed in all of our decisions upon the subject matter. It is proper to say also that the present case is a much stronger one than *Mixer* v. *Howarth*. In this case, the carriage was not only built for the defendant, but in conformity in some respects with his directions, and at his request was marked with his initials. It was neither intended nor adapted for the general market. As we are by no means prepared to overrule the decision in that case, we must therefore hold that the statute of frauds does not apply to the contract which the plaintiff is seeking to enforce in this action.

[The balance of the opinion, holding that enough had been done independently of the statute to vest the general ownership in the defendant, is omitted.]

Judgment entered for the plaintiff.

BAUER *v.* VICTORY CATERING COMPANY

NEW JERSEY COURT OF ERRORS AND APPEALS, 1925

[101 *New Jersey Law Reports*, 364]

KATZENBACH, J. This is an appeal from a judgment of the Supreme Court in an action at law tried at the Essex Circuit.

The Victory Catering Company, the appellant (hereinafter called the Victory Company), is a New Jersey corporation. It operated a restaurant on the boardwalk at Atlantic City. On April 10th, 1921, Milton J. Wolferman, president of the Gotham Silverware Company (hereinafter referred to as the Gotham Company), called at the place of business of the appellant in Atlantic City. He met a Mr. Wyler, president of the Victory Company; Mr. Meyer, the steward, and Mr. Jacobs, the assistant manager. Mr. Wolferman endeavored to interest them in the purchase of new silverware for their restaurant and showed them samples which he had. They became interested. An order was given which Mr. Wolferman at first wrote on the back of a bill of fare. After a selection of styles and the quantity desired had been agreed upon and taken down by Mr. Wolferman on the back of the bill of fare, he packed up his samples and then took out his regular order book and wrote everything which had been ordered down in this book. Three copies of the order were made. The original was given to Mr. Wyler. The two copies were left in the order book. The amount of the order was approximately $8,000. Neither the memorandum on the back of the bill of fare, the original order, or copies were signed in behalf of the Victory Company. The silverware was to be marked with a crest which was to be a wreath with a V in the centre. Certain articles were to be stamped on the bottom "La Victoire." The order stated that certain of the articles were to be shipped between June 15th and July 1st, 1921; balance, August 15th and September 1st.

The Victory Company had on July 7th, 1921, received no part of the order. On that day it wrote a letter to the Gotham Company stating that part of the order given Mr. Wolferman was to have been delivered between June 15th and July 1st, and as the silverware had not arrived they had been obliged to make other arrangements, and to please hold the order until notified to ship the same. On July 15th, 1921, the Victory Company again wrote to the Gotham Company that they did not wish anything shipped to them until the Gotham Company received instructions. No instructions were ever received from the Victory Company. The Gotham Company wrote a number of letters to the Victory Company on the subject, but no shipping instructions were ever received.

The Gotham Company, about March 1st, 1922, prepared the silverware for sale by removing the crest and stamping, and repolishing it. This work cost $650. The goods were sold during the months of March and April, 1922, to restaurants and hotels. The amount realized after deducting the cost of the alteration of the goods for sale was $1,614.96, less than the price the Victory Company were to pay. In order to make the goods the Gotham Company was obliged to purchase some of the metal and obtain the dies for stamping, &c. The claim of the Gotham Company against the Victory Company was assigned to one Henry Bauer, of Bloomfield, Essex county, by the Gotham Company on March 23d, 1923, by an instrument in writing signed by the president of the Gotham Company to which the corporate seal of that company was attached, and attested by its secretary. The execution of the assignment was proved before a notary public of New York county. The assignee then instituted the present suit against the Victory Company upon the claim assigned to him laying the venue of said action in the county of Essex, the residence of the assignee.

The Victory Company set up several defenses in its answer. Among them were the defenses that the contract was within the statute of frauds and that the assignment of the claim to the plaintiff was sham, without consideration, and made for the sole purpose of enabling the Gotham Company to lay the venue in Essex county instead of Atlantic county, where the Victor Company had its principal office and place of business.

At the trial Mr. Wolferman was sworn as a witness. He testified to the facts above stated. A stenographer of the Gotham Company testified that she had written and mailed certain letters to the Victory Company, which were offered in evidence. The plaintiff rested. The defendant then called Mr. Wolferman as its witness and questioned him regarding the assignment of the claim to Mr. Bauer. The questions asked were principally directed to whether the assignment had been made by order of the board of directors of the Gotham Company and why the Gotham Company had not itself sued the Victory Company. Objections to these questions were made and sustained. The trial judge obliged Mr. Wolferman to answer the question as to what the consideration of the assignment was. He testified that it was one dollar. The defendant offered no further testimony and rested. Each side moved for a direction of a verdict. The defendant's grounds were — first, that there was no proof that Mr. Wyler, the president of the Victory Company, had any authority to bind the company; second, that the assignment of the claim was made in bad faith and was a fraud, which disentitled the plaintiff to maintain the action; third, lack of any evidence that the Gotham Company was prepared to perform its contract; fourth, that the contract was within the statute of frauds because there was no memorandum in writing signed by the defendant. The trial judge denied both motions. Exceptions were duly taken.

In deciding the defendant's motion the trial judge stated that whether the case was within or without the statute of frauds was a question of fact for the determination of the jury. In his charge he left to the jury for its decision the questions whether the parties who attempted to contract for the Victory Company had the capacity to do so, whether the goods which were to be made for the defendant came within the statute of frauds, and whether the letters written by the defendant took the case out of the statute of frauds.

In determining whether or not a case is within or without the statute of frauds there may in some instances be disputed questions of fact which must be referred to the jury for determination so that the jury finally decides whether the case is within or without the statute. If, however, there is no disputed question of fact which it is necessary for a jury to pass upon, the question of whether or not a case is within the statute of frauds is a question of law for the determination of the trial judge.

In the present case there could be no dispute as to whether the goods in question were of the character which required a memorandum in writing to be signed by the Victory Company to enable the contract to be enforced.

The law governing this question was decided in this state in 1865 in the case of *Finney* v. *Apgar*, 31 N. J. L. 266, by the late Chief Justice Beasley. In speaking for the Supreme Court he said: "From a careful examination of the English and American authorities and the principles illustrated by them, I think the following general rules may be deduced, viz. — first, that a contract for the sale of goods which is purely executory, is as much within the statute as is one to be executed *in presenti*; second, that where a contract is made for an article not existing at the time *in solido* — to use the expression of the old cases — and when such article is to be made according to order, and as a thing distinguished from the general business of the maker, then such contract is, in substance and effect, not for a sale, but for work and materials.

"The first of the above rules is now received everywhere with entire judicial unanimity.

"With regard to the second rule, much conflict of opinion exists, but I think it is recommended by its evident consonance with the object of the statute, as well as by the decided weight of authority. . . ."

Applying the principle of these cases to the facts of the present case, we find from the testimony that, although the articles for which the order was given were not existing at the time *in solido*, yet they were articles which were made in the course of the general business of the Gotham Company. Consequently, the contract was for a sale and not for work and materials. The contract, therefore, to be enforceable, must be evidenced by a memorandum in writing signed by the Victory Company.

[A page of the opinion is here omitted.]

At the conclusion of the defendant's case the evidence (undisputed) was that the articles contracted for were of such a character as to be the subject-matter of a sale of goods within the statute. There was no memorandum in writing of the contract signed by the Victory Company sufficient to take the case out of the statute of frauds, no part of the goods had been delivered and accepted by the buyer, no earnest to bind the contract had been given by the purchaser, no payment, in part, had been made, and the goods were of a value exceeding the sum of $500. In this state of that evidence there was no question which could properly be submitted to the jury. It was error to have done so. The court should have directed a verdict for the defendant on the ground that the case was one within the statute of frauds. The views thus expressed on this branch of the case make it unnecessary to consider some of the other interesting questions raised in the record.

The judgment is reversed, with costs.

In SACO-LOWELL SHOPS *v.* CLINTON MILLS CO., 277 Fed. 349 (Circuit Court of Appeals, 1st Circuit, 1921), in an action for non-delivery of machinery there was evidence that the machinery in question, although of a standard type supplied by the defendant, was to be manufactured especially for the plaintiff and would be of less value to others. It was held that this was not sufficient to bring the contract within the express exception of the Massachusetts statute.

ATLAS SHOE COMPANY *v.* ROSENTHAL

MASSACHUSETTS SUPREME COURT, 1922

[242 *Massachusetts Reports,* 15]

Contract for $1,095.60 upon an account annexed for shoes alleged to have been sold by the plaintiff to the defendant. Writ dated July 14, 1920.

The answer contained a general denial and an allegation that the action was barred by the statute of frauds, G. L. c. 106, § 6.

In the Superior Court the action was tried before *Fox,* J. Material evidence is described in the opinion. At the close of the evidence, the defendant moved that a verdict be ordered in his favor. The motion was denied. The jury returned a verdict for the plaintiff in the sum of $1,120.98; and the defendant alleged exceptions.

RUGG, C.J. This is an action of contract to recover the price of shoes alleged to have been sold by the plaintiff to the defendant. The plaintiff was not a manufacturer of shoes. It took an order from the defendant for particular styles of shoes, which were to be made especially on the order of the plaintiff by a manufacturer, and were not suitable for sale to others in the ordinary course of the plaintiff's business.

The defence is that part of the statute of frauds contained in St. 1908, c. 237, § 4 (see now G. L. c. 106, § 6). Confessedly that statute is a complete defence unless the facts bring the case within the exception in (2) of said section of the statute, to the affect that "if the goods are to be manufactured by the seller especially for the buyer and are not suitable for sale to others in the ordinary course of the seller's business, the provisions of this section shall not apply."

Manifestly, if this clause is to be construed according to its words, it does not apply to the transaction here in question, because the goods were not to be "manufactured by the seller" but were to be procured by the seller to be made by a manufacturer. It is elementary in the interpretation of statutes that every word, clause and sentence shall be given some force and effect and shall be treated as not superfluous unless absolutely necessary in order to give a rational meaning to the act. *Commonwealth* v.

McCaughey, 9 Gray, 296, 297. Reading the pertinent words of the statute in their ordinary sense, it confines the exception to those instances where the seller is himself the manufacturer and excludes from its scope all cases where the seller procures the goods to be manufactured by another. This conforms to the law of this Commonwealth under the statute of frauds before the enactment of the sales act. *Smalley* v. *Hamblin*, 170 Mass. 380. See *Goddard* v. *Binney*, 115 Mass. 450.

It has been commonly understood that the sales act was intended to be drafted in these respects in conformity to the Massachusetts rules of law. There is every reason for interpreting the statute according to its natural sense and the preexisting law.

So far as we are aware, decisions in other jurisdictions under the sales act are in harmony with this view. *Eagle Paper Box Co.* v. *Gatti-McQuade Co.* 164 N. Y. Supp. 201, 205. *Schneider* v. *Lezinsky*, 162 N. Y. Supp. 769.

The request of the defendant for a directed verdict in his favor ought to have been granted. The case appears to have been fully tried. The exceptions must be sustained and, as the defence of the statute of frauds is decisive, judgment may be entered for the defendant in accordance with G. L. c. 231, § 122.

So ordered.

BECKROGE *v.* SOUTH CAROLINA PUBLIC SERVICE CO.

South Carolina Supreme Court, 1937

[185 *South Carolina Reports*, 210]

The opinion of the Court was delivered by Mr. Justice Fishburne.

This is an appeal from two separate judgments. The actions were commenced separately, but tried together, and separate judgments were entered. The decision in each case depends on the same issues of law and fact. This being true, we will in our discussion specifically refer only to the case of the plaintiff, F. Addie Beckroge.

In her complaint it is alleged that on December 6, 1930, she purchased 37 shares of stock of the Central Public Service Corporation, and paid therefor $2,220.00, and that she paid $720.00, as partial payments on other shares in the same corporation, all of which she purchased and and acquired through the defendant, South Carolina Public Service Company, its agents and servants. That the defendant agreed and promised to refund to her the purchase money of so much of the stock as was paid for in full, and to return all partial payments, with interest at 5 per cent., at any time she requested it. That thereafter the plaintiff tendered to the defendant the stock so purchased by her, and requested the defendant to comply with its agreement and refund to her the money she had paid; that the defendant did return to the plaintiff the sum of $754.39, this being the amount of the partial payments on certain shares of stock, with 5 per cent. interest as agreed, but that it has failed and refused to refund to her the sum of $2,220.00 paid for the aforesaid 37 shares of stock, which are now approximately worthless and unmarketable. The prayer of the complaint is for $2,220.00, and costs.

The defendant denied the material allegations of the complaint, and pleaded the statute of frauds; and further, that the alleged contract, even if made — which it denied — was *ultra vires*, beyond the corporate powers of the defendant, the said capital stock of the Central Public Service Corporation being neither the capital stock of the defendant nor owned by it; and further alleged that under its charter it had no power or authority to engage in the sale of the capital stock of other corporations now owned by it.

[About five pages of the opinion are here omitted.]

The first contention of the appellant is that the Circuit Court erred in holding that the statute of frauds is not applicable, under the facts of this case. The section of the statute of frauds invoked is Section 7045 (1932 Code), and provides as follows: "No contract for the sale of any goods, wares and merchandise for the price of fifty dollars or upwards shall be allowed to be good except the buyer shall accept part of the goods so sold and actually receive the same, or give something in earnest to bind the bargain, or in part payment, or that some note or memorandum in writing of the said bargain be made and signed by the parties to be charged by such contract, or their agents thereunto lawfully authorized."

The position of the respondent is that she is seeking to hold the defendant liable, not on the contract of its principal, but on its independent original agreement, viz.: That, in consideration of the purchase of the stock by the plaintiff through it, the defendant agreed on its own behalf, and not on behalf of the principal, that it would repurchase the stock and refund the money at any time she wished to turn it in. The defendant denies that this agreement was made.

The question of whether or not the sale of existing corporate stock comes within the meaning of the statute of frauds has never been specifically presented nor passed upon by our Court. See *Gadsden* v. *Lance* (1841), 16 S. C. Eq. (McMull. Eq.), 87, 37 Am. Dec., 548; *Kirkpatrick* v. *Hardeman*, 118 S. C., 146, 110 S. E., 119. An examination of the cases, however, shows that the American authorities are practically unanimous in holding that a contract for the sale of existing corporate stock comes within the meaning of statutes equivalent and corresponding to the seventeenth section of the English statute of frauds, which provided that all contracts for the sale of goods, wares, and merchandise within the specified price shall be void, unless made in writing and subscribed by the party to be charged therewith, or unless the party either accepts or receives part of the goods, or at the time pays some part of the purchase price. With this holding we are in full accord. See *Spencer* v. *McGuffin*, 190 Ind., 308, 130 N. E., 407, and the note appended thereto in 14 A. L. R., 394, in which the cases in point are collected.

In *Tisdale* v. *Harris* (1838), 20 Pick. (Mass.), 9, which is a leading and much-cited American case, the Court, speaking through Shaw, C. J., stated: "There is nothing in the nature of stocks or shares in companies, which in reason or sound policy should exempt contracts in respect to them from those reasonable restrictions, designed by the statute to prevent frauds in the sale of other commodities. On the contrary, these companies have become so numerous, so large an amount of the property of the community is now invested in them, and as the ordinary indicia of property, arising from delivery and possession, cannot take place, there seems to be peculiar reason for extending the provisions of this statute to them. As they may properly be included under the term 'goods,' as they are within the reason and policy of the act, the Court are of opinion, that a contract for the sale of shares, in the absence of the other requisites, must be proved by some note or memorandum in writing."

[The balance of the opinion deals with other questions and is here omitted.]

We are of the opinion that the trial Judge committed no error in his refusal to grant a nonsuit, to direct a verdict, or to grant a new trial.

Judgment affirmed.

MR. CHIEF JUSTICE STABLER and MESSRS. JUSTICES BONHAM and BAKER concur.

MR. JUSTICE CARTER did not participate on account of illness.

Compare DUNCUFT *v.* ALBRECHT, 12 Simons 189 (High Court of Chancery, 1841), where a demurrer to a bill for specific performance of an agreement for the sale of shares in a railway company was overruled, the Vice-Chancellor saying: "In my opinion this is a case to which the 17th section of the Statute of Frauds does not apply; because it is impressed upon my mind that, in the decisions which have been made with respect to the 17th section, it has been held to apply only to goods, wares and merchandizes which are capable of being in part delivered. If there is an agreement to sell a quantity of tallow or of hemp, you may deliver a part; but the delivery of a part is not a transaction applicable, as I apprehend, to such a subject as railway shares. They have been decided not to be land. They have been decided to be, in effect, personal estate; but not personal estate of the quality of goods, wares and merchandizes within the meaning of the 17th section."

In FARRELL v. SIMONS, 180 Oklahoma 600 (Oklahoma Supreme Court, 1937), where the question was as to the enforceability of an oral agreement to purchase stock not yet issued, under a statute specifically including "things in action," the Court said: "There is a division of authority as to whether a subscription to the capital stock of a corporation is within the statute of frauds. Plaintiff cites and relies upon the text of Fletcher's Cyc. Private Corporations, vol. 2, page 181, sec. 537, to the effect that it is not. Plaintiff also cites and relies upon 14 C. J. 520, sec. 776, and 25 R. C. L. 617, sec. 231. The text quoted from Fletcher's work, supra, lays down such a rule of law without qualification, as does 14 C. J. supra. But 25 R. C. L., supra, states there are cases to the contrary; and it is significant to notice that Fletcher's Cyc. of Corps. (Permanent Edition) vol. 4, page 152, sec.

1481, departs from the unqualified rule of his earlier edition and states there are cases to the contrary, and in 27 C. J. 238, sec. 264, it is recognized there are two lines of authorities. See, also, 14 A. L. R. 400–401, and 59 A. L. R. 598.

"The cases adhering to the rule contended for by the plaintiff generally are earlier cases, whereas most of the cases holding to the contrary are of more recent date. The older cases pretend to see a difference between a subscription to unissued capital stock and a contract by the corporation for the sale of its issued stock bought back and held in the treasury or a contract between individuals for the sale of issued capital stock. These cases are coeval with the older cases holding that any contract relating to the sale of the shares of capital stock was without the statute of frauds, which rule is now almost wholly departed from in the modern cases. We feel that the tendency of the modern cases to depart from the unqualified rule announced by Fletcher in his earlier edition is a further manifestation of the changing viewpoint of the courts toward the nature of capital stock as property.

Obviously the decisions of those states where by statute the subscription of capital stock is surrounded by certain formalities cannot affect this question. New York state is one such.

"Usually the text-writers and the courts, which say that subscription of unissued capital stock differs from a contract of sale of issued capital stock, will follow such a statement by the statement that such contracts are governed by the same general rules of law. . ...

"We do not believe there is a rational difference between the two contracts — that is, the subscription of the capital stock before issue and the sale thereof after issue — in the light of the statute of frauds. We choose to follow the rule that such a subscription is within the statute."

REISFELD *v.* JACOBS

New York Supreme Court, 1919

[107 *New York Miscellaneous Reports*, 1]

Appeal from a judgment of the Municipal Court of the city of New York, borough of Manhattan, seventh district, after a trial by the court without a jury, dismissing plaintiff's complaint.

Finch, J. The complaint alleges that an agreement was made between the plaintiff and the defendant whereby the defendant should sell and deliver to the plaintiff at the city of New York, on or before the 11th day of November, 1918, 4,000 rubles in 500 ruble denominations, at $21 per 100, and that the plaintiff should pay the defendant the said sum of $21 per 100 upon delivery, amounting to $840. It is further alleged in the complaint that the said rubles were bought for resale by the plaintiff and that the defendant had due notice thereof and that by reason of the defendant's failure to deliver said rubles the plaintiff was compelled to buy said rubles in the open market at the lowest price at which he could, to wit, $24.60 per 100, amounting to $984, and that the plaintiff suffered as damages the difference between the market price at which he purchased the rubles and the contract price. The answer contains a general denial, and for a separate and distinct defense alleges the Statute of Frauds.

As to whether or not there was a sale presented a question of fact which the court below has found in favor of the plaintiff, and the judgment is not against the weight of evidence. The court below has held that the Statute of Frauds applies, and this presents the only question for the consideration of this court. The Statute of Frauds provides: "A contract to sell or a sale of any goods or choses in action. . . ." Pers. Prop. Law, § 85; Laws of 1909, chap. 45. Section 156 of the Personal Property Law defines "goods" as follows: " 'Goods' include all chattels personal other than things in action and money." As noted, the complaint alleges that the rubles were bought for resale and hence they were treated as a commodity and not as money. Our courts have held that even domestic money when dealt in as a commodity and treated as an object of barter and sale, was not within the Statute of Frauds. *Peabody* v. *Speyers*, 56 N. Y. 230, 234; *Fowler* v. *New York Gold Exchange Bank*, 67 id. 138, 146. While the Statute of Frauds has been amended since the decision of these cases so as to specifically except "money" yet it would seem that in order to come within the exception of the statute the article must be money as such and that the meaning and authority of these cases is as applicable now as before the amendment of the statute. There also appears an additional reason for holding the Statute of Frauds applicable. As noted choses in action are expressly placed within the provisions of the statute. Upon this record there is no evidence presented showing that these bank-notes were other than choses in action. The word money may be used in a strict sense as denoting only "legal tender in payment of a debt" (*Legal Tender Cases*, 110 U. S. 421), or it may be used broadly to denote any token of value customarily passing from hand to hand. In the latter sense the word might be used to include foreign coin and foreign bank notes if they were so used in this country. In the case at bar it is undisputed that by rubles was meant bank notes of the Imperial Russian Bank. On their face appears the statement that they are imperial credit notes secured by all the property of the empire on equal basis with gold coin, but there is no evidence in the record supporting this statement or that such notes pass in this country in any wise as money. Also, upon this record, before these notes could be considered as money in any sense this court would have to take judicial notice that they were issued under the authority of and backed by the credit of a responsible government. In view of the fact that these notes were issued by a government now defunct and that the United States at present has no relations with any government in Russia, the court cannot take judicial notice that these notes are backed by the credit of a responsible government or that they even pass current anywhere as money. The plaintiff relies upon the case of *Brown* v. *Perera*, N. Y. L. J. March 2, 1918, opinion of Hon. David Leventritt; affd., without opinion by the Appellate Division, 182 App. Div. 922, but the illuminating opinion in that case concerns the question whether money issued under the authority of a responsible government and used generally for the purpose of convenient transaction is negotiable and this has no application to the question presented in the case at bar.

It follows that the judgment should be affirmed, with twenty-five dollars costs.

LEHMAN and WEEKS, JJ., concur.

Judgment affirmed, with twenty-five dollars costs.

WETKOPSKY v. NEW HAVEN GAS LIGHT COMPANY

CONNECTICUT SUPREME COURT OF ERRORS, 1913

[88 *Connecticut Reports*, 1]

Action to recover damages for an alleged breach of contract, brought to the Superior Court in New Haven County where the plaintiff was non-suited in a trial to the jury before *Bennett*, J., from which judgment he appealed. Error and new trial ordered.

The complaint alleges that the defendant, on March 27th, 1912, being the owner of a dwelling-house situated at number 44 Mill Street in New Haven, which it desired to dispose of and have removed, sold the same to the plaintiff (who then owned a lot on the opposite side of the street to which he intended to remove it) for a good and valuable consideration then paid; that the defendant had knowledge of the purpose for which the plaintiff purchased the house; and that the defendant afterward refused to permit the plaintiff to remove or take possession of the house, or to deliver the same to him.

The answer denied the allegation that the defendant sold the house to the plaintiff, or had knowledge that he intended to remove it across the street to his lot, admitted that the defendant owned the house and the land upon which it stood, and alleged that, being about to construct a tank upon the lot and it being necessary to the progress of such work that the house should be removed from the lot not later than April 2d, the defendant agreed with the plaintiff on March 27th that for the sum of $40, which was then paid by the plaintiff, he might have the materials of which the house was constructed if he would tear it down and entirely remove the materials from the premises on or before the night of April 2d, and that on the following day the plaintiff repudiated this agreement and told the defendant that he did not intend to tear down the house and would not do so, but intended to remove it in its entirety, and that the defendant thereupon, after the plaintiff had again stated that he would not tear down the house, tendered him back the $40 and notified him that the agreement was rescinded, and the defendant afterward tore down the house and removed the materials. The reply denied the allegation that there was an agreement to tear down the house.

Upon the trial the plaintiff introduced in evidence two writings which read as follows: "March 27, 1912. Received of Sylvester Wetkopsky five $\overline{100}$ dollars. Deposit on house No. 44 Mill St. Balance of $35.00/100 to be paid on or before April 1/1912. $5 00/100 The New Haven Gas Light

Company, per J B B. 3:30 p. m. March 27, 1912. Received of Sylvester Wetkopsky thirty-five $\frac{}{100}$ dollars. Balance on house No. 44 Mill St. $35 00/100. The New Haven Gas Light Company, J. B. Byrne." The plaintiff also offered to prove by parol evidence the terms of the contract between the parties. This evidence, upon objection that the contract was within the statute of frauds, was excluded. The appeal assigns as error the action of the court in excluding this evidence, in holding that the above writings were not sufficient memoranda to satisfy the statute of frauds, and in holding that the contract alleged was within the statute.

THAYER, J. The only question which has been argued before us in this case is whether, under the allegations of the complaint, the plaintiff could prove a parol contract for the sale of the dwelling-house therein described. The defendant's counsel in their brief have suggested, without seriously urging the matter, that the complaint treats the contract as one of purchase and sale. We think that it may also be construed as alleging a contract to sell and a breach of the contract by the defendant, the subject-matter being a dwelling-house. The complaint describes the dwelling-house as "situated at number 44 Mill Street," and it appears from the finding that the plaintiff offered evidence tending to prove that it was a two-story, seven room house "on a lot of the defendant" across the street from a lot belonging to the plaintiff. It does not appear, either in allegation or proof, that the house was permanently attached to the realty, or that it was not so detached from it as to be a mere chattel. But it appears from the finding that the trial court, in making its rulings, assumed that the house was attached to the soil, and in this court both parties have argued the case upon the same assumption. We shall assume, therefore, that it was at the time of the alleged contract attached to the real estate in the manner in which such dwelling-houses are ordinarily affixed to the soil, and belonged to the defendant as the owner of the soil.

The plaintiff claims that the sale of a house to be immediately removed from the land on which it stands and to which it is affixed is a sale of personal property and not of an interest in real estate, and so is not within the section of the statute of frauds which prevents the maintenance of an action upon agreements for the sale of real estate unless the same shall be in writing.

Browne, in his first edition, after reviewing the early cases relating to this section of the statute as bearing upon sales of fixtures, buildings, standing trees, growing crops, etc., attached to the soil, drew therefrom the general rule that "if the contract when executed is to convey to the purchaser a mere chattel, though it may be in the *interim* a part of the realty, it is not affected by the statute." Browne on Statute of Frauds (1st Ed.) § 249. Benjamin, after quoting with approval the language of Lord Blackburn (from his work on Sales), lays down the rule that "an agreement to transfer the property in anything attached to the soil at the time of the agreement but which is to be severed from the soil and converted into goods before the property is transferred to the purchaser is an agreement for the sale of goods, an executory agreement." 1 Benjamin on Sales,

§ 133. Williston says: "If the contract is to sell and deliver a house, even though the house is at the time affixed to the realty, it is a contract for the sale of goods, for the parties contract to buy and sell a house separated from the realty and moved from its foundations. On the other hand if the parties attempt to make a present transfer of a building or materials fixed in a building, it is evident that they are attempting to make a sale of realty, even though it is also agreed that the subject-matter of the sale shall be severed in a short time." Williston on Sales, § 66. The Supreme Judicial Court of Massachusetts, speaking in a case where the contract related to growing trees, said: "It may be difficult in many cases to determine, from the terms of the contract, whether the parties intend to grant a present estate in the trees while growing, or only a right, either definite or unlimited as to time, to enter and cut, with title to the property when it becomes a chattel. If the former be the true construction, then it comes within the statute, and must be in writing; if the latter, then, though wholly oral, it may be enforced." *White* v. *Foster*, 102 Mass. 375, 378. There is great conflict in the decisions, but this is the rule in England and in many of our sister States. This is the rule early adopted in this State. *Bostwick* v. *Leach*, 3 Day, 476, 484. We think, notwithstanding the numerous opposing authorities, that this is the better rule.

Counsel for the defendant attempted to distinguish cases of contract to sell mill-stones or other fixtures attached to the realty and belonging to the owner thereof, as was the case in *Bostwick* v. *Leach*, or a case of contract to sell the boards and brick of which a building is composed, where the vendee is to remove the mill-stones in the one case and to tear down the building and remove the materials of which it is constructed in the other, from a contract to sell an entire building to be severed and removed by the vendee. We see no difference in principle between the cases. The brick and materials of which a building is composed are, before the destruction of the building, a part of the realty as much as the entire building is before its severance; indeed they constitute the building. If a vendor contracts to sell a building entire, or to sell the materials of which it is composed, and to sever the building from the land, or tear it down and deliver the materials, it will hardly be claimed that in either case a sale of land or any interest therein is contemplated, or that an action could not be maintained for a breach of the contract; because the intent of the parties in either case to contract with respect to a mere chattel is apparent. Where the intent to sell a building as a chattel is thus apparent from the contract and circumstances attending it, the severance may be made by the vendee. *Marshall* v. *Green*, L. R. 1 C. P. Div. 35, 40. The fact that the vendee is to remove the building is important only as bearing upon the intent of the parties in determining whether the title to the building is to pass at once or only after severance from the realty. When the parties to the contract have in contemplation the sale of a building or a tree as a chattel when it shall be detached from the land, there is no good reason why a court should not give effect to the contract as the parties understood and intended it. In such a case neither party intends that any interest in the real estate shall pass. The very purpose of the contract may be to rid the land of such tree or building. Until detached from the land the thing contracted to be sold would remain a part of the realty, and a conveyance of the realty to a third party would carry it to the purchaser. The implied license to enter and sever the chattel, if this was to be done by the vendee, would be revoked by such conveyance of the land, and the vendee's remedy must be against the vendor for breach of the contract. Growing crops, *fructus industriales*, are an exception to the rule, and may be sold and the title pass to the purchaser before severance from the soil.

In the case before us the complaint alleges that the defendant owned the dwelling-house in question, which it desired to have removed from its lot, and that the plaintiff purchased it with the purpose of removing it across the street to his own lot. The defendant denies this, and by the answer alleges that the contract was that for the $40 paid the plaintiff was to have the materials of which the house was constructed if he would tear down the house and entirely remove the materials. This is denied in the reply. As already intimated, we think that the allegations of the complaint are sufficient to permit proof of an executory contract for the sale of the house as well as a contract of bargain and sale. The parties were at issue as to what the contract was, the plaintiff claiming that it was for the sale of the house severed from the land, the defendant that it was for the sale of the materials of which the house was constructed if the plaintiff would tear it down and remove them.

The two receipts which were in evidence were not sufficient memoranda of any contract to satisfy the statute. They did not show any sale, present or prospective, of the house, and would apply as well to money received on a lease as on a sale of the house. But the plaintiff was entitled to show that the contract was as he claimed, for the sale of the house as a chattel after severance from the soil, and there was error in excluding the evidence offered for this purpose.

There is error, the judgment is set aside and a new trial ordered.

In this opinion the other judges concurred.

HIRTH *v.* GRAHAM

OHIO SUPREME COURT, 1893

[50 *Ohio State Reports*, 57]

BRADBURY, J. The plaintiff in error brought an action before a justice of the peace to recover of the defendant in error damages alleged to have been sustained on account of the refusal of the latter to perform a contract by which he had sold to the plaintiff in error certain growing timber.

The defendant attempted to secure the dismissal of the action on the ground that the justice had no jurisdiction of an action for the breach of such a contract. Failing in this, and the action being tried to a jury, he requested the justice to instruct the jury "that if they find from the evidence that the trees about which this action is brought were at the time of said alleged contract then growing upon the land of defendant, and that no note or contract or memorandum was made of the contract of sale was at the time made in writing the plaintiff cannot maintain this action, and your verdict should be for the defendant"; which instruction the justice refused to give, but on the contrary gave to them the following instructions on the subject: "This is an action for damage, not on the contract nor to enforce the same, and if you find that a contract was made verbal or otherwise and the defendant refused or failed to comply with its terms the plaintiff is entitled to any damage you may find him to have sustained by way of such non-compliance."

The defendant in error, who was also the defendant in the justice's court, excepted, both, to the charge as given and to the refusal to charge as requested; the verdict and judgment being against him he embodied the charge as given, as well as that refused, in separate bills of exceptions, and brought the cause to the court of common pleas on error, where the judgment of the justice of the peace was affirmed; he thereupon brought error to the circuit court, where the judgments of the court of common pleas and that of the justice were both reversed, and it is to reverse this judgment of the circuit court and re-instate and affirm those of the court of common pleas and justice of the peace that this proceeding is pending.

Counsel for plaintiff in error contends that the record contains nothing to show that the trees which were the subject of the contract were standing or growing, and that, therefore, it does not appear that the defendant was injured by the instructions given and refused. The record does not support this contention. During the trial three separate bills of exceptions were taken, and when all of them are considered together, it clearly appears that evidence was given tending to prove that the trees, the subject of the contract, were growing on the land at the time it was made, and that the contract was not evidenced by any note or memorandum in writing. The instruction refused, was, therefore, pertinent, and if it contained a sound legal proposition the refusal to give it in charge to the jury was prejudicial to the defendant. The court however not only refused to give the instructions requested by the defendant, but told the jury in substance that no written memorandum was necessary.

[Two pages of the opinion are here omitted.]

Whether a sale of growing trees, is the sale of an interest in or concerning land has long been a much controverted subject in the courts of England as well as in the courts of the several states of the Union. The question has been differently decided in different jurisdictions, and by different courts, or at different times by the same court within the same jurisdiction. The courts of England, particularly, have varied widely in their holdings on the subject.

Lord MANSFIELD held that the sale of a crop of growing turnips was within this clause of the statute. *Emmerson* v. *Heelis*, 2 Taunt. 38, following the case of *Waddington et al.* v. *Bristow, et al. etc.*, 2 Bos. & Pul. 452, where the sale of a crop of growing hops was adjudged not to have been a sale of goods and chattels merely. And in *Crosby* v. *Wadsworth*, 6 East

601, the sale of growing grass was held to be a contract for the sale of an interest in or concerning land. Lord ELLENBOROUGH saying: "Upon the first of these questions" (whether this purchase of the growing crop be a contract or sale of lands, tenements or hereditaments, or any interest in or concerning them), "I think that the agreement stated, conferring, as it professes to do, an exclusive right to the vesture of the land during a limited time and for given purposes, is a contract or sale of an interest in, or at least, an interest concerning lands." *Id.* 610.

Afterwards, in *Teal* v. *Auty*, 2 B. & B. 99, the court of common pleas held a contract for the sale of growing poles was a sale of an interest in or concerning lands. Many decisions have been announced by the English courts since the cases above noted were decided, the tendency of which have been to greatly narrow the application of the fourth section of the Statute of Frauds to crops, or timber, growing upon land. Crops planted and raised annually by the hand of man are practically withdrawn from its operation, while the sale of other crops, and in some instances growing timber, also, are withdrawn from the statute, where, in the contemplation of the contracting parties, the subject of the contract is to be treated as a chattel. The latest declaration of the English courts upon this question, is that of the common pleas division of the high court of justice, in *Marshall* v. *Green*, 1 C. P. Div. 35, decided in 1875. The syllabus reads: "A sale of growing timber to be taken away as soon as possible by the purchaser is not a contract or sale of land, or any interest therein, within the fourth section of the Statute of Frauds." This decision was rendered by the three justices who constituted the common pleas division of the high court of justice, COLERIDGE, C. J., BRETT and GROVE, JJ., whose characters and attainments entitle it to great weight; yet, in view of the prior long period of unsettled professional and judicial opinion in England upon the question, that the court was not one of final resort, and that the decision has encountered adverse criticism from high authority (Benjamin on Sales, section 126, Ed. of 1892), it cannot be considered as finally settling the law of England on this subject.

The conflict among the American cases on the subject cannot be wholly reconciled. In Massachusetts, Maine, Maryland, Kentucky and Connecticut, sales of growing trees to be presently cut and removed by the vendee, are held not to be within the operation of the fourth section of the Statute of Frauds. . . .

The courts of most of the American states, however, that have considered the question, hold, expressly, that a sale of growing or standing timber is a contract concerning an interest in lands, and within the fourth section of the Statute of Frauds.

The question is now, for the first time, before this court for determination; and we are at liberty to adopt that rule on the subject, most conformable to sound reason. In all its other relations to the affairs of men, growing timber is regarded as an integral part of the land upon which it stands; it is not subject to levy and sale upon execution, as chattel property; it descends with the land to the heir, and passes to the vendor with the soil. *Jones* v. *Timmons*, 21 Ohio St., 596. Coal, petroleum, building-stone, and many other substances constituting integral parts of the land, have become articles of commerce, and easily detached and removed, and, when detached and removed, become personal property, as well as fallen timber; but no case is found in which it is suggested that sales of such substances, with a view to their immediate removal, would not be within the statute. Sales of growing timber are as likely to become the subjects of fraud and perjury, as are the other integral parts of the land, and the question whether such sale is a sale of an interest in or concerning lands, should depend not upon the intention of the parties, but upon the legal character of the subject of the contract, which, in the case of growing timber, is that of realty.

This rule has the additional merit of being clear, simple and of easy application, qualities entitled to substantial weight in choosing between conflicting principles.

Whether circumstances of part performance might require a modification of this rule, is not before the court and has not been considered.

Judgment affirmed.

Compare MARSHALL *v.* GREEN, 1 C. P. D. 35 (Common Pleas Division, 1875), where it was held that a sale of growing timber to be removed by the purchaser as soon as possible was not a contract for an interest in land within the 4th section of the Statute of Frauds, Lord Coleridge, C. J., saying: "I find the following statement of the law with regard to this subject, which must be taken to have received the sanction of that learned Judge, Sir Edward Vaughan Williams, in the notes in the last edition of Williams' Saunders upon the case of *Duppa* v. *Mayo*, p. 395: 'The principle of these decisions appears to be this, that wherever at the time of the contract it is contemplated that the purchaser should derive a benefit from the further growth of the thing sold from further vegetation and from the nutriment to be afforded by the land, the contract is to be considered as for an interest in land; but where the process of vegetation is over, or the parties agree that the thing sold shall be immediately withdrawn from the land, the land is to be considered as a mere warehouse of the thing sold, and the contract is for goods. This doctrine has been materially qualified by later decisions, and it appears to be now settled that, with respect to emblements or *fructus industriales*, &c., the corn and other growth of the earth which are produced not spontaneously, but by labour and industry, a contract for the sale of them while growing, whether they are in a state of maturity or whether they have still to derive nutriment from the land in order to bring them to that state, is not a contract for the sale of any interest in land, but merely for the sale of goods.' The propositions so laid down, as applied to the present case, seem to afford a very clear and intelligible rule. Planted trees cannot in strictness be said to be produced spontaneously, yet the labour employed in their planting bears so small a proportion to their natural growth, that they cannot be considered as *fructus industriales*, but treating them as not being *fructus industriales*, the proposition is that where the thing sold is to derive no benefit from the land, and is to be taken away immediately, the contract is not for an interest in land. Here the contract was that the trees should be got away as soon as possible, and they were almost immediately cut down. Apart from any decisions on the subject, and as a matter of common sense, it would seem obvious that a sale of twenty-two trees to be taken away immediately was not a sale of an interest in land, but merely of so much timber."

B. Non-Enforceability by Action

TAYLOR *v.* GREAT EASTERN RAILWAY COMPANY

King's Bench, 1901

[*Law Reports*, [1901] 1 *King's Bench*, 774]

Trial in the Commercial Court before Bigham J.

On October 19, 1900, a firm of Barnard Brothers sold to one Sanders a quantity of barley at the price of 68*l.* 5*s.* on rail at Elsenham Station on the defendants' railway. Messrs. Barnard gave to Sanders an invoice containing the terms of the contract in the following form: "Newport, Essex. October 19, 1900. Mr. George Sanders. Bought of Barnard Brothers. Per on rail at Elsenham to your order, 52 qrs. 4 bus. barley at 26*s.*, £68 5*s.*" There was no memorandum in writing of the contract signed by Sanders. On October 24 Messrs. Barnard gave a written order to the defendants directing them to transfer the barley to Sanders; and thereupon the defendants sent to Sanders an advice-note informing him that the barley was at the station awaiting his order. After receiving this advice-note Sanders tried to resell the barley, using for the purpose a sample obtained from Barnard Brothers, but he did not succeed in finding a purchaser. He never inspected or sampled the bulk at the railway station. Towards the end of November Sanders committed an act of bankruptcy on which he was subsequently adjudicated, and the plaintiff was appointed trustee. On or about November 30 Messrs. Barnard, as unpaid vendors, claimed to stop the goods *in transitu*, and demanded the barley from the defendants, who gave it up to them. The plaintiff then sued the defendants for conversion.

Bigham J. In this case one of the defences relied upon by the defendants was that although Barnard Brothers had signed a sufficient memorandum of the contract of sale within the meaning of s. 4 of the Sale of Goods Act, Sanders had not; and it was said that he had neither paid any part of the price (which was true) nor accepted any part of the goods. In these circumstances it was argued, as I understand, that the property in the goods had not passed from Barnards to Sanders, and that, therefore, Barnards were entitled to possession. I may say at once that this contention, whatever it may be worth in law, is not well founded in fact. I am of opinion that the goods had been accepted by Sanders.

[A page of the opinion is here omitted.]

The view which I take of the facts makes it unnecessary to consider the point of law, but I should like to say a word or two about it and about the case of *Nicholson* v. *Bower* (1 E. & E. 172), which was cited by Mr. Lush in support of it. I think that the absence of a memorandum in writing, and of the other conditions mentioned in s. 4, sub-s. 1, of the Sale of Goods Act, does not make a contract void or even voidable. The contract is good. The only effect of the non-fulfillment of the statutory conditions is that it is unenforceable. And, the contract being good, all the legal consequences of a contract follow; so that, if the contract is for the sale of specific goods, the property in the goods passes to the buyer. It may be asked, What happens if the buyer, after making the purchase, refuses to fulfil any of the statutory conditions which alone will make the contract enforceable against him? The property in the goods has passed to him, and it may be that he has received the goods themselves, yet he cannot be sued for the price. My answer is that the seller may call on the buyer to pay for the goods, and, if he fails to comply, the seller may treat the contract as rescinded. The effect of such rescission would be to revest the property in the seller and to entitle him to resume possession. As to the case of *Nicholson* v. *Bower* (1 E. & E. 172), it was an issue to try whether certain wheat was the property of the plaintiff, who was the assignee of one Pavitt, a bankrupt, or the property of the defendant who had sold the wheat to Pavitt. Pavitt had not complied with the requirements of the statute, so that the contract of sale never was enforceable against him, and it seems to have been decided that on this ground there was no binding contract between the vendor and the vendee, and that, therefore, the property never legally vested in the buyer. If that is the true ground of the decision, I do not think it was right, nor do I think it is in accordance with the later cases decided under the statute. The seller had sold the goods and was clearly bound by the contract, and the buyer had bought the goods although he could not be sued for the price if he chose to insist on the statutory defence. In such circumstances it would not be true to say that the property had not passed. I think, however, upon a careful examination of the facts of the case, the decision may be justified on the supposition that before the assignee's title could be said to have arisen the vendor and the vendee had rescinded the contract so that the property had revested in the former; and this appears to have been the ground upon which the judgment of Erle J. proceeded. There must be judgment for the plaintiff.

Judgment for the plaintiff.

Note also Edwards Manufacturing Co. *v.* Bradford Co., 294 Fed. 176 (Circuit Court of Appeals, 2nd Circuit, 1923), where there was an action to recover damages for failure to deliver steel under a contract of sale, the damages sought being based on an alleged contract for the resale of the steel to Suzuki & Co. It appeared that this resale contract did not comply with the requirements of the Statute of Frauds. In holding that this did not affect the rights of plaintiff under the contract sued on, Mayer, Circuit Judge, said: "It is contended that the oral modification of the contract between plaintiff and Suzuki & Co. was void under the statute of frauds, and that plaintiff could not have recovered against Suzuki & Co. Therefore, it is argued that, as the basis of plaintiff's recovery is that there was a binding resale contract, that basis is destroyed when it appears that plaintiff's so-called modified contract was not enforceable; for it is urged that in such case the damages at once become uncertain and speculative, depending entirely on the caprice of the purchaser and other 'unpredictable elements.'

"We need not determine what would have been the rights of Suzuki & Co. as against plaintiff, had these two engaged in controversy in respect of the legal effect of the oral modification. The reason is that the defense of the statute of frauds is personal to the contracting parties — here plaintiff and Suzuki & Co.

"As the contract in the case at bar is a New York contract, we look to the New York statute, which no longer uses the word 'void' (although, when the word 'void' was used, see *Crane* v. *Powell*, 139 N. Y. 379, 384, 34 N. E. 91), but reads:

" 'A contract to sell or a sale of any goods or choses in action of the value of fifty dollars or upwards shall not be enforceable by action. * * * ' Uniform Sales Act (N. Y. Personal Property Law [Consol. Laws, c. 41] § 85).

"The principle here concerned is well stated by Judge Speer in *Purdom Naval Stores* v. *Western Union Telegraph Co.* (C. C.) 153 Fed. 327, 330:

" 'The statute merely states that "no action shall be brought." Failure to comply with its terms does not * * * render the contract void, but unenforceable. * * * It is besides true that the benefit of the statute of frauds as a defense is entirely personal, and cannot be set up by third parties. * * * It follows that whether or not the statute was complied with by the parties to the proposed sale, that question cannot now be raised by the defendant company, which was no party to the transaction.'

"It is said by defendant that this is dictum, but, in any event, it states the principle applied to various states of facts in many cases. . . .

"In view of the foregoing, there is no merit in the argument that plaintiff was required to prove, in effect, that Suzuki & Co. would not interpose the defense that the oral modification of the contract avoided it; because the reasoning of these cases is that the contract is valid or at least not void and merely unenforceable at the option of the person against whom it is sought to be enforced."

MILLER *v.* WESTERN UNION TELEGRAPH COMPANY

MISSOURI COURT OF APPEALS, 1911

[157 *Missouri Appeal Reports*, 580]

BROADDUS, P. J. This is an appeal from a judgment of the Jackson County Circuit Court rendered on April 2, 1910, on defendant's appeal from a justice court, in favor of plaintiffs and against defendant.

The action is based on the following facts: On January 16, 1908, and at other times referred to in the testimony herein, the Van Alstyne Elevator Company was engaged in the grain business at Van Alstyne, in the State of Texas. The plaintiffs, Miller Bros. were at said time the proprietors of the 101 Ranch at Bliss, in the State of Oklahoma. The defendant Telegraph Company at such time, operated a line of telegraph between Van Alstyne and Bliss, above mentioned. On said January 16th, the Van Alstyne Elevator Company telephoned to the Telegraph Company at Van Alstyne a message, of which the following is a copy, according to plaintiff's testimony.

VAN ALSTYNE, TEXAS, 1–6, 1908.

To Miller Bros., Bliss, Okla.

Offer fifty there one to five cars bulk mixed corn. White cent over.

VAN ALSTYNE ELEVATOR CO.

This was an offer to buy at fifty cents per bushel for mixed corn and fifty-one cents per bushel for white corn, at Bliss, Oklahoma. On the same day, January 16, 1908, Miller Bros. received from the Van Alstyne Elevator Company, a telegram reading as follows:

VAN ALSTYNE, TEXAS, 1–6, 1908.

To Miller Bros., Bliss, Okla.

Offer fifty-three one to five cars bulk mixed corn. White cent over.

VAN ALSTYNE ELEVATOR CO.

It will be noticed that the message as delivered to the Telegraph Company at Van Alstyne, Texas, read "Offer fifty there," while as received by Miller Bros. at Bliss, Okla., it read "Offer fifty-three." The difference was caused by the transposition of two letters in the word "there." The effect of such change was to make the offer three cents more per bushel than the Van Alstyne Elevator Company actually offered according to their telegram as delivered to the Telegraph Company.

Plaintiff, George L. Miller, in his deposition, testifies that, immediately upon the receipt of the telegram purporting to offer fifty-three cents per bushel for mixed corn, and fifty-four cents for white corn, not having the corn on hand, he arranged with one, W. H. Van Selous, a ranchman living in the vicinity of Bliss, to furnish the corn at fifty-three cents per bushel. As to what passed between Miller Bros. and Van Selous at this time, J. E. Cobb, bookkeeper of Van Selous, testifies in his deposition that Mr. Miller called Mr. Van Selous by telephone, and stated that he could place five thousand bushels of corn at fifty-three cents, and asked whether he could furnish this quantity of corn. Van Selous was not in the office at the time, and the witness Cobb, who received the message, went out and communicated the proposition to him, and on receiving an affirmative answer from Van Selous, Cobb immediately telephoned back to Miller that Van Selous would deliver the corn at Bliss. On receiving Van Selous' reply by telephone, Mr. Miller testifies he at once sent the following telegram to the Van Alstyne Elevator Company, it being only a few minutes after the receipt of their message.

BLISS, OKLA., 1–16, 1908.

To Van Alstyne Elevator Co., Van Alstyne, Texas.
We accept offer on five cars white corn.

MILLER BROS.

Before any further move had been made in the matter by any of the parties, so far as the testimony disclosed, the following letter was received by mail January 18, 1908, by Miller Bros. from the Van Alstyne Elevator Company.

January 16, 1908.

This will be our confirmation of wire to you of even date wherein we offered you 50c for 1 to 5 cars mixed corn f. o. b. your track, one cent more for 1 to 5 cars of white. If we receive your acceptance on any of the above before 6 p. m., this will be our confirmation of purchase to you of 1 to 5 cars on the above terms. If this price is not in line with your market, please wire us on receipt of this letter best offer you can make on any of above.

It thus appears that on January 18, 1908, two days after the receipt of the erroneous telegram, and before anything further had been done towards filling the order than the telephone communication between plaintiff, George L. Miller, and W. H. Van Selous, as already noted, Miller Bros. were fully informed that the error of "fifty-three" for "fifty there" had been made in the transmission of the message.

Miller Bros. elected to fill the order at fifty-one cents a bushel for white corn. The Statute of Frauds of the State of Oklahoma was read in evidence. It is as follows: "Section 3011. What Must be Written. The following contracts are invalid unless the same or some note or memorandum thereof be in writing and subscribed by the party to be charged, or his agent." Among those enumerated is, "An agreement for the sale of goods, chattels or things in action, at a price not less than fifty dollars, unless the buyer accept or receive part of such goods and chattels, or the evidence of some of them, or pay some part of the purchase money." The finding and judgment were for the plaintiff and defendant appealed. . . .

We do not understand that plaintiffs dispute the familiar principle of law requiring the injured party to use all reasonable efforts to mitigate the damage resulting from another's negligence, but they deny that it has any application under the facts of this case. They assert that although the contract they had with Selous for the purchase of the corn was not in writing it was only voidable at the election of the plaintiffs who had the right to waive the necessity of the writing and thereby make it binding. [*Aultman* v. *Booth*, 95 Mo. 383; *Maybee* v. *Moore*, 90 Mo. 340; *R'y Co.* v. *Clark*, 121 Mo. 169.] And it is said that: "It is unquestionably the law of this state that the plea of the Statute of Frauds is not available to a stranger to a contract to show that the contract is invalid because it is within the Statute of Frauds." [*Scudder & Co.* v. *Morris*, 107 Mo. App. 647.]

While it must be admitted that a stranger to the contract cannot be allowed to show that it is non-enforceable under the statute, we are not convinced for that reason that the statute does not apply to the facts of this case. We speak with reference to the Missouri statute.

This is not a suit upon the contract in question, and the appellant does not plead as a defense that it is non-enforceable so far as it was concerned, but that it was not binding on respondents until complied with and that such being the case, it became the duty of the respondents in the exercise of reasonable care in order to mitigate the damages caused by the negligence of appellant to have refused to take the grain. The plea of appellant therefore is but the assertion that respondents wrongfully failed to perform an act wholly within their power, the performance of which would have relieved appellant from all responsibility in the premises, and imposed no burden on respondents.

If we are wrong as to the effect the Missouri Statute of Frauds would have on the case, we think there can be no doubt if the contract be construed according to the statute of Oklahoma, where it is invalid. [*Grant* v. *Milan*, 20 Ok. 672.]

In states where the statute declares such contracts void they are of no effect whatever. [20 Cyc. of Law, 279.] It is held that "a contract which is illegal, as contrary to public policy, is absolutely void, and may be attacked by any one in any proceeding in which it is sought to found rights thereon." And, "In regard to consequences to third persons, the distinction between void and voidable is highly important, because nothing can be founded on what is absolutely void." [*Cumberland Tel. Co.* v. *Evansville*, 127 Fed. 187.] "A void contract is, in fact, no contract, since an instrument of that nature does not alter the relations previously existing between the contracting parties, nor will it serve as the foundation of any right." [*Allen* v. *City of Davenport* 132 Fed. 209; Page on Contracts, sec. 20.]

The position of appellant does not depend upon precedent. The respondents were under no greater legal obligation to Van Selous to accept the grain mentioned than if there had never been any agreement whatever in reference thereto, consequently, the acceptance of the grain by the respondents at the price of fifty-one cents was a new contract under the statute of Oklahoma, with the making of which the said telegram had nothing to do. It was made upon the terms contained in the letter of the Van Alstyne Elevator Company to respondents of January 16, 1908, and on the same terms as contained in said telegram without the error.

The respondents instead of exercising reasonable diligence to mitigate the damages, if any, consequent upon the negligence of appellant in failing to transmit said telegram correctly, voluntarily in effect contracted anew for the grain, the evident purpose of which was to base their claim for the damages in suit. Reversed. All concur.

WEBSTER *v.* CONDON

MASSACHUSETTS SUPREME COURT, 1924

[248 *Massachusetts Reports*, 269]

DECOURCY, J. This is an action of contract brought to recover the loss upon five cars of oats, alleged to have been purchased by the defendants from the plaintiffs on July 22, 1920. The answer set up the statute of frauds, with other defences. At the trial the plaintiffs offered evidence tending to show a custom and usage among grain dealers, which was known to and acquiesced in by the defendants, to disregard and waive the legal rights possessed by them under the statute of frauds. The offer was excluded by the trial judge, and the plaintiffs excepted. The only other exception is to the granting of the defendants' motions that a verdict be directed for them respectively.

The evidence was excluded rightly. The defendants may recognize their obligations under oral contracts, and refrain from setting up the statute of frauds in actions brought against them if they so wish. But if they do rely upon the statute, a custom or usage cannot be allowed to annul the general liabilities of the parties under the established rules of law.

[The balance of the opinion is here omitted.]

C. ACCEPTANCE AND RECEIPT

HILL *v.* DODGE

NEW HAMPSHIRE SUPREME COURT, 1922

[80 *New Hampshire Reports*, 381]

Assumpsit, for breach of a contract to purchase a yoke of oxen. Trial by jury and verdict for plaintiff. At the April term, 1920, of the superior court a bill of exceptions was allowed by *Branch*, J., to the denial of the motions for a nonsuit and for a directed verdict.

April 7, 1919, the plaintiff showed the oxen to the defendant, and made a price for them. The former testified that on the succeeding Friday the following conversation took place: "He [the defendant] said: 'I thought I would stop and see how you stood on the cattle today?' I said [after some preliminary discussion about the ox's condition]: 'What will you give for them just as they stand?' He looked them all over, walked around and [after the ox had eaten some potatoes and saltpeter] said: 'He is all right, I have worked many an ox every day that acted worse than he does.' I said, 'All right, what will you give for them?' He said: '$425 just as I said I would yesterday, for the oxen and everything.' I said: 'By God, you have a yoke of oxen, they are yours.' Nothing further was said about it, only I said: 'You have a yoke of cattle from this moment, they are your oxen from now on.' He said: 'I understand.' I said: 'When will you take them?' He said: 'Monday morning I am coming to Concord with a load and my man is coming over with me and I will take them back.' I said: 'Suppose the ox dies,' and he said: 'He is mine if he dies,' and no more was said about it. That is the trade."

The plaintiff further testified that on Monday, upon inquiry by telephone, the defendant stated that he would be right over, but that shortly after the defendant's foreman telephoned him that the defendant would not take the oxen, and that he could sell them to anyone that he wanted to; that he accordingly sold the oxen for $250.

Snow, J. "No contract for the sale of goods, wares, or merchandise, for the price of thirty-three dollars or more, is valid, unless the buyer accepts and actually receives part of the property sold, or gives something in part payment or in earnest to bind the bargain, or unless some note or memorandum thereof is in writing, and signed by the party to be charged, or by some person by him thereto authorized." P. S., *c.* 215, *s.* 3.

The question presented is whether upon the facts reported, there was any evidence on which the jury could find a receipt and acceptance of the oxen by the defendant to satisfy the requirements of this statute.

The plaintiff contends that manual possession by the defendant was not essential to the acceptance and receipt prescribed by the statute, relying upon *Carter* v. *Willard*, 19 Pick. 1; *Leonard* v. *Davis*, 66 U. S. 476; *Jewett* v. *Warren*, 12 Mass. 300, 302; *Boynton* v. *Veazie*, 24 Me. 286; *Calkins* v. *Lockwood*, 17 Conn. 154; s. c. 42 Am. Dec. 729.

In the first case cited, the goods sold were in the possession of a tenant under a lease and the vendor was not entitled to present possession. In the other cases, the goods consisted of articles of such a ponderous nature that manual delivery was impracticable. Whether in such cases, there may be exceptions to the rule laid down in the statute (*Shindler* v. *Houston*, 1 N. Y. 261, 263; *Shepherd* v. *Pressey*, 32 N. H. 49, 56) is not considered, since the subject of the sale in the instant case was fully in the possession of the vendor and easily capable of manual delivery. Nor is the question of what rule would apply where the buyer is already in possession and control of the goods here involved or considered. See 1 Williston, Contracts, *s.* 554.

The rule in this jurisdiction in the ordinary case is that where receipt and acceptance are alone relied upon to satisfy the terms of the statute, they must be proved by clear and unequivocal acts on the part of the buyer and that no act of the seller alone is sufficient. *Shepherd* v. *Pressey*, *supra*, 55, 56, 57; *Small* v. *Stevens*, 65 N. H. 209, 210; *Clark* v. *Labreche*, 63 N. H. 397, 399. It is not understood that it was intended by *dicta* in the last case to depart from this rule.

In the case at bar, there was no memorandum or payment in part or in earnest. Receipt and acceptance are alone depended upon to satisfy the statute. It is not claimed that there was any physical act or conduct evidencing acceptance and receipt or that anything passed between the parties but mere words. But plaintiff contends that from the words spoken, a delivery of the oxen as they stood in the plaintiff's barn can be found. This he claims can be inferred from the assent of the defendant to plaintiff's statement made "in the presence of the oxen" that they were from that moment the property of the defendant, coupled with defendant's agreement to take them away the following Monday and his further statement, made with reference to the sick ox, "He is mine if he dies." Counsel reasons that this evidence warrants a finding that contemporaneously with acceptance and receipt of the oxen by the defendant, the plaintiff undertook, by a new and collateral contract, to act as bailee, agreeing to hold the oxen for the defendant until such time as he could conveniently take them away; that by consenting to such arrangement, the defendant admitted that title had passed and that there had been an acceptance and receipt by him.

The difficulty with plaintiff's contention lies in the fact that the supposed new contract of bailment, if found, does not prove receipt and acceptance by the defendant but simply presupposes that there had been a completed delivery. At most, it was a verbal admission that there had been a waiver of such delivery. The verbal contract of bailment was not an attesting act. It was not evidence of an actual receipt by the vendee which, standing alone, would satisfy the statute. It cannot be claimed that it was any better evidence of receipt and acceptance than would be the admission of the defendant that there had been a verbal waiver of this requirement. Had the defendant admitted on the witness stand that, at the time of the bargain, he verbally agreed to waive acceptance and receipt, it would not bar his right to set up the statute in defence.

A contract invalid under the statute because none of the alternative requisites provided by the statute have been complied with cannot be made valid by a verbal waiver of such requisites. See 1 Williston, Contracts, *s.* 199. To hold that the statute is avoided by substituting a verbal waiver of a written memorandum, or of the receipt of a part payment, or of the acceptance and receipt of part of the goods is to hold that by verbal agreement the statute may be disregarded. Such a ruling would open the door to every evil the statute was designed to remedy. While a payment in part or earnest, or the receipt and acceptance of a part of the goods sold, may be proven by parol testimony, it does not follow that parol evidence of a verbal waiver of the requirements of the statute may be received to avoid the statute.

In the absence of evidence of a different understanding, a vendor has a lien upon goods sold for the price while they remain in his control and custody. *Williams* v. *Moore*, 5 N. H. 235, 236; *Clark* v. *Draper*, 19 N. H. 419, 421, 422; *Clark* v. *Greeley*, 62 N. H. 394, 395, 396; *Paul* v. *Reed*, 52 N. H. 136. Under a fair construction of the plaintiff's testimony, he was to exchange the oxen for the price on the Monday following the bargain on Friday. There is no evidence from which it can be inferred that the plaintiff had parted with his lien. So long as the plaintiff retained his lien upon the oxen for the price under the original contract for sale, the defendant had not acquired that complete dominion and control over the oxen which an acceptance and actual receipt of the property under the terms of the statute implied. *Shepherd* v. *Pressey, supra,* 56; *Clark* v. *Labreche, supra,* 399.

The irreconcilable conflict in the testimony of the parties to this action, upon whose testimony alone the validity of the sale rests, strikingly illustrates the salutary advantages of the statute, the object of which was not only to guard against the dishonesty of parties and the perjury of witnesses, but against the misunderstanding and mistakes of honest men. *Shindler* v. *Houston, supra,* 263.

Exceptions sustained: verdict set aside: verdict and judgment for the defendant.

All concurred.

Note also MELLEN PRODUCE CO. *v.* FINK, 225 Wisconsin 90 (Supreme Court, 1937), where there was an oral agreement to sell logs to be cut by the seller from a specified tract of land belonging to the seller. After the making of this agreement, and after part of the lumber cut under it had been inspected by the defendant buyer and pronounced satisfactory, the seller executed a chattel mortgage to the plaintiff purporting to cover the same lumber. The defendant subsequently hauled the lumber to his mill, and in an action of replevin the Court said: "The defendant's inspection of the part of the lumber sawed before the mortgage was executed and his announcement that it was satisfactory doubtless constituted an acceptance of a part of the lumber orally agreed to be sold, but the question remains whether there was also an 'actual receipt.'

"The defendant contends that his acceptance of a part of the lumber as above stated also constituted an 'actual receipt' and validated the sale because sec. 121.18, Stats., provides that property in goods sold passes when intended by the parties, and sec. 121.19 (4) provides that the parties intend, unless otherwise provided by the contract, that property in the goods sold passes when the goods are in a deliverable state and are unconditionally appropriated to the contract by the parties. He contends that under this rule the inspection and acceptance of the lumber by the defendant passed the title to the property to the defendant, and that this constituted a receipt of goods to take the sale out of the contract. This might be correct had the contract been enforceable in the first instance. But it is pointed out in *Roberts, Johnson & Rand* v. *Mackowski,* 171 Wis. 420, 422, 177 N. W. 509, that what constitutes delivery in case of an enforceable contract of sale cannot be invoked to validate a contract unenforceable under the statute for want of acceptance of the goods. With like reason the same may be said respecting receipt by the buyer dependent on passing of title. Mere acceptance of goods as conforming to a contract unenforceable in the first instance does not operate to render the contract enforceable even though the parties intended the acceptance as passing the title. There can be no passing of title until there is an enforceable contract of sale. It is held in *Tonkelson* v. *Malis,* 119 Misc. 717, 197 N. Y. Supp. 309, 312, that, while intention of the parties alone may govern as to the time of the passing of title under the Uniform Sales Law, there is no connection between this and the meeting of the requirements of the statute; that, assuming that title would have passed had the contract of sale been without the reach of the statute, such assumption does not avoid the defense of the invalidity of the contract."

MAHER *v.* RANDOLPH

NEW YORK COURT OF APPEALS, 1937

[275 *New York Reports*, 80]

Appeal from a judgment, entered November 16, 1936, upon an order of the Appellate Division of the Supreme Court in the first judicial department reversing, on questions of fact and of law, a judgment in favor of plaintiffs entered upon a verdict directed by the Court at a Trial Term, without a jury, and directing a dismissal of the complaint.

LOUGHRAN, J. As owners of 240 shares of the stock of a corporation formed under a co-operative ownership plan, plaintiffs held a lease of an apartment in a building erected by the corporation. This apartment, with its furnishings, they let to the defendant for a term to expire on May 15, 1935. The furnishings included three pairs of draperies worth about $150.

On May 5, 1935, the parties entered into an oral agreement for sale by the plaintiffs and purchase by the defendant of the 240 shares of stock for $4,000. In the course of this transaction the defendant inquired whether the plaintiffs "would consent to include the draperies in the sale," and the plaintiffs answered: "Very well, the draperies are yours." Before the time fixed for delivery of the stock and for payment of the first installment of the purchase price the defendant withdrew from the transaction.

This is an action for breach of the contract of purchase and sale. The defense is the Statute of Frauds relating to personal property. "A contract to sell or a sale of any goods or choses in action of the value of fifty dollars or upwards shall not be enforceable by action unless the buyer shall accept part of the goods or choses in action so contracted to be sold or sold, and actually receive the same, or give something in earnest to bind the contract, or in part payment, or unless some note or memorandum in writing of the contract or sale be signed by the party to be charged or his agent in that behalf." (Pers. Prop. Law [Cons. Laws, ch. 41], § 85, subd. 1.) The question is whether there was such an acceptance and actual receipt of the curtains by the defendant as to make the contract enforceable.

"The acceptance and receipt are both necessary. The contract is not valid unless the buyer does both. These are two distinct things. There may be an actual receipt without an acceptance, and an acceptance without a receipt. The receipt of the goods is the act of taking possession of them." (*Cooke* v. *Millard*, 65 N. Y. 352, 367, 368.) Prior to the enactment in 1911 of section 85 of the Personal Property Law as part of the Uniform Sales Act, it was settled for us that the mere words of the bargain are not sufficient evidence to satisfy the statute in a case where the buyer already has possession of the goods under some prior and independent transaction of the parties. (*Young* v. *Ingalsbe*, 208 N. Y. 503. See *Matter of Hoover*, 33 Hun, 553; *Dorsey* v. *Pike*, 50 Hun, 534.) Such is this case.

Plaintiffs contend that the law was changed by subdivision 3 of section 85. It is thereby provided: "There is an acceptance of goods within the meaning of this section when the buyer, either before or after delivery of the goods, expresses by words or conduct his assent to becoming the owner of those specific goods." The argument of the plaintiffs, as we understand it, is that acceptance by a buyer in independent possession includes an actual receipt; that an acceptance may now be evidenced by words without an act; and that, therefore, such a transaction, though resting in words alone, is no longer condemned by the statute.

Concededly this construction of section 85 cannot here be adopted consistently with the reasoning of the opinion of this court in a case which was the source of the decisions last cited. What was said in that case is no less true in the case in hand. "The declarations relied upon as evidence of a delivery and acceptance constitute a *part* of the *contract*, and of course are obnoxious to all the evils and every objection against which it was the policy of the law to provide." (*Shindler* v. *Houston*, 1 N. Y. 261, 264.) The validity of this view of the statute, as we are aware, has been doubted and denied. But with the policy of the law as there declared in 1848 the Legislature did not see fit to interfere prior to the enactment of the foregoing subdivision 3 of section 85 of the Personal Property Law in 1911. Under the circumstances we cannot find in section 85 a sufficient expression of intention to overturn so long and so settled a course of decision.

The judgment should be affirmed, with costs.

FINCH, J. (dissenting). We are no longer bound by *Young* v. *Ingalsbe* (208 N. Y. 503). The rule enunciated therein has been the subject of much criticism and is contrary to the great weight of authority. (Williston on Contracts [Rev. ed.], § 554; American Law Institute, Restatement of the Law of Contracts, § 202; Burdick, A Statute for Promoting Fraud, 16 Col. Law Rev. 273.) In 1911 New York adopted the Uniform Sales Act which, in subdivision 3 of section 85 (Personal Property Law; Cons. Laws, ch. 41), provides that "There is an acceptance of goods within the meaning of this section when the buyer, either before or after delivery of the goods, expresses by words or conduct his assent to becoming the owner of those specific goods." Most of the other States which have adopted the Uniform Sales Act construe this to mean that where goods are already in possession of the buyer, acceptance may be evidenced by words. (Williston, *op. cit. supra*, § 557.) The statute having been amended, we are no longer bound by the earlier cases and, especially in view of our adoption of the Uniform Statute, no valid reason appears for continuing to follow a rule which seems to be counter to the new statute and is out of harmony with the rule generally adopted.

The judgment of the Appellate Division should be reversed, and the judgment of the Trial Term reinstated, with costs.

CRANE, Ch. J., LEHMAN, O'BRIEN, HUBBS and RIPPEY, JJ., concur with LOUGHRAN, J.; FINCH, J., dissents in opinion. *Judgment affirmed.*

Compare JAMES MACK CO. *v.* BEAR RIVER MILLING CO., 63 Utah 565 (Supreme Court, 1924). In that case there was an oral agreement to sell to the defendant company a quantity of grain already stored in defendant's warehouse. On the date fixed for payment defendant requested an extension, but at no time took any other action in regard to the plaintiff's order. In an action for the price of the grain the judgment of the lower court for the defendant was reversed, Thurman, J., saying: "The only question is: Was it such a sale as is enforceable under the statute of frauds pleaded by defendant and upon which the court based its conclusion and judgment? In view of this finding of the court and the conclusion reached, it is manifest that the decision of the court turned solely upon the question as to what constitutes accepting and receiving goods in contemplation of the statute, where the goods at the time of the sale are in possession of the vendee, as in the instant case. Here there was no memorandum of the sale in writing, nor anything given in earnest to bind the contract. The amount involved exceeded $500, so that the contract was within the statute unless the buyer accepted and actually received the wheat, or a part thereof, within the meaning of the statute in question.

"The meaning of the terms 'accept' and 'actually receive' in contemplation of the statute are of the first importance in determining the issues involved. The authorities generally agree that these terms, although ordinarily synonymous, do not necessarily mean the same thing in the statute of frauds. Tiedeman on Sales, § 66. 'Receive' seems to imply taking into possession by the buyer, while 'accept' means an assumption of ownership on the part of the buyer, treating the goods as his own. . . .

"In the case at bar, the wheat being in possession of the buyer at the time of the purchase, manual delivery was impracticable and unnecessary, and therefore was not required. It does not follow, however, that, because the buyer was in possession, and for that reason manual delivery was not required, therefore the terms 'accept' and 'actually receive' are of no importance. Something besides being already in possession at the time of the sale is necessary to distinguish the character of the possession. In this case, for instance, at the time of the sale defendant held the wheat in the character of bailee. In order to take the contract out of the statute of frauds something must occur independent of the oral agreement to show that the character of bailee was converted into that of vendee, and that he retained the goods in that capacity. . . .

"It cannot be consistently contended, where the goods are already in possession of the buyer at the time of the oral agreement, that it is necessary for the seller to first take them into his own possession before he can consummate a delivery. Such contention would be absurd on its face and it is only fair to state that respondent makes no such contention in the case at bar. It does insist, however, that there must be some affirmative act on the part of the purchaser manifesting an intention to accept the property under a sale agreement in order to make a transition of title from seller to purchaser. . . .

"As illustrating respondent's position upon this question, it contends that, where the possession is in the buyer as bailee, he must do some act showing acceptance of the property as vendee, for instance, selling, or attempting to sell or dispose of the whole or some portion of it, in order to take the contract out of the statute. . . .

"The proposition that mere words are not sufficient to establish a receipt and acceptance is asserted by some of the authorities. In 27 C. J. 243, hereinbefore referred to and quoted, it is said:

" '*Except as otherwise provided by statute*, as a general rule mere words are not sufficient,' etc. (Italics ours.)

"It will be noted that the statute relied on here (subdivision 3) reads as follows:

" 'There is an acceptance of goods within the meaning of this section when the buyer, either before or after delivery of the goods, expresses by words or conduct his assent to becoming the owner of those specific goods.'

"By the express terms of the statute either words or conduct may be sufficient. Of course the inference to be drawn from either should be clear and unequivocal.

"It is generally held by the authorities that an attempt by the buyer or an offer by him to sell the goods after the contract of sale constitutes an acceptance within the meaning of the statute. It is incontrovertible that an offer to sell may, and generally does, consist of words alone. The question is: Do the words of the buyer in possession imply an assumption of ownership on his part and a recognition of the sale? If so, it seems to the writer it ought to take the contract out of the statute.

"This brings us to a further consideration of the findings. In finding No. 4, after finding that the sale was made and the price settled and agreed upon, the finding reads:

" 'Which price it was then and there agreed was to be paid by the defendant to the plaintiff on or about the 15th day of September, 1920, and that on or about said 15th day of September, 1920, the defendant requested of the plaintiff an extension of the time of payment and promised and agreed to pay the plaintiff the aforesaid purchase price within the period of a week or two weeks after September 15, 1920, to which extension of time plaintiff agreed.'

"By the sales agreement made on September 1, 1920, payment for the wheat was to be made within two weeks, or on September 15th. We omit consideration of this feature inasmuch as it was a part of the sales agreement. But, as the finding shows, on the 15th respondent requested a further extension of a week or two within which to make payment, with which request the plaintiff complied. The sale was manifestly unconditional. There was no understanding that title should not pass until the payment was made. It was simply an extension of credit to a buyer to pay for property he had purchased, which property was already in his possession and under his absolute control and dominion. Is there any doubt whatever when defendant, after the money became due, asked for a further extension of time in which to pay and the extension was granted, that both plaintiff and defendant then and there recognized, signified and understood that defendant was the owner of the wheat? We think not. Furthermore, we are of opinion, if mere words in any case are sufficient to take a contract out of the statute, there ought not be any doubt whatever in the case at bar. The undisputed evidence shows that during the period covered by this transaction the market for wheat was declining. Had the market been advancing it is more than probable this case would not have reached the court at all, or if it had it would have assumed a different form and the position of the parties as to the statute of frauds would have been reversed. The statute was intended to prevent fraud, and not to aid in its perpetration."

MARSHALL *v.* MOULTRIE COTTON MILLS

GEORGIA COURT OF APPEALS, 1936

[52 *Georgia Appeals Reports,* 515]

JENKINS, P. J. This case arose from an action by a vendor against the vendee for $1080, as the "value and agreed purchase-price" of described cotton-mill looms and beams, orally ordered by the vendee for shipment by the vendor on an "order-notify" bill of lading with draft attached. The petition as amended alleged that the plaintiff so shipped the machines to the defendant, and sent the bill of lading with sight-draft attached to the Western Union Telegraph Company at the place of destination; that the defendant refused to pay the draft or receive the machines; that the plaintiff left them in the hands of the carrier, which sold them for freight and demurrage charges; and that the defendant is therefore liable for the value and agreed purchase-price of the machines, interest thereon from the date of shipment, and the freight and demurrage charges after crediting the proceeds from the carrier's sale. There was no averment that the plaintiff exercised the remedy of storing or retaining the property for the vendee under the Code of 1933, § 96–113. The court dismissed the action on the general grounds of demurrer which attacked the remedy seeking to recover the entire purchase-price, and the enforceability of the oral contract under the statute of frauds; and the special ground which attacked the claim of freight and demurrage charges.

[The opinion on the original hearing is here omitted.]

ON REHEARING

When the decision in this case was originally rendered, it was stated that since the general demurrer had been properly sustained, under the rulings made in the preceding divisions of the opinion, the question whether the oral contract would or would not be valid under the statute of frauds, under some new and different form of procedure which might hereafter be adopted, was not for the court to determine on the present pleadings. However, on the grant of a rehearing, in order more thoroughly to consider the rulings as originally made, the case has been reconsidered in its entirety. In adhering to our former rulings, we have reached the further conclusion that since the judgment of the trial court was based upon both grounds of the defendant's demurrer, one of which expressly raised the question as to the statute of frauds, both questions should be adjudicated by this court. Under the statute of frauds (Code of 1933, § 20–401, par. 7), any contract for the sale of goods, wares, and merchandise to the amount of $50 or more, unless the buyer shall accept part of the goods sold and actually receive the same, or give something in earnest to bind the bargain, or in part payment thereof, in order to be binding, must be in writing. The alleged contract of sale, forming the basis of the instant suit for the purchase-price of certain goods, not having been in writing, was invalid under the provisions of the statute of frauds. As was held by this court in *M. C. Kiser Co.* v. *Rosenbloom*, 41 Ga. App. 183 (152 S. E. 273): "A delivery of goods to a common carrier will not, without more, constitute a delivery to the purchaser within the purview of that provision of the statute of frauds which refers to the sale of goods to the amount of more than $50, where the buyer has not accepted and actually received a part of the goods sold, or given something in earnest to bind the bargain or in part payment." In that case it was said by this court that regardless of any possible contrary ruling in *Castlen* v. *Marshburn*, *supra*, the doctrine announced in the *Kiser* case was in accordance with the decision of the Supreme Court in *Denmead* v. *Glass*, 30 Ga. 637 (2). See also *Baer* v. *Hooks*, 40 Ga. App. 425 (supra). In other words, a delivery to a common carrier for even unconditional delivery to a consignee can not, at one and the same time, both create a valid contract and operate as a delivery thereunder. If a contract conforming to the statute of frauds already existed, unconditional delivery to the carrier would amount to delivery to the consignee; but in the absence of such a valid agreement, even an unconditional delivery to the carrier for delivery to the consignee amounts to nothing more than a tender.

Judgment affirmed. Stephens and Sutton, JJ., concur.

Stephens, J., concurring specially. On rehearing I withdraw my dissent from the judgment of affirmance, and now concur in the judgment on the ground that it appears from the petition as amended that the contract was unenforceable by reason of the statute of frauds, and that the demurrer was properly sustained.

Note also Dolan Mercantile Co. *v.* Marcus, 276 Pa. 404 (Supreme Court, 1923), where sugar was sold f. o. b. Chicago to merchants in Pennsylvania, and where it was urged that delivery to the carrier was sufficient to satisfy the Statute. The Court said: "If delivery to a carrier is sufficient to meet the section's requirements, the many difficult situations presented by parol sales would be continued, and such construction would thwart its purposes. . . . To prevent the possibilities that may arise because of these outstanding deficiencies affecting property while in transit, and to shut out questionable receipt and acceptance, which otherwise might be sufficient to bring the contracts within the exemption, the legislature used precise words to interdict such sales. To actually receive necessitates an actual rather than a constructive receipt."

Compare E. A. CLARK & COMPANY *v.* D. & C. E. SCRIBNER COMPANY, 122 Maine 418 (Supreme Judicial Court, 1923), where a carload of cottonseed meal under an oral contract was shipped by rail to the buyer, bill of lading being forwarded with sight draft attached for collection. The Maine statute does not contain the word "actually." The Court said: "Attention is directed to the undisputed fact that the bill of lading never came into the defendant's possession, but was retained by plaintiff to protect its lien for the purchase price. The defendant could not exercise any control over the contents of the car until it paid the draft and thus obtained possession of the bill of lading. This it did not do, and persistently refused to do. These facts are decisive of the case. . . . In the revision of the statutes of Maine in 1857 the word 'actually,' which had been in the statute since 1821 was omitted. . . . We apprehend however that the meaning remains the same as under the readings of the statutes of 1821 and 1841."

BLACK BEAUTY COAL COMPANY *v.* COHEN

MASSACHUSETTS SUPREME COURT, 1929

[267 *Massachusetts Reports*, 98]

SANDERSON, J. The plaintiff seeks to recover in different counts the price of coal sold and delivered, freight and demurrage charges caused by the defendants' failure to discharge the coal from the cars on arrival, damages for breach of the defendants' contract to buy the coal and the reasonable value of services performed, and reimbursement for expenses and liability incurred for freight and demurrage charges in endeavoring to perform the contract. The answer is a general denial; it also sets up the statute of frauds as a defence.

The defendants are copartners doing business under the name Mt. Bowdoin Fuel Company. In January, 1926, the defendant Levine visited Pennsylvania and met one Brennan, the secretary of the Somerset County Coal Operators' Association of which the plaintiff is a member. Thereafter a telegram signed "J. S. Brennan, Secretary Somerset County Coal Oprs. Assn., Somerset, Penna." was sent Levine stating "Can furnish quick eight cars lumpy mine run smokeless two dollars net ton Can you use." Upon receipt of the telegram Levine, in a telephone conversation, asked Brennan to ship the coal, and the plaintiff, in response to a telephone request from Brennan, sent the coal in nine cars to the defendants. The defendants understood that the coal to be shipped belonged to some operator. On the twenty-third day of February Brennan wrote the defendants in confirmation of the telephone conversation stating that nine cars, designated by number, had been shipped to the Mt. Bowdoin Fuel Company at its siding, Dorchester, and describing the kind of coal, stating price per net ton, and when cars would leave the mine. He signed his name "J. S. Brennan Secretary." The letter was written on the letterhead of the Somerset County Coal Operators' Association and a copy of it was sent to the plaintiff. Brennan testified that the defendants were to send a letter of the same purport to the plaintiff but that this was never done. There was evidence that the nine cars had about the tonnage of eight standard cars. One of the cars reached the defendants' siding; the other eight were at the Readville yards. There was evidence that all of the coal was inspected by the defendants. On March 4, a telegram was sent to Brennan by the defendants notifying him of the receipt of a carload of the coal shipped and advising that it contained an excessive amount of impurities and that they were obliged to reject all nine carloads as not high grade fuel. Two days later the defendants sent another telegram to Brennan to the effect that they could not use the grade of coal at any price. The coal was sold by the railroad company in May, 1926, for freight charges, and brought $760.13. The parties agreed that the price for the nine carloads was $1,048.50; that the amount due for freight was $1,975.54, against which the amount received by the railroad company for the coal is credited, and that the demurrage amounted to $2,627, up to May 18, 1926. None of these items has been paid. No demurrage charge was made until after the telegram in which the defendants refused to take the coal had been sent. Notice of this refusal was telephoned to the plaintiff about the fifth or sixth of March, 1926. A claim for freight and demurrage charges has been made against the plaintiff by the carrier. It was agreed that the contract was made in Pennsylvania; that the statute of frauds in that State is the same as in this Commonwealth; and that the case is to be determined as if the contract had been made here.

By consent of the parties, the question, "Was the coal shipped of the quality called for by the contract?" was submitted to the jury; they answered in the affirmative. Thereupon the judge, subject to the plaintiff's exception, allowed the defendants' motion for a directed verdict upon the ground that the contract was within the statute of frauds, with a stipulation of the parties that if this order was wrong and the case should have been submitted to the jury, judgment is to be entered for the plaintiff for the total of such of the foregoing items as the Supreme Judicial Court determines to be proper elements of damages, with interest.

The carloads of coal had been selected by the plaintiff and had been forwarded by a carrier to the defendants. They had reached a place to which the buyers had access, and from which the goods might be taken without the buyers obtaining permission of any one and they were actually examined by the defendants. Their telegram acknowledged the receipt of one car. Upon the evidence a finding could have been made that there had been a sufficient transfer of possession to satisfy the requirement of the statute of frauds as to the receipt of the goods.

By their telegrams the defendants refused to accept the coal after inspection. If they had done no more their defence of the statute of frauds might be maintained as matter of law. But Levine testified that he tried to dispose of the coal to the public; and Brennan testified that Levine told him that he had tried to dispose of it and had received an offer of fifty cents a ton in Boston, but that the price of the coal was $2 a ton and the freight $4.20. G. L. c. 106, § 6 (3) provides that "There is an acceptance of goods within the meaning of this section when the buyer, either before or after delivery of the goods, expresses by words or conduct his assent to becoming the owner of those specific goods." In *Garfield* v. *Paris*, 96 U. S. 557, 563, the court said, ". . . it is well settled that any acts of the parties indicative of ownership by the vendee may be given in evidence to show the receipt and acceptance of the goods to take the case out of the Statute of Frauds." In *Kemensky* v. *Chapin*, 193 Mass. 500, 506, the court stated the ordinary test for determining the question of acceptance to be "whether the conduct of the buyer in dealing with the goods is such as fairly to indicate an assertion of ownership." A resale, mortgage or pledge of the goods by the buyer will be or may be found to be such an exercise of ownership as to be a constructive receipt and acceptance meeting the requirements of the statute of frauds. 1 Williston, Sales, (2d ed.) § 77. *Harrison* v. *Scott*, 203 N. Y. 369, 373.

In *Beedy* v. *Brayman Wooden Ware Co.* 108 Maine, 200, 205, the court said "In reason we fail to distinguish between a sale and an offer to sell. There is no difference in so far as the act of the alleged purchaser is concerned. He does no more than offer the goods in either case. Whether, when he has made the offer, his offer becomes a sale in fact depends upon the action of a party who bears no relation to the parties, *inter se*, to the original alleged sale. In either case his act is equally an assertion of ownership." See also *Shepherd* v. *Pressey*, 32 N. H. 49, 56. There seems to be some conflict of authority on the question whether an offer to resell by the buyer is evidence of acceptance, but in principle, as well as by what seems to be the weight of authority, the legal effect of an offer to sell could be found to be the same as an actual sale of the goods.

Under these circumstances the question, whether the defendants had exercised acts of dominion that were consistent only with ownership and had therefore accepted the coal notwithstanding their statements in the telegraph dispatches, should have been left to the jury to decide.

It follows from the terms of the stipulation that the defendants are liable for the contract price of the coal. . . .

In accordance with the terms of the report, judgment is to be entered for the plaintiff for $4,890.91, being the price of the coal plus the net amount due for freight and demurrage, to which sum interest from the date of the writ is to be added.

So ordered.

BACHMAN, EMMERICH & COMPANY, INC. *v.* MENDELSON

NEW YORK SUPREME COURT, 1922

[120 *New York Miscellaneous Reports*, 52]

LEHMAN, J. The plaintiff has recovered a judgment for the price of goods which it claims its assignor sold to the defendant under an oral contract of sale. The defendant denied the making of the contract and set up as an affirmative defense the Statute of Frauds.

It is undisputed that the plaintiff's assignor delivered the goods which are the subject-matter of the action at the defendant's place of business on or about August 25, 1922, but the defendant claims that the goods were not sold to him and that they were rejected shortly after delivery. The plaintiff claims on the other hand that it received no complaint about the goods nor any offer to return prior to the 21st day of September, 1921.

The trial justice charged the jury in effect that the oral contract even if made was not enforcible unless the defendant accepted the goods, and then stated upon the question of what constitutes an acceptance, "I shall read to you section 129 of the Personal Property Law: 'The buyer is deemed to have accepted the goods when he intimates to the seller that he has accepted them, or when the goods have been delivered to him and he does any act in relation to them which is inconsistent with the ownership of the seller, or when, after the lapse of a reasonable time, he retains the goods without intimating to the seller that he has rejected them.' "

The trial justice also charged the jury that if the plaintiff's testimony was true and the goods were actually delivered on or about August 25, 1921, and were retained without notice of rejection until September 21, 1921, he would hold as a matter of law that defendant had accepted the goods.

It seems to me that the charge incorrectly states the law. The Personal Property Law contains two sections in regard to what constitutes an acceptance. Section 85, known as the Statute of Frauds, provides: "There is an acceptance of goods within the meaning of this section when the buyer, either before or after delivery of the goods, expresses by words or conduct his assent to becoming the owner of those specific goods." We may assume that the legislature intended in providing a test for an acceptance under the Statute of Frauds that this test should be exclusive, and the mere retention of goods for an unreasonable time is not sufficient to take an oral contract out of the Statute of Frauds unless such retention is under circumstances which show an actual assent by the buyer to becoming the owner of the specific goods.

A search of the authorities has not disclosed any case arising under the New York statute in which the court has held that a mere retention of the goods for a period sufficient to constitute an acceptance which would bar the buyer from rejecting the goods for breach of warranty, would as a matter of law constitute an acceptance which would bar the defendant from raising the defense of the Statute of Frauds, though there are a number of cases in this and other jurisdictions in which retention of goods without rejection for a long period has been held to constitute evidence which under the surrounding circumstances took an alleged contract of sale out of the statute.

It may be that the trial justice was correct in holding that retention of goods for twenty-seven days would as a matter of law constitute an acceptance under section 129 of the statute, though it is unnecessary to express any opinion on that point.

A buyer of goods under an enforcible contract must be presumed to know that when goods are delivered under this contract, the seller intends to pass the property in the goods to the buyer, and that the buyer has the right to reject the goods only if upon an examination made within a reasonable time cause for such rejection is disclosed; consequently, a buyer who fails to give notice within a reasonable time that he has rejected the goods may logically be deemed to have accepted them. On the other hand, where goods are delivered and the person who receives them has not made any enforcible contract for their purchase, conduct on his part which consists merely in failing to reject the goods cannot be considered an assent to becoming the owner of those specific goods unless the goods are received under circumstances which place the recipient under some duty to give notice of rejection if he is not the owner of the goods. The acceptance which is sufficient to take a contract out of the Statute of Frauds should at least be some evidence that some contract had been made between the parties, and the mere retention of goods for a month after delivery cannot take the place of the evidence of the contract which the statute would otherwise require.

In the present case there is evidence that the parties had previous dealings together, and if the defendant had knowledge and can be charged with notice that goods were received from the plaintiff's assignor addressed to him, the jury might perhaps infer that from the general course of business between the parties the defendant must have understood that the plaintiff's assignor intended by such delivery to transfer the property in the goods to the defendant, and if the defendant in spite of his previous relations to the plaintiff's assignor remains silent and puts the goods in stock or kept them in reserve or even in his receiving room, the jury might have inferred from his conduct that he assented to becoming the owner of the goods. But at best even though the plaintiff's evidence be entirely true, the circumstances would raise merely a question of fact for the jury, and the retention of the goods would not constitute conduct which would as a matter of law show acceptance under the Statute of Frauds.

The defendant properly raised this objection both by exception to the judge's charge and by a request for a charge which, though not in the same language as the statute, was couched in similar terms.

Judgment should, therefore, be reversed and a new trial ordered, with costs to appellant to abide the event.

McAvoy and Wagner, JJ., concur.

Judgment reversed.

In Klein-Messner Co., Inc. *v.* The Fair Waist & Dress Co., Inc., 217 App. Div. 647 (New York Supreme Court, Appellate Division, 1926), the Court said: "In the case at bar there is evidence that the plaintiff asked the defendant to take the goods, in answer to which request the defendant designated the warehouse, received from the plaintiff warehouse receipts and invoices showing the yardage and the color assortments, kept these for a year and had them at the trial, without at any time offering to return them or expressing any dissatisfaction. In the absence of what the defendant's evidence may disclose, it is not possible to determine whether the issue can be disposed of as matter of law or as a question of fact, namely, did the defendant, by words or conduct, assent to becoming the owner of these goods. Since the complaint was dismissed at the close of the plaintiff's case, the plaintiff is entitled to the benefit of the inferences most favorable to the plaintiff of which the facts proved are susceptible. (*Neville* v. *Morrison Coal & Coke Co.*, 211 App. Div. 282.) At the very least, there was sufficient to submit to the jury as a question of fact whether there had been an acceptance."

Compare JAMES TALCOTT, INC. *v.* COHEN, 226 Wisconsin 418 (Supreme Court, 1938), where it was urged that a contract was taken out of the statute by receipt and acceptance, and where it was said: "The goods in question were shipped October 6, 1933. The defendant reduced them to his possession and stored them in his basement as heretofore stated. He did not notify either the manufacturer or the textile corporation that he declined to accept the goods until February 27, 1934; in other words, there was a lapse of four months during which, so far as the record shows, there was no notification to the vendor that he rejected shipment. These were seasonable goods, and defendant's nonaction puts into operation that portion of sec. 121.48, Stats., which states that the buyer is deemed to have accepted the goods when after the lapse of a reasonable time he retains them without intimating to the seller that he has rejected them. It may be contended that the cancellation by defendant prior to the shipment sufficiently notified vendor that the goods were rejected and gave color to defendant's later inactivity. We think this contention cannot be sustained. A buyer may wrongfully or rightfully cancel an order and later accept the goods. The fact that he has canceled before the goods are shipped throws no light upon his purpose in later retaining possession without any notification to the seller that the goods are not accepted. The statute prescribes the act that takes from retention the consequences of acceptance. It is notification while the goods are in his possession that he rejects them. It is true that the defendant was not obligated to return the goods if they were delivered under circumstances which gave him the right to reject them, but even in this situation sec. 121.50, Stats., which provides that he is not bound to return them to the seller, requires that he notify the seller that he has refused to accept them. The obvious purpose of this requirement is to bring the section into conformity with the provisions of sec. 121.48. We are of the opinion, (1) that defendant retained the goods for an unreasonable length of time without notifying the vendor that he had rejected them; (2) that under sec. 121.48 this constituted an acceptance of the goods; and (3) that, the goods having been delivered and accepted, the statute of frauds is satisfied and the contract enforceable."

Note also GRIGGS-PAXTON SHOE CO. *v.* A. FRIEDHEIM & BRO., 133 South Carolina 458 (Supreme Court, 1925), where it was held as a matter of law that retention of goods for 32 days without effort to inspect them constituted acceptance.

ABBOTT & COMPANY *v.* WOLSEY

COURT OF APPEAL, 1895

[*Law Reports,* [1895] 2 *Queen's Bench,* 97]

Appeal from the judgment of a Divisional Court (Wills and Wright JJ.) allowing an appeal from the Wandsworth County Court.

The action was brought to recover damages for non-acceptance of hay alleged to have been sold by the plaintiffs to the defendant.

The facts so far as material were as follows.

The plaintiffs on July 13, 1894, sold to the defendant twenty tons of Dutch hay, to be delivered at defendant's wharf at Nine Elms, "barge to be alongside on or before July 21, 1894, or order cancelled." There was no memorandum in writing of the contract signed by the defendant, or an agent on his behalf. The barge was not alongside the defendant's wharf by July 21, and on August 4 the plaintiffs sent a messenger to the defendant to ask whether he would then accept the hay. The defendant said he would take the hay if the barge was alongside his wharf by August 8. The barge was alongside on that day, and the plaintiffs' lighterman handed to a servant of the defendant a receiving note for the hay which was not returned. The defendant came on board the barge, took a sample of the hay, and, after examining it, said, "The hay is not to my sample, and I shall not have it." It was contended for the plaintiffs that there was, and for the defendant that there was not, an acceptance by the defendant of the hay within the meaning of the Sale of Goods Act, 1893, s. 4.

The county court judge gave judgment for the plaintiffs, but the Divisional Court on appeal reversed his decision.

LORD ESHER M.R. The question raised in this case was whether there had been an acceptance of the hay within the meaning of the Sale of Goods Act, 1893, s. 4, sub-s. 3. No question was raised as to whether there had been a delivery of the goods or not. On an appeal from a county court the only jurisdiction which the Court has is to determine some question of law which was raised before the county court judge. The only question of law before the Court is, not whether there was an acceptance of the goods within the statute, but whether there was evidence on which the county court judge might properly find that there was such an acceptance. Cases have been cited which were decided before the passing of the Sale of Goods Act, 1893. It may be that the decisions on the subject were not quite consistent; but, assuming that to be so, it is now immaterial, for the legislature have undertaken to determine which of the decisions was correct. The statute was passed to declare the law. We are bound by it, and can look to nothing else. Contrasting s. 4, sub-s. 3, with s. 35 of the Act, the meaning of the former seems to me very clear. The effect of the Statute of Frauds was that certain conditions had to be fulfilled before a contract for the sale of goods of the value of ten pounds or upwards could be enforced by action. If there was no written memorandum of the contract, and if none of the other matters mentioned in the statute existed, the Court could not inquire further into the question whether there was a contract or not. If there was a memorandum in writing of the contract signed by the party to be charged or his agent, the statute was satisfied. There was another way in which the statute might be satisfied, and the Court enabled to hold that there was a contract, although there was no written memorandum, namely, by proof that the goods had been delivered by the seller and accepted by the purchaser. Mere delivery to the purchaser was not equivalent to acceptance by him. But it is clear that the term "acceptance" is used in two senses. The acceptance that satisfies the Statute of Frauds and the acceptance that binds the purchaser to pay for the goods are different things. When s. 4, sub-s. 3, is contrasted with s. 35 of the Sale of Goods Act, 1893, it is obvious that the statute recognises this difference. The acceptance under s. 4 is such an acceptance as will shew the existence of a contract which the Court may enforce. Sub-s. 3 of s. 4 provides that there shall be an acceptance of goods within the meaning of the section when the buyer does any act in relation to the goods which recognises a pre-existing contract of sale, whether there is an acceptance in performance of the contract or not. The acceptance described in s. 35 which is to bind the purchaser to pay for the goods is a different thing. The only question here is as to the existence of the kind of acceptance mentioned in s. 4. Therefore, the observations of judges which have been cited to the effect that a purchaser cannot be held to accept goods when he says that he rejects them seem to me beside the mark. In the case before us the goods are sent to the defendant with a delivery note, which is an intimation by the seller that he is delivering the goods under a contract. The defendant keeps the note, which is a recognition that there is to be such a delivery; and the question is whether there is an acceptance by him. The goods being so delivered, the defendant proceeds to inspect them. It may be that mere inspection would not amount to an act which recognises a pre-existing contract; but, if the defendant does an act, and uses words with regard to that act, those words are material as explaining the act and shewing the nature of it. Here the defendant took what is known in business as a sample. He not only took that sample, but he said that it was not equal to his sample; by which he must have meant some sample previously given to him in connection with a contract for the sale of hay. He did not take the sample merely in order to inspect the quality of the hay, but to see whether it was equal in quality to another sample. I think that that act of taking a sample as explained by the words which accompanied it was an act which recognised a pre-existing contract; at all events, it was evidence upon which the county court judge might properly come to the conclusion that the sample was taken as a bulk sample to be compared with a former sample given in connection with a contract for the sale of the hay, and therefore that the act of taking it was a recognition of an existing contract for the sale of the hay. The only question which we have jurisdiction to determine is whether there was such evidence or not. If there was, we cannot overrule the finding of the county court judge. For these reasons I think the appeal must be allowed.

[Concurring opinions of A. L. Smith, L. J., and Rigby, L. J., are omitted.]

Compare RICHARDSON *v.* SMITH, 101 Maryland 15 (Court of Appeals, 1905). In that case there was an oral agreement for the sale on sight draft with bill of lading attached terms of 633 cases of canned tomatoes. Part of the tomatoes in question were at the seller's cannery, and the rest at a railroad station. The agreement was made at a general store also operated by the seller, and in connection with it the seller took from a shelf several cans just out of the warehouse and gave them to the buyer as samples. The buyer opened one, and took the others away with him. There was held to be no acceptance within the meaning of the Statute of Frauds.

GOODWIN *v.* MARINERS SAVINGS BANK

CONNECTICUT SUPREME COURT OF ERRORS, 1923

[99 *Connecticut Reports*, 169]

Action to recover damages for the nondelivery of shares of stock alleged to have been purchased by the plaintiffs of the defendant and at once resold by them to a customer, brought to and tried by the Superior Court in Hartford County, *Haines*, J.; facts found and judgment rendered for the plaintiffs for $1,371, and appeal by the defendant. No error.

The material facts found are as follows: The plaintiffs are stock brokers doing business as partners in Hartford. The defendant savings-bank was the owner of certain shares of the capital stock of the Hartford-Ætna National Bank of Hartford. On December 16th, 1921, one of the plaintiffs called up Mr. Harwood, the treasurer of the bank, and after some conversation about price told Harwood that he took Harwood's order to sell fifty shares of Hartford-Ætna stock at $215 net to the bank. Within a few minutes the plaintiffs sold the fifty shares of stock to a third party. A few moments later Harwood called the plaintiffs by telephone and stated that he was sorry, but the bank had only forty-five shares of the stock to deliver, and directed the plaintiffs to cover back five shares at $215 in the open market, leaving forty-five shares to be delivered. This the plaintiffs did and reported the fact by telephone to Harwood, who expressed his satisfaction. Shortly afterward another telephone call was received by the plaintiffs from Harwood, saying that the stock in question had been previously placed for sale with another firm of brokers, and that he found it had been already sold and that the bank could not deliver the forty-five shares. Harwood asked what should be done and the plaintiffs replied that it would be necessary to buy the stock in the open market, and asked for a price at which they could buy it. Harwood gave them a limit of $215 per share. These telephone conversations all occurred within the space of one hour. The plaintiffs attempted to execute the order to cover back the forty-five shares at $215, but the market price had risen rapidly, and they were unable to do so. Harwood declined to authorize its purchase at a higher figure, and failed in an attempt to secure the stock himself. The plaintiffs rendered several statements to the bank and made several demands for the delivery of the forty-five shares to which no replies were received until, on December

23d, Harwood absolutely repudiated the transaction. The plaintiffs then notified the bank of their intention to buy in the open market, and, receiving no reply, bought forty-five shares at $241. At the close of the plaintiffs' testimony defendant moved for judgment as of nonsuit, on the ground that recovery was barred under the statute of frauds. The motion was denied, and after defendant's evidence the court gave judgment for the plaintiffs to recover the difference between the contract and the market price of forty-five shares.

BEACH, J. It is not clear from the finding whether the plaintiffs were acting as brokers authorized to sell fifty shares of Hartford-Ætna stock for the account of the defendant, or as buyers of the stock on their own account; but as both parties on their briefs and in argument have treated the transaction described in the finding as evidencing an oral contract for the sale of the stock by defendant to plaintiffs, we accept that construction of the finding. Both parties also agree on their briefs that the appeal is based solely on the ground that recovery on the contract alleged and proved was barred by the statute of frauds. The appellant makes some claims for the correction of the finding, but they do not touch the findings which we regard as decisive. It is admitted that there was no memorandum signed by the defendant, and no partial payment is claimed. The question briefed and argued, is whether there was a partial performance by receipt and acceptance of a part of the stock by the buyer. We think it is quite clear that there was.

If the finding as to the first telephone conversation of December 16th stood alone, it might be difficult to discover in it an unequivocal assent of the defendant to sell; but the findings as to what was said and done shortly afterward make it clear that the defendant had agreed to sell fifty shares of Hartford-Ætna stock at $215 net. Harwood then reported by telephone the defendant could deliver only forty-five shares, and directed the plaintiffs to cover back five shares by buying it in the open market at $215, leaving forty-five shares to be delivered. This the plaintiffs did. That was equivalent to an order to the plaintiffs as brokers to buy five shares for the defendant's account, and to treat the five shares so bought in partial delivery of the fifty shares sold, leaving the other forty-five shares to be delivered thereafter. The plaintiffs in filling that order bought and paid for the five shares in their character as agents for the defendant, and received and accepted them in their character as buyers, as a part performance by the defendant of its contract to sell and deliver fifty shares.

The contract did not limit the defendant to the delivery of the particular certificates which it owned or represented that it owned. If the defendant, owning no Hartford-Ætna stock at all, had directed the plaintiffs as its brokers to go into the market and cover back for its account the whole fifty shares at $215, and the plaintiffs had done it, the contract would have been fully performed on both sides. If that had been done it could hardly be denied that the defendant had made a good delivery of the stock, and that the plaintiffs had actually received and accepted it. So, on this finding, the contract was performed as to five out of the fifty shares, and the practical effect is that the defendant has been discharged *pro tanto*, so that the judgment is for the difference between the contract price and the market price of forty-five shares only. It is quite clear, therefore, that the plaintiffs had actually received and accepted five shares out of the original fifty contracted for.

It is claimed that the direction by Harwood to cover back five shares was a purely verbal act which cannot take the case out of the statute of frauds. It was not, however, an act in the formation of the contract, but an act done in performance of it, and not purely a verbal act, because it created an agency and *qui facit per alium, facit per se.* This part of the transaction falls entirely outside of the statute of frauds, and it resulted in a constructive delivery of five shares of Hartford-Ætna stock by the defendant to the plaintiffs which the plaintiffs actually received and accepted in part performance of the contract sued on. It is therefore unnecessary to discuss the question of constructive acceptance and receipt which is elaborately presented on the briefs.

There is no error.

In this opinion the other judges concurred.

DAVID TAYLOR COMPANY, INC. *v.* FANSTEEL PRODUCTS COMPANY, INC.

New York Supreme Court, Appellate Division, 1932

[234 *Appellate Division Reports*, 548]

Sherman, J. The controlling question is whether or not the amended complaint must meet dismissal upon the ground that the agreement sued on does not constitute an integrated written contract in which are embodied all of the essential terms as required by the Statute of Frauds. The contract is for the sale and delivery of ore containing from thirty per cent to sixty per cent of tantalum oxide, of a value for in excess of fifty dollars, and is not to be performed within a period of one year. Defendant purchased thereunder all of the ore to be used and treated by it during the period of the contract. Deliveries of the ore were to be made from time to time.

Defendant raises the bar of the statute, by reason of the provision of section 31 of the Personal Property Law, that "every agreement * * * is void, unless it or some note or memorandum thereof be in writing" which "By its terms is not to be performed within one year from the making thereof," and, additionally, because section 85 of the Personal Property Law makes an unwritten contract for the sale of goods of the value of fifty dollars and upwards unenforcible. If section 85, alone, be applicable here, part performance, which is here pleaded, would take the case without the statute, but if section 31 also applies, a contract which contravenes its provisions would be void, and part performance would invest it with no validity.

We have concluded that both sections of the Personal Property Law apply here. . . .

The Personal Property Law was amended by chapter 571 of the Laws of 1911, whereby that part of subdivision 6 of section 31 which related to the sale of goods, chattels or things in action for the price of fifty dollars or more, was repealed and substantially re-enacted as part of new section 85. In making that change the Legislature did not manifest an intent to alter the statute so as to exempt such a contract, when not to be performed within one year from its making, from compliance with the requirements of both sections. The footnote (Laws of 1911, p. 1298) denotes that the purpose of the enactment was to make the statute uniform with that enacted in other States.

[The balance of the opinion, and the opinion of Merrell, J., dissenting on other grounds, are omitted.]

A similar result has been reached in England: see *Prested Miners Company, Limited* v. *Garner, Limited,* (1911) 1 K. B. 425 (C.A.), affirming (1910) 2 K. B. 776.

D. Part Payment

HUGH OF CARLISLE *v.* WILLIAM OF HALLING

Fair Court of St. Ives, 1291

[1 *Select Cases on the Law Merchant* (Selden Society, 1908), 47]

Hugh of Carlisle complains of William of Halling, for that whereas he [Hugh] bought from him a pair of tongs for 12*s.* in the vill of St. Ives on Monday last, giving him for the same a God's penny and a drink, of which 12*s.* he was to pay him a half at the fair of Boston on the feast of St. James [1] in the nineteenth year of the reign of King Edward and the other half at the next fair of Winchester, and he was to give him security therefor, the said William unjustly detains the said tongs contrary to their covenant; and thereof he [Hugh] produces suit. The said William is present and denies the words of court, and fully acknowledges the contract between him and the said Hugh touching the said tongs, and [says] that he [William] was always ready to keep the covenant made with him, if the said Hugh would have found security to pay the said 12*s.* at the times stipulated. And [to prove] that this is so, he craves that he may be admitted to his law; pledges of his law, John of Kirkton and Ralph of Armston.

[1] 25 July, 1291.

CHAMBERLAIN *v.* JOHN, PRIOR OF SWAVESEY

FAIR COURT OF ST. IVES, 1295

[1 *Select Cases on the Law Merchant* (Selden Society, 1908), 68]

Walter Chamberlain of London complains of John, prior of Swavesey, for that he unjustly detains from him and does not pay him 5*s.* of silver, and unjustly because whereas on Wednesday[1] before the feast of St. George the Martyr in the nineteenth year of the reign of King Edward a certain Geoffrey, prior of Swavesey, his, John's, predecessor, bought from him, Walter, in the fair of St. Ives two pieces of frieze-cloth for 5*s.* 4*d.*, toward which he [Geoffrey] gave him a God's penny and 4*d.* as earnest money, and whereas he ought to have paid the remaining money to the said Walter on the following Ascension day, he paid him nothing, to his damage 20*s.* etc. The said John, the prior, is present and denies the words of court and all which should be denied, and says that whereas the said Walter counted against him touching a certain contract made between Geoffrey, prior of Swavesey, and himself, as is stated above in his charge, the said Geoffrey, the prior, was at that time[2] dead. And that this is so he craves may be inquired, and the adverse party does likewise; pledges of the prior to come to the inquest on [the following] Monday, Walter Prest and John Humfrey. The inquest comes and says that the said prior [Geoffrey] was not alive at the time when he, Walter, alleges that he was. Therefore the said prior [John] is quit, and Walter is in mercy for his false claim; he is pardoned; pledge ——.

FARR, SMITH AND COMPANY, LIMITED *v.* MESSERS, LIMITED

KING'S BENCH DIVISION, 1927

[*Law Reports*, [1928] 1 *King's Bench*, 397]

Action tried before Wright J. without a jury.

On January 9, 1924, the defendants, who were timber importers, entered into a contract by which they agreed to sell to a partnership firm called Farr, Smith & Co., who were boxmakers, 150 to 200 cubic fathoms of first quality firewood, to be used for boxmaking, according to specification at prices which ranged from 9*l.* 10*s.* to 8*l.* 10*s.* per cubic fathom. Payment was to be made by approved acceptances four months from date of discharge of each parcel.

Farr, Smith & Co. had previously purchased from the defendants and received delivery of another parcel of wood goods. In the early part of 1924 the partnership firm were in some financial difficulty, and from time to time they made payments on account to the defendants, and they informed the defendants of their financial position. The firm desired to obtain fresh

[1] 18 April, 1291.
[2] At the alleged time when the contract was made.

capital and for that purpose the limited company of Farr, Smith & Co., Ld., the present plaintiffs, was formed, and the defendants were notified.

On or about Wednesday, July 9, 1924, Mr. Farr, who was a partner in the old firm and also a director in Farr, Smith & Co., Ld., together with another director of that company, had an interview with Mr. Goff, a director of the defendant company, and discussed the indebtedness of the old firm to the defendants. Eventually it was agreed that Farr, Smith & Co., Ld., should pay by cash and bills the money due to the defendants from the firm of Farr, Smith & Co., and that Farr, Smith & Co., Ld., should have the benefit of the contract for firewood of January 9, 1924. The defendants undertook to perform the contract of January 9, 1924, with Farr, Smith & Co., Ld., instead of with the firm, and to accept the company as buyers of the goods in consideration of receiving from the company a cheque for 200*l.* and three acceptances for 224*l.* 13*s.* 1*d.* in one month, for 225*l.* 19*s.* in two months, and for 227*l.* 5*s.* in three months in respect of the firm's indebtedness to the defendants, in addition to the price of the goods. The defendants received from Farr, Smith & Co., Ld., a cheque for 200*l.* on Monday, July 14, 1924, and also the three acceptances for 224*l.* 13*s.* 1*d.*, 225*l.* 19*s.* and 227*l.* 5*s.*, but the defendants did not deliver the goods under the contract of January 9, 1924, to Farr, Smith & Co., Ld. Requests for delivery were made from time to time and on December 15, 1924, the defendants finally said that they had no contract with Farr, Smith & Co., Ld., for the sale of firewood. The defendants, however, offered to deliver a certain quantity of firewood as under a new contract on certain terms to Farr, Smith & Co., Ld., which offer the company refused.

[One page of the statement is here omitted.]

At the trial the defendants called no evidence to contradict the evidence given by the plaintiffs with reference to the verbal agreement of July 9, 1924, and Wright J. found as a fact that there was such an agreement by which the defendants undertook to perform the contract of January 9, 1924, with the plaintiffs instead of with the partnership firm, and that in consideration of that undertaking the defendants were promised and in fact received from the plaintiffs the cheque for 200*l.* and the three acceptances. Wright J. further found that there had been a breach of that contract and that, subject to the defence raised by the defendants under the Statute of Frauds, the plaintiffs would be entitled to damages.

[Seven pages are here omitted, including part of the opinion holding that there was a sufficient memorandum to satisfy the statute. WRIGHT, J., then continued:]

I think it is desirable, however, that I should deal with the other two points relied upon by Mr. Schiller. One is that there was an earnest given to bind the contract, and the other is, in the alternative, that there was part payment. Dealing with the former of these points, it is somewhat difficult to give a precise definition of the word "earnest." Certain characteristics, however, seem to be clear. An earnest must be a tangible thing, in which definition it may be that a deposit is included, but in the old cases it was always some tangible thing. That thing must be given at the moment at which the contract is concluded, because it is something given to bind the contract, and, therefore, it must come into existence at the making or conclusion of the contract. The thing given in that way must be given by the contracting party who gives it, as an earnest or token of good faith, and as a guarantee that he will fulfill his contract, and subject to the terms that if, owing to his default, the contract goes off, it will be forfeited. If, on the other hand, the contract is fulfilled, an earnest may still serve a further purpose and operate by way of part payment.

In *Howe* v. *Smith* (27 Ch. D. 89, 101) Fry L.J., dealing with a deposit paid upon a contract for the sale of land, says this with reference to a deposit: "Money paid as a deposit must, I conceive, be paid on some terms implied or expressed. In this case no terms are expressed, and we must therefore inquire what terms are to be implied. The terms most naturally to be implied appear to me in the case of money paid on the signing of a contract to be that in the event of the contract being performed it shall be brought into account, but if the contract is not performed by the payer it shall remain the property of the payee. It is not merely a part payment, but is then also an earnest to bind the bargain so entered into, and creates by the fear of its forfeiture a motive in the payer to perform the rest of the contract."

In *Sumner and Leivesley* v. *John Brown & Co.* (25 Times L. R. 745) Hamilton J. said this: "'Earnest' . . . meant something given for the purpose of binding a contract, something to be used to put pressure on the defaulter if he failed to carry out his part. If the contract went through, the thing given in earnest was returned to the giver, or, if money, was deducted from the price. If the contract went off through the giver's fault the thing given in earnest was forfeited."

In Benjamin on Sales, 6th ed., p. 255, there is a definition which is to the same effect. The author says: "The giving of earnest, however common in ancient times, has fallen so much into disuse, that the two expressions in this clause of the Statute of Frauds, identical with that in the Code, 'give something in earnest' or 'in part payment,' are often treated as meaning the same thing, although the language clearly intimates that the earnest is 'something to bind the bargain,' or, 'the contract,' whereas it is manifest that there can be no part payment till after the bargain has been bound, or closed. Earnest may be money, or some gift or token (among the Romans usually a ring), given by the buyer to the seller, and accepted by the latter to mark the final conclusive assent of both sides to the bargain; and this was formerly a prevalent custom in England. And an earnest did not lose its character because the same thing might also avail as a part payment." The learned author refers to what was then the only decided case, not a very clear one, of *Blenkinsop* v. *Clayton* (7 Taunt. 597), where it was held that there must be an actual transfer of the thing which constituted the earnest. I ought to add that in *Sumner and Leivesley* v. *John Brown & Co.* (25 Times L. R. 745) Hamilton J. refused to treat the delivery of certain bags to be loaded with potatoes which had been furnished under the contract, as being in the nature of earnest. He held that the bags were sent to facilitate the performance of the contract, and not to bind it.

I do not think that, on the facts of this case, as I find them, there was anything which can be held to be an earnest within the definition which I have stated. There was nothing given at the time the contract was made to bind the bargain, as I find the facts. There was a promise to give a cheque and a promise to accept and deliver certain drafts, but I think these matters were part of the promise, and, as I shall explain in a moment, in my opinion part of the consideration for the contract. They were not anything given at the time of the conclusion of the contract with the object, or intention, of binding the contract. A few days afterwards the cheque and the drafts were given and the cheque was paid, but I think that was done after the contract was made and in fulfilment and partial performance of the contract.

But there is another contention put forward in the alternative by Mr. Schiller on these facts, and for that purpose he has asked for, and I have given him, leave to add to his statement of claim an alternative allegation of the contract relied upon, setting out all the terms contained in para. 3 of the original defence. I think the contract so stated is the true and complete contract which was entered into on July 9, 1924. Taking that as the complete contract, I hold that the contract was for the sale of goods and that the consideration from the plaintiffs to the defendants was twofold. It was not merely a promise to fulfil the conditions as to payment contained in the original contract, that is to say to pay on certain terms after the goods were delivered and shipped. It was also a promise to pay as part of the consideration for the future delivery of the goods, those amounts which were involved in the cheque for 200*l.* and the three drafts, and I hold that the payment of that cheque and the payment of these drafts was a part payment under the contract for the sale of goods within the meaning of s. 4 of the Sale of Goods Act, 1893.

On these grounds I hold that the technical defences raised to this claim fail, and the only question I have now to consider is the question of damages, which is not free from difficulty and on which the evidence is not at all satisfactory. I intend to arrive at an estimate of damages as if I were a jury, and taking as I do the contract quantity of 150 standards, I shall award as a fair estimate of what the plaintiffs have lost the sum of 300*l.*

Judgment for plaintiffs.

JENNINGS & SILVEY *v.* J. U. DUNHAM

Kansas City Court of Appeals, 1895

[60 *Missouri Appeal Reports*, 635]

Ellison, J. — Plaintiffs sued the defendant for damages in failing to take of them a lot of hogs, according to a contract between them. Defendant prevailed in the trial court. Plaintiffs contracted with defendant to sell him a large number of hogs. Some of them were to be fat, and others stock hogs. They were to be delivered at Seymour. The evidence conflicts as to the exact day of delivery.

The first question presented relates to the statute of frauds. Our statute, section 5187, Revised Statutes, 1889, provides that no sale of personal property of the price of $30 or more, shall be valid, unless the buyer accept and receive a part of the property, "or give something in earnest to bind the bargain, or in part payment," or unless some written memorandum be made. There was no delivery of any part of the hogs at the time of making the contract, nor was there any written memorandum of the sale; and the question arising on the evidence is, was there a part payment? It was shown that plaintiffs and defendant at the making of the contract, each placed the sum of $50 in the hands of a third party, the plaintiffs' theory at the trial being that the sum put up by defendant was to be a part payment; while on the other hand there was evidence in defendant's behalf tending strongly to prove that each party respectively put up these sums as a "forfeit," so that the party failing to perform his contract should forfeit the amount put up by such party; the party not in default should receive the whole sum put up. The trial court instructed the jury, that, if the money was placed in the hands of a third party as money to be forfeited by the defaulting party, it was not a payment and the contract was invalid. A literal reading of the statute undoubtedly makes a distinction between something which is given in earnest to bind the bargain, and that which is given in part payment. Originally this "earnest" was not necessarily a part payment. It was a custom under the common law, and seems also to have been a custom in other countries than England to give something to bind a bargain. In some countries some act was performed. Story on Sales, section 273. Benjamin states in his work on Sales, section 196, that one species of earnest in the Roman law was a payment of a sum which if the sale was carried out was to be credited on the price, but which carried the understanding that it was forfeit money if the sale was not completed by the buyer; and if the contract was not performed by the seller, he was to return to the buyer the money advanced together with a like sum as a forfeit on his part. Whether a sum which is termed forfeit money was ever a species of earnest by the common law need not now be investigated, since it has ceased to be of practical importance. It is now considered, that giving something in earnest to bind the bargain, and giving something in payment mean the same thing; that is, a part payment of the price. Benjamin on Sales, sec. 189; Story on Sales, secs. 273, 275. So, while in some countries in olden times, "earnest to bind the bargain" might consist of forfeit money, it is not so now. In modern times, earnest must be a part payment of the price. And, where the parties to a contract put up a sum of money to be forfeited to the non-defaulting party, it is not a part payment, and therefore does not take the contract out of the statute of frauds.

[More than a page of the opinion is here omitted.]

A full consideration of the points made by plaintiffs, has not led us to the discovery of anything which would justify our interference with the judgment, and it is accordingly affirmed. All concur.

NORTON *v.* DAVISON

COURT OF APPEAL, 1899

[*Law Reports*, [1899] 1 *Queen's Bench*, 401]

[Statement of facts is omitted.]

EARL OF HALSBURY L.C. I regret that I cannot agree with the decision of the Divisional Court. There appears from the notes of the evidence and the findings of the learned county court judge thereon to be no doubt as to the facts of this case. Prior to May 7, 1897, the defendant had ordered certain cabinets of the plaintiffs, which had been duly delivered at various times, and on that day the defendant gave the plaintiffs a further order for an additional number of cabinets. What passed on that occasion was in substance as follows. On receiving the order the plaintiff Steele said that it was a large one, and that he should like something on account; and thereupon the defendant said that the plaintiffs had been overpaid on the previous order to the extent of 1*l.*; and I will take it that, as was argued, the effect of what took place was that it was then agreed that the sum of 1*l.*, which the plaintiffs had already received, should be appropriated to the new order and retained by them as part payment of the price of the cabinets then ordered by the defendant. On these facts the question becomes a dry question of law, namely, whether under the circumstances there has been that which will satisfy the requirements of the 17th section of the Statute of Frauds, or rather of the provisions of the Sale of Goods Act, 1893, which have now taken its place. I am clearly of opinion that there has not. It is not, as it appears to me, very material to consider the policy of the statute. It is enough that the Legislature has provided that, in the case of the sale of goods of the value of 10*l.* or upwards, the contract shall not be enforceable unless either there is a memorandum of it in writing signed by the party to be charged, or his agent, or the buyer accepts part of the goods and actually receives the same, or gives something in earnest to bind the contract or in part payment. The effect clearly is that, where there is no memorandum of the contract in writing, there must be something done in addition to the making of the oral contract in affirmance of the bargain thereby made. The question in this case, therefore, is whether, where there is only an oral contract for the sale of goods of a value exceeding the amount mentioned in the statute, and something which has passed is by a term of that oral contract to be treated as part payment for the goods, the provisions of the statute are satisfied, and a party to the contract may sue upon it by virtue of the mere oral term therein contained without anything actually done which, apart from the contract itself, may testify to its existence. I think that, if such a construction were given to the statute, its provisions would be rendered idle. The intention of the statute obviously being that mere words of mouth should not be sufficient to establish a contract for the sale of goods exceeding the prescribed value, but that something besides should be necessary for that purpose, it would be wholly inconsistent with its provisions to hold that a plaintiff may rely on a mere oral term of the contract as satisfying the requirements of the statute.

[Brief concurring opinions of A. L. Smith, L. J., and Chitty, L. J., are omitted.]

Appeal allowed.

CHARLES R. ABLETT COMPANY *v.* SENCER

CITY COURT OF NEW YORK, 1927

[130 *New York Miscellaneous Reports*, 416]

SHIENTAG, J. Plaintiff and defendant entered into an agreement on April 12, 1927, for the sale of a certain quantity of electric bulbs for the sum of $550. The defendant gave the plaintiff his check on the same day for the full amount of the purchase price and obtained from the plaintiff a receipted bill for the merchandise in question. Subsequently the defendant, the drawer, stopped payment on the check. The plaintiff brings suit on the check, and the only defense with which we are here concerned is that of the Statute of Frauds. There was no acceptance and actual receipt of any part of the goods by the defendant. The plaintiff having made no point of it, I shall assume for the purpose of this motion that there was no memorandum in writing by the party sought to be held on the contract. The plaintiff contends that the defendant's check, although subsequently dishonored, constituted a payment of the purchase price within the meaning of the statute, thus dispensing with the necessity of a writing. This year marks the 250th anniversary of the enactment of the Statute of Frauds in England, section 17 of which, in substantially its original form, is in force in this State to-day (Pers. Prop. Law, § 85, subd. 1). Considering the nature and age of the statute it is not surprising that there has been such a wide difference of opinion among jurists and legal scholars concerning its usefulness and efficacy. These range from the diatribes against the statute by Mr. Justice STEPHEN and Sir FREDERICK POLLOCK in the first issue of the Law Quarterly Review on the one hand to the encomiums heaped upon it by Lord KENYON and Lord ELLENBOROUGH on the other. (1 Law Q. Rev. 1; 43 id. 1; *Chater* v. *Beckett,* [1797] 7 T. R. 201; *Chaplin* v. *Rogers,* [1801] 1 East, 192.) In between there is the comment of a careful student of English law, who says more particularly with reference to the section dealing with the sale of goods: "The prevailing feeling both in the legal and the commercial world is and has for a long time been that these clauses have outlived their usefulness and are quite out of place amid the changed legal and commercial conditions of to-day." (6 Holdsworth, History of English Law, 396 *et seq.*) With the wisdom of legislation, as such, courts can have no concern. It is important, however, in construing the statute in the light of modern conditions, to consider some of the reasons which led to its enactment. The original Statute of Frauds was stated to have been passed "for the prevention of many fraudulent practices which are commonly endeavored to be upheld by perjury and subornation of perjury." Holdsworth points out that in 1677, when the statute went into effect, trial by jury was still in the stage where a jury might decide a case upon its own knowledge of the facts. Furthermore, under the then existing rules of evidence "neither of the parties to an action, nor their husbands or wives, nor any person who had any interest in the result of the litigation, were competent witnesses." (6 Holdsworth, 388.) A man sued on an oral contract, not being permitted to testify himself, was practically helpless in the face of any attempted perjury. The intention of the statute obviously was, as summed up by the EARL OF HALSBURY, L. C., in *Norton* v. *Davison* (L. R. [1899] Q. B. 401), "that mere words of mouth should not be sufficient to establish a contract for the sale of goods exceeding the prescribed value, but that something besides should be necessary for that purpose." (P. 404.) So the statute in the original form provided in substance that no contract for the sale of goods of the value of ten pounds sterling or upwards should be allowed to be good unless some note or memorandum in writing of the bargain be made and signed by the parties to be charged therewith (in New York the party to be charged) or their duly authorized agents. The requirement of a writing was dispensed with if certain acts were performed, viz., (1) if the buyer shall accept and actually receive a part of the goods sold; or (2) if the buyer shall give something in earnest to bind the bargain or in part payment. On this motion I am concerned solely with the second exception. "The giving of earnest, and the part payment of the price, are two facts independent of the bargain, capable of proof by parol, and the framers of the Statute of Frauds said in effect that either of them, if proven in addition to parol proof of the contract itself, is a sufficient safeguard against fraud and perjury to render the contract good without a writing." (Benj. Sales [6th ed.], 255.) To-day the giving of earnest and part payment is practically synonymous. Some overt act is what the framers wanted in addition to words of mouth. The statute places no limitation on the manner in which payment shall be made. The payment may be in the form of any personal property. "The statute requires that he should pay some part of the purchase money. No doubt it must be taken, in its spirit, to mean anything or part of anything given, by way of consideration, which is money or money's worth. But the object was to have something pass between the parties beside mere words; some symbol like earnest money. (2 Black. Com. 448.) . . . One object of the statute was to prevent perjury. The method taken was, to have something done; not to rest everything upon mere oral agreement." (COWEN, J., in *Artcher* v. *Zeh*, 5 Hill, 200, 205. See, also, *Brabin* v. *Hyde*, 32 N. Y. 519.) Is the delivery by the vendee to the vendor of the former's check for the purchase price in and of itself a payment within the statute, regardless of what may thereafter become of the check? What is meant by the term "payment" as used in the statute? "Payment is not a technical term," says Mr. Justice MAULE in *Mail-*

lard v. *Duke of Argyle* (6 M. & G. 40); "it has been imported into law proceedings from the exchange, and not from law treatises." (See *Turney* v. *Dodwell*, [1854] 3 E. & B. 136.) "A check, such as the one in question, is a negotiable instrument. It is a thing of value. It may be the subject of larceny. Checks are in common use, and pass from hand to hand. It is the usual and ordinary way of transacting business of any magnitude, and courts take judicial notice of such custom." (*Rohrbach* v. *Hammill*, 162 Iowa, 131.) In *Gould* v. *Town of Oneonta* (71 N. Y. 298, 307) the court said: "Cash payment of such large sums is usually made by check. In such a case, the check may be regarded as the representative of the money." Since that case was decided it has become the practice in the commercial world to make substantially all payments, large or small, by check. A check bearing the date on which it is issued is regarded in a different light from a promissory note. It is the commonly accepted method of payment in the business world to-day, and has largely supplanted the use of currency as a medium for barter and exchange. The giving of such a check is an overt act more easily proved and less susceptible to misconstruction or perjury than the payment of a sum in currency. (33 Harvard L. Rev. 870.) It is objected that a draft or check of a debtor is only conditional payment and not satisfaction of the debt for which it is given in the absence of some agreement to the contrary. That, it is submitted, has nothing to do with the application of the Statute of Frauds. The statute is not concerned with the legal effect of the payment; it says nothing about the payment being in satisfaction, wholly or in part, of the vendor's claim. The purpose of the statute is fully satisfied by the physical delivery of the instrument, the overt act indicating that there was a bargain between the parties. How is this outward manifestation affected by what may subsequently happen to the instrument or other article that the buyer delivers to the seller at the time of the bargain? The rule as to conditional payment operates solely for the protection of a creditor in the event that the instrument is subsequently dishonored. The learned author of Benjamin on Sales treats the provision of the Statute of Frauds relating to payment as somewhat analogous to a similar provision under the Statute of Limitations Act, holding the term "payment" to have been used in its popular sense. (Benj. Sales [6th ed.], 258; *Marreco* v. *Richardson*, L. R. [1908] 2 K. B. 584.) So in *Turney* v. *Dodwell* ([1854] 3 E. & B. 136) Lord Campbell said: "The statute [relating to limitations of actions] intending to make a distinction between mere acknowledgments by word of mouth and acknowledgments proved by the act of payment, it surely cannot be material whether such payment may afterwards be avoided by the thing paid turning out to be worthless. . . . In mercantile transactions nothing is more usual than to stipulate for a payment by bills where there is no intention of their being taken in absolute satisfaction." (P. 141.) The dictum in *Hunter* v. *Wetsell* (84 N. Y. 549), which emphasizes the necessity of the subsequent payment of the check, is to the contrary. But the entire reasoning of the case is summed up as follows: "The purpose and object of the statute should not be forgotten. Its aim is to substitute some act for mere words, to compel the verbal contract to be accompanied by some fact not likely to be mistaken, and so avoid the dangers of treacherous memory or downright perjury. The delivery of the check was such an act." (P. 554.) The purpose of the statute as so declared is accomplished regardless of what may thereafter happen to the check. It is the delivery and acceptance of the check which constitute the overt act required by the statute. (*McLure* v. *Sherman*, 70 Fed. 190, 192.) *Hessberg* v. *Welsh* (147 N. Y. Supp. 44) is not decisive of the instant case. There the check was given for part of the purchase price, and the court said: "There is no evidence that the check was given under any special agreement that the check should constitute payment rather than the means of payment." In the instant case the check is for the full amount of the purchase price, and when the check was delivered to the seller he gave the buyer a receipted bill for the merchandise sold. Obviously the check in this case was received as a payment. The written exhibits so indicate, and I so find. Giving full effect, therefore, to the actual decision in *Hessberg* v. *Welsh* (*supra*), the vendee's check, although it was subsequently dishonored, was given in payment within the meaning of section 85 of the Personal Property Law. The defense of the Statute of Frauds must, therefore, fail. Motion to set aside the verdict of the jury and for a new trial denied. The defendant is allowed a ten days' stay of execution and thirty days to make a case. Submit order on notice.

Compare the following cases: In GAY *v.* SUNDQUIST, 42 South Dakota 327 (Supreme Court, 1919), it was held that in order to take a case out of the statute it must appear that a cheque was given in absolute payment.

In RABE *v.* DANAHER, 51 Fed. (2nd) 777 (D. C. Conn., 1931), rev. on other grounds in 56 Fed. (2nd) 758 (C. C. A. 2nd, 1932), and in DUTTON *v.* BENNETT, 256 Mass. 397 (Supreme Judicial Court, 1926), it was held that whether a cheque operates as part payment depends on the intent of the parties, and in the latter case the question of intent was said to be one of fact for the jury. In PARKER *v.* CRISP & Co., (1919) 1 K. B. 481 (King's Bench Division), after receiving by mail a cheque "in payment" of saccharine sold by oral agreement, the seller wrote the buyer, mentioning a sudden increase in duty on saccharine, refusing to deliver unless the buyer consented to pay enough to cover this increase, and offering to return the cheque if the buyer did not wish to accede. It was held that there had been an acceptance of part payment within the meaning of the Statute, the earlier case of *Davis* v. *Phillips, Mills & Co.*, 24 T. L. R. 4 (1907), being distinguished on the ground that the cheques there received were returned at once with the statement that there was no contract.

E. The Memorandum

BAILEY *v.* SWEETING

Court of Common Pleas, 1861

[30 *Law Journal* (*New Series*), *Common Pleas*, 150]

This was an action brought to recover 76*l.* 14*s.* 3*d.* for goods bargained and sold.

The defendant paid into court 38*l.* 3*s.* 9*d.*, and pleaded never indebted to the rest of the claim.

The cause was tried, before Erle, C.J., at the London Sittings after Easter Term, 1860. The defendant, a furniture-dealer at Cheltenham, being at the plaintiffs' manufactory, in London, in July 1859, bought of the plaintiffs four old gilt chimney-glasses, at 28*l.* 10*s.*, and a walnut chimney-glass at 6*l.* 6*s.*, to be paid for by a cheque on delivery; and also, on the same occasion, bought of the plaintiffs various other articles (some of which were not then ready, but had to be made), on certain credit terms. The chimney-glasses formed the first parcel of such goods which were sent to the defendant, at Cheltenham. The carrier, however, to whom this parcel was delivered, so damaged it during its carriage, that the defendant refused to receive it when it arrived, and the plaintiffs were at once informed of such refusal. The other goods which had been bought were afterwards sent in different parcels to the defendant, and were duly received by him; and it was admitted at the trial that the value of these was covered by the amount which had been paid into court, and the only question was as to the defendant's liability in respect of the first parcel, the price of which, with the cases in which it was packed, amounted to 38*l.* 10*s.* 6*d.* With reference to the Statute of Frauds, the plaintiffs contended that the sale of all the articles had been under one contract, and that there had been, therefore, a part acceptance; and they also relied on the following letter from the defendant, written in answer to one from the plaintiffs applying for payment, as a memorandum satisfying the statute —

Cheltenham, Dec. 3, 1859.

Gentlemen, — In reply to your letter of the 1st instant, I beg to say that the only parcel of goods selected for ready money was the chimney-glasses, amounting to 38*l.* 10*s.* 6*d.*, which goods I have never received, and have long since declined to have for reasons made known to you at the time; with regard to the other items, viz., 11*l.* 4*s.* 9*d.*, 14*l.* 13*s.* and 13*l.* 13*s.*, for goods had subsequently (less cases returned), those goods are, I believe, subject to the usual discount of 5*l.* per cent., and I am quite ready to remit you cash for these parcels at once, and on receipt of your reply to this letter will instruct a friend to call on you, and settle accordingly. I am yours, &c.,

Geo. Sweeting.

The jury, being of opinion that the chimney-glasses were sold under a separate contract from that under which the other articles were sold, found a verdict for the defendant; leave being reserved to the plaintiffs to move to set the same aside, and to enter a verdict for them for 38*l.* 10*s.* 6*d.*, if the Court should be of opinion that the defendant's letter of the 3rd of December was sufficient to satisfy the Statute of Frauds.

In Trinity Term last Hawkins obtained a rule *nisi* accordingly, to set the verdict aside, and to enter it for the plaintiffs for 38*l.* 10*s.* 6*d.*, pursuant to the leave reserved, or for a new trial on the ground of the verdict being against evidence.

[The arguments of counsel are here omitted.]

ERLE, C.J. — This was an action for goods bargained and sold, and the question was, whether there had been a sale. The defendant relies on the Statute of Frauds, and says that there was no note or memorandum to satisfy the statute. There was a letter, however, written by the defendant, which in effect says this to the plaintiffs: "I made a bargain with you for the purchase of chimney-glasses at the sum of 38*l.* 10*s.* 6*d.*, but I declined to have them because the carrier broke them." Now, the first part of that letter is unquestionably a note or memorandum of the bargain; it contains the price and all the substance of the contract, and there could be no dispute that if it had stopped there it would have been a good memorandum of the contract within the meaning of the statute. I think that what had passed in the first instance orally between the parties on the subject of the purchase was in the nature of an inchoate contract, and which when construed with the letter afterwards written is a good and binding contract. Then the latter part of the letter in effect says, that the goods to which the contract I had made relates were refused by me because the carrier broke them; and it has been contended by the defendant that the letter is not a memorandum of the contract within the statute, because it repudiates the bargain, and the defendant has relied on the passage cited from Mr. Justice Blackburn's book on *Contracts* in support of the proposition that the acknowledgment of the bargain is not within the statute, if it is accompanied by a repudiation of it, and reference has been made to the case of *Rondeau* v. *Wyatt*, where there was a bill of discovery, and it was held that the answer thereto in Chancery was not a sufficient memorandum within the Statute of Frauds. Although I have thus adverted to these authorities, there is in fact no decided authority on the point, and we are therefore referred back to the original Statute of Frauds, and I, for one, am of opinion that the letter of the defendant is a good memorandum of the bargain within the meaning of that statute. The object of the act was to prevent fraud and perjury. That is sufficiently obviated by the letter in question, because the defendant says therein "I made the contract for the goods." The goods and the price are both referred to, and the defendant does not in such letter rely on the Statute of Frauds as making the contract invalid, but he rests his repudiation on the ground of the goods having been broken. That may, I think, distinguish the present case from cases where the party admitting the contract has relied on the statute as a defence. But if there be no such distinction, then, with every respect for that clear-headed and learned Judge, my Brother Blackburn, I cannot assent to the proposition contained in his work on *Contracts* to the extent contended for.

[The concurring opinions of William, Willes, and Keating, JJ., are here omitted.]

Rule absolute to enter verdict for the plaintiffs for 38*l.* 10*s.* 6*d.*

MORRIS FURNITURE COMPANY *v.* BRAVERMAN

IOWA SUPREME COURT, 1930

[210 *Iowa Reports*, 946]

Action at law upon an open account for the agreed price of furniture alleged to have been ordered by defendant and manufactured by the plaintiff in accordance with the order. Defendant, in his answer, denied that he had ordered the goods, and averred, in substance, that the contract is unenforcible, as being in violation of the Statute of Frauds. Verdict and judgment for the plaintiff. The defendant appeals. — Affirmed.

WAGNER, J. — Arnold Davidson is now the owner of the account on which suit is brought, and has been substituted as plaintiff in lieu of the Morris Furniture Company, the original plaintiff. For convenience, we will in this opinion refer to the Morris Furniture Company as the appellee.

In the "errors relied upon for reversal," the appellant contends that the court was in error in refusing to direct a verdict for the defendant upon the ground that the contract is not enforcible because it is within the provision of the Statute of Frauds, and that there is a failure of evidence to take it without said statute; also that the court erred in one of the instructions given.

Appellee's action is founded upon an account for furniture alleged to have been ordered by the appellant and manufactured by the appellee in accordance with the order. The appellee in its petition alleges, in substance, that, on or about the 17th day of September, 1923, the appellant gave to the appellee a written order for furniture, at the prices therein shown, a copy of which order is therein set out; that appellant was given a copy of said written order; that, on September 25, 1923, the appellant acknowledged said written order by a communication in writing, which is as follows:

Cedar Rapids, Iowa.
Sept. 25, 1923.

Morris Furniture Co.,
Chicago, Ill.
Gentlemen:

Will you please hold our order of Sept. 17, until we give further notice?

Yours very truly,
Max Furniture Store, Max.

It is alleged that the appellee has carried out the terms of the contract, and shipped the goods and merchandise to the appellant at Cedar Rapids, and that the appellant has failed and refused to pay for the same. The appellant, by way of answer, denies the allegations of the petition, and avers that the contract is within the Statute of Frauds.

We will first consider appellant's contention relative to the Statute of Frauds. There is no question about the shipment of the furniture by the appellee to the appellant at Cedar Rapids, and that the appellant has refused to accept the same.

[A page of the opinion is here omitted.]

This testimony is uncontradicted. It is to be noted that the order of September 17th is not signed by the appellant, the party to be charged; and, were this all that the record discloses, the appellant's contention that the contract is unenforcible would necessarily have to be upheld. It is the appellee's contention that the aforesaid letter of September 25th, which is signed by the appellant, is sufficient to constitute a "note or memorandum," mentioned in the aforesaid statute. It will be observed that the appellant therein says: "Will you please hold our order of September 17th until we give further notice?" The record discloses that there was only one order by the appellant under date of September 17th. The letter signed by the appellant, the party to be charged, could not refer to any other order. From a reading of the statute it is plain that, in order to take the case without the Statute of Frauds, it is not necessary that the contract be signed by the party to be charged, but only that some note or memorandum in writing of the contract be signed by the party to be charged. The note or memorandum is required only as evidence of the contract, and not to constitute it. Neither is it necessary that the note or memorandum should have been signed by the party to be charged with the intent to comply with the statute. . . .

Obviously, there is sufficient to take the contract without the statute of frauds where the memorandum is made up of several papers which together will furnish the essential terms, and where the separate writing bears internal reference one to the other. See 27 Corpus Juris 262; *Manufacturers L. & H. Co.* v. *Lamp*, 269 Pa. St. 517 (112 Atl. 679); *Mason-Heflin Coal Co.* v. *Currie*, 270 Pa. St. 221 (113 Atl. 202). There are many authorities which hold that oral testimony may be offered, to identify and show the connection between the two writings. This court so held in an early case, *Lee* v. *Mahony*, 9 Iowa 344, wherein it is declared:

"In many [cases] the memorandum is brief, and requires explanation, or else testimony to connect it with something else; and it is not an objection that one paper is to be connected with another by extraneous, and even by parol, evidence."

Also, see *Manufacturers L. & H. Co.* v. *Lamp*, 269 Pa. St. 517 (112 Atl. 679); 27 Corpus Juris 384 and cases therein cited. In the instant case the letter of September 25th in unmistakable language refers to "our order of September 17th." The order of September 17th was in writing, and contained the prices and all the terms relative to the sale. There is in the subsequent letter of September 25th internal reference to the only order given by the appellant on September 17th. Clearly, the letter of September 25th, which is signed by the appellant, the party to be charged, and which unmistakably refers to the order of September 17th, constitutes a memorandum sufficient, within the meaning of the law, to take the contract without the statute of frauds.

[The last page of the opinion is here omitted.]

We find no error in the record, and the judgment of the trial court is hereby affirmed.

Affirmed.

MORLING, C. J., and STEVENS, DE GRAFF, and ALBERT, JJ., concur.

Note also TILTON & KEELER, INC. *v.* BACHRACH, 121 Misc. 708 (New York City Court, 1923). In an action for goods sold but not accepted by defendants it appeared that plaintiff on October 19, 1921, wrote to defendants, "We are herewith enclosing confirmation in duplicate covering goods purchased by you. We would ask you to kindly sign the unsigned copy and return to us at your earliest convenience." No reply was made. On December 27, 1921, defendants wrote to plaintiff: "Please postpone all January deliveries on our orders until February 1, 1922, unless instructed to the contrary." The following day the plaintiff wrote in reply: "We wish to advise that we have looked over our January file and fail to find having received an order from you for delivery during this month." On December 30, 1921, the defendants again wrote: "In answer to your letter of the 28th in reference to our letter of the 27th we should advise that the order referred to calls for 100 pieces of Dunbar Suiting." It was held as a matter of law that the correspondence was a sufficient memorandum under the Statute.

Compare the situation in TAYLOR *v.* SMITH, [1893] 2 Q. B. 65 (Court of Appeal, 1892), where Lord Herschell said: "This action is brought in respect of an alleged contract for the sale of deals, and the question is whether there is a contract complying with the requisitions of the 17th section of the Statute of Frauds. The bargain was made by word of mouth. An invoice was made out which was dated October 21, but not sent to the defendant till October 30, which was in these terms: — 'Mr. John Smith, Manchester. Bought from Messrs. Charles Taylor, Sons & Co., 1060 spruce deals. Free to flat, 100*l.* 11*s.* 4*d.*, per Kenworthy's flat, Arthur.' Kenworthy was a carrier who carried goods to Manchester, and part of the arrangement was that the deals should be sent by Kenworthy's flat. The first question is whether there was a memorandum in writing signed by the defendant of the terms of the contract. No letter was written by him which contained any direct reference to the invoice. He signed the following memorandum on the advice note sent him by the carrier: — 'Refused. Not according to representation. John Smith.' The only other document signed by the defendant was a letter dated November 8, written by him to the plaintiffs, which was as follows: — 'With reference to the deals refused by me now lying at Kenworthy's, they are not according to representation, and much inferior in quality to any St. Johns spruce deals I have seen. I consider them fully 10*s.* per standard below average value, and therefore cannot accept same.' The question is whether either or both of these documents can be said to be, in conjunction with any document incorporated with or referred to in them, or either of them, a memorandum within the statute. It is obvious that the advice note, the indorsed memorandum, and the letter do not by themselves constitute such a memorandum, for the terms of the bargain are not to be found in them. If any of them had referred to or incorporated the invoice I think there would have been a sufficient memorandum; but it is impossible to say that the invoice is incorporated with or referred to in any of them. There is therefore no memorandum to satisfy the statute."

BERMAN STORES CO., INC. *v.* HIRSH

New York Court of Appeals, 1925

[240 *New York Reports*, 209]

Lehman, J. The plaintiff has brought an action to recover damages for the failure of the defendants to manufacture and deliver twenty-two hundred and fifty men's suits of various sizes and models, in accordance with a contract which the plaintiff claims was made between the parties. The defendants pleaded as a defense the Statute of Frauds. At the close of the plaintiff's case the complaint was dismissed on the ground that the plaintiff had failed to show that a memorandum in writing of the contract was signed by the defendants as required by the Statute of Frauds (section 85 of the Personal Property Law [Cons. Laws, ch. 41]).

According to the testimony produced by the plaintiff the defendants are engaged in the business of manufacturing men's suits and overcoats. They have in their place of business models of garments which they manufacture, samples of cloth used and a quantity of "piece goods." They take orders to manufacture garments like the models, from cloth like the samples shown. They accepted an order from the plaintiff for 2,250 suits to be manufactured by them and they signed memoranda which show the number of suits ordered, their size and price. The style and materials of the suits are identified by letters, figures and lot numbers used by the defendants in their business and the memoranda contain all the terms which ordinarily enter into a contract to manufacture and sell except that they contain no statement as to the time of shipment or delivery. Concededly no goods were delivered and no payments made under the alleged contract. The defendants contend and the courts below have held that the contract is unenforcible because the memoranda signed by the defendants do not embody the entire contract which it is said included a definite date for shipment or delivery.

[A page of the opinion is here omitted.]

We have pointed out that the memoranda signed by the defendants contain no provision for the time of shipment or delivery except perhaps that they were to be delivered "when ready." It does not fix any time when the goods were to be ready. The complaint alleges that the parties agreed to deliver the goods within a reasonable time thereafter and in time for it to use in the fall trade of the year 1919. If the parol agreement fixed no time for delivery the memorandum evidencing the contract is sufficient under the statute since it contains all the terms which have been agreed on. In such case the law supplies the missing term and requires delivery within a reasonable time. If, on the other hand, the time was fixed by the parties the memorandum is insufficient. "It is not sufficient that the note or memorandum may express the terms of a contract. It is essential that it should completely evidence the contract which the parties made." (*Poel* v. *Brunswick-Balke-Collender Co.*, 216 N. Y. 310.)

At the trial the plaintiff's secretary testified that he purchased the goods and at that time told the defendants' representative he would have to make them up according to these specifications and deliver them in the usual course for fall. Though asked as to what was said and done he failed to testify that anything further was said as to time of delivery. If there was no further conversation then the defendants would be bound to deliver the goods within a reasonable time and one of the elements of what would constitute a reasonable time would be the fact that they were fall goods. The plaintiff further presented evidence intended to show that a reasonable time for delivery would be somewhere between August first and September fifteenth. On cross-examination he was not asked whether anything further was said between the parties but in answer to questions as to whether the parties "agreed" that the goods should be delivered between August first and September fifteenth, he repeatedly answered in the affirmative. These questions and answers show clearly that he claimed that he was entitled under his contract to delivery between August first and September fifteenth and that he considered that the obligation to deliver within such time constituted a very important part of the contract and because this important part of the contract was omitted from the memorandum the contract has been held unenforcible.

Even if the evidence which the plaintiff produced is sufficient to show that a reasonable time for delivery would be between August first and September fifteenth, it cannot be said that an express agreement that delivery would be made within that time would add nothing to the contract beyond what the law would have supplied if the parties had remained silent. If parties choose to fix a time for delivery instead of leaving the determination of what would constitute a reasonable time to uncertain inference that might be drawn from circumstances which might themselves be disputed, unknown to the parties, or which might even arise thereafter, then the time so fixed becomes an essential part of the contract and must be embodied in the memorandum required under the Statute of Frauds.

The difficulty in the present case is that the evidence does not show conclusively that the parties did fix the time for delivery. If it was fixed by the parties it must have been fixed in the conversations preceding the signing of the memoranda. The silence upon this point of memoranda otherwise complete, is itself not without significance. The testimony of the plaintiff's secretary as to the conversations shows no discussion of such a term. What the parties agreed to is merely a conclusion of law to be drawn from what was said and done by the parties. In answer to questions, for the most part improper in form, the plaintiff's witness, a business man, has drawn the legal conclusion that the agreement included a term that the goods should be delivered between August first and September fifteenth. He had previously testified to a conversation which, if complete, fails to sustain this conclusion. He had further testified to trade customs and circumstances which, even without agreement, would result in an obligation upon the part of the defendants to deliver the goods approximately at that time. A reading of his entire testimony leaves us at least in doubt whether the witness ever intended to testify that any express agreement fixing the time of delivery was made or that the time of delivery was part of the agreement made except in so far as the law would require delivery under the contract within what he claimed to be a reasonable time. It was for the jury who saw and heard the witness to determine whether the witness intended by his answers to say that the parties expressly agreed upon the time of delivery or whether he merely intended to say that the time during which, under the contract, delivery must be made, was between August first and September fifteenth.

The judgments should be reversed and a new trial ordered, with costs to abide the event.

HISCOCK, Ch. J., CARDOZO, POUND and MCLAUGHLIN, JJ., concur; CRANE and ANDREWS, JJ., dissent.

Judgments reversed, etc.

Note also BURLINGTON GROCERY COMPANY *v.* LINES, 96 Vermont 405 (Supreme Court, 1923), where it was held that the memorandum need not name a definite price if none was agreed on by the parties.

DONALD FRIEDMAN & COMPANY, INC. *v.* NEWMAN

NEW YORK COURT OF APPEALS, 1931

[255 *New York Reports*, 340]

Appeal from a judgment, entered July 8, 1930, upon an order of the Appellate Division of the Supreme Court in the first judicial department reversing a judgment in favor of defendant entered upon a decision of the court on trial at Special Term and directing judgment in favor of plaintiff upon new findings.

LEHMAN, J. The plaintiff corporation is a dealer in bank and insurance company stock. As the result of negotiations conducted over the telephone, it agreed to sell to the defendant ten shares of Chase National Bank. Then, in accordance with the usual custom in its business, it prepared a paper known as a "Confirmation of Sale." The "confirmation" was written on the business stationery of the plaintiff, signed by the plaintiff, addressed to the defendant, and thereafter signed by the defendant. At the top appears the word "Confirmation," and it reads as follows:

> We beg to confirm our Sale to you to-day of 10 shares Chase National Bank at 1060 — 10600
>
> Accepted. L. Newman (signed)
> Delivery
> Bank of U. S.
> Pitkin Avenue
>
> Yours truly,
> DONALD FRIEDMAN & CO., INC.
> (signed) by B. WILLUNG.

The plaintiff refused to deliver the stock in accordance with the terms stated in the "confirmation." It claims that in the telephone conversation the parties agreed to a sale at $1,160 per share, and that in the "confirmation" the price of 1060 per share was inserted by mistake. It insisted upon performance by the defendant in accordance with the terms of the alleged oral agreement. The defendant denied the mistake and insisted upon performance of the contract in accordance with the terms contained in the written memorandum or confirmation.

The defendant brought an action in the Municipal Court for damages caused by the refusal to deliver the stock at the price stated in the written confirmation. The plaintiff brought an action in the Supreme Court for reformation of the paper writing, purporting to confirm the sale, and asked damages for the refusal to accept and pay for the stock in accordance with the contract of sale. By order of the Supreme Court the two actions were consolidated and were tried together at Special Term. At the trial the defendant was permitted to amend his answer by inserting a plea of the Statute of Frauds. There was conflicting testimony as to the price at which the parties agreed the sale should be made. The trial judge resolved this conflict in favor of the defendant. The Appellate Division reversed the finding and gave judgment in favor of the plaintiff, decreeing that "the said Confirmation of Sale setting forth the purchase price as $1060 per share for 10 shares Chase National Bank be reformed and corrected so as to express the true agreement between plaintiff and defendant as regards the said purchase price," and awarding to the plaintiff damages for the defendant's failure to accept and pay for the stock at that price.

The contract between the parties was oral. The paper executed thereafter, denominated "confirmation of sale" was, as its name and form clearly indicate, merely intended as a memorandum of the oral contract. It is evidence of an oral contract previously made. The oral contract is unenforceable unless a "note or memorandum thereof be in writing." (Pers. Prop. Law; Cons. Laws, ch. 41, §§ 31, 85.) Neither party may recover damages for the breach of the oral contract unless the paper writing signed by the parties sufficiently evidences the contract actually made.

"It is not sufficient that the note or memorandum may express the terms of a contract. It is essential that it shall completely evidence the contract which the parties made. If instead of proving the existence of that contract, it establishes that there was * * * a contract in terms and conditions different from that which the parties entered into, it fails to comply with the statute." (*Poel* v. *Brunswick-Balke-Collender Co.*, 216 N. Y. 310; *Berman Stores Co.* v. *Hirsh*, 240 N. Y. 209.) The memorandum is not subject to the parol evidence rule, for it does not integrate, but merely evidences, the oral agreement. It "may be shown by parol to be inaccurate or incomplete." (*Mesibov, Glinert & Levy* v. *Cohen Bros. Mfg. Co.*, 245 N. Y. 305, 313.)

The Statute of Frauds merely declares "void" or "unenforceable" a contract not in writing or evidenced by a note or memorandum in writing. It does not declare expressly or by implication that a written note or memorandum of an oral contract is conclusive evidence of the terms of the contract. Doubtless a note or memorandum may constitute an admission of the making of the oral contract and of its terms, but neither the parol evidence rule nor the statute prevents the introduction of evidence contradicting the admission. Except as evidence of the oral contract, the memorandum has no force or effect unless and until the oral contract has been established by a preponderance of evidence. Then, if accurate and complete, it prevents the interposition of the Statute of Frauds as a bar to the enforcement of the oral contract.

Here the Appellate Division has found that the plaintiff sold to the defendant ten shares of Chase National Bank stock for which the defendant agreed to pay to the plaintiff the sum of $11,600. We cannot say that this finding is not in accordance with the weight of evidence. The defendant's cause of action was based upon the allegation that the sale was made at a lower price. He failed to establish that allegation to the satisfaction of the ultimate trier of the fact. The court was not called upon to exercise such equitable powers as it might have to defeat an unconscionable assertion by the defendant of a legal right. Proof that the plaintiff's admission contained in the memorandum was made through mistake justified the court in rejecting the admission. It could not by its fiat change the plaintiff's admission into an affirmation by the defendant of the contrary. Nor was such change necessary to defeat the defendant's cause of action. That cause of action failed when the court rejected the proof intended to establish it.

[More than two pages of the opinion are here omitted.]

Here the parties made their contract by parol. There is dispute as to the terms of the contract. The parol evidence rule does not preclude either party from showing the actual agreement of the parties. A court of law might receive all the relevant testimony and determine what contract was made. No court of equity could change the contract made by the parties or reduce to writing what rested in parol. The parol contract is "void" or "unenforceable" under the provisions of the Statute of Frauds, unless a "note or memorandum thereof be in writing." The parties intended to make a note or memorandum of the contract they had made. By mistake the writing is a memorandum of a contract which in fact was never made. No note or memorandum of the contract which the plaintiff seeks to enforce was ever made. Therefore, that contract is "unenforceable" and no court of equity, by "reforming" the memorandum can give it an effect forbidden by the statute. Mistake by the parties resulting in failure to comply with the statute does not confer upon a court of equity the power to substitute for what they have done that which they should have done. Equity has at times power to reform an instrument which conclusively embodies the intent of the parties; it has no power to reconstitute an evidentiary writing. Though at times the Statute of Frauds may present no bar to the exercise of the court's equitable power to relieve against fraud or mistake, there is no equitable power to enforce a contract which the statute declares void merely because through mistake of the parties their intention to make a valid contract was frustrated.

The judgment of the Appellate Division and that of the Special Term should be reversed and the complaint and counterclaim dismissed, without costs.

CARDOZO, Ch. J., POUND, CRANE, KELLOGG, O'BRIEN and HUBBS, JJ., concur.

Judgments reversed, etc.

In SMITH *v.* SURMAN, 9 B. & C. 561 (King's Bench, 1829), two letters relied on to constitute a memorandum of a sale of timber were inconsistent in that one spoke of the contract as absolute, whereas the other alleged a condition that the timber was to be "sound and good." This was held not to comply with the object of the statute, as the effect was to leave the actual terms of the contract still in doubt.

Compare WATSON & Co. *v.* SHAW, SON & Co., 8 Ll. L. L. R. 227 (King's Bench Division, 1922), where the seller under an oral agreement for the sale of barley, sent a contract note to the buyer for his signature. The buyer replied objecting to certain terms in regard to allowances and refused to sign, later repudiating the bargain altogether. In an action by the seller for non-acceptance, the letter and the contract note were held to constitute a sufficient memorandum.

MESIBOV, GLINERT & LEVY, INC. *v.* COHEN BROTHERS MANUFACTURING CO., INC.

NEW YORK COURT OF APPEALS, 1927

[245 *New York Reports*, 305]

Appeal from a judgment, entered December 17, 1926, upon an order of the Appellate Division of the Supreme Court in the first judicial department, reversing a judgment in favor of plaintiff entered upon a verdict and directing a dismissal of the complaint.

CARDOZO, Ch. J. Plaintiff, wishing to purchase 2,000 pounds of tricolette, received from the defendant the following memorandum:

Acknowledged Date June 28, 1919

COHEN BROTHERS
The Leading Sweater House
16–18–20 West 32nd Street, New York

All contracts subject to strikes, accidents and other unavoidable causes

Sweaters, Fancy Knit Goods

All goods sold and shipped F. O. B. the Mills.

MILLS
Cleveland, Ohio
Brooklyn, N. Y.
Philadelphia, Pa.
West New York, N. J.

Salesman

Filled by
Chg'd by
Date

Make for Mesibov, Glinert & Levy Ship to 104 W. 27th St.

When
Via N. Y. City

	30 32 34 36 38 40 42 44 46	Terms	Price
No.: Style No.: Quantity: Ck: Color:	12 14 16 18 20 22 24 26 28		9.50 a lb
2000 lbs. Raw Trico Cloth		Net 10 days	

Delivery Sept and Oct.
No countermands accepted.

NOTICE.—We hereby agree to accept above order in detail as given and no changes can be made in same unless COHEN BROS. are notified within 10 days from date order is placed.

To facilitate matters this order will be shipped "As ready for express" unless otherwise specified on order. We do not prepay express charges and make no express charge allowance unless shipment of merchandise is routed contrary to written instructions on this order. No goods will be taken back, unless damaged. We ship no goods on consignment.

Accepted

The memorandum was written on a printed order form. The name Cohen Bros. printed in the heading and in the body of the form is that of a partnership to whose business the defendant, Cohen Brothers Manufacturing Co., Inc., had recently succeeded. The plaintiff says that the memorandum was delivered by the defendant with intent to close a contract by the acceptance of an order. The defendant says that it was delivered without contractual intent, and as a memorandum of inquiries to be submitted to the mill. The question is whether the memorandum satisfies the requirements of the Statute of Frauds (Pers. Prop. Law, § 85; Consol. Laws, ch. 41). Criticism is directed to two features of the writing. One is the signature. The other is the description. The two grounds of criticism will be considered in succession.

(1) "The contract," or "some note or memorandum" thereof, shall be "signed by the party to be charged or his agent in that behalf" (Pers. Prop. Law, § 85, subd. 1). There is no longer a requirement that the writing be "subscribed" (*James* v. *Patten*, 6 N. Y. 9). It may be signed at any place, at the top or in the body. A signature, however, there must be, and a name, written or printed, is not to be reckoned as a signature unless inserted or adopted with an intent, actual or apparent, to authenticate the writing (1 Williston, Sales, § 112; Anson, Contracts [Corbin's ed.], p. 106; Benjamin on Sales [6th ed.], p. 308; Browne, Statute of Frauds, § 357). Whether such an intent is to be inferred will be at times a question of law and at others one of fact, according to the circumstances. Thus, a signature is adequate if the party to be charged writes the letters "O.K." in the margin or at the top and adds thereto his name either in full or by initials. A signature is adequate if a letter is written in the third person: "Mr. Stanley begs to inform [the plaintiffs] that he will take an early opportunity of settling their accounts" (*Lobb* v. *Stanley*, 1844, 5 Q. B. [Ad. & Ellis N. S.] 574). The same result has been reached in other cases where intention was more dubious (Benjamin, *supra*, p. 306). The decisions are conflicting whether the name of a seller in the printed heading of a billhead or an order blank is a signing without more. Such a signing was held adequate in *Cohen* v. *Wolgel* (107 Misc. Rep. 505; 191 App. Div. 883); in *Pearlberg* v. *Levisohn* (112 Misc. Rep. 95), and in *Drury* v. *Young* (58 Md. 546), but inadequate in *Lee* v. *Vaughan's Seed Store* (101 Ark. 68), and in *Sutherland* v. *Munsey* (119 Va. 791).

We assume for present purposes that a printed name in such a heading will be treated as a signature if the setting of the occasion gives fair warrant for the inference that it was so intended or adopted. The assumption does not carry us far toward the solution of our problem. The difficulty here is that the imputation of such a meaning to the parties now before us is overcome by tokens of intention too strong to be resisted. Beneath the printed heading is the buyer's order for the goods. Beneath the order is a form wherein the seller accepts the order according to its terms. Beneath this is the printed word "accepted" with a dotted line intended for the signature of the seller, the acceptor. The name was never added.

A memorandum so phrased leaves no basis for the inference, in the absence at all events of other evidence of intention, that the printed heading was adopted as a recognition of the contract. The form shows upon its face that the seller was unwilling to accredit the contract as its own without another signature, separate from the heading, to be placed as a token of validity in a space specially reserved. Even in the English courts, where the rule, it seems, is laxer than with us (Williston, *supra*, § 112), a signature thus disowned would not satisfy the statute. Thus, in *Hubert* v. *Treherne* (3 M. & G. 743) the names of the parties were written in the body of the document, but at the end were the words "as witness our hands," without other authentication. "These words evidently shew that the names of the contracting parties were meant to be subscribed, and that it was not intended that the insertion of the names in the body of the instrument should operate by way of signature" (per TINDAL, C. J., at p. 754; cf. *Hucklesby* v. *Hook*, 82 L. T. 117, and cases there cited; Benjamin on Sales, *supra*). We may, indeed, infer from the delivery of the writing that the defendant intended to assume the obligation of a contract, whether the document was signed or unsigned. It might have intended as much if there had been no writing whatever. It may even have supposed that a writing was unnecessary. Something more must be found before the statutory requirements can be held to be obeyed. The defendant must have intended not merely to contract, but to sign. We see no mark of such a purpose.

The conclusion thus reached is reinforced by other circumstances, if reinforcement be important. The name used in the order blank is not the defendant's name at all. It is the name of a partnership to which the defendant has succeeded. We do not mean that this circumstance, standing alone, would be decisive. If the writing had been signed at the appropriate place, the inference might be permissible that the name had been adopted for the occasion as an informal or abbreviated description of the corporation, just as if the corporation had been designated by the use of its initials. The partnership was no longer in existence, and there is no pretense that the defendant's officers were contracting in behalf of a firm that was extinct. Even so, the use of such a form puts a new strain upon the argument that the heading was adopted as equivalent to a signature. The inference must rather be that the blanks were made use of as a convenient scratch-pad, without thought that they contained a signature, or that signature was necessary.

(2) We pass to a second objection to the note or memorandum. The one already considered is sufficient to sustain the judgment. The second, however, was chosen by the Appellate Division as the basis of its opinion, in misconception, we think, of the effect of our decisions. Our silence might tend to perpetuate the error.

The memorandum is said to be inadequate in its description of the goods that are to be the subject of the contract. Trico cloth, or more properly tricolette, comes in varying widths and weights. The memorandum does not state the widths and weights to be delivered. There might be force in this criticism if the omission were not supplied by the usage of the market. Evidence is in the record that there are standard widths and weights which will be taken to be those intended when the writing is silent as to the delivery of others. A witness for the defendant admits that this is true of widths, though he qualifies his earlier testimony by denying that it is true of weights. On the other hand, there are witnesses for the plaintiff who tell us that it is true of widths and weights alike. If this is so, the goods have been "sufficiently described for reasonable identification" (1 Williston, Sales, § 105-b, p. 198). The memorandum was for the use of merchants. The meaning that the description would have conveyed to them, when they came to read what had been written in the light of the usage of their business, is the meaning to be ascribed to it when scrutinized by courts (*Gumbinsky Bros. Co.* v. *Smalley*, 203 App. Div. 661; 235 N. Y. 619; *Nicoll* v. *Pittsvein Coal Co.*, 269 Fed. Rep. 968). The statute does not abrogate the settled canons of construction that apply to contracts generally (*Marks* v. *Cowdin*, 226 N. Y. 138, 144; *Argus Co.* v. *Mayor*, 55 N. Y. 495, 504; Williston, Sales, § 104, and cases there cited).

Stress is laid by the defendant upon a statement by the plaintiff's agent in the talk that led up to the written memorandum. He said in entering the defendant's office that he wished to buy some more of the same quality of tricolette that had been supplied to him before. The argument is made that the memorandum is an incomplete record of the true agreement between the parties in that it fails to identify the subject-matter of the new deliveries with the subject-matter of the old ones (1 Williston, Sales, § 104). We do not overlook the difference in this connection between a contract in writing, and a note or memorandum of a contract. The one is subject to the parol evidence rule; the other may be shown by parol to be inaccurate or incomplete (Williston, *supra*, § 100; Benjamin on Sales [6th ed.], pp. 264, 267, and cases there cited; *Juilliard* v. *Trokie*, 139 App. Div. 530, 533; 203 N. Y. 604; *Mandel* v. *Guardian Holding Co., Inc.*, 200 App. Div. 767, 769, 770; 234 N. Y. 564). But the goods previously supplied were goods of standard widths and weights. The memorandum did not introduce a variance from the conditions of the order. It put in other words the same thought that would have been expressed if it had identified the new sales by reference to the old ones. A different question would be here if some particular form of expression had been bargained for in advance as an essential term of the agreement. Nothing in the situation justifies an inference that such a bargain was intended. What was said by the plaintiff's agent was merely introductory and preliminary. Indeed, the defendant's argument, if accepted, would lead to the conclusion that the memorandum would be inadequate though it had expressly enumerated the widths and weights to be delivered unless it joined to this a statement that widths and weights were to be identical with those supplied before. Neither reason nor authority constrains to such a ruling. A memorandum expressing the sense of the preliminary agreement is not to be condemned as inadequate for a failure to reproduce the words, unless reproduction of the words was a condition of the bargain. Nothing to the contrary was held in *Berman Stores Co.* v. *Hirsh* (240 N. Y. 209). There the parties had agreed upon a determinate date for the delivery of goods. The memorandum was silent as to this branch of the agreement with the result that delivery might have been made within the flexible and fluctuating limits of a reasonable time (cf. Williston, *supra*, § 104, p. 190). What was written was not fairly the equivalent of what was said. Here equivalence is made out by the usage of the business as soon as usage is established. Equivalence existing, the parties were not insistent that the expression should be in one form to the exclusion of another.

We conclude that the first objection to the writing must be upheld and the second overruled.

The judgment should be affirmed with costs.

POUND, CRANE, ANDREWS, LEHMAN, KELLOGG and O'BRIEN, JJ., concur.

Judgment affirmed, etc.

Compare SCHWARTZ *v.* VIGDEN, 112 Misc. 451 (New York Supreme Court, 1920), where Bijur, J., said: "Plaintiff sues for damages arising out of the failure of defendant to deliver certain furs alleged to have been sold by him to the plaintiffs.

"Defendant, among other things, introduced the defense of the Statute of Frauds. The alleged agreement:

Telephone Madison Square 4253

NEW YORK Aug. 4th, 1919.

M. SCHWARTZ & LERNER
West 29th Street, City:

LOUIS VIGDEN
Importer and Exporter of 1316
FURS AND SKINS

Terms, Net cash 49 West 29th Street.
2103 Raw Damages and Shot rats at 75¢ $1577.25

To be delivered from
Funsten Bros. St. Louis
Mo.

(The name of the defendant apparently being printed on one of his regular billheads.)

"I do not think that this memorandum satisfies the requirements of the Statute of Frauds, in particular because it fails to show or to indicate who is the buyer and who is the seller. Both parties were dealers in furs, occupying, indeed, adjacent premises. It is quite as consistent with the memorandum and the situation of the parties that the defendant was the buyer and plaintiffs the seller as is the converse hypothesis. Although a more liberal rule may possibly be applied toward allowing parol evidence to identify the subject matter of the transaction (see *Marks* v. *Cowdin*, 226 N. Y. 138) a contract of purchase and sale must certainly specify who is the buyer and who the seller."

[This reasoning was disapproved in 210 App. Div. 714 by the Appellate Division, which reinstated a judgment for the plaintiff on the ground that the appearance of both names made the memorandum sufficient even though the parties were not distinguished.]

BACHE *v.* BANKOGRAPH CO., INC.

NEW YORK SUPREME COURT, 1922

[120 *New York Miscellaneous Reports*, 44]

Appeal by plaintiffs from a judgment of the Municipal Court of the city of New York, borough of Manhattan, first district, in favor of the defendant, entered upon the dismissal of the complaint at the close of the plaintiffs' case.

MCAVOY, J. This action is one to recover $925 as damages for breach of contract by which the plaintiffs sold to the defendant and defendant bought from the plaintiffs a check for 1,000,000 German marks. The defense is a general denial and there is a plea of the Statute of Frauds. The conduct of the sale was described as follows in the testimony: One Kahn, who is a foreign exchange broker and has been in the business about fifteen years, was on several occasions during March and April, 1922, called upon by one Lederer, president of the defendant, on the telephone, and quotations on foreign exchange, both marks and francs, were asked for. On one occasion prior to this one the defendant purchased a check for French francs, which was delivered to him in the form of a banker's check for the French francs. The check of the banking house to which the order for the French francs had been given was delivered to the defendant in the customary way, and Lederer, the president of the defendant, paid for the check. On April 24, 1922, Lederer telephoned to Kahn, the foreign exchange broker, that he wanted to buy 1,000,000 German marks and asked for the rate. Kahn informed him that the rate was forty-three and three-fourths, and Lederer said he would take 1,000,000. Kahn is not connected in business with the plaintiffs, but transacts his business in behalf of customers with banking houses generally. Kahn told the defendant's officer to wait until he ascertained what the rate for the mark was, so that he might get the lowest rate for the defendant, and Lederer waited on the 'phone while Kahn called up the plaintiffs on another telephone, received the quotation, and told Lederer that the rate quoted was O. K., and that he had bought a 1,000,000 marks' check on Berlin for the defendant. Lederer told Kahn to have the check drawn to the order of the Bankograph Company, Inc., the defendant here. Kahn then sent a bought note to the defendant and a sold note was delivered to the plaintiffs by him. The sold note recites that the broker had bought 1,000,000 marks from plaintiffs for delivery at forty-three and three-fourths on the order and for the account of the Bankograph Company, Inc. The marks were not delivered that afternoon to the defendant, because the transaction took place after banking hours; but the morning after the contract was made the plaintiffs drew their check on a German bank in Berlin for the 1,000,000 marks. Plaintiffs' messenger took the check for the marks and a bill for $4,375 to the office of the defendant. Lederer refused to accept the check. The marks were sold at the opening of the market on the following morning at thirty-four and one-half, losing nine and one-fourth points, which is the basis of the amount of damage.

The complaint was dismissed at the close of plaintiffs' case on the ground that plaintiffs had failed to prove the cause of action alleged, or any cause of action, and had failed to bring the action within the Statute of Frauds, because there was no writing or note or memorandum in writing of the contract signed by a duly authorized agent of the defendant in his behalf or signed by the defendant, and that no part of the property passed and that no part of the purchase price was paid.

Plaintiffs' claim at the trial was that Kahn was the agent of the defendant, that the customer knew that the broker would purchase the marks from bankers, and would receive his commission therefrom, and that the signing of the bought note by the broker, which was delivered to the bankers, was a sufficient compliance with the requirements of the Statute of

Frauds. It seems fully established in New York that a broker in goods or merchandise who carries on an independent business as a broker and is not a mere employee of the purchaser, is authorized to bind both parties to a transaction by signing a memorandum of purchase in behalf of the buyer; and this rule doubtless applies to the sale of choses in action besides the sale of commodities. It is obvious here that Kahn was not the plaintiffs' employee, that his duties and the defendant's knowledge of them constituted him a broker, who, according to the custom of the trade, was authorized to sign and deliver the bought and sold notes and thus remove the statutory taint of invalidity of a transaction not reduced to writing signed by the party sought to be charged. The defendant's argument is that it would have no cause of action against Bache & Co., the plaintiffs, if the rate of exchange had gone up between the time of purchase and delivery, and Bache & Co. had refused to comply with the contract to furnish the marks to defendant. Whether this be true or not, mutuality of obligation is not essential to the validity of a contract in so far as its compliance with the Statute of Frauds is concerned, and the purchaser may be held notwithstanding the fact that it may not be enforcible against the other party. If the proposal is in writing, signed by the party to be charged, and contains all the terms of the proposed contract the contract as against the party signing is good within the statute. Though a contract by reason of its acceptance being verbal may not be enforcible against the party accepting it, such circumstance is no defense to the party signing the same, the object of the statute being to compel the production of written evidence of the terms of the contract against the party sought to be charged. It is not essential to the liability of the party sought to be charged that there be mutuality of obligation, and the fact that the contract may not be enforcible against one party because not subscribed by him is no defense to the other by whom it is subscribed. *Justice* v. *Lang*, 42 N. Y. 493.

It seems to me that there was a cause of action proved against the defendant in which all the usual elements of a contract were set out, and that the plaintiffs' proof of transaction shows a complete compliance with the Statute of Frauds, and in consequence the judgment should be reversed.

Judgment reversed and a new trial ordered, with thirty dollars costs to the appellants to abide the event.

LEHMAN and WAGNER, JJ., concur.

Judgment reversed.

MADDALONI OLIVE OIL CO., INC. *v.* AQUINO

NEW YORK SUPREME COURT, APPELLATE DIVISION, 1920

[191 *New York Appellate Division Reports*, 51]

Appeal by the defendants, Anielo Aquino and others, from a judgment of the Supreme Court in favor of the plaintiff, entered in the office of the clerk of the county of New York on the 14th day of December, 1918, upon the verdict of a jury, and also from an order entered in said clerk's office on the 20th day of December, 1918, denying defendants' motion for a new trial made upon the minutes.

Since the entry of the judgment and order appealed from Giovanni Aquino, who was the defendant in the action, died and his executors were by order of the court substituted in his place as the defendants in this action.

SMITH, J. This action grows out of a contract between the plaintiff and the defendants' testator for the purchase of 300 barrels of Italian wine. The written contract provided for sixty days' credit. When the wine reached New York the defendant refused to deliver it without payment in cash therefor, and offered to prove a verbal contract subsequent to the written contract and before the wine arrived in New York that the payment should be made in cash and that the sixty days' credit should be waived. Thereafter the plaintiff demanded the wine according to the terms of the original contract. The trial judge refused to allow the defendant to introduce evidence of this oral modification of the written contract upon the ground that the Statute of Frauds required the contract to be in writing and that it could not be altered by parol, and thereupon directed a verdict for the plaintiff for damages resulting from a breach of the original contract by the defendants' testator. From the judgment entered thereupon this appeal is taken.

[After pointing out that an oral agreement may constitute a contract valid for some purposes although not enforceable by action, Smith, J., continued:] There are but very few cases in the English courts which make note of this distinction. The latest case in the House of Lords (*Morris* v. *Baron & Co.*, in 1918) is found in volume 87, New Series of the Law Journal (K. B. Div.), at page 145. In that case it is held: "Under section 4 of the Sale of Goods Act, 1893, an agreement which the law requires to be in writing is merely not enforceable by law if not in writing, but it is not invalid for all purposes, and the law as laid down in section 17 of the Statute of Frauds is altered to that extent; and therefore, although a contract required to be in writing cannot be varied by parol, parol evidence is admissible to prove a total abandonment or rescission of a written contract." The court distinguished between a variation of a contract required to be in writing and a total abandonment or rescission of a written contract, and Viscount HALDANE says at page 152: "Accordingly, while a parol variation of a contract required to be in writing cannot be given in evidence, the very authorities which lay down this principle also lay down not less clearly that parol evidence is admissible to prove a total abandonment or rescission. Now there is no reason why this should not be done through the instrumentality of a new agreement which does not comply with the statutory formalities, just as readily as by any other mode of mutual assent by parol. What is, of course, essential is that there should have been made manifest the intention in any event of a complete extinction of the first and formal contract, and not merely the desire of an alteration, however sweeping, in terms which still leave it subsisting." Upon the distinction made between a rescission of a contract and its variation, Lord PARMOOR, in the same case, says: "It is not possible to lay down any general principle, but where the alteration is such that the conditions of the earlier contract cannot be restored without placing one of the parties under a permanent and substantial disability, there is a strong *prima facie* probability of an intention to rescind."

In *Noble* v. *Ward* (35 L. J. Ex. 81) the change in the contract was as to the date of delivery. The court below held that that amounted to a rescission of the original contract and substituted a new one therefor. The House of Lords upon appeal held that it could not be held as matter of law that that amounted to a rescission of the original contract but that it was, at least, a question of fact for the jury as to whether the intention of the parties was to rescind the original contract. This case is distinguished in *Morris* v. *Baron & Co.*, wherein the distinction as above shown was made between a variation of the original contract which is held invalid by parol and a rescission thereof which might be valid.

In the case of *Morris* v. *Baron & Co.* (*supra*) the new contract in parol was made after the institution of the suit for the breach of the written contract, and it was there held, as matter of law, under the circumstances of that case, that the parol contract was in rescission of and in substitution for the written contract. From the foregoing cases it would appear that it would be competent to show by parol a rescission or abandonment of the written contract and that question under the case of *Noble* v. *Ward* (*supra*) would seem to be a question of fact, but the defendant is in no position to make that claim in this case, because he has not pleaded a rescission or abandonment of the written contract, but only a modification thereof which, under the authorities cited, would seem to be unauthorized as long as the claimed modification was not in writing.

There are many cases, both in this State and elsewhere, holding that where a contract is required to be in writing it cannot be modified by parol. The most prominent case in this State is the case of *Hill* v. *Blake* (97 N. Y. 216). (See, also, *Wright* v. *Weeks*, 25 N. Y. 153; *Clark* v. *Fey*, 121 id. 470; *Stead* v. *Dawber*, 10 Ad. & El. 65; Williston Sales, § 120; *Swain* v. *Seamens*, 9 Wall. 271; *Walter* v. *Bloede Co.*, 94 Md. 80; 50 Atl. Rep. 433.) These are all cases, however, which were decided in actions wherein a party sought to enforce by action a parol modification of an agreement wherein a writing was required by the Statute of Frauds. Under the case of *Morris* v. *Baron & Co.* (*supra*), however, the statute seems to have received a broader interpretation and to have been held to apply where a defendant, sued upon a contract required by law to be in writing, sought to defend upon an oral modification of the contract. . . .

The judgment and order should, therefore, be affirmed, with costs to respondent.

CLARKE, P. J., LAUGHLIN, MERRELL and PHILBIN, JJ., concur.

Judgment and order affirmed, with costs.

BESSELER WAECHTER GLOVER AND COMPANY *v.* SOUTH DERWENT COAL COMPANY, LIMITED

King's Bench Division, 1937

[*Law Reports*, [1938] 1 *King's Bench*, 408]

Goddard J. read the following judgment: The arbitration in which this award in the form of a special case is stated arises out of a contract between the claimants as buyers and the respondents as sellers of 70,000 tons of coal, made in November, 1935. The only question that has to be decided is one under s. 4 of the Sale of Goods Act, and for this purpose the facts can be very shortly stated.

On October 10, 1935, the respondents sold to the claimants 40,000 tons of coal to be delivered in equal monthly quantities from January 1 to June 30, 1936. Soon after this contract was made the claimants' representative asked that deliveries if possible should be expedited, and the respondents' representative, while giving no undertaking, promised to do this if it were possible. Then on November 6 the contract in question was made, providing for equal monthly deliveries between April 1 and December 31, 1936. In April, 1936, while deliveries under the October contract were still being made, and deliveries under the subsequent contract were due to begin, the representatives of the parties met and discussed the situation. Deliveries under the October contract had not been expedited, so that from April to June, 1936, deliveries under both contracts would be due to be made and received.

The representatives came to what the arbitrator refers to as a verbal agreement that deliveries under the later contract should not begin until the deliveries under the former had finished, and that the deliveries should proceed and the coal undelivered under the later contract on December 31 should thereafter be delivered to the claimants under the later contract. But he does not find that the balance should be delivered in monthly or any instalments, finding, as I understand the case, that there was no agreement on this point. This agreement he finds was for the mutual convenience of the parties, and was so considered by them, convenient for the buyers, as their customers had no great amount of storage room, and for the sellers because they were considering closing down one of their pits, in which case it would have been difficult for them to keep up double deliveries, and accordingly no deliveries were made under the later contract till July.

But on December 1, 1936, the sellers wrote to the effect that as the buyers had not taken delivery in accordance with the terms of the contract of November 6, 1935, they declined to deliver any coal after December 31. The buyers claim damages for non-delivery, and the arbitrator has found that as the agreement come to in April, 1936, for postponing delivery was not in writing, s. 4 of the Sale of Goods Act is an answer to this claim, and has awarded, subject to this case, that nothing is due by way of damages. He has also awarded that the buyers cannot claim specific performance of the contract, and that finding is not challenged, as of course coal could have been bought elsewhere, though at a higher price.

Mr. Miller for the claimants, the buyers, took three points: first, that on the findings of what took place in April, 1936, there was not a new contract, but only a postponement of delivery, and that the contract remained in operation subject to a modification as to delivery. Secondly, that if there was a new contract it was not one for sale of goods, but for the delivery of goods already sold. Thirdly, that alternatively, if there was a new contract in April, it had been partly performed by the deliveries that were made between July, 1936 — when deliveries of the 70,000 tons began — and December, 1936, and therefore the provisions of s. 4 are satisfied.

The first two contentions can, I think, be dealt with together, and on this part of the case a large number of cases were cited by either side, those most discussed being *Stead* v. *Dawber* (10 Ad. & E. 57); *Tyers* v. *Rosedale and Ferryhill Iron Co.* (L. R. 8 Ex. 305; L. R. 10 Ex. 195); *Leather Cloth Co.* v. *Hieronimus* ((1875) L. R. 10 Q. B. 140); *Hickman* v. *Haynes* (L. R. 10 C. P. 598); *Plevins* v. *Downing* (1 C. P. D. 220); *Morris* v. *Baron & Co.* ([1918] A. C. 1).

It often happens when either the 4th or the 17th section of the Statute of Frauds, now replaced by s. 4 of the Sale of Goods Act, 1893, has to be considered that the cases are found to be somewhat difficult of reconciliation, and this case is no exception. In *Stead* v. *Dawber* (10 Ad. & E. 57), the Court found it difficult to reconcile *Goss* v. *Lord Nugent* ((1833) 5 B. & Ad. 58) with *Cuff* v. *Penn* ((1813) 1 M. & S. 21), and *Stead* v. *Dawber* (10 Ad. & E. 57), though the facts were very similar, had in turn to be distinguished by the Court in *Hickman* v. *Haynes* (L. R. 10 C. P. 598).

Mr. Miller relied strongly on Martin B.'s judgment in *Tyers* v. *Rosedale and Ferryhill Iron Co.* (L. R. 8 Ex. 305, 316, 317; L. R. 10 Ex. 195), which was upheld when that case went to the Exchequer Chamber. In that case the plaintiffs had requested the defendants to forbear from delivering certain instalments, and accordingly only partial deliveries were made, and then at the end of the contract period the buyers demanded delivery of the residue. Martin B. in a dissenting judgment held that the original contract had not been terminated, and dealt with the objection that the plaintiffs' right to recover was barred by the 17th section as not being in writing by saying: "It (that is the variation) was not a contract for the sale of goods . . . but a contract respecting the delivery of goods already sold, which is not within the section at all." However, when that case went to the Exchequer Chamber counsel for the defendants abandoned this point, because, as I understand the case, if writing were required, there was enough to supply a memorandum, and I feel a difficulty in holding that the approval which the Exchequer Chamber gave to the judgment of Martin B., who had differed from the rest of the Court below on the question as to whether the original contract was rescinded, necessarily extended to this part of his judgment.

With all respect to the high authority of the learned Baron, it seems to me that a term as to delivery is a term of the sale, and if that term be altered it is an alteration of the terms of the contract of sale, and this was, I think, the ground of the decision in *Stead* v. *Dawber* (10 Ad. & E. 57), which Mr. Naisby contended was conclusive in his favour. *Stead* v. *Dawber* (10 Ad. & E. 57) was, however, as I have said, distinguished in *Hickman* v. *Haynes* (L. R. 10 C. P. 598), another case of a verbal request to allow instalments to stand over, where it was held that the Statute was no answer; and in the following year, in *Plevins* v. *Downing* (1 C. P. D. 220), a very similar case, it was decided that it was.

One must therefore try to find the underlying principle which will explain the different results in cases which at first sight appear to be so alike in point of fact. From these two last-cited cases I think it is possible to extract a principle, and it seems to me to be this: If the parties agree to rescind their original contract and to substitute for it a new one, the latter must be evidenced by writing; so, too, if as a matter of contract the parties agree that the terms of the original agreement shall be varied, the variation must be in writing. But if what happens is a mere voluntary forbearance to insist on delivery or acceptance according to the strict terms of the written contract, the original contract remains unaffected, and the obligation to deliver and to accept the full contract quantity still continues. This view is supported by the speech of Lord Atkinson in *Morris* v. *Baron & Co.* ([1918] A. C. 1, 30). . . .

It does not appear to me to matter whether the request comes from one side or the other, or whether it is a matter which is convenient to one party or to both. What is of importance is whether it is a mere forbearance or a matter of contract. This I think is made clear by *Plevins* v. *Downing* (1 C. P. D. 220), where Brett J. emphasizes the distinction between the situation where the party suing was always ready and willing to perform his contract and merely abstained at the request of the other party, and where, if he sued for non-acceptance or non-delivery, he would be driven to rely on the assent of the other party to allow him to vary the terms of the original contract.

If, however, one party asks the other if he would refrain from delivering, and the other party says it would suit him very well to do so, both parties being able and willing to perform their obligations, I think we get the same position as is envisaged by *Hickman* v. *Haynes* (L. R. 10 C. P. 598), and by Lord Atkinson in the passage to which I have referred.

It then has to be determined on which side of the line the present case falls. Mr. Naisby relies on the fact that the arbitrator has found that there was a verbal agreement; but I do not think the use of those words concludes the matter. Whether it be a forbearance or a matter of contract, there is none the less an agreement; there is an agreement between parties, though for want of consideration or because of the provisions of an Act of Parliament their agreement must be regarded as *nudum pactum* or as void. One must have regard to the facts found by the arbitrator, and when one finds that what happened was a conversation which arose, as it seems to me, because one party had not been able to expedite deliveries under an earlier contract which he had promised, but not undertaken, to do if he could, when one finds that neither party thought the matter worth confirming in writing, and that the vendors' representative did not even inform his directors of the matter, and no inquiry was made or pressure applied during the contract period, I think one is driven to the conclusion that this was no more than a mere forbearance, and voluntary in the sense that either party could have rescinded and called upon the other to make or take delivery in accordance with the terms of the written contract. Accordingly I hold that the Statute is not an answer to the buyers' claim.

[The last page of the opinion, holding that part delivery would not be an answer to the Statute, is omitted here.]

PART TWO

THE MAKING OF THE CONTRACT: THE DISTRIBUTION OF RISKS

COMMENT

UP TO THE present point we have been considering what the buyer and seller must do if their bargain is to have any legal effect at all. Emphasis has been laid on the sufficiency of the transaction in general without reference to the particular interests of the parties. Scant thought is necessary however to appreciate that the result so far is merely a framework, albeit an essential one, and that the full sweep of the completed contract is yet to be imposed. From a mercantile point of view indeed the minds of the parties are likely to dwell far less on the formal aspects of agreement than on their respective relations to the incidents, and consequently to the risks, associated with performance.

Modern conditions of trade have tended to multiply these risks. For buyer and seller to meet and chaffer with their wares on view is in the main a thing of the past; the old-fashioned horse trade has become a museum piece. More often than not great distances intervene, and negotiations must be conducted by correspondence, by telegraph, by cable, or perhaps by radio. Buyer and seller may be residents of different countries, accustomed to deal in different currencies. The buyer rarely will have an opportunity to see in advance the actual goods that he is purchasing, and even the seller may be acquainted but indirectly with his own wares. Many a bargain is built around a catalogue number, an item in a stock inventory, or by reference to a standard grade established by a course of dealing or by trade practice. The time element also is a factor. There may be an appreciable interval between the making of the contract and the completion of merchandise to be manufactured or procured, and still more time will elapse from the date of shipment to the final receipt of the goods by the buyer.

These considerations and others of a kindred nature raise questions at once troublesome and important. How may the buyer be assured of getting the goods as and when he wants them and at the place where they will be most useful to him? Must he take the chance that the quantities ordered and furnished may be more or less than those actually required? Which of the parties assumes the risk of depreciation in quality, of shrinkage, and of loss or damage in transit? Is the adventure to be frustrated by obstacles that may hinder or prevent its performance? Must the merchandise supplied correspond exactly to that mentioned in the bargain, being also merchantable and reasonably suited to its intended use; or is the seller excusable for slight or unwitting variations? Who is to forecast the changing factors of supply and demand that will determine the ultimate value of the goods at destination? What is to be done in regard to fluctuations in exchange that may affect the price to be paid and the amount to be received? In what way are credit hazards to be adjusted and financing problems to be solved?

The law, more meticulous in prescribing the form and essentials of the contract, is possibly of less assistance here before the event, although it can and does attempt to interpret the will of the parties in their own silence by reading certain implications into an agreement otherwise sufficient. Inevitably however merchants in their continued dealings with each other have sought ways and means of answering these and similar questions, for the vital difference between profit and loss may hinge on the result. From varying points of view they have fashioned phrases and expressions designed for translation into satisfactory performance. There is ample indication in these clauses of the conflict of interests involved. The entire history of the c.i.f. sale, for example, has been marked by successive attempts by buyers and sellers to shift particular risks from one to the other. In another direction the expanding use of commercial credits has introduced new parties with new interests, not always harmonized readily with those of either the seller or the buyer. On the framework already erected traders thus are engaged constantly in fitting a superstructure, sometimes confused in outline, often discordant in detail, but always responsive in one way or another to the mercantile needs and practices of the time.

In the present section therefore we shall be concerned with the risks of doing business. In the main, the problems raised are problems of construction, but in an atmosphere of performance; for it is usually a dispute in regard to performance that brings the contract before the judicial eye. What did the parties really mean by the words employed, or by their failure to insert any words at all? To what extent will the law give effect to their intention, once interpreted? The usages of merchants march on.

CHAPTER I

Terms and Conditions Relating to the Goods

1. DELIVERY

A. Mode of Delivery

ANDERSON *v.* SCOT

King's Bench, 1806

[1 *Campbell's Reports*, 235]

Special *assumpsit* for the non-delivery of wine bought by the plaintiff of the defendant. It appeared that the plaintiff went into the defendant's cellar, and selected several pipes of wine, for which he agreed, by parol, to pay a certain price: the spills, or pegs by which the wine is tasted, were then cut off; plaintiff's initials were marked on the casks by defendant's clerk in his presence, and plaintiff took the gauge numbers. It was objected that this sale was within the statute of frauds; but Lord Ellenborough held, that the cutting off the spills, and the marking of plaintiff's initials on the casks by defendant's agent, in the presence of all the parties, amounted to a delivery. — It was then contended that this proved the contract laid in the declaration to have been performed. The plaintiff complained of the non-delivery of the wine; whereas he had himself proved that it had been delivered. As to which, Lord Ellenborough observed, that although there had been an incipient delivery, sufficient to take the case out of the statute of frauds, yet that delivery not having been perfected, plaintiff had a right to an action in the present form, to recover damages for the non-completion of the contract.

GROSS *v.* AJELLO

New York Supreme Court, Appellate Division, 1909

[132 *New York Appellate Division Reports*, 25]

Appeal by the defendant, Michele Ajello, from a judgment of the Supreme Court in favor of the plaintiff, entered in the office of the clerk of the county of Kings on the 8th day of May, 1908, upon the verdict of a jury rendered by direction of the court.

Miller, J. The plaintiff seeks to recover the purchase price of two lots of merchandise separately contracted to be sold to the defendant. He declares on two causes of action: (1) The sale and delivery of a quantity of tomato paste; (2) the breach of an executory contract to purchase a quantity of chick peas. The evidence in support of the first cause of action tended to show the sale of 100 cases of tomato paste, to be manufactured and delivered in separate lots; that 15 cases were delivered and paid for; and that thereafter 85 cases were set aside by the plaintiff and marked for the defendant, but never actually delivered. The only evidence to show notice of readiness to deliver or a tender of delivery, not stricken from the record, was the following testimony of the plaintiff's son: "I telephoned him (meaning the defendant) when he would take the rest, and I never received any reply of any kind." . . .

There can be no doubt that both contracts were executory. The obligation of the defendant to pay and of the plaintiff to deliver were mutual and dependent. In the absence of delivery the plaintiff could only recover the purchase price by showing readiness to perform and a tender of performance on her part. . . . But merely setting aside the cases, when prepared, did not constitute a delivery; and in view of the fact that the goods were to be manufactured and delivered in separate lots the inquiry made by the plaintiff's son, as testified to by him, did not amount to a notice that the goods were ready for delivery or to a tender of delivery, at least as matter of law.

But aside from the foregoing, there is still a serious obstacle to the affirmance of this judgment. The defendant rested upon the plaintiff's case, insisting that the plaintiff had failed to establish a sale and delivery as pleaded. There is no doubt that where the vendee has defaulted on an executory contract to purchase personal property, the vendor has a choice of remedies, namely: (a) To keep the goods and sue for damages for breach of contract; (b) to hold them as bailee of the purchaser and recover the contract price; (c) to sell them as agent of the purchaser and recover the difference between the purchase price and the amount realized on such sale. But the plaintiff in this case pleaded an executed, not an executory, contract; and the substantive rules of law hereinbefore referred to have nothing to do with the question of pleading. The plaintiff can only recover the purchase price on the theory that the goods belong to the defendant; but this judgment conclusively establishes the delivery, and could be pleaded as an estoppel in a suit to recover possession of them. At common law the plaintiff could only recover on a declaration for goods sold and delivered by showing an actual delivery. (*Outwater* v. *Dodge*, 7 Cow. 85.) In the cases hereinbefore cited, which permitted a recovery of the purchase price though there was no delivery, no question of pleading was involved; and no reason can be suggested for allowing a recovery for goods sold, but not delivered, on an averment of a sale and delivery, where the point is properly taken on the trial. To constitute a delivery the goods must at least be placed in the power of the vendee. . . .

The judgment must be reversed.

HIRSCHBERG, P. J., WOODWARD, JENKS and RICH, JJ., concurred.

Judgment reversed and new trial ordered, costs to abide the event.

Compare WRIGHTSON *v.* MCARTHUR AND HUTCHISONS, [1921] 2 K. B. 807 (King's Bench Division, 1920), where goods remained on the seller's premises, but were placed by agreement in a room to which the buyer was given the key. In holding that delivery of the key operated to transfer possession of the goods, Rowlatt, J., said: "The actual question was to be considered in the light of the principle that delivery of a key has effect not as symbolic delivery, but as giving the actual control."

WHITTLE *v.* PHELPS

MASSACHUSETTS SUPREME JUDICIAL COURT, 1902
[181 *Massachusetts Reports*, 317]

MORTON, J. This is an action of replevin to recover possession of a quantity of brick. The case was tried by a judge of the Superior Court without a jury, and there was a general finding for the plaintiff. The defendant excepted to the refusal of the judge to rule that it did not appear that there was a sufficient delivery to the plaintiff of the bricks replevied to pass the title, and that on all the evidence the plaintiff could not recover. The principal question relates to the delivery. There was testimony tending to show that one Bailey, the owner of a brick yard in the town of Harvard, agreed with the plaintiff in July, 1899, to furnish him two hundred thousand bricks at $5 per thousand to be delivered in Worcester, and that a few days after, namely, July 11, Bailey executed and delivered to the plaintiff a bill of sale of the bricks in which they were described as "two hundred thousand bricks, more or less as desired, . . . to be shipped from the northerly end of kiln No. 3, consisting of the first ten arches, located in the southerly end of kiln shed." The description in the writ substantially followed this. At the time of the execution of the bill of sale the plaintiff supposed that he was buying merchantable bricks ready for delivery, and it was agreed that he should pay for them at once, and he did so by giving his note for $800, retaining $200 to pay the freight. There was also testimony tending to show that it was agreed that the plaintiff should go to Harvard the following week and take possession of the bricks; that he went to the brick yard as agreed on July 18; that there were nine and a half or ten arches all set up and connected together but not burned; that Bailey put his hand on the arches on the southerly end of the kiln and said, "These are your brick"; "Here are nine and one half arches, and there should be ten arches, which they are drawing in at the present time"; that the plaintiff said that he was not ready to use the brick and would not be probably till the following spring and Bailey said he would let the bricks lie there as long as he pleased; that the plaintiff did not go to the brick yard again till the following April when he went to replevy the brick; and that the bricks that were replevied constituted eight and three quarters of the nine and a half arches of which the plaintiff took possession. It also appeared that shortly after the plaintiff had been to Harvard, namely, July 26, Bailey made a mortgage to the defendant of the personal property in the brick yard which included in its terms the brick in question and on July 31 leased the premises to him for a year; that he told the defendant that he had sold two hundred thousand bricks to the plaintiff; and that more arches were set up and added to those that were there and all were burned by the defendant.

Upon this evidence we think that it was competent for the judge to find that there was a sale and delivery to the plaintiff of the bricks that were replevied. The sale was not a sale of bricks to be manufactured but of the brick in the nine and a half arches in the state in which they were, with the understanding and agreement that they were to be completed by Bailey. At least such could have been found to be the case by the judge. It is true that the plaintiff supposed that he was buying merchantable bricks ready for delivery, and they were described in the bill of sale as at the northerly end, but when the sale was consummated by delivery it turned out to be of unfinished bricks, and to include the nine and a half arches which were there and turned out to be at the southerly end. Until delivery took place, the sale was executory, and it was competent for the parties to agree upon whatever they saw fit as the subject matter of it. The property was bulky in its nature and it was not necessary in order to constitute a delivery that the plaintiff should take manual possession of it. *Parry* v. *Libbey*, 166 Mass. 112. *Jewett* v. *Warren*, 12 Mass. 300. It was sufficient if the delivery was such as the nature of the property admitted of, and the judge must have so found. Assuming that only merchantable brick were to be paid for, there was nothing in that circumstance to prevent the judge from finding that there was a sale and delivery of the nine and a half arches. *Macomber* v. *Parker*, 13 Pick. 175. The description in the writ of the brick as at the northerly end of the kiln was immaterial. It did not affect the identity of the brick that were sold and delivered and that were replevied. The subsequent conduct of the defendant in taking possession of the bricks and completing their manufacture, gave him no rights in or lien on the bricks.

Exceptions overruled.

DUTTON *v.* SOLOMONSON

COURT OF COMMON PLEAS, 1803

[3 *Bosanquet & Puller's New Reports*, 582]

This was an action for goods sold and delivered. At the trial before Lord Alvanley Ch. J. at the Guildhall Sittings after last Trinity term, it appeared that on the 10th of August 1802, the goods in question were purchased by the Defendant of the Plaintiff at Manchester, to be paid for by a bill at two months; that a bill was accordingly drawn upon the Defendant for the amount of the goods, and tendered for acceptance on the 27th of August, which was refused, the Defendant declining to accept any bill except a bill at three months, and that not until after the goods should have arrived. The goods were delivered by the Plaintiff at the common waggon office a few days after the receipt of the order, but did not arrive in London until the 9th of October. The writ was sued out on the 6th of September. The jury found a verdict for the Plaintiff, but liberty was reserved to the Defendant to move that this verdict might be set aside, and a nonsuit entered.

Accordingly a rule *nisi* for that purpose having been obtained on a former day.

On this day the opinion of the Court was delivered by

Lord ALVANLEY Ch. J. who (after stating the case) proceeded thus: The first objection in this case is, that the delivery of the goods to the carrier was no delivery to the person who ordered them, and therefore in that point of view this action was commenced too soon, the writ having been sued out before the arrival of the goods in London. When this point was first mentioned I was surprised, for it appeared to me to be a proposition as well settled as any in the law, that if a tradesman order goods to be sent by a carrier, though he does not name any particular carrier, the moment the goods are delivered to the carrier it operates as a delivery to the purchaser; the whole property immediately vests in him; he alone can bring an action for any injury done to the goods; and if any accident happen to the goods it is at his risk. The only exception to the purchaser's right over the goods is, that the vendor, in case of the former becoming insolvent, may stop them *in transitu*. On this part of the case, therefore, the Court never has entertained any doubt.

EDELSTONE *v.* SCHIMMEL

MASSACHUSETTS SUPREME JUDICIAL COURT, 1919

[233 *Massachusetts Reports*, 45]

This is an action to recover for goods sold and delivered. On December 29, 1916, the defendant at the plaintiffs' place of business in Boston made an agreement to buy of the plaintiffs "ten (10) bales of oil mill motes at 4¼ c. per pound, F. O. B. Boston, terms 1%, 10 net 30 days, to be shipped by the N. Y., N. H. & H. R. R. — to be shipped at once to New York." There was no dispute between the parties as to the terms of this agreement. These goods were shipped to the defendant by the carrier named on December 30, 1916, and a non-negotiable bill of lading was issued on that date, the defendant being named as consignee. This bill of lading was not forwarded to the defendant, but was retained by the plaintiffs, who sent no notice to the defendant respecting it. Owing to other differences between the parties, the plaintiffs on January 11, 1917, and again four days later, wrote in substance to the defendant that they would not deliver to him the oil mill motes unless he accepted and paid demand or sight draft less one per cent discount. The plaintiffs also notified the carrier at Boston, on January 9, not to deliver the mill motes to the defendant. The defendant on January 11, 1917, brought an action in New York City for breach of contract and there attached goods of the plaintiffs alleged to be in the possession of the New York, New Haven, and Hartford Railroad.

The bill of lading is not printed in the record. The plaintiffs testified that the "defendant could get the goods on arrival without bill of lading."

The defendant testified that without the "bill of lading, as matters stood, he could not get possession of the mill motes." The court refused to grant the defendant's sixth request for ruling, which amongst other matters contained a statement of fact to the effect that the defendant could not obtain the possession of the motes without the bill of lading. There was no other evidence and no express finding respecting the bill of lading and its effect on delivery to the defendant in New York. Under the circumstances it must be assumed that mere failure of the plaintiffs to forward it to the defendant had no effect on his right to demand delivery of the goods in New York. See, in this connection, *in Matter of Bills of Lading*, 14 I. C. C. Rep. 346, and *New York Central & Hudson River Railroad* v. *York & Whitney Co.* 230 Mass. 206, 213, 217. It is the general rule that a non-negotiable contract of shipment by a common carrier is discharged by delivery to the consignee without the surrender or production of the bill of lading. The fact that one is consignee is evidence of ownership. *Brown* v. *Floersheim Mercantile Co.* 206 Mass. 373, 375. *Rosenbush* v. *Bernheimer*, 211 Mass. 146, 149, 151.

The contract between the parties was plain. The ordinary rule is that, in case of sales of goods to be shipped by the vendor from one place to another, delivery to the carrier is delivery to the buyer unless there is special agreement to the contrary. *Fechteler* v. *Whittemore*, 205 Mass. 6, 11. *Twitchell-Champlin Co.* v. *Radovsky*, 207 Mass. 72, 75. *Levy* v. *Radkay*, 233 Mass. 29, Sales act, St. 1908, c. 237, §§ 19 and 46. Delivery of the goods to the carrier together with the taking of a non-negotiable bill of lading in the name of the defendant was strong proof of intention by the plaintiffs to transfer the title to the defendant. *Wigton* v. *Bowley*, 130 Mass. 252. The general finding of the trial judge in favor of the plaintiffs imported a finding in their favor on the point of delivery.

The attempt of the plaintiffs by notice to the carrier not to deliver to the defendant was not of decisive consequence. The goods theretofore had been delivered to the carrier; it held as bailee for the defendant to whom the title had passed. The letters of the plaintiffs endeavoring to get the defendant to pay before the due date of the contract were ineffectual to restore to them a title which already had vested in the defendant. These subsequent acts of the plaintiffs had no effect upon substantial elements of the contract which were already executed. *R. H. White Co.* v. *Jerome H. Remick & Co.* 198 Mass. 41, 48. *Daley* v. *People's Building, Loan & Savings Association*, 178 Mass. 13, 18. The finding of fact of the trial judge in favor of the plaintiffs was warranted by the evidence. No error of law is disclosed on the record.

The finding of the judge for the plaintiffs is to stand and judgment is to be entered accordingly.

So ordered.

THE MOTCH & MERRYWEATHER MACHINERY CO. *v.* THE SIDNEY MACHINE TOOL CO.

Ohio Court of Appeals for Shelby County, 1919

[12 *Ohio Appellate Reports*, 266]

Allread, J. The original action was brought to recover the purchase price of certain machinery claimed to have been sold by the plaintiff in error to the defendant in error. The answer, among other things, denies that the property was delivered according to contract.

From the record it appears that the machinery in question was ordered upon open account "Net f. o. b. cars at Cincinnati, Ohio. Delivery October." There is a statement in the order showing that the time of delivery was important. The order was accepted by plaintiff in error subject to the following: "F. O. B. Oakley, delivery October, terms, draft attached to B/L." The added terms were inferentially accepted by defendant in error.

It also appears that the goods were shipped on October 31 from the Cincinnati Planer Company, Oakley, Cincinnati, Ohio, consigned to the order of the plaintiff in error, with direction to notify the defendant in error. The bill of lading was evidently forwarded from Cincinnati to the plaintiff in error at Cleveland, Ohio.

On November 4 the plaintiff in error wrote the defendant in error that the shipment had been made as above stated, and that the bill of lading, duly indorsed, together with a sight draft, had been forwarded by the plaintiff in error to the First National Bank of Sidney for collection.

On November 7 the defendant in error by letter notified the plaintiff in error that the shipment had arrived in Sidney and awaited unloading by the defendant in error, which the defendant in error was prepared to do on the basis outlined in the letter. The substance of the letter was that the defendant would accept the shipment if the terms were changed from a sight draft to a credit of thirty days. This credit was denied by the plaintiff in error, and the defendant in error thereupon canceled the order and refused acceptance of the goods.

The first question for determination is whether there was a delivery within the month of October; the second, whether the delivery as made was accepted by the defendant in error.

It is claimed by counsel for plaintiff in error that delivery was made under the provisions of the Sales Act (99 O. L., 413) when the goods were delivered to the carrier at Oakley, Cincinnati, on October 31.

The defendant in error contends that the delivery to the carrier on October 31 was not a delivery to the defendant in error, and that the goods were for the first time tendered for delivery when the same reached Sidney some days later, and when the bill of lading and draft were presented by the Sidney bank.

The important feature of this transaction is the consignment under a bill of lading to the order of the plaintiff in error instead of to the order of the defendant in error.

[Two pages of the opinion holding that no title passed to the buyer under this disposition of the bill of lading are here omitted.]

Likewise, it may be said that the machinery in the case at bar was not delivered to the common carrier at Cincinnati, Ohio, for delivery to The Sidney Machine Tool Company; but the delivery was to the common carrier for shipment to the plaintiff in error. The delivery to the common carrier was not actual or constructive delivery to the purchaser. There was, within the stipulated period, no delivery, actual or constructive, to the defendant in error. When a delivery was actually tendered subsequent to the month of October the said machine tool company had the right to reject the same.

We think the letter of The Sidney Machine Tool Company of November 7 was not an acceptance of the machinery, but was an offer to accept the same upon certain conditions. When the plaintiff in error rejected the conditions The Sidney Machine Tool Company had the right to unqualifiedly reject the machinery, and this we think it did by its telegram of November 14.

It therefore follows, first, that there was no delivery, actual or constructive, to The Sidney Machine Tool Company within the stipulated period; second, The Sidney Machine Tool Company did not accept, but on the contrary rejected the subsequent delivery of the machinery. The court of common pleas did not err in holding for the defendant.

Judgment affirmed.

Compare ALDERMAN BROTHERS CO. *v.* WESTINGHOUSE AIR BRAKE CO., 92 Conn. 419 (Supreme Court of Errors, 1918). In that case there was an agreement to sell brass chips at 15½ cents per lb. f. o. b. cars Wilmerding, Pa., terms sight draft on arrival at destination. Defendant delivered the brass chips to the carrier at Wilmerding consigned to itself, and took a bill of lading to its own order which it sent to its agent indorsed in blank and attached to a sight draft. In an action by plaintiff to recover a portion of the purchase price because of an alleged shortage the lower court charged the jury that because of the form of the bill of lading the risk of loss in transit rested on the defendant. In disapproving this ruling the upper Court said: "A delivery to a carrier in accordance with §. 46 [of the Uniform Sales Act] is a delivery to the buyer within the meaning of § 22 [of the Uniform Sales Act], notwithstanding the fact that the buyer cannot have possession of the goods until the seller is paid, because the Sales Act contemplates that the seller may at his option reserve the *jus disponendi.* It makes no difference to a buyer who has agreed to pay the freight, whether a sight draft is presented to him attached to a bill of lading drawn to his own order or to a bill of lading drawn to the order of the seller and indorsed in blank. In either case he must pay his draft in order to get possession of the goods, and in either case his rights, on paying the draft, are the same."

See GABARRON *v.* KREEFT, L. R. 10 Ex. 274 (Court of Exchequer, 1875), and contrast with the above argument the remark of Cleasby, B., that "the delivering of goods contracted for on board a ship when a bill of lading is taken is not a delivery to the buyer, but to the captain as bailee to deliver to the person indicated by the bill of lading."

JOHN F. COMSTOCK & CO. *v.* AFFOELTER

MISSOURI SUPREME COURT, 1872

[50 *Missouri Reports*, 411]

BLISS, Judge, delivered the opinion of the court.

This suit was for the price of a bill of goods alleged to have been sold and delivered to defendant, and the only controversy is in regard to the delivery. The plaintiff's salesman and traveling agent testified that he called upon defendant at Carrollton and sold the goods; that the understanding was that they were to be shipped so that they would be received in less time than by river, and that they were shipped at once by the Merchants' Union Express Company. He also spoke of having sold another bill of goods which was paid for, and which had been shipped by the river. The defendant testified that the agreement was to deliver the goods to him at Carrollton within ten days, and that he never received them or heard from them. This was the substance of all the testimony. There was no evidence of any direction in regard to the manner of shipment, or that said express company was a common carrier, or the usual carrier between St. Louis and Carrollton, or that goods were ever shipped by it to that place, or that any notice was given defendant of the shipment.

The plaintiff asked two instructions, which were refused, one of which was to the effect that if the goods were sold at the prices charged, to be shipped to defendant, and were actually shipped by the company named, he is responsible although they were not received; and the other was the same, only that in the latter notice of the shipment was supposed.

When goods are ordered and no specific instructions are given in regard to the shipment, a delivery, with proper directions, to the usual carrier, for the purchaser, is held to be a constructive delivery to him; and the goods become at once his, subject only to the right of stoppage *in transitu*. The purchase with general directions to ship, would authorize a shipment in the usual way, and the carrier would become the agent of the purchaser. (2 Kent, 499 and cases cited; 2 Hilliard Sales, 118, 123.) There are authorities to the effect that the purchaser must designate the carrier in order to make him his agent; but when there is a regular carrier, as a railroad running between the two places, it is believed that a general order would imply an order to send in the usual way, unless another mode is pointed out.

But in the case at bar it does not appear that the express company was the usual carrier, or even a carrier at all, only as might be inferred by its name; nor were any facts shown that would justify a shipment by it. It is not enough for the vendor to forward the goods sold by any person or persons, but they must be forwarded through the usual channels, and channels supposed to be in contemplation of the purchaser.

I think the instructions were properly refused, and that the judgment should be affirmed. The other judges concur.

Note also T. W. RANSON, LTD. *v.* MANUFACTURE D'ENGRAIS, 13 Ll. L. L. R. 205 (King's Bench Division, 1922), where there was a contract calling for the delivery of several thousand tons of basic slag. The contract contained no reference to the mode of delivery. In view of a finding that basic slag shipments usually were made by steamer, it was held that shipment by a sailing vessel did not meet the requirements of the contract. "It seems to me," said Greer, J., "that I must follow what the umpire has found, viz., that the usual thing in this trade is to ship by steamship. When the parties contract without specifying what kind of a vessel they desire the goods to be shipped upon, . . . it seems to me that both of them expect . . . that the ship shall be the usual class of ship that carries these goods, and it is not a sufficient compliance with the contract to ship the goods on a sailing vessel and to say that sometimes it has been known in the trade that such goods have been carried by a sailing vessel."

MILLER *v.* HARVEY

NEW YORK COURT OF APPEALS, 1917

[221 *New York Reports*, 54]

Appeal, by permission, from a judgment of the Appellate Division of the Supreme Court in the first judicial department, entered November 20, 1914, which affirmed a determination of the Appellate Term reversing a judgment of the Municipal Court of the city of New York in favor of plaintiff and directing a dismissal of the complaint.

The nature of the action and the facts, so far as material, are stated in the opinion.

CARDOZO, J. The plaintiff sold to the defendant in the city of New York automobile tires which were to be sent by express to Allenhurst, New Jersey. The price, $95.43, was paid by the defendant in advance. The seller intrusted the tires to an express company without declaring their value. The waybill states that the value was asked and not given. By the contract of carriage the liability of the carrier was limited to $50, unless a greater value was "declared and paid for or agreed to be paid for at the time of shipment." The tires were lost in transit. The defendant notified the plaintiff of the loss and requested a duplicate shipment, which was made. The question to be determined is whether payment must be made again.

The general rule is that delivery to a carrier is delivery to the buyer (Sales of Goods Act, § 127, subd. 1, Pers. Prop. Law, as amended by L. 1911, ch. 571; Cons. Laws, ch. 41). But the rule has its exceptions (Sales of Goods Act, § 100, subd. 5; § 127, subds. 2 and 3). Only one of them will be considered. By section 127, subd. 2, of the Sales of Goods Act it is provided:

"Unless otherwise authorized by the buyer, the seller must make such contract with the carrier on behalf of the buyer as may be reasonable, having regard to the nature of the goods and the other circumstances of the case. If the seller omit so to do, and the goods are lost or damaged in course of transit, the buyer may decline to treat the delivery to the carrier as a delivery to himself, or may hold the seller responsible in damages."

The statute is declaratory of the rule at common law. The seller must not sacrifice the buyer's right to claim indemnity from the carrier. That rule was declared more than a century ago in *Clarke* v. *Hutchins* (14 East, 475). In that case the carrier gave notice that it would not be answerable for any packages above £5 without special entry of value. The seller omitted the entry and was held to have assumed the risk. A more modern instance is a recent decision of the Supreme Court of the United States (*Reid* v. *Fargo*, 241 U. S. 544). An agent delivered an automobile to a carrier and accepted a bill of lading by which liability was limited to $100. The acceptance of such a limitation was held to be a breach of duty. There are other cases of like tenor (*Buckman* v. *Levi*, 3 Camp. 414; *Stafford & Bro.* v. *Walter & Skelton*, 67 Ill. 83; *Lewis* v. *Imhof*, 138 Mo. App. 370; *Gordon* v. *Ward*, 16 Mich. 360). To the same effect are the leading text books (Williston on Sales, §§ 278, 595; Benjamin on Sales [5th ed.], p. 739; 2 Mechem on Sales, 1183; Burdick on Sales, § 694).

Tested by these principles, the plaintiff's case must fail. He limited the carrier's liability to $50. He sacrificed the defendant's right of indemnity to the extent of almost one-half of the value of the shipment. He did this when full indemnity could have been procured by an additional payment of ten cents. That was not a reasonable protection of the interests of his principal. The plaintiff's argument, if sound, would require us to hold that the acceptance of a like limitation would be reasonable if the value had been $1,000. Precedent and reason forbid that conclusion. The seller who puts the buyer at the mercy of the carrier must procure the buyer's approval or assume the risk himself.

Cases such as *Nelson* v. *Hudson River R. R. Co.* (48 N. Y. 498), *Shelton* v. *Merchants' Dispatch Transp. Co.* (59 N. Y. 258), and *Waldron* v. *Fargo* (170 N. Y. 130), cited by the plaintiff, are beside the mark. They deal with controversies between the owner and the carrier. They hold that the principal is not at liberty to repudiate as against the carrier the terms accepted by the agent. They have no bearing upon the measure of diligence owing from the agent to the principal (*Reid* v. *Fargo*, *supra*). It is significant that whenever the plaintiff made shipments C. O. D., he declared the value to the carrier. His duty was to safeguard the defendant's interests as sedulously as his own.

The judgment should be affirmed with costs.

HISCOCK, Ch. J., CHASE, COLLIN, CUDDEBACK and HOGAN, JJ., concur; MCLAUGHLIN, J., not sitting.

Judgment affirmed.

Compare THE SOUTHERN NURSERY CO. *v.* THE WINFIED NURSERY CO., 89 Kansas 522 (Supreme Court, 1913). Burch, J., there said: "The facts are undisputed. In order to obtain a lower freight rate, under a classification permitting it, the plaintiff agreed with the carrier on a valuation of the shipment at three cents per pound, and the bill of lading restricted the liability of the carrier accordingly. At three cents per pound the value of the shipment was $480. Its actual value was $1784. The bill of lading acknowledged notice that the property would be received and transported without limitation as to value under a different classification but at a higher freight rate. It is the custom, understood and agreed upon by nurserymen, for all shipments of nursery stock to be made under a valuation of three cents per pound, for the purpose of saving freight charges, unless positive instruction be given to the contrary. No such instruction having been given to the plaintiff, the goods were billed out according to the custom.

"The defendant requested the court to instruct the jury that the carrier was the seller's agent to make delivery unless the seller took a shipping contract which adequately protected the buyer in case the goods were injured or lost in transit. The instruction was refused and the jury were advised that, if the shipment was made in the ordinary way at the usual rate without instruction from the defendant to do otherwise, the carrier was the agent of the defendant. The defendant contends that a contract to ship at a gross undervaluation to procure the benefit of a lower freight rate, although under a classification permitting it, is contrary to law and public policy, and consequently that a custom among nurserymen to ship under such contracts can not be recognized. . . .

"The seller is authorized, in the absence of special instructions, to ship according to the usual and ordinary method and that he discharges his duty to the buyer when he does so. There is no doubt that such is the law.

"In this case there is no dispute that nursery stock is to be shipped at a valuation of three cents per pound in order to obtain a lower freight rate, under a classification permitting it, unless positive instructions to the contrary are given. The seller's authority, therefore, extends no further than to take a bill of lading of the kind usual to such shipments, if contracts of that character may lawfully be made. . . .

"The result is that the instruction requested was properly refused and the instruction given correctly stated the law."

TAYLOR WHEELHOUSE *v.* PARR

MASSACHUSETTS SUPREME JUDICIAL COURT, 1886

[141 *Massachusetts Reports*, 593]

Contract, upon an account annexed, for goods sold and delivered. The case was submitted to the Superior Court, and, after judgment for the plaintiff, to this court, on appeal, upon agreed facts, in substance as follows:

The plaintiff is a tanner, currier, and leather merchant, having his place of business at Brighouse, England. The defendant is a manufacturer of leather belting in Lowell, in this Commonwealth.

On November 3, 1882, the defendant sent to the plaintiff, by mail, an order for leather goods, with instructions to "ship to care of D. & C. McIver, shipping merchants, Liverpool, as soon as possible, for their next steamer to Boston direct." This order was filled by the plaintiff, and the goods were shipped by the Cunard line by D. & C. McIver, and were duly received by the defendant. On December 16, 1882, the defendant wrote to the plaintiff, acknowledging the receipt of said goods, enclosing sight draft in payment for the same, and ordering the goods described in the plaintiff's declaration, saying: "As regards the shipping of this leather just received, you have done everything satisfactory. Ship this order in like manner."

D. & C. McIver, referred to in the shipping instructions, were at that time shipping merchants and part or sole owners and agents of the Cunard line of steamers.

The goods were properly prepared for shipment, and sent to D. & C. McIver in accordance with the defendant's instructions. D. & C. McIver received them at Liverpool on or about February 1, 1883, and on that day wrote the plaintiff as follows: "The five bales of leather have arrived. Are we to keep them for our steamer sailing 14th inst., or ship by the Glamorgan, which is a very slow steamer sailing 7th inst., and will not, we think, arrive out before our steamer?"

The Glamorgan was a steamer belonging to the Warren line, for which D. & C. McIver were not the agents, and of which steamer they were not the owners.

The plaintiff replied to said letter as follows: "Send the bales by the steamer which will arrive first."

Thereupon, without further instructions of any kind, D. & C. McIver caused the goods to be shipped by the Glamorgan, which foundered in mid-ocean, and the goods were lost. There was no insurance on them.

If, upon these facts, the plaintiff could recover, judgment was to be entered for the amount claimed; otherwise, for the defendant.

DEVENS, J. When goods ordered and contracted for are not directly delivered to the purchaser, but are to be sent to him by the vendor, and the vendor delivers them to the carrier, to be transported in the mode agreed on by the parties or directed by the purchaser, or, when no agreement is made or direction given, to be transported in the usual mode; or when the purchaser, being informed of the mode of transportation, assents to it; or when there have been previous sales of other goods, to the transportation of which in a similar manner the purchaser has not objected, — the goods, when delivered to the carrier, are at the risk of the purchaser, and the property is deemed to be vested in him, subject to the vendor's right of stoppage *in transitu*. This proposition assumes that proper directions and information are given to the carrier as to forwarding the goods.

The defendant had made a purchase of leather in November, previously to the purchase of that the price of which is in controversy, under a direction to the plaintiff to "ship to care of D. & C. McIver, shipping merchants, Liverpool, as soon as possible, for their next steamer to Boston direct." This shipment was made as ordered; and, on December 16, 1884, the defendant sent a further order, saying: "As regards the shipping of the leather just received, you have done everything satisfactory. Ship this order in like manner."

The directions by which the plaintiff was to be controlled must be interpreted as requiring him to forward the goods to D. & C. McIver, to be transported by them by the Cunard line, of which they were managers and agents. The words "their next steamer" could not have meant any steamer which would accept freight from D. & C. McIver. Cases may be readily imagined where these words would be of the highest importance, as if the defendant had an open policy of insurance protecting his goods which might be sent by the Cunard line. It might also be true that the defendant would not deem a policy of insurance necessary when goods were sent by a well-established passenger line, where greater precautions might probably be taken for safety, which he would deem necessary when they were sent by a purely freighting steamer. The goods were actually forwarded to D. & C. McIver, with instructions in conformity with the directions of the defendant; and, had the matter ended there, so far as any directions to D. & C. McIver is concerned, the plaintiff would be entitled to treat them as delivered to the defendant, and to require him to pay the purchase money. If, on the other hand, while the goods were yet in the hands of the carrier, and before transportation of them had commenced, the plaintiff changed the directions given to him by the defendant, or authorized the carrier to transport them in a different mode from that directed by the defendant, and loss has thereby occurred, he cannot contend that they were delivered to the defendant by him. By continuing to exercise dominion over them, and by giving a new direction impliedly withdrawing the directions previously given, he cannot be allowed to assert that he had made a complete delivery by his original act, if a loss has occurred by reason of that which he has subsequently done or directed. The change in the directions given relates back to and qualifies the original delivery.

The plaintiff, in answer to a letter from D. & C. McIver, after the goods had reached them, inquiring whether they were to keep the goods "for our steamer 14th inst., or ship by the Glamorgan," ordered them to be shipped by the steamer arriving out first, presumably the steamer which D. & C. McIver believed would be the first to arrive. The Glamorgan was not a steamer of any line of which D. & C. McIver were owners or agents, and in no way answers the description of "their steamer" as applied to D. & C. McIver. By neglecting to limit the authority of D. & C. McIver to send by a steamer which could be thus described, and by directing them to send by the steamer which would first arrive, the plaintiff had failed to comply with the orders of the defendant as to the shipment of goods, and, if correct directions had originally been given, had withdrawn them and substituted others. When, therefore, exercising the authority thus given by the plaintiff, D. & C. McIver send by the Glamorgan, as being in their judgment the steamer likely to arrive first, and a loss occurs, it should not be borne by the defendant, whose directions have not been followed.

Judgment for the defendant.

Similarly in The Ohio Confection Company *v.* The Eimon Mercantile Company, 154 Minnesota 420 (Supreme Court, 1923), where a contract for the sale of confectionery contained the provision "How Ship: Boat," but where the seller shipped instead by rail. It was held that this was not a delivery to the buyer, the Court, after quoting § 46 of the Sales Act, saying: "The inference is that, if the buyer designates a carrier to whom the goods are to be delivered for transportation, a delivery to another carrier will not be regarded as delivery to the buyer."

Note also Hauptman *v.* Miller, 157 New York Supplement, 1104 (Supreme Court, Appellate Term, 1916), where a contract for the sale of goods contemplated delivery at the buyer's place of business, and where it was held accordingly that delivery to a carrier did not constitute delivery to the buyer, even though the seller had been in the habit of using the same carrier in sending goods to the buyer.

WIMBLE, SONS & CO. *v.* ROSENBERG & SONS

Court of Appeal, 1913

[*Law Reports*, [1913] 3 *King's Bench*, 743]

Appeal from the judgment of Bailhache J.

By a contract dated June 27, 1912, the plaintiffs, as brokers for De Winter, a foreign principal at Antwerp, sold to the defendants 200 bags of rice "f.o.b. Antwerp to be shipped as required by buyers, cash against bills of lading." It was agreed between the parties that the plaintiffs should be treated as being the actual sellers. On August 9 the defendants sent the plaintiffs instructions to ship the rice to Odessa and to pay freight on their account, leaving it to the plaintiffs to select the ship. The printed form of shipping instructions which the defendants ordinarily used contained a request to be informed by the sellers of the name of the ship by which it was proposed to ship the goods and of the date of proposed shipment, but they happened to have temporarily exhausted their supply of those forms and sent their instructions in writing, omitting the customary request above mentioned. The plaintiffs accordingly on the same date sent instructions to De Winter to ship the rice per first steamer to Odessa on account of the defendants and to pay the freight. The rice was shipped on board the steamship *Egyptian* on Saturday, August 24. The ship sailed on Sunday, August 25, and early on the following morning she stranded and became a total loss. The defendants did not receive from the plaintiffs any information of the shipment on the *Egyptian* until August 29, when the plaintiffs presented the bills of lading for payment. The defendants had not insured the rice as it was their practice not to insure until after the receipt of notice of the particular ship on which the goods were loaded. They accordingly refused to pay the price on the ground that the plaintiffs had failed to comply with the provisions of s. 32, sub-s. 3, of the Sale of Goods Act, 1893 (56 & 57 Vict. c. 71, s. 32), and that the rice was consequently at the time of the loss at the plaintiffs' risk. The action was brought to recover the price of the rice and the amount of the freight paid by the plaintiffs on the defendants' account.

The action was tried before Bailhache J. without a jury, and the learned judge held that sub-s. 3 of s. 32 does not apply to a contract for the sale of goods f.o.b. ([1913] 1 K. B. 279).

The defendants appealed.

VAUGHAN WILLIAMS L.J. This is an appeal from the judgment of Bailhache J. sitting without a jury. The case in substance turns on the construction of s. 32 of the Sale of Goods Act, 1893, and in particular of sub-s. 3 of that section. It is to be remembered, I think, throughout the interpretation of this Act that it is a codifying Act and subject, therefore, to the provisions of the Interpretation Act, 1889, and subject also to the canon of construction when dealing with a codifying Act laid down by Lord Herschell, in the House of Lords, in *Bank of England* v. *Vagliano* ([1891] A. C. 107, 144), a case on the Bills of Exchange Act, 1882, which was also a codifying Act: "The proper course is in the first instance to examine the language of the statute and to ask what is its natural meaning, uninfluenced by any considerations derived from the previous state of the law, and not to start with inquiring how the law previously stood, and then, assuming that it was probably intended to leave it unaltered, to see if the words of the enactment will bear an interpretation in conformity with this view." . . .

The defence consists of two parts, in one of which the defendants set up the negligence of the plaintiffs as their agents — that has been abandoned; the other relies upon sub-s. 3 of s. 32 of the Sale of Goods Act, and in effect says that by reason of the notice enabling the defendants as buyers to insure not having been given, the sea transmission was at the risk of the sellers.

An argument before us was on the basis that sub-s. 3 of s. 32 had and could have no application to a contract of sale f.o.b. It was argued also that the buyers did not require a notice, because they might have insured these goods by "a general cover contract" or by a "ship or ships" contract, and the Scottish authority of *Fleet* v. *Morrison* (16 D. 1122) was disposed of on the ground that, although it is mentioned in the argument, the judges of the Scottish Court had not the question of insurance by "cover" or "ship or ships" policies present to their minds, and it is agreed by counsel on both sides that there is no Scottish decision on the point dealing with the case of a contract f.o.b. At the conclusion of Mr. Leck's argument on behalf of the plaintiffs, Mr. Theobald Mathew, his junior, put forward a new point, that notice already had been given, enabling the buyers to insure, for that the contract of purchase itself was notice.

I will now read sub-ss. 1, 2, and 3 of s. 32 of the Sale of Goods Act. [The Lord Justice read the whole section.] I think it is agreed that sub-s. 3, and indeed the whole of s. 32, includes agreements (if any) outside the contract, and includes also the proof of "the circumstances in which it is usual to insure," and I think includes cases where it has been usual *inter partes* to insure although the agreement of sale itself contains no reference to insurance: see *Fleet* v. *Morrison* (*ibid.* at p. 1124).

This case turns to my mind on construction. No facts are in dispute. I am of opinion that sub-s. 3 of s. 32 of the Sale of Goods Act covers an f.o.b. contract. To say generally that sub-s. 3 does not cover an f.o.b. contract seems to me to be a conspicuous illustration of departure from Lord Herschell's canon of construction which I have already quoted. The natural meaning of the words of sub-s. 3 does not exclude an f.o.b. contract. The real ground for the suggested exclusion is that the sub-section, construed according to its natural meaning, is hard to reconcile with some of the previous law laid down in the cases relating to the carriage of goods under an f.o.b. contract, and that it is highly improbable that the Legislature intended to alter or modify law which is the result of a series of decisions laid down by great commercial lawyers.

Mr. Leck, in his excellent argument on behalf of the plaintiffs, to my mind was evidently pressed by a strong desire to avoid a breach of Lord Herschell's canon of construction of codifying statutes and argued that sub-s. 3, read in the light of sub-s. 1, has no application to a case where, in pursuance of a contract of sale, the seller is "authorized or required" to send goods to the buyer, and says that under an f.o.b. contract the seller is never authorized nor required to send the goods to the buyer, but completely performs his duty when he puts the goods on board the steamer. Bailhache J. based his judgment on this contention of Mr. Leck and, as I understand his judgment, in effect held that an f.o.b. contract is excluded unless it includes some words whereby the vendor undertook to send the goods by some ship selected by himself, and that in this case the shipping instructions ought not to be regarded as part of the contract, in which case Bailhache J. thought sub-s. 3 would have applied.

I construe the word "send," both in sub-s. 1 and in sub-s. 3, in the sense of "forward" or "despatch," and in my opinion the word "send" covers every obligation of the seller in reference to effecting or securing the arrival of the goods the subject of sale at the destination intended. It is not true in fact to say that the purchased goods are being sent to the ship on which they are placed for the purpose of delivery at the port of destination. The purchased goods are not the less being sent to the buyer at the port of destination because delivery f.o.b. is *prima facie* delivery to the buyer, or because the property has passed to the buyer. Sub-s. 3, in my opinion, casts a duty on the seller forwarding the goods to the buyer by a route involving sea transit, under circumstances in which it is usual to insure, to give such notice as may enable the buyer (to whom be it observed the property in the purchased goods has passed), to insure them during their sea transit. The penalty for not performing this duty is that goods, though the goods of the buyer, shall be at the risk of the seller during such sea transit. Moreover the same result is arrived at if the words "where goods are sent by the seller to the buyer," at the beginning of sub-s. 3, are construed as describing the whole transaction.

I have already said that I cannot agree with the argument of Mr. Theobald Mathew that the contract of sale itself was notice within the meaning of sub-s. 3, and I have arrived at this conclusion not only on the ground that the contract did not afford sufficient information to enable the buyer to insure the purchased goods during their sea transit, but also on the ground that knowledge of the buyer, actual, inferred, or assumed, which would enable the buyer to insure, does not dispense with the statutory obligation of the seller, where the route involves sea transit under circumstances in which it is usual to insure, to give such notice to the buyer as may enable him to insure the goods during their sea transit. The obligation, unless dispensed with by the agreement, — and in this case there was no dispensing agreement — on the seller is to give such notice, with such details, to the buyer as may be necessary to effect insurance of the goods during sea transit. It is to my mind impossible to construe the words as meaning that the obligation to insure does not arise in case the buyer happens to have sufficient information from some other source than the statutory notice to enable him to insure the goods.

I have only to add that, whichever of the suggested constructions relieving the seller from obligation to give the statutory notice in the case of an f.o.b. contract is adopted, the practical utility and application of sub-s. 3 of s. 32 are reduced to nil.

I think this appeal should be allowed and judgment given for the defendants.

[Buckley, L. J., in holding that the appeal should be dismissed, agreed with Vaughan Williams, L. J., that "send" was to be taken in the sense of "despatch," and was also of the opinion that the sub-section was applicable to f.o.b. contracts. He held further, however, that the seller's obligation to give notice was satisfied, since the buyer was aware of the goods, the port of shipment, and the port of discharge, the name of the ship having been waived. Without reference to these details moreover, he was of the opinion that the contract itself was sufficient notice, since it gave the buyer information on all the necessary points except those to be determined by himself. Hamilton, L. J., in holding that the appeal should be dismissed, argued that the sub-section did not apply to f.o.b. contracts, (1) because in an f.o.b. contract the goods are delivered by the seller to the buyer to be "sent" to their destination by the buyer himself; and (2) because an f.o.b. contract is in effect an agreement "that only certain obligations are incumbent on the seller, and giving notice is not one of them."]

LAW & BONAR, LTD. *v.* BRITISH AMERICAN TOBACCO CO., LTD.

KING'S BENCH DIVISION, 1916

[*Law Reports*, [1916] 2 *King's Bench*, 605]

Action tried by Rowlatt J. as a commercial cause.

By a contract made between the plaintiffs and the defendants on May 6 and 7, 1914, the defendants bought from the plaintiffs a quantity of Calcutta hessian at a price c.i.f. Smyrna to be shipped from Calcutta in time to arrive at Smyrna by September, 1914. The defendants stipulated by a clause in the contract that the goods were to be at the plaintiffs' risk until actual delivery to the defendants. In fulfillment of the contract the goods were shipped by the plaintiffs' correspondents in Calcutta on the British steamship *City of Winchester*, the bill of lading being dated July 20, 1914. The goods were insured by a policy containing the f. c. and s. clause. On August 4, 1914, war was declared between Great Britain and Germany, and on or about August 13, 1914, the *City of Winchester* was sunk by a German cruiser and the goods in question were lost. Neither the fact of the shipment of the goods on the *City of Winchester* nor the fact that that vessel was sunk on the date mentioned were known to the plaintiffs (whose business is in this country) till later. Meanwhile correspondence had passed between the plaintiffs and the defendants on the subject of the insurance of the goods. On July 31 the plaintiffs wrote to the defendants pointing out that war risk was not covered by the insurance under the contract, offering to negotiate such insurance for the defendants at the lowest current rates, and asking for instructions. On August 4 the defendants acknowledged the receipt of the plaintiffs' letter and asked to be advised as to the lowest rates obtainable for war risks, adding that they would give the matter their consideration and advise them accordingly. On August 5 the plaintiffs replied that it would be impossible to insure the goods, as in all probability they would be shipped by an Austrian Lloyd steamer, in which case war risk insurance would not be undertaken by English underwriters.

On August 8 the plaintiffs informed the defendants that they were still without definite advice from Calcutta as to the shipment of the goods, but stating that as the goods were for July shipment the defendants would be quite safe in assuming that they were now on their way, and that from their past experience of similar shipments the goods were almost certain to come forward by an Austrian Lloyd steamer. On August 21 the plaintiffs informed the defendants that they had now received advice from Calcutta that the goods had been shipped by the *City of Winchester*, adding that they gave this information in case the defendants desired to insure against war risk. On the afternoon of the same date the fact of the loss of the *City of Winchester* was reported in London. On August 24 the defendants wrote that as the *City of Winchester* had been sunk it was too late to effect an insurance on the goods and pointing out that the plaintiffs' Calcutta representatives ought to have cabled immediately the goods were shipped, mentioning the name of the steamer, date of sailing, &c. Further correspondence passed between the parties, and in the result the defendants refused to take up the shipping documents and pay for the goods.

The plaintiffs now sued to recover damages for breach of contract by the defendants in refusing to accept and pay for the goods. The defendants denied liability and counterclaimed damages. They alleged that by the letters which had passed between them the plaintiffs became the agents of the defendants to take steps to insure the goods against war risks and that in breach of their duty they had failed to do so; and, further, that it was the plaintiffs' duty to notify the defendants at the earliest possible moment of the name of the steamer by which the goods had been shipped and that in breach of that duty they had failed to do so.

Evidence was given that between August 4 (the date of the outbreak of the war) and August 21, 1914, cargo in British vessels could be insured against war risks.

ROWLATT J. Some points in this case, I think, are quite clear. In the first place, the tender of documents representing goods duly shipped in accordance with the contract and insured against marine risks as required by the contract was not vitiated by the fact that the goods had actually been lost. That is plain. Secondly, the printed clause at the end of the form used in this case stating that the goods are at seller's risk till actual delivery has no application to the present contract. The buyers paying c.i.f. terms were actually paying for the insurance against all contemplated risks from the moment of shipment. It seems to me that a term that, for a period after shipment, the goods were to be at the risk of the seller is repugnant to that, and the clause to that effect printed on the form used in this case is inapplicable to the transaction that actually was entered into.

The next question is whether s. 32, sub-s. 3, of the Sale of Goods Act, 1893, applies to this case. It clearly does not apply to a c.i.f. contract in times when no one contemplates war, and when, therefore, war is not being usually insured against. It does not apply because the contract c.i.f. provides for all the insurance that is contemplated or usual and the seller is to effect it. That was the nature of this contract when made. It dealt exhaustively and expressly with all the insurance that was in view. But now it is said that, on war becoming imminent, another form of insurance emerged and the contract ceased to be one which dealt exhaustively with the question of insurance and a new obligation arose for the seller. I cannot agree. This sub-section annexes a term to the contract, and the question whether it is applicable or not falls to be decided as at the time when the contract is made. I say nothing as to whether the sub-section could apply to a contract c.i.f. made at a time when insurances other than those to be provided by the seller — e.g. against war risks — are usual. That point does not arise. In this case I do not think there is any real evidence that it was usual to insure against war risks at any material time.

Even the buyers themselves in their letter of August 4, referring to the question of insurance against war risks, wrote that, if they were advised of the lowest rates, they would give the matter their consideration. I am not at all certain that they themselves had made up their minds whether they would insure against war risks or not. [His Lordship then dealt with the contention that there was an employment of the plaintiffs by the defendants to effect an insurance against war risks and held that there was no evidence of such an employment.]

In the result, the plaintiffs are entitled to judgment upon the claim and upon the counter-claim.

Judgment for plaintiffs.

ALLEN *v.* BAKER

OREGON SUPREME COURT, 1923

[109 *Oregon Reports*, 443]

RAND, J. — This is an action to recover damages for breach of contract arising from an alleged refusal of the defendant to perform a contract to purchase from plaintiffs certain specific property. The contract was in writing, and by its terms the plaintiffs undertook to sell and deliver to the defendant for a lump sum certain articles which were listed in an inventory prepared by them, and also the furniture, fixtures and equipment, together with the leasehold and goodwill of a business which the plaintiffs were then conducting in Portland, Oregon. . . . Among the articles listed in the inventory and so contracted to be sold and delivered by plaintiffs were 245 service batteries that were appraised as of the value of $15 each, but at the time the plaintiffs were required to make delivery thereof under the contract, the plaintiffs had, in their place of business, and tendered only 141 of these batteries. The contract also provided that in the event the defendant, within ten days after the date of the contract, should fail to take over and pay the sum stipulated to be paid for all of said property, he should forfeit to the plaintiffs the sum of $5,000, which sum, it was stipulated, should be considered as liquidated damages for defendant's failure to perform. This action was brought to recover that sum.

The cause was tried to the court without the intervention of a jury, and from the testimony the court found that the plaintiffs had undertaken to sell and deliver to the defendant, among other things, 245 storage batteries, and had tendered delivery of only 141 thereof, and that, as to the other 104 batteries, plaintiffs had, as a part of their office records, 42 unsigned cards showing that 42 of these missing batteries were in the hands of third parties, customers of the plaintiffs, and that there was no record showing the persons in possession of the remainder, although plaintiffs claimed that these also were in the possession of their customers. The court also found that the plaintiffs had wholly failed to secure or tender to the defendant any acknowledgment, by any of the different bailees in possession of any of the 104 missing batteries, stating that they, or either of them, held said batteries, or any thereof, on behalf of the defendant. The court also found that the defendant did not repudiate or refuse to perform the contract upon his part, and, based upon these findings, the court ruled, as a matter of law, that the plaintiffs, having failed to perform a substantial part of their contract, were not entitled to recover, and gave judgment accordingly. The correctness of this ruling is the only question for determination here.

It appears from the testimony that these missing batteries had not been sold, but were in the hands of third parties, to whom they had been loaned or rented by plaintiffs. These batteries therefore did not come within that provision of the contract which required the plaintiffs to pay for articles sold after the contract date and before the consummation of the sale. The evidence also discloses that the plaintiffs demanded of the defendant the payment of the inventoried price of $15 for each of the missing batteries, and refused to perform the contract upon their part unless the defendant would pay for all of the missing batteries. . . .

In order for the plaintiffs to consummate the sale in accordance with the terms of the contract, it was necessary for them to deliver to the defendant the 245 batteries in question. As 104 of these batteries were in the possession of third parties, who were bailees of the plaintiffs, the plaintiffs could not fulfill their obligation to deliver them without securing from each of these bailees an acknowledgment that he was holding the same on behalf of the defendant. Not having secured the acknowledgment required by statute, the plaintiffs themselves were in default. The result of this was that the plaintiffs, being obligated to deliver 245 batteries, and having tendered delivery of a lesser number, the defendant, under the statute, was authorized to reject the tendered delivery as a noncompliance with the contract. . . .

The judgment is affirmed.

Affirmed.

McBride, C. J., and Burnett and Harris, JJ., concur.

Note also Poulton and Son *v.* Anglo-American Oil Company, 27 T. L. R. 216 (Court of Appeal, 1911), where plaintiffs bought certain boilers from a paper company and resold them, the boilers remaining in possession of the paper company. It was held that the mere fact that plaintiffs notified the paper company of the resale did not preclude plaintiffs from setting up their right of lien as unpaid sellers, as the notification could not be regarded as anything in the nature of a delivery order.

Compare Carter *v.* Willard, 19 Pickering 1 (Massachusetts Supreme Judicial Court, 1837), where there was a sale of furniture and other goods on property being operated by a third person under an agreement with the seller. This third person had written notice of the sale from the buyer, but neither consented nor refused to hold the goods for the buyer, merely continuing in possession as before. The goods subsequently were attached by creditors of the seller, and in a tort action by the buyer against the sheriff who executed the attachment, judgment was given for the plaintiff. The Court said *inter alia*: "Where the goods are in the hands of a custodier or third party, to be kept for the use of the vendor, a notice to such keeper by the parties, of the sale, is held to be a valid constructive delivery. . . . So, in the case at bar, Damon's assent to the sale was not necessary. He had no legal right to prevent the vendor from transferring the right which he had to the goods. . . . If this were otherwise, it would enable one man to exercise a power which he does not possess, over the property of another, to whom the right of disposal belongs. It would fetter and restrain the owner in regard to the beneficial use and appropriation of his property, and be greatly prejudicial to individuals as well as to the community."

J. A. KIRSCH & CO., INC. *v.* ROULSTON, BECKERT & CO., INC.

NEW YORK SUPREME COURT, APPELLATE TERM, 1919

[178 *New York Supplement*, 246]

GUY, J. This is an action for goods sold and delivered, and defendant appeals from a judgment entered upon a verdict directed for plaintiff.

Defendant gave a written order, dated February 14, 1919 (erroneously stated in the record as March 14, 1919), for 300 cases of evaporated milk, Holly brand, to be shipped at once "ex warehouse." On February 17 defendant sent its truckman to plaintiff for the merchandise. The truckman testified that plaintiff's representative, Miss Lobel, gave him an order for 124 cases; that he returned the order to Miss Lobel, whereupon she gave him another order on the Beach street warehouse; that upon presentation of the order at the Beach street warehouse the clerk brought down milk which was not the Holly brand, and on the truckman's refusal to take it the clerk gave him back the order; that the truckman then went back to plaintiff's place of business, gave the last order, which was for Artic brand milk, to Miss Lobel, and after waiting some time he finally got two orders on the York Storage & Warehouse Company, one for the delivery to defendant of 150 cases of milk, and the other for 150 cases of Holly milk. The truckman further testified that at about 4 o'clock in the same afternoon he called with his truck at the York warehouse and presented the orders, but was told he was too late; that there were no other trucks at the warehouse then, and men who looked like workmen were "standing around there"; and that on other occasions he received merchandise from the same warehouse as late as 4:30. At no time afterward did defendant send for the merchandise. On February 19 it returned the two orders to the brokers who made the sale, for the reason, as stated in the letter inclosing the orders, that plaintiff was willing to sell the same brand of milk to defendant through a different broker at 70 cents a case less than the contract price. On or about March 21 the brokers returned the orders to the plaintiff, with a copy of the letter received by them from defendant.

Upon the trial plaintiff produced a receipt from the York Storage & Warehouse Company, dated February 17, 1919, for the merchandise in question, and showed that the milk had not been taken from the warehouse. The warehouse receipt apparently was never delivered to the defendant. At the close of the case, upon defendant's motion to dismiss and plaintiff's motion for the direction of a verdict, the court directed a verdict for the plaintiff, holding that the delivery to and acceptance by the defendant of plaintiff's written orders on the warehouseman was sufficient to place the merchandise in the power of the defendant, and under the authorities delivery was thus established.

In the cases cited by the trial judge in his memorandum there are statements which justify the conclusion reached. For instance, in *Gross* v. *Ajello*, 132 App. Div. 25, at page 27, 116 N. Y. Supp. at page 382, the court says that —

"The delivery of the order on the warehouse for the peas would have justified a recovery of the purchase price" — citing *Salmon* v. *Brandmeier*, 104 App. Div. 69, 93 N. Y. Supp. 273, and *Horst* v. *Montauk Brewing Co.*, 118 App. Div. 300, 103 N. Y. Supp. 381.

In the Salmon Case the court said (104 App. Div. 69, 93 N. Y. Supp. 273):

"Where manual delivery of goods is inconvenient on account of their bulk it is unnecessary, placing the goods in the power of the vendee is sufficient. An actual delivery is not required. A symbolic delivery suffices, and delivery of an order on the warehouseman may be enough." *Dunham* v. *Pettee*, 8 N. Y. 508.

And the court in the Horst Case restates the rule as laid down in the Salmon Case. In the Horst Case, however, there was the additional fact of the vendor sending to the vendee warehouse receipts for the merchandise claimed to have been delivered to the defendant.

An examination of the authority relied upon by the court in the Salmon Case (*Dunham* v. *Pettee*, *supra*) for the doctrine herein stated does not justify the conclusion that the mere giving of a delivery order upon a warehouseman constitutes a delivery of the goods, so as to warrant a recovery for goods sold and delivered. The Dunham Case was not an action for goods sold and delivered. There plaintiffs sold to defendants a quantity of iron stored in public store, upon which the sum of $750 was paid by the buyers; the balance of the purchase price being payable on delivery within 60 days from the date of the contract. The complaint alleged that the plaintiffs were ready and willing to deliver the iron to the defendants and receive the balance of the price therefor, and in all respects to comply with the terms of the contract on their part, and that they within the 60 days mentioned in the contract offered and tendered to defendants the iron, but that the latter were not ready and willing to receive it and pay the balance of the price, and wholly refused to do so. In their answer defendants denied that plaintiffs were ready and willing to comply with the terms of the contract, or that they offered and tendered the iron to the defendants. It appears from the report of the case that a custom house permit addressed to the storekeeper was tendered to the defendants, and that after defendants' alleged default it was agreed between plaintiffs and defendants that the former might dispose of the merchandise to a third party upon a sale which had been agreed upon between the defendants and such party at a fixed price per ton, without prejudice to plaintiffs' claim for the difference between that price and the price fixed in the contract between plaintiffs and defendants, or to defendants' claim for a restoration of the $750 paid. The jury found a verdict for the plaintiffs for the difference between the contract price and the price realized on the resale. The appellate court held that the plaintiffs were excused from doing more than was actually done toward performance; that it was shown that the storekeeper would have delivered the iron without payment of the storage due previous to the date of the contract; that it was not necessary to bring the iron to the defendants' office and tender it there; and that the offer to deliver was made in good faith and in substantial compliance with the contract.

It is clear, therefore, that the Dunham Case is not authority for the proposition that in this case there was a delivery of the merchandise in question. Further, the statute (Personal Property Law [Consol. Laws, c. 41] § 124, subd. 3) provides:

"Where the goods at the time of sale are in the possession of a third person, the seller has not fulfilled his obligation to deliver to the buyer unless and until such third person acknowledges to the buyer that he holds the goods on the buyer's behalf; but as against all others than the seller the buyer shall be regarded as having received delivery from the time when such third person first has notice of the sale. Nothing in this section, however, shall affect the operation of the issue or transfer of any document of title to goods."

Here there was no acknowledgment on the part of the warehouseman that he held the goods on defendants' behalf; and it is evident that the delivery orders, the warehouse receipt having been retained by the seller, were not documents of title within the meaning of the act. It is notable, too, that while one order was for 150 cases of Holly brand milk, the other order for the remaining 150 cases did not designate the brand of milk, and in view of the different attempts of the plaintiff to comply with its contract in February, 1917, this fact may be material, for unless the plaintiff could deliver the 300 cases of Holly brand milk defendant was not obligated to accept a partial delivery.

Judgment and order reversed, and new trial ordered, with costs to appellant to abide the event. All concur.

Delivery orders are used to a large extent to facilitate the apportionment among various consignees of bulk cargo shipped under a single bill of lading, and also in accomplishing the gradual release to the buyer of goods shipped under letters of credit.

Note therefore SOCIÉTÉ COMMERCIALE *c.* THIBOUMERY, 1925 Havre 1.255 (Commercial Court of Havre), where the holder of a bill of lading issued to the plaintiff a delivery order calling for 250 tons of wheat, and where it was held that the plaintiff acquired thereby no claim against the carrying vessel, the Court saying, "A delivery order issued by the holder of a bill of lading, so far as it has not been formally accepted by the ship so as to take the place of the bill of lading, creates no right against the ship."

Compare LLOYD TRIESTINO *c.* GIANNOTTI, 36 Diritto Marittimo, 261 (Court of Cassation, 1934), where the Court said: "The delivery order improperly so-called, that is to say one which is created without the visa of the master and without the corresponding surrender of the bill of lading, is itself indeed a document representing the goods, but unlike a proper delivery order which amounts to a novation of the bill of lading as a document representing the goods, it cannot claim a complete autonomy: it modifies the bill of lading in no degree, and represents the goods only so long as the bill of lading, of which it is merely an accessory, continues to exist."

THE TURNER–LOOKER COMPANY *v.* APRILE

NEW YORK SUPREME COURT, APPELLATE DIVISION, 1921

[195 *New York Appellate Division Reports*, 706]

Motion by the defendant, Antonio Aprile, for a new trial upon a case containing exceptions, ordered to be heard at the Appellate Division, Fourth Department, in the first instance after the direction of a verdict in favor of the plaintiff at the close of the case upon a trial before the court and a jury at the Livingston Trial Term in June, 1920.

HUBBS, J.: On the date of the sale involved in this case the plaintiff was a wholesale dealer in whisky at Cincinnati, O. The defendant was doing business in Rochester, N. Y. On May 8, 1918, the defendant wrote to the plaintiff asking for prices on eighty-proof whisky and on bond whisky. On May tenth the plaintiff telegraphed to the defendant as follows:

CINCINNATI, OHIO, May 10, 1918.

ANTONIO APRILE, 175 Jay St. cor. Kent, Rochester, N. Y.:

Letter received. Best price on Eighty proof six aught five. Can furnish you also fine Kentucky Whiskies Spring Sixteen or Seventeen at Three Ten per gallon in Bond. Spring Thirteen or fourteen at Three Dollars. These prices good today only. Wire us our expense your order. Market will advance again within twenty-four hours and prices will be withdrawn unless we hear from you today Charges Paid. THE TURNER–LOOKER CO.

On the same day the defendant replied by telegram as follows:

GENESEO, N. Y., May 10, 1918.

THE TURNER-LOOKER CO., Cincinnati, O.:

Telegram received. I will take ten Barrel Kentucky Whiskey Spring Thirteen at the price of Three Dollars in Bond per Gallon. ANTONIO APRILE.

On the next day the plaintiff wrote the defendant stating that it inclosed invoice covering ten barrels of spring thirteen Kentucky whisky at three dollars per gallon and stating that it would draw for the amount through the Lincoln National Bank. The defendant testified that he did not receive that letter. On the same day the plaintiff made a draft on the defendant for $1,466.97, and attached to the draft a bill for 503.77 gallons of whisky at $3 per gallon, amounting to $1,511.31, less $44.34, the amount due the warehouse for storage and local taxes, leaving a balance of $1,466.97, the amount of the draft. There were also attached certificates for ten barrels of Kentucky whisky, which certificates were properly indorsed. The certificates described the barrels so that they could be identified. The warehouse stamp number and the serial number of each barrel appeared on the certificates. The certificates were issued in accordance with the provisions of the United States Internal Revenue Law.

On May thirteenth the bank notified the defendant that it held the draft with warehouse receipts attached. The defendant returned the notice indorsed as follows: "Please return this draft back and oblige, A. Aprile." On May twenty-ninth the plaintiff wrote to the defendant demanding pay for the whisky, the defendant did not reply and this action was commenced.

The complaint alleges the agreement to purchase and sell ten barrels of whisky at $3 a gallon in bond and states that the net amount agreed to be paid for said whisky was $1,466.97. It alleges that the plaintiff, through the Lincoln National Bank, tendered to the defendant the warehouse receipts for said whisky upon the payment of said amount and that the defendant refused to accept said receipts and has since refused to accept said whisky and pay for the same; that the plaintiff holds said whisky for said defendant and is ready and willing to deliver the same upon the payment of the purchase price. The answer contains the following admission: "Admits that on or about May 16, 1918, said plaintiff and said defendant entered into an agreement whereby said plaintiff agreed to sell and said defendant agreed to purchase ten barrels of Kentucky whisky, Spring 1913 or 1914, at the agreed price of Three Dollars per gallon." The answer then alleges that the plaintiff has not complied with the terms of the agreement, that it has never delivered or offered to deliver said whisky to the defendant.

At the opening of the case the defendant moved to dismiss the complaint upon the ground that it did not state facts sufficient to constitute a cause of action, first, because there was no allegation as to delivery, and, second, that the complaint did not allege when the contract was to be performed. There is no force in the second ground as the law implies, in the absence of such a term, that delivery was to be made in a reasonable time. The other ground stated involves the question, to be hereafter discussed, as to whether or not the tender of the warehouse receipts constituted a tender of delivery or delivery of the whisky. The motion to dismiss the complaint was denied with an exception. At the close of the plaintiff's case a motion was made for a nonsuit, which was denied, and that motion was renewed at the close of all of the evidence at which time the plaintiff moved for a directed verdict. The defendant then asked to go to the jury upon one question only: "Whether, under all the proof here, there was a delivery of the goods in question under the custom prevailing in regard to the marketing of that particular sort of commodity."

There can be no question but what the telegrams constituted a definite and certain offer and acceptance and, as a result, a contract was completed whereby the plaintiff agreed to sell to the defendant ten barrels of Kentucky whisky, spring thirteen, for three dollars a gallon, in bond. It is undisputed that at the time the plaintiff mailed to the Lincoln National Bank the draft, with the bill and the warehouse receipts, it owned the ten barrels of whisky described in the telegrams and that the same was in bond at New Haven, Ky., in the warehouse of J. N. Blakemore, Incorporated. The receipts in question were regularly issued by J. N. Blakemore, Incorporated. They described the brand of the whisky, the serial number on each barrel, the warehouse stamp number on each barrel, the number of gallons in each barrel, and the receipts had been duly registered on the books of the Equitable Trust Company of New York, and each bore the certificate of the trust company to that effect. They were properly indorsed so that, upon delivery, the defendant could have taken the receipts and identified the whisky. There was nothing more to be done by the plaintiff as vendor. The particular ten barrels had been segregated and identified, the evidence of the same had been forwarded to be delivered to the defendant upon the payment of the price. There was nothing that remained to be done by the defendant, except to pay the purchase price agreed upon. Under such circumstances, the tender of the bonded warehouse receipts constituted a valid tender of delivery of the ten barrels of whisky in question, and the tender of performance, by the tender of delivery of the warehouse receipts, was equivalent to an actual delivery or a tender of physical delivery of the whisky in question.

[Five pages of the opinion are here omitted.]

While the result in this case may seem to be a hardship upon the defendant it is brought about by his own conduct and not by the law. I see no way to relieve him from the penalty that he incurred in violating his contract and I advise that the defendant's exceptions be overruled and a new trial denied and judgment directed for the plaintiff upon the verdict, with costs.

All concur, except KRUSE, P. J., and CLARK, J., who dissent in a memorandum by KRUSE, P. J.

[Dissenting opinion of Kruse, P. J., is omitted.]

Note the remarks of Cardozo, J., in RUMMELL *v.* BLANCHARD, 216 New York 348 (Court of Appeals, 1915) as follows: "The action is replevin. The plaintiffs sold to George A. Alden & Company and the New York Shellac Company two hundred cases of shellac. At the time of the sale the shellac was stored in a warehouse, and the plaintiffs held warehouse receipts, issued in their name, and negotiable in form. These receipts the plaintiffs indorsed and transferred to the purchasers. This was done on February 13, 1913. On February 14, 1913, one of the purchasers, the New York Shellac Company, tendered the receipts to the warehouseman and requested that new receipts be issued. This was refused because the charges of the warehouseman were not paid. A few days later both purchasers became bankrupts. The shellac has never been paid for, and the plaintiffs on learning that the buyers were insolvent paid the warehouse charges and demanded delivery. This demand was refused; an action of replevin against the warehouseman followed; and thereafter the trustees in bankruptcy of the buyers were substituted as defendants. They have demurred to the complaint, the demurrer has been sustained, and the question whether a cause of action has been stated has been certified to this court.

"The plaintiffs insist that the merchandise was never brought into the possession of the purchasers, and, hence, that they have never lost their lien as vendors for the payment of the price. The effect of the indorsement of warehouse receipts is now prescribed by statute. Where the receipts are negotiable in form, the holder to whom they have been negotiated acquires thereby '(a) such title to the goods as the person negotiating the receipt to him had or had ability to convey to a purchaser in good faith for value, and also such title to the goods as the depositor or person to whose order the goods were to be delivered by the terms of the receipt had or had ability to convey to a purchaser in good faith for value, and (b) the direct obligation of the warehouseman to hold possession of the goods for him according to the terms of the receipt as fully as if the warehouseman had contracted directly with him' (General Business Law [Cons. Laws, ch. 20], § 125). Where the receipts are not negotiable the holder 'acquires the right to notify the warehouseman of the transfer to him of such receipt, and thereby to acquire the direct obligation of the warehouseman to hold possession of the goods for him according to the terms of the receipt,' but 'prior to the notification of the warehouseman by the transferor or transferee of a non-negotiable receipt, the title of the transferee to the goods and the right to acquire the obligation of the warehouseman may be defeated by the levy of an attachment or execution upon the goods by a creditor of the transferor, or by a notification to the warehouseman by the transferor or a subsequent purchaser from the transferor of a subsequent sale of the goods by the transferor' (General Business Law, § 126). In brief, the warehouseman who issues a negotiable receipt agrees in advance to hold the goods for the account of any person to whom the receipt is negotiated, and by the very act of negotiation loses his position as bailee for the vendor, and is transformed, without further assent, into a bailee for the vendee. The warehouseman who issues a non-negotiable receipt does not become the bailee for the transferee of the receipt until notice of the transfer. From the moment of the negotiation in the case of a negotiable receipt, and from the moment of notice in the case of a non-negotiable receipt, the holder of the receipt is the bailor, and the warehouseman's possession is for the account of the new owner.

"The significance of this statute will become manifest when we consider the law as it stood before the statute was enacted. It was long a mooted question whether the transfer of a warehouse receipt divested a vendor's lien unless the warehouseman had consented to become the bailee for the vendee. Some courts held the view that such a consent was necessary. It might be given in advance, but unless it was given in some form, either before or after the event, the warehouseman, it was thought, remained the bailee of the vendor, and the transfer of the receipt, though effective to change the title, left the possession undisturbed (Williston on Sales, p. 739; Benjamin on Sales [5th ed.], pp. 216, 846, 853; *Farina* v. *Home*, 16 M. & W. 119; *Bentall* v. *Burn*, 3 B. & C. 424; *Hallgarten* v. *Oldham*, 135 Mass. 1, 9, 10, 11; *Selliger* v. *Kentucky*, 213 U. S. 200, 205; *Union Trust Co. & S. W. Co.* v. *Wilson*, 198 U. S. 530, 536; *Keeler* v. *Goodwin*, 111 Mass. 490). Whether the transfer of bills of lading had any greater effect is a question not before us. It is true that the rule which we have stated has been criticized (see, e.g., *Conrad* v. *Fisher*, 37 Mo. App. 352, 367); indeed, until the enactment of this statute, we may doubt whether it had been fully adopted in this state (*Bank of Rochester* v. *Jones*, 4 N. Y. 497, 503; *Willets* v. *Hatch*, 132 N. Y. 41, 44. See also: *Gibson* v. *Stevens*, 8 How. [U. S.] 384, 399); but in many jurisdictions it was settled law. The critics of the rule maintained that the transfer of a warehouse receipt ought to be deemed equivalent to an actual delivery even without the warehouseman's assent; but never was it doubted that a change of possession resulted where the bailee or agent of the seller had given his assent, and had thereby been converted into a bailee or agent for the buyer. Less may perhaps have been required, but assuredly not more.

"When the statute is read in the light of these decisions, its meaning is not doubtful. It charges every warehouseman who issues a negotiable receipt with a direct obligation to any one and every one to whom the receipt has been negotiated. It charges every warehouseman who issues a non-negotiable receipt with a like obligation after notice of the transfer. In the one case, the holder acquires 'the direct obligation of the warehouseman to hold possession of the goods for him according to the terms of the receipt as fully as if the warehouseman had contracted directly with him.' In the other case, the holder acquires a like right upon giving notice of the transfer. The assent of the warehouseman to act as bailee is thus written by the law into the contract embodied in the receipt. 'By a receipt in that form the bailee assents in advance to becoming bailee for any one who is brought within the terms of the receipt by an endorsement of the same' (*Union Trust Co. & S. W. Co.* v. *Wilson*, *supra*, p. 536; *Selliger* v. *Kentucky*, *supra*). The moment that a receipt, negotiable in form, is indorsed and delivered, a new relation of bailor and bailee springs into being, and with the birth of that relation the possession, once held by the bailee for the account of the vendor, is transmuted into a possession for the account of the vendee. The result 'is a real delivery to the same extent as if the goods had been transported to another warehouse named by the pledgee' (*Union Trust Co. & S. W. Co.* v. *Wilson*, *supra.* See also: *Mills* v. *Charlesworth*, L. R. [25 Q. B. D.] 421, 425)."

SANDERS BROTHERS *v.* MACLEAN & CO.

COURT OF APPEAL, 1883

[*Law Reports*, [1883] 11 *Queen's Bench Division*, 327]

[In this case a contract for the sale of iron rails called for payment in exchange for bills of lading. The seller tendered two bills out of a set of three, and in holding this to be a good tender Bowen, L.J., said ***inter alia***]: "The law as to the indorsement of bills of lading is as clear as in my opinion the practice of all European merchants is thoroughly understood. A cargo at sea while in the hands of the carrier is necessarily incapable of physical delivery. During this period of transit and voyage, the bill of lading by the law merchant is universally recognised as its symbol, and the indorsement and delivery of the bill of lading operates as a symbolical delivery of the cargo. Property in the goods passes by such indorsement and delivery of the bill of lading, whenever it is the intention of the parties that the property should pass, just as under similar circumstances the property would pass by an actual delivery of the goods. And for the purpose of passing such property in the goods and completing the title of the indorsee to full possession thereof, the bill of lading, until complete delivery of the cargo has been made on shore to some one rightfully claiming under it, remains in force as a symbol, and carries with it not only the full ownership of the goods, but also all rights created by the contract of carriage between the shipper and the shipowner. It is a key which in the hands of a rightful owner is intended to unlock the door of the warehouse, floating or fixed, in which the goods may chance to be."

HARPER *v.* HOCHSTIM

UNITED STATES CIRCUIT COURT OF APPEALS, SECOND CIRCUIT, 1921

[278 *Federal Reporter*, 102]

In Error to the District Court of the United States for the Southern District of New York.

Action by J. Ralph Harper and another, copartners doing business as Ralph Harper & Co., against Adolph Hochstim and another, copartners doing business as Hochstim & Bossak. Judgment for defendants on demurrer, and plaintiffs bring error. Affirmed.

The parties hereto entered into a contract evidenced by a document, whereof the material parts are as follows (the italicized portion being written, and the rest a printed form):

New York, February 16, 1920. According to this convention, written and signed in duplicate, the seller, *Ralph Harper & Co., of Tientsin, in China, sells to Hochstim & Bossak* the quantity of about 30,000 *Shantung weasels with tails.* Shipments from *China* per steamer direct or indirect to *New York during March and/or April.* Price: $2.45 *each C. I. F. New York.* Import duty, if any, to be paid by the buyer. Payment: *Four* m/s confirmed banker's letter of credit $73,500 to be opened by the buyer in favor of and to be approved by the seller. Letter of credit to be *telegraphed* within two days *after confirmation.* * * * In case of a c. i. f. sale and the goods are damaged while in transit, the buyer agrees to accept in settlement thereof the same percentage of allowance as the seller may secure from the insurers by way of settlement of recovery.

The sellers were in China; the above contract was signed on their behalf by an agent, and the printed form used was the agent's form.

Plaintiffs (the sellers) never shipped any weasel skins under this contract, but on June 25, 1920, they obtained in New York 10,000 weasel skins of the kind contracted for and tendered them to the buyers, who refused the same. The sellers then brought this action, alleging that the weasel skins tendered had been shipped from China (though not by them) to New York, via Seattle, and further asserting that they "would and could have obtained and delivered to defendants" the remaining weasel skins "within the reasonable time for delivery in New York of March or April shipments by steamer from China."

The complaint further asserted that the weasel skins actually tendered "were insured in the amount and against the risks usual in an ordinary c. i. f. contract under a policy payable to the plaintiffs," and finally alleged a "general custom and usage among the dealers in furs in New York City" to the effect that shipments such as above contracted for permitted "shipments from China by steamer to San Francisco and Seattle and thence overland by freight to New York." This custom is said in the pleadings to have been "well understood by both parties" to the above contract.

The breach alleged is the refusal of the buyers to accept the weasel skins tendered, and their refusal to accept any skins so obtained in New York and tendered as were the 10,000 above mentioned.

To this complaint defendants demurred, on the ground that it did not state facts sufficient to constitute a cause of action. The demurrer prevailed, and to judgment accordingly plaintiffs brought this writ.

HOUGH, Circuit Judge (after stating the facts as above). The allegation of custom, or, properly speaking, of usage (*Eames* v. *Claflin*, 239 Fed. 631, 152 C. C. A. 465), need not be considered; for, if plaintiff did not tender what he agreed to sell, the manner of his shipment is of no importance. The only question in the case is as to the nature of the contract admittedly made.

If that contract is for what is now widely known as a "sale c. i. f.," such sale was by specific agreement to be accomplished or executed by the delivery of documents by vendor to vendee, and not by the physical delivery of the actual goods for which the documents are the evidence of title. The bargain must be kept as made; the buyer can no more refuse the documents and ask for the goods than can the seller withhold the documents and tender the goods; and the documents necessary are a bill of lading and policy of insurance, although additional papers, especially an invoice, are usual.

[The balance of the opinion, holding the contract to be "of the kind known as c. i. f.," is here omitted.]

Judgment affirmed, with costs.

Note also the statement of McCardie, J., in *Manbre Saccharine Co.* v. *Corn Products Co.*, (1919) 1 K. B. 198 (King's Bench Division, 1918), that "the obligation of the vendor is to deliver documents rather than goods — to transfer symbols rather than the physical property represented thereby."

Compare SCRIVEN BROTHERS *v.* SCHMOLL FILS AND COMPANY, 40 T. L. R. 677 (King's Bench Division, 1924), where a contract for the sale of hides on c.i.f. terms contained a clause providing that "no claims shall be valid unless made in writing within two weeks after the goods are delivered." The buyers made a claim more than two weeks after delivery of the documents, but less than two weeks after receiving the goods from the ship. It was held that delivery meant delivery from the ship to the buyer.

Contrast the statement of Ripert, 2 *Droit Maritime* § 1899 (3d ed. Paris, 1929), that "the c.i.f. sale is a sale calling for delivery on shipment . . . the buyer, by using the c.i.f. clause, stipulates that the goods are to be delivered at the moment when they are placed on board the ship which is to carry them to their destination."

B. PLACE OF DELIVERY

FRUIT GROWERS' EXPRESS CO. *v.* PLATE ICE CO.

UNITED STATES CIRCUIT COURT OF APPEALS, FOURTH CIRCUIT, 1932

[59 *Federal Reporter* (*2nd Series*), 605]

SOPER, Circuit Judge. This suit was brought by the Plate Ice Company, a North Carolina corporation, against the Fruit Growers' Express Company, known as the Car Line, a Delaware corporation, for breach of a contract of November 7, 1921, between the parties, whereby the ice company sold and agreed to deliver, and the Car Line purchased and agreed to accept, all the ice that it might require during the period ending October 31, 1926, for the icing of refrigerator cars engaged in the transportation by railroad of perishable commodities originating at railroad stations within an extensive territory to be served from Wilmington, N. C. The contract contained the express statement that the requirements of the Car Line would vary from time to time, depending upon the amount of crops, train schedules, and the number of contracts in force between the Car Line and various railroads operating in North and South Carolina, for the furnishing to them of refrigerating cars and service. It was also agreed that the failure of the ice company to promptly ice the cars, as contemplated by the contract, might result in the spoilage of perishable commodities, and the ice company therefore agreed to indemnify the Car

Line against any loss or damage accruing to the Car Line because of such failure. Reference was made to the plant of the ice company in a provision that the contract should become inoperative if "on account of unavoidable accident, fire or providential cause, the ice manufacturing plant or storage plant of the Ice Company shall be so damaged or destroyed as to render the Ice Company unable to comply with its obligation under this contract." By an addendum to the contract, the Hilton Lumber Company, another North Carolina corporation, largely interested in the ice company, guaranteed the performance of the contract by it.

The case came on for trial before a jury, during which it was determined by the court, with the consent of the parties, that the question of liability should be determined therein, and that the issue of damages, if any should arise, should be referred to a referee. Thereupon testimony was offered, and the following issues were submitted to the jury: (1) Did the defendant wrongfully break its contract with the plaintiff, as alleged in the complaint, and (2) did the plaintiff first fail to perform its contract with defendant, as alleged in the answer? At the conclusion of the testimony the plaintiff moved for a directed verdict, and the court, being of the opinion that under a proper construction of the contract, and in accordance with the testimony, the defendant had broken the contract, and that if there had first been a breach on the part of the plaintiff it had been waived by the defendant, directed the jury to find both issues in favor of the plaintiff. The case was then referred to the referee to fix the damages.

The chief point in controversy relates to the construction of the contract as to the place of delivery of the ice contemplated by the parties, with particular reference to the following paragraphs of the agreement:

> 1. The Car Line shall direct to be iced or re-iced such cars as its business hereunder may require to be iced or re-iced at Wilmington, N. C., and the Ice Company shall ice or re-ice such cars promptly as directed by the Car Line. * * *
>
> 3. It is mutually agreed that such ice is sold to be delivered by the Ice Company in the bunkers of refrigerator cars at Wilmington, N. C., as directed by the Car Line at the following prices. * * *

The ice company contended, and the District Court ruled, that the place of delivery was its plant in Wilmington, N. C., while the Car Line on its part contended that, under the quoted paragraphs 1 and 3 of the contract, the ice company was obliged to deliver the ice at any point in the city of Wilmington, as directed by the Car Line. The dispute on this point between the parties arose by reason of a letter of August 25, 1924, wherein the Car Line notified the ice company that due to the great increase of crops, and the necessity to the railroad company of maintaining adequate and proper train schedules, the Car Line would thenceforth require ice at Wilmington only at the railroad company's Smith Creek yard in that city, delivered in bunkers of refrigerator cars; and the Car Line accordingly directed that all cars should thereafter be iced at the point indicated. This place was about one mile distant from the ice company's plant. The ice company denied the right of the Car Line to shift the point of delivery from the plant in Wilmington, at which deliveries had been made during the prior three years, and signified its refusal to accept the direction referred to. Thereafter, on November 28, 1924, the Car Line formally declared by letter to the ice company that, under the terms of the existing contract, the refusal of the ice company to ice the cars as directed constituted a breach of contract, and that it would thereafter make other arrangements for its supply of ice for the future. The ice company claims damages in this suit for the Car Line's refusal to accept deliveries from it during 1925 and 1926.

Coming to the construction of clauses 1 and 3 of the contract, it should be noted that the contract does not specify any particular place of delivery in the city of Wilmington. The general rule of law is that, where no place of delivery is specified in a contract of sale, the place of delivery is at the seller's place of business, in the absence of facts showing a contrary intention. Williston on Sales, § 450. The Car Line contends that this rule can have no application here because the ice company had no place of business. In fact, the ice was manufactured and delivered at the plant of the Hilton Lumber Company which owned all of the stock of the ice company. Nevertheless, it is obvious that this plant must be taken as the plant of the ice company for the purposes of this suit. The contract refers to the ice company's plant, and the evidence shows beyond question that thereby the parties meant the plant of the lumber company at which deliveries of ice under a previous contract between the parties had been made.

The contract does not lend itself to the interpretation for which the defendant contends. Paragraph 1 contains two correlative obligations: (1) An agreement by the Car Line that it will direct to be iced such cars as its business may require at Wilmington; and (2) an agreement on the part of the ice company that it will ice such cars promptly as directed by the Car Line. Paragraph 3 fixes the price for the ice delivered during the several years covered by the period of the agreement. It also states that the ice is "to be delivered by the Ice Company in the bunkers of refrigerator cars at Wilmington, N. C., as directed by the Car Line." The Car Line contends that the words "as directed" signify the right to designate the place of delivery. We do not think so. If the language be read in the light of the general rule that when no place of delivery is specified, the seller's plant is intended, there is no real uncertainty in the contract. The requirements as to the number and identity of the cars to be iced could not be determined in advance, but only as the business arose. Thereupon it was the privilege of the Car Line to direct the ice company to ice the cars. The words "as directed," in paragraphs 1 and 3, are given full force and effect by making them apply to the identity and number of the cars to be iced, and the time when the work is required to be done. The evidence shows that the plant used by the parties was equipped with platforms and machinery for the loading of ice into the bunkers of railroad cars on sidings provided for that purpose. The substantial additional expenses necessarily involved in the transportation of the ice from the ice company's plant to points distant therefrom, there to be delivered into the bunkers of the cars at the will of the Car Line, makes it unreasonable to suppose that the parties intended the terms of the contract in the sense for which the Car Line contends. It is noteworthy in this connection that, for three years prior to the refusal of the Car Line to proceed under the contract, deliveries were made and accepted at the ice company's plant.

The Car Line's construction of the contract is based not only on the language of the document, but upon circumstances surrounding its execution which it claims should be taken into account. It is urged that the District Court wrongfully refused to receive in evidence two contracts, one of March 7, 1921, between the ice company and the Car Line, and a second of September 27, 1920, between the Atlantic Coast Line Railroad and the Car Line. We need not stop to consider the correctness of the court's rulings in this respect, for, even if the contents of these agreements are considered in connection with the language of the contract in suit, they do not bear out the interpretation for which the Car Line contends. The first of these contracts was preliminary to the contract in suit, and related to prior deliveries of ice into refrigerator cars. It differed from the contract sued upon, in that it was expressly provided that deliveries should be made at the ice company's plant, and it is said that the omission of this clause from the subsequent contract shows that the parties intended therein to change the place of delivery; but this conclusion does not follow when we bear in mind the ordinary rule of delivery at the seller's plant. There is no inconsistency between the two agreements in this respect, and, if the place of delivery had not been expressly designated in the first contract, the result would have been precisely the same.

The contract between the railroad company and the Car Line set out the obligation of the Car Line to furnish the refrigerator cars needed by the railroad company, and the agreement of the Car Line to indemnify the railroad company for any damages to shipments arising from the failure to ice the cars promptly and completely. The Car Line also agreed to erect and maintain upon locations to be mutually agreed upon by the parties, icing stations equipped by the railroad with necessary trackage facilities and buildings for the icing of cars; and it is contended, therefore, that the Car Line could not have intended that all of the ice should be delivered at a single point in the city of Wilmington, for to do this might disable it from carrying out its agreement with the railroad company. The ice company's attention was directed to the existence of contracts between the Car Line and railroads in North and South Carolina, but the evidence does not show that the details of these contracts were brought home to the ice company; and, even if this had been done, the situation would have been the same, for the contract between the railroad company and the Car Line covered the railroad company's requirements for refrigerator cars generally, and was not confined to Wilmington. Nothing in the circumstances surrounding the execution of the contract in suit suggested that delivery at the ice company's plant would not be satisfactory to all parties concerned.

[The balance of the opinion is here omitted.]

The judgment of the District Court is affirmed.

Compare FLANIGAN *v.* WATERMAN, 191 N. Y. S. 646 (New York Supreme Court, 1922), where in the case of a contract for the sale of a lot of potatoes it was held that the place of delivery was a canal boat where the potatoes were known by the parties to be lying.

Refer again to *Turner-Looker Company* v. *Aprile*, *supra*, in which there was a dissenting opinion by Kruse, P. J., on the ground that the place of delivery under the contract should have been the plaintiff's place of business.

MAINE SPINNING COMPANY *v.* SUTCLIFFE & COMPANY

KING'S BENCH DIVISION, 1917

[23 *Commercial Cases*, 216]

By a contract contained in a sold note dated January 22, 1915, the defendants, Messrs. Sutcliffe & Co., of Halifax, sold to the plaintiffs, the Maine Spinning Company, of Boston, U. S. A., 100,000 lb. of merino wool at the price of *27½d.* The contract contained the following clause: — "This order is taken subject to the embargo being removed and your affidavits being accepted. Terms — 90 days London bank credit. Bradford conditioning house certificate. Duty unpaid. Delivery — Liverpool, England, 15,000 lb. weekly, commencing March." The cables and letters which had passed between the parties leading up to and immediately after the contract spoke of the contract being f.o.b. Liverpool.

At the time when the contract was entered into there was an embargo against the export of wool from the United Kingdom, but in the beginning of 1915 the stringency of the embargo, which was at first absolute, had been relaxed, licences being freely granted to export wool particularly to the United States of America. Before such licences could be obtained affidavits were required by the Government department as regards the purposes to which the wool would be put and assurances that it would not reach the enemy. It was the duty of the plaintiffs to procure the necessary licences to allow the wool to be exported, but the course of business between the plaintiffs and the defendants, for reasons of convenience, was for the defendants to obtain such licences although they were not under any obligation to do so, and the plaintiffs, in the present case, left it to the defendants to obtain the necessary licence. The defendants failed to obtain the licence necessary for the exportation of the wool the subject-matter of this contract, but it was not alleged by the plaintiffs that the defendants had not done their best to obtain the necessary licences.

The defendants delivered only 25,000 lb. of the 100,000 lb. of wool sold under the contract, and the plaintiffs brought this action against the defendants claiming damages for their failure to deliver the remaining 75,000 lb. of wool.

BAILHACHE J. stated the facts and continued: — It being the fact, therefore, that licences were necessary for the export of these woollen tops, and it being not now contended that the defendants did not do their best to obtain the licences, the fact that they failed to obtain the licences is a sufficient answer to their failure to make deliveries under this contract subject to one point upon which Mr. Schwabe relies, namely, that under the contract the buyers were entitled to take delivery at Liverpool. The contract says "delivery Liverpool," and Mr. Schwabe says that the buyers were always ready and willing to take delivery at Liverpool, and the question whether or not they could export the goods to the United States was a matter for them and did not concern the defendants, who were bound to hand over the goods to the buyers in Liverpool. The term "delivery Liverpool" is to some extent ambiguous, but when one considers that the wool was bought for export to the United States it is easy to come to the conclusion that "delivery Liverpool" did not mean delivery on rail at Liverpool, but meant delivery in the way in which goods are delivered at Liverpool when they are delivered for export at Liverpool, namely, "delivery f.o.b. Liverpool." If there were any ambiguity as to the meaning of the phrase "delivery Liverpool" I am entitled to look at the cables and letters which passed between the parties at the time the arrangement was made. Apart from those cables and letters, I should have come to the conclusion that the true construction of the words "delivery Liverpool" was "delivery f.o.b. Liverpool." The matter, however, is made abundantly clear when the cables and letters leading up to and immediately following the contract are looked at because they state in express terms that the contract was f.o.b. Liverpool. Mr. Schwabe, however, contends that it was open to the buyers to waive the term "f.o.b. Liverpool" and to take delivery of the goods short of Liverpool, or at Liverpool off rail instead of on board ship. He says that the buyers might even have taken delivery at Bradford, the place when the goods were prepared for the fulfilment of the contract and from which place they were dispatched. In my opinion, however, that is a mistaken view of the law. It is, of course, quite true that where a term of a contract is wholly and entirely for the benefit of one of the parties to the contract it may be waived by the party for whose sole benefit it is inserted in the contract. But a term of the contract as to the mode of delivery is not entirely for the benefit of either party to the contract, and neither party can waive it without the consent of the other; it is a part of the contract which has to be fulfilled by the seller making delivery at that particular place and the buyer receiving delivery there. Of course, if both parties to the contract agree to waive that term there is an end of the matter, but either party is entitled to insist upon making or receiving delivery in strict accordance with the terms of the contract. . . . Mr. Le Quesne has referred to the case of *Wackerbarth* v. *Masson* ([1812] 3 Camp. 270). The headnote in that case is as follows: "Where in a contract for the sale of sugar there is the following term, 'free on board a foreign ship,' the seller is not bound to deliver it into the hands of the purchaser, or to transfer it into his name in the books of the warehouse where it lies, but only to put it on board a foreign ship, which it is the duty of the purchaser to name." That is a decision of Lord Ellenborough as long ago as 1812, and it is directly in point in the present case. I was not aware of that decision, but I was quite prepared, apart from that decision, to hold, applying the rule of law laid down by Lord Watson, that the buyers in this case were not entitled to demand delivery of this wool anywhere except on board ship at Liverpool. That being the only point in the case there must be judgment for the defendants.

Judgment for defendants.

Note also STANDARD CASING COMPANY, INC. *v.* CALIFORNIA CASING COMPANY, INC., 233 New York 413 (Court of Appeals, 1922), where there was a contract in the following terms:

"San Francisco, December 18, 1917.

"THE STANDARD CASING CO., INC.,
"206 East 56th Street,
"New York City, N. Y.:

"We have this day sold you the following:

"Twenty (20) casks of salted pig guts, each about three thousand bundles.

"Shipment: January, February and not later than the fifteenth of March, 1918.

"Quality: Salted pig guts, as previous shipment.

"Price: Eighteen cents United States Gold coin per bundle f. o. b. San Francisco.

"Packing: Bundles of not more than three pieces measuring in all thirteen meters, no piece to be shorter than one meter. Width, 60% from 25/29/m/m and 40% from 29/31/m/m.

"Payment: Sight draft, bill of lading attached with the privilege of examining the goods on arrival.

"CALIFORNIA CASING COMPANY, INC.

"Per B. NEUSTADTER,
"*President.*"

In holding that this contract called for delivery at San Francisco, Cardozo, J., said, speaking for the Court: "We do not overlook the fact that the provision for shipment 'f. o. b. San Francisco,' is found in a paragraph headed, not 'delivery,' but 'price.' The plaintiff argues from this that its only effect was to impose upon the buyer the duty to pay the freight as an addition to the price, and not to fix the point at which delivery would be made. There might be force in this argument if the subject of delivery were covered in other sub-divisions. Without that, little, if any, significance can be accorded to the caption. We think the phrase in question must be deemed to regulate delivery, first, because it has a commercial significance not readily displaced or superseded, and, second, because there is a general presumption, which must prevail as against mere uncertainty or silence, that delivery to a carrier is delivery to the buyer."

UNITED STATES SMELTING CO. *v.* AMERICAN GALVANIZING CO.

District Court, Eastern District of Pennsylvania, 1916

[236 *Federal Reporter*, 596]

At Law. Action by the United States Smelting Company against the American Galvanizing Company. Rule for judgment discharged.

Dickinson, District Judge. The principles of law which control in this case may be thus formulated:

Where either party to a contract gives notice of his refusal to perform, the other may treat this as an anticipated breach, and bring his action, without awaiting the time of performance stipulated.

Delivery contracts, like all others, are to be performed in accordance with their found meaning.

Nondelivery under a contract to deliver and accept may constitute a breach by vendor or vendee. In a case of mere nondelivery, the breach is on the part of the party whose duty it was under the contract to first act.

In contracts to deliver f. o. b. vessel, with or without a designated port of shipment, the vendee is the first actor, and must provide and designate the vessel by proper shipping directions. In a like contract, where the vendor is given optional ports of shipment, the vendor is the first actor, and must name the port before he can require the vendee to provide the vessel.

Where the delivery is f. o. b. cars at the place of shipment, the vendee is the first actor, and must provide the car and give the necessary directions. Where, however, the delivery is to be by carrier at the port or point of destination of the shipment f. o. b. vessel or car, the contract gives the vendor the right, and requires him to select and engage the carrier, and he is thereby made the first actor.

Where the contract itself gives to the party required to act all necessary information to enable him to perform, he cannot excuse performance by proof of the fact that he asked for and was not given, or was refused, further directions.

The following cases were ruled upon some one or more of these propositions and give sanction to them as the law: *Roehm* v. *Horst*, 178 U. S. 1, 20 Sup. Ct. 780, 44 L. Ed. 953; *Kunkle* v. *Mitchell*, 56 Pa. 100; *Dwight* v. *Eckert*, 117 Pa. 490, 12 Atl. 32; *Hocking* v. *Hamilton*, 158 Pa. 107, 27 Atl. 836; *Railway Co.* v. *Steel Co.*, 123 Fed. 655, 59 C. C. A. 419; *Evanston Co.* v. *Castner* (C. C.) 133 Fed. 409. This observation does not in terms apply to the last two propositions, but we think them to be logical corollaries to the others.

When we turn from these general principles to their application to the facts of the instant case, we find this situation and this state of facts: The question is presented as in substance a demurrer question. The plaintiff avers a contract to deliver "f. o. b. cars East St. Louis," or "f. o. b. cars East St. Louis basis." We have stated the place of delivery in the alternative, because there are four suits on four different contracts, three of which follow the one phraseology and one the other, and we wish to dispose of all of them by one opinion. The further averment is made that the plaintiff asked the defendant to designate the place to which the spelter purchased was to be shipped. It affirmatively appears that no shipping instructions were given, and it does not appear that any reply was made by the defendant to the request for them. The position of the plaintiff is that this failure of the defendant was the equivalent of a refusal, and this refusal was in legal intendment a refusal to accept, and a consequent breach of the contract. The position of the defendant is that it was not bound to give shipping directions, and that no inference could be drawn from its refusal to so do, other than one of notice to plaintiff that defendant stood upon the contract and that plaintiff would be held to strict compliance. It should further, perhaps, be stated that nothing appears of the relations of the parties to the contract, except that the plaintiff is a citizen of Maine and the defendant of Pennsylvania.

There is a recognized atmosphere in which the two sides of this case were presented distinctly favorable to the plaintiff. The impression, whether justified or not, could not be resisted that the defendant was seeking to escape the consequences of the bargain into which it had entered. There is a like favorable predisposition in favor of the position of the plaintiff, born of the very clear and forceful argument addressed to us by its counsel and the clear-cut and helpful brief submitted. Counsel for defendant, however, must be freely and fully conceded the right, which may expand into a duty, to protect the defendant in the assertion of every legal right.

To compress the argument for plaintiff into a sentence is to inadequately present it, but the argument essentially is this: The relations of the parties to each other and to the subject-matter of the contract were such that the reference to the place of delivery meant nothing more than a mode of expressing the price. To what place the actual shipment was to be made was determined by the instructions to be given; but, wherever it was, the reference to cars f. o. b. East St. Louis fixed the price, and makes it clear that it was a price term only. The word "basis" in some of the contracts emphasized this.

The fact that there is nothing to show East St. Louis to be the place of manufacture or of final destination — the end of a contemplated carriage — all confirms the view of the contract taken. We are therefore not only justified, but required, to give to the quoted expression its ordinary and recognized meaning. The ordinary meaning of delivery f. o. b. cars is that the vendor is to be at the expense of hauling, loading, etc., or is to pay the freight to the named place, and that no responsibility rests upon the vendee until such delivery is made. It will be seen that this meaning, while clear and unambiguous, may nevertheless apply in whole or in part according to the conditions to which it applies. A contract to deliver f. o. b. vessel at the port of departure would be held to mean that the shipper is to be at the expense of loading. It just as clearly would not be held to mean that he had the right to select or was bound to supply the vessel. If, however, the port is the port of destination of the vessel (which possibly is reached by many vessels), then it would be equally clear that the shipper did have the right to choose the vessel and was bound to provide it. This case really resolves itself into this suggested very narrow question of fact.

The exact bearing point of the controversy can be best found by presenting three supposititious cases: (1) A broker, or other middleman, who buys to sell again, buys for delivery to an unknown consignee at an unknown place. To get a price basis, East St. Louis is named as the place of delivery. It is not in the contemplation of either party that the goods shall be there shipped or received, but they are to go to any place named by the vendee. (2) A vendor has a manufactory in East St. Louis from which he ships. A rate is made for delivery f. o. b. cars East St. Louis, with the expectation of being shipped elsewhere. (3) A vendee buys goods for delivery to himself at East St. Louis, to be there used. The goods are to be shipped in cars to East St. Louis, where the consignee is to receive them. The common-sense as well as legal meaning of these respective contracts is that in the first and second cases the vendee is bound to give shipping instructions. In the third case the vendor has them.

The final question is to which of these three classes does this contract belong? The position of the plaintiff is that it belongs to the first class. The present and real question is not whether it belongs to that class, but whether on the face of the record it is shown to so belong. This must be determined from an inspection of the record alone. The statement of claim avers simply a contract for St. Louis delivery. If this were the real contract, and the vendor was to ship from another place to St. Louis, it would be clear that it was the meaning of the parties that the shipment was to be made by rail to St. Louis and there received. It would be the place of the vendor to pay the freight, and the shipment would belong to him (with all the consequences of this), until delivery at St. Louis. One consequence would be that it would be his right to select the carrier and make his bargain for the shipment. Nothing would be required of the vendee beyond acceptance and payment. A right of action in the vendor could therefore only be based upon a refusal to accept. This refusal is averred, and the case of the plaintiff made out.

The affidavit of defense, however, denies the refusal to accept, although admitting a refusal to give shipping directions. The question then resolves itself into this: Was the defendant bound to give them, or did the plaintiff already have them? On the averments of the pleadings, we cannot find whether the sale called for a delivery f. o. b. cars for shipment from St. Louis, or a shipment by car to St. Louis. Without this finding we cannot determine which of the parties had the right to select, and upon whom was the consequent duty of supplying the car. To find this fact we must go outside the pleadings, and it follows that plaintiff is not presently entitled to judgment. This conclusion eliminates all other questions raised.

Rule discharged.

Compare Colley *v.* Overseas Exporters, [1921] 3 K. B. 302 (King's Bench Division), where there was a contract for the sale of leather f. o. b.

Liverpool. Owing to the unforeseen withdrawal and diversion of several vessels and the owners' inability to substitute others, the buyer failed to name an effective ship. The sellers meanwhile had sent the leather to Liverpool consigned to shipping agents for loading on the ship originally designated. In an action by the seller for the price of the goods, it was held that there could be no recovery as the seller had not met the conditions of the contract as to delivery.

ROYAL ITALIAN GOVERNMENT *v.* NATIONAL BRASS & COPPER TUBE CO., INC.

UNITED STATES CIRCUIT COURT OF APPEALS, SECOND CIRCUIT, 1923
[294 *Federal Reporter*, 23]

In Error to the District Court of the United States for the Southern District of New York.

Action by the Royal Italian Government, to recover moneys paid under an alleged mistake of fact, against the National Brass & Copper Tube Company, Inc. Judgment was rendered for one payment and disallowed on another. Both parties sued out writs of error. Reversed, with directions.

MANTON, Circuit Judge. The parties will be referred to herein as plaintiff and defendant. The plaintiff contracted, through its representative, with the defendant, for the purchase of certain brass discs under terms which are necessary to refer to. The contract was made on July 15, 1917, by one Gen. Tozzi, a member of the Italian Military Mission during the great war, on behalf of the plaintiff. It provided for the sale of 3,000 long tons of discs of certain dimensions and quality. Inspection to take place at the seller's factory by the Italian Mission, and it was to issue, before delivery, an inspector's certificate. The contract also contained the following clauses:

> Delivery. — Delivery shall be made by the seller f. a. s. New York City, or Philadelphia, or Baltimore, in the option of the buyer. In case, however, the buyer directs delivery at any other Atlantic seaboard port of the United States or Canada, seller shall so deliver and buyer shall pay the excess, if any, of the freight to such point over the highest freight to either of such ports; or if the freight be less than the smallest freight to either of said ports named the difference shall be allowed or returned by seller to buyer.
>
> Not less than eight hundred and twenty-five (825) tons of discs shall be delivered in each of the several months of July, August, September, and October, 1917, and delivery shall be completed on or before October 31, 1917.
>
> The deliveries shall be made in approximately equal weekly quantities of about two hundred (200) tons per week.
>
> The seller may in its option anticipate deliveries provided herein.

Payment was to be made under a letter of credit —

> upon presentation of invoices with inland bills of lading and proof of delivery alongside steamer at New York City, Philadelphia, or Baltimore, or other port as above provided, together with certificate of inspection and weight certificate, all of which documents shall be presented to Gen. Pasquale Tozzi, or a person

named by him, at his office in the city of New York, and countersigned by him before payment.

Provision was made for a waiver of the countersignature, upon failure to countersign within three days, and for storage in case of the inability of the shipper, in which event title was to pass to the buyer, but the risk should be that of the seller until delivery f. a. s. New York, Philadelphia, or Baltimore; and it was provided that, in case of delay, only part of the price was to be paid on storage, and the remaining percentage paid on proof of delivery alongside the steamer at designated ports. Time was made the essence of the agreement, and in case the seller failed for any reason to make any of the monthly deliveries of 825 tons or failed to make complete delivery of the whole, on or before October 31, 1917, various options were open to the buyer. The seller agreed to sublet in case of being late in deliveries, and provisions for the termination of the agreement at the end of the war, or at a general armistice, before delivery of all of the discs contracted for had been completed, with provision for payment of expenditures upon the discs, the delivery of which had been canceled. Delivery was to be free alongside steamer, without any name of a steamer being given. After the contract was made, the plaintiff opened an irrevocable letter of credit, providing for payment upon presentation of shipping documents and invoices evidencing a shipment of discs. Payment became subject to the approval of Gen. Tozzi.

Before the shipments in question were made, Gen. Tozzi wrote to the defendant directing it to ship goods to "Gen. Pasquale Tozzi, c/o G. Schiaffino & Co., 220 North Eutaw street, Baltimore," and shipments were made pursuant to these directions on straight bills of lading. The railroad company sent the usual notice of arrival to the consignee, namely, the Italian Mission. There was paid in this manner four payments, aggregating in excess of $800,000. Payments were made in each instance upon presentation of the bill of lading, weigher's certificate, inspector's certificate, and railroad's notice of arrival. On October 30, 1917, there were delivered at a pier of the Baltimore & Ohio Railroad at Locust Point, Baltimore, two different quantities of discs, the first quantity of which was 128 cases, sold at $34,990.04, and the second quantity, 560 cases, sold at $170,709.50. A fire occurred on October 30th, and destroyed all of these cases of discs. On October 25th, the invoices and other documents with reference to the first quantity of discs destroyed were presented to Capt. Savina at New York for approval. By his direction, his assistant countersigned, and payment was made by its bankers on October 26, 1917. It is shown that the plaintiff had actual knowledge of the place on the wharf where the discs were placed at the time of this payment.

The order for payment of the second quantity was drawn October 29, 1917, and on October 31, 1917, documents in connection with this second quantity shipped, and which were also destroyed, were presented and countersigned pursuant to Capt. Savina's instructions. This was the day after the fire, and payment was made on that day. The original authorization of the bank on October 29, 1917, contained no stamp of the Mission, but the copy produced by the Italian government contained at the bottom, "New York, October 31, 1917, Gen. Pasquale Tozzi." The defendant was not requested to, nor did it, furnish proof of the arrival alongside the steamer; and, as was the practice between the parties theretofore, the only notice of arrival at export pier was that given by the Baltimore & Ohio Railroad Company. Upon arrival notices were accepted by Gen. Tozzi. Arrival notices of all the discs in question were sent on October 13, 16, 24, and 29, 1917, and were received by the Mission one or two days after the date of the notice. These cases were unloaded at Locust Point pier, about 6 or 7 feet from the stringpiece of the pier at which the steamer would stand. The railroad company was obliged to furnish lighters to place the goods upon the ships if loaded amid-stream, or at any other place if required. After the fire, the plaintiff filed a claim against the railroad company for the loss. Later the plaintiff sold, and the defendant purchased, some of the salvaged discs. No steamer had arrived at the pier when the fire occurred.

The case was tried before the court and a jury of one. The District Judge thereafter rendered his opinion, in which he denied a recovery to the plaintiff for the value of the first quantity, and granted recovery for the value of the second quantity, destroyed. It was held that "free alongside the steamer" meant free of charges alongside the particular steamer which would take the goods. In his opinion, the District Judge considered the question of a mistake as to the passage of title, a mistake as to the goods, waiver and modification of the terms of the contract, as well as the authority of the agents of the Military Mission.

We think the question here is purely one of whether or not delivery was made as intended by the parties pursuant to the terms of the contract. If such delivery was made, payments made for the discs must stand, and the plaintiff may not succeed on either claim. If not, the plaintiff may succeed as to each payment made. The phrase, we think, means an actual delivery alongside. But it is claimed that there was no steamer at the wharf where the goods were deposited. The cases were actually conveyed to the wharf, removed from the cars, and piled at the wharf stringpiece on October 26th and October 28th respectively. This was a delivery alongside any steamer sent to that point, and when the parties paid for the discs after notices of arrival, as had been their practice in their dealings theretofore, we think that the plaintiff complied with the requirements of the contract, which entitled it to payment on proof of delivery "alongside steamer." Schiaffino & Co. were the agents of the Italian Mission, and were in charge of the disposal of the merchandise which arrived at this pier in Baltimore. The discs were sent to Gen. Tozzi in their care. The contract does not name any particular steamer, but the discs were deposited within reach of the tackle of a steamer. In the absence of the mention of some particular steamer, or other explanatory clause, there were no specific directions as to the point of delivery, and a reasonable interpretation would mean some export pier which was used by the Italian Mission. No expert evidence is offered attempting to show what the phrase "free alongside steamer" meant.

We think the contract itself and the conduct of the parties must be our guide. The intention of the parties must control. The terms of the contract, the conduct of the parties, the usages of the trade, and the circumstances of the case may be considered to ascertain such intention. *Ceballos* v. *United States,* 214 U. S. 47, 29 Sup. Ct. 583, 53 L. Ed. 904; Personal Property Law, § 100, rule 5, as added by Laws 1911, c. 571. The contract contemplated deliveries by the seller running over a period of four months in weekly quantities of 200 tons. The penalties imposed as above referred to contemplated monthly amounts. The parties could not have contemplated a ship which the buyer did not bind itself to furnish, and if the seller placed the discs at a designated wharf, where ships might reach them with their tackle, we think it did all that was required of it within the contemplation of the contract to make delivery. Delivery, under which title would pass, covered acts which were within the power of the seller to perform, and did not rest upon additional acts, which the buyer might or might not perform, and in respect to which it undertook no obligation. In the theretofore business conduct of the parties, it was not insisted upon, as a requirement of payment, that the discs were actually alongside steamer. Indeed, payments both before and after the fire were made upon evidence that the cases were at the wharf ready for ocean shipment.

The bills of lading in the buyer's name were delivered and accepted before the fire. The Mission having possession of them, it could have shipped the cases or not have shipped them as it saw fit. It might have removed the discs or resold them. It was the only one then who was interested. It was within its power to order the ship alongside the wharf, or to have the goods carried by lighter and put aboard in mid-stream. The claim of the plaintiff merely is that the discs must be actually alongside the ship, and that it is not enough to have it within reach of the ship's tackle. The subsequent conduct of the parties is important as showing their intentions. The plaintiff filed its claim with the railroad company for the loss sustained by the destruction of all the cases of discs. Subsequently it made payments upon deliveries such as had taken place in the instant case. If the freight had not been paid, the obligation was made for the seller to pay the freight. But it was undoubtedly the mutual intention to transfer and receive possession at Locust Point pier when payment was made, and then it was that title passed.

[Two pages of the opinion are here omitted.]

Therefore the plaintiff will not prevail on its writ of error, and the judgment on the writ of error of the defendant will be reversed, and the District Court is directed to enter a judgment for the defendant in conformity with this opinion.

Judgment reversed.

Compare CHRISTENSON *v.* GORTON-PEW FISHERIES CO., 8 Fed. (2nd) 689 (Circuit Court of Appeals, Second Circuit, 1925), where there was a contract for the sale of cured codfish f.a.s. New York, and where in an action by the seller against the buyer for breach of contract the buyer contended that the seller had failed to deliver. It was held that the seller "could not carry out the delivery until the shipment order naming the ship and dock was given. It is not an answer to say that instructions would be given after the fish reached New York."

STEIN FORBES AND CO. *v.* COUNTY TAILORING COMPANY

KING'S BENCH DIVISION, 1916

[115 *Law Times Reports*, 215]

ATKIN, J. read the following judgment: —

In this case the plaintiffs are suing the defendants to recover the price of six bales of sheepskins agreed to be sold to the defendants under a contract dated the 17th Sept. 1915. The contract note is as follows. It is dated the 17th Sept. 1915, London.

> The County Tailoring Company Limited, 1 Hoxton-square, London, N. — We beg to confirm having this day sold to you the undermentioned goods of our usual standard assortment and quality, mark: About 12,000 dressed sheepskins for prompt shipment, and about 33,000 ditto for shipment as quickly as possible (September, if possible) at 8*d.* per square foot, c.i.f. London or Liverpool. Payment: Net cash against documents on arrival of the steamer.

Then there is an arbitration clause. That is signed by the County Tailoring Company Limited. The goods were shipped by three different steamers, in lots of ninety-four bales per steamship *Devonian*, 217 bales per steamship *Bohemian*, and six bales per steamship *Den of Glamis*. The first two lots were taken up and paid for by the defendants after some little delay; the question here arises as to the third lot.

The *Devonian* arrived at Liverpool on the 5th Oct., and the goods were paid for about the 11th Oct. The *Bohemian* arrived on the 13th Oct., and the goods were paid for about the 29th Oct. The *Den of Glamis* arrived on the 25th Oct., and the defendants have not taken up the documents. They allege that the documents were never tendered to them, and that they were not informed of the vessel's arrival until the 8th Nov., which date they say was outside the contract date for delivery, which provided for net cash against documents on arrival of steamer.

I am satisfied that the defendants were informed by telephone of the arrival of the steamer immediately after she arrived. It was said, however, that the plaintiffs should have tendered the documents to the defendants at the defendants' office. In the absence of any express stipulation to this effect, or some trade usage or course of business between the parties importing such a stipulation, I doubt whether the obligation on the vendor exists.

Sect. 29, sub-sect. 1, of the Sale of Goods Act 1893 appears to provide the contrary. . . .

But if such an obligation would have existed normally I am satisfied that the defendants by their conduct absolved the plaintiffs of any such duty.

In the other two shipments the defendants desired delay in taking up the documents and expressly promised to come to the plaintiffs' place of business to take up the documents and did in fact take them up there. In the present case I am satisfied that the defendants made the same promises over the telephone. I think this objection fails.

[The balance of the opinion, holding that the seller's remedy lay in a claim for damages rather than in a suit for the price, is omitted.]

Contrast the statement of Lord Atkinson in *Johnson* v. *Taylor Bros. & Co.*, [1920] A. C. 144, 156 (House of Lords, 1920), that the result of the cases is to "establish that if no place be named in the c.i.f. contract for the tender of the shipping documents they must *prima facie* be tendered at the residence or place of business of the buyer."

Compare AMERICAN SUGAR REFINING CO. *v.* PAGE & SHAW, INC., 16 Fed. (2nd) 662 (Circuit Court of Appeals, First Circuit, 1927), where a clause in a c. i. f. contract for the sale of sugar to be shipped from Java to Boston provided: "Delivery of the sugar to be made at a customary safe wharf or refinery, as directed by the buyer." The sugar was shipped on a vessel too large to reach the refinery designated by the buyer. It was held that the clause was not inconsistent with a c.i.f. contract, and that the seller was liable for lighterage and stevedoring charges incurred in removing the sugar from the ship to the refinery.

NEILL *v.* WHITWORTH

EXCHEQUER CHAMBERS, 1865

[18 *Common Bench Reports*, *New Series*, 435]

This was an action for an alleged breach of a contract for the delivery of certain cotton. . . .

The plaintiffs were merchants in London; the defendants were merchants at Manchester; and both dealt largely in cotton. On the 2nd of October, 1863, the defendants, through their brokers, Trueman & Rouse, sold to the plaintiffs 500 bales of cotton, at 15⅛*d.* per lb. The bought-note was as follows: —

Bought for account of Messrs. Neill, Brothers, of B. Whitworth & Brothers, Manchester, 500 bales of cotton, at 15⅛ *d.* per lb., guaranteed October shipment, to arrive in Liverpool per ship or ships from Calcutta.

The cotton guaranteed fair Bengal. Any slight variation in mark not to vitiate this contract. In case of dispute arising out of this contract, the matter to be referred to two respectable brokers, who shall decide as to quality, and the allowance, if any, to be made.

The cotton to be taken from the quay: customary allowance of tare and draft; and the invoice to be dated from date of delivery of last bale.

To be in merchantable condition; the damaged, if any, to be rejected, provided it cannot be made merchantable. Should the cotton be transhipped into other vessels arriving, the contract to hold good: but, if any of the vessels be lost, the contract to be void, so far as regards such ships only.

Payment, cash within ten days, made equal to ten days and three months. Cash on account, before delivery, if required.

Trueman & Rouse.

On the 28th of October, 1863, the plaintiffs re-sold the cotton to one Clarke, through the same brokers, at 18½*d.* per lb.

On the 8th of January, 1864, the defendants declared the Talavera and the Fort George as the ships by which the cotton was to arrive, — 250 bales by each. The Talavera arrived at Liverpool on the 3rd of February, with a cargo of cotton which was landed on the quay there, and subsequently warehoused. Application was made on the part of the plaintiffs for delivery orders, but none were given or tendered until after the cotton had been carried to the warehouse. By the dock regulations at Liverpool, the authorities have power to warehouse all goods after they had been twenty-four hours on the quay.

The Fort George was stranded in Carnarvon Bay, and her cargo was landed there, and forwarded by railway to Liverpool. Arrived there, it was put into the "wreck transit sheds" on the quay, which is considered as part of the quay. The 250 bales ex Fort George were afterwards removed from the wreck transit sheds to the warehouse.

On a subsequent day, the vendors (the defendants) offered to deliver the whole 500 bales from the warehouse, but at quay weights, and without any charge for warehousing, or to cart them back to the quay and deliver them there. The plaintiffs, however, refused to take them, insisting that the defendants had broken their contract by allowing the cotton to be warehoused, instead of delivering it on arrival "from the quay."

A verdict was taken for the plaintiffs, with 2109*l.* 7*s.* 6*d.* damages, leave being reserved to the defendants to move to enter a verdict for them, or to reduce the damages, — the court to be at liberty to draw such inferences of fact as a jury might have drawn, and to make all such amendments as the judge at *nisi prius* might have done.

[Erle, C. J., delivered an opinion in which he said: "The clause in question constitutes an independent stipulation introduced solely for the benefit of the vendors, and therefore is matter on which the vendees cannot rely as amounting to a condition precedent. . . . Looking at the nature of the stipulation itself, I cannot see how it can be of any importance to the vendees whether they receive the cotton from the quay or from the warehouse, provided the warehousing does not impose on them any additional expense or undue delay. It seems to me to be perfectly clear that it was a stipulation inserted for the benefit of the vendors, to enable them to call upon the vendees to take the cotton from the quay, in order to save them expense."]

Williams, J. I am of the same opinion, and for the same reasons.

Willes, J. I am of the same opinion. It struck me at first that the expression "the cotton to be taken from the quay" must be construed as a stipulation on the one hand, accompanied by a corresponding promise on the other, that the delivery should take place upon the quay, and that, unless the vendors were ready to deliver the cotton there, they failed in the performance of their contract, and would be liable for all the consequences of such failure. But, upon consideration, I am satisfied that that literal construction of the words would be an incorrect one. There are several reasons for holding that it could not have been so intended. The stipulation does not affect the identity of the cotton, or its quantity, or its quality, — as, for instance, that it should be cotton from Mobile or from New Orleans, or the like. Then, does it amount to a stipulation as to time. Without it, the contract would stand as a contract for the delivery of the cotton within a reasonable time. The words were evidently introduced with reference amongst other things to who was to be at the charge of the warehouse-rent, insurance, &c. These would otherwise have been at large. There was, therefore, a manifest use for the words "the cotton to be taken from the quay." The meaning of them is, that the quay is to be taken as the place at which the delivery is to be made. This construction is fortified by the provision made for the usual allowances, and the stipulation that the invoice is to date from the delivery of the last bale. That must mean from the time the last bale is landed on the quay. The contract, therefore, stands as a contract for the delivery of the cotton in a reasonable time and under reasonable circumstances, the cotton to be at the buyers' charge from the time it is landed on the quay. That seems to me to be the proper construction; and it is the construction which the sellers have put upon it. They offered to deliver the cotton to the buyers on the same terms as if it had been delivered on the quay: nay, more, the vendors offered to take it back to the quay, so as literally to comply with the words of the contract. For these reasons, I am of opinion that the rule should be made absolute to enter the verdict for the defendants.

KEATING, J. I am of the same opinion. I think, after hearing the argument, it is quite clear that the words in question were introduced as a stipulation in favour of the vendors. The place where they are found seems to me to make this quite obvious. The meaning is, that the vendees shall be bound to take the cotton from the quay, provided the vendors were ready to deliver it there. The words were in all probability introduced in order to get rid of any question as to which party was to bear the expenses to be subsequently incurred. That seems to me to be the only sensible construction of the contract.

Rule absolute accordingly.

In HARRISON *v.* FORTLAGE, 161 United States 57 (United States Supreme Court, 1895), there was a contract for the sale of sugar "to be shipped during this month from the Philippines to Philadelphia, per steamer Empress of India, at 5⅝ c. per pound ex ship." It was agreed that "the words 'ex ship,' as used in this contract, were understood in the trade to mean that the buyer receives the goods at the tackle of the ship, the seller paying the freight and the duty, and the buyer paying all charges of landing after the goods leave the ship's tackle." Citing *Neill* v. *Whitworth*, *supra* the Court stated further of these words that "They do not constitute a condition of the contract, but are inserted for the benefit of the seller."

Compare YANGTSZE INSURANCE ASSOCIATION *v.* LUKMANJEE, [1918] A. C. 585, 589 (Privy Council, 1918), where Lord Sumner remarked: "In the case of a sale 'ex ship,' the seller has to cause delivery to be made to the buyer from a ship which has arrived at the port of delivery and has reached a place therein, which is usual for the delivery of goods of the kind in question. The seller has therefore to pay the freight, or otherwise to release the shipowner's lien and to furnish the buyer with an effectual direction to the ship to deliver. Till this is done the buyer is not bound to pay for the goods."

Note also FISHER, REEVES AND COMPANY, LIMITED *v.* ARMOUR AND COMPANY, LIMITED, [1920] 3 K. B. 614 (Court of Appeal, 1920), where it was held that the buyers were justified in repudiating a contract for the sale of boiled beef "ex store," when it appeared that the beef in question actually was in lighters and never was placed in a store.

C. TIME OF DELIVERY

A. B. MURRAY CO., INC. *v.* LIDGERWOOD MANUFACTURING CO.

NEW YORK COURT OF APPEALS, 1926

[241 *New York Reports*, 455]

Appeal, by permission, from a judgment of the Appellate Division of the Supreme Court in the first judicial department, entered March 2, 1925, unanimously affirming a judgment in favor of plaintiff entered upon a decision of the court at a Trial Term without a jury.

LEHMAN, J. The plaintiff has recovered a judgment for the agreed price of certain tubes. The findings establish that by contract made on the 17th day of April, 1920, the plaintiff's assignor had agreed to have specially cut for, and to sell and deliver to, the defendant certain steel boiler tubes. No time for delivery was expressly fixed in the contract. Delivery of one item of steel boiler tubes included in this contract was made on November 1st, 1920. This item is not included in the tubes for which the plaintiff now seeks payment. No delivery of those tubes or offer to deliver was made until March 26th, 1921, when the plaintiff mailed to the defendant an invoice for them. On April 4th, 1921, the defendant notified the plaintiff by letter that it would not accept delivery of the tubes for which the plaintiff had rendered the invoice. If the defendant's refusal to accept delivery of the tubes was wrongful, the plaintiff is entitled to recover the price of the tubes, for findings to which further reference is unnecessary conclusively establish all the other facts which would entitle the plaintiff to maintain an action for the price of the goods, under subdivision 3 section 144 of the Personal Property Law (Cons. Laws, ch. 41).

The contract to sell does not in express terms fix the time for delivery. The law supplies the missing term and the contract is in legal effect an engagement on the part of the plaintiff to deliver within a reasonable time.

Tender within a reasonable time is a condition which must be complied with by the seller before the buyer can be said to be in default, and performance or waiver of the condition must be pleaded and proved in an action by the seller for the price of the goods or for damages for alleged default by the buyer. (*Pope* v. *Terre Haute Car & Mfg. Co.*, 107 N. Y. 61.) These well-established principles have been reiterated by this court in the recent case of *Trainor Co.* v. *Amsinck & Co., Inc.* (236 N. Y. 392), overruling the contention there made that in the case of *Taylor* v. *Goelet* (208 N. Y. 253) we had laid down a rule which would preclude the buyer from urging that delivery was not tendered or made within a reasonable time unless, by appropriate notice given by the buyer, time for performance was made an essential term of the contract.

In the present case plaintiff by amendment of the complaint made at the trial has pleaded tender within a reasonable time, but the trial judge has not made any direct finding upon that point. He has found a contract made in April, 1920, and no tender of delivery made until more than eleven months thereafter. Even though, as we shall hereafter point out, inference from the testimony produced might perhaps be permissible either that delay was waived or that performance was made within a reasonable time, yet no finding based upon merely permissible inference of fact may be supplied by this court where the court which might have drawn such inference chose not to do so. Certainly the trial judge never intended that such finding should be implied, for he stated his conclusion of the law as follows: "As no time for delivery was mentioned in the contract the plaintiff was bound to deliver within a reasonable time. As the defendant never specified a time within which the plaintiff must deliver and a canceling of the contract would cause the plaintiff the loss of the money it paid for the tubes, the defendant cannot now say that the plaintiff did not deliver within a reasonable time." We may assume that the premises for the conclusion may be regarded as findings of fact but the conclusion of law must be justified, if at all, upon these premises and no others.

The contract fixes the obligations of the parties. Subsequent events may affect the manner of their performance but unless or until waived the duty of the seller, as fixed by the contract to deliver within a reasonable time, is absolute. So we held in the case of *Trainor* v. *Amsinck Co.* (*supra*) and we indicated that the rule applied to executory contracts of sale even of goods which were to be manufactured. The buyer has a right to insist upon such delivery; the seller is bound to make it. The seller's obligation can be no less because remedy for breach of the obligation causes him loss; the buyer cannot be compelled to accept other than the stipulated performance because refusal would leave the seller in a position of hardship. A loss to a party who is in default furnishes no ground in an action at law for depriving the other party of his contractual rights. Unless the buyer has by his own conduct either waived a breach or lulled the seller into inaction, the buyer may insist upon performance by the seller according to the terms of the contract as condition to performance on his part.

What constitutes reasonable time for performance may depend upon many circumstances. Doubtless the attitude of the parties may sometimes be an important factor in determining what is a reasonable time for performance of that particular contract. Good faith may be required of the buyer, and he may be precluded from insisting upon default of the seller when such default is occasioned by his own acts. Sometimes distinction between a waiver of default, or an extension of the time for performance, and acts which enlarge definition of a "reasonable time" as contemplated by the parties beyond the limits which might otherwise be set, is tenuous. Here the contract was made in April, part performance was made and accepted in November. Perhaps a reasonable time for performance had already passed and acceptance of the part performance might then constitute a waiver of the right to insist without further notice upon delivery within reasonable time. Some time thereafter the buyer requested cancellation of the contract. If at that time a reasonable time for delivery had not fully expired, the buyer's indicated desire not to be compelled to take the goods, may lead to an inference that delay thereafter in tendering the goods was due not to fault of the seller but to reasonable consideration for a customer's position and a desire not to press the buyer too hard, and under the circumstances the belated offer to perform in March and April may still have been timely. We indicate these questions; we may not upon the appeal pass upon them. Waiver is not pleaded, and what would constitute delivery within a reasonable time is a question of fact and may depend upon circumstances not shown by the evidence in this record.

We decide only that the seller's obligation to deliver within a reasonable time is fixed by the contract and does not depend upon whether failure to deliver according to the contract causes a loss to the seller. Where, however, failure to deliver within a reasonable time has been waived, or where the buyer has led the seller to the reasonable belief that belated delivery would be accepted as within the terms of the contract, then the buyer may not urge that the subsequent tender was untimely.

The judgment should be reversed and a new trial ordered, with costs to abide the event.

HISCOCK, Ch. J., CARDOZO, POUND, MCLAUGHLIN, CRANE and ANDREWS, JJ., concur.

Judgment reversed.

PEARL MILL CO., LTD. *v.* IVY TANNERY CO., LTD.

KING'S BENCH DIVISION, 1918

[*Law Reports,* [1919] 1 *King's Bench Division,* 78]

Appeal by the plaintiffs from a judgment of the judge of the Oldham County Court.

The action was brought in the county court to recover 70*l.* 10*s.* damages for the defendants' breach of contract in refusing to deliver to the plaintiffs 30 dozen red Welsh roller skins.

On September 26, 1913, a contract in writing was entered into between the defendants by their representative one Mills and the plaintiffs for the sale by the defendants to the plaintiffs of 50 dozen red Welsh roller skins at 27*s*. per dozen, "delivery as required." Under the contract 20 dozen skins were delivered between November 19, 1913, and September 29, 1914, by the defendants to the plaintiffs at their request in 4 lots of 5 dozen each, viz., on November 19, 1913, February 24, 1914, June 24, 1914, and September 29, 1914, respectively, leaving 30 dozen skins undelivered. Mills called on the plaintiffs about twice in 1914 and 1915, but from September 29, 1914, to July 13, 1917, no further deliveries were made by the defendants nor were any requested by the plaintiffs, the plaintiffs' manager having forgotten the existence of the contract and Mills having left the service of the defendants in June, 1915. In July, 1915, the plaintiffs gave Mills a personal order for 50 dozen skins of the same kind and at the same price as that specified in the contract of September 26, 1913, of which they took delivery. Between June, 1915, and April, 1916, one Moorhouse, who had succeeded Mills as the defendants' representative, called upon the plaintiffs and sent in his card to the plaintiffs' managing director with a message that he desired further orders. He however only saw the plaintiffs' lodgekeeper, and the reply sent by the plaintiffs' managing director was that there was nothing for him. On November 15, 1915, the defendants by letter offered the plaintiffs a small parcel of 20 to 30 dozen roller skins similar to those previously supplied and at the same price, but the plaintiffs replied that they had bought some time ago their requirements for the next year. On July 13, 1917, the plaintiffs wrote to the defendants requesting the delivery of the remaining 30 dozen skins under the contract. On July 14, 1917, the defendants replied saying that the plaintiffs had taken delivery at the rate of 5 dozen skins per quarter up to September 29, 1914, and that as there had been no deliveries since then, the contract expired in March, 1916. On July 17, 1917, the plaintiffs replied that the delay was caused by the change in representatives and insisting upon delivery. As the defendants in further correspondence still contended that the contract had expired, the plaintiffs brought the action to recover the 70*l*. 10*s*. damages for breach of the contract, being the difference between the price of 30 dozen skins under the contract and the market price on July 14, 1917.

No evidence was given that the defendants had at any time requested the plaintiffs to take delivery of the remaining 30 dozen skins.

The county court judge found that the plaintiffs had made up their minds to abandon the contract; and, whether his finding on that point was correct or not, that they behaved in such a way that the defendants reasonably believed that the plaintiffs considered that the contract was at an end. He therefore gave judgment for the defendants.

The plaintiffs appealed.

[The opinion of Rowlatt, J., is here omitted.]

McCardie, J. I agree. I think that the point before us is one of considerable commercial importance. The words "as required" appear in a very large number of commercial contracts throughout the country. Those words were interpreted in *Jones* v. *Gibbons* (8 Ex. 920), and it was held that the mere lapse of a reasonable time did not entitle the vendor to put an end to the contract, but that before he could take that course he must give notice to the vendee. I regard *Jones* v. *Gibbons* as a well settled and weighty authority, but in my view it in no way conflicts with other and well known principles of law, such as that which permits parties to rescind, or that which leads the Court to infer the abandonment of contractual obligations. Contracts for the sale of goods frequently require the performance of acts by a vendee before the obligation of delivery falls or becomes imperative upon the vendor — for example, where the class of goods, the size, or the quantities must be specified by the purchaser. In such a contract where the words "as required," or the like words, do not appear, then upon the passing of a reasonable time the vendee will have lost his right to call upon the vendor to deliver; but where the words "as required" appear a particular duty is cast upon the vendor by virtue of the decision in *Jones* v. *Gibbons*. Reasonable time is of course a matter which depends upon the nature of the contract, its terms, the class of goods, the practice of the trade, and the general circumstances of the case. In my opinion, where the contract is one to which *Jones* v. *Gibbons* applies it is clear that the mere lapse of a reasonable time does not *ipso facto* deprive the vendee of his rights, but that rule in no way prevents the operation of the other rules of law which are applicable to contracts. Mere delay or the mere lapse of reasonable time is one thing, but an inordinate lapse of time is wholly different. The former may not give rise to the implication of abandonment, the latter may do so.

In the present case I am satisfied that the learned county court judge came to the conclusion that the lapse of time under the circumstances was so great that the proper inference to draw was that the parties had mutually abandoned the contract. The delay was indeed serious; and the whole circumstances pointed to the conclusion that neither party continued to have the contract in mind. I think there was ample evidence on which the learned county court judge could come to the conclusion he did that the contract had been abandoned.

There is one further ground on which, in my opinion upon the facts and documents proved, he could also give judgment in favour of the defendants, that is, upon the principle of estoppel which is represented by the well-known cases of *Pickard* v. *Sears*, *Cornish* v. *Abington*, and similar authorities. I think, having regard to the documents and to the facts proved before the learned county court judge, that he was entitled to find that the conduct of the plaintiffs was such as reasonably to lead the defendants to the conclusion that the plaintiffs had regarded the contract as at an end. Therefore, whether upon the ground of abandonment or of estoppel, in my opinion the learned county court judge was right in the conclusion at which he arrived.

Appeal dismissed.

Compare American Cotton Oil Co. *v.* Kirk, 68 Fed. 791 (C. C. A. 7th, 1895), where there was an agreement for the sale of 10,000 barrels of oil "deliveries to be made per week as (the buyers) desire," and when in an action for damages for non-delivery a judgment for the plaintiff was reversed, the court holding that the contract was "one-sided and without mutuality," for "if the market price of oil should fall below the contract price, then, according to their contention as to the terms of the contract, the plaintiffs could purchase their supply of oil elsewhere, and at the lower price, resorting to the contract when, and only when, the price stated was lower than the market price."

BRITISH ALUMINIUM CO., LTD. *v.* TREFTS

New York Supreme Court, Appellate Division, 1914

[163 *New York Appellate Division Reports*, 184]

Appeal by the defendant, George M. Trefts, from a judgment of the Supreme Court in favor of the plaintiff, entered in the office of the clerk of the county of New York on the 4th day of December, 1913, upon the decision of the court after a trial before the court, a jury having been waived.

Laughlin, J. The plaintiff is a foreign corporation, and brings this action as vendor of aluminum to recover of the vendee the difference between the contract price and the market price at the time and place of delivery. The action is based upon a contract in writing made between the plaintiff by its agents and the defendants on the 22d day of September, 1910, by which the plaintiff through its agents agreed to sell twenty-five tons, long ton weight, British ingot aluminum, guaranteed ninety-eight to ninety-nine per cent pure, at twenty-two and three-eighths cents per pound The only provisions of the contract with respect to the place and manner of delivery are as follows: "Delivery: f. o. b. New York," and the only provisions with respect to time of delivery follow immediately and are "Shipment: As specified by buyers between October 1910 and April 1911."

The contract next provides that the payments shall be in cash in New York funds fifteen days "from date of invoice." It is further provided that the price was based on the then existing tariff and that in the event of a change in the tariff it should be modified accordingly; and that each delivery should be considered a separate contract, and that "strikes, lockouts, differences with workmen, accidents to machinery, delays en route or other contingencies" beyond the control of the vendor should be "sufficient excuse for any delay traceable to these causes." The clause relating to "shipment" was subsequently modified by substituting the 31st day of December, 1911, for April, 1911, as the final date for delivery. It was stipulated that between the 26th of September, 1910, and the 13th of April, 1911, the plaintiff, pursuant to the contract and at the request of the defendant, duly delivered to defendant twelve long tons of said aluminum, and that the same was duly accepted and paid for in full. The defendant in no manner requested the plaintiff to ship the remaining thirteen tons of aluminum; and the plaintiff neither delivered nor tendered delivery of the same nor did it request defendant for any shipping directions or give defendant notice that it was ready to deliver or call upon defendant to take the aluminum; but it was stipulated that at all times prior to and including the 1st day of January, 1912, "the plaintiff was ready, able and willing to deliver to the defendant thirteen long tons of aluminum of the kind and character mentioned in the contract." . . .

It is contended on the part of the respondent that the plaintiff was under no obligation to deliver or to tender delivery until the defendant specified a time for delivery of the remaining thirteen tons of aluminum which concededly he never did. The parties did not undertake that the vendor need not ship the goods until it received shipping directions from the vendee. The provisions with respect to shipments earlier than the final date were for the benefit of the vendee, and he was required, not to give shipping instructions essential to enable the vendor to make a delivery, but to specify *dates for delivery* in so far as he might desire delivery before the 31st day of December, 1911. The vendor had the right, and I think that it was its duty, if it intended to hold defendant, to deliver or tender delivery of the remaining thirteen tons of aluminum on the 31st day of December, 1911, for the legal effect of the contract was to call for delivery thereof on that day. (See *Sousely* v. *Burns*, 73 Ky. 87; *Chandler* v. *Robertson*, 39 id. 291.) The vendor needed no shipping instructions to enable it to deliver the aluminum, which was to be consigned to the defendant at Buffalo and to be delivered f. o. b. at the city of New York, and if it did it should have asked for them if it desired to perform and to put the vendee in default. (See *Gordon Malting Co.* v. *Bartels Brewing Co.*, 206 N. Y. 528.) The contract merely gave the vendee the right to require delivery of part or all the aluminum prior to the final date of delivery. In so far as delivery was not required to be made before that date, the vendor, if it desired the benefits of its contract, was at liberty without awaiting a request from the vendee to deliver the aluminum f. o. b. New York city consigned to the vendee at Buffalo, and the failure of the vendee to demand delivery did not, in my opinion, excuse the vendor from so delivering or tendering delivery of the remaining thirteen tons. . . .

It follows, therefore, that the judgment should be reversed, with costs to appellant, and the decision modified by eliminating therefrom the conclusions of law and substituting therefor a conclusion of law to the effect that the plaintiff has failed to establish a cause of action and that the defendant is entitled to judgment dismissing the complaint upon the merits, with costs, and granting judgment thereon as amended accordingly.

McLaughlin and Dowling, JJ., concurred; Ingraham, P.J., and Hotchkiss, J., dissented.

[Dissenting opinion of Hotchkiss, J., based on the view that delivery was conditioned on specification of a particular time by the buyer, is omitted.]

Compare Ralph L. Fuller & Co., Inc. *v.* W. H. & F. Jordan, Jr., Inc., 196 App. Div. 114 (New York Supreme Court, 1921), where a contract for the sale of linseed oil f. a. s. New York, to be shipped during August and September 1919, contained the clause "Buyers to furnish marking and shipping instructions in ample time to permit of delivery when desired; and also to furnish G. O. C. permit in order to secure free lighterage to steamer." It was held that "the duty of delivery or a tender of delivery and the duty of furnishing shipping instructions were, therefore, not concurrent duties, but the plaintiff's duty to make tender of delivery was dependent upon the defendant's first furnishing the shipping instructions. Its failure to furnish the same constituted a breach of the contract for which the plaintiff can recover."

Note also AMERICAN SUGAR REFINING CO. *v.* BLAKE, 102 Conn. 194 (Supreme Court, 1925), in which a contract for the sale of sugar f. o. b. Boston contained the provision "Delivery to be during September or as soon thereafter as is possible," with the further clause "Assortment to be furnished to seller by buyer before September 1, 1920." There were at least 15 grades subject to such assortment, and the contract reserved to the seller the right to ship any grades available if the buyer failed to specify his assortments promptly. The buyer furnished no assortments; the seller made no shipments or tenders. In an action by the seller for damages for breach of the contract, the court reversed a judgment for the defendant, saying: "We are of opinion that the contracts do not confer on the buyer a mere privilege of furnishing assortments, which he may or may not exercise at will; and that the clause in question is in form and in substance an obligatory covenant to furnish assortments, upon which the seller's covenant to deliver is dependent in order of performance. It follows that the seller's reserved right to ship available grades in case assortment if not furnished promptly is, in effect, as it is in form, 'a privilege and not a duty'."

C. SHARPE & CO., LTD. *v.* NOSAWA & CO.

KING'S BENCH DIVISION, 1917

[*Law Reports*, [1917] 2 *King's Bench*, 814]

Trial of action before Atkin J. without a jury.

The plaintiffs were seed merchants, of Sleaford in Lincolnshire. The defendants were merchants carrying on business in Japan and having an office in London.

In April, 1914, the parties entered into two contracts for the sale by the defendants to the plaintiffs of two parcels of Japanese peas upon a sample sent to this country. One contract was for 50 tons at 10*s.* 6*d.* a cwt. c.i.f. London May shipment; the second was for 100 tons on the same sample at 10*l.* 15*s.* a ton c.i.f. London June shipment. In respect of the first contract a portion of the goods was shipped by the *Agapenor*, which left Japan on May 24 and arrived on July 21. In the meantime a bulk sample had been sent with the shipping documents and arrived in this country some time before June 16. On comparison of the bulk sample with the contract sample the plaintiffs rejected the goods on the ground that they were not equal to sample. A further shipment consisting of the rest of the 50 tons under the first contract and 6¼ tons under the second contract was sent by the *Phemius*, which left Japan on June 9 and arrived on August 4. In the case of this shipment also a shipping sample was sent forward with the shipping documents and arrived on June 30; and this shipment, like the former, was rejected by the plaintiffs. The parties negotiated with a view to both shipments being accepted with an allowance in the price, and, as the result of an arbitration, the plaintiffs accepted the shipments with an allowance of 1*s*. per ton in the one case and 1*s*. 2*d*. per ton in the other. Neither of the shipments was in fact equal to sample.

As to the balance, 93¾ tons, of the second contract, on June 16 the plaintiffs had cabled to the defendants that they refused to accept the goods as the shipping sample was inferior in every respect. The defendants replied that the quality was equal to sample and that they would cancel the balance. The plaintiffs answered that the quality was not equal to sample, that they refused point blank, and would claim damages. On June 17 they wrote requiring the defendants to send the goods in accordance with the terms of the purchase. On June 18 the defendants, confirming their telegram of June 16, wrote to say that they would cancel the contract. The plaintiffs received this letter on July 6. They replied to it on July 29, asking if they were to understand that the defendants had not shipped the balance of the goods equal to sample and requesting them to cable at once, otherwise they would have to buy against them. The defendants did not answer this letter.

If the goods had been shipped on the last possible day for a June shipment and the shipping documents had been forwarded as they had been in the case of the shipments by the *Agapenor* and the *Phemius*, the documents would have arrived in London on or about July 21, and the goods themselves would have arrived on or about August 30. Neither the documents nor the goods were ever sent. On December 23, 1915, the plaintiffs issued the writ in this action claiming damages for non-delivery of the 93¾ tons. The question was as to the measure of damages. The defendants paid into Court a sum equal to 12*l*. per ton, alleging that to be the value of similar goods procurable in London on July 21. The value of similar goods on August 30 was 17*l*. 10*s*. per ton. The plaintiffs claimed damages on that basis.

Atkin J. The question is whether the damages are to be measured by the price of peas in July, when the documents would have arrived in the ordinary course, or the price in August, when the goods would have arrived on a June shipment, assuming that the voyage took two months. The answer depends upon the true meaning of a c.i.f. contract of this kind. It is reasonably plain that such a contract is performed by the vendor taking reasonable steps to deliver as soon as possible after shipment the shipping documents, including the bill of lading and policy of insurance, and the buyer paying the price against the documents unless there is some other stipulation as to payment in the contract. But performance by the seller is by delivery of the documents which represent the goods, i.e. the bill of lading, which is a constructive delivery. The delivery intended by the contract is a constructive delivery.

[After citing the opinions of Bowen, L.J., and Brett, M.R., in *Sanders* v. *Maclean*, 11 Q. B. D. 327, and of Kennedy, L.J., in *Biddell Brothers* v. *E. Clemens Horst Co.*, [1911] 1 K. B. 934, Atkin, J., continued:]

The right view of that passage is that the Lord Justice intended to adopt the judgment of Brett M.R. in *Sanders* v. *Maclean* (11 Q. B. D. 327) that it is the duty of the vendor to make every reasonable effort to send forward and tender the bill of lading as soon as possible after he has destined the cargo to the particular vendee. He assumes that if there is a mail the vendor will transmit the documents so that they will arrive before the ship. That is clearly the right view. The contract is performed in fact, and the date of its performance is the date when the documents would come forward, the vendor making every reasonable effort to forward them. In this case, on the evidence, such a period would be twenty to twenty-one days after the ship sailed. Not only from the course of business in this case, but from ordinary commercial usage, it would be reasonable for the vendor to send the documents by the mail by the Trans-Siberian Railway as soon as the goods had been shipped. They would have arrived on July 21 — that is, twenty or twenty-one days after the latest possible June shipment. They did not arrive on July 21, and there was consequently a breach of the contract on that date. What, then, is the remedy of the buyer? His remedies are specified in s. 51 of the Sale of Goods Act, 1893. His right is to place himself as nearly as possible in that position in which he would have been if the contract had been fulfilled. . . .

The only other question is as to "the time or times when they" — i.e. the goods — "ought to have been delivered" within the meaning of s. 51 of the Sale of Goods Act, 1893. Those words mean the time or times when they ought to be delivered according to the mode of delivery contemplated by the contract. If the contract provides for delivery of goods by means of documents, or by handing over the key of a warehouse, the date for that event is "the time . . . when they ought to have been delivered." In this case the date on which the documents ought to have arrived, that is to say July 21, is the important date in considering when the plaintiffs ought to have bought in the market. No doubt the plaintiffs ought to have a reasonable time in which to consider their position. The time cannot be indefinitely extended on the assumption that the plaintiffs could waive the term that the shipment should be in June. The matter has to be considered as between vendor and vendee on a contract to be performed strictly as to time. In these circumstances I fix the time for ascertaining the market or current price as somewhere about the last week in July. It is not necessary to fix the price very definitely, because the defendants have paid into Court the equivalent of 12*l.* a ton, and that is a sufficient allowance for all extra considerations. If August is the proper time to fix the market price, the price then was 17*l.* 10*s.* But in my view the end of July is the proper time, and the defendants have paid a sufficient sum into Court. In the result the defendants are entitled to judgment, but the plaintiffs get the costs of the action up to the date of payment into Court by the defendants.

Judgment for defendants.

BOWES *v.* SHAND

House of Lords, 1877

[*Law Reports, 2 Appeal Cases*, 455]

This was an action brought by Shand and others against Bowes and others for not accepting a cargo of rice.

The Plaintiffs carried on business in London and at Madras, and were the charterers of a vessel named the *Rajah of Cochin*. Bowes & Co. were colonial brokers in London.

The declaration stated the contract to be that "the Plaintiffs should sell and deliver to the Defendants, and the Defendants should buy and accept from the Plaintiffs . . . Madras rice, to be shipped at Madras, or coast, for the port of London, during the months of March and/or April, 1874, about 300 tons, per *Rajah of Cochin*," at &c., for "fair pinky." The prompt was to be "one month from breaking bulk." There was another contract for the same number of tons, expressed in the same form of words. The particulars of shipment to be declared when received. Plaintiffs alleged the arrival of the vessel and the refusal to accept.

The Defendants put several pleas on the record. The 5th alleged that the contract was made subject to the condition that the rice should be shipped at Madras, or coast, for the port of London during the months of March and/or April, 1874, and at no other time; that it was not so shipped, but at some other and earlier time, and thereby was rice different in description and character from the rice in the contract mentioned. The 12th plea, which related to the contract for the second 300 tons of rice, repeated this defence.

There was also a denial that the particulars of the shipments had been furnished in due time. Issue on the pleas.

The cause was tried at Guildhall before Mr. Justice Brett and a special jury in the Michaelmas Sittings, 1875.

It appeared in evidence that the loading of the *Rajah of Cochin* was begun on the 17th of February, 1874, and between that date and the 1st of March, 1874, 8150 bags were put on board. On Monday, the 2nd of March, the remaining fifty bags were put on board. Four bills of lading were signed by the master and delivered to the shippers. They were dated on the 23rd, 24th, and 28th of February, and the 3rd of March, and acknowledged the receipt on board on those several days of 1780 bags, 1780 bags, 3560 bags (all in February), and 1080 bags in March. The ship sailed from the Madras coast on the 10th of March, 1874, and arrived at London on the 14th of August. A correspondence took place between the parties, and on the 7th of September Bowes & Co. refused to accept the rice. It was sold in December at a loss, and the action was brought to recover the difference between the contract price and the price obtained at the sale.

Mr. Robinson, one of the Plaintiffs, was called as a witness at the trial, and, on cross-examination, he was asked whether a contract for a March or April shipment of rice did not mean that the rice was to be put on board in March or April, and he said[1] "when we sell rice, March or April shipments, it means that every bag should be put on board in March or April"; but he afterwards added, "there is a difference when the ship is named, in this respect." He stated that the particulars of shipment here were in fact declared as soon as received. On the part of the Defendants, witnesses were called who asserted that it would not be a March or April shipment if a single bag was shipped in February. The Defendant's manager said, "The bill of lading proves the date of shipment in absence of proof to the contrary."

One witness, Mr. Fraser (chairman of the Rice Brokers' Association), said: "The meaning of the phrase, 'Cargo March or April shipment,' is that every bit of the cargo is to be put on board in March or April." The learned Judge left the case to the jury in this form, "Was this cargo, as a cargo, a shipment in March and/or April in the ordinary business sense of the term? If it is for me, I hold the meaning to be, that, if the loading has been conducted consecutively, with ordinary and reasonable dispatch, and is completed in March or April, so that the vessel, so far as the loading of the cargo is concerned, may sail in March or April, that is sufficient." The verdict was found for the Plaintiff, the foreman of the jury adding, "The name of the vessel being given in the contract." Mr. Justice Brett asked, "You agree with me that if the loading has been conducted consecutively, with ordinary and reasonable dispatch, and is completed in March or April, so that the vessel may sail in March or April, that is sufficient?" The foreman answered, "We do, more especially where the name of the vessel is mentioned." Leave to move was reserved.

A motion was made for a new trial, on the ground that the verdict was against the weight of evidence; but the Court, finding that Mr. Justice Brett was satisfied with the verdict on that point, refused that rule. A rule was then obtained to enter judgment for the Defendants; and on the 26th of April, 1876, the Queen's Bench ordered the judgment to be so entered. On appeal that judgment was reversed. This appeal was then brought.

[The opinions of the Lord Chancellor (Lord Cairns), Lord Hatherley, and Lord O'Hagan are here omitted.]

Lord Blackburn. . . . But the parties have chosen, for reasons best known to themselves, to say: We bargain to take rice, shipped in this particular region, at that particular time, on board that particular ship, and before the Defendants can be compelled to take anything in fulfilment of that contract it must be shewn not merely that it is equally good, but that it is the same article as they have bargained for — otherwise they are not bound to take it.

That being so, the question which arises in this case is, whether the rice here tendered was shipped within the period stipulated for or not. That evidently involves in it two questions: first, what is meant by the word "shipped" as used in this contract? and, secondly, the question of fact whether the things which are proved in evidence to have taken place as

[1] Judge's notes of the trial contained in the printed papers.

regards these Defendants did amount to a shipping of the rice within the meaning which ought to be put upon the contract.

Like my noble and learned friend on the woolsack, before saying a word about the evidence which was actually given with regard to usage and custom, I will proceed to consider what is the meaning which your Lordships should, in the absence of any evidence of mercantile usage, put upon the word "shipped" in a contract of this sort. Supposing we had no help from mercantile usage, and had nothing to guide us but that general knowledge of dealings and of what takes place which Judges judicially possess and take notice of, what would that contract mean? It seems to me that where a parcel of goods is begun to be put on board on or after the 1st of March, and they are all finally put on board so that the shipping is entirely completed before the 31st of March, and nothing then remains but to take the bill of lading for them, there can be no doubt that that is a March shipment; the whole shipment is completed in that month. But there would be a good deal more difficulty in saying whether it was a March shipment or not, if the case were this: suppose the shipment of a large parcel of goods goes on, as one transaction, which occupies several days, suppose, for example, the shipment of a large parcel of goods which may take ten days or so to put on board, has been begun before the end of the month of February, and has been proceeded with continuously with reasonable dispatch, and in the ordinary way as a matter of fair dealing, and the completion of the shipment is in March although the commencement was in February, and the bill of lading is taken in March, I think the materiality of the bill of lading would merely be as evidence to shew that the shipment was then completed. I do not think that the delaying of the bill of lading for a fortnight would make the date of the shipment a fortnight later. I think the material thing is the completion of the putting it on board, which would entitle you to the bill of lading; but the bill of lading would be strong, and in most cases conclusive evidence, of the date when the shipment was really completed. I think, in a case of the sort I have supposed, there is a serious and grave question, whether or no the shipment may be considered as being made partly in one month and partly in the other, or whether it may not be considered as made at the time when the one indivisible transaction of putting those bags of rice on board was ended and completed, resulting in the whole parcel being on board, so that there is now a right to say: We have shipped this cargo, or portion of cargo, and we are now entitled to a bill of lading.

That, my Lords, was the case which arose in *Alexander* v. *Vanderzee* (Law Rep. 7 C. P. 530). The majority of the Court of Exchequer, the Lord Chief Baron dissenting, said that that was a sufficiently ambiguous matter to make it a proper question to ask the jury whether this was a shipment in June or not, that being the month when it ended, having begun in May. The decision was, that it was a proper case to take the opinion of the jury upon. I see that I said, standing, as far as I can perceive, alone in that respect, that without the aid of the finding of the jury I should have come to the same conclusion. I do not mean to say more about the case than this, that without saying I was wrong upon that, I have a very considerable hesitation and doubt in saying now that I was right. I pass by that case with merely that observation, and leave it as it stands.

When this case came before the Queen's Bench Division, and I had to give judgment, I could not consider whether the decision in *Alexander* v. *Vanderzee* (Law Rep. 7 C. P. 530) was right or wrong. Being a decision of the Court of Exchequer Chamber, it bound me, and consequently it was absolutely necessary, for the purpose of the decision there, to distinguish the case and shew that it was not the same as *Alexander* v. *Vanderzee* (Law Rep. 7 C. P. 530). Now, when I am advising your Lordships in the House of Lords, that is no longer so; I am not bound to say that the decision in *Alexander* v. *Vanderzee* (Law Rep. 7 C. P. 530) is good; but it is quite enough for the purpose of advising your Lordships what conclusion you should arrive at here to say, that I do distinguish the present case from *Alexander* v. *Vanderzee* (Law Rep. 7 C. P. 530), and that I think it is distinguishable now, for the same reasons as those for which I distinguished it in the Court of Queen's Bench, where it was absolutely necessary to distinguish it.

The facts are here that the great bulk of this rice was put on board during the month of February. For the great bulk, nine-tenths of it, bills of lading were signed in the month of February. With regard to the remaining one-tenth, a large part of that one-tenth was put on board in February, but a small portion amounting, I think, to four tons, was put on board in March, and the bill of lading for the last parcel was signed in March. Under these circumstances, it seems to me, that putting aside the mercantile evidence altogether, or having none, it is quite clear that as far as regards those nine-tenths which were put on board in February, and the shipment of which was completed in February, as was indicated by the taking of the bills of lading then, it was not part of a continuous operation eked out by putting on board four tons more in March. It seems to me that it was so completely a February shipment that, had this contract been slightly differently worded, and had it said "shipped in February," instead of saying "shipped in March and/or April," the Defendants clearly must have taken this as a February shipment — they could not have rejected it. I think that equally applies to the present case; being a February shipment it cannot be a March shipment.

I observe that in delivering the judgment of the Court of Appeal, Lord Justice Mellish — (and I suppose I need hardly say that every word which comes from him I consider with the greatest respect, and do not differ from, without thinking over it very much) — takes a different view of it. He says (2 Q. B. D. at p. 114): "We have therefore to consider whether, having regard to the terms of the two contracts, the circumstance of several bills of lading having been signed for different parcels of rice, instead of the whole being shipped under one bill of lading, makes any difference. A bill of lading is no part of the shipping of a cargo, it is only a declaration that the cargo has been shipped and is to be delivered on certain conditions." I quite agree that a bill of lading is no essential "part of the shipping of a cargo," or rather a parcel of goods, for "cargo" is an inaccurate word to use in reference to this case. A parcel of goods may be put on board a ship without a bill of lading at all; it is no necessary part therefore of the shipment. But when the question is whether there has been a shipment within a particular time or not, the fact that a bill of lading has been made out and signed is, to my mind, evidence, and until a mercantile man appears to tell me that it makes no difference, I should regard it as conclusive evidence that, as far as regards that portion of the shipment for which the bill of lading is signed, it is then completed, and is at an end. It is in that way that I consider it as being a decisive and important question, and I must say that, to my mind, the reasoning of Lord Justice Mellish, and the other learned Justices of Appeal who agreed with him on that part of the case, is not sound.

I think, therefore, that it comes round to this, that *prima facie* in the absence of mercantile evidence, or the like, the true construction of the contract is that "shipped in March" bears such a meaning that the portions or parcels of goods put on board in this case in February, and so completely put on board and shipped that bills of lading were signed for them (I say nothing about the last parcel), were not March shipments, they were not shipped in March, and consequently in the absence of mercantile usage the Defendants are entitled to judgment.

[The last page of the opinion and the opinion of Lord Gordon are here omitted.]

Judgment of the Court of Appeal reversed: Judgment of of the Queen's Bench Division restored: Declared that the appeal from the Queen's Bench Division to the Court of Appeals should have been dismissed with costs, and that the Respondents should pay to the Appellants the costs of the appeal to this House.

THE NATIONAL IMPORTING AND TRADING COMPANY, INC. *v.* E. A. BEAR & CO.

ILLINOIS SUPREME COURT, 1927

[324 *Illinois Reports*, 346]

Per Curiam: The defendant in error filed a suit in the superior court of Cook county against the plaintiff in error company on a contract for the sale and delivery of 225 cases of Chinese crystal hen egg albumen, of about 200 pounds net per case, at the price of $1.54 per pound, duty paid. The contract signed by the parties contained the following specifications:

Shipment from the Orient, 75 cases in April, 50 cases in May and 100 cases in June, 1920. Quality, f. a. q. of the season. To be approved before removal from docks. Terms of payment: Net cash sight draft against bill of lading. Insurance, by seller. Weights, shipping. Tare, shipping. Sample for arbitration to be drawn and sealed in the presence of both buyer and seller or by some persons agreed upon by both.

[The cases comprising the April shipment were put on board the carrying steamer at Shanghai on the last day of March, and the buyer refused to accept a tender by delivery order, at first without ascribing any reason, and later on the ground that shipment had not taken place according to the terms of the contract. The seller sold the goods in the open market, and the present action was to recover the difference between such sale price and the contract price. The jury returned a verdict for the plaintiff for $18,500; the Appellate Court affirmed this judgment, and the cause comes here by writ of *certiorari.*]

The first question involved in the case is whether there was a breach of the original contract by placing the albumen on board ship in the Orient on the 31st of March instead of during the month of April. It is conceded that the boat left Shanghai on April 1. This involves the question of construction of the language, "Shipment from the Orient, 75 cases in April," etc.

It is contended by the plaintiff in error that in contracts of this character time is of the essence of the contract and the buyer may refuse delivery if shipment is not made in strict accordance with the contract, though the difference may be slight; that statements of the date of shipment by the vendor go to the identification or description of the property and are therefore in the nature of warranties, proof of the truth of which is a condition precedent to recovery for failure to accept, and it cites in support of this contention *Bowes* v. *Shand,* 2 App. Cas. 455 (an English case decided in 1877), and cases based thereon. That case cites no authority, and its force as an authority is much weakened by the fact that it is not in harmony with the great weight of authority in this country as to what constitutes a shipment or the time when a shipment is considered as having been made. The contract in the Shand case provided for the sale of rice "to be shipped at Madras, or coast, during the months of March or April, by the steamer Rajah." A portion of the rice was loaded on the steamer in February, but the shipper did not complete the delivery to the vessel until some time in March. It was held that the loading of the vessel constituted the shipment and that the rice loaded in February was shipped in February and not in March, and so constituted a breach of warranty to ship in March or April. In this country a shipment does not consist in loading, alone, but consists in the complete delivery of goods by the shipper to a carrier for transportation, and the shipment is not made until the shipper has parted with all control over the goods and nothing remains to be done by him to complete the delivery, and where goods to be shipped are delivered to a carrier in installments the shipment is not made until the delivery is complete, and until such time the relation of the carrier to the installments delivered is that of warehouseman and not carrier.

Under the above rule, in the absence of a specific contract or of a trade custom to the contrary, the loading of a part of the rice on the steamer in February in the Shand case would not constitute a shipment in February but a shipment in March. There was proof of a trade custom in the case. While there are a few cases which hold that in those particular cases the time of shipment specified in the contract was a warranty as to the identity of the particular goods sold, in this case no particular goods were sold. The evidence shows that vast quantities of albumen are manufactured in the Orient, manufacturing commencing in January and shipments in March, and that there was no difference whatever between shipments made in March and those made in April. The evidence shows that one case of albumen meeting all the other requirements of the contract is just like any other. The time of shipment in the contract was not intended as a warranty of the quality of the albumen, as the contract in detail specifies its quality.

Whether or not time is of the essence of mercantile contracts is a question of fact, to be determined from the language used by the parties, read in the light of the circumstances surrounding them at the time of making the contract. Where a person deals in a particular market he must be taken to deal according to the known general or uniform usages of that market. (*Eau Claire Canning Co.* v. *Western Brokerage Co.* 213 Ill. 561.) Where no particular stipulations are made to the contrary, contracts made in the ordinary course of business are presumed to be made with reference to any existing usage or custom relating to such trade, and it is always competent to resort to such usage or custom to ascertain and fix the terms of the contract (*El Reno Grocery Co.* v. *Stocking*, 293 Ill. 494); and where words are used in a mercantile contract which are susceptible of more than one meaning, it is always competent to prove that in the particular market in which the contract was made according to the known usages of that market such words have a particular meaning. It is therefore competent in this case to prove that in the albumen trade, in the market in which the contract was made, the terms "Shipment from the Orient, 75 cases in April," had a particular meaning.

[A page of the opinion is here omitted.]

China, Japan, Ceylon and Sumatra were customarily known as the Orient, and a shipment of 75 cases of albumen in April from any place in this vast territory, without regard to when it was manufactured, would have technically met the call of this contract, and the evidence shows that the length of time of arrival of shipments made from these various countries would vary greatly. The date of the shipment could in nowise tend to identify the goods shipped and could give only a very indefinite and general idea of the time of arrival. We cannot hold, as a matter of law, that time of shipment was of the essence of this contract and that the vendee had a right to rescind the same for a breach of warranty by reason of the fact that the albumen in question was placed upon the steamer on March 31 instead of April 1.

[The balance of the opinion is here omitted. In the result, judgment for the plaintiff was reversed on other grounds, and the cause remanded for a new trial.]

THOMPSON and DUNN, JJ., dissenting:

The contract in question provided for "shipment from the Orient, 75 cases in April," which, as the authorities hold, means placing on board ship during the month of April. The contract did not say anything about the time of delivery, and a discussion of whether the change in time of shipment affected or might have affected the time of delivery has no place in this case. The parties had the right to contract for shipment in April, and having entered into such a contract the purchaser has the right to insist upon its fulfillment. A shipment on March 31 was no more a shipment in April than a shipment on January 31 or May 31. What was sold was not merely seventy-five cases of albumen of a certain quality, but was seventy-five cases of albumen to be put on board ship in the month of April. Albumen put on board ship in any other month is not the article sold. Where the purchaser contracts to buy rice shipped in March he is not obliged to take rice put on board ship in February, although the ship sails in March. (*Bowes* v. *Shand,* 2 App. Cas. 455.) Where the article sold is pig iron to be shipped from Glasgow, the seller cannot compel the buyer to accept pig iron shipped from Leith. (*Filley* v. *Pope,* 115 U. S. 213.) Where the parties bargained for a "shipment from Java to Philadelphia," the buyer may refuse to accept sugar shipped from Java to New York and later diverted to Philadelphia. (*National Bank* v. *Lamborn,* 2 Fed. — 2d ser. — 23.) The courts have neither the means nor the right to consider whether there is any substantial reason why the parties described the article sold by fixing the time or place of shipment. Merchants usually attach some value to stipulations they place in their contracts, and the purchaser has the right to demand delivery, according to contract, of the article he buys and not some other article. If the article tendered is different in any respect from the article bargained for the purchaser is not bound to take it. Equally good albumen might have been shipped in March or May, but the parties chose, for reasons sufficient to themselves, to contract respecting albumen shipped in April and such albumen is all the purchaser is obliged to take. The only safe rule is to allow competent persons to make their own contracts. It is the duty of the courts to adhere to the terms used and to enforce a contract as it is written.

For these and other reasons unnecessary to set forth we respectfully dissent.

In J. ARON AND COMPANY (INCORPORATED) *v.* COMPTOIR WEGIMONT, [1921] 3 K. B. 435 (King's Bench Division, 1921), a contract for the sale of 20 tons of cocoa powder at an agreed price c.i.f. London called for shipment by steamer from U. S. A. ports during October. The seller delivered the goods to a dock on October 8, but a strike of longshoremen prevented loading in that month, so that the cocoa powder finally was loaded and left port in November. The seller obtained both a dock receipt dated October 8, and a document in the form of a bill of lading dated October 22, the latter reading: "Received in apparent good order and condition . . . to be transported by the good ship Idaho and/or following steamer." In passing on the question of shipment in connection with an award in the form of a special case due to the rejection of the documents by the buyers, McCardie, J., said: "I take in order the questions argued before me. The first was this —namely, whether the goods were 'shipped' in October. Mr. van den Berg for the sellers vigorously argued that shipment in October had actually taken place by reason of delivery at the dock to the agents of the ship in the manner I have stated. The bill of lading — I use the phrase for convenience — is, as I have said, dated October 22, 1919.

"In *Bowes* v. *Shand* ([1877] 2 App. Cas. 455) Lord Blackburn said (*ibid.* 482): 'The bill of lading would be strong, and in most cases conclusive evidence, of the date when the shipment was really completed.' No doubt this was so in 1877, but in view of the changed conditions of recent years I doubt whether the date on a bill of lading is now anything more than *prima facie* evidence of date of shipment. However that may be, it is of course clear that any inference arising from the date of the bill of lading can be displaced by proof or admission of the actual facts. In *In re General Trading Co. and Van Stolk's Commissiehandel* ([1911] 16 Com. Cas. 95, 101) A. T. Lawrence J. said: 'If the bill of lading bears the contract date, but the shipment is not in accordance with the contract, the proof of date afforded by the bill of lading may be displaced by evidence.' Here the actual facts are not in dispute.

"In my opinion those facts do not show 'shipment' in October, 1919, as required by the contract. Delivery at docks to the agents of a ship for the purpose of future shipment is not the same thing as an actual shipment on board. . . . It follows then that as the goods here were not in fact shipped on board in October, 1919, the buyers were *prima facie* entitled to reject the documents and goods."

[The learned judge then stated that this *prima facie* right of rejection was not overthrown by a term of the contract referring to a difference in the shipment from the description of the goods, as "in my humble view the express requirement of a contract that goods shall be shipped at a particular period is a good deal more than a mere description of the goods . . . ; it is an express term of the contract independent of that which is generally known as a description of the goods. It is, I think, a condition precedent."]

The contract of sale often provides that the date of the bill of lading is to be taken as proof of the date of shipment. In such a case, where the contract called for shipment "to be made from Java during September," it was held in *Second National Bank* v. *Columbia Trust Co.*, 288 Fed. 17 (C.C.A. 3d, 1923), that in the absence of fraud "the date in the bill of lading must be construed as absolute proof of the actual date of shipment."

See however OLIVIER STRAW GOODS CORPORATION *v.* OSAKA SHOSEN KAISHA, 27 Fed. (2nd) 129 (C.C.A. 2nd, 1928), where under similar circumstances it was held that such a clause could not be construed "to change a contract which set a definite limit for the date of shipment into an agreement requiring nothing more than 'delivery for shipment' to the carrier within the time. Such an interpretation would contradict the requirement of shipment before a certain date, and would render the time when the goods were likely to arrive doubly uncertain."

For interesting applications, see IN RE THE GENERAL TRADING CO., 16 Com. Cas. 95 (King's Bench Division, 1911), where a contract for the sale of beans c.i.f. Rotterdam contained a clause "shipment made or to be made and bill of lading dated or to be dated during December 1909 and/or January 1910"; and also provided "bill of lading to be considered proof of date of shipment in the absence of evidence to the contrary." Bills of lading were dated February 2, but it appeared that the beans actually had been shipped on January 30 and 31. It was held that the buyer was entitled to have bills of lading of the contract date, as otherwise "there could be no resale with any security."

In UNITED BALTIC CORPORATION *v.* BURGETT & NEWSAM, 8 Ll. L. R. 190 (Court of Appeal, 1921), the contract read "shipment to be made by ocean-going vessel or vessels and bills of lading dated January or February, 1920." The bill of lading was dated January 31, but the goods were not loaded until February 4. The Court of Appeals, reversing the lower Court, held that the shipment was in accordance with the contract.

FRANK E. CHILDS & BRO., INC. *v.* ADOLPH HIRSCH & CO., INC.

NEW YORK SUPREME COURT, APPELLATE TERM, 1923

[202 *New York Supplement*, 226]

Appeal from Municipal Court, Borough of Manhattan, First District.

Action by Frank E. Childs & Bro., Inc., against Adolph Hirsch & Co., Inc., and J. Aron & Co., Inc. From a judgment for defendant Adolph Hirsch & Co., Inc., on its counterclaim, plaintiff appeals. Judgment reversed, and, in accordance with the stipulation of the parties as to the respective amounts to be awarded in case plaintiff is entitled to recover, judgment directed for plaintiff for $437.39 against defendant Adolph Hirsch & Co., Inc., and for that defendant for $816.53 on its counterclaim against J. Aron & Co., Inc.

Per Curiam. The only question under the stipulated facts by all the parties is whether the delivery by plaintiff's consignor of 1,000 bags of cocoa to the steamship line at Bahia, Brazil, and the issuance of a bill of lading therefor on October 31, 1922, for transportation to New York, was a compliance with a contract of purchase by the defendant Adolph Hirsch & Co. from the plaintiff on September 9, 1922, at New York, of "one thousand (1,000) bags good fair Bahia cocoa, for September-October shipment from Bahia at 9 cents per pound."

The court below held that "shipment" meant placing the goods "on board" the steamer, and that the plaintiff had not performed the contract in that respect, and justified the said defendant, and the codefendant as a subpurchaser, in rejecting the cocoa solely on that ground. We are of the opinion that under modern conditions, and in the absence of special circumstances showing a different intention of the parties, the words "for September-October shipment" should be construed as meaning that the goods could be delivered on any day during the specified time to the steamship line for transportation. *Goldenberg* v. *Cutler*, 189 App. Div. 489, 490, 178 N. Y. Supp. 522. The plaintiff was not bound to see that the goods were actually "on board," as there is no fact stipulated tending to show any bad faith upon the part of the plaintiff.

Judgment reversed, with $30 costs to appellant against J. Aron & Co., Inc., and, in accordance with the stipulation of all the parties as to the respective amounts to be awarded in case the plaintiff is entitled to a recovery, judgment directed for the plaintiff for $437.39 against defendant Adolph Hirsch & Co., Inc., and for the defendant Adolph Hirsch & Co., Inc., for $816.53 upon its counterclaim against J. Aron & Co., Inc., the subpurchaser.

Note also STALLMAN *v.* FRANCIS A. CUNDILL & CO., 288 Fed. 643 (S.D.N.Y. 1922), where there was a contract for 30 cases of camphor at an agreed price c.i.f. London, "shipment to be made promptly by steamer from New York to London." The seller tendered a bill of lading which merely acknowledged receipt "for shipment." In holding this a sufficient compliance with the contract, Learned Hand, D.J., said: "I regard the word 'shipment,' when used in such a contract at the present time and for delivery in the port of New York, as subject to the custom of that port, and to require no more than delivery to a carrier in good standing, receiving from him one of the so-called bills of lading which have been put in evidence here."

Compare GEORGE WILLS & SONS, LTD. *v.* LARZELERE, 288 Fed. 559 (C.C.A. 9th, 1923). In that case a contract was entered into for the sale of 75 tons of onions at an agreed price, landed on the dock, duty paid, San Francisco, "shipment to be effected from Australia by steamer on the 10th of March, 1917." In an action by the seller for damages because of refusal to accept delivery, it was held that the contract must be construed as requiring the departure of the onions from Australia on March 10. "It is not shown that this language has a distinctive conventional meaning in commercial usage, and to the common understanding we think it would naturally imply departure."

Similarly in COMMERCIAL UNION OF AMERICA, INC. *v.* ANGLO-SOUTH AMERICAN BANK, 16 Fed. (2nd) 979 (C.C.A. 2nd, 1927), it was held that a contract provision "shipped . . . by steamer . . . direct from New York to Spain, sailing during first half of November, 1920," required that the ship break ground during that period.

To the same effect is STEIN *v.* HAMBRO'S BANK OF NORTHERN COMMERCE, 10 Ll. L. R. 529 (Court of Appeal, 1922), reversing the lower Court, which had held in 9 Ll. L. R. 507 (King's Bench Division, 1921), that the clause "per steamer Caboto leaving Calcutta about the middle of January" was merely descriptive of the vessel named as the carrying vessel.

For the construction of other clauses bearing on shipment, and hence on delivery, see *Bradlee & McIntosh Co.* v. *Frey & Sons, Inc.*, 280 Fed. 375 (C.C.A. 4th, 1922), "expected to arrive"; and *Sanday & Co.* v. *Keighley, Maxsted & Co.*, 91 L. J. K. B. 624 (Court of Appeal, 1922), "expected ready to load."

MOWBRAY, ROBINSON & CO. *v.* ROSSER

COURT OF APPEAL, 1922

[91 *Law Journal, King's Bench*, 524]

Appeal from a decision of Commissioner Sir William Finlay, K.C., at Lancaster.

The plaintiffs were Americans, owners of lumber mills in the United States, and through their broker in Liverpool, an Englishman, they sold timber to the defendant, who was also English. The contract stated that shipment was to be before November 30, 1920, and payment was to be in London against delivery of shipping documents. The documents were presented in due course, but the defendant refused to carry out the contract for various reasons, *inter alia* because the goods had not been shipped by the date specified. The plaintiffs gave evidence that at that date "shipment" had been made in the sense that the timber had been loaded on the railway cars near their mills for transport to New Orleans, and they alleged that in America, and particularly by the custom of that trade, "shipment" meant the loading on railway wagons just as much as the loading on a vessel. Mr. Commissioner Finlay upheld the plaintiffs' contention, and gave judgment for them. The defendant appealed.

LORD STERNDALE, M.R., after stating the facts: There cannot be the slightest doubt that the words "shipment to be made not later than the end of November next" standing by themselves, mean shipment on the ship which is to carry the goods across the Atlantic. But the plaintiffs say that in this trade, by custom — it is not exactly a custom of the trade, but of the way they use words in this trade — "shipment" means shipment on to the car or loading on to the car at the saw-mills from which the lumber comes. The learned Commissioner has held that the evidence established that that is the meaning in the trade, and he has held that the evidence was admissible, and that, therefore, "shipment" in this contract must be taken to mean loading on cars. The defendant, if I remember rightly, said: "Of course what I wanted to know was when I was likely to get these goods, and I should know that if I knew when they were shipped at New Orleans. On the other hand, I should know nothing at all as to when I might get them, if I only knew that they were to be on truck" — perhaps I should say "cars" as we are dealing with America — "at the mills." It does not seem an unreasonable point of view, because, of course he does not know from what mills they are coming, over what line they are coming, or anything about them, or what obstacles, interferences or hindrances may occur in bringing them to the seaboard. On the other hand — and this does not seem unreasonable either — the plaintiffs say: "We have control of the mills; they are our mills; therefore we know that we can control the time at which the goods are put into the cars. But we cannot control, any more than the man on the other side of the Atlantic, the time that those goods will take to get down to the seaboard to be put on board the ship, and therefore we would not take the risk of contracting in respect of a date when they are to be put on board of the ship."

Neither of the positions seems an unreasonable one, in fact both of them seem to me very reasonable, the question being, which is the one which has been expressed in this contract? It seems to me that nobody could possibly say that those words were in the least ambiguous. The expression "shipment" is used in an English contract, made between two English people, in England, although it is true that one of those English people was contracting on behalf of a subject of the United States. There is not the slightest ambiguity in it. No doubt the words "shipped," "shipment," and so on, are sometimes used with meanings that are not the ordinary meanings. There are very few words that have not got some sort of metaphorical sense attached to them by somebody, in some sense, and in some context.

But there is no ambiguity about the ordinary use of the word "shipment." The question is whether a customary meaning can be attached by evidence of people in this particular trade, which makes it mean not "shipment," as anybody in ordinary circumstances would understand it, but "put upon cars at the works." I am not sure that it is a hopeless task, but at any rate it is too difficult a task for me to attempt to undertake to reconcile all the authorities and all the cases that have been decided on the question of the admissibility of custom to alter the ordinary meanings of words. It is enough for me to say that, in my opinion, this case is governed in principle by the last case which was decided in this Court, namely, *The Turid*. That case is standing now for consideration in the House of Lords. It was a case in which the cargo was to be taken from "alongside" the steamer, and it was sought to show that alongside the steamer meant taken from a point some considerable distance from the steamer, to which it was carried by stages which were put up from the vessel to the quay, because there was not enough water for the vessel to put up and lie alongside of the quay. On the authority of *Holman* v. *Wade*, we held that such a custom was inconsistent with the contract as it stood, and could not be admitted. There is, perhaps, a fraction more of ambiguity in the word "shipment" than there is in the words "alongside the steamer," but on the authority of that case, in my opinion, this custom was not admissible to interpret "shipping" as meaning loading on board the cars at the mills. I do not think it is a matter which affects the construction of the document, but perhaps it is a little significant that where the sellers did tender documents, they tendered no document at all which related to any part of the transit except the ocean transit.

Having dealt with other points of no interest to this report, his Lordship said that the appeal succeeded upon the first point, and there must be judgment for the defendants with costs.

[Concurring opinions of Warrington, L.J. and of Scrutton, L.J., are here omitted.]

See also JAMES FINLAY & COMPANY, LIMITED *v.* N. V. KWIK HOO TONG HANDEL MAATSCHAPPIJ, [1928] 2 K. B. 604 (King's Bench Division, 1928), where a contract for the sale of Java sugar c.i.f. Bombay called for September shipment from Java. The carrying vessel arrived at the Java port September 30, but did not load until October 1. A bill of lading was given dated September 30, and in an action by the buyers for damages for breach of contract, the seller alleged a custom in Java to give bills of lading dated on the day of ship's arrival. Wright, J., held that such a custom, even if proved, would have no legal effect, as contrary to the express terms of the contract.

D. IMPOSSIBILITY; FORCE MAJEURE AND COMMERCIAL FRUSTRATION

HUNI & WORMSER, LTD. *v.* E. D. SASSOON & CO.

COURT OF APPEAL, 1920

[5 *Lloyd's List Law Reports*, 199]

Lord Justice BANKES, in giving judgment, said: This is an appeal from a judgment of Mr. Justice Rowlatt upon a special case stated by an Arbitrator, who, we are told, was very greatly experienced in that class of trade in reference to which this dispute has arisen. The facts shortly are these. Messrs. Huni & Wormser, by a contract dated Nov. 25, 1919, sold to Messrs. Sassoon a cargo of 2200 tons of linseed to be shipped per sailing vessel *Fahrwohl*, expected ready to load during February and first half of March, 1920. The seed was to be delivered in sound merchantable condition, and warranted to be about the fair average quality of the season at the time of shipment. The terms were c.i.f. terms, and the sellers in fact chartered this vessel and she was in Buenos Ayres on Feb. 22, in time to take delivery of the cargo. Unfortunately, on Feb. 23 she came into collision with a vessel called the *Hilston*, which she sank. The *Fahrwohl* was herself badly damaged, and the Master on the same day cabled the fact to the owners. The condition of the ship was communicated to the sellers, and on March 11 they wrote to the buyers stating: —

> We have been advised by cable by our Buenos Ayres house that it would be impossible for the vessel to be ready to load during February and first half of March, by reason of the damage sustained, which appears to be so serious that it may be impossible to repair her at Buenos Ayres, and which, in any case, would take several months to carry out.

And under these circumstances they went on to say: —

> In consequence, we regret to inform you that the contract is to be considered as cancelled.

Well, after a little correspondence the buyers took the view that the most sensible thing to do would be to accept the repudiation and to refer the matter to arbitration as to whether or not the sellers were or were not right in their contention that under the circumstances there had been a frustration of the adventure which entitled the sellers to treat the contract as cancelled. The matter was referred to an Arbitrator, and he made his Award in the form of a special case. The important findings seem to me to be those in Para. 6 and Para. 16. In Para. 6 he says: —

"The said telegram was communicated to the sellers, informing them that the ship was unseaworthy and must remain so pending extensive repairs for some months. In so far as it may be a question of fact and not law I find that such a conclusion was reasonable and a necessary inference from the said telegram."

In Para. 16 he says: —

"I find by the same collision it became impossible that the vessel should be ready to load either within the aforesaid period or within a reasonable time thereof." . . .

Now what is the effect of that finding upon the position of the parties, having regard to the contract? They had entered into a contract in which reference was made to the loading time for this particular cargo, and it seems to me that under a contract between buyer and seller reference to loading time may take one of three different forms. There may be a definite undertaking as to the loading date, or there may be a more general statement of what the parties expected might happen in reference to the loading date, or it might take the form of a statement of probabilities as to the loading date on the fulfilment of which the performance of the contract must depend.

Now there is no question here as to any statement containing a positive undertaking as to the loading date, and the question is whether or not the statement of the contract came within the second or third of the three classes I have indicated. As I understand the learned Judge's judgment, he has found that it was a statement of the second class, a mere general statement of possibilities, because he says: — "There is no contract that she will load in fact," and then, at the end of his judgment, he says: —

"And in all the other cases that have arisen since, it was not that the delay would be for more than the reasonable time. It was that the delay would be such as to utterly displace the whole adventure, and make it a different kind of thing altogether. But that does not really arise in this case because the real question was whether the loading was for February and first half of March, or whether the vessel was to be in such a position, at the time of the contract, so that that was likely to happen. Now that was true and there was no breach of the contract on the part of the buyers, and I am of opinion that the buyers are entitled to damages."

And I understand that the Judge thinks that because the vessel had arrived off her loading port in time to take the cargo, there was no breach of contract and no frustration of the adventure, but I cannot at all take that view of this contract having regard to the finding of the Arbitrator, because it seems to me that this statement as to the loading date must involve the implied condition that the vessel should be ready during February and the first half of March, 1920, or within some reasonable time thereafter, to enable this particular contract to be performed, because it was for a shipment warranted fair average quality of the season at the time of shipment.

Now, we have been referred to three decisions, all of which appear to me to be very much in point. First, there was *Jackson* v. *Union Marine Insurance Company*, but the facts there were different from these. The second was *Nichol* v. *Knight Ashton*, a case between buyer and seller, and the only distinction between that and the present case was that in the case of *Nichol* v. *Knight Ashton*, the cargo was to be shipped at Alexandria during the month of January, that is to say, there was a contract as here to ship by a named vessel, the only distinction being that the shipment in that case was to be during the month of January, whereas in this case there was a contract for shipment by the named vessel, but the statement was not that she was to load during February and the first half of March, but expected ready to load.

Does that make any real difference, having regard to the facts of the present case? It seems to me that the answer is to be found by applying the tests and that reasoning which Lord Sumner indicated in a judgment in a case with which he was dealing. He said: "The theory of the dissolution of a contract by frustration of its objects rests on an implication arising from the presumed intention of the parties."

Then he proceeds to consider the various tests that have been applied, and among others he mentions the test which was said to be the correct one to be applied, by Lord Dunedin in *Bush and the Whitehaven Trustees*, and he quotes that statement with approval. Lord Dunedin's statement was this, that interruption may be so long as to destroy the identity of the work or service when resumed with the work or service when interrupted. And Lord Sumner also quotes with approval Lord Watson's statement that there may be many possibilities which would not be actually present to the minds of the parties, and the meaning of the contract must be taken to be not what the parties did intend, but what the parties, as fair and reasonable men, would have agreed upon if, having such possibilities in view, they had made provision for what would have happened in the events of this case.

Now, apply either of those tests to this case, what is the position? What would the parties have agreed upon if, at the time they made this contract, they had been told that on March 11 the probabilities were that the named vessel would not be available to ship the cargo for many months? Or what would anyone conversant with this trade say on the question as to what effect the interruption of the shipment from February-mid-March for many months would have in reference to the destruction of the identity of the work or service when resumed with the work or service when interrupted? And in my opinion the only answer that could really be given under the circumstances is the one given by the Arbitrator. It must be assumed that he applied to that particular question his own knowledge of the trade, and applying his knowledge of the trade to the facts as he found them, it seems to me he was perfectly justified, even if the criticism be correct that his fourteenth finding is a finding in law, in coming to the conclusion that he did. His finding, even if it be a finding of law, is a right and just conclusion of law upon the facts as he stated them, and under these circumstances I am not able to agree with the view of the learned Judge, and I think the question submitted by the Arbitrator must be answered in the sense that the contract was frustrated and that the repudiation was justified. Therefore the appeal must be allowed, with costs.

Lord Justice ATKIN and Lord Justice YOUNGER concurred.

Compare JACOBS, MARCUS & CO. *v.* CREDIT LYONNAIS, 12 Q. B. D. 589 (Court of Appeal, 1884), where there was an action for the non-delivery of esparto under a contract calling for shipment from Algeria. The sellers contended that an insurrection in Algeria, and military operations connected with it, made performance impossible, constituting "force majeure" which would excuse non-delivery under the French Civil Code which was in force throughout Algeria. After deciding that the contract should be governed by English law, the Court affirmed a judgment for the plaintiffs, saying through Bowen, L.J.: "One of the incidents which the English law attaches to a contract is that . . . a person who expressly contracts absolutely to do a thing not naturally impossible, is not excused for non-performance because of being prevented by vis major."

Compare also AMERICAN STEEL CO. *v.* IRVING NAT. BANK, 266 Fed. 41 (C.C.A. 2nd, 1920), in which there was an action by a seller to recover the amount of a dishonored draft drawn on a bank under an irrevocable letter of credit in connection with a contract for the sale of tin plate. This latter contract became impossible of execution because of the inability of the seller to secure an export license from the United States government. A defense to the action based on such impossibility was dismissed as inconsequential on the ground that the liability assumed by the bank to the seller was absolute, and that it was immaterial whether the seller could export the tin or not.

BLACKBURN BOBBIN COMPANY, LIMITED *v.* T. W. ALLEN & SONS, LIMITED

COURT OF APPEAL, 1918

[*Law Reports*, [1918] 2 *King's Bench*, 467]

By a contract made in the early part of 1914 the defendants, who were timber merchants at Hull, sold to the plaintiffs 70 standards of Finland birch timber to be delivered to the plaintiffs free on rail at Hull, deliveries to commence in June or July, 1914, and to continue during the season which would terminate in November, 1914. The contract contained no war or force majeure or suspension provisions. Before the outbreak of war in August, 1914, the practice was to load timber into vessels at Finnish ports for direct sea carriage to England, but this practice was not known to the plaintiffs, nor did they know, as the fact was, that timber merchants in England do not keep Finland timber in stock. Up to the outbreak of the war the defendants had not delivered any of the timber, and after that date, owing to the disorganization of transport caused by the war, it became impossible for the defendants to obtain any Finland timber for delivery to the plaintiffs.

In an action by the plaintiffs claiming damages from the defendants for failure to deliver the timber, the defendants contended that the contract had been dissolved by the outbreak of war.

McCardie J. gave judgment for the plaintiffs, holding (1.) that the contract had not been dissolved, and that the defendants were liable in damages for the non-delivery of the timber; and (2.) that the contract was not one for the supply of materials "for any building or work" within s. 1, sub-s. 1, of the Courts (Emergency Powers) Act, 1917.

The defendants appealed from the decision on the first point.

Pickford L.J. This is an appeal from a decision of McCardie J., and the point raised is whether an implication is to be read into the contract the performance of which has been interfered with or prevented by matters arising out of the war. The contract, which contained no exceptions, was for the sale by the defendants to the plaintiffs of 70 standards of Finland birch timber at the price of 10*l.* 15*s.* per standard free on rail at Hull. Before the war it was the regular practice to load the timber on vessels at ports in Finland for direct sea carriage to English ports, and not to send it by rail across Scandinavia and ship it from a Scandinavian port to England. When war broke out the Germans declared timber to be contraband, but, even before that declaration, sailings from Finnish ports had entirely ceased, and therefore the ordinary and normal method of supplying Finland timber came to an end. I will assume that it was not possible, at first at any rate, to get Finland birch timber to England at all, although it is true that in 1916 a certain amount was sent across Scandinavia and shipped from ports there. In August, 1914, and the following months some correspondence took place between the plaintiffs and the defendants as to the timber, the former asking for supplies, and the defendants taking up the position that all pre-war contracts had been cancelled by the war.

The defendants contend that the contract was at an end because it was in the contemplation of both parties that the defendants should be able to supply the timber according to the ordinary method of supplying it in the trade, and that when that became impossible both parties were discharged from their obligations. We have had a most interesting discussion of the numerous cases where this doctrine has been dealt with, and it is from no disrespect to Mr. MacKinnon's argument that I refrain from going through them, but I refrain from doing so because I accept the principle for which those cases were cited. The principle was thus stated by Lord Haldane in *Tamplin Steamship Co.* v. *Anglo-Mexican Petroleum Products Co.* ([1916] 2 A. C. 397, 406): "The occurrence itself," i.e. the occurrence preventing the performance of the contract, "may yet be of a character and extent so sweeping that the foundation of what the parties are deemed to have had in contemplation has disappeared, and the contract itself has vanished with that foundation." It was also stated thus by Lord Shaw in *Horlock* v. *Beal* ([1916] 1 A. C. 486, 512): "The underlying ratio is the failure of something which was at the basis of the contract in the mind and intention of the contracting parties." In my opinion McCardie J. was right in saying that the principle of these cases did not apply to discharge the defendants in this case. He has found that the plaintiffs were unaware at the time of the contract of the circumstance that the timber from Finland was shipped direct from a Finnish port to Hull, and that they did not know whether the transport was or was not partly by rail across Scandinavia, nor did they know that timber merchants in this country did not hold stocks of Finnish birch. I accept the finding that in fact the method of dispatching this timber was not known to the plaintiffs. But there remains the question, Must they be deemed to have contracted on the basis of the continuance of that method although they did not in fact know of it? I see no reason for saying so. Why should a purchaser of goods, not specific goods, be deemed to concern himself with the way in which the seller is going to fulfil his contract by providing the goods he has agreed to sell? The sellers in this case agreed to deliver the timber free on rail at Hull, and it was no concern of the buyers as to how the sellers intended to get the timber there. I can see no reason for saying — and to free the defendants from liability this would have to be said — that the continuance of the normal mode of shipping the timber from Finland was a matter which both parties contemplated as necessary for the fulfilment of the contract. To dissolve the contract the matter relied on must be something which both parties had in their minds when they entered into the contract, such for instance as the existence of the music-hall in *Taylor* v. *Caldwell* ([1863] 3 B. & S. 826), or the continuance of the vessel in readiness to perform the contract, as in *Jackson* v. *Union Marine Insurance Co.* ([1873] L. R. 8 C. P. 572; [1874] L. R. 10 C. P. 125). Here there is nothing to show that the plaintiffs contemplated, and there is no reason why they should be deemed to have contemplated, that the sellers should continue to have the ordinary facilities for dispatching the timber from Finland. As I have said, that was a matter which to the plaintiffs was wholly immaterial. It was not a matter forming the basis of the contract they entered into.

On the facts the nearest case to this is *Ashmore* v. *Cox* ([1899] 1 Q. B. 436). There shipment was to be made by sailer or sailers from a port or ports in the Philippine Islands between May 1 and July 31, 1898. The Spanish-American war prevented the shipment by sailer between the dates mentioned. Lord Russell of Killowen C.J. held that no implied condition was to be imported that it was possible to ship by sailer between those dates. I think that case was rightly decided, and this is an *a fortiori* case.

For the reasons I have given the defendants have failed on the facts to make out their case that the contract was dissolved. The appeal will be dismissed.

[Concurring opinions of Bankes, L.J., and Warrington, L.J., are here omitted.]

IN RE COMPTOIR COMMERCIAL ANVERSOIS AND POWER, SON AND COMPANY

COURT OF APPEAL, 1919

[*Law Reports*, [1920] 1 *King's Bench*, 868]

[Statement of facts, the opinion of Bailhache, J., below, and the opinions of Bankes, L.J., and Warrington, L.J., are here omitted.]

SCRUTTON L.J. read the following judgment: — In this case I might content myself with saying that with one or two small exceptions I entirely agree with the very careful and closely reasoned judgment of Bailhache J., but as the case may go higher and is of considerable general importance I express my judgment in my own words.

The sellers, the appellants, had eight contracts with the buyers for the supply of wheat from the United States, one contract for Rotterdam and the remainder for Antwerp. Shipment was to be completed at periods between July 1 and September 15, 1914, no contract having an earlier date for completion than August 11. The price was "free on board including freight and insurance," which meant that the sellers had to find the ship and the policy. The policy was only to cover marine risks. Payment was in cash on presentation to buyers (i.e., in Belgium) of bill of lading. There was a provision about insurance of war risk to which I refer later. In shipments from the United States, where payment by the contract is on the other side of the Atlantic, it is very usual, almost universal, for the seller to obtain his money in advance of the contract time by "selling the exchange." I have stated the reasons of this practice, which is also common in the cotton trade, in *Guaranty Trust Company of New York* v. *Hannay & Co.* ([1918] 2 K. B. 623, 659, 660), and Bailhache J. has stated them in his judgment in this case. The only point on which I differ from Bailhache J. is that he treats selling the exchange as a matter arising after shipment and insurance, whereas I think it is generally provided for by contracts of sale, covers or credits effected beforehand by the seller. For instance, in the miscellaneous documents treated as evidence in this case by the arbitrators will be found statements, "Equitable Trust Co. to whom have sold our bills against contracts advised they could not accept bills for the present" — "International bankers will not accept bills in old engagements" — "American Express Company repudiate exchange contract" — "Banks here have refused honour exchange, although war risk covered and exchange sold them prior European hostilities." — "Banks refused accept exchange previously sold." The truth is the system is a way to finance a general selling business, not to render any one transaction possible. Any one transaction could be carried through without exchange, but the seller would be out of money for some time, and so hampered in subsequent operations. Its justification is the general volume of business, not the particular transaction. In this case the sellers had steamers chartered to carry the goods to Antwerp and Rotterdam. There is no finding whether the steamers refused to proceed to Antwerp or Rotterdam, and there are no materials for deciding whether, if they did refuse, they were in the right under their charters. We have had cases in these courts where shipowners have been held to be in the wrong in refusing to proceed to Dutch or Belgian ports for fear of hostilities. But it is proved and found that exchange houses in New York refused to buy exchange on these steamers, and that this inability continued from August 1 till the middle of September, the period of shipment covered by these contracts. There is also a finding that from August 1 to 6, when the sellers cancelled the contracts, no war risk insurance was procurable on these voyages, and this was at any rate one of the reasons why the purchase of exchange could not be effected. We are not told whether the sellers had any general contracts or covers for exchange, and if so whether their terms allowed the bankers or exchange houses to refuse documents in the events that happened. Anyhow the sellers did on August 6 cancel these contracts of sale, and sent the steamers with the goods on board to other destinations.

Thereupon the matter went to the arbitration tribunal of the Corn Exchange who have decided against the buyers, but stated a special case. Anyone who compares the findings of fact in this case with those in the case which came before Sankey J. (*Bassano Zuccotti & Co.* v. *Carruthers*, not reported) will be struck by the way in which findings of commercial custom made by commercial arbitrators grow to meet difficulties raised in the Courts. The arbitrators who have decided in favour of the sellers have apparently rested their decision on three grounds which they treat as findings of fact. (1) That shipment was prevented by hostilities. (2) That the sale of goods provided for in the contracts in question could not be carried out unless (sale of) exchange was possible, and it was an implied term of the contracts that the sellers at all material times should be able to sell exchange. (3) That the commercial purpose of the adventure, so far as the sellers were concerned, was frustrated by this impossibility.

First, as to the prevention of shipment by hostilities, it is remarkable that the arbitrators, who find this as a fact, also find that the sellers shipped all the goods under their contracts in accordance with their tenders. They have obviously in my view put a very wide and erroneous meaning on the word "prevention." Economic unprofitableness is not "prevention," though a very high price for the article sold may be evidence of such a physical scarcity due to hostilities as amounts to prevention by hostilities. They have not considered whether the ships in which the contract goods were placed could physically go to the contract ports, but have rested themselves on the fact that the voyage might be financially unprofitable for the sellers, if they were not insured against war risk and financed from shipment till payment. I agree with the judge below that no facts are found which amount to prevention by hostilities in the true meaning of that term.

Secondly, there is a finding as to an implied term of the contract, that it shall be possible to sell exchange. It was argued that the question, what term was to be implied in the contract or whether the commercial purpose of the adventure was frustrated so that the contract was at an end (a question which again involves what contract on the subject was to be implied), was a question of fact, not of law, and that the decision of the arbitrators on the facts was conclusive. In my opinion the question what contract is to be implied, or whether a term in the contract is a condition precedent so that its untruth invalidates the contract, or is only a promise whose breach gives rise to a claim for damages, is a question of construction and law for the Court, though the circumstances under which the contract was made, which the Court is entitled to know in construing the contract, are facts to be found by the jury, and their importance to the commercial adventure may be a fact which assists the Court materially in coming to a conclusion. . . . Being told the surrounding circumstances and any facts showing their importance, the Court must determine whether the parties must have intended that the contract should only continue in force if certain circumstances continued to exist, which the parties must have treated as essential to performance, or to the necessary common purpose of the parties in performance. I expressed my views fully on this subject in *Metropolitan Water Board* v. *Dick, Kerr & Co.* ([1917] 2 K. B. 1), and do not repeat them.

Now on the facts found by the arbitrators can the Court say that the parties to these contracts must both necessarily have intended that the power to sell exchange was a condition precedent to the continuance of the contract? It seems clear that inability to sell exchange from every cause is not included. The financial weakness or insolvency of the seller can hardly have been meant. Will financial panic in the New York market arising from over-speculation and calling in of loans and preventing exchange being sold put an end to the contract? Can either party insist on the contract being at an end, if exchange cannot be sold? Though the seller is strong enough to finance the particular contract without selling exchange, can the buyer refuse the goods if exchange cannot be sold? One of the counsel for the appellants thought he could; one thought he could not. How can the Court say that the parties to the contract must necessarily have agreed on such a term, and what is the exact wording and extent of the term on which they must have agreed? There is no doubt that, if war breaks out, failure to obtain war risk insurance may be important for both parties. The seller under such a contract usually takes the bill of lading to his own order to keep a proprietary hold on the goods till he is paid, or has a security for payment satisfactory to him; he, therefore, may want war risk insurance to cover his proprietary interest, as of course may the buyer. Now it is important to notice that the parties have thought of this, and have expressed certain terms about it. They have contemplated a war; they have provided that, if the buyer does not provide war risk insurance, the seller may insure, if he can, on buyer's account. But though they have contemplated inability to effect war risk insurance they have said nothing about the effect of that inability on the contract. This may be because they did not think about it; it may be because they could not agree what the effect should be; but why should the Court assume that there is a term which they must have contemplated, rather than a failure on their part to think about or agree on the matter? And if they have not expressed a term about the effect on the contract of inability to get war risk insurance, which they have mentioned, can the Court infer what they would have agreed about a matter they have not mentioned and a more remote result, failure to sell exchange because of failure to obtain war risk insurance? It seems to me one thing to say that the buyer knew that the seller usually made his financial arrangements in a particular way, and quite a different thing to say that the buyer agreed that the contract should be off if the seller could not make his usual financial arrangements. Many buyers arrange to get control of the goods before they pay for them by tendering a bank of first-class standing as acceptor of the documentary bills, but I think sellers would be astonished to hear that their contracts were at an end if their buyers could not make their usual financial arrangements.

The power of implying terms which the parties have not expressed should be exercised by the Courts very sparingly and only in cases of necessity. In this case I agree with the judge below that there are no facts establishing the necessity of such an implication. . . .

Appeal dismissed.

Note also BOLCKOW, VAUGHAN, AND CO. (LIMITED) *v.* COMPANIA MINERA DE SIERRA MINERA, 33 T. L. R. 111 (Court of Appeal, 1916), where there was a contract made in November, 1914, for the sale by a Spanish company of iron ore to be delivered at Middlesbrough, England. In pursuance of this contract the sellers entered into a freight contract at a favorable rate, but owing to threats of German activity against shipping as the war progressed alleged that the shipowners refused to perform, and claimed in their turn to be excused from making further deliveries of ore. In an action for damages for breach of contract a judgment for plaintiffs was affirmed, Swinfen Eady, L. J., saying: "If the shipping company had in fact refused to carry out their freight contract, and had claimed that they were justified in so doing by an excepted peril, and if they could have maintained that position, by reason of the terms of their charterparty, that would not avail the defendants as a defence for not delivering, inasmuch as other tonnage was available, although at an increased rate of freight. It was urged that the rise in freights, owing to the war and to the German notice of February 6, 1915, proclaiming the waters around Great Britain and Ireland a war region, and to the German submarine attacks, was quite abnormal, and far beyond ordinary market fluctuations, and that by 'commercial prevention' the defendants were unable to deliver the ore. That could only mean that the defendants would incur a loss in carrying out their contract. But a mere rise in the price of a commodity to be supplied, or in the rate of freight, was not alone a sufficient excuse for non-delivery. A person was not entitled to be excused from the performance of a contract merely because it had become more costly to perform it.

"This case had nothing to do with the doctrine of frustration of an adventure upon the breaking out of war. The contract was made during the war; iron ore had been declared contraband by the British Government before the date of the contract; and a term was added to the contract immediately after it was made that deliveries would have to be suspended if the North Sea became closed to Spanish tonnage. The parties to the contract were mindful of the existence of a state of war, and contemplated its continuance and contracted with reference to it. In his Lordship's opinion the appeal failed and should be dismissed."

Similarly in BLANC *c.* VALMONT, 1927 Marseille 1.279 (Commercial Court of Marseille, 1927), it was held that a seller who had contracted on terms c.i.f. Marseille to ship egg yolks from Shanghai was not relieved because of circumstances arising out of the existing civil war in China. The Court stated that "the impossibility of making delivery must be absolute, and one cannot consider as such an event which merely makes the carrying out of the bargain more difficult or more burdensome." Moreover, in the present case "the state of civil war relied on existed at the time the agreement was made, and the seller therefore might or should have foreseen the difficulties encountered."

LEBEAUPIN *v.* RICHARD CRISPIN AND COMPANY

KING'S BENCH DIVISION, 1920

[*Law Reports,* [1920] 2 *King's Bench,* 714]

Award in the form of a special case.

The following statement of facts is taken from the judgment: "This award by an umpire in the form of a special case was made by Mr. F. D. Mackinnon K.C. on February 24, 1920. It raises several points of law of novelty and importance. The buyer (M. Lebeaupin) claims damages against the sellers (Richard Crispin & Co.) for breach of contract to deliver a large quantity of tinned salmon.

"There were two contracts; each was dated May 16, 1917, and each was for the supply of 2500 cases of 'British Columbia Fraser river salmon.' The first contract had the following words: 'The salmon to be the first 2500 cases of ½ lb. flat pinks packed by the St. Mungo Cannery, Fraser river, during the season of 1917.' The second contract had these words: 'The salmon to be the first 2500 cases of ½ lb. flat pinks packed by the Acme Cannery, Fraser river, during the season of 1917.' Each contract contained the following exception clause: 'In the event of the destruction, or partial destruction, of the cannery, plant, or material, or the packing being interfered with, or stopped, or falling short through short run of fish, or through strikes or lock-out of fishermen or workmen, or from any cause not under the control of the canners or shippers . . . causing non-arrival at destination, the contract to be cancelled in respect of such non-delivery or part non-delivery as the case may be.' Then appear in large letters the words, 'subject to force majeure.'

"The sellers failed to deliver any part of the above-mentioned goods to the buyer. They asserted that they were saved from liability for several reasons. The umpire negatived their contentions and awarded substantial damages to the buyer." . . .

"The broad facts can be briefly stated. The sellers are merchants in London. To cover themselves upon the present contracts they made contracts with a firm of Evans, Coleman & Evans, also of London, and the latter had in turn made contracts with the St. Mungo Cannery and the Acme Cannery of British Columbia. The terms of the latter contracts were not in evidence before the umpire. The St. Mungo Cannery belongs to the St. Mungo Canning Co. In the season of 1917 there was an excellent run of fish on the Fraser river. The St. Mungo Co. began to pack the salmon into the ½ lb. tins. They then proceeded to prepare the tins as usual by a cooking process, but found that the tins were defective and useless for the desired purpose. Hence they ceased to pack into ½ lb. tins and destroyed the cooking already made. Before they could get a new lot of ½ lb. tins the run of salmon had practically ceased. If they had possessed a sufficient supply of good tins they could have secured fish for 2500 cases of ½ lb. flat pinks. The St. Mungo Co. gave evidence before the umpire to the effect that it was not possible to discover that the tins were defective until pressure was put on them in the process of cooking. Upon this point the umpire says: 'I accept this in the sense that the defects could not be found until the tins were used, and that they had no reason to suspect them until they did use them, but I find that they might have been used and so tested at an earlier date, for example, when they were packing the Toba Inlet fish. There was no evidence of the date or terms of their contract with the American Canning Co., of the date of the delivery of the tins which proved defective. . . .' Apparently the defective tins had been supplied by the American Canning Co.

"The Acme Cannery belongs to the British Columbia Packers' Association. Ample fish existed in the season of 1917 to enable them to pack 2500 cases of ½ lb. flat pinks. They had a full supply of ½ lb. tins. What happened, however, was this. They had a large number of 1 lb. tins. These were getting rusty when the fish began to run. They therefore filled the 1 lb. tins first to the extent of over 3700 cases to avoid the loss of those 1 lb. tins. Then ere they could proceed to fill the ½ lb. tins the run of fish ceased and they were unable to prepare ½ lb. tins at all. The cessation of the run was in no way abnormal. Such are the main facts as to the two contracts."

McCardie, J., read his judgment which, after stating the facts set out above, continued as follows:

[The first two pages of the opinion are here omitted.]

The next point raised by Mr. Raeburn and Mr. Le Quesne in their able arguments turned on the words; "Subject to force majeure." This phrase "force majeure" has been introduced into many English commercial contracts within recent years. It is employed not only with increasing frequency, but without any attempt to define its meaning or any effort to co-ordinate the phrase to the other provisions of documents. It is a phrase employed in the Code de Commerce of France. Thus, for example, article 230 of that Code provides: "La responsabilité du capitaine ne cesse que par la preuve d'obstacles de force majeure." The meaning of the phrase as used on the Continent of Europe is discussed in Calvo's Dictionnaire de Droit International, tit. "Force Majeure," and by Dalloz, Jurisprudence Générale, tom. 24, p. 755, article "Force Majeure." A broad statement on the matter appears in Goirand's French Commercial Law, 2nd ed., p. 854. He says: "Force Majeure. This term is used with reference to all circumstances independent of the will of man, and which it is not in his power to control, and such force majeure is sufficient to justify the non-execution of a contract. Thus, war, inundations, and epidemics, are cases of force majeure; it has even been decided that a strike of workmen constitutes a case of force majeure." This is a wide definition, but I think that it usefully though loosely suggests not only the meaning of the phrase as used on the Continent, but also the meaning of the phrase as often employed in English contracts. That "war" comes within the meaning of "force majeure" would seem to be the opinion of Swinfen Eady L.J. in *Zinc Corporation* v. *Hirsch* ([1916] 1 K. B. 541, 554). That a strike of workmen comes within the phrase was the opinion of Bailhache J. in *Matsoukis* v. *Priestman* ([1915] 1 K. B. 681). That learned judge was, if I may respectfully say so, clearly right when he said that the phrase "force majeure" was not interchangeable with "vis major" or "the act of God." It goes beyond the latter phrases. Any direct legislative or administrative interference would of course come within the term: for example, an embargo. But even such a thing as a breakdown of machinery through accident was deemed by Bailhache J. to come within the words "force majeure." (See *Matsoukis* v. *Priestman* ([1915] 1 K. B. 681, 687)). This opinion is agreeable to the view of Walton J. in *Yrazu* v. *Astral Shipping Co.* ((1904) 9 Com. Cas. 100), where he ruled that though a miscalculation of the master and engineer of a ship causing a ship to leave with insufficient coals whereby she was compelled to call at another port and thereby suffered delay and depreciation of cargo was not a case of "force majeure," yet that it would have been a case of "force majeure" if the deficiency of coal had arisen from some accident or casualty. In *Matsoukis' Case* ([1915] 1 K. B. 681, 687) Bailhache J. seems to have ruled that delay caused by bad weather was not within the "force majeure" clause. But he was there dealing with the particular facts, and I conceive that normal bad weather is one thing whereas abnormal tempest, storm or the like may be another thing and might well fall within the "force majeure" clause. The case of *Dixon & Sons* v. *Henderson, Craig & Co.* ([1919] 2 K. B. 778) throws but little light on the matter inasmuch as the "force majeure" clause there dealt with by the Court of Appeal was defined by the words following the heading of "force majeure." But in *The Concadoro* ([1916] 2 A. C. 199) an interesting question arose as to the meaning of "force majeure" in article 2 of the Hague Convention, No. 6 of 1907. Lord Parmoor, in reading the advice of the Privy Council, said (*ibid.* 202): "The 'force majeure' contemplated in the article is one which renders the vessel unable to leave the port, and cannot be construed to include the circumstance that the master has not been provided by the owners with sufficient financial resources to continue his voyage." I take it that a "force majeure" clause should be construed in each case with a close attention to the words which precede or follow it, and with a due regard to the nature and general terms of the contract. The effect of the clause may vary with each instrument. Now, applying the above observations to the present case, I point out again that there was no failure of fish on the Fraser river in 1917. There was no legislative or administrative interference with the canners or shippers; there was nothing in the nature of *vis major* or *actus Dei*, and nothing in the nature of a strike, or an accident, or a casualty. All that happened as to the St. Mungo Co. was that they were in default with their tins, and if their contractors (the American Canning Co.) had committed a breach of contract in supplying defective tins, they could presumably have secured damages against them. The Acme Co.'s default arose either through their deliberate choice or their own error of judgment. A man cannot rely on his own act, or negligence, or omission, or default, as "force majeure." See the principle stated by Lord Finlay in *New Zealand Shipping Co.* v. *Société des Ateliers* ([1919] A. C. 1, 6). However broadly the "force majeure" clause may be interpreted, it could not exonerate the sellers upon the facts of the present case. I am satisfied that when the parties spoke of "force majeure" they never intended those words to include such a case as this. I therefore think that the learned umpire rightly awarded damages to the buyer.

[The balance of the opinion is omitted.]

ARTICLE 1148 of the French Civil Code has the effect of excusing performance of a contract by reason of "force majeure" or "cas fortuit." In commenting on these expressions Colin et Capitant, 2 *Droit Civil Français* 72 (7th ed. 1932), say: "Most authors see in the words *cas fortuit* and *force majeure* synonyms which may be applied indifferently to any cause foreign to the obligor that prevents the carrying out of the obligation. The compilers of the Code in fact generally use the two terms together or employ them both indifferently to express the same idea (see Arts. 855, 1302, 1722, 1730, 1733, 1769, 1772, 1773, 1784, 1882, 1929, 1934, 1954). Moreover, *cas fortuit* and *force majeure* produce the same liberative effect: they excuse the obligor. Another interpretation has been given to the two expressions according to which *force majeure* would designate an obstacle to performance resulting from an external force, and *cas fortuit* an internal obstacle, that is to say proceeding from the very conditions of the operation, accidents to material, faults of employees, etc. A somewhat different system sees in *cas fortuit* the relative impossibility of performance, that is to say a hindrance personal to the obligor himself but which might be overcome by a will better armed or better equipped — what the Germans call the impotence of the obligor (*Unvermögen*, see Art. 275, sec. 2, of the German Civil Code). *Force majeure* on the other hand would constitute absolute impossibility arising from an obstacle both irresistible, unforeseen, and unforeseeable (a tempest, lightning, earthquakes, war, restraint of princes)."

GEORGE WILLS AND SONS, LIMITED *v.* R. S. CUNNINGHAM, SON AND CO., LTD.

KING'S BENCH DIVISION, 1923

[*Law Reports*, [1924] 2 *King's Bench*, 220]

Action tried before Greer J.

By contracts made in 1922 the plaintiffs, George Wills & Sons, Ld., agreed to buy from the defendants, R. S. Cunningham, Son & Co., Ld., certain steel rods, bars and plates at the prices named therein and within the times thereby prescribed as subsequently extended to May 31, 1923. No particular source from which the goods were to come was indicated. By the terms of the contract the delivery was subject to the condition "U.C.E.," which it was agreed meant "Unforeseen contingencies excepted," and subject to Continental conditions. The defendants failed to deliver part of the goods. They gave evidence that the French occupation of the Ruhr, from which they proposed to procure the goods the subject matter of the contract, had so disorganized industry there as to render the production and supply of those goods impossible. It was not shown that the goods could not be obtained elsewhere.

The defendants alleged that in the above circumstances the U.C.E. clause exempted them from liability to deliver.

GREER J. [after dealing with other contentions, continued]: The defendants relied on another defence. The contract between them and the plaintiffs was expressed to be "U.C.E." The meaning of these letters was admitted to be "unforeseen circumstances excepted" or "unforeseen contingencies excepted," and relying on that provision the defendants contended that they were relieved from liability to deliver the steel goods the subject matter of the contract. The "unforeseen contingency," the occurrence of which the defendants alleged relieved them from liability, was the disorganization of industrial Germany caused by the French occupation of the Ruhr. It appeared that the defendants were to get the goods which they had contracted to supply to the plaintiffs, or part of them, from Germany, and that they would be produced chiefly in the Ruhr district. It was said, probably truly, that the French occupation of this district would render the production and supply of these goods in the Ruhr district impossible. But it was said on behalf of the plaintiffs that although this might be perfectly true, it would have been quite possible to have obtained goods of the contract description elsewhere, though no doubt at an enhanced price, and as the defendants could not show the incorrectness of this contention, I am satisfied that it is the fact. The question is how the exception is to be applied to a contract which does not fix any particular source from which the goods are to come; had it done so the exception would have been much easier to interpret. It is a pity that merchants will continue to use shorthand expressions of this kind, if I may so term them, without any definition of them in the contract, and thus leave them to be interpreted by the Court. It is a difficult matter to determine what the expression was intended to mean in this contract, but I am bound to give it a meaning. After careful consideration I come to the conclusion that the words which the letters U.C.E. stand for mean that unforeseen circumstances must have arisen to render the performance of the contract impossible. It is not enough for the defendants to show that it was impossible for them to get the goods from the particular source they contemplated when entering into the contract. If they could have obtained goods elsewhere which would have satisfied the contract they were bound to do so. In the present case the defendants have failed to prove an absolute prevention, and there must therefore be judgment for the plaintiffs.

Judgment for plaintiffs.

Compare FORD & SONS (OLDHAM) (LIMITED) *v.* HENRY LEETHAM & SONS (LIMITED), 21 Commercial Cases 55 (King's Bench Division, 1915), where a contract for the sale of flour contained the clause "in case of prohibition of export, blockade, or hostilities preventing shipment or delivery of wheat to this country, the sellers shall have the option of cancelling this contract." The export of wheat was prohibited from twenty-one countries, but there was no similar prohibition from the United States, Canada, and the British East Indies, which were the principal sources of supply. The price of wheat rose materially, and the seller claimed the right to cancel. In an action for damages, judgment was given for defendant, Bailhache, J., saying: "In order that this clause may come into operation I think there need not be an absolutely total prohibition of export of wheat to this country; it is sufficient if there is a prohibition of such an extent and such force as that either a considerable source of supply of wheat to this country is shut up thereby or that a very considerable rise in the price of wheat in this country should be occasioned by the prohibition."

In PETER DIXON & SONS, LIMITED *v.* HENDERSON, CRAIG & CO., LTD., [1919] 2 K. B. 778 (Court of Appeal, 1919), there was a contract for the sale of wood pulp at an agreed price c.i.f. Grimsby, to be delivered in quantities of 5000 tons a year over a period of six years from 1911. The contract contained the following clause: "The buyers or sellers may suspend deliveries under this contract pending any contingency beyond their control which prevents or hinders the manufacture of paper or the manufacture or delivery of pulp, namely Act of God, War, etc." The sellers duly made deliveries under the contract until the commencement of the war, when considerable difficulty arose in carrying out the contract. British ships were no longer available for the trade, although foreign shipping could be obtained at increased freights. Admiralty regulations lengthened the voyages, and there was liability to capture by the enemy or loss through mines or submarines, and delay through detention by British or Allied warships. The sellers having failed to deliver the pulp, the buyers bought it in against the sellers at an increased price, and claimed to recover the difference. Judgment for the plaintiffs reversed. The case involved more than a mere rise in price, for the position had been so changed by the war that the sellers, although not "prevented" were "hindered" from carrying out the contract within the meaning of the clause.

In B. P. Ducas *v.* Bayer Co., 163 N.Y.S. 32 (Supreme Court, 1916), there was a contract for the sale of dyestuffs to be delivered in New York with the clause "Sellers not to be held accountable for delays caused by strikes or for any contingencies beyond their control." The parties contemplated that the dyestuffs would be imported from Germany, but the outbreak of war prevented the seller from getting normal supplies. Stocks on hand and imported were prorated by sellers among their regular customers, in some cases against written contracts, in others under oral contracts, and sometimes even in the absence of preexisting contracts of any kind. In these latter cases sellers secured higher prices than those called for under the present contract. In an action by the buyers to recover damages on account of failure to deliver the quantities called for by the contract, judgment for the plaintiff. "The contingency, therefore, which actually caused the non-performance of the contract was not simply the seller's inability to procure adequate supplies of goods, but its own act in distributing the supplies the way it did. . . . The seller has made definite agreements with certain customers; these agreements in terms give those customers a legal right to receive the goods, unless a contingency arises which prevents performance by the seller; the seller has the power to perform these contracts, but voluntarily puts performance out of his power by delivering the goods to other parties who have no legal claim. The defendant did this without legal compulsion, and . . . solely because its officers believed that they had a moral duty to their own customers. I see no reason to question that the defendant was actuated by this motive and made a distribution which was, it believed, fair and equitable under the difficult circumstances, yet where a party has entered into legal obligations which interfere with what he regards as moral obligations, he cannot perform his moral obligations at the expense of the persons who have legal claims against him."

E. Risks of Transit

CASTLE *v.* PLAYFORD

Exchequer Chamber, 1872

[*Law Reports*, 7 *Exchequer*, 98]

Error from the decision of the Court of Exchequer in favour of the defendant on cross-demurrer to declaration and plea.

[The original action was brought by the sellers against the buyer to recover the value of the goods. The following statement of facts is taken from the headnote:

The plaintiffs agreed with the defendant to ship on board a vessel a cargo of fresh-water ice, and to despatch the vessel with all speed to any ordered port in the United Kingdom, "the vendors forwarding bills of lading to the purchaser, and upon receipt thereof, the purchaser takes upon himself all risks and dangers of the seas"; and the defendant agreed to buy and receive the ice on its arrival, and pay for it in cash on delivery, at the rate of 20*s.* a ton of 20 cwt., weighed on board during delivery. The vessel was lost during the voyage by risks and dangers of the seas, within the meaning of the agreement, and after the receipt by the defendant of the bills of lading.]

COCKBURN, C.J. In my opinion our judgment should be in favour of the plaintiffs. I am much disposed to think, though it is not necessary to decide it, that the effect of this contract was, that from the moment the cargo was shipped, and the bill of lading delivered to the defendant, the property passed. I am confirmed in that opinion by the fact that the parties introduced the clause upon which this dispute has arisen, and upon which the present question turns, namely, that from the moment the bills of lading were delivered to the defendant, he should take upon himself all the risks and perils attendant upon the conveying of the cargo by sea to the port of its destination. It seems to me that when one person says to another, "I will ship the cargo upon your account and hand you the bills of lading, (which are the indicia of the property), and give you the control of it, and you are from that moment to undertake all the risks attendant upon its transfer by sea"; it is very strong evidence that it was intended by the parties that the property in the cargo, with all its risks, should pass. However, I do not think it necessary to decide the case upon that ground — I put it only alternatively. If that is not the construction of the contract, I think the true one is this: "If you, the sellers, will undertake to ship me a cargo of ice, and to forward it by a given vessel to London, and hand me the bill of lading, so that I may have the control over the cargo, and the distribution of it, I will engage, when it arrives, to pay you according to what may be its value; and if, in the meantime, while it is upon the seas, it shall perish through the perils of the seas, I will undertake to pay you for it according to what may be estimated to have been its fair value at the time of going down." That I take to be the construction of the contract, and I do not think it was intended to make the stipulation that the cargo should be at the risk of the purchaser contingent upon the fact of the goods arriving or not in this country, which is the proposition contended for on the part of the defendant.

If the first construction that I have been disposed to put upon this contract is right, then, the property having passed, the stipulation as to time and mode of payment seems to have been put in merely with regard to the measure of price; but, as I have observed, I do not think it necessary to rest my view of the case upon that construction of the contract, although I entertain a strong opinion about it. It is enough that the contract is such as would be consistent with the second construction, namely, that the defendant undertook, that if the cargo should be shipped and the bills of lading transferred to him, he would pay for it according to a certain rate; and if it perished, he would pay for it according to what might be a fair estimation of its value at the time it went down.

WILLES, J., concurred.

BLACKBURN, J. My impression is, if it were necessary to decide it now, that the effect of this contract is that the property passed; but I think it is unnecessary to decide the matter. The parties in this case have agreed, whether the property passed or not, that the purchaser should, from the time he received the bills of lading, take upon himself all risks and dangers of the seas; and, according to Mr. Littler's construction, I do not see what risk he took upon himself at all, unless it was this — that he said, "If the property perishes by the dangers of the seas, I shall take the risk of having lost the property, whether it be mine or not." . . .

MELLOR, BRETT, and GROVE, JJ., concurred.

Judgment reversed.

In the CALCUTTA AND BURMAH STEAM NAVIGATION COMPANY (LIMITED) *v.* DE MATTOS, 32 L. J. K. B. 322 (Queen's Bench, 1863), there was a contract for the sale of 1000 tons of coal at an agreed price delivered at Rangoon, half the price to be paid on receipt of bills of lading and insurance policies on shipment, and the balance on right delivery at Rangoon. The carrying vessel became disabled on the voyage, so that the coal never was delivered at Rangoon within the meaning of the contract. The buyer brought an action for damages for non-delivery and to recover the part of the price already paid; and the sellers claimed to recover the balance of the price. In delivering an opinion that subsequently was adopted by the Exchequer Chamber in giving judgment for the defendant in each case, Blackburn, J., said in part: "There is no rule of law to prevent the parties, in cases like the present, from making whatever bargain they please. If they use words in the contract shewing that they intend that the goods shall be shipped by the person who is to supply them, on the terms, that when shipped they shall be the consignee's property, and at his risk, so that the vendor shall be paid for them whether delivered at the port of destination or not, this intention is effectual. Such is the common case where goods are ordered to be sent by a carrier to a port of destination. The vendor's duty is, in such cases, at an end when he has delivered the goods to the carrier, and, if the goods perish in the carrier's hands, the vendor is discharged, and the purchaser is bound to pay him the price. — See *Dunlop* v. *Lambert* (6 Cl. & Fin. 600). If the parties intend that the vendor shall not merely deliver the goods to the carrier, but also undertake that they shall actually be delivered at their destination, and express such intention, this also is effectual; in such a case, if the goods perish in the hands of the carrier, the vendor is not only not entitled to the price, but he is liable for whatever damage may have been sustained by the purchaser in consequence of the breach of the vendor's contract to deliver at the place of destination. . . . But, consistently with this, there might be an intention that there should be a complete vesting of the property in the goods in the company, and a complete vesting of the right to the half of the price in De Mattos; so as in effect to make the goods be at the risk of the company, though half the price was at the risk of De Mattos: so that the goods were sold and delivered, though the payment of half the price was contingent on the delivery. And this, I think, is the true legal construction of the contract. There are, undoubtedly, some expressions in the letters, which may plausibly be said to indicate an intention, that the whole risk shall be on De Mattos up to the time of the contemplated delivery at Rangoon. The coals are *to be delivered* at Rangoon; the whole price is expressed to be '45*s*. per ton of 20 cwt. *delivered* at Rangoon.' I fully admit, that the argument, that these words imply an undertaking that the coals shall be delivered at Rangoon, or, at least, that nothing shall be paid except for such coals as are delivered at Rangoon, is a very forcible one. But then, we must look at the whole contract. We find that the coals when shipped are to be insured, and the policy of insurance is to be handed over to the company. It is consistent with this, that the policy was to be handed over to the company, only to be a collateral security for an advance; but it is more natural that it should be given to them, because the risk which the policy covered was to be theirs. The bill of lading is handed to them so as to give them the actual, *de facto*, dominion over the goods, and to confer upon them the power of giving to a third party, by a sale or pledge of that bill, what that third person would believe to be a rightful dominion over the goods. This, too, is consistent with the bill of lading being delivered to the company merely with a view to give them an effectual security for an advance; but, as before, I think the more natural solution of it is, that it was given to them because, the property being theirs, they were entitled to the control of the goods. It is very true that the company (a steam navigation company, who wanted coals for their own use) probably did not contemplate selling the goods to third parties, and therefore the argument as to the intention of the parties, arising from the possession of the bill of lading, is not so strong as if the purchaser had been an ordinary merchant, who purchased the coals meaning to sell them again, and who, therefore, presumably stipulated for the bill of lading in order that he might be able, without breach of contract or bad faith, to sell them again; but though the company probably did not mean to sell this cargo before it arrived at Rangoon, they had, from the time the bill of lading was put into their hands, power to do so if they thought fit; and it seems to me that the fact, that the contract contains a stipulation for that power in favour of the purchasers, is very strong to shew, that the property, and consequently the risk, was intended to be in them from the time they received the bill of lading. . . .

"It is an intelligible principle, that the handing over a policy of insurance and bill of lading to a purchaser in exchange for a part-payment, is *prima facie* an indication of an intention that the property and risk should be his from that time. If we adhere to this broad ground, merchants will understand what they are about, and will know that in such cases, if they do not mean the risk to go with the indemnity secured by the policy and the control accompanying the bill of lading, they must say so. But if we once enter into refined differences, no man will be able, without unmercantile prolixity, to express his meaning."

MAFFEI *v.* GINOCCHIO

Illinois Supreme Court, 1921

[299 *Illinois Reports*, 254]

Mr. Justice Carter delivered the opinion of the court:

Ginocchio, Costa & Co., of Chicago, executed a contract through a New York agent, R. G. Berlingieri, with H. N. Maffei, of Naples, Italy, a dealer in nuts, for the shipment of 300 bags of No. 1 Sorrento walnuts and 300 bags of Mountain Naples walnuts. The Sorrento walnuts were shipped and received. The Mountain Naples walnuts were shipped on a later vessel, the Ancona, which was sunk by a submarine. The question here in litigation is whether the buyer or the seller should bear the loss of these last named nuts under the terms of the contract and the circumstances of the case. The cause was tried in the municipal court without a jury and a judgment rendered in favor of Ginocchio, Costa & Co., plaintiffs in error here. On appeal to the Appellate Court the judgment of the trial court was reversed and a judgment entered in the Appellate Court for $2545 in favor of defendant in error, and this writ has been sued out to review that judgment.

The parties entered into the contract here in question August 5, 1915. It provided that the terms should be "ninety days confirmed bankers' letter of credit," and shipment was "to be made about the middle of October, 1915, on a direct steamer to New York, in bond to Chicago." It further provided for "marine and war insurance to be covered by consignees," and that defendant in error was "not responsible for failure in shipping goods on account of shortage of tonnage or lack of steamers or other reasons beyond control." A cablegram offer and an acceptance were interchanged between the parties, and the original sales contract went forward from Chicago accompanied by letter of August 13, 1915, in which it was stated that letter of credit would be mailed direct to shipper. On August 14, 1915, the Continental and Commercial National Bank of Chicago issued a letter of credit. . . .

[After holding that shipment had been made according to the contract, Carter, J., continued:]

Plaintiffs in error further argue that the judgment of the trial court should be upheld for the reason that the title to the nuts never vested in them because the bill of lading was not delivered to them, and that in order to pass the title the bill of lading should have been properly endorsed and delivered; that since this was not done plaintiffs in error did not own the nuts at the time the boat was sunk, and therefore the loss is that of defendant in error. Under the common law, when the contract of sale covering the purchase price of merchandise provided substantially for delivery by carrier and payment at the point of delivery and all insurance to be effected by the purchaser, then the beneficial interest in the merchandise passed to the buyer upon delivery of the merchandise to the carrier and the risk of subsequent loss fell upon the buyer. (*Mee* v. *McNider*, 109 N. Y. 500; *Stafford & Bro.* v. *Walter & Skelton*, 67 Ill. 83; *Wheelhouse* v. *Parr*, 141 Mass. 593.) This rule has been substantially formulated in the Uniform Sales act adopted in this State, in paragraph 2 of rule 4 of section 19 of that act. (Hurd's Stat. 1917, p. 2601.) Paragraph (*a*) of section 22 of that act provides: "Where delivery of the goods has been made to the buyer, or to a bailee for the buyer, in pursuance of the contract and the property in the goods has been retained by the seller merely to secure performance by the buyer of his obligations under the contract, the goods are at the buyer's risk from the time of such delivery." (Ibid. p. 2602.) Paragraph 2 of section 20 of the act also provides: "Where goods are shipped, and by the bill of lading the goods are deliverable to the seller or his agent, or to the order of the seller or of his agent, the seller thereby reserves the property in the goods. But if, except for the form of the bill of lading, the property would have passed to the buyer on shipment of the goods, the seller's property in the goods shall be deemed to be only for the purpose of securing performance by the buyer of his obligations under the contract." The Appellate Court so held in its opinion, and we see no reason to reach a different conclusion. If we did, this question being at least a mixed one of law and fact, the judgment of the Appellate Court on this question would be binding on this court. (*Harrison* v. *Thackaberry*, 248 Ill. 512.) It is quite clear from the record that it was the intention of both parties that the bill of lading was not to be delivered up by defendant in error to the Naples bank except upon payment for the nuts, and it is also clear that the bank would have paid defendant in error if the bill of lading and letter of credit had been presented before the closing of the bank on October 30. It would seem, therefore, to follow that the nuts were at the buyer's risk at the time the boat was sunk, and that plaintiffs in error must pay for them unless they are excused, as they claim they are, by the defendant in error's failure to notify them of the date the ship was to sail, so as to enable them to effect war and marine insurance.

[The last two pages of the opinion, holding that defendant in error was not required to give notice of shipment in order that insurance might be effected, are here omitted.]

Judgment affirmed.

STOCK *v.* INGLIS

COURT OF APPEAL, 1884

[*Law Reports*, 12 *Queen's Bench Division*, 564]

(Affirmed by the House of Lords in 10 *Appeal Cases*, 263)

[The following statement of facts is taken from the headnote:

By a contract in writing D. & Co., sugar merchants in London, agreed to sell to the plaintiff, a Bristol merchant, 200 tons of sugar of a certain description, to be shipped from Hamburg to Bristol at the price of 21*s*. 9*d*.

per cwt. net f. o. b. Hamburg; payment by cash in London in exchange for bill of lading. In order to satisfy such contract and also a similar contract for the sale of sugar to another Bristol merchant, D. & Co.'s forwarding agents at Hamburg shipped there about 400 tons in 3900 bags of sugar of the description contracted for, and consigned the same to "order Bristol." It was the usual course of business of D. & Co., as the plaintiff knew, not to appropriate specific bags of sugar to any particular contract at the time of shipment, but to apportion the bags and the bills of lading representing them between their different buyers at the port to which they were shipped after they had been shipped, and after D. & Co. had received the bills of lading.

The *City of Dublin*, on which such shipment was made, was lost with her cargo on the voyage before any appropriation had been so made by D. & Co., but 2000 bags representing 200 tons were subsequently appropriated by D. & Co. to the plaintiff's contract and an invoice of the same sent to the plaintiff, who thereupon paid the contract price, and obtained the bill of lading.

The plaintiff, who had a "floating" policy of insurance on "goods" declared thereunder on the *City of Dublin* in respect of these 200 tons of sugar.]

Upon these facts the plaintiff's right to recover was denied by the defendant on the ground that no property in the sugar had passed to him before the loss; and, secondly, that at the time of the loss he had no insurable interest in the sugar itself, and that even if he had an insurable interest in "profits," he was not entitled to declare the loss in respect of that interest upon a policy on "goods." Field, J., before whom the action was tried, was of opinion on further consideration that the plaintiff had neither property nor insurable interest in the sugar, and that as he was not entitled to recover for a loss of profit under a policy like this on goods, the defendant was entitled to judgment, and he gave judgment for the defendant accordingly. The plaintiff appealed.

BRETT, M. R. . . . Under those circumstances a contract in writing is made for the purchase of a certain quantity of sugar upon the terms "free on board," and the question is, what is the true construction of that contract made between two persons who both knew the course of business which I have described in that trade?

Now if the goods dealt with by the contract were specific goods, it is not denied but that the words "free on board," according to the general understanding of merchants, would mean more than merely that the shipper was to put them on board at his expense; they would mean that he was to put them on board at his expense on account of the person for whom they were shipped; and in that case the goods so put on board under such a contract would be at the risk of the buyer whether they were lost or not on the voyage.

Now that is the meaning of those words "free on board" in a contract with regard to specific goods, and in that case the goods are at the purchaser's risk, even though the payment is not to be made on the delivery of the goods on board, but at some other time, and although the bill of lading is sent forward by the seller with documents attached in order that the goods shall not be finally delivered to the purchaser until he has either accepted bills or paid cash.

Then the question arises, can there be a contract with the terms "free on board" which can be fulfilled without the delivery of specific goods at the time of shipment? Is there any mercantile or legal reason why a person should not agree to sell so much out of a bulk cargo on board or ex such a ship upon the terms that if the cargo be lost the loss shall fall upon the purchaser, and not upon the seller? I can see no reason why he should not; and if such a contract can be made, and in a contract to buy and sell a certain quantity ex ship or ex bulk there is put in the terms "free on board," one must, with regard to that contract, give some meaning to those words "free on board." What meaning can be given to them with regard to the unseparated part of the goods which is the subject-matter of the contract, but the same meaning as is given to those words with regard to goods attributed to the contract? What is there unreasonable or contrary to business or law in those words "free on board," meaning in such a contract "I sell you twenty tons out of fifty upon the terms that you shall pay such a price for those twenty, I paying the costs of the shipment, that is, 'free on board,' and you bearing the risk of whether they are lost or not?" It does not seem to me that there is anything more inconsistent with business or law that parties should make such a contract with regard to a portion of a cargo than that they should make it with regard to a whole cargo or with regard to a specific part of a cargo, and therefore the only question which remains is whether this is such a contract.

Now, taking into account the surrounding circumstances when the contract was made, those circumstances being the course of business known to both buyer and seller, it seems to me that both contracts of Drake & Co., the one with the plaintiff and the one with Beloe, were upon the terms that the buyer should pay for the sugar as it might be distributed or allocated to him when the bills of lading were offered to him, that he should be bound, if the goods arrived, to take those which were allocated to him, with this further term, that the seller should not run the risk of the arrival of the goods here, but that the buyer should be bound to pay the price against that allocation of the bills of lading whether the goods arrived or not. Therefore, if that be true, when Beloe sold to the plaintiff he sold in truth that contract, and then the plaintiff became not directly liable to Drake & Co., but liable to Beloe, to pay for the goods whether they arrived or not, and he was also liable to Drake & Co. to pay whether the goods arrived or not which he had contracted to buy of Drake & Co. If so, then upon the non-arrival of the goods he would suffer a money loss. That is obvious, and therefore the question which has been propounded about *Anderson* v. *Morrice* (Law Rep. 10 C. P. 609; 1 App. Cas. 713) does not arise. It is not only that he would not make a gain, but he would suffer a pecuniary loss.

Under these circumstances it seems to me that he has an insurable interest. The moment one thus arrives at what is the true construction of the contract the case falls within plain insurance rules. It is useless to go through the decisions and authorities in insurance law, because under these circumstances there cannot be a doubt but that there is an insurable interest. Therefore in my opinion our judgment ought to be in favor of the plaintiff.

[Concurring opinions of Baggallay, L.J., and Lindley, L.J., are here omitted.]

Judgment reversed.

Compare J. AND J. CUNNINGHAM, LIMITED *v.* ROBERT A. MUNRO AND CO., LIMITED, 28 Com. Cas. 42 (King's Bench Division, 1922), where there was a contract for the sale of 200 tons of Dutch bran f. o. b. Rotterdam for October shipments. The sellers were obliged to take the bran from their sellers early in October, and sent it to Rotterdam on lighters so that it arrived there on October 14. The buyers were unable to find freight room until October 28, when loading began on their nominated steamer. It then was found that the bran had heated, and the buyers refused to accept it. In a special case under the Arbitration Act, it was held that the bran was at the seller's risk until October 28.

MEE *v.* McNIDER

NEW YORK COURT OF APPEALS, 1888

[109 *New York Reports*, 500]

Appeal from judgment of the General Term of the Supreme Court in the first judicial department, entered upon an order made January 7, 1886, which affirmed a judgment in favor of plaintiff, entered upon a verdict directed by the court. (Reported below, 39 Hun, 145.)

This action was brought to recover damages for the breach of a contract of purchase of a quantity of cocoa.

Upon defendant's refusal to receive and pay for the goods they were sold on his account, and the difference between the purchase-price and the net proceeds of sale plaintiff sought to recover.

The material facts are stated in the opinion.

DANFORTH, J. The agreement between the parties was in these words:

NEW YORK, January 3, 1882.

Sold for account of Mee, Billings & Co., London, to James McNider, five hundred (500) bags prime fermented Bahia cocoa, at 59 s. per cwt., C. F. & I., by steamer to N. Y., buyers to furnish cable credit or pay bankers' commission.

ARTHUR R. KYTE,
Broker.

Plaintiffs proved that 500 bags of cocoa of the quality and description specified were shipped on board a steamer which, on arrival at New York, defendant refused to receive and pay for, because a portion had been wet and damaged on the voyage.

The answer admits that the letters "C. F. & I." mean "to include cost, freight and insurance," and the question is, who, under the contract, took the risk of the voyage? The relation between the parties was that of vendor and vendee. The former, residing in London, undertook to sell, and the latter, residing in New York, undertook to buy the article named. The price is fixed at fifty-nine shillings per cwt., and this is made up of the cost, the freight and the premium of insurance. Thus the purchaser deals with the matter in gross, and not in detail, transacts the various branches of the business with one person instead of three, fixes his liability at a lump sum, and in case of loss will recover the amount of his interest under the policy.

On the other hand, the vendor is to be reimbursed for his advances at the same time and in the same manner that he receives payment for the goods. Only one condition is to be performed, that of shipment by steamer. The case differs in that respect from ***Ireland*** v. ***Livingston*** (L. R. 5 H. L. 395, cited by the appellant from Benjamin on Sales, § 590 [ed. of 1875]), where payment of freight was postponed until the arrival of the goods and the balance of the price, "on having handed to him (the buyer) the charter party, bill of lading and policy of insurance," which might well happen before the arrival of the vessel. But even that case throws the risk of damage at sea upon the buyer, for he engaged to pay a fixed price in consideration of the shipment in a prescribed manner, and except the freight, without reference to its actual delivery.

In the case before us there seems no ambiguity. On the part of the vendor the shipment by steamer was an effectual appropriation of the cocoa to the buyer, and at that moment the agreement on the vendor's part was executed. The plain obligation of the purchaser, as defined by the written contract then attached, and he was bound to accept and pay for the cargo at the price named and in the manner specified. It necessarily follows that injury to the cocoa during the voyage was no excuse for non-performance, and as the amount due, if anything, was conceded, there was no evidence which required the submission of the case to the jury.

It is, however, argued by the appellant, that the trial court erred in overlooking the circumstance that "no bill of lading and no policy of insurance had been delivered to the defendant." If there was default in that respect, the point was not taken at the trial, the only contention upon the facts being "that the goods were not in prime condition, were not merchantable when they came," and a contention upon the law that in consequence of that defect the defendant was relieved from liability.

The judgment appealed from should be affirmed.

All concur except PECKHAM, J., not sitting.

Judgment affirmed.

Note also BIDDELL BROS. *v.* E. CLEMENS HORST CO., [1911] 1 K. B. 934, 955, where Kennedy, L.J., in the course of a dissenting opinion which subsequently was approved by the House of Lords ([1912] A. C. 18), stated that from the time of shipment "the goods are at the risk of the purchaser against which he has protected himself by the stipulation in his c. i. f. contract that the vendor shall at his own cost, provide him with a proper policy of marine insurance intended to protect the buyer's interest, and available for his use, if the goods should be lost in transit."

WILLITS & PATTERSON *v.* ABEKOBEI & CO., LIMITED

New York Supreme Court, Appellate Division, 1921

[197 *New York Appellate Division Reports*, 528]

Appeal by the plaintiff, Willits & Patterson, from an order of the Supreme Court, made at the New York Special Term and entered in the office of the clerk of the county of New York on the 29th day of November, 1920, resettling an order entered in said clerk's office on the 11th day of November, 1920, granting defendant's motion to vacate a warrant of attachment obtained by plaintiff.

Smith, J. The plaintiff is a California corporation. The defendant is a Japanese corporation. Upon the 22d of December, 1919, they entered into a contract on the part of the defendant to sell and on the part of the plaintiff to purchase some soya bean oil. This contract was in the following form:

Kobe Sale No. 84. Kobe, 22nd December, 1919.

Messrs. Willits & Patterson,
San Francisco.

Bought of Abe Kobei Kobe Branch,
Kobe, Japan.

Date	Quantity	Description	Packing	Shipment	Price
	10,000 cases	Bean Oil not exceed 3% of fatty acid Net landed weight	75 lbs. tin in cases	Jan/Feb/ March 1920	$15.00 per 100 lbs. cif San Francisco.

1% of Commission
to Mr. Donkin

Comm. Paid Mar. 27

Confirmed by your Mr. H. Donkin
on the 22nd December 1919

Terms: — as usual

ABE KOBEI KOBE BRANCH
P. P. M. Mori.

It will be noticed that the contract called for 10,000 cases, 75 pounds in each case, which would make 750,000 pounds of this oil. The plaintiff paid the full price for the oil. When the oil arrived in San Francisco, however, there was a shortage of 79,555 pounds. This action is brought by the plaintiff, the buyer, to recover back the proportionate amount of the purchase price paid, which amounts to $11,483. The complaint contained two causes of action. The first cause of action was to recover back the amount paid upon a contract for the delivery of peanut oil, upon which there was a shortage at the time of delivery of the value of $12,864, so that the amount demanded in the complaint was the sum of $24,167, with interest from the 17th day of August, 1920. This included the damages upon both causes of action. An attachment was granted and levied upon property of the defendant in the State of New York. Upon defendant's motion to vacate that attachment, the plaintiff made no claim that the first cause of action was proven, but sought to uphold the attachment as to the second cause of action. The Special Term held, however, that there was no cause of action shown by the papers and granted the order wholly vacating the attachment. The sole question presented for determination here is as to whether the plaintiff has shown by his complaint and affidavit the existence of the cause of action set forth in the complaint as the second cause of action which is upon the contract hereinbefore set forth. The Special Term has held that this contract was simply a c. i. f. contract and that the perils of the voyage from Japan to San Francisco were at the buyer's risk, and for failure to show that this shortage existed at the time of the delivery to the carrier, the plaintiff has failed to show any right of action.

The law is well settled that a simple c. i. f. contract requires the seller to deliver to the carrier and upon such delivery the obligation of the seller is at an end and the risk of the voyage is thereafter with the buyer. These contracts of sale, however, are to be construed according to the intention of the parties. A straight f. o. b. contract is satisfied by the seller's delivery to the carrier for the purpose of shipment, the risk of transportation resting upon the buyer. If, however, there be anything in the contract which shows that such was not the intention of the parties, the contract will be construed according to their intention. This court has lately held in the case of *Standard Casing Co., Inc.* v. *California Casing Co., Inc.* (197 App. Div. 187) that in a contract to ship from California to New York, reserving the right of inspection to the buyer at New York, the liability of the seller was shown by this provision to extend to a delivery in New York city, notwithstanding the contract provided for a price f. o. b. San Francisco. This case followed a decision of this court in the case of *Boss* v. *Hutchinson* (182 App. Div. 88) wherein it was held, notwithstanding a named price f. o. b. at point of shipment that the right of inspection at the destination of the transportation indicated an intention that the delivery was not to be deemed complete until such destination was reached. In the case at bar we find the expression "Net landed weight." This expression can only have one significance and that significance is that the weight at the point of landing, to wit, at San Francisco, must accord with the requirements of the contract. It is true that this expression is put in a column under the word "description," and preceding in that column are the words "Bean Oil not exceed 3% of fatty acid." But the provision "Net landed weight," although appearing in that column, is a distinct expression, not connected with the description in any way. The clause begins with a capital "N," and although it is in the column marked "description," it is between the first column which provides for 10,000 cases and the third column which provides for seventy-five pounds in a case, under which circumstances it may well be held that it was not intended in any way to be a part of the description of the property sold, but was rather intended to be a part of the weight as specified in the first and third columns, although placed in the second column under the word "description" between the first and third columns. Wherever these words might be placed, however, no significance can be given to these words as a part of the description of the article sold. The description in reference to the extent of fatty acid can in no way be determined by weight. It is shown that the amount of fatty acids is determined by chemical analysis and it is not apparent how the net landed weight can in any way qualify the description.

The first cause of action, which has been abandoned, is upon a contract specifying peanut oil "delivered weight," and the contract is defined to be a c. i. f. contract. It might well be held in such a case that "delivered weight" means the weight upon delivery to the carrier. This contract sued upon contains the words "terms as usual." There had been prior contracts between these parties, and one of these contracts not sued upon in this case was for peanut oil not to exceed two per cent fatty acid at arrival. The terms of the contract "net landed weight," can under no conceivable reasoning be held as qualifying the terms of the contract not to exceed three per cent fatty acid, as though they read "on arrival." In no other contract referred to is this expression used and the significance of the expression to my mind is so plain that the only interpretation that can be given to it is that the weight upon arrival at San Francisco should conform to the weight required in the contract. Within the authorities cited construing f. o. b. contracts, I am of opinion that in this contract the expression c. i. f. is deemed modified so as to make the contract one for delivery at San Francisco, and such seems to me to be the plain intention expressed by the contract itself. It is further urged that the letter of credit procured by the plaintiff referred to the contract as a c. i. f. contract, which is deemed to be significant as indicating a practical interpretation by the plaintiff of the meaning of the contract. To my mind that has little significance, however, as the contract was clearly a modified c. i. f. contract, to an extent to fix the liability of the seller to pay the freight and insurance, and to provide for a delivery at San Francisco. If the procurement of the letter of credit be deemed a practical interpretation by the plaintiff of the terms of the contract, the fact that the insurance policy was not attached to the bill of lading, nor sent to the plaintiff, might, on the other hand, be deemed an interpretation by the defendant of its liability for the risk of the voyage, in the retention of this policy of insurance to indemnify the defendant for the risk of transportation. The cases have held that under an ordinary c. i. f. contract, the policy of insurance should accompany the bill of lading, which was not done. In *Ireland* v. *Livingston* (L. R. 5 H. L. 395, 406) Justice Blackburn says: "The invoice is made out debiting the consignee with the agreed price (or the actual cost and commission, with the premiums of insurance and the freight, as the case may be) and giving him credit for the amount of the freight which he will have to pay to the shipowner on actual delivery, and for the balance a draft is drawn on the consignee, which he is bound to accept (if the shipment be in conformity with his contract) on having handed to him the charter party, bill of lading and policy of insurance." Little light, therefore, is thrown upon the interpretation of the contract by any practical interpretation given by the parties, and in view of what I deem to be the plain intendment of the contract as expressed in the words "net landed weight," I deem the right of the buyer established to receive at San Francisco the full weight stipulated for in the contract. . . .

The order should, therefore, be reversed, with ten dollars costs and disbursements, and the motion to vacate the attachment denied, with ten dollars costs.

CLARKE, P. J., DOWLING, PAGE and GREENBAUM, JJ., concur.

Order reversed, with ten dollars costs and disbursements, and motion denied, with ten dollars costs.

Compare ZIGMANT *c.* RENAULT ET CIE., (1928) Havre 1.53 (Commercial Court of Havre), where there was a contract for the sale of lentils c.i.f. Havre "poids brut délivré." The buyer having paid on the invoiced weight claimed reimbursement from the seller because of a deficiency in the landed weight due to the fault of the carrier. Judgment was given for the seller, the court stating that in view of the well understood rule that in a c.i.f. sale the goods were at the risk of the buyer from the moment of shipment, the clause in question must be taken to apply to shortages in weight resulting from the fault of the seller, such as errors in weighing on shipment, abnormal shrinkage, etc., and could not be supposed to refer to shortages due to the fault of the carrier.

Note also SOCIETA ILVA *c.* ZARB, 1931–32 Bulletin de Legislation et de Jurisprudence Egyptiennes 148 (Mixed Court of Appeal of Alexandria). A contract for the sale of goods c.i.f. Leghorn contained a provision that 80 per cent of the price was to be paid on the opening of a credit at Port Said, and that the remaining 20 per cent was to be paid at destination on the basis of weights recognized by the Italian customs. The carrying vessel encountered heavy weather, and part of the goods having been jettisoned the buyer claimed to pay only on actual landed weights. It was held that the clause did not operate to displace the ordinary c.i.f. risks, but only to protect the buyer against excessive shrinkage or against the shipment of quantities less than those indicated by the documents.

KARINJEE JIVANJEE & CO. *v.* WILLIAM F. MALCOLM & CO.

KING'S BENCH DIVISION, 1926

[25 *Lloyd's List Law Reports*, 28]

Mr. Justice ROCHE, in giving judgment, said: This is a case stated by an umpire. The matter arises between buyers and sellers of a quantity of sisal. The umpire has decided the case in favour of the buyers. The sellers submit that the grounds upon which the umpire has decided the case are mistaken and that the decision should be in their favour. . . .

The question arises in the following way. In 1923 the sellers sold and the buyers bought some 600 to 800 tons of East African sisal at an agreed rate per ton,

> cost insurance freight to the U.K. and/or continental port or ports. Insurance without particular average and war risk. Payment by acceptance of sight draft in exchange for shipping documents.

I am now reading the terms of the contract of Aug. 2, 1923. The contract in question further provided as follows: —

> Shipment from Africa gradually between August and December, 1923. Should the goods or any portion thereof not arrive from loss of vessel or other unavoidable cause, this contract to be void for any such portion, but should the goods or any portion be transhipped and arrive in other vessel or vessels the contract to hold good for any such portion.

Those being the provisions of the contract, what happened, as found in the special case, was this. A number of bales, how many tons I know not, of sisal, being a portion of the amount covered by the contract, was in October, 1923, shipped on board a vessel called the *Rijperkerk*. The goods were insured and were, of course, made the subject-matter of bills of lading. The invoice price of the parcel shipped, together with the documents, the bills of lading and the insurance policies, were tendered to the buyers, and they paid the sum demanded by the invoice. The amounts demanded by the invoice were not the whole value of the goods at the agreed price of £36 per ton, because the freight was payable at the port of arrival, and the clear bargain between the parties, in my judgment, was that the buyers might, in part payment of the price, and should, if it was demanded of them, undertake the liability to pay the shipowner the freight. The buyers so undertook in this case.

The *Rijperkerk* caught fire in the course of the voyage, and it not being possible to extinguish the fire she was sunk in order to extinguish it, and there was a total loss of the cargo of sisal in question. The buyers recovered from the underwriters more than they had paid the sellers; and they so recovered partly because there was an addition over and above the invoice price made to the value of the goods in effecting the insurance policy, and in respect of that item, not of over-insurance, but of excess valuation to cover profits and matters of that sort, there is more money in the pockets of the buyers than they took out to pay the sellers; further, for some reason which is a little obscure and is a matter of controversy between the parties, the buyers had not at the time of the award, and have not yet, paid the shipowners the freight.

In those circumstances, the claim of the sellers was to receive from the buyers the amount which the buyers recovered from the underwriters, of course giving credit for the amount which the buyers had paid to them, the sellers. The difference the sellers say was their own and that they are entitled to recover it. They based that contention upon the clause of the contract which I have read, and need not read again, beginning, "Should the goods or any portion thereof not arrive. . . ." The effects of that clause, the sellers say, is to demand and to justify, necessitate and require, the rescission of the contract, a restoration of the parties to the position they occupied before the contract was made, or before it was performed.

The buyers contend, on the other hand, that the clause has a useful and intelligible function, but that that function stops short of the measure which the sellers put upon it. The buyers say that that is a clause under which, if, before the contract had been performed (as it can be performed if it be a c.i.f. contract and according to the terms of this contract) by tender of the documents and payment, there is a loss of goods appropriated to the performance of the contract, thereafter the sellers are neither bound nor entitled to tender, nor are the buyers entitled or bound to accept purported performance or performance by tender of documents in respect of goods which have been lost by loss of the vessel or other unavoidable cause.

The umpire has adopted the construction and contention of the buyers, and, in my judgment, although the matter is not free from difficulty, the umpire's decision is right. I so decide because I think that the construction adopted by the umpire is the more natural construction of the words themselves. They seem to me to be words more apt to the stage of a contract where the performance is still in the future than to a case where performance has been completed as it was completed in this case, when all sorts of rights may have accrued as between the buyers and other parties, strangers to the contract.

Further, the construction of the clause contended for by the buyers, and adopted by the umpire, is in my judgment more consistent with the general scope and effect of the contract. I agree with Mr. Pritt that it is often a mistake to label contracts and to put them, to use his phrase, in watertight compartments. There are many contracts of a mixed nature which contain elements proper to c.i.f. contracts and proper to contracts for actual delivery of goods; but in its general scope this contract partakes far more of the elements and character which belong to c.i.f. contracts than to any other form of contract. It is a contract which is for delivery c.i.f. and in which payment and tender of documents is regulated in a manner which is well known and is applicable to c.i.f. contracts.

[The balance of the opinion is omitted.]

Contrast PRADON ET CIE. c. SALABRAAS, (1920) Marseille 1.84 (Commercial Court of Marseille), where a contract for the sale of tapioca afloat c.i.f. Marseille contained the clause "en cas de sinistre après la designation du vapeur le marché serait annulé." It was held that "inasmuch as this last condition is absolutely incompatible with the basic rules of a c.i.f. contract, one of which is that all the risks of the voyage are for the account of the buyer, it follows that under the erroneous designation of a c.i.f. sale the parties actually have concluded a sale conditioned on safe arrival."

Note also the case of the HALLFRIED, 1927 Am. Maritime Cases 1682 (U. S. District Court S. D. N. Y.), where a contract for the sale of nitrates c.i.f. New York provided as to payment net cash against shipping documents on arrival of the goods. Knox, D.J., stated that the effect of this clause was to deprive the contract of its character as a c.i.f. contract, since "the contract could not have been executed by a delivery of documents by vendor to vendee at any time prior to arrival of the merchandise at the port of destination. If the goods had failed to arrive, the loss would not have been on the purchaser."

Compare RALLI FRÈRES c. SOCIÉTÉ DE L'USINE, (1897) Marseille 1.182 (Commercial Court of Marseille), where a contract for the sale of grain c.i.f. Marseille contained the clause, payment three months from date of arrival. It was held that the clause did not operate to affect the ordinary incidents of a c.i.f. contract, including the obligation to present the documents as soon as possible, but merely to fix the time of payment.

LAW & BONAR, LIMITED v. BRITISH AMERICAN TOBACCO COMPANY, LIMITED

KING'S BENCH DIVISION, 1916

[*Law Reports*, [1916] *2 King's Bench*, 605]

[Refer to the text of this case as printed on p. 225, reading particularly the first paragraph of the opinion by Rowlatt, J.]

Compare BEAU ET CIE. c. TURCAT ET GAUBERT, (1894) Marseille 1.194 (Commercial Court of Marseille), in which there was a contract for the sale of 100 quintals of copra c.i.f. Marseille with a provision that risks of transit were to be for the account of the seller. In holding that the effect of this clause was to transform the contract into something quite different from a c.i.f. contract, the court stated that a sale on c.i.f. terms is essentially characterized by the condition that the goods travel at the risk and peril of the buyer. "It is true that the parties may, in principle, add to a contract so designated particular clauses which modify more or less profoundly its characteristics and extent, but these clauses must not bear on the essential elements without which the contract could not exist."

2. QUANTITY

A. Where the Contract Provisions Are Indefinite

COLD BLAST TRANSPORTATION CO. *v.* KANSAS CITY BOLT & NUT CO.

United States Circuit Court of Appeals, Eighth Circuit, 1902

[114 *Federal Reporter*, 77]

In error to the Circuit Court of the United States for the District of Kansas.

This writ of error challenges a judgment on the pleadings in favor of the defendant in error, who was the plaintiff in the court below. For convenience, the plaintiff in error will be called the "defendant," and the defendant in error the "plaintiff," in this statement, and in the opinion which follows it. The plaintiff's petition stated a cause of action upon a verified account for $5,573.43. The defendant in its answer denied the averments of the petition, and pleaded a counterclaim for $5,341.94 damages for the failure of the plaintiff to deliver to the defendant after June 1, 1899, certain manufactured articles which it ordered and needed, and which the defendant alleged that the plaintiff was bound to deliver under an alleged written contract, which it averred was made and broken in this way: On October 27, 1898, the plaintiff sent to the defendant this letter:

Kansas City, Mo., Oct. 27, '98.

C. S. Ullman, Esq., Purchasing Agent Cold Blast Transportation Co., S. & S. Packing Co.—Dear Sir: We offer to deliver at your works, during six months from November 1st, 1898, the following materials at the prices stated:

Bar iron, $1.20 flat delivered by car, $1.25 by wagon.
Soft steel bars, $1.25 car load, $1.30 by wagon.
Machine bolts, 80 and 10% discount.
U. S. Std. sq. nuts, $6.50 off.
" " hex. " 7.40 off.
70% off extras for tapping.

—and will make in part payment No. 1 wrought scrap at $8.50 net ton, or arch bars and transoms at $10.50 net ton, or wrought iron car axles at $12.50 net ton, delivered your works; the quantity of scrap to be taken not to exceed the weight of materials sold to you.

Yours truly, R. C. HOWES, Secy.

With option of renewal for 6 months from June 1st, 1899.

The K. C. Bolt & Nut Co.,
R. C. Howes, Sec'y.

On receipt of the proposition contained in this letter the defendant accepted it; and between November 1, 1898, and June 1, 1899, it ordered, the plaintiff delivered, and the defendant paid for, nuts, bolts, and bars of the character specified in the letter, under the terms and at the prices there stated. Before June 1, 1899, the defendant notified the plaintiff that it exercised its option to renew the contract evidenced by the letter and acceptance. Between June 1, 1899, and December 1, 1899, the defendant ordered of the plaintiff nuts, bolts, and bars of the character described in the letter, which it needed in its business, which the plaintiff refused to deliver, and which the defendant was forced to purchase of others at prices which, in the aggregate, exceeded those specified in the alleged contract between the parties by $5,341.94. In addition to the counterclaim, which has been stated, the defendant pleaded an offset of $2,727.18, founded on the alleged fact that the plaintiff had charged that amount in excess of the prices specified in the alleged contract for nuts, bolts, and bars which it had furnished to the defendant on its orders between June 1, 1899, and December 1, 1899. The answer of the defendant was not verified. There was a reply to it. But upon this review of a judgment upon the pleadings against the defendant the averments of the reply become immaterial, because the allegations of the answer stand admitted, and those of the reply which assert new matter are denied. The only question for consideration is whether the answer stated any legal defense, counterclaim, or offset to the cause of action pleaded by the plaintiff.

Sanborn, Circuit Judge, after stating the case as above, delivered the opinion of the court.

The main question in this case is whether or not the answer states a legal counterclaim. The basis of this counterclaim is that the plaintiff failed to deliver nuts, bolts, and bars between June 1, 1899, and December 1, 1899, under the alleged renewal of the so-called contract of October 27, 1898. This supposed contract consisted of a written offer to deliver manufactured articles in unnamed quantities at certain specific prices at any time between October 27, 1898, and June 1, 1899, and the acceptance of that offer, without more. The answer contains no averment that either the plaintiff or the defendant paid any consideration or performed any act to induce the contract, except the remitting of the offer by the plaintiff, and the sending of its acceptance by the defendant. There was therefore in the inception of this alleged agreement no consideration for the promise of either of the parties to it, except the promise of the other. Neither the letter nor the acceptance names any quantity or amount of the articles specified that is to be delivered or received under it. The plaintiff does not agree to deliver, nor does the defendant contract to receive or pay for, any quantity or amount whatever of the articles named in the writings. A promise is a good consideration for a promise. But no promise constitutes such a consideration which is not obligatory upon the party promising. It must bind the promisor, so that the promisee may maintain an action for its breach, or it is without legal effect and void. A promise to furnish, deliver, or receive specified articles at certain prices, without any agreement to order or to accept any amounts or quantities of the articles, is without binding force or effect, because neither party is thereby bound to deliver or to accept any quantity or amount whatever. Such promises are void, because they lack one of the essential elements of an agreement, — certainty in the thing to be done. Contracts for the future supply during a limited time of articles which shall be required or needed or consumed by an established business, or used in the operation of certain steamships or other machinery, are no exceptions to this principle, because they fall under the rule, "Id certum est quod certum reddi potest." But an accepted promise to furnish goods, merchandise, or other property, at certain prices, during a limited time, in such quantities as the acceptor shall require or want in his business, is without consideration and void, because the acceptor is not bound thereby to require or take any articles whatever under the supposed agreement. The line of demarkation between valid and invalid contracts here runs between the requirements of machinery, or of an established business, and the wants, desires, or requirements of the tentative vendee; and that because the former are either reasonably certain, or may be made so by evidence, while the latter are conditioned by the will of the tentative vendee alone, and are both uncertain and capable of infinite variation.

It is, however, contended that, even if this alleged contract was void in its inception, it became valid and binding upon the parties when the defendant ordered, and the plaintiff delivered and received payment for, a large quantity of the manufactured articles at the prices and in accordance with the terms of the letter of October 27, 1898. But the fatal defect in the alleged contract was that the plaintiff was not bound to deliver, nor the defendant to take and pay for, any specific quantity of the offered articles. As to all undelivered articles, that defect still inheres in the agreement. The plaintiff is not bound to deliver, nor the defendant to take and pay for, any articles that have not been delivered, because there is no specification in the alleged contract of the amount or quantity which the one is to deliver and the other to receive. The orders for these articles which have been filled by their delivery specified the amounts so delivered, and thus effected contracts for their sale. But these orders and deliveries have in no way remedied the fatal defect of the offer and acceptance regarding those articles which the defendant has ordered, and the plaintiff has refused to deliver. The defendant never agreed to order or to pay for any quantity of these undelivered articles. If it had refused to order and take them, no action could have been maintained for its failure, because no court could have determined what amount it was required to take. Nor can an action be better maintained against the plaintiff for its failure to deliver the articles which the defendant has ordered, because the offer contains no measure of the quantity which the plaintiff was to deliver, and consequently no agreement on its part to deliver any whatever. As the contract was void in its inception, and has continued to be void as to all undelivered goods, the notice of its renewal which was delivered by the defendant was futile, since the renewal of a void contract but continues its invalidity.

It is said that the intention of the parties was to make an agreement that the plaintiff should sell and deliver, and the defendant should buy, all the articles of the character specified in the offer which should be needed or required by its business between October 27, 1898, and June 1, 1899; that the purpose of the construction and interpretation of contracts is to ascertain the intention of the parties; and that this contract should be interpreted to effect this intent. The answer is that, while ambiguous terms and doubtful stipulations may be interpreted to carry out the intention of the parties when they fairly evidence it, their secret intention cannot be imported into contracts whose terms and meaning are plain and unambiguous, and do not express it. It is only the intention of the parties which the contract itself expresses that the courts may enforce. In the case at bar the offer of the plaintiff is nothing but a price list. The acceptance of the defendant contains no agreement to buy any of the articles specified in the list, and there is no ambiguity in the terms, or doubt in the meaning, of the writings in issue. To give effect to the intention of the parties which the defendant now alleges would be to ascribe to them a purpose, and to make and enforce for them a contract, which their writings neither express nor suggest; and this is beyond the province of the courts.

The rules applicable to contracts of this class may be thus briefly stated: A contract for the future delivery of personal property is void, for want of consideration and mutuality, if the quantity to be delivered is conditioned by the will, wish, or want of one of the parties; but it may be sustained if the quantity is ascertainable otherwise with reasonable certainty. An accepted offer to furnish or deliver such articles of personal property as shall be needed, required, or consumed by the established business of the acceptor during a limited time is binding, and may be enforced, because it contains the implied agreement of the acceptor to purchase all the articles that shall be required in conducting his business during this time from the party who makes the offer. But an accepted offer to sell or deliver articles at specified prices during a limited time in such amounts or quantities as the acceptor may want or desire in his business, or without any statement of the amount or quantity, is without consideration and void, because the acceptor is not bound to want, desire, or take any of the articles mentioned. Accepted orders for goods under such void contracts constitute sales of the goods thus ordered at the prices named in the contracts, but they do not validate the agreements as to articles which the one refuses to purchase, or the other refuses to sell or deliver, under the void contracts, because neither party is bound to take or deliver any amount or quantity of these articles thereunder.

Tested by these rules, the accepted offer of October 27, 1898, was void in its inception for want of consideration and mutuality. No quantity of nuts, bolts, or bars was named in the offer or in the acceptance. The defendant was not bound to order, to receive, or to pay for any of the articles named in the offer; and there was therefore no consideration for the offer itself, and no mutuality in the supposed agreement. The orders which were made and filled prior to June 1, 1899, constituted valid contracts for the purchase and sale of the goods so ordered at the prices named in the offer. But they effected no agreement on the part of the defendant to order, or on the part of the plaintiff to deliver, any other goods under the offer, because the amount of goods whose delivery was contemplated was still unnamed. The defendant was not legally bound to order, to receive, or to take any articles which it had not ordered, so that there was still no consideration and no mutuality in the contract as to any articles which the defendant had not ordered, or which the plaintiff had not delivered. The refusal of the plaintiff to honor the orders of the defendant was therefore no breach of any valid contract, and formed no legal cause of action for the counterclaim.

It is specified as error that the court refused to permit the defendant to amend its answer at the trial so as to allege that it orally, and by the written contract, agreed to purchase all of the goods of the kinds mentioned in the offer of October 27, 1898, "that it might use or desire to use during the times mentioned in the contract"; but no argument is presented in support of this specification, and no plausible reason for its assignment is suggested. If the amendment had been allowed, the alleged contract would still have been void, because, under the agreement stated in the amendment, the defendant would not have been bound to desire to use, or to use, any of the articles mentioned in the price list, and there would still have been no mutuality in the contract. Moreover, the granting of the motion was discretionary with the court below, and it was made so late that it would have been no abuse of discretion to have denied it if the amendment had been material. It was properly denied because the amendment was immaterial, because if it had been allowed the answer would not have stated facts sufficient to constitute a legal counterclaim, and because its allowance was discretionary, and there was no abuse of that discretion. . . .

The judgment below was right, and it is affirmed.

In Midland Steel Sales Co. *v.* Waterloo Gasoline Engine Co., 9 Fed. (2nd) 250 (Circuit Court of Appeals, Eighth Circuit, 1925), a letter from the buyer to the seller read in part as follows: "As per conversation we agree to purchase from you all your surplus stock of cold rolled steel, mild steel bars, angles, and sheet steel. Quantities as specified on list you are to furnish." At the bottom of the letter appeared the word "Accepted," followed by the seller's signature. In subsequent correspondence the seller wrote: "The list is all ready with the exception of checking over to determine what we will retain"; and later: "will mail list what we have for disposal early as possible." No such list however was furnished, and an action was brought by the buyer for damages for breach of the alleged contract. The court below directed a verdict for the defendant. In affirming judgment on the verdict, Kenyon, Circuit Judge, said in part: "It is frankly conceded by counsel for plaintiff that, if it conclusively appear 'that what the plaintiff bought was to be determined by what the defendant might will, want, or wish,' the judgment was right and should be affirmed; in other words, the contract would be unenforceable, because of lack of mutuality. It seems to us that this is exactly what the evidence shows. What specific material could plaintiff claim it had purchased? What particular bars of steel could plaintiff take from defendant's place of business by virtue of the contract? Clearly none, until such time as a list had been furnished. Plaintiff by the agreement itself, without the list subsequently to be furnished, bought nothing. It could not have taken Exhibit D to defendant's place of business and have insisted upon the turning over to it of a single bar of steel. The list to be furnished was an essential and determinative part of the agreement, and defendant was under no obligation to list therein any material, except such as it might desire to dispose of as its surplus."

Note also GROSS *v.* STAMPLER, 165 N. Y. S. 214 (Supreme Court, Appellate Term, 1917), in which there was an action to recover damages for breach of an alleged contract to furnish bread to the plaintiff under an oral agreement to supply plaintiff daily with such quantities of bread as he might order. A judgment for the plaintiff was reversed, Finch, J., saying: "The plaintiff did not obligate himself to purchase any bread or to do anything else. All that he agreed to do was to pay the stipulated price in case he should order some bread."

A CONTRACT which leaves the quantity sold entirely subject to the will of one of the parties involves what is known in the Civil Law as a potestative condition, as mentioned in Arts. 1170 and 1174 of the French Civil Code, the latter of which provides expressly that any obligation is null if contracted under a potestative condition on the part of the obligor. See Colin et Capitant, 2 *Droit Civil Français*, Sec. 393 (7th ed., 1932), for a discussion of the French law.

THE GREAT NORTHERN RAILWAY COMPANY *v.* WITHAM

COURT OF COMMON PLEAS, 1873

[*Law Reports*, 9 *Common Pleas*, 16]

[In response to an advertisement for tenders defendant sent in a tender in which he undertook "to supply the Great Northern Railway Company for twelve months . . . with such quantities of each or any of the several articles named in the attached specification as the company's storekeeper may order from time to time at the price set opposite each article respectively. . . ." The tender was accepted. Several orders were given and executed, but ultimately the defendant refused to supply further, and an action was brought for breach of contract. Verdict for plaintiffs, and motion to enter a nonsuit. Rule refused. The opinion of Keating, J., is omitted.]

BRETT, J. The company advertised for tenders for the supply of stores, such as they might think fit to order, for one year. The defendant made a tender offering to supply them for that period at certain fixed prices; and the company accepted his tender. If there were no other objection, the contract between the parties would be found in the tender and the letter accepting it. This action is brought for the defendant's refusal to deliver goods ordered by the company; and the objection to the plaintiffs' right to recover is, that the contract is unilateral. I do not, however, understand what objection that is to a contract. Many contracts are obnoxious to the same complaint. If I say to another, "If you will go to York, I will give you 100*l.*," that is in a certain sense a unilateral contract. He has not promised to go to York. But, if he goes, it cannot be doubted that he will be entitled to receive the 100*l.* His going to York at my request is a sufficient consideration for my promise. So, if one says to another, "If you will give me an order for iron, or other goods, I will supply it at a given price"; if the order is given, there is a complete contract which the seller is bound to perform. There is in such a case ample consideration for the promise. So, here, the company having given the defendant an order at his request, his acceptance of the order would bind them. If any authority could have been found to sustain Mr. Seymour's contention, I should have considered that a rule ought to be granted. But none has been cited. *Burton* v. *Great Northern Railway Co.* (9 Ex. 507; 23 L. J. (Ex.) 184) is not at all to the purpose. This is matter of every day's practice; and I think it would be wrong to countenance the notion that a man who tenders for the supply of goods in this way is not bound to deliver them when an order is given. I agree that this judgment does not decide the question whether the defendant might have absolved himself from the further performance of the contract by giving notice.

GROVE, J. I am of the same opinion, and have nothing to add.

Rule refused.

Compare MILLER *v.* THOMASON, 229 Alabama 267 (Supreme Court, 1934), where there was an action in *assumpsit* on the common count for merchandise, goods and chattels sold by the plaintiff to the defendant under an agreement by which the plaintiff undertook to furnish to the defendant "all the fertilizer that he desires to sell at Albertville," at prices as low as those obtainable from certain named suppliers. Defendant bought and received 100 tons of fertilizer under this agreement, but owing to a dispute about the price plaintiff refused to deliver a further 100 tons which was ordered. Defendant pleaded in recoupment, claiming damages for this refusal. In correcting and affirming a judgment for the plaintiff, Brown, J., said in part: "Under the terms of the alleged contract, the defendant was not obligated to order, purchase, or receive any amount of fertilizer from the plaintiff. This feature of the contract was left solely to the desire and will of the defendant, and was wanting in mutuality of obligation, and will not support an action for its breach, or for a breach of any warranty embodied therein, by the party not bound thereby.

"The fact that the defendant, after a slump in the market price of fertilizers, ordered a definite quantity of such fertilizers, which plaintiff declined to sell, did not constitute such performance of the contract as supplied the element of mutuality. The contract being void *ab initio*, the plaintiff had the right to disregard it and refuse the shipment.

"This does not impinge the well-settled principle, that in so far as the unilateral obligation is performed, it becomes a binding obligation. In such a case the performance supplies the element of mutuality necessary as a consideration to support the obligation."

Note also TEXARKANA CASKET Co. *v.* BINSWANGER & Co., 3 Fed. (2nd) 611 (District Court, E.D. Texas, 1924), where defendant proposed to sell to plaintiff "all of the glass that plaintiff might desire to purchase that was manufactured by the Libby-Owens Sheet Glass Company" at prices reflected by the "regular list price" of that company. The proposition was accepted, and plaintiff "agreed that thereafter the plaintiff would order such glass or glass products of the Libby-Owens make or manufacture as it desired from and through the defendant." On various later dates four carloads of glass were ordered and paid for at prices that subsequently were discovered to be in excess of the Libby-Owens list price. In each case the order was given in reliance on the original agreement, but each of the first three orders was given after request for and receipt of a definite quotation. Following judgment on a verdict for the plaintiff, a motion for a new trial was granted on the ground that the transaction was not conducted by both parties with the contract in mind, but that the defendant was not pretending to fill the orders except at the prices actually quoted.

CABOT *v.* WINSOR

MASSACHUSETTS SUPREME JUDICIAL COURT, 1861

[1 *Allen's Reports*, 546]

Contract to recover the price of four hundred and seventy-five bundles of gunny bags, sold and delivered by the plaintiff to the defendants.

At the trial in the superior court, the defendants admitted their liability to pay for two hundred bundles, but denied their liability to pay for any more. The plaintiff introduced in evidence a paper, of which the following is a copy: "Boston, Sept. 4, 1858. Sold to Nath'l Winsor Jr., & Co., for account of Stephen Cabot, Esq., five hundred (500) bundles, more or less, gunny bags at 10*c.* per bag. Terms, 6 months. Simeon Sowle & Co., Brokers for the parties. Accepted, Nath'l Winsor Jr., & Co." The execution and delivery of this paper were not denied.

The plaintiff offered evidence to show that, at the time when this paper was signed, he had about five hundred aind twenty-one bundles of gunny bags, of fifty bags each, all of which, on the day before, were at the Grand Junction Wharf in East Boston, and that he had given orders to one Sullivan, who was a compresser of gunny bags, and had a store on India Wharf, to take them to his store and there compress them into bales; that, when the paper was executed, some of the bundles were at the Grand Junction Wharf, and some of them had already been taken to Sullivan's store, and others were on the way thither, and that forty-five bundles had been compressed into bales and put into the store, and orders were at once given by the plaintiff to Sullivan not to compress any more of them. These facts, except the number already compressed by Sullivan, were known to both parties; and the plaintiff claimed and introduced evidence, under objection, to show that it was the uncompressed gunny bags which were the subject of the contract.

It appeared in evidence that both parties knew that the object of the defendants in making the purchase was to fill the ship Hesperus, then lying at India Wharf, and about to sail, and that at the time of the purchase it was uncertain what number of bundles would be needed for that purpose; and it was verbally agreed that they should be removed to the ship at the defendants' expense by the truckman already employed by Sullivan. Only two hundred bundles were actually taken on board of the Hesperus, that being all that proved to be necessary to fill the ship; and, of the remainder, amounting to two hundred and seventy-five bundles, some were left by the truckman in a storehouse on the wharf, which, by permission of the wharfingers, was temporarily used by various persons having business there, and the residue were taken into Sullivan's store, to keep them from the rain.

The defendants claimed that under the contract they were to have five hundred bundles, or more or less than that number, as might reasonably be found necessary to fill the ship; or at their election; and that, as they did not require any more than the two hundred bundles for that purpose, and as they never in fact received any more than that number, they were only bound to pay for two hundred. But Lord, J., ruled that there was no latent ambiguity in the contract, and that its construction was for the court; and he instructed the jury that the contract covered all the gunny bags which had not been compressed, and that a delivery of a part of the lot, under and in pursuance of the contract, was a delivery of the whole.

The defendants then offered to prove by parol that both parties understood the contract differently, and that it was not intended to cover more than enough to fill the ship; and they offered to prove the declarations and acts of the plaintiff, before, at the time of, and after the making of the contract, for the purpose of showing that he so construed it; but the judge excluded the evidence.

The defendants, in view of the construction put upon the contract by the judge, requested him to instruct the jury that a delivery of four hundred and seventy-five bundles, or a readiness to deliver that number, was not a compliance with the contract, which called for a delivery of five hundred bundles, more or less, unless the defendants knew that the number was so much less than five hundred, and accepted the same as a compliance with the contract, or waived the non-compliance. But the judge declined so to rule, and instructed the jury that, if in point of fact the lot respecting which the parties were negotiating consisted of four hundred and seventy-five bundles, neither party knowing the precise number, there was no such discrepancy between the actual number and that stated in the contract, as to avoid the operation of the contract, and that the plaintiff was bound to deliver, and the defendants were bound to receive, the four hundred and seventy-five bundles, in execution of the contract.

The plaintiff was called as a witness in his own behalf, and testified that the defendants were to take delivery of the property where it was.

The defendants claimed the right in cross-examination to put in the whole conversation in which this agreement was made, to affect the construction of the contract, as well as the question of delivery. The court ruled that it was not competent for the former purpose, but was competent for the latter purpose. The whole conversation was then put in, and the plaintiff testified that it was then agreed that the defendants were to return what they did not want to fill the ship; and the broker who made the agreement testified to the same effect; and the judge instructed the jury that this evidence could not be considered as controlling or affecting the construction of the contract as to the amount of goods sold.

The jury returned a verdict for the plaintiff, for the price of four hundred and seventy-five bundles, and interest; and the defendants alleged exceptions.

BIGELOW, C. J. The paper or writing on which the plaintiff relies in support of his case is not a mere bill of parcels, designed to specify only the quantity and price of articles sold, nor was it so intended and understood by the parties. It is a written memorandum or contract of sale, drawn up by a broker as the agent of both parties, in the form of what is usually termed a "sold note," and designed to embody the terms and conditions of a bargain for the sale of merchandise, so as to bind the parties by an agreement valid and sufficient under the statute of frauds. To this contract, the defendants have bound themselves by their written acceptance of its terms.

We are unable to perceive any ground on which it can be held that this contract falls within any of the exceptions to the familiar and well established rule which excludes all parol evidence in the construction of the written agreements of parties. The language in which it is expressed is not technical, nor is it alleged to have any peculiar or local signification, or to have been used with reference to any custom or usage, which would vary or change its natural and ordinary meaning. Nor are the terms of the contract rendered uncertain or doubtful by reference to extrinsic facts, so as to create a latent ambiguity. The words "more or less," which seem to have given rise to the contention between the parties, have a plain, ordinary, and popular signification, and are often used in contracts relating both to real and personal estate. As applied to quantity, they are to be construed as qualifying a representation or statement of an absolute and definite amount, so that neither party to a contract can avoid it or set it aside by reason of any deficiency or surplus, occasioned by no fraud or want of good faith, if there is a reasonable approximation to the quantity specifically named as the subject of the contract. In sales of merchandise, especially in large quantities, where it is impossible to ascertain with precise accuracy the number or weight of the articles before concluding the contract for their purchase, it is necessary and usual to insert the words "more or less" or "about" in connection with the specific amount, which forms the subject of the contract, in order to cover any variation from the estimate, which is likely to arise from differences in weight, errors in counting, diminution by shrinking, or other similar causes. But in such cases, parol evidence is not admitted to show that the parties intended to buy and sell a different quantity or amount from that stated in the written agreement. On the contrary, it is held to be a contract for the sale of the quantity or amount specified; and the effect of the words "more or less" is only to permit the vendor to fulfill his contract by a delivery of so much as may reasonably and fairly be held to be a compliance with the contract, after making due allowance for an excess or short delivery arising from the usual and ordinary causes, which prevent an accurate estimate of the weight or number of the articles sold or as it is sometimes briefly expressed, it is "an absolute contract for a specific quantity within a reasonable limit." What is a reasonable limit and a substantial compliance with such contract, if the facts are not in dispute between the parties, is a question for the determination of the court. *Cross* v. *Eglin*, 2 B. & Ad. 106. *Moore* v. *Campbell*, 10 Exch. 323. *Bourne* v. *Seymour*, 16 C. B. 336. *Stebbins* v. *Eddy*, 4 Mason, 414, 419. *Pembroke Iron Co.* v. *Parsons*, 5 Gray, 591. Applying these rules to the contract in question, its construction is clear and unambiguous. It was an agreement for the sale of five hundred bundles of gunny bags, under which, by the term "more or less," the plaintiff had a right to deliver a number which should reasonably approximate to that number; and, in the opinion of the court, a variation of five per cent. in so large a quantity was not such a deficiency as to fall outside of the fair and reasonable limit of short delivery. By proof of a delivery of a portion of the four hundred and seventy-five bundles, and a readiness to deliver the residue of the lot, the plaintiff proved a full compliance with the terms of his contract. . . .

Exceptions overruled.

SOCIÉTÉ ANONYME L'INDUSTRIELLE RUSSO–BELGE *v.* SCHOLEFIELD AND SON

Court of Appeal, 1902

[7 *Commercial Cases*, 114]

Appeal by the plaintiffs from the judgment of Mathew J. given on November 23, 1901. The action was brought by the plaintiffs, a Belgian company, to recover damages for breach of contract. By a contract dated April 21, 1899, the defendants, who were a firm of Newcastle coal merchants, sold to the plaintiffs about 10,000 tons of Northumberland small coals and about 2500 tons of Northumberland Duff coal, c.i.f. Antwerp. The coal was to be shipped over a period of twelve months from September, 1899, in as nearly equal monthly instalments as the sellers could arrange; the sellers were to endeavour to effect monthly shipments, yet if for any reason whatever they were unable to do so then they were to be at liberty to ship two months' supply in one month. By a second contract dated October 31, 1899, the defendants sold to the plaintiffs on substantially the same terms a further quantity of about 6000 tons of Northumberland Duff coals in ten monthly instalments from November, 1899.

Monthly deliveries were made under the contracts in approximately equal quantities until August, 1900, when, the last instalment becoming due, the defendants delivered a shipment which, with the previous shipments under the two contracts, brought the total deliveries up to 9592 tons of small coal and 8453 tons of Duff coal, being a shortage on the quantities of 10,000 tons, 2500 tons, and 6000 tons of 455 tons, or about 2½ per cent.

The plaintiffs claimed damages as for 445 tons short delivered.

At the trial before Mathew J. the defendants gave evidence of a custom in the Newcastle coal trade that in contracts such as those in question the word "about" allowed to the vendors a margin of 5 per cent. either way at their option. Mathew J. held that the custom was proved and gave judgment for the defendants. The plaintiffs appealed.

VAUGHAN WILLIAMS L.J. The appeal must fail. The sole question is whether there is a custom of the Newcastle coal trade that the word "about" gives to the vendor at his option a margin of 5 per cent. above or below the specific quantity named. Whether there is such a custom is a question of fact, and I think here the evidence was all one way. I think the custom was fully proved and that the learned Judge arrived at the right conclusion. A distinction must be made. No evidence is admissible to explain the general meaning of the word "about" — that is a question of construction for the Judge — but evidence is admissible to prove that by the custom of a particular market or trade or locality the word "about" has a special meaning, as has been proved in this case. It is clear that "about" refers to the total amounts, and not to the monthly instalments. No question was raised in the Court below as to the unreasonableness of the custom, but I think there is nothing unreasonable in such a one-sided option. For these reasons I think the appeal must be dismissed.

STIRLING L.J. and COZENS-HARDY L.J. concurred.

Compare CROSS *v.* EGLIN, 2 B. & Ad. 106 (Court of King's Bench, 1831), in which there was a contract for "about 300 quarters, more or less," of rye. The buyers refused a tender of 345 quarters, and in an action to recover part of the price already paid offered evidence that where the words "more or less" were used in a grain contract, it was contrary to the custom of merchants to require the buyer to accept so large an excess. The evidence was admitted with leave to move, and when the rule was argued the Judges thought it immaterial whether the evidence was properly received or not, but were of the opinion that its admissibility was doubtful. Said Littledale, J.: "It is true such evidence is often received to explain mercantile terms; but 'about' and 'more or less' seem to be words of general import, and I should have much difficulty in saying that evidence ought to be received to ascertain their meaning."

IN RE AN ARBITRATION BETWEEN HARRISON AND MICKS, LAMBERT & CO.

KING'S BENCH DIVISION, 1917

[*Law Reports*, [1917] 1 *King's Bench*, 755]

Special case stated by the Appeal Committee of the Hull Corn Trade Association.

Harrison (hereinafter called "the seller") carried on business as a corn merchant at Liverpool, and Micks, Lambert & Co. (hereinafter called "the buyers") were corn merchants carrying on business at Hull. Prior to April 27, 1916, the seller sold to various persons, including the buyers, part of a cargo of wheat ex *Clodmore*. On April 27 the buyers verbally agreed with the seller to purchase the remainder of the cargo, which the seller estimated at 5400 quarters. At the time of the verbal agreement the buyers stipulated that they should have the whole of the remainder of the cargo, and on the same day the seller sent by post from Liverpool a contract in writing, bearing the date April 27, 1916, by which he sold to the buyers "the remainder (more or less about) 5400 quarters Manitoba wheat . . . at Hull ex *Clodmore*." The buyers accepted delivery of about 5400 quarters. The seller had, in fact, made a miscalculation, and at the time of the sale he had 574 quarters more than 5400 quarters in hand. He contended that the effect of the contract was that the buyers were liable to take delivery of the 574 quarters in addition to the 5400 quarters. The buyers contended that the word "remainder" was governed by the words "about 5400 quarters," and that they could not be compelled to take more than "about 5400 quarters," and that any excess remaining must be held by the seller on his own account. The seller admitted that the dispute had arisen owing to his mistake in calculating the quantity of wheat which he had disposed of. The contract was in the printed form of the Hull Corn Trade Association, Limited, and was headed "No. 1 Spot Contract." Rules and conditions were indorsed on the contract, of which condition 3 was as follows: "The word 'about' when used in reference to quantity shall mean within 5 per cent. over or under the quantity stated." In view of that clause the buyers contended that at the most they could be compelled to accept 5400 quarters plus 270 quarters, i.e. 5 per cent., on the 5400 quarters. The question for the opinion of the Court was (*inter alia*) whether on the true construction of the contract the buyers were liable to take delivery of the whole of the remainder beyond 5400 quarters.

BAILHACHE J., having stated the facts, continued: The question is whether on the true construction of the contract the buyers are liable to take delivery of the remainder, the 574 quarters, and the point for our determination is whether under the contract there was a sale of 5400 quarters "more or less about" — the words "more or less about" merely giving a 5 per cent. margin within which the buyer or the seller were bound to accept or deliver as the case might be — or whether the quantity "5400 quarters more or less about" are words of estimate; and the subject-matter of the sale is the remainder of the cargo ex *Clodmore.* I have come to the conclusion that upon the true construction of the contract the subject-matter of the sale was the remainder of the cargo ex *Clodmore.*

In my judgment the words "5400 quarters more or less about" are, as they *prima facie* appear to be, words of estimate and of estimate only, and the ruling words are "the remainder of the cargo." We could not hold otherwise without departing from the reasoning in *Levi* v. *Berk* (2 Times L. R. 898, 899) and *Borrowman* v. *Drayton* (2 Ex. D. 15). . . .

The conclusion at which I have arrived is that the parties in the present case were dealing with — they were buying and selling — so much of the cargo ex *Clodmore* as happened to be left, and the words "5400 more or less about" were the seller's estimate of what that remainder of the cargo was. The estimate was exceeded, but, notwithstanding the excess, the buyer is, in my judgment, bound to take the 574 quarters, or whatever the excess may turn out to be. That conclusion is, I think, very strongly borne out by *McLay & Co.* v. *Perry & Co.* (2 Ex. D. 15), where the parties were dealing with a heap of scrap iron in a yard. There it was clear that the subject-matter of the bargain was the heap of scrap iron. It is true that the estimate of the heap given was very much greater than the heap turned out to be; but, inasmuch as it was held that what they were really bargaining about was the heap, the fact that the estimate of what was in the heap was incorrect was immaterial.

ATKIN J. I agree. I think that in all these cases one has to look to the particular contract and construe it. It is difficult to lay down a general rule, but it is quite plain that one must apply the ordinary principles of construction and try to give the words in the contract their reasonable and ordinary meaning. In a commercial contract for the sale of goods it is quite usual to define the subject-matter, after the description of quality, in terms of quantity. On the other hand, it is not at all uncommon to define the subject-matter of the sale by reference to attributes other than mere quantity — for instance by relation to its locality past or future, its ownership, manufacture, or other respect. And if it is defined by each party saying in effect "I bargain to bring into the contract those relations" they must be given effect to. In the present case the contract begins by saying that the seller has sold the "remainder," and, omitting for the moment the words of quantity, that would be the remainder of Manitoba wheat ex *Clodmore.* That, so far, seems to be a description of the subject-matter as far as the amount is concerned. It is not expressed in the ordinary terms of quantity by reference to weight or number; but after "remainder" the contract contains the term "more or less about 5400 quarters." Having already defined what it is to be, namely, "remainder," it appears to me that the full and proper effect is given to the words which follow by treating them as terms of estimate. No language could more clearly point to something in the nature of an estimate than those words "more or less" and "about"; and it appears to me on the true construction of this contract, and following the lines of reasoning suggested by the authorities to which my brother has referred, that that is the right view to take in this case.

It is true that when a person buys a remainder he may be buying a quantity which may vary within quite large limits; but it is perfectly possible for him to adopt words in the contract of sale which would prevent him from being exposed to any extreme variation, because he can quite easily say "not to exceed so much," or "not to be less than so much." If he says so, of course that would define the subject-matter. Moreover, it might very well be that in entering into such a contract as this a seller might have made representations which, if untrue, would entitle the buyer to rescind his contract if he discovers the misrepresentations in time. That has not been suggested, and the buyers have in fact taken delivery of the great bulk of the remainder. It is not necessary in the present case to define the precise meaning of the expression "remainder," nor to ascertain precisely how much is now left; but we have to decide whether on the contract the buyers were obliged to accept the remainder, even although it amounted to more than 5400 quarters with a margin of 5 per cent. In my view they were, and I think we ought to answer the question by saying that on the true construction of the contract the buyers are bound to take delivery of the whole or the remainder.

Compare the remarks of Atkin, J., in MARX *v.* AMERICAN MALTING Co., 169 Fed. 582 (Circuit Court of Appeals, Sixth Circuit, 1909), where there was a contract for all the buyer's requirements of malt to a certain date with the following clauses: "Amount of malt to be used will be between 15,000 and 20,000 bushels. . . . No privilege, option or refusal on an additional quantity will be recognized unless special and definite mention thereof is made on this order blank." Reversing the lower court, it was held without reference to the latter clause that the controlling factor was the requirements of the buyer, the amounts named being purely by way of estimate.

Note also WADDELL *v.* PHILLIPS, 133 Maryland 497 (Court of Appeals, 1919), where a contract read: "We have this day sold to (the buyers) their requirements of cans for the 1916 packing season . . . as follows: About 500,000 No. 3 cans and about 200,000 No. 2 cans." The buyers' actual requirements ran much in excess of the figures mentioned, but after supplying 330,240 No. 2 cans and 509,536 No. 3 cans, the seller refused to furnish any more. Against the amount due the seller, the buyers sought to recoup the expense of purchasing in the open market the additional cans required for the season. A judgment for the seller for the full contract price was affirmed, the court holding that the seller had complied sufficiently with the contract terms. "The defendants have only themselves to blame for any additional expense they may have been put to, as they knew better than anyone else what their plans and engagements for the coming packing season were."

NEW YORK OVERSEA CO., INC. *v.* WARFIELD–PRATT–HOWELL CO.

CALIFORNIA DISTRICT COURT OF APPEAL, 1925

[70 *California Appellate Reports*, 724]

LANGDON, P. J. — This is an appeal by the plaintiff from a judgment against it in an action brought to recover something over $5,000, damages suffered by reason of the failure of defendant to accept and pay for twenty tons of sugar, alleged to have been purchased by said defendant from the plaintiff. The only question presented at the trial and upon appeal is as to whether the quantity of sugar in question was purchased by defendant under the admitted contract between the parties. This contract contained the following provisions pertinent to our inquiry: After naming the buyer and seller, and the commodity sold, it continued: "Quantity: (About) two hundred (200) tons (each 2240#)." The price was then specified and other conditions, immaterial here, after which appears the following: "It is understood that where the word 'about' appears in this contract, it shall mean 10% over or under."

Many of the facts were agreed to by stipulation of the parties. No question is made as to the quality of the sugar nor as to the fulfillment of any of the conditions binding upon the seller, and it is agreed that upon the arrival of the vessel containing the sugar, the plaintiff tendered to the defendant 220 tons of the same. Two hundred tons were accepted and paid for by the defendant. However, the price of sugar had decreased between the time of the signing of the contract and the arrival of the sugar in San Francisco, and the defendant objected to accepting the maximum amount called for by the contract. It was agreed that the twenty tons of sugar in dispute should be sold at the market price and the defendant's liability for the difference between that amount and the price it had contracted to pay for the sugar should be submitted to the court.

The trial court concluded that the contract provisions hereinbefore quoted obligated the defendant to accept only 200 tons of sugar. Respondent seeks to support this decision by citing cases in which such terms as "about" and "more or less" were used in connection with the specification of an amount of merchandise, but in all of those cases the definition of such terms was not agreed upon by the parties and, therefore, the contracts presented some ambiguity, some opportunity for judicial construction. Such cases are not in point here, because, as appellant points out, the parties have exactly defined their terms, and such definition is as binding a part of their contract as any other part. There is no situation presented in the instant case which invites construction of the contract. The contract is simple and unambiguous, and the invariable rule in this and every other jurisdiction, under such circumstances, is to give full effect to the agreement of the parties.

It is appellant's position that the contract in this case gave the seller an option to deliver any amount of sugar between 180 and 220 tons.

[After reviewing a number of cases, Langdon, P.J., continued:]

It seems well settled by the foregoing authorities that where parties make a contract for the purchase and sale of merchandise between certain limits, the option is with the seller to determine the amount to be delivered by him within those limits. Upon the same principle, when parties have used the word "about" in their contract and have exactly defined such term, the option is with the seller to deliver within the quantitative limits expressed by the definition of such term.

[A page of the opinion is here omitted.]

It would seem that the citation of further authority is unnecessary, but it is interesting in considering the question before us to find our position sustained by an English case closely analogous to the instant case (*In re Thornett and Fehr, etc.* [1921], 1 K. B. 219). There the contract was for the sale of "200 tons, five per cent more or less" of tallow. The court said:

"The third question is whether as a matter of law the arbitrators ought to treat the contract as being a contract for 200 tons, or whether they are at liberty at their discretion to treat it as a contract for 190 tons or 210 tons or any number of tons falling between those limits. The answer to that question is that the contract is for the number of tons specified in the document — that is, for '200 tons, 5 per cent more or less.' That means that the sellers would be performing their obligation under the contract if they delivered 5 per cent less than the 200 tons or 5 per cent more than the 200 tons. It is a provision which is inserted into the contract for the sellers' protection, and it gives them a margin within which to deliver, so that they are not bound to deliver exactly 200 tons, but within 5 per cent of the quantity, whether more or less. . . ."

The contention of the respondent in the case before us that the tender of the maximum amount of sugar after the price had decreased was evidence of bad faith is without legal force. The most that can be said of this aspect of the case is that it indicated a lack of generosity, but we cannot charge a seller with bad faith in a legal sense because he insists upon the full benefit of a contract which he has made. Such procedure is the usual course of business and the buyer must have known when he signed the contract that the seller would probably elect to furnish the minimum or maximum amounts called for thereunder according to whether the price of sugar increased or declined. There is no element of either good or bad faith involved in the transaction since the seller is merely insisting upon the express and unambiguous provisions of his contract with the defendant.

The findings of fact are such as to warrant the entry of a judgment thereon for the appellant herein, the plaintiff in the trial court. They follow, for the most part, the stipulation of the parties as to the matters therein recited, including the making of the contract, its terms, the tender of 220 tons of sugar and payment for 200 tons; the difference of $5,095.94 between the contract price of twenty tons of sugar and its selling price in the open market after the refusal of the defendant to accept the same. The finding that 2,009 bags of sugar, containing approximately 200 tons were marked with certain letters, while the remaining twenty tons tendered to defendant were marked with different letters is immaterial. Respondent urges this circumstance upon our attention as an evidence of bad faith; but, as we have stated, we do not consider such an issue involved in the case. The statement in the findings that the sale between the parties provided for by the terms of the contract was for 200 tons of sugar is a conclusion of law. We are of the opinion that no judicial construction of this contract was permissible since its terms are clear and unambiguous, and it is also true that any conclusion as to its legal effect is not binding upon this court as a finding of fact.

The findings of fact binding upon appeal demand a judgment for the appellant for $5,095.94. The judgment is reversed, with directions to the trial court to enter a judgment for plaintiff in accordance with the views herein expressed.

Sturtevant, J., and Nourse, J., concurred.

SOUTHERN PUB. ASS'N. *v.* CLEMENTS PAPER CO.

TENNESSEE SUPREME COURT, 1917

[139 *Tennessee Reports,* 429]

MR. JUSTICE WILLIAMS delivered the opinion of the Court.

This case was disposed of in the court below on bill of complaint and demurrer; the chancellor overruled the demurrer, and defendant paper company has appealed. The grounds of demurrer are sufficiently indicated in the discussion which follows:

The complainant is a publishing concern, requiring large amounts of paper for use in its business. Defendant is engaged in the buying and selling of paper. Both concerns are located in the city of Nashville.

The publishing association submitted to the defendant an offer in letter form, which on acceptance constituted the contract, as follows:

Nashville, Tennessee, August 5, 1915.

Clements Paper Co., Nashville, Tenn. — Gentlemen:

You may enter our contract for a minimum quantity of one hundred twenty tons, maximum quantity of one hundred forty-five tons, M. F., Eggshell, and S. and S. C. book paper, stock to be in every way equal to samples bearing your O. K., this paper to cost us $3.70 on Machine Finish and Eggshell, and $3.95 on the S. and S. C., paper to be packed soft fold and all prices to be F. O. B. Nashville. . . .

Terms: Three per cent. for cash when paid by the tenth of the month following shipment, or ninety days net from date of shipment.

This contract takes effect January 1, 1916, and terminates on December 31, 1916.

SOUTHERN PUBLISHING ASSOCIATION,
R. L. PIERCE, Manager.

Accepted by CLEMENTS PAPER CO.,
R. M. CLEMENTS, Pres.

We are of opinion that, on reason and by the decided weight of modern authority, such a contract is not void either for uncertainty or for lack of mutuality. *Cherry* v. *Smith*, 3 Humph. (22 Tenn.), 19, 39 Am. Dec., 150; *Walker Mfg. Co.* v. *Swift & Co.*, 200 Fed., 529, 119 C. C. A., 27, 43 L. R. A. (N. S.), 730, and note.

The main controversy is as to which of the contracting parties had the option in respect of the margin of twenty-five tons between the minimum and maximum limits specified, of one hundred and twenty and one hundred and forty-five tons. The rapid and pronounced rise in the price of print paper due to conditions incident to the Great War manifestly gave rise to the contention just stated.

The bill states the course of previous dealings, the circumstances in which the contract was made, and the situation of the parties as aids in determining the meaning of the contract. These are matters proper to be looked to by the court in arriving at the intention of the parties to the contract.

The option, being a limited one, in that either a minimum or maximum quantity is specified, the option might be with the seller or the purchaser as the language used, read in the light of the surrounding circumstances, may indicate. If the option was with the seller, it was bound to deliver at least the minimum quantity of paper, and might deliver any additional quantity it might choose up to the maximum limit. If it lay with the purchaser, it was compelled to accept the minimum, and might require deliveries up to the maximum quantity limit. 2 Mechem on Sales, 1170, 1171.

Looking for aid, in construction respecting the option, to the situation of the parties: Which of the two in ordinary course would stipulate for its protection by way of such a margin of safety? As between a wholesale dealer and a purchaser who is to consume, so to speak, the commodity so sold, more frequently it is the case that such a hedge is incorporated for the benefit of the latter. A wholesaler, generally speaking, is bent on swelling the bulk of his sales, and has not the incentive or intent to stipulate for a minimum and maximum limit. He has other methods of hedging, such as the placing of covering orders in the markets; whereas, a purchaser who is not himself a seller of the commodity, as such, may stand to carry the overplus into another season or year.

The primary consideration in determining in whom is lodged the option seems to us to be: For whose protection was the provision made? . . .

One of the *indicia* (subordinate to this primary consideration just noted) may be that the offer comes (1) from the purchaser, and the language used being his may relate to his needs, which are uncertain within certain limits of quantity; or (2) from the seller who may be stipulating against a contingency that may have bearing upon his ability to produce or furnish.

In the instant case the offer was the purchaser's, and we are of opinion that the incorporation of the minimum and maximum provision was meant to be its factor of safety. The letter of August 5, 1915, should be read as if it stated, "having looked into the matter of our requirements as publishers for the year 1916, enter our contract," etc. The ultimate option, therefore, was with the purchaser; it being its needs that were gauged.

The defendant contends that another rule is applicable, and should, when taken into consideration, deflect the decision in its favor. It is argued that the option was with the seller, it being the first actor, as deliverer of the paper. . . .

In our opinion the test of first actor should be treated as only one among the *indicia*. It is more artificial or less substantial than the others, and is to be applied only when the others may not be brought into play.

The case of *Small* v. *Quincy*, 4 Me. 497, perhaps best illustrates its proper application. There the transaction was between two dealers in the same commodity living in the same city. The memorandum contract was in duplicate. One copy, signed by the purchaser, recited, "We agree to receive," and the other, by the seller, reciting, "We agree to sell and deliver." The case, therefore, was one where there was no order proceeding from the one party to the other, and where there appeared no difference in the attitude of the parties, to raise a presumption of a stipulation for the requirements of the one or the inability of the other to deliver. The case was one solvable by the application of the test last referred to.

But if this were a case for the application of that test, it seems that the first actor would be the publishing association, since it must have made specification of qualities and amounts of paper before deliveries could be made.

The defendant paper company was bound to furnish the maximum quantity, on complainant's clear election to that effect.

[After concluding that in view of other facts there was no matured cause of action when the suit was brought, a demurrer relying upon prematurity of suit was sustained.]

IN RE UNITED CIGAR STORES CO. OF AMERICA

UNITED STATES DISTRICT COURT, SOUTHERN DISTRICT, NEW YORK, 1934

[8 *Federal Supplement*, 243]

PATTERSON, District Judge. The Consolidated Dairy Products Company filed a claim against the bankrupt estate. The trustee moved to expunge the claim, but the referee held the claim valid. The trustee brought the matter here on petition to review.

The claim is based on a "requirements" contract made by the bankrupt with a predecessor of the claimant which will be referred to as Consolidated. The bankrupt owned and operated a chain of retail stores. The contract is dated May 3, 1928. It is a long document and bears the marks of careful draftsmanship. Under it the bankrupt agreed for ten years to buy from the Consolidated all ice cream "required for its stores." The contract contains apt provisions relative to quality, price, and deliveries. By another clause the Consolidated agreed to sell 15,000 shares of its stock to the bankrupt at $18.50 a share (the stock was then selling on the Stock Exchange at $38 a share), and to give an interest in a certain option on stock of another corporation. The bankrupt was to cause certain subsidiaries similarly to agree to purchase their requirements of ice cream from the Consolidated.

The contract was performed by the bankrupt until August 29, 1932, when it filed a voluntary petition in bankruptcy because of insolvency. It was duly adjudicated bankrupt, and a receiver took possession of its stores and other property. Subsequently the trustee in bankruptcy notified the Consolidated that the contract was not adopted. As a result of the bankruptcy, the bankrupt ceased doing business and has not purchased any ice cream.

The trustee takes the position that the bankrupt lived up to the contract; that its only obligation was to purchase its requirements from the claimant and that it did so as long as it had requirements; that there was no undertaking by it that it would continue in business for ten years; that consequently the cessation of business on bankruptcy was not a breach. The claimant, on the other hand, insists that, although there is no express obligation on the bankrupt's part to stay in business and to have requirements for ten years, such an obligation is to be implied, and that the abandonment of business on bankruptcy was a breach. The sole issue is whether there was an obligation on the bankrupt to have requirements for ten years.

Contracts whereby a buyer undertakes to buy his entire requirements of a commodity from a seller, and also contracts whereby a seller agrees to sell his entire output to a buyer, have been a frequent source of litigation. There is no difference in the legal principles applicable to the two types of contracts. At one time the view was taken in some quarters that such agreements were lacking in consideration. The promise was thought illusory because the buyer in a requirements contract might refrain from having requirements or the seller in an output contract might have no output. Latterly it has been generally recognized that this view is erroneous. The buyer in a requirement contract surrenders his right to buy from any one he pleases. If he has requirements, he is bound to satisfy them through the seller alone. So, too, of the seller in an output contract; he has given up his right to sell at large. In both cases the obligation is a real and not an illusory one. In the present case both sides concede the validity of the contract. The question is its interpretation.

On the effect of such agreements there are two lines of authorities. The view has been taken that, where the buyer engages to buy from the seller all his requirements of an article for a definite period, the seller agreeing to sell on agreed terms, the subject-matter of the contract is the buyer's actual requirements during the period. If his requirements taper off or altogether cease, either because of a change in his needs or because of a sale or discontinuance of his whole business, there is no default. He did not agree to buy any specific quantity, but only his requirements. No promise to continue to have requirements will be read into the contract. Subterfuges or evasions would doubtless not be tolerated, but the buyer's conduct in good faith determines his requirements. The same effect is given to output contracts; if the seller cuts down his manufacture or even closes up his plant in good faith, he has still performed his undertaking. The weight of authority supports this construction of the ordinary requirements contract and the ordinary output contract.

In other cases a stricter view of the buyer's undertaking in a requirements contract has been adopted. There has been read into such a contract an obligation on the part of the buyer to have requirements to substantially the same extent as were his requirements when the contract was made. In one or two instances courts have been prompted to take this interpretation by the older and now discarded notion that otherwise the agreement would be a mere option and lacking in mutuality. On principle this view of the ordinary requirements contract and the ordinary output contract is difficult to justify. When a buyer agrees to buy his requirements from a seller, he means his requirements whatever they may be. If the parties had intended that the buyer should be bound to take goods according to his requirements in the past, they would have expressed that intention or would have inserted a specific quantity as the amount to be purchased. If they had intended that the buyer should be obligated to have future requirements, they presumably would have inserted a minimum quantity as is quite usual in contracts of this character (see *Wigand* v. *Bachmann-Bechtel Brewing Co.*, 222 N. Y. 272, 118 N. E. 618; *Louisville Soap Co.* v. *Taylor*, 279 F. 470 (C. C. A. 6)), or in some other manner have indicated that the buyer must continue to buy throughout the term. There is another consideration. No case, so far as I know, has gone so far as to hold that the buyer is liable in case his requirements slump off in the course of the contract to one-half, one-third, or one-tenth of his former needs; and yet, if he is not liable in such a case, it is hard to see how he can be held liable where in good faith he ceases business altogether and thereafter has no requirements. The incongruity of this was commented on by the Montana court in *Helena Light & R. Co.* v. *Northern Pacific R. Co.*, 57 Mont. 93. The moment we depart from the plain meaning of the words used and begin to imply condition and covenants into the contract, we run into perplexing inconsistencies. In *Wells* v. *Alexandre*, 30 N. Y. 642, a case frequently cited, the defendant made a contract to buy from the plaintiff all coal required for his three steamers for one year. In the middle of the year he sold the steamers and thereafter required no coal for them. The plaintiff was allowed to recover; the court viewing the contract as one to take all coal "which the ordinary and accustomed use of the steamers" required for one year. But the New York courts have since recognized that there is more elasticity in the usual requirements contract, and that the buyer is not limited to "the ordinary and accustomed" volume of his supplies; on doubling his business, he may call on the seller to fill his double needs. *New York Central Iron Works Co.* v. *United States Radiator Co.*, 174 N. Y. 331, 66 N. E. 967; *Fuller & Co.* v. *Schrenk*, 58 App. Div. 222, 68 N. Y. S. 781, affirmed in 171 N. Y. 671, 64 N. E. 1126. In *Edison Electric Illuminating Co.* v. *Thacher*, 229 N. Y. 172, 178, 128 N. E. 124, Judge Crane referred to *Wells* v. *Alexandre* as presenting "an exceptional form of contract." In none of the cases that take the minority view has it been held that the buyer in a requirements contract incurs liability on ceasing business altogether because of financial inability to keep going.

On principle and the weight of authority, therefore, it seems clear that, where the buyer makes a contract to purchase his requirements of a commodity for a term, he has not broken his contract when his requirements diminish or when he ceases to have any requirements by reason of retirement from business, voluntary or involuntary. A provision that he shall continue to have requirements is not ordinarily implied.

Other provisions of the requirements contract may be strong enough to indicate an agreement that the buyer was to remain in business and continue to have requirements. The claimant insists that the provision requiring it to sell 15,000 shares of its stock to the bankrupt at a figure which was one-half the market price is such an indication. There is force in the argument. But the transfer of stock, giving the bankrupt an interest in the claimant's business, is not the same as a cash payment. The transfer of stock to the bankrupt was doubtless intended to stimulate the purchase of ice cream by the bankrupt by giving it an interest in the claimant's business. This feature of the contract is not enough to warrant the court in importing into the contract a provision that is not there, that the bankrupt must continue in business for the ten year term. On familiar principles, the implication of such a covenant can be resorted to only in a case so plain that no doubt can exist as to the real intention of the parties. The fact that this agreement was a deliberately prepared document, as is manifest from the reading of it, must not be lost sight of. In the *Pfann Case*, 194 Fed. 69, the contract was one for the seller's output, and the buyer as part of the contract agreed to make a loan to the seller. This circumstance did not render the seller liable for selling his plant before the expiration of the contract and thus terminating his output. . . .

I am of opinion that the bankrupt performed its contract with the claimant, and that the latter has no claim for damages. The order of the referee will accordingly be reversed.

HAMLYN & CO. *v.* WOOD & CO.

COURT OF APPEAL, 1891

[*Law Reports,* [1891] 2 *Queen's Bench,* 488]

Action for breach of contract.

The facts as proved at the trial before Mathew, J., with a jury, were as follows. The defendants formerly carried on a large business as brewers under the firm of Wood & Co. The plaintiffs and defendants had entered into a written contract as follows: "Wood & Co." (the defendants) "agree to sell, and Hamlyn & Co." (the plaintiffs) "agree to buy, all the grains made by the said Wood & Co., at the current rates charged each year by the following firms [then followed the names of certain firms of brewers] from the 10th July, 1885, until the 30th September, 1895, inclusive. In the event of there being any difference in the rates of the above firms, then the average price charged by them shall be taken as the current rate. The quantity of grains to be calculated monthly, and payment for the same to be made at the brewery on or before the last day in the month following delivery. The said Hamlyn & Co." (the plaintiffs) "to throw the grains out of the mash-tub, and empty and clear away the same in a proper and workmanlike manner at their sole expense on the day on which they are made, and to pay for any damage done by carelessness of the persons employed by them, otherwise the said Wood & Co." (the defendants) "to be at liberty to cart away and dispose of the grains in the best manner they in their opinion can, and such carting and disposal to be made at Hamlyn & Co.'s cost, and any loss made by such sale to be sustained by them." In August, 1890, the defendants sold their business to Watney & Co., who did not adopt the contract; thereupon the plaintiffs brought an action against the defendants for refusing to continue to perform the agreement, and to sell grains to the plaintiffs pursuant to the terms thereof.

The plaintiffs contended that it was an implied term of the agreement that the defendants would not by any voluntary act of their own prevent themselves from continuing the sale of grains under it for the period specified, and that the sale of their business was a breach of such implied term. The jury assessed the damages at 350*l*., and Mathew, J., gave judgment for the plaintiffs for that amount. The defendants now moved for judgment or a new trial, on the ground that the learned judge's ruling was erroneous.

Lord ESHER, M.R. The question is whether we can agree with the implication that Mathew, J., has made in this case. A large number of cases have been cited, in some of which the Court implied a stipulation, and in others refused to do so. In my opinion, it is useless to cite such cases, so far as they merely shew that in the particular case an implication was or was not made. The only use of citing such cases is where they lay down the rule as to such implications, upon which the Court will act in dealing with the particular case before it. I have for a long time understood that rule to be that the Court has no right to imply in a written contract any such stipulation, unless, on considering the terms of the contract in a reasonable and business manner, an implication necessarily arises that the parties must have intended that the suggested stipulation should exist. It is not enough to say that it would be a reasonable thing to make such an implication. It must be a necessary implication in the sense that I have mentioned. In the case of *The Moorcock* (14 P. D. 64), Bowen, L.J., laid down the principle upon which such implications must be made in terms which seem to me to be really an expansion of the terms I have used, and with which I entirely agree. He said, in that case (at p. 68): "An implied warranty, or, as it is called, a covenant in law, as distinguished from an express contract or express warranty, really is in all cases founded on the presumed intention of the parties and upon reason. The implication which the law draws from what must obviously have been the intention of the parties, the law draws with the object of giving efficacy to the transaction and preventing such a failure of consideration as cannot have been within the contemplation of either side; and I believe, if one were to take all the cases, and they are many, of implied warranties or covenants in law, it will be found that in all of them the law is raising an implication from the presumed intention of the parties, with the object of giving to the transaction such efficacy as both parties must have intended that at all events it should have."

It is admitted in the present case that there has been no breach of any express stipulation of the agreement, and therefore we are asked to imply a stipulation of which there has been a breach. The stipulation we are asked to imply is, not that the defendants contracted to carry on their business for ten years, but that they contracted that they would not during that period wilfully do anything to prevent their so doing. If you cannot imply the first of these stipulations as a matter of business, I should think it would be very difficult to imply the second. The express contract is not that the defendants will sell the plaintiffs' grains for ten years; it is that the defendants will sell, and the plaintiffs will buy, all grains made by the defendants for ten years. What was the object of those parties as business men in entering into this agreement? The last stipulation of the contract shews that it was an advantage to the defendants to get the grains carried away from their brewery. Then what was the advantage which the plaintiffs as business men sought to gain? If the contract is construed against their contention, do they still gain something? It must be assumed that they must have thought that they would gain a profit by buying the grains at the agreed price; and therefore it was an advantage to them to have the right of purchasing any grains the defendants might make in preference to any other purchaser for ten years. The agreement is not that they are to pay a sum down and then to have the grains for ten years, so that, if they did not get grains for ten years, they would not get what they had paid for. That would be a different case. In that case they would have paid money for nothing, unless the implication were made that the other party had stipulated that they would not voluntarily discontinue the business during ten years. The agreement is to pay a price to be ascertained from time to time, as provided by the contract, for the quantity of grains which they from time to time obtain. Therefore, it cannot be said that, unless the implication suggested is made, they will have paid money for nothing. Such being the terms of the contract, the question is whether we can say, looking at the contract in a reasonable and business way, that it is a necessary implication that both parties contemplated an undertaking by the defendants not voluntarily to discontinue the business for ten years, at whatever loss they might carry it on, or however advantageously they might be able to sell it. It seems to me that such an implication is tremendously strong, and one which is beyond all bounds. I cannot come to the conclusion that the defendants ever contemplated such a thing, or that the plaintiffs were entitled to suppose that they did so.

I do not think it necessary to go into the various cases which have been decided in regard to other contracts. In this case I decline to make the suggested implication. For these reasons I think that the defendants are entitled to judgment.

[Concurring opinions of Bowen, L. J., and Kay, L. J., are here omitted.]

Appeal allowed.

Compare WISEMAN *v.* DENNIS, 156 Virginia 431 (Supreme Court of Appeals, 1931), where there was a contract for the sale to a filling station owner of all his gasoline requirements for a period of five years. The filling station business was sold within that period and the contract was not included in the sale. In affirming judgment for the plaintiff in an action for damages for breach of contract, Epes, J., said: "The contract presupposes that Wiseman would have a business for the time agreed, and it cannot be avoided by a sale of his business within that time."

CHALMERS & WILLIAMS *v.* WALTER BLEDSOE & COMPANY

ILLINOIS APPELLATE COURT, 1920

[218 *Illinois Appellate Reports*, 363]

Mr. Presiding Justice THOMSON delivered the opinion of the court.

The plaintiff, Chalmers & Williams, is a corporation engaged in the manufacture of machinery and the defendant is a corporation engaged in the business of mining and selling coal. The plaintiff brought this action on a contract, under which it was provided that the plaintiff would buy and the defendant sell all of the plaintiff's "consumption requirements" of coal for a period of 2 years, from May 1, 1914 to May 1, 1916, and that the plaintiff might have an option of renewing the contract for an additional period of 2 years, thus extending it to May 1, 1918. In its statement of claim the plaintiff alleged that it had exercised its option and had made demands on the defendant for coal during the period from November, 1916, to April, 1918; that the defendant refused to sell or deliver the coal, as thus demanded; and that the plaintiff was thus obliged to purchase the coal required, on the open market, as a result of which the plaintiff was put to additional cost in the sum of $2,974.24.

In its amended affidavit of merits the defendant set up the following matter by way of defense: (1) It admitted the execution of the contract and the exercise of the option by the plaintiff extending the contract to May 1, 1918. (2) It denied any breach by the defendant and charged a breach by the plaintiff. (3) It alleged that at the time of the execution of the original contract the plaintiff was, and for a long period prior thereto had been, engaged in the manufacture of certain kinds of machinery; that for the purpose of supplying the motive power for the manufacture of such machinery, the plaintiff maintained, and for a long period prior thereto had maintained, a power plant of its own, wherein it generated steam power through the exclusive use of coal; that in order to maintain that power plant throughout the year and also heat its buildings during the winter, the plaintiff had for a number of years required 60 to 70 cars of coal per year in nearly equal monthly instalments of 4 to 6 cars, or approximately 300 tons, throughout the year. (4) It alleged that, as a result of their prior dealings, the defendant knew of the character and magnitude of the plaintiff's coal requirements as above set forth, and that their nature was fully discussed and understood by the parties at the time of the execution of the original contract, and that the contract was executed in contemplation of a continued existence of the known facts and circumstances therein set forth, and in contemplation that the plaintiff would continue to generate its motive power by the exclusive use of coal in its own power plant, in the same way it had in the past. (5) It alleged that some time in the early part of 1916, without its knowledge, the plaintiff discontinued the use of its power plant and entirely abandoned the use of steam as a motive power with which to run its machinery and substituted electrical power in lieu thereof; that ever since that time the plaintiff had not required or used any coal whatsoever for the purpose of generating power but used coal for heating purposes only; that because of said substitution of electrical power for steam, the plaintiff, although often requested by the defendant to take the coal contracted for, neither ordered nor used any coal from April 1, 1916 until October 19, 1916; that because of said substitution of electrical power for steam, the plaintiff used and required, during the period of the contract as extended by the exercise of the option from May 1, 1916 to May 1, 1918, only 38 cars of coal, whereas during the 2 years preceding, from May 1, 1914 to May 1, 1916, the plaintiff used and required 132 cars of coal, and that it had required this in approximately equal monthly instalments throughout that period. (6) It alleged that the defendant did not know of the said substitution of electrical power for steam until on or about October 1, 1916. (7) It alleged that at no time before it acquired the knowledge of the substitution of electrical power for steam did it refuse to sell any coal to the plaintiff. (8) It alleged that ever since it acquired knowledge of the substitution of electrical power for steam the defendant refused to sell the plaintiff any coal under the contract. (9) It alleged that at all times after such substitution the plaintiff continued its business as usual. (10) It admitted that plaintiff bought coal in the open market during the period referred to in the statement of claim and that plaintiff was compelled to pay more for such coal than it would have been obliged to pay for the same coal under the contract but that such additional cost amounted to $2,332.58 and no more. (11) It alleged that by virtue of the facts thus set forth there was no sum due to the plaintiff from the defendant.

On motion of the plaintiff the court struck from the files all of the matter set forth in the amended affidavit of merits except that contained in paragraph 10. The defendant thereupon elected to stand upon its amended affidavit of merits, following which the court found the issues for the plaintiff and assessed its damages in the sum of $2,332.58, from which judgment the defendant has perfected this appeal. . . .

The real issue in this case is, did the plaintiff breach the contract when it changed its motive power from steam to electricity and thus reduce its "requirements" for coal from approximately 66 cars a year, distributed nearly equally throughout the year, to approximately 19 cars a year, for use in heating their plant only, in the cold months of the year.

The plaintiff contends that the defendant was the one who broke the contract when it refused to deliver the coal ordered by the plaintiff in the fall of 1916. Apparently plaintiff's contention is that it did not breach the contract when it ceased operating its steam power plant and changed its motive power to electricity. Counsel for plaintiff admit in their brief that plaintiff "was bound to carry out its contract no matter what changes it made in its plant, even if it sold its plant." But it also seems to be plaintiff's contention that the contract would be carried out on its part if it bought of defendant during the contract period, all the coal it "needed" in connection with the operation of its plant. On this theory the contract would be fulfilled on plaintiff's part if all the coal it "needed" during the contract period was (for example) 500 tons a month to be used for heating purposes, although at the time the contract was entered into, its "requirements" were, and for sometime had been, 2,000 tons a month, for use in its power plant, as well as for heating purposes, this average monthly requirement running throughout the year. The inconsistency of plaintiff's position is shown by the last phrase of its admission as we have quoted it. It is admitted plaintiff was bound to carry out its contract, "even if it sold its plant." What interpretation should be placed upon the term "requirements" under this contract in such an event? Certainly not the plaintiff's needs for it would have none at all.

Of course, plaintiff "was bound to carry out its contract," as counsel admit. The question is, what was its contract? It was, to buy its "requirements" in coal, for a given period, from the defendant. What does that mean? If "requirements," as that term is used in this contract, means "needs" in the sense that if plaintiff's plant is shut down or so altered that it needs no coal at all to operate it, then plaintiff is not obliged to order or buy any coal, then the contract must be held void for want of mutuality. But if the "requirements" of plaintiff is to be given such a meaning as will make the contract valid and a mutually binding agreement, then that term must be given the meaning the parties may be shown to have had in mind when they executed the contract. . . .

Plaintiff has called our attention to that part of the contract providing that, "it is understood that this contract is to cover the entire consumptive requirements of the party of the first part (plaintiff), and it is also understood and agreed that should the party of the first part so desire, in the fall of the year to lay aside a pile of coal against any contingencies through the winter, it will be furnished in accordance with the terms of this contract." In our opinion there is no merit to plaintiff's contention that this language in the contract negatives the theory that prior dealings or past requirements were in contemplation of the parties as defining the amount of coal covered by the contract.

For the reasons stated, the trial court erred in allowing plaintiff's motion to strike the paragraphs of defendant's amended affidavit of merits referred to and in entering judgment for the plaintiff and therefore the judgment of the municipal court is reversed and the cause is remanded to that court for further proceedings not inconsistent with this opinion.

Reversed and remanded.

Mr. Justice O'Connor concurs. Mr. Justice Taylor dissents.

Compare Ives *v.* Willimantic, 121 Conn. 408 (Supreme Court of Errors, 1936). The city of Willimantic owned a reservoir, ice houses, and equipment for harvesting ice. A contract was made by which the city agreed to sell to plaintiff at a fixed price "such quantity of ice as the City owns or shall harvest in the ice houses" for a period of years. During the contract period the ice houses were destroyed by fire and were not rebuilt, so that the city ceased to harvest ice. Plaintiff brought an action for damages for breach of contract. On affirming judgment for defendant, the Court said: "The contract here did not in express terms or by necessary implication bind the city to harvest any ice, and, when none was harvested, it was under no obligation to furnish any to the plaintiff, since the contract provided for the sale only of such ice as the city actually harvested."

T. W. JENKINS & CO. *v.* ANAHEIM SUGAR CO.

United States Circuit Court of Appeals, Ninth Circuit, 1918

[247 *Federal Reporter*, 958]

In Error to the District Court of the United States for the Southern Division of the Southern District of California; Benj. F. Bledsoe, Judge.

Action by T. W. Jenkins & Co., a corporation, against the Anaheim Sugar Company, a corporation. Defendant's demurrer having been sustained, and the action dismissed (237 Fed. 278), plaintiff brings error. Reversed and remanded, with directions.

This was an action upon a contract by Jenkins & Co., plaintiff below, an Oregon corporation, wholesale grocers, and engaged in buying and selling and dealing in sugar, against the Anaheim Sugar Company, a California corporation, engaged in manufacturing and refining sugar. The contract is as follows:

San Francisco, Calif., June 13, 1914.

A contract is hereby entered into between Anaheim Sugar Company, party of the first part, and T. W. Jenkins & Co., party of second part, to wit: Party of first part sells and party of second part buys August requirements bags fine granulated beet sugar at $4.20 per bag less 2% cash 8 days, f. o. b. San Francisco, August shipment. It being understood and agreed that party of the first part guarantees the price up to time of refusal against decline only to the base of C. & H. and Western Sugar Refining Co.

Plaintiff alleges that the contract price was less than the prevailing market price in San Francisco when the contract was entered into, and that the price was fixed by defendant in consideration of the plaintiff's agreement with defendant that it would buy "exclusively from defendant all * * * granulated beet sugar required in its business during the month of August, 1914." It is alleged that the plaintiff relied upon the agreement, and made no other arrangements for its August requirements; that thereafter, in August, plaintiff required in its business and ordered 4,800 bags of sugar, and there was shipped and delivered from time to time during August by defendant to plaintiff 600 bags of sugar and no more; that it had many thousand customers to whom it sold sugar and merchandise and that much of its business was wholesaling to customers sugar in bag lots; that the method of dealing in sugar was this: Plaintiff would contract with a sugar producer or refiner for the sale to it, covering a specified period, of such sugar as it would require for its sale to its customers, and plaintiff would thereupon receive from and solicit from its customers orders for sugar in bag lots at a stipulated price, based on the contract price between plaintiff and the producer or refiner, delivery to be made to its customers at a future time agreed upon between the plaintiff and its customers at the time of sale, all of which was well known to the defendant when the contract herein involved was made. It is alleged that defendant in its business usually and ordinarily required in August of each year sugar in excess of 4,800 bags, and that, relying upon the contract, plaintiff solicited and received from many of its customers orders for 4,800 bags of sugar, which it intended to deliver to said customers from the sugar to be delivered under the terms of the contract; that when the contract was entered into defendant knew the nature of plaintiff's business and the manner in which it was conducted, and what plaintiff's requirements for sugar would be during the term of the contract entered into with plaintiff; that because of the refusal of defendant to deliver 4,200 bags of sugar plaintiff lost its profits on the resale thereof, and had to buy in the open market sugar in excess of the price stipulated for with defendant and was damaged in the sum of $13,020.

By demurrer these questions were presented: (1) Does the complaint state facts sufficient to constitute a cause of action, and (2) is the complaint uncertain, ambiguous, or unintelligible? The District Court sustained the demurrer, plaintiff declined to amend, and judgment was entered, dismissing the action, whereupon plaintiff sued out writ of error.

Hunt, Circuit Judge (after stating the facts as above). The District Court was of the opinion that the contract as entered into was not supported by sufficient consideration to make it valid; that it lacks mutuality, in that defendant under any circumstances could be compelled to furnish the sugar covered by the contract, but that plaintiff could not be compelled by defendant to order and accept any sugar thereunder. In support of this view the learned judge distinguishes between cases which uphold contracts binding one party to sell and the other party to buy all of the requirements of the latter's established business as to a given commodity, and those where the contract is between parties, one of whom is in the business, not of manufacturing the commodity involved, but only of selling the same at wholesale; that is to say, where the purchase and use of the commodity becomes not an incident to the principal business of the buyer, but is his main business, a contract of the general character of the one here in question will be held invalid as unilateral and void for want of mutuality.

The difference between a contract which does not obligate a buyer to take any specified quantity of the seller's product and one where in consideration of the seller's promise to sell the buyer promises to buy all the produce it may require for its own use for a definite period of time is substantial. In the one instance there would be no consideration, while in the other there would be a mutual obligation to perform which is a consideration for the promise of each. A mere option to buy is readily distinguishable from an agreement to buy all to be required. Suppose, for instance, the plaintiff herein had bought sugar from any other sugar dealer for sale to its customers during August, it must be that if loss had occurred, action in damages for breach of contract would have been sustainable, and damages could have been ascertained by extrinsic evidence. Failure in the contract to fix any requirements on the part of the Jenkins Company for August, 1914, does not seem to us to call for a nullification of the contract upon the ground of want of mutuality. The complaint charges that the contract was made with the knowledge on the part of the defendant of how plaintiff's business was conducted, and that plaintiff made contracts with customers for sale and delivery of sugar to be acquired under the contract with defendant, and knowing what the probable requirements of plaintiff would be. We think that upon demurrer the presumption is that the parties made their agreement with regard to the knowledge as alleged, and that the defendant intended to sell and deliver the quantity of sugar which the plaintiff needed for its August business. . . .

It does not seem that necessarily there is a substantial basis for a distinction between the needs or requirements of a wholesale dealer in sugar and a manufacturer who uses sugar. Ascertainment of the requirements of the one may be as capable of estimation as the other. The temptation to speculate may be greater on the part of the dealer than of the manufacturer, but if the contract is honestly entered into the law ought not to refuse to enforce its terms for any such reason as possible misuse of its purposes. The presumption is in favor of integrity of conduct. Furthermore, in the present case, defendant knew of probable requirements, and by the terms of the contract temptation to cut down requirements because of falling market was reduced, in that it was expressly agreed that the Anaheim Sugar Company, manufacturer, guaranteed the price up to time of refusal against decline only to the base of price charged by the manufacturer to certain buyers.

Our construction of the several averments of the complaint is that Jenkins & Co., dealer, agreed to confine its purchases to the sugar company, manufacturer; that its normal requirements were alone involved, and that they were known approximately by the manufacturing company; that there was a safeguard against inducement to eliminate requirements should prices fall, by stipulating for protection in the event of such contingency.

It follows that the court should have overruled the demurrer and required the defendant, to answer.

We must reverse the judgment and remand the case, with directions to overrule the demurrer.

ASAHEL WHEELER COMPANY *v.* MENDLESON

NEW YORK SUPREME COURT, APPELLATE DIVISION, 1917

[180 *New York Appellate Division Reports*, 9]

LYON, J. This is an action to recover damages for breach of a contract entered into between the parties hereto of date November 1, 1914, by which the defendants agreed to sell and the plaintiff agreed to buy "their supply of Caustic Soda packed in barrels, 76 per cent test at $2.30 per cwt. * * * Challenge Lye, 2 doz. case * * * Hudson Lye, 2 doz. case. * * * Quantity not to exceed 25 tons delivered. Prices guaranteed from any decline on our part. * * * Time of delivery during 1915. * * * Terms. Payable at 30 days from date of invoice * * *."

Concededly, the term of the running of the contract was from January 1, 1915, to January 1, 1916. The plaintiff gave the defendants no orders for any of these products until November 30, 1915, at which time the price of caustic soda had advanced from the contract price of $46 per ton to $110 per ton, and the advance in price of the other products amounted to $15. By letter of date November 30, 1915, and by letters during December, the plaintiff directed shipment to it of 24 tons, 250 pounds of caustic soda and 1,750 pounds of lye. The defendants refused to make the shipment, and early in 1916 this action was brought. The trial resulted in a decision in favor of the plaintiff for the difference in the prices of the products at the date of the contract and of the demand, that is, for $1,559.

It is the defendants' contention that the contract of November 1, 1914, is invalid by reason of want of mutuality. To the extent of "their supply" it was certainly mutual and valid, as the defendants agreed to sell and the plaintiff agreed to buy such supply during the year 1915. The important question in the case, therefore, is as to the construction which should be given the words "their supply."

The plaintiff was engaged in a general paint, drug and chemical business, and the defendants in a general wholesale and retail paint and drug business. There had been dealings between them for twenty years. By reason thereof the defendants must have been informed in a general way of the probable demands of plaintiff's trade and the methods of its doing business, and in the absence of other evidence the parties may be presumed to have contracted with that in mind. The nature and extent of these dealings were, therefore, doubtless important as bearing upon the construction to be given to the words "their supply." Such dealings were not shown excepting as to the year 1914. In August of that year the plaintiff bought of the defendants eight barrels of caustic soda, thirty-five cases of Challenge lye, and ten cases of Hudson lye, aggregating approximately 5,080 pounds. During the first eleven months of the year 1915 the plaintiff ordered none of the contracted products of the defendants. In December, 1915, the plaintiff still had on hand 2,000 pounds, or four of the eight barrels, of caustic soda which it had bought of the defendants more than a year before, and as the plaintiff had bought no lye of the defendants up to that time in 1915 and was bound by the contract of November 1, 1914, to buy of the defendants all those brands of lye necessary to supply its trade, it may be presumed that up to November 30, 1915, the plaintiff had in stock sufficient of the lye purchased of defendants in August, 1914, to supply its trade. Unquestionably the contract should be given a reasonable construction. This would allow the plaintiff to call for shipments of sufficient of the products to fill its orders and to keep in stock a reasonable supply for its trade. However, as to an executory contract which is indefinite as to the quantity of goods to be furnished, the obligation of good faith and fair dealing towards each other is implied, and a party to a contract has no right to use it for a purpose not within the contemplation of the parties, as for speculative, as distinguished from regular and ordinary business purposes. (*New York Central Iron Works Co.* v. *United States Radiator Co.*, 174 N. Y. 331; *Moore* v. *American Molasses Co.*, 179 App. Div. 505.)

It was the manifest intention of the parties to limit the operation of the contract as to both parties to the plaintiff's supply. There is nothing whatever in the evidence tending to show that the demand for the whole 50,000 pounds of products during the final month of the year the contract was to be in force was necessary to supply the legitimate demands of plaintiff's trade. I think the plaintiff was in good faith required to make such proof if such fact existed, and in the absence of any evidence upon the subject the inference is under the circumstances practically irresistible that the demand made by the plaintiff upon the defendants was for the purpose of speculation, and was born of the extraordinary increase in the value of caustic soda. Instead of definite evidence as to the delivery of the products being required to supply the needs of plaintiff's business, there is only the testimony of plaintiff's vice-president that at various times the plaintiff had demand for such goods from its customers, but when and in what quantities does not appear. The fact that 2,000 pounds of the defendants' caustic soda bought by plaintiff in August, 1914, was sufficient to supply plaintiff's trade until November 30, 1915, a period of over fifteen months, while the remaining 2,000 pounds of the 1914 purchase on hand December 4, 1915, was insufficient to supply the plaintiff's trade until January first, but 50,000 pounds additional of product was demanded during the remaining period of less than one month, would seem to call for some explanation in order to bring the plaintiff's demands of November and December, 1915, within the contemplation of the parties at the time they entered into the contract. We do not say that the production of such evidence as to the requirements of plaintiff's business would entitle the plaintiff to a recovery, but we call attention to the fact as one of the reasons why the judgment should be reversed. Unfortunately, the record is bare of much evidence which is necessary to enable a court to properly decide the rights of the parties, and hence a new trial should be had to the end that each party may furnish such additional proofs as counsel may advise.

All concurred.

Judgment reversed and new trial granted, with costs to abide the event.

Compare NEW YORK CENTRAL IRON WORKS *v.* UNITED STATES RADIATOR CO., 174 New York 331 (Court of Appeals, 1903), where there was a contract to supply plaintiff "with their entire radiator needs for the year 1899." Plaintiff never before had required more than 48,000 feet of radiation in a year, but under the contract in question sent in orders that would bring the total for the year to 100,000 feet. Defendant declined to fill orders for more than 48,000 feet, claiming that a limitation to the amount usually called for was necessarily to be imported into the contract. In affirming a judgment for plaintiff in an action for damages for breach of contract, O'Brien, J., said: "The defendant bound the plaintiff to deal exclusively in goods to be ordered from it under the contract and to enlarge and develop the market for the defendant's wares so far as possible. Hence, the parties left the contract open and indefinite as to the quantity of goods that the plaintiff might order from time to time. It is quite probable that this controversy originated in a circumstance which the defendant, at least, had not anticipated or provided for. After the execution of the contract there was a large advance in the market price of iron and the manufactured products of iron, and, consequently, the value and selling price of the goods covered by this contract advanced in the same or possibly in a greater proportion. The needs of the plaintiff could be indefinitely enlarged when the market was in such a condition as to enable it to undersell its competitors in the same business in consequence of a favorable contract with the manufacturer of the goods. If a party contracts for goods upon a rising market he is ordinarily entitled to such profits as may accrue to him by reason of a prudent or favorable contract. We cannot perceive that there is any error of law in this judgment, although the plaintiff has recovered a considerable sum in damages for the breach. The case in its general features is the same as another case which was recently before this court, where there was a similar recovery that was sustained. . . .

"But we do not mean to assert that the plaintiff had the right under the contract to order goods to any amount. Both parties in such a contract are bound to carry it out in a reasonable way. The obligation of good faith and fair dealing towards each other is implied in every contract of this character. The plaintiff could not use the contract for the purpose of speculation in a rising market since that would be a plain abuse of the rights conferred and something like a fraud upon the seller. The plaintiff's claim for damages in this case might have been affected by the condition and customs of the trade, and any breach of good faith on its part could be taken into account. In such a case it would be competent for the defendant to plead and prove facts to show that the orders were in excess of the plaintiff's reasonable needs and were not justified by the conditions of the business or the customs of the trade. In other words, that the plaintiff was not acting reasonably or in good faith, but using the contract for a purpose not within the contemplation of the parties; that is to say, for speculative as distinguished from regular and ordinary business purposes. But no defense of this kind was either pleaded or proved in this case, and so the judgment must be affirmed, with costs."

B. Where the Contract Provisions are not Met

HARLAND AND WOLFF LIMITED *v.* J. BURSTALL AND CO.

King's Bench Division, 1901

[84 *Law Times Reports*, 324]

Bigham, J. read the following judgment.—This is an action brought to recover damages for the breach of a contract by which the plaintiffs bought of the defendants 500 loads of timber on c.i.f. terms. The facts are as follows: The defendants are timber merchants trading at Quebec. In the autumn of 1899 they had in stock a quantity of about 600 loads of Waney timber. On the 9th Aug. the plaintiffs, who are shipbuilders at Belfast, telegraphed to the defendants' London house asking if they had any Waney timber to offer. The answer to the inquiry was contained in a letter from defendants of the 17th Aug. saying: "We can offer you about 500 loads first-class Waney for shipment as soon as tonnage is procurable." The letter then described what the size of the timber would be, and mentioned the terms of sale and of payment. On the 13th Sept. the defendants telegraphed to the plaintiffs that they had an offer of freight room for 500 loads, and asking whether they would buy. On the 14th Sept. the plaintiffs telegraphed that they would take 500 loads, and thereupon the defendants engaged room for that quantity in a ship called the *Merrimac*. The bargain was reduced into the form of a contract note on the 20th Sept., and, so far as is material, the terms were as follows: "Sold 500 loads prime Waney pine, cost, freight, and insurance, freight to be deducted from the invoice, and paid by buyers in terms of charter-party, and the balance to be paid in cash ten days after final delivery in Belfast." The note also described the sizes of the timber to be shipped. The defendants then proceeded to select from their stock timber to answer the contract, but apparently they were unable to collect as much as 500 loads of the required description, and they, in fact, only collected 470 loads. This quantity they shipped, taking bills of lading to their own order. The ship sailed on the 24th Oct., but was lost on the voyage to Belfast. The bills of lading were never tendered to the plaintiffs, nor was the shipping invoice sent to them, but no doubt the defendants intended that the shipment should be applied to the plaintiffs' contract. The insurance of the goods was effected by the defendants in the following manner: They had a floating policy open with underwriters upon which they were in a position to declare 92 per cent. of the value of their risks; as to the remaining 8 per cent., the defendants took the risk themselves. By arrangement with their underwriters the defendants were also entitled to declare on each adventure a further 20 per cent. for what they called "profit." Accordingly, when the shipment by the *Merrimac* was made, they declared the invoice price as the value (about 2000*l.*), and they also declared 400*l.* for the "profit." The question is whether by what they have done the defendants have performed their contract. They say they have; they contend that by the sale itself, or, if not by the sale, then by the shipment, they vested the property in the 470 loads of timber in the plaintiffs, and that, having insured it and arranged for the freight, they did all that the contract required them to do. Perhaps if these contentions were well founded the defendants would be right; but, in my opinion, they are not well founded. No shipment within the meaning of the contract was ever made. The contract was to ship 500 loads; a shipment of 470 loads does not comply with the requirement. Nor does it satisfy the contract *pro tanto*. The shipment cannot be made piecemeal; it must be in one parcel. Some evidence was given before me to show that in a contract of that kind it is open to the vendor to deliver about the quantity named, and that "about" means 10 per cent. more or less; and reliance was placed on the fact that during the negotiations leading up to the contract note the word "about" was used. I am quite satisfied, however, that no such custom as that contended for in fact exists, and I think the use of the word "about" in the negotiations has no significance, and cannot be allowed to qualify the reading of the document into which the contract was finally reduced. Of course, in carrying out a commercial contract such as this some slight elasticity is unavoidable; no one supposes that the delivery is to be within a cubic foot of the named quantity, but it must be substantially of the quantity named; and in my judgment 470 loads is not substantially 500. It was a shipment which the plaintiffs would have been entitled to reject if it had been tendered to them as a shipment under the contract. . . .

Judgment for 175*l. for the plaintiffs.*

Compare MUTUAL CHEMICAL COMPANY OF AMERICA *v.* MARDEN, ORTH & HASTINGS CO., INC., 235 N. Y. 145 (Court of Appeals, 1923), where there was a contract for the sale at an agreed price of six carloads of bichromate of potash f. o. b. seller's works, "carloads to be 36,000 pounds each." A carload tendered under the contract contained 36,418 pounds, and was refused by the buyer. In an action by the seller for breach of contract, it was held that evidence was competent to show that "under a well-known and long-established custom of the trade a delivery of 36,418 pounds of bichromate of potash was a proper delivery under a contract calling for 36,000 pounds."

E. E. HUBER & CO. *v.* LALLEY LIGHT CORPORATION

MICHIGAN SUPREME COURT, 1928

[242 *Michigan Reports*, 171]

Assumpsit by E. E. Huber & Company against the Lalley Light Corporation for breach of a contract of sale. Judgment for defendant. Plaintiff brings error. Affirmed.

CLARK, J. In 1920, defendant, Lalley Light Corporation, a Delaware corporation, manufactured farm lighting plants in Detroit. Plaintiff, E. E. Huber & Company, a Salvador corporation, was then and is now foreign representative in Central America of certain American manufacturers, and then was defendant's exclusive distributor. In April, 1920, a new distributor's contract was made in Detroit by the parties, estimating plaintiff's requirements for the remainder of the year. The contract contemplates forwarding plants to plaintiff from Detroit on plaintiff's orders thereafter to be received. Mr. Huber, president of plaintiff company, before leaving United States, caused a credit to be established at the Commercial Bank of Spanish America, Limited (New York Agency), which bank on June 25, 1920, wrote defendant as follows:

LALLEY LIGHT CORPORATION,
Detroit, Michigan.
Attention Export Dept.

Dear Sirs: We beg to advise you that in accordance with cable request from our Guatemala office, we have established a credit in your favor for the amount of about $5,000 to cover an order for 30 lighting plants on account of Mr. E. E. Huber.

We are not yet advised as to where the goods are to be shipped but we presume they are intended for the Guatemala district. You will please note that in any case they must be consigned to the order of this bank on the ocean shipping documents. Payment will be made as usual against delivery of full set ocean shipping documents, certificate of insurance and commercial invoice.

Yours very truly,
COMMERCIAL BANK OF SPANISH AMERICA, LTD.,
S. C. DOBSON, Agent.

Defendant replied, suggesting mistake, as the cost of 30 plants was nearly $11,000. The matter had not been cleared up on July 22d when defendant cabled plaintiff as follows:

Commercial Bank advises credit established covering order plants Guatemala. Have not received order. Advise details.

On July 26, 1920, the bank again wrote defendant:

LALLEY LIGHT CORPORATION,
Detroit, Michigan.
E. E. HUBER.

Dear Sirs: Referring to our letters dated June 25th and July 17th respecting the credit established in your favor on account of above to cover thirty lighting plants, we have now received the expected letter from our Guatemala office. From this letter it appears that a cash payment of $5,000 is required by you, the balance of the order to be paid within 120 days.

Please note, therefore, that we have amended to cover cash payment of $5,000 against your delivery to us of the ocean shipping documents, and we will be responsible to you for the payment of balance of your invoice 120 days from the date of our initial payment, interest to be added at the rate of 6% p. a.

We await to hear from you that you are in accord with this arrangement, and remain,

Yours very truly,
COMMERCIAL BANK OF SPANISH AMERICA, LTD.,
S. C. DOBSON, Agent.

This was later modified to provide for payment of full amount in cash on delivery of required documents. On July 28, 1920, defendant shipped 30 plants, f. o. b. Detroit, invoiced to plaintiff and consigned to the bank on bill of lading. The shipment cleared New York on August 27th. Defendant presented required shipping documents to the bank and was paid in full.

Mr. Huber, returning from United States, reached his office in San Salvador about July 23d, when he received defendant's cablegram of July 22d. He testified that he replied by letter, which defendant denies having received. On August 7th, plaintiff ordered by mail 10 plants from defendant. On September 3d, defendant cabled plaintiff:

30 plants Puerto Barrios cleared Steamer Lake Flattery August 27th.

Plaintiff insists that from this cablegram it first learned that defendant intended to ship 30 plants and that the shipment had been made. The 30 plants reached Guatemala in due course. Plaintiff accepted 10 of them and demands of defendant refund of the value of 20, plus expense. Defendant refused. The 20 plants are in a warehouse in Guatemala and are held by the bank to secure plaintiff's indebtedness to it. The trial was without a jury. Upon findings, duly excepted to, defendant had judgment on April 5, 1926. Plaintiff brings error.

The bank that issued the letter of credit is not affected by this litigation between buyer and seller. It was not concerned with the provisions of the sales contract not incorporated in the letter of credit. It paid on the required documents as it had a right to do. *Maurice O'Meara Co.* v. *National Park Bank*, 239 N. Y. 386 (146 N. E. 636, 39 A. L. R. 747); 30 A. L. R. 353, 1310, notes; and 22 Columbia Law Rev. 311. Plaintiff concedes that the bank followed its instructions.

The theory of plaintiff's case as presented is that it ordered 10 plants and was shipped 30; that defendant upon advice of the letter of credit had no right to ship except upon plaintiff's order; and that there is no contract relation between the parties respecting the 20 plants; that plaintiff has not accepted but has rejected them; that defendant has its money; and that plaintiff is therefore entitled to recover. Assuming that plaintiff ordered but 10 plants and was shipped 30 as it contends, upon arrival at destination it might accept all, reject all, or accept the 10 it had ordered and reject the rest. Section 11875, 3 Comp. Laws 1915 (uniform sales act); 2 Commerce Clearing House, U. S., Unit. § 1699. But if it exercised acts of ownership, or acts inconsistent with seller's ownership, it may be held to have accepted. 2 Williston on Sales (2d Ed.), § 483.

The claim of the bank on the goods is valid. Neither party can question it. It secured and still secures a debt of plaintiff. The bank might have sold the rejected goods and applied the avails in reduction of plaintiff's debt to it. It may be observed that the bank, in the trade sense, was plaintiff's bank. It owed him the duty of service, and it is not unlikely that it would have sold the goods had it been requested to do so. *Imbrie* v. *D. Nagase & Co.*, 196 N. Y. App. Div. 380 (187 N. Y. Supp. 692). It is not suggested in the record that the bank agreed to do so. It has not sold the plants or any of them. Without resorting to the collateral it had, and it seems now has, the right to proceed against plaintiff to recover. . . .

It may be that plaintiff under the sales act had right of a lien on the rejected goods to secure the amount it has paid, unwittingly, as it contends. But such right is wholly apart from its right to use the goods as security for its debt to another. Conceding the amount of the bank's claim to be larger and to cover more goods than plaintiff intended, and that the situation has been produced by defendant's wrong, it is still the bank's security and the plaintiff's debt. Defendant is not to be penalized by being deprived of both the money and the goods. Plaintiff had right to be compensated in damages. It seems clear that in rejecting the goods and to bring this action plaintiff within a reasonable time ought to have freed them from the hold of the bank. And by a timely sale of the goods by the bank and credit of the avails on plaintiff's debt to it, the way for this suit might have been opened. Counsel insist that this may work a hardship, but our attention is called to no rule which permits escape from it. See American Commercial Credits, chap. 14, by Ward, Ronald Press, N. Y., relating to the mercantile risk and the buyer's dilemma, and see The Trust Receipt as Security, by Frederick (reprint Columbia Law Review) and Commercial Letters of Credit, by McCurdy (reprint Harvard Law Review). Plaintiff may not have judgment against defendant for the money paid and at the same time have the property held by the bank to secure the debt. At the time of the trial the goods had been so held for more than six years. We are constrained to agree with the trial court that plaintiff must be held to have accepted the goods. . . .

That plaintiff is not damaged until it is out of pocket, until it has paid the bank, is a question not necessary to decision. That the result would be different if there had been no bargain and sale, if defendant had sent the goods and taken the money as a mere intermeddler, need not be considered.

Judgment affirmed.

FELLOWS, WIEST, McDONALD, and SHARPE, JJ., concurred.

The late Chief Justice FLANNIGAN and the late Justices SNOW and BIRD took no part in this decision.

ROCK GLEN SALT COMPANY *v.* SEGAL

MASSACHUSETTS SUPREME JUDICIAL COURT, 1918

[229 *Massachusetts Reports*, 115]

Contract for $322.56 as the price of certain salt, as described in a paragraph of the report which is quoted in the opinion, alleged to have been sold to the defendant. Writ in the Municipal Court of the City of Boston dated April 28, 1913.

The evidence at the trial in the Municipal Court is described in the opinion. The defendant asked the judge to make certain rulings, among which were the following:

"8. Where the seller delivers to the buyer goods which he contracted to purchase mixed with goods of a different description not included in the contract the buyer may reject the whole.

"9. The defendant was not bound to accept a greater quantity of goods than he ordered.

"10. The plaintiff by appropriating a greater quantity of goods than the defendant contracted to buy did not perform his contract and therefore cannot maintain this action."

The judge made the following findings and rulings: "I find that the invoice dated February 14 was received by the defendant on or before February 18; that the car containing four hundred bags and fifteen barrels of salt arrived in Boston February 18; that the Boston and Maine Railroad had then received the bill of lading indorsed by the plaintiff to the defendant's order; and that said company on or about February 19 sent notice to the defendant and that the salt was damaged February 26. I rule that the title had passed to the defendant before February 26, and that the salt was then at his risk. I refuse to give the rulings requested by the defendant."

The judge found for the plaintiff in the sum of $344.19, and at the request of the defendant reported the case to the Appellate Division. The Appellate Division made an order that judgment be entered for the defendant, and the plaintiff appealed.

PIERCE, J. "This is an action of contract to recover the purchase price of 300 burlaps 70/2s Table Salt at $1.05, 50 burlaps 50/3s Table Salt at $1.02 and 50 burlaps cotton 200s V.C.F. Salt at $0.74, amounting in all to $403, less freight, $80.44, net amount $322.56."

A "Memorandum of agreement" for the purchase and sale of "a supply of salt numbering five to ten cars" fixed the prices to be paid for different kinds of salt F. O. B. cars, Boston. The shipment in question was the last to be made under this contract and no question as to previous shipments is involved.

The defendant had previously ordered and received at different times during the period covered by the contract and the time following its extension, nine carloads of salt, and each time paid freight on the goods that he had ordered and deducted the freight charges from his invoice when he paid such invoice. It was understood between the parties that the goods were to be invoiced "less freight" and that the defendant should pay the freight charges on his goods when they arrived and deduct the amount from the bill when remitting.

On February 8, 1913, the plaintiff purchased of the Watkins Salt Company, Watkins, New York, the salt in bags ordered by the defendant. Two days later the plaintiff purchased fifteen barrels of salt ordered by another of its customers. The salt in bags and barrels was placed in a car and shipped at the plaintiff's request from Watkins, New York, to the Rock Glen Salt Company, Boston. The plaintiff took from the carrier a non-negotiable bill of lading. The salt was not consigned to the defendant, but on the contrary was consigned to the plaintiff itself, and was described in the bill of lading as "15 Bbls. 400 Sax Weight 64600 lbs." "Destination, Boston State of Mass." "Route B. & M. Car Initial Erie Car No. 111529." This bill of lading was indorsed "Deliver to order of Segal Bros. Rock Glen Salt Co. F. W. Relyea, Treas." It was then sent to and received by the Boston and Maine Railroad at Boston, but it was never delivered to or accepted by the defendant.

The car containing the bags and barrels of salt arrived in Boston at the Boston and Maine freight house on February 18, 1913. On February 19, 1913, the Boston and Maine Railroad notified the defendant in writing of the arrival of freight consigned to the Rock Glen Salt Company and stated that it was ready for delivery. The notice gave the "Car Initial and Nos." as "E 111529" and the "Original Point of Shipment" as "Watkins, N. Y. via ER." It described the "Articles and Marks — Weight — Rate — Freight — Advances" as

"15 Bbl.
400 sx. } Salt   64600   90.44   Total, 90.44."

Neither the bill of lading nor the notice stated the different kinds of salt that made up the four hundred bags nor the quantity of each kind. Nor did the defendant know that the fifteen barrels of salt had been put into the car with the four hundred bags to fill an order of another customer of the plaintiff.

When the defendant received the notice he had already received an invoice for salt as ordered, which showed a shipment over the Boston and Maine Railroad in "Car No. 111529 Erie," the amount of said invoice being $403 "less freight" $80.44, or $322.56. He compared the notice with the memorandum of his order, found that the salt stated in the notice did not correspond to the order given by him to the plaintiff, noticed that the freight charges were excessive for the quantity of salt ordered by him, and that they covered the whole quantity of salt contained in the car. He thereupon returned the notice to the "railroad's messenger." Without contradiction, so far as the record discloses, he testified "that there was no way in which the freight charges could have been apportioned or separated and if [he] the defendant had accepted any part of this car of salt he would have been obliged to pay the full amount of the freight charges on said car." He also testified that "he had a charge account with this railroad for freight due the railroad on shipments, and that actual payment by him to the railroad at the time of receiving possession of shipments was not necessary to receive such possession."

On February 26, 1913, the car of salt was damaged by fire at the Boston and Maine freight house and the defendant refused to receive the salt. The presiding judge ruled "that the title had passed to the defendant before February 26, and that the salt was then at his risk," and found for the plaintiff. Upon report, the Appellate Division of the Municipal Court of the City of Boston, ordered "Judgment for defendant," and the case is before this court on appeal from that decision.

We think the forwarding of the salt to Boston at the seller's expense, the taking of a bill of lading running to itself as consignee, and the provision in the contract "sells . . . at the following prices F. O. B. cars, Boston," indicate an intent of the seller to reserve to itself the *jus disponendi* of the salt until the railroad company in Boston on behalf of the plaintiff, and in the exercise of the authority conferred by the indorsement upon the bill of lading, should appropriate and deliver to the defendant from the mass the quantities and kinds ordered by the defendant. *First National Bank of Cairo* v. *Crocker*, 111 Mass. 163, 167. *Sawyer Medicine Co.* v. *Johnson*, 178 Mass. 374. St. 1908, c. 237, § 19, Rule 5. The question is, Was the notice of the Boston and Maine Railroad an appropriation and proper tender on behalf of the plaintiff of the salt to the defendant in performance of the contract?

In this regard it is to be noticed that the railroad company was not instructed by the bill of lading or otherwise of the kind or quantity of salt required to fill the defendant's order. Nor, so far as appears, was there anything about the bags or barrels to indicate the quality of their contents. What the railroad did was to tender the contents of a car, — a quantity of goods larger than the defendant agreed to purchase and on which the defendant would have been obliged to advance freight charges in excess of the amount he agreed to advance. . . .

In the case at bar the defendant, upon receiving the notice and invoice, could have assumed properly that the fifteen barrels of salt had been sent by the seller to be delivered by the railroad to him. The bill of lading in terms directed the railroad company to do so. Upon this assumption, if he did not intend to pay for the whole car, he must have determined whether to take a part and reject a part, or reject the whole. If he desired to have the part only which he had ordered, it remained to determine whether he would become responsible for the entire freight charges and look to the purchaser of the fifteen barrels or to the seller for his repayment. If it were a fact that the defendant could have paid the proportionate charges, that fact does not appear in the report and cannot be assumed. We are of opinion that the severance of the four hundred bags from the fifteen barrels involved pecuniary "trouble" or "risk" to the defendant.

It follows that the title never passed to the defendant.

Judgment for the defendant affirmed.

BROWNFIELD *v.* JOHNSON

PENNSYLVANIA SUPREME COURT, 1889

[128 *Pennsylvania Reports,* 254]

[Eleven pages dealing with the facts of the case, proceedings in the lower court, etc., are here omitted.]

Opinion, Mr. Justice CLARK: A complete understanding of the rules of law governing this case involves a brief statement of the material facts. On the second day of December, 1866, Brownfield & Co., the defendants, gave an order to Lawrence Johnson & Co. to purchase for them in Brazil 300 bags best quality of new brazil-nuts of the first receipts; payments to be made in cash on arrival, or by sixty day note, etc., at the defendants' option; the plaintiffs to cable price at the time of shipment. On the same day the plaintiffs replied, stating that brazil-nuts were not bought by the bag, but by hectolitres, a measure which in past years averaged from 100 to 120 pounds; that the nuts came in bulk in the steamer, and the defendants would have to furnish the bags on arrival in New York; and as "the out-turn of the measure is uncertain" they proposed to order 450 hectolitres, etc. To this the defendant replied by telephone, "Order 400 hectolitres and buy only the very best nuts obtainable."

The plaintiffs placed the order in the hands of their correspondents, La Roque, Da Costa & Co., Para, Brazil, who undertook the purchase, and on the 9th of February following advised the plaintiffs of shipment per steamer Portuense, upon board of which were nearly 6000 hectolitres of brazil-nuts for other parties. Of this shipment and of the price, notice was on the same day given to the defendants. Upon the arrival of the Portuense in New York, Lawrence Johnson & Co. handed to the defendants a delivery order for 400 hectolitres brazil-nuts, in bulk, in separate hold, on board the Portuense, with copy of original invoice and the plaintiffs' bill, amounting to $3,441:18.

The invoice was for 312 hectolitres at 15,150 reis each and 88 hectolitres at 14,000 reis each; showing that the nuts had been originally purchased in two separate lots, and at different prices. The defendants, with the delivery order in their possession, proceeded to New York and went on board the Portuense, where they found no consignment of nuts in the name of Brownfield & Co., but the plaintiffs' store-keeper informed them that the 400 hectolitres in question, were embraced in a consignment of 582 hectolitres of brazil-nuts, in separate hold, in the name of the plaintiffs. The defendants thereupon refused to receive any portion of these nuts as an execution of their order. The plaintiffs tendered to the defendants the whole 582 hectolitres, or 400 hectolitres thereof, at their option, at the invoiced prices, which tender in either alternative the defendants declined to accept. The plaintiffs afterwards tendered 400 hectolitres at the average price, which the defendants also declined; subsequently, the plaintiffs, separated the 400 hectolitres from the lot and notified the defendants of their weight, but the defendants absolutely declined to accept the nuts on any of the several propositions made by the plaintiffs.

The 582 hectolitres were made up of two lots, one of 312 hectolitres, invoiced at 15,150 reis; the other of 270 hectolitres, invoiced at 14,000 reis; 88 hectolitres of the latter were invoiced to the defendants, and the residue, being 182 hectolitres, to Lawrence Johnson & Co. for account of La Roque, Da Costa & Co., who, it is said, according to the method of dealing in Brazil, in order to get 88 hectolitres to fill the order were obliged to buy a larger lot. That all parties acted in good faith is a fact found by the jury, and the case turns upon the question whether the defendants' order was properly and legally executed. . . .

The only question, therefore, would seem to be upon the effect of the shipping of the whole lot of 582 hectolitres in one hold. It was shown that this was the usual method of shipping, especially when the orders were small. There was no effort to establish a custom of this kind, but simply to show that this was the usual and ordinary method pursued in the shipping trade. The defendant had a right to suppose these goods would be shipped in the usual manner, unless he directed otherwise, and that although intermingled with others in the forward hold of the vessel for transportation, they would be separated at the place of delivery. The nuts in question were of the same quality; they were bought at different prices, but the evidence is clear that they were of uniform quality. The weight of American authority supports the proposition that when property is sold to be taken out of a specific mass of uniform quality, title will pass at once upon the making of the contract, if such appears to be the intent. Oil in a tank and grain in an elevator may serve as illustrations of this rule. Where, however, the property is sold as part of a mass made up of units of unequal quality or value, such as cattle in a herd, selection is essential to the execution of the contract, and of course the rule cannot apply: Benj. on Sales, 477–531, and cases there cited. The storage of oil in tanks and of grain in elevators, although not universal, is the usual and ordinary means employed by large dealers in those commodities, and, whilst no custom of that kind, technically speaking, could be established, the usage of the trade and general course of business in this country is well known. In view of the necessities which grow out of such usage, the American courts have departed from the rule adhered to in England, and have recognized a rule for the delivery of this class of property more in conformity with the commercial usages of the country. A distinction is made between those cases where the act of separation is burdensome and expensive or involves selection, and those where the article is uniform in bulk and the act of separation throws no additional burden on the buyer. In the latter class of cases a tender of too much, from which the buyer is to take the proper quantity, is a good delivery. . . .

We are of opinion that when the nuts were delivered on board the Portuense at Para, the title to 400/582 of the bulk belonged to the defendants, and that upon the arrival of the vessel at New York the tender of the

582 hectolitres from which the defendants were invited to take their share was a good delivery.

The judgment is affirmed.

MOORE & COMPANY *v.* LANDAUER AND COMPANY

KING'S BENCH DIVISION, 1920

[*Law Reports,* [1921] 1 *King's Bench,* 73]

[Affirmed by the Court of Appeal in [1921] 2 K. B. 519]

ROWLATT, J. In this case there was a contract for the sale of a large number of tins of canned fruits of various kinds, to be packed in cases, each case to contain thirty tins, the price being payable at per dozen tins. At the date of the contract the steamship *Toromeo* with the goods on board had already sailed, but she did not arrive until a wholly unreasonable time afterwards, owing to causes for which the sellers were not responsible. It turned out, as to about one-half of the cases, that they contained twenty-four tins only instead of thirty. The award was in favour of the sellers, subject to the question (*inter alia*) whether the fact that some of the goods were packed in cases containing twenty-four tins instead of thirty entitled the buyers to reject the whole consignment or only the cases containing twenty-four tins. The arbitrator, in dealing with this question, seems to have brushed it aside as an afterthought of the buyers. But it seems to me clear that on the construction of the contract the buyers were entitled to say: "We must have the goods packed in the way we have contracted for." I cannot speculate as to the effect this alteration in the mode of packing would have in the trade; the buyers may have their particular reasons for preferring to have their goods packed in a certain way, and I cannot see on what grounds it is said that they are bound to take them packed in another way. The fact that in this case the value of the goods on the market, so packed, was unaffected, makes no difference.

The point remains whether the buyers were entitled to reject the whole consignment, or whether they were bound to take those cases which were packed in accordance with the contract. I do not think they were bound to accept them. Sect. 30 of the Sale of Goods Act, 1893 (56 & 57 Vict. c. 71), deals with three cases. In the first, sub-s. 1 enacts that where the seller delivers to the buyer a quantity of goods less than he contracted to sell, the buyer may reject them. The second case is not here material. In the third case sub-s. 3 enacts that where the seller delivers to the buyer the goods he contracted to sell mixed with goods of a different description not included in the contract, the buyer may accept the goods which are in accordance with the contract and reject the rest, or he may reject the whole. The words "mixed with" in sub-s. 3 cannot refer to physical confusion but are equivalent to "accompanied by." In the present case, if half only of the goods — namely, those properly packed — had been tendered, the buyers could have refused to accept them under s. 30, sub-s. 1.

It is said that because they were accompanied by something else not in the contract — namely, the goods improperly packed — the buyers were bound to accept the goods properly packed. I cannot agree with that contention. [The learned judge proceeded to deal with further contentions of fact by the buyers.]

On these grounds I think the award must be in favour of the buyers.

Judgment for buyers.

Compare WILLIAM BARKER (JR.) AND COMPANY, LIMITED *v.* EDWARD T. AGIUS LIMITED, 33 Commercial Cases 120 (King's Bench Division, 1927). In that case there was a contract for the sale of coal briquettes, size two inches, which were shipped in part above and in part below deck. On removal of the deck cargo it appeared that although the briquettes stowed on deck were of the right size, those stowed below were not. A special case was stated by an arbitrator relating to the right of the buyer to reject, and on the question of applicability of sub-section 3 of the Act, Salter, J., said: "If I were free to read that section as *res nova* I should have thought it referred only to the goods of surplus delivery and admixture. I should be disposed to give to the word 'mixed' a much more definite meaning than was given to it by Rowlatt J. in the case of *Moore and Co.* v. *Landauer and Co.* reported in the Court below in 1921, 1 K. B. 73. He said in that case that he thought it meant no more than 'accompanied by.' I should have thought that it meant much more than 'accompanied by.' If a man buys a horse and the seller delivers a horse and a donkey it would not require an Act of Parliament, I should think, to say he must keep the horse and return the donkey. I think that a good deal was meant to depend here on the word 'mixed.' I should have thought that it refers to the case, and only the case, where the seller has delivered the whole of the goods he contracted to deliver, the whole quantity and all of the right description and quality, but he has intermixed with those goods goods which are wholly alien to the contract, goods of a different description not included in his contract. Then the position is that the goods which are in accordance with the contract mixed with those which are not, cannot be separated out without trouble and expense, and then the section would simply say if the buyer chooses to go to that trouble and expense he can accept the goods which are in accordance with the contract and reject those which are not, but that he need not go to that trouble and expense. The seller cannot say to him, 'All the goods I contracted to sell of the agreed quantity are there and, therefore, you must take them and sort them out for yourself.' He cannot say that. The buyer may, if he pleases, reject the whole."

PORTFOLIO *v.* RUBIN

NEW YORK COURT OF APPEALS, 1922

[233 *New York Reports*, 439]

CRANE, J. This action was brought in the Municipal Court to recover the sum of $638.99, the price of four pieces of goods suitable to be manufactured into cloaks and suits. The defendant accepted two of the pieces and tendered the amount due for them, $311.91, which sum he deposited into court. The remaining two pieces he rejected as not in accordance with the order and notified the seller to that effect. It was conceded on the trial that under the contract the purchase price of the two accepted pieces was $311.91 and of the two rejected pieces $327.08. It was also stipulated that the goods sold were to be first grade regulation goods.

The plaintiff's counsel in reply to the court stated that the only issue was whether or not the goods were shaded. Shaded goods would not be suitable for cloaks and suits, neither would they be in conformity with the contract of sale. There was ample evidence that the two pieces rejected were shaded goods.

The Municipal Court decided that under section 156 of the Personal Property Law (Cons. Laws, ch. 41) the contract of sale was divisible and that the defendant could accept part and reject the portion which did not comply with the contract. He gave judgment for the defendant.

The plaintiff, insisting that the sale constituted an entire contract and that the defendant having accepted part accepted all, appealed to the Appellate Term which held with him in this view and reversed the judgment of the Municipal Court.

Upon further appeal the Appellate Division reversed the Appellate Term and reinstated the verdict of the Municipal Court in favor of the defendant. It was, however, inclined to the view of the law taken by the Appellate Term that the Personal Property Law did not cover this case; that the contract was an entire contract, and that the defendant was obliged to accept all or none of the goods. The reversal by the Appellate Division and the affirmance of the judgment for the defendant was on the question of waiver and practice.

We are of the opinion that the judgment and rulings in favor of the defendant were correct, but not upon the ground stated by the Appellate Division, adopting rather the view that this case is covered by the Personal Property Law. . . .

The fact is that the defendant received less in quantity of the goods he had ordered than he had contracted to purchase. Of the first grade regular goods, he only received two pieces. The other two pieces, shaded goods, were not part of the purchase, or goods for which he had contracted. He thus received less than the quantity ordered and subdivision 1 of section 125 gave the defendant the right to accept these and pay for them according to the contract price.

We think that subdivision 3 of this section also applies to the case. The two pieces rejected by the defendant were of a different description from those purchased by him. (*Waeber* v. *Talbot*, 167 N. Y. 48.) It was stipulated by counsel at the opening of the case as above stated, that the goods purchased were supposed to be first grade regular goods and that the only issue was whether or not the two pieces rejected were shaded. That issue was tried out. The witnesses differed in their testimony as to the shading. It seems to have been conceded, also, that if the goods were shaded then they were not of the kind or description ordered by the defendant, and he was justified in rejecting them. The plaintiff's counsel stated to the court: "That is really the only issue whether they are shaded or not."

As shaded goods did not answer the description of the goods purchased, the buyer, the defendant in this case, was entitled to reject them and accept the goods which were in accordance with his contract.

[The balance of the opinion, holding that the Municipal Court was right in deciding this to be a divisible contract, is omitted.]

We agree with the Appellate Division that the judgment of the Municipal Court was right, and affirm the judgment appealed from on the reasons here stated, with costs.

HISCOCK, Ch. J., HOGAN, CARDOZO, POUND, MCLAUGHLIN and ANDREWS, JJ., concur.

Judgment affirmed.

HOLLIS BROS. & CO. LTD. *v.* WHITE SEA TIMBER TRUST, LTD.

KING'S BENCH DIVISION, 1936

[56 *Lloyd's List Law Reports*, 78]

This was a case stated for the decision of the Court pursuant to Sect. 9 (1) (b) of the Arbitration Act, 1934, and concerned the construction of a contract for the shipment of timber from Igarka, North Russia, to Hull. The case was stated by Mr. Harold French as umpire in an arbitration arising out of a dispute as to allowances claimed by buyers. The parties to the contract were Messrs. Hollis Bros. & Co., of Hull, the buyers, and the White Sea Timber Trust, Ltd., of London, the sellers. The contract provided for the sale of Siberian redwood, sawn parquet blocks from the Kara Sea, totalling about 50 standards in all. The buyers, on arrival of the cargo at Hull, claimed compensation for excess delivery of short lengths and also for non-delivery of long lengths, as well as compensation for admixture of sizes. The sellers contended that the contract was conditional, and they sold only such goods as were actually shipped, goods not shipped being cancelled. The question for the Court was whether the buyers were entitled to an allowance for non-shipment of long lengths. . . .

The contract was in the ordinary c.i.f. form, and the clause referred to was in typewritten matter, below the printed conditions. It was for about 30 standards of 1 in. by 3 in. by 9¼/9½ in., and for about 20 standards of 1 in. by 3 in. by 18½/19 in., each at £11 per standard. There was no dispute about the dimensions. It was not a sale of a cargo but of two parcels, which could be shipped in one or more steamers at shippers' option. The contract provided that

In the event of over-shipment of any item of the contract or of the total contract quantity buyers shall not be entitled to reject the entire shipment but shall have the option to be exercised without delay of taking up the bills of lading and paying for the whole quantity shipped or of taking up the bills of lading and paying only for the contract quantity rejecting the balance. . . . If buyers elect to take the contract quantity only the sellers shall pay all extra expenses incurred by buyers in consequence of the over-shipment. In the event of under-shipment of any item, buyers are to accept or pay for the quantity shipped, but have the right to claim compensation for such short-shipment. Each item of this contract to be considered a separate interest.

The following typewritten clauses were also included in the contract: —

All the goods under this contract are subject to a variation of 25 per cent. more or less, in shippers' option.

This contract is subject to sellers making necessary chartering arrangements for the expedition, and sold subject to shipment: any goods not shipped to be cancelled. . . .

Mr. Justice Porter, in giving judgment, said: . . . The sale was a sale of two parcels of goods, one of which was just half the length of the other. All the goods were small in size and short in length, the largest length specified being 19 in. Though there were two parcels, the parcels, I think, must be considered as separate interests. That was provided for by the provision in the printed part of the contract: "Each item of this contract to be considered a separate interest." . . .

So far as the larger size of goods is concerned — the 1 in. by 3 in. by 18½/19 in. — there was a considerable shortage in the delivered quantity even if one takes into consideration the fact that there is a provision for a variation of 25 per cent. The actual amount delivered was about one-half — it is not necessary for me to put it with accuracy. Of course, if the original provisions of the printed contract had remained in existence, the buyers would have been entitled to compensation under the words, "In the event of under-shipment of any item, buyers are to accept or pay for the quantity shipped, but have the right to claim compensation for such short-shipment." That provision, however, did not remain in those terms, because it is at least modified, and possibly altered, by the third clause, in the typewritten words, "sold subject to shipment: any goods not shipped to be cancelled." I need not trouble, except for the purpose of illustrating the meaning of the contract, with the earlier portion of the words, "Subject to sellers making necessary chartering arrangements for the expedition." The expedition sailed, and certain goods were put on board. The primary matter which I have to consider is the meaning of the words "Sold subject to shipment: any goods not shipped to be cancelled."

It is said on behalf of the sellers that the words in that portion of the contract mean that the obligation of the seller is subject to a double condition; the first condition being that the necessary chartering arrangements are made and the second condition being that the goods must be shipped, and any goods not shipped are to be cancelled. In other words, unless the goods are shipped the sellers are not obliged to tender the documents or goods, this being a c.i.f. contract, though on the other hand they could tender what was shipped, but any goods not shipped are to be cancelled. I do not, for this purpose, intend to decide that which may well arise in another case, namely, whether, supposing there to be a short shipment beneath the minimum quantity, the buyers are obliged to take the smaller quantity. In fact they have taken the smaller quantity, and that particular question does not arise in this case. I have merely to determine, they having taken that portion, whether the sellers are excused from paying compensation for the short shipment.

Now, it is said here by Mr. McNair, on behalf of the buyers, that I must read the contract as a whole, and that it is possible to give effect both to the printed words and the written words of the contract. He says in effect, first of all, that in this case the buyer made provision for two types of goods, and that you must not ship one type of goods so as to prevent the shipment of the other; you must not fill up your space with the smaller goods so as to shut out the larger goods. And he says that they are entitled, looking at the contract, to infer that the smaller goods are less valuable than the larger goods. All I can say about that is that there is no such finding in the case as stated, and I do not think I am entitled to speculate as to which of the goods was the more valuable.

He says, secondly, and it is true, that when one is considering the construction of a contract containing both written and printed words one must as far as possible give effect to both the written and printed words. The authorities state with accuracy the proposition which one has to bear in mind when construing documents in these cases. Nevertheless, though that is so, there are cases in which it is not possible to give effect to both the printed and the written words, and in such a case the written words must prevail. The case that was quoted to me was *Hadjipateras and Others* v. *S. Weigall & Co. and Another*, 34 T. L. R. 360, which I do not use for any purpose except to show that there may be cases where you can and must disregard the printed words altogether and take the written words only.

In the present case, Mr. McNair points out, it is true to say that it might have been possible to leave out the words, "This contract is subject to sellers making necessary chartering arrangements for the expedition" if it is true to say that "sold subject to shipment any goods not shipped to be cancelled" means that it is left to the sellers to ship or not to ship, and that if the goods are not in fact shipped, the bargain is that they are under no obligation to deliver the goods at all. That is true, but I do not think that that is the conclusion of the case, because one knows that in mercantile contracts one does from time to time get repetition of provisions, some of which may not be necessary, but which are thought to be desirable in order to point out the exact position in which the parties stand, one to the other.

Then is it possible to take the second part of the words "sold subject to shipment: any goods not shipped to be cancelled," and give them a meaning which is consistent with the words "in the event of under-shipment of any item buyers are to accept and pay for the quantity shipped but have the right to claim compensation for such short shipment"? I do not think it is.

At one time I thought it might be possible to say that "Sold subject to shipment" means "subject to some shipment taking place," and that it might be possible to say that "any goods not shipped to be cancelled" merely provided that there was no obligation upon the sellers to ship, at a future date, any goods left on their hands. I do not think that is consistent. It seems to me to be inconsistent with the whole scheme of the arrangement by which the expedition is to start, and which merely gives a latitude of 21 days for shipping.

I thought also that it might be possible to say that "subject to shipment: any goods not shipped to be cancelled" might be construed as meaning "sold subject to the possibility and the ability of the sellers to ship, and sold subject to any goods not able to be shipped to be cancelled." I do not think that that is the natural meaning of the words, and I do not think I ought to speculate as to what was in the minds of the parties when they made the contract.

In my view, "subject to shipment" means "provided the sellers in fact ship," and that meaning must be read with the phrase "any goods not shipped to be cancelled." Reading the two phrases together the meaning is not "subject to some shipment taking place," but is "sold subject to these goods being shipped" and the clause provides that if a portion of the goods is shipped that does not prevent the sellers from saying that that portion may be delivered in accordance with the contract though the rest is not.

I agree that the actual provision itself is not very happily drawn, because one finds that it says that this contract is "subject to sellers making necessary chartering arrangements for the expedition," and it goes on "and sold subject to shipment." The proper meaning of that, and its accurate meaning, would be that the contract was sold subject to shipment. I do not think that this looseness of language makes any difference. I think one must say, particularly in regard to the fact that "any goods not shipped to be cancelled" follows "sold subject to shipment," that it means the goods and not the contract are sold subject to shipment.

I think I can get some assistance — in spite of the differences rightly pointed out by Mr. McNair — from the "to arrive" cases. Just as in the "to arrive" cases there is no sale of the goods until the goods arrive in the ship and that leaves it at the option of the sellers to ship or not to ship as they please, so here the words "subject to shipment" seem to me to leave it at the option of the sellers whether they intend to ship or not.

I think it is too late in the world's history now to make any criticism of the construction put upon the words "to arrive." I think it is an old-established principle how those words are to be construed. It is true that those were not c.i.f. contracts and that these are, but I think that the two cases are to some extent analogous. The words "to arrive" mean that if the goods do not arrive there is no sale, and here the words "sold subject to shipment" mean that they are sold if they are shipped, but if they are not shipped then there is no sale. It is quite true that that puts it at the option of the sellers to ship or not to ship, but the words in my opinion bear that plain meaning, and I do not think that the objection raised ought to prevail. . . .

For these reasons I think the alternative is the correct award and I find in accordance with the alternative award, which is, I understand, that the sellers pay the buyers £13 *2s. 6d.*

The costs of the arbitration would remain as awarded in the special case, said his LORDSHIP, but the sellers must have the costs of the proceedings before the Court.

Compare the following examples of sellers' clauses in regard to quantity:

In HARROWER, WELSH & Co. *v.* McWILLIAM & SONS, 30 Ll. L. R. 182 (Court of Sessions, 1928), a contract for the sale of 750 tons of coal on c.i.f. terms contained the clause: "Payment according to bill of lading weight in net cash in exchange for bill of lading and insurance certificate." Only 712 tons of coal were delivered from the carrying ship. It was held that the clause in question could not be construed to prevent the buyer from having the price adjusted to conform with the quantity actually received.

In GREEN *v.* ARCOS, LTD., 47 T. L. R. 336 (Court of Appeal, 1931), a contract for the sale of a quantity of timber to be shipped from Russia allowed a variation of 10 per cent at seller's option, and contained the following clause: "Buyers shall not reject the goods herein specified but shall accept or pay for them in terms of contract against shipping documents." When the cargo arrived it was found that there was an excessive shipment in some classes of timber, short shipment in others, and in some no shipment at all. The buyer claimed to reject the whole cargo. It was held that the clause quoted had no application, as the goods received were not those "herein specified."

See also ANGLO-CHINESE EASTERN TRADING Co. *v.* ROYAL COMMISSION, 10 Ll. L. R. 667 (King's Bench Division, 1922), where a contract for the sale of wheat provided that the certificate of Lloyd's agent should be final as to quantity. A document was tendered in which the manager of the railway company at the port of shipment certified as to quantity, his signature being certified by Lloyd's agent with the statement that "every confidence may be placed in the said certificate." It was held that in the absence of a usage to the contrary, this document was not a certificate of Lloyd's agent.

As to buyers' quantity clauses, refer again to WILLITS & PATTERSON *v.* ABEKOBEI & Co., *supra*, p. 306 (net delivered weight). See also DWANE *v.*

WEIL, 199 App. Div. 719 (New York Supreme Court, Appellate Division, 1922), where there was a contract for the sale of green calfskins, "all 6/12 lbs. average 9½/10 lbs. c.i.f. New York, invoice weight, shrinkage guaranteed not to exceed 5% where reweighed on dock on arrival in New York." It was held that this clause had nothing to do with delivery, but was merely indicative of an allowance to be made to the buyer.

C. INSTALLMENT CONTRACTS

NATIONAL KNITTING COMPANY *v.* BOUTON & GERMAIN COMPANY

WISCONSIN SUPREME COURT, 1909

[141 *Wisconsin Reports*, 63]

Appeal from a judgment of the municipal court of the city and town of Ripon: J. J. FOOTE, Judge. Affirmed.

The plaintiff corporation is a manufacturer and dealer in knitted goods at Milwaukee, and the defendant corporation is a jobber in the same line of goods at Ripon. In November, 1905, the defendant ordered of the plaintiff, in writing, a quantity of gloves of different kinds at fixed prices, aggregating $322.86, delivery to be made in the following May, bill to be dated as of November 1, 1906, payable in thirty days. The order was accepted, and in April the plaintiff delivered the greater part of the goods ordered, but never delivered one item of eighteen dozen gloves and another item of six dozen gloves. The plaintiff sues to recover for the goods actually delivered at contract prices. The defendant contends that the contract is entire, and hence that nothing is due, because the contract has never been fully performed. The defendant also sets up a counterclaim for damages because of nondelivery of said two items, in case the court should hold the contract to be severable. The trial court held the contract to be severable, and awarded judgment for the plaintiff for the contract price of the items delivered, less damages, consisting of the loss of profits on the items not delivered. From this judgment defendant appeals.

WINSLOW, C. J. We think that the business world would be astonished to learn that whenever an order for a bill of merchandise is accepted the contract thus made is entire, and requires delivery of every article before there can be recovery of any part of the purchase price. Such would be the practical effect of the defendant's contention here, if it should be upheld. We cannot so hold. The question of entirety is a question of intention; severability of the subject matter and measurement of consideration by units may assist in determining, but do not of themselves necessarily determine, the question.

In case of a contract naturally and accurately severable (such as a contract for the sale of a bill of goods at certain prices for each article), courts incline to hold the contract severable, and to grant a recovery for that portion of the goods actually delivered, less damages for the nondelivery of any portion not delivered. Under all ordinary circumstances this course will result in exact justice. The vendor will receive pay for his goods which the vendee has retained, and the vendee will receive compensation for any damage which he has actually suffered.

If, however, it appears by express terms or by necessary implication from the terms of a contract that the intention of the parties was to make payment of the consideration depend upon delivery of all the articles, the contract will be held entire, though the consideration may be measured in units and be actually severable. *Goodwin* v. *Merrill*, 13 Wis. 658; *Shinn* v. *Bodine*, 60 Pa. St. 182. Thus, when a contract required the delivery of 2,000 yards of crushed stone for the purpose of building a bridge, it was held to be entire, notwithstanding the payment was to be at a certain rate per yard. *Prautsch* v. *Rasmussen*, 133 Wis. 181, 113 N. W. 416. So contracts to tow a given quantity of logs at so much per thousand feet, and to carry 5,000 barrels of salt at so much per barrel, have been held entire, upon the idea that the terms of the contract, in the light of the surrounding facts, showed that the parties evidently intended to contract for one entire job, and only used the unit of measurement of the consideration for convenience and not as indicating any contemplation of severability. *Boutin* v. *Lindsley*, 84 Wis. 644, 54 N. W. 1017; *Warehouse & B. S. Co.* v. *Galvin*, 96 Wis. 523, 71 N. W. 804. See, also, *Widman* v. *Gay*, 104 Wis. 277, 80 N. W. 450.

The principle here decided is that contracts for the sale of goods like the present, which are naturally severable, will not be held entire contracts, in the absence of express or implied provision to that effect in the contract, or persuasive circumstances showing the intention of the parties to make it entire.

By the Court. — Judgment affirmed.

Note also HOWELL *v.* EVANS, 42 T. L. R. 310 (King's Bench Division, 1926). In that case the plaintiffs were publishers of engravings, and the defendant signed an order for a set entitled "The Cries of London," to be sent to him as published, the price of each plate to be £10 10*s*. The plaintiffs delivered the first four plates, but the defendants refused to pay for them until the complete set was published and delivered, and returned the plates received. In an action for the price of the four plates received, it was held that the words "to be sent to me as published" made it clear that the contract was an installment contract, and that the plaintiffs accordingly could recover.

Compare BEHREND & CO., LTD. *v.* PRODUCE BROKERS CO., LTD., [1920] 3 K. B. 530 (King's Bench Division, 1920). In that case there were two contracts in identical terms for the sale of 200 tons of Egyptian cotton seed at £32 per ton, and for 500 tons of Egyptian cotton seed at £26 per ton, the seed to be shipped from Alexandria and delivered in London, payment net cash against shipping documents. The sellers gave notice of 176 tons and of 400 tons shipped by a certain steamer, and the buyers accepted this notice, paying against the documents. A portion of the seed was delivered into the buyers' barges, but the ship then left for Hull with the rest of the seed on board in order to discharge other cargo. On the return of the ship to London in fourteen days the buyers refused a tender of the balance, claiming to keep the part already delivered and to be entitled to repayment for the part rejected. It was held that as each parcel of goods was indivisible, an award in favor of the buyers was right.

MAPLE FLOCK CO., LTD. *v.* UNIVERSAL FURNITURE PRODUCTS (WEMBLEY), LTD.

COURT OF APPEAL, 1933

[*Law Reports*, [1934] 1 *King's Bench*, 148]

[Three pages of the preliminary statement are here omitted.]

Lord HEWART, C.J. The judgment which I am about to read is the judgment of the whole Court.

The appellant company are manufacturers of rag flock, and the respondents are manufacturers of furniture and bedding for which they use such flock. The action was brought by the appellants for breach by the respondents of a contract in writing, dated March 14, 1932, for the sale by the appellants to the respondents of 100 tons of black lindsey flock at 15*l.* 2*s.* 6*d.* per ton, to be delivered in three loads per week as required. It was further stipulated that there should be a written guarantee that all flock supplied under the contract should conform to the Government standard. The load was 1½ tons or 60 bags. The Government standard was that required under the Rag Flock Act, 1911, which had been fixed by regulation under the Act at not more than 30 parts of chlorine in 100,000 parts of flock. The Act made it a penal offence punishable by fine for any person (*inter alia*) to sell or have in his possession for sale or use or to use flock not conforming to that standard. A person charged under the Act might, however, if he could prove that he bought it from some one resident in the United Kingdom under a warranty that it complied with the Government standard, and that he had taken reasonable steps to ascertain and did in fact believe in the accuracy of the warranty, bring the seller before the Court by information and transfer the burden of the offence to him.

The appellant company duly gave a written guarantee as required by the contract and deliveries were at once commenced and continued of 1½ tons each. The sixteenth of these deliveries was made on April 28, 1932, and, according to the respondent's evidence, was duly accepted and the stuff put into use; a further delivery was made on April 29, 1932, and another on May 2, 1932. On that latter date the respondents notified the appellants that a sample drawn from the delivery of April 28, 1932, had been analysed and showed a contamination of 250 parts of chlorine, instead of the maximum allowed by law of 30 parts. The respondents thereupon claimed to rescind the contract; the appellants protested, and some negotiations took place, during which two more deliveries were tendered and taken, each of 1½ tons. Eventually the respondents adhered to their claim that they were entitled to rescind, and the writ was issued by the appellants claiming damages on the ground that the refusal of the respondents to take further deliveries was wrongful.

No complaint is made in respect of the 15 deliveries made before April 28, 1932, or in respect of the four deliveries made after that date. The respondents made no claim for damages in respect of the delivery said to be defective, because it had all been used before the report was received on the sample. The learned Judge finds that the sample was taken in the usual way — namely, one handful drawn from one bag of the 60 bags which constituted the delivery, and he held that the respondents were entitled, applying the ordinary rules of probability, to say that such must be the condition of the whole or substantially the whole of that delivery of 1½ tons. On the other hand the appellants produced analyses of the flock they had in store from time to time, including an analysis dated April 29, 1932, all of which showed percentages of chlorine well below the Government maximum, though they could not identify any sample as drawn from the flock actually delivered to the respondents. In their evidence they described the process of manufacture by washing which they used. The learned Judge finds that it would be quite wrong to make any general criticism at all of the way in which the appellants conducted their business; he was very favourably impressed, he said, by the evidence of Mr. Jebb, who gave evidence for them; he seemed to the Judge a careful, scrupulous and honourable man. Mr. Jebb could give no explanation of so gross a degree of contamination and was disposed to think some mistake had been made as to the sample. The learned Judge, however, finding that the sample must be taken as a fair test of the delivery, held that the defendants, as prudent traders, could properly say to themselves, in regard to the defective delivery, "it might happen again." He nowhere finds that it was a reasonable inference that it would happen again. His conclusion appears to us to be that there was a mere possibility, not a reasonable probability, that it would happen again. On the contrary, he finds that the occurrence was a very extraordinary thing. We think that on the evidence, and the findings of the learned judge, the true inference of fact is that there was no reasonable probability of any such improper delivery being repeated under the contract.

The decision of this case depends on the true construction and application of s. 31, sub-s. 2, of the Sale of Goods Act, 1893. . . . That subsection was based on decisions before the Act, and has been the subject of decisions since the Act. A contract for the sale of goods by instalments is a single contract, not a complex of as many contracts as there are instalments under it. The law might have been determined in the sense that any breach of condition in respect of any one or more instalments would entitle the party aggrieved to claim that the contract has been repudiated as a whole; or on the other hand the law as established might have been that any breach, however serious, in respect of one or more instalments should not have consequences extending beyond the particular instalment or instalments or affecting the contract as a whole. The sub-section, however, which deals equally with breaches either by the buyer or the seller, requires the Court to decide on the merits of the particular case what effect, if any, the breach or breaches should have on the contract as a whole. . . .

Since the Act, the sub-section has been discussed by a Divisional Court in *Millars' Karri and Jarrah Company* (1902) v. *Weddel, Turner & Co.* (14 Com. Cas. 25), where the contract being for 1100 pieces of timber, the first instalment of 750 pieces was rejected by the buyers; and arbitrator awarded "that the said shipment was, and is, so far from complying with the requirements of the said contract as to entitle the buyers to repudiate and to rescind the whole contract and to refuse to accept the said shipment and all further shipments under the said contract." The Court upheld the award. Bigham J. thus stated what in his opinion was the true test. "Thus if the breach is of such a kind, or takes place in such circumstances as reasonably to lead to the inference that similar breaches will be committed in relation to subsequent deliveries, the whole contract may there and then be regarded as repudiated and may be rescinded. If, for instance, a buyer fails to pay for one delivery in such circumstances as to lead to the inference that he will not be able to pay for subsequent deliveries; or if a seller delivers goods differing from the requirements of the contract, and does so in such circumstances as to lead to the inference that he cannot, or will not, deliver any other kind of goods in the future, the other contracting party will be under no obligation to wait to see what may happen; he can at once cancel the contract and rid himself of the difficulty" (14 Com. Cas. 29). Walton J. concurred.

This ruling was more recently applied in *Robert A. Munro & Co.* v. *Meyer* ([1930] 2 K. B. 312), where under a contract for the sale of 1500 tons of bone meal, 611 tons were delivered which were seriously adulterated. The sellers were middlemen, who relied on their suppliers, the manufacturers, for correct delivery; when the buyers discovered that the deliveries did not conform to the contract they claimed that they were entitled to treat the whole contract as repudiated by the sellers. It was held that they were right in so claiming, on the ground that "in such a case as this, where there is a persistent breach, deliberate so far as the manufacturers are concerned, continuing for nearly one-half of the total contract quantity, the buyer, if he ascertains in time what the position is, ought to be entitled to say that he will not take the risk of having put upon him further deliveries of this character" ([1930] 2 K. B. 331, per Wright J.). On the other hand in *Taylor* v. *Oakes Roncoroni & Co.* (27 Com. Cas. 261), Greer J., as he then was, and the Court of Appeal, declined to hold that the buyers were entitled to refuse to go on with the contract, but held that the breach was a severable breach, as it was a case "where the instalment delivered failed in a slight but appreciable degree to come up to the standard required by the contract description."

With the help of these authorities we deduce that the main tests to be considered in applying the sub-section to the present case are, first, the ratio quantitatively which the breach bears to the contract as a whole, and secondly the degree of probability or improbability that such a breach will be repeated. On the first point, the delivery complained of amounts to no more than $1\frac{1}{2}$ tons out of a contract for 100 tons. On the second point, our conclusion is that the chance of the breach being repeated is practically negligible. We assume that the sample found defective fairly represents the bulk; but bearing in mind the judge's finding that the breach was extraordinary and that the appellants' business was carefully conducted, bearing in mind also that the appellants were warned, and bearing in mind that the delivery complained of was an isolated instance out of 20 satisfactory deliveries actually made both before and after the instalment objected to, we hold that it cannot reasonably be inferred that similar breaches would occur in regard to subsequent deliveries. . . . We think the deciding factor here is the extreme improbability of the breach being repeated, and on that ground, and on the isolated and limited character of the breach complained of, there was, in our judgment, no sufficient justification to entitle the respondents to refuse further deliveries as they did.

The appeal must accordingly be allowed and judgment entered for the appellants, with costs here and below, for damages for their breach of contract in refusing further deliveries.

HELGAR CORPORATION *v.* WARNER'S FEATURES

NEW YORK COURT OF APPEALS, 1918

[222 *New York Reports*, 449]

CARDOZO, J. The plaintiff's assignor made a contract with the defendant for the sale of films for moving pictures. At least one film was to be delivered every month. Deliveries were to begin in November, 1913, and to end in October, 1914. The price was fixed at eight cents per foot; and payment for each film was to be made within thirty days after exhibition to the public. By way of additional compensation, the defendant was also to pay one-half of the net profits realized by it as the result of foreign sales.

The plaintiff, having received an assignment of the contract, delivered pictures of the value at the contract rate of nearly $10,000. The price was payable on December 24, 1913. The finding is that payment was then demanded, and that "the defendant refused and neglected to pay the same or any part thereof, nor did the defendant offer or tender a part payment of said amount or offer to pay the same in installments." Two days later this action was begun. The plaintiff alleged its election to terminate the contract by reason of the breach. Judgment was demanded for the price of the films delivered, and also for the profits that would have been gained through the completion of the contract. The referee gave judgment for the price, but refused to award the profits. In his opinion, he put his refusal upon the ground that the failure to make punctual payment was not accompanied by acts or words evincing repudiation or abandonment. The Appellate Division added $2,000 to the judgment. This was the estimated value of foreign rights which attached to the sales already made. That value was thought to be recoverable as an incident to the price. With this modification, the judgment was unanimously affirmed. There are cross-appeals in this court.

The rights of vendor and vendee upon the breach of an installment contract are now regulated by statute. The rule is to be found in section 126, subdivision 2, of the statute governing sales of goods (Personal Prop. Law, Consol. Laws, ch. 41; amd. L. 1911, ch. 571). . . .

The statute thus establishes a like test for vendor and for vendee. The earlier cases may not be wholly uniform (*Wharton & Co.* v. *Winch*, 140 N. Y. 287; *Kokomo Strawboard Co.* v. *Inman*, 134 N. Y. 92; *Wolfert* v. *Caledonia S. I. Co.*, 195 N. Y. 118). We do not need to reconcile them. We have departed from the rule of the English statute (56 & 57 Vict. ch. 71, § 31, subd. 2), which keeps the contract alive unless the breach is equivalent to repudiation (Note of Commissioners on Uniform Laws, American Uniform Commercial Acts, p. 98; Williston on Sales, pp. 809, 810; 25 Halsbury, Laws of England, p. 220). We have established a new test, which weighs the effect of the default, and adjusts the rigor of the remedy to the gravity of the wrong. "It depends in each case on the terms of the contract and the circumstances of the case" whether the breach is "so material" as to affect the contract as a whole.

The answer to that question must vary with the facts (Williston on Sales, p. 810). Default in respect of one installment, though falling short of repudiation, may under some conditions be so material that there should be an end to the obligation to keep the contract alive. Under other conditions, the default may be nothing but a technical omission to observe the letter of a promise (Williston on Sales, p. 823; *Nat. Machine & Tool Co.* v. *Standard S. M. Co.*, 181 Mass. 275, 279; *Wharton & Co.* v. *Winch*, *supra*). General statements abound that, at law, time is always of the essence (Williston, *supra; Norrington* v. *Wright*, 115 U. S. 188; *Booth* v. *S. D. Rolling Mills Co.*, 60 N. Y. 553; *Schmidt* v. *Reed*, 132 N. Y. 108). For some purposes this is still true. The vendor who fails to receive payment of an installment the very day that it is due, may sue at once for the price. But it does not follow that he may be equally precipitate in his election to declare the contract at an end (Williston, p. 823; *Beatty* v. *Howe Lumber Co.*, 77 Minn. 272, and cases there cited; *Graves* v. *White*, 87 N. Y. 463, 466). That depends upon the question whether the default is so substantial and important as in truth and in fairness to defeat the essential purpose of the parties. Whatever the rule may once have been, this is the test that is now prescribed by statute. The failure to make punctual payment may be material or trivial according to the circumstances. We must know the cause of the default, the length of the delay, the needs of the vendor, and the expectations of the vendee. If the default is the result of accident or misfortune, if there is a reasonable assurance that it will be promptly repaired, and if immediate payment is not necessary to enable the vendor to proceed with performance, there may be one conclusion. If the breach is willful, if there is no just ground to look for prompt reparation, if the delay has been substantial, or if the needs of the vendor are urgent so that continued performance is imperilled, in these and in other circumstances, there may be another conclusion. Sometimes the conclusion will follow from all the circumstances as an inference of law to be drawn by the judge; sometimes, as an inference of fact to be drawn by the jury.

The findings in this case do not enable us to say that the plaintiff was justified in its precipitate election to declare the contract at an end. There is a finding that payment was refused. That is inconclusive by itself. The refusal may have been nothing more than a declaration of inability to make payment on the instant. There is a finding that the defendant did not offer part payment or payment in installments. That again is inconclusive. It is not an ultimate, but at most an evidentiary fact. The circumstances may none the less have indicated a temporary default to be followed promptly by full payment. The referee must have interpreted the situation in that way for he states in his opinion that the default was not accompanied by any act or declaration that would indicate abandonment. If we were at liberty to look into the evidence and draw our own inferences, we might reach a contrary conclusion. But the evidence is not open to our scrutiny. The plaintiff has not requested the referee to find the ultimate fact on which the right to the recovery of profits depends. It has not requested a finding that the breach was so material as to justify its hasty election to declare the contract at an end. It has not requested a finding of the circumstances preceding or accompanying the default. There is not even a request which brings before us in due form the ruling that all profits must be excluded. The only request made specifies the extent of the loss, and includes elements of damage which the referee, in any view of the breach, was at liberty to reject. In these circumstances, we must hold the plaintiff to the rule which requires a request to find and an exception (*Sherman* v. *Foster*, 158 N. Y. 587, 597; *Ostrander* v. *Hart*, 130 N. Y. 406, 414; *Burnap* v. *Nat. Bank of Potsdam*, 96 N. Y. 125, 131; *Thomson* v. *Bank of B. N. A.*, 82 N. Y. 1; *Drake* v. *N. Y. Iron Mine*, 156 N. Y. 90). The findings as made leave the character of the default equivocal. In the absence of an appropriate request for other findings, the evidence is not before us. The rule would be different if we were asked to go behind the findings for the purpose of affirmance (*Ogden* v. *Alexander*, 140 N. Y. 356; *Ostrander* v. *Hart*, *supra*). The plaintiff asks us to go behind them for the purpose of reversal. Its appeal must, therefore, fail.

The defendant complains of the increase of the judgment directed at the Appellate Division. We think the increase was erroneous. We have seen that the plaintiff was not at liberty to treat the entire contract as broken. Its cause of action was limited to the recovery of payments in default. But there has thus far been no default in respect of foreign sales. No foreign sales have yet been made. The award in that respect is an estimate of sales to be made hereafter. Until the conditions prescribed by the contract have been satisfied, the extra compensation is not payable. The plaintiff's recovery must be limited to payments already due.

The judgment of the Appellate Division to the extent that it modifies the judgment entered on the report of the referee should be reversed, and the judgment entered upon such report affirmed, with costs in this court to the defendant.

HISCOCK, Ch. J., CHASE, HOGAN, POUND, McLAUGHLIN and ANDREWS, JJ., concur.

Judgment accordingly.

CZARNIKOW-RIONDA CO. *v.* WEST MARKET GROCERY CO.

UNITED STATES CIRCUIT COURT OF APPEALS, SECOND CIRCUIT, 1927

[21 *Federal Reporter* (*Second Series*), 309]

In Error to the District Court of the United States for the Southern District of New York.

Action by the West Market Grocery Company (formerly known as the Sheppard Strassheim Company) against the Czarnikow-Rionda Company. Judgment for plaintiff, and defendant brings error. Affirmed.

The parties will be referred to as plaintiff and defendant, in accordance with their relation to the litigation in the trial court.

The plaintiff was an Illinois corporation, engaged in business as a wholesale grocer in Chicago. The defendant was a New York corporation, engaged in the business of selling sugar. In April, 1920, the parties entered into a contract for the sale by defendant to plaintiff of a quantity of sugar described as "4,200 bags, eastern cane fine granulated Federal Sugar Refining Company brand." The price was $17 net per bag of 100 pounds, and delivery was to be f. o. b. refinery, New York. Shipments were to be made at seller's option during August, 1920. The contract provided that the buyer should establish in New York an irrevocable letter of credit, to be drawn against by the seller upon presentation of bills of lading.

Some time prior to August 18, 1920, defendant shipped at plaintiff's request one carload of 600 bags of the sugar to a company in Dayton, Ohio, to which plaintiff had sold this quantity. Payment for this carload was obtained by defendant by draft drawn against the aforesaid letter of credit. The remainder of the sugar, 3,600 bags (except for the shortage of one bag, of which no point is made), was shipped by defendant in six carloads, delivered to the railroad on several dates between August 20 and 24. The bills of lading were made to the order of defendant as consignee, notify plaintiff. Drafts for $61,183, the aggregate price of the 3,599 bags, were drawn by defendant and paid under the letter of credit. The six carloads of sugar arrived at Depot Harbor, Ontario, at various times, and were there placed on one boat and transported to Chicago where they arrived September 9, 1920.

Upon being notified of their arrival, plaintiff promptly made inspection, samples being drawn from many bags, and determined that the sugar was not merchantable or marketable as a standard eastern cane fine granulated sugar. Thereupon plaintiff promptly notified defendant of its rejection of the sugar and offered to return it. Defendant refused its return, and it was sold by plaintiff at the best price obtainable. The proceeds, subject to deductions for expenses, were credited to defendant, leaving a balance of approximately $27,000, which plaintiff claimed to be due and owing on account of its payments of the drafts drawn against the letter of credit when the sugar was shipped. The plaintiff made no offer to return to defendant the 600 bags previously shipped to plaintiff's Ohio customer.

After demand for payment and refusal by defendant, this suit was brought; jurisdiction of the federal court resting upon diversity of citizenship. By stipulation a jury was waived and the issues referred to a referee, to hear evidence and report findings of fact and conclusions of law. The referee found in favor of the plaintiff. The District Court, without opinion, confirmed the report, and judgment was entered accordingly.

Swan, Circuit Judge (after stating the facts as above). The main question presented on this writ of error raises an interesting point of law, but before reaching it the sufficiency of the evidence to prove one essential fact must be considered.

[One column of the opinion, holding that there was adequate proof of the inferior quality of 3,599 bags of sugar, is omitted here.]

This brings us to the proposition upon which the defendant places chief reliance for reversal of the judgment, namely, that the plaintiff could not rescind its contract as to the 3,599 bags complained of without returning also the 600 bags previously shipped under the contract to plaintiff's customer in Ohio. Argument has been ably presented by learned counsel to the effect that the contract for 4,200 bags was an entire and indivisible contract; that the common law of New York requires a buyer under such a contract to rescind *in toto,* if at all; and that the Uniform Sales Act (Consol. Laws N. Y. c. 41, art. 5), which is embodied in the Personal Property Law of the state, has not changed the common-law doctrine.

The plaintiff meets this argument by referring to section 125 of the Personal Property Law (Consol. Laws, c. 41) and the decision of *Portfolio* v. *Rubin,* 233 N. Y. 439, 135 N. E. 843. . . . The defendant contends, however, that section 125 and the Portfolio decision relate only to a single mixed delivery, of which part conforms to the contract and part does not, and that the statute and the decision have no bearing upon a contract which contemplates delivery in installments. It must be conceded that the Portfolio Case involved only a single mixed delivery. But that a different result would have been reached, had the four pieces of cloth been delivered at different hours of the day, and the first two pieces been accepted before the two defective pieces arrived, seems to us most unlikely. No adequate reason can be advanced for permitting rejection of the defective goods in the one case, but not in the other.

Section 125 was held applicable to an installment contract in *Guaranty Trust Co.* v. *Gerseta Corporation,* 212 App. Div. 76, 208 N. Y. S. 270. In fact, an installment contract, particularly where it is contemplated that a large total quantity shall be shipped at different times in carload lots, and to parties to whom the buyer may resell, as well as to the buyer himself, and that the seller shall draw drafts for the purchase price of each consignment as soon as shipped, seems to present a far stronger case for holding the contract divisible than did the facts in the Portfolio Case. That the doctrine there laid down should be so narrowly limited as to apply only to a single mixed delivery we cannot believe.

In this conclusion we are fortified by the English case of *Jackson* v. *Rotax Motor Co.*, [1910] 2 K. B. 937. The sellers (plaintiffs) were manufacturers of motor horns, in Paris. The buyers (defendants) were dealers in motor accessories in London. The buyers ordered from the sellers some 600 motor horns of various descriptions and prices. The order provided: "Delivery as required, usual terms 2½ per cent. franco franco London." At the buyers' request the goods were delivered to a particular firm of carriers. They were delivered in 19 cases at various dates in May and June, 1909. The first installment of four cases was accepted by the buyers, who had resold the goods in one of the cases. The cases shipped in subsequent installments were rejected when inspection, on the arrival of the last consignment, disclosed that a large portion were defective. The sellers sued for the full purchase price. The buyers paid into court the sum due for the first four cases. The trial court held for the plaintiffs, allowing a deduction to defendants for damages for the defective goods. In the Court of Appeals the judgment was reversed, all of the judges agreeing that the contract was divisible, and that acceptance of the first installment did not preclude rejection of the later defective installments. . . .

That interpretation of the contract seems to us equally applicable to the case at bar. The contract is divisible in the sense defined in the Portfolio Case; that is, the part to be performed by the seller consists of several distinct and separate items (installments), and the price to be paid by the buyer is apportioned to each item.

None of the later New York cases appear to us to be inconsistent with this view. While a contract for installment deliveries may be treated as an entire contract, when the issue is whether a failure by the seller or the buyer in respect to an early installment may be so material a breach of the contract as to justify the other party in refusing to perform in respect to later installments, as held in *Bahnsen & Co.* v. *Gerst*, 235 N. Y. 426, 139 N. E. 563, and *Ferguson* v. *Chuck*, 236 N. Y. 149, 140 N. E. 225, it does not necessarily follow that the contract is to be deemed entire when the issue is whether acceptance of an early installment precludes rejection of a later defective installment. Where this is the issue, we hold the contract before us divisible.

If the buyer is under no duty to accept and pay for a defective installment, it can hardly be doubted that, if he had paid for it in advance, he would have a right to recover such payment on the theory of failure of consideration.

It is urged that the plaintiff cannot recover its payment for the second installment without rescinding *in toto* and returning the 600 bags shipped to its Ohio customer. The argument is highly technical, for the seller is better off by retaining the contract price paid him for the 600 bags than he would be if they were returned and he were obliged to refund the price, which exceeded the market value, as found by the referee, at the date of the seller's default and continuously thereafter until September 18, 1920. Under such circumstances it may perhaps be doubted whether a rescinding buyer must return in kind the first installment, even if the contract were nondivisible. See *Norrington* v. *Wright*, 115 U. S. 188, 205, 6 S. Ct. 12, 29 L. Ed. 366. But this need not be decided, because, as we have held above, the contract for the sugar is divisible in respect to the installments. Under such circumstances, the power of rescission exists as to each installment. . . .

The judgment is therefore affirmed, with costs.

BALLANTINE AND CO. *v.* CRAMP AND BOSMAN

KING'S BENCH DIVISION, 1923

[129 *Law Times Reports*, 502]

[Only the opinion is given.]

McCARDIE, J. This is a special case stated by the parties under Order XXXIV. of the Rules of the Supreme Court, and it raises several points of practical interest upon the effect in law of a contract made between the parties. The bargain related to the sale of frozen meat. It was made in writing on the 8th Dec. 1920, when the plaintiffs sold to the defendants a quantity of 2500 carcases of New Zealand sheep. The material terms of the contract are these: first, the weight of the carcases was to be under 72 lb.; secondly, the average was not to exceed 60 lb.; shipment to be not later than the 30th June 1921. Amongst the further terms were these: "Each month's or steamer's contract to be considered as a separate contract"; and insurance was to be effected at a certain amount; and then "payment net cash against documents on arrival of steamer or steamers at port of discharge." Then, omitting several immaterial provisions, there is this further statement, that "Notices of claims, if any, to be handed to us" that is, the vendors, "in writing within twenty-one days after final discharge of vessel carrying the goods." Now that is the bargain, and the facts are most concisely stated in this special case. What happened was that the vendors sent forward a quantity of meat in two ships; the first was the *Whakatane* steamship, and she carried 1092 carcases of a total weight of 68,597 lb. at an average of 62.81 lb. per carcase. The other vessel was the *Port Caroline*, and she carried 1494 carcases of a total weight of 79,820 lb. at an average per carcase of 53.43 lbs. If you take the two ships together, the average per carcase was 57.77. But now what happened was this, that the *Whakatane* arrived in London in the month of Aug. 1921; all her goods had been shipped within the contract period, and the day after the arrival of that vessel the plaintiffs tendered certain documents to the defendants and required the defendants to pay 2500*l.* 18*s.* 7*d.* for them. The contract, as is clear, was c.i.f. contract. The documents revealed the fact that the meat upon the carcases was of the average weight of 62.81 lb. per carcase. That is above the average of 60 lb. mentioned in the contract; and thereupon for that reason the buyers refused the documents. They alleged that the tender was bad. The plaintiffs did not accept the view of the buyers. They sold the goods, with the result that a loss accrued of 510*l.* 1*s.* 3*d.*, which is now sought as damages against the buyers. That is what occurred with regard to the *Whakatane.* Two months later, namely, on the 4th Oct. 1921, the *Port Caroline* arrived, and she carried on board the goods I have mentioned of the average weight of 53.43 lb. per carcase. The plaintiffs tendered the documents to the defendants; the defendants took them up and paid for them, and no further question arises as to those.

The serious question at issue is whether or not the buyers were entitled to refuse the tender of the *Whakatane* documents and goods. The argument for the sellers is that the court must look, not at the average weight of the goods on board the *Whakatane,* but must look also at the average weight of the goods on the *Port Caroline* which arrived a couple of months later. The buyers, on the other hand, say that upon the proper interpretation of this bargain regard must be had to the average weight of the meat upon the *Whakatane* as tendered to them in August, 1921. The point at issue, in my view, is not peculiar to this contract at all, because it is a point that is common to a vast number of contracts of this description. The question is, what is the proper meaning of this bargain? In the first place I take it to be clear that the words "average not to exceed 60 lb." constitutes a part of the description of the goods. That seems clear upon the cases of *Manbre Saccharine Company* v. *Corn Products Company* (120 L. T. Rep. 113; (1919) 1 K. B. at p. 20), and *Moore and Co. Limited* v. *Landauer and Co.* (125 L. T. Rep. 372; (1921) 2 K. B. at p. 524).

The next question is as to whether this contract is to be deemed a divisible contract and divisible in the sense that with respect to each part of the contract, each stage of performance, the sellers must comply with their obligations. In my view, this contract is in substance an instalment contract. The effect of the words "each month's or steamer's contract to be considered as a separate contract" is to provide that under the one contract there may be different stages of performance. It is for practical purposes to be deemed an instalment contract within sect. 31 of the Sale of Goods Act 1893. With regard to a contract of that description, I think Mr. Benjamin's book rightly describes it at p. 816 of the sixth edition as a contract which is a contract for the whole quantity, though it is divisible in performance. If it be a divisible contract, then there arises a question as to the obligations of the vendors with regard to each stage of the performance, and in my opinion the burden rests upon the vendor, if he elects, as he may, to fulfil his contract by different steamers, to provide that the shipment on each steamer shall comply with the requirement that the average is not to exceed 60 lb. Unless that effect be given to it, I am unable to see how the contract could satisfactorily work in practice. It is to be noticed that the last clause of the contract is "notice of claims, if any, to be handed to us in writing within 21 days after final discharge of vessel carrying the goods," and it is very difficult to see how that clause could apply at all if the contention of the vendor is correct. Further, if one takes another illustration, namely, the case where goods are delivered in five instalments, it would be of interest to reflect upon the position of the buyer if the contention of the vendor is correct. Suppose the first instalment was 65 lb., that second, third and fourth instalments a like weight, what is the buyer to do? Is he merely to hope that the average may conceivably be made up by the fifth instalment to be delivered by the vendor? Quite apart from such an illustration as that, it seems to me that one must look at the practical working of this matter. The buyer would resell; he would make a sale to arrive. And it seems to me that if, as is quite common, those resales are to be made the buyer would require with respect to each shipment the fulfilment of the obligation that the average is not to exceed 60 lb. Both upon the wording of the contract and upon the practical considerations applicable to it, illustrated by what I have just said, I am of opinion that the buyers were right in this case in rejecting the goods.

[The last page of the opinion is omitted.]

The result is, therefore, upon these questions put before me, I am of opinion that there must be judgment for the defendants with costs.

Action dismissed.

In ROBERT A. MUNRO AND COMPANY, LIMITED *v.* MEYER, [1930] 2 K. B. 312 (King's Bench Division, 1930), which was summarized briefly in *Maple Flock Company, Limited* v. *Universal Furniture Products (Wembley) Limited*, *supra*, p. 367, the contract contained the following clause: "Each delivery or shipment shall be treated as a separate contract, and the failure to give or to take any delivery or shipment shall not cancel the contract as to future deliveries or shipments." The sellers claimed that the effect of this clause was to prevent the buyers from repudiating as to subsequent shipments despite defects in shipments already made. Wright, J., said on this point: "The next contention of the plaintiffs is based upon the provision in the contract that 'Each delivery or shipment shall be treated as a separate contract, and the failure to give or to take any delivery or shipment shall not cancel the contract as to future deliveries or shipments.' That is a clause which is often found in contracts of this description and which is very difficult to construe, or at least to apply to all possible emergencies. It seems to me, however, that whatever effect it may have — and I am not going to attempt to exhaust the possibilities of this clause — it cannot be construed so as to defeat the rights of the buyer under s. 31 of the Sale of Goods Act. The matter can be tested by a very simple illustration. Suppose the seller in the middle of performing the contract said in terms that he would not in any circumstances make any further deliveries, would the buyer then be bound to wait until each delivery became due, and then, if and when it was not delivered, and then only, be entitled to bring his action? In my opinion this clause could not operate so as to prevent the buyer in such circumstances from bringing his action, if he were so minded, so soon as the complete and positive refusal to fulfil the contract was expressed; but the rule under s. 31, sub-s. 2, of the Sale of Goods Act is only a method of giving effect to the same principle as would arise in the case of a definite and express refusal; because the acts of the seller in such a case are treated as being equivalent to declaring that he will not fulfil the contract, that is, a refusal. It appears to me, therefore, that this clause, whatever it may mean, has nothing to say to the particular question at issue here."

Compare Higgin *v.* Pumpherston Oil Company, Limited, 20 Session Cases 532 (Court of Session, 1893), where a contract for the sale of twenty tons of paraffin wax in twelve monthly shipments contained a similar clause. One ton was delivered after six months, and two tons more after eight months. At the end of a year the buyer demanded delivery of the remaining seventeen tons, and on refusal of the sellers to deliver more than two tons brought an action for damages. In giving judgment for the sellers the Court held that the effect of the clause was that if the sellers failed to deliver a monthly quantity it became the duty of the buyer to buy in against them for the quantity in question.

3. QUALITY

A. Implied Warranties and Conditions

EICHHOLZ *v.* BANNISTER

Exchequer Chamber, 1864

[17 *Common Bench* (*New Series*), 708]

[Preliminary statement of facts and arguments of counsel are omitted.]

Erle, C. J. I am of opinion that this rule should be discharged. The plaintiff brings his action to recover back money which he paid for goods bought by him in the shop of the defendant, which were afterwards lawfully claimed from him by a third person, the true owner, from whom they had been stolen. The plaintiff now claims to recover back the money as having been paid by him upon a consideration which has failed. The jury at the trial found a verdict for the plaintiff, under the direction of the learned judge who presided; and a rule has been obtained on behalf of the defendant to set aside that verdict and to enter a nonsuit, on the ground that it is part of the common law of England that the vendor of goods by the mere contract of sale does not warrant his title to the goods he sells, that the buyer takes them at his peril, and that the rule *caveat emptor* applies. The case has been remarkably well argued on both sides; and the court are much indebted to the learned counsel for the able assistance they have rendered to them. The result I have arrived at, is, that the plaintiff is entitled to retain his verdict. I consider it to be clear upon the ancient authorities, that, if the vendor of a chattel by word or conduct gives the purchaser to understand that he is the owner, that tacit representation forms part of the contract, and that, if he is not the owner, his contract is broken. So is the law laid down in the very elaborate judgment of Parke, B., in *Morley* v. *Attenborough,* 3 Exch. 500, 513, where that learned judge puts the case upon which I ground my judgment. A difference is taken in some of the cases between a warranty and a condition (see *Bannerman* v. *White,* 10 C. B. (N. S.) 844): but that is foreign to the present inquiry. In *Morley* v. *Attenborough,* 3 Exch. 513, Parke, B., says: "We do not suppose that there would be any doubt, if the articles are bought in a shop professedly carried on for the sale of goods, that the shopkeeper must be considered as warranting that those who purchase will have a good title to keep the goods purchased. In such a case the vendor sells 'as his own,' and that is what is equivalent to a warranty of title." No doubt, if a shopkeeper in words or by his conduct affirms at the time of the sale that he is the owner of the goods, such affirmation becomes part of the contract, and, if it turns out that he is not the owner, so that the goods are lost to the buyer, the price which he has received may be recovered back. I ventured to throw out some remarks in the course of the argument upon the doctrine relied on by Mr. Holker, which he answered by assertion after assertion coming no doubt from judges of great authority in the law, to the effect that upon a sale of goods there is no implied warranty of title. The passage cited from Noy certainly puts the proposition in a manner that must shock the understanding of any ordinary person. But I take the principle intended to be illustrated to be this, — I am in possession of a horse or other chattel: I neither affirm or deny that I am the owner: if you choose to take it as it is, without more, *caveat emptor*: you have no remedy, though it should turn out that I have no title. Where that is the whole of the transaction, it may be that there is no warranty of title. Such seems to have been the principle on which *Morley* v. *Attenborough* was decided. The pawnbroker, when he sells an unredeemed pledge, virtually says, — I have under the provisions of the statute (39 & 40 G. 3, c. 99, s. 17) a right to sell. If you choose to buy the article, it is at your own peril. So, in the case of the sale by the sheriff of goods seized under a *fi. fa.*, — *Chapman* v. *Speller*, 14 Q. B. 621. The fact of the sale taking place under such circumstances is notice to buyers that the sheriff has no knowledge of the title to the goods; and the buyers consequently buy at their own peril. Many contracts of sale tacitly express the same sort of disclaimer of warranty. In this sense it is that I understand the decision of this court in *Hall* v. *Conder*, 2 C. B. (N. S.) 22. There, the plaintiff merely professed to sell the patent-right such as he had it, and the court held that the contract might still be enforced, though the patent was ultimately defeated on the ground of want of novelty. The thing which was the subject of the contract there was not matter, it was rather in the nature of mind. These are some of the cases where the conduct of the seller expresses at the time of the contract that he merely contracts to sell such a title as he himself has in the thing. But, in almost all the transactions of sale in common life, the seller by the very act of selling holds out to the buyer that he is the owner of the article he offers for sale. The sale of a chattel is the strongest act of dominion that is incidental to ownership. A purchaser under ordinary circumstances would naturally be led to the conclusion, that, by offering an article for sale, the seller affirms that he has title to sell, and that the buyer may enjoy that for which he parts with his money. Such a case falls within the doctrine stated by Blackstone, and is so recognized by Littledale, J., in *Early* v. *Garrett*, 9 B. & C. 928, 4 M. & R. 687, and by Parke, B., in *Morley* v. *Attenborough*, 3 Exch. 513. I think justice and sound sense require us to limit the doctrine so often repeated, that there is no implied warranty of title on the sale of a chattel. I cannot but take notice, that, after all the research of two very learned counsel, the only semblance of authority for this doctrine from the time of Noy and Lord Coke consists of mere dicta. These dicta, it is true, appear to have been adopted by several learned judges, amongst others by my excellent Brother Williams, whose words are almost obligatory on me: but I cannot find a single instance in which it has been more than a repetition of barren sounds, never resulting in the fruit of a judgment. This very much tends to shew the wisdom of Lord Campbell's remark in *Sims Marryat*, 17 Q. B. 291, that the rule is beset with so many exceptions that they well nigh eat it up. It is to be hoped that the notion which has so long prevailed will now pass away, and that no further impediment will be placed in the way of a buyer recovering back money which he has parted with upon a consideration which has failed.

[Concurring opinions of Byles, J., and Keating, J., are here omitted.]

Rule discharged.

JONES *v.* JUST

QUEEN'S BENCH, 1868

[*Law Reports,* 3 *Queen's Bench,* 197]

The judgment of the Court (Cockburn, C. J., Blackburn and Mellor, JJ.), was delivered by

MELLOR, J. In this case, on the trial before Blackburn, J., at Liverpool, it appeared that the plaintiffs, through Messrs. Beneke & Co., their brokers, entered into a contract with the defendant for the purchase of a quantity of Manilla hemp, to arrive.

The sold note was in the following terms: —

Liverpool, 19th Oct., 1865.

We have this day sold for you the following goods to Messrs. J. A. Beneke & Co. J.H.V. 200 bales Manilla hemp, expected to arrive p. *Richard Cobden,* @ Singapore, for Liverpool, . . . 309 . . . expected to arrive pr. *Christopher Newton,* @ Singapore for Liverpool, . . . 209 . . . expected to arrive pr. *Fortitude* . . . @ Singapore for London, {H 193 / H H 1} . . . expected to arrive pr. *Opher,* @ Singapore for Liverpool, @ 38*l.* 10*s.* pr. ton of 2240 lbs., cost freight and insurance. Shipping weights. Payment, cash against shipping documents on 21st Oct. 1865, less 2½% discount.

The shipping documents were duly delivered to the plaintiffs, and the price was paid. All the vessels named in the contract arrived in due course, with the respective numbers of bales of hemp having marks corresponding to those specified in the contract on board; and the bales were delivered to the plaintiffs. On examination of the bales it was found that the whole of those marked J.H.V. were in such a state as to afford strong evidence that they had at sometime, probably from a shipwreck when on the voyage from Manilla to Singapore, been wetted through with salt water, had afterwards been unpacked and dried, and then repacked in the bales which were afterwards shipped at Singapore.

Manilla hemp is divided into several qualities. The hemp in the bales in question, if in good condition, would have been what is called "fair current Manilla hemp," which is not the lowest quality; but in all the bales the hemp was damaged to some extent, though not so far as to make it lose the character of hemp.

After some correspondence between the parties, the hemp was sold by auction by the plaintiffs' orders as "Manilla hemp, with all faults," and at the auction it realised about 75 per cent. of the price which similar hemp would have fetched if undamaged. The price of hemp had risen considerably since the contract, so that the proceeds of the sale were very nearly equal to the invoice price. There was no attempt to shew that the defendant knew of the state in which the hemp had been shipped at Singapore.

At the close of the plaintiffs' case, Mr. Brett, for the defendant, contended that, in point of law, under this written contract, there was no further condition of warranty than that the bales on their arrival should answer the description of bales of Manilla hemp, which they did, as was proved by the fact that the hemp, though sold with a stigma upon it, fetched a price only 25 per cent. below that of sound hemp; and that as to quality or condition there was no warranty; that consequently the maxim *caveat emptor* applied.

The learned judged expressed an opinion adverse to this view. He said: —"I think that the question is for the jury, whether what was supplied under this contract was, when shipped at Singapore, such as to answer the description of reasonably merchantable Manilla hemp, that being the warranty which, I think, the law implies in a contract to supply, as this is: though it would be different in a sale of specific things which the purchaser might examine, or of things sold by sample. And I think the question whether it is fairly and reasonably merchantable, is a question of more or less, which must be left to the jury as reasonable men to determine." The judge then reserved leave to move to enter the verdict for the defendant, if there was no evidence to go to the jury of a breach of warranty.

Upon this intimation of opinion, the counsel addressed the jury, and the case was left to them substantially to the effect above stated; and the jury were further told that if they found for the plaintiffs, the damages should be measured by the rate which the hemp was worth when it arrived compared with the rate which the same hemp would have realised had it been shipped in the state in which it ought to have been shipped: thus, in effect, giving the plaintiffs the benefit of the rise in the market.

The jury found for the plaintiffs, damages 756*l.*

Mr. Brett, in the ensuing Term, obtained a rule to enter the verdict for the defendant, pursuant to the leave reserved; or for a new trial, on the ground of misdirection as to the measure of damages, which he contended ought at most to have been the difference between the value of the article actually delivered, *viz.*, fair average Manilla hemp in a damaged state, and the value of sound Manilla hemp of the lowest quality which might have been supplied at Singapore under this contract. The other objections to the direction were substantially only varied modes of putting the point reserved.

We thought that if the contract had the effect which the direction stated it to have, the true measure of the damages was given, as it put the plaintiffs in the position in which they would have been if the contract had been fulfilled; but we took time to consider the question as to what the contract really was, which is no doubt one of importance and difficulty.

After careful consideration, we are of opinion that Blackburn, J.'s direction was substantially correct. On the argument before us, it was contended that the contract was performed on the part of the defendant by the shipping at Singapore of an article which answered the description of "Manilla hemp," although at that time it was so damaged as to have become unmerchantable. It was said that there being no fraud on the part of the vendor, and both parties being equally ignorant of the past history and actual condition of the article contracted for, and neither of them having had the opportunity of inspecting it, it was the duty of the vendees to have stipulated for a merchantable article if that was what they intended to contract for. In other words, it was said that the maxim, *caveat emptor*, applied in such a case, in the same way as on a sale of a specific article by a person not being the manufacturer or producer, even though the defect was latent and not discoverable upon examination.

We are of opinion that there is a great distinction between the present case and the sale of goods *in esse*, which the buyer may inspect, and in which a latent defect may exist, although not discoverable on inspection. The cases which bear upon the subject do not appear to be in conflict, when the circumstances of each are considered. They may, we think, be classified as follows: —

First, where goods are *in esse*, and may be inspected by the buyer, and there is no fraud on the part of the seller, the maxim *caveat emptor* applies, even though the defect which exists in them is latent, and not discoverable on examination, at least where the seller is neither the grower nor the manufacturer: *Parkinson* v. *Lee* (2 East, 314). The buyer in such a case has the opportunity of exercising his judgment upon the matter; and if the result of the inspection be unsatisfactory, or if he distrusts his own judgment he may if he chooses require a warranty. In such a case, it is not an implied term of the contract of sale that the goods are of any particular quality or are merchantable. So in the case of the sale in a market of meat, which the buyer had inspected, but which was in fact diseased, and unfit for food, although that fact was not apparent on examination, and the seller was not aware of it, it was held that there was no implied warranty that it was fit for food, and that the maxim *caveat emptor* applied: *Emmerton* v. *Mathews* (7 H. & N. 586; 31 L. J. (Ex.) 139).

Secondly, where there is a sale of a definite existing chattel specifically described, the actual condition of which is capable of being ascertained by either party, there is no implied warranty: *Barr* v. *Gibson* (3 M. & W. 390).

Thirdly, where a known described and defined article is ordered of a manufacturer, although it is stated to be required by the purchaser for a particular purpose, still if the known, described, and defined thing be actually supplied, there is no warranty that it shall answer the particular purpose intended by the buyer: *Chanter* v. *Hopkins* (4 M. & W. 399), *Ollivant* v. *Bayley* (5 Q. B. 288).

Fourthly, where a manufacturer or a dealer contracts to supply an article which he manufactures or produces, or in which he deals, to be applied to a particular purpose, so that the buyer necessarily trusts to the judgment or skill of the manufacturer or dealer, there is in that case an implied term or warranty that it shall be reasonably fit for the purpose to which it is to be applied: *Brown* v. *Edgington* (2 Man. & G. 279), *Jones* v. *Bright* (5 Bing. 533). In such a case the buyer trusts to the manufacturer or dealer, and relies upon his judgment and not upon his own.

Fifthly, where a manufacturer undertakes to supply goods, manufactured by himself, or in which he deals, but which the vendee has not had the opportunity of inspecting, it is an implied term in the contract that he shall supply a merchantable article: *Laing* v. *Fidgeon* (4 Camp. 169; 6 Taunt. 108). And this doctrine has been held to apply to the sale by the builder of an existing barge, which was afloat but not completely rigged and furnished; there, inasmuch as the buyer had only seen it when built, and not during the course of the building, he was considered as having relied on the judgment and skill of the builder that the barge was reasonably fit for use: *Shepherd* v. *Pybus* (3 Man. & G. 868).

If, therefore, it must be taken as established that, on the sale of goods by a manufacturer or dealer to be applied to a particular purpose, it is a term in the contract that they shall reasonably answer that purpose, and that on the sale of an article by a manufacturer to a vendee who has not had the opportunity of inspecting it during the manufacture, that it shall be reasonably fit for use, or shall be merchantable, as the case may be, it is difficult to understand why a similar term is not to be implied on a sale by a merchant to a merchant or dealer who has had no opportunity of inspection. . . .

We are aware of no case in which the maxim, *caveat emptor*, has been applied where there has been no opportunity of inspection, or where that opportunity had not been waived. . . .

In general, on the sale of goods by a partciular description, whether the vendee is able to inspect them or not, it is an implied term of the contract that they shall reasonably answer such description, and if they do not, it is unnecessary to put any other question to the jury. . . .

It appears to us that, in every contract to supply goods of a specified description which the buyer has no opportunity to inspect, the goods must not only in fact answer the specific description, but must also be saleable or merchantable under that description. In the words of Lord Ellenborough in *Gardiner* v. *Gray* (4 Camp. at p. 145), "Without any particular warranty this is an implied term in every such contract." In the present case the question appears to be, was the article as delivered at Singapore merchantable or saleable in the market under the description of "Manilla hemp"? Blackburn, J., appears to have divided that question into two, *viz.*: — Was the article, in fact, Manilla hemp? Secondly, was it merchantable? The precise mode of submitting the question is not material, provided the substantial direction was correct, as we think it was. . . .

It was contended further by the defendant's counsel that the shippers at Singapore were the persons who selected the goods in question, and that the defendant, who merely sold them to arrive, was as little aware of their true condition when shipped as the plaintiffs; but it is clear that the defendant, if not directly connected with the shippers as his correspondents, must at least have purchased from them, and had recourse against them for not supplying an article reasonably merchantable.

The remarks of Cockburn, C. J., on the argument in *Bigge* v. *Parkinson* (H. 7 & N. at p. 959), though not in terms repeated by him in delivering the judgment of the Court of Exchequer Chamber, are really involved in it, and are very closely in point here.

We are therefore of opinion that Blackburn, J.'s direction was right, and that this rule must be discharged.

Rule discharged.

Chalmers, *Sale of Goods Act*, 203 (11th ed., 1931), writes as follows: "The term 'warranty' seems to have been imported into the law of contract from the old law of conveyancing, where it signified an express or implied covenant by the grantor of real estate, to indemnify the grantee if he should be evicted.

"Its meaning has been considerably widened in the law of contract, and it is now a term of very uncertain signification.

"It is sometimes used as strictly equivalent to condition precedent, though it is sometimes sought to contrast it with condition precedent, or rather with a certain kind of condition precedent, namely, a promissory condition precedent. When used in the latter sense the distinction between 'condition' and 'warranty' corresponds with the distinction drawn by the older cases between what were known as 'dependent' and 'independent' covenants or promises.

"In insurance law its use is curious. When it relates to any undertaking by the assured it is used to denote a condition precedent of the strictest kind, the breach of which destroys the contract, as in the case of a sailing warranty. But the term is also used as a mere term of exclusion or limitation, as where goods are insured, warranted free from particular average under 3 per cent.

"The chief controversy over the proper meaning of the term 'warranty' has arisen in the law of sale, and the ambiguity of its use appears to result from the want of clear distinction in English law between sale — *i.e.* the transfer of property in a thing — and the contract by which that transfer is effected. The term is used in two different senses, and judges and text writers continually oscillate between them.

"First, the term 'warranty' is opposed to the term 'condition precedent,' and denotes a stipulation in a contract of sale, the breach of which gives rise to a claim for damages, but not to a right to reject the goods and treat the contract as repudiated. This is the meaning which, after much consideration, has been adopted by the Act as regards England and Ireland (see sects. 11 and 62) (but note the saving for Scotland in those sections). The objection to this use of the term appears to be that it does not cover the whole field of independent stipulations. For instance, where there is a contract for instalment deliveries the obligation to pay for a particular instalment may be an independent promise, but it would not ordinarily be called a warranty.

"Secondly, the term 'warranty' is used to denote any auxiliary stipulation in a contract of sale, and in particular a stipulation relating to the title to, or the quality, condition, or fitness of, goods contracted to be sold. In this sense of the term a breach of warranty may give rise either to a mere claim for damages, or to a right to reject the goods, and treat the contract as repudiated according as the goods may have been accepted or not.

"The weight of judicial authority is in favour of the first meaning, though etymologically and historically the second meaning appears more correct. [Warranty = Guarantee.] The objection to this use of the term is that it does not mark the distinction between a condition precedent and a collateral promise or undertaking. Using the term in the first sense, it is to be noted that many stipulations which in their inception are conditions (*i.e.* the implied undertakings as to merchantableness and fitness for a particular purpose) may become contracted into warranties by virtue of subsequent events, and this fact doubtless explains much of the confusion of language which the term has given rise to."

In notes to CUTTER *v.* POWELL, 2 Smith's Leading Cases at p. 20 (8th American edition, 1885), the annotator says: "A warranty properly so called, can only exist where the subject-matter of the sale is ascertained and existing, so as to be capable of being inspected at the time of the contract, and is a collateral engagement that the specific thing so sold possesses certain qualities; but the property passing by the contract of sale [*Dixon* v. *Yates*, 5 B. &. Ad. 313; *Gilmour* v. *Supple*, 11 Moo. P. C. C. 551], a breach of the warranty cannot entitle the vendee to rescind the contract, and revest the property in the vendor, without his consent; the vendee must therefore resort to an action for such breach, or give it in evidence in reduction of the price, or as an answer to the action if the breach renders the article wholly worthless.

"But where the subject-matter of the sale is not in existence, or not ascertained at the time of the contract, an engagement that it shall, when existing or ascertained, possess certain qualities, is not a [mere] warranty but a condition, the performance of which is precedent to any obligation upon the vendee under the contract, because the existence of those qualities being part of the description of the thing sold, becomes essential to its identity, and the vendee cannot be obliged to receive and pay for a thing different from that for which he contracted."

In T. & J. HARRISON *v.* KNOWLES & FOSTER, [1917] 2 K. B. 606 (King's Bench Division), Bailhache, J., said: "I proceed, therefore, to the difficult task of deciding between condition and warranty, and I have come to the conclusion that the rule to apply is that where the subject-matter of a contract of sale is a specific existing chattel a statement as to some quality possessed by or attaching to such chattel is a warranty, and not a condition, unless the absence of such quality or the possession of it to a smaller extent makes the thing sold different in kind from the thing as described in the contract."

In CHANTER *v.* HOPKINS, 4 M. & W. 399 (Exchequer, 1838), Lord Abinger, C. B., said: "A good deal of confusion has arisen in many of the cases on this subject, from the unfortunate use made of the word 'warranty.' Two things have been confounded together. A warranty is an express or implied statement of something which the party undertakes shall be part of a contract; and though part of the contract, yet collateral to the express object of it. But in many of the cases, some of which have been referred to, the circumstance of a party selling a particular thing by its proper description, has been called a warranty; and a breach of such contract, a breach of warranty; but it would be better to distinguish such cases as a non-compliance with a contract which a party has engaged to fulfil; as, if a man offers to buy peas of another, and he send him beans, he does not perform his contract; but that is not a warranty; there is no warranty that he should sell him peas; the contract is to sell peas, and if he sells him any thing else in their stead, it is a non-performance of it. So if a man were to order copper for sheathing ships — that is a particular copper, prepared in a particular manner; if the seller sends him a different sort, in that case he does not comply with the contract: and though this may have been considered a warranty, and may have been ranged under the class of cases relating to warranties, yet it is not properly so."

Williston, 1 *Sales* 331 (2nd ed., 1924), comments as follows: "It will be noticed that Lord Abinger does not make use of the word 'condition,' he is concerned in defining warranty, and endeavoring to bring out the point that a warranty is collateral to the express object of the contract in modern parlance. The obligation of the seller in such a case as that which is put by Lord Abinger is now, however, frequently called a condition, and this terminology is made use of in the Sale of Goods Act. It is obvious in the case supposed of a contract to buy and sell peas, if the buyer authorizes the seller to appropriate peas to the bargain, and thereby transfer the property in them, it is a condition precedent to the transfer of title that the goods which the seller attempts to appropriate to the bargain shall be peas, in the same sense that it is a condition precedent to the formation of a simple contract that the parties assent to the same thing; or in the same sense that it is a condition precedent to the liability of a principal that an agent act within the scope of his authority. It is not, however, properly a condition of the buyer's obligation to accept peas or to pay the price; beans are simply not within the terms of the buyer's contract, as Lord Abinger says. Still less is the obligation of the seller either a condition or subject to a condition. He has promised to sell peas, and the failure to perform that promise, whether accompanied with an offer to furnish beans or any other vegetable, is a breach of his promise. It is unnecessary to argue at this point whether this promise of the seller is properly called a warranty. The essential thing to bring out is that it is a promise. The buyer's promise is indeed impliedly conditional on the performance by the seller of his promise, and this is so provided in subsection (2) of the section of the Sales Act under consideration, but this is the general rule in the law of sales, and to call the seller's obligation in this kind of case a condition merely because of the mutual dependency of the buyer's and seller's promises is wholly to confuse legal terminology. In the Sales Act, therefore, and in this book, the word condition is never used in the sense of promise."

Continuing, Williston, *supra*, says of warranty: "There is no more troublesome word in the law than the word 'warranty.' It is constantly used in different senses. It is a common term in the law of insurance, the law of charter parties, and the law of sales. In an insurance policy, the insured can hardly be regarded as making any promises, yet certain provisions in insurance policies are commonly denominated warranties. The effect of calling a provision in an insurance policy a warranty is not that the insured can be sued for breaking a promise, but that the insurer is excused from the performance of his promise; that is, the so-called warranty is in fact a condition qualifying the liability of the insurer.

"In the law of charter parties, warranty has a wider sense. If a vessel is warranted seaworthy or warranted to be at a certain place, and the vessel is not seaworthy or is not at that place, the effect is two-fold. The charterer may sue the owner of the vessel for breach of a promise and, furthermore, the charterer is himself excused from performing his promise; that is, warranty means not only a promise but also that the promise is so essential that performance of it is a condition precedent to the obligation of the other party. Where the word is used in mercantile contracts other than contracts to sell or sales, this is the meaning ordinarily given to it.

"In the law of sales in England a third meaning is given to warranty; namely, 'an agreement with reference to goods which are the subject of a contract of sale but collateral to the main purpose of such contract, the breach of which gives rise to a claim for damages but not to a right to reject the goods and treat the contract as repudiated.' That is, the warranty is a promise, but performance of the promise is not a condition.

"This variety of meaning attached to the word 'warranty' is a source of confusion, and it is obviously a service to the law to limit the word to one meaning. Accordingly in the Sales Act the word is limited to what is probably its essential meaning — a material promise. It makes no difference under the Sales Act whether this promise is or is not collateral, and as provided in a later portion of the Sales Act, a breach of warranty in a contract to sell or a sale is followed by the same consequences as the breach of a material promise in other contracts; namely, the innocent party has a right to rescind or repudiate the transaction. What promises may be called collateral is indeed so difficult a question that the results reached under the English law cannot always be reconciled with the general statements of the rules of that law. It is believed that no greater simplification can be made in the law of sales than to make it of no importance whether an obligation which forms part of a bargain is collateral or not; and that this simplification is obtained without danger of injustice."

BENABU AND CO. *v.* THE PRODUCE BROKERS' COMPANY, LIMITED

COURT OF APPEAL, 1921

[37 *Times Law Reports*, 851]

This was an appeal from a decision of Mr. Justice Shearman in favour of the buyers, the Produce Brokers' Company, Limited (37 The Times L. R., 609).

On August 19, 1918, the sellers, Messrs. Benabu and Co., sold to the buyers 85 tons of Portuguese locust beans in bags, per steamship Luzo, afloat from Portugal, payment by cash in London on arrival of steamer against documents. In fact the vessel had, without the knowledge of either sellers or buyers, arrived and discharged the goods before the date of the contract. The buyers took up the documents and afterwards discovered that the Luzo had arrived and discharged her cargo some days before the date of the contract. Thereupon they claimed to reject the goods. When the matter was referred to arbitration an award was made in favour of the buyers, but on appeal to the Board of Appeal this decision was reversed, the Board holding that the buyers were not entitled to reject the goods, but that the sellers must pay certain landing and warehousing charges. A case was stated for the opinion of the High Court, and Mr. Justice Shearman held (*inter alia*) that the contract was perfectly free from ambiguity and that the word "afloat" was clearly intended to be a condition and not a mere warranty, with the result that the buyers were justified in rejecting the goods.

From this decision the sellers appealed to the Court of Appeal.

The Court dismissed the appeal.

Lord Justice BANKES said that two short points were raised in this appeal — first, as to the true construction of the contract; and, secondly, assuming the construction contended for by the buyers to be the correct one, whether the expression in the contract "afloat" was a condition precedent. On the question of construction the contract was fairly plain to anyone reading it, and as to the word "afloat" it was used in reference to the goods and not to the ship. The question, therefore, was whether the buyers were entitled to reject the goods or whether they had a right only to damages. In his opinion, looking at the contract itself, the word "afloat" constituted a condition precedent, for the fact that the goods were at sea would make a difference in various ways, as, for example, there might be a necessity of taking out a policy of insurance. In the present case the sellers endeavoured to correct the mistake by paying the charges for warehousing, but that did not alter the matter or prevent the buyers from saying that they were entitled to reject the goods. The decision of the learned Judge was right and the appeal must be dismissed with costs.

Lord Justice SCRUTTON and Lord Justice ATKIN agreed.

Note also MONTAGUE L. MEYER, LIMITED *v.* TRAVARU A/B H. CORNELIUS, OF GAMLEBY, 46 T. L. R. 553 (King's Bench Division, 1930), where timber was shipped on deck although the contract specified shipment under deck, and where Rowlatt, J., said: "That he was clearly of opinion that the words 'under deck' were a condition of the contract. Generally speaking, he thought that the question whether goods were to be carried on deck or under deck went to the whole performance of such a contract, just like provisions as to the time or place of shipment. It was a material term of the contract. And, further, where provisions were set out in a specification, these provisions became the description of the thing which was the subject of the sale, and if the goods did not comply with the specification they did not comply with the contract description."

In *Bowes* v. *Shand*, *supra*, p. 267, Lord Cairns spoke of the contract provision in regard to time of shipment as being "part of the description of the subject matter of what is sold." Compare the observation of McCardie, J., in *J. Aron & Co.* (*Incorporated*) v. *Comptoir Wegimont*, as quoted *supra*, p. 274.

DAVID SASSOON & CO., LTD. *v.* LINDSAY, BENDIX & CO.

KING'S BENCH DIVISION, 1922

[13 *Lloyd's List Law Reports*, 280]

Mr. Justice BAILHACHE, in giving judgment, said: In this case certain beer was bought and ordered as English Pilsener lager beer, and it was sold under the same nomination. It was rejected because the label on the bottle contained the words "British lager," but did not contain the words "British Pilsener lager." In my judgment, when the beer was sold in bottles, which by common consent are deemed to have a label on them, it is necessary that the labels should have the same description upon them as the description in the contract between the parties. The labels omitted the word "Pilsener," a very unfortunate thing, because I understand and believe that the beer that was in the bottles was English Pilsener lager; and the buyers were, I think, technically right in rejecting on the ground that they did not contain the word "Pilsener," although I have no doubt that the ground of their objection is to be sought elsewhere. In the circumstances, there must be judgment for the plaintiffs for £1000 with costs.

Refer again to *Moore & Co.* v. *Landauer & Co.*, *supra*, p. 357 (goods to be put up thirty tins in a case).

LOOSE *v.* FLICKINGER

CALIFORNIA DISTRICT COURT OF APPEAL, FIRST APPELLATE DISTRICT, 1932

[121 *California Appellate Reports*, 77]

SPENCE, J. Plaintiff brought this action seeking damages and the rescission of a contract to purchase 500 cases of dates. Defendants answered and filed a cross-complaint seeking damages for breach of the contract. The cause was tried by the court sitting without a jury and from a judgment in favor of defendants, plaintiff appeals.

The sale was negotiated by a Mr. Hatton, who had originally imported the dates from England and sold them to defendants. Mr. Hatton appears to have acted as a volunteer without compensation in the present transaction. He told plaintiff of these dates and after bringing him a sample, invited plaintiff to the cold-storage warehouse to inspect and examine them. Plaintiff went to the warehouse and examined some of the cases and three days later entered into a written contract with the defendants. The contract called for "five hundred (500) cases of 1927 crop 'Sayers' Dates of T. G. & Co. Brand as per samples inspected at the Growers Cold Storage Company." Pursuant to the contract the first 50 cases were delivered and paid for. Thereafter plaintiff, claiming the dates delivered to be of an inferior quality and "inferior in all respects to said samples," brought this action. Upon the trial plaintiff sought to show that the dates delivered were inferior to those originally exhibited to him by Mr. Hatton, but refused to state whether there was any difference between the dates delivered and those inspected at the warehouse. The trial court found that the dates were purchased by plaintiff as a result of the inspection of the dates at the warehouse and that plaintiff did not rely upon any alleged warranty upon the part of defendants.

Appellant's attack upon the trial court's findings and rulings upon evidence all center around appellant's contention that this was a sale made with reference to the original sample and that respondents thereby warranted the bulk to be equal to that sample. (Civ. Code, sec. 1766.) We find no merit in appellant's contention. In order to constitute a sale by sample so as to give rise to a warranty it must appear that the parties contracted solely with reference to the sample exhibited. (55 Cor. Jur. 416.) Here, even though a sample was originally exhibited, appellant was given the opportunity to inspect the bulk and availed himself of that opportunity. In our opinion the evidence was ample to sustain the trial court's findings that the sale resulted from said inspection and not from reliance on any warranty express or implied and the maxim *caveat emptor* was properly applied.

We find no error in the record and accordingly the judgment is affirmed.

Nourse, P. J., and Sturtevant, J., concurred.

In L. A. LOCKWOOD, JR., INC. *v.* E. GROSS AND COMPANY, INC., 99 Conn. 296 (Supreme Court of Errors, 1923), there was a contract for the sale of paperstock sweepings collected during the year 1920. In the course of telephone negotiations leading up to the contract the buyers requested a sample, and the sellers agreed to send one, stating further however that the sweepings were low-grade stock and that they would not sell by sample. A sample was sent, and some days later the buyer signed a sales note bearing the notation "Quality: As seen and agreed." The market price for sweepings declined steadily during the year, and after June 1 the buyers, although repeatedly asked, gave no shipping instructions, claiming that the sweepings already shipped had not been equal to sample. In an action by the sellers for damages for wrongful refusal it was held that the contract was not for a sale by sample, for "the sample was intended merely as a representation as to the bulk of the sweepings," and "if a representation, express or implied, is not made a part of the contract, we do not see how it can affect the sale, unless, indeed, it was a fraudulent representation."

Compare S. Stroock & Co., Inc. *v.* Joseph Lichtenthal, Inc., 224 New York App. Div. 19 (Supreme Court, Appellate Division, 1928), where there was a written contract for "La Parisienne" cloth, with no reference to a sample, although a sample had been exhibited prior to the reduction of the contract to writing. The buyer claimed the right to reject the goods delivered because of variation from the sample. In reversing a judgment for the seller on other grounds, the Court said: "Likewise we overrule the defendant's contention that this was a sale by sample. The contracts were in writing. They made no reference to a sample. Oral evidence was not admissible to prove a warranty that the bulk should correspond with the sample. And the mere exhibition of a sample during the preliminary negotiations offers no basis for the conclusion that the seller made such warranty. . . . Either party had a right to offer oral evidence to elucidate the meaning of the phrase 'La Parisienne.' This was not a recognized trade name; it was an appellation given by the plaintiff to a new cloth which it had just devised. . . . If a sample itself was used and referred to in the course of such conversation, it would necessarily be admissible in evidence. It should be made clear, however, that the court upon a new trial would not be justified in requiring proof from the plaintiff that the merchandise delivered conformed with this sample in quality. The maximum of plaintiff's duty with respect to the sample would be to deliver in merchantable condition goods of the general character indicated by the sample. It made no warranty that the goods would conform with the sample and it is not obliged to show that the merchandise tendered was the equivalent in excellence of the sample."

Contrast Bradford *v.* Manley, 13 Mass. 139 (Supreme Judicial Court, 1816), in which the buyer sought to recover the difference in value between two casks of cloves alleged to be sold by sample and the cloves actually delivered. The bill of parcels mentioned cloves generally, without designation of kind, but a sample had been shown when the buyer was asked if he wished to purchase cloves, and the jury found expressly that those delivered were different from the sample and inferior in value. In giving judgment on a verdict for the plaintiff, Parker, C. J., said: "The fair import of the exhibition of a sample is, that the article proposed to be sold is like that which is shown as a parcel of the article: it is intended to save the purchaser the trouble of examining the whole quantity. It certainly means as much as this, 'The thing I offer to sell is of the same kind, and essentially of the same quality, as the specimen I give you.' I do not know that it would be going too far to say that it amounts to a declaration, that it is equally sound and good. . . . Indeed the exhibition of a sample must, in all fair dealing, stand in lieu of a warranty or affirmation. It is a silent, symbolical warranty, perfectly understood by the parties, and adopted and used for the convenience of trade. . . .

"We are all decidedly of the opinion, that a sale by sample is tantamount to an express warranty that the sample is a true representative of the kind."

Note further NIEHOFF-SCHULTZE GROCERY COMPANY *v.* GROSS, 205 New York App. Div. 67 (Supreme Court, Appellate Division, 1923). In March, 1917, the buyer purchased from samples a lot of 100 bags of beans. In April, 1917, the buyer placed a repeat order for 400 bags of beans of the same kind. It was held that the second sale was a sale by sample.

F. A. D. ANDREA, INC. *v.* DODGE

UNITED STATES CIRCUIT COURT OF APPEALS, THIRD CIRCUIT, 1926

[15 *Federal Reporter* (*Second Series*), 1003]

DAVIS, Circuit Judge. This was a suit at law for damages for an alleged breach of a contract for 20,000 cabinets for radio sets. The contracts consisted of proposals in the form of orders by the defendant and acceptances by the plaintiff. Each order contained in substance the following provision: "These cabinets to have best quality lacquer finish equal to our sample. The color must be identical with our sample." Some of the orders contained the provision: "These cabinets to have best quality lacquer finish that will not change color or turn white."

The cabinets were shipped from plaintiff's factory in Philadelphia to defendant's plant in New York, where they were fitted out with other parts of a radio set and forthwith sent out to the trade. After delivery, white spots and blemishes developed on them. This caused, not only numerous complaints to defendant from its customers, but also the return of many cabinets. The plaintiff refinished these returned cabinets, and, in order to save freight charges from New York to Philadelphia and return, it sent a man to New York to refinish them at defendant's plant. There is a dispute as to how many defective cabinets there were. Defendant says there were about 3,500, or nearly one-third of the number delivered, but plaintiff denies this.

There is no question about the good faith of the parties to the contract. The cause of the trouble seems to have been the use of a process in finishing known as "padding." This process is used with beneficial results in varnish finish, but in lacquer finish produces a whitened effect, which, however, does not appear for some time. The evidence indicates that the officers of the plaintiff company did not know that this process was being used on this lacquer finish by its employees, and did not discover it until some time after the contract was canceled, when a new superintendent was secured at the plant. Because the defects did not appear immediately, they were not discovered by plaintiff's factory, where defendant had an inspector in accordance with the terms of the contract. The return of the cabinets to the plaintiff's plant began early in December, 1924, and continued until March 6, 1925, when defendant wrote plaintiff as follows:

"The dissatisfaction with these cabinets has become so general that some dealers are threatening or indicating an intention of discontinuing selling our productions, so you can readily appreciate our good will with the trade and the purchasing public is seriously jeopardized. Since our complaints have not resulted in any improvement in the conditions, and the protests of dealers are increasing, we have arrived at the conclusion that you are either unable or unwilling to produce cabinets for us in accordance with the specifications upon which the order was placed with you; in consequence we have concluded to cancel the order and in future will accept no further cabinets from you."

On March 9, 1925, the plaintiff replied, and among other things said: "Unless your letter of March 6th is formally withdrawn on or before March 11, 1925, we will on that date stop work on all of your orders, prepare and render you as promptly as possible a statement of your indebtedness to us, and place the account for collection if not settled promptly." The letter was not withdrawn and the plaintiff ceased manufacturing on March 11th. This suit was begun on the 18th of June following, and was tried to by the court and jury, which rendered a verdict for the plaintiff, and the defendant has brought it here on writ of error.

The essence of defendant's complaint is that the learned trial judge erred in defining the word "bulk," as used in sections 14 and 16 of the Uniform Sales Act of Pennsylvania of May 19, 1915. . . .

In his charge to the jury the learned trial judge said: "There is no provision in the law that, where there is a sale by sample, every individual article sold must conform to the sample; and it is a question, then, whether the bulk of these cabinets delivered to the plaintiff did or did not correspond to the sample.

"If from the evidence in the case you are satisfied that a very large percentage of the cabinets delivered did not correspond with the sample, then, of course, the bulk of those delivered did not correspond. You will take into consideration the large number of cabinets that were delivered — I think over 11,500 cabinets were delivered — and take into consideration the evidence as to the number of cabinets which did not correspond to the sample, and then determine from that whether or not from the evidence in this case you believe that the defendant had a right to cancel the contract. The law does not lay down any definite percentage or *pro rata* number of individual articles to be delivered that must correspond with the sample, but it does say that there is a warranty that the merchandise delivered shall correspond in bulk. So that it would be for you to determine what proportion of the merchandise delivered did not correspond to the sample, and when you have determined that, considering a reasonable definition of the word 'bulk,' whether you consider that the goods delivered did or did not correspond in bulk."

Did the word "bulk," as used in this portion of the charge, correspond with the word as used in the Uniform Sales Act? In section 14 of the act, the word "bulk" is used to denote the goods as distinguished from the sample with which they must correspond. "Goods," in the phrase "bulk of the goods," is an appositional genitive defining "bulk." Similarly we say "city of Philadelphia," or "the city, Philadelphia." "Philadelphia" is in apposition with "city." So the word "goods" is in apposition with "bulk," and means the bulk, to wit, the goods.

The Legislature did not intend to distinguish between "the bulk of the goods" and "the goods" themselves. When goods are sold by both sample and description, "the bulk of the goods" — that is, the goods themselves — must correspond with the sample, and the same "goods," without the mention of "bulk," must also correspond with the description. The "bulk of the goods" and "the goods" are one and the same thing.

In section 16 the word "bulk" is used without the addition of the words "of the goods." "There is an implied warranty that the buyer shall have a reasonable opportunity of comparing the bulk with the sample," and thus satisfy himself that all the goods he has purchased are as warranted.

"Bulk," as used in the charge, means something less than all the goods. This thought ran through the charge. In the opinion refusing a new trial the definition of "bulk" in Webster's and the Century Dictionaries is cited in support of this view: "The main mass of the body; the largest or principal portion; the majority, as the bulk of a debt."

The contract in question expressly provided that: "These cabinets to have best quality lacquer finish, equal to our sample." "Bulk" is not used. "These cabinets," in the contract, mean all the cabinets embraced within it, and not "a very large percentage" of them.

However, it is the growing policy of the law not to take notice of trifling matters. "De minimis non curat lex" is a maxim which has greater force to-day than ever. Courts in different jurisdictions have taken opposite views of what constitutes a breach. Some hold that nothing short of an intent totally to repudiate the contract is a breach, while others hold that any failure or defect, though immaterial, is a breach. The better and prevailing view is that anything "so material and important as in truth and fairness to defeat the essential purpose of the parties" is a breach. . . .

The real question in issue was whether or not the number of defective cabinets was so material as in truth and fairness to defeat the essential purpose of the parties, and this fact was to be found by the jury, unless no reasonable person could have drawn more than one inference from the facts or the defects were so slight that they could not possibly be regarded as vital. 2 Williston on Sales (2d Ed.) pp. 1180, 1181; *Truitt* v. *Guenther Lumber Company*, 73 Pa. Super. Ct. 445; *Du Pont* v. *United Zinc* Co., 85 N. J. Law, 416, 89 A. 992; *Ferguson* v. *Chuck*, 194 App. Div. 583, 185 N. Y. S. 800; *C. Bahnsen* v. *Gerst*, 235 N. Y. 426, 139 N. E. 563; *Roach* v. *Lane*, 226 Mass. 598, 116 N. E. 470; *Monroe* v. *Diamond*, 279 Pa. 310, 123 A. 817. In *Paulson, Linkroun & Co.* v. *Bidwell* (C. C. A.) 278 F. 381, we said that a breach justifying cancellation must be "substantial."

As above quoted, the charge contained the following statement: "If from the evidence in the case you are satisfied that a very large percentage of the cabinets delivered did not correspond with the sample, then, of course, the bulk of those delivered did not correspond." Every positive implies a contrapositive or obverse. The contrapositive of the above statement in the charge is that, unless a very large percentage of the cabinets did not correspond with the sample, the bulk and sample did sufficiently correspond, and there was no ground for the cancellation of the contract by the defendant. This is an incorrect statement of the law, but is doubtless the conclusion which the jury drew from the language of the charge.

If the number of defective cabinets shipped to defendant by plaintiff was material, when all the facts and circumstances were considered, the bulk did not legally correspond with the sample, and the defendant was justified in canceling the contract. If, on the other hand, that number, in the light of all the facts, was immaterial, the bulk did substantially correspond with the sample, and the defendant was not justified in canceling the contract. Materiality is the test that justifies cancellation, and not "a very large percentage"; for something less than "a very large percentage" might, under the circumstances, be material. The charge did not clearly declare the law, and was susceptible of an erroneous conclusion, which was prejudicial to the defendant.

Therefore the judgment is reversed, and a *venire facias de novo* is awarded.

STEWART *v.* VOLL & SON

New Jersey Court of Errors and Appeals, 1911

[81 *New Jersey Law Reports*, 323]

Bergen, J. The plaintiff brought this suit in the District Court to recover for the breach of an implied warranty that two hundred and fifty bags of potatoes sold him by the defendant were merchantable, and he had judgment, from which defendant appeals.

We find from the evidence that the defendant had a large quantity of potatoes in bags on a public wharf which he was offering for sale; that he called upon the plaintiff and solicited him to buy, saying that he had a fine lot of potatoes and asked plaintiff to go and look at them, which he did, by examining five or six bags, some of which were opened and some he opened; that after plaintiff had examined the samples the defendant assured him that the lot were all like the sample, and were a fine lot of potatoes, saying, "They ran like that all through," referring to the sample. As the sample appeared to be sound and merchantable, the plaintiff bought two hundred and fifty bags, most of which he resold the same day. Within forty-eight hours it was discovered that the potatoes were diseased, for which reason the sales by the plaintiff were rescinded by his vendees, and the potatoes being worthless plaintiff suffered a total loss. We also find that the defect in the potatoes was one not apparent on a reasonable examination of the sample, but although latent, when the sample was examined was of a character likely to develop within forty-eight hours when they would be worthless, and that they were so afflicted when sold to plaintiff was known to the defendant. We base defendant's knowledge of the defect upon the fact that on the day of the sale, and immediately thereafter, the defendant gave to a general teamster two orders on the transportation company, in whose charge the potatoes were, for delivery to him of the potatoes sold, to be carted by him to the plaintiff, and each of the orders contained an endorsement indicating that they were not sound, one "sold as they are, not guaranteed to be sound," and the other "sold not to be sound," nor did the defendant, as a witness, deny that he knew they were unsound, his defence being that he did not warrant, and produced the two orders, which plaintiff never saw until at the trial, as evidence that they were sold as unsound. The conclusion we reach is that the goods were sold by sample, and that under section 16 of "An act concerning the sale of goods and to make uniform the law relating thereto" (Pamph. L. 1907, p. 311), there was an implied warranty that the goods were free from any defect, rendering them unmerchantable, which was not apparent on reasonable examination of the sample. There being an implied warranty, and a breach thereof, the plaintiff is entitled to recover his damages.

[The last two pages of the opinion are here omitted.]

The judgment will be affirmed, with costs.

Note also THE NIXA CANNING COMPANY *v.* THE LEHMANN-HIGGINSON GROCER COMPANY, 70 Kansas 664 (Supreme Court, 1905), where the Court said: "The apples were put up in cans by the defendant for the purpose of selling them to merchants, and were bought by plaintiff, as defendant knew, to be resold to its customers. The sale was made by sample, the sample cans being opened and examined by the plaintiffs before the purchase. The samples were apparently sound and fit, and were not in fact subject to any defect that could have been discovered by any reasonable examination. The goods sold were in all respects like the sample, but by reason of the character of certain substances that had been employed in the canning process they spoiled and became unmerchantable within a few months, and before they could have been disposed of in the usual course of trade.

"Plaintiff in error contends that where goods are sold by sample there is, in effect, an express warranty of conformity to the sample, and no other warranty as to quality can be implied. This may be granted to be the ordinary rule as to transactions between merchants, but where the seller is also the manufacturer, there is an implied warranty that the sample and goods sold are alike free from latent defects not discoverable upon ordinary examination."

In JAMES DRUMMOND & SONS *v.* E. H. VAN INGEN & CO., 12 A. C. 284 (House of Lords, 1887), there was a contract for the sale of "worsted coatings" to correspond in quality and weight with patterns which had been supplied by the seller. The buyer had purchased worsted coatings from the seller the previous year which had been satisfactory. Owing to the mode of manufacturing the coatings for the current contract, however, there was so serious a tendency in the warp to slip that the material could not be made up in the ordinary way. The coatings nevertheless corresponded in every way with the patterns, and the seller maintained that this was a complete answer to any claim by the buyer. An order in favor of the buyer was affirmed, and Lord Herschell said *inter alia*: "When a purchaser states generally the nature of the article he requires, and asks the manufacturer to supply specimens of the mode in which he proposes to carry out the order, he trusts to the skill of the manufacturer just as much as if he asked for no such specimens. And I think he has a right to rely on the samples supplied representing a manufactured article which will be fit for the purposes for which such an article is ordinarily used, just as much as he has a right to rely on manufactured goods supplied on an order without samples complying with such a warranty.

"I adopt what was said by Willes, J., in *Mody* v. *Gregson* (Law Rep. 4 Ex. 49, 53): 'The object and use of either inspection of bulk or sample alike are to give information, disclosing directly through the senses what any amount of circumlocution might fail to express. It seems difficult, therefore, to ascribe any greater effect to a sample in excluding implication than would be ascribed to express words in the contract giving, as far as words could give, the same amount of information; and as to such words, the doctrine that an express provision excludes implication, does not affect cases in which the express provision appears on the true construction of the contract to have been superadded for the benefit of the buyer.'

"There is no doubt that the implied warranty will be excluded as regards any defects which the sample would disclose to a buyer of ordinary diligence and experience. The inquiry, therefore, arises whether the defendants by 'due diligence in the use of all ordinary and usual means' would have detected in the patterns the defects of which they now complain. I think not. What is 'due diligence' must depend upon the circumstances. Having regard to the order given in the previous year, and the mode in which that order was fulfilled, I think that when the defendants made the contract there was nothing which could reasonably lead them to anticipate that the patterns represented goods possessing the defect which was, in fact, inherent in them. And I am satisfied upon the evidence that the defendants who, undoubtedly, did not discern the defect, did not fail to do so from neglecting to use the means usually adopted by buyers under like circumstances."

MANCHESTER LINERS, LTD. *v.* REA, LTD.

House of Lords, 1922

[*Law Reports,* [1922] 2 *Appeal Cases,* 74]

Appeal from an order of the Court of Appeal reversing a judgment of Salter J.

The appellants, who were shipowners of Manchester, owned the steamship *Manchester Importer.* The respondents were coal merchants of Liverpool and had a dockside office at Manchester and they supplied coal for the bunkering of steamers.

On October 8, 1919, it was verbally agreed between the appellants through their agent Mr. Watts and the respondents through their agent, Mr. Edwards, that the respondents should supply to the appellants 500 tons South Wales coal for the steamship *Manchester Importer* at Partington, and this agreement was confirmed by a letter of the same date. The coal supplied was unsuitable for the bunkering of the steamer, which was a natural draught steamer, and as a consequence the steamer was obliged to return to port. Thereupon the appellants brought an action against the respondents for damages for breach of the agreement. The appellants by their statement of claim alleged that it was an implied term of the contract that the coal supplied by the respondents should be fit for the purposes for which it was to be used, and claimed damages for the delay occasioned to the *Manchester Importer* by reason of the unsuitability for bunkering that vessel of the coal supplied. The respondents by their defence alleged that the coal supplied was suitable for bunkering steamers and, alternatively, that, as the appellants well knew, the only coal available to the respondents for supply as bunker coal to steamers was coal requisitioned by the Coal Controller; that it was an implied term of the contract that the coal supplied by the respondents to the appellants should be coal so requisitioned and made available; that by reason of the premises no other warranty was implied by statute or otherwise on the sale of the said coal except that the coal had been requisitioned by the Coal Controller and made available for bunkering purposes.

The facts are fully stated in the opinion of Lord Buckmaster and are summarised in the headnote.

Salter J. found as a fact that the coal supplied was not suitable for the purpose for which it was bought and that a warranty ought to be implied that the goods were fit for that purpose and he gave judgment for the appellants. The Court of Appeal (Bankes, Warrington and Atkin L.JJ.) reversed this decision and ordered judgment to be entered for the respondents on the ground that in the special circumstances of the case the statutory warranty ought not to be implied.

Lord Buckmaster. My Lords, when the circumstances in which this appeal has arisen are examined, it will be found that its determination really depends upon the proper aspect of the facts rather than on an examination of uncertain principles of law.

The appellants are the owners of the steamship known as the *Manchester Importer*, and the respondents are coal merchants of Liverpool, who are in the habit of supplying coal for bunkering steamers.

In the autumn of 1919 the position of shipowners anxious to obtain coal for their steamers was one of peculiar difficulty. The coal supply was in the hands of the Coal Controller who had authority to restrict and direct supplies as he thought right, and, in addition, a railway strike had begun on September 27, lasting until October 7, with the result that the loading of vessels in the South Wales ports ceased, so that in October the only coal available for bunkering purposes at Manchester was the coal in stock at Partington or on vessels then at sea.

In October the appellants' steamer was at Partington waiting to be coaled, and shortly before October 7 one of the directors of the appellant company saw Mr. Bradley, who was agent for the Controller, and discussed with him the position of supplies. He was told as to the stock that was then in hand, which was 300 tons of South Wales coal, and 300 local tons, and that it was quite inadequate to satisfy the demand; he was also informed that the Coal Controller was doing his best to divert a collier that would bring some 4000 to 5000 tons more coal into the port. Relying upon the prospect of this latter source, a form was obtained by the appellants from the Coal Controller known as a "pre-entry form," without which they would be unable to obtain coal. That was dated October 8 and was passed, entitling the appellants to obtain Welsh coal at Partington.

On the same day, following a telephonic communication, they sent an order to the respondents in these terms: "Referring to conversation with Mr. Edwards please supply five hundred tons South Wales coal for the steamship *Manchester Importer* at Partington on Friday, and oblige."

This order was accepted and coal was delivered under it which had been brought in by the vessel referred to by Mr. Bradley, which turned out to be steamship *Penrhys*; unfortunately the furnaces of the *Manchester Importer* were natural draught furnaces, for which the coal supplied was wholly unsuitable, so that the steamer was obliged to return to port. An action was then brought by the appellants claiming damages against the respondents for breach of implied warranty as to the character of their goods, which succeeded before Salter J., and failed in the Court of Appeal.

The grounds on which the judgment of the Court of Appeal depend are these: That the agent for the plaintiffs, who acted for them in obtaining the contract, knew, both by general knowledge and by special information, all about the coal position at the time when he made the contract, and knowing that the only coal that could be obtained was the coal from the steamship *Penrhys*, his order must be regarded as an order for satisfaction from that source, and this order was satisfied.

Both these propositions need to be modified in the light of the evidence. The knowledge possessed by the plaintiffs was undoubtedly that the coal supplies in Manchester were short and inadequate to the demand, and that a steamship, which turned out to be the *Penrhys*, was expected into port containing coal. What the quality or character of that coal was they did not know, and they certainly did not order any coal as coal from that steamship.

It then remains to be considered whether in the circumstances there was any warranty that the coal was suitable for the purpose for which it was required. It is plain that the order was expressed for the use of a particular steamship, and it must, therefore, be assumed that the respondents knew the nature of her furnaces and the character of the coal she used, for it was this coal they contracted to supply.

On this assumption, however, the respondents have argued that by virtue of s. 14 of the Sale of Goods Act, 1893, no warranty can be implied unless "the buyer expressly or by implication makes known to the seller the particular purpose for which the goods are required, so as to show that the buyer relies on the seller's skill and judgment," and this the order in question fails to effect. This is, in my opinion, a misunderstanding of the statute, for the section embraces and restates the common law doctrine in the form which was clearly derived from the case of *Jones* v. *Just* (L. R. 3 Q. B. 197). If goods are ordered for a special purpose, and that purpose is disclosed to the vendor, so that in accepting the contract he undertakes to supply goods which are suitable for the object required, such a contract is, in my opinion, sufficient to establish that the buyer has shown that he relies on the seller's skill and judgment.

The view taken by Lord Russell C.J. in *Gillespie Bros. & Co.* v. *Cheney, Eggar & Co.* ([1896] 2 Q. B. 59) appears slightly at variance with this conclusion though the result is the same, for he regards the common law as partly incorporated in the statute and partly remaining outside. In my opinion, the section completely incorporates the common law, and in no way limits its operation. There, therefore, was a warranty in this case, and the circumstances from which it is suggested that such a warranty can be negatived cannot be found. At the best the facts amount to no more than this — that the buyer knew that the sources of supply of the vendor were limited, and they might, indeed, be confined to the cargo of a particular vessel. That does not negative an implication drawn from the face of the contract that the coal supply must be of a certain quality or it would be useless for the purpose in hand. The respondents themselves may well have been unaware of what was the character of the coal in the *Penrhys* until her cargo was discharged, but its general description of South Wales coal certainly included coal that might be suitable and would have satisfied the contract, and if the respondents found that its actual cargo was unsatisfactory for this purpose it was their duty to have informed the vendor at once.

I think the judgment of Salter J. is correct, and I think the judgment of the Court of Appeal should be reversed.

[Concurring opinions of Lords Dunedin, Atkinson, and Sumner, are omitted. Lord Carson also agreed.]

In PREIST *v.* LAST, [1903] 2 K. B. 148 (Court of Appeal), the plaintiff, a draper, went to the shop of the defendant, a retail chemist, and asked for a hot-water bottle. An article was shown to him as such. He inquired whether it would stand boiling water, and was told that it would not, that it was meant for hot water. He then purchased it. Some days later the bottle burst while in use by the plaintiff's wife, and she was scalded. In an action for breach of warranty the jury found that the bottle was not fit for use as a hot water bottle, and that this was the cause of its bursting. In affirming a judgment for the plaintiff, Collins, M. R., said: "The argument appears to be that the purpose for which this article was sold was merely the ordinary purpose of use as a hot-water bottle, and, that being its ordinary purpose, the case is not brought within the words 'makes known to the seller the particular purpose for which the goods are required.' I do not think that this contention is sound. I think that, regard being had to the state of the law as it existed previously to the passing of the Act, the object with which those words were introduced is clear. There are many goods which have in themselves no special or peculiar efficacy for any one particular purpose, but are capable of general use for a multitude of purposes. In the case of a purchase of goods of that kind, in order to give rise to the implication of a warranty, it is necessary to shew that, though the article sold was capable of general use for many purposes, in the particular case it was sold with reference to a particular purpose. But in a case where the discussion begins with the fact that the description of the goods, by which they were sold, points to one particular purpose only, it seems to me that the first requirement of the sub-section is satisfied, namely, that the particular purpose for which the goods are required should be made known to the seller. The fact that, by the very terms of the sale itself, the article sold purports to be for use for a particular purpose cannot possibly exclude the case from the rule that, where goods are sold for a particular purpose, there is an implied warranty that they are reasonably fit for that purpose. The sale is of goods which, by the very description under which they are sold, appear to be sold for a particular purpose."

Compare COUNTRY CLUB SODA COMPANY, INCORPORATED *v.* JOHN ARBUCKLE, 279 Mass. 121 (Supreme Judicial Court, 1931), where a manufacturer of beverages ordered from a sugar refiner a car load of "fine granulated sugar" under such circumstances that it made known to the seller that the sugar was intended for use in the manufacture of syrups. The sugar supplied under the contract contained foreign matter including insects, and was unfit for human consumption in consequence. In an action for damages resulting from breach of warranties, it was held that the words "fine granulated" were words of description and not a patent or trade name; that this fact did not preclude an implied warranty of fitness for a particular purpose, as the description was not so exact as to control evidence of the buyer's reliance on the skill and judgment of the seller; but that since "the plaintiff ordered fine granulated sugar and to that extent made its own decision without reliance on the skill or judgment of the defendants, the warranty of fitness did not extend to a warranty that sugar of that description would make good syrup."

In Keenan *v.* Cherry & Webb, 47 R. I. 125 (Supreme Court, 1925), plaintiff after trying on numerous coats, bought a French Coney which defendant represented as "a good coat" which would "wear very good." As a matter of fact the stitches sewing the pelts together had cut through one of the skins, so that the coat ripped when first worn and could not be repaired. Inspection by one having no knowledge of furs would not have revealed the danger of tearing. In an action for breach of warranty a new trial was ordered on the ground that the real issue had not been presented to the jury, the Court saying: "Prior to the enactment of the Uniform Sales Act in the United States it was commonly held that inspection of goods bought from a dealer, which inspection took place before the bargain was made, precluded the implication of warranty of quality whether or not the defect was latent. . . . Inasmuch as the fundamental test under the implied warranty is 'whether the buyer justifiably relies on the seller's skill and judgment,' Williston § 234, at p. 455, the Sales Act leaves inspection as an important but not conclusive element to be considered in determining the question of reliance. It treats reliance as a question of fact."

RINALDI *v.* THE MOHICAN COMPANY

New York Court of Appeals, 1918

[225 *New York Reports*, 70]

Andrews, J. We have held as to a sale of food for immediate consumption made before September 1st, 1911, by a dealer who makes or prepares the articles sold that there is an implied warranty of wholesomeness. (*Race* v. *Krum*, 222 N. Y. 410.) That is as far as any decision of ours has gone. In *Maxwell* v. *Marsh* (173 App. Div. 1003; affirmed, without opinion, 225 N. Y. —), where tainted meat was sold in 1913, a charge to the jury that such a warranty was to be implied was made without objection. It became, therefore, the law for that case. Yet in *Race* v. *Krum*, in an opinion in which all the members of the court concurred, there was a full discussion of the rule in this state and the conclusion was reached deliberately "that accompanying all sales by a retail dealer of articles of food for immediate use there is an implied warranty that the same is fit for human consumption." This was an exception to the general rule regarding the sale of other chattels based on grounds of public policy. The opinion, however, expressly refused to consider whether such a warranty existed in the case of hotel proprietors or those engaged in a similar business.

On September 1st, 1911, section 96 of the Personal Property Law (Cons. Laws, ch. 41) took effect. It provided that there is no implied warranty or condition as to the quality or fitness for any particular purpose of goods sold except, among other cases, "where the buyer, expressly or by implication, makes known to the seller the particular purpose for which the goods are required, and it appears that the buyer relies on the seller's skill or judgment (whether he be the grower or manufacturer or not)." If, however, the buyer has examined the goods there is no implied warranty as regards defects which such an examination should have revealed.

Article 5 of the Personal Property Law is not merely a codification of the existing rules regarding sales in this state. It was the design as far as possible to make our law uniform with the legislation and laws on this subject existing throughout the country. To this end changes were made in what had previously been here the law. In section 96 itself, for instance, the distinction between the liability of sellers who were growers and manufacturers and others was ended. A warranty may now be established by proof of the usage of trade. Although an express warranty of quality is given, one not inconsistent with it may also be implied. Having in view the purpose of the article and the fact that in some states no implied warranty based on grounds other than those which affect every sale of a chattel was enforced, we have no doubt that section 96, expressed as it is in general terms, applies to all sales, including sales of food, and that any rules hitherto applied inconsistent with this section are abolished.

In a sale of food, therefore, there is no longer an implied warranty of fitness unless the buyer expressly or by implication acquaints the seller with the purpose of the purchase and unless it appears that the buyer relies on the seller's skill or judgment. Even then if the buyer has examined the goods and should have discovered the defect there is no warranty. The burden of showing that he has made known his purpose and that he has relied upon the seller is on him who claims the existence of an implied warranty. If either of these two facts do not appear he fails in his claim. Whether they exist or not may often become a question of fact to be solved by the jury. But often also, where the facts are undisputed, and no differing inferences may be drawn from them, the question becomes one of law for the court; and we have to determine just what and how much evidence is necessary to show conclusively the existence of these essential elements.

We think that the mere purchase by a customer from a retail dealer in foods of an article ordinarily used for human consumption does by implication make known to the vendor the purpose for which the article is required. Such a transaction standing by itself permits no contrary inferences. In this we agree with the courts of Massachusetts. (*Farrell* v. *Manhattan Market Company*, 198 Mass. 271–279.) But we think further that such a purchase, where the buyer may assume that the seller has the opportunity to examine the article sold, unexplained, is also conclusive evidence of reliance on the seller's skill or judgment. We here limit the rule. We do not pass upon the question as to whether it applies to a sale in the original package bought by the vendor from others. In such circumstances it is possible that the inference of reliance would not be properly deduced from the purchase alone. But on the other hand we do not lay stress on the question as to whether the particular article was selected by the buyer or by the seller. That may or may not be important. If the buyer selects one chicken from twenty offered him, exercising his judgment as to its wholesomeness, clearly he does not, or at least may not rely upon the dealer's skill. But where the buyer selects one of the twenty for some reason unconnected with its fitness for food and exercising and having no judgment on that question — makes the selection because the color is pleasing or the weight suitable, then he is relying upon the dealer no less than when the selection is made by the latter. He assumes that the dealer knows and has the means of knowing that all are fit for food. It is a matter about which ordinarily the purchaser knows and can know nothing.

Therefore, in case of a purchase of unwholesome meat from a market after section 96 went into effect, where all that appears is the ordinary transaction between dealer and customer, a charge to the jury that on every sale of food by a dealer for immediate human consumption there is an implied warranty of its wholesomeness, while inaccurate is harmless. If it does not appear that the buyer has examined the goods or, having examined them, has failed to discover defects which he should have found, precisely such an implied warranty exists as the court said existed in all cases whenever a dealer sold food.

Such is the case before us. On December 16th, 1915, the plaintiff bought a loin of pork at a market owned by the defendant. The meat was infested with trichinæ. She cooked and ate it and was made ill. The action was brought to recover for the resulting damages. It was not tried on any theory of negligence or fraud but upon that of implied warranty. The jury found a verdict for the plaintiff and the judgment has been affirmed in the Appellate Division. The plaintiff found no defect in the meat. The court submitted to the jury the question as to whether she could have found such a defect if she had used reasonable care. And finally the defendant insists strenuously that no such defect could have been discovered.

There is no question but what such an action for damages caused by the breach of the implied warranty with regard to food may be maintained, at least by him to whom the warranty is made. Whether in favor of others we do not determine. (*Gearing* v. *Berkson*, 111 N. E. Rep. 785.)

The judgment of the Appellate Division should be affirmed, with costs.

HISCOCK, Ch. J., COLLIN, CUDDEBACK, CARDOZO, POUND and CRANE, JJ., concur.

Judgment affirmed.

Compare CANAVAN *v.* CITY OF MECHANICVILLE, 229 N. Y. 473 (Court of Appeals, 1920), where it was held that "a taker of water from the pipes of a system of water works of a water corporation or a municipality does not by the mere taking make known, either expressly or by implication, to the seller of the water the particular purpose for which the water is required, and cause it to appear that he relies as to the wholesomeness of the water on the seller's skill or judgment."

Note WARD *v.* GREAT ATLANTIC & PACIFIC TEA CO., 231 Mass. 90 (Supreme Judicial Court, 1918), where the plaintiff bought from the defendant a sealed tin can of baked beans bearing the label "Grandmother's Brand A & P Beans & Pork with Sauce." The beans were purchased by the defendant from the Thomas Canning Company of Grand Rapids, after canning, labels being supplied by the defendant and affixed by the manufacturer. The plaintiff broke his tooth on a pebble in the beans, although there was no visible indication of such a defect. The case was reported for determination on a case stated, and in ordering judgment for the plaintiff the Court said: "The defendant was a dealer, the plaintiff a buyer at retail. There arises inevitably the implication that the plaintiff made known to the defendant that he was purchasing the beans for consumption as food and that he was relying, because from the character of the transaction he was bound to rely, upon the skill of the defendant in selecting the can which was offered to him.

"It is not expressly stated in the agreed facts that the defendant selected the can for delivery to the plaintiff, or that the latter relied upon the skill and judgment of the defendant in selecting the can for delivery. But that he did so rely seems an almost irresistible inference from the facts stated. The cans in the defendant's stock were all alike in label and in general appearance. The cans were sealed. Their contents could not in the nature of things be open to inspection before the sale. There could be no intelligent selection based upon any observation by the purchaser. There is no room for the exercise of individual sagacity in picking out a particular can. The customer at a retail store is ordinarily bound to rely upon the skill and experience of the seller in determining the kind of canned goods which he will purchase, unless he demands goods of a definite brand or trade name. . . . The case at bar must be treated on the footing, as matter of necessary inference arising from the relation of the parties, so far as that is material in view of the other facts, that the plaintiff relied upon the knowledge and trade wisdom of the defendant in purchasing the can of beans. In the absence of an express statement to the contrary, this must be regarded as a necessary inference from the relation of the parties.

"There appears to us to be no sound reason for engrafting an exception on the general rule, because the subject of the sale is canned goods, not open to the immediate inspection of the dealer, who is not the manufacturer, any more than of the buyer. It doubtless still remains true that the dealer is in a better position to know and ascertain the reliability and responsibility of the manufacturer than is the retail purchaser."

Crosby, J., dissented on the ground that there was no reliance by the buyer on the seller, since the article purchased was in a sealed can and it was hence impossible for the seller to have any more knowledge of the contents than the buyer had.

Note further KANSAS CITY WHOLESALE GROCERY CO. *v.* WEBER PACKING CORPORATION, 93 Utah 414 (Supreme Court, 1937), in which catsup supplied by the manufacturer to a wholesaler was condemned by an inspector of the Federal Food and Drug Administration. In an action to recover the price paid on the ground of breach of an implied warranty, it was held that when "goods are sold for shipment in interstate commerce, the implied warranty that the goods are fit for the purpose for which they were manufactured and sold should meet the test of the federal pure food act."

In GEDDING *v.* MARSH, [1920] 1 K. B. 668 (King's Bench Division), plaintiff kept a small shop and was supplied by defendant with mineral water in bottles under an arrangement by which she was charged three pence for the water in each bottle and one penny for the bottle, the latter being refunded on return of the bottle. The County Court judge found that under this arrangement there was no sale of the bottles to the plaintiff. One of the bottles so supplied burst and injured the plaintiff, the accident being due to a defect in the bottle. In dismissing an appeal by the defendant in an action for damages, Bray, J., said: "This was a contract of sale none the less because there was a special provision with regard to the bottles. The section, in my opinion, extends not only to the goods actually bought under the contract but to goods 'supplied under the contract of sale.' This particular bottle was thus supplied 'under a contract of sale,' and it follows that it should be reasonably fit for the purpose for which it was supplied. In fact it was not reasonably fit and in consequence of that unfitness the plaintiff was injured."

BALDRY *v.* MARSHALL

COURT OF APPEAL, 1924

[*Law Reports,* [1925] 1 *King's Bench,* 260]

Appeal from Greer J.

The plaintiff, who was dissatisfied with a motor car which he then possessed, on the ground that it was uncomfortable and an unsuitable one in which to take out his wife, wrote on April 13, 1923, to the defendants, motor car dealers, "Can you tell me if the Bugatti eight cylinder is likely to be on the market this year and if so will you send particulars." The defendants, in reply, sent full particulars and a specification, and added, "As no doubt you are already aware, we specialize in the sale of these cars, and are in a position to supply you with all information necessary." The plaintiff knew nothing about Bugatti cars, except what he had read in newspapers. At an interview with the defendants he informed them that he wanted a fast car, which would be flexible and easily managed, and that would be comfortable and suitable for the ordinary purposes of a touring car. The defendants said that they thought a Bugatti car would satisfy those requirements, and showed him a specimen. He then gave them an order on one of the defendants' printed order forms: "Please supply me, on the terms and conditions hereinafter specified, with one eight cylinder Bugatti car, fully equipped and finished as per car inspected." Among the terms and conditions were the following: "The company reserve the right to withdraw any model or alter specifications and prices without notice. Illustrations and specifications must be taken as a general guide and not as binding in detail," and "Guarantee the same as received by us from the manufacturers." The guarantee given by the manufacturers was for twelve months against breakage of parts due to faulty material, there being a stipulation that the said guarantee, if accepted, "expressly excludes any other guarantee or warranty, statutory or otherwise." An eight cylinder Bugatti car was eventually delivered by the defendants to the plaintiff in pursuance of that order, but it was found that the car was not a comfortable one or suitable for touring purposes. The plaintiff claimed to reject the car, and brought the action to recover back the purchase money which he had paid. Greer J. held that an implied condition arose under s. 14, sub-s. 1, of the Sale of Goods Act, that the car should be reasonably fit for touring purposes, and that on the principle of *Wallis* v. *Pratt* that condition was not excluded by the terms of the contract, which was expressed only to exclude warranties and not conditions. He accordingly gave judgment for the plaintiff.

The defendants appealed.

Bankes, L. J. . . . The mere fact that an article sold is described in the contract by its trade name does not necessarily make the sale a sale under a trade name. Whether it is so or not depends upon the circumstances. I may illustrate my meaning by reference to three different cases. First, where a buyer asks a seller for an article which will fulfill some particular purpose, and in answer to that request the seller sells him an article by a well-known trade name, there I think it is clear that the proviso does not apply. Secondly, where the buyer says to the seller, "I have been recommended such and such an article" — mentioning it by its trade name — "will it suit my particular purpose?" naming the purpose, and thereupon the seller sells it without more, there again I think the proviso has no application. But there is a third case where the buyer says to a seller, "I have been recommended so and so" — giving its trade name — "as suitable for the particular purpose for which I want it. Please sell it to me." In that case I think it is equally clear that the proviso would apply and that the implied condition of the thing's fitness for the purpose named would not arise. In my opinion the test of an article having been sold under its trade name within the meaning of the proviso is: Did the buyer specify it under its trade name in such a way as to indicate that he is satisfied, rightly or wrongly, that it will answer his purpose, and that he is not relying on the skill or judgment of the seller, however great that skill or judgment may be? Here there is nothing to show that the plaintiff when describing the car in the contract as an "eight cylinder Bugatti car," after he had communicated to the defendants the purpose for which he wanted it, meant to intimate that he was not relying on their skill and judgment. The evidence seems to be all the other way. In my opinion the appeal must be dismissed.

Atkin L.J. I agree, though I am bound to say that, as in other cases, I have considerable difficulty in construing the proviso to s. 14, sub-s. 1. What is meant by "a sale of a specified article under its trade name"? What is the meaning of "a specified article"? and what is meant by "a sale under a trade name"? Where a person buys an article like a motor car of a named make upon a particular specification, after he has inspected a specimen and has informed the seller that he desires a car to satisfy certain requirements, and the design is capable of being adapted to meet those requirements, I think it would be very difficult to suggest that he bought it under its trade name. It would seem rather to be bought under the specification with a condition as to adaptation. And if so the case would not fall within the proviso. Take again the case put by my Lord of a buyer who goes to a dealer in motor vans and tells him that he wants a motor van for the purposes of his business, that it must not be too heavy, because of the nature of the roads over which it will have to travel, and that it must be sufficiently powerful to enable it to climb a particular hill, and the dealer says that under the circumstances he cannot do better than buy "an X van," and he accordingly buys an X van. In such a case is the implied condition of fitness excluded? I do not think so. The real object of the proviso was to meet a case like that in *Chanter* v. *Hopkins* ((1838) 4 M. & W. 399), where the defendant sent to the plaintiff, who was the patentee of an invention known as "Chanter's smoke consuming furnace," the following order: "Send me your patent hopper apparatus to fit up my brewing copper with your smoke consuming furnace," and upon the plaintiff supplying what was ordered it was found to be unsuitable for a brewery. There the defendant took the risk of the apparatus being suitable for his particular purpose, and having got what he ordered he was held bound to pay for it. *Prideaux* v. *Bunnett* ((1857) 1 C. B. (N. S.) 613, 616) is to the same effect. There the defendant sent to the plaintiff, the patentee of an invention called "Prideaux's Patent Self-closing Valve," who carried on business as "The Smoke Prevention Company," an order, "Please prepare us a smoke preventing valve." The valve supplied was found to be useless for the purpose for which it was designed, but the defendant was held liable to pay the price. In the course of argument Cockburn C.J. said: "The defendant intended to purchase the very thing," and Cresswell J. said: "Taking all the evidence together, is it not clear that the order was given for the patented, the ascertained article?" It appears to me that the right view of the matter is that when the proviso speaks of "the sale of a specified article under its patent or other trade name," it means an article specified by the purchaser as being the article which he wishes to buy. If he so specifies the article and it is sold to him under its trade name it seems clear that the condition is excluded, even though he made known to the seller the purpose for which he intended to use it. But if on the other hand he buys the article in reliance on the seller's assurance that it will answer his purpose, the fact that it is described in the contract by its trade name will not have the effect of excluding the condition. And upon the evidence I think that the present case falls within the latter proposition. . . .

SARGANT L.J. I am of the same opinion, and I will confine my observations to the meaning of the proviso to s. 14, sub-s. 1. It seems to me that the articles which are dealt with in that proviso are primarily things like patent medicines and common articles sold under well-known trade names.

In my judgment the proviso does not apply to an article like a motor car, which is sold under a very elaborate and specific description. The proviso rather applies to a "sale of a specified article under its patent or other trade name," and it seems to me that the sort of mischief it was intended to prevent was this: — It is well known that patent medicines and articles sold under trade names are often sold under puffing or laudatory names, which imply that the article will perform a definite function satisfactorily. Suppose a hosier were to offer for sale some hose as "holeproof hose," and a purchaser were to send him an order for holeproof hose, I think it is clear that the purchaser would under ordinary circumstances be relying on the skill and judgment of the vendor to sell him an article which would have the quality implied in its name. But if there is on the market a well-known article known as holeproof hose, then it seems to me that the proviso is aimed at preventing an order of that article under its laudatory name from raising the implication that the buyer is asking the seller to supply him with something which will fulfil the requirements indicated by the name. I do not say that that is the only purpose of the proviso, but I think it is the main purpose.

But apart from that I think that too much importance has been attached to the proviso in the argument for the appellant, because it seems that it is only to apply in the absence of anything to the contrary, that is to say, it is only on the mere ordering of an article by its trade name that the implied condition is excluded. In my judgment, although a person may order an article under a patent or trade name within the meaning of the proviso, yet if at the same time that the order is given he makes it clear to the vendor that he is relying on his skill and judgment to ensure that the article shall be fit for the particular purpose, the proviso has no application, and the buyer is entitled to the benefit of the provisions of sub-s. 1. I agree that the appeal should be dismissed.

Appeal dismissed.

Compare Whitty Manufacturing Company, Inc. *v.* Clark, 278 Mass. 370 (Supreme Judicial Court, 1932), where there was a written contract for the sale of a "#10 Whitty Automatic Coal Burner." In an action to recover a balance due on the purchase price, the defendant filed a declaration in set-off seeking to recover the amount paid on the ground that he had rescinded the contract. At the trial the defendant offered to prove (1) that he bought the burner not because of its trade name, but because plaintiff told him that it would run automatically all night without attention; (2) that he signed the contract relying on plaintiff's skill and judgment to provide a burner fit for the particular purpose which he had made known to plaintiff; and (3) that the burner was not contracted for or delivered in fulfilment of an offer to purchase goods by a name known to the trade. These offers of proof were excluded. The defendant then requested a ruling that "if the defendant contracted to buy the burner, not because of its trade name, if any, or in reliance upon its trade name, if any, but because he was told . . . that it would run automatically all night without attention, the sale is not a sale under a trade name" within the Statute. The request was refused. The defendant next requested a ruling that "The sale of an article which is referred to in the contract by a trade name is not necessarily a sale under its trade name." This request also was refused. The defendant saved exceptions, and the exceptions were overruled. "The name itself from its designating title necessarily implies as matter of law that it was a trade name." There was no warranty in the contract except those expressly included.

Note also Ryan *v.* Progressive Grocery Stores, Inc., 255 N. Y. 388 (Court of Appeals, 1931), where plaintiff went into a chain grocery store and asked for a loaf of "Ward's Bread." The loaf, sold in a sealed package, contained a pin which injured the plaintiff's mouth. It was held that there was no implied warranty of fitness for a particular purpose, for "There is no room for a holding that choice shall be imputed to the seller when the transaction shows upon its face that the judgment of the seller was superseded, and choice determined by the buyer."

CANADA ATLANTIC GRAIN EXPORT COMPANY (INC.) *v.* EILERS

King's Bench Division, 1929

[35 *Commercial Cases*, 90]

Award stated in the form of a special case by arbitrators appointed in accordance with contract form No. 3 of the London Corn Trade Association. The case was a test case, many others depending on the decision.

The arbitration arose out of a dispute between buyers and sellers of a quantity of North American barley. The sellers were American grain exporters, and the buyers were merchants carrying on business at Bremen in Germany. In July and August, 1928, the sellers entered into contracts to sell to the buyers a quantity of No. 2 Barley, Federal Standard, c.i.f. Bremen, shipment in October. Each contract contained a number of conditions, of which the following were here material:

> Official certificate of inspection to be final as to quality.
>
> The grain is not warranted free from defect rendering the same unmerchantable which would not be apparent on reasonable examination, any statute or rule of law to the contrary notwithstanding.
>
> Shipment in good condition.
>
> Should any of the above-mentioned quantity form part of a larger quantity of the same or a different period of shipment . . . of similar quality in bags or in bulk no separation or distinction shall be necessary.

The barley was shipped from New York, in bulk except so far as bags were needed for stiffening, on October 4, 1928, and reached Bremerhaven on October 15. From Bremerhaven it was sent on in lighters to Bremen, arriving there on October 17. The buyers, however, refused to take up the documents on the ground that the barley did not comply with the contract.

It appeared that barley of this type was principally used for feeding pigs, and was largely used by smallholders in Germany for that purpose. When shipments of the 1928 crop began to arrive from America they were given to pigs as usual, but in many cases the animals would not eat it, or if they did eat it they became ill. The matter became so notorious that on September 27 the German Government issued a decree, to come into force on October 4, that no No. 2 Federal Standard barley except that coming from certain specified States should be allowed to pass beyond the port of importation until an analysis had been made and the Government was satisfied that it was harmless. In these circumstances when the barley the subject of this case arrived in Germany the buyers refused to take up the documents. The sellers then resold the documents for what they would fetch, and in the arbitration they claimed the difference between the contract price and the sum realized on resale. The barley was analysed by the Bremen health authority and was condemned, as it was found to be infected by a fungus growth known as *fusarium roseum*. The genus *fusarium* contained various species, not all of which were harmful; the existence of the genus could be discovered by microscopical examination, but whether the particular species present was or was not of the harmful variety could only be discovered by a further process of gelatine culture.

The buyers contended that they were not bound to accept the barley, as it did not comply with the contract; the sellers contended that as the defect was not discoverable by reasonable examination the barley was in accordance with the contract and the buyers must accept. The dispute was referred to arbitration, and the arbitrators awarded in favour of the sellers, subject to the opinion of the Court on a special case.

The special case now came on for argument.

WRIGHT, J. . . . In particular, two main questions emerge: (1) What are the determinant factors which the contract requires to be considered in order to decide what is a reasonable examination? (2) What is the true definition of "merchantable quality"?

Such questions, in any case very difficult, are particularly so when the Court has only before it the words of the contract and findings of fact of the arbitrators, which are undoubtedly clear and precise, but somewhat summary and lacking in life and colour, as indeed is inevitable.

The barley was admittedly of the contract description, that is to say, Barley No. 2 Federal Standard, official inspection; and the official certificates were in order. The questions turned on the clause which I have already read: "The grain is not warranted" . . . and so on. That clause is negative in form, because it is to cut down the warranty, or more correctly the condition, otherwise implied by section 14, subsection (2) of the Sale of Goods Act, 1893, which is in these terms: "Where goods are bought by description from a seller who deals in goods of that description, whether he be a manufacturer or not, there is an implied condition that the goods shall be of merchantable quality, provided that if the buyer has examined the goods there shall be no implied condition as regards defects which such examination ought to have revealed." Under that section, the warranty of merchantable quality, subject to the proviso, is absolute, and applies to defects rendering the goods unmerchantable, whether latent or patent.

The contract clause may be thus paraphrased: "The barley is warranted to be merchantable unless it is unmerchantable through defects which would not be apparent on reasonable examination."

[Three pages of the opinion dealing with the question of reasonable examination are here omitted.]

The second question, whether the finding of the deleterious fungus rendered the barley unmerchantable, must now be considered. Mr. Vaughan-Williams has contended that the fungus which produces toxalbumens, which are poisonous, must in law render a feeding-stuff, such as this barley, unmerchantable. There is some plausibility in this argument on the face of it, but as Blackburn J. told the jury in the case of *Jones* v. *Just* ([1868] L. R. 3 Q. B. 197), at page 200: "I think the question whether it is fairly and reasonably merchantable is a question of more or less, which must be left to the jury as reasonable men to determine."

The Court in the present case is not trying the facts *ab initio*, but merely seeing whether the arbitrators, who have held or found that the barley was at all material times merchantable, can be shown to have proceeded on a wrong principle of law, or arrived at a conclusion which in law is without evidence, or contrary to the evidence; a position which, while it gives the Court less freedom, also imposes on it less responsibility, and is not such as always to enable the Court to arrive at an independent judgment.

The precise meaning and application of the words "merchantable quality" in section 14, subsection (2), is not defined in the Act, and is not easy to define or ascertain from the authorities, and its application must vary with the circumstances; and that presumably is the reason why Blackburn J. in the case cited before the Act left the question to the jury in the terms which he used.

It has sometimes been expressed as merely meaning "saleable under the description." (See per Willes J. in *Wieler* v. *Schilizzi* ([1856] 17 C. B. 619).) His words are "not a perfect article, but an article which would be saleable in the market" under the contract description. (See also *Jones* v. *Just* ([1868] L. R. 3 Q. B. 197), referred to above.) But "saleable" must, I think, mean "properly saleable," and is little more than a definition *idem per idem*. Lord Ellenborough in *Gardiner* v. *Gray* ([1815] 4 Camp. 144) told the jury: "The purchaser cannot be supposed to buy goods to lay them on a dunghill. The question then is whether the commodity purchased by the plaintiff be of such a quality as can reasonably be brought into the market to be sold as waste silk," which was the quality in question there. . . . "The witnesses describe it as unfit for the purpose of waste silk and of such a quality that it cannot be sold under that denomination." Best C.J. in *Jones* v. *Bright* ([1829] 5 Bing. 533), at p. 546, says: "The law then resolves itself into this, that if a man sells generally, he undertakes that the article sold is fit for some purpose; if he sells it for a particular purpose, he undertakes that it shall be fit for that particular purpose." The

Chief Justice is there pointing to the distinction afterwards more fully developed in section 14, subsection 1, as contrasted with section 14, subsection 2, of the Sale of Goods Act.

Similarly in *Jones* v. *Padgett* ([1890] 24 Q. B. D. 650), woollen cloth was held not to be unmerchantable because it was unfit to be sold to tailors, it being fit for various other purposes to which such cloth might be applied. In *Drummond* v. *Van Ingen* ([1887] 12 App. Cas. 284), some of the expressions used seem to approximate to the implied warranty under section 14, subsection 1, of the Sale of Goods Act, rather than to that under section 14, subsection 2; no doubt because the material in that case was sold as coatings, and hence the scope of the implied warranty was construed with reference to that limited description. Lord Macnaghten, indeed, said the question is "not were they saleable, but were they fit for the purpose for which they were known to have been ordered."

It seems to follow that if goods are sold under a description which they fulfil, and if goods under that description are reasonably capable in ordinary user of several purposes, they are of merchantable quality within section 14, subsection 2, of the Act if they are reasonably capable of being used for any one or more of such purposes, even if unfit for use for that one of those purposes which the particular buyer intended. No doubt it is too wide to say they must be of use for some purpose, because that purpose might be foreign to their ordinary user. Thus in *Asfar* v. *Blundell* ([1896] 1 Q. B. 123; 1 Com. Cas. 185) (a case of freight) dates were held to be unmerchantable as dates because they had been submerged in the Thames and become impregnated with sewage, though they were of considerable value for distillation into vinegar.

To turn to the findings of the arbitrators in this case; they find that the documents, after rejection, were sold to Dutch buyers as No. 2 Barley, Federal Standard, c.i.f., at the ruling market price of this date. They do not find whether the buyers, who I must infer took up the documents, raised any objection afterwards to the goods; but it is difficult to think that when they bought they were not aware of the complaints current in Germany, and the arbitrators may have thought that the resale in these circumstances was some evidence that the goods were reasonably saleable as such. Apart from the evidence of general complaints and of the character and effect of *fusarium roseum*, the only findings of the arbitrators are those in paragraphs 10, 11 and 12, which deal with the results of the feeding and weighing tests and laboratory tests.

The award finds that this barley is recognized in the grain trade as a feeding barley, and the great bulk of its use is as a feeding barley for pigs; but it is also used for cattle, horses, and poultry. There is no finding that the samples of this cargo were tested on any animals but pigs, and the tests on pigs and their results are set out in paragraph 11. If the barley was of such a character that it was impossible to tell without trial whether it would poison or fatten any particular pigs, it would be difficult to say that it was fit for use for feeding pigs generally. But the arbitrators may have thought that on the evidence as a whole, as it stood, they were justified in finding that the barley was merchantable, and were not satisfied that it was unmerchantable, and they may have attached importance to the occasional use for malting or distilling. I do not feel able to say, on the materials before me, that their finding can be upset on grounds of law, though I do not say I should have arrived at the same conclusion.

In any case, their finding that the defects were not discoverable on reasonable examination is enough to support their award. I therefore give judgment upholding the award, and the claimants will have the costs of the hearing before me.

Award confirmed.

In SUMNER PERMAIN AND COMPANY *v.* WEBB AND COMPANY, [1922] 1 K. B. 55 (Court of Appeal, 1921), the defendants, manufacturers of mineral waters, sold to the plaintiffs a quantity of tonic water, under the description of "Webb's Indian Tonic," to be delivered f.o.b. London. The water, as the defendants knew, was bought for the purpose of shipment to the Argentine. Among the ingredients of the water there was, unknown to the plaintiffs, a certain percentage of salicylic acid. By the law of the Argentine the sale of any article of food or drink containing salicylic acid was prohibited, but the defendants had no knowledge of that law. On the arrival of the water in the Argentine the authorities condemned it as unfit for human consumption. In an action for breach of the contract of sale the plaintiffs contended that the impossibility of legally selling it in the market for which it was intended constituted a breach of the implied condition that the goods should be of merchantable quality. An appeal from a judgment for the plaintiffs was allowed. Bankes, L. J., said: "I emphasize the fact that the condition is not that the goods shall be 'merchantable,' but that they shall be of 'merchantable quality,' and that it is more restricted than it would have been if it had required that the goods should be merchantable. On the other hand the statute by the definition clause, s. 62, somewhat extends the natural meaning of the word 'quality,' for it defines it as including the 'state or condition' of the goods. Now I do not propose to attempt a definition which would include every possible case; it is enough for me to say that in my opinion it is impossible to bring within the expression 'merchantable quality,' even as extended by the definition clause, the capability of the goods being lawfully resold according to the law of the country in which it is known that the resale is intended to take place. The terms, 'quality,' 'state,' and 'condition,' seem to me to refer to something essentially different in their nature from that."

Scrutton, L. J., added: "In my view 'merchantable quality' means that the goods comply with the description in the contract, so that to a purchaser buying goods of that description the goods would be good tender. It does not mean that there shall in fact be persons ready to buy the goods. For instance take the case that I put during the argument; if you sell 'vestings' of a particular fancy pattern for sale in China, you do not warrant that the Chinese buyer will like that pattern and will buy it when it goes out there; if the goods are vestings of the pattern contracted for, they are merchantable though nobody likes the pattern or is willing to buy. Similarly I do not think 'merchantable quality' means that there can legally be buyers of that article. If the goods are of the contract description the possibility of legally making a sale of them does not in my view come within the expression 'merchantable quality.' "

Atkin, L. J., said, with reference to the obligation to insure that the goods shall be of merchantable quality, that "it is a warranty that the goods delivered shall be the goods described in the contract, and that they shall not differ from the normal quality of the described goods, including under the term 'quality' their state or condition as required by the contract, to such an extent as to make them unsaleable."

Compare NIBLETT *v.* CONFECTIONERS' MATERIALS COMPANY, [1921] 3 K. B. 387 (Court of Appeal), where there was a contract for the sale of "3000 cases of sweetened full cream condensed 1919 season's milk, quality equal to federal standard," at an agreed price c.i.f. London net cash against documents. The buyers received the documents and paid the price. The goods arrived bearing the name or brand "Nissly," an infringement of the registered trade mark of another manufacturer, at whose instance the goods were detained by the Commissioners of Customs. The buyers were obliged to remove the labels to get possession of the goods, and could sell them only at a loss without any distinctive marking. In an action by the buyers against the sellers for breach of warranty, it was held by Bankes and Atkin, L.JJ., that the sellers had broken the implied condition that the goods should be of merchantable quality, the former saying: "Quality includes the state or condition of the goods. The state of this condensed milk was that it was packed in tins bearing labels. The labels were as much part of the state or condition of the goods as the tins were. The state of the packing affected the merchantable quality of the goods." Bankes, Atkin, and Scrutton, L.JJ., all were of the opinion that the sellers also had broken the implied condition of having a right to sell.

Refer again to *Ryan* v. *Progressive Grocery Stores, Inc.* (*supra*, p. 412). In that case, after holding that there had been no reliance on the seller's judgment, Cardozo, Ch. J., concluded that there nevertheless had been a breach of the implied warranty of merchantable quality, saying: "Dealer as well as manufacturer or grower affirms as to anything he sells, if purchased by description, that it is of merchantable quality. The burden may be heavy. It is one of the hazards of the business.

"Most of the sales of defective food stuffs have been dealt with by the courts as if subdivision 1 of the section defining warranties gave the exclusive rule to be applied. In some instances the goods were not purchased by description. In others, the courts may have been unmindful of the fact that the warranty of merchantable quality is no longer confined to manufacturers or growers. Innovations of this order are slow to make their way. Gradually, however, as the statute has become better known, the bearing of subdivision 2 upon sales of food in sealed containers has been perceived by court and counsel. The nature of the transaction must determine in each instance the rule to be applied. There are times when a warranty of fitness has no relation to a warranty of merchantable quality. This is so, for example, when machinery competently wrought is still inadequate for the use to which the buyer has given notice that it is likely to be applied. There are times on the other hand when the warranties coexist, in which event a recovery may be founded upon either. . . .

"Loaves baked with pins in them are not of merchantable quality. The dealer is thus charged with liability though the buyer selects the brand, just as he would be liable for concealed defects upon a sale of wool or silk. Assume that the sale had been made by a manufacturer or a grower, and that there had been a request for a special brand. There would then be no warranty of fitness for any 'particular' purpose. Would any one dispute, however, that a defect of this order, destroying value altogether, would be covered by the warranty of merchantable quality? The question carries its own answer. The rule is different, to be sure, upon a sale of specific goods, not purchased by description (*Hight* v. *Bacon,* 126 Mass. 10). It may even be different, though the purchase is by description, if the goods are subject to inspection and the defects are of such a nature that inspection will reveal them (Williston, Sales, § 234; Pers. Prop. Law, § 96, subd. 3). Here the sale was by description, the defect was wholly latent, and inspection was impossible. In such circumstances, the law casts the burden on the seller, who may vouch in the manufacturer, if the latter was to blame. The loss in its final incidence will be borne where it is placed by the initial wrong."

B. Express Warranties and Conditions; Limitations and Disclaimers

CHANDELOR *v.* LOPUS

Exchequer Chamber, 1625

[*Croke's Reports, tempore James I,* 4]

Action upon the case. Whereas the defendant being a goldsmith, and having skill in jewels and precious stones, had a stone which he affirmed to Lopus to be a bezar-stone, and sold it to him for one hundred pounds; *ubi revera* it was not a bezar-stone: the defendant pleaded not guilty, and verdict was given and judgment entered for the plaintiff in the king's bench.

But error was thereof brought in the exchequer-chamber; because the declaration contains not matter sufficient to charge the defendant, *viz.* that he warranted it to be a bezar-stone, or that he knew that it was not a bezar-stone; for it may be, he himself was ignorant whether it were a bezar-stone or not.

And all the Justices and Barons (except Anderson) held, that for this cause it was error: for the bare affirmation that it was a bezar-stone, without warranting it to be so, is no cause of action: and although he knew it to be no bezar-stone, it is not material; for every one in selling his wares will affirm that his wares are good, or the horse which he sells is sound; yet if he does not warrant them to be so, it is no cause of action, and the warranty ought to be made at the same time of the sale; as F. N. B. 94. c. & 98. b. 5. Hen. 7. pl. 41. 9. Hen. 6. pl. 53. 12. Hen. 4. pl. 1. 42. Ass. 8. 7. Hen. 4. pl. 15. Wherefore, forasmuch as no warranty is alleged, they held the declaration to be ill.

Anderson to the contrary; for the deceit in selling it for a bezar, whereas it was not so, is cause of action. — But, notwithstanding, it was adjudged to be no cause, and the judgment was reversed.

POWER *v.* BARHAM

King's Bench, 1836

[4 *Adolphus & Ellis's Reports*, 473]

Assumpsit. The declaration stated that, in consideration that the plaintiff, at the defendant's request, would buy of him four pictures at a certain price, to wit, &c., the defendant "promised the plaintiff that the said pictures were painted by a certain artist or master in painting, called or named Canaletti, otherwise Canaletto." Breach, that the said pictures "were not, nor was either of them, painted by the said artist or master called or named Canaletti, otherwise Canaletto," whereby the said pictures were and are of little or no use, &c., and the plaintiff lost the benefits, &c. Plea, *non assumpsit.* On the trial before Coleridge J. at the sittings in Middlesex after last term, it appeared that the defendant sold the pictures to the plaintiff for 160*l.*, and, at the time of the sale, gave the following bill of parcels and receipt: —

Mr. N. Power.

Bought of J. Barham.

May 14th 1832.

Four pictures, Views in Venice, Canaletto,		£160 0 0
Settled by two pictures	£ 50 0 0	
And a bill at five months	110 0 0	
	£160 0 0	

J. Barham.

A carver and gilder, who had been employed by the plaintiff to procure original pictures for him, gave evidence of previous representations by the defendant to him and to the plaintiff, that the pictures were genuine; some doubt, however, was raised as to the expressions actually used. The witness stated that the pictures were in the manner of Canaletti, and, at the time of the sale, appeared to him worth the money. A witness experienced in paintings stated that he considered the pictures not to be Canaletti's, and valued them at about 8*l.* each; and some other evidence was given on this point. For the defendant it was contended that the bill of parcels was not a warranty, but only an expression of opinion; and *Jendwine* v. *Slade* was cited. The learned Judge, in summing up, told the jury that the pictures were admitted not to be Canaletti's, and that the only question on the pleadings was, whether the promise was made; and he submitted to their consideration, upon the whole of the evidence, whether the defendant had made a representation, as part of his contract, that the pictures were genuine, not using the name of Canaletti as matter of description merely, or as an expression of opinion upon something as to which both parties were to exercise a judgment, but taking upon himself to represent that the pictures were Canaletti's. His Lordship noticed the argument on behalf of the defendant, as to the bill of parcels; and said that the words of Lord Kenyon, in the case referred to, must be considered, not as a general rule of law, but as a direction to the jury on the circumstances of that case. The jury found a verdict for the plaintiff, saying, "We think the bill of parcels is a warranty."

Lord DENMAN, C. J. I think that the case was correctly left to the jury. We must take the learned Judge to have stated to them that the language of Lord Kenyon in *Jendwine* v. *Slade* (2 Esp. N. P. C. 572) was merely the intimation of his opinion upon such a contract as was then before him. It may be true that, in the case of very old pictures, a person can only express an opinion as to their genuineness; and that is laid down by Lord Kenyon in the case referred to. But the case here is that pictures are sold with a bill of parcels, containing the words "Four pictures, Views in Venice, Canaletto." Now words like these must derive their explanation from the ordinary way in which such matters are transacted. It was, therefore, for the jury to say, under all the circumstances, what was the effect of the words, and whether they implied a warranty of genuineness, or conveyed only a description, or an expression of opinion. I think that their finding was right: Canaletti is not a very old painter. But, at all events, it was proper that the bill of parcels should go to the jury with the rest of the evidence.

LITTLEDALE, J. The case was rightly sent to the jury; though, as to their decision, I think that all the auctioneers in London would be alarmed if they thought that such words as these were to be understood as a warranty.

WILLIAMS, J. The words in question might be a mere expression of opinion, or might amount to a warranty; it was for the jury to say which they imported. The language ascribed to Lord Kenyon seems to imply that, if a master is very old, there can be no means of saying that a certain picture is his, and, therefore, no warranty. The Attorney-General admits that this is not correctly applicable to the present case. If a person will undertake to sell these things as the productions of a particular master, he must take the consequences.

COLERIDGE J. concurred.

Rule refused.

Compare JENDWINE *v.* SLADE, 2 Esp. 572 (Nisi Prius, 1797), where there was an action to recover damages on the sale of two pictures sold under a catalogue in which appeared opposite the pictures the names of the respective artists. It was contended by the plaintiff that the name of the artist put opposite any picture in a catalogue was a warranty. Lord Kenyon said: "It was impossible to make this the case of a warranty; the pictures were the work of artists some centuries back, and there being no way of tracing the picture itself, it could only be a matter of opinion whether the picture in question was the work of the artist whose name it bore, or not. What then does the catalogue import? That, in the opinion of the seller, the picture is the work of the artist whose name he has affixed to it. . . . The catalogue of the pictures in question leaves the determination to the judgment of the buyer, who is to exercise that judgment in the purchase."

HEILBUT, SYMONS & CO. *v.* BUCKLETON

House of Lords, 1913

[*Law Reports,* [1913] *Appeal Cases,* 30]

Appeal from an order of the Court of Appeal affirming a judgment of Lush J.

The action was brought by the respondent against the appellants, originally for damages for false and fraudulent representation whereby the respondent was induced to purchase 6000 shares in a company called the Filisola Rubber and Produce Estates, Limited, but by his statement of claim the respondent added an alternative claim for damages for breach of warranty, the alleged warranty being that the company was a rubber company the main object of which was to produce rubber. This appeal is concerned with the question of warranty only. . . .

Viscount Haldane L.C. My Lords, the appellants, who were rubber merchants in London, in the spring of 1910 underwrote a large number of shares in a company called the Filisola Rubber and Produce Estates, Limited, a company which was promoted and registered by other persons about that time. They instructed a Mr. Johnston, who was the manager of their Liverpool business, to obtain applications for shares in Liverpool. Johnston, who had seen a draft prospectus in London but had at the time no copy of the prospectus, mentioned the company to several people in Liverpool, including a Mr. Wright, who sometimes acted as broker for the respondent. On April 14 the respondent telephoned to Johnston from Wright's office. As to what passed there is no dispute. The respondent said "I understand you are bringing out a rubber company." The reply was "We are." The respondent then asked whether Johnston had any prospectuses, and his reply was in the negative. The respondent then asked "if it was all right," and Johnson replied "We are bringing it out," to which the respondent rejoined "That is good enough for me." He went on to ask how many shares he could have, and to say that he would take almost any number. He explained in his evidence in chief that his reason for being willing to do this was that the position the appellants occupied in the rubber trade was of such high standing that "any company they should see fit to bring out was a sufficient warranty" to him "that it was all right in every respect." Afterwards, as the result of the conversation, a large number of shares were allotted to the respondent.

About this time the rubber boom of 1910 was at its height and the shares of the Filisola Company were, and for a short time remained, at a premium. Later on it was discovered that there was a large deficiency in the rubber trees which were said in the prospectus to exist on the Filisola Estate, and the shares fell in value. The respondent brought an action against the appellants for fraudulent misrepresentation, and alternatively for damages for breach of warranty that the company was a rubber company whose main object was to produce rubber.

The action was tried at Liverpool Assizes before Lush J. and a special jury. The jury found that there was no fraudulent representation by the appellants or Johnston, but they found that the company could not be properly described as a rubber company, and that the appellants or Johnston, or both, had warranted that the company was a rubber company.

The only evidence of warranty before the jury was the conversation I have quoted above. Lush J. gave judgment for the respondent for 406*l*. 5*s*., being the agreed amount of damages. The appellants appealed to the Court of Appeal, consisting of the Lord Chief Justice and Vaughan-Williams and Farwell L.JJ., on the ground that both findings ought to be set aside on the ground of want of evidence to go to the jury, or as being against the weight of evidence, and that the appellants were consequently entitled to judgment. The Court of Appeal dismissed the appeal on the ground that the evidence entitled the jury to find as it did.

As the case, so far as based on fraudulent misrepresentation, has been decided in favour of the appellants, who acted honestly, it is not necessary to consider whether the company was improperly described as a rubber company, unless the finding of the jury that there was a warranty can stand. For the warranty had become the sole ground on which the respondent could succeed. As I have already stated, the whole of the evidence of the conversation out of which the warranty alleged is said to have arisen is contained in the passages I have cited from the respondent's evidence in chief, and this conversation is not in dispute.

Now it is true that, when a jury has found facts, a Court of Appeal is not free to review unfetteredly the reasoning by which the jury has arrived at its conclusion. When evidence has been properly submitted to the jury, that body is entrusted with a duty which in large measure limits the province of the judge. If there was evidence on which the jury could properly find, its finding cannot be set aside, merely because if the Court had been dealing with that evidence the Court would have found otherwise. So far I agree with the Court of Appeal in the present case. But the question always remains whether the evidence was, so far as the relevant issue is concerned, of a character so insufficient as to render it wrong in law for the judge to have submitted it to the jury as material on which to base a finding on that issue.

My Lords, as neither the circumstances of the conversation nor its words were in dispute, I think that the question of warranty or representation was one purely of law, and that it ought not to have been submitted to the jury.

As soon as fraudulent representation was negatived, it seems to me that as to this there was no question of fact. The words of Mr. Johnston in the conversation proved by the respondent were words which appear to me to have been words not of contract but of representation of fact. No doubt this representation formed part of the inducement to enter into the contract to take the shares which was made immediately afterwards, and was embodied in two letters dated the next day, April 15. But neither in these letters nor in the conversation itself are there words either expressing or, in my opinion, implying a special contract of warranty collateral to the main contract, which was one to procure allotment.

It is contrary to the general policy of the law of England to presume the making of such a collateral contract in the absence of language expressing or implying it, and I think the learned judge who tried the case ought to have informed the jury that on the issue of warranty there was no case to go to it, and that on this issue he and the Court of Appeal ought to have given judgment for the appellants. The strongest presentation of the case for the respondent seems to me that of Farwell L.J. to the effect that there was a contract that the shares should be shares in a rubber company, and that the jury has found that the company was not a rubber company. But even on the basis of this finding I do not think that the account given by the learned Lord Justice of the transaction properly describes it. The respondent did not ask the technical question whether the company of which he had heard vaguely was correctly described as a rubber company. That he was not thinking of this point seems to me clear from the fact that when he received the letters informing him that he was to have shares in the Filisola Rubber and Produce Estates (a description which was in accordance with that in the prospectus) he made no further inquiry. What he from the first wanted to know was whether Johnston thought the company was "all right," a question to which Johnston simply replied that the appellants were bringing it out, an answer which, to my mind, simply conveyed that a firm of their standing would not be bringing it out if they did not believe it to be all right. From the evidence of the respondent, which immediately follows in the passage I have quoted, it seems to me plain that this was accepted by the respondent as the answer he wanted.

My Lords, words which on the face of them appear to be simply representations of fact may, if the context so requires, import a contract of warranty. The judgment of Lord Blackburn in *Brownlie* v. *Campbell* ((1880) 5 App. Cas. 925, at p. 953) is instructive on this point. But I cannot find in the words under construction, or in the circumstances, any context which required the Court to put upon them any interpretation beyond the natural one which I have stated. This interpretation I think they naturally bore, and the parties themselves appear to have put it upon them.

I wish to add that I entirely agree with the observations made by Lord

Moulton in the judgment which he is about to deliver, and which I have had the advantage of reading, on the authorities as to the test of whether words can be interpreted as giving rise to a warranty. Considerable confusion has arisen from failure to keep in view the simple principle to which he refers as enunciated by Holt C.J. that an affirmation can only be a warranty provided it appear on evidence to have been so intended. The words of Holt C.J. are cited with approval by Buller J. in *Pasley* v. *Freeman* ((1789) 3 T. R. 51). Not the least interesting of the older authorities which laid down the general principle, even in days when the action of *assumpsit* was by no means clearly marked off from that of case, is *Chandelor* v. *Lopus* ((1603) Cro. Jac. 4). It was there decided that the plaintiff, who was suing the defendant for misrepresentation as to the character of a precious stone sold to him, must declare on a contract, or if he declared in tort for a misrepresentation must aver a *scienter*. Had a moral of this decision, with its firm distinction between two wholly different causes of action, been steadily kept in view, there would have been less disposition than the Law Reports disclose to slip, by the easy process of leaving a supposed question of fact to a jury, from one legal conception into another which is totally distinct.

Neither the respondent nor Johnston appears to have had any question in his mind other than whether some company dealing with rubber, as to the identity of which there was no question raised, was being brought out by the appellants. For the respondent says that the position of the appellants in the rubber trade was such that "any company that they should see fit to bring out was a sufficient warranty" to him "that it was all right in every respect." His interest was in the shares for which he was minded to apply, and all he was really asking for was the assurance I have mentioned. Had Johnston thought that he was being asked to do anything else than answer the question whether the appellants were bringing out the company, he might well have refused to pledge himself, and I do not believe that either he or the respondent, regard being had to the character of the conversation, was thinking of any other question. But if not, there was in point of law no evidence to go to the jury on the issue as to warranty, and this issue ought not to have been submitted to it. In reality the only contract entered into seems to have been the contract reduced into writing by the two letters of April 15 for procuring an allotment of shares in what was described as the Filisola "Rubber and Produce Estates" Company.

It is with great reluctance that, in a case where the Court of Appeal has agreed with the verdict of a jury and the judgment of the judge who tried the case, I feel myself bound to come to a different conclusion. But I cannot, on the facts of this case, take any other view than that the appeal ought to be allowed. Judgment should, in my opinion, be entered in the action for the appellants, and the respondent ought to pay the costs here and in the Courts below. I move accordingly.

[Concurring opinions of Lord Atkinson and of Lord Moulton are here omitted.]

Order of the Court of Appeal reversed and judgment entered for the appellants. The respondent to pay the costs in the Courts below and of the appeal to this House.

Note also McFarland *v.* Newman, 9 Watts 55 (Pennsylvania Supreme Court, 1839) where the Court said: "Though to constitute a warranty requires no particular form of words, the naked averment of a fact is neither a warranty itself, nor evidence of it. In connection with other circumstances, it certainly may be taken into consideration; but the jury must be satisfied from the whole, that the vendor actually, and not constructively, consented to be bound for the truth of his representation. Should he have used expressions fairly importing a willingness to be thus bound, it would furnish a reason to infer that he had intentionally induced the vendee to treat on that basis; but a naked affirmation is not to be dealt with as a warranty, merely because the vendee had gratuitously relied on it; for not to have exacted a direct engagement, had he desired to buy on the vendor's judgment, must be accounted an instance of folly. Testing the vendor's responsibility by these principles, justice will be done without driving him into the toils of an imaginary contract."

Compare McClintock *v.* Emick, Stoner & Co., 87 Ky. 160 (Court of Appeals, 1888), where there was an action for damages resulting from the unsoundness of a lot of mules, the petition averring that the seller represented the mules to be all right. In upholding the sufficiency of the petition in this respect Holt, J., said: "It may be regarded as settled law, that no particular form of words is necessary to constitute a warranty, and that the mere expression of an opinion does not make one a warrantor. Some of the cases, however, seem to make the existence of a warranty depend upon the intention of the vendor; and it is urged in this case that the petition is defective in failing to aver that the appellant expected or intended the appellee to rely upon his representation in making the purchase. If the true construction of this class of cases is that the decision did not turn upon whether the party intended to be held by a warranty, but whether he intended to affirm a fact or merely express an opinion, then they are reconcilable with the cases which, in our opinion, correctly hold that if one even supposes that he is not making himself liable upon a warranty, yet if he makes a positive affirmation as to the condition of the property, or utters what is equivalent to a promise as to it, instead of expressing a belief merely, then such affirmation or promise amounts to a warranty, and he is liable upon it. It does not depend upon whether the vendor intends to be bound by his warranty or not, but upon whether he made an affirmation as to the condition of the article or merely expressed an opinion as to it."

JOHNSON *v.* CITY CO. OF NEW YORK, INC.

United States Circuit Court of Appeals, Tenth Circuit, 1935

[78 *Federal Reporter* (*Second Series*), 782]

Bratton, Circuit Judge. This is an action at law to recover damages. Plaintiff instituted the suit in two counts against the National City Company, a corporation organized under the laws of the state of New York with an office in Denver, Colorado. The corporate name of the defendant was changed during the pendency of the suit to the City Company and that substitution was made of record.

It was alleged in the first count that on November 1, 1929, plaintiff purchased from defendant at Denver 200 shares of capital stock of the National City Bank of New York at $450 per share, aggregating $90,000; that as a part of the sale defendant warranted that by November 4th — three days thereafter — the market price of the stock would be $650 per share; that the warranty was a material consideration for the making of the purchase and that plaintiff would not have bought without it; that the market value of the stock did not reach $650 per share at the specified date, but instead it dropped materially below the purchase price; that on November 6th he sold 100 shares at $295 per share less brokerage charge and on the next day he sold the remaining 100 shares at $270 per share less brokerage charge, each sale being made at the best price then obtainable and to avoid further loss; that the loss directly sustained upon the stock was $33,573.20; that the purchase and subsequent decline in value of the stock placed plaintiff under a financial obligation which forced him to sell other stock at a loss of $10,295.12 in order to protect himself.

The second count charged that defendant was an affiliate of the National City Bank, the two having certain officers and directors in common; that for more than five years prior to the transaction in question defendant represented and held itself out to plaintiff and others as being peculiarly fitted and situated to advise prospective purchasers with respect to the purchase of stocks and their value; that at the time of the transaction an arrangement existed between defendant and the bank through which each purchaser of stock in the bank thereby obtained a beneficial interest in the shares of stock of the defendant; that by reason of these facts defendant was well fitted to know the value of the stock being offered plaintiff; that defendant represented to plaintiff that the stock then had a value of $650 per share; and that plaintiff would be able to sell it for that price on November 4th. The other material allegations were similar to those contained in the first count. Judgment was prayed for $43,863.32, that sum represented the loss sustained on the stock in question and on the other stock which was sold.

The court sustained a demurrer to the second count and at the conclusion of plaintiff's evidence directed a verdict for the defendant on the first count. Judgment was entered accordingly, and plaintiff appealed.

Adopting the order in which the parties present the questions, we first consider the action of the court in sustaining the demurrer to the second cause of action. Two statements made by the defendant in connection with the sale are the foundation of the action. They were that the stock then had a value of $650 per share and that it could be sold for that price three days later. The statement respecting value necessarily had reference to its intrinsic value, because it was a listed stock of wide circulation and plaintiff knew that its then quoted market value was $450 per share. Ordinarily, a statement with respect to the intrinsic value of property which is the subject of barter and sale constitutes a mere expression of opinion and consequently will not support an action for breach of warranty. *Kimber* v. *Young* (C. C. A.) 137 F. 744; *Zimmern* v. *Blount* (C. C. A.) 238 F. 740. There is one well-recognized exception to that general doctrine. It is that where the seller makes a statement of that kind which he knows to be false to one who is ignorant of the facts and has no means of ascertaining them, under circumstances reasonably indicating that the statement is being relied upon, it becomes a deliberate affirmation of fact and may be the basis for recovery. *Kershaw* v. *Julien* (C. C. A.) 72 F.(2d) 528; *Dye* v. *Farm Mortgage Inv. Co.* (C. C. A.) 74 F.(2d) 395. But this case does not come within the exception. The subject-matter of the transaction was stock sold daily on the open market throughout the country. It was quoted currently and its market value was known on that day. It was not alleged that plaintiff lacked experience in the purchase of stocks or was unfamiliar with the means of ascertaining their worth and that defendant wrongfully took advantage of that situation in making statements which amounted to an affirmation of value upon which he had a right to act. That controlling fact distinguishes this case on clear ground from many upon which plaintiff relies, in which an ignorant and confiding purchaser without available means of knowledge relies upon statements of that nature made by the seller.

That part of the statement that the stock could be sold three days later at $650 per share was merely the expression of opinion, prophecy, or prediction. Even though such a statement is positive and emphatic, it lays no foundation for action since one must know that another cannot penetrate the future and forecast with reasonable certainty the course which the many fluctuating factors entering into value of stock will take. For that reason, one who gives credence to such statements and acts upon them does so as his peril and cannot have recourse in law for the recovery of damages if they fail to materialize. *Crosby* v. *Emerson* (C. C. A.) 142 F. 713; *Towle* v. *Maxwell Motor Sales Corp.* (C. C. A.) 26 F.(2d) 209. We think the court was right in sustaining the demurrer.

Was it error to direct a verdict for defendant on the first cause of action? It appears from the complaint and the proof that in the course of the negotiations an agent for defendant stated that it would guarantee that the stock would sell for the increased price three days thereafter, but no promise was made or even suggested that defendant would take it back if it failed to reach that figure. In the absence of extraordinary circumstances, a statement made in connection with the sale of property concerning its value must relate to a present, existing fact in order to constitute a contract of warranty. The word guarantee or warrant has no magic within itself. Use of either does not convert a statement in respect of future value into a contract of warranty upon which recovery may be had. If the statement relates to value at a future time, it is an expression of opinion, prophecy, or prediction, although it may embrace either of those words. A false statement or representation as to what the declarant expects to occur in the future, made by one having peculiar or extraordinary contacts and professing to have superior knowledge as the result, may constitute a representation of an existing condition which will support recovery for fraud. *Seimer* v. *James Dickinson Farm Mortgage Co.* (D. C.) 299 F. 651; *Wendell* v. *Ozark Orchard Co.* (Mo. App.) 200 S. W. 747; *State* v. *Taylor* (Mo. Sup.) 73 S. W.(2d) 378, 95 A. L. R. 476. But this case falls well outside the boundaries of that rule. Plaintiff was a business man of wide experience. He had dealt extensively in stocks and bonds. He had conducted 129 transactions with defendant alone covering a period of about ten years and aggregating more than $340,000 in amount. In addition, he had invested large sums in stocks for several oil companies with which he was associated and most of such investments were made through brokers. He usually visited the offices of defendant two or three times daily; he maintained an active account with a brokerage company in New York and he was conversant with the manner in which listed stocks and bonds were sold. He knew that the stock in question was listed throughout the country; that it was quoted daily on the market and he must have known that any statement with respect to its market value three days in the future was in essence and effect a mere expression of opinion or prediction. In these circumstances, he cannot be heard to say in a court of law that the statement was a warranty upon which he relied and acted. . . .

Concluding that there was no error in the trial proceedings, the judgment is affirmed.

In IRELAND *v.* LOUIS K. LIGGETT CO., 243 Mass. 243 (Supreme Judicial Court, 1922), Jenney, J., said: "The evidence warranted the following findings: The plaintiff's intestate, Inez M. Ireland, hereinafter called the plaintiff, went to a store of the defendant to purchase a jar of cold cream, and having asked for a particular kind that she had used, was informed by the clerk who waited upon her that the defendant did not have it in stock, but had 'a cream of their own . . . which was superior to the one she had been using' and which was 'pure and healthful'; relying on his recommendation she purchased two jars placed in cartons. Both cartons and jars were labelled 'Riker's Violet Cerate for the Complexion, a Soothing, Healthful Face Cream. Riker Laboratories, Inc., Distributor.' The plaintiff while using the cream rubbed some of it in her hand, and a piece of glass contained therein lodged in her palm.

"The plaintiff bases the right to recover for the injury so sustained solely upon alleged breaches of the contract of sale, having waived any right to recover in tort. No question of pleading is raised.

"The statement that the cream was 'pure and healthful' was an affirmation of fact and, having a natural tendency to induce the buyer to purchase the goods, it could have been found that she relied thereon; hence there was an express warranty that the cream was as stated. G. L. c. 106, § 14. *Henshaw* v. *Robins*, 9 Met. 83, 88. *Brown* v. *Bigelow*, 10 Allen, 242. *Cavanaugh* v. *D. W. Ranlet Co.* 229 Mass. 366. *Morse* v. *Moore*, 83 Maine, 473.

"A warranty of purity is broken if some foreign substance is contained in the merchandise rendering its normal use dangerous. *Flynn* v. *Bedell Co. of Massachusetts*, 242 Mass. 450, and cases collected. It follows that the motion for a directed verdict was properly denied, and the request for an instruction that the plaintiff on all the evidence was not entitled to recover was rightly refused. . . .

"In the charge the judge in substance instructed the jury that if the defendant's clerk at the time of the sale said to the purchaser that the merchandise furnished was 'very good, very popular, you will like it, we sell a great deal of it, and people don't find fault with it, they seem to be satisfied with it,' and if 'she relies upon what the clerk said in praising the goods, then there is a warranty in such a case that the goods are fit for the purpose for which they are sold, so that if there is any defect in them, glass or anything . . . then the seller is responsible for that defect.' And later continued: 'If you find that the facts warrant your finding the issue as claimed by the plaintiff, namely, that the deceased . . . asked for a kind of cream that wasn't in the store, and she was told they didn't have it, but they had this other kind, just as good, popular, recommended it, and the deceased girl relied upon that, relied upon the seller's talk about it, his recommendation, then there would be a warranty and the plaintiff would be entitled to recover.' The defendant's exception to these instructions must be sustained. They permitted the jury to find an express warranty of fitness because of representations in substance that the cream was good, popular, largely sold, that the plaintiff would like it, that fault had not been found with it, and that purchasers were satisfied; and the jury were told that if the plaintiff relied upon what the clerk said in praise of the goods and upon 'seller's talk' about the cream there would be a warranty. If we assume that these instructions related to statements that were in evidence, it is clear that they were erroneous because they disregarded the well settled distinction between affirmations of fact which may constitute a warranty and what is included in the term 'seller's talk,' puffing of wares, and expressions of opinion."

Refer also to *Keenan* v. *Cherry & Webb* (*supra*, p. 404), where it was held that "the language used when the coat was sold did not constitute an express warranty. To so hold would preclude fair commendation by a shopkeeper of his goods or expressions of honest opinion about their value or wearing qualities. Perhaps modern conceptions of business exact from a store keeper a larger degree of frankness than did those in the day when the doctrine of *caveat emptor* first appeared, but as yet general expressions of commendation as distinguished from statements of fact have not been held to be warranties. Such expressions as occurred in this case are still recognized as proper dealer's talk."

KRAIG *v.* BENJAMIN

CONNECTICUT SUPREME COURT OF ERRORS, 1930

[111 *Connecticut Reports*, 297]

MALTBIE, J. This is an action based upon a claimed breach of warranty growing out of a misrepresentation as to a used automobile purchased by the plaintiff from the defendant. From a judgment for the defendant the plaintiff has appealed. The plaintiff examined and rode in the car and was satisfied with it. Thereafter he purchased it. At the time of purchase the defendant or his salesman told the plaintiff that the car was a 1927 model; and the conditional bill of sale then executed so described it. In its conclusions, however, the trial court has found that the plaintiff did not rely upon this statement as the inducing cause of his purchase but rather relied upon the appearance of the car, its demonstrated condition, and the fairness of the purchase price. Whether this finding be regarded as a statement of a primary fact, out of place among the conclusions, as it apparently is, or as a fact deduced from the subordinate facts elsewhere stated, it must stand, if for no other reason, because the appeal in no way attacks it. The trial court was correct in its ruling that if the plaintiff did not rely upon the oral representation it would not constitute a warranty. General Statutes, § 4678; *Smith* v. *Reed*, 141 Wis. 483, 124 N. W. 489; *Richardson* v. *Coffman*, 87 Iowa, 121, 54 N. W. 356; 1 Williston on Sales (2d Ed.) § 206. In this case upon the finding we cannot say that the reference in the conditional bill of sale to the model of the car was more than mere description, and hence would not in itself constitute a warranty. *Hellman* v. *Kirschner*, 191 N. Y. Supp. 202; *Anthony & Dakota Elevator Co.* v. *Princeton Roller Mill Co.*, 104 Minn. 401, 116 N. W. 935; 1 Williston on Sales (2d Ed.) § 205, p. 396. As upon the record no warranty has been proven there is no occasion to examine the other claimed errors, except to note that the ruling on evidence, of which complaint is made, was so clearly right as not to justify discussion.

There is no error.

In this opinion the other judges concurred.

In HELLMAN *v.* KIRSCHNER, 191 N. Y. S. 202 (Supreme Court, Appellate Term, 1921), a written memorandum described the car sold as a "Cadillac sedan, model 57–V." It was in fact a model 57–J. The buyer had inspected the car before purchase, and the car delivered was the one which he had seen and agreed to buy. In an action for damages for breach of warranty the trial justice repeatedly stated to the jury that the memorandum incorporated an express warranty, and that the only question was whether there had been a breach of that warranty. A judgment for the plaintiff was reversed on the ground that the real issue to be submitted to the jury was whether the words used were of such a nature that the buyer relied on them in making the purchase.

CAMMELL LAIRD & CO., LTD. *v.* THE MANGANESE BRONZE & BRASS CO., LTD.

HOUSE OF LORDS, 1934

[*Law Reports,* [1934] *Appeal Cases,* 402]

Lord MACMILLAN. . . . The respondents are specialists in the manufacture of ships' propellers. The appellants, who are shipbuilders, placed an order with them for a propeller for a ship which the appellants were building. The order stated the dimensions and other particulars of the propeller required, and referred for further particulars to a print containing detailed drawings. It was stipulated that the propeller should be to the entire satisfaction of the building owners' representative and of the appellants. The propeller when supplied and fitted to the ship was found on trial to be so noisy as to be quite unserviceable. The respondents supplied a second propeller which proved little better. Finally they supplied a third propeller which worked quite satisfactorily. The question is who is to bear the loss consequent upon the respondents having supplied to the appellants the two propellers which had to be discarded.

If there is one thing clear it is that the two discarded propellers were certainly not to the entire satisfaction either of the appellants or of the building owners' representative. There is no suggestion that their dissatisfaction was unreasonable or expressed otherwise than in good faith. There would thus seem to have been a plain breach of a specific stipulation of the contract. The respondents do not dispute that they undertook to supply a propeller to the entire satisfaction of the appellants and of the building owners' representative, but they say that this requirement had reference not to the working of the propeller but only to its manufacture. The stipulation, they submit, was met if the propeller as delivered at the appellants' premises was satisfactory to them as regards material and workmanship and conformity with the order and if no dissatisfaction with it was then expressed.

My Lords, so narrow an interpretation of the stipulation appears to me to rob it of all business efficacy. The appellants wanted a propeller that would work. How could they know whether it was satisfactory until they had tried it? It has been proved that the unsatisfactory operation of the two discarded propellers was not due to the terms of the specification or to the way in which they were fitted to the ship or to any peculiarity in the ship itself or its engines, for at the third attempt the respondents supplied a propeller made to the same specification, which, when similarly fitted to the ship, worked satisfactorily; and a propeller made by the respondents to a practically identical specification for a sister ship also worked satisfactorily. The experts appear to have found great difficulty in ascertaining why the first two propellers worked unsatisfactorily; but it is, I think, demonstrated that the cause resided in the propellers themselves. I accordingly share the view of my noble and learned friends that the respondents are responsible for the loss occasioned by their failure at their first two attempts to supply a propeller to the satisfaction of the building owners' representative and the appellants.

[The balance of the opinion, dealing with the application of sec. 14, sub-sec. 1, of the Sale of Goods Act is here omitted. Concurring opinions of Lord Tomlin, Lord Warrington of Clyffe, and Lord Wright, also are omitted. Lord Russell of Killowen said in part:] Neither of those propellers was "to the entire satisfaction of the owners' representative."

There was therefore, according to the plain *prima facie* meaning of the words used in the contract, a breach of one of its express terms. I confess that I share Greer L.J.'s difficulty in seeing what answer there can be to the claim for breach of this express term. Both Roche J. and Scrutton L.J. dispose of this part of the case by saying that if the article is manufactured in accordance with the specification and is of good material and workmanship, the buyer has no right to express dissatisfaction about something else which is not in the contract, and thereby add a term to the contract. They both seem to overlook the fact that this contract requires the satisfaction of a third party who is a stranger to the contract, and who may know nothing of its terms. Lawrence L.J., although he does at one point refer to the owners, deals with the clause upon substantially the same footing, for he says ([1933] 2 K. B. 185): "The satisfaction of the person ordering the article must . . . be limited to satisfaction with something which under the contract the manufacturer has bound himself to do."

Whether or not this view is correct as regards the buyer (as to which I express no opinion), I can see no ground for so limiting the clause as regards a stranger to the contract. In terms there is an obligation on the respondents to make a propeller which will satisfy a third person. No doubt the third person must act in good faith and not capriciously. But that is only to say in other words, that he must in fact be dissatisfied with the propeller before it can be alleged that the express term has been broken. I can find no justification for modifying the absolute nature of this term of the contract. Even if its operation were limited to satisfaction in respect of matters not specifically covered by the contract, the facts of this case fall within it, because, as indicated above, the cause of the noise must be some feature or property not covered by the specified particulars and details.

Nor can I see any ground for limiting the operation of the clause to satisfaction with the propeller as a manufactured article, and saying that it does not include satisfaction with the propeller in operation. But even so limited, the clause would apply here. The owner is dissatisfied with the propeller, not with its propelling; the dissatisfaction is with the propeller because it contains some feature or property which results in excessive noise. The dissatisfaction is with the propeller because, as manufactured, it contains that undesirable feature or property.

In my opinion the appellants are entitled to succeed on this ground alone.

In BROWN *v.* FOSTER, 113 Mass. 136 (Supreme Judicial Court, 1873), Devens, J., said: "There was evidence at the trial to show that the contract between the parties was an express contract, and by the terms of it the plaintiff agreed to make and deliver to the defendant upon a certain day a suit of clothes, which were to be made to the satisfaction of the defendant. The clothes were made and delivered upon the day specified, but were not to the satisfaction of the defendant, who declined to accept and promptly returned the same. If the plaintiff saw fit to do work upon articles for the defendant and to furnish materials therefor, contracting that the articles when manufactured should be satisfactory to the defendant, he can recover only upon the contract as it was made; and even if the articles furnished by him were such that the other party ought to have been satisfied with them, it was yet in the power of the other to reject them as unsatisfactory. It is not for any one else to decide whether a refusal to accept is or is not reasonable, when the contract permits the defendant to decide himself whether the articles furnished are to his satisfaction. Although the compensation of the plaintiff for valuable service and materials may thus be dependent upon the caprice of another who unreasonably refuses to accept the articles manufactured, yet he cannot be relieved from the contract into which he has voluntarily entered."

Compare FECHTELER *v.* WHITTEMORE, 205 Mass. 6 (Supreme Judicial Court, 1910), where a contract for the sale of transfer signs provided for cancellation if "after a thorough trial we find that they do not work satisfactorily." In an action for the price the trial judge refused certain rulings requested by the defendant, and in overruling exceptions to this refusal and to the charge given, Morton, J., said: "The contract was partly in writing and partly oral, and it was rightly left to the jury to determine what the contract was and whether it had been performed by the plaintiffs. The jury were also rightly instructed that the defendants were not bound to accept and pay for the goods until they had had a reasonable opportunity to test and examine them, nor unless they were satisfactory to them, if they acted in good faith and did what they ought reasonably to have done to decide whether the goods were or were not satisfactory. In other words, the substance of the instructions in regard to the question of satisfactoriness was that the defendants were not bound to accept and pay for the goods unless they were satisfactory, and that they were entitled to sufficient time 'whether . . . three, or four, or six months, or a year,' to determine whether they were satisfactory, and that it was for the jury to say, taking all of the circumstances into account, whether the defendants had had a reasonable time to test and examine the goods, and, if that were so, then whether as reasonable men acting in good faith towards the plaintiffs the goods should have been accepted as satisfactory, and if they should have been, then the defendants were liable; otherwise not. This was correct and afforded the defendants no just ground for complaint."

In GUMBINSKY BROS. COMPANY *v.* SMALLEY, 203 App. Div. 661 (New York Appellate Division, 1922), a contract for the sale of paper stock provided that the quality was to be satisfactory to the sub-purchaser. The price of paper stock fell off, and the sub-purchaser refused the goods, stating that they were unsatisfactory, although there was sufficient evidence to justify a finding that this refusal was arbitrary and capricious. In affirming a judgment for the plaintiff in an action for the price, Greenbaum, J., said: "The second point made by appellant is that the quality of the stock was not satisfactory to [the sub-purchaser]. But they could not arbitrarily refuse to accept the shipment by merely stating that the quality was not satisfactory to them. It must appear that some fair basis exists for rejecting the shipment."

GLACKIN *v.* BENNETT

MASSACHUSETTS SUPREME JUDICIAL COURT, 1917

[226 *Massachusetts Reports,* 316]

CARROLL, J. In October, 1912, the plaintiff bought from the defendants a second hand 1907 Peerless motor car, for which he paid $600. At this time a written agreement was executed, a copy of which is printed above. This action is to recover for the breach of an oral warranty (made during the negotiations resulting in the sale), that the motor car could be operated twelve miles on one gallon of gasoline. There was no evidence of fraud nor of a breach of any of the terms of the written contract. On the cross-examination of the plaintiff, when the written contract for the first time appeared in evidence, he testified that when it was delivered he inquired concerning the warranty; thereupon the defendant Doane wrote what appears on the agreement in pencil, namely: "Guarantee as to parts same as with a new car." "I asked him to give me the guaranty that went with a new car. If that is the guaranty that goes with a new car I got all I asked for." He also testified that he did not know what Doane wrote. In the Superior Court the verdict was for the plaintiff.

When it is apparent that the writing contains only a part of the agreement and does not purport to set forth all its terms, or when it is a reasonable inference that it was not intended to be a full and final statement of the entire transaction, the existence of a separate agreement, not inconsistent with its terms and relating to some subject on which the written instrument is silent, may be shown by parol. *North Packing & Provision Co.* v. *Lynch,* 196 Mass. 204, 206. *Green* v. *Danahy,* 223 Mass. 1, 4. See also *West End Manuf. Co.* v. *P. R. Warren Co.* 198 Mass. 320; *Davis* v. *Cress,* 214 Mass. 379; *Lyman B. Brooks Co.* v. *Wilson,* 218 Mass. 205. But where a writing shows on its face that it includes the whole agreement of the parties and comprises all that is necessary to constitute a contract, it is presumed that they have placed the terms of their bargain in this form to prevent misunderstanding and dispute, intending it to be a complete and final statement of the whole transaction. And all their stipulations relating to its subject matter are to be found within the written instrument.

"The rule forbidding the introduction of parol testimony to vary or contradict a written agreement is not merely one of evidence, though commonly, perhaps, so spoken of, but one of substantive law, and rests on the doctrine that when parties have deliberately put their agreements in the form of a written contract they shall not be allowed to show that the agreement was something else." *Mears* v. *Smith*, 199 Mass. 319. *Butterick Publishing Co.* v. *Fisher*, 203 Mass. 122. *Fairfield* v. *Lowry*, 207 Mass. 352, 358. *Rochester Tumbler Works* v. *Mitchell Woodbury Co.* 215 Mass. 194, 197. *Goldenberg* v. *Taglino*, 218 Mass. 357, 359. By deciding to put in writing all their promises they made the writing the sole record of their agreement; they agreed to this by the execution of the contract. Its terms and conditions therefore must be sought in the instrument wherein they are recorded, and to modify, enlarge or contradict them, would violate the substantive rights of the parties. The instrument was complete in itself, — it showed on its face that it denoted a complete legal obligation and contained all the conditions of the contract: it gave the name of the buyer and of the seller, the make and kind of automobile, the price paid, the acknowledgment of payment, and the specific warranty "as to parts same as with a new car." In view of this it is unnecessary to consider the testimony of the plaintiff, and what inferences, if any, were to be drawn from it, showing his acceptance of the writing as a final and complete account of the agreement.

Although the plaintiff testified that he did not know what Doane wrote when the addition in pencil was made, there was no fraud practised upon him. He accepted the instrument as a final statement definitely fixing the terms of the agreement; and even if he did not sign it, no question under the statute of frauds arising, he is bound by it. See *Old Colony Railroad* v. *Evans*, 6 Gray, 25, 32, and cases cited.

There are no obscure words in the document requiring explanation, and oral evidence cannot be resorted to for this purpose. *Waldstein* v. *Dooskin*, 220 Mass. 232, 235.

An express warranty which is an affirmation of fact inducing the sale (sales act, St. 1908, c. 237, § 12), cannot be added to the written agreement under the rule permitting an agreement by parol which is collateral to the contract and on a distinct subject to be proved. *Durkin* v. *Cobleigh*, 156 Mass. 108. *Keith* v. *Radway*, 221 Mass. 515, 517, and cases there collected. *Dawson* v. *Grote*, 222 Mass. 240. If the terms of the sale are in writing, extrinsic evidence of an express warranty not referred to in the writing is not admissible, subject of course to the exception that the document is not a mere bill of parcels or other imperfect and incomplete record of the agreement. *Whitmore* v. *South Boston Iron Co.* 2 Allen, 52, 58.

Neale v. *American Electric Vehicle Co.* 186 Mass. 303, and cases cited. *Frost* v. *Blanchard,* 97 Mass. 155. *Scholl* v. *Killorin,* 190 Mass. 493. *Leavitt* v. *Fiberloid Co.* 196 Mass. 440, 445.

It is also to be mentioned that the contract was not silent on the question of warranting the motor car. When some particular subject is dealt with in the writing, it is presumed that the complete engagement on that subject is contained in the written contract. When the plaintiff asked for a warranty one was inserted. "By requiring a warranty, he is to be understood as excepting against all terms but such as are stipulated in the bargain." *Yeats* v. *Pim,* Holt, N. P. 95. *Webb* v. *Plummer,* 2 B. & Ald. 746, 750. The contract expressly provided that "Guarantee as to parts same as with a new car," and an additional warranty guaranteeing the extent of the consumption of gasoline in its operation could not be added by parol. The defendants' request, that the oral statements of warranty introduced before the written agreement was in evidence be stricken out, should have been granted.

As there was no breach of the written agreement and it could not be changed by parol, it is unnecessary to consider the other questions raised by the defendant.

Under St. 1913, c. 716, judgment should be entered for the defendant. Exceptions sustained.

Judgment for the defendant.

In Seitz *v.* Brewers' Refrigerating Machine Company, 141 U. S. 510 (U. S. Supreme Court, 1891), a contract was in the following terms:

"This agreement, made this 11th day of January, A.D. 1879, between the Brewers' Refrigerating Machine Company of Alexandria, Va., party of the first part, and Michael Seitz, of Brooklyn, N. Y., party of the second part, witnesseth:

"That the party of the first part hereby agrees and contracts to supply the party of the second part with a No. 2 size refrigerating machine, as constructed by the said party of the first part, by the 15th day of March next, or as soon thereafter as possible, the machine to be delivered at the depot or wharf in Philadelphia, Penn., and to be put up and put in operation in the brewery of the said party of the second part at 258–264 Maujer street, at Brooklyn, E. D., N. Y., under the superintendence of a competent man furnished by the said party of the first part.

"The party of the second part hereby agrees and contracts to pay to the said party of the first part for said machine the sum of nine thousand four hundred and fifty dollars ($9450.00)."

Further details followed as to the manner of payment. It was held that evidence was inadmissible tending to show a collateral parol warranty that the apparatus would cool a space of 150,000 cubic feet to the desired temperature.

Compare Gilmore *v.* Wingate, 21 Ariz. 542 (Supreme Court, 1920), where a contract read as follows: "Hay, 12 calves, 70 cows, 10 heifers, 2 mowers, 1 rake, 1 derrick, 1 separator can, 1 bull. Building feed rack bull pen to be left on place. I have received check for 200.00 Balance of 10,560 to be paid Oct. 16, 1917." It was held that evidence was admissible of an express oral warranty that the cattle were free from a certain disease.

BURKETT *v.* OIL AUTOMATIC HEATING CORPORATION

MICHIGAN SUPREME COURT, 1928

[241 *Michigan Reports*, 634]

FELLOWS, J. Supported by the evidence and not against its weight, the trial judge found that plaintiff made known the purpose for which he desired an automatic heating device to the defendant, a manufacturer of such a device using oil as a fuel and having a thermostatic control, and that he relied on defendant's skill and judgment in furnishing him a heating plant adaptable to his purpose, and that the plant furnished by defendant totally failed in its purpose. The testimony shows that plaintiff owns a house having several apartments, some of which are rented. Both he and his wife are employed and away from home during the day and he desired an automatic heating device which would not need constant attention to keep the rented appartments warm during their absence. The defendant first installed a so-called "Breeding" oil burner, but it was unsatisfactory and at an added price it installed an "Electro." There is no doubt on this record that defendant knew of plaintiff's purpose, and that plaintiff relied on defendant's skill and judgment in furnishing a device that would effectuate such purpose. There is an abundance of testimony that the device installed did not accomplish its purpose, and that plaintiff's tenants during the day, and he and his wife when at home suffered much from a want of heat. There is testimony that the service department of defendant frequently went to plaintiff's home to make adjustments and there is some testimony that requests for such service were met by undue delay. The parties came to the parting of the ways when an explosion and resultant fire endangered plaintiff's home and he ordered the outfit taken out.

Plaintiff claims that under the uniform sales act (Act No. 100, Pub. Acts 1913 [3 Comp. Laws 1915, § 11832 *et seq.*]), there was under the facts an implied warranty of fitness, while defendant contends that there was an express warranty and that none can be implied. We need not quote the "guarantee" found in the contract between the parties. For the purposes of the case we assume it to be an express warranty warranting that the equipment is free from defect in material and workmanship, and agreeing that defendant will replace any defective parts within the period therein stated. It does not go further than this. . . .

In the instant case the express warranty that the equipment was free from defects in material and workmanship is in no way inconsistent with the implied warranty of fitness provided for in the statute. Both counsel call our attention to numerous cases but neither of them cited *Pentland* v. *Jacobson*, 189 Mich. 339, which to our mind is decisive of the question. In that case it was held (quoting from the syllabus):

"Under Act No. 100, Pub. Acts 1913, § 15, and subd. 6, an express warranty does not preclude the existence of and reliance upon an implied warranty unless the two are inconsistent."

As this case follows the unambiguous language of the statute and is controlling, we need not take time to discuss and distinguish the numerous cases cited.

The judgment must be affirmed.

WIEST, CLARK, MCDONALD, and SHARPE, JJ., concurred. NORTH, J., did not sit.

Chief Justice FLANNIGAN and the late Justice BIRD took no part in this decision.

Compare WHITTY MANUFACTURING COMPANY, INC. *v.* CLARK, *supra*, p. 411, where a contract for the sale of an automatic coal burner contained express warranties with reference to conformity to the local smoke ordinance and that the burner would burn efficiently 100 tons of coal per hour. It was held that evidence was inadmissible to establish reliance under an implied warranty of fitness for a particular purpose.

S. F. BOWSER & COMPANY, INC. *v.* MCCORMACK

NEW YORK SUPREME COURT, APPELLATE DIVISION, 1930

[230 *New York Appellate Division Reports*, 303]

CROSBY, J. Plaintiff, appellant, brought this action to recover the balance of the purchase price of a so-called "oil fountain," which consisted of a series of storage tanks to be located inside defendants' service station and connected, by underground pipes, with a structure out of doors, called the fountain, where the oil was drawn near the customer to be served. The storage tanks and the fountain were furnished by the plaintiff, and defendants furnished the piping to connect the tanks with the fountain, and defendants also did the work of installation. Concededly there were no defects in the materials furnished by plaintiff, and concededly there was no fault with the manner of installation.

The defendants made an initial payment of $65.10 on the day of the sale, and, by the terms of the contract of sale, the $581 balance of the purchase price became due on May 7, 1928, when defendants defaulted in the payment of the installment then coming due.

The answer of defendants sets up, by way of counterclaim, a breach of express warranty as well as a breach of implied warranty of fitness for the purpose for which the fountain was intended. Under this counterclaim the jury awarded to defendants a verdict for the down payment made by them, plus the cost of installation. No fault is found with the amount of this verdict, provided defendants were entitled to recover on their counterclaim.

The fault that defendants find with the fountain is that oil will not, during the cold winter months, flow through the underground pipes and out through the spigots. An air pressure pump, furnished by defendants, was used to force the oil from the tanks through the pipes and out through the spigots. During cold weather the oil would not flow to advantage, even under pressure.

The written contract of sale contains no warranty that the oil will flow properly in cold weather. The only express warranty in the contract is that the materials are free from defects in materials and workmanship, and no such defects are claimed by defendants. The written contract contains a stipulation that "it covers all agreements between parties hereto relative to this transaction, and that [plaintiff] shall not be bound by any representation or promise made by any agent relative to this transaction which is not embodied herein."

Defendants offered to prove oral representations by plaintiff's agent that the oil would flow in the coldest weather. The trial court properly held that, under the clause of the written contract above quoted, defendants were precluded from reliance upon any express oral warranty. But the court also held that all these oral representations might be proven by defendants, together with all the talks between defendants and plaintiff's agent, for the sole purpose of showing that defendants made known to plaintiff the particular purpose for which the fountain was required, and relied on plaintiff's skill and judgment in relation thereto, and then submitted to the jury the question of implied warranty arising from such proof. (Pers. Prop. Law, § 96, subd. 1, as added by Laws of 1911, chap. 571.) In this, too, we think the trial court was quite right. Implied warranties may arise under written, as well as oral, contracts. (See *Carleton* v. *Lombard, Ayres & Co.*, 149 N. Y. 137.) That case holds, however, that parties may so frame their contracts as to preclude implied warranties. The question here is — does the stipulation that the written contract "covers all agreements" between the parties preclude implied warranties? We think not. We are persuaded that the implied warranty is not a part of the agreement, although necessarily connected with it. As was said in the opinion in *Matter of Casualty Co.* [*Bliss Co. Claim*] (250 N. Y. 410), the implied warranty "enters into or attends the contract" (p. 416). And in *Oetjen* v. *Whitehead Metal Products Co., Inc.* (126 Misc. 369) it was stated that "the statute itself fastens the implication upon the transaction." (See, also, *Dexter & Carpenter, Inc.* v. *Bliss Buildings, Inc.*, 123 Misc. 379, and *Cohan* v. *Markel*, 215 App. Div. 435.) Still the implied warranty is not an integral part of the agreement that gives rise to it. The following is the language of the opinion in *Hoe* v. *Sanborn* (21 N. Y. 552, 559), in speaking of implied warranties: "The civil law holds that the warranty enters into and forms an integral part of the contract of sale itself. * * * But the common law with, as I conceive, better logic, derives the obligation from the general doctrine which holds vendors responsible for every species of deception." This is another way of saying that the implied warranty, instead of being a part of the contract to which it attaches itself, is the law's contribution to the welfare of the parties beyond the terms of the contract itself. Or, to put it another way, the implied warranty is not read into the contract as a part and parcel thereof, but is a legal fiction invented to prevent the seller from loading a fraud onto a contract which, by its terms, would not be able to combat the fraud.

[The balance of the opinion holding as a matter of law that there was no reliance on plaintiff's skill and judgment is here omitted.]

All concur. Present — SEARS, P. J., CROUCH, TAYLOR, EDGCOMB and CROSBY, JJ.

Judgment and order reversed on the law and facts, with costs, and counterclaim dismissed, and judgment directed for the plaintiff for the sum of $581, with interest thereon from May 7, 1928, with costs.

Compare S. F. BOWSER & CO., INC. *v.* INDEPENDENT DYE HOUSE, INC., 276 Mass. 289 (Supreme Judicial Court, 1931), where a contract for the sale of "1 complete continuous white solvent circulating system for 8 washers" contained a clause identical with that in the principal case. In an action for a balance due on the purchase price the defendant sought to establish breach of an implied warranty of fitness for a particular purpose, but in ordering a new trial following a directed verdict for the plaintiff, Pierce, J., said: "We think there was no implied warranty of fitness upon the facts presented by the report, for the reason that the parties to a contract of sale of goods may expressly stipulate that the contract covers all agreements between them, and that such a stipulation, when made, as here, in the absence of fraud should be held to cover the implication which the law reads into the contract, as well as any special agreement between the parties which is outside the terms of the written contract."

In BEKKEVOLD *v.* POTTS, 173 Minn. 87 (Supreme Court, 1927), a contract for the sale of a tractor and truck contained a clause that "no warranties have been made in reference to said motor vehicle by the seller to the buyer unless expressly written hereon at the date of purchase." None were written thereon. It was held that this clause did not exclude an implied warranty of fitness, Wilson, C. J., saying: "It is only when an implied warranty is inconsistent with an express provision of the contract, that all implied warranties are merged in or superseded by the express provisions of the contract. In other words, warranties are not implied in conflict with the express terms of the contract. It has always been competent for the parties to put their entire agreement in writing and to expressly stipulate that no obligation arising out of an oral agreement, imposition of law, or otherwise shall rest upon either save as defined by their written agreement. If the parties wish to avoid the implied warranty they must in form or in substance contract against it.

"An implied warranty is not one of the contractual elements of an agreement. It is not one of the essential elements to be stated in the contract nor does its application or effective existence rest or depend upon the affirmative intention of the parties. It is a child of the law. Because of the acts of the parties, it is imposed by the law. It arises independently and outside of the contract. The law annexes it to the contract. It writes it, by implication, into the contract which the parties have made. Its origin and use are to promote high standards in business and to discourage sharp dealings. It rests upon the principle that 'honesty is the best policy,' and it contemplates business transactions in which both parties may profit. Defendants' claim does not commend itself to us as consistent with the honesty of purpose with which they are entitled to be credited in their dealings with their customers. The doctrine of implied warranty should be extended rather than restricted."

Contrast LANDES & Co. *v.* FALLOWS, 81 Utah 432 (Supreme Court, 1933), where a contract for the sale of a harvester contained a clause in substantially the same terms, and where it was held that the effect was to preclude an implied warranty of fitness.

INDUSTRIAL RAYON CORPORATION *v.* CLIFTON YARN MILLS, INC.

PENNSYLVANIA SUPREME COURT, 1933

[310 *Pennsylvania Reports*, 322]

Opinion by Mr. Justice SIMPSON:

This is an action to recover the price of certain inferior rayon yarn, sold by plaintiff to defendant. The principal issue between the parties was whether the sale was "as is and not returnable and without price guarantee," as plaintiff averred, or according to "sample," as defendant asserted. The trial judge told the jury that plaintiff could not recover unless they found the contract to be an "as is" contract. Their verdict for plaintiff, which was, as to this point, justified by the evidence, was, therefore, a finding that the sale was "as is and not returnable and without price guarantee"; and hence, unless defendant shows there was error in the admission or rejection of evidence, or some mistake in the manner of submitting that question to the jury, the judgment must be affirmed, since all other errors, if any, were harmless *quoad* the main point on which the verdict turned.

Viewed thus, the principal error alleged was that the trial judge submitted to the jury the determination of whether or not defendant was bound by a letter written on its behalf by one "B. Sherman." On this question, the record showed that after a consultation between plaintiff's Philadelphia representative and defendant's general manager, plaintiff sent to defendant, on request from the latter, five tubes weighing half a pound each of thirty filament inferior rayon yarn. Defendant, in turn, sent it to a prospective customer, and the latter agreed to take 50,000 lbs. of it, at 60 cents a pound. Defendant then sent to plaintiff, at its home office in Cleveland, Ohio, a purchase order for the 50,000 lbs. at 55 cents à pound, to which plaintiff, through its sales manager, wrote to defendant an acceptance of the order, directed to the "Attention of M. A. Price," defendant's general manager, saying therein: "It is further understood that this product is sold 'as is' and not returnable and without price guarantee." When the letter arrived at defendant's place of business, the general manager was absent, and the reply to it was signed "Clifton Yarn Mills, Inc., Rayon Plant, B. Sherman." It stated "The only change we wish to make in connection with your acknowledgment is that you omitted specifying net weight." The next day plaintiff wrote, agreeing to that change, and thus the contract upon which plaintiff relied was made.

Defendant contends, however, that "B. Sherman," who signed the second of the above letters, had no authority to act for defendant, and hence the contract relied on by plaintiff was not made, though the receipt of the 50,000 lbs. of inferior rayon yarn was admitted. This question was submitted to the jury, and their verdict in favor of plaintiff concludes this point also, if there was evidence justifying its submission.

[A page of the opinion, holding that there was such evidence, is here omitted.]

With these questions resolved in plaintiff's favor, the assignments of error raise but one other point which needs consideration. Defendant, in one of its points for charge, asked the court to say that a sale "as is . . . refers simply to the condition of the goods and not to their quality," and hence does not affect the question as to whether or not the "as is" sale was also to be according to a sample which had been submitted. The trial judge decided otherwise; but told the jury that if, as defendant alleged, plaintiff, in order to induce defendant to make the contract in suit, alleged the "goods were a reject of the coneing department . . . and the defendant purchased the yarn relying on that statement, and the statement was untrue because the delivered yarn was not a reject from the coneing department, then, even though it was an 'as is' contract, the defendant would have had a right to reject the goods, because while I said that 'as is' means you take the goods as is, that is subject to the doctrine that if there is an actual description or statement made of a fact, the purchaser has the right to rely on that statement or description, and in that case . . . the goods must be within the description." There is nothing in this of which defendant can justly complain, and the verdict in favor of plaintiff therefore determines that it made no false statement in regard to the yarn, and defendant's sole remaining contention must be that the court erred in deciding that if the yarn delivered was inferior rayon, "sold 'as is' and not returnable and without price guarantee," plaintiff had complied with its agreement.

Defendant correctly asserts in its brief: "The uncontradicted testimony is that there are only two standard grades of rayon yarn, first and second grade. . . . All rayon below these standard grades, down to waste, falls under the category of 'inferior rayon.'" Defendant also admits that the yarn it was to get was to be inferior rayon, and that it did get inferior rayon, but alleges that it was not of as high a quality as the five tubes which were sent to it before the contract was made. Perhaps, therefore, this complaint of defendant might be considered as having been answered by defendant itself, when it says in the letter of April 3, 1931, written by the sales manager: "I understood fully that the yarn was inferior and sold 'as is.' Inasmuch as there was no guarantee on the yarn, we accepted it 'as is' and based the quality of the yarn on the eight or ten [actually five] tubes that you submitted for approval."

Defendant cites a number of cases which it alleges bear out its contention as to the meaning of the words "as is" in a contract of sale; but a consideration of them shows that none of them does. In *Savage* v. *Z. S. Vertner Motor Sales Co.*, 3 Pa. D. & C. 505, it is simply decided that the language of a contract, which a vendor relies on to compel a vendee to accept a machine "absolutely incapable of performing its usual and customary functions," should "be clear and unequivocal and apply to the purchase in no uncertain terms." Here, the language of the contract falls within this requirement. In *United States* v. *Atlanta Wrecking Co.*, 8 Fed. (2d) 542, it is held that where at an auction sale the article was sold "as is and where is," and not by sample — although samples were submitted — its purchaser is bound to take the article he purchased though "on inspection [it] proved to be practically worthless." This antagonizes defendant's contention. In *W. H. Hedger Co.* v. *United States*, 42 Fed. (2d) 553, it is said that where the identity of articles sold is fixed, the "as is, where is" of the bill of sale refers only to the condition of the article. The court there relied on *Shepherd* v. *Kain*, 5 Barn. & Ald. 240, where the sale of an article was "with all faults," and it was held that this means all faults consistently with its being the thing described. Substantially the same conclusion was reached in *Whitney* v. *Boardman*, 118 Mass. 242, where it was held that "A sale of goods with 'all faults' covers, in the absence of fraud on the part of the vendor, all such faults and defects as are not inconsistent with the identity of the goods as the goods described." Fraud is not even averred in the instant case. In *Schwartz* v. *Kohn*, 155 N. Y. Supp. 547, "pussy willow taffeta was sold by sample 'as is,'" and it was held that "the seller cannot recover the purchase price where the goods delivered were not of the kind sold." *Morris Run Coal Co.* v. *Carthage Sulphite Pulp & Paper Co.*, 206 N. Y. Supp. 676, was decided under the provisions of the Personal Property Law of New York; and in *Stroock & Co.* v. *Lichtenthal*, 229 N. Y. Supp. 371, the contract construed was not an "as is" contract.

It will be observed that none of those cases defeats the construction of the court below in the present case. The jury have resolved in plaintiff's favor all questions touching statements made in regard to the goods; it is admitted that the yarn sold and the yarn received was inferior rayon yarn, taken from the same general lot as that from which the five tubes were taken; and the only question was as to whether or not defendant had the right to return what was delivered, because it was not as good in quality, and hence not as valuable as that contained in the five tubes. This objection is unavailing to defendant, under the contract provision "that this product is sold 'as is' and not returnable and without price guarantee."

Admittedly, the yarn delivered was thirty filament inferior rayon yarn, as the contract required it to be; and, this being so, the contract also said it was not to be returnable, and its price was not guaranteed. We regret defendant's loss, but this gives us no right, without plaintiff's consent, to do other than construe the contract which was made.

The judgment of the court below is affirmed.

ANDREWS BROTHERS (BOURNEMOUTH), LTD. *v.* SINGER AND COMPANY, LTD.

COURT OF APPEAL, 1933

[*Law Reports*, [1934] 1 *King's Bench*, 17]

Appeal from a decision of Goddard J.

The plaintiffs sued the defendants, claiming damages for breach of contract in respect of the sale of a motor-car.

By what was described as a "Main Dealers' Agreement," dated August 1, 1931, the defendants appointed the plaintiffs their sole dealers within a named area "for the sale of new Singer cars," and the plaintiffs agreed to purchase from the defendants a certain number of those cars. Clause 5 of the agreement was in these terms: — "All cars sold by the company [the defendants] are subject to the terms of the warranty set out in Schedule No. 3 of this agreement, and all conditions, warranties and liabilities implied by statute, common law or otherwise are excluded."

The warranty set out in Schedule No. 3 was as follows: — "We warrant that in the manufacture of new vehicles we have taken all precautions which are usual and reasonable to secure excellence of material and workmanship, and we undertake that if any defect is disclosed in any part of a new vehicle within twelve months of the date of delivery of such vehicle we will (provided such defective part is returned to our works, carriage paid) examine the part alleged to be defective, and if, on such examination, the fault is due to defective materials or workmanship, for which we are responsible, we will repair or replace the defective part free of charge. The foregoing warranty is limited to new vehicles manufactured by us, and is in lieu of any warranty (or condition) implied by common law, statute or otherwise, as to the quality or fitness for their purpose of any goods manufactured, replaced or repaired by us, every such implied warranty (or condition) being in all cases excluded, and our liability under the terms of this warranty is strictly limited to the replacement or repair and despatch to the sender, carriage forward, of the part replaced or repaired. . . ."

In pursuance of the agreement the plaintiffs sent an order to the defendants, for one 18 h.p. 6-cylinder Singer saloon car, and the defendants agreed to deliver it on March 9, 1932. The plaintiffs alleged that it was an express term and/or an implied term that the car should be a new car of the defendants' manufacture. Delivery of the car was taken at the defendants' works at Birmingham by the plantiffs' managing director, who noticed that the speedometer bore the reading 550 odd miles, and who found in the pocket of the car a parking ticket issued at Leicester, and from these he knew, as the judge found, that the car had run a considerable distance. The plaintiffs' representative at the time asked no questions regarding this, and the car was delivered to the plaintiffs at Bournemouth.

It appeared from the evidence at the trial that before its purchase by the plaintiffs the car had been sent to Darlington to be shown to a prospective customer, but, as he did not buy it, it was driven back to Birmingham, where it was adjusted, and was, at the time of the sale to the plaintiffs, as the judge found, in good mechanical condition.

The plaintiffs alleged that by reason of what had taken place the car was not a new car; that they had lost the profit on resale of a new car, and had been put to expense in and about taking delivery and examination of the car; and in respect of this they claimed damages.

The defendants pleaded that the plaintiffs' representative in the exercise of his own skill and judgment took delivery and paid for the car as a new car. They denied that they were guilty of any breach of agreement, and, further, they pleaded that if the car was in fact depreciated or was defective in any way (which they denied) their liability was limited to the repair or replacement of defective parts, and as these had not been returned they were under no liability to the plaintiffs.

Goddard J. held that the car was not a new car when sold to the plaintiffs; that the defendants' obligation was to sell and deliver a new car; and that as a new car had not been delivered the plaintiffs were entitled to damages, which he assessed at 50*l.*, and in addition he gave them certain expenses to which they had been put.

The defendants appealed.

[The opinion of Scrutton, L. J., upholding the judgment of Goddard, J., is here omitted.]

Greer L.J. I agree. There are two facts that form more or less firm ground on which the judgment can be based. First, it is not disputed that by the terms used in the contract the sale is to be of a new Singer car, and secondly, it was found by the judge, and is not now disputed, that the car delivered and as to which damages are claimed was not a new Singer car. It is said, however, by Singers that inasmuch as the car has been delivered to and accepted by the plaintiffs, and as the time for its rejection has passed, there is a clause in the contract which deprives the buyers of any remedy. It is contended that they are not liable for this breach of contract in delivering an old car instead of a new one, by the express terms of clause 5 of the contract, which says that "all cars sold by the company are subject to the terms of the warranty set out in Schedule No. 3 of this agreement, and all conditions, warranties and liabilities implied by statute, common law or otherwise are excluded." Scrutton L.J. has pointed out that sellers who desire to protect themselves against liability for damages for breach of condition or warranty were probably alarmed by the decision in *Wallis, Son & Wells* v. *Pratt & Haynes* ([1910] 2 K. B. 1003;

[1911] A. C. 394), and so the vendors in this case have endeavoured to escape the effect of the decision by phrasing the exempting clause differently. In *Wallis, Son & Wells* v. *Pratt & Haynes* ([1910] 2 K. B. 1003; [1911] A. C. 394) the clause was in these terms: "Sellers give no warranty express or implied as to growth, description, or any other matters, and they shall not be held to guarantee or warrant the fitness for any particular purpose of any grain, seed, flour, cake, or any other article sold by them, or its freedom from injurious quality or from latent defect." In that clause the sellers had not inserted, in addition to the word "warranty" the words "or condition," and inasmuch as compliance with the description in the clause was held not to be a warranty but a condition, the sellers failed to gain the protection they claimed they had from the clause. In one respect that clause was wider than that in the present case because there the sellers protected themselves against any express warranty that there might be in the contract, while those responsible for the wording of the clause in this contract, though they inserted the word "condition" left out the word "express." It seems to be an odd thing to say with respect to the description of an article sold that the vendor's obligation to deliver something which is the article sold and which complies with its description in the contract is an implied condition or warranty. It is quite true that by s. 13 of the Sale of Goods Act, 1893, the words "implied condition" are used, the section providing that "where there is a contract for the sale of goods by description, there is an implied condition that the goods shall correspond with the description. . . ." The Sale of Goods Act was intended to be a code for the purpose of removing all difficulties with regard to the interpretation of contracts of sale, as well as to provide for what might be determined to be the legal consequences of such contracts. It may be right to say that the descriptive terms of the contract, though they are express terms, are not expressly made conditions of the contract, and by using the expression "implied condition" in s. 13, those responsible for the statute did not mean to say that the obligation to supply the thing described is not an express obligation; they merely meant to say that the description is not a mere term or a mere warranty but is a condition of the contract by implication of law.

Looking at this contract it seems quite plain that it is one for the sale of a new Singer car and the phrase "new Singer car" is an express and not an implied term. Not only is that the case with regard to the body of this contract, but when we look at the guarantee which is to take the place of all warranties and liabilities implied by statute or common law which are excluded by clause 5, we find that the guarantee is to apply to any goods delivered under the contract and is a warranty expressly relating to new vehicles. It cannot be applied to a case where there is no new vehicle at all, because by its very terms the guarantee applies only to repairs to be done within twelve months after the delivery of a new Singer car, and if I did not take the view I have expressed with regard to the contract, apart from the guarantee, I should be prepared to say that the guarantee in itself contains a warranty that the goods which are to be delivered, and in respect of which the warranty is to apply, are to be new Singer cars. For those reasons I think the judgment of Goddard J. was right, and that this appeal should be dismissed.

EVE J. I am of the same opinion and I need add nothing to what has been said.

Appeal dismissed.

In WALLIS SON & WELLS *v.* PRATT & HAYNES, [1911] A. C. 394 (House of Lords), referred to in the principal case, there was a sale by sample of seed described as "common English sainfoin," the contract containing the clause quoted above. The seed produced a crop of giant sainfoin, an entirely different thing. It was held that the clause in question did not protect the sellers, for they had excluded liability for breach of warranty only, and warranties and conditions were *ab initio* entirely different.

LUMBRAZO *v.* WOODRUFF

NEW YORK COURT OF APPEALS, 1931

[256 *New York Reports*, 92]

CRANE, J. The plaintiff is a farmer living in Canastota, N. Y., and the defendants are growers of, and dealers in, seeds in the State of Connecticut. On May 14, 1926, the defendants sold to the plaintiff 300 bushels of Japanese onion sets at $3.50 per bushel. The sales contract contained a disclaimer of warranty clause reading: "We give no warranty, express or implied, as to description, quality, productiveness, or any other matter, of any seeds sent out, and will be in no way responsible for the crop, and the purchaser hereby waives the right of refusal and return of goods which is usually connected with the non-warranty."

The peculiarity of the Japanese onion sets is that under favorable conditions they produce a very large crop. The year previous, out of a purchase from the same defendants of one hundred bushels of Japanese onion sets, the plaintiff had raised twenty-two hundred bushels. While the Japanese onion may be of a somewhat better quality than others, "its productive ability is the greatest characteristic." The small bulb onion, or set, about one-half inch in diameter, has no distinguishing features which from inspection will indicate its vitality. From the fact that the planting of these three hundred bushels of sets produced about eighty per cent of seed stalks, and only one thousand bushels of onions, the conclusion has been reached that the sets could not have been Japanese onion sets, but those of an inferior grade or quality. The plaintiff has brought this suit for breach of warranty, in which he has recovered a judgment of $661.58. The Appellate Division, in affirming, has certified that a question of law is involved which should be reviewed by this court. The question is the validity and scope of the disclaimer of warranty clause.

Prior to the Uniform Sales Act, adopted in this State September 1, 1911, article 5 of the Personal Property Law (Cons. Laws, ch. 41), a sale by description was supposed to be an inherent part of the contract separate and distinct from any agreement, express or implied, amounting to a warranty. If the goods purchased were not of the kind ordered, it was the buyer's duty to return them within a reasonable time, and no cause of action for damages survived acceptance. In *Reed* v. *Randall* (29 N. Y. 358, p. 362) this rule was stated in the following language: "In cases of executory contracts for the sale and delivery of personal property, the remedy of the vendee to recover damages, on the ground that the article furnished does not correspond with the contract, does not survive the acceptance of the property by the vendee after opportunity to ascertain the defect, unless notice has been given to the vendor, or the vendee offers to return the property. The retention of the property by the vendee is an assent, on his part, that the contract has been performed."

Where the defendants purchased No. 1 extra foundry pig iron of the Coplay Iron Company, Ltd., make and received iron of a different make and inferior quality, but failed to return or offer to return the delivery after the facts became known, this court said: "Here there was no collateral warranty or agreement as to the quality of the iron. The representation as to the kind and quality of iron was part of the contract of sale itself, descriptive simply of the article to be delivered in the future; and clearly within the cases cited an acceptance of the property by the defendants, without any offer to return the same at any time, deprives them of any right to make complaint of its inferior quality." (*Coplay Iron Co.* v. *Pope*, 108 N. Y. 232.)

The words of description or of identification of a kind or class of property purchased have been considered not as warranties, but conditions precedent to any obligation on the part of the vendee, since the existence of the qualities indicated by descriptive words, being part of the description of the things sold, becomes essential to its identity, and the vendee cannot be obliged to receive and pay for a thing different from that for which he contracted. (*Carleton* v. *Lombard, Ayres & Co.*, 149 N. Y. 137, p. 148; Williston on Sales, vol. 1, §§ 179, 180, 205, 224.)

The distinction between a description amounting to a condition in the contract, or an essential part of the article sold, and a warranty, was quite important. As stated, when description was a condition, no right of recovery survived acceptance, whereas, for breach of warranty the buyer could retain the goods and sue to get his damage. Some confusion in the use of these terms arose, as is evident by the language of the opinion in *White* v. *Miller* (71 N. Y. 118, 129). The plaintiffs, who were market gardeners, purchased of the defendants market cabbage seeds of a variety known as Large Bristol Cabbage. The seeds were impure and of different variety, so that the plants raised therefrom were worthless. This court said: "A dealer who sells an article, describing it by the name of an article of commerce, the identity of which is not known to the purchaser, must understand that the latter relies upon the description as a representation by the seller that it is the thing described; and this constitutes a warranty."

In my judgment, the sounder view, however, was later expressed in the opinion by placing the decision upon the further ground that there always was an implied warranty that the thing sold was free from any latent defect arising from the mode of cultivation or the manner of manufacture, citing *Hoe* v. *Sanborn* (21 N. Y. 552). With cabbage seed no inspection could have disclosed its kind or purity so as to permit the purchaser to return the article under the condition precedent rule, relating to sales. The discovery of the kind and nature of the seed could only be disclosed by the crop, but it would then be too late to return or offer to return the seeds. The warranty was, therefore, applied to an inherent defect which no inspection would disclose. This distinction runs through such cases as *Hawkins* v. *Pemberton* (51 N. Y. 198), and *Van Wyck* v. *Allen* (69 N. Y. 61). No doubt it was difficult at times to distinguish between description and assertions as to quality or condition.

All these distinctions causing more or less confusion and uncertainty in the law have been swept away by the Uniform Sales Act, and we now have in section 95 of the Personal Property Law the provision that where there is a contract to sell, or a sale of goods by description, there is an implied warranty that the goods shall correspond with the description. This warranty, like the other warranties at common law, survives acceptance. The remedies are alike for all breaches of warranty, even those including what was formerly known in our State and at common law as the description of property, constituting a precedent condition authorizing rejection. The conditions in a contract of sale referred to in section 92 of the Personal Property Law are of a different nature altogether from those we are here discussing.

When, therefore, in the contract of sale made between the plaintiff and the defendants in this case, the word "warranty" is used, it has reference to those warranties defined in the Uniform Sales Act, unless it is otherwise expressed or restricted. The parties in the disclaimer of warranty clause exercised a right and privilege expressly reserved to them by section 152 of the Personal Property Law, which reads: "Where any right, duty or liability would arise under a contract to sell or a sale by implication of law, it may be negatived, or varied by express agreement or by the course of dealing between the parties, or by custom, if the custom be such as to bind both parties to the contract or the sale."

In raising Japanese onion sets the result is not always certain, and the examination of the bulbs will not disclose their inherent vitality. The business is more or less an undertaking to bargain with nature; the elements are not always the same. Therefore, the defendants were unwilling to assume the risk of the implied warranty connected with the sale of Japanese onion sets, as enacted in section 95 of the Personal Property Law, and insisted that if the plaintiff purchased three hundred bushels of these sets, he must take the risk of the crop, provided, of course, that the defendants had resorted to no fraud, unfair dealing or negligence amounting to undue enrichment. This clause was, therefore, made a part of the contract: "We give no warranty, express or implied, as to description, quality, productiveness, or any other matter, of any seeds sent out, and will be in no way responsible for the crop." The words cover the facts of this case. The defendants did not warrant that the seeds or sets were Japanese onion sets; neither did they warrant their productiveness. As stated above, the principal quality of Japanese onion sets is their ability to multiply, or their productiveness. There was to be no guarantee of these qualities. The plaintiff's only damage consisted in the failure to get the crop he expected or as many bushels of onions as the purchase should have produced.

Neither party was obliged to enter into this contract, and there is no public policy which prevents adult persons of sound mind making such agreements as they please, not prohibited by statute, or contrary to natural justice and good morals. This court and other courts have recognized the validity of agreements limiting or excluding implied warranties. (*Plimpton* v. *Brown Bros. Co.*, 224 N. Y. 724; *Kibbe* v. *Woodruff*, 94 Conn. 443; *Leonard Seed Co.* v. *Crary Canning Co.*, 147 Wis. 166; *Blizzard Bros.* v. *Growers' Canning Co.*, 152 Ia. 257; *Larson* v. *Inland Seed Co.*, 143 Wash. 557.)

Much reliance has been placed upon *Wallis* v. *Pratt* ([1911] App. Cas. [H. L.] 394, reversing [1910] 2 K. B. 1003), and *Howcroft* v. *Laycock* (14 Times L. R. 460). In reading these cases, the distinction between conditions precedent arising out of description and a true warranty, which has been referred to in the beginning of this opinion, must be remembered. The distinction apparently still exists in England; in fact, the English Sale of Goods Act, section 13, uses the word "condition" in place of the word "warranty," contained in our law, which has important consequences. Under that law breach of warranty does not justify rescission of an executed sale, and apparently does not even justify rejection of goods under an executory contract to sell. A "condition," on the other hand, not only justifies rejection of goods, but permits an action as in warranty, not formerly existing. (Williston on Sales, vol. 1, § 223-a.) *Wallis* v. *Pratt*, therefore, was governed by these distinctions and determined that the words, "sellers give no warranty expressed or implied as to growth, description or any other matters" relating to common English sainfoin, had no reference to condition or description. By this terminology, as heretofore stated, a sale by description constituted a sale upon condition, and did not constitute a warranty. A recovery could be had as on warranty for breach of a condition.

The judgment of the Appellate Division and that of the Trial Term should be reversed, and the complaint dismissed, with costs in all courts. (See 256 N. Y. 640.)

CARDOZO, Ch. J., POUND, LEHMAN, KELLOGG and O'BRIEN, JJ., concur; HUBBS, J., not sitting.

Judgments reversed, etc.

C. Privity

CHYSKY *v.* DRAKE BROTHERS COMPANY, INC.

New York Court of Appeals, 1923

[235 *New York Reports*, 468]

McLaughlin, J. The plaintiff was employed as a waitress in a lunch room run by one Abraham, for which she was paid thirty dollars a week and furnished board and lodging. On the 4th of May, 1918, she received from her employer, as part of her lunch, a piece of cake which had been made and sold to him by defendant. While she was eating it a nail, baked into the cake in such a way that it could not be discovered by inspection, stuck in her gum, which became so infected as to necessitate the removal of three of her teeth. She brought this action against the maker of the cake to recover the damages alleged to have been sustained, upon the theory it was liable to her, since it had impliedly warranted, when the cake was sold, that it was fit for human consumption and that such implied warranty inured to her benefit. This was the cause of action alleged in the complaint, as amplified by the bill of particulars, and this was the theory upon which the action was tried and submitted to the jury. She had a verdict and the judgment entered thereon was unanimously affirmed by the Appellate Division. Appeal to this court followed.

In *Race* v. *Krum* (222 N. Y. 410) we held that accompanying all sales by a retail dealer of articles of food for immediate use there is an implied warranty that the same is fit for human consumption. We did not consider or pass upon, as will appear from the opinion, whether such a warranty existed in the case of hotel proprietors or those engaged in a similar business. The cause of action arose before section 96 of the Personal Property Law took effect. (Cons. Laws, chap. 41.) In the present case the cause of action arose after the section took effect. This section provides that "there is no implied warranty or condition as to the quality or fitness for any particular purpose of goods supplied under a contract to sell or a sale, except as follows: 1. Where the buyer, expressly or by implication, makes known to the seller the particular purpose for which the goods are required, and it appears that the buyer relies on the seller's skill or judgment (whether he be the grower or manufacturer or not), there is an implied warranty that the goods shall be reasonably fit for such purpose."

If there be any liability, therefore, it must be under this section and the jury was so instructed.

In *Rinaldi* v. *Mohican* (225 N. Y. 70), where the cause of action arose after the section of the Personal Property Law quoted took effect, we held "that the mere purchase by a customer from a retail dealer in foods of an article ordinarily used for human consumption does by implication make known to the vendor the purpose for which the article is required. Such a transaction standing by itself permits no contrary inferences."

Under the section of the Personal Property Law referred to and the *Rinaldi* case, an action may be maintained to recover damages caused by the breach of an implied warranty in the sale of food to a consumer for immediate consumption. Whether this warranty extends to a wholesaler was expressly reserved in the *Rinaldi* case, but is now squarely presented.

The plaintiff received the cake from her employer. By reason of its condition it was not fit for human consumption. Her employer bought the cake from the defendant. Is it liable to the plaintiff for the injury sustained? We do not think so. If there were an implied warranty which inured to the benefit of the plaintiff it must be because there was some contractual relation between her and the defendant and there was no such contract. She never saw the defendant, and so far as appears, did not know from whom her employer purchased the cake. The general rule is that a manufacturer or seller of food, or other articles of personal property, is not liable to third persons, under an implied warranty, who have no contractual relations with him. The reason for this rule is that privity of contract does not exist between the seller and such third persons, and unless there be privity of contract, there can be no implied warranty. The benefit of a warranty, either express or implied, does not run with a chattel on its resale, and in this respect is unlike a covenant running with the land so as to give a subsequent purchaser a right of action against the original seller on a warranty.

It may be assumed that under certain facts and conditions the manufacturer of an article would be liable to a third person, even though no contractual relation existed between them, if the article sold were negligently prepared or manufactured. (*MacPherson* v. *Buick Motor Co.*, 217 N. Y. 382, and authorities there cited; Williston on Sales, sec. 244; *Thompson* v. *Quaker Oats Co.*, 239 Mass. 147; *Gearing* v. *Berkson*, 223 id. 257; *Tomlinson* v. *Armour & Co.*, 75 N. J. L. 748; *Johnson* v. *Cadillac Motor Car Co.*, 261 Fed. Rep. 878; *Haley* v. *Swift & Co.*, 152 Wis. 570.) But the recovery in the present case was not based upon the negligence of the defendant. Plaintiff limited her right to recover to a breach of warranty. She specifically stated in her bill of particulars "such breach of warranty by defendant she makes the issue in this action." I have not been able to find any authority, in this state at least, which would permit a recovery upon that ground and the great weight of authority in this country and England is directly to the contrary. (See *Ketterer* v. *Armour & Co.*, 247 Fed. Rep. 921, and authorities there cited.)

The judgments appealed from, therefore, should be reversed and the complaint dismissed, with costs in all courts.

HISCOCK, Ch. J., CARDOZO, POUND, CRANE and ANDREWS, JJ., concur; HOGAN, J., dissents.

Judgments accordingly.

Note also CARLSON *v.* TURNER CENTRE SYSTEM, 263 Mass. 339 (Supreme Judicial Court, 1928), where Braley, J., said: "The defendant corporation, engaged in the business of bottling and selling milk in quart and pint glass bottles, sold to one Holden, a retail dealer and its largest bottle customer, a quart bottle of milk with the name 'Turner Centre System' blown in the glass, which was purchased by the plaintiff of one Roberts, a storekeeper, to whom one Holden sold milk. It could be found on the evidence, that at the time of purchase there was a small piece of glass in the milk which lodged in the throat of the plaintiff while she was using it for food, causing injuries for which she seeks damages. A witness for the defendant stated, that he was in charge of the process of bottling the milk, which he described. It appeared that in washing the bottles before filling them with milk, the bottles were heated to a point just short of breaking, and that the bottles often broke while being washed, and sometimes pieces of glass flew into bottles that were being filled.

"The first count of the declaration, which is in tort for negligence, is not before us. It is contended by the plaintiff under the second count, in contract, upon which she elected to rely, that while there was no express warranty, there was an implied warranty by the defendant that the milk in question was wholesome and fit for human consumption. But there was no contractual relation between the defendant and the plaintiff, who dealt only with the retailer. . . .

"The verdict for the defendant in the case at bar was ordered rightly."

In GIMENEZ *v.* GREAT ATLANTIC & PACIFIC TEA CO., 264 N. Y. 390 (Court of Appeals, 1934), a married woman bought a can of crabmeat at a shop operated by the defendant company, and both she and her husband became ill because of the unfitness for human consumption. It was held that the husband had no action against the defendant in contract, the presumption being that the wife bought on her own account and not as an agent.

Note also PRINSEN *v.* RUSSOS, 194 Wis. 142 (Supreme Court, 1927), where three tourists went into a restaurant and ate ham sandwiches paid for by one of them. All three developed trichinosis. In an action against the owner of the restaurant by one of the tourists who had not paid for the sandwiches, it was held that no liability arose on an implied warranty because there was no privity of contract.

Compare COCA COLA BOTTLING WORKS *v.* LYONS, 145 Miss. 876 (Supreme Court, 1927), where two women parked in front of a wayside stand and ordered Coca Cola, one of them paying for the bottles that were brought. The other woman suffered severe internal injuries as a result of swallowing broken glass which was in the bottle from which she drank. The injured woman was allowed to recover on the ground that the bottle was at least a gift, which carried with it the title and consequently the implied warranty of fitness. An alternative theory was suggested but not relied on that the drinks were sold to both women, and that it hence was immaterial which one paid as the contract of sale already had arisen and payment was merely the settlement of an obligation incurred by both.

NOCK *v.* COCA COLA BOTTLING WORKS

PENNSYLVANIA SUPERIOR COURT, 1931

[102 *Pennsylvania Superior Court Reports,* 515]

Opinion by BALDRIGE, J.

The plaintiff purchased from a retailer a bottle of coca cola which was produced from an ice chest, the cap removed therefrom by the use of an opener attached underneath the counter, and the bottle then handed to the plaintiff. She had consumed a portion of the contents, when she was conscious of a creeping sensation on her lips, which proved to be due to a worm that had been in the bottle. She brought this action in *assumpsit* against the defendant who had manufactured and sold the product to the retailer, and recovered a verdict for $500. . . .

There is considerable confusion in the decisions as to the theory of the liability of the defendant in this class of cases. Some of them hold that an action is based upon negligence alone; others that it may be founded on an implied warranty; and still others that where an implied warranty exists, it does not extend to third parties. Undoubtedly, an action in tort could have been brought, but in determining whether or not that form is exclusive, one is confronted by a conflict of authorities which is confusing. The question whether an *assumpsit* under a contract of implied warranty of fitness, etc., may be maintained is, in many instances, so closely related to the question of negligence that the decisions are not always susceptible of clear classification. . . .

We think the sounder reasoning is in support of the theory that a sale of food or beverage impliedly warrants that it shall be free of a foreign matter which may be injurious to the well-being of the consumer. Nor do we see any just reason, from a public policy standpoint, as the health or human life may be involved, why a sale of food or beverage intended for human consumption should not carry with it an implied warranty that it is suitable and wholesome. Our Sales Act of May 19, 1915, P. L. 543, Section 15, provides that an implied warranty as to the quality or fitness for a particular purpose may be annexed by the usage of trade. Of course, there could have been no question as to the particular purpose for which the coca cola was to be used. It can hardly be conceived that it was for any other than drinking purposes and the implication is so strong as to be almost conclusive. . . .

That brings us to the question whether or not there was a privity of contract which created a liability. If the buyer has an opportunity to examine the article, as in *Wiedeman* v. *Keller,* 171 Ill. 93, where the product sold was meat, there may not be a liability, but when there is a sale in the original package, the rule now seems to be recognized that there is a privity of contract. In 11 R. C. L. 1122, it is stated, "In the case of articles of food sold in cans, bottles and sealed packages, some of the earlier decisions denied the right of the consumer to recover from a manufacturer, it appearing the goods were purchased through the medium of a retail dealer." In 17 A. L. R. 688, this principle is recognized in the following language: "The decided weight of authority is to the effect that an ultimate consumer may bring an action directly against a negligent manufacturer or packer for injuries from the use of a dangerous article, such as unwholesome food or beverages, though there is no contractual relation between the parties." A manufacturer may not ordinarily be liable to those with whom he has no contractual relation, but if he puts goods upon the market in a bottle or original package, he, in effect, represents to each purchaser that the contents thereof are wholesome and suitable for the purpose for which they are sold, and the common law doctrine of *caveat emptor* does not prevail. If the purchaser is without opportunity to examine for himself, as when he buys a bottle of beverage or a can of food, he had a right to rely upon the assurance of the manufacturer that the contents are fit and wholesome, and it is only just and reasonable to hold him responsible. We conclude, therefore, that there was an implied warranty for the plaintiff to found his action.

[The last two pages of the opinion are here omitted.]

The foregoing reasons lead us to hold that there is no merit in the assignments of error. Judgment affirmed.

Note also ANDERSON *v.* TYLER, 274 N. W. 48 (Iowa Supreme Court, 1937), where plaintiff bought a bottle of Coca Cola from the refreshment stand operated by a country club. The bottle contained a mouse, and plaintiff became so ill from drinking part of the contents of the bottle that he was obliged to leave his work and lost twenty pounds in weight. Recovery against the wholesalers supplying the bottle to the country club was allowed on the view that "the implied warranty that such products are fit for use runs with the sale, and to the public, for the benefit of the consumer, rather than to the wholesaler or retailer, and that the question of privity of contract in sales is not controlling and does not apply in such a case."

In WARD BAKING CO. *v.* TRIZZINO, 27 Ohio App. 475 (Court of Appeals, 1928), the original plaintiff purchased from a retail grocer a cake wrapped in thin waxed paper labeled "American Beauty Cake" together with the name of the Ward Baking Co. The cake contained a needle which the plaintiff swallowed, with resulting injury. Plaintiff was allowed to recover damages from the manufacturer of the cake on the ground of an implied warranty in his favor arising as a result of a contract between the grocer and the manufacturer for the benefit of the ultimate consumer.

BAXTER *v.* FORD MOTOR COMPANY

WASHINGTON SUPREME COURT, 1932

[168 *Washington Reports*, 456]

Appeal from a judgment of the superior court for Lewis county, Simpson, J., entered December 4, 1931, dismissing an action for damages for breach of warranty, upon sustaining a challenge to the sufficiency of the evidence. Reversed as to Ford Motor Company; affirmed as to St. John Motors.

HERMAN, J. During the month of May, 1930, plaintiff purchased a Model A Ford town sedan from defendant St. John Motors, a Ford dealer, who had acquired the automobile in question by purchase from defendant Ford Motor Company. Plaintiff claims that representations were made to him by both defendants that the windshield of the automobile was made of non-shatterable glass which would not break, fly or shatter.

October 12, 1930, while plaintiff was driving the automobile through Snoqualmie pass, a pebble from a passing car struck the windshield of the car in question, causing small pieces of glass to fly into plaintiff's left eye, resulting in the loss thereof. Plaintiff brought this action for damages for the loss of his left eye, and for injuries to the sight of his right eye. The case came on for trial, and, at the conclusion of plaintiff's testimony, the court took the case from the jury and entered judgment for both defendants. From that judgment, plaintiff appeals.

Appellant's first assignment of error is: The court erred in allowing the respondents to introduce in evidence, over the objection of appellant, the written contract of agency between the respondents. An investigation of the record discloses that A. C. St. John, the president of St. John Motors, was called as a witness by appellant's counsel, and was questioned with reference to his relationship with respondent Ford Motor Company. On cross-examination by counsel for the Ford Motor Company, this contract was offered in evidence for the purpose of showing the relations between respondents. The ruling was correct.

The second assignment of error is that the court refused to admit in evidence certain catalogues and printed matter furnished by respondent Ford Motor Company to respondent St. John Motors for distribution and assistance in sales.

When the car was sold to appellant, a written purchase order was entered into between the seller and the purchaser. Ford Motor Company was not a party to this agreement. Certain reading matter was printed on the back of the purchase contract, which printing purported to tell what constituted the Lincoln Motor Company warranty and the Ford Motor Company warranty. There was nothing in connection with the sales agreement which indicates that either the Lincoln Motor Company warranty or the Ford Motor Company warranty there set forth was made to, or accepted by, appellant or any other person.

The instrument in question was devoid of any provision which would have given appellant the right to sue the Lincoln Motor Company or the Ford Motor Company, if privity of contract be a condition precedent to a suit predicated on misrepresentations perpetrated by a manufacturer upon the public, resulting in the sale of products put forth as possessing qualities which the victim of such misrepresentations later discovers, to his damage, were lacking. Hence, respondent Ford Motor Company cannot successfully maintain that, so far as appellant is concerned, its warranties to appellant were set forth in the purchase agreement between appellant and the respondent dealer.

So far as that respondent, St. John Motors, is concerned, the written contract limits its responsibility to appellant. The purchase order stated that it contained the entire contract, and there was contained therein the following agreement:

"It is further agreed that no warranty either express or implied is made by the dealer under this order or otherwise covering said car."

To have permitted the introduction of the testimony in question as against respondent St. John Motors, would have been to have countenanced an attempt to vary the terms of the written instrument by parol testimony. Such evidence was not competent against respondent St. John Motors, and there was not sufficient evidence against that respondent to justify submission of the cause to the jury. Judgment was properly entered for respondent St. John Motors.

The principal question in this case is whether the trial court erred in refusing to admit in evidence, as against respondent Ford Motor Company, the catalogues and printed matter furnished by that respondent to respondent St. John Motors to be distributed for sales assistance. Contained in such printed matter were statements which appellant maintains constituted representations or warranties with reference to the nature of the glass used in the windshield of the car purchased by appellant. A typical statement, as it appears in appellant's exhibit for identification No. 1, is here set forth:

Triplex Shatter-Proof Glass Windshield. All of the new Ford cars have a Triplex shatter-proof glass windshield — so made that it will not fly or shatter under the hardest impact. This is an important safety factor because it eliminates the dangers of flying glass — the cause of most of the injuries in automobile accidents. In these days of crowded, heavy traffic, the use of this Triplex glass is an absolute necessity. Its extra margin of safety is something that every motorist should look for in the purchase of a car — especially where there are women and children.

Respondent Ford Motor Company contends that there can be no implied or express warranty without privity of contract, and warranties as to personal property do not attach themselves to, and run with, the article sold. . . .

In the case at bar, the automobile was represented by the manufacturer as having a windshield of non-shatterable glass "so made that it will not fly or shatter under the hardest impact." An ordinary person would be unable to discover by the usual and customary examination of the automobile whether glass which would not fly or shatter was used in the windshield. In that respect, the purchaser was in a position similar to that of the consumer of a wrongly labeled drug, who has bought the same from a retailer, and who has relied upon the manufacturer's representation that the label correctly set forth the contents of the container. For many years, it has been held that, under such circumstances, the manufacturer is liable to the consumer, even though the consumer purchased from a third person the commodity causing the damage. *Thomas* v. *Winchester*, 6 N. Y. 397, 57 Am. Dec. 455.

The rule in such cases does not rest upon contractual obligations, but rather on the principle that the original act of delivering an article is wrong, when, because of the lack of those qualities which the manufacturer represented it as having, the absence of which could not be readily detected by the consumer, the article is not safe for the purposes for which the consumer would ordinarily use it.

The vital principle present in the case of *Mazetti* v. *Armour & Co.*, 75 Wash. 622, confronts us in the case at bar. In the case cited, the court recognized the right of a purchaser to a remedy against the manufacturer because of damages suffered by reason of a failure of goods to comply with the manufacturer's representations as to the existence of qualities which they did not in fact possess, when the absence of such qualities was not readily discoverable, even though there was no privity of contract between the purchaser and the manufacturer.

Since the rule of *caveat emptor* was first formulated, vast changes have taken place in the economic structures of the English speaking peoples. Methods of doing business have undergone a great transition. Radio, bill boards and the products of the printing press have become the means of creating a large part of the demand that causes goods to depart from factories to the ultimate consumer. It would be unjust to recognize a rule that would permit manufacturers of goods to create a demand for their products by representing that they possess qualities which they, in fact, do not possess; and then, because there is no privity of contract existing between the consumer and the manufacturer, deny the consumer the right to recover if damages result from the absence of those qualities, when such absence is not readily noticeable.

"An exception to a rule will be declared by courts when the case is not an isolated instance, but general in its character and the existing rule does not square with justice. Under such circumstances, a court will, if free from the restraint of some statute, declare a rule that will meet the full intendment of the law." *Mazetti* v. *Armour & Co.*, 75 Wash. 622, 135 Pac. 633.

We hold that the catalogues and printed matter furnished by respondent Ford Motor Company for distribution and assistance in sales (appellant's exhibits for identification Nos. 1, 2, 3, 4 and 5) were improperly excluded from evidence, because they set forth representations by the manufacturer that the windshield of the car which appellant bought contained Triplex non-shatterable glass which would not fly or shatter. The nature of non-shatterable glass is such that the falsity of the representations with reference to the glass would not be readily detected by a person of ordinary experience and reasonable prudence. Appellant, under the circumstances shown in this case, had the right to rely upon the representations made by respondent Ford Motor Company relative to qualities possessed by its products, even though there was no privity of contract between appellant and respondent Ford Motor Company.

[The last page of the opinion is here omitted.]

We have considered the other assignments of error, and find them to be without merit.

Reversed, with directions to grant a new trial with reference to respondent Ford Motor Company; affirmed as to respondent St. John Motors.

MILLARD, BEALS, and MAIN, JJ., concur.

Compare ROBERTS *v.* ANHEUSER-BUSCH BREWING ASS'N, 211 Mass. 449 (Supreme Judicial Court, 1912), where plaintiff's wife and child became very ill through drinking a bottle of Malt Nutrine purchased by plaintiff from a druggist. There was evidence that the defendant had represented by advertisements that this product was healthful, free from all injurious substances, beneficial to women and children and to those needing strength and nourishment, and that it was compounded with great care. It was held that no action could be maintained on the ground that there was any warranty of good quality by the defendant, for there was no contractual relationship between plaintiff and defendant; but since the declaration was in tort, there was a question for the jury in the light of other circumstances on the points of knowledge and reliance.

In TURNER *v.* EDISON STORAGE BATTERY COMPANY, 248 N. Y. 73 (Court of Appeals, 1928), Pound, J., said: "The complaint alleges that the defendant is a manufacturer of storage batteries and that plaintiff purchased from the Fisher Hardware Company a battery manufactured by the defendant. Plaintiff attempts to state two causes of action against the defendant, one in negligence (*MacPherson* v. *Buick Motor Co.*, 217 N. Y. 382) and one for breach of warranty. In pleading the second cause of action he alleges that defendant warranted the battery to be safe, that he relied on the warranty, and that injury was sustained by breach of warranty. Warranty is an incident of a sale. (*Levis* v. *Pope Motor Car Co.*, 202 N. Y. 402; Pers. Prop. Law [Cons. Laws, ch. 41], § 93.) The complaint negatives a sale by the defendant to the plaintiff and any contractual relation between the plaintiff and the defendant. There can be no warranty where there is no privity of contract. A cause of action for breach of warranty, either express or implied, is not, and cannot be, stated. (*Chysky* v. *Drake Brothers Co.*, 235 N. Y. 468, 472.) The goods may have been sold to the Fisher Hardware Company with a so-called written and continuing warranty for the benefit of the ultimate purchaser. A cause of action for deceit conceivably might arise from such a transaction

(*Roberts* v. *Anheuser Busch Brewing Assn.*, 211 Mass. 449) or for negligent words (*International Products Co.* v. *Erie R. R. Co.*, 244 N. Y. 331), but no suggestion is made of an attempt to plead such a cause of action."

HAWKINS *v.* ALFALFA PRODUCTS CO.

KENTUCKY COURT OF APPEALS, 1913

[152 *Kentucky Reports*, 152]

Opinion of the Court by Judge CARROLL — Affirming.

The appellant, Hawkins, purchased from the appellee, Alfalfa Products Co., a Nebraska corporation, a carload of meal. The contract of purchase stipulated that the meal should be delivered to him in good order at Paducah, Kentucky. The Alfalfa Products Co. delivered in the state of Nebraska to the railroad company the carload of meal ordered by Hawkins and received from the railroad company a bill of lading therefor. This bill of lading showed that the meal was consigned to the Alfalfa Products Co., Paducah, Kentucky, and stipulated that H. P. Hawkins should be notified. In other words, it was that character of bill of lading commonly known as a "shipper's order bill of lading."

When the Alfalfa Company received from the railroad company the bill of lading, it drew its draft for $430, the purchase price of the meal, on H. P. Hawkins, payable to the Freemont National Bank and then attached the draft to the bill of lading and discounted the draft to the bank, with the bill of lading as collateral security. Hawkins paid to the bank in Paducah, to which the bill of lading and draft had been sent for collection by the Freemont bank, the amount of the draft and took possession of the bill of lading. After obtaining the bill of lading, which he could not secure until he paid the draft, he examined for the first time the carload of meal and discovered that it was worthless.

As the bill of lading stipulated that before the property covered by it was delivered to or inspected by the consignee the bill of lading should be surrendered to the carrier, Hawkins had no opportunity to learn of the condition of the meal until he obtained the bill of lading upon the payment of the draft; but when he discovered the worthless condition of the meal, he immediately brought suit against the Alfalfa Products Co. and the Freemont National Bank, and attached in the hands of the collecting bank the money he had paid it for the draft, his right to attach the proceeds of the draft being rested on the ground that the bank was responsible to him for the performance of his contract with the Alfalfa Co., and therefore liable to him in damages in the amount of the draft.

In answer to this suit the Freemont National Bank averred that it did not sell or deliver to Hawkins the carload of meal, and was not the owner, or in possession of the carload of meal at any time except as the owner and holder of the bill of lading given for same. It further averred, "That by virtue of the discounting and sale of said draft to it by the Alfalfa Products Co., it had a lien upon the said carload of meal and upon the proceeds of said draft for the satisfaction and payment of the said sum of $429.55, paid by it in discounting of said draft and bill of lading. It further says that, at the time of the payment of the said draft on the 21st day of March, 1912, to the First National Bank of Paducah, by plaintiff, the plaintiff had no lien upon said carload of meal, or upon the proceeds of said draft, and that it did have a lien upon all of the proceeds of said draft and the money paid in satisfaction therefor for the sum of $429.55, which said lien was prior and superior to the claims of all persons whatsoever, including the plaintiff herein, and that it is entitled to the proceeds of the draft as against the attachment sued out by the plaintiff herein."

Some evidence was taken by the parties, but as there is really no issue of fact involved in the case, it is not necessary to notice the evidence. We may, however, observe that the evidence does not show that the bank had any information of the conditions of the contract between the Alfalfa Co. and Hawkins, or that there was any collusion or bad faith in the transaction so far as it was concerned. It simply discounted the draft and took the bill of lading as collateral security in the ordinary and usual course of banking business. It had no contract relations with reference to the meal with Hawkins or anything to do with the quantity or quality of the meal shipped to him by the Alfalfa Co.

When the case came on for hearing the court adjudged that the lien of the Freemont National Bank was superior to the attachment lien of Hawkins, and directed the garnishee to pay the proceeds of the draft to the Freemont bank. On this appeal it is insisted by counsel for Hawkins that the Freemont National Bank, in accepting the bill of lading, which not only transferred to it during transit the title but the constructive possession of the meal, obliged itself to deliver the meal according to the terms of the contract between Hawkins and the Alfalfa Products Co., or, in other words, assumed the contract and took the place of the Alfalfa Products Co. in the transaction, and hence Hawkins had the right to subject to his claim for damages for breach of contract the money he paid in satisfaction of the draft, to compensate him for the injury he sustained by the delivery to him of the worthless carload of meal.

For the Freemont National Bank the argument is made, that it was not a party to the contract between Hawkins and the Alfalfa Co., and had nothing to do with and knew nothing about the condition of the carload of meal.

That it simply discounted the draft drawn by the Alfalfa Co. on Hawkins, which was secured by the pledge of the bill of lading. That it had no contractual relations with Hawkins, and did not warrant or guarantee the quantity or quality of the meal, or in any manner assume the performance of the contract.

If the Freemont National Bank, by its acceptance of the bill of lading as security for the money it advanced on the draft, put itself in the attitude of guaranteeing the contract made between Hawkins and the Alfalfa Co., or assumed the obligation of performing this contract, the attachment lien of Hawkins should be adjudged superior to the lien of the bank, as Hawkins was damaged by the breach in the amount paid for the draft.

On the other hand, if the acceptance by the Freemont National Bank of the bill of lading, as security for the money advanced on the draft, did not have the effect of substituting it to the obligations assumed by the Alfalfa Co. in its contract with Hawkins, or of creating any contract relations between it and Hawkins, except such as might arise in the collection of the draft, Hawkins could not rely on the breach of contract made with the Alfalfa Co. to defeat the collection of the draft, or look to the bank for compensation for the damage he sustained, his remedy being a suit against the Alfalfa Co.

The rights and liability of the assignee of a bill of lading with a draft attached, as in this case, have been before us several times, but in no one of the cases was the exact question here presented involved.

[Several cases were here mentioned.]

While the cases we have referred to cannot be regarded as controlling the disposition of this case, there are many from other courts that do, but before referring to some of the representative cases that sustain the judgment below, we will notice the authorities relied on by counsel for Hawkins.

The principal case is *Russell* v. *Smith Grain Co.*, 80 Miss. 688, 32 Sou. Rep. 287. The opinion in that case, which was rested entirely on the case of *Landa* v. *Lattin Bros.*, 19 Texas Civil Appeals, 246, fully supports the position taken by counsel. In that case the Mississippi Court held that a bank buying a draft from the shipper, with a bill of lading attached to secure it, became responsible for the performance of the contract between the buyer and the seller of the goods mentioned in the bill of lading, and hence, when the buyer and consignee paid the draft and took possession of the goods, he had a right upon finding that they did not come up to the contract, to maintain an action against the holder and owner of the draft for a breach of his contract with the seller, and to attach the money he paid on the draft in the hands of the collecting bank to secure him in the damages growing out of the breach of the contract.

We find, however, that *Landa* v. *Lattin Bros.*, was impliedly, if not expressly, overruled by the Texas court in *S. Blaisdell, Jr., Co.* v. *Citizens National Bank of Tyler*, 96, Texas, 626, 75 S. W., 292, 62 L. R. A., 968, 97 Am. St. Rep. 944. *First National Bank of Chicago* v. *Mineral Wells & L. P. St. Ry. Co.* ——— Tex. ———, 133 S. W., 1099. In these cases the court held in substance that a bank in purchasing a draft with bill of lading attached, did not assume the contract between the seller and the buyer, or become responsible to the buyer for a breach of its conditions, and so the buyer could not maintain an action for a breach of his contract against the owner of the draft, or attach the money he had paid for the draft.

The case of *Finch* v. *Gregg*, 126 N. C., 176, also relied on by counsel, was overruled in *Mason* v. *Cotton Co.*, 148 N. C., 492, 18 L. R. A. (n. s.) 1221. *Hass* v. *Citizens Bank*, 144 Ala., 562, 1 L. R. A. (n. s.) 242, also giving support to the contention of counsel, was in effect overruled in *Cosmos Cotton Co.* v. *First National Bank of Birmingham*, 171 Ala., 392, 32 L. R. A. (n. s.) 1173.

The result of this change of position on the part of the Texas, North Carolina and Alabama courts puts these courts in line with the current of opinion, which is that the holder of the draft is not liable for a breach of the contract between the seller and the buyer, and cannot reclaim from the holder of the draft the money paid for it. This leaves the Mississippi court, so far as our investigation goes, alone in holding to the doctrine that, a bank discounting for the seller a draft with a bill of lading attached, assumes the position of the seller in his contract with the buyer, and becomes responsible to the buyer for the seller's breach of contract.

But aside from the cases in conflict with the views announced by the Mississippi court, we are not disposed to adopt the reasoning of that court. We think the fundamental error in the position assumed by it consists in the fact that it seeks to make the transferee of the bill of lading liable for the performance of a contract that he had no part in making and no connection with. The transfer of the bill of lading does not transfer the contract between the seller and the buyer, or in any manner effect the rights of the parties to that contract. *Cox* v. *Central R. R.*, 170 Mass., 129.

The transferee of a bill of lading only acquires title during transit to the goods for which the bill of lading was issued in the condition they were at the time of its issue. His acceptance of the bill of lading as security for a loan does not create any contract relation between him and the consignee, or make him either a guarantor or a warrantor of the quality or quantity of the goods, or impose on him the duty of undertaking that they will be delivered in good order. In short, the transfer of a bill of lading is nothing more or less than a constructive delivery to the transferee of the goods mentioned in it. The transferee, with the bill of lading in his possession, has, in the eyes of the law, the possession of the goods until they are delivered to the consignee. *The Carlos F. Roses*, 177 U. S., 655, 44 Law Ed., 929; *Means* v. *Bank of Randall*, 146 U. S., 620, 36 Law Ed., 1107.

In paying the draft and taking possession of the goods the right of the buyer to enforce compliance with his contract by the party with whom the contract was made is unimpaired, and to the party with whom the contract was made he must look for damages for its breach. If the goods do not fulfill the contract, the buyer must look to the seller for compensation or recoupment, and if they are damaged in transit by the fault of the carrier, he must look to the carrier for indemnity. When the buyer in a case like this pays the draft, the transaction between him, and the owner and holder of the draft, is a closed incident. His acceptance of the draft creates a new and independent contract and the only one that exists between him and the bank, and when he has paid the draft this contract is fully executed and the bank released from all liability to him.

The buyer can neither attach the money paid on the draft nor maintain an action against the owner of the draft for a breach of the contract committed by the seller. Of course if the buyer could attach the money paid on the draft he could likewise, after paying the draft, and without seeking to hold the money by attachment, bring an independent action against the owner of the draft and substitute him to the full liability of the seller for a breach of the contract.

To impose upon the transferee of a bill of lading, who takes it in good faith, for a valuable consideration, the duty of fulfilling the contract between the seller and the buyer, would impair, if not destroy, the value of bills of lading as instruments of trade and commerce, in the transaction of which they play so useful a part. No bank would feel safe in advancing or lending money on a bill of lading if the law burdened it with the performance of the contract between the seller and the buyer that it was not a party to.

It may be true to some extent, as argued by counsel, that if the buyer is compelled to pay the draft before he can obtain the attached bill of lading and inspect the goods, it will subject him to probable loss, and, in the case of a non-resident seller, leave him without a convenient forum in which to recover the damage he has sustained by the seller's failure to deliver the goods according to contract. But this circumstance should not be permitted to lead to the adoption of a rule that would work infinitely more harm than the occasional damage resulting from a breach of the contract.

The judgment is affirmed.

Note also FIRST NATIONAL BANK *v.* TCHULA COMMERCIAL CO., 132 Miss. 58 (Supreme Court, 1923), where a similar result is reached under the Federal Bills of Lading Act (1916) on the ground that the effect of that Act is to free the innocent holder of a draft and bill of lading from any liability on the contract between the shipper and the purchaser.

In MARTIN *v.* AUTO FINANCE CO., 25 S. W. (2nd) 919 (Texas Civil Appeals, 1930), a financing company purchased from the seller notes given by the buyer to cover a sale of machinery. In an action against the buyer by the finance company on the notes, the buyer pleaded breach of an implied warranty of fitness. It was held that the finance company, not having been the seller, could not stand in the relation of warrantor to the buyer.

Note also WILLIAM J. BITTLES COMPANY, INCORPORATED *v.* PELLEGRINO REALTY COMPANY, 109 N. J. L. 520 (Court of Errors and Appeals, 1932), where it was held that the purchaser of a buyer's note from the seller assumed no liability in regard to a warranty of proper performance of refrigerating equipment, and that knowledge of the warranty by the purchaser was immaterial in the absence of notice that the consideration of the note might be affected.

CHAPTER II

Terms and Conditions Relating to the Documents

1. SHIPPING DOCUMENTS

DIAMOND ALKALI EXPORT CORPORATION *v.* FL. BOURGEOIS

King's Bench Division, 1921

[*Law Reports,* [1921] 3 *King's Bench,* 443]

Award in an arbitration stated in the form of a special case.

By a contract in writing dated August 7, 1920, the Diamond Alkali Export Corporation of New York agreed to sell to Fl. Bourgeois of Great St. Helens in the City of London, 50 tons of soda ash for September/October shipment from American seaboard at $4.70 per hundred pounds c.i.f. Gothenburg. Terms of payment were cash against documents under confirmed banker's credit at London.

Among the conditions contained in the contract was the following: "Seller not liable for failures or delays in delivery due to strikes, lockouts, fire, accident, embargoes, stoppage of navigation, lack of transportation, war restrictions or seizures by any governmental agency or any contingencies whatever beyond seller's control. In case any deliveries are delayed owing to any such contingency, the delayed shipments shall be made as soon as possible after such contingency has been removed or such shipments may be cancelled at seller's option. Date of bill of lading is to be considered date of payment."

The sellers arranged for the goods to be carried in the Swedish steamship *Anglia,* which was originally scheduled to leave Philadelphia for Gothenburg on October 13, 1920, and obtained the necessary permit for shipment from the Traffic Control Manager in New York. The date of sailing was, however, delayed, and the date of the bill of lading which, according to the contract, was to be considered the date of shipment, was November 8, 1920. This delay arose from causes which were, as the arbitrator found, beyond the seller's control.

The original documents were tendered in London with an invoice for the goods to the buyer on November 24, 1920. The documents were rejected by the buyers and payment was refused on the grounds (1.) that the sellers had not shipped the goods until November 8 and 9, 1920: (2.) that a proper bill of lading was not presented, the goods being described in the document presented to the buyers as "received in apparent good order and condition to be transported by the S.S. *Anglia*" instead of as "shipped per S.S. *Anglia*": (3.) that a proper policy of insurance was not presented them, but a document described as a "certificate of insurance."

As to (1.) the sellers contended that the non-shipment of the goods in September/October, 1920, was met by the above strike clause in the contract.

The questions for the opinion of the Court were (1.) whether the "strike clause" applied, and (2.) whether under the contract, and according to the law of England, the documents presented by sellers — namely, the bill of lading and certificate of insurance — were, together with the invoice for the goods, valid and sufficient to entitle sellers to payment of the price. It was admitted that these points were to be decided according to English law and the award so stated.

The arbitrator made an alternative award to meet the decision of the Court, according as it should be in favour of the sellers or the buyers. The terms of the documents and the arguments are sufficiently set out in the judgment.

McCardie, J. [His Lordship first decided that the effect of the strike clause was to enable the sellers to ship at a later date, and then continued:]

It thus becomes my duty to consider the serious and powerfully argued contention of the buyers, that the documents tendered did not conform to the contract. I will deal with those documents separately. It is admitted that the points are to be decided by English law and the award so states. I take first what I will call for convenience the bill of lading. That document was issued by the Swedish America Mexico Line, Ld., of Gothenburg, Sweden. It is dated November 8, 1920. It contains many clauses. The arguments before me turned on the earlier words of the bill of lading, and those only I set out. They are these: "Received in apparent good order and condition from D. A. Horan to be transported by the S.S. *Anglia* now lying in the port of Philadelphia and bound for Gothenburg, Sweden, with liberty to call at any port or ports in or out of the customary route or failing shipment by said steamer in and upon a following steamer, 280 bags Dense Soda." Perhaps I should add that the first of the many clauses in the bill of lading is this: "It is mutually agreed that this shipment is subject to all the terms and provisions of and all the exemptions from liability contained in the Act of Congress of the United States approved on the 13th day of February, 1893, and entitled 'An Act for the navigation of vessels.' " This Act of 1893 provides by s. 4: "That it shall be the duty of the owner or owners, master or masters or agent of any vessel transporting merchandise or property from or between ports of the United States and foreign ports to issue to shippers of any lawful merchandise a bill of lading or shipping document stating, amongst other things, the marks necessary for identification, number of packages or quantity, stating whether it be the carrier's or shipper's weight, and apparent order or condition of such merchandise or property delivered to and received by the owner master or agent of the vessel for transportation, and such document shall be *prima facie* evidence of the receipt of the merchandise therein described." I call attention to the words "bill of lading or shipping document." The Act recognizes that there may be shipping documents fulfilling the requirements of the section and yet not bills of lading.

Now the buyers strongly contend that the document here tendered was not a bill of lading at all, and that in any event it was not such a bill of lading as was required by the contract. They call attention to the fact that the document does not acknowledge the goods to have been actually placed on board. It merely says that the goods have been received "to be transported by the S.S. *Anglia*." They further call attention to the words "or failing shipment by said steamer in and upon a following steamer." I need scarcely say that I appreciate the vital nature of the buyer's contention, inasmuch as the form of document now before me is of frequent use at American ports. In order to test the matter it is necessary in the first place to consider the rights of a buyer under a c.i.f. contract. The strike clause here is a mere accident, and does not seem to affect the point at issue. For inasmuch as the duty of the vendors was to ship as soon as the contingency ceased to operate, and inasmuch as they were able to ship on November 8 and 9, 1920, it follows that the time of shipment under the contract was that date.

What then are a seller's duties and buyer's rights under a c.i.f. contract? They were stated by Lord Blackburn in *Ireland* v. *Livingston* ((1872) L. R. 5 H. L. 395, 406), where he refers to a "bill of lading." So, too, the well-known judgment of Hamilton J. in *Biddell Brothers* v. *E. Clemens Horst Co.* ([1911] 1 K. B. 214, 221), where he says: "It follows that against tender of these documents, the bill of lading, invoice, and policy of insurance, which completes delivery in accordance with that agreement, the buyer must be ready and willing to pay the price." So Kennedy L.J. says in his judgment in the same case in the Court of Appeal ([1911] 1 K. B. 934, 956): "How is such a tender to be made of goods afloat under a c.i.f. contract? By tender of the bill of lading, accompanied in case the goods have been lost in transit by the policy of insurance. The bill of lading in law and fact represents the goods": see too the judgment of Scrutton J. in *Landauer & Co.* v. *Craven* ([1912] 2 K. B. 94, 107). The latest statement is the opinion of Lord Birkenhead in *Johnson* v. *Taylor Bros. & Co.* ([1920] A. C. 144, 149), where he says in speaking of the duties of a vendor under a c.i.f. contract: "He is bound in the second place to tender to the purchaser within a reasonable time after shipment the shipping documents, for example, the bill or bills of lading and a policy of insurance reasonably covering the value of the goods." I should mention also the notes to Scrutton on Charterparties, 10th ed., Art. 59. If then a vendor under an ordinary c.i.f. contract is bound to tender a bill of lading, the question next arising is: What is meant by a bill of lading within such a contract?

The contract decides the rights of the buyer. The question is not as to the meaning of the phrase in a particular Act of Parliament or as to the possible meaning under other forms of contract. Nor is it material that a buyer objects to the documents for ulterior motives: see, for example, Lord Cairns' judgment in *Bowes* v. *Shand* ((1877) 2 App. Cas. 455, 465, 476) and Lord Hatherley's judgment in the same case. A buyer, as these noble Lords pointed out, is entitled to insist on the letter of his rights. As Lord

Hatherley said: "If you seek to fasten upon him the engagement, you must first bring him" — the buyer — "within the four corners of the contract." A buyer, moreover, may have obvious business reasons for so insisting, as he may have to implement his own bargain with rigorous subvendees. Now I consider that the phrase "bill of lading" as used with respect to a c.i.f. contract means a bill of lading in the sense established by a long line of legal decisions. Unless this meaning be given the matter is thrown into confusion.

In Art. 3 of Scrutton on Charterparties, 10th ed., is a definition which says: "A bill of lading is a receipt for goods shipped on board a ship signed by the person who contracts to carry them or his agent and stating the terms on which the goods were delivered to and received by the ship." This statement suggests at once an obvious and serious distinction between a receipt for goods actually shipped on board a particular ship and a receipt for goods which are at some future time to be shipped on board either a particular ship or an unnamed ship to follow her. The business distinction and varying results of the two seem to me to be plain. The legal distinction seems to me to be equally plain.

From the earliest times a bill of lading was a document which acknowledged actual shipment on board a particular ship. In Bennett's History of the Bill of Lading (Cambridge Press, 1914), at p. 8, is this passage: "Desjardins says that towards the close of the 16th century the use of the Bill of Lading was widespread — he quotes a definition from Le Guidon de la mer, a document of that epoch, which defines the Bill of Lading as 'the acknowledgment which the master of the ship makes of the number and quality of the goods loaded on board' ": see Desjardin's Traité de Droit Commercial Maritime, Tome 4, Art. 904 (Paris, 1885). It is clear, I may add, that the bill of lading sprang from the ship's book of lading, which was a document of recognized importance showing the goods actually put on board.

The famous case of *Lickbarrow* v. *Mason* ((1794) T. R. 685) was decided in 1794. It decided that bills of lading were transferable by the custom of merchants. The finding of the jury as to the custom is set out as follows: It begins: "By the custom of merchants, bills of lading, expressing goods or merchandises to have been shipped by any person or persons to be delivered to order or assigns, have been, and are, at any time after such goods have been shipped, and before the voyage performed, for which they have been or are shipped, negotiable and transferable by the shipper or shippers of such goods." The word "negotiable" in that special verdict really means no more than the word "transferable" or "assignable": see Scrutton on Charterparties, Art. 56 (note).

I am not aware of any decision which has modified the finding of the jury in *Lickbarrow* v. *Mason* ((1794) T. R. 683, 685) as to the subject-matter to which alone the custom of transferability applied. Apparently that custom, and that custom only, was operative when the Bills of Lading Act, 1855 (18 & 19 Vict. c. 111), was passed. Now that Act expressly recites the custom found in *Lickbarrow* v. *Mason* ((1794) T. R. 683, 685), and then proceeds: "And whereas it frequently happens that the goods in respect of which bills of lading purport to be signed have not been laden on board." It thus seems plain that the Act was referring to documents acknowledging an actual shipment on board a specified ship. I need not refer to ss. 1 and 2 of the Act. But s. 3 says: "Every bill of lading in the hands of a consignee or endorsee for valuable consideration representing goods to have been shipped on board a vessel shall be conclusive evidence of such shipment as against the master or other persons signing the same." It seems clear that no assignee can invoke the benefits, for example, of s. 3 of the Act, unless the document actually asserts the goods to have been shipped on board.

The whole point of the section seems to go if the document does not contain such an assertion. I will refer to this Act later.

Now in Blackburn on Sale, 3rd ed. (1910), p. 421, is this statement. "A bill of lading is a writing signed on behalf of the owner of the ship in which goods are embarked, acknowledging the receipt of the goods, and undertaking to deliver them at the end of the voyage (subject to such conditions as may be mentioned in the bill of lading)." The common form of a bill of lading is given in Carver on Carriage by Sea, 6th ed., Sect. 54. It is worthy of observation that in an American case, *Rowley* v. *Bigelow* ((1832) 12 Pick. 307 (Mass.)), Shaw C.J. said: "The bill of lading acknowledges the goods to be on board and regularly the goods ought to be on board before the bill of lading is signed": see note (3.) in Parsons on Shipping (Boston), vol. i., p. 187, where the learned author somewhat pointedly says: "It is a fraud on the part of the Master to sign the bills before the goods are on board." In Benjamin on Sale, 6th ed., p. 846, is this passage, giving the result of the cases: "When delivery is to be made by a bill of lading the rule is that the seller makes a good delivery if he forward to the buyer, as soon as he reasonably can after the shipment, a bill of lading, whereunder the buyer can obtain delivery, duly indorsed and effectual to pass the property in the goods, made out in terms consistent with the contract of sale, and purporting to represent goods in accordance with the contract, and which are in fact in accordance therewith." Apart from any authority to the contrary it seems to me that I must hold that the document here is not a bill of lading within the c.i.f. contract before me. It does not acknowledge the goods to be on board a specific ship, nor does it acknowledge a shipment on board at all. It leaves it uncertain as to whether the goods will come by the *Anglia* or some following ship. The word "following" is loose and ambiguous in itself. The document does not even say "immediately following," nor does it indicate that the "following ship" will belong to or be under the control of the person who issues the bill of lading. The document seems to me to be (in substance) a mere receipt for goods which at some future time and by some uncertain vessel are to be shipped. It is not even in the form of the New York Produce Exchange bill of lading set out in Carver, 6th ed., Appendix A, p. 971. The buyer is left in doubt as to actual shipment and actual ship.

The sellers, however, submit that I am bound by the opinion of the Privy

Council in *Marlborough Hill* (*Ship*) v. *Cowan & Sons* ([1921] 1 A. C. 444). The buyers, on the other hand, contend that that opinion is erroneous and that I ought not to follow it. I need scarcely state the deep diffidence and embarrassment which I feel in discussing that weighty opinion. As Lord Phillimore himself, however, pointed out in *Dulieu* v. *White & Sons* ([1901] 2 K. B. 669, 683), a Privy Council advice is not binding on the King's Bench Division even as to the *res decisa.* I wish to point out first that the actual decision in the *Marlborough Hill Case* ([1921] 1 A. C. 444) was merely that the bill of lading there in question (which closely resembles the one now before me) fell within s. 6 of the Admiralty Court Act, 1861. It may be that the phrase "bill of lading" in that section permits of a broad interpretation. I point out next that there is no express statement in the *Marlborough Hill Case* ([1921] 1 A. C. 444) that the document there in question actually fell within the Bills of Lading Act, 1855. In the third place it seems to me to be clear that the Board did not consider the nature and effect of an ordinary c.i.f. contract or the decisions thereon in relation to the question before them. The case of *Bowes* v. *Shand* (2 App. Cas. 455) moreover was not even cited to the Board. Lord Phillimore, in reading the advice of the Privy Council, said ([1921] 1 A. C. 451): "There can be no difference in principle between the owner, master, or agent acknowledging that he has received the goods on his wharf, or allotted portion of quay, or his storehouse awaiting shipment, and his acknowledging that the goods have been actually put over the ship's rail." With the deepest respect I venture to think that there is a profound difference between the two, both from a legal and business point of view. Those differences seem to me clear. I need not state them. If the view of the Privy Council is carried to its logical conclusion, a mere receipt for goods at a dock warehouse for future shipment might well be called a bill of lading. Again the Board say ([1921] 1 A. C. 444, 452): "Then as regards the obligation to carry either by the named ship or by some other vessel; it is a contract which both parties may well find it convenient to enter into and accept. The liberty to tranship is ancient and well established, and does not derogate from the nature of a bill of lading, and if the contract begin when the goods are received on the wharf, substitution does not differ in principle from transhipment." I do not pause to analyse these words. I only say that in my own humble view substitution and the right of transhipment are distinct things, and rest on different principles. The passage last cited can, I think, have no application at all to a c.i.f. contract, which provides for a specific date of shipment. It will suffice if I say two things. First, that in my view the *Marlborough Hill Case* ([1921] 1 A. C. 444) does not apply to a c.i.f. contract such as that now before me. Secondly, that grounds for challenging the dicta of the Privy Council will be found in Art. 22, and the notes and cases there cited, in Scrutton on Charterparties, 10th ed., as to what are called "through bills of lading," in the lucid article in the Law Quarterly Review of October, 1889, vol. v., p. 424, by Mr. Bateson, K.C.; and of July, 1890, vol. vi., p. 289, by the late Mr. Carver, and in Carver on Carriage, 6th ed., notes to Sect. 107. I do not doubt that the document before me is a "shipping document" within the U.S.A. Harter Act, 1893. I feel bound to hold, however, that it is not a bill of lading within the c.i.f. contract of sale made between the present parties.

[The balance of the opinion, holding that no proper policy of insurance was tendered, is here omitted.]

For the reasons given I find in favour of the buyers with the results stated in the award. The sellers must pay the costs of the proceedings before me.

Appeal dismissed.

In BANCA COMMERCIALE ITALIANA *c.* DITTA MAGLI E TIBERINI, 35 Temi Genovese 127 (Court of Cassation, 1925), a c.i.f. buyer refused to reimburse his bank under a letter of credit arrangement because the bank had accepted from the seller a received for shipment bill of lading. In upholding the buyer's contention the Court said:

"Although a regular bill of lading is an admission of the actual loading of merchandise on a ship, an admission guaranteed by the signature of the person charged with the transport, a document made out as received for shipment not only does not admit that the goods have been loaded on a designated ship, but does not admit any shipment at all. In fact it is a mere receipt for goods intended for shipment at some later date on a ship not yet determined. So far as concerns the value of such instruments in the practice of maritime commerce, some importance is to be attached to the rules recommended by the Committee on Maritime Law and adopted unanimously by the International Law Association at its Congress at the Hague in September, 1921, a meeting at which Italy was represented and at which one of the questions most carefully examined was with reference to received for shipment bills of lading. However, following a long discussion the Hague Rules were limited to noting the existence of these documents in practice, and to preventing, in Rule 3, the simultaneous issue and transfer of both a received for shipment and an on board bill of lading; thus affirming the right of the shipper to have delivered to him a regular bill of lading when the goods are loaded on board, on the well understood condition that he surrenders the received for shipment bill. . . . As a result of the adoption of this rule it should be noted that the banker who accepts such a document knows perfectly well that it does not mean that the goods are on board the ship, but simply that they have been received by the agent of the shipping company for loading at some later date. . . . It should be noted further that since the present case involves a c.i.f. sale, in which the seller assumes the obligation of shipping the goods on board a vessel and consequently of tendering an on board bill of lading, he cannot furnish proof that such shipment has been made and that he has carried out his obligation."

Note also SOCIÉTÉ FRANCO-COLONIALE ANTILLAISE *c.* MIGUOT & CIE., Revue de Droit Maritime Comparé Supplement 3, 458 (Commercial Court of Havre, 1925), where the right of a c.i.f. buyer to refuse a tender of a received for shipment bill of lading was upheld on the ground that the result otherwise would be to throw on the buyer risks prior to actual shipment.

Compare WEIS *v.* PRODUCE BROKERS CO., 7 Ll. L. R. 211 (Court of Appeal, 1921), where a bill of lading reading "shipped or delivered for shipment" was deemed to be a good tender under a c.i.f. contract, Bankes, L. J., observing that the form was "quite usual in the trade, not universal, but quite usual." Scrutton, L. J., added: "There is very good reason why it is framed in that way. The ship wants to have a bill of lading beginning with the time delivered for shipment because it wants the time delivered for shipment covered by the exceptions. The shipper wants it in that form because he wants to be protected from the time he has given the goods into the hands of the ship for shipment."

Note also VIETOR *v.* THE NATIONAL CITY BANK OF NEW YORK, 200 App. Div. 557 (New York Supreme Court, Appellate Division, 1922), where evidence of custom was held to be admissible to justify the tender of a received for shipment bill of lading under a c.i.f. contract, even though the contract called for shipment by October 15, and the bill of lading was dated October 11, on which date the vessel in question had not reached port so that a sailing by October 15 was impossible.

HEILBERT, SYMONS & CO., LTD. *v.* HARVEY, CHRISTIE-MILLER & CO.

KING'S BENCH DIVISION, 1922

[12 *Lloyd's List Law Reports*, 455]

Mr. Justice BAILHACHE, in giving judgment, said: This is an action brought by Heilbert, Symons & Co., against Harvey, Christie-Miller & Co., relating to a contract for the sale of some balata, which I understand is a substance which is dealt with in conjunction with the rubber business, although it is not india rubber. The contract is contained in bought and sold notes of Nov. 5, 1921; and was for the sale of 15 tons f.a.q. sheet balata, cost, insurance, freight London; insurance was to be warehouse to warehouse with a further 10 days after discharge at destination, and payment was to be cash against documents in London, buyers' option, on or before arrival of vessel at port of discharge. There were printed at the bottom the terms of the contract of the Rubber Trade Association of London. By these terms it is provided that

On final declaration reaching last buyer, he shall complete and forward to first selling broker with due dispatch the special counterfoil provided for the last buyer on the declaration form. Delay or nonfulfilment of this condition renders last buyer liable to a penalty. On receipt of the counterfoil, first selling broker shall permit buyer to inspect the documents. In the event of documents not being in first selling broker's possession that first selling broker shall arrange a time within 24 hours for last buyer to inspect the documents at first selling broker's office. Within two hours of inspection of documents last buyer shall deliver to first selling broker either (1) a memorandum in the form laid down by the Association that he has inspected the documents and that same are in order, or (2) notice in writing specifying any objection to the validity of the documents. In the event (2) first selling broker shall take the necessary steps to remove buyer's objection and obtain buyer's memorandum of approval.

The facts of the case are that the plaintiffs, having bought a quantity of balata, had shipment of it as to 10 tons under a bill of lading, dated Mar. 3, 1922. They were going to deliver five tons to the defendants and five tons elsewhere; and the result of that was that the quantity that was contained in the bill of lading was split into two equal parts; and the first question that arises is, what is to be done in these circumstances in respect of the inspection of documents? The terms of the Rubber Trade Association contemplate the splitting of parcels; and the forms provided indicate this — there are pink and green forms to be used, and it is contemplated that the quantity mentioned in the bill of lading will be split. The documents that were tendered to the buyers in this case were not the bill of lading but the ship's release and in addition certificates of insurance. By the terms of the contract I am satisfied that this particular form was not quite satisfactory in that it did not cover the 10 days: but it was a small error and not a matter of moment. The real controversy raises the question of what ought to be tendered in the way of a bill of lading or in substitution for a bill of lading. It appears that this was a second delivery of balata under the contract between the parties; and on the first delivery the delivery order or ship's release was tendered and was accepted after some grumbling: but it is clear that it was conveyed to the plaintiffs in this case that what the defendants required was the bill of lading.

There has been some evidence before me that where these parcels are split as here, it being highly inconvenient to procure two bills of lading, a practice has grown up whereby one of the purchasers gets the bill of lading and the other purchaser of the split parcel gets the ship's release; and if he requires it in addition to the ship's release he gets a satisfactory form of guarantee. That is how the difficulty is normally got over; and I have to consider whether, assuming that custom to be proved, how the facts of the case fit in with that suggested custom.

By the terms of the Rubber Trade Association contract it is provided the buyer must inspect documents before arrival and if not satisfied he must inform the seller that he is not. Upon the plaintiffs' evidence the buyers did not go to inspect documents, but conveyed to the seller that what they required was the bill of lading. The seller therefore knew that he would be expected to tender the bill of lading. He did not in fact tender the bill of lading, but he tendered the ship's release; and in tendering the ship's release he did not tender with it a guarantee. These documents were rejected; and upon rejection the seller's attitude was this — not, "I will put my tender in order," but "my tender is a good one and I stand by it; and if you do not accept the documents as tendered I will sell against you." Now, in that, I think, the seller was clearly wrong. Even assuming that the practice which has been spoken to is a good practice of delivering the ships' release and guarantee instead of a bill of lading, in this case the only thing tendered was the ship's release; and, clearly, when one looks at the ordinary meaning of shipping documents, the ship's release, by itself, was not a shipping document in the ordinary meaning of the contract: it was not a tender that could be forced by custom upon an unwilling purchaser without the guarantee. The tender, therefore, was a wrong tender whichever way you look at it. Mr. Mackinnon has urged that this was a matter that could have been put right in a few minutes or hours, and I think he is right about that; and he says that defendants are not entitled to insist on their objection because they did not come round to inspect; and I think he would have been right on that but for the plaintiffs' own attitude, for upon these objections being made the plaintiffs did not say, "Well, we will put the matter right and give you your guarantee or get for you the bill of lading." If they had said that there would have been a good deal to be said for them, but that was not their attitude. They said, "No, these documents are in order and we stand by our tender." Having taken that attitude they are wrong in this case, and they are also wrong about the certificate of insurance: but I do not attach any importance to that, because I am certain that was a detail that had escaped attention. I am not purporting here to decide whether the tender of a ship's release plus guarantee is a good tender or not; I say that in no case can the delivery of the ship's release to an unwilling purchaser without the guarantee be a good tender. That is all that I am deciding. In the event of the matter of whether the tender of a ship's release plus guarantee is good having one day to be decided, I should like to point out to those interested in this trade that there may be a serious difficulty in law in holding that these two documents are a good tender; and I say that for two reasons. (1) In the ordinary c.i.f. contract, speaking only about the bill of lading, the purchaser is entitled to the bill of lading which was issued upon the goods being put on board; and obviously the ship's release fails in that respect. (2) He is entitled to a document which will give him a direct action against the shipowner or carrier of the goods from the time that they were loaded until the time they were discharged; and it is clear that a ship's release does nothing of the kind. All that the ship's release does is to bind the shipowner to hand over to the person to whom the release is given the goods which are mentioned in the release: but it does not make the shipowner liable for any acts of negligence on his part in the carriage of the goods from port of loading to the port of destination. I point this out to the gentlemen here who deal with this trade, because in the event of the matter arising to be tested one way or another it has to be borne in mind that there are material differences between a ship's release, even accompanied by a guarantee, and a bill of lading.

For the reasons that I have given, based upon the documents tendered plus the attitude taken by the plaintiffs when the documents were objected to, I have come to the conclusion that the plaintiffs have failed to make out their case; and there must be judgment for the defendants, with costs.

In Chegaray et Cie. *c.* Nizard Frères, 1926 Havre 2.74 (Rouen Court of Appeal), there was a contract for the sale of sugar on c.i.f. terms. The seller shipped under one bill of lading a quantity of sugar sufficient to take care of sales to various buyers, and tendered to the buyer in question a delivery order covering his portion. It was held that this did not constitute a good tender unless so signed by the master of the ship as to give the buyer rights equal to those he would have had under a bill of lading.

SKANDINAVISKA KREDITAKTIEBOLAGET *v.* BARCLAYS BANK

King's Bench Division, 1925
[22 *Lloyd's List Law Reports*, 523]

Mr. Justice Greer, in giving judgment, said: This is an action brought by a Scandinavian credit bank against Barclays Bank, Ltd., for, in form, the sums of £2177 *5s. 6d.* and £76 *0s. 8d.*; and as to the £2177 *5s. 6d.* it is claimed as money to cover their right to be indemnified against the consequences of following out the defendants' instructions with regard to the opening of a credit in favour of a foreign seller to a Hull buyer in these circumstances.

Barclays Bank at Hull were approached on May 1, 1922, to get opened an irrevocable credit in respect of 6000 bags of potatoes, 1¾ in., Hull or Middlesbrough — and this is a matter that we have to consider in the present case — and a credit with the Scandinavian Bank, the plaintiffs, at Malmo, of £2175 in favour of Beldring & Co., Copenhagen, against the documents. The documents described in the first part of the instructions are bills of lading, special health and quality certificate and policy of insurance. Further correspondence took place in reference to this matter; and on May 1 Barclays Bank telegraphed to the plaintiffs: —

> Open irrevocable credit 30628 extent twenty-one hundred seventy-five pounds sterling favour Beldring Company Copenhagen against full set clean blank endorsed on board bills of lading official health and quality certificate marine war risks insurance policy in sterling covering six thousand bags potatoes one and three-quarter inch to Hull or Middlesbrough account Nellist Company reimbursement will credit you Vostro will advise expiry date later.

Then they telegraph to the plaintiff bank to accept Nellist's instructions with reference to the credit regardless of other conditions if within the credit amount; and on May 15 Nellist sent forward instructions to the plaintiffs in these words, after some preliminary observations: —

> I now beg you to kindly open a new irrevocable credit in favour of Messrs. Beldring & Co. or order for an amount of until £2175 for until 6000 bags at 51 kilos net "Magnum Bonum" and/or "Up to Date" and/or "Imperator" potatoes 1¾ inches, shipped from Reval to Hull, the credit negotiable against full set blank endorsed bills of lading, health certificate, way bill and invoice, expiration date May 31 this year.

By a subsequent letter the expiry date was extended to June 7, and such documents as were presented to the plaintiff bank were presented before June 7, and therefore no question arises of the presentation being out of date.

But the question arises between the parties in this way. When the documents were presented to the plaintiff bank they did not appear to be in order, and in consequence of that the plaintiff bank declined to part with their money until they got from Messrs. Beldring, who were shipping at any rate part of the goods, a guarantee against their acting on the credit without having had the proper documents; and they desired to have from Messrs. Beldring a similar document as to the balance of the cargo and the balance of the credit. Messrs. Beldring would not give them that; and they accordingly refused to advance under the credit to Messrs. Beldring the balance over and above the sum of £2175 which they had advanced to the shipper of the bulk of the goods. . . .

The first thing to be observed is that this is a credit which is opened against delivery of documents, and the documents are the security of the bank for the money covered by the credit. It is of vital importance that they should be in what I may call good merchantable order, so that if anything happened to the parties mainly concerned and the money was not forthcoming to the bank, the bank would have realisable documents from which they could reimburse themselves against the risk that they had undertaken. In looking at the documents which were delivered I find that the bill of lading is a bill of lading which does not name the shipper; it is a bill of lading "to order," and it is a document as to which, from the document itself, no one could ascertain who was the person entitled to endorse the document; and it would have been a document of very little value in the hands of the bank if they had had to realise the security they obtained by means of it. It is not in my judgment what is called for by the letter of instructions from Mr. Nellist. It is not a blank endorsed bill of lading. It has some writing on the back of it as to which the term "hieroglyph" has been used. It is impossible for anyone to read what purports to be somebody's signature; and all one can say with regard to it is that one can come to the negative conclusion that it is not the endorsement of the shipper or of Messrs. Beldring or of Messrs. Trier.

In those circumstances in my judgment the document is one which would not have been available for the bank to realise. It is not a blank endorsed bill of lading within the meaning of the instructions of May 15, and in accepting it the plaintiff bank were accepting something which they were not entitled to accept under the instructions they had; and the risk they ran was one in respect of which they are not entitled to be indemnified by those instructing them. That would be sufficient to dispose of the plaintiffs' claim in this case, because the other claim for £76 depends upon the validity of the indemnity.

[The balance of the opinion is here omitted.]

For these reasons I think the plaintiffs' claim fails in this case and would equally have failed if a plea of waiver or estoppel had been put upon the record.

My judgment will be for the defendants, with costs.

In Westminster Bank *v.* Banca Nazionale di Credito, 31 Ll. L. R. 306 (King's Bench Division, 1928), the defendant Italian bank under an arrangement with an Italian buyer instructed the plaintiff English bank to pay for a shipment of frozen beef against full sets of bills of lading. The plaintiff paid out £74,000 against the bills of lading that were presented but the defendant refused to take up these bills of lading and to reimburse the plaintiff on the ground that the bills of lading were not in order. In upholding this contention Roche, J., said: "Now these bills of lading were six in number and four of them contained what are called clauses, that is to say, stamped clauses — I do not mean mere clauses or conditions printed on the bills of lading, but stamped clauses referring to the condition of the goods and referring to them in the sense of indicating that the ship said they were out of order when they were received on board. The banking evidence contends for a simple proposition that whether the instructions that they got are express or not as to the necessity of the bills of lading being what is called 'clean,' it necessarily implied that they are not either bound or entitled to accept as bills of lading within those instructions bills of lading which are claused and in that sense not 'clean.' As to that there has been apparently in the past a difference of opinion between eminent Judges; Mr. Justice Bailhache, on the one hand, who held that 'clean' bills of lading were required; and the Court of Appeal who thought that it might depend on circumstances and you could not lay down any such definite rule. That difference of view is expressed in the case of the *National Bank of Egypt* v. *Hannevig's Bank, Ltd.*, reported not in the regular Law Reports, but in a useful publication, 1 Ll. L. Rep. 69. Far be it from me to enter on this controversy in a case where I conceive that it is entirely unnecessary that I should do so. What I do find is this, that assuming for this purpose that the view of the Court of Appeal is the correct one and that it depends upon the circumstances, I find in the circumstances of this case there was so much wrong with these bills of lading that the acceptance of them would not have been in compliance with the instructions given by the Banca Nazionale to the plaintiff bank.

"The witnesses for the plaintiff bank spoke of them most frequently as 'detrimental clauses'; some of the witnesses and more than one witness, I think, for the defendants, the Union Cold Storage Company, spoke of 'deleterious clauses.' In other words, there were clauses which so dealt with the condition of the meat or with what the ship said as to the condition of the meat for shipment as to seriously affect its price and its acceptability."

Compare Romariz and Pistacchini *v.* Zeyen and Co., 35 T. L. R. 299 (King's Bench Division, 1919), where contracts for the sale of 1100 cases of sardines on c.i.f. terms provided for payment against delivery orders.

Subsequently it was agreed that payment should not be made against delivery orders, but should be made by the buyer's bankers against dock warrants. The dock warrants presented bore the notation "cases frail, not accountable for quantity of contents," and the bankers thereupon refused to accept them. Judgment was given for the sellers in an action for damages against the buyers on the ground that if clean warrants were desired, a stipulation to that effect should have been included in the contract.

RE AN ARBITRATION BETWEEN KEIGHLEY, MAXTED AND CO. AND BRYAN, DURANT AND CO.

COURT OF APPEAL, 1894

[70 *Law Times Reports* (*New Series*), 155]

This was an appeal by Bryan, Durant, and Co. from an order of the Divisional Court (Wills and Wright, JJ.) upon a special case stated by arbitrators.

The appellants, Messrs. Bryant, Durant, and Co. sold to the respondents, Messrs. Keighley, Maxted, and Co., a quantity of East Indian wheat under a written contract.

By the contract Keighley, Maxted, and Co. bought of Bryan, Durant, and Co., on the printed rules indorsed on the back of this contract, about 3000 tons Karachi wheat (10 per cent. more or less), to be shipped per first-class steamer from Karachi, shipment to be made, and bill or bills of lading to be dated, during July or August. Payment, cash in London, within seven days from the day on which invoice is handed, in exchange for bill or bills of lading and policies of insurance.

On the margin of the contract was indorsed a clause as follows:

> Sellers have option of shipping less than the minimum quantity, in which case the price of the quantity short shipped of the medium quantity will be settled at the value of the day of the appropriation. Sellers can also exceed the maximum quantity, in which case the excess over the medium quantity will remain for their account.

The appellants wrote to the respondents saying that 3800 tons of wheat had been shipped on the s.s. *Bombay*, "3000 tons of which we beg to appropriate against our contract with you." No reply was made to that letter.

On the 23rd Aug. the appellants wrote to the respondents with provisional invoice for 3000 tons of wheat *ex Bombay*.

On the 23rd Aug. the respondents inspected the documents, including four bills of lading, two for 1750 tons each, and two for 250 tons each.

The appellants were willing to deliver to the respondents either all the bills of lading, or the two for 1750 tons each, against payment of the amount of the invoice, leaving 800 tons, or 500 tons, as the case might be, balance of the cargo in the buyer's possession, but the property of the sellers.

The respondents rejected this tender, and refused to pay the amount of the invoice or any part thereof, or to make any deposit.

The question whether the buyers were bound to accept the shipment was referred to arbitration under the provisions of the contract, and an award was made in favour of the buyers, and this award was confirmed by the appeal committee of the London Corn Trade Association.

The sellers, the appellants, applied to the Queen's Bench Division to have the award remitted, and obtained an order remitting the award.

This order was affirmed by the Court of Appeal (68 L. T. Rep. N. S. 61).

The appeal committee reheard the matter and made an award in favour of the sellers, Bryan, Durant, and Co. This award was made in the form of a special case.

The Divisional Court (Wills and Wright, JJ.) held that the arbitrators were wrong, and set aside the award in favour of Bryan, Durant, and Co.

Bryan, Durant, and Co. appealed.

Lord HALSBURY. I am of opinion that the decision of the arbitrators was wrong, and that the order of the Divisional Court was right. I feel compelled to say that the arbitrators were wrong because of the observations which have been made during the argument that these arbitrators were commercial men familiar with contracts of this kind. Parties ought either to be content with their decisions and not come to a court of law, or else be satisfied with a decision according to law in a court of law. In this case the arbitrators did not act upon any fixed principles of law. As to the question which arises for our decision here, whether there was a good tender by the sellers, when the facts are properly understood and made plain, it is not at all difficult to see what our decision must be. The contract is for the sale and delivery of wheat, the amount of which is to be ascertained thus: there is in the contract what is called a "maximum" and "minimum" clause, which provides that the sellers may ship less than the minimum quantity, in which case the price of the quantity short shipped of the medium quantity is to be settled at the value of the day of the appropriation; or that the sellers may ship more than the maximum quantity in which case the excess over the medium amount will remain for their account. The only question really is, whether there were shipping documents corresponding to the amount bought which the purchasers could have to deal with as they pleased. It has been argued that the seller could give a bill of lading for as much wheat as he liked under this contract. That, however, can only be so if contradictory words are added to the contract. It seems to me, therefore, that the purchasers had a right to have a bill of lading for the amount which they bought, 3000 tons. Such a bill of lading was not offered to them, and the tender by the sellers was therefore bad, and the purchasers are not liable. The appeal fails, and must be dismissed.

[Concurring opinions of Lopes and Davey, L. JJ., are omitted.]

In BANK OF ITALY *v.* MERCHANTS NATIONAL BANK, 236 N. Y. 106 (Court of Appeals, 1923), defendant bank guaranteed payment of the purchase price of two carloads of dried grapes on presentation of bills of lading. Plaintiff bank made advances against bills of lading which described the goods as raisins. It was held that defendant bank was justified in refusing to pay against these bills of lading.

Note also LAMBORN *v.* LAKE SHORE BANK & TRUST CO., 231 N. Y. 616 (Court of Appeals, 1921), where the action was upon a letter of credit under the terms of which drafts could be drawn against bills of lading for "Java White Granulated Sugar." It was held that the absence of the word "granulated" from the bill of lading accompanying plaintiff's draft was a bar to plaintiff's recovery.

HANSSON *v.* HAMEL AND HORLEY, LIMITED

HOUSE OF LORDS, 1922

[*Law Reports,* [1922] 2 *Appeal Cases,* 36]

[Detailed statement of facts and brief opinions of Lord Buckmaster and Lord Atkinson are here omitted.]

Lord SUMNER. My Lords, the only question argued on this appeal was whether the respondents were right in refusing to take up and pay for certain shipping documents tendered to them, on the appellant's behalf, by his bankers in London. The bill of lading was the actual document in dispute. Why the respondents really refused the documents does not matter, nor does the case turn on the particular objection put forward by them at the time.

It was common ground that the whole transaction is governed by English law. The cargo — cod guano in bags — was sold c.f. and i., Kobe or Yokohama, to be shipped from Norway, the first instalment March/April, and the balance May/June. There was no stipulation as to the months within which the bill of lading itself must be dated, or as to the date of the bill of lading being conclusive evidence of the date of the shipment. The bags in question were shipped at Braatvag in Norway. A direct steamer to Japan was not available from Braatvag, nor do I imagine that the buyers supposed that it would be, and the seller shipped the consignment at Braatvag on board the *Kiev,* a steamer belonging to a Norwegian company, to be carried to Hamburg, where it was to be transhipped into the Osaka Shosen Kaisha's steamship *Atlas Maru* for Yokohama. The appellant had made a contract, partly expressed in a "Freight Contract" and partly in correspondence, with a Mr. Lind, of Hamburg, the representative of the Osaka Shosen Kaisha, for the conveyance of the cod guano from Hamburg to Japan on the terms, among others, that bills of lading to Japan should be signed in Hamburg on presentation of the local bill of lading — that is, the bill of lading for carriage by the *Kiev* — as soon as the goods were in Mr. Lind's possession, being there either taken over in lighters on the appellant's behalf or direct into the steamer for Japan. If they arrived in Hamburg too late for the steamer scheduled, the appellant reserved to himself the right to ship them by the next steamer of the line.

The first, or local, bill of lading was signed on behalf of the master of the *Kiev* on April 22, 1920, and acknowledged receipt of the cod guano from the appellant, to be delivered to "order Yokohama," the *Kiev* being bound for Hamburg, with the right to tranship and send on the goods by another steamer, freight prepaid to Hamburg, the *Kiev's* destination.

At Hamburg there was issued to the appellant an ocean bill of lading, signed by Mr. Lind on behalf of the captain of the *Atlas Maru* and dated May 5, 1920. The respondents were named in it as the shippers in accordance with a stipulation they had made, and the cod guano was made deliverable to order at Yokohama. . . . The document was headed: "Through Bill of Lading," and it contained in the margin these statements: "from Braatvag to Yokohama" and "shipped from Braatvag according to bill of lading on the 22nd April, 1920," and it began thus: "Shipped in apparent good order and condition by Messrs. Hamel and Horley, Ltd., on board the steamship 'Kiev,' lying in or off the port of Braatvag and bound to Hamburg for transhipment into the Osaka Shosen Kaisha's Steamship 'Atlas Maru' . . . (1500) One thousand and five hundred bags cod guano . . . to be delivered . . . at the port of Yokohama . . . unto 'order.' "

This bill of lading accordingly was itself dated after the contract time of shipment — March/April, but it stated in the margin, and truly so, that, according to a bill of lading (that is, the local one), shipment at Braatvag was within the contract time. It stated further that the goods, when shipped in the *Kiev,* were in apparent good order and condition, but it was silent as to their condition at Hamburg. There was no express statement that any goods had been shipped in the *Atlas Maru* at all, or, if so, in what order and condition they were when shipped, and it was reasonably plain that the *Kiev* did not belong to the Japanese owners of the *Atlas Maru.* The undertaking to deliver in Japan would, in the absence of special authority to those signing the bill of lading, apply only to such cargo as might, in fact, have been shipped at Hamburg on board the *Atlas Maru,* and no one would assume, without actual evidence of it, that a person like Mr. Lind, signing on behalf of the captain of the *Atlas Maru,* had any authority to bind her owners for the carriage by the *Kiev* or the owners of the *Kiev* for anything at all. The question is whether this ocean bill of lading was a good tender under the contract of sale and whether the respondents were bound to take it up and pay for the consignment.

A c.f. and i. seller, as has often been pointed out, has to cover the buyer by procuring and tendering documents which will be available for his protection from shipment to destination, and I think that this ocean bill of lading afforded the buyer no protection in regard to the interval of thirteen days which elapsed between the dates of the two bills of lading and presumably between the departure from Braatvag and the arrival at Hamburg. The initial words, on which the matter depends, may be put as a mere recital of a fact, or as words of contract. . . .

My Lords, with all deference to the very weighty opinion of Bailhache J. to the contrary, in my judgment these words are mere words of recital, but, even if they were what the appellant contends that they are, I think it is clear that they do not make the ocean bill of lading a good tender in this case. The bill of lading by the *Kiev* was originally a contract with the appellant himself, and never was, nor in any normal course of business ever would be, tendered to the respondents. As there were not, I suppose, to be two contracts for carriage as far as Hamburg, this is strong to show that the appellant never intended the ocean bill of lading to be a contract of carriage from Braatvag to Hamburg. When documents are to be taken up the buyer is entitled to documents which substantially confer protective rights throughout. He is not buying a litigation, as Lord Trevethin (then A. T. Lawrence J.) says in the *General Trading Co.'s Case* (16 Com. Cas. 95, 101). These documents have to be handled by banks, they have to be taken up or rejected promptly and without any opportunity for prolonged inquiry, they have to be such as can be re-tendered to sub-purchasers, and it is essential that they should so conform to the accustomed shipping documents as to be reasonably and readily fit to pass current in commerce. I am quite sure that, under the circumstances of this case, this ocean bill of lading does not satisfy these conditions. It bears notice of its insufficiency and ambiguity on its face: for, though called a through bill of lading, it is not really so. It is the contract of the subsequent carrier only, without any complementary promises to bind the prior carriers in the through transit. The appellant's contract with Mr. Lind was not transferable by indorsement and delivery, nor was it tendered; the *Kiev* bill of lading he kept to himself, and endorsed to Mr. Lind under his own contract with him. I do not suggest that tender of either document would have carried matters any further, but, as things stood, the buyer was plainly left with a considerable lacuna in the documentary cover to which the contract entitled him.

The point is also put in a slightly different way, which equally relates especially to bills of lading. Scrutton J. points out in *Landauer & Co.* v. *Craven* ([1912] 2 K. B. 94), that in a sale of goods c.f. and i., the contract of affreightment must be procured "on shipment." Of course this is practicable and common even when a through bill of lading is necessary, containing provision for transhipment at an intermediate port from a local to an ocean steamer not in the same ownership. I do not understand this proposition as meaning that the bill of lading would be bad, unless it was signed contemporaneously with the actual placing of the goods on board. "On shipment" is an expression of some latitude. Bills of lading are constantly signed after the loading is complete and, in some cases, after the ship has sailed. I do not think that they thereby necessarily cease to be procured "on shipment," nor do I suppose that the learned judge so intended his words. It may also be that the expression would be satisfied, even though some local carriage on inland waters, or by canal, or in an estuary by barge or otherwise, preceded the shipment on the ocean steamer, provided that the steamer's bill of lading covered that prior carriage by effectual words of contract. "On shipment" is referable both to time and place. In principle, however, and subject to what I have said, I accept this opinion of so great an authority, and I am quite sure that a bill of lading only issued thirteen days after the original shipment, at another port in another country many hundreds of miles away, is not duly procured "on shipment." Indeed the ocean bill of lading was not procured as part of this c.f. and i. shipment at all, and "on shipment" does not at any rate mean on re-shipment or on transhipment. It is not enough that at the time of the initial shipment the c.f. and i. seller procured a contract by correspondence with Mr. Lind for the forwarding of the goods by an ocean steamer, for that was not procuring a bill of lading. If the *Kiev* had been lost with the cod guano on the coast of Norway, no contract of affreightment to Japan would have been procured or forthcoming at all. The matter was well tested thus in the Court of Appeal. In the absence of express stipulation, shipping documents under a contract of sale on c.f. and i. terms must be tendered by the seller as soon as possible after shipment: Kennedy L.J. in *Biddell Bros.* v. *Horst Co.* ([1911] 1 K. B. 934, 958). If, then, the port of transhipment was late on in the through voyage, a seller might be entitled to tender the documents long before any through bill of lading to Japan had been signed or procured at all, and when there was no bill of lading in existence except that to the intermediate port. This ocean bill of lading was, therefore, on this ground also, in my opinion, a bad tender.

[Two pages of the opinion are here omitted.]

I would suggest to your Lordships that the appeal should be dismissed with costs.

My Lords, my noble and learned friend Lord Wrenbury desires me to add that he concurs in this opinion.

Lord Carson. My Lords, I also concur.

Order of the Court of Appeal affirmed and appeal dismissed with costs.

See also Landauer & Co. *v.* Craven & Speeding Bros., [1912] 2 K. B. 94 (King's Bench Division), where there was a c.i.f. contract for the sale of Manila hemp to be shipped from a port in the Philippine Islands or from Hongkong by steamer or steamers direct or indirect to London between October 1 and December 31, 1909, payment cash in exchange for documents. The sellers purchased hemp shipped at Manila under bills of lading dated December 28, 1909, for delivery at Hongkong to the order of the shippers. The hemp was transhipped at Hongkong for London under bills of lading dated March 25, 1910. The buyers refused a tender of the Hongkong bills of lading, and it was found by an arbitrator that the usual practice in shipping goods from Manila to London was to take out a through bill of lading at Manila. It was held that the tender of the Hongkong bills was bad, first because of the date of the bills of lading, and secondly because it did not cover the carriage from Manila to Hongkong.

In Sutro & Co. *v.* Heilbut, Symons & Co., [1917] 2 K. B. 348 (Court of Appeal), a c.i.f. contract for the sale of rubber provided that it was to be shipped "by vessel or vessels (steam or motor) from the East to New

York, direct and/or indirect, with liberty to call and/or tranship in other ports." Shipment was made at Singapore under a through bill of lading which stated that the goods were shipped at Singapore for New York via Seattle, whence they were to go by rail. Owing to the difficulty in obtaining freight space for New York on through steamers, this had become a usual route for rubber sold under similar contracts. It was held however that the usage was inconsistent with the terms of the contract, and that the buyer was justified in objecting to a declaration under this form of bill of lading. Scrutton, L. J., dissented on the ground that the finding as to the route being a usual one should be conclusive.

In L. M. FISCHEL & CO. *v.* R. KNOWLES SPENCER, 12 Ll. L. R. 36 (King's Bench Division, 1922), there was a c.i.f. contract for the sale of copra with a stipulation as to shipment per steamer from port or ports in the Philippine Islands to Rotterdam. The bill of lading contained this provision: "Having liberty as regards the whole or any part of the goods and at the risk of the owners thereof, before shipment or any time during the transit as may be deemed expedient to ship by or tranship to any other vessels, or land or store or put into other hulk craft or lighter or tranship or reship in vessel proceeding by any route or forward by lighter rail or any other conveyance." There was a finding of fact that "where a seller desires to have the power to tranship it is usual and customary for him to insert in the contract a clause authorizing transhipment." It was held that the bill of lading was not a good tender.

In PACIFIC RICE MILLS *v.* WESTFELDT BROS., 31 Fed. (2nd) 979 (Circuit Court of Appeals, Fifth Circuit, 1929), a contract for the sale of 1000 bags of rice c.i.f. Sagua La Grande contained the following provision: "Shipment: February/March from Orient; transhipment at Havana or San Francisco, sellers option. If the latter, transhipment must be effected not later than two weeks after arrival of goods at San Francisco." The bill of lading tendered provided for shipment from San Francisco by rail to Mobile and thence by steamer to Sagua La Grande. The buyer refused to accept the bill of lading. In an action by the seller for damages for breach of contract, a judgment for defendant was affirmed on the ground that the contract in terms permitted only one transhipment, whereas the bill of lading showed on its face that there would be two.

2. INSURANCE DOCUMENTS

KUNGLIG JARNVAGSSTYRELSEN *v.* DEXTER & CARPENTER, INC.

DISTRICT COURT, SOUTHERN DISTRICT, NEW YORK, 1924
[299 *Federal Reporter*, 991]

LEARNED HAND, District Judge. The declaration is for breach of a contract for the sale of coal. It alleges, stripped of irrelevant matter, that the defendant sold and the plaintiff bought a cargo of coal at $31.90 per ton, "said price including cost, insurance and freight upon said coal prepaid to the port of Malmo," the price "to be paid against delivery in the city of New York of shipping documents, including insurance policies, bills of lading, and invoice"; that the plaintiff established a letter of credit with a New York bank, which it instructed to pay the price on receipt of the invoice, shipping documents, and "policy or policies of insurance"; that the bank, contrary to instructions, paid the purchase price without demanding policies of insurance, and received in lieu thereof only a "certificate of insurance," declaring under the hand of the defendant's insurance broker that insurance had been underwritten in London for account of the defendant; that under the law of England such a certificate was not a policy of insurance within the meaning of such a contract of sale; that the coal was lost at sea and that the plaintiff has paid the bank; that the insurance broker had not taken out any insurance when the certificate of insurance was delivered to the bank.

The plea makes profert of the contract, which was parol, and which provided for the sale of 150,000 tons of coal at various prices for various points of delivery, in all cases "c.i.f." (the letters being so written), of which 30,000 were to be delivered at Malmo. It alleged that the cargo in question was shipped under the contract; that it was a universal custom in the United States, in cases of "c.i.f." sales, for the seller to have the option of New York or London insurance; that in case of London insurance the seller might procure it through an American broker, who would in turn through a London broker secure the actual policy, who cabled back when he had fixed it; that on receipt of such a cable the New York broker would issue such a certificate of insurance as the plea made profert of; that this custom was followed in the case at bar, the defendant paid the New York broker, indorsed the certificate, and the bank accepted the papers on tender. The certificate of insurance in question recited that insurance of necessary amount had been issued by "London underwriters" for the account of the defendant on the shipment in question; that policies of London underwriters would be exchanged on demand for the certificate as soon as practicable; that the insurance was placed subject in all respects to English laws and customs governing marine and war risk insurance. Various conditions applicable specifically to coal cargoes were contained in an annexed rider.

The purpose of the demurrer is to secure a ruling consonant with those recent English cases under which such a certificate would not be a valid tender of insurance, and under which apparently, even after acceptance, substantial damages may be recovered. Under the declaration at bar it may well be argued that only nominal damages can in any aspect be recovered, without some allegation that the plaintiff has been unable to collect from the London underwriters under the certificate of insurance. That is quite another question from whether the tender could have been refused and damages recovered for the breach. However, since the tender, if bad, was a breach, I suppose that nominal damages, at least, were recoverable, and, if so, the declaration is not demurrable. Hence the demurrer raises the validity of the plea.

Before reaching this question, there is one preliminary matter, to wit, whether the acceptance by the bank of the certificate without reservation still left it within the power of the plaintiff to treat it as an insufficient tender. The bank was the plaintiff's agent for that purpose, and it is a matter of no moment to the defendant if it disobeyed its instructions. That question I mention only to pass, assuming merely for argument that, though acceptance would bar the right to reject, it did not prevent an action for damages on breach of the promise to deliver insurance.

Thus I am brought squarely to the question whether, if there be a uniform usage in this country to treat such certificates as performance of a contract "c. i. f.," the tender was good. I must start by observing that the plea varies from the declaration, the latter alleging that the contract stipulated for "policies of insurance," while the contract contained only the words:

"We offer * * * the quantity indicated herein at the following prices: * * * $31.50 per gross ton c. i. f. Malmo."

On demurrer the plea controls, and the case is at once distinguished from the only case in the English Court of Appeal, and that last decided in order of time, *Donald H. Scott & Co.* v. *Barclay's Bank*, [1923] 2 K. B. 1. There action was brought on by the seller on a letter of credit, upon the bank's refusal to accept the tender of a certificate of insurance completer in detail than that at bar, but still referring to the policy for part of the contract. The letter of credit had prescribed among the necessary documents an "approved insurance policy." Bankes, Scrutton, and Atkin, L. JJ., held that, as the buyer must look to another policy to ascertain all the terms of insurance, the tender was bad. There was no proof of usage, and the certificate did not declare that a specific policy had been taken out on the cargo in suit, but it was merely a coverage slip on a floating policy. However it specifically provided against any broker's lien for premiums paid.

In *Diamond, etc., Co.* v. *Fl. Bourgeois*, [1921] 3 K. B. 443, the next most recent case, McCardie, J., had before him an action on the refusal by the buyer to accept under a contract of sale "c. i. f." A certificate of insurance was tendered similar to that in *Scott* v. *Barclay's Bank*, *supra*, which the learned judge held insufficient. His reasons were three: First, the same as that later adopted by the Court of Appeal; second, that the certificate was not a classifiable legal document at all; and, third, that it was very doubtful whether such a certificate would support an action under the British statute. McCardie, J., expressed a faint doubt whether a uniform usage might not have made good such a tender.

In *Wilson, etc., Co.* v. *Belgian, etc., Co.*, [1920] 2 K. B. 1, Bailhache, J., also had a case of suit upon the buyer's refusal under a usual "c. i. f." contract. There the tender had been of a broker's coverage note. This was not identical in form with the certificate of insurance in the two later cases, but so far as I can see was the same in substance, except for the absence of a provision relating to the broker's lien for premiums, a circumstance on which Bailhache, J., in part relied in his judgment. There was some proof of custom, but the witnesses could recall no instance where such a note had been forced upon an unwilling buyer, a defect that, with deference, it seems to me was scarcely of moment, if none had never been refused. Bailhache, J., in declaring that the certificate was not a good tender of insurance, said that he did not mean to include in his decision American certificates of insurance, a reservation which, however, the two cases already cited declined to accept. The custom he thought insufficiently proved for the reason given. How far a custom might have controlled does not definitely appear.

The first case was also a judgment of McCardie, J., in *Manbre Saccharine Co.* v. *Corn Prod. Co. Ld.*, [1919] 1 K. B. 188. The suit was by the buyer, who had accepted the documents under a "c. i. f." contract, one of which was a letter of the seller stating that the goods were insured by it under a general policy covering these and more, and in substance that the policy was *pro tanto* for the benefit of the buyer. Having paid, the buyer sued for breach of contract as in the case at bar. McCardie, J., thought that custom might have made such a tender good, but found none such. It did not appear whether the buyer's efforts, if any, to collect on the insurance, had proved vain, but damages in full were allowed on the theory that only a separate policy of insurance, uncomplicated by sharing with other goods, was a proper tender.

Such is the law at present in England, so far as I have found, and it is clear that no case is like that at bar. The contract did not here prescribe a policy of insurance, but left the obligations to be determined from the letters "c. i. f." There was a specific London policy underwritten on this cargo alone; the usage in New York was universal to accept such certificates as performance; the policy as underwritten is valid under the laws of England, where it was made. Candidly, it seems to me probable that a tender even under all these circumstances would at present be held bad in England, but any conclusion is as yet doubtful, and the results so far have been reluctantly reached. However that may be, and much as I should hesitate to diverge from the settled law of so great a commercial country, it seems to me, in the language of a great English judge:

"It is the business of courts reasonably so to shape their rules of evidence as to make them suitable to the habits of mankind." *Humfrey* v. *Dale*, 7 E. & B. 266, 278.

When a usage of this kind has become uniform in an actively commercial community, that should be warrant enough for supposing that it answers the needs of those who are dealing upon the faith of it. I cannot see why judges should not hold men to understandings which are the tacit presupposition on which they deal. From Lord Holt's time on they have generally in one way or the other been forced in the end to yield to the more flexible practices of commercial usage. So far as I know, the results have been generally acceptable to every one, once they were settled.

The objections to this specific usage are that it is unreasonable, and that it contradicts the contract. The first objection may be divided into two parts: First, that it compels the buyer to take insurance the full terms of which he has no opportunity to see; and, second, that it exposes him to a broker's lien. As to the first, it would be formidable if the contract prescribed the terms of the policy to be delivered, but it does not. Any policy would do which was adequate marine protection within tolerable limits. The certificate at bar contains some of the terms of the policy actually underwritten, and for the balance refers to "English law and customs." Now it is quite true that such a reference leaves much uncertain, but can any one say that it is less certain than the permissible latitude in the provisions of a policy which the seller might tender and the buyer must accept? That law is a standard of reference as definite as the contract prescribed, and I can see no ground for declaring a usage unreasonable which substituted one for the other. Certainly the situation is *toto cœlo* different from such a tender under a contract which stipulated for the delivery of an approved policy of insurance.

The other supposed unreasonable feature of the usage is that there might be a broker's lien upon the policy for premiums. The New York broker could have none, because the lien is possessory (*Spring* v. *So. Car. Ins. Co.*, 8 Wheat. 268, 285, 5 L. Ed. 614; *Rose* v. *Shinasi*, 168 App. Div. 93, 153 N. Y. Supp. 734), and he has given up the certificate. The London broker might indeed have a lien for the premium paid by him, even though the seller paid the New York broker (*Fisher* v. *Smith*, L. R. 4 App. Cas. 1); but he would have no general lien (*Manss* v. *Henderson*, 1 East, 335), because he knew that the policy was for a third person. Therefore the objection comes to this: Though the seller pays the premium to the New York broker, a usage is unreasonable which exposes the buyer to the possibility of a lien for that premium in favor of the London broker, whom the New York broker does not pay. In the first place, is it altogether clear that the London broker could hold his lien, if he knew that the certificate was to pass to a third person and would represent the policy which he retained? Assuming that he could, and that the usage leaves the buyer exposed to such a risk, it does not on that account appear to me to be beyond reasonable limits because of that possible injustice. Usages are never of importance, unless they modify rights which would otherwise result. The fact that the usage imposes a risk upon the buyer, which he would not incur if a policy were delivered, is not, I think, so vital to the substance of the contract that it may not be interpolated into the contract by implication.

This raises the general question of how far the usage contradicts the language of the contract. "Insurance" certainly does not literally mean a "policy of insurance." When the buyer has a policy of insurance awaiting his demand and covering the loss, and that alone, why should the situation be thought to contradict a contract giving him only "insurance"? Is it less insurance because, though he has received symbolic delivery of the policy and actual delivery of the document which controls its production, he has not the policy itself? I must own that I cannot see why.

But the conventional statement of the rule is really not susceptible of consistent application anyway, and has been recognized not to be by the best writers. Words mean what the parties who use them want them to mean, and it makes no difference how widely their meaning in a special case varies from their common meaning. It is true that, in deciding how far any specific usage can be supposed to vary that normal meaning, the extent to which that meaning is set awry ought to be an important consideration, but that is all. At least that, I am glad to say, is the authoritative rule in this court. . . .

The demurrer is overruled.

In PHOENIX INSURANCE CO. *v.* DE MONCHY, 141 L. T. R. (N. S.) 703 (House of Lords, 1929), the right of the holder of a marine insurance certificate to claim under it as on the contract of insurance was accepted without question, thus resolving the doubts voiced by McCardie, J., in *Diamond Alkali Export Corporation* v. *Fl. Bourgeois*, as cited in the principal case.

YUILL & CO. *v.* SCOTT ROBSON

COURT OF APPEAL, 1907

[*Law Reports*, [1908] 1 *King's Bench*, 270]

Appeal of the defendant from the judgment of Channell J. in an action tried in the Commercial Court without a jury (reported [1907] 1 K. B. 685).

The action was brought to recover damages for breach of a stipulation in a contract for the sale of bullocks under the following circumstances. The contract was contained in two letters, dated April 4, 1903, written at Buenos Ayres by one Miskin, the plaintiffs' agent, and the defendant respectively, by which the defendant agreed to sell, and the plaintiff to buy, 250 bullocks at 17*l.* a head, to include cost, freight, and insurance, for shipment by the steamer *Abbey Holme* to Durban; the contract contained a stipulation that the bullocks were to be insured by the defendant "against all risks." The bullocks were duly shipped by the defendant and the price paid by the plaintiffs. On the voyage of the *Abbey Holme* to Durban foot-and-mouth disease broke out among the cattle, with the result that on arrival at Durban the authorities forbade the landing of the cattle, which were consequently slaughtered and their carcases sold at 5*l.* a head. The plaintiffs thereupon gave notice of abandonment to the underwriters, alleging a constructive total loss of the bullocks, but the underwriters refused to pay the plaintiffs' claim, amounting to 3829*l.*, on the ground that the policy taken out by the defendant for the plaintiffs under their contract contained an exception of losses occasioned by "capture, seizure and detention and the consequences thereof."

An action by the plaintiffs on the policy was compromised for 990*l.* (representing principally the value of cattle which had died on the voyage), and the plaintiffs sought in the present action to recover the difference of 2839*l.*, with the costs of the action against the underwriters, making a total of 2986*l.*, as damages for the breach by the defendant of his undertaking to procure for the plaintiffs an insurance of the bullocks against all risks. The defendant contended that he had procured a policy which satisfied the terms of the contract, and which had been accepted by the plaintiffs and by their agent to whom it was delivered. The policy procured by the defendant was an ordinary Lloyd's policy with special clauses attached. The clause in controversy was printed in italics, but by a note was to be construed as if it had been written, and was in these terms: "Warranted nevertheless free of capture, seizure and detention, and the consequences thereof, or of any attempt thereat, piracy excepted, and also from all consequences of hostilities or warlike operations, whether before or after declaration of war." Certain typewritten clauses, called "All risks live stock clauses," were attached to the policy, of which the important one ran: "To cover mortality, jettison, washing overboard, and risks of every kind from time of arrival at wharf and until delivered to consignees, but free of all claim for particular average and depreciation of animals which walk ashore (or after release from the slings) at destination, unless caused by or in consequence of the vessel craft or cargo being stranded, sunk, burnt, or on fire or by collision or by disablement of steamer. . . ." The defendant further pleaded that, in the absence of special instructions, it was a usual and well-known custom to include in marine policies against all risks the warranty "free of capture, seizure or detention," and that the custom was, or ought to have been, well known to the plaintiffs. The defendant took out a summons for leave to take evidence on commission in Buenos Ayres as to the meaning of the expression "insurance against all risks," as understood by persons in the cattle trade. No order was made on the summons, but it was reserved for the judge at the trial to say whether the commission should be granted. At the trial Channell J. refused to allow the commission. Evidence was given on behalf of the defendant by several London underwriters and insurance brokers to prove the custom with regard to a policy "against all risks," and to shew that the usual course was to effect a separate insurance against the risk of the landing of cattle being prohibited by the authorities of the country or place to which they were consigned.

Channell J. gave judgment for the plaintiffs.

The defendant appealed.

Lord ALVERSTONE C.J. In my opinion the conclusion at which Channell J. arrived in this case was perfectly right. The question turns on the meaning of the stipulation in the contract that the cattle were to be insured by the defendant against all risks. It is contended on behalf of the defendant that the expression "all risks" must be subject to some limitation. Speaking for myself, I do not think that it is necessary, in deciding this case, to say whether or not that proposition might not be correct in certain cases, but when considering the meaning of the words as used in this contract I cannot do better than adopt the language of Channell J. He said: "No doubt the evidence clearly shews that an insurance broker would expect a policy against all risks to contain the warranty against capture, seizure, and detention; but the question as between the buyer and seller of goods is a very different one indeed, and I very much doubt the admissibility of the evidence given on behalf of the defendant. I think that in the present case the expression covers insurance against a risk so obvious to parties buying and selling live cattle for shipment as that of the cattle being prevented from landing at their destination by reason of the apprehension of the authorities of the importation of disease. Such a prohibition is very usual, and the risk would naturally be present to the minds of persons in the position of the plaintiffs and the defendant." I can only say that I entirely agree with that statement. But it is said that in the cattle trade the words "insurance against all risks" have acquired a secondary and special signification, and that the parties to this contract must be taken to have known that an insurance against all risks would not include all risks, but would exclude the particular risk of a prohibition against the landing of the cattle by an order of the authorities in the country to which they were to be sent.

It is said that there are two kinds of policy in use, one of which does not contain the free of capture, seizure, and detention warranty, and that, if a policy in that form is desired, an additional premium has to be paid. We are also told that if the slip does not contain the words "no free of capture, seizure, and detention warranty," it is the practice for underwriters to insert the clause in the policy. That may be a very reasonable and proper practice, but to my mind it to a great extent negatives the suggestion that the words "all risks" have acquired a special secondary meaning binding on the parties to this action. Throughout Mr. Hamilton's argument I had great difficulty in seeing how any question could be framed which would establish that the words had acquired a secondary meaning in the cattle trade. He contended that the words must be subject to some limitation because otherwise they would be wide enough to cover loss due to inherent vice. I do not follow that argument. The policy, which was tendered and which was assumed by both parties to be an all risks policy, contained what are known as the "all risks live stock clauses," one of which, the "mortality" clause, contained certain stipulations limiting the insurer's liability in certain events. The argument for the defendant has not satisfied me that the words "insurance against all risks" in this contract must be read subject to a limitation; but, in any case, I agree with Channell J. that it was necessary in order to comply with the contract to tender a policy which would protect the assured against the whole venture being frustrated by reason of a prohibition against the landing of the cattle at Durban. The policy which was in fact tendered contained the warranty against capture, seizure, and detention, and the cattle having been prevented from landing by the authorities at Durban, the case of *Miller* v. *Law Accident Insurance Co.* decides that that loss was not recoverable under a policy in that form. For the reasons which I have given I am of opinion on the main point that the plaintiffs were not bound to accept the policy which was tendered.

[The last paragraph of the opinion, and concurring opinions of Buckley and Kennedy, L.JJ., are omitted.]

In VINCENTELLI & Co. *v.* JOHN ROWLETT & Co., 16 Commercial Cases 310 (King's Bench Division, 1910), a contract for the sale of citrons c.i.f. per steamer from the Piraeus to Antwerp contained the words "Insurance to be effected by [sellers] all risks." It appeared from correspondence that the buyers wanted a policy insuring against total loss, no partial loss however small to be excluded under an f.p.a. clause or otherwise. The citrons were shipped at Piraeus on an English steamer under an ordinary form of bill of lading, but on arrival at Antwerp it was discovered that part of the citrons were damaged. The damage was caused by their having been stowed, without the knowledge of the sellers, on deck instead of below deck. The insurance taken out by the sellers was in the form of an ordinary Lloyds "all risks" policy, which did not cover goods carried on deck. The buyers, having failed in an action against the shipowners brought in Belgium, and having compromised a suit against the underwriters, sued the sellers for failing to insure the goods against all risks. Two underwriters testified that the premium for "on deck" insurance under the circumstances would be prohibitive, as no company would care to take such a risk. This testimony was not contradicted. Defendants argued that under a c.i.f. contract all that the sellers needed to procure at their own expense was contractual protection against all risks partly under the contract of carriage, and partly under the contract of insurance, and that it should be sufficient if under the one or the other there was a cause of action for all kinds of damage. Without deciding this point, Hamilton, J., held that on its true construction the contract was that the insurance should cover all risks in the sense of the entire quantum of damage, and not that it should cover the plaintiffs effectively against all causes of accident.

Compare SCHLOSS BROTHERS *v.* STEVENS, [1906] 2 K. B. 665 (King's Bench Division), where in an action by the insured against the insurer it was held that the phrase "all risks by land and water" in an ordinary

Lloyds policy must be read literally as covering all risks whatsoever, and as intended to cover all losses by any accidental cause of any kind. The policy accordingly covered damage caused by abnormal exposure to damp and accidental wetting due to extraordinary delay.

Note also VALE *v.* VAN OPPEN, 37 T. L. R. 367 (King's Bench Division, 1921), where a seller arranged for shipment of two bales of gabardine through a forwarding agent, and instructed the forwarding agent to insure against all risks. Insurance was effected against marine risks, "to include theft, pilferage, fresh water and war." One bale was not delivered at destination, and the seller, being unable to show how the bale was lost, could not recover under the policy. In an action for damages against the forwarding agent for failing to insure according to instructions, it was held that defendant had acted reasonably in taking out a policy covering the goods against all the risks covered by the ordinary marine policy.

BELGIAN GRAIN AND PRODUCE COMPANY, LTD. *v.* COX & COMPANY (FRANCE) LTD.

COURT OF APPEAL, 1919

[(1919) *Weekly Notes*, 308]

Appeal from Rowlatt J.

On September 28, 1918, the plaintiffs sold to French purchasers 100 tons of Japanese green peas, hand sorted, of fair average quality, in bags, to be shipped from Japan during September, October, and November, 1918, for Marseilles direct or indirect with or without transhipments, at the price of 300 francs per 100 kilos gross weight delivered; cost, freight, and insurance to Marseilles. Payment was to be by net cash at Marseilles against bills of lading and policies of insurance, and the buyers were to furnish an irrevocable bank credit in favour of the plaintiffs at the time of the signature of the contract. On October 3, 1918, the French purchasers wrote to the defendants informing them of this contract, and asking them to open a firm credit in favour of the plaintiffs for the sum of 300,000 francs payable to the plaintiffs' agent, one Ivan Rossius, representing the purchase of the Japanese peas. On October 5 the defendants wrote to I. Rossius informing him that they had opened a documentary confirmed credit in favour of the plaintiffs for 300,000 francs against surrender of full set of bills of lading, invoice, and policies, certificates and letters of insurance, marine and war, at the arrival of the steamer at the port of discharge, and delivery orders at Marseilles; the whole relating to 100 tons of Japanese green peas hand picked in bags to be shipped, etc., following the terms of the contract of September 28 as stated above. The plaintiffs shipped the goods, and on February 6, 1919, tendered to the defendants documents relating to 82,296 kilos, being the balance of the 100 tons, and demanded payment of 9,495*l.* 14*s.* The defendants refused to pay on the ground that the proper documents had not been tendered to them.

The bill of lading, dated September 14, 1918, declared that there had been shipped in apparent good order and condition on board the steamship *Koyei Maru*, lying in or off the port of Yokohama, having liberty to deviate for the purpose of saving life or property, to call at any ports in or out of the customary or advertised route in any order, to discharge and receive goods and passengers and to take in coal and other necessary supplies at any port or ports, to sail without pilots, and to tow and assist vessels in distress, 896 bags green peas only being marked and numbered as per margin, and to be carried upon the steamer to the port of Kobe and thence to be carried upon any vessel or vessels belonging either to the shipowners or any other company or individual to the port of Bombay and thence again to be transhipped to the port of Marseilles. In the margin was written "From Yokohama to Marseilles, to be transhipped at Kobe and at Bombay." The bill of lading contained numerous clauses, of which one numbered 12 was as follows:

> The company reserve the right of forwarding the goods to their destination by any other vessel belonging either to this or any other company or individual, subject to all conditions which may be exacted by the companies or individuals who may complete the transit. . . .

The invoice was for

> 896 bags (81 tons) green peas from Japan per the steamship *Koyei Maru/Kasado Maru*, partial execution of the contract of September 28 . . . R.M./M.Y. green peas from Japan hand sorted from Yokohama via Kobe to Marseilles. 896 bags, namely, 81 English tons at 1,016 kilos — 82,296 kilos at 300 francs per 100 kilos c.i.f. Marseilles 246,888 francs. Bill of lading dated September 14, 1918. . . . Payable at the Bank Cox & Co. (France), Ltd. . . .

The 896 bags of peas were insured by three policies, one of which contained the words, "at and from Yokohama to Marseilles via Kobe . . . in the good ship or vessel called the s.s. *Kasado Maru* and s.s. *Koyei Maru*." The policies of insurance included the Institute Cargo Clauses (F. P. A.), 1919, of which the following are material: —

> 4. Held covered, at a premium to be arranged in case of deviation or change of voyage or of any omission or error in the description of the interest vessel or voyage. 5. Including (subject to the terms of the policy) all risks covered by this policy from shippers' or manufacturers' warehouse until on board the vessel, during transhipment, if any, and from the vessel whilst on quays, wharves, or in sheds during the ordinary course of transit until safely deposited in consignees' or other warehouse at destination named in policy. . . . 7. Including all liberties as per contract of affreightment. . . .

The goods arrived at Marseilles on board a vessel named the *Saigon Maru*. The French purchasers objected that this was not in accordance with the contract inasmuch as the policy of insurance above specified, made no mention of the *Saigon Maru*. They therefore served upon the defendants a formal document forbidding them to pay the plaintiffs the amount claimed by them, and warning the defendants that if they did pay they would do so at their own risk. The defendants accordingly refused to pay the plaintiffs. The facts were that the 896 bags of peas were loaded on the *Koyei Maru* at Yokohama and carried by her to Kobe; there they were transhipped on board the *Kasado Maru,* and carried by that vessel from thence to Bombay, where they were again transhipped and carried to Marseilles on the *Saigon Maru.*

The plaintiffs brought an action to recover the amount claimed. The case was heard before Rowlatt J., who gave judgment for the defendants on the ground that the policy of insurance was not sufficient.

The plaintiffs appealed.

The Court (Bankes, Warrington and Scrutton L.JJ.) held that the policy of insurance was sufficient. The words "all liberties as per contract of affreightment" included the rights reserved by Clause 12 of the bill of lading enabling the shipowners to forward the goods by other vessels, as well as the liberty to deviate, call at ports in any order, sail without pilots, etc. The policy therefore covered the goods on the *Saigon Maru.* The appeal was allowed, and judgment was entered for the appellants.

In HICKOX *v.* ADAMS, 29 L. J. Exch. 36 (Court of Appeal, 1876), there was a contract for the sale of 1000 quarters of wheat, c.f.i. Bristol. The sellers shipped 2000 quarters to business acquaintances in Bristol, to whom were sent an insurance policy covering the entire parcel, bills of lading, one draft on themselves for the full amount of the 2000 quarters, and a separate draft on the buyers for 1000 quarters with instructions to attach this latter draft to a bill of lading and present it to the buyers. The buyers refused the draft on the ground that no proper policy of insurance was tendered. In an action by the sellers against the buyers it was held that a tender of the policy on 2000 quarters of wheat did not satisfy the requirements of a contract for the sale of 1000 quarters.

LANDAUER *v.* ASSER

KING'S BENCH DIVISION, 1905

[*Law Reports,* [1905] *2 King's Bench,* 184]

Motion to set aside an award.

By a contract dated November 3, 1903, Messrs. Landauer bought from Messrs. Asser 250 bales of Manila hemp to arrive at the price of 35*l.* 10*s.* per ton cost, freight, and usual f.p.a. insurance. The contract contained the following clause: "Insurance for 5 per cent. over net invoice amount to be effected by sellers for account of buyers under an f.p.a. policy on usual Lloyd's conditions at Lloyd's, or with a London insurance company having a responsible and well-known London agent." The 250 bales were invoiced to Messrs. Landauer on May 3, 1904, as shipped per SS. *Peleus.* The hemp had been bought by Messrs. Asser from Messrs. F. E. Coney & Co., the shippers, who had insured it under a floating policy of insurance dated April 29, 1904, for 25,616*l.* on hemp per steamers from Philippines to United Kingdom, by a declaration thereunder of even date of 1280*l.* on

250 bales of hemp so valued per SS. *Peleus* to London. On May 4 Messrs. Landauer paid to Messrs. Asser the invoice amount of 1054*l.* 13*s.* 9*d.*, and received in exchange the shipping documents, together with the above declaration of insurance. The *Peleus* arrived in London about May 4, 1904, and discharged the said 250 bales in due course into the dock company's sheds, and while there about 160 bales, part of the 250 bales, were destroyed by fire. Messrs. Landauer claimed under the insurance as for a total loss of the 160 bales. The underwriters were prepared to pay the claim upon basis of the insurance being for 1280*l.* But Messrs. Asser claimed to be entitled to a share of the insurance money to the extent to which 1280*l.* exceeded the amount of the net invoice plus 5 per cent. Messrs. Landauer disputed this claim, and the matter was referred to arbitration. The two arbitrators, being unable to agree, nominated Mr. H. K. Bibby as umpire, who made his award in the following terms: "Having been asked to act as umpire on the question as to the liability and interest in the policy of insurance appertaining to 250 bales Manila hemp per *Peleus*, I decide that as the parties to the contract dated November 3, 1903, were by the terms thereof principals thereto, their interest and liability in insurance is defined to be the value of the invoice plus 5 per cent., and that the buyers are therefore entitled to and only to the said amount, the balance one way or the other being due from or to the sellers." Messrs. Landauer moved to set aside the said award upon the ground that it was bad on the face of it.

Lord Alverstone C.J. This was a motion to set aside an award made by Mr. Bibby, an umpire appointed under an arbitration clause in a contract of sale of November 3, 1903. The only ground on which it is alleged that the award should be set aside is that the arbitrator has gone wrong in point of law, and that the error in law appears upon the face of the award. There is no doubt whatever that if this can be established the award ought to be set aside.

[Two pages of the opinion are here omitted.]

It is alleged on behalf of Messrs. Landauer & Co. that the award is bad because it decides that the buyers are only entitled under the contract to such amount of the insurance money as represents the net price plus 5 per cent., and that the balance is due to Messrs. Asser. It is alleged on behalf of Messrs. Asser that the question to be decided by the umpire was one of mercantile usage, and that he was entitled to say, under the contract, that the interest of Messrs. Landauer was limited to the extent of the purchase-money plus 5 per cent., and that as against Messrs. Landauer the sellers, Messrs. Asser, were entitled to receive from the underwriters and retain the difference between the amount of the insurance and the amount of the net price plus 5 per cent. The umpire appears to have decided, so far as we can gather from his award, that under the contract of November 3 the purchasers are, as against the sellers, not entitled to claim more than 1107*l.*, even though the policies handed over in pursuance of the contract were intended to be so handed over as a discharge of the sellers' obligation to deliver the policy of insurance. This seems to me to be an error in point of law. If policies are handed over by the sellers under such a contract, the interest in them passes wholly to the purchasers, and, assuming the underwriters to pay on those policies the amount insured, I do not see under what right the sellers are entitled to claim that the purchasers are trustees for them of any portion of the money so recovered. The sellers, Messrs. Asser & Co., had at the time of the loss no interest in the subject-matter of the insurance, and could not upon the facts assumed have made any valid claim against the underwriters, and if the underwriters pay they must be taken to have paid to the persons who were entitled to the goods at the time of the loss. The only reason stated in the award for a different conclusion is that the parties to the contract were principals and not brokers, and the award states that the buyers are therefore entitled only to the value plus 5 per cent. This seems to me to be immaterial except possibly for the purpose of excluding any question of the right of the sellers, or purchasers, respectively to represent the interests of third parties. I can see no other bearing that it has upon the question. Although not directly in point, the case of *Ralli* v. *Universal Marine Insurance Co.* supports the contention that under such a contract policies, which are in fact handed over in discharge of the sellers' obligations, are to be treated as belonging to the purchasers. For these reasons I think the award should be set aside and the appeal allowed.

[Concurring opinions of Kennedy and Ridley, JJ., are omitted.]

In KARINJEE JIVANJEE & CO. *v.* MALCOLM (*supra*, p. 310), the sellers sold a quantity of sisal c.i.f. a port in the United Kingdom, documents against acceptance. Insurance was affected for the invoice price plus an extra insurance of £444. The buyers took up the documents, and learned two days later that the cargo had been lost. The buyers claimed the right to retain the full insurance collected, including the excess. The sellers relied on a provision in the contract of sale that "should the goods or any portion thereof not arrive . . . this contract to be void for such portion," and claimed the benefit of the documents and of the insurance. It was held that the buyers were entitled.

Compare BUCKERFIELD'S LTD. *v.* SMITH, 54 Ll. L. R. 304 (King's Bench Division, 1936), where there was a contract for the sale of bran c.i.f. Hull, with a provision that "the amount insured in excess of 2 per cent of invoice amount to be for seller's account." The seller took out insurance for the c.i.f. value of the bran plus 2 per cent. The goods were sent forward upon a bill of lading under which freight was to be collected on arrival. The ship was a total loss. The buyers, having taken up the documents, accordingly collected insurance which included the amount of the freight, although the freight had not been earned and was not payable. The seller claimed the benefit of this windfall. In an action by the seller against the buyer, judgment was given for the plaintiff.

LODERS AND NUCOLINE, LIMITED *v.* BANK OF NEW ZEALAND

King's Bench Division, 1929

[45 *Times Law Reports*, 203]

This special case stated by arbitrators raised a question as to the proper form of the policy of insurance in a c.i.f. contract.

The facts out of which the special case arose were as follows: —

By two contracts dated November 21, 1927, and December 12, 1927, a firm, Fischel and Co., bought from the Bank of New Zealand 200 and 100 tons of copra at £27 5*s*. a ton, "cost freight insurance shipped or to be shipped per steamer and/or steamers from Australasia to London . . . during December, 1927, and/or January, 1928." Fischels sold to Loders, the buyers in this case, and dropped out of the transaction. The case was, therefore, an arbitration between first seller and last buyer.

On December 10, 1927, the 300 tons of copra in question were shipped on the Clan Macwilliam, which then left for Europe. On the voyage she called at one of the Tonga islands to pick up further cargo, and there she took fire and with her cargo became a total loss. By the bill of lading the freight for the copra was payable only if and when the vessel arrived at the place of destination. Accordingly, the freight did not and would not become payable.

In February, 1928, after the loss had become known, the shipping documents were presented to Loders, the documents consisting of (1) invoice; (2) bills of lading; and (3) three insurance policies all in the same form and for the same amounts, each being for £2,862 10*s*., as follows: —

Copra.	
1,510 sacks — 100 tons at £25 7*s*. 6*d*. per ton	£2,537 10 0
Freight payable at destination at £3 5*s*. per ton	325 0 0
So valued	£2,862 10 0

The policies all had a clause in the margin known as the "freight contingency clause," which read as follows: —

> On freight payable at destination valued at £325, being increased value of copra through payment of freight or from such time as freight becomes due at destination, this insurance being deemed to be part of the total amount insured on the copra valued at such total amount. . . .

The contract contained an insurance clause as follows: —

> Insurance including war risk on free from particular average terms to be effected by sellers at the contract price plus 5 per cent. on the net shipping weight. . . . Such insurance to cover the copra until delivered in the ordinary course of transit into warehouse at the port of destination.

When the documents were presented Loders objected to the policies as not being in accordance with the contracts, in that they did not constitute an insurance "at the contract price," part of such price, representing the freight, being separately valued in the policy and covered only on the terms of the freight contingency clause set out above.

They claimed under their policies and the insurance company paid £7,612 10*s*., but refused to pay the balance of £975 representing freight, on the ground that in the circumstances the freight had never become covered by the terms of the freight contingency clause. Loders accepted payment from the company without prejudice and claimed from the sellers damages for breach of the contracts by reason of the policies being in a form which did not comply with the terms of the contracts.

The dispute was referred to arbitration. At the hearing Loders contended that under the contracts they were entitled to receive from the sellers valued policies on the copra for a single amount representing the contract price on a c.i.f. basis plus five per cent. thereon, but that the policies tendered failed to comply with the contracts in that an amount representing the freight was separately insured on the terms of the freight contingency clause. The bank contended that the policies were in accordance with the contracts as they covered the price of the goods, together with a contingent insurance of the increased value represented by the freight attaching to the goods as soon as the freight became payable. The bank further contended that in any event Loders had suffered no damage because even if the policies tendered had been in the form contended for by Loders — namely, valued policies for the full c.i.f. contract price plus 5 per cent. — yet, as the goods had been lost before freight became payable the insurance company would have been entitled to reopen the valuation and to refuse to pay such part of the amount insured as represented the freight, which had never been at risk.

The arbitrators found as a fact that the policies tendered to Loders were not in the form customary in the copra trade under contracts on the terms here in question.

The questions of law for the opinion of the Court were: —

"(*a*) On a true construction of the contracts, did the policies tendered to Loders comply with the contracts, or were Loders entitled to demand valued policies for the full c.i.f. price plus 5 per cent. thereon, without any freight contingency clause and without any separate valuation of the freight?

"(*b*) If Loders were so entitled had they suffered any damage, or would the insurance company even on a policy in the form contended for by Loders have been entitled to reopen the valuation, and to refuse to pay such part of the claim as represented the freight on the copra?"

Subject to the opinion of the Court the arbitrators awarded that the policies were not in accordance with the contracts, or, alternatively, were not in the form customary in the trade, and that by reason thereof Loders had suffered damage to the extent of £975, and that the bank must therefore pay Loders £975 with interest.

Mr. Justice WRIGHT, in giving judgment, stated the facts and said that it was necessary to look at the contracts, the bills of lading, and the policies. He discussed the provisions of the documents, and said that the intention was to have valued policies and the insurance was to cover the contract price. The contract price was an indivisible sum, but the policies as taken out distinguished between the price of the goods and the freight and made two subjects of insurance with a different valuation for each. Instead of insuring at the contract price the sellers made separate insurances on the goods and on the freight. The buyers objected to the policies when presented, and, in his view, they were right. The contract was absolutely clear, and separate insurances did not satisfy it. It was unnecessary to consider the point that those policies were not in accordance with the customary form of insurance in the copra trade, for by the express terms of the contract they were clearly wrong in form.

But it was said that, even if the policies were not such as were required by the contracts, the buyers had really no claim for damages because even if policies which did satisfy the contract had been tendered the insurance company on learning the facts could have reopened the valuation, and could have refused to pay the part of the insurance representing freight. He thought the sellers must fail on that point also. The policies were valued policies, and, as laid down by section 27 (3) of the Marine Insurance Act, the value fixed by them was conclusive. It was of primary importance in business that the value fixed in a valued policy should be binding and conclusive, though in case of fraud the whole policy could be set aside. In this case there were to be policies on goods valued at the contract price, and if in the particular circumstances the buyers made a profit on the insurance because they did not in fact have to pay freight that was only an ordinary incident of business life. There was nothing to be objected to in the valuation and the insurance company could not have reopened it.

It was said that, in fact, the freight in this case was never at risk. But the subject-matter of the insurance should have been the goods and nothing else; and there was no right to split up the insurance. It should have been for one indivisible subject, and the buyers would have had the right to recover under it. The claim of the buyers, therefore, must succeed and the award must be confirmed.

YANGTSZE INSURANCE ASSOCIATION, LIMITED *v.* LUKMANJEE

PRIVY COUNCIL, 1918

[*Law Reports,* [1918] *Appeal Cases,* 585]

Lord SUMNER. In this case Mr. Adamjee Lukmanjee sued upon a policy of marine insurance to recover a loss in respect of 144 logs of teak-wood, which, after being discharged overside ex steamship *Hild* at Colombo, were lost in a gale while still in raft. He succeeded, though on somewhat different grounds, both in the District Court of Colombo and in the Supreme Court of Ceylon. The insurance company now appeals.

The policy was effected at their own expense by the Bombay, Burmah Trading Corporation, Limited, "as well in his or their own name as for and in the name and names of all and every person or persons, to whom the same doth, may, or shall appertain in part or in all," following the company's usual form of policy, and under these words Mr. Lukmanjee claims to have been assured under the policy from the beginning, and entitled to sue as a party to it, subject to his having an insurable interest at the time of loss. There is no question here of any assignment of the policy. In fact he had such an interest; for the logs, when lost, were his, so the question is whether he was a party insured under this policy in respect of that interest, or, in other words, whether the Bombay, Burmah Trading Corporation effected it in any measure on his behalf.

The Bombay, Burmah Trading Corporation, by its agents at Colombo, had sold to Mr. Lukmanjee, who was also at Colombo, "200 tons of Indian first-class teak squares at Rs.175 per ton ex ship. Shipment November-December at the rate of 100 tons monthly. . . . Payment cash against documents." The 144 logs constituted the first instalment under this contract, and it is common ground that when they were discharged ex ship into the water they had been paid for and had become the property of the respondent.

Except in so far as it can be inferred from the transaction itself and the documents by which it was effected and carried out, there is no evidence to show with what intention the Bombay, Burmah Trading Corporation effected the insurance, nor was there any evidence of any course of business or of any customary understanding of any of the terms employed. What is significant about the policy itself is that it covered 382 pieces of teak, all particularly marked, of which only 144 were for Mr. Lukmanjee and the remainder were for the account of the Bombay, Burmah Trading Corporation. There was a separate bill of lading made out to the order of the shippers, the Bombay, Burmah Trading Corporation, for the 144 logs, and in it they were identified by the same marks as in the policy. Among the marginal clauses in the policy was one covering the ancillary risk between ship and shore, namely, "all risk of craft and/or raft from land to land," but it was admitted that such a clause would be included almost as a matter of course, and that, although it was only under this clause that Mr. Lukmanjee could recover, the fact of its insertion in the policy threw little or no light on the question whether the policy was effected on his behalf as one of the original assured.

The trial judge was of opinion that the property in the goods passed to the buyer before shipment, and that in shipping them the sellers had acted as his agents. Hence he inferred that the insurance was effected for him. The Supreme Court apparently treated the contract as if it contained an implied obligation on the seller's part to insure the buyer in respect of such contingent interest in the goods as he might have while they were at sea. Neither view was, or indeed could be, sustained on appeal, nor had the attention of either Court been directed to the true question, whether the evidence showed that the insurance was effected on the buyer's behalf.

It is clear that the policy itself evidences no such intention. The sellers, and the sellers alone, were throughout interested in the major part of the cargo. Even as to the 144 logs, until the ship arrived and came to deliver overside they, and they alone, had the interest properly describable by the words used in the policy, namely, "upon goods." If the buyer were to fail to pay for the timber in accordance with the contract, their interest in it would continue after discharge overside, for it would remain their property. Even if these logs were paid for against documents, as was the case, the inclusion in the policy of cover against raft and craft risk was necessary as to the residue, and was of no significance in the present connection.

Two suggestions were made in argument; one was that "against documents" means in the language of commerce against a policy of insurance and sundry other documents; the other, that an obligation, binding the sellers to insure on the buyer's behalf, might be inferred because the effect of the contract was to require payment not merely against goods delivered ex ship in a state corresponding to the contract description, but also against documents representing the goods, even though, through sea perils, they were no longer in a state corresponding to the contract description.

The first point fails because there is no evidence to show that the word "documents" in such a connection includes a policy of insurance. A contract of sale, at a price c. f. and i., is so well understood that no proof is needed that one of the documents which it contemplates is a policy. It may be that, detached from any context, the mere expression "shipping documents" would suggest that one of them is a policy. When, however, the expression is found in a contract, and there is nothing but the language of the contract to determine its meaning, it must be construed as meaning such documents as are appropriate to the contract. In the case of a sale "ex ship," the seller has to cause delivery to be made to the buyer from a ship which has arrived at the port of delivery and has reached a place therein, which is usual for the delivery of goods of the kind in question. The seller has therefore to pay the freight, or otherwise to release the shipowner's lien and to furnish the buyer with an effectual direction to the ship to deliver. Till this is done the buyer is not bound to pay for the goods. Till this is done he may have an insurable interest in profits, but none that can correctly be described as an interest "upon goods," nor any interest which the seller, as seller, is bound to insure for him. If the seller insures, he does so for his own purposes and of his own motion.

Again, the mere documents do not take the place of the goods under such a contract. They are not the subject-matter of the sale. If an indorsed bill of lading is delivered to the buyer it is given as a delivery order and not with any intention of making him a party liable upon it, or of vesting him with the property in the goods by the mere delivery of the document. As the goods are not at the buyer's risk during the voyage, there is nothing from which to infer an obligation on the seller, and therefore an intention on his part, to effect an insurance on the buyer's behalf.

It was said that "cash against documents," first of all, implied some document other than a delivery order because of the use of the plural, and, secondly, must have reference to the risks of the voyage so as to make the contract analogous to a c. f. and i. sale, since if "documents" only meant "delivery of the goods" this would be implied by law. The answer seems to be, on the first point, that the plural "documents" would be satisfied either by two delivery orders, one for each shipment, or by two documents, a delivery order and a receipt for the freight, in the case of each shipment. On the second point there is nothing surprising if such a contract is found to express something which the law would imply, and certainly there is nothing in it to compel a Court to give simple and well-known words a meaning which does not belong to them, and which does belong to other words or letters equally well known though not so simple. In truth, however, "cash against documents" does carry the matter beyond "cash on delivery," that is, delivery of the goods, for it imports a convenient mercantile way of effecting the same object without the inconvenience of a payment at or contemporaneous with the discharge overside. It was admitted that payment could not be demanded, even "against documents," till the ship had arrived with the goods. The provision enables payment to be made in a counting-house and in the ordinary course of business, without reference to the precise stage which the process of tumbling the logs into the water may happen to have reached.

Their Lordships are therefore of opinion that there was no evidence on which it could be found that the policy was effected on behalf of the respondent, or to cover his interest in the goods, and that he could not sue on it. They will therefore humbly advise His Majesty that the appeal should be allowed, and that both judgments should be set aside with costs here and below.

Compare IONIDES *v.* HARFORD, 29 L. J. Exch. 36 (Court of Exchequer, 1859). In that case a ship under charter was loaded with grain at Galatz, to proceed to Emden for orders, and to discharge at a port in the United Kingdom. The owners took out insurance on the grain from Galatz to Emden, and thence to a port of discharge in the United Kingdom. The grain was sold afloat while on the voyage from Galatz to Emden, the contract stating "including freight and insurance to Emden." The bill of lading and the insurance policy were delivered to the buyer. The grain was subsequently lost between Emden and the United Kingdom. It was held that the buyer of the grain had no claim for the loss under the insurance policy.

CHAPTER III

Terms and Conditions Relating to Price and Payment

INTERSTATE ELECTRIC CO. *v.* RADIO CORPORATION OF AMERICA

Louisiana Supreme Court, 1932

[174 *Louisiana Reports*, 200]

Rogers, J. The Interstate Electric Company, a domestic corporation, brought suit against the Radio Corporation of America, a non-resident corporation, for the recovery of $2,617.57, alleged to be the balance due on certain credit memoranda and invoices and for rebates growing out of a price reduction on radio products. Jurisdiction was obtained by attachment process. The defendant bonded the attachment, joined issue on the merits, and reconvened for $2,315.73, which defendant alleged was transmitted to plaintiff to be distributed by it to its dealers, but which plaintiff retained. The court below awarded plaintiff judgment for $2,416.36, maintaining the attachment and dismissed the reconventional demand. Defendant has appealed from the judgment.

The record discloses that in marketing its products the Radio Corporation of America appoints distributors to whom it makes its sales. The distributors, in turn, sell to the dealers; and the dealers, in turn, sell to the consumers.

In 1921 or 1922 the Interstate Electric Company, of New Orleans, became one of the distributors of the Radio Corporation of America. The business relations between the parties continued until May 1, 1925, when they ceased pursuant to a notice given to the Interstate Electric Company on March 17, 1925.

On various occasions prior to January 1, 1925, the Radio Corporation of America, according to agreement, guaranteed the Interstate Electric Company, as one of its distributors, and its dealers against price reductions. These agreements, following the established policy of the Radio Corporation of America, were effectuated by telegrams containing the guaranties for short periods. The record shows that this method fo dealing with its distributors was adopted by the Radio Corporation of America, in lieu of extending them guaranties for longer periods, in order to protect and stabilize its prices.

On January 31, 1925, the Radio Corporation of America sent telegrams to all its distributors, including the Interstate Electric Company, guaranteeing price reductions up to July 1, 1925, on all radios and accessories which the distributors and their customers had on hand.

A price reduction was also granted by the Radio Corporation on September 1, 1925, and, according to its usual practice, on November 21, 1925, it sent the Interstate Electric Company a check for $2,315.73 covering rebates for that company's dealers on radios and accessories remaining unsold in their stock as of date August 31, 1925, as certified by them.

The Interstate Electric Company contends that the price reduction effective September 1, 1925, applied to the stock it had on hand on that date, and therefore it was entitled to the rebates the Radio Corporation of America was allowing its distributors. The correctness *vel non* of this contention is the sole question presented for decision.

The original claim of the Interstate Electric Company on these rebates was $4,432.08. On this alleged indebtedness it credited the Radio Corporation of America with the $2,315.73 received for distribution among its dealers, leaving a balance of $2,116.35, which is set forth as one of the items of indebtedness for which judgment is sought in this suit.

The Radio Corporation of America contends that the price reduction which it granted on September 1, 1925, was not applicable to the Interstate Electric Company, because that company prior to the reduction had ceased to be one of its distributors. . . .

Our conclusion is that the defendant's guaranty against the decline in prices of its goods was indivisible. It must stand or fall as a whole. It cannot be valid so far as it requires the distributors to pay their dealers an amount equivalent to the reduction in prices and invalid so far as it requires the Radio Corporation of America to pay an amount equivalent to the reduction in price to its distributors. This conclusion is supported, not only by nature of the agreement, but also by the position assumed by defendant in the letters which it wrote to the plaintiff's dealers, an extract from one of which letters is hereinabove quoted. In this letter, plaintiff's dealers were expressly notified that the credit was issued to the Interstate Electric Company for their stock on hand "in accordance with the conditions of the rebate"; thus disclosing plaintiff's own understanding that, in the event of a decline in prices, it was a condition precedent of plaintiff's paying its dealers that defendant should pay plaintiff. The Radio Corporation of America was to deal directly with the Interstate Electric Company, and that company, in turn, was to deal directly with its own customers. The record shows that the amount accruing to the dealers of the Interstate Electric Company under the price reduction declared by the Radio Corporation of America on September 1, 1925, imposed the burden upon the Interstate Electric Company of paying its dealers approximately 23 per cent. more than $2,315.73, the remittance received by it for that purpose.

It seems plain to us that, while the business relations between the plaintiff and defendant companies were severed as of date May 1, 1931, the severance applied only to their future relations, and had no application whatever to the rights and obligations growing out of their past relations. Plaintiff remained a distributor of defendant's goods, so long as it had any of those goods to distribute. As such distributor it was entitled to all the benefits of the agreement by virtue of which the relation was established.

In view of the conclusion we have reached and expressed on the main demand, we do not find any merit in the reconventional demand.

The judgment of the court below was made up of two items, namely, an admitted indebtedness of $300 and $2,116.35, representing the difference claimed by plaintiff under its agreement with defendant and the amount of $2,315.73 remitted by defendant to plaintiff. In rendering the judgment, the court overlooked a credit of $99.21 due the defendant, which credit accrued subsequent to the filing of the suit. The judgment will have to be amended accordingly.

For the reasons assigned, the judgment appealed from is amended by reducing the principal amount thereof from $2,416.35 to $2,317.14, and, as thus amended, it is affirmed; defendant and appellant to pay the costs of appeal.

In HAIGH HALL STEAMSHIP COMPANY, LIMITED *v.* ANDERSEN, 246 Mass. 34 (Supreme Judicial Court, 1923), a contract for the sale of coal to be supplied to plaintiff's vessels contained a clause reading: "Should the general current price for bunker coals as contracted for herein delivered to steamers at port of supply be below those herein named on day of coaling buyers to have benefit of such lower price." The clause was construed to carry the implication that the seller was to bear the loss of a rise in such general current price.

In CUB FORK COAL CO. *v.* FAIRMOUNT GLASS WORKS, 33 Fed. (2nd) 420 (Circuit Court of Appeals, Seventh Circuit, 1929), a contract for the sale of 17,500 tons of coal provided: "It is expressly understood that the price or prices named herein are based on existing rates of pay for all mine labor and the price or prices will be subject to readjustment in event existing rates of pay are changed." The wages paid to miners were raised during the period covered by the contract, but the seller nevertheless made no move to increase the price to the buyer. The latter, however, telegraphed to the seller to stop shipments under the contract, and in an action for damages for breach attempted to defend on the ground of non-compliance with the clause in question. It was held to be error to submit this issue to the jury: "Obviously defendant cannot avoid its contract because of an unexercised right of the seller to increase the price."

Note also HANSEN *v.* FRESNO JERSEY FARM DAIRY CO., 220 Calif. 402 (Supreme Court, 1934), where a contract for the sale of milk to a dealer fixed a basic price founded on the butter-fat content of the milk, and with the following provision: "It is furthermore agreed that whenever and whilst buyer reduces its price to customers in order to meet competition, or on account of a milk price war in Fresno, said basic price for milk hereinabove fixed shall stand reduced for the time of continuance of buyer's said reduced price, in an amount equal to one-half of said reduction." At the time the contract was made the buyer's business was almost entirely retail, but circumstances later changed so that the business became 85 per cent wholesale. It was held that the clause quoted applied to price reductions to wholesale as well as to retail customers.

GRAWITZ ET FILS *c.* TURNER ET CIE
COMMERCIAL COURT OF MARSEILLE, 1924

[1926 *Marseille* 1.151]

[A contract for the sale of 25 tons of Australian lard was made on September 26, 1922, and fixed the price at 36 shillings per cwt. c.i.f. Marseille, payment against sight draft on arrival of the steamer. On the date when the contract was made sterling was quoted at 58 francs, the contract price on that basis working out at Fr. 205.50 per kilo. The rate of exchange subsequently fluctuated so that more francs were required to buy the same quantity of sterling. In regard to the obligation of the buyer under such circumstances the Court said:]

It results from the very terms of the contract that the price was payable in English currency on the arrival of the ship carrying the merchandise, and not in francs on the day when the agreement was made. It follows that Grawitz et Fils would have been bound, if the appropriation of 25 tons of Australian lard had been duly made, to pay to the sellers the sum of £943.5.0, and that in default of English currency, payment being effected in France, they would have been under an obligation to settle in French money at the rate of exchange current on the day of the ship's arrival. In other words, the buyer who engages to pay his debt in foreign money on a fixed day must take the chance of a rise or fall in value of the money by means of which he will provide the sum due to his creditor, where the money of payment is not that which has been stipulated in the contract. The creditor has the right to receive the amount due him either in the money agreed or in some other money which is its equivalent on the day of payment; he accordingly is not concerned in the question of whether the debtor has or has not arranged in advance for the agreed money of payment.

Compare SOCIÉTÉ COMMERCIALE *c.* AUGUSTIN, 4 Revue de Droit Maritime (Supplement) 485 (Commercial Court of Marseille, 1927), where there was a contract for the sale of goods c.i.f. a French port in which the price was fixed in French francs. At the time when payment was due exchange had fluctuated to a point where the number of francs named would buy more of the seller's currency than at the time when the contract was made. The buyer claimed to be entitled to a corresponding reduction in the price. It was held, however, that the apparent purpose of the parties in fixing the price in francs was to avoid exchange risks, and that it was the duty of the buyer to pay the price fixed.

In VACCA *c.* PARODI, 1925 Temi Genovese 230 (Court of Appeal of Genoa), there was a contract for the sale of goods to be shipped from England to Italy. The price was fixed in pounds, and payment was to be against surrender of the bill of lading. The seller was more than six months late in making shipment, notwithstanding which the buyer took delivery of the goods but claimed to pay on the basis of the exchange current when the goods would have arrived had they been shipped within the contract time. In an action by the seller for the price, it was held that in the absence of force majeure exchange should be calculated as of the day when the goods ought to have been shipped.

HODGSON & CO. *v.* WIGGLESWORTH & CO., LTD.

KING'S BENCH DIVISION, 1920

[3 *Lloyd's List Law Reports*, 106]

It appeared from the case that on June 5, 1919, Messrs. Hodgson & Co., sold to Messrs. Wigglesworth & Co., Ltd., 500 bales of jute on c.i.f. terms, shipment between June 1 and Aug. 31, 1919, to Dundee. On June 6 there was a sale of a further 500 bales and the sale prices depended upon a variable factor expressed in the words "Exchange rate 1*s.* 8⅝*d.* Any rise or fall on buyers' account." The Committee's interpretation of these words was that in order to establish the price payable by the buyers there would have to be an Exchange transaction in India, whereby the shippers would obtain rupees in India in exchange for their sterling drafts on the buyers; that if the rate at which the Exchange transaction took place were such that the contract basis of 1*s.* 8⅝*d.* sterling was the Exchange price of each rupee which the shipper so obtained, then the price to be paid by the buyers for the goods was £41 per ton and £42 10*s.* as named in the contracts, but if the Exchange rate were higher so that a larger sum in sterling was the exchange price of each rupee, then the sterling price per ton to be paid by the buyers for the goods would be proportionately higher than the figures of £41 and £42 10*s.* respectively. On the other hand if the Exchange rate were lower than the basis, so that a smaller sum in sterling was the Exchange price of each rupee, then the sterling price per ton to be paid by the buyers would be proportionately lower. The sterling value of all jute was affected in Great Britain by an "extra consideration" that the shippers were having to pay to holders of rupees in India, in order to induce them to let the Indian banks have those rupees at the official rate, as cover for the necessary Exchange transactions. In the present case the rate of "extra consideration," including the Exchange broker's commission, was 4½ per cent. on £2870 12*s.* 2*d.*, for which cover was required, that is to say £129 3*s.* 6*d.*

The sellers had claimed and the buyers had refused to pay the £129 3*s.* 6*d.*, and this the sellers claimed to recover in the arbitration. The sellers said that the £129 3*s.* 6*d.* was part of a rise over the Exchange of 1*s.* 8⅝*d.*, which was the contract basis for calculation of the price to be paid by the buyers, and that the buyers were legally liable for the amount. The buyers said that the only Exchange rate that concerned them was the actual Exchange rate at which the Bank bought the shippers' sterling drafts, viz., 1*s.* 10 15-32*d.*, and that when the contracts were made the existence and the policy of what was known as the "official rate" were known to both parties, and no one had heard of any extra expense being required to obtain cover, and that the "official rate" was a factor easily to be ascertained, and buyers were content to buy jute subject to the rise or fall of such a factor, but not subject to such an uncertain factor as the varying cost of obtaining cover, and that the buyers never authorised the sellers or the shippers to incur the expense in question. . . .

Mr. Justice ROWLATT, in giving judgment, said: This at first sight seemed to be a very puzzling point, and a difficult point. Mr. Leck has put his point of view extremely clearly, but I now have no doubt myself about it. The contract between the buyers and the sellers provided that the sellers should draw on the buyers — of course, in sterling. It is obvious that they would require to exchange the sterling draft for rupees in India, and at the bottom of the contract there are these words: — "Exchange rate 1*s*. $8\frac{3}{8}$*d*., any rise or fall on buyers' account." It is the application of these words to the facts that have arisen that gives rise to the present difficulty. At the date when the contract was made there existed Exchange rates which were called "official rates," as I understand it. They were not free rates obtained by the ordinary play of the laws of exchange, but they were controlled rates, or rates arrived at by some arrangement with or through interference by the Government, but they existed, and they were the rates at which the Bank did buy drafts in sterling of this country.

Prima facie, therefore, this Exchange rate which is referred to in the contract refers to the Exchange rate which the parties knew at the time, viz., this rate, varying, of course, from time to time, which became known as the "official rate." Afterwards, when this draft came to be negotiated in August, a new development had occurred. There was still the "official rate," but there was another thing to be considered, for although it was the "official rate," the Banks would not deal at it — that is what it comes to — unless they were provided with cover to balance the transaction, and to provide that cost money, and that was a new expense to the buyers. In the view I take of it — which is the view that has also prevailed with the Arbitrator — that was money not provided for, it was not foreseen, and it was not provided for. A variation in the "official rate" was provided for, but this was a new thing that was not provided for and, therefore, was not covered.

Mr. Leck, in his argument, put it in the most telling way it could be put, by saying that the purport of this clause was to ensure the sellers against bearing the *de facto* variation in the exchange, and this is all part of it. Well, it is true that is what they thought they were doing by the clause, but in the event that happened after they had put their hands to the clause it turned out that the clause had not covered the whole ground, and that often happens, and every time a position like that occurs where something new has occurred, which prevents the party being put into the position which he aimed at being put into by means of the stipulations he has put into the contract, whenever that occurs, it is always said "the object of the contract was to put him in such and such a position so he ought to have had this advantage," but it does not prevail. I think that is the way contracts are construed, but it does not prevail if the new circumstance that has arisen is one which is not provided for by the contract, and he has failed to cover himself in respect of that new danger. The Courts have to look to see what the parties have done and give effect to what is provided by the language of the contract, and I do not think they can extend it to make the contract cover new things merely to produce the effect which the parties, not being able to foresee, thought they were securing by the clause that they did insert. Therefore, I think I must affirm this award, I am quite clear about that, and I must affirm it with costs.

In ROYAL COMMISSION ON WHEAT SUPPLIES *v.* BULLOCH BROS. & CO., 13 Ll. L. R. 290 (Court of Appeal, 1922), contracts for the sale of rice at 8 shillings per cwt. on an f. o. b. basis provided for payment in net cash in London against bills of lading, and contained the following clause: "Rate of exchange for the purpose of this transaction is fixed at 1*s.* 5 7-32*d.*, fluctuations being on buyers' account." After several contracts had been entered into with the sellers, it was found that the original basis on which the price had been fixed required readjustment. A new price basis was reached by mutual agreement, but adjustment was not possible until the end of the year, and it was then found that the sellers had been underpaid by a sum expressed in terms of rupees of 188,644. The parties could not agree as to the rate of exchange. The rate at the date of adjustment was much higher than the rates at the dates when bills of lading had been presented, or than an average rate over the whole year. It was held that the sellers were entitled to the rate current at the date of adjustment.

In PEYRAE *v.* WILKINSON, [1924] 2 K. B. 166 (King's Bench Division, 1923), the action was brought by the plaintiff to recover the balance of the price of goods sold and delivered. The defendants in 1921 agreed to purchase certain goods of the plaintiff, who carried on business at Lyons, France. The agreed price was 10,630 francs, and should have been paid on December 10, 1921. A part payment was made some months later. The plaintiff sued in 1923 to recover the balance of 8017 francs. The question for the Court was whether in converting that sum into English currency the rate of exchange current on December 10, 1921 should prevail, or whether the rate should be taken as at the date of judgment in the action. Between those two dates the value of francs reckoned in sterling had fallen considerably. It was held that the rate on December 10, 1921, should be taken, that being the date of the breach.

In MULLER MACLEAN & CO. *v.* S. S. ATAULLA & CO., 51 Ind. L. R. Calcutta Series 320 (High Court, 1923), drafts drawn on an Indian buyer in dollars and in sterling bore the notation "draft to be paid at the current rate for bank demand draft at date of payment." The drafts were dishonored, and in an action on them against the buyer it was held that the clause was to be construed as meaning the rate on the date of maturity for payment rather than on the date of actual payment.

BANK OF TAIWAN, LTD. *v.* SCHILD

NEW YORK SUPREME COURT, APPELLATE DIVISION, 1932

[236 *New York Appellate Division Reports*, 128]

MERRELL, J. The action is brought by plaintiff, as assignee of S. Nagasaku, of Yokohama, Japan, to recover the purchase price of 15,000 raw white Japanese rabbit skins sold to defendant by plaintiff's assignor. Among other things, the contract for the purchase of the rabbit skins provided that payment should be made in the following manner: "By your establishing by cable (within three days) an approved irrevocable Letter of Credit at 4 Months Sight in favor of S. Nagasaku, Yokohama, Japan, negotiable against documents. Letter of Credit to expire September 25th, 1930." The contract further provided: "These goods are bought with the understanding that the title to same shall not pass until the goods are paid for in full." Pursuant to the provisions of the contract the defendants, who were engaged in the business of importing and merchandising skins and have their office in the city of New York, applied to the Bank of United States for the letter of credit, which was issued on September 12, 1930, by that bank. S. Nagasaku shipped the goods ordered by defendants on or about September 20, 1930, insuring them, paying the freight and obtained a bill of lading for the rabbit skins. Plaintiff's assignor drew his draft for $6,300 upon the Bank of United States and on the same day said draft, with documents attached, was purchased by plaintiff, plaintiff paying Nagasaku the full amount of the draft. Plaintiff forwarded the draft, with documents attached, to the Bank of United States, which accepted it on or about October 9, 1930. The documents of title and, later, the goods themselves were received by defendants under a trust receipt delivered to the bank. Before February 9, 1931, the date when the draft became due, the Bank of United States was taken over by the Superintendent of Banks and the draft was not paid at its maturity. S. Nagasaku, on March 4, 1932, assigned to plaintiff all his right, title and interest in the money due from defendants on account of said contract, and on the same day plaintiff brought the present action.

In the answer the defendants deny knowledge or information of the negotiation of the draft to plaintiff and of the assignment. The answer also denies that S. Nagasaku performed all the conditions precedent, and denies that the goods were unpaid for. As a separate defense of payment the answer alleges the terms of the contract, the issuance of the letter of credit, the drawing of the draft thereunder, the sale of the draft to plaintiff, and the acceptance thereof by the Bank of United States.

The affidavit of Irving Schild, one of the defendant copartners, read in opposition to plaintiff's motion for summary judgment, sets forth substantially the same facts as are alleged in the answer. In this affidavit the provision of the contract of sale that "these goods are bought with the understanding that the title to same shall not pass until the goods are paid for in full," is set forth. Said affidavit further states that no demand has ever been made by the seller for the return of the goods, or that defendants have improperly received the same on the ground that title had not passed to them.

The appellant contends that the answer and the affidavit in support thereof do not present any issue to be tried. The court at Special Term held otherwise. The question presented upon this appeal is whether the facts set forth in the answer of defendants and in the affidavit of defendant Schild are sufficient to present the issue that Nagasaku, the seller of the goods, had received payment therefor, and that plaintiff, in March, 1932, took nothing by its purported assignment of the seller's right, title and interest in the money due from defendants. It seems to us that under the terms of the contract as to the manner of payment for the goods and the retention of title until the same had been paid in full, coupled with the drawing of the draft, its discounting, and the unconditional delivery of the merchandise by the seller, evidenced the fact that the parties intended that the seller should receive the acceptance of the Bank of United States in payment for the goods. The contract expressly states how payment should be made, to wit, by the establishing of an approved irrevocable letter of credit in favor of the seller negotiable against documents. The law seems to be fairly well settled that where a buyer of merchandise procures, at the instance of the seller, the obligation of a third party agreed to be accepted in payment, and such obligation is accepted by the seller as payment for the goods sold, the obligation of the buyer is discharged. (*Wise* v. *Chase*, 44 N. Y. 337; *Gibson* v. *Tobey*, 46 id. 637.) In the latter case the buyer of a quantity of hogs procured, at the request of the seller, a draft drawn on a third party, payable to the seller's order. The hogs had previously been delivered to the buyer. The draft was later dishonored and the seller sued the buyer for the purchase price of the goods, having first unsuccessfully offered to deliver up the draft upon payment of the purchase price. The question was tried out before a referee, who held as a matter of law that the price was unpaid and that the draft was not a satisfaction of the purchase price of the hogs. The Court of Appeals reversed the decision of the referee. The Court of Appeals said that the sale was for cash, and that the delivery was impliedly, if not expressly, made conditional upon payment. The Court of Appeals (at p. 642) stated: "The presumption of law that the draft was received as payment therefore applies, and the plaintiff cannot maintain the action." At page 643 the Court of Appeals further said: "For the purposes of this question the transaction is the same as if it had all taken place at the same time, and in construing it we must observe the rule applicable to all contracts, that the intent of the parties is to be effectuated. If the plaintiff had not intended to have received he draft in payment he would have said so, or required an indorsement. (*Darnell* v. *Morehouse*, Court of Appeals, not reported.) And when a creditor has an option to receive money or a note of a third party, and he accepts the latter, it will be presumed that he receives it with the same effect as if he had received the money. (*St. John* v. *Purdy*, 1 Sand., S. C. R., 9 [3 N. Y. Super. Ct.].)" (See, also, *Hall* v. *Stevens*, 116 N. Y. 201.) In the case last mentioned the seller of some cattle accepted a bank draft in payment therefor. The draft was deposited for collection and dishonored due to the insolvency of the bank upon which it was drawn. Action was brought to recover the price and plaintiff asked to go to the jury on the question whether the draft had been received in payment. The trial court refused such request and directed a verdict for defendants. The Court of Appeals held that such direction was proper. At pages 205 and 206 the Court of Appeals said: "If it had been a part of the original agreement between the parties that the plaintiff should take a draft in payment for his cattle, that would have been conclusive and would have left no question for discussion." In the case at bar the agreement was that payment should be effected by obtaining an approved irrevocable letter of credit. The approval of the letter of credit obtained is evidenced by the fact that it was accepted by the seller in payment, indorsed over to plaintiff, which in turn drew a draft thereon for the amount of the purchase price of the rabbit skins, and which draft was accepted by the drawee bank. (See, also, *Dibble* v. *Richardson*, 171 N. Y. 131, 138.) The Court of Appeals by the decisions mentioned held that the obligation of a third party procured by the buyer and accepted by the seller as a part of the transaction by which it was created is presumably accepted as payment and in discharge of the buyer's obligation. In the instant case the goods were surrendered by the seller when the draft was drawn and discounted. The contract provided that title should not pass until the goods were paid for in full. Therefore, the facts here present a question as to whether the parties intended that the obtaining of the approved irrevocable letter of credit should be in full payment for the goods. The court properly denied plaintiff's motion for summary judgment, and that sufficient facts were set forth in the answer and answering affidavit to present an issue for determination at the trial.

The order appealed from should be affirmed, with ten dollars costs and disbursements to defendants, respondents, against plaintiff, appellant.

FINCH, P. J., MCAVOY and TOWNLEY, JJ., concur.

Order affirmed, with ten dollars costs and disbursements.

In LAMBORN *v.* ALLEN, KIRKPATRICK & CO., INC., 288 Pa. 114 (Supreme Court, 1927), there was a contract for the sale of 300 bags of Java sugar at a fixed price ex dock New York. The contract provided: "Payment to be made by net cash on presentation of sight draft, with invoice, and bill of lading attached in New York. Buyers to open within five (5) days confirmed irrevocable letter of credit in favor of [the seller]." A letter of credit as specified was duly issued, but acting on instructions from the buyer the bank declined to honor drafts drawn under it. In an action by the seller against the buyer for damages for breach of contract, it was held that the seller was not limited in remedy to an action against the bank under the letter of credit.

Compare BANK OF UNITED STATES *v.* SELTZER, 233 App. Div. 225 (New York Supreme Court, Appellate Division, 1931), where a contract for the purchase of raw silk provided for the establishment of a ninety-day letter of credit. A letter of credit was issued by agreement between the defendant buyer and the plaintiff bank, and the seller drew drafts under the credit which were accepted by the plaintiff. The defendant secured the goods under trust receipt, and the plaintiff, before payment of the accepted drafts, became unable to meet its obligations. In an action for the proceeds of the goods held under trust receipt, it was held that "the issuance of such letter of credit was obviously not a payment of defendant's debt to [the seller], but merely provided means by which the latter could obtain payment."

In GREENOUGH *v.* MUNROE, 53 Fed. (2nd) 362 (Circuit Court of Appeals, Second Circuit, 1931), two contracts of sale provided respectively "Terms of Payment: Letter of credit to be established in favor of [the seller]"; and "Payment: Draft at 4 m/s under letter of credit." Under circumstances similar to those in the preceding case it was said by the Court: "There does not seem to be much basis of fact for inferring an intention to accept the banker's letter of credit as absolute payment. . . . We conclude that the authorities favor the view that there is no presumption that the seller takes a draft drawn under a letter of credit in absolute payment of the buyer's obligation to pay for the merchandise."

MAINE LUMBER CO., LTD. *v.* MARYLAND CASUALTY CO.

NEW YORK SUPREME COURT, APPELLATE DIVISION, 1926

[216 *New York Appellate Divisions Reports*, 35]

MERRELL, J. The action was brought to recover the sum of $86,000 upon a bond given by the respondent, Maryland Casualty Company, to secure the performance by the defendants, Tazewell Timber Corporation and W. & S. Job & Co., Inc., hereinafter referred to as the Tazewell Corporation, of a contract with the plaintiff. The plaintiff, appellant, is an English Corporation, having its principal office at Liverpool, Eng. The Tazewell Timber Corporation was organized in March, 1920, in the State of Virginia. It acquired a tract of timberland of approximately 5,600 acres and had entered upon lumbering operations thereon. At first the Tazewell Timber Corporation manufactured lumber by the rather primitive means of a circular-saw mill. Desiring to increase its output it began, in July, 1920, to erect what was known as a band-saw mill. The improved mill was completed in December, 1920. In January, 1921, the Tazewell Timber Corporation entered into negotiations with the plaintiff for the sale of its lumber. A written contract was finally entered into between the parties. The contract was negotiated by means of cable communication. The plaintiff, as a condition to entering into a contract with the Tazewell Timber Corporation, required that the timber corporation furnish a surety company bond for the faithful performance of its contract with the plaintiff. . . .

The bond for which the timber company applied was executed by the respondent, and together with the proposed contract, which, until then, the plaintiff had never seen, was then sent to the plaintiff at Liverpool, where the contract was executed by the plaintiff and returned to New York in the latter part of March, 1921. The defendant W. & S. Job & Co., Inc., a New York corporation, joined with the Tazewell Timber Corporation in making said contract with the plaintiff, and the bond of the respondent, Maryland Casualty Company, as surety, joins both the Tazewell Timber Corporation and W. & S. Job & Co., Inc., as principals. The contract thus entered into between the plaintiff and the defendants, other than the respondent, was for the purchase by the plaintiff from the Tazewell Timber Corporation of 1,800,000 feet of lumber of certain specified grades at a total price of $86,000. Delivery of the lumber was to be F. O. B. cars at Burkes Garden, a railroad siding some five or six miles from the mill of the defendants. As to the manner in which payment for the lumber thus sold and to be delivered to the plaintiff was to be made, the contract provided that the plaintiff was to advance to the Tazewell Timber Corporation and its associate, W. & S. Job & Co., Inc., from time to time as requested, amounts sufficient to meet the payrolls and current bills of the lumber manufacturers. Such advances were to be made by the plaintiff by accepting upon presentation drafts or trade acceptances drawn by the Tazewell Timber Corporation or by payment of cash or assignment of customers' trade acceptances as might be mutually agreed upon between the parties. The contract further states that such advances on drafts were to be debited by plaintiff to a special account with the Tazewell Timber Corporation and W. & S. Job & Co., Inc. Shipments of the lumber were to be made on orders of the plaintiff and were to be credited by the plaintiff against such advancements made by it and when the amount of lumber shipped was equivalent to the amount advanced, thereafter the lumber manufacturers were to draw at sight with documents attached to cover the amount of each shipment. . . . The Tazewell Timber Corporation requested of the plaintiff advances from time to time in the months of April, May and June, 1921, pursuant to the provisions of the contract. Drafts and trade acceptances were drawn by the Tazewell Timber Corporation and the same were accepted by the plaintiff, appellant. These acceptances were used by the timber corporation in the ordinary course of business and were negotiated through the Greenwich Trust Company. In all, the advancements and trade acceptances thus made by the plaintiff aggregated $86,000, the entire purchase price of the lumber contracted for. The Tazewell Timber Corporation received from the Greenwich Trust Company in cash upon such trade acceptances the full sum of $86,000. The business enterprise of the Tazewell Timber Corporation was a failure. Its timber turned out to be of inferior quality, and not up to the character of the lumber for which the plaintiff had contracted. Out of 1,000,000 feet of various kinds of lumber which were put into the warehouse of the Gratton Storage Company there were only about 25,000 feet of prime lumber, and 62,000 feet of No. 1 common and selects of oak, poplar and chestnut. This comparatively small amount of lumber up to contract was all that was sufficiently dry and delivered prior to September, 1921. On September 1, 1921, the Tazewell Timber Corporation went into the hands of a receiver. A large part of the lumber manufactured was low-grade, wormy and of different varieties of wood from those called for by the contract. The tract upon which the lumbering was done appears to have been cut over without regard to the kind of timber cut. Notwithstanding the fact that the plaintiff had advanced the full purchase price of the lumber for which it had contracted of $86,000, there was only delivered to the plaintiff 25,000 feet of prime lumber out of 800,000 feet provided in the contract and 62,000 feet of No. 1 common and selects out of 1,000,000 feet covered by the contract. After the affairs of the Tazewell Timber Corporation were taken over by the receiver the latter made no effort to perform the contract. The contract provided that the lumber covered thereby should be delivered to the plaintiff within eight months from the date of the contract, February 28, 1921. The plaintiff at once applied for an injunction restraining the receiver from shipping any lumber which the defendants had on hand. As soon as the receiver was appointed the Tazewell Timber Corporation notified the plaintiff in writing that it would be unable to perform the contract. The respondent, Maryland Casualty Company, also was notified of the situation at and before the appointment of the receiver, and was requested to look into the matter with a view of carrying out the lumber contract under the provisions of the bond which authorized the casualty company to perform the contract in the event of its principals' default. The respondent took no steps to protect itself or to carry out the contract for which it stood surety.

On August 18, 1921, the plaintiff notified the respondent of the default of its principals and of the fact that the plaintiff would hold the respondent upon its bond. To such notification the respondent replied, by letter dated August 22, 1921, waiving its option under the terms of the bond to complete the work. Action was thereafter brought upon the bond to recover the sum of $86,000, the amount limited by the bond. . . .

The questions presented by this appeal are as to the nature of the liability of the Maryland Casualty Company upon its bond, and as to what damages the plaintiff should recover thereunder. The trial court held, and it is the contention of the respondent, that the bond upon which the plaintiff sued was one of indemnity, and that the plaintiff, in order to recover of the surety company, was required to first show that it had paid a loss.

[Nearly five pages of the opinion, holding the bond to be one of surety rather than of indemnity, are here omitted.]

It is the contention of the respondent that the plaintiff did not actually pay for the lumber. Such is not the fact. Under the terms of the contract the lumber was to be paid for by the plaintiff advancing amounts sufficient to meet payrolls and current bills of the Tazewell corporation. By the terms of the contract these advances were to be made by the plaintiff "accepting upon presentation drafts or trade acceptances drawn by the Tazewell." Such advances or drafts were to be debited by the plaintiff to a special account of the Tazewell corporation and shipments made by it were to be credited against such advancements. In short, the moneys advanced were to be repaid by lumber shipped. There is no dispute in the evidence but that the Tazewell corporation drew on the plaintiff to the amount of $86,000; that the drafts in such amount were accepted by the plaintiff, appellant, and that the Tazewell corporation cashed such drafts thus accepted with the Greenwich Trust Company. There can be no question but that the plaintiff in accepting the drafts became primarily liable to the holder and that the drawer after acceptance is only secondarily liable. I think it is quite immaterial whether the drafts were paid upon maturity or were renewed. Sooner or later these drafts, amounting to $86,000, accepted by the plaintiff, must be met and paid. There is no reasonable ground for saying that the plaintiff did not pay for the lumber for which it contracted, but which it did not receive. . . .

The judgment and order appealed from should be reversed, with costs, and the plaintiff should have judgment against the defendant Maryland Casualty Company for the sum of $86,000, with interest thereon from September 28, 1921, amounting to the sum of $102,398.90, and with costs, together with interest thereon from the date of the entry of the judgment appealed from.

DOWLING, FINCH, MCAVOY and MARTIN, JJ., concur.

Compare BUSCH *v.* MANAHAN, 56 N. D. 491 (Supreme Court, 1928). The plaintiff was the owner of certain grain stored in defendant's elevator. Plaintiff sold the grain to defendant, and the local elevator agent delivered in payment two drafts for the amount of the price drawn on the defendant principal. Payment of the drafts was refused on presentation. In an action for the purchase price defendant maintained that payment had been made. Judgment for plaintiff was affirmed, the Court saying that "in the absence of a special agreement to the contrary, it must be assumed that plaintiffs accepted the bills of exchange merely as conditional payment of the purchase price, defeasible on the nonpayment of the instruments."

See also TOWEY *v.* ESSER, 133 Calif. App. 669 (District Court of Appeal, 1933), a ranch superintendent sold a hundred head of cattle to defendant, it being understood that the superintendent was authorized to sell only for cash. After the cattle had been weighed and loaded into railroad cars consigned to a live-stock company, defendant gave the superintendent a draft for the price drawn on the consignee in exchange for a signed bill of sale. The superintendent forwarded the draft to the San Francisco office of his employer, and it was deposited for collection. In the meantime the cattle arrived at destination and were resold by the consignee. The draft however was refused payment. It was held that the draft was not accepted as absolute payment, but was taken merely in accordance with the custom followed in similar commercial transactions.

In ROSTEIN *v.* HINES, 115 Wash. 644 (Supreme Court, 1921), a contract for the sale of used rails contained the following sentences: "Payment in full received from J. Rostein with Alaska Junk Co.'s trade acceptances for 30 days and 60 days. Rails examined and accepted O.K. by Mr. J. Rostein for the Alaska Junk Co." After taking the trade acceptances the seller found that they were not bankable. He accordingly returned them to the buyer, and refused to deliver the rails except on payment of cash. In an action by the buyer to obtain possession of the rails, it was held that this was not a sale of goods for cash, but a sale on credit. The fact that the trade acceptances could not be discounted at a bank did not affect the duty of the acceptor to pay them when presented.

In JEFFERSON MOTORS CO. *v.* WILLIAMS, 227 Ala. 432 (Supreme Court, 1933), a motor car was sold on cash terms. The buyer gave the seller her check for the price, and the seller indorsed the signed order for the car "paid in full by check." The next day the buyer offered to return the car, and stopped payment on the check. In an action by the seller to recover the price of the car, a judgment for defendant was reversed, Bouldin, J., saying: "A check given in payment for a cash purchase of this character . . . is, in the absence of other agreement, a conditional payment only, to become effective as a satisfaction of the original demand, when and if the check is cashed. . . . The burden is upon the party claiming the check was given and accepted as absolute satisfaction of the original demand to prove an agreement to that effect. A receipt 'paid by check' does not evidence such agreement. It merely imports the kind of payment usual to such transaction, conditional payment. Nor does the acceptance of such check, whether directly expressed, or implied from the fact of acceptance, import anything more than such conditional payment."

GREAT WESTERN ELECTRO CHEMICAL CO *v.* WEISENTHAL

DISTRICT COURT, SOUTHERN DISTRICT OF NEW YORK, 1925

[6 *Federal Reporter* (*Second Series*), 934]

Upon the trial of this action the parties stipulated that the case should be tried with one juror, and, at the close of the testimony, that a verdict should be directed by the court. Pursuant to this stipulation, both parties moved, at the close of the testimony, for the direction of a verdict. The action is brought by the plaintiff to recover of the defendant damages for breach of a contract for the sale of 75 tons of bleach, in three carload lots of 25 tons each; one car to be shipped each month during January, February, and March, 1921. The agreement, which is dated September 2, 1920, at San Francisco, Cal., reads as follows:

Memorandum of agreement by which Great Western Electro Chemical Company of San Francisco agrees to sell, and Weisenthal & Co., New York City, N. Y., agrees to buy:
Material: 35/37% Bleach.
Quantity: 75 tons (2,000 lbs. each net weight) 3 cars of 25 tons each.
Duration of contract: April 1, 1921.
Time of Shipment: One car each month, during Jan., Feb., and Mar., 1921.
Price: $86 per ton, f. o. b. Pittsburgh, Cal.
Terms: Net cash against shipping documents prior to establishment of irrevocable letter of credit for 25 per cent. of purchase price with bank here.

Stipulations: It is to be forfeited to us in case of failure of buyer to take and pay for entire quantity covered by this contract.

To be packed in 800 lb. drums.

Great Western Electro Chem. Co.
[Signed] J. F. C. Hagens.
Weisenthal & Co.
[Signed] P. Weisenthal.

[One column of the statement, giving details as to the letter of credit, is here omitted.]

On January 28, 1921, the plaintiff shipped to Weisenthal & Co., of New York, 50,286 pounds of bleach, the price of which, under the terms of the contract, was $2,162.30. On the following day the plaintiff presented to the Crocker National Bank of San Francisco, Cal., railroad bills of lading issued to order and indorsed in blank covering this shipment, together with invoice, certificate of analysis, and weight certificate, and at the same time presented to the bank a draft drawn upon it in the sum of $500, together with a draft drawn on Weisenthal & Co. for the balance of the purchase price of the shipment, namely, $1,662.30, requesting payment of the first draft, and further requesting that they deliver the documents to Weisenthal & Co., only upon collection of the second draft covering the balance of the purchase price of the shipment, specifying that this collection should be made through the Irving National Bank of New York City. The officials of the Crocker National Bank refused to make payment of the $500 draft under the letter of credit, if the plaintiff directed that the documents could not be delivered without payment of the second draft of $1,662.30. After this refusal the plaintiff drew a draft for $1,500, the entire amount of the letter of credit, presented this to the Crocker National Bank, together with all of the documents, and demanded payment thereof. Payment of the draft for $1,500 was refused on the ground that not more than $500 on any one shipment could be paid under the terms of the letter of credit. Thereafter some efforts were made by the plaintiff to collect a draft for the full amount of the purchase price of this shipment through its own bank, but the proof does not disclose that the documents were ever formally presented to the defendants in New York, or any further demand or tender made. The breach alleged in the complaint as amended is the refusal of payment of the two drafts first presented. It was shown that the shipment was not received or accepted in New York by the defendants, but was sold by the plaintiff. During February the defendants were advised that the plaintiff regarded their failure to accept and pay for the bleach tendered in January as a breach of the entire contract, and that the defendants would be held in damages accordingly.

The plaintiff seeks to recover as its damages the difference between the contract price and the market value of the 75 tons of bleach called for under the terms of the contract.

THACHER, District Judge (after stating the facts as above). The phrase in the contract of sale, "net cash against shipping documents prior to establishment of irrevocable letter of credit for 25 per cent. of purchase price with bank here," is undoubtedly the product of stenographic error arising from the misuse of the word "prior" in place of the word "buyer." If the contract had read "buyer to establish" instead of "prior to establishment of," the manifest intention of the parties would have been accurately and precisely expressed; but in this case it is not necessary to correct what appears to be a manifest clerical error, as was done in *O'Brien* v. *Miller*, 168 U. S. 287, 297, 18 S. Ct. 140, 42 L. Ed. 469. Taking the words as written, the clause, "prior to establishment of irrevocable letter of credit," simply limits the preceding clause, "net cash against shipping documents," thus leaving the agreement silent as to the terms of payment if payment be made after the establishment of the credit. In such case, with respect to 25 per cent. of the purchase price, payment was provided for under the letter of credit. With respect to the balance, there being no agreement that the buyer was to have credit, the law requires payment to be made on delivery. In this case the delivery contemplated was f. o. b. at point of shipment, and the shipping documents were required to be "surrendered" to the Crocker National Bank. Under these circumstances the seller adopted the only course open to it in order to carry out the agreement. Having made delivery in accordance with the agreement (*Rosenberg Bros. & Co.* v. *Buffum Co.*, 234 N. Y. 338, 137 N. E. 609), it presented the documents with two drafts to the Crocker National Bank — one for approximately 25 per cent. of the purchase price, payment of which was demanded under the credit; the other for the balance of the purchase price, requesting the bank to surrender the shipping documents to the buyer only upon payment of the latter draft. The bank, however, refused to pay the drafts or to accept the documents with any strings, probably mindful of the provision of the letter of credit requiring "surrender" of the documents against payment under the credit. If the bank could thus rightfully refuse payment under the credit in the absence of an unconditional surrender of the documents, the primary duty of the buyers to make payment upon presentation of the documents nevertheless remained. *Rosenberg Bros. & Co.* v. *Buffum Co., supra.* Under these circumstances the office of the bank, being the only place where the documents could be presented, in view of the contract provisions and the terms of the credit, must be regarded as the place of payment, and by failing to provide payment there the buyers failed to pay for the merchandise as they were obligated to do. For this breach of the agreement the seller elected to regard the contract as at an end and sue for its damages.

A verdict in favor of the plaintiff is directed for $4,225, with interest on $1,325 from January 31, 1921, on $1,450 from February 28, 1921, and on $1,450 from March 31, 1921.

In IN RE INDEPENDENT COAL CORPORATION, 18 Fed. (2nd) 1 (Circuit Court of Appeals, Second Circuit, 1927), there was a contract for the sale of 3200 tons of coal. The contract provided that "terms of payment" should be "of the essence of the contract," but nowhere in the contract was there any statement as to what the terms of payment were to be. In a reclamation proceeding evidence was given showing a uniform custom or usage in the New York coal trade that sales such as this contemplated payment in 30 days from delivery, with a discount usually allowed for prior payment. It was held therefore that the sale was not for cash but was on credit.

Compare J. W. ELLIOTT & CO. *v.* THE CANDOR MANUFACTURING COMPANY, 3 Ll. L. R. 105 (King's Bench Division), where a contract for the sale of cotton cloth c. i. f. Tunis provided for payment cash against documents. There was evidence of a custom in Tunis that buyers should take up goods against documents within a reasonable time after the arrival of the steamer bearing the goods. It was held that the alleged custom could not alter an express provision of the contract.

In RYAN *v.* RIDLEY & CO., 19 T. L. R. 45 (King's Bench Division, 1901), there was a c. i. f. contract for the sale of a cargo of codfish "cash in exchange for shipping documents." The sellers tendered the documents on October 24, the day on which the cargo arrived. No payment had been made by November 1, and the sellers resold the cargo, claiming what they had lost on the sale as damages. In giving judgment for the sellers, Kennedy, J., said: "The words 'cash against documents' mean that when the documents are tendered the cash must, in a practical and business sense, be ready. They do not mean that if the seller walks into the buyer's office and offers the documents the buyer will have committed a breach of contract because he does not at once tender money or a cheque in payment. That would not be business. The clause means that the payment against the documents must be made within a reasonable time from their presentation."

Note also WEYERHAUSER TIMBER CO. *v.* FIRST NATIONAL BANK OF PORTLAND, 150 Ore. 172 (Supreme Court, 1935), where there was a contract for the sale of lumber, payment to be cash in exchange for documents. In such a contract, said the court, "there is necessity for sufficient time to examine or check the documents, ascertain if the invoice corresponds with the order, if the inspection certificate is in proper shape and if the mate's receipt covers all the lumber described in the invoice."

COPPOLA *v.* THE MARDEN, ORTH & HASTINGS COMPANY

ILLINOIS SUPREME COURT, 1917

[282 *Illinois Reports*, 281]

MR. JUSTICE FARMER delivered the opinion of the court:

G. S. Coppola, plaintiff in error, gave his written order to a solicitor of the Marden, Orth & Hastings Company, defendant in error, on July 9, 1914, for forty barrels of a certain brand of olive oil at $1.30 per gallon, said oil to be delivered within one year, terms sixty-day draft with shipment. On August 10, following, the plaintiff in error (hereafter called plaintiff) called upon defendant in error (hereafter called defendant) for five barrels of olive oil. Defendant on August 13 by letter acknowledged receipt of the said order for five barrels of the forty barrels ordered July 9, stating the European situation had affected the market in olive oil, and that the oil quoted plaintiff at $1.30 was then worth $2.50 per gallon. The letter stated: "However, your order was taken for forty barrels, and, subject to immediate acceptance, we shall deliver this quantity net spot cash. It is the request of our credit department that we allow no credit on oil sold at this low price, and we shall therefore be obliged to give you this oil on these terms." Plaintiff called upon defendant to deliver him, as per the terms of his contract, ten barrels of oil on October 12, 1914, ten on May 14, 1915, and fifteen on July 2, 1915. Defendant refused in each instance to sell him the oil on credit but offered him the same for cash at the contract price of $1.30 per gallon. Plaintiff refused to pay defendant cash for the oil and purchased it of other firms, the ten barrels purchased May 14, 1915, costing $1.85 per gallon and the other thirty barrels costing $2.20 per gallon, this being the market price at that time. Plaintiff brought suit in the municipal court of Chicago against defendant for the difference between the contract and market price at the place and on the different times purchased and recovered a judgment for $1537.50. On appeal to the Appellate Court the judgment was reversed and a judgment entered against defendant for $21.67, this being interest at the legal rate upon the price of the oil for a period of sixty days, — the length of credit extended by the contract. Plaintiff has brought the record to this court for review by writ of *certiorari*. . . .

The plaintiff contends, and the trial court held, he was entitled to the difference between the contract price and the market price of the oil at the place and within the time mentioned in the contract, which was found to be $1537.50. Defendant contends, and the Appellate Court held, plaintiff was only entitled to interest on the amount of the contract price for sixty days, amounting to $21.67. While it is true that upon a breach of a contract of sale by the seller the buyer is required to do what is reasonable to minimize or reduce his loss, he is not required to do all that is possible. (Sutherland on Damages, — 3d ed. — sec. 90; 24 Am. & Eng. Ency. of Law, 1156.) The proof showed the securing of sixty days' credit to pay for the oil was one of the considerations moving plaintiff to enter into the contract for the purchase of the oil from defendant. Plaintiff testified he would not give defendant's agent an order for the oil when first offered thirty days' credit but insisted upon and was given sixty days' time in which to pay for the oil. Time in which to pay, or credit, was clearly a material element of the contract. Defendant refused to perform its contract to deliver the oil on sixty days' credit. It is apparent from the evidence that the advance in price was the reason for its refusal, but the reason assigned was that the contract was not for a sale on credit but was for cash. Plaintiff contended the contract gave him sixty days' time and insisted upon its performance according to its terms. Whatever may have been plaintiff's reason for wanting sixty days in which to make payment, the contract gave him that privilege and he was entitled to it. Although there are some authorities to the contrary, we do not think he was required to pay defendant or anyone else cash for oil to take the place of oil he had contracted to pay for in sixty days. To have done so with defendant would have been, in effect, acquiescence in defendant's contention of what the contract was. We do not consider it important whether plaintiff could have borrowed the money to pay cash for the oil. He contracted for it on credit for reasons sufficiently important to him, and if he had not been given the credit he would not have contracted to purchase the oil of defendant, and he was under no obligation to pay cash for the oil in order to lessen the damages resulting from defendant's failure to keep its promise and perform its contract. Pertinent and applicable to this discussion is language of the Supreme Court of Iowa in *Cook Manf. Co.* v. *Randall*, 62 Iowa, 244. The court there said: "It is true, as said by counsel for plaintiff, that defendants were required to do all they reasonably could to prevent damages, but to require them to pay cash when they had contracted for credit is not within the bounds of reason. The condition as to credit was an important and essential provision of the contract."

It cannot be denied that there are authorities of high respectability sustaining, directly or indirectly, the measure of damages contended for by defendant, but the contrary authorities seem to us to be supported by sounder policy and reason. It is a sound and wholesome rule which makes it the duty of one damaged by the unlawful act of another to use reasonable diligence to prevent or lessen the damage, but to construe that rule to apply to a case of this character would be to impose a burden on the vendee of doing what the contract relieved him from, in order that the guilty party might be saved from the full consequences of his willful wrongdoing. We believe it to be sound both in law and morals that commercial contracts of a lawful character, knowingly and understandingly entered into, are binding obligations on both parties to them, and, as said in substance in *Illinois Central Railroad Co.* v. *Cobb, Christy & Co.* 64 Ill. 128, it comes with an ill-grace from a party who has refused to perform the agreement to demand that the other party, who has not been at fault, should do something contrary to the terms of the contract to mitigate or lessen the damages resulting from the refusal to perform the contract.

The judgment of the Appellate Court is reversed and the judgment of the municipal court affirmed.

Judgment of Appellate Court reversed.
Judgment of municipal court affirmed.

Note also PLESOFSKY *v.* KAUFMAN & FLONACKER, 140 Tenn. 208 (Supreme Court, 1918). In that case a retail clothier contracted to purchase on credit a quantity of Palm Beach suits for delivery some months later. Near the date set for delivery the seller notified the buyer that "the reason your order has not been shipped is that we have been unable to get our credit department to approve same. The only way we can have same approved for shipment is on a cash basis, allowing you six per cent discount in lieu of the terms. If this will be satisfactory to you, let us have your check for $100 to apply on the account and we will let the goods go forward without delay, bill of lading attached." The buyer refused to agree, and sued the seller for breach of contract. There was no proof that the buyer could pay cash, or that he could borrow funds in order to do so. In giving judgment for plaintiff, Williams, J., said: "Here, the offer to deliver was not for cash, but on prepayment of $100, and balance cash on delivery, and with bill of lading attached, radical changes in the original contract. The sellers, not being willing to credit the buyer as they had contracted to do, demanded that he credit them to the extent of $100; and, harder still, they would even then ship the goods only on bill of lading attached to a draft. This was a stipulation that the buyer was not compelled to submit to. If the law should require him to do so in order to mitigate damages, it would require a small retailer, struggling to build up his credit, by his own hand to put the bar sinister on that credit by holding himself out as one who must buy his goods under the imposed safeguard of a bill of lading attached. The agents of the carrier or of the bank who should handle the papers would become aware of the plight of the buyer. The law will never place such a distasteful and hurtful burden on a confessedly wronged buyer at the instance of those who stand as guilty breachers of their contract with him. . . .

"Many tradesmen, especially small retailers, must operate on the capital of others. They must have a period of credit for the goods within which they may make sales of them and use the proceeds toward liquidation. Such a buyer enters into a contract for his supplies, disclosing that he must have credit. What fairness could there be in a rule which would permit the vending wholesaler or manufacturer at a late and critical date, when the buyer must have goods, to say:

" 'Pay cash; if you haven't it, use your credit and find it in bank. We tender you the equivalent or better for the discount you will have to pay.'

"That would be to mock the buyer, who frankly and confessedly from the outset was never able to pay cash and was in need of the credit. The breaching sellers in this case would be in the attitude of saying to buyer that he did not have and was not worthy of credit from them, but that he must procure it from another."

In HAZEL HILL CANNING CO., INC. *v.* ROBERTS BROTHERS, 129 Md. 306 (Court of Appeals, 1916), a contract for the sale of 5000 cases of tomatoes specified "terms, less 1½%, 10 days." Being in need of funds, the seller shipped the tomatoes to the buyer under bill of lading with a draft attached for the contract amount less 1½ per cent, payable 10 days after sight. The buyer refused to accept. Stoppage of the goods in transit by the seller and refusal to deliver were held to amount to a breach of contract.

Compare, however, H. MUEHLSTEIN & CO., INC. *v.* HICKMAN, 26 Fed. (2nd) 40 (Circuit Court of Appeals, Eighth Circuit, 1928), where a contract for the sale of fifty tons of crude rubber provided "Terms: 30-day trade acceptance from date of shipment, without interest." Prior to the date set for delivery the seller discovered that the buyer was heavily involved, and at about the same time the board of directors of the buyer passed a resolution declaring its inability to pay its debts and its willingness to be declared a bankrupt on the ground of insolvency. The seller thereupon refused to ship on the contract terms, but offered to ship the rubber with sight draft attached to bill of lading. The buyer was willing to take the rubber on the contract terms; but not on those proposed. The seller then sold the rubber elsewhere, and, the market price having declined, brought an action against the buyer for the difference between the contract price and the amount realized. It was held that the seller under the circumstances was entitled to demand payment on delivery, and that the refusal of the buyer to accept justified the seller in treating the contract as broken.

MIDLAND LINSEED PRODUCTS CO. *v.* CHARLES R. SARGENT CO.

UNITED STATES CIRCUIT COURT OF APPEALS, SIXTH CIRCUIT, 1922

[281 *Federal Reporter*, 704]

DONAHUE, Circuit Judge. These two cases were heard and submitted together. The Midland Linseed Products Company brought an action in the District Court against the Charles R. Sargent Company for the recovery of damages for the breach of five separate contracts for the sale and delivery of specified quantities of pure linseed oil, and for a sixth cause of action averred that defendant was indebted to it in the sum of $806.76 upon an account for oil sold and delivered.

The defendant, for answer to plaintiff's first five causes of action, admitted that it had entered into the contracts described in the petition and denied any breach thereof on its part. For answer to the sixth cause of action it denied each and every statement therein contained. Defendant also filed a cross-petition, containing five separate causes of action based upon an alleged breach of each of these same contracts by the plaintiff. After the plaintiff had introduced these contracts in evidence, the trial court sustained a motion by the defendant to direct a verdict in its favor upon the first five causes of action set forth in plaintiff's petition, and also sustained a motion by the plaintiff to direct a verdict in its favor upon defendant's cross-petition.

No. 3645 is a proceeding in error to reverse the judgment of the trial court in directing a verdict for defendant upon plaintiff's first five causes of action. No. 3646 is a cross-petition to reverse the judgment of the trial court directing a verdict in favor of plaintiff upon defendant's cross-petition. The five separate contracts sued upon are identical, except as to dates and quantities, and it will be sufficient to state the terms and conditions of the first of these contracts pertinent to the questions involved.

The several provisions of this first contract, bearing date of January 29, 1920, that have application to the questions presented by the record, read as follows:

The seller hereby sells and agrees to deliver, and the buyer hereby purchases and agrees to receive, 500 barrels, containing about 50 gallons each (7½ pounds in a gallon), of pure linseed oil, for shipment in quantities as follows: 500 barrels May, 1920, for shipment from seller's factory in car lots. Raw linseed oil at $1.61 per gallon, f. o. b. shipping station, freight allowed to Cleveland, Ohio. . . .

Buyer to furnish specifications for shipment, in writing, to seller's office at Minneapolis, Minn., in ample time to enable the seller to execute order within the period or periods above mentioned. . . .

Buyer agrees to pay invoices within 10 days from date of shipment, less a discount of 1 per cent., or to give a 30-day trade acceptance for the full amount of such invoices.

In case of default in payment of any installment of purchase money when due, or in case the credit of the buyer becomes unsatisfactory to the seller, the whole sum owing by the buyer shall become due at once, and further deliveries shall be made only for cash.

In the first cause of action based upon this contract it is averred that —

"The plaintiff during the latter part of the month of May and the early part of the month of June, 1920, acting in good faith, and upon facts and circumstances arising subsequent to the making of such contract, became dissatisfied with defendant's financial condition, and defendant's credit so became unsatisfactory to plaintiff, and plaintiff so advised defendant, and finally, on or about June 9, 1920, plaintiff advised defendant that it would not ship or deliver any further oil under said contract, except for cash, and offered to ship the balance of the oil under this contract to defendant, or its order, upon payment for such being made in cash, and that on June 9, 1920, the defendant advised plaintiff that it would not accept from plaintiff any oil to be paid for in cash, and later notified plaintiff that its refusal so to do was final."

There is also a similar averment in each of the other four of the first five causes of action.

It is contended upon the part of the plaintiff that the provision of the contract authorizing it to demand cash upon delivery whenever it shall become dissatisfied with the buyer's credit is solely for the protection of the plaintiff, that its exercise of that right to demand cash does not release the buyer from its obligation to receive and pay for the quantity of oil named in the contract, and that its refusal to accept any further deliveries and pay cash therefor constituted a breach of this contract. It is the claim of the defendant that the election of the seller to demand cash upon delivery released the buyer from its unconditional contract obligation to accept delivery of this oil, and conferred upon the buyer the right to accept or refuse further delivery upon the terms of payment demanded by the seller. The sole question presented by this record is the construction of this provision of the contract.

This provision must, of course, be construed in harmony with the other terms and conditions of this contract. The basic fundamental provision covering the subject-matter of the contract, in plain, positive, and unambiguous language, required the seller to furnish and deliver to the buyer

500 barrels of pure linseed oil within the month of May, 1920, and required the buyer to accept this quantity of oil and pay for it at $1.61 per gallon, less freight to Cleveland, Ohio. The contract in this respect is absolute and unconditional, and unless further provisions, in equally plain and unambiguous language, are found in this contract, modifying or qualifying the obligation of the parties hereto, then the plaintiff must, under its terms, sell and deliver, and the buyer must accept and pay the price named, and that, of course, would imply cash upon delivery, in the absence of a provision covering time and manner of payment.

There are, however, a number of provisions in this contract relieving the seller from this unconditional agreement on its part to deliver, if prevented from so doing by causes beyond its control; but there would seem to be nothing written therein releasing the buyer from his absolute obligation to accept and pay for the quantity of oil named in the contract. This, taken in connection with the fact that these contracts are on blank forms evidently very carefully prepared by the seller to protect its rights under practically every possible condition that might arise, would not only justify, but require, the application of the rule that a contract so prepared will be construed more strictly against the party to the contract preparing the same. Nevertheless the language used is so plain and unequivocal, and the relations of the several provisions of this contract to each other are so evident, that the application of this rule to the construction of this contract is not helpful to the buyer. There are also provisions in this contract with reference to the payment of the purchase price of this oil, and these provisions are found in the two other paragraphs of this contract above copied.

The first of these paragraphs provides that the buyer may pay cash in 10 days, less 1 per cent. discount from the invoice price, or it may give 30-day trade acceptances for the full invoice price. This modifies the basic provision covering the subject-matter of the contract in respect to time and terms of payment only. It modifies in no respect whatever the absolute obligation of the seller to deliver and the buyer to accept the 500 barrels of oil named therein. This provision as to payment, however, is materially modified by the succeeding paragraph, which in no uncertain terms provides, in part, that, upon default in the payment of any installment of purchase money when due, the whole sum owing by the buyer shall become due and payable, and further deliveries shall be made only for cash. If this were all of this paragraph, it would hardly be contended that it could in any way affect any provision of this contract, other than the provision relating to payment. Certainly nothing is found in this provision as to terms of payment that would relieve the seller from delivering or the buyer from accepting the balance of this 500 barrels of oil not delivered at the time such default occurred.

It is equally clear that the further provisions of this paragraph that, "in case the credit of the buyer becomes unsatisfactory to the seller, the whole sum owing by the buyer shall become due at once, and further delivery shall be made only for cash," does not, nor does it purport to, release or relieve either of the contracting parties from their respective obligations, the one to deliver, the other to accept, the full quantity of oil named in the contract. On the contrary, it relates solely and only to that provision of the contract in reference to time and manner of payment. This entire paragraph must be read as a modification of the provision relating to payment only. It is not subject to the construction that, upon the happening of one or both of the conditions named therein, either the seller will be released from its obligation to deliver or the buyer will be released from its contract obligation to accept the balance of the oil due on the contract, but may at its election demand or refuse further deliveries for cash. . . .

Construing these two paragraphs of the contract relating to payment and to payment only, the conclusion necessarily follows that it was the purpose and intent of the contracting parties that the buyer should have the right and privilege to pay cash in 10 days, with discount of 1 per cent. from invoices, or give 30-day trade acceptance for the full invoice price upon two conditions: First, that the buyer should not default in the payment of any installments due on the purchase price; second, that the credit of the buyer should continue to be satisfactory to the seller until the relative obligations of the parties to the contracts should be fully performed and discharged. If the buyer had defaulted in the payment of any installment of the purchase price when the same became due, it would hardly be contended that it could plead its own default as a release of its further contract obligations; yet this provision must be construed the same, regardless of whether further credit was refused by reason of such default or by reason of the fact that the credit of the buyer had become unsatisfactory to the seller, so that upon the happening of either of these conditions subject to which credit was extended to the buyer, the provision relating to such credit must fail, except, of course, the provision relating to discount, being based upon cash or substantially cash payment, will apply to a cash payment whether made voluntarily or otherwise.

For the reasons stated, the judgment of the District Court directing a verdict for the defendant upon the first five causes of action stated in the plaintiff's petition is reversed.

[The balance of the opinion is omitted.]

Compare Raw Silk Trading Co., Inc. *v.* Katz, 201 App. Div. 713 (New York Supreme Court, Appellate Division, 1922), where there were contracts for the sale of raw silk, in some cases providing "90 days, less 1½%. Settlement within 30 days by cash or trade acceptance," and in another "4 months' trade acceptance, less 1%." All the contracts contained the clause: "Subject to credit limit at seller's discretion." In connection with each contract the seller tendered the goods upon immediate cash payment, claiming the right to do so under the clause in question. The buyer refused the goods on such terms. In an action by the seller for breach of contract, it was held that the facts did not show a cause of action. The act of the seller could not be regarded as a limitation of credit in any sense, for the result was to give no credit whatever.

In Fidelity Fuel Co. *v.* Martin Howe Coal Co., 15 Fed. (2nd) 470 (Circuit Court of Appeals, Seventh Circuit, 1926), a contract for the sale of coal contained the clause "subject to our satisfaction as to your financial responsibility." After various orders had been placed and accepted under the contract, the seller refused to proceed, and there was evidence that the real reason was ability to get a higher price elsewhere. The buyer brought an action for damages for breach of contract. A judgment for the defendant on a directed verdict was reversed and a new trial ordered on the ground that under the satisfaction clause quoted the seller must not act abritrarily or capriciously, and that there was a question for the jury on that point.

DERY *v.* BLATE

New York Court of Appeals, 1924
[239 *New York Reports*, 203]

Pound, J. Defendants have judgment on the pleadings dismissing the complaint. The question is whether the complaint states facts sufficient to constitute a cause of action. (Civil Practice Act, § 277 *et seq.*)

The action is brought by the seller against the purchasers on a written contract for the purchase and sale of silk goods — satin and taffeta — to recover damages for non-acceptance of such goods. The goods were to be delivered one-fifth of each quantity in May, June, July, August and September, 1920, on terms indicated as follows: "Term: 6/10/60," which means six per cent discount, ten days, sixty days extra, and would have given defendants seventy days to pay for the goods. But below the signature to the contract in fine type are these words: "Subject to the Rules of the Silk Association of America as printed on back," and among the rules thus printed is the following:

"8. The amount of credit to be extended to buyer may be determined at any time by seller."

The complaint alleges that this was one of the terms of the contract and that it was further intended and understood thereby that a financial statement should be furnished by the buyers to determine the amount, if any, of credit to be extended; that before the delivery of any goods under the contract a financial statement was demanded and refused, whereupon plaintiff canceled the terms of payment and credit provided in the agreement and demanded payment in cash for the delivery of the goods; that defendants then refused to take the goods, to plaintiff's damage.

The point is whether plaintiff, having contracted to sell and deliver the goods on credit, the amount alone of such credit to be determined by him at any time, may for any reason determine not only that the amount of credit shall be nothing but also that the purchasers must take the goods and pay cash therefor.

While the pleading is to be liberally construed, we are at liberty to consider that the result of plaintiff's contention would be, by a dubious incorporation and a far-stretched interpretation which have been put in issue by the answer, to convert a sale on credit into a cash sale at the option of the seller. On a fair construction of the complaint the question presents itself, to what extent did the purchasers put themselves to the mercy of the seller? The language of the agreement plainly implies a promise and creates an obligation to sell on credit. The term of credit is fixed. The amount of credit is to be determined by the seller. If the seller chose to limit the amount of credit, the purchasers might have offered cash for the goods and compelled their delivery but they were not bound to take and pay cash for them. The seller's option was to fix the term credit bargained for at such amount as he should determine or to keep his goods. The purchasers' option was to take the goods on the term credit bargained for or to refuse them.

The principle of mutual assent should be applied. The contract is drawn on one of plaintiff's order blanks. Its ambiguities should be resolved against him. In fairness it can be said to serve no useful purpose except to protect him from an extension of credit on the terms specified therein in an amount deemed by him unsafe.

The judgment appealed from should be affirmed, with costs.

HISCOCK, Ch. J., CARDOZO, MCLAUGHLIN, ANDREWS and LEHMAN, JJ., concur; CRANE, J., absent.

Judgment affirmed.

Bei Fragen zur Produktsicherheit wenden Sie sich bitte an:
If you have any questions regarding product safety,
please contact:

Walter de Gruyter GmbH
Genthiner Straße 13
10785 Berlin
productsafety@degruyterbrill.com

PART THREE

THE FINANCING OF THE CONTRACT: THE AUXILIARY INSTRUMENTS OF THE LAW MERCHANT

COMMENT

UNDER modern conditions of doing business the extension of some sort of credit to the buyer is the rule rather than the exception. Rarely indeed is the buyer called on to make advances. Even in cases where credit seems to be negatived by a provision for cash on delivery, for cash against documents, or for cash on arrival of vessel, it is noteworthy that nothing is put up before shipment. From the point of view of the buyer there may be no arrangement for credit; but from that of the seller there still remains a period of greater or less duration in which the seller has an investment in the goods balanced only by a promise. In the vast majority of instances the initial financing burden is thus thrown on the seller, and his specific problem is to realize on the promise of payment which he has received from the buyer.

The solution of the problem is implicit in its statement. The situation plainly calls for the intervention between the buyer and the seller of a third party to whom the seller can, in effect, sell the buyer's promise. Reduction of that promise to a tangible and ambulatory form is inherent in the idea. In the simplest type of case, therefore, the seller draws a draft on the buyer, or takes a note from the buyer, and discounts the instrument with a bank. The immediate load on the seller is lightened, and the buyer continues to enjoy the provisions for payment written into the original contract. In due course his promise will be presented to him for redemption.

The practical difficulty with the operation is that its final issue is a question mark. The assumption is that the buyer will honor this concrete evidence of his undertaking, but there is always the possibility that he may not do so. The bank must protect itself against this contingency, and the precise terms of intervention thus may vary widely under differing circumstances. Even under the best of conditions the seller takes the chance of having to return the amount of the discount to the bank: his hold on the purchase price is by no means definitive. In order to improve the position of the seller in this respect some assurance is needed that the commercial paper which he is about to launch will make port safely. It has become common practice therefore for another bank to enter the picture by arrangement with the buyer, and to convey this assurance through the medium of a letter of credit. The tacit understanding that drafts drawn on the buyer represent a *bona fide* transaction which the buyer will delight to honor gives way to the definite engagement of a bank that bills drawn in accordance with the terms of the credit will be accepted and paid. Bills so drawn command a ready market and can be negotiated with a maximum of confidence; often indeed the seller is privileged to discount them without recourse.

The background is not yet complete. The original promise of the buyer to pay for goods has been converted with a bank's blessing into a negotiable commodity. The bank thus extends credit to the buyer in a form which involves its commitment to honor drafts drawn by the seller. No bank, however, is likely to extend credit without security, and in an operation built around a transaction of sale no security could be more obvious or more appropriate than that afforded by the goods sold. It is natural therefore to look for such security in the bill of lading which represents the goods in transit. The participation of the bank is normally in the knowledge that the seller will attach to his bill of exchange the relative bill of lading. The former carries the personal responsibility of those whose names it bears; the latter adds the physical backing of the merchandise. In the last analysis therefore it would appear that the seller may obtain the amount of the purchase price in reasonably final form practically as soon as the goods are shipped, although the buyer is untouched by any demand for accelerated payment.

Our present purpose is to look more closely at the financing operation and to examine in some detail the instruments by which it is accomplished. The apparent simplicity of the basic outline is perhaps misleading, for in few fields have the efforts of merchants to keep abreast of the times been more productive of legal problems. The growth of international and of branch banking has been a comparatively recent development. The swiftly moving current of world affairs creates for each transaction individual requirements in themselves an invitation to complexity. There have been, moreover, profound changes and developments in the instruments of trade finance. Around bills of exchange has been erected a body of law that has resulted not merely in one but in three general codifications, no two precisely alike. Promissory notes have been added to the family, and more recently checks and trade acceptances, each in turn bringing its own problems. It has taken over seven hundred years to develop the modern irrevocable letter of credit from the letter of credit with which King John raised money in Italy; and still other modifications are in use for special purposes in such forms as the revolving credit, the anticipatory credit, and the authority to purchase. Letters of credit also have been associated to a large extent with the growth of the trust receipt, an instrument once used primarily in connection with import transactions, but later as an important adjunct to the conditional sale. The bill of lading too has assumed new functions. Starting as an entry in the ship's register it has become successively a receipt for the goods shipped, evidence of the contract of carriage, if not the contract itself, and a document of title, hovering on the verge of negotiability.

In all these directions, as in others, merchants are engaged constantly in plotting new courses for the law to follow, but progress is sometimes erratic and fixed sights are not always available. A great deal of ground has to be covered by dead reckoning. It remains to be seen what the law can do with the charts provided.

CHAPTER I

Letters of Credit

1. THE LETTER OF CREDIT CONTRACTS

FIRST WISCONSIN NATIONAL BANK OF MILWAUKEE *v.* FORSYTH LEATHER COMPANY

Wisconsin Supreme Court, 1926

[189 *Wisconsin Reports*, 9]

Action by the plaintiff, First Wisconsin National Bank of Milwaukee, against the defendant, the Forsyth Leather Company, for the amount of a draft drawn against the plaintiff in connection with a letter of credit issued by the plaintiff at the request of the defendant.

The issues may be briefly stated as follows: The plaintiff was engaged in the banking business in the city of Milwaukee. The defendant was engaged in the manufacture of patent leather at Wauwatosa. At the request of the defendant the bank issued a letter of credit in favor of Persson & Company of New York. In due course of business the bank was drawn upon by draft pursuant to the letter of credit, and the draft was honored and paid. Before the draft was paid the defendant sought to have the bank cancel its letter of credit and refuse payment of the draft. The bank refused. The defendant refused to reimburse the bank, and the bank sued.

The case was tried before the court without a jury. The court made its findings of fact and conclusions of law, and entered judgment thereon in favor of the plaintiff. Defendant appeals. The pertinent facts are stated in the opinion.

Crownhart, J. On March 1, 1922, the defendant wrote to the plaintiff as follows:

> Confirming telephone conversation of this morning, we are inclosing herewith two copies of contract, for which kindly open letters of credit as follows:
>
> 1. . . .
>
> 2. Ninety-day letter of credit in favor of Persson & Company for $12,500 covering purchase of 3,500 B. A. Matadero Kips; this letter of credit to expire May 1, 1922.

Inclosed with this letter was a contract between the defendant company and Persson & Company of New York, which contract read as follows:

Forsyth Leather Co., Feb. 21, 1922.
Wauwatosa, Wis.

Contract.

Gentlemen: We confirm our sale and your purchase of the following:
Kind: Wet salted washed B. A. Matadero Kips, Frigorifico type, ranging from

7/15 kilos per kip, averaging about 11/12 kilos, all short-haired, fresh, clean stock.

Quantity: About 3,500.

Price: 13½¢. per lb. shipping weight, c. i. f. New York; shrinkage in transit guaranteed not to exceed 10%.

Shipment: Prompt shipment from Buenos Aires.

Terms: Ninety days' confirmed letter of credit to be opened in our favor with a New York bank for $12,500, and available by our ninety days' drafts with ocean documents and invoice attached. Same to remain in force until May 1, 1922.

Any discrepancy in the quality to be settled in the usual manner by New York arbitration.

The fulfilment of this contract is subject to contingencies beyond our control.

Very truly yours,
PERSSON & CO.
By C. Persson.

The Forsyth Lea. Co.
E. H. Graber, Treas.

Pursuant to such request, on March 2d the plaintiff issued its letter of credit to Persson & Company as follows:

We hereby authorize you to value on the First Wisconsin National Bank of Milwaukee, Wis., for account of the Forsyth Leather Company, Wauwatosa, Wisconsin, for any sum or sums not exceeding in all twelve thousand five hundred dollars ($12,500), by bills at ninety (90) days' sight, against shipment of about 3,500 wet salted washed B. A. Matadero Kips, Frigorifico type, ranging from 7/15 kilos per kip, averaging about 11/12 kilos, all short-haired, fresh clean stock, @ 13½¢. per lb., to Wauwatosa, Wis.

The bills of lading must be issued to the order of the First Wisconsin National Bank of Milwaukee, Wis.

Terms: Cost, insurance, freight New York. Shrinkage in transit guaranteed not to exceed 10%.

The shipment must be completed and the bills drawn on or before May 1, 1922, accompanied by bills of lading and abstract of invoice, on receipt of which documents the bills will be duly honored. Advice thereof to be sent to the foreign department of the First Wisconsin National Bank of Milwaukee, Wis.

We hereby agree with the drawers, indorsers, and *bona fide* holders of drafts drawn under and in compliance with the terms of this credit that the same shall be duly honored at the office of the First Wisconsin National Bank of Milwaukee; payable when due at the First Wisconsin National Bank of Milwaukee.

Drafts drawn under this credit must be marked "Drawn under First Wisconsin National Bank of Milwaukee Credit C-558."

On the same day it advised the defendant by letter of the issuance of the letter of credit, inclosing a copy thereof, and also inclosing an obligation or guaranty to secure the plaintiff for any payment made under the letter of credit, which obligation the defendant was requested to execute and return to the bank. The plaintiff in the same letter also inclosed a formal application in duplicate for the issuance of the letter of credit, to be signed by defendant and returned. The obligation and the application were both promptly executed by the defendant and returned to the plaintiff.

The first contention of the defendant is that the letter of credit constituted merely an offer by the plaintiff to Persson & Company, which was not binding upon the plaintiff until Persson & Company should accept the offer by performing its obligation thereunder. In other words, it is claimed on the part of the defendant that the letter of credit was revocable, and that the defendant had demanded that the letter of credit be revoked prior to such acceptance. The plaintiff's contention is that the letter of credit was irrevocable, and that it was under obligation to accept and pay the draft when accompanied by the proper documents, irrespective of the demands of the defendant to cancel the letter.

It is undisputed that both irrevocable and revocable letters of credit are issued in the ordinary course of banking business. It seems to be the practice to issue such letters by expressly designating therein their character, as "irrevocable" or "revocable," but it also appears that letters of credit are issued without such designation. Where letters are so issued without express designation, there is authority to the effect that they are revocable. 6 Ruling Case Law, 606; *Moss* v. *Old Colony T. Co.* 246 Mass. 139, 140 N. E. 803; *Banco Nacional Ultramarino* v. *First Nat. Bank*, 289 Fed. 169. And other authority to the effect that they are irrevocable: *American S. Co.* v. *Irving Nat. Bank*, 266 Fed. 41; *Maurice O'Meara Co.* v. *Nat. Park Bank*, 239 N. Y. 386, 146 N. E. 636, 39 A. L. R. 747, and note. This question has never been passed upon in this state, and we approach it as a case of first impression.

A letter of credit is a contract, to be construed as other contracts. *Moss* v. *Old Colony T. Co.* 246 Mass. 139, 140 N. E. 803. Where a contract is indefinite or uncertain as to its terms, resort is had to all the surrounding facts and circumstances to determine its proper construction. 6 Ruling Case Law, p. 850, § 240. Here the contract was entered into through communications by mail, pursuant to the ordinary course of business. We think there can be no doubt but that the various letters and inclosures are to be construed together as one transaction.

In the formal application for the letter of credit, it will be noted that the request was to establish a "documentary letter of credit under our guaranty." In the contract between the defendant and Persson & Company accompanying the request to issue the letter of credit, defendant was required to furnish "ninety days' confirmed letter of credit to be opened in our favor with a New York bank for $12,500, and available by our ninety days' draft with ocean documents and invoice attached," and in the guaranty by defendant to plaintiff it is recited:

> Whereas, the First Wisconsin National Bank of Milwaukee, Wisconsin, did at our request, on March 2, 1922, open its irrevocable Credit No. C–558, in favor of Messrs. Persson & Company. . . .

It appears by the contract between defendant and Persson & Company that the defendant agreed to purchase certain hides from Persson & Company, who in turn were to purchase the hides at Buenos Aires, South America. The contract provided for a letter of credit to be drawn against when accompanied by "ocean documents and invoice." This would indicate that the contract price was payable as soon as the goods were loaded on ship at Buenos Aires and the proper documents attached to the draft. However, the letter of credit issued by the bank, as interpreted by Persson & Company, provided for inland bill of lading instead of ocean bill of lading, and in order that Persson & Company might finance the shipment from Buenos Aires to New York, Persson & Company wrote the plaintiff:

> Inasmuch as this credit calls for "inland" bill of lading instead of ocean bill of lading from Buenos Aires to New York as stipulated in our contract to Forsyth Leather Company, and said inland bill of lading not being obtainable until the actual arrival and reshipment of the goods at this port, we have today wired the Forsyth Leather Company to kindly have the credit extended to June 1 and to ask you to kindly advise us of this fact by special-delivery letter.

The defendant requested the extension of time of the plaintiff accordingly, and the letter was extended pursuant to such request to June 1st.

In order to finance the shipment from Buenos Aires to New York, Persson & Company assigned its rights under the contract, accompanied by a draft in blank covering the shipment, to Levison & Company of New York, and Levison & Company thereupon procured an irrevocable letter of credit to be issued in favor of the consignor of the hides at Buenos Aires.

It would seem plain from these transactions that all the parties considered the letter of credit to be irrevocable. The guaranty by defendant to the plaintiff expressly so recited, and as between the plaintiff and defendant they are bound by such recital. Here was a case where Persson & Company were required to make large commitments, and in order to finance the transaction they expressly requested of the defendant a letter of credit to be used accordingly. It would seem to be wholly unreasonable to say, under the circumstances, that such letter of credit should be treated merely as an offer, which might be revoked at any time before the goods were actually loaded on cars in New York. Persson & Company would be obliged to receive and pay for the goods in New York, and then if the letter of credit were treated as revocable the defendant might revoke the same and Persson & Company would be left with the goods on their hands without security.

We think there is a further reason why the defendant is held liable under its guaranty. The contracts between the plaintiff and defendant were Wisconsin contracts and are governed by the Wisconsin law. It is the well settled law of this state that a contract made between two parties for the benefit of a third party is enforceable by such third party according to its terms. *Sedgwick* v. *Blanchard*, 164 Wis. 421, 160 N. W. 267, and cases there cited. The letter of credit here issued was unquestionably for the benefit of Persson & Company. It was issued upon sufficient consideration, and the plaintiff was liable to Persson & Company under its contract with the defendant.

For the reasons stated, we must hold that the letter of credit was irrevocable, and that the plaintiff was bound to accept the draft of Persson

& Company when accompanied by the proper documents. The attempt of defendant to have the letter of credit canceled was wholly unavailing. . . .

We think that, under all the circumstances, the plaintiff bank was liable under its letter of credit to accept and pay the draft drawn pursuant thereto, and the judgment of the circuit court must be affirmed.

By the Court. — The judgment of the circuit court is affirmed.

Compare Moss *v.* Old Colony Trust Company, 246 Mass. 139 (Supreme Judicial Court, 1923), where the letter of credit was in the form of a cable message as follows: "Advise Moss & Co. we open irrevocable credit No. 1475 their favour $2.150.000. U. S. Currency account E. R. Sherburne Company Boston available sight drafts on ourselves covering shipment from Buenos Aires during June July of 5000 tons sugar net shipping weights price $430.u/s/Currency per 10.000 Kilos C. I. F. New York export duty and all taxes payable by shippers credit expires 30th. October. Documents required commercial and consular invoices inspection certificate of United States Chamber of Commerce Buenos Aires certifying sugar equal to fine American Standard granulated sugar, negotiable B/Ladings showing Argentine Government Export License marine war risk insurance certificate showing loss payable in New York — one consular invoice and B/Lading to be forwarded by Bank negotiating direct to us and certificate attached to draft."

In an action by the seller against the issuing bank for refusal to honor drafts drawn under the credit, Rugg, C. J., said: "A letter of credit is a well known instrumentality of commerce. No particular form is prescribed for it. It is a contract in writing. It is governed by the same general principles of law as are all other contracts in writing. To attempt a comprehensive definition applicable to all appropriate cases and not exclusive of others in use or likely to come into use with changes in commercial and banking methods would be difficult. It has been said that it is not 'the business of practical jurisprudence to give definitions or lay down abstract propositions, but to give the rule applicable to the facts proved.' *Lee* v. *Kilburn*, 3 Gray, 594, 599. Moreover, letters of credit are extensively used in commerce. Their nature and use ought to be kept as free as possible from narrowing statements of limitations and from judicial dicta not necessary to a particular decision. They should not be bound by definition so as to become incapable of growth and change in accordance with the development of legitimate business practices.

"It is sufficient for present purposes to say that a letter of credit is an offer by a bank or other financial agency to be bound to the person to whom it is directed, when accepted and acted upon by the latter according to its stipulations. It commonly is issued at the request of a third person who in some way indemnifies the bank against its obligations incurred or to be incurred under the letter of credit, and who gives directions to the bank as to its terms. Although not a party to the letter of credit, he is the one behind the transaction. It is in his interest or for his benefit that the business or other financial adventure is to be undertaken, to which the addressee of the letter of credit is invited. He usually is relieved of all liability to the bank unless it conforms strictly to the terms of the letter of credit in dealing with the person to whom it is directed. If that person is not satisfied with its terms he is under no obligation to act upon it but is entirely at liberty to decline. If he accepts it and acts under it, he is bound to conform to its requirements in every particular. It is in substance an authority to him to draw on the bank in accordance with the terms stated, and a promise by the bank to accept and pay at maturity bills or drafts so drawn. There is no promise to pay unless drafts are in strict conformity to the authority conferred. The letter of credit, when so accepted and acted upon by the person in whose favor it is issued, becomes a contract between them wholly independent of the relation between the writer of the letter of credit and its customer by whose procurement the letter was issued except perhaps in so far as these may be incorporated in the letter. The writer of the letter of credit also has no immediate concern with the relations between the person to whom it is addressed and by whom it is accepted on the one side and the person with whom he has commercial transactions on the other side. The writer of the letter is bound strictly to the terms of his contract as expressed in its letter. The bank as the writer of the letter of credit will not be bound to accept and pay bills or drafts drawn against it unless the holder of the letter pursues and conforms in every material particular to the authority conferred therein. It therefore has come to be the law that letters of credit are construed with some strictness to the end that the rights of those directly parties to them and of those remotely concerned with them as purchasers or indemnitors of the bank respecting its obligations under them may be preserved and the interests of no one of them put in jeopardy."

BANCO NACIONAL ULTRAMARINO *v.* FIRST NATIONAL BANK OF BOSTON

District Court, Massachusetts, 1923

[289 *Federal Reporter*, 169]

Peters, District Judge. This is a suit on a bill of exchange drawn by Magalhaes & Co., of Rio de Janeiro, Brazil, on the First National Bank of Boston, in favor of the plaintiff, for $43,674.54, dated July 28, 1920, at 15 days' sight, protested for nonacceptance on August 30th, and for nonpayment on September 30th.

There are two counts in the writ. The first declares on the draft as an accepted draft by virtue of a promise to accept; the second, on the promise itself. The facts from which the plaintiff claims to recover for a breach of contract on the part of the defendant are substantially as follows:

On May 11, 1920, the Holbrook Grocery Company, of Keene, N. H., made a contract with Magalhaes & Co. for the purchase of some 300 tons of Brazil white crystal sugar, to be shipped from Rio to New York, about 100 tons in July and the balance a little later. The costs and freight to New York were to be paid by Magalhaes & Co., the sellers; insurance to be effected by Holbrook Grocery Company, the buyers, who agreed to take out a banker's letter of credit in favor of the sellers, covering the shipments, under which drafts were to be drawn at 15 days' sight, with complete shipping documents attached.

On June 29, 1920, the defendant bank, at the request of the buyer, mailed to the British Bank of South America, at Rio de Janeiro, the following letter of credit:

The First National Bank of Boston

Boston, Mass., U. S. A., June 29, 1920.

Messrs. Magalhaes e Company, Rio de Janeiro, Brazil — Dear Sir: We hereby authorize you to draw on the First National Bank of Boston, Massachusetts, at fifteen days' sight for any sum or sums not exceeding in total forty-five thousand dollars, for account of the Holbrook Grocery Company, for invoice cost of about 100 tons Brazil white crystal sugar @ 19½¢ per pound c. & f. New York, freight insurance here, including war risk, to be shipped from Rio de Janeiro, Brazil, to New York. Bills of lading for such shipments must be made to the order of the First National Bank of Boston, Boston, Massachusetts, and together with the invoices must accompany the drafts.

A duplicate of such invoices with consular certificate attached, together with one copy of bills of lading and insurance certificates where required, must be sent by the bank or bankers negotiating drafts direct to Mr. E. H. Leland, Room 1800, 14 Wall street, New York City, by first mail, attaching to the draft a statement that such documents have been so forwarded.

Bills of lading must be dated on or before September 15, 1920, and drafts must be drawn on or before September 15, 1920, and each and every draft under this credit must bear upon its face the clause "Drawn under credit No. 8451, dated June 29, 1920, of the First National Bank of Boston, Boston, Mass."

The amount of each and every draft negotiated and date of negotiation must be indorsed hereon.

We hereby agree with the drawers, indorsers, and *bona fide* holders of bills drawn and negotiated in compliance with the terms of this credit that said bills will be duly honored on presentation at our counter in Boston.

Yours very truly, The First National Bank of Boston,
[Signed] C. C. McCauley, Asst. Mgr. For Dept.
[Signed] Charles E. Spencer, Jr., Vice President.

On the same day, prior to the mailing of the letter of credit, the defendant bank cabled to the British Bank of South America, as follows:

June 29th, 1920.

To the British Bank of South America, Rio de Janeiro, Brazil:

Open credit $45,000 favor Magalhaes e Company account Holbrook Grocery Co. drafts 15 days' sight drawn on us shipment about 100 tons Brazil white crystal sugar at 19½ cents per pound c. & f. New York Insurance here war risk included bladings to our order one set documents to E. H. Leland 14 Wall street New York expires September 15th Number of credit 8451 notify beneficiary.

On July 8th the British Bank of South America wrote Magalhaes & Co., at Rio, advising them of the receipt of the cable message and inclosing a copy.

On July 30th the British Bank of South America, having received the letter of credit of June 29th, from the defendant bank, mailed it to Magalhaes & Co., at Rio.

Meanwhile, on July 28, after the cablegram had been received, but before the letter of credit had arrived, Magalhaes & Co. drew on the defendant bank by the draft in question, discounted it with the plaintiff bank, and received credit for the proceeds, being a regular customer of that bank. No documents accompanied this draft which was sent by the plaintiff by mail to its agents or branch in New York.

On July 29th Magalhaes & Co. shipped from Bahia about 100 tons of sugar consigned to the defendant at New York. Certain shipping and other documents were prepared on account of this shipment and mailed by the plaintiffs' agents or branch at Bahia to the plaintiffs' branch in New York, where they were received on August 28th and forwarded to the National Shawmut Bank of Boston, to which bank, also, had been forwarded just previously the draft itself. Thereupon the Shawmut Bank, on August 30th, presented to the defendant bank for acceptance the draft in question, accompanied by the following supporting documents:

[The documents were a bill of lading, a consular invoice, a commercial invoice, a certificate of quality, and an inspection certificate.]

The draft itself presented for acceptance with the documents mentioned was refused and protested, the entry in the notice of protest reading:

> Refuse. Shipment from Bahia, instead of Rio de Janeiro. Invoice does not call for Brazil white crystal sugar. Our customer refuses consent to our acceptance.

On September 30 the draft was presented for payment, accompanied by the same papers with the addition of a memorandum by a warehouse administrator to the effect that from his books it appeared that 1,693 bags of superior crystal sugar, marked "G," went forward in the steamer *Virgil* bound for New York.

Payment was refused, and the draft protested for nonpayment, the reason as given in the notice of protest being, "Same reason existing for nonpayment as for nonacceptance."

It should be mentioned that, on August 30, 1920, E. H. Leland, 14 Wall street, New York City, agent in New York of the defendant, and referred to in the letter of credit, received by mail a nonnegotiable copy of the bill of lading and a copy of the consular invoice.

This action being for the breach of a contract, it is important at the outset to consider what the contract is, and with whom made.

1. Taking these questions in inverse order, with whom was the contract made?

The obligation of the defendant is contained in a cable message of June 29. The more full and detailed letter of credit, in common form and sent by mail, did not reach the beneficiary until after the negotiation of the draft which was negotiated, according to the testimony of the plaintiff's submanager, wholly on the strength of the cablegram and information received from its branch at Bahia that the shipping documents were in order. The only function of the letter of credit as a piece of evidence, as I view it, is to throw light on any obscurity in the cablegram as to the intent of the sender.

The defendant suggests, and asks for a ruling, that the cablegram was a request to the British Bank of South America to open a credit, and was not a letter of credit, that the plaintiff could act upon.

The ordinary commercial letter of credit contains an authority to draw, given the beneficiary, and a promise to honor the draft, given either generally to *bona fide* holders or to some particular person. If the letter shows that it was written for the purpose of being shown in order to obtain credit, and the purchaser is within the terms of the letter, it amounts to an offer that, if he purchases the draft, it will be honored. That offer or promise becomes a contract when the draft is negotiated.

If the letter designates a particular person to whom the promise is made, it has been held that no other can take advantage of it, on the principle that a person has the right to select his own promisee.

This was the principle followed in *Bank of Buchanan County* v. *Continental National Bank* (C. C. A.) 277 Fed. 385, relied upon by the defendant, where a guaranty that a draft would be paid was addressed to a particular bank.

The reasoning of that and similar cases is that the intent of the guarantor to confine his promise to the person addressed is inferred from the fact of the address, and sometimes from other circumstances supposed to throw light upon the intent. In the last-mentioned case it is said:

"It is to be observed that in most of the cases cited the intention of the guarantor to confine his engagement to the person named is shown, not only by the formal address or superscription at the beginning of the writing, but is also shown by the use of some pronoun in the body of the guaranty, in phrases such as 'if you will furnish,' or 'which you may supply.' "

In the instant case there is no occasion to grope around to ascertain the intent of the issuing bank. Its written letter of credit and cabled authority relate to the same transaction, and were written and sent the same day to the same person. The letter was full and explicit, and was an offer or promise to any *bona fide* holder of the draft. The cable message was an abridgment in terse language. Without the letter it might be reasonably argued that the intent of the sender of the cable message was to confine the offer to the addressee; but with the letter it is clear that any *bona fide* holder was intended, as is customary in such transactions.

The plaintiff has a right to rely upon the cablegram, if he brings himself within its terms.

2. What was the promise made by the defendant, which ripened into a contract when accepted according to its terms?

The cable message, freed from its abbreviations and interpreted in the light of the custom of merchants, may be fairly described as an offer to honor a draft of not exceeding $45,000, drawn on 15 days' sight against a shipment of about 100 tons of Brazil white crystal sugar at 19½ cents per pound, costs and freight paid to New York, shipping documents to accompany draft, with duplicate set to be sent to Leland in New York. Shipping documents in such a case according to the custom of merchants include a negotiable bill of lading, a consular invoice, and usually a commercial invoice. These documents are commonly in triplicate, sometimes in duplicate. In this case they would be at least in duplicate, as one set was to be sent to Leland in New York. The cable letter of credit amounted to an offer to purchase such documents.

[The balance of the opinion, holding that the documents supplied did not comply with the terms of the offer, is omitted.]

DOELGER *v.* THE BATTERY PARK NATIONAL BANK

NEW YORK SUPREME COURT, APPELLATE DIVISION, 1922

[201 *New York Appellate Division Reports*, 515]

GREENBAUM, J. The plaintiff entered into an agreement to sell to the corporation known as the Machinery and Metals Sales Company 800 tons of round shell discard steel bars, which required the buyer to provide an irrevocable domestic documentary letter of credit from a responsible bank in New York, covering the purchase price of the merchandise available against the sight drafts accompanied by railroad bills of lading and commercial invoices. In accordance with this agreement the defendant issued its irrevocable letter of credit on October 14, 1918, in which it authorized the plaintiff to draw on it for the account of the Machinery and Metals Sales Company up to an aggregate amount of $65,410 for the invoice cost of "800 ton Round Shell Discard Steel Bars, conforming to Machinery & Metals Sales Company's orders Nos. 3229, 3230, 3232, 3233 and 3235," available by sight drafts accompanied by railroad bill of lading and commercial invoice (in duplicate) shipment from Pittsburgh District to Seattle, Washington, bills of lading to be drawn "to the order of order (*sic*) and endorsed in blank and dated not later than November 1st, 1918," which will be honored on presentation at the office of the defendant "on or before November 3rd, 1918." On October 28, 1918, the defendant wrote to the plaintiff as follows:

> Referring to our letter of credit No. 536 issued in your favor for $65,410, kindly note that same has been increased $600, making the total credit to read $66,010. We also wish to inform you that this credit has been extended to expire December 1st, 1918. All documents pertaining to the above must be in our possession on or before this date. All other terms and conditions of this credit remain the same as heretofore.

The extension mentioned in the foregoing letter was made at the request of the Machinery and Metals Sales Company as evidenced by the following letter written by it to the defendant:

> GENTLEMEN. — Referring to your letter of credit No. 536, would thank you to increase this L/C in the amount of $600, making a total of $66,010. Also extend

this credit until December 1st, 1918. All other terms and conditions are to remain unchanged.

Yours very truly,
(signed) MACHINERY & METALS SALES COMPANY,
J. J. WHITEHEAD, *Pres.*

On November 25, 1918, the plaintiff, having shipped a carload of the steel, presented to defendant a sight draft for $2,920, the purchase price thereof, accompanied by an invoice and railroad bill of lading dated November 20, 1918. Defendant refused payment of the draft for the reason stated in the following letter addressed to plaintiff, dated November 25, 1918:

Answering your letter of the 23rd inst. referring to our credit No. 536, dated October 14th, 1918, for $66,010 and assigned by you to the Guaranty Trust Company of New York, we have to advise you that payment under this credit is declined in accordance with instructions from the Machinery & Metals Sales Company, as per their letter of the 15th instant — copy of which is herewith attached.

Very truly yours,
E. B. DAY
Vice-President.

It thus appears that the defendant refused to honor plaintiff's draft solely because the buyer requested it so to do. The learned counsel for the appellant conceded in open court that such a request in itself was not a legal justification on the part of the defendant to refuse payment of the draft.

[The balance of the opinion is omitted.]

Note also BANQUE DE MARSEILLE *c.* DELAMARE ET INGELBRECHT, 1926 Dalloz 1.201 (Court of Cassation), where there was a contract for the sale of 3000 bags of Santos coffee under a confirmed credit. The credit was duly issued to the seller. Subsequently however the issuing bank notified the seller that the credit was to be considered as cancelled because the buyer had not carried out the arrangements made with the bank. In an action by the seller against the bank, it was held that the default of the buyer on his contract with the bank could not affect the contract between the bank and the seller.

BANK OF EAST ASIA, LIMITED *v.* PANG

WASHINGTON SUPREME COURT, 1926

[140 *Washington Reports*, 603]

MAIN, J. — The complaint in this action is based upon two drafts for the sums of twelve thousand five hundred dollars and seven thousand five hundred dollars respectively. To the amended complaint, which will be referred to as the complaint, a demurrer was interposed and sustained. The plaintiff declined to plead further and elected to stand upon the complaint, with the result that judgment was entered dismissing the action, from which it appeals.

The facts, as stated in the complaint, essential to present the law question to be determined, may be summarized as follows: The appellant, the Bank of East Asia, Ltd., was located at Shanghai, China, and will be referred to as the bank. The Sang Lee Company was engaged in business at the same place. The respondents Herbert Archie Pang and Law Wing Woo did business under the name of Union Trading Company at Seattle, Washington. The Sang Lee Company purchased steel products from the Union Trading Company and to facilitate the matter of payment the bank issued two letters of credit, the first of which was for twelve thousand five hundred dollars and was in words and figures as follows:

American Express Company, Seattle, Washington.
Mr. Grimmig, Building.
Mr. Eberle, For. Traff. Dept.
Aug. 9, 1923,

Union Trading Company,
Seattle, Washington

Irrevocable Export Credit.
No. 17196
Mention this Credit Number on all communications.

Dear Sir:

For account of our correspondent, named below, as ordered by cablegram we herewith open an IRREVOCABLE CREDIT in your favor as follows:
Amount $12,500. (Twelve thousand five hundred dollars)
Expires Sept. 30th, Draft must be presented on or before that date.
For account of Sang Lee Company
Covering shipment of Steel products.
Destination Shanghai direct.
Insurance-marine to be effected by shippers
available by draft on us at Sang-Lee Co., Shanghai at 90 d/a (in dup)
accompanied by following shipping documents (in form satisfactory to us).
Complete set of steamer B/L to order Bank of East Asia, Ltd., Marine and War risk Insurance Certificates in duplicate. Notify consignee.
Invoice in triplicate.
P. S. Draft should bear the clause reading: "Payable with interest added at 7% from date of draft until approximate date of arrival of cover in New York."

Above Credit opened by
Bank of East Asia, Ltd.,
Shanghai, China.

Yours truly,
Assistant Treasurer

This letter of credit by its terms is made irrevocable and was for the purpose of covering a shipment of steel products to the Sang Lee Company. The American Express Company was the agent of the bank for the purpose of making payment. On September 5, 1923, the Union Trading Company made a shipment of steel products and drew a draft in accordance with the letter of credit, as follows:

Seattle,
Exchange for $12,500.00 September 5th, 1923.

AT NINETY DAYS SIGHT............................of this FIRST OF EXCHANGE (SECOND UNPAID) pay to the order of BANK OF EAST ASIA, LTD., SHANGHAI, CHINA.
TWELVE THOUSAND FIVE HUNDRED DOLLARS ONLY......................
Value received, and charge the same to account of

Drawn under your Irrevocable Export Credit No. 17196. "Documents against payment." Payable with interest added at 9% from date of draft until approximate date of arrival of cover in New York, U. S. A.

UNION TRADING CO.,
By Archie Pang,
Manager.

To MESSRS. SANG LEE COMPANY,
Shanghai,
China.

This draft with the documents attached was presented to the American Express Company and paid. The draft calls for acceptance at sight and payment in ninety days. It, together with the bill of lading and invoice, was transmitted to the bank and was by it presented to the Sang Lee Company and accepted. On the due date, the latter company was unable to take up the draft and it was duly protested and demand made upon the Union Trading Company to reimburse the bank. This demand was refused and the present action followed. The second draft and the proceedings thereunder was the same as that upon the first.

The bank claims, and so alleges in the complaint, that the steel products were not of the kind and quality which had been contracted for by the Sang Lee Company and that therefore it has a right, having paid the draft through its agent, to maintain an action directly against the Union Trading Company. The question is, whether the bank, having issued the letter of credit providing that payment would be made when certain documents were presented, can now rely upon the claimed fact that the steel products were of an inferior quality. The contract for these products was between Sang Lee Company and the Union Trading Company. The letter of credit was a contract between the bank and the Union Trading Company. There is no claim that the documents presented when the payment was made by the express company did not conform to the requirements of the letter of credit. The bank was dealing in documents and not merchandise. . . .

A bank, when it issues a letter of credit, has the right to write into it such requirements and conditions as it sees fit. If it does not do so and, as in this case, simply issues the letter of credit obligating itself to pay when certain documents are presented, then the terms of the contract are satisfied when documents conforming to the requirements of the letter of credit are presented.

It is alleged in the complaint in the present case that there was failure of consideration and fraud, but these allegations are based upon the fact that the products shipped were not of the kind and quality contracted for by the Sang Lee Company. As already pointed out, this is a question which cannot be inquired into when the action is by the bank against the seller of the product or by the seller of the product against the bank. . . .

The judgment will be affirmed.

TOLMAN, C. J., MITCHELL, PARKER, and MACKINTOSH, JJ., concur.

In URQUHART, LINDSAY AND COMPANY, LIMITED *v.* EASTERN BANK, LIMITED, [1922] 1 K. B. 318 (King's Bench Division, 1921), the defendant bank issued to the plaintiff seller a "confirmed irrevocable credit" in connection with a contract for the sale of machinery. This contract contained terms in regard to the prices to be invoiced which were not included in the letter of credit, the latter merely stipulating for "signed invoices in duplicate." In drafts and invoices presented to defendant under the credit, plaintiffs named amounts which the buyer claimed were in violation of the terms of the sale contract. Defendant thereupon refused to honor the drafts, contending that the letter of credit must be taken to incorporate the contract between plaintiff and the buyer. In an action for damages for breach of contract judgment was given for plaintiff on the ground that defendant undertook without qualification to pay the invoice amounts, and the contract could not be affected by the contract of sale.

Note also BANK OF TAIWAN, LIMITED *v.* UNION NATIONAL BANK, 1 Fed. (2nd) 65 (Circuit Court of Appeals, Third Circuit, 1924), where a contract for the purchase of 360 tons of copra provided for the opening of a confirmed irrevocable credit, and stipulated for shipment during September or October, 1920. The defendant bank issued to the seller a letter of credit undertaking to honor bills accompanied by full sets of bills of lading dated during September or October, 1920. The letter also contained the usual statement that defendant "hereby agrees with the drawers, indorsers, and bona fide holders of bills, drawn in compliance with the terms of this credit, that the same shall be duly honored on presentation to us." The seller discounted with the plaintiff bank drafts drawn under the credit accompanied by bills of lading dated October 30, 1920. Defendant refused payment on the ground that shipment had not been made in September or October. In an action for damages for breach of contract the lower court admitted the terms of the sale contract in evidence and judgment was given for defendant. Error. Judgment reversed.

Compare ARTIC ICE & COAL CO. *v.* SOUTHGATE, 287 Fed. 48 (Circuit Court of Appeals, Fourth Circuit, 1923), where the sale contract called for presentation of dock receipt or bill of lading and where the letter of credit mentioned merely "shipping documents." It was held that this general description should be read in the light of the more precise language of the sale contract.

Refer again to AMERICAN STEEL CO. *v.* IRVING NATIONAL BANK, *supra*, p. 283.

MAURICE O'MEARA COMPANY *v.* THE NATIONAL PARK BANK OF NEW YORK

New York Court of Appeals, 1925

[239 *New York Reports*, 386]

McLaughlin, J. This action was brought to recover damages alleged to have been sustained by the plaintiff's assignor, Ronconi & Millar, by defendant's refusal to pay three sight drafts against a confirmed irrevocable letter of credit. The letter of credit was in the following form:

The National Park Bank
of New York

Our Credit No. 14956 October 28, 1920.

Messrs. Ronconi & Millar,
49 Chambers Street,
New York City, N. Y.:

Dear Sirs — In accordance with instructions received from the Sun-Herald Corporation of this City, we open a confirmed or irrevocable credit in your favor for account of themselves, in amount of $224,853.30, covering the shipment of 1322 2/3 tons of newsprint paper in 72½" and 36½" rolls to test 11–12, 32 lbs. at 8½¢ per pound net weight — delivery to be made in December 1920 and January 1921.

Drafts under this credit are to be drawn at sight on this Bank, and are to be accompanied by the following documents of a character which must meet with our approval:

Commercial Invoice in triplicate
Weight Returns
Negotiable Dock Delivery Order actually carrying with it control of the goods.

This is a confirmed or irrevocable credit, and will remain in force to and including February 15th, 1921, subject to the conditions mentioned herein.

When drawing drafts under this credit, or referring to it please quote our number as above.

Very truly yours,
R. STUART,
Assistant Cashier.
(R. C.)

The complaint alleged the issuance of the letter of credit; the tender of three drafts, the first on the 17th of December, 1920, for $46,301.71, the second on January 7, 1921, for $41,416.34, and the third on January 13, 1921, for $32,968.35.

[The accompanying documents complied with the requirements of the credit.]

The complaint also alleged defendant's refusal to pay; a statement of the amount of loss upon the resale of the paper due to a fall in the market price; expenses for lighterage, cartage, storage and insurance amounting to $3,045.02; an assignment of the cause of action by Ronconi & Millar to the plaintiff; and a demand for judgment.

The answer denied, upon information and belief, many of the allegations of the complaint, and set up (a) as an affirmative defense, that plaintiff's assignor was required by the letter of credit to furnish to the defendant "evidence reasonably satisfactory" to it that the paper shipped to the Sun-Herald Corporation was of a bursting or tensile strength of eleven to twelve points at a weight of paper of thirty-two pounds; that neither the plaintiff nor its assignor, at the time the drafts were presented, or at any time thereafter, furnished such evidence; (b) as a partial defense, that when the draft for $46,301.71 was presented, the defendant notified the plaintiff there had not been presented "evidence reasonably satisfactory" to it, showing that the newsprint paper referred to in the documents accompanying said drafts was of the tensile or bursting strength specified in the letter of credit; that thereupon an agreement was entered into between plaintiff and defendant that the latter should cause a test to be made of the paper represented by the documents then presented and if such test showed that the paper was up to the specifications of the letter of credit, defendant would make payment of the draft; (c) for a third separate and distinct defense that the paper tendered was not, in fact, of the tensile or bursting strength specified in the letter of credit; (d) for a fourth separate and distinct defense that on or about January 15, 1921, and after the respective drafts referred to in the complaint had been presented to defendant for payment and payment refused, and at a time when the paper was owned and possessed by plaintiff or Ronconi & Millar, the Sun-Herald Corporation, in accordance with whose instructions and for whose account the letter of credit was issued, offered to the plaintiff that it would accept the newsprint paper referred to and pay for the same at a price of eight and one-half cents per pound, provided the plaintiff or its assignor would promptly and reasonably satisfy the Sun-Herald Corporation that the newsprint paper tested as much as eleven points to thirty-two pounds as specified in the letter of credit, and was of the sizes specified therein; that the plaintiff refused to accept said offer; and (e) as a fifth separate and partial defense, all of the allegations of the fourth defense were repeated.

After issue had been joined the plaintiff moved, upon the pleadings and affidavits, pursuant to rule 113 of the Rules of Civil Practice, to strike out the answer and for summary judgment.

The claim for damages for the non-payment of the third draft was, apparently, abandoned at or prior to the time the motion was made. It is unnecessary, therefore, to further consider that and it will not be again referred to in the discussion as to the first two drafts.

The motion for summary judgment was denied and the defendant appealed to the Appellate Division, where the order denying the same was unanimously affirmed, leave to appeal to this court granted, and the following question certified: "Should the motion of the plaintiff for summary judgment herein have been granted?"

It is unnecessary to consider the denials contained in the answer, since in the answering affidavits defendant raised no issue as to any of the facts alleged in the complaint and in the plaintiff's affidavits upon which the motion was based. Defendant's affidavits used in opposition to the motion merely repeat the various denials contained in the answer. These denials were insufficient to raise an issue on a motion for summary judgment, since, under the rule, facts must be presented rather than mere general or specific denials in order to defeat a motion. (Rules Civ. Prac., rule 113; *General Investment Co.* v. *Interborough R. T. Co.*, 235 N. Y. 133, 139.)

I am of the opinion that the order of the Appellate Division and the Special Term should be reversed and the motion granted. The facts set out in defendant's answer and in the affidavits used by it in opposition to the motion are not a defense to the action.

The bank issued to plaintiff's assignor an irrevocable letter of credit, a contract solely between the bank and plaintiff's assignor, in and by which the bank agreed to pay sight drafts to a certain amount on presentation to it of the documents specified in the letter of credit. This contract was in no way involved in or connected with, other than the presentation of the documents, the contract for the purchase and sale of the paper mentioned. That was a contract between buyer and seller, which in no way concerned the bank. The bank's obligation was to pay sight drafts when presented if accompanied by genuine documents specified in the letter of credit. If the paper when delivered did not correspond to what had been purchased, either in weight, kind or quality, then the purchaser had his remedy against the seller for damages. Whether the paper were what the purchaser contracted to purchase did not concern the bank and in no way affected its liability. It was under no obligation to ascertain, either by a personal examination or otherwise, whether the paper conformed to the contract between the buyer and seller. The bank was concerned only in the drafts and the documents accompanying them. This was the extent of its interest. If the drafts, when presented, were accompanied by the proper documents, then it was absolutely bound to make the payment under the letter of credit, irrespective of whether it knew, or had reason to believe, that the paper was not of the tensile strength contracted for. This view, I think, is the one generally entertained with reference to a bank's liability under an irrevocable letter of credit of the character of the one here under consideration. (See Commercial Letters of Credit, 35 Harvard Law Review, 730, 734, 735, and authorities there cited; *National City Bank* v. *Seattle National Bank*, 121 Wash. 476; *Bank of Plant City* v. *Canal-Commercial Trust & Savings Bank*, 270 Fed. Rep. 477; *International Banking Corp.* v. *Irving National Bank*, 274 Fed. Rep. 122, 125; affd., 283 Fed. Rep. 103; *Harper* v. *Hochstim*, 278 Fed. Rep. 102; *Horst Co.* v. *Biddell Brothers*, [1912] App. Cas. 18, revg. [1911] 1 K. B. 934; *Brown* v. *Raritan Chemical Works, Inc.*, 188 App. Div. 578, 584.)

The defendant had no right to insist that a test of the tensile strength of the paper be made before paying the drafts. Nor did it even have a right to inspect the paper before payment, to determine whether it in fact corresponded to the description contained in the documents. The letter of credit did not so provide. All that the letter of credit provided was that documents be presented which described the paper shipped as of a certain size, weight and tensile strength. To hold otherwise is to read into the letter of credit something which is not there, and this the court ought not to do, since it would impose upon a bank a duty which in many cases would defeat the primary purpose of such letters of credit. This primary purpose is an assurance to the seller of merchandise of prompt payment against documents.

It has never been held, so far as I am able to discover, that a bank has the right or is under an obligation to see that the description of the merchandise contained in the documents presented is correct. A provision giving it such right, or imposing such obligation, might, of course, be provided for in the letter of credit. The letter under consideration contains no such provision. If the bank had the right to determine whether the paper were of the tensile strength stated, then it might be pertinent to inquire how much of the paper must it subject to the test? If it had to make a test as to tensile strength, then it was equally obligated to measure and weigh the paper. No such thing was intended by the parties and there was no such obligation upon the bank. The documents presented were sufficient. The only reason stated by defendant in its letter of December 18, 1920, for refusing to pay the draft, was that "there has arisen a reasonable doubt regarding the quality of the newsprint paper. . . . Until such time as we can have a test made by an impartial and unprejudiced expert we shall be obliged to defer payment." This being the sole objection, the only inference to be drawn therefrom is that otherwise the documents presented conformed to the requirements of the letter of credit. All other objections were thereby waived.

[Four pages of the opinion are here omitted.]

The orders appealed from should, therefore, be reversed and the motion granted, with costs in all courts. The question certified is answered in the affirmative.

CARDOZO, J. (dissenting). I am unable to concur in the opinion of the court.

I assume that no duty is owing from the bank to its depositor which requires it to investigate the quality of the merchandise (*Laudisi* v. *American Ex. Nat. Bank*, 239 N. Y. 234). I dissent from the view that if it chooses to investigate and discovers thereby that the merchandise tendered is not in truth the merchandise which the documents describe, it may be forced by the delinquent seller to make payment of the price irrespective of its knowledge. We are to bear in mind that this controversy is not one between the bank on the one side and on the other a holder of the drafts who has taken them without notice and for value. The controversy arises between the bank and a seller who has misrepresented the security upon which advances are demanded. Between parties so situated, payment may be resisted if the documents are false.

I think we lose sight of the true nature of the transaction when we view the bank as acting upon the credit of its customer to the exclusion of all else. It acts not merely upon the credit of its customer, but upon the credit also of the merchandise which is to be tendered as security. The letter of credit is explicit in its provision that documents sufficient to give control of the goods shall be lodged with the bank when drafts are presented. I cannot accept the statement of the majority opinion that the bank was not concerned with any question as to the character of the paper. If that is so, the bales tendered might have been rags instead of paper, and still the bank would have been helpless, though it had knowledge of the truth, if the documents tendered by the seller were sufficient on their face. A different question would be here if the defects had no relation to the description in the documents. In such circumstances, it would be proper to say that a departure from the terms of the contract between the vendor and the vendee was of no moment to the bank. That is not the case before us. If the paper was of the quality stated in the defendant's answer, the documents were false.

I think the conclusion is inevitable that a bank which pays a draft upon a bill of lading misrepresenting the character of the merchandise may recover the payment when the misrepresentation is discovered, or at the very least the difference between the value of the thing described and the value of the thing received. If payment might have been recovered the moment after it was made, the seller cannot coerce payment if the truth is earlier revealed.

We may find persuasive analogies in connection with the law of sales. One who promises to make payment in advance of delivery and inspection may be technically in default if he refuses the promised payment before inspection has been made. None the less, if the result of the inspection is to prove that the merchandise is defective, the seller must fail in an action for the recovery of the price. The reason is that "the buyer would have been entitled to recover back the price if he had paid it without inspection of the goods" (2 Williston on Sales [2d. ed.], §§ 479, 576).

I think the defendant's answer and the affidavits submitted in support of it are sufficient to permit a finding that the plaintiff's assignors misrepresented the nature of the shipment. The misrepresentation does not cease to be a defense, partial if not complete, though it was innocently made (*Bloomquist* v. *Farson*, 222 N. Y. 375; 2 Williston on Sales [2d ed.], § 632).

The order should be affirmed and the question answered "no."

HISCOCK, Ch. J., POUND and ANDREWS, JJ., concur with McLAUGHLIN, J.; CARDOZO, J., reads dissenting opinion in which CRANE, J., concurs; LEHMAN, J., not sitting.

Orders reversed, etc.

Note also CONTINENTAL NATIONAL BANK *v.* NATIONAL CITY BANK OF NEW YORK, 69 Fed. (2nd) 312 (Circuit Court of Appeals, Ninth Circuit, 1934), where the defendant bank issued a confirmed irrevocable credit "against shipment of twelve thousand (12,000) Barrels Portland Cement. . . . Cement to be of a sound merchantable quality and standard of same shall meet with the requirements of the American Society for testing materials." Drafts drawn by the seller under the letter of credit were purchased by the plaintiff bank, and were refused acceptance by defendant because the character of the cement did not comply with the specifications in the letter of credit. Part of the cement shipped under previous credits had been of inferior quality, and the cement in question, stored until after the arrival of the documents, was tested while in storage and found to be below standard. In an action for damages, a judgment for plaintiff was affirmed.

Compare OLD COLONY TRUST CO. *v.* LAWYERS' TITLE & TRUST CO., 297 Fed. 152 (Circuit Court of Appeals, Second Circuit, 1924), where an irrevocable letter of credit issued in connection with a contract for the sale of Java sugar required drafts to be drawn against net landed weights. The sugar was not weighed until several days after drafts were tendered, so that it was obvious that statements in the invoices accompanying the drafts referring to weights as net landed weights were false. The credit further required tender of negotiable warehouse receipts, and the receipts tendered were issued while the sugar was still afloat. The defendant issuing bank refused to honor the drafts. In an action by the presenting bank, which had discounted the drafts in good faith, a judgment for defendant was affirmed, Mayer, Circ. J., saying: "Obviously, when the issuer of a letter of credit knows that a document, although correct in form, is, in point of fact, false or illegal, he cannot be called upon to recognize such a document as complying with the terms of a letter of credit."

2. THE ISSUING BANK AND THE BUYER

FREY & SON, INC. *v.* E. R. SHERBURNE CO. & THE NATIONAL CITY BANK OF NEW YORK

NEW YORK SUPREME COURT, APPELLATE DIVISION, 1920

[193 *New York Appellate Division Reports*, 849]

GREENBAUM, J. This action is brought in equity by the plaintiff, a buyer of Java sugar, permanently to enjoin the defendant Sherburne Company, the seller, from drawing or negotiating drafts upon a letter of credit issued by the National City Bank to the Sherburne Company to secure the payment of the purchase price of the sugar and permanently to enjoin the defendant bank from honoring or paying any drafts which may have been drawn and which now may be in the hands of third parties.

The facts, so far as material on the appeal, are that the plaintiff, a Maryland corporation, entered into a written contract in New York with the defendant Sherburne Company, a Massachusetts corporation, under which the plaintiff bought from that defendant 350 tons of Java sugar, shipments to be made from the Island of Java by steamer or steamers to New York in five separate shipments. Payment for the sugar was to be made in cash in New York on presentation of a warehouse receipt or delivery order and the plaintiff was to furnish an irrevocable letter of credit for the full amount of the invoice. The contract also provided as follows: "Should any unforeseen circumstances such as accidents, stress of weather, etc., prevent the steamer or steamers hereafter declared against this contract from clearing within the time specified above, and the sellers or their agents be unable to supply other tonnage of equal character and capacity, the buyer has the option of cancelling such portion of this contract, as has not cleared within the time specified above or taking the sugar for later shipment without claiming damages and their decision is to be given immediately on advice from sellers that delay has occurred."

Carrying out the terms of the contract, the plaintiff procured a letter of credit from the defendant National City Bank, under which the bank authorized the Sherburne Company to draw on it, in the aggregate sum of $164,640, on sight drafts accompanied by delivery order or warehouse receipt, invoice and weigher's certificate covering 350 tons of sugar, shipment of which was to be made in the quantities and during the months as specified in the letter of credit which were the same specifications of the sugar as those appearing in the contract. The letter of credit contains the following provision: "We hereby agree with *bona fide* holders that all drafts issued by virtue of this credit and in accordance with the above stipulated terms, shall meet with due honor upon presentation at our Export Commercial Credit Department if drawn and negotiated not later than period indicated."

The provision in which reference is made to the plaintiff's right of cancellation which appears in the contract between the plaintiff and the defendant was not embodied in the letter of credit.

It is alleged that on August 28, 1920, the defendant Sherburne Company notified the plaintiff that the forty-five tons of sugar referred to in the contract to be shipped in July had in fact been shipped on the steamer *Karimoen* and that the steamer was expected to arrive in the second week of September; that as matter of fact the steamer did not clear from Java in July but that it did clear about August fifteenth and that, therefore, the plaintiff elected to cancel the contract. Based upon the foregoing alleged facts, the complaint states that notwithstanding the exercise of said option by the plaintiff as aforesaid the defendant Sherburne Company threatens to negotiate or present for payment a sight draft upon the defendant bank for the purchase price of the said forty-five tons and the defendant National City Bank threatens to pay such draft if so presented or negotiated. It is also alleged that the defendant Sherburne Company refused to notify plaintiff Frey as to the names of the vessels for the next shipments for one hundred tons for July or August and that the defendant National City Bank acknowledged the right of the defendant Sherburne Company to negotiate or present for payment drafts for the purchase price of the remaining quantities of merchandise mentioned in the letter of credit to be delivered on the presentation of the documents required by that letter.

The contentions of the defendants are, *first*, that according to the complaint there existed two distinct contracts, one between plaintiff and the Sherburne Company, being the contract of purchase and sale, and the other between the National City Bank and the defendant Sherburne Company and the holders of drafts, drawn in reliance on the letter of credit under the terms of which the defendant bank agreed to pay drafts drawn in accordance with the letter of credit regardless of the terms of the contract between the plaintiff and the Sherburne Company as to the right to cancel the contract and which are not mentioned or referred to in the letter of credit; *second*, that the plaintiff has a full and adequate remedy at law; *third*, that no injunction may issue against the bank paying drafts in the hands of third parties, which were drawn in accordance with the terms of the letter of credit, regardless of any other terms embodied in the contract between plaintiff and defendant Sherburne Company; *fourth*, that as matter of fact there was no breach of the contract between the plaintiff and defendant which gave plaintiff the right to cancel it. And, finally, that the contract did not require the Sherburne Company to make a declaration at any time as to the steamer upon which the various shipments were to be made.

From our view of the case it is not important to discuss the rights of the plaintiff under the contract with the defendant Sherburne Company. In the case before us the letter of credit was an irrevocable one.

In the recent case of *American Steel Co* v. *Irving National Bank* (266 Fed. Rep. 41) the court held that a letter of credit was "a complete and independent contract."

In *Benecke* v. *Haebler* (38 App. Div. 344; affd., 166 N. Y. 631) the buyer had notified the banker who issued a letter of credit that the merchandise was not equal to sample. The court said: "I cannot see that the fact that the beans sent forward by Strauss were inferior in quality to those contracted for at all affects the question of the defendants' liability for moneys paid by the plaintiffs in discharge of an obligation assumed by them at the defendants' request. The kind or quality of the beans to be shipped by Strauss was not defined in the defendants' letter asking for a credit, and no duty devolved upon the plaintiffs to ascertain, before accepting, whether the goods shipped corresponded in quality with the goods ordered."

In *Matter of Agra and Masterman's Bank* (L. R. [1867] Ch. App. 391) it was held that holders in good faith of drafts upon a letter of credit were entitled to the absolute benefit of its terms and are not concerned with differences existing between the parties to the contract out of which the letter of credit was issued.

It is equally clear here that the bank issuing the letter of credit is in no way concerned with any contract existing between the buyer and seller. The bank may only be held liable in case of a violation of any of the terms of the letter of credit. It would thus follow that if the bank paid any drafts violative of the terms of the letter, the buyer would have recourse to the bank in an action for damages for the breach of its contract. Similarly, if the defendant Sherburne Company violated its contract with the plaintiff, the latter has a remedy in an action at law for damages against the defendant. It is not alleged in the complaint that the National City Bank is in financial difficulties. Nor is it alleged that the Sherburne Company is not financially able to respond to damages. Our attention has been called to *Higgins* v. *Steinhardter* (106 Misc. Rep. 168). We are of opinion that the facts appearing in the opinion of that case did not warrant the granting of an injunction. Interests of innocent parties who may hold drafts upon the letter of credit should not be made to suffer by reason of rights that may exist between the parties to the contract of sale in reference to which the letter of credit was issued. It would be a calamity to the business world if for every breach of a contract between buyer and seller a party may come into a court of equity and enjoin payment on drafts drawn upon a letter of credit issued by a bank which owed no duty to the buyer in respect of the breach. The parties should be remitted upon their claims for damages to an action at law.

We think the order should be affirmed, with ten dollars costs and disbursements.

CLARKE, P. J., LAUGHLIN, DOWLING and MERRELL, JJ., concur.

Order affirmed, with ten dollars costs and disbursements.

Note also LAUDISI *v.* AMERICAN EXCHANGE NATIONAL BANK, 239 N. Y. 234 (Court of Appeals, 1924), where there was a contract for the purchase of grapes which were to be shipped from California. The transaction was financed under a letter of credit by the terms of which a draft was drawn by the seller on the issuing bank. Before the draft matured the buyer notified the issuing bank that the grapes shipped did not comply with the requirements of the sale contract, and requested the bank not to pay the draft. The bank nevertheless paid, and it was held that "the bank has the right to pay the draft no matter what may be the defects in the goods which have been shipped. The bank is not obliged to assume the burdens of a controversy between the vendor and vendee and incur the responsibility of establishing as an excuse for not paying a draft that the vendee's version is the correct one."

In Grillo *v.* Banca America e Italia, 1936 Foro Italiano 1.604 (Court of Cassation), there was a contract for the sale of a quantity of hides under a confirmed credit. Drafts under the credit were to be drawn on a correspondent of the issuing bank. The drafts were duly drawn and accepted, and the buyer reimbursed the issuing bank under the terms of the credit agreement. Before the drafts fell due for payment however the buyer sought to attach the funds paid to the issuing bank by way of reimbursement on the ground that the seller had shipped inferior goods. It was held that no attachment would lie, as the contract between the bank and the buyer was entirely distinct from that between the buyer and the seller, and the payment had been made to the bank as to a creditor, not for the account of the seller.

BROWN *v.* C. ROSENSTEIN COMPANY

New York Supreme Court, 1923

[120 *New York Miscellaneous Reports,* 187]

Burr, J. Motion for summary judgment, under rule 113 of the Rules of Civil Practice. The plaintiffs are copartners carrying on business as bankers under the firm name of Brown Brothers & Company. Plaintiff's complaint for a first cause of action alleges: On or about the 26th day of August, 1922, at defendant's request they issued a letter of credit authorizing Georges Vemian, of Varna, Bulgaria, to draw upon plaintiffs at three months' sight for account of defendant for any sum or sums not exceeding in all $4,500 for eighty-five per cent cost of merchandise to be shipped to New York, the bills to be drawn and shipments completed on or before September 30, 1922. At defendant's request and risk the issue of said credit was advised by telegraph through Brown, Shipley & Company of London to said Georges Vemian, Varna, Bulgaria. A copy of the said letter of credit is attached to the complaint. In order to induce the plaintiffs to issue the said letter of credit the defendant executed and delivered to the plaintiffs prior to the issue of the letter of credit a receipt and obligation by the terms of which the defendant agreed to provide plaintiffs previous to the maturity of all drafts drawn under said credit with sufficient funds in cash to meet the payment of the same, together with a commission of three-eighths per cent on the drafts so drawn. A copy of the receipt and obligation is attached to the complaint. On or about September 25, 1922, Georges Vemian drew upon the plaintiffs under the said letter of credit, at three months' sight, a draft for $4,500. A photostat of the draft is annexed to the complaint. The said draft was accompanied by all the documents specified in the letter of credit, including a bill of lading and properly certified invoice covering fifty tons millet seed and fifty tons canary seed and a marine policy satisfactory to plaintiffs. A photostat of the bill of lading, invoice and insurance policy is attached to the complaint. On or about October 13, 1922, said draft, with the accompanying documents, was presented by the holders thereof, Messrs. John Munroe & Company, to the plaintiffs for acceptance, and plaintiffs thereupon accepted said draft and obtained from the holders for account of defendant the said accompanying documents. On or about October 13, 1922, plaintiffs notified the defendant that the said draft had been drawn by Georges Vemian under said letter of credit and that plaintiffs had accepted same and had obtained for defendant's account the accompanying documents. At defendant's request the plaintiffs thereupon delivered to defendant a trust receipt, a copy of which is attached to the complaint. The plaintiffs thereafter and prior to the maturity of the said draft requested the defendant pursuant to the terms of the said obligation to provide plaintiffs with funds sufficient to meet the payment of the said draft, together with the plaintiffs' commission. At the maturity of the said draft on or about January 15, 1923, the same was presented to plaintiffs for payment by the Federal Reserve Bank of New York, the then holder thereof, and thereupon plaintiffs paid the same. Defendant has refused and neglected to provide plaintiffs with the amount of the said draft at or prior to the maturity thereof and the agreed commissions of plaintiffs. For a second cause of action plaintiffs allege the issuance of another letter of credit at defendant's request on or about September 12, 1922, authorizing the said Georges Vemian to draw upon plaintiffs at three months' sight for account of defendant for any sum not exceeding $2,750 in the same manner and under the same conditions, under which letter of credit the said Georges Vemian drew upon the plaintiffs at three months' sight a draft for $2,735, which was presented and paid in the same way as was the draft in the first cause of action. Copies of all the papers are attached to the complaint in the same way as the first cause of action. The total amount claimed to be due under both drafts from defendant is $7,262.13. The defendant in its answer admits the obtaining of the letter of credit for $4,500 and that it executed the receipt and obligation as alleged. It denies upon information and belief that Georges Vemian drew upon the plaintiffs under the said letter of credit at three months' sight a draft for $4,500; denies knowledge or information sufficient to form a belief of the presentation of said draft to plaintiffs by John Munroe & Company; admits the notification set forth in the complaint, but denies that the documents referred to were delivered at defendant's request and denies the implication therein contained that in said alleged "trust receipt" the defendant receipted for actual merchandise; and alleges that said "trust receipt" only applies, if at all, to the documents received, "which said documents as hereinafter alleged being fraudulent, cannot create any legal or equitable obligation upon the defendant herein."

Defendant admits the notification and request to provide the funds to meet the draft; denies any knowledge that said draft was presented to plaintiffs for payment and that plaintiffs paid same; denies that it "neglected" to provide the plaintiffs with the amount of the said draft and admits it has not paid plaintiffs, although duly demanded, the sum of $4,516.88 claimed by plaintiffs, representing the amount of said draft and plaintiffs' commissions. Defendant's answer to plaintiffs' second cause of action is similar to the answer to the first cause of action. "For a complete defense" to each cause of action defendant alleges that all the terms and conditions stated in the letter of credit set forth in the complaint were not and have not been duly performed at any time prior to or since the alleged acceptance and alleged payment of the draft; that all the terms and conditions upon which the guaranty worked alleged to have been executed by the defendant have not been performed or complied with at any time prior to or since the alleged payment of the said draft; that none of the merchandise described in the complaint has ever been shipped or attempted to be shipped by any one and never has been received by the defendant; that the alleged bill of lading is fraudulent, void and of no effect, the same being a forgery, never issued by the Cunard Steamship Company, Ltd., and never signed by any officer, agent or employee of said company; and said company never acquired possession of any of the merchandise described in said forged bill of lading and never shipped any of the said merchandise; that the alleged guaranty is and was at the date of the execution of the same and is now wholly without consideration; that at the time of the alleged issuance of the letter of credit, the alleged acceptance and payment of the draft the plaintiffs had in their possession the knowledge and information that said Georges Vemian, the drawer of said draft and who forged the bill of lading, was dishonest and a criminal, and upon information and belief had been guilty of forgery similar in manner to the forgery committed in the transaction set forth in the complaint; that such knowledge was then unknown to the defendant, was not disclosed by the plaintiffs to defendant at the time of or prior to the issuance of the said letter of credit; that prior to the alleged payment of said draft the defendant having discovered the fraud and forgery above set forth, notified the plaintiffs thereof and demanded that said plaintiffs should not pay said draft; that plaintiffs refused to comply with said demand not to pay, assigning as reason therefor that they were advised by their attorneys that such refusal would only subject plaintiffs to an action to which no defense could be made; that upon information and belief "marine insurance including war risk" was never effected, and that the alleged policy of insurance set forth in the complaint is not a genuine document, but is, in its entirety, a forgery.

[About four pages of the opinion are here omitted.]

When the drafts with these specified documents were presented to the plaintiffs on October 13, 1922, by John Munroe & Company, the plaintiffs accepted the drafts payable at the Bank of America, on January 15, 1923. The shipping documents so obtained by plaintiffs were delivered to the defendant on October 14, 1922, as the trust receipt (Exhibit D) bearing that date acknowledged. The documents so delivered were held by the defendant for nearly six weeks without objection or criticism. Section 224 of the Negotiable Instruments Law allows but twenty-four hours to the drawee within which to act upon a draft presented for acceptance. The photostats clearly show that the documents were regular in form and appearance and were those prescribed by the credits. Upon acceptance by plaintiffs the drafts became current in the discount market, and, as the indorsements indicate, were transferred by John Munroe & Company to the First Federal Foreign Banking Association, and thereafter were presented by the Federal Reserve Bank in New York. The plaintiffs became bound by their acceptance to pay the drafts at maturity. . . . Vemian's alleged fraud in forging the shipping documents would have been no defense. . . . The execution and delivery of the trust receipt (Exhibit D) was an approval by defendant of the acceptance of the Vemian drafts under the credits. This trust receipt, as already pointed out, acknowledges the delivery of the bills of lading and refers to the acceptance of the plaintiffs under the first and second letters of credit. It also refers at the foot to the amount of the drafts, aggregating $7,235. No question was raised as to the regularity of the documents until six weeks after the delivery of this trust receipt. The trust receipt was a plain approval by defendant of plaintiffs' acceptance of the drafts. None of the matters pleaded in the so-called "complete defense" to the first and second causes of action is sufficient in law. The allegations pleaded in each of these "complete defenses" are either wholly irrelevant to the causes of action stated in the complaint or insufficient in law to constitute a defense. The documents submitted show that the plaintiffs accepted the Vemian drafts, which is all that they contracted to do, and having accepted them, the drafts being within the terms of the credit, the defendant's obligation to reimburse was fully established. There is no term or condition expressed in Exhibit A–2 to be performed by the plaintiffs. All of the obligations and covenants are those of the defendant. The plaintiffs were solely concerned with documents and the defendant expressly assumed all risk of Vemian's acts and absolved plaintiffs from responsibility for the genuineness or correctness of documents. Whether the merchandise was or was not shipped is a matter wholly between Vemian and the defendant. The allegation that the Exhibit A–2 by which defendant agreed to pay plaintiffs the amount of all drafts accepted by them under the letter of credit was without consideration is contradicted by the terms of the contract itself, which shows that the consideration for defendant's obligation to reimburse the plaintiffs was the issue of the credit to Vemian, which obligated the plaintiffs to honor drafts drawn within the terms of the credit. The credit having been issued and the plaintiffs having accepted the Vemian draft, the defendant is bound by its contract to reimburse the plaintiffs. Even without the express provisions of the credit agreements Exhibits A–2 and E–2, which relieve plaintiffs from all responsibility, plaintiffs would not have been responsible for the forged documents. . . . The defendant has failed to show facts sufficient to entitle it to defend and the motion for summary judgment is, therefore, granted, with ten dollars costs. Summary judgment granted, with costs. Order signed.

Ordered accordingly.

Compare CHABRIÈRES MOREL ET CIE *c.* MERCANTILE BANK, 1929 Marseille 1.100 (Commercial Court of Marseille), where the credit agreement preliminary to the issue of a confirmed credit covering a shipment of seeds contained a provision that the bank was not to be responsible for the regularity or genuineness of documents apparently in good order. Two bills of lading were presented to the bank on the same day, one genuine and the other forged, covering the same lot of seeds, the former naming a third party as consignee, and the latter naming the present buyer. There were at least three marked differences in the form and manner of signature on the two bills. The bank accepted the forged bill under the credit, and the buyer, having reimbursed the bank, sought to recover the amount paid. Judgment was given for the buyer. "The clause quoted did not relieve the bank from the duty of using care in the examination of documents."

CHAPTER II

Bills of Exchange

1. THE CONTRACT OF THE ACCEPTOR

A. Formal Aspects

BELTON NATIONAL BANK *v.* ARMOUR & CO.

United States Circuit Court of Appeals, Fifth Circuit, 1926

[11 *Federal Reporter* (*Second Series*), 929]

Foster, Circuit Judge. Plaintiff in error, hereafter called plaintiff, brought suit in the district court of Bell county, Tex., against defendant in error, hereafter called defendant, and the firm of Bassel Bros., to recover on five certain drafts, aggregating $51,039.20, drawn by said firm on defendant and discounted by plaintiff, which defendant had refused to accept and pay. The suit as to defendant was removed to the District Court for the Western District, on the ground of diversity of citizenship and that the controversy was separable. At the close of the case, the District Court directed a verdict in favor of defendant. Error is assigned to this.

It appears that in the early part of November, 1922, Bassel Bros. entered into an agreement to ship to defendant their entire output of Thanksgiving turkeys, including outside purchases, on a consignment basis, defendant to receive 5 per cent. commission. Drafts were to be drawn for shipment for the value of the turkeys, less the commission and certain charges. This contract was carried out with satisfaction to both parties. Later another agreement was made for what may be called Christmas turkeys, on the same basis, but with the change made by telegram that the drafts were to be drawn at a flat price of 40 cents per pound. This contract was also carried out with satisfaction, except as to the last five cars shipped. Some 17 cars were shipped under the first contract and 55 or 56 were shipped under the second. Negotiations for both of these contracts were had between Neal Bassel, representing his firm, and J. C. Orear, representing defendant. Prior to any shipment under the first contract, a letter was written to Bassel Bros. on November 8, 1922, signed Armour & Co., by J. C. Orear, the material part of which is this:

Referring to our visit with you yesterday, it is now our understanding that you are arranging to give us your entire output of Thanksgiving turkeys on consignment basis, and that you are expecting to have at least 10 cars, including outside purchases. It will be satisfactory with us for you to draw for 80 per cent. of the market value of these turkeys date of shipment, using the regular Urner-Barry quotations on Texas stock as your guide. These drafts will be taken up upon presentation, providing cars have been inspected by our inspector. If it is necessary to ship any cars that cannot be inspected by us, drafts will be taken up on receipt and inspection of the car at destination. However, if you will keep Mr. Nickerson, of the Fort Worth office, closely advised as to where and when your cars are ready to ship, he will arrange to have inspector on the ground in plenty of time.

With regard to the second contract, there was an exchange of telegrams as to the amount to be drawn for, terminating with a telegram of December 6, 1922, which is as follows:

Ar Union Stockyards Ills 1040 A Dec. 6 1922 Bassel Bros Belton, Tex. Answering while we would much prefer have you draw thirty eight on these drafts if absolutely necessary satisfactory draw forty give us as much advanced notice as possible on these cars now looks like market will be around fifty fifty two do not want to see it go too high J C Orear

Neal Bassel testified in substance that his firm was engaged in the produce business in 1922, and during that year they handled some 75 or 76 cars of turkeys through Armour & Co., amounting in value to between $800,000 and $1,000,000, all of which were inspected before shipment; that Orear, representing defendant, came to Belton, where his firm was doing business, about November 5th, and they arranged for the shipment of turkeys; that in the course of his conversations, before the letter of November 8th was written, he had a discussion with Orear as to whether he could finance the handling of the turkeys, and he asked Orear about a bank guaranty, and was told by him, "Well, Bassel, we can give you a bank guaranty, but we can give you a guaranty by Armour & Co., which is bigger than any bank, and you can take this to the Belton National Bank, or any other bank, and do business with them, and get any amount of money you want"; that at that time he was unable to finance the business without the aid of a bank and that he discussed that with Orear; that on receiving the letter of November 8th he called on Mr. James, president of the Belton National Bank, and asked him if he could finance the transaction, and told him that all the cars would be inspected by Armour & Co., as to quality and as to what they had agreed to do. After the receipt of the telegrams on the December business, he showed them to James and explained his agreement. James corroborates Bassel as to the exhibition of the letter and telegrams to him as president of the plaintiff, and also testifies his bank bought the drafts on the faith of the guaranty by Armour & Co. Orear denies that Bassel asked him for a bank guaranty, and denies that he told him he would give a written promise to pay the drafts on presentation, that he could take to the bank.

The letter and telegrams above quoted are susceptible of the construction that they were intended to guarantee the payment of Bassel Bros.' drafts drawn on defendant. If they were intended to be communicated to plaintiff, they constitute a contract between it and defendant to pay drafts drawn by Bassel Bros., and would have the same effect as a more formal letter of credit. In *Coolidge* v. *Payson*, 2 Wheat. 66, 4 L. Ed. 185, the Supreme Court said this: "Upon a review of the cases which are reported, this court is of opinion that a letter written within a reasonable time before or after the date of a bill of exchange, describing it in terms not to be mistaken, and promising to accept it, is, if shown to the person who afterwards takes the bill on the credit of the letter, a virtual acceptance binding the person who makes the promise." The doctrine thus announced has been followed in numerous cases, and we regard it as the law applicable to this case. See, also, *Border Nat. Bank* v. *Am. Nat. Bank* (C. C. A.) 282 F. 73.

With regard as to whether it was the intention of defendant that its letter and telegrams were to be communicated to plaintiff there was material conflict in the evidence, sufficient to go to the jury with proper instructions, and it was therefore error to direct a verdict in favor of the defendant. It follows that the judgment must be reversed, and the case remanded for a new trial.

Reversed.

In Ensign *v.* Clark Brothers Cutlery Company, 195 Missouri App. 584 (Kansas City Court of Appeals, 1917), a prospective buyer sent an employee to Watertown, Conn., to effect certain purchases. In order to facilitate negotiations, the buyer sent a telegram to his employee reading: "Will honor your draft fifteen hundred dollars telegram attached." The employee thereupon drew a draft for the amount named, and presented it to a bank with the telegram attached. The bank gave the employee full value for the draft, which subsequently was dishonored by the buyer. In an action by the bank against the buyer, it was held that the telegram was an unconditional acceptance of the draft.

In Wilson & Co. *v.* Niffenegger, 211 Mich. 311 (Supreme Court, 1920), a packing company sent a letter to a bank saying "It will be satisfactory for you to honor drafts against us by F. M. Sauer covering shipments of poultry, provided drafts have bill of lading or express receipts attached, until further notice." The bank showed this letter to defendant who thereupon took a draft from Sauer for a shipment of chickens, cashing the draft with the bank. The drawee packing company refused to honor the draft on the ground that Sauer already had been paid for the chickens. In a subsequent transaction defendant held back the amount of the Sauer draft in paying the packing company. In an action to recover, a judgment for defendant was affirmed. At the time presented for payment the draft was an accepted draft by virtue of the earlier letter to the bank.

Compare Bank of Ireland *v.* Archer, 11 M. & W. 383 (Exchequer Chamber, 1843). The drawers, having shipped a quantity of corn to defendants, proposed to draw on them against it, and defendants agreed to the arrangement. The plaintiff bank discounted the draft in reliance on this agreement, but defendants then refused to honor the draft. In an action on the bill as accepted Parke, B., said:

"The point reserved by my Brother Coltman in this case was, whether a parol promise to accept a foreign bill of exchange before it was drawn, amounted to an acceptance, such promise having been communicated to the indorsees, the plaintiffs, and the bill having been taken by them on the faith of it. The learned Judge thought not; and we agree in this opinion, and think there should be no rule.

"The case of *Pillans* v. *Van Mierop* appears to be the authority on which the doctrine, that a person can be bound by a promise to accept a future bill, is rested. It is not quite clear from the report of that case, on what ground the defendant was held liable to the plaintiffs, the drawers; whether on his special contract with them to accept, or as actual acceptor. Some of the Judges rest his liability on the ground of special contract, considering that the doctrine of *nudum pactum* does not apply to written or to mercantile contracts; a doctrine which is now entirely exploded. Mr. Justice Yates, as well as Lord Mansfield, expresses an opinion that he was liable, on the authority of the cases which laid it down that an acceptance need not be on the bill itself; not adverting to the distinction between existing and non-existing bills. In Beawes' Lex Mercatoria, p. 466, pl. 112, a promise to accept is apparently put on the ground of a contract, for a breach of which an action lies, and not as being an actual acceptance. In *Pierson* v. *Dunlop* (Cowp. 571), the supposed rule, that a promise to honour was equivalent to an acceptance, was qualified by Lord Mansfield; and he said that it was not, unless accompanied with circumstances which might induce a third person to take the bill by indorsement; if there were such circumstances, it might amount to an acceptance, though the answer were contained in a letter to the drawer. His Lordship was then speaking of a promise to honour an existing bill; a doctrine which is not now disputed, the case of *Wynne* v. *Raikes* (5 East, 514) having established that a promise to the drawer, after a bill is drawn, operates as an acceptance in favour of an indorsee, such promise having not only been communicated to him, but made long after the indorsement. In this state of the authorities, it was not surprising that the case of *Johnson* v. *Collings* decided that a promise to accept a non-existing bill was no acceptance. Mr. Justice Le Blanc alludes to the qualification by Lord Mansfield of the previous doctrine, and supposes it to be meant to apply to non-existing bills only; which is inaccurate: and Lord Kenyon expresses what may be termed a strong opinion, that such a promise would not amount to an acceptance, even with the qualification that the bill is taken on the faith of it.

"This opinion, we believe, has been generally acquiesced in, and the doctrine is reasonable, simple, and convenient. For reason points out that, in order to constitute an acceptance, there ought to be a bill in existence which could be accepted; and to hold that the same act would be an acceptance or not, according to the subsequent contingency of the holder of the bill having notice of it, would introduce a strange anomaly and confusion into the relation of the parties to the bill, the drawee being an acceptor as to some and not as to other indorsees. No subsequent case appears to have cast any doubt upon the propriety of Lord Kenyon's dictum. That of Lord Chief Justice Gibbs, in the case of *Miln* v. *Prest*, which was quoted in support of this application, amounts, according to the report in 4 Campb. 393, merely to this, that the authority of

Johnson v. *Collings* was directly in point, there being no evidence of any communication to the plaintiff of the promise to accept. The report in Holt's Nisi Prius Cases is evidently inaccurate.

"It is said, however, that in America the rule is otherwise; and if it had appeared from the decisions in other countries, that this was a part of the law merchant, we should have given due weight to them. In different countries, however, a different rule seems to prevail; and even in America, it appears, from Mr. Justice Story's book on Bills of Exchange, s. 249, p. 275, that in order to constitute an acceptance, the promise is required to be in writing, describing the bill to be drawn in terms not to be mistaken, so as to identify it, and distinguish it from all others, and that the bill should be drawn in a reasonable time afterwards; — circumstances which do not occur in this case."

Compare Secs. 134 and 135 of the Uniform Negotiable Instruments Law with Sec. 17 (2a) of the Bills of Exchange Act and with Art. 25 of the Geneva Law.

LEMON IMPORTING CO. *v.* GARFIELD SAVINGS BANK CO.

NEW YORK SUPREME COURT, APPELLATE TERM, 1919

[105 *New York Miscellaneous Reports*, 627]

DELEHANTY, J. The question presented herein is one of law, there being no dispute as to the facts which were stipulated and are briefly as follows:

On July 28, 1916, one Grice sent a telegram to plaintiff asking for a quotation on a brand of lemons known in the trade as "Fancy Verdillis 300." In reply thereto plaintiff wired Grice on July 29, 1916, as follows:

We offer two hundred boxes 300 size, same quality as last, seven fifty. Balance to fill car 360 size, same brand six dollars. Must have quick answer. Bank guarantee.

On July 31, 1916, plaintiff wired Grice as follows:

Telegram received. To-morrow our last lemon sale this week. If we receive your order and bank guarantee on time will accept one car, 360, six dollars.

On the same day in answer to that offer Grice wired plaintiff as follows:

Book United Fruit & Vegetable Co. Amber Mob Ike (translated means 250 boxes 360 fancy Verdillis), same brand. Wiring guarantee.

Later on same day plaintiff wired Grice as follows:

Telegram received late. We have only 120 boxes same brand. Will substitute balance for brands equally good. On receipt of bank guarantee will ship car.

Pursuant to the foregoing correspondence, defendant on July 31, 1916, wired plaintiff as follows:

Will honor your draft on United Fruit and Vegetable Company for fifteen hundred dollars.

On August 3, 1916, plaintiff sent defendant a sight draft, bill of lading attached, for the lemons referred to. On August 8, 1916, Grice notified plaintiff that the lemons had arrived but were found on examination to be imperfect, not what had been ordered and that he could not use them. On the same day plaintiff wired Grice as follows:

> Car arrived Cleveland last Friday. You should have informed us sooner. Absolutely refuse to make allowance. If car intact forward to G. Catanzara Sons Pittsburg. Produce Yards Delivery. Our market today for 360, fifty cents to a dollar higher. Rush answer.

On same day Grice wired plaintiff that car had been diverted to Pittsburg as directed. Thereupon defendant refused to accept the draft in question and returned same to plaintiff. The lemons were sold by Catanzara Sons at a loss of $430.92, for which amount the learned court below directed judgment against defendant with interest and costs, and from which judgment defendant appeals. It was agreed by the parties hereto for the purpose of this suit that the shipment of lemons in question was not up to standard and did not conform to the contract and that the United Fruit and Vegetable Company, defendant's client, was justified in refusing to accept the same. The basis of this action is section 223 of the Negotiable Instruments Law which provides that: "An unconditional promise in writing to accept a bill before it is drawn is deemed an actual acceptance in favor of every person who, upon the faith thereof, receives the bill for value." This provision of law is a re-enactment of 2 Revised Statutes (6th ed.), 1160, section 8, and has been construed as not penal in nature and entitled to a reasonable interpretation with a view to accomplish the purpose intended. *Louisiana Nat. Bank* v. *Schuchardt*, 15 Hun, 405, 409. In the consideration of the case at bar it is well to remember that the original parties to the transaction in question are the only parties now involved. No intervening rights such as innocent holder for value or third parties' claims are concerned. Plaintiff was the drawer of the draft, the United Fruit and Vegetable Company the drawee and defendant the acceptor thereof. In view of the conceded fact that the lemons in question were not up to standard and failed to conform to the contract and that the United Fruit and Vegetable Company was justified in refusing to accept same in performance thereof, it must be held that plaintiff did not "receive the bill for value." This is clearly apparent not alone from the facts stipulated but from the very intent of the parties based thereon. The acceptance and honoring of the draft were dependent on plaintiff's performance of its contract in the terms mentioned and its conceded failure so to do strips the transaction of any consideration moving to defendant by plaintiff which would justify the claim of plaintiff as a holder of the draft for value.

It follows that the judgment appealed from must be reversed and judgment directed for defendant on the merits with costs.

Guy and Bijur, JJ., concur.

Judgment reversed, with costs.

In CITIZENS BANK *v.* HENRY J. PERKINS CO., 250 Mass. 156 (Supreme Judicial Court, 1924), a fruit dealer in Massachusetts wrote to a Georgia bank promising to honor drafts drawn by a certain buyer covering peaches purchased for the account of the dealer. In replying, the bank wrote: "You, of course, know that we expect immediate payment upon presentation regardless of arrival or condition of fruit. Any differences or adjustments are to be made between you and Mr. James, and payment of drafts not delayed nor based upon same, as the bank is a party neither to the purchase nor the sale of the fruit."

EXCHANGE BANK OF ST. LOUIS *v.* RICE

MASSACHUSETTS SUPREME JUDICIAL COURT, 1867

[98 *Massachusetts Reports*, 288]

GRAY, J. The plaintiffs in this action seek to recover the amount of a bill of exchange for $3300. The material facts appearing by the report of the judge before whom (a trial by jury having been waived) the case was tried in the superior court are as follows:

The bill was drawn by John P. Hill at St. Louis on the 8th of March 1865 upon the defendants at Boston, "against twelve bales of cotton," (as was stated in a memorandum at the foot of the bill), and payable in thirty days from date to the order of Pitman & Co., and on the day of its date was discounted by the plaintiffs and indorsed to them by the payees. On the same day Hill wrote to the defendants informing them of the drawing of the bill and the forwarding of the cotton. On the 14th of March the defendants wrote in reply, saying, "Your shipment of twelve bales of cotton will receive due attention. Bill of lading not at hand. Your draft for $3300 is excessive, particularly as we shall have no margin on previous shipments as the market now looks. We will honor the same, but shall expect you, on receipt of this, to make us shipment of cotton to cover the margin." On the 15th of March the bill was presented by the plaintiffs to the defendants and noted for non-acceptance, and the defendants wrote to Hill that this had been done because they had received no bill of lading, and added, "When bill of lading is received, will accept draft." The bill of lading was in terms for the delivery of the twelve bales to the defendants or order, and was sent on the 12th and received by them on the 17th of March. The defendants, on the same day, wrote to Hill and to Pitman & Co. that they should not honor the bill unless additional cotton should be sent them to meet unaccepted bills, and informed Pitman & Co. that they had telegraphed to Hill; and on the same day Pitman & Co. wrote to the defendants that they were advised of the protest for non-acceptance of this bill. On the 22d of March the defendants' letter of March 15 was shown by Pitman & Co. to the plaintiffs, who procured of them the letter and the duplicate bill of lading, and on the 27th of March again presented the bill, with these documents, to the defendants, and protested it for non-acceptance, and on the 10th of April for non-payment. The defendants subsequently received the cotton, sold it, and credited Hill with the amount in general account.

The judge found, as matter of fact, that the plaintiffs, in discounting the bill, relied on the memorandum thereon, as well as on the names of the parties thereto; and held, as matter of law, that the defendants by their letter of March 15, whether taken by itself or in connection with the whole correspondence, absolutely promised to accept the bill, when the bill of lading should be received; and that upon the receipt of the bill of lading the defendants became liable as acceptors of the bill; and gave judgment for the plaintiffs for the amount thereof, with interest. The defendants alleged exceptions.

It has long been well settled, though it has often been regretted that it should not originally have been held otherwise, that, in the absence of any statute prescribing a different rule, the acceptance of a bill of exchange need not be by writing upon the bill itself, but that a separate written or even oral promise by the drawee to the holder binds the drawee as an acceptance which he is estopped to deny. *Wilkinson* v. *Lutwidge*, 1 Stra. 648. *Lumley* v. *Palmer*, Cas. temp. Hardw. 74; S. C. 2 Stra. 1000. *Ward* v. *Allen*, 2 Met. 53. *Wells* v. *Brigham*, 6 Cush. 6. It is equally well settled that an acceptance, otherwise sufficient, is not the less so by reason of a previous refusal to accept and protest for non-acceptance. *Grant* v. *Shaw*, 16 Mass. 344. And an acceptance may be conditional, and become absolute when the condition is performed. *Coolidge* v. *Payson*, 2 Wheat. 72. *United States* v. *Bank of the Metropolis*, 15 Pet. 394, 395. *Grant* v. *Shaw*, 16 Mass. 344.

Under what circumstances a promise to accept, contained in a letter to the drawer, will enure as an acceptance to the benefit of the holder, is a question upon which there has been a divergence between the English and American courts since the time of Lord Mansfield.

Where drawees were sought to be charged as acceptors of a bill of exchange by reason of a letter from them to the plaintiffs, to whom the bill had been previously indorsed, Lord Mansfield said, "It has been truly said as a general rule that the mere answer of a merchant to the drawer of a bill, saying he will duly honor it, is no acceptance, unless accompanied with circumstances which may induce a third person to take the bill by indorsement." *Pierson* v. *Dunlop*, Cowp. 573, 574. And in an action against the drawees as acceptors on a promise to accept in a letter written to the drawer before the drawing of the bill sued on, he said, "There is no doubt but an agreement to accept may amount to an acceptance, and it may be couched in such words as to put a third person in a better condition than the drawer. If a man, to give credit to another, makes an absolute promise to accept his bill, the drawer or any other person may show such promise upon the exchange, to get credit, and a third person, who should advance his money upon it, would have nothing to do with the equitable circumstances which might arise between the drawer and acceptor." *Mason* v. *Hunt*, 1 Doug. 299. See also *Pillans* v. *Van Mierop*, 3 Burr. 1667, 1669, 1672, 1673.

These cases were formerly supposed to have settled the rule in England to be that a promise to accept even a bill not yet drawn would sustain an action by one who afterwards took the bill on the credit of the promise. Beawes Lex Merc. Bills of Exchange, pl. 112. Kyd on Bills (1st Am. ed.) 72, 74. Byles on Bills (6th ed.) 145. But from the time of Lord Kenyon the tendency of the English decisions has been to hold any promise to accept a non-existing bill of exchange insufficient to support an action by an indorsee of the bill. *Johnson* v. *Collings*, 1 East, 98. *Ex parte Bolton*, 2 Deacon, 537; S. C. 3 Mont. & Ayrt. 367. Opinions of English counsel in 2 Story, 219, 220. *Bank of Ireland* v. *Archer*, 11 M. & W. 383.

On the other hand, in the case of a promise to accept a bill already drawn, the later decisions in England have established the rule there to be that such a promise, oral or written, either to the drawer or the payee, is an acceptance upon which an indorsee who has taken the bill before the making of such promise, and of course therefore not upon the faith of it, may maintain an action; even if the drawer does not receive the letter containing the promise until after the bill becomes due, or is dead before it is written. *Wynne* v. *Raikes*, 5 East, 514. *Rees* v. *Warwick*, 2 B. & Ald. 115. *Fairlee* v. *Herring*, 3 Bing. 625; S. C. 11 Moore, 520. *Billing* v. *Devaux*, 3 M. & G. 565; S .C. 4 Scott N. R. 175. *Grant* v. *Hunt*, 1 C. B. 44. These cases are all founded upon that of *Powell* v. *Monnier*, 1 Atk. 611, in which Lord Hardwicke is reported to have held that a letter written by the drawee to the drawer, saying that the bill should be duly honored and placed to his debit, showed an acceptance upon which a previous indorsee might maintain an action. It is to be observed that it does not appear, either by the report in Atkins, or by that since published with additions from Lord Hardwicke's own note book in West Ch. 68, that any objection on the ground that the promise was not made or communicated to the plaintiffs was raised or considered; and that the earlier cases to which Lord Hardwicke referred as conclusive authorities were of oral or written promises made directly to the holder. If the decision went as far as has been understood in the later English cases, it is somewhat remarkable that it was not cited in any of the cases before Lord Mansfield, and that he laid down a narrower rule.

In *Coolidge* v. *Payson*, 2 Wheat. 66, Chief Justice Marshall, who delivered the unanimous opinion of the supreme court of the United States, affirming the judgment of Mr. Justice Story in 2 Gallison, 238, after carefully examining the opinions of Lord Mansfield, and alluding to a distinction suggested between bills drawn before and after the date of the promise, said, "The court can perceive no substantial reason for this distinction. The prevailing inducement for considering a promise to accept as an acceptance is, that credit is thereby given to the bill. Now this credit is given as entitrely by a letter written before the date of the bill as by one written afterwards. It is of much importance to merchants that this question should be at rest. Upon a review of the cases which are reported, this court is of opinion that a letter written within a reasonable time before or after the date of a bill of exchange, describing it in terms not to be mistaken, and promising to accept it, is, if shown to the person who afterwards takes the bill on the credit of the letter, a virtual acceptance binding the person who makes the promise." This rule has since been repeated in the same words by the supreme court, and by Justices Story, McLean and Nelson on the circuit. *Schimmelpennich* v. *Bayard*, 1 Pet. 284. *Boyce* v. *Edwards*, 4 Pet. 121. *Wildes* v. *Savage*, 1 Story, 27. *Russell* v. *Wiggin*, 2 Story, 234–237. *Bayard* v. *Lathy*, 2 McLean, 463. *Cassel* v. *Dows*, 1 Blatchf. C. C. 341. As applied to non-existing bills, it corresponds with the rule previously stated and since affirmed by this court, and by the supreme court of New York. *Wilson* v. *Clements*, 3 Mass. 10, 11. *Storer* v. *Logan*, 9 Mass. 58, 59. *M'Evers* v. *Mason*, 10 Johns. 207. *Goodrich* v. *Gordon*, 15 Johns. 6. *Parker* v. *Greele*, 2 Wend. 545; S. C. 5 Wend. 414. *Carnegie* v. *Morrison*, 2 Met. 406. *Murdock* v. *Mills*, 11 Met. 5. It is true that all these cases were of promises to accept non-existing bills, and did not necessarily involve any question upon promises to accept bills already drawn. But the general rule laid down by the supreme court of the United States in terms includes letters written within a reasonable time "before or after" the bill; is adopted in the same form by Chancellor Kent in his Commentaries; has been applied with all its limitations, as a rule of the general law merchant, to promises of the drawee to the drawer to accept bills already drawn, by the supreme courts of New York and New Jersey, and, with some qualification, Pennsylvania; and has been affirmed in New York and Missouri, and perhaps in other states, by statute. 3 Kent Com. (1st ed.) 55; (6th ed.) 84. *Ontario Bank* v. *Worthington*, 12 Wend. 593. *Bank of Michigan* v. *Ely*, 17 Wend. 510, 511. *Oderman* v. *Hoboken City Bank*, 1 Vroom, 68. *Howland* v. *Carson*, 15 Penn. State, 453. *Steman* v. *Harrison*, 42 Penn. State, 49. Rev. Sts. of N. Y. (5th ed.) pt. 2, c. 4, tit. 2, §§ 6–10. Gen. Sts. of Missouri, c. 86, §§ 1–5. The only American case to which we have been referred, in which an action has been maintained by the holder of a bill upon a separate promise to accept, made not to him, after he took the bill, is that of *Read* v. *Marsh*, 5 B. Monr. 8.

The rule generally adopted by the American courts in such a case is analogous to that by which the signer of a letter of credit has been held liable to those drawing bills or advancing money upon the faith of it. Molloy, bk. 2, c. 10, § 36. *Pillans* v. *Van Mierop*, 3 Burr. 1663. *Boyce* v. *Edwards*, 4 Pet. 111. *Russell* v. *Wiggin*, 2 Story, 213. *Carnegie* v. *Morrison*, 2 Met. 381. *Barney* v. *Newcomb*, 9 Cush. 45. *In re Agra & Masterman's Bank*, Law Rep. 2 Ch. 397.

The difference of opinion between the American and the English courts upon a question of commercial law, affecting the right of action upon negotiable instruments which pass freely between the two countries, is much to be regretted. But in view of the peculiar importance of maintaining consistency and harmony in the decisions of the various courts, state and national, throughout the United States, it is clearly our duty to follow the rule deliberately announced by the supreme court of the United States more than half a century ago, and ever since recognized and affirmed by the American authorities, with hardly an exception. The American rule has the advantages of being uniform in its application to all promises to accept a particular bill, not made to the holder or written on the very bill, whether made before or after it is drawn; and of restricting within the narrowest limits the anomalous doctrine of liability to an action upon negotiable paper, by reason of anything not appearing on the face of the paper itself.

In this case, the bill of exchange, when negotiated to the plaintiffs, was not accompanied by the bill of lading of the goods consigned to the defendants. The memorandum at the foot of the bill of exchange, that it was drawn against twelve bales of cotton, can have no more effect to charge the defendants as acceptors, than the mere signature of the drawer, which of itself always implies a promise by him that he has funds in the hands of the drawee. The letter of March 15, having been written after the plaintiffs took the bill of exchange now sued on, and not addressed to them, did not make the defendants liable to them as acceptors of the bill. The ruling of the superior court was therefore erroneous, and, as it appears to have been based exclusively upon the assumption that the defendants were liable as acceptors, its finding must be set aside.

Upon the question whether the defendants, by reason of the subsequent receipt of the bill of lading and of the cotton therein mentioned, or of any other facts which were or might be proved, can be held liable in any other form, and, if so, for what amount, no ruling appears to have been made by the court below, and no opinion is expressed by this court.

Exceptions sustained.

In COLCORD *v.* BANCO DE TAMAULIPAS, 181 App. Div. 295 (New York Supreme Court, Appellate Division, 1918), a draft on defendant was presented to plaintiff for purchase. Plaintiff wired defendant asking if it would pay the draft. Defendant replied, saying "Draft . . . is good." It was held that this did not constitute an acceptance, as it meant merely that the drawer "then had on deposit with defendant at least the sum of 5,000 Mexican dollars, but gave the [plaintiff] no right to assume that defendant would hold the funds to meet the draft or would itself accept or pay the draft. On the contrary, the very form of the reply . . . was sufficient to put the [plaintiff] on its guard."

LAWLESS *v.* TEMPLE

MASSACHUSETTS SUPREME JUDICIAL COURT, 1925

[254 *Massachusetts Reports*, 395]

PIERCE, J. This is an action by the payee of a bill of exchange against the drawee. The bill is as follows:

Natick, Sept. 24, 1923.

Maurice E. Temple
Please pay to the order of Hazel Lawliss $351.50/100 three hundred and fifty one dollars & 50/100

Norris J. Temple
Maurice E. Temple

The answer raised the question of the sufficiency of the acceptance under G. L. c. 107, § 155, which is as follows: "The acceptance of a bill is the signification by the drawee of his assent to the order of the drawer. The acceptance must be in writing and signed by the drawee. It must not express that the drawee will perform his promise by any other means than the payment of money." The specific contention of the defendant is that the mere signature of the name of the drawee on the bill cannot fulfil the requirement of the statute that the signification of the assent of the drawee must be in writing and must also be signed. Before the passage of the negotiable instruments act, an oral acceptance of an existing bill of exchange was generally valid in this country and formerly was so in England. *Putnam National Bank* v. *Snow*, 172 Mass. 569, and cases cited at page 576. The reason for the adoption of the rule requiring acceptance in writing, like the underlying reason for the statute of frauds and similar statutes, "is that sound policy requires some substantial evidence of the contract and more reliable in its nature than the statement or recollection of witnesses." *Selma Savings Bank* v. *Webster County Bank*, 182 Ky. 604; 2 Am. L. R. 1136. See *Clarke* v. *Cock*, 4 East, 57, 72.

The common practice before the act was to write the word "accepted" on the face of the bill, followed by the signature of the acceptor. *Barnet* v. *Smith*, 30 N. H. 256; 64 Am. Dec. 290. But such was not necessary, as Sewall, J., said in *Storer* v. *Logan*, 9 Mass. 55 at page 59: "An acceptance entered upon a bill generally, or the blank endorsement of the name of the drawee, holds him absolutely as the acceptor; and no conditions or stipulations, which he may have connected with his acceptance, unless expressed upon the bill, will avail him against an endorsee or payee, to whom the bill has been negotiated, and who had received the bill as accepted, without notice of the conditions."

It was said by Cowen, J., in *Spear* v. *Pratt*, 2 Hill, 582, in considering the legal valuation of the mere signature by the drawee on the bill, under a statute of New York which required the acceptance to be in writing and signed by the acceptor or his agent, "The acceptance in question was, as we have seen, declared by the law merchant to be both a writing and signing. The statute contains no declaration that it should be considered less. An endorsement must be in writing and signed; yet the name alone is constantly holden to satisfy the requisition." . . .

We are of opinion that under G. L. c. 107, § 155, a drawee may be charged as acceptor although he writes merely his name upon the bill, and that any one taking the bill has the right to fill up a blank acceptance on the same principle that any holder may fill up a blank endorsement. *Storer* v. *Logan*, *supra*, *Spear* v. *Pratt*, *supra*.

The instrument in question was legally accepted. It follows in accordance with the terms of the stipulation that judgment is to be "entered for the plaintiff for the full amount of the bill and interest thereon from the date of demand as set forth in the second count."

So ordered.

Compare Sec. 132 of the Uniform Negotiable Instruments Law with Sec. 17 (2a) of the Bills of Exchange Act and with Art. 25 of the Geneva Law.

LOCKHART *v.* MOSS

St. Louis Court of Appeals, 1893

[53 *Missouri Appellate Reports*, 633]

The cause was tried in the circuit court without the intervention of a jury. The evidence tended to prove that the order sued on was given in payment of a cow sold and delivered by the respondent, was drawn upon the appellant by Isaac Cardwell, who was then engaged in doing work for appellant, and was expressed in language, to-wit: "Please pay to the order of James Lockhart the amount of $18, and charge to the account of."

The evidence further tended to prove that this order was taken by the respondent to the store owned by the appellant and handed to his clerk or agent, who took it and said it could not be paid until next pay day; that the order was never returned to the respondent, although demanded by him when he had a settlement of his running account at the store owned by the appellant; that the amount of the order was deducted by the appellant when he subsequently settled with the drawer, Isaac Cardwell, but no part of the amount drawn for was allowed the respondent on his said settlement with appellant. It may be conceded that the order sued on is embraced in the definition of bills of exchange, the proof showing that it was an unconditional written order by one person on another for the payment of a certain sum of money to a third person or his order (Tiedeman on Commercial Paper, sec. 2, and notes); and that, therefore, the rights of the payee (respondent) are determined by the provisions of our statutes as to the liability of acceptors in his suit against the drawee. While the general statutory rule requires acceptances to be in writing (Revised Statutes, 1889, sec. 719) in order to charge any person as acceptor of a bill of exchange, another section (Revised Statutes, 1889, sec. 724) prescribes a modification of the requirement as to writing, when the drawee "shall refuse * * * within such period as the holder may allow, to return the bill accepted or non-accepted to the holder." In such cases the drawee shall be deemed to have accepted the bill. Under the facts in this case there was ample evidence to meet this statutory exception to the rule as to the necessity of a written acceptance of the order or bill of exchange drawn upon appellant.

[The balance of the opinion is omitted.]

Note also Harvey *v.* Martin, as reported in 1 Campbell 425 (1807). Plaintiff transmitted a bill by post to defendant drawee, asking him to accept and hand it over to plaintiff's agent in London, which was the usual mode of dealing between the parties. Hearing nothing of the bill from his agent, plaintiff wrote to defendant remonstrating with him for the delay. The defendant answered that he had retained the bill because he had once meant to accept it, which he now declined doing. In an action on the bill Lord Ellenborough said: "This is clearly an acceptance. If a bill is left for the express purpose of being accepted, and is retained by the drawee, such retention is as much an acceptance as if he had written his name upon the face of it."

In WISNER *v.* FIRST NATIONAL BANK, 220 Pa. 21 (Supreme Court, 1908), it was held that the presentation of a bill for acceptance is a demand for acceptance which, if the bill is retained, implies a demand for its return if acceptance is refused; failure to return therefore amounts to acceptance.

BAILEY & CO. *v.* SOUTHWESTERN VENEER CO.

ARKANSAS SUPREME COURT, 1916

[126 *Arkansas Reports*, 257]

I. W. Saxon was indebted to appellant in the sum of $84.96, and on the 22d day of March, 1915, gave an order drawn on appellees for said sum in payment of said indebtedness. This order was immediately presented to appellees for acceptance. They did not accept it in writing, but stated to the appellant that the order was all right. Subsequently thereto and within a few days, they confirmed the oral acceptance of the order over telephone. Later, they refused to pay the order. On the 12th day of April thereafter appellant demanded a return of the order. Appellees stated that the order had been thrown in the waste basket and burned up. The return of the order was refused.

The record fails to disclose why the order was thrown into the waste basket and burned. No explanation appears in the record as to why appellees refused to pay it. The order was never paid by either I. W. Saxon or appellees.

This cause was tried in the circuit court on appeal and after the evidence was closed, the court gave the following peremptory instruction to the jury:

"Gentlemen of the jury, under the law and testimony in this case, you are instructed to return a verdict for the defendant."

Thereupon the jury returned in open court the following verdict: "We, the jury, find for the defendants. V. O. Richey, Foreman."

Appellant filed his motion for a new trial, which was overruled. Judgment was rendered on the verdict, and this cause was brought here on appeal.

HUMPHREYS, J. (after stating the facts). Section 126 of Act 81 of the Acts of Arkansas, 1913, known as the Law of Negotiable Instruments, defines a bill of exchange as "an unconditional order in writing, addressed by one person to another, signed by the person giving it, requiring the person to whom it is addressed, to pay on demand or at a fixed or determinable future time a sum certain in money to order or bearer."

So far as disclosed in this record, the order in question in form and substance conforms to this definition and is an inland bill of exchange. By another section of the same act, a written acceptance is necessary to bind the drawee. By still another section, if the drawee destroys the bill he will be deemed to have accepted the same. Section 137, Act 81, Acts of Arkansas, 1913.

The evidence in this case is undisputed that appellees destroyed this bill and are silent as to why they did so. No excuse is rendered by them for not paying the order. Certainly it is not the privilege of a drawee to put the holder to sleep by an oral acceptance, then afterward to destroy the order or bill of exchange and refuse to pay same without rendering any kind or character of explanation or excuse, for destroying it.

An accidental destruction of the bill could not amount to an acceptance, but a wilful destruction of the bill would. Under all the circumstances in this case, we are of the opinion that the question of fact as to why the order was destroyed should have been submitted to the jury under proper instructions. Throwing the order in the waste basket and permitting it to burn and refusing to pay it without explanation, after having orally accepted same, indicates a negligent and reckless manner of handling bills of exchange. If wilful, then appellee herein became responsible. For this error, this case must be reversed and remanded for a new trial. It is so ordered.

In First National Bank *v.* Whitmore, 177 Fed. 397 (Circuit Court of Appeals, Eighth Circuit, 1910), four sight drafts on the president of a bank were forwarded to the bank for collection. The president absconded. The drafts were not returned, and it did not appear what became of them. A claim against the estate of the drawee was disallowed on the ground that the drafts were presented for payment and not for acceptance.

Compare Sec. 137 of the Uniform Negotiable Instruments Law with Sec. 17 (2b) of the Bills of Exchange Act and with Art. 25 of the Geneva Law.

SMITH *v.* ABBOT

King's Bench, 1741

[2 *Strange's Reports*, 1152]

The defendant accepted a bill of exchange to pay it when goods consigned to him, and for which the bill was drawn, were sold. And the plaintiff counted upon the custom of merchants. After a verdict for the plaintiff, it was moved in arrest of judgment; that this acceptance depending upon the contingency of the sale of the goods was not within the custom of merchants, or negotiable. But the court (upon consideration) held it good. For though the plaintiff might have refused to take such an acceptance, and have protested the bill; yet no body can say he might not submit to it. And it will affect trade, if factors are not allowed to use this caution, when bills are drawn before they have an opportunity to dispose of the goods: a man who is drawn upon to pay at ten days sight may accept for thirty, *Molloy* 304, though the other might protest the bill. *Salk.* 129. *Cumb.* 452.

In SMITH *v.* VERTUE, 30 L. J. C. P. 56 (Common Pleas, 1860), Erle, C. J., said:

"The question raised in this case is, whether the plaintiffs, the holders of a bill of exchange, are entitled to recover from the acceptors, upon an acceptance in these terms: 'Accepted payable, on delivering bill of lading, at the London and Westminster Bank'; the material fact which has led to the discussion being, that on the day of maturity the holders of that bill did not present it together with the bill of lading, but did on the following day; and the acceptors have contended that, under these circumstances, they are not liable. I am of a contrary opinion. The matter to be decided, according to my view of the case, is, the meaning of the qualified acceptance the defendants came under. I am clearly of opinion that it is a conditional acceptance. The words are, 'accepted payable on the delivery of the bill of lading'; and I think the defendants could not be called upon to pay unless the bill of lading was delivered to them. But they contend that the qualification was, that the bill of lading should be delivered to them on the day on which the bill of exchange came to maturity, and that if not delivered to them on that day, they should be entirely discharged from their liability. Now I do not so construe the words of the qualification which they have attached to their acceptance. It was within their power to have so stipulated. They might have said, 'Accepted payable, if on the day of maturity the bill of lading is delivered.' If they had so stipulated, I believe their contention would have been supported in any court. The question is not what it would be the duty of the holder to do if he wished to have recourse to the drawer; for the contract here is the contract of the acceptor. Now, as a general rule, the contract of the acceptor is to pay on the day when the bill falls due; or on any future day when the holder chooses to call upon him. He in effect, by his acceptance, says, 'I will have funds on the day of the maturity of the bill, and I will keep those funds ready for the holder of the bill when he shall choose to call for payment.' That being the case with respect to an ordinary acceptance, many, which have been held to be qualified acceptances, are of the same nature; for instance, where the acceptor has said, 'Accepted payable when I shall be in funds from such a ship,' or 'Accepted payable when I shall have received the proceeds of a certain cargo.' In all those cases, I am inclined to think that where the acceptor intended that the holder should understand that the acceptor's liability was postponed until the funds came to the acceptor's hands, the contract did not stipulate for a presentment on any particular day; but that under a contract so qualified the acceptor would be bound, when the funds did come to his hands, to keep them for some time at least, during which the holder might resort to him. I think the holder would not be bound to come to him on the particular day on which the funds came to the acceptor's hand; for it could not be reasonable so to bind the holder, it being obvious that the holder might have no notice when the funds did come to the acceptor's hands. I felt a great deal the force of the argument of the defendants' counsel, that the condition here is a condition to be performed by the holder of the bill. That the acceptance is of this nature, 'I will pay you provided you deliver to me the goods which are really the consideration for which I am making myself liable'; and there is no doubt that in mercantile transactions, — contracts for the purchase of a cargo, — time may very frequently be of the essence of the contract, and there may be a great deal of reason for the defendants saying, as is said in the second plea, 'we stipulated for receiving the cargo of clover-seed on the day of the maturity of the bill. As the cargo was not delivered to us on that day we have been disappointed in delivering it to our sub-vendee; our speculation, therefore, is entirely thwarted through your delay in presenting the bill of exchange with the bill of lading; and for those reasons we refuse to pay.' There seems to me to be a good deal of truth in that, but the inconvenience suffered does not, in my mind, authorize me to say that the words in which the defendants have expressed the qualification to their acceptance, are, 'We will pay you provided the cargo and the bill of exchange are delivered to us on the very day when the bill falls due, and if you fail to deliver them to us on that day we shall be entirely discharged.' I have, therefore, come to the conclusion, that the construction to be put upon this qualified acceptance is such as entitles the plaintiffs to our judgment."

H. MEYER & CO., LIMITED *v.* JULES DECROIX, VERLEY ET CIE

House of Lords, 1891

[*Law Reports,* [1891] *Appeal Cases,* 520]

Appeal from an order of the Court of Appeal (25 Q. B. D. 343) upon a special case of which the following are the material parts: —

The action was brought by the respondents as indorsees against the appellants as acceptors of a bill of exchange. The bill was drawn by L. Delobbel Flipo upon the defendants, a company carrying on the business of merchants and agents in London, as follows: —

"Roubaix, Sept. 12th, 1889.

"On October 31st after date pay to order Mr. L. Delobbel Flipo £778 4*s.* 2*d.* Value received." The defendants accepted the bill as follows: — Across the face of the bill they stamped in printed letters the words "Accepted payable at Alliance Bank London for H. Meyer and Co. Limited." Then followed the signatures of two directors of the defendant company countersigned by the secretary. Above the word "accepted" the defendants wrote the words "In favour of Mr. L. Delobbel Flipo only," and between those words and the word "accepted" they wrote "No. 28." The word "order" was struck out, but when or by whom did not appear.

Flipo on receiving the bill sent it to the plaintiffs, bankers at Lille in

France, who discounted it for him. It was not noticed by the plaintiffs that the bill had been accepted in any unusual form. They did not understand the English language, and their attention was not called to the form of the acceptance until after the dishonour of the bill at the Alliance Bank. It was not suggested that there is any custom amongst merchants upon which the acceptors could rely by which the addition of the words "In favour of Mr. L. Delobbel Flipo only" restricts the negotiability of the bill. The defendants relied solely on the provisions of the Bills of Exchange Act 1882. The question for the opinion of the Court was whether the plaintiffs were entitled to recover in the action. Judgment to be entered accordingly. The Divisional Court (Cave and A. L. Smith JJ.) held that the acceptance was a qualified acceptance, rendering the bill not negotiable, and gave judgment for the defendants, the present appellants. The Court of Appeal (Lord Esher M.R., Lindley and Bowen L.JJ.) reversed that decision and entered judgment for the plaintiffs, the present respondents, for the amount claimed (25 Q. B. D. 343).

Lord Halsbury L. C.: My Lords, I am of opinion that in this case the judgment of the Court of Appeal ought to be affirmed.

The action was brought by the plaintiffs, who are bankers at Lille, against the defendants, a limited company, carrying on business in London, upon a bill drawn by one Flipo, and accepted by the defendants. The only question is whether the bill, as accepted, was a negotiable instrument.

My Lords, I think it is impossible adequately to discuss the questions that arise in this case without having a facsimile of the bill before you. As to the form which purports to be the acceptance, no one can doubt that it was an ordinary mercantile form accepted and payable at the Alliance Bank with the proper signatures. But the question arises by reason of some words written above that which every mercantile man would look upon as the acceptance, and these words are "In favour of Mr. L. Delobbel Flipo only. No 28." These words are written above what I have called the acceptance, and I think any mercantile man would regard the words I have quoted as something apart from and not forming any portion of the acceptance itself. Nor is it easy to construe them as giving any qualification to the acceptance. I think much depends upon the exact form, an apparently complete stamped acceptance being found in its usual place on the bill.

A known mercantile instrument with the word "accepted" printed by a stamp, and in ordinary mercantile form, is sought to be cut down and qualified by some words written, it is true, on the same piece of paper, and above the acceptance, but which to my mind, even now that I have heard the argument, convey no particular meaning.

I am not certain that I understand what is the true meaning of the words, treated as separate writing, "In favour of Mr. L. Delobbel Flipo only." The form of the instrument, so far as the ordinary mercantile language is concerned, is quite intelligible. The bill is accepted, payable at a particular bank. It is suggested in the argument that it was intended that these words should tell the holder of the bill that it was only payable to the drawer himself. I am not certain that I can even now gather the meaning of the words themselves, but I am quite certain that any ordinary mercantile man, looking at the stamped acceptance in ordinary form and stamped across the bill, would assume that it was a clean acceptance, and that the words written above it, whatever the meaning they might convey to the immediate parties, would certainly not convey anything which would qualify or cut them down to a person who had nothing before him but the bill itself.

I am happy to think that the decision in this case involves nothing more than the proposition that if a person writes across a bill that which unqualified would, in ordinary course, import a clean acceptance of a bill, and intends to qualify its operation, he must do so by plain and intelligible language, and make that qualification sufficiently part of the acceptance itself to be intelligible in the ordinary course of business. If any other principle were laid down I think it would be fatal to the convenience of trade and the conduct of mercantile affairs, which demand for their transaction convenient and compendious forms, to which the law merchant has attached a definite meaning. Such ambiguous and inappropriate language as is sought to make here a qualification of an ordinary mercantile instrument would defeat the very object which mercantile instruments are intended to effect.

I move your Lordships that the judgment of the Court of Appeal be affirmed and this appeal dismissed with costs.

[Concurring opinions of Lords Watson and Herschell, and dissenting opinions of Lords Bramwell and Morris, are omitted.]

Compare Secs. 139–142 of the Uniform Negotiable Instruments Law and Secs. 19 and 44 of the Bills of Exchange Act with Arts. 26 and 27 of the Geneva Law.

COX *v.* TROY

King's Bench, 1822

[5 *Barnewall & Alderson's Reports*, 474]

Assumpsit upon a bill of exchange for 938*l.*, dated 20th May, 1820, drawn by Stephen and James Roch, upon the defendant and W. T. Robarts, since deceased, by the names and firm of Messrs. W. T. Robarts and Co. London, payable 61 days after sight to Michael Murphy, and indorsed by him to the plaintiffs, and alleged to have been accepted by the defendant and W. Tierney Robarts, payable at Messrs. Robarts, Curtis and Co. The first count stated these facts, and a presentment for payment when due, and refusal to pay at Messrs. Robarts, Curtis, and Co. The second count was on a general acceptance; and the third was special, stating that the bill was delivered to the defendant and W. T. Robarts, to determine, within a reasonable time, whether or not they would accept the same; and that they promised to take due care of the same, and return the same without defacing or spoiling it, which they did not do, but returned the same bill in a defaced and injured state. The declaration also contained the usual money counts. Plea, general issue. The cause was tried at the sittings after Trinity term 1821, before Abbott C. J. when a verdict was found for the plaintiffs, subject to the following case. It was admitted on the trial, that the bill of exchange mentioned in the declaration was drawn by Messrs. T. and J. Roch on the defendant and W. T. Robarts, since deceased, as stated in the declaration, and that the same was duly indorsed to the plaintiffs by the payee. The plaintiffs in London received the bill from Cork on the 24th May, 1820; and on the same day their clerk, by their directions, left it for acceptance at the defendant's counting-house in Old Broad-street, London, in the usual way. He did not call for it until Saturday the 27th May, upon which day one of the defendant's clerks delivered back the bill of exchange to him without any observations being made at the time. The words "24 May, 1820, at Messrs. Robarts, Curtis, and Co., W. T. Robarts and Co." were written upon the bill by the defendant, or some one authorized by him, whilst the same was in his custody; and the jury found by their verdict that the defendant and the said W. T. Robarts did accept the bill of exchange; but at the time the clerk redelivered the bill of exchange to the clerk of the plaintiffs, the words "24th May, 1820, at Messrs. Robarts, Curtis and Co., W. T. Robarts and Co." were inked and written over, so as with great difficulty to be deciphered. The defendant did not offer any evidence to account for the obliteration of the acceptance. The bill itself was not obliterated, or any part of it rendered illegible.

Abbott C. J. I am of opinion, that, in this case, the defendant is entitled to judgment. It is true, that the jury have found that he did accept the bill; but connecting that finding with the other facts of the case, it does not seem to me that it means more than that, at one period, the defendant, or some one in his behalf, did write an acceptance on it, and at that time was minded to accept it. The question will then be, whether, having that intention at the time, and having written his acceptance, he was at liberty, on an alteration of circumstances, to erase those words, before he delivered out the bill to the holder. Upon that question, there appears, in the books, to be some difference of opinion. In *Bentinck* v. *Dorrien*, Lawrence J. says, "When the general question shall arise, it will be worth considering how that which is not communicated to the holder, can be considered as an acceptance, while it is yet in the hands of the drawee, and where he obliterates it before any communication made to the holder." That expression was used after the decision, in the cases of *Thornton* v. *Dick* and *Trimmer* v. *Oddy*. And at a later period, in *Raper* v. *Birkbeck* (15 East, 20), Lord Ellenborough says, "I remember Pothier, in his treatise on bills of exchange, speaking of an acceptor who has put his signature to a bill, but has not parted with it, says, that before he does part with it, 'il peut changer de volonté, et rayer son acceptation'; *a fortiori*, then, a third person who cancels an acceptance by mistake, shall not be held thereby to make void the bill, but shall be at liberty to correct that mistake, in furtherance of the rights of the parties to the bill." The manner in which Lord Ellenborough quotes the treatise of Pothier, seems to indicate, that, at that time, he did not retain the opinion which he had delivered in the case of *Thornton* v. *Dick*. In a case like the present, which depends on the law merchant, the opinions of learned lawyers and the practice of foreign and commercial nations, though they cannot, strictly speaking, be quoted as authorities here, yet are entitled to very great weight and attention. When I find, therefore, that it is laid down in Pothier's treatise, that a party who has given an acceptance may erase it before the bill goes out of his hands, it affords a strong argument in support of the view which I take of the question. I think the rule there laid down is far better than the one contended for by the plaintiff. I cannot perceive how the holder of a bill, or any antecedent party, is prejudiced by it; for it is to him the same thing, whether when the drawees give it back, they deliver it to him unaccepted, or whether he finds that the drawees have withdrawn their acceptance, having at one time intended to accept it, but having subsequently changed their mind. Thinking, as I do, that no prejudice can arise to the holder, or any other parties to the bill, and that they are placed in precisely the same situation as if no acceptance was given, it seems to me, that it was competent for the acceptors to erase their acceptance before they delivered out the bill, and therefore that the defendant is entitled to our judgment.

[Concurring opinions of Bayley and Holroyd, JJ., are here omitted.]

BEST J. This is a question on the law merchant, and it is desirable, that that law should be the same in this as in every other commercial country. We ought, sitting here, to act according to the judgments of the courts in our own country, but in the absence of these authorities, we may with great advantage take into our consideration the opinions of learned writers on this point. There seems to be no authority in the English law, except the case of *Thornton* v. *Dick*. I agree with my Lord C. J., that Lord Ellenborough seems to have changed the opinion which he is reported to have delivered in that case. The passage in Molloy is probably applicable to the case where the bill has been delivered out, for it does not speak of cancellation, but revocation. But the authority of Pothier is expressly in point. That is as high as can be had, next to the decision of a court of justice in this country. It is extremely well known that he is a writer of acknowledged character; his writings have been constantly referred to by the Courts, and he is spoken of with great praise by Sir William Jones in his *Law of Bailments*, and his writings are considered by that author equal in point of luminous method, opposite examples, and a clear manly style, to the works of Littleton on the laws of this country. We cannot, therefore, have a better guide than Pothier on this subject. As to the opinion of Pardessus, I should understand him as rather speaking of bills delivered out, accepted, and not erased. That seems to me perfectly clear from the next passage, where he says, that though a man does accept a bill, still if he cancels that acceptance before he delivers it out, that is sufficient. But considering this as a question merely of common sense, and judging by analogy, is it not clear that the party is not bound in such a case as this? It may be said, that the defendants here ought to have shown that this was done by mistake. How is it possible to do that? The thing looks like a mistake. He may have written an acceptance, and afterwards find when he has written it, that it is on the wrong paper; and not meaning to accept that bill, he does that which shews, that it was his intention not to enter into such a contract. Nobody can be injured by it. When the bill goes back it is in as good a state as it came. The party is still placed in the same situation. It appears to me, therefore, not only on authority, but on the principles of common sense, that the defendant was not bound by this as an acceptance, and that our judgment ought to be in his favour.

Judgment for the defendant.

In WILDE *v.* SHERIDAN, 30 L. J. Q. B. 260 (Bail Court, 1852), a bill drawn in Norwich was accepted in London, and in an action by the drawer against the acceptor in Norwich the question of jurisdiction was raised. In holding that the County Court in Norwich had no jurisdiction, Coleridge, J., said: "One purpose of an indorsement is to pass the property in the bill, and that purpose is not effected until actual or constructive delivery. But the acceptor has no property in the bill either before or after acceptance; he must be supposed to receive the drawer's paper, and on it to write his promise without in any way altering the property in the bill. He may, indeed, before any communication to the drawer of the act done, revoke it, according to *Cox* v. *Troy* (*supra*) and modern authorities; but his promise, unless so revoked, is complete, and takes effect from the time when it was made."

In THE BANK OF VAN DIEMEN'S LAND *v.* THE BANK OF VICTORIA, L. R. 3 P. C. 526 (Privy Council, 1871), a draft was presented to the drawee for acceptance on Friday afternoon. The holder returned for the draft Saturday morning, but it had been mislaid, although actually accepted the day before. On Monday morning, before the holder called again for the bill, the drawee learned of circumstances affecting remittances that were expected to cover the bill, and cancelled the acceptance. It appears to have been assumed by all the parties and by the Privy Council that the cancellation was effective.

Compare Sec. 16 of the Uniform Negotiable Instruments Law with Sec. 21 of the Bills of Exchange Act and with Art. 29 of the Geneva Law.

B. OBLIGATIONS AND ADMISSIONS

THE NATIONAL CITY BANK OF CHICAGO *v.* THE NATIONAL BANK OF THE REPUBLIC

ILLINOIS SUPREME COURT, 1921

[300 *Illinois Reports*, 103]

Mr. Justice THOMPSON delivered the opinion of the court:

On January 4, 1915, the Jackes-Evans Manufacturing Company of St. Louis purchased a draft for $629.80 from the Broadway Savings Trust

Company of St. Louis drawn on the National City Bank of Chicago and payable to the order of the American Sheet and Tin Plate Company of Pittsburgh. On the same day the St. Louis company enclosed the draft in a letter addressed to the Pittsburgh company and deposited the letter in a mail-box. Andrew H. Manning rifled this mail-box and stole the draft. He substituted his name for the name of the American Sheet and Tin Plate Company. The alteration of the draft was done with such skill that it could not be detected by inspection. January 9 Manning appeared at Barnett Bros. jewelry store, in Chicago, and selected and agreed to purchase certain diamonds for $600. In payment of the purchase price Manning tendered to P. Barnett the altered draft for $629.80. Manning, in the presence of Barnett, endorsed the draft in blank, and Barnett, with the consent of Manning, took the draft to the drawee, the National City Bank of Chicago, and personally presented it to that bank for acceptance. The bank accepted the draft by writing across the face of the draft these words and figures: "Accepted, payable through Chicago clearing house 55055, Jan. 9, '15 — The National City Bank of Chicago, per G. D. Grim, Paying Teller." The drawee also entered in its records the following notation:

THE NATIONAL CITY BANK OF CHICAGO.

Certification Debit. $629.80

As shown by teller's stamp we certify & charge to the account of Broadway Sav. Trust Co. St. Louis, Makers number or date 5584 Order of Andrew H. Manning.

No. 55055 Asst payer Jan 9, 1915

Customer will please call at bank & exchange this slip for check described above.

N. C. B. 1/9/15

The draft, with the acceptance written thereon, was returned to Barnett, who returned to his place of business. Barnett delivered the diamonds, of the fair retail market value of $600, and $29.80 in money, and retained therefor, with the consent of Manning, the draft so endorsed and accepted. Thereafter Barnett endorsed the draft to the order of the National Bank of the Republic, and January 11, 1915, deposited the draft to the credit of his account with said bank. January 12, 1915, the National City Bank, the drawee, through the Chicago clearing house, paid the National Bank of the Republic the sum of $629.80 in payment of the draft. February 4, 1915, the National City Bank returned to its customer, the Broadway Savings Trust Company, this draft along with other canceled paper for January. The draft was received in St. Louis the following day, and the St. Louis bank at once notified its Chicago correspondent, the drawee, that the draft had been altered by changing the name of the payee, and asked that its account be credited with the amount of the draft. The drawee in turn notified the National Bank of the Republic of the alteration and asked for reimbursement, which was refused. The drawee voluntarily credited the account of the St. Louis bank with the amount of the draft and brought suit in the circuit court of Cook county against the National Bank of the Republic to recover the amount paid on this draft. Judgment was rendered in favor of the drawee, and that judgment was affirmed, on appeal, by the Appellate Court for the First District. That court granted a certificate of importance, and this appeal followed.

In its last analysis the question presented for decision is the liability of the acceptor of a negotiable instrument under section 62 of the Negotiable Instruments law, which provides: "The acceptor by accepting the instrument engages that he will pay it according to the tenor of his acceptance, and admits: 1. The existence of the drawer, the genuineness of his signature, and his capacity and authority to draw the instrument; and, 2. the existence of the payee and his then capacity to endorse." The question presented, so far as we have been able to determine, is one that has not been passed upon by any court of last resort in this country. Judging from the able briefs filed, counsel have given this case much thought, and they say that they have been unable to find a case exactly in point. . . .

Illinois adopted the Negotiable Instruments law in 1907. This law was the result of an effort to codify the law of negotiable instruments and to establish uniformity in this important branch of the law by securing the adoption of the code by all the States of the Union. In 1896 the commissioners appointed by the several States finally agreed upon a draft of a bill to be recommended to the several legislatures. This law, in a few cases with some modifications but generally in the form recommended, has been adopted in forty-six of the forty-eight States of the Union. Prior to the adoption of the act by the various States there was lack of uniformity in the statutes of the States and in the decisions of the courts with reference to the law merchant. This led to great confusion in the conduct of business among the merchants of the several States and prompted the effort to establish uniformity. The aim was to codify the law rather than to reform it. In order to establish uniformity it was necessary to change the law in some States, but where these changes were made the Negotiable Instruments law generally lays down the rule which conforms to the weight of authority. The confused state of the law before the adoption of the Negotiable Instruments law would naturally bring some of its provisions in conflict with the statutes and decisions of the several States. In construing the act the language ought to be interpreted in such a way as to give effect to the beneficent design of the legislature in passing an act for the promotion of harmony in the law regarding negotiable paper. The court must take the act as it is written and should give to the words used their natural and common meaning. The law was enacted for the purpose of furnishing in itself a certain guide for the determination of all questions covered thereby relating to commercial paper, and, so far as it speaks without ambiguity as to any such question, reference to case law as it existed prior to the enactment is more likely to be misleading than beneficial. If the provisions of the act harmonize with the general principles of commercial law in force before its enactment those principles should be followed, but if the language of the act conflicts with statutes or decisions in force before its enactment the courts should not give the act a strained construction in order to make it harmonize with earlier statutes or decisions. If this is done the very purpose of the act is defeated. In order to keep the law as nearly as may be uniform, the courts of all the States should keep in mind the spirit and object of the law and should give to the language of the act a natural and common construction, so that all might be more likely to come to the same conclusion.

Section 62, hereinbefore quoted, so far as it applies to the facts in this case, declares that the acceptor by accepting the instrument engages that he will pay the instrument which he has accepted according to the tenor of his acceptance and admits the existence of the payee and his then capacity to endorse. The instrument which appellee accepted was payable "to the order of Andrew H. Manning." By its acceptance it admitted that Andrew H. Manning was in existence, and that Andrew H. Manning at the time of acceptance was not suffering any legal disability which would affect his ability to pass title to the instrument accepted by means of endorsement. According to the plain language of this section appellee by its general acceptance bound itself to pay a draft for $629.80 payable to the order of Andrew H. Manning. After the draft was accepted by appellee the drawer was discharged from liability thereon. When appellant took the draft it was complete and regular upon its face. It had been duly accepted by the drawee. It was taken in good faith and for value, and appellant then had no notice of any infirmity in the instrument or defect in the title of the person negotiating it, and appellant was therefore a holder in due course. It relied upon the general acceptance of appellee and under the Negotiable Instruments law was protected by it. This construction of section 62 is in accordance with that sound principle which declares that where one of two innocent parties must suffer a loss the law will leave the loss where it finds it. . . .

Appellee contends that the drawee by accepting this draft admitted the existence of the payee named in the draft by the drawer, — that is, the American Sheet and Tin Plate Company, — and that it admitted the capacity of the American Sheet and Tin Plate Company to endorse the draft. We cannot agree with this contention. The drawee knew nothing of the American Sheet and Tin Plate Company and could have admitted nothing regarding its existence or its capacity to endorse. If section 62 means anything it means just what it says — that is, by accepting this draft appellee admitted the existence of the payee then named in the draft and the capacity of the named payee to endorse the draft. . . .

The judgments of the Appellate and circuit courts are reversed.

Judgment reversed.

Note also WELLS FARGO BANK & UNION TRUST COMPANY *v.* BANK OF ITALY, 214 Calif. 156 (Supreme Court, 1931), where the drawee bank sought to recover the amount paid to a holder in due course on a certified check in which the name of the payee had been altered prior to certification. In affirming a judgment for defendant, the Court said: "The wording of the act suggests that a change in the common law was intended. A careful reading thereof, independent of any common law influence, requires that the words 'according to the tenor of his acceptance' he construed as referring to the instrument as it was at the time it came into the hands of the acceptor for acceptance, for he accepts no other instrument than the one presented to him — the altered form — and it alone he engages to pay. This conclusion is in harmony with the law of England and the continental countries. . . . It makes for the usefulness and currency of negotiable paper (31 Yale Law Journal 522, 527) without seriously endangering accepted banking practices, for banking institutions can readily protect themselves against liability on altered instruments either by qualifying their acceptance or certification or by relying on forgery insurance and special paper which will make alterations obvious."

In SCHOLFIELD *v.* THE EARL OF LONDESBOROUGH, [1896] A. C. 514 (House of Lords), a bill of exchange for £500 was accepted by the drawee, and was subsequently raised to £3500 by the drawer, the alterations being facilitated by spaces left at the time of the original drawing. In an action by a holder in due course against the acceptor on the bill, as on a bill for £3500, the acceptor paid £500 into court, and a judgment in his favor on that basis was affirmed. An acceptor owes no duty to potential holders in due course to see to it that the bill accepted is in a form not susceptible of fraudulent alteration. Said Lord Watson: "In many if not most cases which occur in the course of business, the bill is written out by the drawer, and sent by him to the acceptor, who is under an obligation to sign it. Assuming the appellant's argument to be well founded, it would be within the right of the acceptor to return the bill unsigned, if it were not drawn so as to exclude all reasonable possibilities of fraud or forgery. The exercise of that right might lead to very serious complications in commercial transactions."

PRICE *v.* NEAL

KING'S BENCH, 1762

[3 *Burrow's Reports*, 1354]

This was a special case reserved at the sittings at Guildhall after Trinity term 1762, before Lord Mansfield.

It was an action upon the case brought by Price against Neal; wherein Price declares that the defendant Edward Neale was indebted to him in 80*l.* for money had and received to his plaintiff's use: and damages were laid to 100*l.* The general issue was pleaded; and issue joined thereon.

It was proved at the trial, that a bill was drawn as follows — "Leicester, 22d November 1760. Sir, Six weeks after date pay Mr. Roger Ruding or order forty pounds, value received for Mr. Thomas Ploughfor; as advised by, Sir, your humble servant Benjamin Sutton. To Mr. John Price in Bush-lane Cannon-street, London"; indorsed "R. Ruding; Antony Topham, Hammond and Laroche. Received the contents, James Watson and son: witness Edward Neale."

That this bill was indorsed to the defendant for a valuable consideration; and notice of the bill left at the plaintiff's house, on the day it became due. Whereupon the plaintiff sent his servant to call on the defendant, to pay him the said sum of 40*l.* and take up the said bill: which was done accordingly.

That another bill was drawn as follows — "Leicester, 1st February 1761. Sir, Six weeks after date pay Mr. Rogers Ruding or order forty pounds, value received for Mr. Thomas Ploughfor; as advised by, Sir, your humble servant Benjamin Sutton. To Mr. John Price in Bush-lane, Cannon-street, London." That this bill was indorsed, "R. Ruding, Thomas Watson and son. Witness for Smith, Right and Co." That the plaintiff accepted this bill, by writing on it, "accepted John Price"; and that the plaintiff wrote on the back of it. — "Messieurs Freame and Barclay, pray pay forty pounds for John Price."

That this bill being so accepted was indorsed to the defendant for a valuable consideration, and left at his bankers for payment; and was paid by order of the plaintiff, and taken up.

Both these bill were forged by one Lee, who has been since hanged for forgery.

The defendant Neale acted innocently and *bona fide,* without the least privity or suspicion of the said forgeries or of either of them; and paid the whole value of those bills.

The jury found a verdict for the plaintiff; and assessed damages 80*l.* and costs 40*s.* subject to the opinion of the court upon this question —

"Whether the plaintiff, under the circumstances of the case (see 12 *Mod.* 494. *Str.* 648. *Salk.* 344. *Carth.* 357. *Str.* 1154. 2 *P. Wms.* 76. *Doug.* 618. *Plowd.* 166. 1 *H. Bl.* 590. 4 *Durn.* 325) can recover back, from the defendant, the money he paid on the said bills, or either of them."

Mr. Stowe, for the plaintiff, argued that he ought to recover back the money, in this action; as it was paid by him by mistake only, on supposition "that these were true genuine bills"; and as he could never recover it against the drawer, because in fact no drawer exists; nor against the forger, because he is hanged.

He owned that in a case at Guildhall, of *Jenys* v. *Fawler et al.* (an action by an indorsee of a bill of exchange brought against the acceptor), Lord Raymond would not admit the defendants to prove it a forged bill, by calling persons acquainted with the hand of the drawer, to swear "that they believed it not to be so": and he even strongly inclined, "that actual proof of forgery would not excuse the defendants against their own acceptance, which had given the bill a credit to the indorsee."

But he urged, that in the case now before the court, the forgery of the bill does not rest in belief and opinion only; but has been actually proved, and the forger executed for it.

Thus it stands even upon the accepted bill. But the plaintiff's case is much stronger upon the other bill which was not accepted. It is not stated "that that bill was accepted before it was negotiated"; on the contrary, the consideration for it was paid by the defendant, before the plaintiff had seen it. So that the defendant took it upon the credit of the indorsers, not upon the credit of the plaintiff; and therefore the reason, upon which Lord

Raymond grounds his inclination to be of opinion "that actual proof of forgery would be no excuse," will not hold here.

Mr. Yates, for the defendant, argued that the plaintiff was not intitled to recover back this money from the defendant.

He denied it to be a payment by mistake: and insisted that it was rather owing to the negligence of the plaintiff; who should have inquired and satisfied himself "whether the bill was really drawn upon him by Sutton, or not." Here is no fraud in the defendant; who is stated "to have acted innocently and *bona fide*, without the least privity or suspicion of the forgery; and to have paid the whole value for the bills."

Lord Mansfield stopt him from going on; saying that this was one of those cases that could never be made plainer by argument.

It is an action upon the case, for money had and received to the plaintiff's use. In which action, the plaintiff can not recover the money, unless it be against conscience in the defendant, to retain it: and great liberality is always allowed, in this sort of action.

But it can never be thought unconscientious in the defendant, to retain this money, when he has once received it upon a bill of exchange indorsed to him for a fair and valuable consideration, which he had *bona fide* paid, without the least privity or suspicion of any forgery.

Here was no fraud: no wrong. It was incumbent upon the plaintiff, to be satisfied "that the bill drawn upon him was the drawer's hand," before he accepted or paid it: but it was not incumbent upon the defendant, to inquire into it. Here was notice given by the defendant to the plaintiff of a bill drawn upon him: and he sends his servant to pay it and take it up. The other bill, he actually accepts; after which acceptance, the defendant innocently and *bona fide* discounts it. The plaintiff lies by, for a considerable time after he has paid these bills; and then found out "that they were forged": and the forger comes to be hanged. He made no objection to them, at the time of paying them. Whatever neglect there was, was on his side. The defendant had actual encouragement from the plaintiff himself, for negotiating the second bill, from the plaintiff's having without any scruple or hesitation paid the first: and he paid the whole value, *bona fide*. It is a misfortune which has happened without the defendant's fault or neglect. If there was no neglect in the plaintiff, yet there is no reason to throw off the loss from one innocent man upon another innocent man: but, in this case, if there was any fault or negligence in any one, it certainly was in the plaintiff, and not in the defendant.

Per Curiam.

Rule — That the *postea* be delivered to the Defendant.

Note also Dedham National Bank *v.* Everett National Bank, 177 Mass. 392 (Supreme Judicial Court, 1900), where the drawee bank sought to recover the amount of two forged checks from a holder in due course to whom payment had been made. In affirming a judgment for the defendant, Holmes, C. J., said in adopting the rule laid down in *Price* v. *Neal*: "Probably the rule was adopted from an impression of convenience rather than for any more academic reason; or perhaps we may say that Lord Mansfield took the case out of the doctrine as to payments under a mistake of fact by the assumption that a holder who simply presents negotiable paper for payment makes no representation as to the signature, and that the drawee pays at his peril."

In SANDERSON *v.* COLLMAN, 4 Man. & G. 209 (Court of Common Pleas, 1842), a bill of exchange purporting to be drawn by a firm in Rio de Janeiro was presented to and accepted by defendant in London. The bill then was purchased by the plaintiff, a holder in due course. It subsequently appeared that the bill was a forgery, and defendant refused to pay it. In an action for non-payment, judgment was given for plaintiff, Tindal, C. J., saying "an acceptor cannot set up a want of authority, or a want of identity, as to the party by whom the bill professes to have been drawn. And this doctrine is of the greatest importance as applicable to bills drawn abroad, which obtain their credit and currency here on the faith of the acceptance, and not on the signature of the drawer." Coltman, J., added: "I think it may be taken as settled that the acceptor of a bill of exchange is not at liberty to show that it was not drawn by the party who appears to be the drawer."

The following variants of the general situation presented should be noted:

WILLIAMSBURGH TRUST COMPANY *v.* TUM SUDEN, 120 N. Y. App. Div. 518 (Supreme Court, Appellate Division, 1907): Action to recover money paid by mistake. Four checks purporting to be drawn by L. F. Rand and payable to bearer were indorsed by Tum Suden, who had been in the habit of cashing checks for Rand; and who took the checks in question from a maid in the employ of Rand. Tum Suden presented the checks to the drawee bank and they were paid. It subsequently appeared that they were forgeries. The bank was allowed to recover the amount paid on the ground that under the circumstances "it was but natural for the bank to assume that Tum Suden's indorsement warranted the genuineness of the signature."

SOUTH BOSTON TRUST COMPANY *v.* LEVIN, 249 Mass. 45 (Supreme Judicial Court, 1924): Action to recover the amount of ten checks payable to cash and paid by the drawee bank to the indorser. The checks purported to be drawn by a depositor in the bank, but in reality were forgeries. Recovery was denied under the common law rule of *Price* v. *Neal*, and sec. 62 of the Uniform Negotiable Instruments Law was held to be inapplicable to such a situation, the Court saying: "It cannot be successfully contended that it is a necessary implication of [Sec. 62] that the drawee of a bill is to be held to the same admissions when he pays the bill that are expressly provided for when he accepts it. . . . There is no similarity between acceptance and payment: payment discharges the instrument, and no one else is expected to advance anything on the faith of it; acceptance contemplates further circulation, induced by the fact of acceptance. The rule, that the acceptor makes certain admissions which will inure to the benefit of subsequent holders, has no applicability to payment of the instrument where subsequent holders can never exist."

The First State Bank and Trust Company v. The First National Bank of Canton, 314 Ill. 269 (Supreme Court, 1925): A forged check was presented to the defendant bank by a person who represented himself to be the payee and who indorsed the check as such. Defendant gave cash to the indorser for part of the amount and credit for the balance in an account opened in the payee's name. Defendant then indorsed the check, and it was presented to the drawee bank through the local clearing house and paid. The forgery was not discovered by the drawer for three months. The drawee then recredited his account, and demanded payment of the amount from defendant. At that time the amount credited to an account in the name of the payee remained intact. There was no evidence that the person who indorsed and deposited the check was not the payee; nor was there any evidence that there was in fact any such person as the one named as payee. The indorser never had been seen in the defendant bank before, and never was seen again. The teller who took the check believed that he had been introduced by some officer of the bank. It was held that the drawee could recover the amount still lying at credit, as with respect to that the defendant had not parted with anything of value; but that the drawee could not recover the amount paid out in cash because of its own negligence in failing to report the forgery for three months.

National Union Fire Insurance Co. v. Mellon National Bank, 276 Penn. 212 (Supreme Court, 1923): Drafts drawn by an insurance agent to cover losses were accepted by the insurance company after receiving the purported indorsements of the payee policy holders. These indorsements were forged. It was held that the company did not admit the genuineness of the payee's signature by acceptance.

Compare Sec. 62 of the Uniform Negotiable Instruments Law with Sec. 54 of the Bills of Exchange Act and with Art. 28 of the Geneva Law.

2. THE CONTRACT OF THE DRAWER AND OF THE INDORSERS

MAZUKIEWICZ *v.* THE HANOVER NATIONAL BANK

NEW YORK COURT OF APPEALS, 1925

[240 *New York Reports*, 317]

ANDREWS, J. Having purchased from the defendant as drawer in 1914 two foreign drafts or bills of exchange aggregating 15,000 rubles the plaintiff duly presented them for payment to the drawee in Lomza, Russia, but payment was refused. No notice of dishonor of either draft was given to the defendant. The plaintiff was detained in Russia by the war and subsequently by lack of funds but he returned to New York in 1921 and in April of that year presented the original drafts to the defendant. He then asked for the money which he had paid for them but this was refused. The present action was then begun to recover that sum and at the close of the evidence, both parties having moved for a directed verdict, the court directed a verdict for the plaintiff and the judgment subsequently entered has been unanimously affirmed by the Appellate Division. The question for us to consider is whether there is any evidence to justify the verdict so directed by the trial court.

Section 111 of the Negotiable Instruments Law (Cons. Laws, ch. 38) provides that the drawer of such instruments as are involved in this action engages that upon due presentment the same will be accepted and paid, or both according to the tenor, and if they are dishonored and the necessary proceedings on dishonor are duly taken he will pay the amount thereof to the holder. Section 160 of the same law provides that unless notice of dishonor be given to the drawer he is discharged unless it is one of the cases specified in section 185. These exceptions, so far as applicable here, are where the drawer has countermanded payment or where he has no right to expect or require that the drawee or acceptor will honor the instrument.

In his complaint the plaintiff alleges that the defendant had countermanded payment and later he was allowed to amend by alleging that at the time the drafts were drawn the defendant had no funds with the drawee.

As to the question of countermand we find no evidence that would permit a finding in favor of the plaintiff. He testifies that when the drafts were presented the drawee told him that the Hanover National Bank had notified him not to pay. As to the defendant this evidence was purely hearsay. The drawee was not the agent of the defendant in any such sense that his statements were competent as against it. (*Carle* v. *White*, 9 Me. 104; *Forbes* v. *Eldridge*, 9 Mass. 497; *Baldwin's Bank of Penn Yan* v. *Smith*, 215 N. Y. 76, 82.) Indeed, neither of the courts below seem to have placed their decision upon any such theory.

It is quite true that the defendant at the time it drew the drafts had no funds with the drawee. It might not, therefore, require their payment. But if it had a right to expect that they would be paid it was entitled to notice of dishonor. The uncontradicted evidence is that it was in correspondence with the Commerce Bank of Warsaw, with whom it had a sufficient balance on deposit. The bank in Lomza was in turn one of the correspondents of this latter bank. The agreement and practice was for the defendant to draw a draft directly upon such correspondents, notify the latter that the draft had been drawn, ask them to charge it against the Commerce Bank of Warsaw and the latter bank, being also notified that the draft was drawn, instructed its correspondents to honor the draft and charge it to the Warsaw bank which bank in turn charged it against the account of the Hanover National Bank with it. Following this procedure, drafts had been previously drawn on this very bank in Lomza and it seems to have been the regular course of New York banks with relation to foreign drafts and the only practicable course. They could not keep accounts with banks in each of the smaller foreign towns and if all they could do would be to draw upon the central banks in each country, business transactions would be impeded. In view of this uncontradicted evidence the only possible inference is that the defendant had a right to expect that these drafts would be paid when presented and that is sufficient. (*Robinson* v. *Ames*, 20 Johns. 146; *Rucker* v. *Hiller*, 16 East, 43; *Knickerbocker Life Insurance Company* v. *Pendleton*, 112 U. S. 696; *Simonoff* v. *Granite City National Bank*, 279 Ill. 248.) It, therefore, was entitled to notice of dishonor.

The judgments appealed from must be reversed and, as it is possible that upon a new trial the plaintiff may show by competent evidence that payment was countermanded, a new trial must be granted, with costs to abide the event.

CRANE, J. (dissenting). The bank at Lomza, Russia, was the agent of the defendant; the first communication to pay the plaintiff was from the defendant to this bank in Lomza. The refusal of the agent in Lomza to pay the plaintiff and the statements of the reason for its refusal that payment had been countermanded by the defendant were competent evidence in my judgment, and sufficient to make the defendant liable; that is, as the defendant through its agent had refused to pay, notice of nonpayment was unnecessary.

HISCOCK, Ch. J., CARDOZO, MCLAUGHLIN and LEHMAN, JJ., concur with ANDREWS, J.; CRANE, J., dissents in memorandum; POUND, J., absent.

Judgments reversed, etc.

Compare WOOD *v.* MCMEANS, 23 Texas 481 (Supreme Court, 1860), where in an action by the payee against the drawer of a bill of exchange the defense was that the bill had not been protested and that notice had not been given to the drawer. On proof that at the date of the draft and at the date of its presentation the drawer had no funds in the drawee's hands, it was held that notice was unnecessary, the Court saying that the drawer "is rendered primarily liable, by the fact of having drawn where he had no funds in the hands of the drawee, and no reasonable expectation that his draft would be honored."

In USHER *v.* A. S. TUCKER COMPANY, 217 Mass. 441 (Supreme Judicial Court, 1914), a check drawn by defendant was indorsed in blank by the payee, who was a holder in due course, and came to the drawee bank through the clearing house. The defendant meanwhile had stopped payment on the check, but through an oversight it was paid and defendant's account debited. The drawee bank recredited defendant's account, and charged the amount of the check to the clerk responsible for the oversight. Defendant closed its account. The clerk took an assignment from the bank of all the right, title or interest the bank had in and to the check "or the funds evidenced thereby or the amount paid thereon." In an action by the clerk on the check, it was held that "where the payment has been stopped, as above stated, the relations between the drawer and the payee become the same as if the check had been dishonored and notice thereof given to the drawer. And hence the effect so far as respects the drawer is to change his conditional liability to one free from this condition, and his situation is like that of the maker of a promissory note."

In WHITEHEAD *v.* WALKER, 9 M. & W. 506 (Exchequer of Pleas, 1842), Parke, B., said: "The question raised by the pleadings in this case is, whether, if the indorsee of a foreign bill of exchange has presented it for acceptance, and (acceptance having been refused) has duly presented it and given notice to the drawer, (for the defendant, the indorser, is in the same situation), and so has acquired a right of action against him by reason of the non-acceptance, a new right of action afterwards accrues to him on the subsequent presentment of the bill for payment, and non-payment according to its tenor. . . . The practical importance of the point in the present case arises from the delay of the holder in bringing his action. The non-acceptance and the protest thereon occurred in September 1834. The bill, according to its tenor, would not be payable till the subsequent month of December, and this action was commenced in November 1840; so that if a right of action accrued in December 1834, the Statute of Limitations cannot be successfully pleaded; whereas, if there was no right of action accruing subsequently to the protest for non-acceptance in September 1834, the statute is a bar.

"On the part of the plaintiff it was contended, that although he undoubtedly might have brought an action in the month of September 1834, founded on the non-acceptance, yet it was optional with him to do so or not; that he might, if he thought fit, waive that action, and proceed merely on the ground of the subsequent non-payment in December 1834. For the drawer of a bill, it was contended, enters into a double engagement with the payee, and through him with the successive holders of the bill, namely, first, that the drawee shall accept the bill when regularly presented to him for acceptance; and secondly, that he shall pay the bill when regularly presented to him for payment. And if this be a correct representation of the engagement entered into by the drawer, the conclusion seems unavoidable, that whatever right of action the holder might have acquired by the non-acceptance, he certainly is not precluded from suing in respect of the default of payment. But we are of opinion that the contract entered into by the drawer is not such as is contended for by the plaintiff, and that he in fact enters into one contract only; namely, in the case of a bill made payable after sight, that the drawee shall, on the bill being presented to him in a reasonable time from the date, accept the same, and having so accepted it, shall pay it when duly presented for payment according to its tenor; and in the case of a bill payable after date, that the drawee shall accept it if it is presented to him before the time of payment, and having so accepted it, shall pay it when it is in due course presented for payment; or if it is not presented for acceptance at all, then that he shall pay it when duly presented for payment. . . .

"In spite of the non-acceptance, the drawer still may pay the bill when at maturity, and the holder having by protest and notice on non-acceptance put himself in a condition to sue the drawer, may very reasonably, as a matter of prudence, retain the bill, and endeavour to obtain payment when the bill is at maturity, and not involve himself in litigation until there has been a failure of payment as well as of acceptance. It by no means, however, follows, because this is spoken of as being, what probably it still is, the usual course, that any second right of action arises on the second default. For let us consider what is the nature of the right which the holder acquires on the default of the drawee to accept. It is clear (whatever might formerly have been considered on the subject), that by the non-acceptance, followed by the protest and notice, the holder acquires an immediate right of action against the drawer — a right of action, be it observed, not in respect of any special damage from the non-acceptance, but a right of action on the bill, i.e. a right of action to recover the full amount of the bill. The effect of the refusal to accept is (according to the language of the Court of King's Bench in *Macarty* v. *Barrow*, as quoted by C. J. Wilmot, in 3 Wils. 16), that the drawee says to the holder, 'I will not pay your bill; you must go back to the drawer, and he must pay you.' The holder thus acquires by the non-acceptance the most complete right of action against the drawer which the nature of the case admits, and no subsequent act or omission of the drawee can give him a more extensive right against the drawer than he has already acquired. But further, on failure of acceptance, the holder is bound to give immediate notice to the drawer, and if he omits to do so, he forfeits all right of action against him, not only in respect of the default of acceptance, but also in respect of the subsequent non-payment."

RICE *v.* STEARNS

MASSACHUSETTS SUPREME JUDICIAL COURT, 1807

[3 *Massachusetts Reports*, 225]

Assumpsit by the endorsee of a promissory note against the promisors. The note was originally made payable to Jonathan Symonds, or his order, who endorsed it to the plaintiff in these words: "For value received, I order the contents of this note to be paid to Merrick Rice, at his own risk."

Upon the trial, at the last April term, in this county, before Sedgwick, J., two of the defendants denied the signature of their names to the note. The plaintiff thereupon offered Symonds, the promisee named in the note, to prove that he, as a deputy sheriff, having an execution in his possession against the defendant James Stearns, and having arrested the said James thereon, took the said note in satisfaction of said execution, which he afterwards endorsed in manner aforesaid, to the present plaintiff, as attorney to the creditor in said execution, which was discharged. The defendants objected to the competency of Symonds to testify to the said facts, on the ground that he was interested. The judge overruled the objection, and the plaintiff had a verdict. The defendants moved for a new trial, because Symonds was admitted, and the cause was continued to this term.

PARSONS, C. J. The interest of Symonds must depend on the effect of his endorsement.

A security, negotiable in its creation, must, during its negotiation, preserve its negotiable quality; otherwise, when assigned, the assignee would hold a contract by the assignment different from the contract assigned. It is for this reason settled, that a negotiable note endorsed in blank, or by a direction to pay the contents to A. B., omitting the words, "or his order," is further negotiable by the holder under such endorsement. It is also settled that when a negotiable security is endorsed, "Pay the contents to my use," or, "to the use of a third person," or, "Carry this bill to the credit of a third person," such an endorsement is not an assignment of the security, but is only an authority to pay the money agreeably to the direction of the endorsement. There are other restricted endorsements also made; as, "Pay the contents to A. B. only." Whether this endorsement is only an authority to A. B. to receive the money for the use of the endorser, or for his own use, if made for value received, or whether in this last case the restriction is not void, and A. B. may further negotiate it, seems not to be settled. If the property of the note be vested in A. B., perhaps he will hold it with its negotiable quality, notwithstanding the restriction. But of this we give no opinion.

The case at bar is a restricted endorsement of another kind, and which in practice is very common. The promisee of a negotiable note endorses it to a third person, or his order, for value received, stipulating that the endorser is not to be responsible, if the maker does not pay it. If, notwithstanding this stipulation, the endorser is answerable, if the maker do not pay the note, then the witness, Symonds, is interested, and ought not to have been sworn.

Upon consideration, we are of opinion that the promisee, endorsing the note under this express stipulation, is not eventually holden to pay the note, if the maker should not. As the promisee had the property of the note, he might dispose of it on what terms he pleased, with the assent of the purchaser, and the latter cannot complain of the necessary effect of his own agreement; and the endorser cannot be charged upon his own contract, directly against the express intent of it. If this opinion is correct, Symonds, after this restricted endorsement, had no interest in the event of the suit, and was a competent witness.

Another point of some importance arises, which involves the question, whether, by this restricted endorsement, the property of the note passed to the endorsee, so that he may sue upon it in his own name. If the restriction applied to the quality of the contract, so as to render a negotiable security no longer negotiable, there would be some difficulty in allowing, consistently with legal principles, an endorsement of this effect to operate as a transfer of the note. But this is not the effect of the restriction; the note remains negotiable in the hands of the endorsee, although he has no remedy against the endorser; and in whose hands soever the note may come, the maker is still liable, according to the terms of his original contract, to pay to the promisee or his order. The note, therefore, being the absolute property of the plaintiff, and Symonds being a competent witness, the verdict must stand, and judgment be entered accordingly.

Compare the modern practice illustrated in the following clause from an "Irrevocable Advice to Purchase" dated January 4, 1939: "We have been requested by the ——— Bank, Hongkong, to purchase your documentary bills without recourse to you to the extent of $29,600 U. S. Currency drawn as follows and accompanied by complete sets of documents as specified."

DUBLER *v.* TOSCANA STRAW GOODS CORPORATION

CITY COURT OF NEW YORK, 1932

[142 *New York Miscellaneous Reports*, 369]

WENDEL, J. Motion for reargument. While ordinarily the court would not entertain an application for rehearing at this late day, special circumstances, as disclosed by the record of the proceedings heretofore taken in this action, exist for a departure from the usual procedure.

The action is to recover on five trade acceptances dated February 28, 1928, executed by plaintiffs to the order of themselves and accepted by defendant, payable, respectively, on July, August, September, October and November 12, 1928. The answer sets up as a separate defense that the trade acceptances were made payable at the Amalgamated Bank of New York, and that by reason thereof they became in legal effect and operation of law the checks of defendant with the defendant as maker and the bank as drawee and the plaintiffs as payees (paragraph 17); that the trade acceptances were not presented for payment on the due date and that no notice of presentment or non-payment was given to the defendant (paragraph 18); that by reason of said non-presentment of said trade acceptances and the failure of the plaintiffs to give notice of such presentment and non-payment, this defendant was legally discharged from all liability thereunder (paragraph 18). This defense is attacked as insufficient. Eliminating therefrom the legal conclusions contained in paragraphs 17 and 18, the question for determination is whether or not the failure of plaintiffs to present the trade acceptances for payment and to give notice of such presentment and non-payment to defendant is a good defense.

A trade acceptance is a draft or bill of exchange drawn by the seller on the purchaser of goods sold and accepted by such purchaser. (*Atterbury* v. *Bank of Washington Heights*, 241 N. Y. 271.) Upon acceptance by the drawee it becomes in effect a promissory note, the acceptor standing in the place of the maker and becoming primarily liable. (*Anglo & Paris Nat. Bank* v. *Jacobson*, 187 N. Y. Supp. 508.) Being primarily liable, notice of presentment of the instrument and demand for payment are not necessary. (Neg. Inst. Law, § 130.)

Defendant not having pleaded ability and willingness to pay at the place of payment at maturity, it is unnecessary to now pass upon the effect of failure of presentment in such case. Defendant's contention that notice of the presentment is necessary is based upon section 147 of the Negotiable Instruments Law, which provides as follows: "Where the instrument is made payable at a bank it is equivalent to an order to the bank to pay the same for the account of the principal debtor thereon." While, so far as the requirement of payment is concerned, the trade acceptance may be equivalent to a direction to the bank to pay it for the account of the debtor, it nevertheless does not convert the instrument from a bill of exchange or trade acceptance to a check to the extent of requiring presentment thereof to be made. The essential characteristic of a check is that it shall be instantly payable on demand, and also that it shall be drawn on a bank, and accordingly before action may be brought thereon by the payee against the maker there must be presentment to the bank for payment, and in the event of dishonor notice thereof must be given to the maker. (Neg. Inst. Law, § 160.) The acceptor of a trade acceptance is not entitled to notice any more than is the maker of a promissory note. It is only where a bill of exchange is drawn on a bank payable on demand that it is a check. (Neg. Inst. Law, § 321.)

The defense is stricken out. Order signed.

In Rowe *v.* Young, 2 Bligh 391 (House of Lords, 1820), Bayley, J., said at page 467 in answering a question put to the Judges for the information of the House: "The acceptor is, by the law and custom of merchants, considered as the principal debtor; the drawer and indorser as sureties only, liable on his default, and not otherwise. His engagement is general, that he will pay; that of the drawer and indorsers is conditional, namely, that if due diligence be used, they will pay, if the acceptor does not. The engagement of the acceptor is, either that he has effects in hand, or that he is secure of having them by the time the bill becomes due. In the language of the Lord Chief Justice Eyre, 'The theory of a bill of exchange is, that the bill is an assignment to the payee of a debt due from the acceptor to the drawer, and the acceptance imports that the acceptor is a debtor to the drawer, or at least has effects of the drawer's in his hands.' The acceptor, therefore, has, or ought to have, in his hands, or under his control, the fund by which payment ought to be made; and it is his duty so to apply it. The drawer or indorsers have no control over the fund, and consequently no duty with respect to it. This difference of situation and character between the drawer and indorsers and acceptors, has produced a settled distinction in the manner of suing them. The action against drawer and indorser invariably shows that due diligence has been used; the action against the acceptor invariably omits it. In an action against the drawer and indorsers the declaration invariably avers presentment of the bill, its dishonour, and notice thereof to the defendant. In an action against the acceptor no such averments are made. Every bill is to be properly presented for payment; and in an action thereon against the drawer or indorser, a presentment according to the usage and custom of merchants must be averred and proved. In an action thereon against the acceptor, presentment (generally speaking) need not be averred or proved. This is clear, settled, undisputed law. Not that in practice such presentment is likely to be omitted: the risk of losing the responsibility of the drawer and indorsers generally secures it: but if there were to be an omission, that is no reason why the acceptor, who has, or ought to have, funds to discharge it, should keep those funds to himself, or should refuse so to apply them."

In In re Francke *v.* Rasch, [1918] 1 Ch. 470 (Chancery Division), bills accepted payable in an enemy country after the outbreak of war had been drawn by an enemy firm carrying on business in England, and purchased from the firm before the war by an English bank, in whose hands they remained unpaid. The due date according to the tenor had passed, but presentment had not been made. Emergency legislation of the enemy country since the war postponed the maturity of bills until further notice. On a claim by the bank against the assets in a winding up of the business of the firm, it was held that the due date of the bills had not yet arrived, and that the claim therefore failed.

Compare Engle *v.* Shepherd, 100 Okl. 200 (Supreme Court, 1924), where the acceptor of a bill became bankrupt, so that on due date his business had ceased to operate and was in the hands of a liquidating agent. Under such circumstances presentment for payment was held to be excused.

In Pittsburgh Steel Company *v.* Hollingshead & Blei, 202 Ill. App. 177 (Appellate Court, First District, 1916), defendant sent to plaintiff in settlement of invoices covering a purchase of hoop and band steel two bills of exchange drawn on and accepted by a third company and indorsed by defendant. Plaintiff mislaid the drafts, and they were not presented for payment at maturity. The acceptor later became bankrupt. Plaintiff claimed against the estate on the basis of the two drafts, and received a dividend. Defendant made a payment to plaintiff to cover the difference between this dividend and the amount of the drafts, but in a later action to recover on invoices of shipments subsequent to the settlement attempted to set off the amount so paid. A judgment allowing the set-off was affirmed. Plaintiff was negligent in failing to present the drafts for payment. Presentment was necessary in order to charge the defendant as indorser. Under the circumstances the account was paid, and plaintiff had no legal right to demand payment again.

In SPENCER *v.* BURAKIEWICZ, 288 Mass. 85 (Supreme Judicial Court, 1934), a check drawn on a Worcester bank was given to plaintiff in a town twelve miles from Worcester on December 13. On December 14 plaintiff took the check to a bank in a neighboring town, indorsed it, and received cash for the amount. On the morning of December 15, before the check was presented for payment, the drawee bank closed its doors. In an action by the plaintiff, who took back the check, against the drawer, Donahue, J., said:

"The defendants would be discharged from liability as drawers to the extent of any loss suffered by them which was caused by delay in the presentation of the check for payment if it were not presented within a reasonable time after its issue, G. L. (Ter. Ed.) c. 107, § 209, that is, within a reasonable time after its delivery to the plaintiff (§ 18). The statutory rule for the determination of what is a reasonable time, providing that 'regard is to be had to the nature of the instrument, the usage of trade or business, if any, with respect to such instruments, and the facts of the particular case' (§ 20), is in substance the common law rule. *Seager* v. *Dauphinee*, 284 Mass. 96. By our decisions, in general accord with decisions elsewhere, what is a reasonable time in certain circumstances as to the residence or business location of the drawer, drawee and payee of a check and as to the time intervening between its delivery and its presentation for payment, has been determined. Thus 'where the drawer and drawee and the payee are all in the same city or town, a check, to be presented within a reasonable time, should be presented at some time before the close of banking hours on the day after it is issued, and . . . its circulation from hand to hand will not extend the time of presentment to the detriment of the drawer.' *Lowell Co-operative Bank* v. *Sheridan*, 284 Mass. 594, 598. Where, however, a check is received by the payee at a place distant from the place of payment, there is presentment within a reasonable time if the payee, on the next secular day after its receipt, forwards it to some person at the place of payment and that person presents it to the drawee for payment on the next secular day after his receipt of the check from the payee. *Seager* v. *Dauphinee*, 284 Mass. 96. In the present case the drawers and the drawee had their places of business in the city of Worcester but the payee lived on his farm in a town twelve miles distant from and not adjoining that city. The delivery of the check was made to the payee at his farm. On Monday, the next secular day following the delivery of the check, the payee negotiated it at a savings bank in a neighboring town and on the morning of the following secular day, Tuesday, the drawee bank was closed. There is no sound reason for holding that the savings bank in these circumstances should be in any worse position with regard to presentment for payment within a reasonable time than a bank located in the city of Worcester which under like circumstances had, on Monday, received the check from the plaintiff for collection. Under the rule last stated we do not think that it could be said as matter of law that such Worcester bank would not have had until the close of banking hours on Tuesday to make presentment to the drawee bank. The defendants delivered to the plaintiff an instrument which by its terms they made negotiable. He had the right to negotiate it. Its negotiation cannot be permitted to extend what was otherwise a reasonable period of time for its presentment for payment to the detriment of the drawers. On the other hand there is no reason why the mere fact of negotiation should be held to shorten the period of reasonable time for its presentment. On the facts in this particular case it cannot be said that the trial judge erred in finding that presentment of the check for payment by the savings bank at any time during banking hours on Tuesday would have been within a reasonable time.

"The matter of the presentment of the check for payment in the circumstances of this case has significance not because that step was necessary in order to create a liability on the part of the defendants, who as makers had become parties primarily liable on the instrument (§ 93), but because if the check should not be presented for payment within a reasonable time after its issue the defendants to the extent of a resultant loss, if any, would be discharged from their already existing liability. Inasmuch as the trial judge might properly have found that, before a reasonable time after the issuance of the check had elapsed, the doors of the bank had been closed, and that within the balance of such reasonable time no presentment could have been made, the fact that no presentment was ever made is of no consequence (§ 105). The conclusion that loss to the defendants did not result from delay in the presentment of the check for an unreasonable time was warranted. The savings bank, a holder in due course, acquired the right to recover on the check and that right now rests in the plaintiff."

FRY *v.* HILL

COURT OF COMMON PLEAS, 1817

[7 *Taunton's Reports*, 397]

This was an action for goods sold and delivered; and upon the trial before Park, J., at the sittings after Michaelmas term, 1817, it appeared that the Defendant having occasion to pay the Plaintiff 134*l.* 18*s.*, for goods, early on Friday the 9th day of the month, the Defendant's bankers, on his account as to 134*l.* 18*s.*, (parcel) and receiving from the plaintiff the difference in cash, delivered at Windsor to the Plaintiff's servant, a bill to which the Defendant was no party, drawn by themselves upon their own corresponding banker in London, at one month after sight, for 140*l.* The bill was presented for acceptance on the 13th of the same month, and the country bankers having failed on that same day, acceptance was refused. Shepherd, Solicitor-General, contended, that as well by this course of dealing, which the Plaintiff himself had elected, as by his laches in presenting the bill, the Plaintiff had made the bill his own, and was paid for the goods. The jury, however, under the direction of Park, J., who relied on *Goupy* v. *Harden* (7 Taunton 159), found a verdict for the Plaintiff.

The Solicitor-General now moved to set it aside, and enter a nonsuit, renewing the same objections. He insisted that it was the duty of the Plaintiff, receiving a bill payable at a certain time after sight, to present it for acceptance as soon as he conveniently could: if the Plaintiff had forwarded this bill for acceptance on the Friday, Saturday, Sunday, or Monday, he would thereby have enabled the Defendant to withdraw his funds from his banker's hands. The necessity is more urgent to present for acceptance a bill payable after sight, than a bill payable after date, because by deferring it, the holder protracts the period of that payment, whereby the drawer proposes to withdraw his effects from the hands of the drawee. Secondly, it was for the Plaintiff's own convenience of remittance, that, instead of taking a check for the sum which the Defendant proposed to pay, he had commuted it for a bill; and this was strongly evinced by his taking a bill, not for 134*l.* 18*s.*, but for 140*l.*, paying the difference, and therein blending his own property with this payment, whereby he had rendered the bill completely his own, and was paid for his goods.

GIBBS, C. J. The Defendant's argument on the first point would go to the extent, that the holder of a bill payable after sight is bound to transmit it for acceptance, without putting it into circulation at all. But even if it were a case in which it was required to give instant notice, it has been repeatedly determined, that the holder of a bill is not bound to send it on the same day that he receives it; and there was no post to London on the Saturday. He might have sent it on the Sunday. But I do not go upon that ground. The holder must present a bill payable after sight within a reasonable time; but it is in the power of the holder to postpone the day of payment, by postponing the date of the presentment for acceptance; and he certainly may put the bill into circulation if he will. In the recent case of *Goupy* v. *Harden*, the bills were put into circulation; here it does not appear what was done with the bill in the interval. The question on these bills drawn at sight certainly is left very loose by the cases. The result of the cases undoubtedly is that which I have stated; and Eyre, C. J., says, in *Muilman* v. *D'Eguino* (2 H. Bl. 565), that it is under all circumstances a question for the jury to determine, whether such a bill was presented in reasonable time. Buller, J., in the same case, rather narrows that doctrine, and though he agrees, that if it were in circulation a twelvemonth, there would not be laches; but he says, that if, instead of putting it into circulation, the holder were to lock it up for any length of time, he would be guilty of laches. Is this, therefore, a case, in which the Plaintiff can be said to lock up this bill for any length of time? If we were to grant a new trial, the result would come at the last to this; it would be a question for the jury, whether there has been a default to present the bill within a reasonable time. That question has already been left to the jury, and they have found that the bill was presented in a reasonable time. We think, as the matter stands, it is perfectly right.

Rule refused.

Compare THE N. Y., N. H. AND H. RAILROAD COMPANY *v.* THE FIRST NATIONAL BANK OF BRIDGEPORT, 105 Conn. 33 (Supreme Court of Errors, 1926). A milling company in Minnesota shipped a carload of flour to a grain dealer in Bridgeport, and at the same time, through its Minnesota Bank, forwarded to a Bridgeport bank the bill of lading and a draft on the consignee "payable thirty days after arrival," together with written instructions to "surrender documents upon drawee's acceptance of draft payable thirty days after arrival of car." The papers were received on November 10, and the draft was accepted on November 12. The car did not arrive until November 27. There was a custom among Bridgeport banks to treat the acceptance of such a draft as establishing the arrival of the car and as fixing the due date of the draft. The consignee received the bill of lading on acceptance, and became bankrupt on November 22. The consignee contended that the bank had violated its instructions in regard to the surrender of documents. It was held that there was nothing in the instructions making it incumbent on the bank to depart from the general rule of presentment for acceptance within a reasonable time, and that the banking custom in question was not inconsistent with the instructions.

In NEEDERER *v.* BARBER, 17 Fed. Cas. 10,079 (Circuit Court, Southern District of New York, 1843), in an action by the payee against the drawer of a bill of exchange it appeared that after the bill was drawn the drawer gave orders to the drawee not to accept it. Under such circumstances it was held that the question of the sufficiency of the protest when the bill was dishonored was immaterial, "because the drawer by his own act excused the payee from the necessity of presenting for acceptance or payment."

Compare HALL *v.* CRANE, 213 Mass. 326 (Supreme Judicial Court, 1913), where the indorser of a note wrote above his signature the words "Waive demand." In an action by a subsequent holder against the indorser it was held that this operated only to excuse the holder from making demand on the maker for payment, and not as a waiver of notice.

BEECH–NUT PACKING COMPANY *v.* THE NATIONAL CITY BANK OF NEW YORK

NEW YORK MUNICIPAL COURT, 1933

[149 *New York Miscellaneous Reports*, 682]

WATSON, J. Edward Bach and Isaac Grenthal were copartners under the firm name and style of Edward Bach & Co. As such, they were lessees of certain premises in the borough of Manhattan, city of New York. On or about July 3, 1930, Edward Bach, on behalf of the partnership, entered into a lease, in his own name, as landlord, with the plaintiff, as tenant, of a certain sign space on those premises.

Edward Bach died July 6, 1931, leaving a last will and testament, naming Flora Bach sole legatee and sole executrix. The will was duly admitted to probate on August 17, 1931, and letters testamentary thereon were issued to Flora Bach, who qualified and has since acted as executrix. The estate of Edward Bach is solvent and all his debts have been paid.

Subsequent to the death of Edward Bach, Flora Bach entered into partnership with Isaac Grenthal in the firm of Edward Bach & Co.

On August 30, 1932, plaintiff drew its check on defendant bank, wherein it was a depositor, to the order of Edward Bach, for the sum of $225. This check was in payment of semi-annual rent under the aforesaid lease, and recites on its face that it is "in settlement of sign rent." This check was received by Isaac Grenthal and Flora Bach about August 31, 1932, and with the knowledge and express consent of Flora Bach was, about September 13, 1932, indorsed by Isaac Grenthal in the names of Edward Bach and E. Bach & Co., and deposited in the account of Edward Bach & Co. with the Chemical Bank and Trust Company, which thereafter collected the amount thereof from the defendant and paid such proceeds over to Edward Bach & Co. The defendant, having paid the check, charged the amount thereof to the account of the plaintiff.

The plaintiff seeks to recover this amount on the ground that the check was neither indorsed by nor paid to Edward Bach, the payee therein named; that the indorsement of his name was a forgery, and payment thereon was unauthorized.

The relation between a bank and its depositor is that of debtor and creditor, and the law implies a contract on the part of the bank to disburse the money standing to the depositor's credit only upon his order and in conformity with his directions; no payments can be charged against a depositor unless made to such persons as the depositor directed. (*Shipman* v. *Bank S. N. Y.*, 126 N. Y. 318.) Such is the law; how are we to apply it?

Edward Bach, the individual named in the check as payee, was dead when the check was drawn. He was a non-existing person. If that fact was known to plaintiff at that time, the check would be regarded as payable to bearer. (Neg. Inst. Law, § 28, subd. 3.) But, although Edward Bach died more than a year before, it does not appear that such fact was known to plaintiff. However, section 111 of the Negotiable Instruments Law provides that "The drawer by drawing the instrument admits the existence of the payee and his then capacity to indorse." I find no reported decision in this State passing upon the effect of this provision. In *McCornack* v. *Central State Bank* (203 Iowa, 833; 211 N. W. 542; 52 A. L. R. 1297) a bare majority of the court, against a vigorous dissent by the minority, expressed the opinion that such a provision does not inure to the benefit of the drawee; but the argument turned rather upon the question whether payment had been made to one to whom the drawer did not intend the payment to be made. The distinction between the admission and its operation is observed in *Robertson Banking Co.* v. *Brasfield* (202 Ala. 167; 79 So. 651), also decided by a divided court, in which the majority held that the statute does not make the drawer admit that any one other than his named payee could properly and legally indorse the check.

That there may be instances in which a bank may, upon the principle of estoppel, claim protection against its depositor for payments made upon forged indorsements, is recognized by the authorities. (*Shipman* v. *Bank S. N. Y.*, *supra*.) In my opinion, this statutory admission operates by way of estoppel, and runs as well to the drawee as to a holder in due course; the former is as much entitled to rely upon it as the latter.

The question remains, whether payment has been made to one to whom the drawer did not intend the payment to be made. This is not a case, such as those which have received the attention of the courts, wherein the depositor, in drawing the check, has been the victim of a swindler or an impostor. When the plaintiff drew this check to the order of Edward Bach, it intended thereby to pay rent due under a hiring from him. Can it be said that plaintiff intended to make this payment only if he was then living, but not if he were dead? Concededly, if he were then living, but died without having indorsed or deposited the check, his executrix could have collected it. There is no reason why the same should not be true, where, as here, the person named as payee was dead when the check was drawn. Plaintiff, by drawing the check, admitted the existence of the payee and that payee did exist in the person of the executrix of Edward Bach; by her authority this check was indorsed and collected and payment was thus properly made.

[The balance of the opinion is omitted.]

Compare Secs. 61, 66, 67, 70, 79, 80, 82, 84, 87, 89, 109, 111, 114–118, 143, 144, 150–152, and 186 of the Uniform Negotiable Instruments Law with Secs. 39–52, 55, 56, and 73–75 of the Bills of Exchange Act and with Arts. 9, 21, 22, 38, and 53 of the Geneva Law.

3. NEGOTIABILITY

A. Formal Requisites

TRADERS SECURITIES CO. *v.* KALIL

Pennsylvania Superior Court, 1932

[107 *Pennsylvania Superior Court Reports*, 215]

Opinion by Parker, J., October 10, 1932:

This is an action by the holder against the acceptor of five trade acceptances all in the same form, maturing over a period of from three to twelve months. On the oral argument in this court it was agreed that there were but two questions for determination, — the negotiability of the instrument and the right of this court to grant a new trial.

The trade acceptances were in the following form:

Trade Acceptance

$59.60 St. Louis, Mo., Nov. 11, 1927. No. 1.

Three months after date pay to the order of ourselves at our office at St. Louis, Mo., fifty-nine and 60/100 dollars.

The obligation of the acceptor hereof arises out of the purchase of goods from the drawer.

Report by
No. 21645

To G. Kalil,
Meadville, Pa.
Due Feb. 11, 1928.

Arch Manufacturing Co.

Signed: Accepted Geo. Kalil.

Endorsements:

Without recourse on us, pay to the order of Traders Securities Company.
Arch Manufacturing Co. Per W. A. Blackstad.
Pay to the order of any bank or attorney for collection.
Traders Securities Co.

It was contended by defendant that the promise to pay was not "an unconditional promise to pay" and the notes were therefore not negotiable. The trial judge supported this contention.

The third section of the Uniform Negotiable Instruments Act of 1901 provides that "an unqualified order or promise to pay is unconditional within the meaning of this act though coupled with a statement of the transaction which gives rise to the instrument." Under the plain terms of that act, the paper in question was therefore an unconditional promise to pay. The statement that "the obligation of the acceptor hereof arises out of the purchase of goods from the drawer" would not have destroyed its negotiability prior to the passage of the Negotiable Instruments Act: *Devenny* v. *League Island Loan and Building Assn.*, 9 W. N. C. 127;

Citizens National Bank v. *Piollet*, 126 Pa. 194. In the case of *Panati* v. *Booth*, 95 Pa. Superior Ct. 238, we held that placing on the face of an instrument the words "as per contract" did not destroy its negotiability. It would follow that the mere statement that the bill arose out of the purchase of goods from the drawer would not make the instrument conditional. It is not unreasonable to assume that the words were inserted to make the paper eligible for rediscount in a Federal Reserve Bank, rather than to suggest anything that created a necessity for inquiry. The same construction has been given to the act in many other jurisdictions.

[The balance of the opinion is omitted.]

In OKLAHOMA STATE BANK *v.* HANOVER FIRE INS. CO., 169 Okl. 116 (Supreme Court, 1934), a draft drawn by an insurance agent on his company in settlement of an automobile policy read as follows:

"550.00 Claim No. 87733 Chicago 14, 1928.

"To The Hanover Fire Insurance Company

1105–175 Jackson Boulevard, Chicago, Ill.

"Pay to the order of L. P. Shaw & Moore Motor Company, five hundred fifty-five dollars, dollars, in full payment, satisfaction, compromise and discharge of all claims for loss and damage by fire which occurred on the 4 day of August, 1928, to the property insured under policy No. A363 issued at Ada, Okla., Agency, and in consideration of said payment the policy is hereby cancelled and surrendered herewith.

"W. K. Maxwell, Agt.

"Payable through Chicago Trust Co., in Chicago, Chicago, Ill., U. S. A.

"No Protest.

"This draft must be indorsed by all parties in interest and if indorsed by an attorney, the original power of attorney or a certified copy of same must accompany draft to be filed with this company, prior to the presentation of draft for acceptance and payment."

The draft was held to be negotiable.

In SHAWANO FINANCE CORPORATION *v.* JULIUS, 214 Wis. 637 (Supreme Court, 1934), a note was signed by the purchaser of an automobile under a conditional sales contract. The note and the contract were on a single piece of paper, separated only by a perforated line, and the note contained the following clause: "This note covers deferred instalments under a conditional sale contract made this day between the payee and the maker hereof." The note was held to be negotiable.

Compare HEIMAN *v.* MURPHY, 143 Misc. 81 (New York Municipal Court, 1932), where a note similarly attached to a conditional sale contract provided: "If any instalment of this note is not paid at the time, manner and place specified herein and/or as provided in the conditional sale contract executed herewith, the entire amount unpaid shall become due and payable forthwith." It was held that the note was not negotiable.

In HUBBARD BROS. & CO. *v.* SOUTHERN PAC. CO., 256 Fed. 761 (Circuit Court of Appeals, Fifth Circuit, 1919), a draft drawn in connection with a sale of 214 bales of cotton read as follows: "Pay to the order of T. E. Flourney, cashier, nine thousand dollars, value received, and charge the same to account of against 214 B/C." It was said that "the insertion of '214 B/C' cannot be held to be more than an indication of a particular fund out of which reimbursement is to be made."

Compare GLENDORA BANK *v.* DAVIS, 204 Calif. 220 (Supreme Court, 1928), where a note contained the following clause: "This note is given in payment of merchandise and is to be liquidated by payments received on account of sale of such merchandise." The note was held to be not negotiable.

In ROBERTS & CO. *v.* MARSH, [1915] 1 K. B. 42 (Court of Appeal), a buyer, not having his checkbook at hand, drew a bill of exchange on a blank piece of paper on his banker for £100. As he did not wish a check in this form to go through his bank account, he wrote across the face of the instrument "to be retained." It was held that this did not destroy the negotiability of the instrument, as it was merely a direction to the payee.

Compare Secs. 1 (1) and (2), 3 and 4 of the Uniform Negotiable Instruments Law with Sec. 3 of the Bills of Exchange Act and with Art. 1 of the Geneva Law.

MASON *v.* LACK.

KING'S BENCH DIVISION, 1929

[140 *Law Times Reports, New Series*, 696]

The plaintiff Mason claimed from the defendant Lack 125*l.* 7*s.* 4*d.* on an alleged bill of exchange drawn by the plaintiff, and accepted by the defendant, payable on the 31st Dec. 1928. The alleged bill was in the following form: "125*l.* 7*s.* 4*d.* On December 31st 1928 pay to my order the sum of one hundred and twenty-five pounds seven shillings and four pence for value received. Accepted payable at Lloyd's Bank Limited, High-street Branch, Shoreditch, London, E.C. 2. John H. Lack." At the time when the defendant accepted the bill there was, therefore, no other name upon it. The defendant had no account at the above bank. The defendant denied liability on the grounds (1) that the document sued on was accepted by him as an accommodation bill for which there was no consideration, and (2) that after the acceptance of the bill by him it was drawn by the plaintiff without his authority, the defendant's case being that the only person who could be authorised to draw the bill was the plaintiff's son. The defendant relied on the following further defence in law — that the instrument in question was not a bill of exchange at all, because it was not drawn upon one person by another, and had not complied with the requirements of the Bills of Exchange Act 1882.

HUMPHREYS, J. In this action the plaintiff, Mr. Harry Mason, by a specially endorsed writ, sues the defendant, Mr. John H. Lack, as the acceptor of a bill of exchange. The defendant set out his defence in an affidavit sworn by him asking for unconditional leave to defend. He set up three defences which he alleged that he had to the action: (1) The document sued on was accepted by him as an accommodation bill for which there was no consideration; (2) after the acceptance of the bill by him it was drawn by the plaintiff without his authority, the defendant's case being that the only person who could be authorised to draw the bill was the plaintiff's son; and (3) a defence, which raised an interesting question of law, namely, that the instrument in question was not a bill of exchange at all because it had not complied with the provisions of the Bills of Exchange Act 1882.

[After holding that the first two defenses must fail, his Lordship continued]:

I now come to the main defence, which depends upon the form of the instrument. When it was accepted by Mr. Lack there was no other name upon it at all. There was no name, and there was only an indication of a name in this sense, that the bill is payable at Lloyd's Bank, High Street, Shoreditch, and the bill was not addressed to any person. At a subsequent date Mr. Mason, the plaintiff, put his name to the bill as drawer. In these circumstances it is submitted that this instrument is not a bill of exchange within the meaning of sect. 3 of the Bills of Exchange Act 1882, which defines the expression "bill of exchange" as " . . . an unconditional order in writing addressed by one person to another, signed by the person giving it, requiring the person to whom it is addressed to pay on demand or at a fixed or determinable future time a sum certain in money to or to the order of a specified person, or to bearer." And it is further provided in sub-sect. 2 that: "An instrument which does not comply with these conditions, or which orders any act to be done in addition to the payment of money, is not a bill of exchange." Sect. 6 of the Act provides in sub-sect. 1: "The drawee must be named or otherwise indicated in a bill with reasonable certainty." Now in the last edition of Chalmers' Bills of Exchange as a note to sect. 6, sub-sect. 1 of the Act of 1882, it is stated by way of illustration: "Instrument in the form of a bill, but addressed to no one. B. writes an acceptance thereon. This is not a bill, and B. is not liable as an acceptor, but he may be liable as the maker of a note." Reference is there made to the case of *Peto* v. *Reynolds* (1854, 9 Exch. 410, and 11 Exch. 418). The decision in that case is clearly no authority for that proposition, because the learned judges expressly withheld from deciding that question. But when one looks at the report of the case in the court below it does appear that some of the judges expressed tolerably strong views that a bill which is not addressed to anybody was not a bill of exchange according to the law as it existed at that date in 1854. The document in that case was drawn by a person named, and purported to be accepted by Samuel Reynolds, but it was not addressed to anyone. In giving judgment in that case Chief Baron Pollock abstained from expressing any opinion on the matter of law because in his view there ought to be a new trial. Baron Parke said this: "I cannot, however, help observing that, with the exception of *Reg.* v. *Hawkes* (2 Moo. C. C. 60) there is no case in which it has ever been decided that an instrument could be a bill of exchange where there was not a drawer and a drawee." In the same case Baron Alderson said: "With respect to the question whether this instrument is or is not a bill of exchange, the case of *Reg.* v. *Hawkes* (*supra*) is undoubtedly in point. I must own, however, that I now think that I was wrong on that occasion. This case seems to have been decided on the ground that *Gray* v. *Milner* (8 Taunt. 739) governed it; and the fact was not adverted to, that *Gray* v. *Milner* (*supra*) may be thus explained; that a bill of exchange, made payable at a particular place or house, is meant to be addressed to the person who resides at that place or house." Baron Martin said that if it were necessary to express a decided opinion on the matter of law, he should agree with the views of the two previous judges on that question. "It seems to me," he said "that it is absolutely essential to the validity of a bill of exchange that it should have a drawer and a drawee. . . ."

Therefore it is right to say that these three judges expressed their views that a bill in the form in which the instruments are in this case was not such an instrument as could be sued upon as a bill of exchange at that date. In the case of *Gray* v. *Milner* (*supra*) the document in question was accepted by Milner and drawn by one, W. Sustanance, and was in this form: "May 20th, 1813: Two months after date pay to me, or my order, the sum of thirty-two pounds two shillings. — W. Sustanance." And then there was written on it: "Payable at No. 1 Wilmot-street, opposite the Lamb, Bethnal-green, London," and it appeared that No. 1, Wilmot-street was in fact the address of the acceptor, and that being so, Dallas, C.J. said (8 Taunt. at p. 741): " . . . it was not necessary that the name of the party who afterwards accepted the bill should have been inserted, it being directed to a particular place, which could only mean to the person who resided there." Now, that case is not of any assistance to the plaintiff in this case because the bill in question here is made payable at Lloyd's Bank, High-street, Shoreditch, where it was proved that the defendant had no account at all. Therefore it was not addressed to any place which could be said to be the address of the defendant.

There is one other case, that of *Fielder* v. *Marshall* (3 L. T. Rep. 858), where the decision was to the effect that the document there sued upon was not given as a bill of exchange, but was valid as a promissory note. All that the judges said was that it was right to treat that document as a promissory note, and that judgment might properly be asked upon it as a promissory note; but it seems to me that that judgment assumes that that document was not valid as a bill of exchange. It had a drawer and an acceptor, but no addressee.

In those circumstances it appears to me clear that at least up to the time of the coming into force of the Bills of Exchange Act 1882 this document in the present case would not have been held to be a bill of exchange. And when I come to look at the language of the Act, and the definition of the term "bill of exchange" which it includes, I find myself unable to hold that this instrument is a bill of exchange, and, therefore, the defence must succeed upon that issue.

The application was made to me for leave to amend so as to make the claim against the defendant not as acceptor of a bill of exchange but as the maker of a promissory note. But since the amendment asked for is a technical matter I thought it right to give leave to amend the statement of claim, which must be that the claim is against the defendant as the maker of a promissory note signed by the defendant and payable on the 31st Dec. 1928. And the defendant, as the maker of that promissory note, must be held liable. I have no doubt that up to 1882 this document would have been held to be a good promissory note, and I turn to the Act to see what is the definition of a promissory note, and I find in sect. 83 (1) that: "A promissory note is an unconditional promise in writing made by one person to another, signed by the maker, engaging to pay, on demand or at a fixed or determinable future time, a sum certain in money, to, or to the order of, a specified person or to bearer." In my opinion this document fulfils all the requirements of that definition and, therefore, the plaintiff is entitled to judgment upon the footing of this document being a promissory note. . . .

Judgment for plaintiff.

Note also McIntosh *v.* Lytle, 26 Minn. 336 (Supreme Court, 1880), where an instrument read: "Pay to the order of, on sight, two hundred dollars, in current funds." In an action on the writing by a holder against the drawer, a judgment for defendant was affirmed. "The drawer undoubtedly meant to draw a check, but having left out the payee's name, without inserting in lieu thereof words indicating the bearer as payee, it is as fatally defective as it would be if the drawer's name were omitted."

Compare American National Bank *v.* Kerley, 109 Ore. 155 (Supreme Court, 1923), where in the case of an instrument payable "to the order of the bearer," it was held that the word "bearer" indicated the payee with reasonable certainty.

In Dugane *v.* Hvezda Pokroku, 119 N. W. 141 (Iowa Supreme Court, 1909), an order to pay was addressed to no one in particular but in general terms to anyone who might owe money to the drawer. In an action by a holder it was held that the instrument "was too indefinite and uncertain to be binding on anyone."

In Renfrow *v.* Citizens State Bank, 87 Ind. App. 318 (Appellate Court, 1928), drawee was named as "Bank of Stilesville" instead of correctly as "Citizens Bank of Stilesville." It was held that the description was sufficient.

KRAMER *v.* MID-CITY TRUST & SAVINGS BANK

ILLINOIS APPELLATE COURT, FIRST DISTRICT, 1922

[225 *Illinois Appellate Reports*, 575]

Mr. Presiding Justice BARNES delivered the opinion of the court.

This appeal is from a judgment entered upon a verdict in favor of defendant bank in a suit brought by appellants, a copartnership which had a checking account therein, claiming a wrongful deduction of $3,000 from their account, and refusal to pay them when requested so to do. The bank denied any indebtedness and claimed justification for the so-called deduction, which consisted in the payment of two drafts for $1,000 and $2,000, respectively, drawn upon plaintiffs.

As we view the case the essential facts the evidence tended to establish are about as follows:

Plaintiffs were in the commission business in Chicago. For some years the firm Goldstein Brothers, of Benton Harbor, Michigan, had been buying produce for them. Mannie Goldstein, the son of one of them, was in their employ buying for plaintiffs. In the fall of 1919, an arrangement was made between Goldstein Brothers and plaintiffs for Mannie to go to northern Michigan and buy potatoes and ship them to plaintiffs. Mannie was to draw a draft on plaintiffs for everything he shipped. Plaintiffs and Goldstein Brothers were to divide profits equally. Mannie purchased the potatoes, deposited drafts on plaintiffs in a Charlevoix bank, which gave him credit thereon and forwarded the drafts to a Chicago bank, which in turn sent them through a clearing house to defendant bank, as, pursuant to the arrangement, the drafts were made chargeable to plaintiffs at said bank. These drafts were not sent through for collection and were treated as cash items in accordance with a custom among Chicago banks. Several similar drafts, so drawn before those in question, were paid by defendant and deducted from plaintiffs' account without objection and with plaintiffs' knowledge and consent. But it was claimed by plaintiffs that there was no authorization for the deduction of the two drafts in question.

These two drafts were sight drafts payable to the order of the Charlevoix bank, dated October 16 and 20, 1919, respectively. Each was paid the second day after its date through the Chicago clearing house. The account was overdrawn on the 21st to the extent of $1,349.49, which was after the $1,000 draft had been honored. On each occasion of the receipt by the bank of the drafts in question it called up plaintiffs' firm by telephone and was advised by its bookkeeper that it was all right to pay such drafts, and that the balance of the account would be made good. The record supports the inference that one of the plaintiffs knew of such authorization and promise. At the end of October defendant bank returned said paid drafts to plaintiffs with the statement of their account. At the time the bank notified plaintiffs that the account was overdrawn, one of plaintiffs talked with its bookkeeper in charge of the account and not until November 7, after some disagreement between plaintiffs and the Goldsteins, was any question made as to the authority of the bank to pay the drafts.

We deem it unnecessary to go into further details. Appellants seek a reversal on the ground that there was no written acceptance of the drafts, as required by the Negotiable Instruments Act, and that the court erred in not giving instructions to that effect. . . .

Where the drawer and drawee are the same person, then under section 129 of the Negotiable Instruments Act [Cahill's Ill. St. ch. 98, par. 151] the holder may treat the instrument either as bill of exchange or a promissory note. The drafts in question were drawn by Mannie Goldstein. He was plaintiffs' recognized agent to purchase the potatoes, and authorized by them to draw on them to pay for the same. The drafts seem to have been cashed by the Charlevoix bank upon knowledge of the relation of the parties to the draft. In such a case it has been held that the draft is equivalent to one drawn by the principal upon himself and need not be accepted by the drawee to bind it under the Negotiable Instruments Act. . . .

Affirmed.

In BEADALL *v.* MOORE, 191 N. Y. S. 826 (Supreme Court, Appellate Division, 1922), a bill read as follows:

"London, Nov. 16, 1919.

"George G. Moore.

"Pay A. Mark & Co. or order nine hundred and fifteen pounds (£915).

"George G. Moore"

It was held that the holder had the right to elect to treat the instrument as a negotiable promissory note.

Compare GORDON *v.* LONDON, CITY AND MIDLAND BANK, LTD., [1903] A. C. 250 (House of Lords), where drafts payable to plaintiff's order and drawn on the head office by the branch office of defendant bank were stolen, and were deposited by the thief under forged indorsements in an account with defendant. The account was closed before the fraud was discovered, and in an action by the payee against the bank for conversion it was held that the bank was not entitled to treat the drafts as bills of exchange, since they were not addressed by one person to another. The bank accordingly could not rely on Sec. 60 of the Bills of Exchange Act in defense of the action.

In CHAMBERLAIN *v.* YOUNG, [1893] 2 Q. B. 206 (Court of Appeal), the action was brought by the indorsee against the drawer and indorser of an instrument reading as follows: "Five months after date pay to ——— order the sum of one hundred and fifty pounds for value received." The trial judge decided that the document was not a bill of exchange, but an application for a new trial was granted, Bowen, L.J., saying: "The bill in its present form in effect directs payment 'to my order,' and this is a form of bill which is perfectly well known in the law, and perfectly consistent with its being a negotiable instrument from the moment when it was issued."

Compare Secs. 1 (1) and (5), 8, 126, 128, and 130 of the Uniform Negotiable Instruments Law with Secs. 3, 5, 6, and 7 of the Bills of Exchange Act and with Arts. 1, 2, and 3 of the Geneva Law.

INCITTI *v.* FERRANTE

BERGEN COUNTY COURT OF COMMON PLEAS, 1933

[12 *New Jersey Miscellaneous Reports*, 840]

DELMAR, C. P. J. This action was brought by the plaintiff against the defendants upon a promissory note alleged to have been made by the defendants for the sum of "15,400 Italian lires." The complaint does not allege any consideration for the note and concludes with a prayer for judgment against the defendants for said sum of 15,400 Italian lires, or its equivalent in lawful money of the United States. The note is dated at Hackensack, New Jersey, and is made payable at the Bank Italia Company, and neither the complaint nor the note sets forth the address of said company, so that the presumption, therefore, is that the note is payable in the State of New Jersey.

Defendants moved to strike out the complaint on the ground that the same does not set forth a cause of action; and in the argument on said motion they contended that the note in question is not negotiable and that the complaint, therefore, must allege a consideration, which it does not do.

Upon the argument the point made by defendants' counsel was that the note was not made for money, but for a commodity and that, therefore, there is no presumption that it was made upon a legal consideration. In support of this contention counsel cites *Thompson* v. *Sloan et al.*, 23 Wend. 71.

Whether the note in question is or is not negotiable must be determined by the laws of this state. *Story Confl. L.* (2d ed.), § 317; *Thompson* v. *Taylor*, 66 N. J. L. 253; 49 *Atl. Rep.* 544; *Campbell* v. *Nichols*, 33 N. J. L. 81.

The note in question is negotiable in form unless the provision for the payment of the sum named in Italian lire makes it non-negotiable. . . .

If it had been the intention of the legislature to provide that a note in order to be negotiable must be payable in lawful money of the United States, or in legal tender, it would have been a simple matter to have used language appropriate for that purpose. The use of the words, "money and current money," indicate that such was not the purpose.

The question arises — what is money? Money is purely a legal institution; it is impossible without law. "Money is what the law or custom makes receivable for payments, taxes and debts." See Delmar, *The Science of Money* (3d ed.) 25, 46. "Money by itself is but a mere device. It has value only by law and not by nature. So that a change of convention between those that use it is sufficient to deprive it of its value and of its power to purchase our requirements." Aristotle's *Politica.*

What then does our law provide?

The constitution of the United States, article 1, section 8, provides that the "congress shall have power to coin money, regulate the value thereof, and of foreign coin," "and under the power vested in it by this section of the constitution the congress has from time to time established the value of foreign coins. It is a matter of common knowledge that foreign coins of various nations such as England, Spain, France, Portugal and Mexico, passed as currency in the United States prior to the civil war. (Sometimes as legal tender under acts of congress.) In fact, they constituted at that time, with the exception of the note issues of the state banks, the bulk of the currency then in circulation. The congress from the earliest times has fixed the values of various foreign coins by statute. One of these statutes, namely, act of August 27th, 1894, chapter 349, section 25, provides, 'The value of foreign coin as expressed in the money of account of the United States shall be that of the pure metal of such coin of standard value, and the values of the standard coins in circulation of the various nations of the world shall be estimated quarterly by the director of the mint and be proclaimed by the secretary of the treasury immediately after the passage of this act and thereafter quarterly on the 1st day of January, April, July and October in each year.' "

It is well established that a bill or note may be payable in the money of any country, that is to say in its coins, "such as guineas, ducats, louis d'ors, doubloons, crowns or dollars; or in the known currency of a country, as pounds sterling, livres, tournoises, francs, florins, &c.; for in all these cases the sum of money is fixed by the par exchange on the known denomination of the currency with reference to the par." *Story Bills,* § 43; *Daniell Neg. Inst.,* § 58; *Edw. Bills* 137, 138. See, also, *King* v. *Hamilton,* 12 Fed. Rep. 478, the material facts in which case are similar to those in the case at bar.

The law merchant is international in its character and was developed for the purpose of facilitating trade in commerce between different countries. It seems clear, therefore, that where a note is made payable in a country in the money or coins of another country, which money or coins have a value fixed by the law or under the authority of the law of the country where the note is payable, and which value can by a simple mathematical calculation be expressed in the value of the lawful money of the latter country, that such note by the rules of the law merchant and under the Uniform Negotiable Instruments act is negotiable. There is a scarcity of decisions in this country touching this question. The following cases, most of which have been cited by counsel for the plaintiff as authorities, bear on the point: *Black* v. *Ward,* 27 Mich. 193. In this case, however, the note was made in Michigan but was payable in Canada in Canada currency. It was decided that the note was payable in money and, therefore, negotiable. This can hardly be considered a precedent, because the note being payable in Canada was governed as to its negotiability by the law of that country, and, therefore, was payable in its own currency. *Hogue* v. *Williams*, 85 Tex. 553; 22 *S. W. Rep.* 580; 20 *L. R. A.* 481. The note in this case was made at Saltillo, in Mexico; no place of payment was specified but it was payable in one thousand Mexican silver dollars. The case was decided on the theory that Mexican silver dollars were recognized by the United States laws as money of the Republic of Mexico, and that, therefore, the note was negotiable; but since no place of payment was specified the note should have been construed under the laws of Mexico, and since it was payable in Mexican money, it was not an authority on the point in question.

In *Thompson* v. *Sloan, supra*, decided in 1840, the note was made and dated at Buffalo, New York, in the year 1836, for $2,500, payable in Buffalo, "in Canada money." This case is cited by counsel for the defendants as authority for the point argued by them that a note payable here in the coin of a foreign country is not negotiable. The court said: "A promissory note must in order to come within the statute * * * be payable in money only, in current specie * * * ; or, at least, in what we can judicially notice as equivalent to money. * * * Admitting that the note in question imports an obligation to pay in gold and silver current in Canada, I do not see on what principle we can pronounce it to be payable in money within the meaning of the rule. It is not pretended that coins current in Canada are, therefore, so in this state. As gold and silver they might readily be received and so might the coin of any foreign country, Germany or Russia for instance, but the creditor might, and in many cases doubtless would refuse to receive them because ignorant of their value. In law they are all collateral commodities like ingots or diamonds, which, though they might be received and be, in fact, equivalent to money are not yet goods and chattels. A note payable in either would, therefore, be no more negotiable than if it were payable in cattle or other specific articles. The fact of Canada coins being current here is not, at any rate, so notorious that we can judicially notice them as a universal customary medium of payment in this state, and if not, they are no more a part of our currency than Pennsylvania bank bills. * * * Nor do I perceive in the case any proof or offer to prove that such coins were of universal currency."

It must be borne in mind that at the time of this decision there was no country or province known as "Canada." "There were at that time the provinces of Upper Canada [Ontario], and the province of Lower Canada [Quebec], and it was not until the year 1841 that they were united into a single province, and not until many years later that the present Dominion of Canada was formed. At that time and for many years afterwards there was no currency issued in Canada. Both English and American coins circulated. The standard was gold, but there were different methods of counting, namely, English currency, Halifax currency and Canadian sterling, the respective ratios being 100:120:108. So that even if the note were held to be payable in gold coin current in Canada there was no way to determine the weight and fineness of the coin.

"It must also be remembered that prior to the civil war the circulating medium of the United States consisted almost entirely of bank notes issued by numerous independent corporations variously organized under state legislation of various degrees of credit and very unequal resources. 'Acts of congress prohibited the receipt of disbursement in the transactions of the national government of anything except gold and silver and the laws of the states required the redemption of bank notes in coin on demand. There was no national currency excepting coin. There was no general regulation of any other by national legislation.' *Veazie Bank* v. *Fenno*, 8 Wall. 539; 75 U. S. 482. The bulk of the currency circulating in New York in 1836 consisted of bank bills issued by various state banks and coins issued by the United States and a few foreign countries and the power of congress to issue paper currency had not then been determined. I do not, therefore, consider the decision in this case to be adverse to the contention of the plaintiff but rather as supporting it, especially so, as the court further stated, "this view of the case is not incompatible with a bill or note payable in money of a foreign denomination or any other denomination being negotiable, for it can be paid in our own coin of equivalent value to which it is always reduced by a recovery."

In *Hebblethwaite* v. *Flint*, 173 N. Y. Supp. 81, the note was made in Brazil and payable in the national currency of that country stabilized by a specific rate of exchange into British sterling. It is not stated where the note was payable. The court held that the note was negotiable by the law merchant, distinguishing this case from *Thompson* v. *Sloan*, *supra*, because the note in this case was made abroad, the court saying, "that cannot apply to notes made abroad which incidentally come before our courts."

In the case of *Reisfeld* v. *Jacobs*, 176 N. Y. Supp. 223, involving a contract for the purchase of Russian bank notes, it was held that such notes were not money. The court said, "in view of the fact that these notes were issued by a government now defunct and that the United States at present has no relations with any government in Russia, the court cannot take judicial notice that these notes are backed by the credit of a responsible government or that they even pass current anywhere as money." The court, therefore, found that the contract in question was a contract for the sale of goods.

A year prior to this decision, however, the same court in the case of *Brown* v. *Perera*, 176 N. Y. Supp. 215, affirmed an opinion of a referee holding that "foreign money is not, in legal contemplation, a legal commodity or article of merchandise, but that it was money, the title to which was acquired by the innocent holder, even though he purchased it from one who had no title. As was said in the former case (*Reisfeld* v. *Jacobs*), the opinion in the latter case "concerns the question whether money issued under the authority of a responsible government and used generally for the purpose of convenient transaction is negotiable, and this has no application to the question presented in the case at bar."

The contract sued on here is a contract for the payment of money and not a commodity. It is also a contract for the payment of Italian lire and, therefore, within the purview of the act of 1879, *supra*, under which act the value of this foreign coin in money of the United States is established by the director of the mint and proclaimed by the secretary of the treasury. This note was made for a sum certain, because a note for any number of Italian lire is only another form of expression for the equivalent in dollars, which equivalent is now established under the authority of the legislation previously referred to. See *King* v. *Hamilton*, *supra*.

The motion to strike out the complaint is, therefore, denied.

In COHN *v.* BOULKEN, 36 T. L. R. 767 (King's Bench Division, 1920), the action was against the drawer by the indorsee of a check "for 7,680 francs (Paris)" drawn in London on a London bank. It was objected that this was not a bill of exchange as no rate of exchange was indicated and no direction was given on the cheque from which the rate of exchange could be ascertained. The objection was overruled. The rate of exchange was sufficiently indicated on the face of the cheque, or in any event by banking practice (which had been proved) to pay at the rate current on presentation.

In KLAUBER *v.* BIGGERSTAFF, 47 Wisconsin 551 (Supreme Court, 1879), Ryan, C. J., said: "The controlling question in this case is whether the certificate of deposit stated in the proceedings is negotiable. . . . The learned counsel for the respondents . . . takes the position that the certificate of deposit in question is not a promissory note, because it is not payable in money. It is for so many dollars, payable in currency; and the learned counsel contends that the word *currency* does not express or imply money. . . . Money is a generic and comprehensive term. It is not a synonym of coin. It includes coin, but is not confined to it. It includes whatever is lawfully and actually current in buying and selling, of the value and as the equivalent of coin. By universal consent, under the sanction of all courts, everywhere, or almost everywhere, bank-notes lawfully issued, actually current at par in lieu of coin, are money. The common term, paper money, is in a legal sense quite as accurate as the term, coined money. . . . To be money, part of the circulating medium, it is not essential that currency should be legal tender against the wishes of the person to whom it is tendered. Even coined money is not, under all circumstances, legal tender. But paper currency, bank-notes which are current *de jure et de facto*, are legal tender unless specially objected to at the time of tender, for the reason that they are money, though not absolutely legal tender. With some exceptions this doctrine is general in this country. . . . In fact almost all civilized countries, including this country, have a mixed circulation of coin and bank-notes. These constitute the currency of the country — its money; and the general term, currency, includes both. Currency, therefore, means money — coined money and paper money equally. But it means money only; and the only practical distinction between paper money and coined money, as currency, is that coined money must generally be received, paper money may generally be specially refused, in payment of debt; but a payment in either is equally made in money — equally good. The confusion in the cases appears to have arisen for want of proper distinction between money which is current and money which is legal tender. The property of being legal tender is not necessarily inherent in money; it generally belongs no more to inferior coin than to paper money. . . . The certificate of deposit in this case calls for so many dollars; that is to say, for so much money. It makes them payable in currency, which also means money. It could be paid only in money. It was, therefore, clearly negotiable."

In ROBERTS *v.* SMITH, 58 Vt. 492 (Supreme Court, 1886), a note reading "Two years from date for value received I promise to pay J. S. King or bearer one ounce of gold" was held to be a simple contract for the delivery of merchandise, and not a promissory note.

In PRATT *v.* HIGGINSON, 230 Mass. 256 (Supreme Judicial Court, 1918), a 4 per cent convertible gold bond of the American Telephone and Telegraph Company provided that the holder at maturity might receive the face of the bond in money, or at his option an equivalent in stock of the company. The bond was held to be a negotiable instrument.

In LESSEN *v.* LINDSEY, 238 App. Div. 262 (New York Supreme Court, Appellate Division, 1933), a note contained a promise to pay $625.00 "with interest thereon at the rate of eight per cent per annum from date until fully paid. Interest payable semi-annually. . . . Deferred payments to bear interest from maturity at ten per cent per annum semi-annually." In holding the note to be for a sum certain the Court referred to *First National Bank of Miami* v. *Bosler*, 297 Penn. 353, and said: "It was reasoned in that case that the notes carried eight per cent interest on the principal sum secured up to the time when the principal or any part thereof was paid, whether at or after maturity, that 'deferred payments' bearing ten per cent interest referred to payments of principal as well as interest and that thereby uncertainty of amount to be paid resulted. We disagree with this reasoning. The applicability of the provision as to payment of eight per cent interest on principal seems clear. It covers all principal unpaid and as long as it is unpaid, whether at or after the maturity date of the notes. The 'deferred payments' refer only to payments of interest accrued and unpaid at and at any time after the maturity date of the notes. Thus construed the notes present no ambiguity or inconsistency."

Compare Secs. 1 (2), 6 (5) and 17 (1) and (2) of the Uniform Negotiable Instruments Law with Secs. 3 (1) and (2), and 9 of the Bills of Exchange Act, and with Arts. 1, 5, and 33 of the Geneva Law.

PIERCE, BUTLER & PIERCE MANUFACTURING CORP. *v.* DANIEL RUSSELL BOILER WORKS, INC.

MASSACHUSETTS SUPREME JUDICIAL COURT, 1927

[262 *Massachusetts Reports*, 242]

BRALEY, J. These four actions of contract, which were tried together, are brought to recover the amount of certain "trade acceptances" identical in form except as to dates, the amount, the time of payment, and the drawee. The declaration in each case consisted of three counts upon a separate trade acceptance, and, the plaintiff having waived the first count in one of the actions, the trial proceeded upon the remaining eleven counts. The answers were a general denial with averments of payment, and that the indorsements were *ultra vires* as to the defendant corporation, as well as the want of authority of its treasurer to make the indorsements. A copy of one of the acceptances as shown by the record, which is typical of all of them, is in these words.

TRADE ACCEPTANCE

Boston, Mass., Mar. 24, 1922 $525.00

Sixty Days after date Pay to the Order of Ourselves

Five hundred twenty-five.................................00/100 Dollars

As per invoice of Your Account With Exchange and interest

The obligations of the acceptor hereof arises out of the purchase of goods from the drawer and such goods remain the property of said drawer, until this acceptance is paid.

Value received and charge the same to the account of

COMMONWEALTH PIPE & SUPPLY CO. INC.
By: Earle L. Wheeler, Asst. Treas.

To Economy Plb. & Htg. Co.,
72 Middle St., Lowell, Mass.

Accepted Mar. 24, 1922, Payable at Lowell Trust Co., Lowell, Mass.

ECONOMY PLUMBING & HEATING CO., N. P. Nelson, Treas.

It appears that each acceptance was signed by authority of the "Commonwealth Pipe & Supply Company," as drawer, and was made payable to the order of "Ourselves." It was conceded that each instrument had been accepted by the drawee prior to its delivery by the drawer, who was also the payee, to the plaintiff. The indorsements were in the following order: "Commonwealth Pipe & Supply Company by Earle L. Wheeler, Asst. Treas. Daniel Russell Boiler Works, By: Daniel Russell, Treas. Manton A. Wood." We shall hereinafter refer to the "Commonwealth Pipe & Supply Company" as the drawer, and to the defendant, the Daniel Russell Boiler Works, Incorporated, as the indorser.

While the "trade acceptances" are to be considered as bills of exchange under G. L. c. 107, § 149, *Jones* v. *Revere Preserving Co.* 247 Mass. 225.

227, the question of liability between the indorser and the plaintiff is governed by the same rules as if the acceptances or bills of exchange were promissory notes. *Grant* v. *Wood*, 12 Gray, 220.

It is provided in each acceptance that "The obligations of the acceptor hereof arises out of the purchase of goods from the drawer and such goods remain the property of said drawer, until this acceptance is paid"; and each instrument shows upon its face that the acceptances were given in payment for goods bought under a contract of sale wherein the drawer was the conditional vendor and the acceptor, the Economy Plumbing & Heating Co., was the conditional vendee. It is settled by *Sloan v. McCarty*, 134 Mass. 245, that at common law the acceptances were "something more than a promise to pay money, and the promise to pay money is not a promise to pay it absolutely and at all events." The words of the acceptances as quoted incorporated the contingency that title to the goods was to remain in the drawer until the acceptances were paid. The time fixed for payment consequently might be shortened or prolonged beyond sixty days from the date of the acceptance, when it matured and became payable. The time of payment was indefinite and uncertain. The acceptances accordingly were not negotiable instruments at common law.

The plaintiff, however, presses the argument that "G. L. c. 107, §§ 25–46 inclusive," has changed the common law, and this defence has been abrogated. But a full review of these sections and their application in connection with the present record is unnecessary. In *Central National Bank* v. *Hubbel*, 258 Mass. 124, the note in suit contained a statement, that it was "one of a series . . . given . . . as per contract for certain apparatus, it is hereby agreed that the ownership and title of said apparatus remain in . . . [payee] until this note is fully paid. . . ." It was held that, "The negotiable instrument law affords no ground for reaching any different conclusion from that reached before it was enacted." And the cases in other jurisdictions in accordance with this result are there collected. If in that case the note was nonnegotiable under the act, because G. L. c. 107, § 23, among other provisions requires, that to be negotiable, a note or bill "Must be payable on demand, or at a fixed or determinable future time," the acceptances in the cases at bar also come within the rule. The plaintiff therefore took them subject to all the equities.

[The balance of the opinion is omitted.]

In MILLS *v.* CHARLSON, 201 Minn. 167 (Supreme Court, 1937), a note reading "after date, for value received, we promise to pay, etc.," was held to be negotiable on the ground that in the absence of an expressed due date the instrument was to be construed as payable on demand.

In GRANT *v.* WOOD, 12 Gray 220 (Massachusetts Supreme Judicial Court, 1858), a bill drawn under a contract for the sale of coal read as follows: "At sight after the arrival and discharge of coal per Brig Wm. M. Groton, bill lading dated Philadelphia, Nov. 30, 1854, pay to the order of myself fifteen hundred dollars, value received." The instrument was held to be not negotiable, as payable on a contingency.

In NORTHRIDGE *v.* GRENIER, 278 Mass. 438 (Supreme Judicial Court, 1932), Rugg, C.J., said:

"This is an action to recover an instalment due on a written instrument, with interest. The instrument was duly protested and the action is against the indorser. The instrument, otherwise a promissory note payable to the defendant in quarterly specified instalments, contained these words: '. . . with the right to anticipate any or all payments at any time. . . .' The single question for decision is whether an instrument payable in instalments, indisputably a promissory note in every other particular, is rendered nonnegotiable by reason of the right reserved to anticipate payments.

"The decision of that question depends upon the correct interpretation of the relevant sections of the negotiable instrument law which is found in G. L. c. 107. . . . Interpreting these words according to the common and approved usage of the language, there is no doubt of their significance. An instrument payable at a stated time or times with the privilege on the part of those liable on it to anticipate any or all payments at any time cannot reasonably be thought to be payable in any other way than on or before a fixed or determinable future time.

"Before the passage of any controlling statute and under the common law of this Commonwealth a written promise to pay in the terms of the one here in suit was not negotiable. *Stults* v. *Silva*, 119 Mass. 137. *Mahoney* v. *Fitzpatrick*, 133 Mass. 151. It is not necessary to revert to the common law and those decisions do not state the present law of the Commonwealth in view of the explicit provisions of G. L. c. 107 already quoted. It is our duty to construe the provisions of the negotiable instrument act in conformity to their obvious meaning without regard to the previous law of the Commonwealth unless necessary to resolve some doubt or obscurity. . . .

"It follows that the instrument in question is negotiable, the defendant is liable upon it as indorser and judgment is to be entered for the plaintiff. The exact amount for which judgment is to be entered is to be determined in the Superior Court.

"So ordered."

Compare PEOPLE'S FINANCE & THRIFT CO. *v.* SHAW-LEAHY CO., 214 Calif. 108 (Supreme Court, 1931), where a trade acceptance contained the following clause: "The obligation of the acceptor of this bill arises out of the purchase of goods from the drawer. Upon the acceptor hereof suspending payment, giving a chattel mortgage, suffering a fire loss, disposing of his business or failing to meet at maturity any prior trade acceptance, this trade acceptance, at the option of the holder, shall immediately become due and payable." The drawer sold this acceptance for value. Subsequently the contract of sale between drawer and acceptor, on which the acceptance was based, was cancelled. In an action by the holder against the acceptor it was contended that in order to preserve negotiability the events and contingencies specified in the acceleration clauses must be such in their nature that the happening thereof will be brought about by some act or omission on the part of the acceptor, and must relate to some business act incidental to the collection of the instrument. It was held that the instrument was negotiable.

Compare Secs. 1 (3) and 4 of the Uniform Negotiable Instruments Law with Secs. 3 and 11 of the Bills of Exchange Act and with Arts. 1 (4), 2, and 33 of the Geneva Law.

HAGGARD *v.* MUTUAL OIL & REFINING COMPANY

KENTUCKY COURT OF APPEALS, 1924

[204 *Kentucky Reports*, 209]

Opinion of the Court by Judge CLARKE — Affirming.

The single question presented by this appeal is whether or not the following check is a negotiable instrument:

Winchester, Ky., July 10, 1920.

$2,500.00

THE WINCHESTER BANK,
of Winchester, Ky.

Pay to Arco Refinery Construction Co. [The printed words "or bearer" in the form used had been stricken out by a line drawn through them.] Twenty-five Hundred and no/100 Dollars. For a/c Constructing Refinery, switch & loading racks, Win., Ky.

MUTUAL OIL & REFINING CO.,
By C. L. Bell, Pres.

. . . .

Since, as the check itself shows, and as is admittedly true, the maker, in issuing the check, drew a line through the printed words "or bearer," we need only to examine it to ascertain whether or not it was "payable to the order of a specified person," for unless so, it lacked one of the essentials prescribed for negotiability. . . .

It will be noticed that the above check is not payable to the order of the payee, nor to the payee or its order, but is payable simply to the payee. It therefore seems to us too clear for dispute that this check is not payable to order, and is, therefore, as the lower court held, not negotiable.

In other words, we think it is clear that subsection 8 means, as it says, that the instrument must be payable either (1) to the order of the payee, or (2) to the payee or order, and that it does not permit of the construction that the instrument may be payable (1) to the order of the payee, (2) or to the payee, or (3) to his order.

To give the section the latter of these two constructions rather than the former makes the first and third alternatives identical, and this plainly was never intended. Not only is this conclusion unavoidable from a consideration simply of the language of the section, but it has uniformly been so construed by this and other courts. *Wettlaufer* v. *Baxter*, 137 Ky. 362, 125 S. W. 741; *Kerr* v. *Smith*, 142 N. Y. S. 57; *Johnson* v. *Lessiter*, 155 N. C. 47, 71 S. E. 23; *Gilley* v. *Harrell*, 118 Tenn. 115, 101 S. W. 424;

Cowan v. *Hallack*, 9 Colo. 572; *Fawsett* v. *U. S. Nat. L. Ins. Co.*, 97 Ill. 11, 37 Am. R. 95.

In England and Canada the rule is otherwise, but this is due to the fact that the Bills of Exchange Act expressly provides that a bill or note is payable to order where expressed to be payable to a particular person and not containing words prohibiting transfer or indicating an intention that it should not be transferable. 8 C. J. 153.

Counsel for appellant concede that this section has been construed by this court and others in the above cases to require the use of the words "order, or bearer," or other words of similar legal import in order to make a note or other bill negotiable, but they insist that there is such a material difference between a note and a check as that these cases are not applicable to one in which, as here, the bill is a check.

But in this they are clearly mistaken. Section 185 of the act expressly declares that a check is a bill of exchange payable on demand, and that, except as otherwise therein provided, the provisions of the act applicable to a bill of exchange payable on demand shall apply to a check, and as it is not otherwise therein provided, it is clear that sections 1 and 8 of the act apply to a check as well as to any other bill of exchange, and to be negotiable it also must employ some such words as "order" or "bearer" indicating negotiability.

It results therefore that a check, just as any other bill of exchange that is made payable simply to the payee and not to his order or to bearer, is not negotiable, and that appellant, to whom this check was assigned by the payee, took same subject to all defenses which were available between the original parties.

The lower court therefore did not err in overruling appellant's demurrer to appellee's answer pleading want of consideration, etc., or in dismissing his petition upon his refusal to reply thereto.

Judgment affirmed.

In Charleston National Bank *v.* Lemkuhl, 97 W. Va. 284 (Supreme Court, 1924), a completed note read as follows: "*One month* after date I promise to pay to the order of *Gordon S. Seal One Hundred Dollars*, negotiable and payable at the Charleston National Bank." The italicized words were written in the blanks of a printed form by the maker who at the same time drew a line through the words "the order of." It was held that the note was not negotiable.

Compare Essig *v.* Porter, 63 Ind. App. 318 (Appellate Court, 1916), where the instrument read: "One day after date I promise to pay S. J. Porter the sum of $318, negotiable and payable at the Union Bank." The note was held to be negotiable.

In First National Bank of Sidney *v.* Greenlee, 102 Neb. 180 (Supreme Court, 1918), a note was in the following form: "One year after date I promise to pay to the order of L. F. Closman only one thousand dollars." The words "to the order of" were part of a printed form, but the word "only" was written by the maker. The note was held to be non-negotiable.

THE MECHANICS' BANK OF THE CITY OF NEW YORK *v.* STRAITON

NEW YORK COURT OF APPEALS, 1867

[3 *Keyes's Reports*, 365]

Appeal from a judgment of the Supreme Court, rendered at General Term, in the second district, affirming a judgment at Special Term overruling a demurrer.

The action was brought by the respondents as the holders of a check payable to "bills payable or order" against the appellants as drawers.

The complaint alleges that the appellants drew the check, and that it was afterward, for a valuable consideration, transferred and delivered to the respondents, whereby they became and are the holders and owners of it.

The appellants demurred on the grounds — first, that the check is an irregular instrument, not negotiable and void; second, that the complaint does not state facts sufficient to constitute a cause of action.

SCRUGHAM, J. The rules which establish the negotiability of commercial paper apply to bank checks as to other bills of exchange, and the doctrine that when such instruments are made payable to the order of a fictitious payee, they are to be construed and treated as payable to bearer, is too well settled to admit of serious question.

In the great case of *Minet* v. *Gibson* (1 H. Bl. 569), the determination proceeded upon the ground that according to the true intent and meaning of the parties the bill was intended to be made payable to bearer.

The words "or order," "or bearer," and "bearer," in notes or bills are words of negotiability, without which or other equivalent words the instrument will not possess that quality, and therefore the use of either of these expressions by the drawer of a bill or maker of a note must be regarded as indicating his intention that the paper shall be negotiable.

By naming the person to whose order the instrument is payable, the maker manifests his intention to limit its negotiability by imposing the condition of indorsement upon its first transfer. But no such intention is indicated by the designation of a fictitious or impersonal payee, for indorsement under such circumstances is manifestly impossible; and words of negotiability, when used in connection with such designation, are capable of no reasonable interpretation except as expressive of an intention that the bill shall be negotiable without indorsement; i.e., in the same manner as if it had been made payable to bearer. . . .

The judgment should be affirmed.

All the judges concurring,

Judgment affirmed.

In AMERICAN NATIONAL BANK *v.* KERLEY, 109 Oregon 155 (*supra* p. 612), where the instrument was payable "to the order of the bearer," the Court said ***inter alia***: "We cannot agree with the contention of the plaintiff that the instrument may be treated as one payable to bearer without the condition of indorsement, on the theory that it is payable to a fictitious payee; nor can we accept the view suggested by the plaintiff that the paper may be deemed payable to bearer on the theory that the name of the payee does not purport to be the name of any person within the meaning of Section 7801, subdiv. 4, Or. L. The rule, recognized by the law-merchant and by the statute, which declares that an instrument made payable to the order of a fictitious person is payable to bearer, and the likewise recognized rule which declares that a writing payable to the order of an impersonal or inanimate payee, as, for example, 'cash,' 'bills payable,' and the like, is payable to bearer, are based upon the idea that the maker, although knowing in one case that the payee is fictitious and therefore cannot indorse and in the other case knowing that the impersonal payee is neither a natural nor an artificial person and therefore is not a payee who can indorse, intends by the use of the word 'order' to make the instrument negotiable, and since that intention cannot be effected by the indorsement of the fictitious or nonexisting payee or by the indorsement of the inanimate payee, the intention will in each of such two instances be given effect by treating the instrument as one payable to bearer. The reason upon which these two rules are based cannot be said to be present in the instant case; and, the reason failing, the rule fails. A fictitious or nonexisting person cannot be the 'bearer' of a paper; nor can an inanimate payee be the 'bearer'; but a natural or artificial person may be the 'bearer' of paper."

THE GOVERNOR AND COMPANY OF THE BANK OF ENGLAND *v.* VAGLIANO BROTHERS

House of Lords, 1891

[*Law Reports*, [1891] *Appeal Cases*, 107]

Lord Herschell. My Lords, I propose to deal at the outset with the question of the construction of the Bills of Exchange Act, which gave rise to a difference of opinion in the Court below.

The facts material to this part of the case I take to be these. The bills in question purported to be drawn by Vucina, but were, in fact, entirely the production of Glyka, a clerk in the service of Vagliano Brothers, the respondents. He fraudulently procured the necessary forms to be printed and filled them up, inserting the name of Vucina as drawer and of C. Petridi & Co. as payees. A firm of C. Petridi & Co. carries on business at Constantinople, and had been the payee of some genuine bills previously drawn by Vucina upon Vagliano Brothers. I think there can be no doubt that this fact suggested to Glyka the insertion of the name of C. Petridi & Co.; but I do not believe that he made this choice with the idea that it would assist his fraud. I entertain no doubt, under the circumstances disclosed by the evidence, that Vagliano Brothers would equally have accepted the bills if any other name had been inserted, and that Glyka knew this. It was of course never intended by Glyka that Petridi & Co. should be the persons to whom the bill should be paid. The name was inserted merely to make the bills complete in form. The bills were accepted by Vagliano Brothers, payable at the Bank of England, who were requested by Vagliano Brothers to pay them at maturity. They were presented for payment with indorsements to all appearance regular, these having been written by Glyka, and were paid to the persons presenting them at maturity.

The conclusion at which the majority of the Court of Appeal arrived with reference to the construction of the sub-section of the Bills of Exchange Act with which your Lordships have to deal is thus stated: "The word 'fictitious' must in each case be interpreted with due regard to the person against whom the bill is sought to be enforced. If the drawer is the person against whom the bill is to be treated as a bill payable to bearer, the term 'fictitious' may be satisfied if it is fictitious as regards himself, or in other words fictitious to his knowledge. If the obligations of the acceptor are in question, and the acceptor is the person against whom the bill is to be so treated, 'ficitious' must mean fictitious as regards the acceptor, and to his knowledge. Such an interpretation is based on good sense and sound commercial principle."

The conclusion thus expressed was founded upon an examination of the state of the law at the time the Bills of Exchange Act was passed. The prior authorities were subjected by the learned Judges who concurred in this conclusion to an elaborate review, with the result that it was established to their satisfaction that a bill made payable to a fictitious person or his order was, as against the acceptor, in effect a bill payable to bearer, only when the acceptor was aware of the circumstance that the payee was a fictitious person, and further, that his liability in that case depended upon an application of the law of estoppel. It appeared to those learned Judges that if the exception was to be further extended, it would rest upon no principle, and that they might well pause before holding that sect. 7, sub-sect. 3, of the statute was "intended not merely to codify the existing law, but to alter it and to introduce so remarkable and unintelligible a change."

My Lords, with sincere respect for the learned Judges who have taken this view, I cannot bring myself to think that this is the proper way to deal with such a statute as the Bills of Exchange Act, which was intended to be a code of the law relating to negotiable instruments. I think the proper course is in the first instance to examine the language of the statute and to ask what is its natural meaning, uninfluenced by any considerations derived from the previous state of the law, and not to start with inquiring how the law previously stood, and then, assuming that it was probably intended to leave it unaltered, to see if the words of the enactment will bear an interpretation in conformity with this view.

If a statute, intended to embody in a code a particular branch of the law, is to be treated in this fashion, it appears to me that its utility will be almost entirely destroyed, and the very object with which it was enacted will be frustrated. The purpose of such a statute surely was that on any point specifically dealt with by it, the law should be ascertained by interpreting the language used instead of, as before, by roaming over a vast number of authorities in order to discover what the law was, extracting it by a minute critical examination of the prior decisions, dependent upon a knowledge of the exact effect even of an obsolete proceeding such as a demurrer to evidence. I am of course far from asserting that resort may never be had to the previous state of the law for the purpose of aiding in the construction of the provisions of the code. If, for example, a provision be of doubtful import, such resort would be perfectly legitimate. Or, again, if in a code of the law of negotiable instruments words be found which have previously acquired a technical meaning, or been used in a sense other than their ordinary one, in relation to such instruments, the same interpretation might well be put upon them in the code. I give these as examples merely; they, of course, do not exhaust the category. What, however, I am venturing to insist upon is, that the first step taken should be to interpret the language of the statute, and that an appeal to earlier decisions can only be justified on some special ground.

One further remark I have to make before I proceed to consider the language of the statute. The Bills of Exchange Act was certainly not intended to be merely a code of the existing law. It is not open to question that it was intended to alter, and did alter it in certain respects. And I do not think that it is to be presumed that any particular provision was intended to be a statement of the existing law, rather than a substituted enactment.

Turning now to the words of the sub-section, I confess they appear to me to be free from ambiguity. "Where the payee is a fictitious or non-existent person" means, surely, according to ordinary canons of construction, in every case where this can, as a matter of fact, be predicated of the payee.

I can find no warrant in the statute itself for inserting any limitation or condition. I am putting aside for the present the question by whom a bill answering the description of the sub-section may be treated as payable to bearer, and I am accepting too for the moment the meaning attributed by the majority of the Court of Appeal to the word "fictitious," *viz.* a creation of the imagination, confining myself to the question in what cases a bill purporting on the face of it to be payable to order may be treated as payable to bearer. I find it impossible without doing violence to the language of the statute to give any other answer than this — In all cases in which the payee is a fictitious or non-existent person. The majority of the Court of Appeal read the section thus: Where the payee is a fictitious or non-existent person, the bill may, as against any party who had knowledge of the fact, be treated as a bill payable to bearer. It seems to me that this is to add to the words of the statute and to insert a limitation which is not to be found in it or indicated by it. It is said that when the acceptor is the person against whom the bill is to be treated as payable to bearer, " 'fictitious' must mean fictitious as regards the acceptor, and to his knowledge." With all respect, I am unable to see why it must mean this. I confess I cannot altogether follow the meaning of the words fictitious "as regards" the acceptor. I have a difficulty in seeing how a payee, who is in fact a "fictitious" person in the sense in which that word is being used, can be otherwise than fictitious as regards all the world — how such a payee can be "fictitious" as regards one person and not another. The truth is the words, "as regards" the acceptor, are treated as equivalent to the words, "to the knowledge of" the acceptor. But I do not think these expressions are synonymous. It seems to me that to import into the statute after the words "fictitious person" the words "as regards" the acceptor or drawer, as the case may be, and then to interpret those words as meaning "to the knowledge of," only tends to obscure the fact that the condition that the payee must be fictitious to the knowledge of the person sought to be charged as upon a bill payable to bearer is being introduced into the enactment.

For the reasons I have given I find myself compelled to the conclusion, notwithstanding my respect for those who have expressed a contrary view, that in order to establish the right to treat a bill as payable to bearer it is enough to prove that the payee is in fact a fictitious person, and that it is not necessary if it be sought to charge the acceptor to prove in addition that he was cognisant of the fictitious character of the payee.

[Three pages of the opinion, arguing that the interpretation adopted is in accordance with sound commercial principle, are here omitted.]

Even assuming, it is said, that where the payee is a "fictitious" person the bill may be treated as against the acceptor as a bill payable to bearer, the word "fictitious" is only applicable to a creature of the imagination, having no real existence, whilst in the present case "C. Petridi and Company" was the name of a firm having a real existence, so that the payee here cannot be termed a fictitious person. But are the words "where the payee is a fictitious person" incapable of legitimate application in any other case than that suggested? The first observation I have to make is, that, if so, there was no necessity for the introduction of the word "fictitious" in the enactment; the word "non-existent" would have sufficed. It was argued that whilst a fictitious person is one who has never existed, a non-existent person is one who has existed but whose existence has ceased. But even if this be admitted, the word "non-existent" would have sufficed, for it can hardly be doubted that it is employed as suitably in reference to that which has never existed as to that which, having existed, exists no longer.

Without however dwelling too much on this point, which may perhaps have a historical explanation, let me call attention to the inconvenient complexity and strange and unmeaning distinctions to which, as it seems to me, the construction adopted by the Court of Appeal would give rise. If, for example, a drawer inserts after the words, "Pay to the order of," a name which he invents, himself indorses that name, and puts the bill into circulation, it is within the terms of the statute, and may be treated as a bill payable to bearer. But if he inserts the first name that occurs to him, though he never intends a bearer of that name to be the payee, or that title shall only be made through him, but himself indorses this bill and puts it into circulation just as he did the other, this bill, as I understand the Court below, stands in a different position. The case is not within the statute, and if the bill can be treated, even as against the drawer, as a bill payable to bearer, this does not depend upon the words of the enactment, but must result from the rules of the common law, which, in so far as they are not inconsistent with the express provisions of the Act, are by sect. 97, sub-sect. 2, still to apply to bills of exchange.

It follows that, according to the view of the majority of the Court of Appeal, the legislature has dealt by express enactment with one case of estoppel — that is to say, where the payee is a "fictitious person" in the sense which they attribute to those words — but has left the analogous case, where, though the payee was not fictitious in that sense, the name was inserted as a mere pretence, and without any intention that payment should be made to the person designated, undealt with, and the rights and liabilities upon the bill to be ascertained by an appeal to the rules of the common law. Certainly a strange proceeding in a code of this description, and one for which it would be difficult to find a satisfactory explanation.

But this is not all. If I am right in thinking that in the case of a payee who is a fictitious person (whatever be the meaning of that expression) a bill may, as against the acceptor, be treated by a lawful holder as payable to bearer whether the acceptor knew of the fiction or not, why should this right and liability differ according as the name inserted as payee be a creature of the imagination or correspond to that of a real person, the drawer in neither case intending a person so designated to receive payment, and in each case himself indorsing the bill in the name of the nominal payee before putting it into circulation? I am at a loss for any reason why this distinction should exist. It is true that there is this difference between the two cases — that in the one an indorsement by the named payee is physically impossible, whilst in the other it is not. But I do not think this difference affords a sound basis for a distinction between the respective rights and liabilities of the drawer, acceptor, and holder. It seems to me that it would in each case be reasonable, and on the same grounds, that the acceptor should be liable to the holder of the bill, indemnifying himself out of the funds of the drawer or obtaining reimbursement from him.

It must be admitted, of course, that if the language of the statute is not reasonably capable of any other interpretation than that adopted by the majority of the Court of Appeal, if it will not allow of a construction which would cover the case we have been considering, then one must submit to the conclusion that the legislature has left the law in this respect in an unsatisfactory position and full of distinctions devoid of any sound principle. But are we compelled to this conclusion? Do the words, "where the payee is a fictitious person," apply only where the payee named never had a real existence? I take it to be clear that by the word "payee" must be understood the payee named on the face of the bill; for of course by the hypothesis there is no intention that payment should be made to any such person. Where, then, the payee named is so named by way of pretence only, without the intention that he shall be the person to receive payment, is it doing violence to language to say that the payee is a fictitious person? I think not. I do not think that the word "fictitious" is exclusively used to qualify that which has no real existence. When we speak of a fictitious entry in a book of accounts, we do not mean that the entry has no real existence, but only that it purports to be that which it is not — that it is an entry made for the purpose of pretending that the transaction took place which is represented by it. . . .

Turning to the interpretation of the word "fictitious" in Dr. Johnson's Dictionary, I find amongst the meanings given are "counterfeit," "feigned." It seems to me, then, that where the name inserted as that of the payee is so inserted by way of pretence only, it may, without impropriety, be said that the payee is a feigned or pretended, or, in other words, a fictitious person. Stress was laid upon the fact that the words of the statute are, "where the payee is a fictitious person," and not "where the payee is fictitious." There is not, to my mind, any substantial difference in the meaning of the two phrases; and I cannot think that the legislature intended the rights and liabilities arising upon mercantile instruments to depend upon nice distinctions such as this.

For the reasons with which I have troubled your Lordships at some length, I have arrived at the conclusion that, whenever the name inserted as that of the payee is so inserted by way of pretence merely, without any intention that payment shall only be made in conformity therewith, the payee is a fictitious person within the meaning of the statute, whether the name be that of an existing person, or of one who has no existence, and that the bill may, in each case, be treated by a lawful holder as payable to bearer. . . .

Assuming, then, that the bills in question are within the sub-section of the Bills of Exchange Act which we are considering, and may therefore be treated as bills payable to bearer, the question remains, By whom may they be so treated? By a *bona fide* holder for value, certainly; and in considering the construction of the section, I have thus far limited my attention to the case of such a holder. It is the case which ordinarily arises in the course of commercial transactions with negotiable instruments, and it is the one, therefore, which must be taken to have been primarily had in view in framing a law to determine the rights and liabilities in respect of such instruments. But I can see nothing in the words of the enactment to confine their application to this case.

It appears to me that the natural answer to the question which I have proposed is this: a bill, within the sub-section, may be treated as payable to bearer by any person whose rights or liabilities depend upon whether it be a bill payable to order or to bearer. I, of course, exclude the case of one who is a party to, or who has notice of, a fraud. At all events, I can see no reason why a banker who has been requested to pay the bill by his customer, the acceptor, may not so treat it. Where the bill is, in truth, payable to order — that is to say, where the drawer intends that payment should be made only to the person named as the payee, or to someone deriving title through him — then the direction to the banker must, since the decision in *Robarts* v. *Tucker*, be taken to be a direction to pay to such person only. But where the payee is a fictitious person within the meaning of the sub-section, I think the direction to the banker must be taken to be to pay the bearer. It is by reason of his filling that character that the holder is entitled to demand payment of the acceptor. And when a banker has been instructed by the acceptor to pay such a bill on his behalf, it is to the person filling that character that he must be taken to have intended the payment to be made. If the holder were a *bona fide* holder for value who, if payment had been refused, could hold the acceptor liable, I do not think this could be doubted; and where the bill is one which might be treated as payable to bearer by a *bona fide* holder, so that the direction to the banker to pay the bill is a direction to pay the bearer, I do not think that the banker is any the less entitled to charge the payment of the bill against his customer, because the bearer to whom payment is made holds it under such circumstances that the acceptor could successfully resist a claim for payment by him. It cannot be doubted that this would be so where a bill was in terms payable to bearer, and I do not think there is any sound distinction in the relative position of banker and customer between this case and that of a bill which may be treated as payable to bearer. . . .

The conclusion which I have indicated is sufficient to determine the case in favour of the appellants.

[Lords Morris, Halsbury, Selborne, Watson, and Macnaghten delivered concurring opinions, the last four also advancing reasons based on the conduct of the parties. Lords Bramwell and Field delivered dissenting opinions, holding that since the name inserted as payee was that of a real firm, the payee was not fictitious.]

In JACOBY *v.* KLINE BROS. CO., INC., 241 App. Div. 470 (New York Supreme Court, Appellate Division, 1934), a clerk induced his employer to sign checks by representing that they were in payment of invoices for merchandise delivered by Tri Rite Dresses. The invoices were fictitious, no such merchandise had been delivered, and there was no such firm as Tri Rite Dresses. The fraudulent employee indorsed the checks in the name of the purported payee, and they were cashed by plaintiff. In an action against the employer on the checks, it was held that plaintiff could not recover without proof of indorsement by the payee.

Compare RANCHO SAN CARLOS, INC. *v.* BANK OF ITALY NATIONAL TRUST AND SAVINGS ASSOCIATION, 69 Calif. App. Dec. 656 (District Court of Appeal, First District, 1932). Plaintiff corporation was in the habit of delivering to a clerk checks signed in blank for the purpose of enabling the clerk to pay current bills. The clerk filled in such a check for the sum of $10,000, inserted the name of another employee as payee, forged the indorsement, and so procured payment by defendant bank. In an action to recover the money paid, a judgment for defendant was affirmed.

Compare also GOODYEAR TIRE & RUBBER CO. OF CALIFORNIA *v.* WELLS FARGO BANK AND UNION TRUST COMPANY, 1 Calif. App. (2nd) 694 (District Court of Appeal, Second District, 1934). A clerk who was in charge of plaintiff's returned goods department created on the books a number of fictitious accounts and prepared checks purporting to discharge the balances thus shown. Plaintiff's system required checks to be signed by two persons, and the clerk in question was one of those having authority to sign. The checks thus drawn were signed by the clerk and taken to a co-signer who signed without question in the belief that the supporting accounts and documents were in order. In some cases the co-signer signed without reference to any supporting papers, merely on the strength of the signature already attached by the clerk. The clerk then took the checks, indorsed the names of the payees appearing therein, and obtained payment from the drawee bank by cashing the checks with a third person who deposited them for collection. In an action to recover from the drawee bank the amounts so paid, a judgment for plaintiff was reversed.

Compare Secs. 1 (4), 8, and 9 of the Uniform Negotiable Instruments Law with Secs. 3, 7 (3), and 8 of the Bills of Exchange Act and with Art. 1 (6) of the Geneva Law.

B. INCOMPLETE AND IRREGULAR INSTRUMENTS

LINICK *v.* A. J. NUTTING & COMPANY

NEW YORK SUPREME COURT, APPELLATE DIVISION, 1910

[140 *New York Appellate Division Reports*, 265]

BURR, J. On July 20, 1909, plaintiff signed his name to a blank check. Thereafter David Ryckoff and Benjamin Silberman stole the check, filled in the name of F. A. Mann as payee and the sum of $147.87 as the amount thereof, and presented it to the State Bank, where plaintiff kept his account, and procured it to be certified. Thereafter they indorsed said check with the name of F. A. Mann and passed it to defendant for value, who collected the amount thereof from the said bank. Plaintiff, having taken up said check from the bank now sues defendant as for money had and received for the amount of the check.

The question submitted, and which we are called upon to decide, is whether defendant obtained any title to the check which, as against the plaintiff, was a valid obligation for $147.87. As a general rule, one can only part with title to personal property by his voluntary act, or by conduct sufficient to create an estoppel. In the case of commercial paper it was long ago held that when by voluntary act a party intrusts another with such paper with a blank thereon designed to be filled up with a stipulated amount, such party is liable to a *bona fide* holder of the instrument, although the amount inserted was larger than that agreed upon. So, if the place of payment is left blank when the maker delivers it, the insertion of a different place of payment than that agreed upon will not avoid such paper in the hands of an innocent holder for value. (See *Van Duzer* v. *Howe*, 21 N. Y. 531; *Redlich* v. *Doll*, 54 id. 234.) The authorities are not harmonious as to the basis of this liability. Some deem that it rests upon an implied authority conferred by the maker upon the person to whom it was delivered to fill in the blanks, and others upon estoppel by reason of negligence. (*National Exchange Bank* v. *Lester*, 194 N. Y. 461, 465.) Upon neither of these grounds can the plaintiff be charged in this case. Certainly not upon the ground of implied authority, for that doctrine grows out of the relation of principal and agent, and there is no such relation between a thief and his victim. There is a vast difference in the rule of liability upon negotiable instruments between a case where the possession has been parted with by the affirmative act of the maker in an incomplete state, and one where his parting with such possession is the result of a crime. The rule that the *bona fide* holder of an incomplete instrument, negotiable but for some lack capable of being supplied, has an implied authority to supply the omission, and to hold the maker thereon, only applies where the latter has by his own act, or the act of another, authorized, confided in or invested with apparent authority by him, put the instrument in circulation as negotiable paper. (*Ledwich* v. *McKim*, 53 N. Y. 307; *Davis Sewing Machine Co.* v. *Best*, 105 id. 59, 67.)

None of the circumstances connected with the theft of this paper appear, except that it was stolen and that the persons guilty of the crime have been tried, convicted and sentenced for the same. Plaintiff, therefore, cannot be charged with negligence giving rise to an estoppel, unless a man is guilty of negligence in writing his name upon a piece of paper which by some possibility may afterwards be stolen from him, which paper afterwards comes into the hands of a third person who is an entire stranger to the transaction, with words written over the signature which are sufficient in form to make it a check or note. Actionable negligence involves, first, the existence of a duty; second, the omission to exercise ordinary and reasonable care in connection therewith, and third, injury resulting in consequence thereof. In view of the contractual relation existing between the bank and its depositor, some duty of care may be owing to it. The bank. by the terms of its contract with him, is bound to pay on his account to the holder of paper bearing his genuine signature the amount called for, if such amount is to his credit. But a third person is under no obligation to honor his paper. He can take it or not as he pleases, and as a rule such paper is accepted in reliance upon the immediate transferrer thereof. (*Trust Co. of America* v. *Conklin*, 65 Misc. Rep. 1.) What duty, therefore, is owing to him? Again, at the risk of being charged with lack of ordinary care and prudence, must one guard against the possibility of a crime being committed? It has been held that where the maker of a completed negotiable instrument has parted with its possession, but it is in such form that it is possible to make alterations in it, he is not guilty of negligence in thus delivering it, for the reason that he is not bound to assume that the person to whom he delivers it will be likely to commit a crime because it is apparently easy to do so. (*National Exchange Bank* v. *Lester*, *supra.*) The drawer of a check is not bound so to prepare it that nobody else can successfully tamper with it. (*Critten* v. *Chemical Nat. Bank*, 171 N. Y. 219, 224.) Much less can a party be held liable for negligence because it is possible that he may be deprived of the possession of an incomplete negotiable instrument by a crime. He is not bound to anticipate nor guard against such an act. No case has been cited holding a maker liable under such circumstances. We have found two well-considered cases to the contrary. (*Burson* v. *Huntington*, 21 Mich. 415; *Baxendale* v. *Bennett*, L. R. 3 Q. B. Div. 525.) . . .

This rule of law has now passed into the statute. . . .

We conclude, therefore, that the delivery of a promissory note by the maker is necessary to a valid inception of the contract. The possession of such a note by the payee or indorsee is *prima facie* evidence of delivery, but if it appear that the note has never been actually delivered and that without any confidence, or negligence, or fault of the maker, but by force or fraud, it was put in circulation, there can be no recovery upon it, even when in the hands of an innocent holder. . . .

The judgment appealed from must be reversed and a new trial ordered, costs to abide the event.

[Dissenting opinion of Woodward, J., holding that a valid delivery should be conclusively presumed since the instrument had come into the hands of a holder in due course, is omitted.]

Compare Joseph Heimberg, Inc. *v.* Lincoln National Bank, 113 N. J. L. 76 (Supreme Court, 1934), where the president of a corporation signed a corporation check in blank, the date, amount, and name of the payee being omitted. The check was placed in a safe from which it was stolen, completed by the thief as payable to cash, indorsed in the name of Jack Cohn, and cashed at the drawee bank with the statement that the bearer was an employee of the corporation. In an action by the corporation against the bank, a judgment for plaintiff was affirmed, Perskie, J., saying: "As we have said the authorities are not in accord. The conflict seems to arise out of the fact that at least three different theories or principles of law have been applied by these varying jurisdictions in construing and determining the rights and liabilities as between a depositor and his bank under the circumstances presented in the case at bar. They are as follows: First, a strict and literal construction of section 15 of the act aforesaid. A construction that is all inclusive. This results in liability on the part of the bank towards a depositor whenever the former pays on a check of the latter which comes within the provision of the act. Second, that as between the two innocent parties, the bank and depositor, liability should be borne by the one, the depositor, who made the loss possible. Such conclusion is based on the breach of a duty which it is held a depositor owes to his bank and that a depositor violates that duty when he signs a check in blank. Third, that the right of recovery shall be based on the doctrine of negligence and estoppel.

"The latter construction was the one adopted by the court below. The subject being one of first impression it is open to us to adopt what we believe to be the soundest view.

"It is urged very strongly that to adopt the third construction would, in these modern times, work great hardship and greatly interfere with the custom prevailing in modern banking. We are not prepared to say that this is so. We are, rather, of the firm opinion that the facts as proven in the instant case constitute an exception rather than the usual or ordinary case. The very fact that we have no like adjudicated case in our state tends to greatly lessen the force of defendant's contention. At all events if there may be a recovery under the act, and there may be under certain circumstances, for example, as in alteration cases under sections 124 and 125, and in forgery cases, under section 23, &c., we are inclined to adopt the view that in so far as a bank is concerned it should not be immune from the operation and liability of section 15 of our Negotiable Instruments act, under the proven facts of the instant case. It appears to us that the application of construction three, negligence and estoppel, is the soundest of the three constructions. It permits of the consideration of the particular facts of a given case and the working out of substantial justice."

In S. S. ALLEN GROCERY COMPANY *v.* BANK OF BUCHANAN COUNTY, 192 Mo. App. 476 (Kansas City Court of Appeals, 1916), the president of a corporation before going on vacation signed a number of checks in blank and left them with the general manager who kept them in a check book on top of his desk. Some of the checks were stolen by a traveling salesman, filled up for varying amounts, and cashed at different places. The checks were paid by the drawee bank, the effect of paying the last two being to overdraw the corporation's account. In an action by the corporation against the bank, it was held that with reference to the check cashed before the overdraft the relationship was that of depositor and banker; that with reference to the checks cashed subsequently the bank was an innocent holder for value; and that in either case the loss should fall on the plaintiff.

In FIRST NATIONAL BANK OF GRAND HAVEN *v.* ZEIMS, 93 Ia. 140 (Supreme Court, 1894), defendant signed a blank piece of paper under the impression that he was giving a specimen signature for purposes of identification. The paper was completed as a promissory note, and came into the hands of the plaintiff, a holder in due course. In holding that plaintiff could not recover, Deemer, J., said: "No doubt, if one signs a blank promissory note, and intrusts it to another, whether it be to accommodate him to whom it is intrusted or to be used for his own benefit, such instrument carries on its face an implied authority to fill up the blanks and perfect the instrument. Of if one should execute a commercial instrument in blank, and deliver it to an agent to be filled up in accordance with certain specific directions, and this agent should fill them up for larger amounts or on different terms, the maker would be bound by the instrument as filed, if it should come into the hands of a *bona fide* holder, on account of having reposed trust in the agent. But in each of these cases it is the intent of the signer that the paper shall become operative as a promissory note or other contract. In one case he has given the holder implied authority to fill up the note, and in the other has given express authority which has been exceeded. There is a sharp distinction between cases where the signer of the paper executes an instrument intending it to be a contract in some form and where he merely signs a paper to furnish the means of identification."

Compare THE STATE BANK OF KANSAS CITY *v.* HARFORD, 116 Kansas 262 (Supreme Court, 1924), where defendant signed a trade acceptance in blank in the belief that it was a merchandise order receipt and in no way negotiable. The blanks were filled in by the person to whom it was delivered, and it was sold on the following day to the plaintiff bank, a holder in due course. In an action on the instrument, judgment was given for plaintiff.

BLOOM *v.* HORWITZ

NEW YORK SUPREME COURT, APPELLATE TERM, 1917

[100 *New York Miscellaneous Reports*, 687]

LEHMAN, J. The plaintiffs sued on a note made by the defendant Horwitz, indorsed by both defendants and delivered to one Sol Brill. The answer contains a general denial and three affirmative defenses. It is conceded that any defense to the note which the defendants could prove against Brill may be proven against the plaintiffs who are apparently not holders for value. The second affirmative defense contained in the answer is clearly insufficient on its face and was stricken out on plaintiff's motion in accordance with the opinion of this court written upon a previous appeal. 97 Misc. Rep. 622. Upon this trial the plaintiffs rested after producing the note and notice of protest and the defendants then attempted to show that the note was without consideration and that a blank left for the time of payment was filled in by Brill without authority. The trial justice at the close of the defendants' case directed a verdict in favor of the plaintiffs and the defendants appeal.

The note in its present form reads as follows:

NEW YORK, February 23, 1915.

Five months after date I promise to pay to the order of myself One Thousand Three Hundred and seventy-five 00/100 dollars. Payable at 43 W. 16th Street, New York City.

Value received with interest.

No. xxx Due July 23, H. HORWITZ.

The defendant Horwitz testified, and for the purpose of this appeal we must accept his testimony as true, that when he delivered the note to

Brill on February 23, 1915, there were no words or figures in the blank before the words "after date" or after the word "due." The note when delivered was, however, entirely complete except that no time for payment was expressed. The holder of the note had *prima facie* authority under section 33 of the Negotiable Instruments Law to fill in these blanks and thereby to make the note payable at a fixed time and even if he filled them in without authority the note would be enforcible in the hands of a *bona fide* holder for value. Evidence may, however, always be given to show that the holder did not have actual authority to fill in the blanks. Ordinarily of course where a holder wrongfully fills in blanks to complete an instrument he does not technically "alter" an instrument but he puts the instrument so completed into existence either without any authority or not in accordance with the authority given. In the present case, however, the note was probably enforcible as a demand note even if no blank had been filled in. Neg. Inst. Law, § 26. If then the note was given to Brill without any actual authority to fill in the blanks and upon the understanding that it was a completed note payable on demand, then Brill had no right to fill in the blanks and make it a note payable at a definite time. Such act does actually alter a demand note into a note payable at a fixed time. If an instrument has been altered in this way such alteration would constitute a defense to the instrument if it is material. It is claimed, however, that the alteration of a demand note into a note payable five months after date is not a material alteration in the sense that it increases the obligation of the maker, for the holder of a demand note may at any time demand payment and by inserting a definite time for payment merely limits the date on which he can make such demand. This contention, however, seems to me without merit. If the note was payable on demand and thereafter altered into a note payable in five months, such alteration would certainly be a material alteration as against the indorser who would be discharged from his liability on a demand note unless presentment is made within a reasonable time after its issue. Neg. Inst. Law, § 131. Even as against the maker, however, such alteration would be material for the maker of a note payable at a definite time cannot pay the note previous to that time and thereby stop the running of interest, and the Statute of Limitations only begins running from the date on which the note becomes due and at least in these particulars such an alteration would materially change the effect of the note.

In the present case the defendant Horwitz, in addition to the proof that the note was not in the condition in which it was delivered, testified that prior to the delivery he arranged with Brill that he should give him a note payable on demand but that the note should not become due until a building which Horwitz was preparing to erect was completed. The trial justice struck out this testimony and all testimony of a similar kind on the ground that this court had decided upon the previous appeal that evidence to establish that the note was delivered conditionally was not admissible unless such condition was pleaded. Evidence to establish that a note on its face payable on demand was payable only after the happening of an event not named in the instrument is, of course, inadmissible, for such evidence would tend to vary the written instrument. See *Reinhandler* v. *Lowenthal*, 159 N. Y. Supp. 695; *Sheldon* v. *Heaton*, 88 Hun, 535. It was, however, admissible in my opinion to show that Brill had no authority to fill in the blanks in the manner he has done.

It is true that the evidence offered by the defendant upon this point is perhaps open to the construction that while Horwitz called the note a demand note it was really the intention of the parties that the note should remain an incomplete note until the theatre was completed and that the holder should then have authority to complete the instrument by filling in the blank. Such a construction of the conversation might be reasonable in view of the fact that the note bore an indorsement and that presumably the parties intended that the indorser should be held even though demand was not made till months thereafter. Even such a construction, would not, however, in my opinion, aid the plaintiff. If this testimony failed to show that the note was altered it would rebut the *prima facie* authority of the holder to complete the note in the manner he has done and would show that the holder filled in the blanks without authority. It is urged, however, that the defendant has pleaded only alteration and not that the holder filled in the blanks without authority. It seems to me quite evident that the defendant has a right to show such facts without pleading them. The *prima facie* authority to fill in blanks in an incomplete instrument may be rebutted by affirmative proof which the defendant has the burden of presenting. Logically it would seem that such proof was admissible under a general denial. The respondent claims, however, that under authority of *Madden* v. *Gaston*, 137 App. Div. 294, the defendant must plead affirmatively that the note has not been completed in accordance with the holder's actual authority. In that case the court merely said that the "statute imposes the burden upon the defendant to show the agreement, and that its terms have been violated," and it is no authority for the view that the defendant has any greater burden than producing evidence to rebut the *prima facie* case made by the plaintiff and it does not even discuss whether the defendant must affirmatively plead the actual agreement. In the case of *Schwarz* v. *Oppold*, 74 N. Y. 307, the Court of Appeals held that the defendant may even show an alteration under a general denial and *a fortiori* it seems to me he may show that the instrument sued on was issued incomplete and never completed in accordance with the authority given.

I agree with Mr. Justice Bijur that there is doubt whether evidence that the payee had "authority to fill in the blanks in manner or tenor inconsistent with the remaining text of the note" would be admissible but I cannot find that any evidence was offered for such purpose. The defendant offered evidence to show that the note was delivered with blanks for the time of payment. If as a matter of law the note was then payable on demand any change in the note without authority would constitute an alteration. On the other hand if the note was incomplete and the plaintiffs' assignor thereof filled in the note contrary to the intent of the parties he acted without authority and the plaintiff cannot enforce the note so filled out. The evidence excluded was apparently offered for no other purpose and was, therefore, in my opinion, clearly admissible.

[A page of the opinion is here omitted.]

Judgment should therefore be reversed and a new trial ordered, with costs to appellant to abide the event.

[Dissenting opinion of Bijur, J., is here omitted.]

Compare Wilson *v.* Stark, 146 Miss. 498 (Supreme Court, 1927), where notes given as part of the purchase price of a safe contained no date of maturity, there being an oral understanding between the parties that the notes were to be paid on delivery of the safe. The payee inserted a date in the notes, and sold them to a holder in due course. In an action by the holder against the maker, it was held that the holder could recover as on an instrument payable on demand.

In Imperial Bank of Canada *v.* Bank of Hamilton, [1903] A. C. 49 (Privy Council, 1902), a check for $5.00 was certified by a bank, and subsequently was raised to $500, negotiated to a holder in due course, and paid before the alteration was discovered. In an action by the certifying bank against the holder, plaintiff was allowed to recover $495.00.

MORRIS PLAN CO. OF NEW YORK *v.* EPSTEIN

New York Municipal Court, 1933

[147 *New York Miscellaneous Reports*, 164]

Bissell, J. This is an action to recover the balance of $120 owing on an amount advanced by the plaintiff against defendants' promissory note. It appears that on February 26, 1931, the plaintiff advanced $200 against a $480 promissory note executed by the defendants herein. The defendants claim as their defense a material alteration of the note in question, which is in evidence.

On the face of the note the words, "Four hundred eighty Dollars" clearly appear, and in the upper left-hand corner of the note at the margin in numerals "$480. — " appear, and above this, in pencil, the figures "200." The testimony of the defendant Harry S. Schorr is that at the time the promissory note was signed there was no pencil notation of the numerals above the figures $480. — in the upper left-hand margin; and it would appear that, at the time of the making of the loan, plaintiff's representative, who was in charge of the making of the loan, struck through the numerals $480. — and inserted, in pencil, the 200 above it. This line does not now appear; but evidences of an erasure remain.

The question before the court is whether the foregoing state of the instrument constitutes a material alteration. Section 206 of the Negotiable Instruments Law provides what constitutes a material alteration, and constitutes as such any alteration which changes "2. The sum payable, either for principal or interest."

There appears to be no reported case in New York which is directly in point in this matter. The general rule is, however, that changes "which in no manner alter the identity or legal effect of the instrument are not material, as where the change is in the marginal numerals, which form no part of the instrument, leaving the amount expressed in the body of the instrument intact." (2 Cyc. 196.) . . .

Under the facts in the instant case, it does not appear that a material alteration has been made in the note in question, inasmuch as the amount written in the body of the note remains unchanged. Accordingly, judgment is given for the plaintiff against the defendants in the sum of $120. Five days stay.

In JONES *v.* JONES, 254 Ky. 475 (Court of Appeals, 1934), notes were altered by changing the interest rate from 6 per cent to 8 per cent. Under a state law a rate of interest of more than 6 per cent was usurious, so that the payee could not collect 8 per cent in any event. A judgment rendered on the notes against the maker was held to be error.

In KELLER *v.* ROCK ISLAND STATE BANK, 292 Ill. 553 (Supreme Court, 1920), a check was drawn with no designation of payee or amount. The holder calculated the amount necessary to close out the account, and filled up the check for the appropriate figure, but owing to a mistake in the calculation the check was returned because of insufficient funds. The holder then altered the amount to correspond to that remaining on deposit, and the check was honored. In an action against the bank on account of the payment, it was held that the alteration was material. "It is immaterial whether the alteration is injurious or beneficial to the party who is liable on the instrument. Reducing the amount without the maker's knowledge will avoid the instrument. The question is not whether the change is injurious or beneficial to the maker of the instrument but does it materially affect his rights? Is the changed instrument the contract which he made?"

In LONDON JOINT STOCK BANK, LIMITED *v.* MACMILLAN AND ARTHUR, [1918] A. C. 777 (House of Lords), a firm who were customers of a bank entrusted to a confidential clerk, whose integrity they had no reason to suspect, the duty of filling in their checks for signature. The clerk presented to one of the partners of the firm for signature a check drawn in favor of the firm or bearer. There was no sum in words written on the check in the space provided for the writing and there were the figures "2 .0 .0" in the space intended for figures. The clerk subsequently added the words "one hundred and twenty pounds" in the space left for words, and wrote the figures "1" and "0" respectively on each side of the figure "2" which was so placed as to leave room for the interpolation of the added figures. The clerk presented the check for payment at the firm's bank, and obtained payment of £120 out of the firm's account. In an action by the firm against the bank, a judgment for plaintiff in the Court of Appeal was reversed.

Compare BROAD STREET BANK *v.* THE NATIONAL BANK OF GOLDSBORO, 183 N. C. 463 (Supreme Court, 1922). Four New York Exchange checks in amounts of a few dollars each were issued by a bank on the lithograph forms ordinarily used for that purpose. The payee erased the amounts and inserted others aggregating $40,000, leaving no visible trace of the change. The checks then were negotiated to another bank for value. In an action by the second bank against the drawer it was held that plaintiff could recover only the original amounts of the checks; that the drawer owed no duty on which negligence could be predicated to use sensitized paper and a protectograph.

Contrast SECOND NATIONAL BANK *v.* CAMPBELL, 4 Ohio App. 158 (Court of Appeals, 1914), where a check for $3.60 was stamped by protectograph "not over $500." The check was raised to $360 and negotiated to a holder in due course who was allowed to recover the full altered amount from the drawer.

COLUMBIA GROCERY COMPANY *v.* MARSHALL

TENNESSEE SUPREME COURT, 1914

[131 *Tennessee Reports*, 270]

Mr. Justice FANCHER delivered the opinion of the Court.

The case was brought to collect on an open account. Notes had been executed by defendant covering the account but materially altered by complainants. The case involves the question as to whether suit can be maintained on the original account.

The Columbia Grocery Company is a partnership composed of Mose and Ben Lazarous, doing a wholesale grocery business at Columbia, Tenn. Defendant O. M. Marshall was a retail merchant at Campbell's Station, in Maury County, and for several years had purchased goods of the complainants, and a running account had existed for considerable time. Complainants sold this business and desired to close out their accounts. They urged defendant to pay his indebtedness, and he disputed a large part of the account. After some considerable dispute about this, he finally agreed to give his interest-bearing notes, which he did, covering the account of $1,073.78 and $45 of interest. The notes were eleven in number, bearing date February 2, 1914 — nine for $75 each, and one for $200, and another for $242.88. One note fell due each two months during the years 1914 and 1915. The notes were prepared by complainants some days before execution and handed to defendant. They were actually executed February 21st and delivered to complainants. That evening Ben Lazarous discovered that the bookkeeper had left out a clause they usually inserted in serial notes of this character, and they had it filled in with a typewriter on each note; the first being as follows:

"This is note one of a series of eleven, default in payment of any note of this series all notes become due and payable."

Defendant's attention was not called to this alteration. The notes were then put in a box with other notes and papers and placed in the vault in the bank for safe-keeping.

Complainants say it was not their intention to keep these notes, but this is hardly to be credited, for they did keep them after voluntarily making the unauthorized change until it was discovered by defendant about seventeen days after the execution. He had called to pay the first note, and, when the note was produced, he noticed the typewritten alteration, and thereupon refused to pay. He was urged to pay notwithstanding, and, upon refusal, Mose Lazarous says that he proposed that they would destroy the notes and let the account stand. Some days afterwards the complainants mailed to the defendant all the notes.

It was customary for the bookkeeper to write this clause into notes of this character, and some notes had been so fixed after their execution, in other instances.

This suit was brought to recover on the original account. The defendant resists a recovery on the ground:

First. That the notes were intended and did extinguish the original indebtedness, being taken in settlement and closing out of the account; and that, the notes being void because of the alteration, no recovery can be had.

Second. That, the alteration being fraudulently made, no recovery can be had, regardless of whether the original account was extinguished.

The chancellor dismissed the bill on the trial.

[Over two pages of the opinion are here omitted.]

It does not clearly appear in the present case that there was an intention, at the time these notes were executed, that they were to settle and extinguish the original demand for goods, wares, and merchandise sold and delivered. And the modern rule being that this intention must appear or else the creditor can sue upon the original debt when he loses his right innocently or without fraud, we reach the conclusion that the case must turn alone on whether the complainants have lost that right on account of their own wrongs. We think the chancellor correctly found that the notes were accepted by the complainants.

The question in the case then is: What is the degree of the wrong or the effect of the material alteration made in each of these notes?

Very able and exhaustive briefs have been furnished on the questions involved, and we find no material difference in the position of counsel either as to the facts or the law. It is the conclusion from the facts upon which counsel differ. The complainants maintain that these insertions in the notes were made innocently and in accordance with complainants' custom, and do not affect the right to sue on the original debt.

The defendant says that though he did not owe the complainants as much as they claimed in order to get time, and prevent them from closing him out in business, he gave these notes; that the insertion of a stipulation after delivery, without his assent or knowledge, that default in the payment of any one note would cause all the notes to become due and payable, was a material change in the contract; that such a change, which the chancellor mildly termed constructive fraud, was in reality an intentional and subtle fraud and deception, for which the punishment will be inflicted to the extent that they will lose their right to sue on the original contract.

The modern rule, as expressed in many authorities touching this whole question, may be stated as follows: The intent with which an alteration of an instrument is made is not of material consequence in determining the effect upon the immediate instrument, but the intent or motive is of great importance in determining whether a recovery can be had upon the original debt or consideration.

If the alteration of a written instrument is made by the holder with a design and intent to defraud the maker, it extinguishes the debt. This rule is founded on public policy, and in order to preserve the integrity of valid legal instruments, by providing a punishment for the wrong, and to deter the holder from tampering with it. If, however, the alteration is without fraudulent intent, while it will destroy the instrument, it will not destroy the right to recover on the original consideration, of which the instrument is a mere evidence. Thus, if a holder of a promissory note makes a material alteration in it after its execution but without any design to defraud, and in the belief that he had a right to alter it in order to make it conform to the original agreement of the parties, such alteration does not deprive the holder of the right to elect to disregard the note and to sue on the original obligation, provided the note was not accepted as payment thereof.

There is some authority that although the alteration be material and fraudulent, since a bill or note suspends and is not absolute payment of the debt for which it was given, such alteration only extinguishes the security, and the original consideration remains, but this is not sound doctrine. The correct rule undoubtedly is that, when a party to a bill or note fraudulently alters its legal effect, he not only destroys the instrument, but he also extinguishes the debt for which it was given. Daniel on Negotiable Instruments, vol. 2, secs. 1410 to 1416.

We think the chancellor very mildly termed this act of the complainants a constructive fraud. It was more than that. It was not made in an innocent effort to conform the instrument to the true intention and agreement of the parties or through ignorance, or any other simple, guileless motive. It was a secret and stealthy attempt to gain an advantage. The defendant says that he would not have executed the papers with stipulations that, in the event of default of one, all would become due and payable, and it is reasonable to believe he would not. He was attempting to get a breathing spell between payments so he could meet them, one by one, through a period of two years. His wife had been sick in the hospital, and he was embarrassed financially. His debts were pressing him. These insertions in the notes destroyed the whole advantage he had gained by closing the account and substituting time notes, if he should be so unfortunate as to fail in one small payment. He went to make a payment before it was due and discovered the change, and thereupon promptly refused to pay.

The law on the subject is founded on wise public policy, and we are not at liberty to disregard it.

Affirmed.

Compare BORN *v.* LAFAYETTE AUTO COMPANY, 196 Ind. 399 (Supreme Court, 1925). Defendant bought a motor car from plaintiff under an agreement that he was to sign a four-months note with interest at 6 per cent from date. The note actually signed contained a provision for "interest from maturity until paid, at the rate of eight percent per annum." Intending to change this to conform to the original agreement, the secretary of the plaintiff company some time later drew a line through the words "maturity" and "eight," and wrote in the words "date" and "six" without defendant's knowledge. It was held that the alteration, although material, did not discharge defendant from his obligation to pay the purchase price of the motor car, as the change was made in the honest belief that the party making it had the right to do so.

COMMERCE SECURITIES CORPORATION *v.* HAYS

TEXAS COURT OF CIVIL APPEALS, 1933

[60 *Southwestern Reporter*, (*Second Series*) 335]

BOND, J. This is a case originating in the county court of Dallas county at law No. 1. Appellant brought the suit against appellee, W. S. Hays, claiming to be a holder in due course of a negotiable note executed by appellee to McLendon Radio Shop, and purchased before maturity, without notice of any defect or vice therein. The defences relied upon by appellee in the trial court were: (1) The failure of consideration; (2) fraud in the inducement and factum of the note; (3) that the instrument sued upon is not a negotiable instrument; and (4) forgery by material alterations, the negotiation and completion of the instrument by payee, without authority or consent of the maker.

The issues raised by the pleadings were submitted to a jury, and it found that appellant was an innocent purchaser of the note for value before maturity; that the execution of the note was induced by fraud, signed in blank, and altered after its execution without the maker's knowledge or consent. Accordingly, the court entered judgment against appellant and in favor of appellee. . . .

The evidence shows that one H. B. McLendon was operating a radio establishment under the name and style of McLendon Radio Shop, and solicited appellee to purchase a radio; McLendon did not have in stock the particular model which appellee wanted, and induced appellee to sign the instrument sued upon, on the assurance that it was a sales application. At the time it was presented to and signed by appellee, the instrument had not been completed. The blank spaces in the printed form had not been filled in, and appellee did not authorize it to be completed in the form it was afterwards found, and never signed the instrument with the intention to be bound thereby. Appellee was not to sign a promissory note and was advised that the instrument was only necessary to enable McLendon to secure from another dealer the radio desired. Relying upon such recitations, appellee failed to read the blank form of the instrument, signed it, and thereafter, without his knowledge or consent, the amount, payee, date of execution, and date of payment were placed in the blank spaces therein provided, and transferred to appellant.

The jury in such cases being the arbiters of all controverted issues arising from pleadings and supported by evidence, under the legal observation of a trial judge, appellate courts are not authorized to disturb such findings, except in cases where a miscarriage of justice is shown. The conclusion reached is that the execution of the instrument by appellee was induced by fraud, and that the filling in of the instrument with covenants of liability, without the authority, knowledge, or consent of the maker, is forgery and subject to attack in the hands of any subsequent holder. It is well settled in this state, we think, founded upon reason and justice, that, where a person, by fraudulent representation, is induced to sign an instrument, and which, after transfer of possession, is filled in as to payee, amount, and dates of maturity, such alterations amount to forgery, and, when it is proven that the maker was not negligent in signing his name to the instrument, the same is unenforceable, even in the hands of a holder in due course.

We have considered all assignments presented, and, while some may be subject to appellant's contention, yet no such assignment is germane to the issues above quoted, therefore immaterial to the conclusion we have reached. From what we have said herein, all assignments of error are overruled. The judgment of the lower court is affirmed.

Affirmed.

Compare FIRST NATIONAL BANK OF GRAND HAVEN *v.* ZEIMS, and STATE BANK OF KANSAS CITY *v.* HARFORD, *supra*, pp. 637–638.

In THE PEOPLE *v.* LEWINGER, 252 Ill. 332 (Supreme Court, 1911), a check in which the figures read "25.00," the words "twenty-five hundred dollars," and an indented stamp "Not over $2500," was altered by the holder by changing the figures to "$2500." It was held that the alteration did not amount to a forgery, as it was not a material alteration changing the character and legal effect of the check.

GREENWOOD *v.* MARTINS BANK, LIMITED

COURT OF APPEAL, 1931

[47 *Times Law Reports*, 607]

This was an appeal by the defendants, Martins Bank, Limited, from a decision of Mr. Commissioner du Parcq, K.C., in an action tried by him at Manchester Assizes.

The plaintiff, Mr. Bertie Greenwood, of Vicarage-lane, Blackpool, who had a banking account with the defendants and was a customer at the defendants' branch in Clifton-street, Blackpool, claimed that the defendants had wrongfully and without his authority paid £410 6*s*. on cheques which had been forged, and that he was entitled to be credited with that sum by the defendants.

In November, 1928, an account was opened with the defendants in the plaintiff's name, and on that account he drew 19 genuine cheques, but 44 forged cheques, amounting in all to £410 6*s*., were drawn by his wife. Some of the husband's forged signatures on these 44 cheques looked very suspicious, and the Commissioner, after examining the cheques and hearing the evidence of the bank officials, found that the 44 signatures were not genuine and were honoured through carelessness of the bank officials.

In October, 1929, the plaintiff asked his wife to get his cheque book, as he wanted to draw some money from the bank. She then told him that there was no money left in his account at the bank, as she had drawn it all out to lend to her sister, who was involved in some litigation. The plaintiff's wife appealed to the plaintiff not to go to the bank. She told him that he was certain to get his money back when the litigation ended favourably for her sister. He did not go to the bank or inform them about the forgeries. There were no more forged signatures after October, 1929.

On June 5, 1930, the plaintiff's wife told him that she wanted a further £60 for her sister's litigation. The plaintiff declined to give it her and said that he was going to the bank. That night his wife shot herself.

The plaintiff then went to the bank and told the manager about the forged cheques. The manager asked, "Why did you not let us know before?" The plaintiff replied that he did not want to give his wife away. He admitted that if he had got his money back from the result of the litigation he would not have done anything in the matter.

The bank, by their defence, pleaded: — (1) acquiescence, adoption, or ratification; and (2) estoppel.

The Commissioner gave judgment for the plaintiff for the amount claimed, and the defendants appealed.

Lord Justice SCRUTTON, in his considered judgment, said that in this case the learned Commissioner on the Northern Circuit had given against Martins Bank, Limited, in a claim against them by one Greenwood for £410 6*s*., being the amount of 44 forged cheques which he alleged to have been wrongly debited to his account. The bank had alleged that Greenwood's conduct had estopped him from alleging that the cheques were forgeries. The Commissioner, however, held that the circumstances did not raise such an estoppel. Counsel for the bank had argued that the husband by his silence had ratified or adopted the forged cheques as his own, and that he was estopped by his silence from alleging that the signatures were forgeries. Disputing both these allegations, counsel for the plaintiff argued that the negligence of the bank in carelessly honouring the signatures prevented any question of estoppel from arising.

The argument started with forged signatures which could not authorize the bank to honour the cheques, whether or not the bank could by reasonable care have detected the forgeries. He did not think that "ratification" had any applicability to a forged signature. For ratification to be effective the act ratified must purport to be done by an agent for the person who ratified. It was true that Lord Blackburn, in *McKenzie* v. *British Linen Company* (6 App. Cas., 82), said that in civil cases a man might ratify a forgery, but in *Brook* v. *Hook* (L. R., 6 Ex., 89) the majority of the Court pointed out that a forgery which did not profess to be executed by a person as agent could not be ratified by the alleged principal, and in his (Lord Justice Scrutton's) opinion that was the correct view of the law.

A forgery could, however, be adopted. The supposed signer might say, "I will recognize this signature as my own; you may debit my account with these cheques," and in such a case a bank which had acted on that statement could successfully object to the customer's endeavouring to withdraw his adoption. There was no evidence in this case that the husband ever adopted the cheques as his own. He delayed in telling the bank that they were forged, but never said that they were his. He never had a pass book for that account. That, however, was getting near to the defence of estoppel.

Estoppel was a rule of evidence which prevented the person estopped from telling the truth or from proving a state of things inconsistent with a previous statement or attitude of his own. The classic exposition of the principle of estoppel was that given by Baron Parke in *Freeman* v. *Cooke* (2 Ex., 654, at p. 663), which was cited with approval by Lord Haldane in *London Joint Stock Bank, Limited* v. *Macmillan* (34 *The Times* L.R. 509; [1918] A.C., 777). That case had laid stress on the relations of banker and customer as executor and giver of a mandate, and the duties, which were, he thought, mutual, to use reasonable care in the execution of the mandate. The customer was held bound to use reasonable care in drawing the cheque so that the banker might not be misled. But the relation did not merely refer to one cheque; it was a continuing relation where the customer might draw cheques from time to time and the banker was under a continuing duty to honour mandates.

That involved a continuing duty on either side to act with reasonable care to ensure the proper working of the account. The banker, if a cheque was presented to him which he rejected as forged, would be under a duty to report that to the customer, to enable him to inquire into and protect himself against the circumstances of the forgery. That would involve a corresponding duty on the customer, if he became aware that forged cheques were being presented to his banker, to inform the banker, in order that the banker might avoid loss in the future. If that were correct there was in the present case silence, a breach of a duty to disclose, which might give rise to an estoppel. . . .

The customer was not made liable by silence for the forged cheques, because the payment of the forged cheques preceded and was not caused by the customer's silence. The customer would not be liable for his silence if the bank had not lost any right of action thereby. But if the silence of the customer had caused the bank to lose their right of action, the customer was estopped from alleging the fact which he ought to have disclosed — namely, that the cheques were forged.

If the claim of the bank were for damages for failure to disclose, it might be that the improbability of recovering anything on the cause of action might be taken into account; but the authorities showed that in a question of estoppel, where the question was whether the customer was estopped from alleging that the bills were forgeries, if the bank had lost something the value of that something was not the measure of their claim, but, the customer being estopped from proving the bills forgeries, the bank gained by the amount of the bills.

The plaintiff relied on two passages in Paget on The Law of Banking (4th Ed., pp. 330, 345) that neither estoppel nor adoption could be relied on if the banker's negligence had in part contributed to the loss. No English authority was cited for that. The American authority was explained by the fact that the United States law had gone much farther than English law as to the mutual duties of banker and customer. But in the present case, while the carelessness of the bank was a proximate cause of the bank's loss in paying the forged cheques, it was not the proximate cause of the bank's losing its right of action against the forger. That was caused by the failure of the husband to inform the bank of the forgery till his wife was dead and the cause of action was lost.

The appeal would be allowed, the judgment for the plaintiff set aside, and judgment entered for the defendants with costs here and below.

Lord Justice GREER and Lord Justice ROMER also delivered judgments allowing the appeal.

CHALMERS, *A Digest of the Law of Bills of Exchange* (10th Ed., 1932), says at page 87: "A forger does not act, and does not purport to act, on behalf of the person whose name he forges. There is, therefore, nothing on which ratification can be grounded."

Compare dissenting opinion of Martin, B., in BROOK *v.* HOOK, L. R. 6 Exch. 89 (Court of Exchequer, 1871), pointing out that the alleged illegality or voidness of the initial contract is the very thing that is cured by the subsequent act of ratification, so that it is not a question of ratifying an illegal contract but of remedying the defect that made it illegal.

In STUMPP *v.* FARMERS' LOAN AND TRUST COMPANY, 109 Misc. 24 (Supreme Court, 1919), a confidential bookkeeper forged a check on defendant bank, signing with a clumsy imitation of his employer's signature. The employer was in the habit of going over monthly bank statements in the company of the bookkeeper, who so manipulated the examinations that the fraud was not discovered for two months. The employer brought an action to recover the money paid on the check, and it was contended by the drawee bank that there had been ratification and a failure to exercise ordinary care in checking the monthly statements. Judgment was given for plaintiff.

COHEN *v.* LINCOLN SAVINGS BANK

NEW YORK COURT OF APPEALS, 1937

[275 *New York Reports*, 399]

LEHMAN, J. A check for $4,500, drawn upon Irving Trust Company by Lincoln Savings Bank to the order of the plaintiff, a depositor of the savings bank, was indorsed in blank by the plaintiff and handed by her to her husband, Samuel Goldberg, with authority to use the check in payment for the assignment to her of a half interest in an award of $10,000 made in proceedings for the condemnation of a parcel of real property. An attorney, William L. Abrams, had previously offered to sell the award to Goldberg at a discount. After some negotiations they agreed that the sale should be made at a discount of ten per cent. Goldberg at that time did not, so far as appears, know or care who was the owner of the award. What he wanted was, of course, a valid assignment by the owner of record of the award which Abrams had agreed to sell and he retained an attorney, Feinstein, to search the title so that he might know who the owner of record was.

On the day set for the closing, Goldberg, accompanied by this attorney, went to Abrams' office. There he met Kurtz, another attorney, who claimed that he represented the owner of the award. A man who came into the office a little later was introduced by Kurtz as Harry Wolter, the owner. Goldberg told Abrams, that he was in a hurry and wished to leave. Abrams, Goldberg and Goldberg's lawyer, Feinstein, then went into another room. Goldberg had arranged that the plaintiff, his wife, should buy and pay for half the award and Samli Building Corporation, of which he was president, the other half. He had checks from both in his possession. He handed them indorsed in blank to Abrams and said to him: "Assign these checks to the proper owner and deliver to Mr. Feinstein the assignment of the papers to be recorded." He saw Abrams write over the blank indorsements the words "Pay to the order of Harry Wolter." Then Goldberg left the office.

The man introduced as Harry Wolter was in fact an impostor named Dennis. He executed and acknowledged an assignment of the award in the name of Harry Wolter. It was a forgery and resulted in no transfer of title to any award. Because Goldberg, Feinstein and Abrams believed that the stranger was Harry Wolter, the record owner of the award, and that his written assignment would pass good title to the award, the impostor received the checks which were payable only to the order of Harry Wolter. The impostor then indorsed the checks in the name of Harry Wolter and induced the defendant Jacoby to believe that he was in fact Harry Wolter, the payee named in the check obtained from the plaintiff, and to discount the check. Jacoby deposited the check in his own bank. Bearing Jacoby's indorsement as well as the indorsement of two banks, it was presented at the Irving Trust Company, upon which it was drawn, and there paid in due course. The fraud was revealed some months thereafter. The plaintiff has received nothing for her check because no assignment by Dennis could transfer title to an award for property belonging to Harry Wolter as record owner. Her account in the savings bank has been charged with the amount of the check which was intended as payment for an assignment from Harry Wolter and which was payable only to the order of Harry Wolter, though Harry Wolter never indorsed or transferred the check. She has recovered judgment for the amount so charged against her, upon a finding that the signature of Harry Wolter, placed upon the check by an impostor, who has no right to that name, is a forgery just as the same signature placed by the same impostor upon the assignment is a forgery. Under the judgment the loss must ultimately fall upon the impleaded defendant Jacoby who paid value for it. . . .

We have said recently: "In determining whether there was a forgery the true test is whether or not the indorsement of the name of the payee was made by the person who was intended by the drawer to be the payee. If such person indorsed, there is no forgery." (*Halsey* v. *Bank of New York & Trust Co.*, 270 N. Y. 134, 138.) We apply that test here. It is indeed the test which is almost universally applied in determining whether there has been a forgery. It is to be noted, however, that both at common law and under the statutory rule, a signature which is "forged or made without authority of the person whose signature it purports to be" may not be wholly "inoperative," but, on the contrary, may confer a right against a party to a negotiable instrument if "the party, against whom it is sought to enforce such right, is precluded from setting up the forgery or want of authority." A distinction between a case where there has been no forgery or want of authority and a case where a party against whom it is sought to enforce a right is "precluded from setting up the forgery or want of authority" seldom carries any practical consequences; and the courts may at times ignore distinctions in thought which carry no practical consequences. Thus sometimes a confusion seems to creep unnoticed into many opinions which discuss the effect of a signature on a negotiable instrument made by a party who has been given possession of the instrument but is not named therein. The question of whether a challenged indorsement of the name of the payee has been made by the person who was intended by the drawer to be the payee then becomes obscured and confused with the question of whether a party against whom a right is asserted is "precluded" from setting up the forgery.

Where a person has been induced by fraud to draw a check to the order of an existing person, whose name and identity has been fraudulently assumed by another, and to deliver the check to the impostor, it has been held by most courts that an indorsement by the impostor is not a forgery and the bank upon which it is drawn may pay it upon such indorsement. . . .

An academic legal problem may be greatly simplified by excluding, in its formulation, all facts which might introduce conflicting considerations to be weighed in the balance in reaching a sound conclusion. Legal problems, as presented in actual litigation, are seldom free from such complications. The rule that the payee of the check is the particular person who was intended by the drawer to be the payee can hardly be questioned. The name by which he is designated is merely the tag by which the intended person may be identified. A person, though bearing that name, if not the person intended, has no title to the check and cannot indorse or transfer title to it. . . .

Every valid instrument which is not payable to bearer must be payable to a determinate payee and where it appears that the maker intended a particular person to be the payee, the payee so intended even though designated by a wrong name and even though he induced the maker to deal with him through fraudulent misrepresentation as to his responsibility, character or name, is the real payee and can by indorsement transfer title to the instrument. "Although one may be deceived as to the name of the man with whom he is dealing, if he dealt with and intended to deal with the visible person before him the check may properly be indorsed by the impostor." (*Halsey* v. *Bank of New York & Trust Co., supra*, p. 139.)

Thus if we assume the premises of the problem as formulated by the author of the article, viz., that the maker of a check though "deceived as to the man he was dealing with" yet "intended to deal with the visible man who stood before him, identified by sight and hearing," and if "thinking that this man's name was B., he drew the check to B.'s order intending thereby to designate the person standing before him," then there can be little if any room for disagreement with the conclusion, generally accepted by courts and academic writers, that a drawee bank which pays the check upon the indorsement of the person intended to be the designated payee "has simply paid the money to the person for whom it was intended."

In any examination of the cases which have considered the problems arising from false impersonation of a named payee, it quickly appears that the real difficulty has been in determining whether the intended payee was in truth the person bearing the name by which the payee was designated or was the visible person who had assumed that name in order to misrepresent his responsibility or character. Seldom, if ever, is possible argument excluded that the payee named and not the visible person, who by fraud obtains the instrument, was the payee actually intended, and "there are border cases where the line is hard to draw between the impostor who appropriates what is intended for another, and the impostor who deceives by misrepresenting his responsibility or character." (*Strang* v. *Westchester County Nat. Bank*, 235 N. Y. 68, 72.)

It has been said that "In these fraudulent impersonation cases, the maker or drawer of the instrument may be said to have a double intent. First, he intends to make the instrument payable to the person before him or to the person writing at the other end of the line, in case the negotiation is by correspondence. Second, he intends to make the instrument payable to the person whom he believes the stranger to be. The courts have almost unanimously held that the first is the controlling intent except where the named payee was already known to the maker or drawer, as in *Cundy* v. *Lindsay*, 3 A. C. 459, and *Rossi* v. *Nat. Bank*, 71 Mo. App. 150, or was more particularly identified in some manner, e.g., by some designation, description or title, as in the case of *Mercantile Nat. Bank* v. *Silverman*, 148 App. Div. 1; 132 N. Y. Supp. 1017, in which cases the courts treat the second as the controlling intent." (Brannan on the Negotiable Instruments Law [5th ed.], pp. 310, 311.)

Perhaps, in truth, both intents are so inseparable that the choice of one intent rather than the other is purely arbitrary — an example of rationalization, perhaps unconscious, to reach a desired result. (Cf. *Keel* v. *Wynne*, 210 N. C. 426, and note in 15 N. C. L. Review 186 [1937].) Nevertheless an examination of the cases in other jurisdictions can leave no doubt that, as Brannan points out, in most jurisdictions it has been held that "the first is the controlling intent." . . . We do not attempt in this opinion to analyze these cases in detail. In none are the facts exactly similar to those presented in the case under consideration. It is sufficient to point out that even in those cases which apply the so-called "majority rule" there was proof of an antecedent fraud by which a stranger induced a person to deal with him by masquerading as another and the negotiable instrument was made payable to the impostor as a result of the antecedent fraud and the negotiations induced thereby; and it appeared that the instrument was delivered to consummate the dealings with the stranger and with intent that it should be paid to him, though that intent may have been coupled with a second intent of the drawee "to make the instrument payable to the person whom he believes the stranger to be." It was the finding of this first intent which has dictated the conclusion in every case where a bank has been exonerated of fault in the payment of a negotiable instrument to a person not named in the instrument. . . .

In every case in this court where the loss has been imposed upon the drawer there has been proof of dealings between the drawer and another person who deceived the drawer as to his name and identity and there has been a finding that the drawer delivered the instrument to the impostor as the consummation of such dealings or negotiations and with intent that the instrument should be paid to the person with whom such dealings were previously had even though that person was designated by a name he did not bear. (Cf. especially *First Nat. Bank* v. *American Exchange Nat. Bank*, 170 N. Y. 88.) No person can become a "holder for value" of a negotiable instrument by transfer from a person not named therein and who has no title thereto or authority to transfer it. A person who pays value for an instrument takes the risk that the person named therein as payee is not the person designated and intended as payee, at least where the party to the instrument against whom a right thereunder is asserted has not by act or default contributed to the deception. He may protect himself against such risk by requiring sufficient identification or guaranty by others upon whom reliance can be placed. The drawer of an instrument payable to a named payee is under no duty to assure himself that the person to whom it is delivered is the payee so named or is entitled to receive it in his behalf. Though Goldberg erroneously believed that the visible person was in fact Harry Wolter, the person entitled to the check as consideration for the promised assignment of the award, reasonable care did not require that he determine it. He and Abrams were justified in delivering to him the check made out to Harry Wolter in reliance on the fact that the check could not be transferred except by Harry Wolter, the named payee, or paid except upon an order made by him. (*Mercantile Nat. Bank* v. *Silverman*, 148 App. Div. 1; affd. on opinion below, 210 N. Y. 567.) That may be true, indeed, even where there is some doubt in the mind of the drawer whether the person to whom the check is delivered may not be masquerading as the named payee. (*Gallo* v. *Brooklyn Sav. Bank*, 199 N. Y. 222.) Unless the evidence in this case dictates the inference that Goldberg or Abrams had the actual intent that the visible person, though masquerading as Wolter, should receive payment of the check, there can be no ground for reversing the judgment.

We have pointed out at the beginning of the opinion that the negotiations for the purchase of the award were conducted by Goldberg entirely with Abrams. The plaintiff and Goldberg, her representative, had no dealings or communications of any kind with the impostor or indeed with the owner of the property until the moment that the impostor came into the room, and even thereafter, so far as appears, their only dealing with him was, through their agent, to hand him the check indorsed to the order of Harry Wolter. The absence of all prior dealings differentiates this case from every case which has been cited to sustain the contentions of the appellants. The premises fall upon which the conclusion in those cases rested that the drawer must bear the loss. Here there was no antecedent fraud by which the drawer was induced to enter into a transaction with the impostor. At the time when Goldberg left the office knowing that the checks were payable only to the order of Harry Wolter, the assignment had not been executed, delivered or examined. The impostor did not deceive "by misrepresenting his responsibility or character." He deceived by inducing Goldberg and Abrams to believe that he was Harry Wolter who, as they thought, was assigning an award which he owned, and thus he succeeded in appropriating what was intended for another. (*Strang* v. *Westchester County Nat. Bank*, *supra*.)

Physical presence is, as we have said, "often a surer means of identification" than a designated name (*Halsey* v. *Bank of New York & Trust Co.*, *supra*, p. 139), but as we also pointed out in the same case, only where physical presence is combined with antecedent dealings and intention "to deal with the visible person." "The fact that the vendor deals with the person personally rather than by letter is immaterial, except in so far as it bears upon the question of intent." (*Phelps* v. *McQuade*, 220 N. Y. 232, 234.)

The appellants stress testimony of Goldberg that he intended that the checks should be delivered to Kurtz or his client. Of course Goldberg so intended. He accepted the introduction of the impostor as Harry Wolter, the true owner. He had no reason to suspect fraud. There was no reason to require further identification. He named as payee the person whom he intended, i.e., Harry Wolter, the owner, from whom he expected to receive an assignment. He authorized delivery to the impostor because he believed that he was the person so intended. Under these circumstances it certainly cannot be said as matter of law that the payee intended was the visible person with whom there had been no previous dealings and who could have no possible right to the check unless he was, as he claimed, Harry Wolter, the payee named therein. Any question of fact that may exist has been resolved in favor of the plaintiff. The only case in this State which in some aspects might seem to support the plaintiff's case is *Hartford* v. *Greenwich Bank* (157 App. Div. 448; affd., 215 N. Y. 726). After labored attempts to distinguish that case in *United Cigar Stores Co.* v. *American Raw Silk Co.* (184 App. Div. 217), and to limit it in *Strang* v. *Westchester County Nat. Bank* (*supra*), this court definitely overruled the case in *Ulmann Co.* v. *Central Union Trust Co.* (257 N. Y. 563), and thus definitely established the rule that only a payee named in the instrument or identified by previous dealings and intended to be described by that name can transfer title to the instrument.

It has been said that "both commercial practice and legal theory tend more and more to disregard everything except that which actually appears on the instrument." (McKeehan, The Negotiable Instruments Law, 41 American Law Register [N. S.], p. 449.) Only in that way can merchants rely upon the rule that a negotiable instrument in the hands of an innocent purchaser will be paid according to its tenor and intent and will not be paid otherwise. The judgment in favor of the plaintiff enforces rights in accordance with the written instrument and in accordance with commercial practice and especially the practice upon the closing of title, and it accords with the decisions of this and other States.

The judgment should be affirmed, with costs.

[Dissenting opinion of Hubbs, J., is here omitted.]

In MONTGOMERY GARAGE COMPANY *v.* MANUFACTURERS LIABILITY INSURANCE COMPANY, 94 N. J. L. 152 (Supreme Court, 1920), one Ennis, representing himself to be N. K. Turner, went to the insurance company and delivered to it a check for $5,000, which turned out to be bogus, and received from the company its check for $1,500. On the same day the latter check was indorsed and delivered to the plaintiff for value. The check was promptly presented to the drawee bank for payment, but payment had been stopped. In an action against the insurance company judgment for plaintiff was affirmed on the ground that the money was paid to the person intended by the drawer.

Compare MERCANTILE NATIONAL BANK *v.* SILVERMAN, 148 App. Div. 1 (Supreme Court, Appellate Division, 1911), where a private banker received a letter written by an impostor and signed in the name of an army officer asking the banker to discount pay vouchers. The banker agreed, and mailed a check to the supposed officer payable to him under his official title. The check was indorsed by the impostor in the name of the payee, and was paid by the drawee bank. In an action by the private banker against the drawee bank, judgment for plaintiff was reversed.

GUSTIN BACON MANUFACTURING CO. *v.* FIRST NATIONAL BANK OF ENGLEWOOD

ILLINOIS APPELLATE COURT, FIRST DISTRICT, 1922

[224 *Illinois Appellate Reports,* 457]

Mr. Justice MATCHETT delivered the opinion of the court.

The defendant below, First National Bank of Englewood, appeals to this court from a judgment in favor of Gustin Bacon Manufacturing Company, a corporation, plaintiff. The judgment was entered on the finding of the court.

The plaintiff's statement of claim alleged that on the 18th day of October, 1919, it was the owner and lawful possessor of a certain check drawn by it on the New England National Bank of Kansas City, Missouri, payable to the order of John Lord's Sons, dated October 10, 1919, for the sum of $2,175.92; that the defendant wrongfully and without authority from the plaintiff procured possession of the check without the indorsement of the payee, the said "John Lord's Sons," or by their authority, and converted said check and amount of money represented by it to its own use; that the indorsement appearing on the check was a forgery and was placed thereon before it came into possession of defendant; that plaintiff has demanded payment by the defendant of the amount of the check, which has been refused.

To this statement the defendant bank filed an affidavit of merits, alleging a good defense to the whole of the demand, which was stated to be that the defendant was the owner of the check on October 18, 1919, and lawfully possessed of it; that it did not wrongfully procure possession of the check without authority and that the indorsement was not a forgery.

The affidavit further alleged that the plaintiff did not exercise due diligence in notifying the drawee bank of any irregularities in the transfer or indorsement of the check, or of its objection to the payment of the check, and that plaintiff was negligent in failing to stop payment thereon. The court found the issues against the defendant and assessed the damages at the sum of $2,298.23, the amount of the check with interest thereon. Findings of fact and propositions of law were submitted to the court by the respective parties, and the rulings of the court thereon appear in the record.

As to the material facts there seems to be little dispute. Harry and Charles Lord were a copartnership, doing business under the name of John Lord's Sons. Their principal office and place of business was in Philadelphia, Pennsylvania. The business of the copartnership was the manufacture and sale of cotton and woolen waste. The copartnership at the time this transaction occurred had an office at 939 West Van Buren street, Chicago. The manager of the Chicago office at that time was one Melvin. He employed as a clerk in his office Walter J. Riddle, who at a prior time had been a member of a copartnership consisting of himself and one Rivet, which did business under the name of John Lord's Sons, and which represented the Philadelphia copartnership as its agent in Chicago and contiguous territory. This copartnership, however, had ceased to act for John Lord's Sons prior to the transaction out of which this controversy arose. Riddle was afterwards employed by Melvin on account of his knowledge of the trade and business. Neither he nor Melvin had authority to indorse checks which were payable to the order of John Lord's Sons, the members of the copartnership reserving the right to themselves; and all checks were indorsed by them. These checks were usually indorsed with a rubber stamp, which read, "For deposit only to the credit of John Lord's Sons."

A carload of waste was sold to plaintiff through Riddle. After giving the order for the carload of waste the plaintiff on October 10, 1919, drew its check to the order of John Lord's Sons on the New England National Bank, Kansas City, Missouri, and mailed this check in an envelope addressed to John Lord's Sons at the Chicago office. Later plaintiff rejected the car of waste and it was returned to Chicago, placed in the warehouse and afterwards sold to other parties. The notice that the waste was rejected reached the Chicago office prior to the arrival of the check. The manager, Mr. Melvin, directed Riddle to mail the check to the Philadelphia office. Riddle took the check but did not send it to Philadelphia. He had an account with the defendant bank. He indorsed the check John Lord's Sons and W. J. Riddle, and so indorsed deposited it in his account with the defendant bank, which received the same for collection, and about two weeks thereafter the amount of the check was by the defendant bank credited to Riddle's account. Thereafter, and before the defendant bank had any actual notice of irregularity, Riddle checked out the proceeds with the exception of $18.54.

November 19, defendant was informed that Riddle had no authority to indorse the check.

[A page of the opinion is here omitted.]

The indorsement of Riddle being unauthorized, unless some other defense is made to appear, the defendant was, under the authorities, liable in trover for the conversion of the check upon payment by defendant to Riddle.

The copartnership of which Riddle was a member had nothing to do with the sale of the goods to plaintiff, and there is not a scintilla of evidence in the record that the plaintiff ever knew of the existence of any such a partnership doing business as John Lord's Sons. Plaintiff therefore could not have intended to make payment to that copartnership, and could not have intended to make that copartnership the payee of the check, all of which Riddle well knew. It is therefore unnecessary for us to discuss propositions of law and cases cited in support of them that are based on this untrue assumption as to the facts.

Appellant says that this action in trover will not lie because plaintiff did not have the title and right to possession of the check at the time of bringing suit; that the check had been delivered to John Lord's Sons at the time of its alleged conversion; that they were payees named therein and therefore having title and possession any right of action for the conversion of the check was in John Lord's Sons and not in plaintiff; further, that a payee to whom a check has been delivered is the owner and entitled to possession of it; that the mere failure of consideration would not revest the maker of the check with title, and especially would this be true where, as here, there has been no demand upon the payee for the return of the check; and that demand for the delivery of the check to the maker in such a case is clearly essential.

We think these contentions also are based on assumption of facts which are not sustained by the evidence in the case. Whether the check was in fact delivered depends in the last analysis upon the intention of the parties in that respect. This check was issued in payment for goods. These goods were rejected and returned. The notice of such rejection reached the manager of John Lord's Sons of Philadelphia in Chicago prior to the receipt of the check. Under the circumstances disclosed it was the duty of the payee to return the check to the plaintiff, as it must have been apparent that it was mailed by mistake. John Lord's Sons at no time have made any claim against plaintiff on account of the transaction.

[A page of the opinion is here omitted.]

We think the undisputed evidence in this case tends to show that the plaintiff was the true owner of the check and of the fund represented by it at the time when defendant received the proceeds thereon and paid the same to Riddle. As it was the true owner, it was therefore the proper party to bring action.

But appellant further says that, conceding the foregoing, the check had not been indorsed by the payee and was therefore worthless; that if the maker had been sued on it, he could have successfully defended on the ground that the consideration had failed; that the check did not operate as an assignment of the fund since the enactment of the present Negotiable Instruments Law, and that the drawee bank would not be liable until it had accepted the check; that an innocent holder could get no title by means of a forged indorsement; that the check was returned to plaintiff before it was indorsed by the true payee and before this suit was brought; and that there is therefore no damage.

Appellant further says that there is no proof of a demand of the check and that no special damages are alleged; that the proof that the goods were returned and accepted shows affirmatively the worthlessness of the check, because the debt it was intended to pay was canceled by the return of the goods, and the check could be applied to no valuable purpose. It says if plaintiff did not pay the check it is not damaged; that if it wishes both to return the goods and to pay the check, it may do so, but cannot thus augment the damages which defendant would be required to pay.

In the first place, we think there is evidence in the record tending to show that the check was in fact paid. The indorsements thereon indicate that it was so paid and defendant's affidavit of merits affirmatively avers that the check was collected by the defendant. Plaintiff's statement of claim avers not only the conversion of the check, but of the amount or money represented by the face of it.

The value of the property in the action for conversion is fixed as of the date of the conversion, and on that date this check was *prima facie* worth its face value. If the face value of the check was paid, as we think must be inferred from the evidence, then clearly the plaintiff was damaged to that amount.

Appellant further contends that under the facts as set forth the plaintiff is estopped to maintain the action by reason of its negligence; that plaintiff knew the goods were returned and that the consideration therefor had failed; that he knew defendant might become secondarily liable upon its indorsement of the check; that an order from plaintiff stopping payment of the check, which it had a right to do, would have prevented damage both to plaintiff and defendant, and in this connection the defendant invokes the rule of law that where one of two innocent parties must suffer loss, he who is the cause or occasion of that confidence by which the loss has been brought about ought to bear it. We do not think there is any merit in these contentions. Plaintiff owed no legal duty to the defendant bank. It was not bound to assume that a depositor in defendant's bank would forge an indorsement on the check, or to presume that defendant, without taking precautions, would collect and pay the amount of the check, relying on such a forged indorsement. The rules of estoppel are not applicable to the facts in this case. On the question of authority of Riddle to indorse paper for the real payee, estoppel might be invoked if there were facts making it applicable; or if there were facts tending to show that a depositor was negligent, after receiving his returned checks, in notifying his own bank of a forgery, which, in the exercise of reasonable care, he should have learned of, then as between such depositor and the bank the doctrine of estoppel might be invoked; but beyond this the courts have not gone in this class of cases.

Contributory negligence is not, generally speaking, a defense in this class of cases. On the contrary, defendant was bound to ascertain the genuineness of the indorsement upon this check at its peril. The rule rests upon public policy, and is necessary for the security of commercial transactions, although hardship often results from its application. *Hamlin's Wizard Oil Co.* v. *United States Exp. Co.*, 265 Ill. 156 [7 N. C. C. A. 638].

For the reasons indicated the judgment is affirmed.

Affirmed.

Dever, P. J., and McSurely, J., concur.

In SLATTERY & CO. *v.* NATIONAL CITY BANK, 114 Misc. 48 (New York Municipal Court, 1920), a brokerage firm sold securities for Harold E. Richards of Oklahoma and by mistake mailed check in settlement to Harold E. Richards of Texas, who formerly had had an account with the bank. The Texas Richards indorsed and cashed the check, although it was accompanied by a statement showing the transaction out of which it arose. In an action by the drawer as assignee of the Oklahoma Richards against a collecting bank for conversion, it was held that the indorsement was not a forgery, as "the intent to make the check payable to Harold E. Richards, Bartlesville, Okla. was superseded and blotted out by the actual delivery of the check to Harold E. Richards, Rockdale, Tex."

In DEFIANCE LUMBER COMPANY *v.* THE BANK OF CALIFORNIA, 180 Wash. 533 (Supreme Court, 1935), the day foreman of a lumber company manipulated time cards in such a way as to induce the company to execute pay checks in the names of nonexistent workmen. The foreman then obtained payment on the checks by indorsing them in the names of the payees. In an action by the company against the drawee bank to recover the amount of the checks the trial court found that the company was negligent in its methods of time keeping and paying employees, and in entrusting the foreman with all details in connection with such matters. A judgment for the defendant was affirmed.

Compare Secs. 13–15, 17, 23, and 124 of the Uniform Negotiable Instruments Law with Secs. 9 (2), 20, 24, 60, and 64 of the Bills of Exchange Act, and with Arts. 6, 10, and 69 of the Geneva Law.

4. NEGOTIATION

A. In General

HERDMAN *v.* WHEELER

King's Bench Division, 1901

[*Law Reports*, [1902] 1 *King's Bench*, 361]

[Defendant, requiring a loan, signed and handed to one Anderson a blank stamped paper with authority to fill it up as a promissory note payable to Anderson and for the amount of £15 only. The stamp however was sufficient to cover a note for £75. Anderson filled up the note for £30, and made it payable to plaintiff, to whom he handed it for value and without notice of any breach of authority. Anderson misappropriated the proceeds. In an action by the plaintiff on the note, Channell, J., said in upholding a judgment for defendant:]

The real point in the present case after all is, Can we hold that this note was "negotiated" to the plaintiff within the meaning with which the words are used in the proviso to the 20th section? And as to this, we certainly have the opinion of the late Lord Chief Justice that a delivery to a payee for value is not a "negotiating" within the meaning of the Act. In the 31st section it is said, "a bill is negotiated when it is transferred from one person to another in such a manner as to constitute the transferee the holder of the bill." Does this mean only from one person who is holder to another, or may the person transferring be an agent in possession of the bill otherwise than as holder, whose delivery constitutes the receiver a holder? And even if that cannot be the meaning in the 31st section, may it not be possible to say that in the 20th section "negotiated to a holder in due course" means no more than delivered to a person in such a way that he thereupon becomes a holder in due course? This is the argument of Mr. Arthur Powell for the plaintiff, and he quotes from the Imperial Dictionary a meaning of "negotiate" which might cover the present case. He also points out that, if this note had been payable to Anderson's order and indorsed by him to the plaintiff, or if it had been by the form in which it was drawn, or by a blank indorsement, payable to bearer, the plaintiff could clearly have recovered on it. If the production by Anderson of the promissory note in either of those forms would have made it unnecessary for the plaintiff to inquire into Anderson's authority to deal with it, it certainly is odd that the production of a note with plaintiff's own name in as payee should be a matter which plaintiff must inquire into and ascertain the extent of Anderson's authority before he could safely take it. The fact that plaintiff's name was there would be more likely to lull suspicion on his part than to arouse it. Mr. Powell contends that the present case clearly comes within the mischief which the proviso in the 20th section was intended to meet, and suggests that we should not be straining the words in putting on them the meaning for which he contends. On the other hand, we have to deal with the points raised by Mr. Bruce Williamson, in his argument for the defendant, that the issuing of a bill or note to the first holder stands on a different footing altogether from the transfer of it from one holder to another, because, when the first holder takes it, it has not become part of the mercantile currency of the country, to use an expression found in some of the cases. He contends that the rule that one holder of a negotiable instrument can give a better title to it than he himself possessed is based upon the view that negotiable instruments are currency, and that it is on their passing from hand to hand, and not on their coming into being, that negotiable instruments acquire their special validity in the hands of a holder in due course. Even if the payee of a note may be a holder in due course, the question whether he is or not depends upon the actual state of facts as between him and the maker of the note; and the contract between the payee and the maker, though no doubt it has some incidents, such, for instance, as days of grace written into it by the law merchant, yet is governed more by the ordinary law of contracts than by the law merchant, and in particular that the element of negotiability in no way enters into the contract between maker and payee. There is much to support this argument in the Bills of Exchange Act. For instance, delivery to the payee being required to complete the contract, it is said in s. 21, sub-s. 2, that "as between immediate parties, and as regards a remote party other than a holder in due course, the delivery (*a*) in order to be effectual must be made either by or under the authority of the party drawing, accepting, or indorsing as the case may be." Payees and holders not in due course are, therefore, put on the same footing as regards proof of authority of the person handing them the bill. In the present case, therefore, the delivery of the note to the plaintiff must, in order to enable him to recover, be under the authority of the defendant. It certainly was not so delivered by the defendant's actual authority, and cannot be said to have been delivered under his authority by reason of the ostensible authority with which Anderson had been clothed (to use Lord Bowen's words) by the signature in blank. . . . Anderson, if agent of the defendant at all, was only agent to fill up the paper, and, if the question were to be determined altogether apart from the law merchant and the Bills of Exchange Act, we should have to say that there was here no binding contract at common law whereby the defendant promised the plaintiff that, if the plaintiff would give 25*l.* to Anderson for the defendant, he, the defendant, would pay 30*l.* to the plaintiff in a month.

We have been very reluctant to come to the conclusion that the judgment in favour of the defendant in this case was right, because it appears dangerous even to cast any doubt upon a payee's right to recover when he has taken a bill or note complete and regular on the face of it honestly and for value; but, after carefully considering the matter, we have come to the conclusion that we should be unfairly straining the words if we did not hold that "negotiated" in the proviso at the end of the 20th section meant transferred by one holder to another. It is to be observed that the Bills of Exchange Act in s. 2 defines "issue" as meaning "the first delivery of a bill or note complete in form to a person who takes it as holder." Here Anderson clearly issued the note to the plaintiff within the meaning of this definition. There is therefore a technical word defined and used in the Act to mean that which Anderson did here, and the appropriate words to have used in the proviso to s. 20, if it had been intended to include this case, would have been "if such instrument after completion is issued or negotiated to a holder in due course." Those are not the words, and, although we think that the present case might possibly have been decided in the plaintiff's favour before the Bills of Exchange Act was passed, we think that we cannot consistently with the meaning of "issue" and "negotiate" in the Act say that the present case is covered by the words used in the proviso. That being so, it falls within the first part of the 2nd subsection of s. 20; and as the authority of the defendant was not strictly followed he is not liable.

We think, therefore, that the appeal must be dismissed.

Appeal dismissed.

In LLOYD'S BANK, LIMITED *v.* COOKE, [1907] 1 K. B. 794 (Court of Appeal), Fletcher Moulton, L. J., said that "when the definition of 'negotiation' given by s. 31, sub-s. 1, is looked at, it appears clear that the Legislature intended to make it apply also to the original operation of transferring the bill to the payee." This dictum was expressly disapproved by the House of Lords in *R. E. Jones, Limited* v. *Waring and Gillow, Limited*, [1926] A.C. 670, Viscount Cave, L. C. pointing out that under s. 31 a bill is negotiated by being transferred from one person to another and (if payable to order) by indorsement and delivery.

Compare LIBERTY TRUST COMPANY *v.* TILTON, 217 Mass. 462 (Supreme Judicial Court, 1914), where the maker of a promissory note delivered it to the payee for value in violation of an agreement with an accommodation indorser that it should be for a less amount and signed by another indorser. In holding that the instrument had been negotiated to the payee, Rugg, C.J., said: "A promissory note complete as to form and payable to a named person may be negotiated to that person by being sold to him or taken by him for value. This is the common and popular signification of the word. It was the sense in which it was used in the law merchant before the negotiable instruments act. Its meaning has not been changed by the act. That was in substance the decision in *Boston Steel & Iron Co.* v. *Steuer*, 183 Mass. 140

"The soundness of that decision in this respect is confirmed by other provisions of the act. 'Negotiation' is defined by § 47, whereby it is provided that 'an instrument is negotiated when it is transferred from one person to another in such manner as to constitute the transferee the holder thereof.' 'Holder' is defined in § 207 to be 'the payee or indorsee of a bill or note, who is in possession of it.' The remaining sentence of § 47, *viz.*,

'If payable to bearer it is negotiated by delivery; if payable to order it is negotiated by the indorsement of the holder completed by delivery,' was not intended to include all the ways in which an instrument might be negotiated, nor to restrict the comprehensive terms of the preceding sentence. Plainly under these two sections a negotiable instrument payable to a named payee is negotiated when the physical possession of it is handed for value to the person named as payee. One effect of the last sentence of § 47 is to describe the method by which the person who first becomes holder may pass title. It does not comprehend all the ways by which an instrument may be negotiated.

"The word 'negotiate,' being defined thus in the act and being given a definition in conformity to that attached to it by the common law before the passage of the act, it must be held to have the same meaning throughout the statute in the absence of a strongly countervailing context requiring a different signification. There is nothing in § 31 to indicate that it there was used in any different sense. . . .

"The conclusion follows that the payee named in a promissory note, who purchases it complete in form for value before maturity, in good faith and without notice of any infirmity in title or otherwise, is a person to whom it has been negotiated as holder in due course, notwithstanding it was signed in blank by the party to be charged, whose instructions as to the filling of blanks and the delivery have not been followed by the one to whom it was intrusted by him in its incomplete state."

STATE SAVINGS BANK OF LEAVENWORTH *v.* KRUG

KANSAS SUPREME COURT, 1920

[108 *Kansas Reports*, 108]

[In part payment of an ice making machine the buyer gave a note to the seller. The seller sold the note to the plaintiff bank. In an action on the note by the bank against the buyer, Porter, J., having stated the facts, continued:]

In our view, the principal question involved is whether the manner in which the note came into the hands of the bank amounts to a commercial indorsement as defined by the negotiable-instruments law. The indorsement was by rubber stamp. Defendant insists that this was not sufficient and that it requires a signature of the indorser in writing. Section 37 of the negotiable-instruments act (Gen. Stat. 1915, § 6557), provides that where the instrument is payable to order "it is negotiated by the indorsement of the holder completed by delivery," and section 38, (Gen. Stat. 1915, § 6558), declares that the "indorsement must be written on the instrument itself or upon a paper attached thereto." The precise question has never been before the court. In *Flanders* v. *Snare*, 37 Pa. Sup. Ct. 28, decided in 1898, it was held that there was nothing in the negotiable-instruments law which prevents the use of a rubber stamp in the indorsement of drafts, checks and notes. In the opinion it was said:

"Of course, we are not to be understood as saying that an indorsement made by the use of a rubber stamp, any more than one made in manuscript, proves itself." (p. 31.)

It was held, however, that the testimony of the indorser showing that he had adopted that method of entering into the contract of indorsement was sufficient.

In the case just cited, the court reached the conclusion that an indorsement of a negotiable instrument made by the use of a rubber stamp would be valid and binding on the indorser before the passage of the negotiable-instruments law and that the legislature did not intend by the adoption of the act to make any change in that respect. And in the opinion it was said:

"Of course, the legislature knew that the necessities of trade had long before brought about the fact that almost the entire bodies of the various forms of commercial contracts in ordinary use were printed. But it would hardly be contended that after the maker of a note or the drawer of a bill had, for his own convenience and in accord with almost universal usage, selected such printed form and launched his obligation on the sea of commerce, he could thereafter be heard to deny his responsibility for it on the ground that the instrument was not 'in writing' within the meaning of the act of assembly." (p. 30.)

The only testimony introduced by the plaintiff was upon this point. After identifying the note in question, Mr. Fisher, the president of the company, stated that the indorsement was stamped on it with his authority by Mr. Masterson and in his presence.

[The balance of the opinion is omitted. Judgment for defendant was reversed and the case remanded with directions to enter judgment for plaintiff for the amount of the note and interest.]

See also Pingree National Bank *v.* McFarland, 57 Utah 410 (Supreme Court, 1921), where a typewritten indorsement was held to be adequate.

BARKLEY *v.* MULLER

New York Supreme Court, Appellate Division, 1914

[164 *New York Appellate Division Reports,* 351]

Dowling, J. The complaint herein, after setting forth that the defendant Muller made his promissory note in writing on a certain date, whereby he promised to pay to the order of George B. Burch, at the Hudson Trust Company in the city of New York, the sum of $2,500 four months after said date, further proceeds to allege: "That the defendants George B. Burch and Sarah M. Burch, thereafter and before maturity of said note, for value, indorsed the one-half interest therein to and delivered the same to this plaintiff, who is now the owner and holder thereof."

By section 62 of the Negotiable Instruments Law (Consol. Laws, chap. 38; Laws of 1909, chap. 43) it is required that an indorsement must be of the entire instrument and that an indorsement which purports to transfer to the indorsee a part only of the amount payable is declared not to operate as a negotiation of the instrument. By section 60 of the same law, "negotiation" is defined as the transfer of an instrument from one person to another in such manner as to constitute the transferee the holder thereof; where an instrument is payable to order it is negotiated by the indorsement of the holder completed by delivery. By section 2 of the same law the holder is defined as the payee or indorsee of a bill or note who is in possession of it, or the bearer thereof. In *King* v. *King* (37 Misc. Rep. 63; affd., 73 App. Div. 547; appeal dismissed, 172 N. Y. 604) it was held that in an action at law upon a promissory note the obligation of the defendant is single and cannot be divided into parts, and that only one action can be maintained for the debt in its entirety. The present action being one at law, and containing no averments or prayer for relief appropriate in an action in equity, it follows that the complaint set forth no cause of action, and that the order appealed from should, therefore, be reversed, with ten dollars costs and disbursements, and the demurrers of the defendants sustained, with ten dollars costs, with leave to the plaintiff to serve an amended complaint within twenty days upon payment of said costs.

INGRAHAM, P. J., LAUGHLIN, SCOTT and HOTCHKISS, JJ., concurred.

Order reversed, with ten dollars costs and disbursements, and motion denied and demurrers sustained, with ten dollars costs, with leave to plaintiff to amend on payment of costs.

BYERS *v.* THE BELLAN-PRICE INVESTMENT CO.

COLORADO COURT OF APPEALS, 1897

[10 *Colorado Appellate Reports*, 74]

THOMSON, P. J., delivered the opinion of the court.

This suit was brought by the appellee before a justice of the peace, upon a contract of the appellant guarantying the payment of a promissory note. The following is the note:

$3000.00 DENVER, COLO., January 18, 1895.

Sixty days after date we, or either of us, promise to pay to the order of ourselves, three thousand and no 100ths dollars, for value received, at the office of The Bellan-Price Investment Company, Denver, Colo., with interest at 10 per cent. per annum from maturity until paid.

In case suit is brought hereon, we agree that $200 attorney's fees shall be taxed as a part of the costs in the case.

(Signed)

THE DENVER HARDWARE MANUFACTURING CO.,

By WM. N. BYERS, *President.*

Attest:

R. A. GUTSCH, *Secretary.*

On the back of the note appears the following:

Pay to the order of , to whom, for value received, we, or either of us, hereby guarantee the payment of the within note at maturity, or any time thereafter, with interest at the rate of 10 per cent. per annum from maturity until paid, waiving demand, notice of non-payment and protest.

(Signed)

THE DENVER HARDWARE MANUFACTURING CO.,
By WM. N. BYERS, *President*.
WM. N. BYERS,
FRANK N. BRIGGS,
ARTHUR HATCH,
R. A. GUTSCH

Attest:
R. A. GUTSCH, *Secretary*.

Between the date of the note and the commencement of the suit, there was paid upon the note, at various times, as shown by indorsements on its back, the aggregate sum of $2,806.80. The amount claimed before the justice to be due, as shown by his transcript, was $275. The justice gave the plaintiff judgment for $246.80, from which the defendant appealed to the county court, where judgment was awarded against him for $274.20. He has brought the case here by appeal. . . .

It is said that the legal title to the note could be transferred only by indorsement, and that this note was not indorsed, so that the plaintiff, not being the payee, could maintain no action on it in his own name; therefore, it is argued, the note was improperly admitted in evidence. It is probably true that an indorsement was necessary to enable the plaintiff to maintain the action before the justice in his own name, because the code provision that actions shall be prosecuted in the names of the real parties in interest, has no application to proceedings in justices' courts. But on the back of the note are the words, preceding the guaranty: "Pay to the order of ," and below is signed the name of the payee. If the space left blank had been filled with the name of some person, this would have been an indorsement in full. There was no need of the payee's signature to the contract of guaranty, because it was the maker of the note, and a guaranty of payment by it would not increase, or in any way alter, the liability it assumed by executing the note. Only the payee could indorse the note so as to transfer the title, its signature to the guaranty of payment was meaningless, and the use of words of transfer, lacking only the name of the indorsee to make the note the property of a particular individual, evidences the intention of the payee, and explains its signature below. If the name of the indorsee had been inserted, the indorsement would have been full; but as it was omitted, and the intention to indorse is evidence from the words which were used, we must hold that the signature of the payee on the back of the note amounts to an indorsement in blank, and that the plaintiff, having possession of the note, was *prima facie* its legal owner.

[The balance of the opinion is omitted. The judgment of the court below was affirmed.]

Compare GAYLORD *v.* NEBRASKA SAVINGS AND EXCHANGE BANK, 54 Neb. 104 (Supreme Court, 1898), where it was held that in the case of a note payable to Mary W. Gaylord an indorsement reading "Pay to the order of ...... Mary W. Gaylord" was ineffectual and vested no legal title in the transferee.

In CHANDLER *v.* SMITH, 147 Ga. 637 (Supreme Court, 1917), it was held that an indorsement by the payee "to J. A. Smith," omitting the words "or order," was a general indorsement which did not restrict the negotiability of the paper.

HENDRIX *v.* BAUHARD BROTHERS

GEORGIA SUPREME COURT, 1912

[138 *Georgia Reports*, 473]

LUMPKIN, J. Bauhard Brothers brought suit against the makers of a promissory note payable to the order of Bridges & Flora. On the back of it was this entry: "For value received, we hereby warrant the makers of this note financially good on execution. Bridges & Flora." The defendants demurred to the petition on the grounds, that it set out no cause of action; that it showed on its face that the plaintiffs had no legal title and were not *bona fide* holders for value; and that the entry on the note by the payees was not a formal indorsement, but only a guaranty that the makers of the note were good for the amount thereof. The presiding judge overruled the demurrer. The defendants filed an answer to the petition, denying its allegations; but they wtihdrew the denial of the paragraph in which the plaintiffs alleged that they bought from the payees the note for value, before due, and without notice of any defense. The presiding judge thereupon, on motion, struck the answer and, after the introduction of evidence, directed a verdict for the plaintiffs. Defendants excepted. . . .

On the subject of indorsements like the one here involved there are two conflicting lines of authority. On the one hand, it has been held by the Supreme Court of the United States and some inferior Federal courts, and by the courts of two or three States, that an entry of a guaranty followed by the signature of the payee on the back of a note payable to order does not amount to such an indorsement as to carry title and cut off defenses existing against the payee. *Central Trust Co.* v. *First National Bank*, 101 U. S. 68 (25 L. ed. 876); *Snevily* v. *Ekel*, 1 Watts & S. 203; *Edgerly* v. *Lawson*, 176 Mass. 551 (57 N. E. 1020, 51 L. R. A. 432), though some of the earlier decisions in Massachusetts seem inclined to take a contrary view. The leading case on this side of the question (discussing it with reference to the common law) is the one decided by the Supreme Court of the United States. It cites the *Snevily case*, *supra*, and two cases from New York. The reasoning on which this class of cases is based is, that the indorsement is not in blank, but is filled up; that it expresses fully the contract, and can raise no implication of another. Opposed to this view are the decisions in a very large number of States. Numerically, the latter class of decisions greatly preponderates, and we think the reasoning on which they are based is sounder than that contained in the class first mentioned.

At common law (though not so under the statute of this State) the general rule was that choses in action were not assignable so that the assignee could sue in his own name. He acquired only an equitable title, had to sue in the name of the assignor for his use, and was subject to the defenses which could be made against the assignor. Growing out of the necessities of commerce, there was an exception to this rule in favor of negotiable instruments. They were transferable by indorsement and delivery, and the indorsee could sue in his own name. Those payable to bearer required no indorsement. A *bona fide* indorsee for value, before maturity, and without notice of any defense, was protected. No particular form was necessary to constitute an indorsement. The mere signing of the name of the person to whose order the note was payable, upon the back of it, was sufficient.

[A page of the opinion is here omitted.]

We now come to consider more particularly the statute and decisions in this State. By the Civil Code, § 4275, it is declared that "any person indorsing or transferring a negotiable instrument may limit his own liability upon such indorsement or transfer, by express restrictions therein." This declares a general rule, and expressly recognizes the right in this State of a person indorsing a negotiable instrument to limit his liability. If there is no limitation, but a mere indorsement in blank, the general liability resulting therefrom applies. No reason appears why an indorser may not enlarge his liability as well as limit it. The writing of his name upon the back of a negotiable note by the payee thereof constitutes an indorsement. The addition of a limitation or enlargement of liability does not make it cease to be an indorsement sufficient to carry title to the note, although it may restrict or enlarge the liability of the indorser. From an early date it has been recognized in the decisions of this court that no express form of words was necessary to constitute an indorsement which would operate to convey title.

[Over two pages of the opinion are here omitted.]

It has been suggested that an indorsement of the character of the one now under consideration, accompanied by a physical transfer of the paper, may operate to pass title to the instrument and give the holder the right to treat the payee as an indorser, with a prescribed liability; but that such an indorsement, without express words of transfer or assignment, does not constitute the holder such a purchaser for value as to protect him from defenses already accrued to the maker against the original payee. In this distinction we can not concur. An entry on the back of a note payable to order, signed by the payee, is either an indorsement or it is not an indorsement, in the legal sense of the term. Of course, an entry may be physically indorsed or written on the back of a note, without being in the legal sense an indorsement; but we are unable to accede to the proposition that it may be both an indorsement and not an indorsement. If it is such an indorsement of a negotiable note as will pass the legal title to it upon delivery, and will place on the indorsee the duty of recognizing the indorser as such and of treating him as an indorser under the law merchant, it would be peculiar if it were an indorsement to the holder for burdens, but not for benefits. We can not concur in the argument that the indorsement under consideration is an indorsement sufficient to carry legal title upon delivery, but not sufficient to give the corresponding benefit to him who thus acquires it, arising from being a *bona fide* taker before due, and for value. In some of the cases before this court, and other courts, the question has been not whether the addition of words of transfer or assignment and warranty to the indorsement aided it, but whether they prevented its being an indorsement in the legal sense, on the ground that they were not words strictly descriptive of that relation. Of course there must be delivery of the instrument in order to carry title, even with the most formal or general indorsement.

The note now under consideration was payable to the order of the payees. When they wrote upon the back of it that for value received they warranted the makers of the note financially good on execution, and sold and delivered it for value to a third person, with no other indorsement (save an entry of a credit), it must be assumed that they intended to accomplish something by so doing. They did not intend to warrant to themselves the financial standing of the makers, nor did they mean that they had received value from themselves for so doing. If not to themselves, then to whom did they make such warranty? Clearly to some other person who should be the owner of the note. Moreover, the statement that the financial status of the makers was warranted "good on execution" indicates the expectation that execution would issue in favor of some person other than themselves against the makers. But unless this indorsement and delivery for value carried the legal title to the note to the person to whom it was so delivered, it would remain in the payees, and no execution could issue in favor of another person. Nor can we agree with the statement made in *Lamourieux* v. *Hewitt*, 5 Wend. (N. Y.) 308, which is cited by the Supreme Court of the United States in the Trust Company case to which reference has already been made, that the payee making such an indorsement on a note would be liable upon his guaranty, not as an indorser of negotiable paper, but as a party to a special contract "which might have been written on a separate piece of paper as well as on the back of the note." In that clause inheres the fallacy of the argument. There is a wide difference between writing on a separate piece of paper and a payee's writing something over his name on the back of a promissory note. If he should simply write his name on a separate sheet of blank paper, it would bind him to nothing; but if he writes his name on the back of a promissory note payable to his order, he becomes an indorser. So, if he should write an assignment, or a guaranty, on a separate sheet of paper and sign it, that would be a distinct contract; but when he writes his name upon the back of a note payable to his order, the addition of words which either limit or enlarge the usual liability on his part which would arise from a blank indorsement does not destroy the fact that the entry is an indorsement upon a negotiable paper, or prevent its efficacy as a method of passing the legal title upon negotiation, at least unless there is something in the indorsement to show an intention to destroy the negotiable character of the paper. . . .

Judgment affirmed. All the Justices concur.

In JONES COUNTY TRUST & SAVINGS BANK *v.* KURT, 192 Iowa 965 (Supreme Court, 1921), the following appeared on the back of a note: "For value received I do hereby assign the within note to the Jones County Trust & Savings Bank, Monticello, Iowa, and guarantee the payment of same when due or at any time thereafter and consent to any extension of time or renewal waiving demand, notice, and protest." This writing, signed by the payee, was held to be a regular indorsement.

In INTERNATIONAL HARVESTER COMPANY *v.* WATKINS, 127 Kan. 50 (Supreme Court, 1928), notes given for the purchase of a tractor and harvester-thrasher bore an unconditional indorsement for value received, together with a guarantee of payment. This portion was printed, but was followed by the words "without recourse" in writing before the signature. Answering the contention that the indorsement was inconsistent, it was held that the written words controlled the printed ones, and that the indorsement was a qualified indorsement which did not impair the negotiability of the notes.

RANDLES *v.* GULLY

OKLAHOMA SUPREME COURT, 1927

[128 *Oklahoma Reports,* 220]

HEFNER, J. E. I. Gully, as plaintiff, brought suit in the district court of Beaver county against O. J. Budd and Lula Randles, as administratrix of the estate of W. T. Randles, as defendants. The suit was based upon a promissory note executed by the defendant Budd in favor of W. T. Randles, who sold the note to the plaintiff. The parties will be referred to herein as they appeared in the trial court.

On October 18, 1917, the defendant O. J. Budd delivered his promissory note to W. T. Randles in the sum of $1,500, due January 1, 1919. As a part of the same transaction; the parties executed a contract for the sale by Randles to Budd of a threshing machine. A portion of the written contract is as follows:

That the note shall be paid by 40 per cent. of the gross earnings of said machine, and any time that the machine will not make expenses he has the privilege of bringing in the machine.

On June 1, 1918, the plaintiff purchased said note, and, the written indorsement on the back of the note is as follows:

This indorsement is made subject to all the conditions of the separate contract in writing of which this note is a part of the same transaction.

W. T. Randles. Gully's Garage, by E. I. Gully.

The plaintiff introduced the note sued on, and it was admitted that he became the owner thereof before the final due date. The defendant offered in evidence the written contract executed at the same time the note was executed. This is all the evidence that was introduced.

On this evidence, the court rendered judgment for the plaintiff and against the defendant for the full amount shown to be due on the note. The defendant appealed to this court and contends, as a defense, that the note and contract together constitute one contract, which is nonnegotiable, and that the transfer of the note was simply an assignment of the contract.

When the plaintiff purchased the note he took it subject to all the conditions of the separate contract. This is shown by a mere reference to the contract of indorsement on the back of the note. It is, therefore, plain from the indorsement that the note and the contract must be taken together.

The note in itself was a negotiable instrument; but in the indorsement the parties by their contract expressly made the written contract and the note one and the same transaction. It must follow that the plaintiff took the note subject to the conditions of the contract.

Under these facts, we do not think the evidence is sufficient to sustain the judgment of the trial court, and the same is, therefore, reversed and remanded for a new trial.

BRANSON, C. J., and HARRISON, LESTER, HUNT, CLARK, and RILEY, JJ., concur.

FIRST NATIONAL BANK OF SIOUX CITY *v.* JOHN MORRELL & COMPANY

SOUTH DAKOTA SUPREME COURT, 1928

[53 *South Dakota Reports*, 496]

BROWN, J. Defendant conducts a packing plant industry in Sioux Falls and sells its products in different parts of the United States, receiving in payment checks from its customers on banks in their respective localities. It deposited those checks in Sioux Falls National Bank, indorsed as follows:

"Pay to the order of Sioux Falls National Bank, for deposit only.

"John Morrell & Co."

By agreement with the bank defendant was credited conditionally in its checking acount with the amount of the checks, but the bank was at all times to retain a minimum balance of $20,000, to take care of what was known as "the float," being checks in process of collection, which might not be paid. Between plaintiff and Sioux Falls National Bank, mutual accounts had been maintained for a number of years. In the early part of January, 1924, defendant deposited in Sioux Falls National Bank 20 checks, aggregating about $3,900, all bearing the indorsement hereinbefore quoted, receiving credit for such checks under the agreement already referred to. The Sioux Falls National Bank, on January 8th, 9th, and 10th, transmitted these checks to plaintiff at Sioux City, indorsed:

"Pay to the order of the First National Bank of Sioux City, Iowa. Sioux

Falls National Bank 98–1. Thomas A. Wadden, Vice President and Cashier."

And each was transmitted in a letter reading:

"We inclose herewith for collection and return items listed below"—followed by a list of the checks inclosed.

Plaintiff, in accordance with a custom between it and the Sioux Falls Bank, credited the latter conditionally with the amount of the checks, and forwarded them for collection to banks in the localities on which they were drawn. On the morning of January 11th the Sioux Falls Bank failed to open, and was taken over by the Comptroller of the Currency for liquidation.

The vice president of the John Morrell & Co., who was also a director of Sioux Falls National Bank, telegraphed to the various makers of the checks and had payment of them stopped, and the makers of the checks thereafter paid the accounts represented by the checks direct to defendant. The dishonored checks were returned to plaintiff, and plaintiff brings this action, claiming that defendant is liable to it as indorser of the checks. The action was tried by the court without a jury, and from judgment on a decision in favor of defendant, and an order denying a new trial, plaintiff appeals.

Appellant contends that, because defendant received credit in his account in the Sioux Falls National Bank for the amount of the checks, the relation of debtor and creditor existed between defendant and the bank; that the bank became the owner of the checks, and that, by its indorsement of them to plaintiff, plaintiff became the owner of the checks, with a right of recourse, in the event of their dishonor, against any prior indorser. But this contention entirely ignores the contract between defendant and the Sioux Falls bank, created by the indorsement on the checks. The indorsement "for deposit only" is a restrictive indorsement (R. C. § 1740), and clearly vests title in the indorsee in trust for the indorser. Such an indorsement confers upon the indorsee the right to transfer its rights as indorsee, because the indorsement authorized payment "to the order of Sioux Falls National Bank"; but the subsequent indorsee (in this case, plaintiff) acquires only the title of the first indorsee under the restrictive indorsement (R. C. § 1741), and, irrespective of the directions contained in the letters or transmittal, plaintiff could only have the rights of an agent or trustee for the defendant, clothed with authority to collect the checks. *Haskell* v. *Avery*, 181 Mass. 106, 63 N. E. 15, 92 Am. St. Rep. 401. Appellant says that:

"It is frankly conceded that the sole and only purpose of stopping payment of these checks was to enable defendant to reduce its balance in the Sioux Falls bank when the same closed, and, by collection of the items through other channels, thus to realize 100 cents on the dollar, instead of taking the proportion of loss, if any, which other depositors may sustain through failure of the bank."

But this is just what defendant had a lawful right to do. It had a right at any time to revoke the agency of plaintiff for collection of the checks, and to avoid loss by collecting through other channels the accounts due from the makers of the checks. Had the checks been collected through the medium of the banks, and the money had reached the Sioux Falls National, the relation of debtor and creditor between the bank and defendant would then, and not until then, have arisen.

The rights of an indorsee under a restrictive indorsement are not those mentioned in section 1770 of the Code, but only those enumerated in section 1741, among which is not the right to recover from the indorser on dishonor of the instrument.

The judgment and order appealed from are affirmed.

BURCH, P. J., and POLLEY and SHERWOOD, JJ., concur.

CAMPBELL, J., concurs in result.

In GULBRANSON-DICKINSON COMPANY *v.* HOPKINS, 170 Wis. 326 (Supreme Court, 1919), notes given by defendant to a manufacturing company in connection with the purchase of advertising material were transferred to plaintiff by the company with the following indorsement: "Pay to the order of Iowa City State Bank, Iowa City, Iowa, for credit account of Gulbranson-Dickinson Co." The Iowa bank indorsed the notes to the First National Bank of Chicago, and they were returned dishonored at maturity. In an action against defendant on the notes, plaintiff claimed to be a holder in due course. Judgment for plaintiff was reversed. The notes ceased to be negotiable with the restrictive indorsement.

Compare NATIONAL CITY BANK OF ST. LOUIS *v.* MACON CREAMERY COMPANY, 329 Mo. 639 (Supreme Court, 1932). A seller drew drafts on buyers payable to the order of a bank, and deposited them with the bank under an agreement by which the bank gave the seller immediate credit for the amounts with the understanding that any drafts dishonored would be charged back. The bank indorsed such drafts "Pay any bank or banker or order; previous indorsements guaranteed," and sent them to plaintiff bank for collection. By arrangement between the two banks plaintiff credited the account of the indorsing bank with the amounts of the drafts immediately on receipt. While drafts were in the hands of plaintiff bank for collection, the indorsing bank closed its doors, and the seller thereupon instructed the buyer not to honor the drafts. In an action against the seller, judgment for plaintiff was affirmed. A restrictive indorsement carries title to the paper when made in pursuance of an understanding whereby the paper is taken, credited, and treated as a cash deposit subject to check.

In FIRST NATIONAL BANK OF FORT SMITH *v.* BRUNK, 170 Ark. 583 (Supreme Court, 1926), it was held that the indorsement on a draft "To any bank, banker, or trust company" was not a restrictive indorsement.

NATIONAL SALES CORPORATION, LIMITED *v.* BERNARDI

KING'S BENCH DIVISION, 1931

[47 *Times Law Reports*, 380]

Mr. Justice WRIGHT delivered judgment as follows: — These are two consolidated actions. In the first the National Sales Corporation, Limited, are plaintiffs, and G. Bernardi is defendant; and in the second Bernardi is plaintiff and the corporation are defendants. In the first the claim was on three specified bills of exchange, but at the hearing the corporation admitted that they could not recover by reason of failure to give notice of dishonour. In the second, Bernardi claimed a declaration that three specified bills of exchange were void as against him, and should be delivered up, while the corporation counterclaimed for the amount of those three bills, which were drawn by the corporation to their own order on Allday's Commercial Motors, Limited, accepted by the drawees and indorsed by Bernardi and by the corporation, the indorsement of the corporation being written below that of Bernardi. Each of the bills bore date December 12, 1929, and was for £52 10*s*., and they were payable respectively four, five, and six months after date. It was agreed that presentation and notice of dishonour should be deemed to have been waived.

The facts concerned with the making and signing of the bills were, as I find, as follows. Allday's Commercial Motors, Limited, were liable to the corporation for £478. It was agreed that the corporation should give time to Allday's on the terms that they gave a cheque for £178, and for the balance gave six bills of exchange, to be drawn by the corporation on Allday's and accepted by them while Bernardi, who was associated with Allday's, agreed to "back" (that is, to indorse) them in consideration of time being given, and so as to render himself liable to pay if Allday's did not. The bills were to be dated when the corporation made certain payments amounting to £478 to a third party, that being the money which Allday's were liable to reimburse to the corporation.

This was arranged as between all parties at a meeting on November 21, 1929, at which the corporation and Allday's were represented, and Bernardi was present. At that meeting the six bills were prepared, signed by the corporation as drawers and by Allday's as acceptors, and indorsed by Bernardi, who put his signature on the back of the bills close to the top. It was arranged that the bills should only become effective, that is, be deemed to be delivered, and the corporation should only give time to Allday's, if the latter sent a cheque for £178. That cheque was sent, and, in my judgment, was accepted by the corporation, and time thereupon given, so that the bills there and then became effective and were notionally delivered as between all parties, though the cheque, in fact, was not honoured. The bills were duly dated in accordance with the authority given — namely, as on December 12, 1929, on which day the corporation paid the third party £478. . . .

The defence principally relied on was that, notwithstanding all these facts, the bills were not enforceable against Bernardi, because, when the corporation indorsed them, which they did after receiving them from Allday's and Bernardi, they did so below instead of above Bernardi's signature. It was not suggested that the indorsements by the corporation were not made in a reasonable time, or that these indorsements were not made with the intention of completing the bills and rendering them enforceable, if necessity arose, against Bernardi and thus giving effect to the intention that he should be liable in the event of default by Allday's. This default, in fact, happened, because Allday's had gone into liquidation and could not pay.

On the facts as I have found them the case would be precisely covered by *McDonald and Co.* v. *Nash and Co.* (40 *The Times* L.R., 530; [1924] A.C., 625) but for the relative positions of the signatures on the back. The House of Lords held in that case that a bill to the drawer's order, indorsed by a third party before any indorsement by the drawer, was a bill of exchange, though an incomplete bill, and could be completed by the drawer afterwards indorsing his name, which, in fact, he did above that of the third party. The view taken was that the third party having indorsed the bill in order to make himself liable to the drawer, he had impliedly authorized the drawer to give effect to that purpose by adding his own indorsement, that is, to "fill up the omission" as is provided by section 20, subsection (1), of the Bills of Exchange Act, 1882. There is an omission in such a case, because before the third party indorsed the bill there should have first appeared on it the indorsement of the drawer, who was also payee (since a bill to drawer's order is payable to the drawer), which would operate as an indorsement from the payee to the third party, even though the third party only held the bill in the act of indorsing it, and never had any property or rights in it. Lord Dunedin, in *McDonald and Co.* v. *Nash and Co.* (*supra*, at p. 636): "Now, on the hypothesis that Nash intended to become liable, which we have found is a fact, then it seems to me that the second part of subsection (1) of section 20 precisely applies; for *ex hypothesi* the material particular that is wanting is that very indorsation which was afterwards filled in, and this is done as conditioned by subsection (2) of section 20 in accordance with the authority given." And Lord Sumner (at p. 648) says that the bill in such a case is incomplete till it is filled up, and when filled up, though not before, becomes retrospectively enforceable, as if it had been complete throughout. Thus a holder who takes a bill not complete and regular on its face can turn himself retrospectively into a holder in due hourse by virtue of section 20 if he fulfills the conditions of the section.

In the present case it cannot be doubted that the corporation, in indorsing, intended to do what was necessary to complete the bill, which, till then, was lacking in their indorsement, and it would be curious if their rights were defeated by a mere blunder committed in putting their name in the wrong place on the back. Such a result would falsify the intention of the parties, and would not readily be upheld by any Court unless compelled so to do by principle or authority; and, on general principles, evidence, in my judgment, is admissible to explain the intention with which a signature is added to a bill, since the order of the indorsements as they physically appear on the back is not conclusive. It was so held in *Penny* v. *Innes* (1 C., M. and R., 439) and the same principle was recognized in *Macdonald* v. *Whitfield* (8 App. Cas., 733). In my judgment, effect can here be given to the necessary inference that the corporation indorsed the bills to complete them by adding the necessary indorsement between themselves as drawers and Bernardi as indorser, and on that basis the position of the signatures is immaterial, and the result is just as if the indorsement by Bernardi had been added to the indorsement of the corporation, after in time and below in space.

[After reviewing other cases in which the point had arisen directly or indirectly, his Lordship concluded:]

It is true that in *McDonald and Co.* v. *Nash and Co.* (*supra*) no point was expressly considered as to the order of the signatures on the back, but I think that the House must, in approving these cases, have been conscious that the point of the order of the indorsements was involved, and hence, on the authorities I have cited, in such a case as the present, and on such facts as I have found, the mere order of these indorsements should be held not to nullify the intention of the parties, but to be a mere inadvertence, not changing the rights of the parties, and I hold that the corporation are entitled to recover.

HADDOCK, BLANCHARD AND COMPANY *v.* HADDOCK

NEW YORK COURT OF APPEALS, 1908

[192 *New York Reports*, 499]

CHASE, J. The plaintiff is a foreign corporation authorized to do business in this state and engaged as a wholesale dealer in coal at Binghamton. The Plymouth Coal Company, a corporation, was engaged in the operation of coal mines in Pennsylvania prior to March, 1902, at which time it went into the hands of a receiver. The defendant was the president and manager of said coal company and the owner of substantially all of its stock.

The defendant was, until May, 1902, the president of the plaintiff and during all the times herein mentioned had charge of plaintiff's New York office. At the time when the note and bills hereinafter mentioned were given the plaintiff was engaged in selling on commission at wholesale, the coal mined by the Plymouth Company or its receiver, under a contract made with said coal company. One B., the vice-president of the plaintiff prior to May, 1902, and its president thereafter, passed upon the financial responsibility of persons seeking credit with the plaintiff, and he arranged with a trust company at Binghamton to discount commercial paper of the plaintiff's customers. The Lenape Coal Company, the Living Stone Coal Company and the Montauk Coal Company were severally organized as corporations and engaged in the business of retailing coal in or near the city of New York and the defendant was the owner of substantially all of the stock of each. Soon after the organization of such corporations to retail coal, they sought credit with the plaintiff and their financial responsibility was investigated by B. The responsibility of each was found to be unsatisfactory and B. so reported to the defendant, and the defendant replied that said companies were his companies and he would guarantee their credit by indorsing their paper. On February 13, 1902, said Lenape Coal Company for value received executed and delivered to the plaintiff as payee its certain promissory note for $880.96, dated on that day, payable four months after date at a bank in the city of New York.

On and between January 27, 1902, and May 13, 1902, the plaintiff for value received made thirty several drafts each on either said Lenape Coal Company, said Living Stone Coal Company or said Montauk Coal Company, payable to the order of itself as payee, which drafts aggregated $26,833.15 each of which drafts was for value received accepted by the coal company on which it was drawn payable at a place and on a day in each respectively specified.

The drafts or bills were all similar in form, and the following is a copy of one of said bills:

1327.41–100

COAL OFFICE OF HADDOCK, BLANCHARD & CO.
INCORPORATED.

NEW YORK, Apl. 28, 1902.

Four months after date pay to the order of ourselves Thirteen hundred twenty-seven and 41/100 Dollars. Value received and charged the same to account of Haddock, Blanchard & Co., Incorporated. C. N. BLANCHARD,
Asst. Treas.

TO MONTAUK CO.,
BROOKLYN, N. Y.

Indorsed across the face:

Accepted. Payable at The Binghamton Trust Co., Binghamton, N. Y. The Montauk Coal Co.

CHAS. B. SMITH, *Treas.*

Indorsed on the back:

Haddock, Blanchard & Co., Incorporated. C. N. Blanchard, Assistant Treasurer.
JOHN C. HADDOCK.

Said note after it had been signed by said Lenape Coal Company and each of said bills after they had been accepted by the corporation on which they were severally drawn were indorsed by the defendant before delivery, and thereafter each of them so indorsed was before maturity delivered to the plaintiff as payee, and the plaintiff thereafter and prior to their maturity severally indorsed and procured them to be discounted at a trust company at Binghamton.

Said note and each of said bills were given and delivered to the plaintiff for the purchase price of coal sold and delivered by the plaintiff to the acceptors respectively of said bills and the maker of said note, or in renewal in whole or in part of prior notes or bills given or accepted for the purchase price of coal so sold and delivered.

Said note and each of said bills were so indorsed by the defendant for the accommodation of the maker of said note and the acceptor of said bills respectively and for the purpose of giving such maker and acceptors credit with the plaintiff, and in pursuance of an agreement between the defendant and the plaintiff by which the plaintiff agreed to sell coal on credit to the acceptors of said bills and to the maker of said note upon the defendant's guaranteeing the credit of said companies respectively, and the plaintiff was induced to take said accepted bills and said note and each of them for such coal by reason of the indorsement of the said defendant and pursuant to said agreement that the defendant would be liable thereon to the plaintiff in case the respective corporations primarily liable thereon should make default in payment thereof.

The proceeds of said bills and note were remitted to the defendant at the New York office of the plaintiff to provide funds to pay for coal and other current expenses. At the time when said note and bills respectively became due they were presented for payment at the place where they were respectively made payable and payment duly demanded, which was refused, and thereupon each was duly protested for non-payment, and notice thereof given to the plaintiff and to said defendant. Thereafter the plaintiff was compelled to take up said note and drafts and pay the amount due thereon respectively and became the owner and holder thereof and of each of them.

This action is brought to compel the defendant to pay to the plaintiff the amount of said note and bills pursuant to his said agreement with the plaintiff when they were severally indorsed by him and the facts upon which the plaintiff's claim is based are stated in the complaint.

The defendant denies that he indorsed the note and bills for the accommodation of and as surety for the retail coal companies respectively, but the evidence is sufficient to sustain the findings of the court from which the statements of fact in this opinion have been taken.

As the facts are found, if the intention of the parties is to prevail, the defendant should be required to pay to the plaintiff the amount of such note and bills as established by the judgment.

The defendant contends that the position of his name upon the note and bills conclusively establishes that he indorsed the several instruments without liability to the plaintiff and that parol evidence should not have been received to affect or overcome the alleged conclusive presumption arising from his indorsements as made. . . .

There has always been conflict among the courts of the several states both in asserting the principles upon which irregular indorsers upon commercial paper are to be held and in the conclusion arrived at in particular cases litigated. The number of cases is so great, and the possibility of even a partial reconciliation of them so remote, that we will confine our citation of authorities wholly to those in this state.

It was well settled in this state for many years prior to the enactment of the Negotiable Instruments Law that a person who puts his name on the back of a bill or note before its delivery, is presumably a second indorser and not liable to the payee, but the presumption could be rebutted by parol evidence to show that the intention of the indorser was to become surety for some prior party to the instrument.

[The learned judge quoted sec. 113 of that law (Sec. 63, U.N.I.L.), holding that defendant was within this definition an indorser of each of the instruments in question, and then quoted Sec. 114 (Sec. 64, U.N.I.L.)]

By this section of said law the presumption as established by the courts in this state was changed, and an irregular indorser is now presumed to be liable in accordance with the express language of the statute. Questions relating to the sufficiency of the pleadings are settled by the statute. A complaint upon a note or bill without alleging a collateral agreement between the parties whose names are on the instrument seeking to recover against a person except as provided by the statute, would clearly be demurrable.

The note of the Lenape Coal Company was payable to the plaintiff, a third person, and the defendant, according to the provisions of said section 114, is liable to the plaintiff, the payee therein. No serious contention has been made to the contrary. The serious question for consideration arises from the fact that the bills were payable to the maker and drawer thereof respectively and the defendant as an indorser thereon before delivery is not under the statute *prima facie* liable thereon to the plaintiff. Should parol evidence have been allowed to show the intent of the parties? We have not discovered any exception to the rule as established by the courts of this state allowing parol evidence as between the parties whose names appear on the bill or note to determine their liability as between themselves. It is frequently stated that where a note is payable to a person other than the maker and is indorsed by a third person before delivery the intention of the indorser is ambiguous and uncertain on the face of the paper and such uncertainty justifies the receipt of parol evidence to determine the true intention of the parties. We do not see that any greater certainty exists upon the face of a bill as to the true intention of the parties where it is drawn to bearer or to the order of the maker, and it is indorsed by a third person after acceptance by the acceptor and before delivery to the payee and maker. There is a certain rule of presumption determined by common law or by statute, but the alleged reason for the rule in either case is not very apparent. The long-established rule to allow parol evidence that the intention of the parties may prevail seems to have met with somewhat general approval without discussing specifically the principles upon which such evidence is admitted. . . .

It must constantly be borne in mind that the acceptance of a bill makes the acceptor the principal debtor. A bill when accepted becomes similar to a promissory note, the acceptor being the promisor and the drawer standing in the relation of an indorser. (Daniel on Negotiable Instruments [5th edition], section 532.) There is nothing in the Negotiable Instruments Law to indicate an intention on the part of the legislature to change the rule as established in this state relating to the receipt of parol evidence to determine the primary liability as between the persons whose names appear upon the instrument or as between those secondarily liable thereon. [Sec. 55 (Sec. 29, U. N. I. L.) was quoted.]

Parol evidence is necessary to determine whether a party to an instrument, including an indorser thereon, is an accommodation party, and also to determine which other party to the instrument he had accommodated. The plaintiff was the holder of the note for value, and the evidence showed that the defendant was an accommodation indorser for the benefit of the acceptor.

The last subdivision of section 114, as we have quoted, makes parol evidence necessary to establish whether the indorser signed the instrument for the accommodation of the payee. It is true that this section does not expressly state that if the indorser signed for the accommodation of the acceptor he is liable to all parties subsequent to the acceptor, but the fact that such a provision is not included in section 114 does not prevent the admission of parol evidence to determine generally the questions relating to an accommodation party as provided by section 55. [Secs. 7 and 118 (Secs. 196 and 68, U. N. I. L.) were here quoted.]

As we have seen, upon the acceptance of the bill the acceptor becomes the principal debtor and the one primarily liable to pay the amount of the bill, and all other parties to the instrument, including the maker and indorser, are secondarily liable. We are of the opinion that the maker of the bill is in legal effect and within the intention of this section an indorser, and that as between the plaintiff and the defendant parol evidence is authorized to determine the liability as between them.

[Secs. 130, 139, 140, 160, and 186 (3) (Secs. 70, 79, 80, 89, and 115 (3), U. N. I. L.) were then cited.]

There is no reason that we can conceive why the legislature should intend to change the rule in regard to the admission of parol evidence as it had existed in this state for many years. All of the quotations that we have made from the Negotiable Instruments Law show that it has enlarged rather than restricted the rules allowing parol evidence to show the true liability and relation of the parties whose names appear upon the bill or note in all actions between themselves. It is certainly very material to the drawer of a bill whether an indorser signs it at his request or at the request and for the benefit of the acceptor. We do not think it was the intention of the legislature by the enactment of section 114 of the Negotiable Instruments Law to establish a rule as to the liability of an irregular indorser conclusive on the parties to the instrument as between themselves in an action where the facts showing a different intention are fully alleged. All of the decisions of our courts since the enactment of the Negotiable Instruments Law tend to sustain the views herein expressed. . . .

The judgment should be affirmed, with costs.

Cullen, Ch. J., Haight, Vann, Werner, Willard Bartlett and Hiscock, JJ., concur.

Judgment affirmed.

In FRANKLIN *v.* KIDD, 219 N. Y. 409 (Court of Appeals, 1916), a note was indorsed by plaintiff before delivery to the payee, and on non-payment the holder recovered a judgment against plaintiff. The payee obtained an assignment of the judgment. In an action to restrain the enforcement of the judgment, it was held that although the indorsement of the note gave rise to a presumption that the indorser was liable to the payee, the presumption could be rebutted by evidence that the indorsement was in truth for the accommodation of the payee.

Compare Secs. 30–50 of the Uniform Negotiable Instruments Law with Secs. 31–37 of the Bills of Exchange Act, and with Arts. 11–18 of the Geneva Law.

B. HOLDERS IN DUE COURSE

STANDARD ACCEPTANCE CORPORATION *v.* CHAPIN

MASSACHUSETTS SUPREME JUDICIAL COURT, 1931

[277 *Massachusetts Reports*, 278]

WAIT, J. The plaintiff sues upon a promissory note dated June 11, 1930, made by the defendant payable to the order of The Maykel Automobile Company and indorsed without recourse by the payee to the plaintiff for value. At the trial the judge denied a motion to direct a verdict for the plaintiff; the jury found for the defendant, and answered "Yes" to the question: "Did the plaintiff at the time of the negotiation of the note in suit have knowledge of such facts that its action in taking the note amounted to bad faith?" Under leave reserved, pursuant to G. L. c. 231, § 120, the judge subsequently granted the plaintiff's motion to order a verdict for the plaintiff. The case is before us upon the defendant's exceptions to this ruling and order.

The only matter argued is whether there was evidence sufficient to justify finding that the plaintiff had knowledge of such facts that its action in taking the note amounted to bad faith. No contention is made that it had actual knowledge of infirmity or defect in the title of its indorser; and it is not disputed that there was no error in the ruling and order if the plaintiff was a holder of the note in due course.

There was evidence as follows: The defendant, an architect, signed the note and an agreement of conditional sale with The Maykel Automobile Company to accommodate his brother who was a salesman for that company and who represented that he wished to purchase the automobile described in the agreement but could not buy in his own name because the seller refused to accept a salesman's note. The defendant had no intention of purchasing for himself or of taking delivery. He did not know that the note was to be discounted with the plaintiff. The brother represented, and the sales manager of The Maykel Automobile Company, in writing, agreed, that no liability on note and agreement should attach to the defendant. No delivery of the automobile was made. In fact the machine described in the agreement had been sold and delivered to another customer several months before June 11, 1930. The agreement signed by the defendant contained the statements: "The purchaser hereby acknowledges receipt of said motor vehicle"; and, in italics and heavy print just below the place for signature: "Purchaser sign here if motor vehicle is actually in your possession, but do not sign here unless you have actually received motor vehicle, since by doing so you might place yourself in position of being party to a fraud." The plaintiff, when note and agreement were delivered to it and when it paid the amount of the discount to The Maykel Automobile Company, did not know that no car had been delivered to the defendant. It did not check to see if cars were delivered in such transactions as such a practice "would be a physical impossibility."

The plaintiff specialized in financing the notes and "leases" of automobile dealers. It had an office in Worcester where The Maykel Automobile Company was a large dealer. Prior to 1930 it had refused to finance notes and leases of the Maykel company because it had heard that other finance corporations had had troubles in dealings with it and that it had been irregular in its transactions. But plaintiff had heard, in 1929, that the Maykel company had sold and delivered cars and later had obtained money from finance corporations on leases of the same cars executed by its salesmen. In January, 1930, it began to do business with the Maykel company. Its treasurer told the assistant treasurer and general manager of the Maykel company: "I will forget what happened between you and the other finance companies if you go straight with me. That is all right, but if you don't you will find me a pretty tough fellow." From January to June, 1930, it discounted about forty-five conditional sale contracts and notes and up to June 13, 1930, found only one matter to be wrong, and that was explained. It refused to take leases and notes assigned by salesmen. It had refused to finance a "lease" to be signed by the defendant's brother. Later when application was made for discount on a conditional sale to the defendant, the plaintiff had inquired why he was buying another car when he already owned one and was told by the sales manager of the Maykel company, "of course, he is signing for his brother."

On May 28 or 29 the plaintiff discovered that the Maykel company had made sales of cars in violation of mortgage agreements, and had the first definite knowledge of the company's failure to live up to its agreement. On June 13 it had its first definite knowledge of the company's obtaining discount on notes and agreements of salesmen for cars previously sold and delivered to other purchasers. This agreement and note were signed by the defendant on June 11, and, on the same day, the plaintiff discounted the note and received the agreement. On June 23 or 24 The Maykel Automobile Company was petitioned into bankruptcy.

The judge was right in ruling that this evidence does not justify a finding of bad faith toward the defendant in the transaction. *Russell* v. *Bond & Goodwin Inc.* 276 Mass. 458. See *Reynolds* v. *Park Trust Co.* 245 Mass. 440; *Paika* v. *Perry,* 225 Mass. 563; *Beacon Trust Co.* v. *Barry,* 260 Mass.

449. The note was perfect on its face. There was nothing to warn the plaintiff that the title of the payee was defective. If it were believed that the plaintiff had reason to suspect that the ostensible purchaser of the machine was not buying for himself, there nevertheless was nothing to show that he had been tricked or deceived into executing the papers. Knowledge that the maker is an accommodating party does not deprive an indorsee of his right as a holder in due course. G. L. c. 107, § 52. *Beacon Trust Co.* v. *Barry*, 260 Mass. 449, 452. Information that the would-be seller of a negotiable instrument is unscrupulous and has been concerned in shady or illegal transactions is not enough of itself to render the purchaser from him one who does not take in due course. *Estabrook* v. *Boyle*, 1 Allen, 412. *Setzer* v. *Deal*, 135 N. C. 428. As was pointed out in *Fillebrown* v. *Hayward*, 190 Mass. 472, 480, "neither knowledge of suspicious circumstances, nor doubts as to the genuineness of the title, nor gross negligence on the part of the taker either singly or together are sufficient to defeat the holder's recovery, unless amounting to proof of want of good faith." There is here a complete absence of any evidence to show participation in any scheme of deceit on the part of the plaintiff, or of any act on its part calculated to mislead the defendant, or of knowledge of any fact which should have led it to believe that the defendant had been defrauded by the holder or any prior party to the note. The only element even of suspicion of genuineness of the transaction resulting in the note — the participation of one who did not intend to be the real buyer of a motor vehicle — was deliberately connived at by the defendant. It gives no strength to his claim of bad faith in discounting the note. The plaintiff thus on the evidence was a holder in due course.

There was error in refusing, at the trial, to direct a verdict in its favor. The motion to enter a verdict for the plaintiff was granted properly under the leave reserved.

Exceptions overruled.
Judgment for the plaintiff.

In KELSO & COMPANY *v.* ELLIS, 224 N. Y. 528 (Court of Appeals, 1918), a dealer in advertising specialties developed a plan for piano contests, whereby merchants would offer pianos to be voted for by their customers and given to the contestant receiving the highest number of votes. In connection with the operation of this plan defendant contracted for a piano and in consideration therefor gave the dealer six negotiable promissory notes payable to the order of the dealer. In accordance with his usual procedure the dealer then wrote to plaintiff, a piano manufacturer who had shipped many pianos in this way to other merchants, ordering a piano to be shipped at once to defendant. The piano was not shipped. Some weeks later the dealer transferred defendant's notes to plaintiff, and plaintiff credited him with the amounts on general account. In an action on the notes, judgment for plaintiff on a directed verdict was reversed. The question whether plaintiff took the notes in good faith was one of fact for the jury, and there was evidence on which a finding of bad faith might have been based.

In GERSETA CORPORATION *v.* WESSEX-CAMPBELL SILK CO., 3 Fed. (2nd) 236 (Circuit Court of Appeals, Second Circuit, 1924), trade acceptances drawn by and payable to the order of an importing company were accepted by defendant under an agreement that they were to be used to secure the release of imported silks held by banks, and that on the subsequent sale of such silks the acceptances of the vendees were to be substituted for those of defendant. In violation of this understanding the importing company indorsed the trade acceptances to plaintiff in part payment of an indebtedness. In an action on the trade acceptances defendant requested a charge that not only must plaintiff show that "it had no actual knowledge, but that it had no knowledge of facts sufficient to put it on notice of the agreement." The court ruled: "You may infer knowledge; there are two ways of showing knowledge, one is by a man admitting that he had knowledge, and the other is that the circumstances under which he acts make the jury believe that he had knowledge whether he admits it or not; you may infer knowledge from the circumstances." Defendant excepted. In upholding the ruling, Hough, Circ. J., said: "We conclude that the statute means and says that under section 91 [sec. 52, U. N. I. L.] a holder must take in good faith, and if he does not take in bad faith, his good faith is sufficiently shown, and bad faith under section 95 [sec. 56, U. N. I. L.] means that he must have knowledge of facts which render it dishonest to take the particular piece of negotiable paper under discussion. Knowledge, not surmise, suspicion, or fear, is necessary; not knowledge of the exact truth, but knowledge of some truth that would prevent action by those commercially honest men for whom law is made."

Compare HARTFORD NATIONAL BANK & TRUST COMPANY *v.* CREDENZA, 119 Conn. 368 (Supreme Court of Errors, 1935), where a note for $5000 was obtained by the payee from the maker, who could neither read nor write, by representing that it was for a few hundred dollars only. The payee indorsed the note and discounted it with the plaintiff bank, the bank making no inquiries beyond ascertaining that the maker owned real estate. In an action against the maker it was contended that the facts shown imposed upon the plaintiff an active duty to investigate the circumstances, and that such an inquiry would have disclosed the infirmity in the note. In affirming a judgment for plaintiff the court said: "The doctrine of notice as it affects the good faith of transactions generally does not apply to negotiable instruments. No duty rests upon the purchaser to make inquiry as to the purpose for which the paper was given, the responsibility of the maker or indorser, or the existence of possible defences. Suspicious circumstances sufficient to put a prudent man on inquiry and negligent failure to make such inquiry will not necessarily bar a recovery by the holder. The test is not whether the plaintiff was negligent in acquiring the paper but whether he acted in good faith. It is not the failure to inquire but the dishonest purpose which establishes bad faith."

THE BATH NATIONAL BANK *v.* ELY N. SONNENSTRAHL, INC.

NEW YORK COURT OF APPEALS, 1925

[249 *New York Reports*, 391]

LEHMAN, J. Early in February, 1926, the Bath Produce Company shipped by rail two lots of beans. In each case it received a uniform order bill of lading showing that the beans were consigned to its order at New York, with instructions to notify the defendant. It then drew two drafts on the broker, payable at sight or on arrival of shipments to the order of the plaintiff, and attached thereto the bills of lading indorsed without restriction. These were deposited to its credit in the plaintiff's bank and duly credited to the Produce Company which subsequently drew checks against this credit and these checks were paid.

The plaintiff promptly sent the drafts with bills of lading attached to a New York bank for collection, but when presented to defendant payment was refused. On learning this fact the plaintiff sent an agent to New York to make the collection or if he could not do so to sell the beans on its account. This agent, however, was also one of the principal officers of the Produce Company. He delivered the bills of lading to the defendant — whether saying that he represented the plaintiff or claiming to act for the Produce Company is disputed. The beans were then delivered to the defendant and it sold them. If at the time the bills of lading were delivered to the defendant the plaintiff bank was a holder for value of the drafts and bills of lading, then the defendant must account to it.

We assume that the plaintiff received the drafts merely for collection, and did not become the owner of the drafts at the time the deposit was made. The plaintiff by failure to move for the direction of a verdict or to except to the portions of the charge in which such question of fact was submitted to the jury is not in a position to urge now that there is no evidence to sustain the finding of the jury in that regard. The trial judge erred, however, in his refusal to charge that: "If the Bath National Bank, after crediting the amount of the drafts to the account of the Bath Produce Company, the Bath Produce Company drew on it by checks, then value was passed for the bills of lading." That request, even if inartificially drawn, was clearly intended and understood to mean that if the bank, though merely an agent for collection, advanced the amount of the drafts to its customer before the collection was made, then it became a holder for value of such drafts and the accompanying bills of lading. That proposition of law is established by an overwhelming mass of authority in this country, both judicial and extra-judicial.

Even where a depositor delivers to a bank a negotiable instrument without restrictive indorsement and the amount of the face value of the instrument is placed to the depositor's credit without special contract that the credit is only provisional, the bank does not become a holder for value until the depositor has actually availed himself of the credit so given by draft upon it. (*Citizens' State Bank* v. *Cowles*, 180 N. Y. 346; *Shawmut National Bank* v. *Manson*, 168 Mass. 425.) The beneficial title of a bank receiving an instrument for collection only may be more restricted. That we need not now decide. None the less, the bank becomes a holder for value when it makes advances upon the instrument in advance of collection. At least it may then hold the instrument as collateral security.

Though title to a draft left by a depositor with the bank for collection does not pass absolutely to the bank where the full amount of the draft was credited to the depositor, "for convenience and in anticipation of its payment," and "the bank could have cancelled the credit, as it clearly accepted no risk on the paper," yet if the depositor "had overdrawn, and this draft had been credited to cover the overdraft, or if the company had drawn against the draft, the bank could hold the paper until the account was squared." It would then be a holder for value. . . .

For these reasons the judgment of the Appellate Division and that of the Trial Term should be reversed and a new trial granted, with costs to abide the event.

CARDOZO, Ch. J., POUND, CRANE, ANDREWS, KELLOGG and O'BRIEN, JJ., concur.

Judgments reversed, etc.

Thus in FOURTH NATIONAL BANK *v.* BRAGG, 127 Va. 47 (Supreme Court of Appeals, 1920), a seller drew a sight draft for $1740 on a buyer and attached to it a bill of lading covering the goods sold. The draft was deposited with seller's bank. It was not entered for collection, but was treated as cash, bringing the amount to the credit of the seller to $1875. Checks subsequently reduced the account to less than $25. The proceeds of the draft were attached in the hands of the collecting bank by a creditor of the seller. The original bank intervened, claiming to be the owner of the draft by purchase, and the contention that the bank would have recourse on the seller was dismissed as immaterial in that connection.

In THE WORTH COMPANY *v.* INTERNATIONAL SUGAR FEED NO. 2 COMPANY, 172 N. C. 335 (Supreme Court, 1916), a bank discounted a seller's draft, and placed the amount to the credit of the seller with the right to draw on it. There was some evidence of an agreement to charge the amount of the draft back to the seller if it was dishonored. In an action against the seller in which the bank intervened to claim ownership of the proceeds of the draft, the court said: "The rule prevails with us, and it is supported by the weight of authority elsewhere, that if a bank discounts a paper and places the amount, less the discount, to the credit of the indorser, with the right to check on it, and reserves the right to charge back the amount if the paper is not paid, by express agreement or one implied from the course of dealing, and not by reason of liability on the indorsement, the bank is an agent for collection and not a purchaser."

In NATIONAL BANK OF COMMERCE *v.* MORGAN, 207 Ala. 65 (Supreme Court, 1921), although the bank, in discounting the seller's draft, credited his account with the amount and gave him the privilege of checking against the credit, the evidence showed that the seller had on deposit with the bank a balance in excess of the amount of the draft continuously from the negotiation of the draft to the commencement of the present action. Checks, however, were drawn against the account during that period, and if fresh deposits had not been made from time to time these checks would have been sufficient to exhaust the credit from the draft. It was held that under such circumstances the bank was not a purchaser for value.

In ASHLEY & RUMELIN *v.* BRADY, 41 Ida. 160 (Supreme Court, 1925), where a bank discounted a note and credited the account of the person from whom it was purchased with the amount, it was held that the bank became a purchaser for value only to the extent that the credit was exhausted before maturity of the note or before notice of defenses.

In FIRST NATIONAL BANK OF SHREVEPORT *v.* CAPITOL CITY PETROLEUM PRODUCTS CO., INC., 13 La. App. 498 (Court of Appeal, First Circuit, 1930), a trade acceptance was discounted and the amount credited to the account of the seller. No evidence was offered that any checks were drawn on the account following the credit. In an action by the discounting bank against the acceptor, it was held that the bank was not a purchaser for value on such a showing, and the case was remanded for evidence as to whether the seller drew out any or all of the proceeds of the discount.

PROGRESSIVE FINANCE AND REALTY COMPANY, INC. *v.* STEMPEL

ST. LOUIS COURT OF APPEALS, 1936

[231 *Missouri Appeals Reports*, 721]

SUTTON, C. — This action is founded on a promissory note dated October 23, 1929, for $2703, payable in monthly installments of $225.25 each, the first installment being payable on November 23, 1929. The note was given to the North American Sound and Talking Picture Equipment Corporation, for a part of the purchase price of one Type 1 M. D. Tone-O-Graph Reproducing Unit, consisting of two turn tables, two pick ups, one Double Channel Amplifier, one Monitor Horn and two Dynamic Speakers, one Fader and one Sound-on-Film equipment, sold by the North American Sound and Talking Picture Equipment Corporation, to the defendant on October 23, 1929, for the price of $3050, plus a carrying charge of six per cent. At the time of the purchase defendant paid the North American Sound and Talking Picture Equipment Corporation $500 in cash. This left a balance due, including the carrying charge, of $2703, for which the promissory note was given. On February 7, 1930, defendant paid to the North American Sound and Talking Picture Equipment Corporation the first installment of $225.25, which according to the terms of the promissory note fell due on November 23, 1929. The sale, which was a conditional one, was evidenced by a written contract, of even date with the promissory note, executed by the North American Sound and Talking Picture Equipment Corporation and the defendant. On March 1, 1930, plaintiff notified defendant that the contract of sale and the promissory note had been assigned to plaintiff by the North American Sound and Talking Picture Equipment Corporation, and that the balance due thereon was $2447.75.

The petition alleges the execution of the note and contract, and the assignment of them to plaintiff by the North American Sound and Talking Picture Equipment Corporation, and prays judgment for $2703, together with interest.

Defendant in his answer pleads breach of warranty, failure of consideration, and rescission.

The trial was had before the court without a jury, and resulted in a judgment for the defendant. Plaintiff appeals.

[The court held first that undisputed evidence showed clearly that there had been a breach by the seller of an implied warranty that the machine was fit for the purpose for which it was intended, and that defendant had rescinded the contract as entitled.]

We are unable to agree to the suggestion of plaintiff that it is protected as an innocent purchaser of a negotiable instrument. Three installments of the promissory note in suit were past due and unpaid at the time plaintiff purchased it. Plaintiff knew this. Its letter of March 1st to defendant so shows. It is true that in this letter plaintiff stated that the balance of $2447.75 started with the installment of March 23, 1930. Plaintiff says that this shows an extension of the time for the payment of the installments, so that the December installment did not become due until March 23, 1930. We are unable to see that this letter shows anything more than the willingness of the plaintiff to so extend the time of payment, but we are unaware of any rule of law permitting the endorsee of a past due promissory note to thus restore the negotiability of the note after purchasing it, so as to make himself a purchaser in due course. Moreover, in this case there is no showing whatever that plaintiff at the time it purchased the note had no knowledge of the existing defenses thereto.

The Commissioner recommends that the judgment of the Circuit Court be affirmed.

Per Curiam: — The foregoing opinion of SUTTON, C., is adopted as the opinion of the court. The judgment of the Circuit Court is accordingly affirmed. HOSTETTER, P. J., BECKER and MCCULLEN, JJ., concur.

Compare SINGER *v.* KOHLMAN, 170 La. 598 (Supreme Court, 1930), where the maker of a note indorsed it after maturity, extending the time of payment for ten years. It was held that a person taking the note subsequently, but before the expiration of the ten years, was a holder in due course.

In GEORGE *v.* WILLIAMS, 27 Colo. App. 400 (Court of Appeals, 1915), a note payable one year from date was followed on the same paper by an agreement signed by the payee and the maker that payment was to be made from certain dividends, and that in the absence of such dividends "the same may be extended for the period of one year." It was held that a holder to whom the note was negotiated nearly three months after the original maturity date was not a holder in due course, as the provision in question did not operate to extend the note automatically.

In GROSSMAN *v.* CHECHILA, 127 Misc. 151 (New York Supreme Court, Appellate Term, 1926), a demand note was given on the representation that the payee would produce certain credentials. The credentials were not forthcoming, but about one year from the date of issue the payee transferred the note to plaintiff. It was held that plaintiff was not a holder in due course.

In GERMAN AMERICAN BANK *v.* WRIGHT, 85 Wash. 460 (Supreme Court, 1915), a check given on February 21 in part payment of stock was handed by payee to a bank on March 30 as security for a loan on the understanding that the bank would hold the check for twenty days. On April 22, the loan being unpaid, the bank took steps to secure payment of the check, but learned that payment had been stopped because of non-delivery of the stock. In an action by the bank against the drawer of the check, judgment for plaintiff was affirmed. Although not an unqualified holder in due course, the bank was such a holder except in so far as the drawer of the check could show that he had been injured by the delay.

Compare Secs. 52–59 of the Uniform Negotiable Instruments Law with Secs. 29, 30, 36 (3), 38, and 90 of the Bills of Exchange Act, and with Arts. 16 and 17 of the Geneva Law.

C. WARRANTIES

KLAR *v.* KOSTIUK

NEW YORK SUPREME COURT, APPELLATE TERM, 1909

[65 *New York Miscellaneous Reports*, 199]

GILDERSLEEVE, J. This action is brought on a promissory note for the sum of $1,500, payable in six months, with interest, made by the defendant Goodman Kostiuk to the order of the defendant Kamber, and indorsed by the said Kamber and the defendants Samuel Kamlet and Morris Kostiuk.

The action was defended by Goodman Kostiuk, the maker, and Morris Kostiuk, an indorser. These defendants answered jointly and set up the defense of usury. A usurious agreement is alleged between Goodman Kostiuk and the defendant Samuel Kamlet, whereby $150 was paid by the borrower and received by the lender as interest on the loan in addition to the regular interest. A trial was had before a court and jury. The jury rendered a verdict for the amount claimed. From the judgment entered thereon against said defendants Goodman Kostiuk and Morris Kostiuk, and the order denying their motion for a new trial, the appeal herein is taken.

The defendants offered ample evidence, if believed by the jury, to support findings that the plaintiffs were holders in due course and that there was usurious interest taken at the inception of the note. The learned trial justice charged the jury that, if the plaintiffs were holders in due course, the defense of usury was not available against them. To this instruction the appellants duly excepted, and they now claim it constitutes error that requires a reversal of the judgment. No other question is involved in the appeal.

Until the enactment of section 96 of the Negotiable Instruments Law, in respect to notes having a usurious inception, and the decisions in *Schlesinger* v. *Gilhooly*, 189 N. Y. 1; *Schlesinger* v. *Lehmaier*, 191 id. 69, and *Schlesinger* v. *Kelly*, 114 App. Div. 546, there was no uncertainty about the law in this State in respect to notes usuriously given. It was plainly declared in *Claflin* v. *Boorum*, 122 N. Y. 385. The court said: "A note void in its inception for usury continues void forever, whatever its subsequent history may be." Section 96 of the Negotiable Instruments Law provides as follows: "A holder in due course holds the instrument free from any defect of title of prior parties and free from defenses available to prior parties among themselves and may enforce payment of the instrument for the full amount thereof against all parties liable thereon."

We think it was the purpose of the Legislature in enacting this provision to make a radical change in the law of this State affecting negotiable paper, and that the law now is that a *bona fide* holder in due course holds the note free from any taint of usury. The Schlesinger cases, *supra*, unmistakably and specifically declare the law to be that a bank acquiring in good faith, for value, commercial paper, void between the parties for usury, may recover thereon. We see no reason why the provision under consideration does not apply to, and may not be invoked by, individuals as well as banks. In *Wirt* v. *Stubbefield*, 17 App. Div. 283, the court, in construing the same provision enacted by Congress for the District of Columbia as the Negotiable Instruments Law, took the view that we have adopted and made no distinction between individuals and banks.

We think Mr. Justice Laughlin, in *Schlesinger* v. *Kelly*, *supra*, correctly stated the law of this State, when he said: "The usury laws remain in full force, but to facilitate the free circulation of negotiable paper by protecting holders thereof in due course for value in their right to enforce the same, the usury laws are to that extent superseded by the provisions of section 96 of the Negotiable Instruments Law."

We see that the alleged error in the judge's charge affords no ground for reversal in behalf of the appellant, the maker of the note.

An indorser cannot successfully raise the defense of usury against a holder in due course. Section 116 of the Negotiable Instruments Law provides: "Every indorser who indorses without qualification warrants to all subsequent holders in due course * * * that the instrument is at the time of his indorsement valid and subsisting." See *Horowitz* v. *Wollowitz*, 59 Misc. Rep. 520, and cases there cited. The charge in question was certainly correct as to the indorser.

The judgment and order should be affirmed, with costs to the respondent.

[Concurring opinion of Seabury, J., is here omitted.]

LEHMAN, J. (dissenting). Before the Negotiable Instruments Law was passed, the law of this State was clear that a note, void for usury in its inception, was void forever and could not be enforced, even by a purchaser in good faith and for a valuable consideration. While the term "holder for value," or "holder in due course," has been applied to such a person in the cases, I do not think that this term is technically correct, because the instrument, never having come into existence, had no negotiable character and a purchaser could never be a "holder in due course." See *Eastman* v. *Shaw*, 65 N. Y. 522. On the other hand, if a note had a valid inception, no defense by which the liability of any party thereon could be avoided could be raised against a *bona fide* holder.

I believe that section 96 of the Negotiable Instruments Law was intended, simply, to put into the form of a statute the law of negotiable instruments as established by commercial custom and as declared by the courts. . . .

Judgment and order affirmed.

Note also WACHOVIA BANK AND TRUST COMPANY *v.* CRAFTON, 181 N. C. 404 (Supreme Court, 1921). The action was brought by a holder in due course on a note given to defendant for money won by defendant in a card game, and indorsed by defendant to plaintiff bank. The defendant denied liability, alleging that the note was void in its inception. Judgment for defendant was reversed. The indorsement of the note created a new and independent contract in which the indorser warranted the validity of the instrument.

In SHEPHERD *v.* MORTGAGE SECURITY CORPORATION, 139 Va. 274 (Supreme Court of Appeals, 1924), the indorser of a note secured the indorsement of defendant by agreeing to sign as maker. Instead, the first indorser forged the name of the defendant accommodation indorser as maker, and sold the note to plaintiff, who took it as a holder in due course. In an action on the note judgment for plaintiff was affirmed. The forgery of the maker's signature was immaterial, as the plaintiff was relying on defendant's liability as indorser, not as maker.

In LOUISA NATIONAL BANK *v.* KENTUCKY NATIONAL BANK, 239 Ky. 302 (Court of Appeals, 1931), a forged check was indorsed by the holder and presented to the drawee bank for payment. In an action by the drawee against the holder for a refund of the amount so paid, it was held that the indorsement did not, as to the drawee, warrant the genuineness of the drawer's signature.

ATLAS ACCEPTANCE CORPORATION *v.* DAVIDSON BROTHERS MOTOR COMPANY

KANSAS SUPREME COURT, 1934

[139 *Kansas Reports*, 118]

JOHNSTON, C. J.: Davidson Brothers were automobile dealers in Kansas City. In 1929 the defendant, E. T. McAbee, purchased a Hudson automobile from them for the sum of $1,375. McAbee was given an allowance of a small sum for an old car which was traded in, paid a small amount in cash and there remained a balance due Davidson Brothers of $1,258. McAbee asked for a credit to that extent, and it was granted to him after an investigation by the Atlas Acceptance Corporation, to which the Davidson Brothers applied in order to carry the loan. After it had investigated McAbee and his wife, it informed Davidson Brothers that it would purchase the note if the wife of McAbee also joined in the execution of it. The note was then obtained with a chattel mortgage on the automobile and appeared to have been signed not only by McAbee but by Ethel McAbee, his wife. Davidson Brothers gave a restricted indorsement of the note to the Atlas Acceptance Corporation. Thereafter it found that the signature of Ethel McAbee had been forged. There was a delay in payments made by McAbee, and when the automobile was taken by him into New York state, the plaintiff, relying on the terms of the chattel mortgage, repossessed itself of the car in New York and returned it to Wyandotte county, at an expense of $265.22. The car was later sold at public sale for the sum of $850, and thereafter the Atlas Acceptance Corporation brought this action against E. T. McAbee and the Davidson Brothers to recover the sum of $604.20, including the expense incurred in returning the automobile from New York.

Issues were joined, and when the case came on for trial before the jury the counsel for the plaintiff made his opening statement of the facts to the jury, after which counsel for defendants, Davidson Brothers, the qualified indorsers of the note and chattel mortgage, moved for judgment on the pleadings and the opening statement of counsel. The trial court held that on the pleadings and opening statement, the writings, including the note and chattel mortgage, were to be construed together and that Davidson Brothers, to whom the note was given and who transferred it to plaintiff "without recourse," were qualified indorsers, and as the action was brought on the instrument, the Davidson Brothers were no more than mere assignors of the title to the note.

[Over a page of the opinion is here omitted.]

The motion for judgment on the pleadings and the opening statement of counsel for plaintiff was made by Davidson Brothers Motor Company and was sustained by the court, giving judgment in their favor. They claimed that they had acquitted themselves of liability on the note which they indorsed and transferred to the plaintiff without recourse. They concede that they are qualified indorsers of the note and cite *Challis* v. *McCrum*, 22

Kan. 157, to show that in an indorsement without recourse they expressly declined to assume the liability of an indorser and that the effect was to do away with an indorser's liability on the note and place them in the position of a vendor. That authority was announced before the negotiable-instruments act was passed. In that act, under which this action was brought, the legislature declared in specific terms that —

"Every person negotiating an instrument by delivery, or by a qualified indorsement, warrants: (1) That the instrument is genuine and in all respects what it purports to be; (2) that he has a good title to it; (3) that all prior parties had capacity to contract; (4) that he has no knowledge of any fact which would impair the validity of the instrument or render it valueless; but when the negotiation is by delivery only, the warranty extends in favor of no holder other than the immediate transferee. . . ." (R. S. 52–606.)

Thus it is provided that a qualified indorser as well as one who negotiates by delivery specifically warrants four different propositions. He warrants that the instrument is genuine and is what it purports to be. Here, it was not genuine and was not what it purported to be. One of the signatures of a maker attached to the instrument was a forgery, and, further, Davidson Brothers warranted that they had no knowledge of anything which would impair the validity of the instrument, and yet the allegations of the petition are that Davidson Brothers knew that a maker's name was forged when the transfer was made. These warranties and promises of the payee are prescribed by the statute. While the payee purports to transfer it without recourse, it was a qualified indorsement, and the law itself attaches the warranty that the note was genuine and not a forgery, that it was signed by two makers, whereas it was in fact only signed by one of them and therefore it is not in all respects what it purports to be.

According to the petition that contract was broken when it was negotiated. When the payee indorsed the note as was done, it was the equivalent of writing over the name the words "without recourse," except that I am liable on such obligations as are specified in the statute (R. S. 52–606), and in such cases the holder may look to and recover from qualified indorsers. The statutory warranties of R. S. 52–606 apply to all transfers of those classes of paper; it says every person negotiating an instrument by delivery or qualified indorsement. As to these classes there are no exceptions, and evidently the design of the lawmakers was to cut off those defenses. (See *Foley* v. *Hardy*, 122 Kan. 616, 253 Pac. 238.) In effect the law writes the warranties into every transfer of a qualified indorser, and he cannot set aside the law nor make it ineffective. The restriction "without recourse," which qualified the transfer, is in fact the foundation for the mandatory warranties which the law writes into the contract of indorsement. . . .

It follows that the ruling of the district court must be reversed and remanded for further proceedings. It is so ordered.

Note also Commercial Credit Co. *v.* Ward & Son Auto Co., 215 Ala. 34 (Supreme Court, 1926), where a motor-car dealer took a note from the purchaser of an automobile, and indorsed the note without recourse to a financing company for value. The purchaser of the car was a minor having no capacity to contract. In an action by the financing company against the dealer on the note, the lower court sustained a demurrer to the complaint, and was upheld in the court of appeals. An application for a writ of *certiorari* to the court of appeals to review and revise its judgment was granted.

In QUEENSBORO NATIONAL BANK *v.* KELLY, 48 Fed. (2nd) 574 (Circuit Court of Appeals, Second Circuit, 1931), certain bills of exchange were assigned by plaintiff to defendant without indorsement under a written agreement stating that they were assigned without recourse. It did not appear whether these bills were order or bearer paper. The present action was on a note made by defendant in consideration of the assignment. It was stipulated at the trial that the bills in question were worthless at the time the note was executed due to prior payment. The trial court, in directing a verdict for defendant, excluded evidence that defendant had been aware when making the note of the invalidity of the bills assigned. Judgment reversed and cause remanded for a new trial. Whether the bills were order or bearer paper, plaintiff at the most warranted under sec. 65 only against its own knowledge and not against the fact of invalidity. Parol evidence of defendant's knowledge of the invalidity was admissible to negative the implication of any such warranty by plaintiff.

Compare HOUSTON *v.* LAWHEAD, 116 W. Va. 652 (Supreme Court of Appeals, 1935). A township note, invalid because not executed in conformity with law, was indorsed without recourse by the holder to the plaintiff. In an action on the note against the indorser it was held that the implied warranty that the note was genuine and in all respects what it purported to be amounted also to an engagement that it was valid.

GUARANTY TRUST COMPANY OF NEW YORK *v.* HANNAY & CO.

COURT OF APPEAL, 1918

[*Law Reports,* [1918] 2 *King's Bench,* 623]

[Detailed statement of facts, and opinion of Pickford, L. J., are omitted.]

WARRINGTON L.J. read the following judgment: — After many days' discussion the result, in my opinion, is that the real question is a short one, namely, whether the plaintiffs, on presenting to the Liverpool bank for acceptance on behalf of the defendants a draft drawn upon them by Knight, Yancey & Co. accompanied by what purported to be a bill of lading of certain cotton, warranted the genuineness of the bill of lading, and are therefore liable in damages for breach of such warranty, the bill of lading having turned out to be forged, and the amount of the draft having been paid to the holders in due course. The answer to this question does not, in my opinion, depend upon the negotiability or otherwise of the draft, and is to be decided in accordance with English law. In this view the discussion as to the American law is largely, if not wholly, irrelevant, but as Bailhache J. has decided against the plaintiffs on the footing that the negotiability or otherwise of the draft is the determining factor, that this depends on American law, and that under that law it was not negotiable, and in deference to the elaborate argument addressed to us on the point, I propose to deal with it hereafter.

The facts are not in dispute, and there is no occasion to state them in detail, as they are fully and accurately stated in the judgment of Bailhache J. It is enough to say that the plaintiffs were the indorsees for value and in good faith of a draft drawn by Knight, Yancey & Co., of Decatur, Alabama, upon the Bank of Liverpool pursuant to a contract between the drawers and the defendants for the sale and purchase on credit of certain cotton. The draft ended with the words "and charge the same to account of 100/R.S.M.I. bales of cotton," being part of that included in the contract, and there was a reference in the margin to the date of sale and the grade of cotton. Documents purporting to be a bill of lading and certificate of insurance relating to the cotton were attached to the draft. The draft was presented to the bank by the plaintiffs for acceptance in the ordinary course and under no special circumstances. It was accepted by them, and the bill of lading and certificate of insurance were detached and retained by them. It was subsequently negotiated by the plaintiffs, and ultimately found its way into the hands of the London City and Midland Bank as holders in good faith and for value. It became due on April 27, and was paid by the Bank of Liverpool. It was at this time suspected, and was afterwards discovered, that the so-called bill of lading was a forgery, and that no cotton had been shipped as represented by it.

[Two pages of the opinion are here omitted.]

I propose now to deal with what I have stated above to be the real question, namely, whether under the circumstances there must be implied a warranty by the plaintiffs that the so-called bill of lading was a genuine document. There is clearly no express warranty, nor is there any express representation that the bill of lading was genuine, which, if acted on, might result in a warranty to the same effect. The defendants are driven to insist on an implied warranty. Whether there was or was not such a warranty depends on the intention with which certain acts were done: *Heilbut, Symons & Co.* v. *Buckleton* ([1913] A. C. 30). Moreover, "in business transactions, what the law desires to effect by the implication is to give such business efficacy to the transaction as must have been intended at all events by both parties who are business men": per Bowen L.J. in *The Moorcock* ((1889) 14 P. D. 64, 68). There appears to be some difference of opinion between the noble and learned Lords who sat to consider *Heilbut's Case* ([1913] A. C. 30) as to whether the question of intention is for the jury (compare the speeches of Lord Haldane and Lord Atkinson). In the present case, if it be a question for the jury, they have negatived the alleged warranty, but without insisting on this as conclusive, and treating the question as one for the Court, or at all events as one which ought to be withdrawn from the jury on the ground that there is no evidence of warranty, I am clearly of opinion that the alleged warranty ought not to be implied.

I will first consider the case on the assumption that the draft was a bill of exchange in the proper sense, i.e., a negotiable instrument. The plaintiffs receive from the drawer the bill of exchange with the bill of lading attached. They are the indorsees of the bill, and have become so for value and in due course. They then present the bill to the drawee for acceptance. The consideration for the acceptance moves from the drawer to the acceptor, not from the indorsee, even in a case in which the indorsee requests the drawee to accept: *Robinson* v. *Reynolds* (2 Q. B. 196). That is to say, the drawee accepts the bill, not in performance of any new engagement made between him and the indorsee, but by virtue of the arrangement he has with the drawer. But in truth the plaintiffs did not request the bank to accept; they only desired to know whether the bank would acknowledge their liability to do so and perform it or not, with an intimation that in the latter case a well-known step would be taken. It is quite clear that in such a case there is no warranty of the genuineness of the signature of the drawer: *East India Co.* v. *Tritton* (3 B. & C. 280, 289), the principle of which, though dealing directly with the signature of the indorser, applies also, with at least equal force, to that of the drawer. I can see no ground on which any such warranty should be implied as to the bill of lading. It is contended that by surrendering the bill of lading on acceptance the plaintiffs purported to transfer the property represented by it to the acceptors, and that it must be taken that they warranted the existence of such property and that the bill of lading represented it. The answer is that the indorsee of a bill of exchange with the bill of lading attached obtains a special property only in the goods defeasible upon acceptance, and on that event the property in the goods passes, not by virtue of the surrender to the acceptor of the bill of lading, but by virtue of the contract between the drawer as vendor of the goods and the acceptor as the purchaser thereof: *Mirabita* v. *Imperial Ottoman Bank* ((1878) 3 Ex. D. 164). The bill of lading is surrendered, not by virtue of any contractual obligation between the indorsee and the drawee, but by virtue of the obligation he assumed towards the drawer. Under such circumstances I can see no room for any implication of warranty as to the genuineness of the bill of lading.

I have so far considered the question as if there were no direct authority on the point. But this is by no means the case. The precise question was decided by Malins V.-C. in *Leather* v. *Simpson* (L. R. 11 Eq. 398). This case has been known to the profession since 1871, it has been treated in textbooks as expressing the law, it has never been questioned, and in America, at all events, there are many cases reported in which it has been followed. I do not say this intending to throw any doubt on the correctness of the decision, with which, as will have been seen, I entirely agree, but only as indicating that, even if I did not, I should hesitate now to overrule it. In my opinion, therefore, if the draft be a bill of exchange, there is no such warranty as alleged.

But suppose it be not, that is to say, suppose it is a conditional order to pay and therefore not negotiable, and suppose the condition be that the bill of lading is genuine and that the goods have been shipped, with all respect to the learned judge and others who seem to have assumed that this would bring about a different result, I really fail to see how it would affect the question. The consequences of non-negotiability would be that the holder would be in the position of an ordinary assignee holding subject to any equities between the parties to the original contract, and if the drawer could not require payment unless he gave the acceptor the goods, the holder could not do so either, but this is not a circumstance leading to the inference of an implied warranty that the drawer has performed or will perform his obligation; if anything there is less ground for implying the warranty in the case now under consideration than in the case of a negotiable instrument, inasmuch as the acceptor is in a stronger position as regards the holder than if the draft were negotiable, for he is not bound to pay even a *bona fide* holder if the drawer's contract with himself is broken.

The result is that the plaintiffs are not, in my opinion, under any liability to the defendants, and are entitled to the direction they ask, and to have the counter-claim dismissed.

[The balance of the opinion and concurring opinion of Scrutton, L.J., are here omitted.]

Note also Springe *v.* The Hanover National Bank, 209 N. Y. 224 (Court of Appeals, 1913), where a similar result was reached, Hiscock, J., saying:

"In these cases the argument has been made on which plaintiffs in this case must finally rely, that a party accepting or discounting drafts accompanied by purported bills of lading upon the faith and security of which he more or less relies and which prove to be forgeries has acted under a material mistake of fact which entitles him to be relieved from his acceptance of payment. To this argument, however, the answer in substance has been made by the courts with almost unvarying uniformity, that the mere attachment of bills of lading to a draft does not make the former a part of the latter; that one who accepts or pays such a draft must be assumed in the absence of special circumstances to do so on the faith of the draft itself and that reliance upon the bills of lading is not a fact which enters into the substance of the real transaction in accepting or paying the draft, but is an extrinsic fact; that if the rule were established that relief should be afforded against the acceptance or payment of a draft because of mistaken belief in the genuineness of attached bills of lading, such rule logically would apply to other cases, as that the drawee had entertained a mistaken notion as to the financial standing and responsibility of the drawers or as to the value of security for the draft, and thus lead to an instability and confusion in transactions involving negotiable paper which would be intolerable; that as between the innocent holder for value of a draft and the drawee who has accepted or paid the same in reliance upon forged bills of lading there is no reason why the drawee should be permitted to shift the burden of loss to the holder."

Compare GUARANTY TRUST COMPANY *v.* GROTRIAN, 187 Fed. 686 (Circuit Court, S. D. New York, 1911), where a draft payable 60 days after sight contained the following words: "and charge same to account of 8417.50 bushels of flax seed." The acceptance read: "Accepted, payable at Lloyd's Bank, Ltd., London, against indorsed bills of lading for 8417 bushels of flax seed, per Buffalo S. S. at New York." The bills of lading were forged, and the acceptor was allowed to recover from the holding bank the amount paid on the draft on the ground that the acceptance was conditional on the delivery of genuine bills of lading.

Refer again to BROWN *v.* C. ROSENSTEIN COMPANY, *supra*, p. 558.

Compare Secs. 65 and 66 of the Uniform Negotiable Instruments Law with Secs. 55 (2) and 58 of the Bills of Exchange Act and with Art. 15 of the Geneva Law.

5. PAYMENT AND DISCHARGE

ALLENBERG *v.* RAPKEN & COMPANY, LIMITED

CALIFORNIA COURT OF APPEAL, FIRST APPELLATE DISTRICT, 1930

[108 *California Appellate Reports*, 99]

THE COURT. — An action by an assignee against the acceptor of a draft to recover the amount thereof. A judgment was entered for the plaintiff, from which the defendant appealed.

A draft for $1800 was drawn upon defendant by Caroni Products Company, a New York corporation. It was accepted by defendant on January 3, 1928, and was payable on March 10, 1928, at the Anglo & London-Paris National Bank in San Francisco. The evidence shows that the drawer, after acceptance and before maturity, indorsed the draft for value to Aetna Finance Company, a corporation. It is not claimed that the acceptance was without consideration or was induced by fraud, but at the time the draft was presented for payment the defendant claimed a set-off as against the drawer in the sum of $108.12. This amount represented the freight charges paid by defendant upon the purchase price of certain merchandise for which the acceptance was given, and which it was alleged the drawer agreed to pay. The instrument before its maturity was sent to the Federal Reserve Bank at San Francisco for collection, and about March 1, 1928, the evidence shows that defendant was so notified by the bank. Defendant thereupon offered to pay the draft less the freight charges, which offer the bank refused. The defendant then communicated with the drawer and made the same offer to it. The drawer accepted the offer and, according to defendant's witnesses, agreed to procure the return of the draft, at the same time requesting that the amount be remitted to it by telegraph. The defendant, however, mailed a check for the amount to the drawer, but on the receipt of a second request by the latter to remit by telegraph this was done on March 16, 1928, and payment of the check was stopped. It appears that this amount was retained by the drawer and not paid to the indorsee. In the meantime the draft was presented for payment, which was refused, and the instrument was duly protested. Defendant alleged collusion between the drawer and the indorsee in this transaction, and that the amount remitted constituted payment of the draft. The trial court found in accordance with the allegations of the complaint and against the defenses set up by the defendant. As grounds for the appeal it is contended that the decision is unsupported.

While defendant claimed that it was not advised of the indorsement to Aetna Finance Company before remitting the amount to the drawer, it made not request for an inspection of the instrument, which would have disclosed the facts. It further appears that the remittance by telegraph was made on March 16, 1928, although a notice of protest showing the name of the indorsee of the draft was mailed to defendant by a notary in San Francisco on March 13, 1928. It is a fair inference from the evidence that the notice was received by defendant before the date of the telegraph remittance and this was not denied. . . . The rule is well settled that from the nature of the obligation the principal debtor is protected only where payment is made to the holder or his agent (8 Cor. Jur., Bills and Notes, sec. 828, p. 593). Under this rule payment by the acceptor to the drawer will not discharge the bill. (*Woodward* v. *Elliott*, 13 Ind. 516.) Likewise, payment to one not in possession is at the risk of the payor (*Herron* v. *Gear*, 26 Cal. App. 18 [145 Pac. 731]), and payment to the payee without requiring the production and surrender of the instrument is insufficient as against a transferee who is a holder in due course. . . .

The judgment is sufficiently supported, and no error is shown which would justify a reversal.

The judgment is affirmed.

In MUNDET CORK CORPORATION *v.* GRUPP, 154 Misc. 798 (New York Supreme Court, Appellate Term, 1935), the court said: "The holder of a note in due course is not bound by a payment made to a prior holder after the transfer of the note. Such a payment is made at the peril of the one making it."

In FEDERAL RESERVE BANK OF PHILADELPHIA *v.* GETTLEMAN, 117 N. J. L. 416 (Court of Errors and Appeals, 1937), four notes discounted with the payee bank were pledged by the payee with plaintiff. The defendant maker paid the amount of the notes to the payee, and obtained a receipt. In an action on the notes a judgment for defendant was reversed. "Their obligation was to pay the holder or one with authority to collect for the holder. No agency to collect arises from the fact that payee bank was a member of the Federal Reserve Bank of Philadelphia. The Federal Reserve Bank and its member banks are separate and distinct corporate entities and no relationship of agency exists between them except such as arises from contract."

Note also COMMERCIAL CREDIT CO. *v.* MAXEY, 289 Ill. App. 209 (Illinois Appellate Court, Second District, 1937). The purchaser of an automobile gave a note for the price to the seller, who indorsed it without recourse to the order of the plaintiff. Through a mistake in plaintiff's office the note was stamped paid. In some unexplained way the note in this condition was wrongfully acquired by an unidentified third person and presented to the maker, who paid it without question or investigation. Plaintiff subsequently repossessed the automobile and claimed payment on the note. Judgment for plaintiff affirmed.

GROUF *v.* STATE NATIONAL BANK OF ST. LOUIS

CIRCUIT COURT OF APPEALS, EIGHTH CIRCUIT, 1935

[76 *Federal Reporter* (*Second Series*), 726]

BOOTH, Circuit Judge. . . .

The action was upon a letter of credit and drafts drawn upon the faith of the same.

A jury was duly waived and the case tried to the court.

The letter of credit was issued August 13, 1915, by appellee, addressed to Anglo-Austrian Bank, whose name was subsequently changed to Anglo-Austrian Bank, Limited (hereinafter called the Austrian Bank). The beneficiaries of the letter of credit were Francis L. Stuever and Celia M. Stuever, his sister, American citizens then temporarily residing in Vienna, Austria.

Upon the faith of and pursuant to said letter of credit, the Austrian Bank cashed, and paid in kronen, drafts drawn by the Stuevers as follows:

To Francis L. Stuever, February 1, 1916	$ 100.00
To Celia M. Stuever, March 10, 1916	400.00
To Celia M. Stuever, March 13, 1916	400.00
To Celia M. Stuever, March 17, 1916	400.00
To Celia M. Stuever, March 24, 1916	400.00
To Celia M. Stuever, March 29, 1916	400.00
To Francis L. Stuever, April 7, 1916	100.00
To Celia M. Stuever, April 26, 1916	3100.00
To Francis L. Stuever, April 28, 1916	4150.00
	$9450.00

Owing to the World War then existing, it was not feasible for the Austrian Bank to transmit some of the drafts drawn; and in December, 1916, it had in its possession five of them, of the face amount of $8,150.

[Specific findings of the Court below are here omitted.]

The situation disclosed is, accordingly, somewhat as follows: The Austrian Bank held five drafts amounting to $8,150, which it had cashed for the Stuevers on the faith of the letter of credit in their behalf from the appellee Bank in St. Louis. The Austrian Bank, finding it not feasible to forward the drafts to St. Louis on account of war conditions, requested the Stuevers to personally reimburse it for the drafts so held, and the Bank agreed that if the Stuevers would pay the equivalent of said drafts in kronen, the same would be accepted by it in payment of the drafts. The Stuevers accepted the proposal and agreed to instruct their agent in St. Louis to forward to the Austrian Bank the amount in kronen. A list of the drafts with dates and amounts was furnished by the Bank to the Stuevers. The total amount so furnished was $8,100. The true amount of the drafts held by the Bank was $8,150; but by an error of the Bank, the amount was stated to the Stuevers as $8,100.

The Stuevers carried out their part of the agreement, and the result was that there were placed in the hands of the Austrian Bank 69,528 kronen, the equivalent at that time of $8,100.

The Austrian Bank refused to apply these kronen as a payment on the drafts on the sole ground, as stated at that time, that it was entitled to receive dollars; but the Austrian Bank retained the kronen and refused to deliver to the Stuevers either the drafts or the kronen.

No mention was made at that time of the shortage of $50 worth of kronen.

The market value of kronen thereafter declined to almost nothing while they were still held and controlled by the Austrian Bank.

After the war the Austrian Bank brought the present suit, through appellant, against the appellee, the St. Louis Bank, for the full amount of the drafts cashed and unpaid under the letter of credit.

The trial court entered judgment for $1,350, which was the amount of the drafts concededly unpaid, plus the $50 also concededly unpaid under the agreement between the Austrian Bank and the Stuevers, on account of the error above mentioned.

Appellant presents and argues in its brief four points.

"1. Payment by the beneficiary of a letter of credit to the addressee is not a defense in a suit by the addressee against the issuer of the letter.

"2. Finding No. 12 is insufficient as a finding of payment by the Stuevers to the Anglo-Austrian Bank."

[The two remaining points are omitted. The pertinent part of Finding 12 was that 69,528 kronen had been delivered to and retained by the Anglo-Austrian Bank, being the equivalent at that time of the $8,100 demanded by the Bank. One column of the opinion is here omitted.]

On the second trial, the court has made (in Finding 12) what we shall for the moment assume to be a sufficient finding of payment by the Stuevers to the Austrian Bank.

We are thus squarely presented with the question whether such payment is a defense which can be set up by the writer of the letter of credit (the St. Louis Bank) when sued by the addressee.

It is to be noted in the first place that the defense thus set up is not an equity in favor of the beneficiary and against a third party such as a seller of goods to the beneficiary. The defense, therefore, does not come strictly within the rules above noted. Payment as a defense is not an equity but a strictly legal defense. The question, therefore, is whether payment by one not primarily liable on the obligation can be set up as a defense by the party primarily liable.

It must be remembered that the Stuevers were not strangers to the transaction between the St. Louis Bank and the Austrian Bank. By reason of that transaction, the Stuevers had received moneys from the Austrian Bank. Because they had received the moneys, and because the Austrian Bank could not avail itself of the usual means for obtaining payment, that Bank requested the Stuevers to make payment in part of the debt owing by the St. Louis Bank. The Stuevers agreed to do so.

We see nothing invalid in such an agreement; and if the payment was in fact made, we see no good reason why it should not be set up as a defense by the St. Louis Bank when sued by the Austrian Bank. Such we understand to be the law in Missouri where the obligation was to be paid by the St. Louis Bank under the letter of credit [see *Bacon* v. *Reichardt* (Mo. Sup.) 208 S. W. 24; *Stark* v. *Scherf* (Mo. App.) 207 S. W. 863]; and such we understand from the testimony in the record to be the law in Austria where the alleged payment by the Stuevers was made. The general law is in accord.

In Restatement of the Law of Contracts by the American Law Institute, the law applicable to the case at bar is thus stated (section 421): "A payment or other performance by a third person, accepted by a creditor as full or partial satisfaction of his claim, discharges the debtor's duty in accordance with the terms on which the third person offered it. But the debtor on learning of the payment or other performance has power by disclaimer within a reasonable time to make the payment or other performance inoperative as a discharge."

In the case at bar, the payment by the Stuevers to the Austrian Bank was made, not in satisfaction of the whole debt owed by the St. Louis Bank to the Austrian Bank, but in part satisfaction. It was retained by the Austrian Bank and kept under the control of the Bank, although the Stuevers offered to receive it back.

There was no disclaimer by the St. Louis Bank. . . .

As to the second point urged by appellant, it is contended that Finding 12 is insufficient as a finding of payment, first, because there was no acceptance of the amount furnished by the Stuevers; second, because the amount was insufficient.

We do not agree with these contentions. We think the finding was sufficient as a finding of payment. It is true that the letter of credit called for payment of dollars by the St. Louis Bank. But the medium of payment can be waived by the creditor, and the Austrian Bank, by its agreement with the Stuevers, agreed to accept kronen instead of dollars. The medium of payment provided in the letter of credit was therefore waived. The Austrian Bank had full knowldge of its rights. See *Rand* v. *Morse*, 289 F. 339 (C. C. A. 8); *Mitchell* v. *Kemp & Burpee Mfg. Co.* (C. C. A.) 218 F. 843; *G. Amsinck & Co.* v. *Springfield Grocer Co.*, 7 F.(2d) 855 (C. C. A. 8). That Bank's verbal refusal to accept the kronen was, under the circumstances, of no avail. Acceptance of an offer may be by exercise of dominion over the thing offered.

In Restatement of the Law of Contracts, the law is thus stated (section 72): "Where the offeree exercises dominion over things which are offered to him, such exercise of dominion in the absence of other circumstances showing a contrary intention is an acceptance. If circumstances indicate that the exercise of dominion is tortious the offeror may at his option treat it as an acceptance, though the offeree manifests an intention not to accept."

See *Beck Elec. Const. Co.* v. *Nat. Contracting Co.*, 143 Minn. 190, 173 N. W. 413.

The Bank's exercise of dominion over the kronen was an acceptance.

As to the discrepancy in amount, it is to be noted that the record shows no mention of this by the Bank at the time. The sole objection was as to the medium of payment. . . .

This contention of appellant as to shortage in effect is an attempt to "mend the hold" of the Austrian Bank long after the transaction occurred and after litigation had been begun. We think it should not be allowed. . . .

Our conclusion is that the judgment entered was right, and the same is accordingly affirmed.

Compare BANK OF UNITED STATES *v.* ABRAHAMS, 144 Misc. 308 (City Court of New York, 1932), where, in an action against the maker of a promissory note, it was pleaded that the maker had paid the indorser, that the indorser had sufficient moneys on deposit with plaintiff to offset the amount of the note, and that such an offset had been made. A motion to strike out this defense was granted. "The mere direction by the indorser to offset against his indebtedness on the note sued on the amount on deposit with the plaintiff does not constitute a payment for the benefit of, or as agent for, the makers. More is required; there must be a mutual agreement or understanding that the payment or setoff was thus made."

In NELEN *v.* SMITH BROS. AUTO SALES, INC., 45 R. I. 245 (Supreme Court, 1923), plaintiff loaned defendant $2,200 and received in return a note for the amount secured by a mortgage on two cars. Defendant, without plaintiff's consent, sold one of the cars to one Devine and thereafter paid plaintiff $1,700 on account of the note. After suit for the balance had been commenced Devine, fearing an action of replevin with attendant annoyance and expense, paid plaintiff the amount due on the note under an agreement that he would be reimbursed after collection. Exceptions saved by defendant on a directed verdict for plaintiff were overruled. Defendant was not entitled to the benefit of the payment made by Devine.

Note further HOOPER *v.* HERRING, 14 Ala. App. 455 (Court of Appeals, 1915). Plaintiff drew a check on defendant, a banker, in favor of a creditor. The check was refused payment on presentation, and was protested for non-payment. In an action claiming damages for the refusal to pay, it was held that plaintiff had the right to intervene and pay the amount of the check to the payee for the protection of his honor.

CRAINE, INC. *v.* ANDERSON

NEW YORK SUPREME COURT, APPELLATE DIVISION, 1936

[246 *New York Appellate Division Reports,* 102]

RHODES, J. The action is brought to recover the purchase price of a silo sold by the plaintiff to the defendant. The defense is payment.

The sale in question was evidenced by a conditional sales agreement entered into between the plaintiff and the defendant upon a form prepared by plaintiff, by which plaintiff agreed to sell to the defendant f. o. b. factory, the silo in question. Among the terms, were the following:

"Net cash on arrival.

"Shipment will be made on order bill of lading with either sight draft or settlement papers attached. * * *

"Send papers to Conewango Valley National Bank; Address, Conewango Valley, N. Y."

The court below found: "That the phrase 'Papers be sent to Conewango Valley National Bank' meant and was intended to mean that when the silo was shipped to defendant an endorsed bill of lading with sight draft attached would be sent by plaintiff to such bank and defendant would go to the bank and pay the bank the amount of the draft, and the bank would then release the bill of lading so that defendant could get silo from the R. R. Co."

The court further found: "That silo was shipped by plaintiff to defendant on or about February 18, 1933, and letter was written to and mailed to defendant on or about said 18th day of February, 1933, advising defendant of such shipment and directing defendant to go to such bank and pay said draft."

The letter of the plaintiff to the defendant above referred to contained the following: "According to the terms of your contract, settlement of this invoice is to be net cash upon the arrival of the material. We are, therefore, forwarding an endorsed Bill of Lading with the Sight Draft attached to the Conewango Valley National Bank, Conewango Valley, New York. Upon receiving notice from the bank of the arrival of the papers, if you will kindly go there and pay the Sight Draft, the bank will release the Bill of Lading. This will enable you to secure your shipment from the Railroad Company."

There is also the finding: "That at about the time of the shipment the plaintiff forwarded to the Conewango Valley National Bank a sight draft upon the defendant with endorsed bill of lading attached, said bank having been designated in said written contract as the bank to which said draft and bill of lading should be sent, the letter of transmittal directing the bank to deliver the bill of lading upon payment of the draft and remit the proceeds."

Pursuant to the instructions contained in said letter, the defendant went to the bank where he had and continued to keep on deposit more than sufficient to pay the amount of said draft and drew a check thereon, payable to said bank for the amount of the draft.

Upon receiving defendant's check the bank stamped the draft as paid, and delivered it with the bill of lading to the defendant, who thereupon went to the railroad station and received the silo.

After receiving defendant's check, the bank held it and did not charge it upon the books to his account; neither did the bank in any manner remit or attempt to remit the amount of the draft as directed. Shortly thereafter the bank holiday was declared by presidential proclamation, the bank ceased to do business and was not reopened; a conservator was appointed, who was succeeded by a receiver; the assets of the bank, together with those of another bank in the vicinity, were acquired by a reorganized institution.

The learned court below correctly stated that the question here is whether the bank acted as agent for the plaintiff, and whether delivery to it of a check that was perfectly good upon an account in such bank, relieved the defendant from all further liability.

The defendant requested the court to hold, as a conclusion of law, "That by the terms of said contract the plaintiff made and constituted said Conewango Valley National Bank its agent to collect said draft." This request was refused.

Beyond question, the instructions to the bank were given by plaintiff in connection with and in furtherance of plaintiff's business, which is but another way of saying that the bank was acting by command of plaintiff in connection with and in furtherance of plaintiff's business; therefore, the bank was acting as plaintiff's agent.

Section 147 of the Negotiable Instruments Law declares that "Where the instrument is made payable at a bank it is equivalent to an order to the bank to pay the same for the account of the principal debtor thereon."

It follows that the transaction between the bank and defendant constituted payment of the draft, and the bank, as plaintiff's agent, having received defendant's check as payment, the plaintiff is bound thereby; hence the claim sued upon herein has been paid and discharged. (*Baldwin's Bank* v. *Smith,* 215 N. Y. 76.) (See, also, *Heinrich* v. *First National Bank,* 219 N. Y. 1; *Davison Coal Co., Inc.* v. *National Park Bank,* 201 App. Div. 309; *Jones* v. *Board of Education, Town of Pelham,* 242 id. 17.)

The judgment should, therefore, be reversed on the law and the facts, with costs, and the complaint dismissed, with costs.

Hill, P. J., Crapser, Bliss and Heffernan, JJ., concur.

Judgment reversed on the law and the facts, with costs, and complaint dismissed, with costs.

The court makes the finding of fact and finds as a conclusion of law that by the terms of the contract between plaintiff and defendant, the plaintiff made and constituted said Conewango Valley National Bank its agent to collect the draft in question; that the same has been paid, and that there is no sum due plaintiff from defendant on its claim herein. The court disapproves of the conclusions of law contained in the decision to the effect that the plaintiff is entitled to a judgment against the defendant, with costs.

Note also Terminal Gas & Supply Company *v.* Medford Auto Company, 285 Mass. 528 (Supreme Judicial Court, 1934). In payment for merchandise defendant mailed to plaintiff three checks drawn on the Medford Trust Company. Plaintiff deposited the checks in the Charlestown Trust Company and they were forwarded by that bank to the Atlantic National Bank and thence to the Federal Reserve Bank. The last-named bank sent the checks by messenger to the drawee bank, and received in return a cashier's check on the National Shawmut Bank. This check was refused payment, and an hour later the drawee bank closed its doors. The checks on return were charged to plaintiff. In an action of contract for merchandise sold and delivered, a judgment for defendant was affirmed, Rugg, C.J., saying:

"The case has not been argued on the footing that the Charlestown Trust Company received the checks indorsed without restriction and gave credit for them to the plaintiff as its regular depositor as cash in a drawing account without further understanding and thereby became the purchaser of the checks. *Taft* v. *Quinsigamond National Bank*, 172 Mass. 363. *Burton* v. *United States*, 196 U. S. 283, 302–303. Neither party has relied upon that principle. This decision has been rendered without consideration of that principle and without determining whether the facts would warrant its application.

"It is plain that so far as concerns the defendant the checks were paid. When the checks were presented by the Federal Reserve Bank to the Medford Trust Company, the latter was conducting business as usual. If cash had been demanded for them, it would have been given, because the defendant had to his credit in the Medford Trust Company funds in excess of the total of the checks. The checks were surrendered to the Medford Trust Company, and the Federal Reserve Bank received, instead of cash, a cashier's check of the Medford Trust Company for the total sum due on its clearings. The checks of the defendant were thereupon by the Medford Trust Company stamped as paid, charged to the account of the defendant and delivered to it. The Federal Reserve Bank was not the agent of the defendant. It is not necessary to determine whether the Federal Reserve Bank was the agent of the plaintiff as owner of the checks, *Lord* v. *Hingham National Bank*, 186 Mass. 161, or whether the Charlestown Trust Company had become owner of the checks, *Salem Elevator Works, Inc.* v. *Commissioner of Banks*, 252 Mass. 366, 370. In any event, the Federal Reserve Bank was rightfully in possession of the checks for collection in behalf of the owner. For its own convenience it chose to accept the cashier's check of the Medford Trust Company instead of demanding and receiving money. If it had demanded and received cash, the defendant would have been discharged of all liability because its checks would have been paid. So far as concerns the defendant, the duty of the Federal Reserve Bank was to accept cash, and acceptance of anything else was at its peril. By receiving a cashier's check instead of cash in the circumstances, the Federal Reserve Bank became the owner of the proceeds of the collection and as owner had mingled the proceeds with its other funds. The checks of the defendant were paid."

Compare LLOYD MORTGAGE COMPANY *v.* DAVIS, 51 N. D. 336 (Supreme Court, 1924). Defendant, owing $360 to plaintiff on a note, purchased a cashier's check for that amount from a bank in which he was a depositor. His account was debited when the check was issued. The check was sent to plaintiff who indorsed and deposited it with his own bank. After passing through two other banks the check came into the hands of a bank in the town of issue, but by that time the issuing bank had closed its doors, and the check could not be presented. In an action on the note, it was held that the note had not been paid. The note was payable in money, whereas defendant delivered to plaintiff a cashier's check. Mere acceptance of this check did not amount to payment, nor did the surrender of the note indicate otherwise.

In CIE YOUROVETA *c.* BARTHELEMY ET CIE., 1927 Havre 1.213 (Commercial Court), a bill of exchange covering a sale of coffee was drawn in dollars. It was held that the seller could insist that the bill be paid in dollars, and that the drawee buyer could not pay in francs, leaving the conversion to the seller.

Compare Secs. 50, 51, 88, 119–123, and 161 of the Uniform Negotiable Instruments Law with Secs. 38(3), 59–63, and 68(1) of the B. E. A., and with Arts. 40, 50, and 55 of the Geneva Law.

CHAPTER III

Trust Receipts

IN RE CATTUS

United States Circuit Court of Appeals, Second Circuit, 1910

[183 *Federal Reporter*, 733]

Ward, Circuit Judge. This is a petition of a trustee in bankruptcy to revise an order of the District Court confirming the report of the special master in reclamation proceedings awarding to the London & Hanseatic Bank, Limited, certain goods and proceeds of certain goods now in the hands of the trustee, covered by trust receipts given it by the bankrupt, Cattus, and authorizing the bank to sell certain other goods covered by bills of lading in its hands and to apply the proceeds to repayment of advances made by it on account of the bankrupt. The course of dealing between the bank and the bankrupt is according to commercial usage of long standing, under which by a loan of credit a vast amount of business is rapidly and safely done. The particular steps of the method followed are not always the same, but the substantial feature which makes the banker the owner of the goods until the purchase price of them advanced by him is paid is always present. One common method, which seems to have been adopted in this case, is as follows: A merchant who wishes to import goods for which he has not funds to pay obtains credit from a bank to a fixed amount, against which he draws for the price of the goods to the order of the vendor or the vendor draws for the price to his own order. The draft with bill of lading indorsed in blank or to the order of the bank is forwarded by the vendor to the banker for acceptance. The banker accepts the draft payable in one, two, three, or four months, as the case may be, forwards the bill of lading indorsed in blank to his agent in New York, who delivers the same to the importer against a receipt called a trust receipt, whereby he agrees to sell the goods for account of the banker, to pay him the proceeds and so put him in funds to take up the acceptance at maturity.

In this case the bank had accepted drafts to the amount of some £5,000, had delivered the bills of lading for most of the goods to Cattus against his trust receipts before his adjudication as a bankrupt, and still has in its hands bills of lading for other goods not so delivered.

The form of the trust receipt in this case is as follows:

New York, ..., 190..

Received from ...... through their representatives Messrs. G. Amsinck & Co., of New York, the following goods and merchandise, their property, specified in the bill of lading per shipped by under credit No. ...... and in consideration thereof, we hereby agree to hold said goods in trust for the above named bankers, and as their property, with liberty to sell the same for their account, and in case of sale to give Messrs. G. Amsinck & Co. the name of the buyers, and to hand them the avails, as soon as received, as security for due provision for the acceptance of the said bankers, on our account, noted at foot; and we further pledge to them said goods and the proceeds of such as security for the payment of any and every other indebtedness of ours to the aforesaid bankers, whether matured or unmatured according to its terms. In case the above mentioned goods are not sold we agree to store and fully insure the same, and hand the storage and insurance papers to Messrs. G. Amsinck & Co., of New York. It is also understood that ...... of Messrs. G. Amsinck & Co., as their representatives, may at will cancel this trust at any time, and repossess themselves of their said property in whatever condition it may then be, or of the proceeds of such of the same as may then have been sold, wherever the said goods or proceeds may then be found, and in the event of any insolvency, suspension, or failure, or assignment for benefit of creditors on our part, or of the non-fulfillment of any obligation, or of the non-payment, either at maturity or upon previous demand by the said Messrs. G. Amsinck & Co., of any acceptance made for us under said credit or any other credit issued by ...... or G. Amsinck & Co., on our account, or of any indebtedness on our part to either of them, all obligations, acceptances, indebtedness and liabilities whatsoever shall thereupon (with or without notice) mature and become due and payable.

We further agree to keep said property fully insured against fire, payable in case of loss to Messrs. G. Amsinck & Co., as representatives of said bankers, we to pay any expenses incurred thereon, the intention of this arrangement being to protect and preserve unimpaired their lien on said property as security for any and all obligations on our part then outstanding.

£......

Due ......

The structure of the instrument indicates that it has grown gradually, being altered to meet new exigencies, just as we find in many commercial documents like charter parties, masters' drafts, and riders on policies of fire and marine insurance inartistic and inconsistent provisions. This trust receipt contains clauses some of which describe the right of the banker in the goods as property or title and others as a lien. But the inconsistency is apparent rather than real, because, as Judge Hough pointed out in the court below, it admits easily of division into two parts: First, an acknowledgment that the bankers are owners until payment of the acceptance for the purchase price of the specific goods and thereafter they are lienors for any other balance of indebtedness due from the bankrupt, however arising. Inasmuch as the proceeds of all the goods as well as all the goods in specie now in the hands of the trustee and of the banker are insufficient to pay the acceptances for the price of the specific goods covered by the bills of lading attached to the acceptances, we need not consider the clauses of the trust receipt relating to liens for general indebtedness or determine whether such pledge or lien would be good against the trustee.

The purpose of the parties, describe the trust receipt as you will, was to keep the title to the goods in the bankers until their acceptances for the price of the goods were paid. The courts, without always defining exactly what the relation between the parties is or always defining it in the same way, still are astute to protect the rights of the banker in such case. *Moors* v. *Kidder,* 106 N. Y. 32, 12 N. E. 818; *Drexel* v. *Pease,* 133 N. Y. 129, 30 N. E. 732; *National Bank* v. *Rogers,* 166 N. Y. 380, 59 N. E. 922; *Moors* v. *Drury,* 186 Mass. 424, 71 N. E. 810; *New Haven Wire Co. Cases,* 57 Conn. 352, 18 Atl. 266, 5 L. R. A. 300.

It would be most inequitable that the bankrupt or his trustee should escape from the performance of this obligation for the benefit of any one except a bona fide purchaser for value or creditors protected by statute. Extended discussion of the authorities is not necessary. They are considered in the report of A. L. Everett, Esq., as special master, in the case of *Charavay & Bodvin* v. *York Silk Mfg. Co.* (C. C.) 170 Fed. 819.

The order is affirmed, with costs.

CHARAVAY & BODVIN *v.* YORK SILK MFG. CO.

United States Circuit Court, Southern District of New York, 1909

[170 *Federal Reporter,* 819]

The following is the opinion of A. L. Everett, Special Master:

This proceeding is brought to determine the right to a certain fund deposited in bank pursuant to order by the receivers of the York Silk Manufacturing Company. The German Bank of London claims the fund, and the claim is disputed by the receivers.

The receivers were appointed in an action brought in this circuit, entitled "Charavay & Bodvin, Complainant, v. York Silk Manufacturing Company, Defendant." This cause was ancillary to one in the court of common pleas for York county, Pa., in which the Western National Bank and others were the complainants and the York Silk Manufacturing Company the defendant.

The facts which give rise to the dispute are these: The York Silk Manufacturing Company imported raw silk from China, its agents in Hongkong being Arnhold, Karberg & Co. For this purpose the silk company had applied to the German Bank of London (through the latter's agent, the Bank of New York, N. B. A.) in New York, and obtained from it a letter of credit in favor of Arnhold, Karberg & Co. for account of the silk company, amounting to £5,000, "for the cost of raw silk to be shipped from Hongkong to New York." This letter of credit provided that the bills of lading should be made out to the order of the German Bank of London, and that the bill of lading used for forwarding to the bank's agent in New York should be accompanied by an invoice properly certified. At the same time the silk company signed an agreement, of which the following provisions are material:

> We will place your bank, previously to the maturity of the bills that may be drawn under the credit, in possession of sufficient funds in cash or in bankers' bills of exchange at not exceeding sixty (60) days' sight, indorsed by us and approved of by you to meet the payment of the said bills, etc.

Upon receipt from you of the possession of the said merchandise shipped under such credit or the bills of lading or other documents of title thereto, we will sign and deliver a receipt therefor in such form as you may require and will give such security as you may demand, and the said merchandise, after delivery of the custody thereof to us, and the proceeds thereof, if sold by us, shall be held subject to your order on demand as your property, with authority to take possession of and dispose of the same at any time by public sale or otherwise, for your reimbursement or protection and to charge all expenses, including commissions for sale and guaranty, the bank being free from all responsibility whatever in respect of such sale. Said merchandise shall be covered by insurance at our expense, loss, if any, payable to the German Bank of London, Limited.

All questions arising under this agreement or the credit issued in connection herewith shall be determined according to the law of the State of New York.

The agreement also provides that, in the event of a decline in the market of such merchandise, additional security shall be deposited.

The letter of credit and agreement in question are dated July 5, 1907. Thereafter, from time to time, silk was bought and drafts were drawn under this credit. The drafts were accepted and paid by the bank. The bills of lading for the silk were duly made out to the bank's order. The invoices stated the value of the silk as $4 per pound. As it arrived, the bank permitted the silk company to take and hold it upon signing what are known as "trust receipts." By these trust receipts the York Silk Manufacturing Company agreed to hold the merchandise on storage as the property of the German Bank of London, Limited, with liberty, however, to manufacture it and to sell it, accounting for the proceeds to the Bank of New York, as the attorney of the German Bank of London, Limited, until all of the said bills of exchange should have been paid or provided for, "the intention of this agreement being to protect and preserve unimpaired the ownership and rights of the said bank in and to said property in whatever form or condition it may be, and the proceeds thereof, and to give said bank all rights in respect to said property and proceeds as provided in the agreement signed by us in connection with the credit under which said property was imported." The silk company failed to place the bank in funds to meet the drafts, and thereupon, under the credit agreement, all the obligations of the silk company immediately became due. The silk company having gone into the hands of receivers, the bank tried to recover from them the silk which had been obtained by the company in the way described, and it made petition to the court of common pleas of York county, Pa., where the receivers had been appointed and where the silk, or some of it, was, to be permitted to retake such silk as had been taken under the trust receipts and could be identified. A certain amount was so identified. The court then made an order, upon consent of the receivers, directing them to deliver to the petitioner such merchandise, and ordering also that the receivers have authority to purchase the silk at $3 per pound. The order also contained this provision: "This order is made without prejudice to any existing right of the petitioners to present any additional claim or claims which they may have against the York Silk Manufacturing Company, defendant, or its receivers." From a receipt annexed to the order it appears that the silk was sold to the receivers for the sum of $5,207.05, which amount, less a charge of $500 of the attorneys for the petitioner in that proceeding, was received by the bank. At that time the bank had accepted or paid drafts amounting to a sum which, together with interest to July 1, 1908, aggregated £4,507 18*s.* 8*d.* Against this is to be credited the proceeds of the silk mentioned (less the attorney's fees), amounting to £966 10*s.* 10*d.*, leaving a balance due and unpaid on July 1, 1908, of £3,541 7*s.* 10*d.*, with interest from July 1st to September 1st; this amounts to £3,577 9*s.* 7*d.*, or $17,458.10. In the proceedings in this circuit $15,222.40 was admitted by the receivers to be due to the bank, and, in accordance with the resumption agreement executed by the silk company and its creditors, the bank received satisfaction for that amount. It now claims the difference, amounting to $2,235.70, as of September 1, 1908.

Counsel for the receivers show that this is the difference between the invoice value (at $4 per pound) of the silk which was retaken in Pennsylvania and the amount (at $3 per pound, plus attorney's fees) which it actually realized, and they assert that the bank is not entitled to this difference, it having, by the retaking of the property, elected to satisfy itself from this source, and thereby abandoning the right to recover the full amount advanced by it for the purchase of the silk in China. This is on the theory that the transaction between the bank and the silk company constituted a conditional sale, and they invoke the familiar doctrine of election of remedies which obtains in connection with such transactions. Unless this applies, the bank must prevail, because it has admittedly advanced (with interest) the full amount of $17,458.10, and has only received satisfaction to the extent of $15,222.40. It is not necessary to consider the claim made against the receivers otherwise than as a claim against the silk company itself, nor do I understand it to be asserted by either side that the receivership introduces any distinguishing element.

In considering the nature of the relation between the parties, it must first be determined under what law the case is to be decided. The credit agreement provides that all questions under it shall be decided according to the laws of New York. The retaking of the property under the order of the York county court took place in the state of Pennsylvania. In the proceeding in Pennsylvania the credit agreement was before the court, and the silk must be presumed to have been surrendered in consequence of this credit agreement. The court made a special proviso that the order was made without prejudice to any existing right of the petitioners to present any additional claims which they might have against the York Silk Manufacturing Company or its receivers, and this, I think, must be construed as including the right to sue in this case upon the agreement as construed by the New York law. If this case were not to be decided by New York law, the result would, however, be the same, according to the view which I take of the Pennsylvania law and which I shall later briefly consider.

[Nearly three pages of the opinion are here omitted.]

The result of the cases is that, when a banker advances money for the purchase of goods and takes the goods as security, the contract of the parties in respect to the title and disposition of the goods will be recognized and enforced. If the banker stipulates for the legal title, that stipulation will be enforced to the extent necessary for his protection. The title is, in its nature, at all times a security title, and no more; and it is incident and subordinate to the general obligation of the purchaser to repay the banker his advance.

In this connection the difference between these transactions and true conditional sales is apparent. In cases of true conditional sale, where it has been held that the vendor having reclaimed and sold the goods cannot afterwards sue for his deficiency, it is pointed out by the courts that by retaking the goods the whole consideration has failed or been terminated, and that there is no further consideration upon which to sue. *Earle* v. *Robinson*, 91 Hun, 363, 36 N. Y. Supp. 178. When a banker advances money for the purchase of goods the result is different, because the consideration is different. The consideration is not the supplying of goods, but the supplying of funds. The goods themselves are no essential element in the contract, being merely security for its execution. The claim of the German Bank of London is not upon a cause of action for goods sold and delivered, but for money lent to or furnished for the silk company.

Certainly a banker never intends that the amount of his recovery shall depend upon the value of the goods. He is concerned only with getting back his advance, with interest and commissions. That is his business. Just as he has to return any surplus after a sale of the security, so he has a right of action for any deficiency which may result. It is clear enough that in the ordinary case, where the banker has not parted with possession of the goods under trust receipt or otherwise and is forced to realize upon them at a loss, he is entitled to claim for a deficiency, and there is no reason why, because he has given them up and retaken them, his rights should be any less.

If further illustration were needed of the difference between the transaction in question and a conditional sale, it can be found in this view of it: At whose risk is the property from the inception of the transaction? No one will pretend that if the goods were destroyed at sea without insurance (there being no agreement for insurance) the loss would fall upon the bank. Yet, if the transaction were a conditional sale, the risk of loss would be upon the bank until it delivered the goods to the importer.

The application of the analogy of conditional sale to its remote consequences would produce here a great injustice. There is no authority, which necessitates such a holding, and, indeed, the cautious expressions of the courts leave it to be inferred that they do not intend this analogy to be pushed farther than the case requires. The transaction is not actually a sale, and that word is used only by fiction or analogy. It is not necessary to find in the nomenclature of security relations a category in which to place this one. It is governed by the contract of the parties, and the contract will only be disturbed by courts for illegality. It is not pretended that this contract is illegal. My conclusion is that the bank is not precluded by the retaking of the silk from recovering the loss which it has suffered by reason of the sale of the silk below the invoice valuation. . . .

WARD, Circuit Judge. The exceptions to the report of the special master are overruled, and the report confirmed on his opinion.

Compare IN RE BETTMAN-JOHNSON CO., 250 Fed. 657 (Circuit Court of Appeals, Sixth Circuit, 1918), where the holding bank claimed from the receiver of the buyer the full purchase price (which had been set apart) of cherries imported under a letter of credit and trust receipt arrangement. It was held that the transaction fell within the terms of the Ohio statute relating to conditional sales, and that the bank accordingly was entitled to no priority since the trust receipt had not been recorded.

IN RE DAVID ALLESTER, LIMITED

CHANCERY DIVISION, 1922

[*Law Reports,* [1922] 2 *Chancery,* 211]

Summons.

The above company (now in liquidation) had carried on the business of wholesale seed merchants. In connection with this business it constantly borrowed money from Barclays Bank, among others, by way of overdraft, depositing as security from time to time the bill of lading and other documents of title to seed which it had bought for resale, generally from abroad.

When the company was in a position to sell the seed so pledged with the bank it communicated with the bank to that effect and in accordance with the well-established mercantile practice in these transactions obtained the invoice, bill of lading and copy of insurance policy for realization on the terms stated in the ordinary letter of trust of which the following is an example: —

February 1, 1921.

To BARCLAYS BANK, LIMITED.

GENTLEMEN,

I/we have to acknowledge receipt of invoice, bill of lading, and copy of insurance policy representing: — 100 bags alsike and white clover, loan 271, January 11, 1921.

I/we receive the above in trust on your account, and I/we undertake to hold the goods when received, and their proceeds when sold as your trustees. I/we further undertake to keep this transaction separate from any other and to remit you direct the entire net proceeds as realized, but not less than 1200*l.* within 28 days from this date.

I/we undertake to cover the goods by insurance against fire and to hold the policy or policies on your behalf.

Yours faithfully,

For and on behalf of David Allester, Ld.

HENRY F. MILLS, *Secretary.*

The loan in the above instance was 1200*l.*, but at the date of the liquidation — namely, February 25, 1921, several of these documents were outstanding, the goods not having been sold, or the proceeds not having reached the bank.

The question therefore arose whether the bank was entitled to priority in respect of its claims for (*a*) the full amount of the proceeds of sale of goods pledged to the bank by the company before the liquidation and released by the bank for sale by the company or (*b*) the amount of moneys standing to the credit of the company or the liquidator in any bank representing those proceeds of sale.

On July 19, 1921, the liquidator issued this summons to determine these points.

Business experts on behalf of the bank proved that the custom or practice whereby goods pledged with a bank were released for purposes of sale under a letter of trust was very well known and generally adopted and made use of in banking business. It had been in existence for twenty years and upwards and during that period the letters of trust had always been considered and treated as being documents used in the ordinary course of business as proof of the possession or control of goods and accordingly excepted from the operation of the Bills of Sale Acts, and an enormous number of transactions had been carried out by banks on that basis.

Astbury J. [after stating the facts]. The real question is whether these letters of trust are valid documents because, if so, the bank's right cannot be contested. The only ground upon which the liquidator is entitled to defeat the bank's claim is by showing that these documents were given subsequent to the respective pledges are invalid under the Companies (Consolidation) Act, 1908, s. 93, sub-s. 1 (*c*), (*e*).

The liquidator puts his case on two grounds. He says in the first place that each letter of trust was "a mortgage or charge created or evidenced by an instrument which, if executed by an individual, would require registration as a bill of sale" and therefore within clause (*c*); and, secondly, that it was a mortgage or charge on the book debts of the company within the meaning of clause (*e*).

With regard to the first point the liquidator contends, though I think without much confidence, that these letters of trust would, if executed by an individual, require registration as bills of sale. He relies on the definition in the Bills of Sale Act, 1878, s. 4, and contends that the letters of trust are "declarations of trust without transfer" within that Act, and that they are not covered by the exception "documents used in the ordinary course of business as proof of the possession or control of goods."

In my judgment these letters of trust do not fall within the bills of sale definition at all. The pledge rights of the bank were complete on the deposit of the bills of lading and other documents of title. These letters of trust are mere records of trust authorities given by the bank and accepted by the company stating the terms on which the pledgors were authorized to realize the goods on the pledgees' behalf. The bank's pledge and its rights as pledgee do not arise under these documents at all, but under the original pledge: see *Ex parte Hubbard* (17 Q. B. D. 690, 697). The bank as pledgee had a right to realize the goods in question from time to time, and it was more convenient to them, as is common practice throughout the country, to allow the realization to be made by experts, in this case by the pledgors. They were clearly entitled to do this by handing over the bills of lading and other documents of title for realization on their behalf without in any way affecting their pledge rights. . . .

The second point taken by the liquidator is a more difficult one. Sect. 93, sub-s. 1 (*e*), of the Companies (Consolidation) Act, 1908, provides that "a mortgage or charge on any book debts of the company" shall so far as any security on the company's property or undertaking is thereby conferred be void against the liquidator unless the prescribed particulars are registered. The object of that addition to the mortgage registration section in the Companies Act is perfectly plain and well known; and the liquidator did not disguise the fact that if he succeeds he will succeed under the language of the section, quite irrespective of any intention of the Legislature to upset a long-established course of business in the City and elsewhere under which merchants are financed by financial and other people. The answer however to this point is, that these letters of trust really create no mortgage or charge on book debts in any true sense of the word at all. The bank had its charge before these letters came into existence. The object of these letters of trust was not to give the bank a charge at all, but to enable the bank to realize the goods over which it had a charge in the way in which goods in similar cases have for years and years been realized in the City and elsewhere.

It is suggested that the letters of trust come within the judgment of Pickford J. in the *Ladenburg Case* ([1912] 3 K. B. 275). In that case: "The defendant company, carrying on business as merchants in Manchester, consigned goods to their customers in South America, and, in order to obtain advances from the plaintiffs, who were bankers, wrote to the plaintiffs enclosing for their acceptance the company's drafts drawn in respect of specified shipments then being made and copies of the bills of lading and of the invoices relating thereto, and stating that the defendant company hypothecated the goods or the proceeds thereof to the plaintiffs. As between the defendant company and their customers the terms of sale were such that the property in the goods passed on shipment to the customers to whose orders the bills of lading were drawn. The plaintiffs having accepted drafts in the above circumstances, and the defendant company having gone into liquidation, the plaintiffs claimed to be entitled to the proceeds of the goods as against the liquidator: — Held, that the effect of the transaction was that the defendant company had created a charge on the company's book debts" within the meaning of s. 93, sub-s. 1 (*e*), and that the charge not having been registered was void.

Now in that case the bank had no pledge or other right in the goods at all before the transaction in question; the transaction was one which notwithstanding its form could not and did not give the bank any right except a charge over the company's book debts, and as Pickford J. pointed out, it was simply and solely a mortgage or charge on the company's book debts, and as such was avoided by the Act. There was, as I have stated, no previous right in the bank at all under which they could claim as against the liquidator. The charge was explicit, and there was nothing at the date of the charge that the company could charge except its book debts, which it expressly and plainly charged to the bank as security. That case does not appear to me to have any bearing upon the present case at all. Here, if I may repeat myself again, the bank as pledgee created a trust agency in the company for the purpose of the realization of the bank's security. That trust agency was acknowledged and recorded in the letters of trust. That is the whole of the transaction. The letters of trust are neither bills of sale within s. 93, sub-s. 1 (*c*), nor are they in any sense mortgages or charges on book debts within clause (*e*) or any other clause of the section.

On these grounds there will be a declaration on the summons that the letters of trust are good and valid documents, and that the bank, as against the liquidator, is entitled in priority to the goods mentioned therein or their proceeds so far as they can be traced.

The bank's costs will be paid out of the assets and the liquidator's costs will be costs in the liquidation.

Compare In re A. E. Fountain, Inc., 282 Fed. 816 (Circuit Court of Appeals, Second Circuit, 1922), where an importer borrowed $3000 from a bank, giving as security a trust receipt covering a stock of manufactured dolls owned by and in the possession of the importer. The trust receipt recited that certain described quantities of dolls had been set aside in accordance with its terms, and provided that the importer might sell the dolls, any proceeds to be handed to the bank for application against the loan and any other indebtedness. Where the importer subsequently became bankrupt a considerable quantity of dolls was found in his stock in trade, although less in some descriptions than those mentioned in the trust receipt. The bank demanded these dolls from the receiver and was refused. In a reclamation proceeding it was held by Augustus Hand, District Judge, "that the holder of a trust receipt has no better standing than the holder of an unfiled chattel mortgage, unless he derives his security title from a person other than the one responsible for the satisfaction of the obligation which the property secures"; for "this arrangement seems more nearly to resemble a chattel mortgage than any other form of security. It is dependent on title rather than possession, and originates out of a loan of money rather than through a purchase and sale of goods. . . . If the present trust receipt can prevail against a trustee in bankruptcy, it is hard to say what protection exists against secret liens."

Note also In re Schuttig, 1 Fed. (2nd) 443, (District Court, New Jersey, 1924), where automobiles bought by a dealer were shipped by the manufacturer under negotiable bills of lading to the order of the buyer, these bills being sent to a bank with sight drafts attached. A financing company advanced to the dealer 80 per cent of the amount of the drafts in return for his check for 20 per cent and trust receipts covering the cars.

The financing company then paid the bank, and obtained the release of the bills of lading to the dealer. The dealer became bankrupt. The financing company claimed from the trustee the three cars covered by the trust receipts. The findings of a referee in favor of plaintiff were affirmed on the ground that plaintiff never had title, but merely loaned money to the dealer to take up documents. The transaction amounted to an unrecorded chattel mortgage.

CENTURY THROWING CO. *v.* MULLER

UNITED STATES CIRCUIT COURT OF APPEALS, THIRD CIRCUIT, 1912

[197 *Federal Reporter*, 252]

GRAY, Circuit Judge. The defendants in error, Muller, Schall & Co. (hereinafter called the plaintiffs) brought an action in trover in the court below against the Century Throwing Company, the plaintiff in error (hereinafter called the defendant). At the conclusion of the evidence, and before the case was submitted to the jury, both the plaintiffs and the defendant moved for the direction of a verdict. The learned judge of the court below refused the motion of the defendant and granted that of the plaintiffs, and from the judgment upon the verdict so directed (which was for damages amounting to $3,516.51) this writ of error was sued out by the defendant.

The action was for the recovery of damages for the detention of 888.9 pounds of raw silk, which plaintiffs claim as their property and allege that the defendant had converted. The material facts are as follows:

Vivanti Bros. were purchasers or brokers in the purchase and sale of raw silk, doing business in New York City and Yokohama, Japan. Neuberger-Phillips Silk Company was a New Jersey corporation, manufacturing silk goods in Paterson. The defendant company was engaged in throwing raw silk, an operation which consisted of twisting, spinning and preparing the raw silk for manufacture. This operation was well known in the silk trade, and carried on by various concerns, for manufacturers, at a certain price per pound.

Wishing to purchase raw silk in Japan, the Silk Company arranged with Vivanti Bros., in January, 1910, for the purchase of a quantity of the same at Yokohama, and in February, 1910, the Silk Company were notified by the said silk brokers that the purchase had been made as ordered. Under this arrangement, the shipment was to be made on the basis of a six months' sight draft drawn against the silk, provided that payment of the same should be guaranteed by a banker's letter of credit. Such letter of credit, in order to accomplish this importation, was obtained by the Silk Company from the plaintiffs, who were bankers doing business in New York. . . .

Relying upon the plaintiffs' guaranty, as set forth in this letter of credit, Vivanti Bros., on February 15, 1910, shipped the silk to New York, taking a bill of lading, deliverable to the order of plaintiffs. The duplicate bills of lading, with the consular invoice, were sent direct to the plaintiffs and in due course received by them, as was also the original bill of lading attached to the draft. About March 11, 1910, the goods themselves arrived in New York, and on the same day the plaintiffs indorsed the bill of lading and delivered it to Mr. Neuberger, president of the Silk Company, receiving from him at the same time the so-called trust receipt, signed on behalf of his company. This trust receipt read as follows:

Received from Messrs. Muller, Schall & Co. the merchandise specified in the Bill of Lading per S. S. "Inaba Maru" to N. Y. via Seattle.

F V
206/235 30 bales raw silk.

imported under the terms of their Letter of Credit No. 6169 issued for our account, together with Consular Invoice, Invoice and Insurance Policy; and in consideration thereof, we agree to hold the said merchandise, on storage, as the property of Messrs. Muller, Schall & Company, and subject to their order, with liberty to sell the same for cash, and in case of sale to pay over to them the proceeds as soon as received, to be held and applied by them against the acceptances of Direction der Disconto Gesellschaft, London, on our account under the terms of the said Letter of Credit and to the payment of any other liability or indebtedness of ours to Messrs. Muller, Schall & Company or to Direction der Disconto Gesellschaft, London, the intention being to protect and preserve unimpaired the title of the said Muller, Schall & Company to the said merchandise and the proceeds thereof. It is further agreed that the undersigned shall keep said merchandise insured against fire at its full value, loss, if any, payable to Messrs. Muller, Schall & Company, and that said Muller, Schall & Company shall not be chargeable with any storage, insurance premiums or other expenses incurred thereon, and that nothing in this Receipt contained shall impair or alter any of the provisions or obligations of the said Letter of Credit or of our agreement accepting the same.

New York, 3/11/10.

Neuberger-Phillips Co., by J. Neuberger, Pst.

The draft drawn on the London bankers for the purchase price, with bill of lading attached, payable six months after sight, was presented and accepted in London on March 8, 1910, in accordance with the stipulations of the letter of credit, thus becoming payable in London September 8, 1910. On March 17, 1910, the plaintiffs made the following written statement to the Silk Company:

Muller, Schall & Co., 44–46 Wall Street.

To the Neuberger-Phillips Silk Co., New York City.

New York, March 17, 1910.

Dear Sir: We have received from Direction der Disconto Gesellschaft, the following advice of maturities for your account.

Under No.	L/c	Amount	Due in London	Due in N. Y.	Valued Against
6169	6m/s	3,137.11/-	Sept. 8, '10	Aug. 27, '10	30 bales raw silk per S. S. "Inaba Maru"

Yours truly,

Muller, Schall & Co.

When the plaintiffs handed over to the Silk Company the possession of the silk, by indorsing and delivering the bill of lading, there is no direct evidence that it was for the purpose of passing title to the Silk Company, or waiving or abandoning any of their rights of property, as security for the liability incurred by reason of their acceptances of the purchase money drafts, which were to be cared for at maturity by the Silk Company. On the contrary, that there was no such purpose may legitimately be inferred from the facts as testified to and from the stipulations of the letter of credit, apart from the trust receipt. The trust receipt, however, given by the Silk Company expressly negatives such purpose, by setting forth the nature and character of the transaction under which the silk was delivered by the plaintiffs to the Silk Company, and closing with the stipulation "that nothing in this receipt contained shall impair or alter any of the provisions or obligations of the said letter of credit or of our agreement accepting the same."

Shortly after receiving the bill of lading from the plaintiffs, which was necessary in order to enable it to receive possession of the goods from the carrier, the Silk Company handed over a portion of the importation of 30 bales to the defendants, as throwsters, to be thrown by them. It seems that before the silk here in question was offered to the defendant to be thrown, the defendant had had deposited with it other silk for the same purpose, which had been already thrown. The Silk Company, desiring to get possession of this silk, found that the defendant was unwilling to deliver the same without payment of a claimed lien thereon for an indebtedness which amounted to several thousand dollars. It was then agreed that the defendants should deliver this thrown silk to the Silk Company, and should receive the raw silk here in question from the Silk Company, and hold the same as security, not only for the throwing of it, but for this past indebtedness.

Shortly after the defendant got possession of the silk in question, the Silk Company was adjudicated a bankrupt, on a petition filed April 12, 1910. On April 13, 1910, a receiver of the alleged bankrupt was appointed and duly qualified, and on April 18, 1910, plaintiffs preferred their petition to the District Court, in bankruptcy, for the Southern District of New York, stating the fact of the petition in bankruptcy and the appointment of a receiver, as also the facts in relation to the transaction between the plaintiff and the Silk Company as to the raw silk here in question, and stating that part of the same was in possession of the receiver and the remainder in the possession of the defendant and other throwsters; also that plaintiffs had demanded of the receiver that he deliver up to them all of the said 30 bales of silk, or any part thereof in his possession or control; and that the said receiver had refused so to do.

[About two pages of the opinion are here omitted.]

A strong *prima facie* case, establishing the plaintiffs' title to the goods in question, was made by the documents above referred to and by the history of the transaction between the plaintiffs and the Silk Company, as disclosed by the evidence. From this evidence, it appears that the financing of such importations has for years constituted a regular part of the plaintiffs' business, and that this transaction was begun and carried through in the regular form. The papers used were filled up printed blanks, thereby showing the customary character of the transactions embodied therein, and that the method of procedure was the usual and customary one. There were no special agreements between the parties, and no arrangements or understandings of any kind, except those embodied in the papers mentioned. The plaintiffs were conducting a conservative foreign banking transaction in the usual and customary way, their compensation being a small commission of about 1¼ per cent., and amounting to less than $200 for a transaction extending over six months and for a liability of about $16,000, the smallness of the commission being due to the reliance placed upon the security afforded by title to the goods until this liability had been discharged.

The customary character of the transaction is attested, not only by the record before us, but by the judicial notice elicited in many modern cases more or less similar to the present one. We can readily understand how the business of foreign importation by merchants, and especially by manufacturers, is facilitated and enlarged by making available to those of small means the credit of banking capital. The business of importation is thus extended, by not being confined to those concerns having large capital and established foreign credit.

The exigencies of trade and commerce have caused many exceptions to be made to the rigid rule founded on the policy underlying the statute of frauds, by which the divorce of title from possession is declared either evidence of fraud or to be fraudulent *per se.* Accordingly, courts consistently recognize and protect the title of the real owner of goods placed by him in the hands of a bailee for a legitimate purpose, and will protect it, even where such bailee is clothed with all the indicia of ownership that physical possession can give, and undertakes, in violation of his contract, to dispose of the goods to an innocent purchaser. Cases of conditional sale and other bailments, where title has never passed from the real owner and where the possession of the bailee is not inconsistent with the real contract between the parties, are familiar illustrations of the law in this regard. In the present case, there can be no doubt that the title to the goods in question passed from the original vendors to the plaintiffs for a well recognized and lawful purpose, *viz.*, to secure the plaintiffs by the acquirement and retention of said title against failure on the part of the Silk Company to make good the acceptance by the plaintiffs of the purchase money draft at its maturity. Nor can it be seriously questioned that the plaintiffs could legally deliver possession of these goods to the manufacturer, for whose benefit the purchase had been made in Japan, without parting with the title to the same, and measurably retain the security intended to be given the plaintiffs by virtue of the original undertaking, provided always that the possession be consistent with the agreement between the parties for that purpose. The law has long been settled that such title and ownership will be recognized, so far as they are necessary to the security they were intended to give for the payment of the purchase money of the goods bailed, and this, although a dishonest bailee is thereby enabled, by violating his contract of bailment, to avail himself of such possession to represent the property as his own, and thus practice a fraud on third persons with whom he deals in respect thereto. . . .

There is no doubt at all that the understanding of the parties, as evidenced by what they did, the documents passing between them, the evident purpose of the transaction, and the well understood commercial custom above referred to, was that the title to the goods in question should pass from the vendor directly to the plaintiffs, and should there remain for his protection until the payment had been made for the invoices by the Silk Company. . . .

Where the real nature of the transaction upon which the banker's credit is advanced for the purchase of goods on another's account is apparent, courts will sustain the title and property of the banker as security for his advances, even where the goods have been allowed to go into the possession of the one upon whose account they were purchased, though no trust receipt, as in this case, or other document, specifically stated the agreement upon which they were so delivered. Such a case was that of *Farmers' Bank* v. *Logan*, 74 N. Y. 568, where there was no trust receipt or no letter of credit or letter of obligation, but upon the advances made by the bank and the nature of the transaction the court sustained the bank's title. . . .

The plenary protection afforded by this customary banker's title, where the goods have been delivered to the one on whose account they have been purchased under circumstances like those of the present case, has been often sustained by courts of the highest authority, as attested by the numerous cases cited by the defendant in error. The courts have not attempted to define exactly what the relation between the credit-lending banker and the merchant is, as to the goods. In the language of the court in *Charavay* v. *York Silk Co.* (C. C.) 170 Fed. 819:

"It is not necessary to find in the nomenclature of security relations a category in which to place this one. It is governed by the contract of the parties, and the contract will only be disturbed by courts for illegality."

[About two pages of the opinion, holding that a New Jersey statute giving a lien to throwsters had no application here as the Silk Company was not the owner of the silk in question, are here omitted.]

The defendant, however, urges that, even if the documentary evidence, consisting of the letter of credit, the letter of obligation, the trust receipt, and such open conduct of the parties in conformity thereto by themselves, might serve to establish the title of the plaintiffs, nevertheless all the steps in this transaction, though on their face regular and legitimate for the purposes had in view, were but a mask for a secret and fraudulent understanding between the plaintiffs and the Silk Company, by which it was permitted to have such a possession and control that enabled it to deceive the defendant into believing that it was the real owner of the silk in question, and had the right to dispose of it as such. For establishing the existence of such an understanding, which it contends was a "tacit" one, defendant asserts that the plaintiffs had knowledge that the Silk Company was a manufacturing concern when defendant delivered to it the goods in question and took the trust receipt, and that therefore, although no expression was given to such understanding, either orally or in writing, it must have been contemplated that the goods were to be put in the course of manufacture and sale. A "tacit" understanding is somewhat elusive as a subject of proof. In this case it seems to us to rest simply upon the assertion of defendant that there must have been such an understanding as above stated. This assertion so grounded cannot be accepted as a sufficient basis for evading seriously the character of the transaction between the plaintiffs and the Silk Company. We do not find that the transfer of the bill of lading by the plaintiffs to the Silk Company served to clothe the Silk Company with a title contradicting that explicitly set forth and stated in the trust receipt, and, independently of that receipt, inherent in the character of the transaction between the parties. It is true, the indorsement of the bill of lading was a symbolical delivery of the goods. In this case, however, it cannot amount to more than the physical delivery of the goods themselves would have amounted to. It did not import anything more than a possessory title, even if it had been exhibited by the Silk Company to the defendant, which the defendant does not claim to have been the case. . . .

After a careful examination, we see nothing in the evidence in this case that shows any conduct or act on the part of the plaintiffs by which they would be estopped to assert their title and ownership to the goods in question, so far as the same would serve to protect them in respect to the liability incurred by them for the acceptances made in the purchase of such goods. To hold otherwise would be to strike down a *bona fide* and honest transaction of great commercial benefit and advantage and founded upon a well recognized custom by which banking credit is efficiently mobilized for manufacturers and importers of small means.

It only remains to say that we find no ground upon which we can hold that the transaction here in question was tantamount to a mortgage, equitable or otherwise.

The judgment of the court below is therefore affirmed.

Note also Essex County Acceptance Corporation *v.* Pierce-Arrow Sales Co., 288 Mass. 270 (Supreme Judicial Court, 1934). An automobile dealer, while a car was in his possession under a trust receipt arrangement for the purpose of making a sale, mortgaged the car with a bank by pretending to be the owner. The dealer becoming bankrupt, the wholesaler repossessed the car, and the bank sought to recover possession of it in an action of replevin. An order dismissing a report in favor of defendant was affirmed.

Compare Jones *v.* Commercial Investment Trust, 64 Utah 151 (Supreme Court, 1924), where, following initial facts substantially similar to those in *In re Schuttig, supra*, the dealer exhibited for sale in his show room and sold the car held under trust receipt. The dealer failed before the purchaser of the car had taken delivery. The financing company took the car, and in an action to recover possession a judgment for the purchaser was affirmed on the ground that the financing company was estopped from setting up any rights under the trust receipt.

In COMMERCIAL CREDIT CORPORATION *v.* NORTHERN WESTCHESTER BANK, 256 N. Y. 482 (Court of Appeals, 1931), the dealer, holding six cars under trust receipt from the financing company, executed certain promissory notes to a bank, and as security for payment delivered to the bank bills of sale covering the six cars in question. The dealer defaulted in payment of the notes. The bank took possession of the cars, and the financing company replevied them. A judgment for the bank was reversed on the ground that no facts appeared on which to raise an estoppel, and further that there was no evidence of a present advancement of money sufficient to bring the bank under subdivision 1 of the Factors' Act.

PERKINS *v.* LIPPINCOTT CO.

PENNSYLVANIA SUPREME COURT, 1918

[260 *Pennsylvania Reports*, 473]

Opinion by Mr. Justice FRAZER, March 11, 1918:

Plaintiff sued in *assumpsit* to the use of the Bank of Commerce as assignee for the price of dry goods alleged to have been sold and delivered by Perkins to defendant. The latter refused payment alleging, *inter alia*, that the right of action for the value of the merchandise was in the Philadelphia National Bank, which institution had issued to plaintiff a letter of credit covering the price of the goods, and had retained title to them up to the time of their delivery to defendant. The case was tried before the court without a jury and, from judgment entered in favor of defendant, plaintiff appealed.

Perkins, the legal plaintiff, an importer, on December 24, 1914, received an order from defendant for certain enumerated dry goods, which provided that upon their delivery payment should be made to the Philadelphia National Bank. At the same time, and to finance the transaction, arrangements were made with that bank for a letter of credit whereby the bank agreed to accept drafts to the extent of two thousand pounds sterling, drawn on a London bank, the merchandise to be shipped to the order of the Philadelphia National Bank, with bills of lading and drafts attached. Upon their arrival the bank authorized the custom house broker to deliver the goods to Perkins, taking from him a trust receipt in which he agreed to hold the consignment in trust for the bank, and, in the event of sale, collect the proceeds and deliver same to the bank.

Subsequent to the above negotiations, a second order was given by the bank to Perkins, and an arrangement made for an additional letter of credit on which defendant became surety for plaintiff. All goods included in both orders on arrival were in fact delivered directly to defendant, though plaintiff, in each instance, was required to sign the trust receipt. Subsequently, Perkins assigned the account represented by the sale of the goods to the Bank of Commerce as security for advances, that bank having no notice of any defect in the title of Perkins.

The facts are not in dispute and are quite similar to those in Perkins to use of *Bk. of Commerce* v. *Halpren et al.*, 257 Pa. 402, upon which appellants rely for reversing the court below. In that case, upon execution of the trust receipts, the goods were sent to a warehouse in the name of the custom house broker, for the use of the plaintiff, and allowed to remain there until defendant, the purchaser, to whom plaintiff sold and billed the goods pursuant to the power given by the trust receipt, was ready to use them. In the meantime they continued in storage subject to the control of the purchaser, to be delivered to him from time to time upon payment of the duty. The principal question involved, was whether there was delivery sufficient to pass the title from the vendor to the vendee. The bank made no claim to the proceeds. We there said (page 407): "Whether or not title passed to defendants . . . depends upon the intention of the parties as indicated by the course of dealing with each other"; and on page 410: "The course of dealing between the parties, the method of purchase and subsequent disposition of the merchandise on its arrival in a bonded warehouse, wherein it was set apart subject to withdrawal at the pleasure of defendants, and the actual withdrawal of part, together with the delivery of the invoices, all tend to support the conclusion of the trial judge, and furnish ample foundation to sustain his decision.

"The fact that plaintiff failed to transfer the proceeds of the sale to the Philadelphia National Bank, conformably to his obligation under the trust receipt to deliver to the latter, has no bearing on the present discussion. The trust receipt authorized plaintiff to sell the merchandise, consequently an exercise of the power of sale, so far as the purchaser is concerned, divests the title of the bank: *Canadian Bank of Commerce* v. *Baum & Sons*, 187 Pa. 48."

In the present case while the goods under one order were marked "for account of" plaintiff, no delivery was made to him, but, under direction from the bank, were delivered directly to defendant. The other order did not contain a stipulation that defendant should pay the bills direct to the bank; it, however, agreed to become surety for the payment of the draft negotiated under the letter of credit, and in turn was assured by the bank that the goods would be consigned to it, and that delivery would be made to no one else, which arrangement was carried out. No actual delivery of the goods under either consignment was made to plaintiff. He had neither title nor possession with right of disposal at any time, though the trust receipt contemplated possession by him and sale for the account of the bank. Aside from this, however, there is no denial that title to the goods passed to defendant, and it is immaterial whether it passed through plaintiff or through the bank. The sole question is whether plaintiff or the bank is entitled to the proceeds. The power given by the trust receipt to sell the goods did not include the power to dispose of the proceeds, and the only way in which plaintiff could acquire such right was by paying his indebtedness to the bank. Until that was done he had no title to the proceeds, and the Bank of Commerce, the use plaintiff, succeeded to only such rights as plaintiff possessed.

The judgment is affirmed.

In ASSETS REALIZATION CO. *v.* SOVEREIGN BANK OF CANADA, 210 Fed. 156 (Circuit Court of Appeals, Third Circuit, 1914), an importer holding wool under a trust receipt resold the wool to a subpurchaser who became bankrupt before paying. The trust receipt was held by the bank which had financed the import transaction, and in whose name bills of lading had been taken covering shipment of the wool. Both the bank and the importer filed claims for the price against the estate of the bankrupt. It was held that only the bank was entitled.

Compare IN RE CANAL BANK & TRUST CO.'S LIQUIDATION, 178 La. 575 (Supreme Court, 1933), GREENOUGH *v.* MUNROE, 53 Fed. (2nd) 362 (Circuit Court of Appeals, Second Circuit, 1931), and BANK OF UNITED STATES *v.* SELTZER, 233 App. Div. 225 (New York Supreme Court, Appellate Division, 1931), in all of which the banks holding the trust receipts became unable to meet their obligations subsequently to their acceptance, but prior to payment, of drafts drawn by the original sellers under the relative letters of credit. In each case the claim of the bank to take into its general assets the proceeds in the hands of the buyer of the goods covered by trust receipt was denied. In each case it was held that the proceeds in question must be applied in payment of the seller's drafts.

CHAPTER IV

BILLS OF LADING

1. THE BILL OF LADING AND THE CONTRACT OF CARRIAGE

A. IN GENERAL

JOHN VITTUCI CO. *v.* CANADIAN PACIFIC RAILWAY CO.

DISTRICT COURT, W. D. WASHINGTON, N. D., 1917

[238 *Federal Reporter*, 1005]

NETERER, District Judge. The plaintiff predicates his action upon an oral agreement for the transportation of commodities by the defendant, a common carrier. A demurrer has been filed to the complaint. I think the demurrer must be sustained. While it is stated on the face of the complaint that an oral agreement for the transportation was made, it is likewise stated that the defendant issued "its receipt or bill of lading for said shipment," and that the bill of lading was assigned to the plaintiff by the shipper. An oral contract for the transportation of commodities may be made. *Mobile & Montgomery Ry. Co.* v. *Jurey*, 111 U. S. 584, 4 Sup. Ct. 566, 28 L. Ed. 527; *The Jeannie* (D. C.) 225 Fed. 178. But where it is apparent upon the face of the complaint that a bill of lading was issued for the transportation of the commodities, the presumption is that the contract was merged in the bill of lading, which must be the basis of the plaintiff's rights, unless there is some fact pleaded to negative such presumption.

A bill of lading is a contract to transport and deliver the goods to the consignee upon the terms therein specified. The Supreme Court of the United States, in *The Delaware*, 81 U. S. (14 Wall.) 579, at page 601, 20 L. Ed. 779, speaking of a bill of lading, said:

"Such an instrument is twofold in its character; that is, it is a receipt as to the quantity and description of the goods shipped, and a contract to transport and deliver the goods to the consignee or other person therein designated, and upon the terms specified in the same instrument. Beyond all doubt a bill of lading, in the usual form, is a receipt for the quantity of goods shipped and a promise to transport and deliver the same as therein stipulated."

The Circuit Court of Appeals of the Second Circuit (*Vanderbilt* v. *Ocean S. S. Co.*, 215 Fed. 886, 132 C. C. A. 226), speaking through Judge Rogers, said:

"A bill of lading has a twofold character. It is a contract to transport and deliver the goods to the consignee upon the terms specified in it; and it is also a receipt as to the quantity and description of the goods shipped. So far as it embodies the terms of the contract, it is not to be varied by parol evidence."

A bill of lading is a contract for the carriage of goods reduced to writing, and is the only evidence of the contract. Aspinall's Reports of Maritime Cases, vol. 6 (N. S.) 1886–90.

The plaintiff may not sue upon "a special oral agreement," where the oral agreement is merged in a written bill of lading for the shipment of the goods. His right of action must be based upon the bill of lading. *Indianapolis & Cincinnati Ry. Co.* v. *Remmy et al.*, 13 Ind. 518; *Sun Mutual Ins. Co. et al.* v. *Mississippi Valley Transportation Co.* (D. C.) 14 Fed. 699. The cause of action arising from a breach of a written contract of affreightment, evidence could not be received of an oral contract or agreement. The complaint, therefore, does not state a cause of action.

The demurrer is sustained.

Compare ARMOUR AND COMPANY, LIMITED *v.* LEOPOLD WALFORD (LONDON), LIMITED, [1921] 3 K.B. 473 (King's Bench Division), where a shipper was given a bill of lading containing a clause that "The Company has the right to carry the goods below deck and/or on deck." The goods were carried on deck and were damaged in consequence by sea water. In an action by the shipper against the carrier, plaintiff contended that this clause "was unusual, that it was not specifically drawn to their attention, that they were not aware of it and therefore are not bound by its provisions." In rejecting this contention, McCardie, J., said: "In my view a bill of lading is not, as between shipper and shipowner, conclusive of the true contract. It may, e.g., be inconsistent with a prior overriding, and express written bargain as to the terms on which goods shall be carried or the form in which bills of lading shall be issued. . . . Whatever the prior express bargain has been, a shipper is free to accept any bills of lading he chooses. If therefore he has chosen to accept without protest a bill of lading in a certain form he should ordinarily be bound by it, for as Mr. Carver well observes in sec. 56 of his book: 'Where that has been done it is difficult to suppose that the document can be treated as not being what it seems to be. . . . The practice of looking to it as the contract may be said to be uniform and indeed has been adopted by the Legislature (Bills of Lading Act, 1855); and the scarcity of authority is in truth a strong confirmation of the view that it is the contract: for it shows that in practice the point has not been considered open to question.' "

In TRANSMARINE CORPORATION *v.* CHARLES H. LEVITT & CO., INC., 25 Fed. (2nd) 275 (Circuit Court of Appeals, Second Circuit, 1928), an oral contract was made for the carriage of 75 cases of knit goods from Newark to Havana. Subsequently, while the goods were still lying on the wharf, a received for shipment bill of lading was issued to the shipper. Failing actual shipment, the goods later were recalled by the shipper and sent by another line. In an action on the oral contract, L. Hand, Circuit Judge, said: "We agree that the bill of lading was the only contract between the parties, and that it took the place of the prior oral contract as the final memorial of the parties' obligations. When the goods have once been dispatched under an oral contract and are beyond recall, the issuance and acceptance of a bill of lading has been treated not to substitute it as the contract. But this was not such a case. The goods still remained within recall, and indeed the plaintiff later recalled them."

In NORTHERN PACIFIC RAILWAY COMPANY *v.* AMERICA TRADING COMPANY, 195 U. S. 439 (Supreme Court, 1904), goods were shipped under a written contract providing for shipment from Newark to Tacoma and thence to Japan by steamer sailing on a specified date. After the goods had been shipped the shipper was given a bill of lading of the railroad company which he did not read, but which contained a clause stating that the railroad was not liable beyond its own line. The shipper used this bill of lading at his bank as collateral for an advance. The goods were not shipped by the specified steamer, and in consequence were sold in Tacoma at a loss. In an action by the shipper against the railroad it was held that the no liability clause of the bill of lading could not displace the specific provision of the earlier written contract. Mere acceptance of the bill of lading did not indicate consent to alter the existing contract.

Note also THE ARCTIC BIRD, 109 Fed. 167 (District Court, N. D. California, 1901), where under substantially similar circumstances it was held that the terms of the subsequently issued bill of lading cannot affect the provisions of the earlier written contract unless it is shown that they were called to the attention of the shipper so that his consent could be presumed.

LEDUC *v.* WARD

COURT OF APPEAL, 1888

[*Law Reports*, 20 *Queen's Bench Division*, 475]

Appeal by the defendants from the judgment of Denman, J., at the trial without a jury.

The action was by indorsees of bill of lading against shipowners for non-delivery of goods, and the facts were in substance as follows. The plaintiffs had purchased goods from merchants abroad to be shipped from a foreign port. The payment of the price was to be made in exchange for shipping documents, and, the price of the goods having been paid, the bill of lading, signed by the defendants' captain upon the shipment of the goods, had been indorsed to the plaintiffs. The ship was a general ship. The bill of lading as far as material was as follows: "Shipped in apparent good order and condition on the steamship *Austria*, now lying in the port of Fiume, and bound for Dunkirk, with liberty to call at any ports in any order, and to deviate for the purpose of saving life or property; 3123 bags of rape seed, being marked and numbered as per margin, and to be delivered in the like good order and condition at the aforesaid port of Dunkirk unto order or assigns." Then followed the usual clause excepting perils of the sea, &c. The vessel, instead of proceeding direct to Dunkirk, sailed for Glasgow and was lost, with her cargo, near Ailsa Craig, off the mouth of the Clyde, by perils of the sea.

Evidence was given at the trial by the defendants, the effect of which was contended to be that the shippers of the goods, who were alleged to be, under the circumstances, the agents of the plaintiffs for shipment of the goods, knew, at the time when the goods were shipped, that the vessel was intended to proceed to Dunkirk via Glasgow, and in substance agreed to her so proceeding.

The learned judge admitted the evidence *ex majori cautelâ,* expressing an opinion, however, that it was not admissible: but he found that it did not prove any agreement on the shippers' part that the ship should proceed via Glasgow. He accordingly held that there had been a deviation, and gave judgment for the plaintiffs.

[Arguments of counsel and the opinion of Lord Esher, M. R., are here omitted.]

FRY, L.J. In my opinion many of the points argued are concluded by the provisions of the Bills of Lading Act as applied to the facts of the case. Here the contract made between the merchants abroad and the plaintiffs being that the goods were to be paid for in exchange for shipping documents, the property in the goods passed to the plaintiffs upon the indorsement of the bill of lading. The Bills of Lading Act, 18 & 19 Vict. c. 111, s. 1, says that "every indorsee of a bill of lading to whom the property in the goods therein mentioned shall pass upon or by reason of the indorsement shall have transferred to and vested in him all rights of suit, and be subject to the same liabilities in respect of such goods as if the contract contained in the bill of lading had been made with himself." Here is a plain declaration of the legislature that there is a contract contained in the bill of lading, and that the benefit of it is to pass to the indorsee under such circumstances as exist in the present case. It seems to me impossible therefore now to contend that there is no contract contained in the bill of lading, whatever might have been the case before the statute. The Master of the Rolls has referred to the language used by Blackburn, J., in *Fraser* v. *Telegraph Construction Co.* (Law Rep. 7 Q. B. 566), by himself in *Chartered Mercantile Bank of India* v. *Netherlands India Steam Navigation Co.* (10 Q. B. D. 521), and by Lord Selborne in *Glyn, Mills & Co.* v. *East and West India Dock Co.* (7 App. Cas. 591), as to the contract contained in the bill of lading. The contract of carriage is therefore to be sought for in the bill of lading; and it cannot be doubted that one of the most important terms of that contract is as to the course by which the goods are to be carried to their destination. The question, therefore, becomes simply one of the construction of this contract as to that; and, so far as that is concerned, I entirely agree with the Master of the Rolls. The bill of lading states that the goods are shipped on board the steamship *Austria,* now lying in the port of Fiume and bound for Dunkirk. It further declares that the goods are to be delivered at Dunkirk. As a matter of construction I cannot doubt that the power to deviate from the voyage so described must be confined to that given by the bill of lading in terms, *viz.*, a power to deviate in order to call at any ports in any order, or for the purpose of saving life or property. The question is whether that power includes a power of going to Glasgow, which appears to be, to and fro, somewhere about 1200 miles out of the ordinary course of the voyage. I think the meaning of the clause with regard to calling at ports is what the Master of the Rolls has stated, and that it cannot include a right to go to Glasgow. It is said that there is an American authority which shews that notice to the shipper of the route by which the ship is going to sail will rebut what is said to be an implied term of the contract, *viz.*, that the vessel will proceed by the direct route to the port of destination. In the first place it should be observed that this seems to have been a mere *obiter dictum*; but assuming that, apart from the Bills of Lading Act, such notice would have had any such effect, which I am far from saying, I think it impossible, having regard to the provisions of that Act, to suppose that any effect could be produced by such notice to the shipper with respect to a contract by bill of lading which is by statute made assignable to a third person; for to hold that it could have such effect would be to hinder that assignability of the contract which the legislature designed to effectuate. The contract as contained in the bill of lading expressly gives certain powers of deviation, and the possibility of the existence of any other power to deviate is according to the ordinary rule governing the construction of written documents thereby repelled. If it were necessary to decide the point, I should be disposed to agree with the learned judge who tried the case, that the evidence given at the trial fell short of proving that there was any understanding between the shippers and the shipowner that the vessel was to go to Glasgow before going to Dunkirk; but I prefer to rest my judgment on the view that the provision of the statute making the contract contained in the bill of lading assignable is inconsistent with the idea that anything which took place between the shipper and shipowner, not embodied in the bill of lading, could affect the contract. For these reasons I think the appeal should be dismissed.

[Concurring opinion of Lopes, L. J., is here omitted.]

Appeal dismissed.

Note also THE EMILIEN MARIE, 32 L. T. 435 (Admiralty Court, 1875), where a bill of lading for 40 tons of palm kernels was given to the shipper on the understanding that no delivery was to be made under the bill until delivery had been made under two bills of lading previously given for portions of the same cargo, delivery then to be made only if any kernels were left. There were not enough kernels to satisfy all the bills of lading. It was held that an indorsee of the third bill of lading was entitled to claim full delivery of 40 tons from the carrier.

COMPARE SEARS, ROEBUCK *v.* SOUTH ATLANTIC STEAMSHIP COMPANY, [1934] Am. Maritime Cases 532 (U. S. District Court, Southern District, Georgia), where it was held that the assignee of a bill of lading who purchases and presents the bill of lading and receives delivery of the goods is not bound, either as a party to the bill of lading contract, or as one who adopted it and acted upon it, by a clause in the bill of lading stating that shipper and receiver are liable for damage caused by dangerous and smelly goods, where it is not shown that the assignee was either the shipper or the consignee named in the bill.

BRANDT *v.* LIVERPOOL, BRAZIL AND RIVER PLATE STEAM NAVIGATION COMPANY, LIMITED

COURT OF APPEAL, 1923

[*Law Reports*, [1924] 1 *King's Bench*, 575]

[Plaintiffs were correspondents in London of a Buenos Aires firm, selling the goods of this firm in return for a commission and financing the transactions by accepting bills of exchange for 90 per cent of the invoice price of the goods on receipt of the bill of lading for the goods, the bill of lading or the proceeds of the goods being their security for advances thus made. The Buenos Aires firm shipped a quantity of zinc ashes, drew a draft at sight on plaintiffs, indorsed the bill of lading, and sold the draft with the bill of lading attached to a bank in Buenos Aires. Plaintiffs took up the documents in the ordinary course. The bill of lading recited that the ashes had been received in apparent good order and condition, but they were in fact wet on shipment and had to be unloaded and reconditioned. As a result, there was great delay in shipment, and plaintiffs were obliged to pay nearly £750 for the cost of the reconditioning. Plaintiffs brought this action as indorsees of the bill of lading against the shipping company, claiming damages for breach of the contract contained in the bill of lading.]

BANKES L.J. This is an appeal from a judgment of Greer J. in an action raising an interesting and important question with which the learned judge dealt in a very clear and exhaustive manner and in my opinion quite correctly. Indeed it is only in deference to the arguments which have been addressed to us that I do not content myself by saying that I agree with the judgment delivered by the learned judge.

The action was brought by Brandt & Co., and alternatively by F. W. Vogel trading as Vogel & Cia. at Buenos Aires. The claim was for delay in the delivery of some 5620 bags of zinc ashes and for the return of 748*l.*, the amount they had to pay the appellants, the shipowners, for reconditioning these goods.

The main question raised in the Court below was whether Brandt & Co. had a cause of action arising from the fact that they were the holders of the bill of lading and had presented it. They claimed to have a right of action on one or both of two grounds. One was that the general property in the goods had passed to them, and the other was that from the fact of their presenting the bill of lading, paying the freight and taking delivery of the goods there was to be inferred a contract by the defendants to make delivery upon the terms of the bill of lading so far as they were applicable to the circumstances at the time when the plaintiffs took delivery. Greer J.

decided against Brandt & Co.'s contention founded upon the general property in the goods having passed to them, and I agree with that view, and it is unnecessary to express any opinion about it, or to go into the facts in relation to it.

The argument in this Court has been mainly directed to the question whether there was a contract between Brandt & Co. and the shipowners which entitled Brandt & Co. to sue for damages for the delay in delivery of these goods and for the return of the money they had had to pay for reconditioning them. Now, it is quite true that there is no authority expressly covering the question how far, that is to what extent, the shipowner is bound by the contract which may be inferred from the offer made by the holder of a bill of lading to take delivery of the goods, which offer is accepted by the shipowner. Is his obligation merely to deliver the goods which he has on board, or is he bound to the extent of the contract contained in the bill of lading so far as its terms are applicable to the circumstances of the case. We have been referred to three authorities: *Stindt* v. *Roberts* (5 D. & L. 460); *Young* v. *Moeller* (5 E. & B. 755); and *Allen* v. *Coltart & Co.* (11 Q. B. D. 782). By those authorities it has been clearly established that where the holder of a bill of lading presents it and offers to accept delivery, if that offer is accepted by the shipowner, the holder of the bill of lading comes under an obligation to pay the freight and to pay the demurrage, if any, and there are general expressions in all those three cases, I think, in which the learned judges have said that the contract so made by that offer and acceptance covers, so as to include, the terms of the bill of lading. In my opinion in this particular case the contract must include the terms and conditions of the bills of lading and for this reason. In this case the bill of lading holder offered the freight before the goods were delivered; and in fact paid it, and under those circumstances it seems to me that by the acceptance of the freight and the subsequent delivery the shipowners undertook an obligation to deliver the goods as described in the bill of lading. I think from the shipowner's point of view it must necessarily include the whole of the terms of the bill of lading, because he must desire that he should be covered by the exceptions in the bill of lading. I think, therefore, that the learned judge is right when he states his conclusion that on the facts in this case it is sufficient to say there was a promise by the shipowners to deliver the goods to Brandt & Co. in the condition in which they ought to be delivered under the bill of lading. So much for the scope and extent of the contract. I entirely agree with the learned judge's conclusion upon this very important matter.

[The balance of the opinion, holding that plaintiffs were entitled to damages for the delay and to the return of the amount paid for reconditioning, is here omitted.]

SCRUTTON L.J. I substantially agree with the judgment of Greer J., and I only give in my own words some reasons for agreeing, because some of the matters involved are of considerable commercial importance. [His Lordship then pointed out that by putting into circulation a bill of lading stating the goods to have been received "in apparent good order and condition," although as a matter of fact they were externally wet, the shipowners might be estopped from setting up the bad condition of the shipment against a person taking the bill of lading for value in reliance on its statements.]

The first line of defence made was that Messrs. Brandt were not in any way parties to the bill of lading so as to be able to rely on the estoppel contained in it. This raises a novel point which has not in terms been considered in the authorities, as far as I know. Before the Bills of Lading Act, 1855, was passed, by the custom of merchants the indorsement of the bill of lading passed the property in the goods contained therein, but it did not assign the contract contained therein, and therefore the person who by indorsement became the owner of the goods did not by the same indorsement acquire a right to sue the shipowner upon his contract, which was evidenced in the bill of lading; and before 1855 a long series of decisions had been given, of which perhaps two of the leading cases are *Sanders* v. *Vanzeller* (4 Q. B. 260) and *Cock* v. *Taylor* ((1811) 13 East, 399), the general effect of which was that, while it could not as a matter of law be said that by presenting a bill of lading the person who presented it became liable to the terms of the bill of lading, there might as a matter of fact be inferred a contract from presenting the bill of lading and taking the goods. In every case that has been reported the question which was discussed seems to have been, Was the person who presented the bill of lading and took the goods bound to comply with the conditions which had to be performed by the owner of the goods; was he bound to pay freight, or demurrage, or any other specific charge mentioned in the bill of lading? The question of his rights against the shipowner, as far as I know, was never expressly raised, and I think there is a reason why it should not be so. If he had any property in the goods he could sue the shipowner in tort, and it was to the interest of the shipowner to say that the person who took the goods was bound by the whole bill of lading, including those terms which had to be performed by the shipowner and those exemptions from liability which were contained for the benefit of the shipowner. But when one comes to consider the contract to be inferred from the fact of taking delivery and the promise by the person who takes delivery to perform the terms of the bill of lading, and one asks what was the consideration moving from the shipowner for that promise, one sees it was to deliver the goods on the terms of the bill of lading. That document contains the terms on both sides which were implied from presenting the bill of lading and taking delivery under it. When the Bills of Lading Act, 1855, was passed this difficulty was so far remedied that when the whole property passed by the indorsement to the indorsee, the contract also passed. That left untouched the question where the whole of the property did not pass to the indorsee, but only some property which would enable him to sue in tort for damage to his goods or conversion or detinue of his goods. In *Sewell* v. *Burdick* (10 App. Cas. 74) the question was raised: What is the position of bankers who have taken a bill of lading as a pledge, as security for an advance, and who never present the bill of lading because their advance is small, and the presenting of the bill of lading would render them liable for a much larger amount, and the House of Lords has decided that bankers who are pledgees not having the whole property and not presenting the bill of lading, and not taking delivery under it, are not liable to perform the conditions of the contract in the bill of lading? Lord Selborne expressed the view that if the bankers did present the bill of lading they might then be liable on the contract contained in the bill of lading. It seems to me that such a case is to be governed by the old law which existed before the passing of the Bills of Lading Act. When a holder of a bill of lading, who has some property in the goods, presents the bill of lading and accepts the goods, can there be inferred a contract on each side to perform the terms of the bill of lading? The view that Greer J. has taken is that such a contract can and ought to be implied in this case, and I take the same view. It follows, therefore, that Brandt & Co. may enforce the terms of the bill of lading and are entitled to the benefit of the estoppel which is contained in the statement, "In apparent good order and condition."

[The balance of the opinion is here omitted.]

Atkin L.J. I agree. I assume for this purpose that Brandt & Co. are not in a position to sue the shipowners under the Bills of Lading Act; that is to say, they cannot prove that the property in the goods passed to them by indorsement of the bill of lading. The question then is whether any and what contract arises between them and the shipowners in the circumstances in which they did in fact take delivery. I am inclined to agree with the criticism addressed by Greer J. to the dictum of Lord Selborne in *Sewell* v. *Burdick* (10 App. Cas. 74), and for my part I have great difficulty in seeing how a pledgee of the goods who under the decision in *Sewell* v. *Burdick* (10 App. Cas. 74) does not under the Bills of Lading Act get the right to sue on the contract in the bill of lading, can improve his position by doing that which it was necessary he should do as pledgee of the bill of lading — namely, taking delivery of the goods when the ship arrives. That seems to me to be merely asserting his limited right of possession in order to continue to act as pledgee. But his position may for all that be very much strengthened by the circumstances under which he takes delivery. Before the Bills of Lading Act a series of cases had been decided gradually extending the liability of the indorsee of a bill of lading who came to the shipowner and claimed delivery under it. The first class of decisions I think arose by reason of the terms of the bill of lading which made the goods deliverable to order, or his assigns, he or they paying freight. It was said that if a person came to the shipowner and said to him, "Deliver the goods to me as an assign," the shipowner was entitled to insist that as a condition of receiving the goods the assign should in the terms of the bill of lading pay the freight; and therefore he was held bound to pay the freight in an action of *assumpsit* on the delivery of the goods. Later on that obligation was extended to paying charges other than freight in cases where those other charges were not specified in the contract expressly as being payable by an assignee, as, for instance, to payment of demurrage or other charges, and there the contract obviously becomes a contract to be implied from the circumstances of the delivery being taken by the assignee of the bill of lading. Then is there any corresponding obligation on the part of the shipowner in that contract? It appears to me that just as plainly as the assignee is bound by an implied contract, so is the shipowner, and the shipowner's obligation in the case where freight has in fact been paid by the holder of the bill of lading, is that he will deliver the goods. What other contract could be inferred from the fact that an assignee of a bill of lading goes to the shipowner's representative and offers him the freight, which is accepted by the shipowner? The necessary implication when the shipowner says, "Yes, I will take the bill of lading freight," is that he undertakes in consideration of that to deliver the goods which he has received on board under the bill of lading. Is it a contract to deliver the goods on the terms of the bill of lading? Shipowners would be surprised to hear it suggested that having undertaken to carry goods upon terms in their bill of lading qualifying and limiting their liability they are nevertheless under an absolute obligation to deliver the goods and not an obligation qualified by the exceptions in the bill of lading. They are not accustomed to having a burden put upon them in reference to the carriage of goods except accompanied by the qualification of exceptions, and no other contract could properly be inferred. The bill of lading freight has been assessed and calculated upon the footing of a contract of carriage, qualified by exceptions from liability, and it would be very unfair to say to a shipowner: "You have received the bill of lading freight which is based upon an obligation to carry qualified by all the exceptions, and now having taken it you must accept an obligation to deliver the goods unqualified by any of the exceptions." I have no doubt at all that the obligation on the shipowner is to deliver on the terms of the bill of lading. It follows that the contract to be inferred in cases such as this is that the holder of the bill of lading and the shipowner make a contract for the delivery and acceptance of the goods on the terms of the bill of lading, so far as they are applicable to discharge at the port of discharge. In these circumstances it appears to me that the indorsee of the bill of lading is substantially in the same position as though he came under the Bills of Lading Act.

[The balance of the opinion is here omitted.]

Appeal dismissed.

In DELAURIER *v.* WYLLIE, 27 Sc. L. R. 148 (Court of Session, 1889), iron was shipped to a buyer to whom title already had passed, and the bill of lading was indorsed subsequently by the shipper to the buyer. The iron was lost owing to negligent navigation. It was held that the buyer had no action against the shipowner under the bill of lading as the goods already belonged to him before the indorsement.

Compare Secs. 31 (b) and 32 of the Federal Bills of Lading Act with Sec. 1 of the English Bills of Lading Act (1855).

POLLARD *v.* VINTON

UNITED STATES SUPREME COURT, 1881

[105 *United States Reports*, 7]

Mr. Justice MILLER delivered the opinion of the court.

The defendant in error, who was also defendant below, was the owner of a steamboat running between the cities of Memphis, on the Mississippi River, and Cincinnati, on the Ohio River, and is sued on a bill of lading for the non-delivery at Cincinnati of one hundred and fifty bales of cotton, according to its terms. The bill of lading was in the usual form, and signed by E. D. Cobb & Co., who were the general agents of Vinton for shipping purposes at Memphis, and was delivered to Dickinson, Williams & Co. at that place. They immediately drew a draft on the plaintiffs in New York, payable at sight, for $5,900, to which they attached the bill of lading, which draft was duly accepted and paid. No cotton was shipped on the steamboat, or delivered at its wharf or to its agents for shipment, as stated in the bill of lading, the statement to that effect being untrue.

These facts being undisputed, as they are found in the bill of exceptions, the court instructed the jury to find a verdict for the defendant, which was done, and judgment rendered accordingly. This instruction is the error complained of by the plaintiffs, who sued out the present writ.

A bill of lading is an instrument well known in commercial transactions, and its character and effect have been defined by judicial decisions. In the hands of the holder it is evidence of ownership, special or general, of the property mentioned in it, and of the right to receive said property at the place of delivery. Notwithstanding it is designed to pass from hand to hand, with or without indorsement, and it is efficacious for its ordinary purposes in the hands of the holder, it is not a negotiable instrument or obligation in the sense that a bill of exchange or a promissory note is. Its transfer does not preclude, as in those cases, all inquiry into the transaction in which it originated, because it has come into hands of persons who have innocently paid value for it. The doctrine of *bona fide* purchasers only applies to it in a limited sense.

It is an instrument of a twofold character. It is at once a receipt and a contract. In the former character it is an acknowledgment of the receipt of property on board his vessel by the owner of the vessel. In the latter it is a contract to carry safely and deliver. The receipt of the goods lies at the foundation of the contract to carry and deliver. If no goods are actually received, there can be no valid contract to carry or to deliver.

To these elementary truths the reply is that the agent of defendant has acknowledged in writing the receipt of the goods, and promised for him that they should be safely delivered, and that the principal cannot repudiate the act of his agent in this matter, because it was within the scope of his employment.

It will probably be conceded that the effect of the bill of lading and its binding force on the defendant is no stronger than if signed by himself as master of his own vessel. In such case we think the proposition cannot be successfully disputed that the person to whom such a bill of lading was first delivered cannot hold the signer responsible for goods not received by the carrier.

Counsel for plaintiffs, however, say that in the hands of subsequent holders of such a bill of lading, who have paid value for it in good faith, the owner of the vessel is estopped by the policy of the law from denying what he has signed his name to and set afloat in the public market. However this may be, the plaintiffs' counsel rest their case on the doctrine of agency, holding that defendant is absolutely responsible for the false representations of his agent in the bill of lading.

But if we can suppose there was testimony from which the jury might have inferred either mistake or bad faith on the part of Cobb & Co., we are of opinion that Vinton, the shipowner, is not liable for the false statement in the bill of lading, because the transaction was not within the scope of their authority.

If we look to the evidence of the extent of their authority, as found in the bill of exceptions, it is this short sentence: —

"During the month of December, 1873" (the date of the bill of lading), "the firm of E. D. Cobb & Co., of Memphis, Tennessee, were authorized agents of the defendant at Memphis, with power to solicit freights and to execute and deliver to shippers bills of lading for freight shipped on defendant's steamboat, 'Ben. Franklin.' "

This authority to execute and deliver bills of lading has two limitations; namely, they could only be delivered to shippers, and they could only be delivered for freight shipped on the steamboat.

Before the power to make and deliver a bill of lading could arise, some person must have shipped goods on the vessel. Only then could there be a shipper, and only then could there be goods shipped. In saying this we do not mean that the goods must have been actually placed on the deck of the vessel. If they came within the control and custody of the officers of the boat for the purpose of shipment, the contract of carriage had commenced, and the evidence of it in the form of a bill of lading would be binding. But without such a delivery there was no contract of carrying, and the agents of defendant had no authority to make one.

They had no authority to sell cotton and contract for delivery. They had no authority to sell bills of lading. They had no power to execute these instruments and go out and sell them to purchasers. No man had a right to buy such a bill of lading of them who had not delivered them the goods to be shipped.

Such is not only the necessary inference from the definition of the authority under which they acted, as found in the bill of exceptions, but such would be the legal implication if their relation to defendant had been stated in more general terms. The result would have been the same if it had been merely stated that they were the shipping agents of the owner of the vessel at that point.

[The balance of the opinion is omitted.]

Judgment affirmed.

Note also THORMAN v. BURT, BOULTON AND CO., 54 L. T. (N.S.) 349 (Court of Appeal, 1886). A bill of lading in terms certified to the receipt of 7497 pieces of timber. There was a shortage on delivery of 216 pieces, due to the fact that 216 pieces had been lost in some way while being floated to the ship on rafts, and never had been loaded on board. In an action by the indorsee of the bill of lading against the shipowner, it was held that the indorsee could claim only under the contract in the bill of lading, and that contract only bound the shipowner as to the timber actually put on board.

Compare OLIVIER STRAW GOODS CORPORATION v. OSAKA SHOSEN KAISHA, 27 Fed. Rep. (2nd) 129 (Circuit Court of Appeals, Second Circuit, 1928). Hemp braid was delivered by the seller to a steamship line for transport to the buyer, and an on board bill of lading was issued calling for delivery to the order of the financing bank, although the braid as a matter of fact had not been loaded on the ship but was in warehouse. Owing to the Japanese earthquake of 1923 the braid never was shipped. The buyer acquired the bill of lading as an indorsee, and filed a libel against the steamship line to recover damages for non-delivery. A decree in favor of respondent was reversed, Augustus Hand, Circuit Judge, saying: "It is true that it has for years been held by the English and Federal courts that the master of a vessel has no apparent authority to sign bills of lading when he has not possession of the goods, and the same doctrine has been applied to railroad freight agents. But here the merchandise was in the hands of the carrier, and it cannot be, and we understand is not, contended that the bill of lading was issued without apparent authority. . . . We can see no difference in principle between a misrepresentation as to the condition of merchandise and a misrepresentation that it is on board, when it is not. Either furnishes a basis for an estoppel."

B. PARTICULAR CLAUSES

T. M. DUCHE & SONS, INC. v. COMPANIA TRASATLANTICA

DISTRICT COURT, S. D. NEW YORK, 1931

[46 *Federal Reporter* (*Second Series*), 693]

WOOLSEY, District Judge. I sustain the exception to the libel herein on the ground that it does not state a cause of action against the respondent.

As an amendment would not serve any purpose in the case, I will enter a decree dismissing the libel with costs to the respondent.

I. The libelants herein are purchasers for value of three order bills of lading issued by the respondent for the carriage to New York of 500 boxes of shelled almonds shipped on the respondent's steamship Buenos Aires at Alicante, Spain, on or about March 20, 1930.

The three bills of lading, photostat copies of which are annexed to the libel, are alike in terms. They each acknowledge the receipt of a certain number of boxes of almonds of which the weight and contents were noted as declared by the shippers. On the face of each bill of lading also appeared a notation, "Weight and contents unknown." In the body of each bill of lading was the provision that the carrier was "also not responsible for the contents, weight and quality of the packages."

The libel is supplemented by a stipulation between counsel for the respective parties, made only for the purpose of argument on this exception. Annexed to the stipulation is a translation of the bills of lading issued for the shipments in question here.

It is stipulated (*inter alia*).

(1) That neither the boxes in question herein, which were received, transported, and delivered by the respondent, nor their contents, sustained any physical damage while in the possession of the respondent, or prior thereto, nor was there any shortage in the contents of any of the said boxes upon delivery thereof by the respondent to the libelants at New York, and the libelants make no such claim herein.

(2) That the bills of lading attached to and made a part of the libel herein acknowledged the receipt of 500 boxes of shelled almonds, and that the respondent delivered to the libelants at New York the same 500 boxes of shelled almonds that it received from the shippers at Alicante, Spain, and in the same order and condition as when received.

(3) That the capacity of a standard box for the carriage of almonds, as referred to in article sixth of the libel therein, is 28 pounds net of shelled almonds, and that the dimensions of such a box are as follows: Length, $23\frac{1}{16}$ inches; width, $11\frac{1}{16}$ inches; and depth, $6\frac{7}{8}$ inches.

(4) That the capacity of the boxes in question, which were received, transported, and delivered by the respondent herein, was 20 pounds net of shelled almonds, and that the dimensions of such boxes were as follows: Length, $22\frac{7}{8}$ inches; width, $10\frac{5}{16}$ inches; and depth, $5\frac{5}{8}$ inches.

The real gravamen, therefore, of this libel is that the libelant consignees did not receive as many pounds of almonds as they thought they were buying.

II. The question herein is whether the libelant consignees were deceived by the shipowner respondent so that it is precluded by any estoppel or otherwise from showing the facts of this case which obviously will prevent recovery from it; for there was no shortage of, no outage from, no damage to, these shipments. The shipments here involved were received and delivered in the same condition. If these facts can be brought out, the respondent shipowner must obviously prevail.

The libelants allege and contend that, because the bills of lading recited the receipt of boxes of almonds, it meant boxes of the usual size containing about 28 pounds each, and that consequently, as the boxes did not and could not contain so much, the shipowner is estopped to show that the boxes received and delivered as received were of the size received.

I think there is not any basis for such a contention. The receipt in the bill of lading was not in any way untrue. Guarded with the clause "weight and contents unknown," and accompanied by the recital, weight and contents declared by shipper, and the provision that the carrier was "not responsible for the contents weight and quality of the packages," the bills of lading could not properly have misled any purchaser thereof or justified his claiming that he was lulled by the terms thereof into thinking he was buying anything except a document of title for a certain number of boxes supposedly containing almonds, but for the weight and contents of which the shipowner was unable and, consequently, unwilling to vouch.

[More than two columns of the opinion, referring particularly to *The Querini Stamphalia*, 19 Fed. 123, and to the citation therein of *Jessel* v. *Bath*, L. R. 2 Exch. 267, are here omitted.]

The instant case involves a controversy in international trade solely between the foreign seller and the domestic buyer of goods, in which the shipowner is wholly innocent of the breach of any duty laid on him by the law.

A final decree dismissing the libel, with costs, may be presented for settlement on two days' notice.

In New Chinese Antimony Company, Limited *v.* Ocean Steamship Company, Limited, [1917] 2 K. B. 664 (Court of Appeal), a bill of lading for antimony oxide ore shipped by plaintiffs from Hankow to London with transhipment at Shanghai stated that 937 tons had been shipped on board. In the margin was a typewritten clause "A quantity said to be 937 tons," and in the body of the bill of lading was printed in ordinary type "weight, measurement, contents and value (except for the purpose estimating freight) unknown." Only 861 tons were delivered in London. In an action against the shipowners to recover the value of 76 tons, the trial court treated the matter as if there were a presumption against the shipowner because of the statement in the bill of lading that 937 tons had been shipped. An appeal from a judgment for plaintiffs was allowed. In view of the clauses quoted the bill of lading was not even *prima facie* evidence of the quantity shipped, but the *onus* was on plaintiffs to prove that 937 tons had been shipped.

Note further Pendle & Rivet, Limited *v.* Ellerman Lines, Limited, 33 Comm. Cas. 70 (King's Bench Division, 1927). Goods were shipped on defendants' ship by plaintiffs under a bill of lading describing them as "2 cases of wool and silk piece-goods Nos. 6854 and 6855. Gross weight 7 cwt. 3 qr. 12 lb." In addition were the words "Weight unknown," and a provision that the bill of lading should be subject to the Rules of the Carriage of Goods by Sea Act. Case No. 6855 was found on arrival at destination to show signs of tampering, to be empty of goods, and to contain only old magazines. It was apparent that if the statement of weight in the bill of lading was correct the case was not empty on shipment as on arrival.

Plaintiffs sued for damages for loss of the goods. In giving judgment for plaintiffs, Mackinnon, J., after reviewing evidence indicating on the one hand that the case in question had been received full by the Superintendent of the West India Docks and by the mate of the carrying vessel, and on the other that it could not have been tampered with during the voyage, continued, quoting Rules 3 and 4 of Article III:

"Now it is said for the plaintiffs that this bill of lading does more than was perhaps necessary — whereas it might have been obligatory to show only either the number or the weight, and they here have done both — they have shown two cases whose weight is 7cwt. 3qr. 12lb., and as they have done that, there is *prima facie* evidence of the receipt of two packages of that weight. Mr. Dickinson, on the other hand, says that that is only to look at part of the bill of lading, and that you must take in addition to that the added words in the body of the bill of lading, 'Weight unknown'; that though in discharging the obligation under Rule 3 of stating the weight, if the number of packages had not been stated as well, then it might be that he could not have relied on 'Weight unknown,' because that would be an unlawful thing to add, in view of the obligation to state the weight. But he says, 'if I have fulfilled the obligation under Rule 3 by stating the number of packages, then it is only a voluntary thing for me to add a statement of the weight; I can qualify that by saying "Weight unknown." That addition of "weight unknown" is not beyond my powers, and "weight unknown" qualifies and negatives the admission of weights.' It is a very subtle point. On the whole, I am inclined to think that perhaps Mr. Dickinson is right as regards that; and that the mere fact that, having said in the bill of lading that he had received two cases, he has then added the weight, with the qualification 'weight unknown,' does not bring him under the liability under Rule 4 of having that weight treated as *prima facie* evidence against him. But there is another aspect of it. Quite apart from the statement in the bill of lading, there is the various other evidence that I have referred to. As I have pointed out, if it were not for the subsequent history of these goods that the ship seeks to offer, no one could doubt that there was not merely *prima facie* but there was conclusive evidence that this case, weighing 2cwt., or whatever it was, was shipped. But there is one link in that chain of evidence that seems to me of the greatest significance, and that is the fact that the agent of the defendants signs the mate's receipt for these three cases, and signs it without any qualification for three cases weighing 10cwt. and 17lb. It may be that he did not weigh them. It may be that it was merely copied down by the Port of London Authority from the shipping notes. I should think that is very likely; but the mate is there to acknowledge the receipt of goods, and he has authority to do so; and if he chooses to acknowledge the receipt of cases of a certain weight, I think it certainly binds the defendants to the extent of being very clear *prima facie* evidence against them that they received on board the ship cases of that weight. In other words, that that which is provided by Rule 4 of Article III does arise by virtue, not of the provision of Rule 4 itself, but by proof of these other facts, and there is *prima facie* evidence that the ship did receive the cases as acknowledged. If that be so, then under Article IV, Rule 2, the burden of proof should be on the person claiming the benefit of the exception to show that these goods were lost, taken out of the case, without fault or privity on the part of the carrier, or of his servants or agents. Now, have they discharged that? As I say, if I accepted all their evidence, in a sense they have; but in another sense they have not, because that which they seek to prove is plainly inconsistent, and wholly irreconcilable, with the evidence of the plaintiffs. There is, in truth, a complete mystery about it. If I accepted all the evidence for the defendants it is quite a mystery. In those circumstances, one side or the other must win, and one side must fail. I cannot give victory to both, and I think the only logical result is that defeat must be upon that side on which lies the burden of explaining what would be otherwise inexplicable. In this conflict of evidence on both sides I think I must hold that the defendants have not discharged the burden which is put upon them by Clause (*q*) of Rule 2 of Article IV."

THE NIEL MAERSK

CIRCUIT COURT OF APPEALS, SECOND CIRCUIT, 1937

[91 *Federal Reporter* (*Second Series*), 932]

AUGUSTUS N. HAND, Circuit Judge. This is a suit in admiralty to recover damages in the sum of $2,600 to 6,000 bags of Japanese sardine meal shipped on board the Danish motorship Niel Maersk from Kobe, Japan, in February, 1935, by Mitsubishi Shoji Kaisha, Limited. Of these 6,000 bags, 4,000 were consigned to the libelants Bradley & Baker, and 2,000 to the libelants the Fox Company. Five bills of lading were issued, each of which recited that the goods were "shipped on board in apparent good order and condition." The libel alleges that the Niel Maersk was a common carrier, that each lot of merchandise was shipped thereon in good order and condition for carriage to various ports in the United States, but that upon delivery of each lot the merchandise was "not in like good order and condition as when received, but on the contrary the bags were torn and otherwise damaged and the meal caked, lumpy and otherwise damaged and depreciated in value."

Interrogatories were propounded by the respondents to the libelants regarding the history of the merchandise prior to shipment, what had been done by way of processing or drying the sardine meal, where it was packed, and whether it was taken to be laden upon the vessel on undecked lighters, to which the libelants answered that they were the consignees of the merchandise and had no knowledge of matters occurring prior to or at the time of shipment. There was nothing on the outside of the bags to indicate that the meal was not in good order. Upon later examination at the ports of discharge, however, the meal in question was discovered to be in a somewhat damaged condition.

Respondents based their defense on the failure of the libelants to prove the actual condition of the merchandise at the time of shipment and also on the exceptions in the bills of lading, of which inherent vice, heating, decay, putrefaction, sweat, rain or spray, change of character and the nature of the goods were the most important.

The District Court found that the meal was not in as good condition when discharged as when received on board and that this deterioration was due to heating and sweating caused by the carrier's failure to provide ample ventilation and furnish the character of stowage which fish meal requires, at least for a long voyage. After a careful examination of the entire record and the contradictory statements of the witnesses as to the stowage, we do not feel justified in differing with the trial court in its conclusion that the stowage and ventilation were not adequate for the protection of a cargo so easily damaged as fish meal. The Nichiyo Maru (C.C.A.) 89 F.(2d) 539. The questions on which the conclusion of the court below was based were purely of fact, and though we perhaps may doubt whether the stowage was not adequate, we should not reverse the findings of an experienced judge when the facts and the permissible inferences are not more certain. And, even if the cargo had inherent defects when laden on board, as seems exceedingly probable, the conditions of the stowage may have aggravated the damage during transit, though the extent of the damage, if any, which occurred on the voyage is impossible to determine from the record.

Assuming that the findings of the District Court as to stowage and ventilation and as to the condition of the meal when delivered were correct, we differ with the result it reached because there was no proof that the meal when shipped was merchantable or in a condition fit for transportation. Indeed, we find no competent proof in the record as to what was its condition. The tendency of fish meal to deteriorate depends on whether it contains an excess of moisture or oil. There was no proof whatever as to the oil content of the bags, and the only attempt to prove the water content was by the certificates by the Fish Meal Producers & Exporters Association of Japan. That association certified the moisture content at 7.29 per cent., which, according to the testimony of Manning who seems to have been the most disinterested and credible witness on the subject, was above the water content proper for transportation. But the certificates of the Exporters Association were surely not competent proof. They were in no way official documents entitled to be received in evidence, and without them there was nothing to show the condition of the fish meal when shipped. The recitals of "apparent good order and condition" in the bills of lading furnished only *prima facie* proof of the external condition of the bags. But their external condition would not show whether the contents were potentially subject to decay or had begun to heat up or deteriorate owing to excess of moisture or other causes such as excess of oil. Excess of moisture would cause the meal to cake or perhaps even to char, though a fish meal having a proper percentage of moisture might not heat so as to cake under the conditions of stowage in the Maersk.

It may be argued that some of the testimony indicated that the bags were soft when shipped and that this tended to show that the cargo was then in good condition. There is, however, much reason to believe that the bags did not externally show any caking, even when unloaded, but though they did, and had appeared soft and not caked when placed on board, that fact did not show that they did not contain too much oil or moisture when shipped or that deterioration from inherent defects had not then begun. The shippers had the burden of establishing that their merchandise was in actual good order and condition at the time of shipment. This burden was not sustained, and libelants accordingly must fail in their effort to recover damages against the carrier.

[The case of *Schnell* v. *The Vallescura*, 293 U. S. 296, was then distinguished on the ground that in that case the merchandise was assumed to be in good order when shipped.]

The libelants have not sustained the initial burden of proving the condition of the shipments when made so that they have not established a cause of action.

Decree reversed, with costs, and cause remanded, with directions to dismiss the libel.

[Chase, Circuit Judge, dissented on the ground that the trial judge was justified in treating good condition on shipment as established.]

Compare THE AKI MARU, 255 Fed. 721 (Circuit Court of Appeals, Ninth Circuit, 1919). Fifteen hundred cases of eggs were shipped from Shanghai under a bill of lading reciting that they were received "in apparent good order and condition." They were discharged in bad condition at Seattle. In a libel against the ship for damages, libellants introduced evidence of candling to show that the eggs were in good condition when shipped. Appellant, the owner of the ship, asserted that the eggs were in bad condition when shipped, and offered the testimony of Chinese merchants that the months in question were unfavorable for shipment because of their heat, many eggs being brought long distances to Shanghai over rough roads. In affirming a decree for libellants, Hunt, Circuit Judge, held, quoting the words of the court in *Nelson* v. *Woodruff*, 66 U. S. 156, that "in case of such loss or damage the presumption of law is that it was occasioned by the act or default of the carrier, and of course the burden of proof is upon him to show that it arose from a cause existing before his receipt of the goods for carriage."

In H. MUEHLSTEIN & CO., INC. *v.* SILVER LINE, LTD., [1935] Am. Maritime Cases 1229 (New York Municipal Court), rubber was shipped from Penang to New York under a bill of lading stating that it was received "in apparent good order and condition." On arrival at New York both the burlap coverings of the bales and the rubber within were wet. In an action by the shipper against the shipowner for damage to the rubber, judgment was given for the plaintiff although no evidence was offered that the rubber was in good condition when shipped. "Where the wrappings at the time of delivery were in such condition as to account for the damage to the contents, proof of good condition at the time of shipment need not be given."

Refer again to Brandt and Company *v.* Liverpool etc. Steam Navigation Company, *supra*, p. 735.

Note also The Carso, 53 Fed. (2nd) 374 (Circuit Court of Appeals, Second Circuit, 1931), where 1050 cases of cheese were shipped from Naples to New York under clean bills of lading reciting that they were received "in apparent good order and condition." The cheese in all cases arrived damaged by reason of having lost butter fat and being covered by maggots. A libel was filed by the consignees who had taken up drafts covering the shipment in reliance on the clean bills of lading. It appeared that all the cheese was damaged when shipped. As to 168 cases no evidence was offered that they were in apparent good order when received by the ship. As to 420 cases the mate's receipts contained the notation "broken, not answerable for contents," but there was nothing to indicate that the breakage was responsible for the damage. As to the remaining 468 cases the mate's receipts bore the notation "stained by the contents," thus indicating an exudation of butter fat from the cheese. A decree in favor of libellant was reversed as to the first two groups and affirmed as to the third.

Note further Silver *v.* Ocean Steamship Company, Limited, [1930] 1 K. B. 416 (Court of Appeal, 1929). Frozen eggs were shipped in cans from Shanghai to London under a bill of lading stating that the cans were "shipped in apparent good order and condition." On arrival many of the cans were damaged by perforations, some being gashes and others merely pinholes. In an action for damages by plaintiff as indorsee of the bill of lading against the shipowner, the trial court allowed recovery only for damage due to negligent discharge of the goods. Appeal by plaintiff allowed. Defendant was estopped from alleging that the cans were not in good condition on shipment so far as the gashes were concerned but was not estopped as to the pinholes, since these were not easily visible because of being covered with rime and because of night loading by inadequate light.

THE KERLEW — THE METTE JENSEN

United States District Court, Southern District of New York, 1924

[(1924) *American Maritime Cases*, 560]

Goddard, D. J. These are two libels *in rem* by J. Aron & Company, a New York corporation, against the steamships *Kerlew* and *Mette Jensen* to recover the sums of $204,332.49 and $85,775.16 respectively, for damages to shipments of refined sugar in cases delivered by said steamers to the libellant in New York, short and in a badly damaged condition during July, August and September, 1920.

[Both libels alleged in substance that the sugar was shipped in good order and condition at Hamburg, that it was not delivered in like good order and condition, and that libellant was indorsee of the bills of lading.]

To the libel of the *Mette Jensen*, an answer was filed by George Johannes Ingerslov Nielson as master and claimant.

To the libel of the *Kerlew*, an answer was filed by the American Ship and Commerce Navigation Corporation, as owner and claimant.

The answers are substantially identical.

They admit the shipment in each case and the issuance and delivery in each case of bills of lading to the shippers, Cohrs & Amme, and that upon delivery at New York, some of the cases of sugar were broken and some cases were slack.

In each answer the claimants allege that the cargo was well and carefully loaded, delivered and cared for; each answer sets up that the bills of lading, pursuant to which the cargo was shipped, provided, among other things:

"Second: The Shipowner is not responsible for damage, injury and loss arising from: * * * perils of the sea * * * shrinkage, breakage * * * or consequences resulting from these causes, * * * or damage of any kind brought about by the inherent nature of the goods loaded or by the packing being insufficient, weak or contrary to regulations." * * *

The answers then allege that if the libellants sustained any damage, which each claimant denies, same was due to perils of the sea, shrinkage, breakage or insufficient or weak packages and neither said steamships or the claimants are liable therefor under said bills of lading and under the Act of Congress of February 13th, 1893, known as the Harter Act.

On May 8th, 1920, the libellant J. Aron & Company, Inc. of New York, entered into a written contract, with Czecho-Slovak Sugar Export Company, Ltd., for the purchase of 1,000 tons of cube sugar in cases of 50 Kilos net. The price of the sugar was $44. per hundred kilos net, f. o. b. Hamburg, by cable transfer against ocean bills of lading. The contract further provided that the payment was to be effected through irrevocable credits of a New York Bank, which credits were to be confirmed to the seller by the Bank. Pursuant to these provisions, the libellant opened the two credits, each one covering 500 tons of sugar purchased. The total quantity of 1,000 tons was to be packed in cases of 50 kilos net, which would amount to 20,000 cases.

On or about June 25th, 1920, at Hamburg, 14,279 cases were loaded on the *Mette Jensen* and two bills of lading, dated June 25th, 1920 were issued for the master by the Hamburg-American Line; one bill of lading was for 10,000 cases and the other bill of lading was for 4,279 cases. The remainder of the 20,000 cases, amounting to 5,721 cases, were loaded on the steamship *Kerlew*. On June 30th, 1920, a bill of lading was duly issued for the master by the agents, the Hamburg-American Line for 5,721 cases. The bills of lading recited that the sugar was "shipped, in apparent good order and condition by Cohrs & Amme" and agreed to deliver the merchandise in like good order and condition at New York unto the order of the shipper. At the top of the bills of lading are printed in large letters the words — "Kerr Steamship Co., Inc." and beneath these words are printed in slightly smaller letters — "Hamburg-American Line, Agents." The three bills of lading in question are signed with a printed stamp, as follows:

For the Captain, Hamburg-American Line, Freight Department.

Beneath the printed stamp is an illegible signature.

Thereafter, the clean ship's bills of lading were presented by the shippers to the Hamburg Banks, which were acting correspondents of the New York Banks under the letters of credit previously opened, and on or about July 7th, 1920, libellant was informed by the New York banks that the bills of lading had been received by the Banks in Hamburg; that the Banks in Hamburg had paid the shippers for the sugar against the clean bills of lading. In response to this notice of July 7th, 1920, J. Aron & Company, Inc. paid their Bankers in New York the sum of $221,837.75 representing the purchase price paid to the sellers by one of the Hamburg Banks for the clean *Kerlew* bill of lading for 5,721 cases, and the clean *Mette Jensen* bill of lading for 2,279 cases.

On July 13th, 1920, J. Aron & Company, Inc. paid the New York Bank $221,100. representing the purchase price paid by the other Hamburg Bank for the *Mette Jensen* clean bill of lading for 10,000 cases. Subsequently the original clean bills of lading covering the shipments of the *Kerlew* and *Mette Jensen* were delivered by the Banks to Aron & Company, Inc. in New York.

The representatives of Aron & Company, Inc., did not see the sugar before it left Germany.

The *Mette Jensen* arrived in New York on July 19th, 1920 and docked at the pier on 57th Street, Brooklyn; the *Kerlew* also arrived on July 19th, 1920, and docked at pier 4, Army Base, Brooklyn.

Upon discharging the cargo from the *Jensen* and also from the *Kerlew*, it was found that many of the cases either came apart or were broken, and that the contents had come out. The evidence is convincing that the cases were made of too light material and were insecurely fastened, and were too frail to stand ordinary handling and stowage incidental to an ocean voyage.

It also appears that the shippers, in exchange for clean bills of lading incorrectly setting forth the apparent good order and condition of the sugar, gave letters of indemnity holding the steamers harmless against loss owing to the cases being of too frail a nature to stand an ocean voyage.

On July 27th, 1920, the libellant made claim to the steamers' New York agent for the damage, and on the same day received the following letter from the Kerr Steamship Co., Inc.:

July 27, 1920.

Messrs. J. Aron & Company, Inc.,
95 Wall Street,
New York, N. Y.

Dear Sirs:

We beg to acknowledge receipt of your favor of July 27th in which you state that the sugar tablets ex the S. S. *Mette Jensen* and S. S. *Kerlew* are being discharged, instead of in cases as called for in the bill of lading, in bulk and put into bags, and that you intend to hold this Company responsible in the event of any loss.

While we regret that this sugar is being discharged in that condition, nevertheless, our agents at Hamburg have received from the shippers letters of indemnity holding the steamers harmless in the event of this sugar being discharged in the manner which you describe owing to the cases being of too frail a nature to stand an ocean voyage.

This seems to be a matter, which should be adjusted between your goodselves and the shippers.

Will you please advise from whence you received the information that our employees are discharging this sugar without any regard for the protection of the goods.

Very truly yours,
Kerr Steamship Co. Inc.,
W. Goeppert,
Manager Inward Freight & Claim Dept.

The bills of lading, which are admitted by counsel for claimants to be the ship's bills of lading have printed on the top — "Kerr Steamship Co., Inc., Hamburg American Lines, Agents." The Kerr Steamship Co., Inc., entered the *Kerlew* and *Jensen* in the New York Custom House under their own name on July 19th. The master of the *Kerlew*, in an official manifest, filed in the New York Custom House, made oath that the Kerr Steamship Co., Inc. was the owner of the Kerlew. It is admitted by the claimants that the Kerr Steamship Co., Inc. was operating the *Kerlew*. The Kerr Steamship Co. Inc. advertised the *Kerlew* and *Jensen* as general ships in the New York newspapers over the name, Kerr Steamship Co., Inc. They demanded and received payment of the freight on each vessel. The claim agent of the Kerr Steamship Co., Inc. admitted that the Kerr Steamship Co., Inc. were the agents of the *Kerlew*. The Kerr Steamship Co., Inc. and the Kerr Navigation Co., the latter being the registered owner of the *Kerlew*, had offices together in New York, and called no witnesses to deny the relationship. The Hamburg-American Lines were the agents of the ships at Hamburg. It was the charterer of the *Jensen*. The Hamburg-American Lines was advertised in the Hamburg papers as the agent of the ships.

The evidence is also conclusive that the ships were negligent with respect to the stowage, care and delivery of the shipments in view of the known frail condition of the cases. The sugar which was in cases, the side boards of which were only ⅜ inch in thickness and the end pieces ¾ inch, each case containing 128 lbs. of sugar, were about 30 inches long, 14 to 16 inches wide and 9 to 10 inches deep. Such handling and stowage as they received would have been likely to cause the cases, which were of very light material and fastened together with too few and too small nails, to break and come apart, and an unusually large number of them did. I think not only is the testimony of witnesses convincing, but it is reasonable to assume that it was their stowage and handling that caused this, for it is hardly to be supposed that the ship received a cargo with so many cases broken and contents loose, as were discharged on the dock in Brooklyn. Moreover, their bills of lading state that they were in good condition.

"* * * A carrier who accepts goods of a nature which requires special care in their stowage must exercise such care, and failing to do so, is liable for the damage caused thereby, even where the character of the damage is within the exception from liability contained in the bill of lading." *The San Guglielmo*, 241 Fed. 969, 977. *Doherr* v. *Houston*, 123 Fed. 334, affirmed 128 Fed. 594.

There is no testimony to show that the claimants used more care than is ordinarily used in stowing or discharging the cargo, notwithstanding they knew of the frail condition of the cases. Possibly this can be explained by the fact that the ship had obtained letters of indemnity from the shippers to protect them from any claims.

Libellant's claim for loss of damages having been repudiated on July 27th, 1920, on the ground that the shippers had given letters of indemnity holding the ships harmless in the event of the sugar being discharged in a damaged condition, owing to the cases being too frail, seems to me to bring them under the rule laid down in the case of *Railway Company* v. *McCarthy*, 96 U. S. 258; *Luckenbach Steamship Company, Inc.* v. *W. R. Grace & Company*, 267 Fed. 676, 679; and *Robertson* v. *Garvan*, 270 Fed. 643, at p. 649.

Claimants contend that this rule does not apply to the case at bar for the reason that the Kerr Steamship Co., Inc. was not the proper party to address any claim for damage to, or had authority to bind claimants in this respect, but the record fully justifies the conclusion that the Kerr Steamship Co., Inc. was the agent of the steamers, was the proper party to whom the claim should be submitted, and did have the authority to repudiate the claim.

It is also to be noted that the claimants contend that no one had authority to bind the steamers by the issuance of a false bill of lading, yet the claimants themselves set up the same bills of lading as contracts limiting the steamers' common law liability. They contend that the ships were relieved from liability as common carriers for losses and particularly for the damage sustained in the present instances by reason of the second paragraph of the bills of lading, releasing them from damage as a result of insufficient packing, breakage, etc., and the Act of Congress dated February 13th, 1893 (quoted *supra*).

The libels are ordinary libels *in rem* to recover for damage to cargo and are not brought on the theory of fraud. It is the ships themselves which endeavor to take advantage of the false statements in their bills of lading. The shipments were refused by the ships because of the frail nature of the packages until the letters of indemnity were given to them; so they certainly knew that the statements in the bills of lading "shipped in apparent good order and condition" were not true and considered the sugar to be in such an unsatisfactory condition and likely to become seriously damaged, that they wanted protection. Certainly the libellant should not be prejudiced because the ships delivered to them false bills of lading which they relied on and acted upon, and which the ships knew were false. To hold otherwise, would be putting a premium on false bills of lading. *Higgins* v. *Anglo Algerian S. S. Co., Ltd.*, 248 Fed. 386; *N. Y. Millinery & Supply Co.* v. *Hamburg-Amerika P. A. G.*, 171 Fed. 577.

The ships were not compelled to accept a cargo insecurely packed; if they did so, and as a result of their handling the goods were damaged, certainly as between this libellant and themselves, it is only fair that they should stand such loss. They apparently preferred to assume this risk with an indemnity from the shippers, for they issued clean bills of lading.

Furthermore, the claimants could not claim the benefit of the exemptions in the bills of lading since they themselves had breached this very contract. *The St. Johns*, N. F. 280 Fed. 553; affirmed 263 U. S. 119, 1923 A. M. C. 1131; *The Sarnia*, 278 Fed. 459; *Niles-Bement-Pond Co.* v. *Dampskibsaktieselskabet Balto. et al.*, 282 Fed. 235; *St. Paul*, 277 Fed. 99, 106.

Accordingly, a decree may be entered in favor of the libellant in each action and against the respondent in each action, with a reference to a commissioner to ascertain the damages.

Compare AUSTIN NICHOLS & COMPANY *v.* STEAMSHIP "ISLA DE PANAY," 267 U. S. 260 (Supreme Court, 1925). Olives were shipped from Seville to New York in casks so weak that the agent of the shipowner refused to give a clean bill of lading without a letter of indemnity.. The shippers provided such a letter, and a bill of lading was issued which not only bore no notation as to the frailty of the casks, but contained no references of any kind to the order or condition of the merchandise. One of the clauses in the bill of lading expressly exempted the vessel from damages resulting from fragile containers. The consignees, who were the buyers of the olives, had directed their Seville bankers to pay the purchase price against clean bills of lading. The consignors thus obtained payment on presentation of the bill of lading in question, though there was nothing to show that the ship or its owner was aware of this arrangement between buyer and seller; nor was there any evidence that the bank was not aware of the circumstances. The olives were damaged on the voyage because of the weakness of the casks, and proceedings *in rem* were brought by the consignees against the vessel. A decree dismissing the libel was affirmed. The bill of lading did not affirmatively represent good order and condition, and there was nothing requiring that it should be given a different effect, either by construction or by estoppel.

KILTHAU *v.* INTERNATIONAL MERCANTILE MARINE COMPANY

New York Court of Appeals, 1927

[245 *New York Reports*, 361]

Lehman, J. The defendant carrier received in San Francisco several thousand bags of flour consigned to New York. The plaintiff is the owner of the flour through purchase of the bills of lading. The flour was stowed in a cargo space in defendant's steamer *Kroonland*. Part of the flour was found on delivery in New York "to be tainted with the odor of said shingles, and was thereby damaged." The defendant does not dispute liability for such damage. The controversy concerns the measure of its liability. The parties have submitted the controversy upon agreed facts.

The plaintiff was entitled to receive the flour in New York in good condition. He received it in damaged condition. It is not questioned that in the absence of stipulation in the bill of lading fixing other measure of recovery, the plaintiff should recover damages computed on the basis of market value of the flour at destination. (*St. Johns N. F. Shipping Corp.* v. *Companhia Geral, etc.*, 263 U. S. 119, and cases there cited.) In the present case the bill of lading does contain such stipulation. It provides that "The freight on the cargo carried hereunder is regulated in consideration of all the terms of this contract and is based purely on the value of the cargo. Unless a greater value shall be declared and written in the bill of lading as a basis for adjustment of freight and freight paid thereon accordingly, the value of general cargo does not exceed $100 per package, and of household goods or personal effects does not exceed $5 per 100 lbs., and in computing any liability of the carrier, no value shall be placed thereon higher than $100 per package of general cargo or $5 per 100 lbs. of household goods or personal effects (but in no case higher than invoice value) or the proportionate part of such value in case of any partial loss or damage." According to the statement of agreed facts "the plaintiff's damages computed on the basis of market value at destination amount to $1,802.08," while plaintiff's damages computed on the basis of invoice value in accordance with the terms of the bill of lading hereinbefore set forth amounts to $832.58. The Appellate Division upon the submission of the controversy has given judgment for the plaintiff for damages suffered, computed on the basis of the market value of the flour at destination, and has held that the clause of the bill of lading providing for lesser damages may in this case be given no effect. We are in accord with its conclusion.

The clause of the bill of lading now under consideration provides for limitation of damages to $100 per package unless greater value is declared. The defendant offered shippers of commodities of greater value than $100 per package, two different rates of freight; "a lower one based on the bill of lading valuation and a higher *ad valorem* rate applicable if the shipment is declared to be of a value higher than the bill of lading valuation." Here the value of the flour was much less than $100 per package. For shipments of goods of value less than $100 per package, the defendant had in effect only one rate, applying to shipments between San Francisco and New York, namely, 30 cents per hundredweight, the rate paid in this case. The limitation of value, for the purpose of fixing damages, to $100 per package was inconsequential here, since the goods were in fact worth less than that sum. Higher rates for carriage, if paid, were intended as consideration for assumption of greater risk. No alternative rate was made for restriction of liability below the limit of value of $100 per package. The recital in the bill of lading that the freight is based partly on the value of the cargo may be given no other effect. We are concerned upon this appeal only with the question whether in such circumstances a restriction of recovery to the invoice value of the goods, though actual damage suffered is determined by the value of the goods at the point of destination, is enforcible.

The rule is well established, at least in this State, that a carrier may limit its liability for damages caused even by its own negligence if the parties agree that recovery shall be limited to an agreed valuation which forms the basis of the charges fixed by the carrier, or where limitation is the consideration for other benefit to the shipper. (*Boyle* v. *Bush Terminal R. R. Co.,* 210 N. Y. 389; *Tewes* v. *North German Lloyd Steamship Co.,* 186 N. Y. 151.) Here the agreement that liabilities shall not exceed the invoice value of the goods did not result in a reduction of charges to the shipper. Limitation imposed without choice of rates between limited and unlimited liability is not valid. (*Union Pacific R. R. Co.* v. *Burke,* 255 U. S. 317.) At least in the absence of other special consideration moving to the shipper for a limitation of liability for negligence on the part of the carrier, such limitation is without effect.

Here the effect of the valuation clause is solely to limit liability. If market value at place of destination should prove less than the invoice value, the shipper could not under its terms recover larger damages. It provides no new measure of damages of which either party may claim the benefit; it leaves the usual measure of damages unaffected, except that the damages so measured may not exceed the invoice value or its proportionate part in case of partial loss or damage.

It is urged, however, that such limitation is not invalid unless it is arbitrary, and that here the limitation is based upon an actual valuation of goods shipped as stated in the bill of lading and is, therefore, not arbitrary though that valuation is different from market value at point of destination. Undoubtedly in some cases the courts have based decisions refusing to enforce a clause of limitation to a stipulated valuation on the ground that the valuation was "arbitrary." If the parties here had agreed that such invoice value should be the basis for fixing damages in all cases, it might perhaps be said that the valuation and consequent limitation was not arbitrary and should be enforced. Where, however, the parties by their contract have not changed the measure of damages, except to provide that liability may not exceed a sum fixed or ascertainable upon a different basis from that which is used to determine the actual damages, it seems impossible to say that such limitation is not in real sense an arbitrary limitation. The valuation used as a basis for limitation of liability bears no relation to the valuation used as a basis for the determination of damages. An agreement for such limitation should be founded upon special consideration or choice.

We recognize that in a considerable number of cases in the United States District and Circuit Courts, clauses which are in many respects similar to the clause under consideration by us have been held valid and enforcible. We need not consider those cases where the parties provided not merely for a limitation of liability, but for a new measure of damages, or have stipulated a valuation of goods shipped for the purpose of adjusting any loss that might arise thereafter. Such cases present, as we have already pointed out, a different question, and are governed by other considerations. There remain, however, a number of cases where the clauses provide only for a limitation of liability based on invoice value.

The line of Federal cases which have reached the conclusion that such clauses are enforcible begin with *The Hadji* (18 Fed. Rep. 459; affd., 20 Fed. Rep. 875) and *Pearse* v. *Quebec Steamship Co.* (24 Fed. Rep. 285). In both those cases the courts construed the clause as creating a basis for the measure of damages and not merely a maximum limit of damages. Based upon that construction, the court in those cases held that the agreement was valid and enforcible. In *The Styria* (101 Fed. Rep. 728) the court pointed out that the construction placed upon this clause in these earlier cases was erroneous, and discarded it. Apparently, however, the court did not consider whether under the correct construction a different conclusion as to its validity was not dictated. It merely assumed validity of the limitation so created. Similar assumption seems to have been made in *The Aline* (25 Fed. Rep. 562) and *U. S. Lace Curtain Mills* v. *Oceanic Steam Navigation Co.* (145 Fed. Rep. 701) and *U. S. Willow Furniture Co.* v. *La Compagnie Generale Transatlantique* (271 Fed. Rep. 184). In other cases the validity of the limitation was apparently either conceded or not regarded as in controversy. (*Phœnix Insurance Co.* v. *Erie Transportation Co.*, 117 U. S. 312; *Anchor Line* v. *Jackson*, 9 Fed. Rep. [2d] 543; *The Bencleuch*, 10 Fed. Rep. [2d] 49; *The Ellerdale*, 10 Fed. Rep. [2d] 53.)

In no case cited has any court given effect after reasoned consideration to a clause which provided for invoice value merely as a maximum limit of liability where no special consideration moved to the shipper for such limitation. In the case of *Union Pacific R. R. Co.* v. *Burke* (255 U. S. 317) the court stated: "To allow the contention of the petitioner, would permit carriers to contract for partial exemption from the results of their own negligence without giving the shippers any compensating privilege." We hold that such contract for partial exemption is invalid whether created by limitation of liability to "invoice value" or by similar limitation to any other value different from the value which forms the basis for determination of actual damages.

The judgment should be affirmed, with costs.

CARDOZO, Ch. J., POUND, CRANE, ANDREWS, KELLOGG and O'BRIEN, JJ., concur.

Judgment affirmed, etc.

In F. A. STRAUS & CO., INC. *v.* CANADIAN PACIFIC RAILWAY COMPANY, 134 Misc. 439 (New York Supreme Court, New York County, 1929), a through bill of lading covering a shipment of silk from Shanghai to New York contained the following clause: "All claims for loss or damage or injury to any of the goods . . . shall be adjusted upon the basis of the market value of the said goods . . . at the place and time of the original shipment, unless the invoice or declared value of the goods shall be less than such market value in which case such invoice or declared value shall be the maximum, and in any case not exceeding $100 for any one package, unless a higher value shall have been declared in writing at the time of shipment and *ad valorem* freight paid thereon." It was held that this clause was void because it did not offer the shipper any choice of rates.

Compare VENEZUELAN MEAT EXPORT COMPANY, LTD. *v.* UNITED STATES OF AMERICA, 12 Fed. Supp. 379 (District Court, Maryland, 1935), where a cargo of hides was shipped from Puerto Cabello to Havre under a bill of lading containing the following clause: "It is mutually agreed that, unless a higher value be stated herein and an increased freight rate specially arranged therefor, the value of the merchandise hereby receipted for does not exceed $250.00 per freight ton, and relatively for any portion thereof, or exceed $100.00 per package, and that the freight has been adjusted on such valuation. . . . In the event of any liability . . . in respect to the merchandise, no value shall be placed on such merchandise higher than the invoice cost, not exceeding $250.00 per freight ton, and relatively for any portion thereof, or exceed $100.00 per package, or such other value as may be expressly stated herein and agreed to." In holding that the liability of the shipowner was properly limited under this clause, the Court said:

"Although a much higher value is actually written on the bills of lading ($691,600), no higher rate of carriage was actually paid. Both the bills of lading and the stipulation make no mention of any freight rate, prepaid or to be collected; and, therefore, with the total absence of any evidence that a rate higher than the usual one was understood to apply, it is accepted as a fact that there was no understanding as to a higher rate. Libelant's contention is that, because the limitation of liability in the second sentence of article 5 (above quoted) is not expressly conditioned on the choice of rates recited in the first sentence, it is void; in other words, that the second sentence must be interpreted as if it stood alone, unqualified by anything in the preceding sentence, and that so interpreted it is invalid; and that therefore the entire article 5 is invalid. But the second sentence of paragraph 5 is qualified by the first, and we believe that the correct meaning of paragraph 5, in view of the valuation written into the bills of lading, which was very much greater than $250.00 a ton (nearly three times as great, in fact, on the basis of slightly more than 988 tons — that is,

$681,600 against $249,000), is that, although the value exceeded $250 a ton, and although the libelant had the option of paying a higher freight rate than it did pay and thereby making the carrier liable for a greater amount, it never negotiated for, or agreed upon, such higher rate, and therefore is to be considered as having elected to avail itself of the benefit of the lower freight rate, in consideration of which it is to be considered as having agreed with the representative of the vessel's owner that $250 a ton should be the limit of the latter's liability. Thus interpreted, such a limitation is valid."

In THE CAYO MAMBI, 62 Fed. (2nd) 791 (Circuit Court of Appeals, Second Circuit, 1933), a quantity of gunnies were shipped from Calcutta under a bill of lading which provided that the goods were to be carried to New York and forwarded from there to Cuba "subject to the terms and conditions of the local bill of lading." The original bill of lading limited liability to £100 for any one package. The local bill of lading limited the value of the gunnies to $100 per package. The gunnies were damaged by sea water owing to the unseaworthiness of the forwarding vessel. In libel proceedings against both vessels, a decree allowing recovery from the original carrying vessel on the basis of the £100 clause was affirmed. A general reference to the terms of the local bill of lading was insufficient to justify a limitation fundamentally inconsistent with the original one and injurious to the interests of the shipper.

Note the provisions of Sec. 4 (5) of the Carriage of Goods by Sea Act.

VITA FOOD PRODUCTS, INC. *v.* UNUS SHIPPING COMPANY, LTD.

PRIVY COUNCIL, 1939

[63 *Lloyd's List Law Reports*, 21]

This was an appeal by the Vita Food Products, Inc., from an order of the Supreme Court of Nova Scotia *en Banc*, affirming a decision of Sir Joseph Chisholm, Chief Justice of Nova Scotia, sitting in the Supreme Court, dismissing their claim against the Unus Shipping Company, Ltd. (in liquidation), owners of the motor vessel *Hurry On*, in respect of damage to a cargo of herrings shipped in that vessel.

The claim arose out of the stranding of the *Hurry On* at Grady's Point, Chedabucto Bay, N. S., on Jan. 18, 1935. The vessel was bound from Middle Arm (N. F.) to New York, and she had on board 1806 barrels of Scotch cured herrings, 133 barrels of round herrings and 37 half barrels of Scotch cured herrings belonging to appellants, who carried on business at New York. After a time, the ship was salved and towed to Guysboro, where the cargo was unloaded and forwarded to its destination. Between Mar. 6 and Mar 8, 1935, the herrings were delivered in a damaged condition to the appellant firm, and subsequently appellants lodged a claim for damages against the shipowners. The claim was tried by the Chief Justice of Nova Scotia on agreement by Counsel that the question of liability should be first determined, and that if the shipping company were held liable, the damages should be assessed later.

The short question raised in the appeal was whether the shipowners, as carriers by sea, were entitled to rely upon the exemptions from liability contained in the bills of lading, though the bills of lading issued by them and accepted by the owners of goods shipped from Newfoundland failed to contain, in accordance with the specific requirement of the Newfoundland Carriage of Goods by Sea Act, 1932 (which was similar in terms to the English Act of 1924), an express statement that the bills of lading were to have effect subject to the provisions of the rules contained in the Act.

None of the bills of lading contained any clause paramount incorporating the Newfoundland Carriage of Goods by Sea Act, 1932, or indeed contained any reference to the Act. The bills, therefore, failed to comply with the provisions of the Act.

The learned trial Judge, Sir Joseph Chisholm, in giving judgment, found that the *Hurry On* was a common carrier at all material times and therefore that the respondents were liable as insurers of the cargo unless they had contracted out of such liability; that the claims were founded on contract and not in tort; that the contract was wholly embodied in the bills of lading; that the mandatory words "shall contain" as used in Sect. 3 must be construed as meaning "shall be deemed to contain"; that notwithstanding the non-inclusion of the clause paramount in the bills of lading they were effective documents to which were incident the freedom from liability prescribed in the Rules; and that the claim accordingly failed.

On appeal, the Supreme Court of Nova Scotia *en Banc* upheld the decision of the learned trial Judge, but on different grounds. But although they gave various reasons for their conclusion they were all of opinion that the omission of the clause paramount rendered the bills of lading illegal and void, and that, the parties being *in pari delicto*, the claim failed.

LORD WRIGHT [after stating the facts]:

The bills of lading are in identical terms except as to the description of the goods included in each parcel, and it will be convenient to begin by stating briefly the substance of them and of the Act. The bills of lading contained, as already stated, an acknowledgment that the goods had been received on board for carriage to New York, with a proviso that they should be at shipper's risk while at the dock pending loading. There was a later clause by which in accepting the bill of lading the shipper, consignee and holder of the bill of lading agreed to be bound by all its stipulations as fully as if the shipper, consignee or holder had signed it. The bill of lading set out in detail the "terms and conditions of this contract bill of lading which are hereby mutually agreed upon as follows."

These terms and conditions, so far as material, may be briefly summarised. There were the usual exceptions of sea and other perils, and the usual exemptions of specified classes of damage such as leakage, breakage and so forth. Of these latter, Clause 7 is specially material in this case.

It contains a general exemption in respect of the goods carried from liability for all damage capable of being covered by insurance, and from liability above a certain value per package unless a special declaration is made. There follows a wide general exemption of loss or damage due to negligence of the shipowners' servants at or after the commencement of the voyage, or to unseaworthiness provided all reasonable means had been taken to provide against it. General average was to be settled according to York-Antwerp Rules, 1924, and adjusted in the country selected by the owners. The same clause also provided that "This contract shall be governed by English law." By Clause 8, the liability of the goods to contribute to general average and similar charges was not to be affected though the necessity for that contribution was due to negligence or unseaworthiness, however, that due diligence was exercised to make the ship seaworthy and properly manned, equipped or supplied. By Clause 22 no claim was to be admitted unless made in writing within 15 days after delivery or failure to deliver the goods. Provision was also made that in the case of shipments from the United States the Harter Act of 1893 was to apply. It was also stipulated that save as so provided, the bill of lading was subject to the terms and provisions of and exemptions from liability contained in the then unrepealed Canadian Water-Carriage of Goods Act, 1910, and the clause of that Act which declared illegal, null and void any clauses exempting the shipowners from liability save in accordance with the provisions of that Act was specifically incorporated. The Canadian Act only applies to shipments of goods from any port in Canada, whether to ports in Canada or ports outside Canada, and accordingly *prima facie* would not apply to a shipment from Newfoundland. In any event, the incorporation of the Canadian Act, like the incorporation of the Harter Act, would only have effect as matter of contract on the principles laid down in *Dobell & Co.* v. *Steamship Rossmore Company, Ltd.*, [1895] 2 Q.B. 408.

The Newfoundland Act, passed in 1932, recited that it is expedient that the rules agreed to as a draft convention for the unification of certain rules relating to bills of lading by the delegates of a number of States, including the delegates representing His Majesty at the International Conference on Maritime Law held at Brussels in October, 1922, and afterwards amended at a further conference at Brussels in October, 1923, should, subject to the provisions of the Act, "be given the force of law with a view to establishing the responsibilities, liabilities, rights and immunities attaching to carriers under bills of lading."

Of the sections of the Act, it is necessary to set out Sects. 1 and 3 in full. They are as follows:

(1) Subject to the provisions of this Act, the rules shall have effect in relation to and in connection with the carriage of goods by sea in ships carrying goods from any port in this Dominion to any other port whether in or outside this Dominion.

(3) Every bill of lading, or similar document of title, issued in this Dominion which contains or is evidence of any contract to which the

rules apply shall contain an express statement that it is to have effect subject to the provisions of the said rules as applied by this Act.

Sects. 4, 5 and 6 (3) contain certain provisions to which the rules are subject. Sect. 7 gives any Court in Newfoundland having jurisdiction to the amount claimed power to try any action for loss or damage to goods carried by sea to or from the Dominion of Newfoundland, notwithstanding any stipulation in the bill of lading or similar document.

The rules which are thus given the force of law are set out in full in the schedule to the Act. These rules, often called the Hague Rules, are identical with those scheduled to the British Sea Carriage of Goods Act, 1924, and have now been adopted with or without modifications by certain foreign States, including recently the United States, and also by the Crown Colonies, by Australia, by Canada, and by New Zealand. They confer rights and immunities and also impose liabilities upon the shipowner — liabilities which he cannot escape, since Art. III (8) avoids any clause or agreement relieving the carrier from the liability for negligence imposed by the rules or lessening that liability. But the Act and rules only apply where a bill of lading is issued and there is no provision making it imperative for the carrier to issue a bill of lading save on demand of the shipper.

If the rules are compared with the provisions of the bills of lading in suit, they agree in substance in respect of the relevant matters, viz., liability in respect of negligence and unseaworthiness. In some respects the rules go beyond the bills of lading, as for instance where they provide that the carrier is to be released from liability if suit is not brought within one year after delivery has been or should have been made. In other respects the bills of lading contain provisions which are outside the scope of the Act and rules. The bills of lading are furthermore documents of title which define the contractual voyage and provide for general average and for the obligation to deliver the goods which are received at the dock and actually loaded. Moreover, they expressly stipulate that the proper law of the contract is to be English law. It is necessary to bear such matters in mind when the central questions in the case are being considered, that is, the questions whether the failure to obey Sect. 3 of the Act is illegal under the law of Newfoundland, the place where the contract was made, and whether that failure renders the contract void in the Courts of Nova Scotia, and in either event what is the resultant legal position. . . .

Their Lordships are of opinion that the bills of lading were not illegal, and must be accepted as valid documents by the Courts of Nova Scotia. The precise meaning of this statement, however, and the reasoning on which it is based require elucidation.

The first question to determine is the true construction of Sects. 1 and 3 of the Act. Sect. 1 provides for the application of the rules to every bill of lading for the carriage of goods by sea in ships from any port in Newfoundland to any other port, whether in or outside that Dominion. The appellant contended that since Sect. 1 only provided that the rules should have effect "subject to the provisions of this Act," the rules could not apply to a bill of lading unless the terms of Sect. 3 were complied with. Their Lordships do not so construe the section. In their opinion, the words "subject to the provisions of this Act" merely mean in this connection that the Rules are to apply but subject to the modifications contained in Sects. 2, 4, 5 and 6 (3) of the Act. To read these words as meaning that the rules are only to have effect if the requirements of Sect. 3 are complied with, would be to put an unnecessarily wide interpretation upon them instead of the narrower meaning, which is more natural and obvious. In their Lordships' judgment, Sect. 1 is the dominant section. Sect. 3 merely requires the bill of lading to contain an express statement of the effect of Sect. 1. This view of the relative effect of the sections raises the question whether the mandatory provision of Sect. 3, which cannot change the effect of Sect. 1, is under Newfoundland law directory or imperative, and if imperative whether a failure to comply with it renders the contract void, either in Newfoundland or in Courts outside that Dominion.

It will be convenient at this point to determine what is the proper law of the contract. In their Lordships' opinion, the express words of the bill of lading must receive effect, with the result that the contract is governed by English law. It is now well settled that by English law (and the law of Nova Scotia is the same) the proper law of the contract "is the law which the parties intended to apply." That intention is objectively ascertained and if not expressed will be presumed from the terms of the contract and the relevant surrounding circumstances.

[About two columns of the opinion are here omitted.]

There is, in their Lordships' opinion, no ground for refusing to give effect to the express selection of English law as the proper law in the bills of lading. Hence, English rules relating to the conflict of laws must be applied to determine how the bills of lading are affected by the failure to comply with Sect. 3 of the Act.

If, however, by reason of this failure to obey the Act the bills of lading were illegal in Newfoundland, it would not follow as a necessary consequence that a Nova Scotian Court, applying the proper law of the contract, would in its own forum treat them as illegal, though the position of a Court in Newfoundland might be different if it held them illegal by Newfoundland law. A Court in Newfoundland would be bound to apply the law enacted by its own Legislature, if it applied, and thus might treat the bills as illegal, just as the Supreme Court in the United States treated as void an exemption of negligence in a bill of lading issued in the United States, though in relation to the carriage of goods to England in an English ship (the *Montana* (*Liverpool and Great Western Steam Company* v. *Phenix Insurance Company*), 129 U.S. 397). Such a clause, it was held, was against public policy and void by the law of the United States, which was not only the law of the forum but was also held to be the proper law of the contract. This decision may be contrasted with *In re Missouri Steamship Company*, 42 Ch. D. 321, where in similar circumstances the Court of Appeal, holding the proper law of the bill of lading to be English, held that English law did not apply the American rule of public policy though the shipment took place in America and the bill of lading was issued there, and that the clause being valid in English law must receive effect.

With these considerations in mind it is necessary first to consider if the bills of lading are illegal by Newfoundland law. If they are not, the question of illegality cannot arise in the Courts of another jurisdiction, e.g., those of Nova Scotia. Illegality is a concept of so many varying and diverse applications that in each case it is necessary to scrutinise the particular circumstances with precision in order to determine if there is illegality and if so what is its effect. . . .

Each case has to be considered on its merits. Nor must it be forgotten that the rule by which contracts not expressly forbidden by statute or declared to be void, are in proper cases nullified for disobedience to a statute, is a rule of public policy only, and public policy understood in a wider sense may at times be better served by refusing to nullify a bargain save on serious and sufficient grounds.

Are there such grounds for holding that the Newfoundland law does in Newfoundland nullify bills of lading such as those in question? In their Lordships' opinion there are not. The matter can be tested by asking what would be the position if a bill of lading set out *in extenso* the exact provisions of the rules, but failed to contain an express statement in compliance with Sect. 3, that the provisions of the rules applied to it. Surely such a bill of lading could not be regarded as illegal. Or again, what is the position where not only is a shipment made in a Newfoundland port but the port of delivery also is in Newfoundland? In such a case Sect. 1, by its own force, imports the rules and Sect. 3 is merely an intimation of what, if the parties concerned are all residents or natives of Newfoundland and bound by that law, they must be taken to be aware. At least this is the position if Newfoundland law governs the contract. It seems impossible to hold that in such cases the bills of lading would be illegal and void. If that is so of a transaction beginning and ending in Newfoundland, and if such a transaction is not illegal, their Lordships do not think that such a transaction is to be treated as illegal because the place of delivery is outside Newfoundland and the parties or some of them are outside that Dominion and are not bound by its laws.

It is said that the rules are not made part of the contract save when there is an an express clause in the contract stating that they are to apply as provided in Sect. 3, and that to hold the bills of lading legal and effective documents without such a clause would frustrate the purpose of the Hague Rules and of the International Conference, which aims at an obligatory unification of bills of lading all over the world, at least so far as particular nations adopt them. The Act, however, does not in terms provide that the bill of lading is to be deemed illegal and void merely because it contravenes Sect. 3, nor does it impose penalties for failure to comply with Sect. 3, nor does it in terms expressly prohibit the failure. Indeed, there is nothing to prevent a contract of sea carriage in respect of which there is no bill of lading at all: see *Harland & Wolff, Ltd.* v. *Burns & Laird Lines*,

[1931] Sess. Cas. 722 (40 Ll. L. Rep. 286). The inconveniences that would follow from holding bills of lading illegal in such cases as that in question are very serious. A foreign merchant or banker could not be assumed to know or to inquire what the Newfoundland law is, at any rate when the bill of lading is not expressed to be governed by Newfoundland law and still less when it provides that it is governed by English law, and it would seriously impair business dealings with bills of lading if they could not be taken at their face value, and as expressing all the relevant conditions of the contract. It was partly for that reason that in *Dobell & Co.* v. *Steamship Rossmore Company, Ltd.*, [1895] 2 Q. B. 408, the Court of Appeal refused to treat the Harter Act as having any effect as a foreign law affecting the validity of the contract but treated it only as part of the English contractual document which expressly embodied it. A bill of lading fulfils other functions than merely that of setting out the conditions of carriage. It is a document of title which, if indorsed, passes the property, and which, if money is advanced upon it, as is done in ordinary course of business, passes a special property by way of pledge to the banker or other lender. It would be a grave matter if business men when dealing with a bill of lading had in a case like the present to inquire into the foreign law ruling at the port of shipment.

All these reasons seem to justify the conclusion that the omission of what is called the clause paramount does not make the bills of lading illegal documents, in whole or in part, either within Newfoundland or outside it. Sect. 3 is, in their Lordships' judgment, directory. It is not obligatory nor does failure to comply with its terms nullify the contract contained in the bill of lading. This, in their Lordships' judgment, is the true construction of the statute, having regard to its scope and its purpose and to the inconvenience which would follow from any other conclusion. If that is so, the bills of lading are binding according to their terms and consequently the respondent is entitled to succeed in its defence.

But on the basis that the bills of lading were illegal in Newfoundland in that their issue without the clause paramount was prohibited by the law of that country, it was argued that no Court in any country would enforce their terms and exemptions and the carriage would therefore be upon the terms implied where goods are taken for carriage by a common carrier, i.e., subject only to the exception of the act of God and the King's enemies. No further terms, it was said, could be implied nor could any reliance be put upon the provisions of the Hague Rules since they had not been incorporated in the bills of lading by the insertion of the clause paramount. The appellant contended that unless the clause was inserted, no contract between carrier and shipper which included the provisions of the Hague Rules was entered into. Nor could the Act be said to have incorporated them even in Newfoundland itself, since Sect. 1 only provided that the Rules should have effect "subject to the provisions of this Act," a phrase which the appellants maintained meant (*inter alia*) that the Rules were not incorporated unless the provisions of Sect. 3 were complied with. For reasons already explained their Lordships do not so construe the section.

But whatever view a Newfoundland Court might take, whether they would hold that the contracts contained in the bills of lading must be taken to have incorporated the Hague Rules or whether they would hold them to have been illegal, the result would be the same in the present case, where the action was brought not in a Newfoundland but in a Nova Scotian Court. It may be that if suit were brought on these bills of lading in a Newfoundland Court and the Court held they were illegal, they would refuse to give effect to them, on the basis that a Court is bound to obey the laws of its own Legislature or its own common law, as indeed the United States Supreme Court did in the *Montana*, *sup.* But it does not follow that any other Court could properly act in the same way. If it has before it a contract good by its own law or by the proper law of the contract, it will in proper cases give effect to the contract and ignore the foreign law.

[The balance of the opinion, amplifying the last paragraph, and refusing to follow or apply the reasoning of the Court of Appeal in *The Torni*, [1932] P. 78, is here omitted.]

Their Lordships are of opinion that the appeal should be dismissed with costs and will humbly so advise His Majesty.

In THE TORNI, *supra*, oranges were shipped from Palestine to England under bills of lading which provided that they were "to be construed in accordance with English law." The Palestine Ordinance contained in Sec. 4 a provision corresponding to that of Sec. 3 of the Newfoundland Act, but adding "and shall be deemed to have effect subject thereto, notwithstanding the omission of such express statement." In an action by indorsees of the bills of lading for damage and short delivery, it was held that the bills were subject to the provisions of the Palestine Ordinance.

Compare AMERICAN TRADING COMPANY *c.* QUEBEC STEAMSHIP COMPANY, LIMITED, [1910–1911] Revue Internationale du Droit Maritime 439 (Court of Cassation, France, 1910). A quantity of flour was shipped from New York to Guadaloupe under a bill of lading denying liability for negligence on the part of captain or crew. Such a clause was "null and void and of no effect" under Sec. 1 of the Harter Act. The clause was held to be valid. The inclusion of such a clause in a contract calling for the transport of goods to French territory, where clauses of the kind are permitted, shows that the parties intended the contract to be governed by French law.

Contrast COSULICH FRÈRES *c.* BARBER ET CIE., [1902] Havre 2.262 (Rouen Court of Appeal), where on substantially similar facts it was held that the clause in question, being prohibited under the Harter Act, was invalid.

2. THE BILL OF LADING AS A DOCUMENT OF TITLE

SEWELL *v.* BURDICK

HOUSE OF LORDS, 1884

[*Law Reports*, 10 *Appeal Cases*, 74]

Appeal by the defendants from an order of the Court of Appeal (13 Q. B. D. 159) reversing a decision of Field J. The facts are fully set out in the judgment of Field J. (10 Q. B. D. 363). Briefly they were as follows: —

In September 1880 Nercessiantz shipped machinery on the respondent's ship to be carried from London to Poti in the Black Sea, under bills of lading whereby the goods were made deliverable to the shipper or assigns, freight, primage, and disbursements to be paid at destination, in default the owners or agents to have an absolute lien on the goods and liberty to sell by auction and retain freight and all charges. The bills of lading indorsed in blank were in November 1880 deposited by Nercessiantz with the appellants, bankers in Manchester, as security for a loan of £300 advanced by them to Nercessiantz. The ship meanwhile had arrived at Poti in September, and the goods were landed and warehoused at the Russian custom-house in October. Nercessiantz disappeared, and after a year the goods in accordance with Russian law were sold to pay custom-house duty and charges, and realized no more than enough for that purpose. Meanwhile the appellants had indorsed the bills of lading to their agents at Tiflis with instructions to protect their interests, and had informed the shipowners that if the goods were sold to pay freight &c. the appellants claimed all the proceeds over and above the amount due to the shipowners for freight &c., but the appellants never claimed delivery of the goods. The respondent having brought an action for £174 8*s.* 9*d.* for freight and charges, against the appellants as indorsees of the bills of lading, Field J. who tried the case without a jury gave judgment for the defendants (10 Q. B. D. 363). The Court of Appeal (Brett M.R. and Baggallay L.J., Bowen L.J. dissenting) set aside this judgment and gave judgment for the plaintiff for the amount claimed (13 Q. B. D. 159). The defendants appealed.

EARL OF SELBORNE L.C. My Lords, this appeal raises the question whether under the Bills of Lading Act of 1855 (18 & 19 Vict. c. 111) every holder of a bill of lading, indorsed in blank, who has taken it by way of security for an advance of money (and has not afterwards parted with it) is liable, by reason of such indorsement only, to an action for freight by the shipowners; although he may not have obtained delivery of the goods or derived any other benefit from his security.

The goods in this case were, by the terms of the bill of lading, deliverable at Poti, a Russian port on the Black Sea, and had been landed and warehoused there in a public warehouse (no one appearing to claim or take charge of them) before the date of the indorsement. This was their position when the present action was brought by the respondent, the shipowner, against the appellants, who are bankers at Manchester, and who had advanced £300 to the shipper upon the security of the bill of lading. In his statement of claim the plaintiff alleged that the goods still remained at Poti under the care of the Russian authorities; that the plaintiff had under Russian law no power of selling them for the purpose of paying himself the amount claimed in the action (£174 8*s.* 9*d.* and interest); and that the Russian authorities were about to sell the same for a sum barely sufficient to cover the Customs duties and Government charges thereon. They were, in fact, sold by the Russian authorities, and did not realise more than the amount of those duties and charges.

Under these circumstances, Field J. (who tried the case without a jury) gave judgment for the defendants (the appellants here). That judgment was reversed by a majority (Brett M.R. and Baggallay L.J.) of the judges in the Court of Appeal, Bowen L.J. dissenting.

The difference between those learned judges mainly (if not altogether) turned upon the question, whether, according to the authorities from *Lickbarrow* v. *Mason* (1 Sm. L. C. 753, 8th ed.) downwards, the effect of an indorsement and deposit of a bill of lading, while the goods are *in transitu*, by way of security for a loan, is to pass the whole legal title to the goods, or only to pledge them, passing at law a "special property" and leaving the "general property" in the shipper. That question was much debated in *Glyn Mills & Co.* v. *East and West India Dock Company* (6 Q. B. D. 475) where Brett L.J. expressed the same opinion on which he acted in the present case, Bramwell L.J. taking the opposite view. My noble friend Lord Blackburn, in his opinion on that case, when it reached this House adverted to the point but thought it unnecessary to express any opinion upon it (7 App. Cas. 606).

In the present case the true question is whether "the property" in the goods "passed to the indorsee upon or by reason of the indorsement," within the meaning of those words, as used in the Bills of Lading Act of 1855? It was considered by Brett M.R. and Baggallay L.J. that if the effect of the indorsement and deposit was (as they thought) to pass the whole legal title to the goods to the appellants as indorsees, leaving an equitable interest only in the shipper, it was a necessary consequence that "the property passed" to them within the meaning of the statute, and that the respondent, the shipowner, was entitled to recover under the statute in this action. They clearly used the words "legal" and "equitable" in that technical sense which they have acquired in English law.

I am not myself satisfied that this consequence is necessary; but I admit that there are difficulties in the way of the contrary view; as there are also difficulties (arising from the strong and unqualified language used by judges of great authority, from the time when *Lickbarrow* v. *Mason* (5 T. R. 683) was decided downwards) in the way of the opinion that an indorsement and deposit of a bill of lading in a case like the present operates by way of pledge, and not as an assignment of the whole legal title to the goods. The facts here are simply an indorsement in blank and deposit of the bills of lading, so indorsed, by way of security for money advanced. There are no special circumstances, except that the indorsee never did obtain, and that it was never possible for him (in fact) to obtain, delivery of the goods.

I should not feel greatly embarrassed (if there were no other authority) by the mere terms in which the custom of merchants was found in *Lickbarrow* v. *Mason* (5 T. R. 683); namely, that "bills of lading are after the shipment, and before the voyage performed, negotiable and transferable by the shipper's indorsement and delivery, . . . and that by such indorsement and delivery the property in such goods is transferred." This, it may be said, is the language of the Bills of Lading Act. But I do not understand it is necessarily meaning more than that "the property" which it might be the intent of the transaction to transfer, whether special or general, passes by such an indorsement, according to the custom of merchants. The finding must be reasonably understood; it cannot (for instance) mean that the property will be transferred when there is no consideration.

[After reviewing the cases, the Lord Chancellor continued:]

In such a conflict, not of decisions but of judicial phraseology, if not doctrines, it becomes important to remember that it is often dangerous to infer, even from very strong words, when used *diverso intuitu,* conclusions on other subjects which if they had been present to the minds of the speakers, might perhaps have led to their being more guarded or qualified. None of the cases to which I have referred arose upon the statute with which your Lordships have now to deal, they related, some to the right of stoppage *in transitu,* some to competing claims between holders for value of different parts of the same set of bills of lading. It may well be that, as against all such claims, and against parties setting up interests adverse to the title of the indorsee for value, such words as "the legal ownership," "the legal right," "the right of property in the goods," might be used, and the property which passed to the indorsee might be described as "absolute" in a sense substantially true, even though such property might, as between the indorsee receiving and the shipper depositing the bill of lading by way of security, be special only and not general; and though the most apt term for a scientific definition of the transaction as between the borrower and the lender, may be, not assignment or transfer, but pledge.

In such a state of authority it is important to see how the matter stands in principle.

In principle the custom of merchants as found in *Lickbarrow* v. *Mason* (5 T. R. 683) seems to be as much applicable and available to pass a special property at law by the indorsement (when that is the intent of the transaction) as to pass the general property when the transaction is, e.g., one of sale. In principle also there seems to be nothing in the nature of a contract to give security by the delivery of a bill of lading indorsed in blank, which requires more in order to give it full effect, than a pledge accompanied by a power to obtain delivery of the goods when they arrive, and (if necessary) to realize them for the purpose of the security. Whether the indorsee when he takes delivery to himself may not be entitled to assume, and may not be held to assume towards the shipowner, the position of full proprietor, is a different question. But, so long at all events as the goods are *in transitu*, there seems to be no reason why the shipper's title should be displaced any further than the nature and intent of the transaction requires. This is not inconsistent with what was said by Erle C.J. in *Meyerstein* v. *Barber* (Law Rep. 2 C. P. 45), that "the indorsement and delivery of the bill of lading while the ship is at sea, operate exactly the same as the delivery of the goods themselves to the assignee after the ship's arrival would do." That learned judge cannot have meant that possession of the symbol is for every purpose the same thing as actual possession of the goods; what he did mean was, that the indorsement and delivery of the bill of lading by way of pledge (which he considered to be the effect of the transaction in that case) was equivalent, and not more than equivalent, to a delivery by way of pledge of the goods themselves. Lord Hardwicke (1 Atk. 249) thought that there was a difference between an indorsement of a bill of lading in blank and a personal indorsement, and (for some purposes) I think there is much reason for that opinion. If, from a personal indorsement, the inference might properly be drawn that a title by assignment, as distinguished from pledge, was meant to pass to the indorsee, it would not, in my opinion, follow that the same inference ought to be drawn from an indorsement in blank. Part of the custom of merchants, found in *Lickbarrow* v. *Mason* (5 T. R. 683), was that "indorsements of bills of lading in blank may be filled up by the person to whom they are delivered or transmitted, with words ordering the delivery of goods to be made to such person; and, according to the practice of merchants, the same when filled up have the same operation as if it had been done by the shipper." Whether it is or is not usual in practice to fill up the blank with any name before taking delivery, it is certainly not to be implied from the custom as thus found that the operation of the indorsement, while it remains in blank, is necessarily to all intents and purposes the same as if it were filled up with the holder's name. So long as it remains in blank it may pass from hand to hand by mere delivery, or it may be redelivered to the shipper without any new transfer or indorsement, which would not be the case if there were a personal indorsement. It would be strange if the Bills of Lading Act has made a person whose name has never been upon the bill of lading, and who (as between himself and the shipowner) has never acted upon it, liable to an action by the shipowner upon a contract to which he was not a party.

I am not however sure, that, for the decision of the present appeal, it is really necessary to rely, either upon any difference between a personal indorsement and one in blank, or upon the distinction between such a form of security as (in English law) might be held to pass the whole legal title, and a simple pledge. . . .

The statute contemplates the passing of "the property in the goods" by the indorsement of the bill of lading, as a thing which may, or may not, happen, according to the nature and intent of the contract or dealing, for the purpose of which that indorsement is made; and it seems to provide for those cases only in which the property so passes, as to make it just and convenient that all rights of suit under the contract contained in the bill of lading should be "transferred to" the indorsee, and should not any longer "continue in the original shipper or owner." One test of the application of the statute may perhaps be, whether, according to the true intent and operation of the contract between the shipper and the indorsee, the shipper still retains any such proprietary right in the goods, as to make it just and reasonable that he should also retain rights of suit (the word is suit, not action) against the shipowner, under the contract contained in the bill of lading. If he does, the statute can hardly be intended to take from him those rights, and transfer them to the indorsee. If they are not transferred to the indorsee, neither is the indorsee subjected to the shipper's liabilities.

It is very difficult to conceive that when the goods are still *in transitu*, when the substance of the contract is not sale and purchase, but borrowing and lending, and when the indorsement and deposit of the bill of lading is only by way of security for a loan, it can be the intention of either party thereby, without more, to divest the shipper of all proprietary right to the goods, and to take from him and transfer to the indorsee all rights of suit under the contract with the shipowner. That some proprietary right (his original right, subject only to the creditor's security) remains in him is indisputable. If that proposition needed illustration from authority it would be found in the cases of *Re Westzinthus* (5 B. & Ad. 817), *Spalding* v. *Ruding* (6 Beav. 376), and *Kemp* v. *Falk* (7 App. Cas. 573). Can it be that he is by the statute deprived of all remedies, legal and equitable, under the bill of lading, as long as it remains in the hands of the secured creditor? The creditor, in the ordinary course of things, will do nothing until the time for payment or delivery of the goods arrives. Can it then be material whether the proprietary right, thus remaining in the shipper while the goods are *in transitu*, is legal or equitable? The statute relates to a subject of general mercantile law, in which not Englishmen only but foreigners also may be, and often are, concerned. Foreign as well as British indorsements of bills of lading by way of security for advances (which may be made abroad, perhaps in countries not governed by English laws) are liable to be affected by it, whenever recourse must be had to British Courts. It seems to me to be inconceivable that the construction of the words "the property in the goods," in such a statute can have been intended to depend upon any such technical distinction as that made in English law (but by no means in the laws of all other countries in which the customs of merchants prevail) between legal and equitable titles.

It is to be observed further that the statute contemplates *beneficium cum onere* and not *onus sine beneficio*. It may be reasonable if the indorsee has the benefit (as he would if he were a purchaser out and out, or if under his title as indorsee of the bill of lading he obtained delivery of the goods to himself), that he should take it with its corresponding burden, quoad the shipowner. But it would be the reverse of reasonable to impose upon him such a burden, when he has neither entered into any contract of which it might be the natural result, nor (having taken a mere security) has obtained any benefit from it. This observation is fortified by the fact that the statute does not appear to distinguish between indorsement subsequent and those anterior to its enactment.

On the other hand it seems impossible to suppose the legislature to have passed this statute without some reference to the custom proved in *Lickbarrow* v. *Mason* (5 T. R. 683), and to the law (whatever may be the true view of it) established on the same subject by later authorities in the English Courts. And if (as I think) it ought to be understood with some reference to that custom and to those authorities, I cannot persuade myself that its operation is altogether restricted to cases of out and out sale, or that an indorsee of a bill of lading by way of security, who converts his symbolical into real possession by obtaining delivery of the goods, ought never to derive any benefit from it. The authorities decided upon the statute itself appear to me to be most easily reconciled with its apparent objects, and with each other, by a view which, if hardly consistent with expressions to be found in some other cases, nevertheless seems to me to have a real and substantial foundation in reason and good sense; viz. that the indorsee by way of security, though not having "the property" passed to him absolutely and for all purposes by the mere indorsement and delivery of the bill of lading while the goods are at sea, has a title by means of which he is enabled to take the position of full proprietor upon himself, with its corresponding burdens, if he thinks fit; and that he actually does so as between himself and the shipowner, if and when he claims and takes delivery of the goods by virtue of that title.

[Three pages of the opinion are here omitted.]

Upon the whole I cannot dissemble that this case appears to me to be attended with some considerable difficulties. But those difficulties are mainly technical, arising out of a comparison of the language of the statute with various and not always consistent forms of expression found in authorities not decided with a view to any such consequences as those which the statute would produce. They deal with questions between unpaid vendors of goods comprised in bills of lading and *bona fide* indorsees of the same bills of lading for value, or between competing and adverse claimants to priority as *bona fide* holders for value of the bills of lading themselves. The statute, on the other hand, deals with questions between shippers and indorsees of bills of lading claiming under them, and between indorsees and shipowners. The preponderance of principle and reason appears to me to be against the proposition, that, as between those parties, it can have been intended by, or can be the effect of, the statute to make the creditor of the shipper liable (in effect) as his surety to the shipowner (with whom he was never brought in contact), by reason only of the deposit with him, by way of security, of a bill of lading indorsed in blank; his right under that deposit, being (whether at law or in equity) special and not general, and the shipper retaining (whether at law or in equity) the real and substantial property in the goods, subject to the security. It had not, until the present case, been directly or indirectly determined by any authority that such is the effect of the statute.

My conclusion is, that the appellants ought to be exonerated by your Lordships' judgment from the respondents' action; and that the order of the Court of Appeal ought to be reversed, with costs.

[Concurring opinions of Lords Blackburn, Bramwell, and FitzGerald, are omitted.]

CHASE NATIONAL BANK *v.* SPOKANE COUNTY

WASHINGTON SUPREME COURT, 1923

[125 *Washington Reports*, 1]

BRIDGES, J. The validity of a tax, levied by the authorities of Spokane county, in this state, against certain personal property, is the only question involved in this appeal.

Chronologically, the facts are as follows: The Bethlehem Motors Corporation, of Pennsylvania, sold eight auto trucks to the Northwestern Auto Company, of Portland, Oregon, for shipment to Spokane. These were shipped according to program. The Motors Corporation drew two drafts on the Northwestern Auto Company, one dated June 14, 1920, and the other June 30, 1920, for the total purchase price of the trucks. These drafts were made payable to the respondent, Chase National Bank of the City of New York. Attached to the drafts were the bills of lading. The respondent purchased these drafts, paying the full amount thereof, and credited the account of the Motors Corporation therewith. The respondent forwarded the drafts and bills of lading to its correspondent at Portland, for collection. The Northwestern Auto Company failed or refused to pay the drafts and they were returned, together with the bills of lading, to the respondent. In August, 1920, a receiver was appointed for the Motors Corporation. On September 3, 1920, the railroad still having possession of the trucks, warehoused them in the city of Spokane, and on September 22, 1920, a written arrangement was made between the respondent and the receiver of the Motors Corporation whereby the latter was to undertake to sell the trucks for the account of the respondent. On March 9, 1921, the trucks were assessed for general taxes as the property of the Motors Corporation. They were then in the warehouse where they had previously been put. The receiver, being advised of the assessment, wrote the appellant that he had no interest in the trucks and that they belonged to the respondent. On April 30, 1921, the respondent paid the taxes under protest, because the public officers of the appellant were threatening to distrain and sell the trucks for the taxes. Later it brought this action to recover the amount so paid. The lower court found that, at the time of the taxation, the trucks belonged to, and were the property of, the respondent, and concluded therefrom that the taxes were illegal, and entered judgment for the respondent.

The respondent contends that it owned the trucks at the time they were taxed, and that it being a national bank, incorporated and doing business under and by virtue of the national banking act, the appellant had no authority to levy the tax. On the contrary, the appellant contends that the respondent was at no time the owner of the property.

[A page of the opinion, pointing out that states have no power to tax the property of national banks except as authorized by Congress, is here omitted.]

But, to our mind, the more serious question is whether respondent was such an owner of the trucks as deprived the appellant of power to tax them.

The respondent, in its brief, asserts its ownership because "title to the trucks vested in respondent immediately upon the discount of the drafts and the endorsement of the bills of lading." After supporting the foregoing assertion with argument and authorities, it says: "But it is unnecessary to determine whether the legal title thus transferred was absolute and unqualified in respondent from the moment of discount and endorsement. If the property was special at that juncture, it became absolute when the Northwestern Auto Co. refused payment of the drafts."

[After reviewing cases cited on this proposition, the Court continued]:

Expressions may be found in a good many cases to the effect that, under the circumstances existing in the case at bar, the taker of the bill of lading obtains title to the property covered thereby. . . . Indeed, a few cases have gone so far as to hold that the purchaser of a draft with bill of lading attached, so far becomes the owner of the property shipped as that he steps into the shoes of the shipper and is liable in damages or otherwise to the purchaser to the same extent that the shipper would have been. *Haas* v. *Citizens Bank of Dyersburg*, 1 L. R. A. (N. S.) 242, and cases therein cited. But the great weight of authority has entirely repudiated this doctrine. See note to case last cited.

Generally speaking, in the cases where it is said that, when a bank purchases a draft with bill of lading attached, it becomes the owner of the property covered by the bill of lading, it will be found that the goods have been attached by some third person as the property of the shipper, or the money paid in discharge of the draft has been garnished. In our cases, heretofore cited, we have held that such attachments or garnishments could not affect the rights of the bank.

We do not deny that a bill of lading may be transferred under such circumstances as to conclusively show that the intention was that the shipper's title to the property covered by the bill of lading should vest in the transferee; but where, as here, a bank has bought the draft of the shipper and the bill of lading is attached, it seems to us manifest that the bank does not become the absolute owner of the property covered by the bill of lading — in other words, does not become a common purchaser of the property, but does acquire some kind of character of special property, claim or lien upon that property to protect it in the payment of the draft which it had purchased. Whatever interest it has is held only as security.

Some of the authorities hold that, by taking the bill of lading, the bank acquires a "special property" in the thing covered by the bill of lading for the purpose of protection or security. Others hold it thereby acquires a "lien or security" to protect its draft. 4 R. C. L. 33, says:

"A well established custom has grown up in commercial circles by which bills of lading as the symbols of title to the property in transit, are taken as security for money advanced, and indorsed and delivered as a transfer of the property, generally in connection with, and as security for, the payment of drafts attached thereto. . . . Such transfer of the bill of lading is regarded as equivalent to investing the pledgee with the actual possession of the property, and as long as he retains the possession of the property, either actual or symbolical. . . . It is a well established rule of law that after the holder of a negotiable draft with bill of lading attached has secured an acceptance of such draft from the drawee and consignee, he is unaffected by any equities originally existing between such consignee and the original seller of the goods. . . . It has been said that a special property passes to the transferee when a bill of lading with draft attached is delivered subject to be divested by the acceptance and payment of the draft; but until the draft is accepted and paid the possession of the transferee is good as against all parties. Opposed to the great weight of authority there are some cases holding that a transfer of bill of lading with a draft attached operates as a complete and absolute transfer of the goods and places the transferee in the position of the drawer in every respect."

In note 56, 7 C. J. 716, many authorities are cited in support of the assertion that "If a draft to which a bill of lading properly indorsed, is discounted by a bank, a special property in the merchandise described therein passes to the bank as security, which is preserved until the draft is accepted and paid." . . .

After all, this court probably stated the doctrine correctly in the case of *Wickens* v. *Scheuer*, 118 Wash. 614, when it was said that whether the purchase of a draft, with the bill of lading attached, will transfer the absolute title to the property depends upon the intention of the parties. If we adopt that rule as a guide, it seems that we must hold that, in this instance, it was not the intention of the parties to vest in the respondent the absolute title to the property covered by the bill of lading.

It is unnecessary to cite authorities in support of the statement that a national bank has absolutely no power to buy, trade and deal in ordinary personal property, and that it acts *ultra vires* when it so does. Of course, this is not to say that a national bank may not, under some circumstances, become the owner of ordinary personal property. Unquestionably, such ownership is authorized where it is obtained for its financial protection and its taking grows out of legitimate transactions. Such a bank may take a mortgage or pledge upon personal property, and if for its protection it is required to take over the property, the law will not forbid such act. If we accept the argument advanced by respondent, then it seems to logically follow that the bank here actually purchased these eight auto trucks, a transaction directly in violation of its authorized powers. It will not, therefore, be presumed that the bank intended to take the title to the property in violation of statute. On the contrary, it will be presumed that whatever interest it took in the trucks was for security only, or, as some authorities hold, a "special property." But probably this special property is nothing more than a pledge or mortgage or other kind of security with the exclusive right of possession.

If it be said that only the United States government may raise the question of *ultra vires*, our answer is that appellant has a right to raise it in so far as it tends to indicate the intention of the parties when the bill of lading was taken.

As before noted, the state has no authority to tax the personal property of a national bank. But this must mean such property as is owned entirely and exclusively by the bank, and not such as it may hold for the purpose of security. Our view, then, is that, by purchasing the draft with the bill of lading attached, the respondent did not become such an owner of the property covered by the bill of lading as deprived the authorities of the county of the right to tax it. It is not necessary for us to decide the exact character of the interest which the respondent acquired in the trucks—whether it was in the nature of a mortgage, pledge, or other kind of security. What we do hold is that, whatever its interest, it was held merely for security and that it did not become the unconditional owner.

[The last page of the opinion is omitted.]

Having concluded that the bank was not such owner of the trucks as deprived appellant of the right to tax them, it must follow that the judgment must be reversed and the respondent's action be dismissed. It is so ordered.

MAIN, C. J., HOLCOMB, and MITCHELL, JJ., concur.

Note also COCHRANE *v.* FIRST STATE BANK, 198 Mo. App. 619 (Kansas City Court of Appeals, 1918). Three carloads of peaches were shipped by a seller under a bill of lading to the order of the shipper. The seller attached the bill of lading to a draft drawn on the buyer and payable to a bank, the amount of the draft being credited to the seller's checking account. The buyer, having obtained the peaches without payment of the draft or production of the bill of lading, sold them and received payment. These proceeds were attached in the hands of the buyer by plaintiff in an action against the seller. The draft then being presented to the buyer was refused payment. The bank at first charged the amount of the draft against the seller's account, which was at all times in ample funds, but later recredited the account. The bank interpleaded, claiming to have been the owner of the peaches at the time they were sold by the buyer. In discussing this contention the Court said:

"Now, it is undoubtedly true that by the delivery to the bank of the bills of lading to shipper's order, the legal title to the peaches was put in the bank; but this may have been done, not to effect a sale of the peaches to the bank but merely to afford it security, just as the legal title to property is put in another by way of mortgage, so that whether the transaction was a sale of the peaches to the bank or was merely a transfer of the legal title as security, would depend upon the intention of the parties to be determined in the light of all the circumstances and their conduct in the premises. Now, the evidence is in such shape that different inferences might be drawn from the transaction. In one view of the evidence it might be taken to mean that Walters contracted for a sale of the peaches to Ward Brothers but before delivery he sold the peaches to the Bank and that at the time they were delivered to Ward Brothers the Bank was the owner thereof and was entitled to the proceeds. In which case, such proceeds could not be subject to garnishment for Walters' debt. On the other hand, the circumstances tend very strongly to show that, in the transaction between Walters and the Bank, a sale of the peaches to the bank was not thought of. In fact, it is hardly probable that the bank understood or thought it was buying peaches. The assumption would be rather that it was dealing in commercial paper — the objects of its usual and ordinary business. However, whether there was a sale of the peaches to the bank, depends upon what was the intention of the parties to the transaction at the time, and this intention is not determined merely by what they now say about it, but also by the transaction itself viewed in the light of their acts and course of conduct under all the circumstances. We cannot say, as a matter of law, that there was no sale of the peaches to the bank. Hence, we cannot, upon a reversal of the judgment, direct a judgment to be rendered in plaintiffs' favor. Neither can it be said, as a matter of law, that there was a sale of the peaches to the bank. Indeed, a large portion of interpleader's case rests upon the oral testimony of the bank's cashier, and, as his credibility was a matter for the jury to pass on, the trial court could not direct a verdict in interpleader's favor. Nor does the testimony offered by plaintiffs conclusively show a sale of the peaches to the bank. It shows rather a sale to Ward Brothers and Walters' testimony that he refused to consent to the charging of the drafts back to his account may be referred as well to his view of the law as to the bank's right to do so, as to the view that he knew he had sold the peaches to the bank. In fact, he never at any time said he sold the peaches to the bank but did say he sold the peaches to Ward Brothers subject to their guarantee to the bank that they would pay so much per bushel for them.

"We are, therefore, of the opinion that the case should have been submitted to the jury, under proper instructions, leaving it to them to say what was intended in the transaction between Walters and the Bank and who was the owner of the peaches at the time Ward Brothers received them. If the Bank took the bills of lading as mere security, then it released that security when it authorized the railroad to deliver the peaches without payment of the drafts. On the other hand, if it bought the peaches and paid for them by depositing the amount of the drafts to Walters' credit, then it was the owner of the peaches at the time of their delivery to Ward Brothers and consequently the owner of the proceeds of said fruit; and if the bank bought the peaches, it could not thereafter charge the drafts against Walters' account, thus rescinding the sale, without the latter's consent."

Compare COMMERCIAL SAVINGS BANK *v.* MANN, 200 N. Y. S. 587 (Supreme Court, Appellate Division, 1923). A seller in Michigan entered into a contract to sell a cargo of beans to a buyer in New York. The seller shipped the beans, took out a bill of lading to its own order, and drew a draft on the brokers who arranged the sale, the draft being sent through the seller's bank for collection with bill of lading attached. The brokers paid the draft by check, received the bill of lading, attached to it another draft drawn on the buyer, and deposited the duly indorsed bill of lading and the draft in its general account with the plaintiff bank. After the brokers' account had been thus credited, it was charged by the bank with the amount of a note held by the bank, with the result that the check given to pay the original draft was dishonored. On arrival of the beans at destination they were seized by a sheriff under a writ in a replevin action brought by the bank which had received the original draft from the seller for collection. The present action was in conversion. Judgment for defendant reversed. Plaintiff was an absolute purchaser of the draft and bill of lading, and in the absence of notice of any infirmity acquired an absolute title to the beans.

In DAVIS *v.* CARROLL, 30 Ga. App. 719 (Court of Appeals, 1923), an owner of cotton entered into an agreement with a broker for an advance to be made against the cotton of an amount less than the market price. The broker undertook to store the cotton subject to the direction of the owner, and to remit to the owner the difference between the amount advanced and the sale price when the cotton should be finally sold. In pursuance of this agreement the owner shipped the cotton to the broker under a bill of lading to shipper's order and attached a draft on the broker for the amount of the advance. After the draft had been duly paid, the cotton was damaged in transit by negligence. In an action by the shipper against the carrier, the defense was that the shipper was not the owner of the cotton at the time of the damage. Judgment for plaintiff affirmed. Title did not pass to the broker under the circumstances disclosed.

Compare Sec. 31 (a) of the Federal Bills of Lading Act with Sec. 1 of the English Bills of Lading Act.

LONDON JOINT STOCK BANK (LTD.) *v.* BRITISH AMSTERDAM MARITIME AGENCY (LTD.)

KING'S BENCH DIVISION, 1910

[16 *Commercial Cases*, 102]

Action tried by CHANNELL J. without a jury.

The plaintiffs claimed £258 8*s.* 10*d.* as damages for wrongful conversion and non-delivery of linseed oil which they alleged was their property. By their defence the defendants denied that the plaintiffs had or ever had acquired any property in the linseed oil.

The facts of the case were as follows: — The oil in question was shipped by Messrs. J. E. de Beer and Zoon on the S.S. *Maesstroom* for carriage from Amsterdam to London under a bill of lading dated April 29, 1910, which was made out in the name of P. H. Palmer and Co., as shippers, and which made the oil deliverable to their order or assigns. The oil was sold f.o.b. in Palmer's drums, cash against documents, and it was arranged that the sellers should retain possession of the bill of lading until the draft was paid. The oil was poured into drums belonging to the buyers. The draft and the bill of lading were then sold by the vendors of the oil to certain bill brokers and they sold them to an Amsterdam bank, who had an account with the plaintiffs. The Amsterdam bank sent the bill of lading, with the draft attached, to the plaintiffs for collection, and the plaintiffs on receiving same credited on May 2 the Amsterdam bank with the amount of the draft. When the vessel arrived in London on May 2, Palmer and Co. approached the defendants, who were the London agents of the Holland Steamship Company, the owners of the *Maesstroom*, and informed them that they had not then received the bill of lading for the oil, but that if they could have delivery of same, they (Palmer and Co.) would give an indemnity; and on these terms delivery of the oil was given to Palmer and Co. Thereafter Palmer and Co. went to the plaintiffs (with whom they had business connexions) and asked for an advance on the consignment of oil, and on May 4 this loan was arranged, and Palmer and Co. endorsed the bill of lading, which was still in the plaintiffs' possession, and gave them a charge. Some days later, on the plaintiffs' representative applying to the defendants for the oil, they were informed that it had already been delivered to Palmer and Co., who had disposed of it.

Channell J. In this case the defendants are the agents of shipowners running a line of ships from Amsterdam to this country, and Messrs. Palmer came to them and said: — "There are certain drums of oil for us; we have not yet got the bill of lading for them; it has been delayed in the post. Please deliver the oil to us, and we will give you an indemnity"; and in this way they got the oil. Those who so gave the oil may be taken to have known from their captain's copy of the bill of lading that the bill of lading was in Messrs. Palmer's name as shippers, and that the bill of lading made the oil deliverable to their order here; but Palmers did not have the bill of lading. What risk did the shipowners thereby take? If Messrs. Palmers were the persons entitled at that time to have the goods delivered to them, it seems to me that the bill of lading would be exhausted; its function would be over by the delivery to the right person, and that when that person afterwards got the bill of lading he could not by it convey an effective title to the goods. If it had been true that the bill of lading was delayed in the post, and that it came to Palmers the next day, after they had, in fact, got the goods, they could not thereafter by endorsement of the bill of lading to a bank, or anybody else, have conveyed any title to the goods, because, as I have said, the bill of lading would then have been exhausted. But whether it was exhausted depends entirely upon whether the delivery was to the persons entitled to it.

When the case was before me in the first instance all I knew was that the bill of lading had come from a foreign bank attached to a draft, and in a letter which contained no special instructions except to place the draft to the credit of that foreign banker. So coming without special instructions, the draft and the bill of lading coming attached to each other, of course the instructions would be to collect the draft, and not to part with the bill of lading except against payment of the draft. That is the effect of attaching the documents to each other. I knew that much, and there was in addition the invoice for the goods, but there was nothing to show how the matter had arisen, and it seemed to me that it would be unsatisfactory to dispose of the case without further information. It now appears that Palmers bought the oil from a Dutch firm upon the terms that they should pay for it against documents — that is to say, that the very practice I have referred to should be followed — viz., that the documents should be sent over here, and against those Palmers should pay. Palmers requested that the bill of lading should be made out in their name, and either they requested, or it was arranged between the parties, that the oil should be put into drums of theirs. Under those circumstances, the sellers shipped the goods themselves, but took the bill of lading in the name of Palmers, and they put the oil into the drums of Palmers. I think that the effect of that would be to pass the property in the oil when it was put into Palmers' drums and shipped in their name in that way, but the arrangement then was that, although the bill of lading was to be in Palmers' name as shippers, yet that the vendors were to retain the physical possession of the bill of lading until the draft was paid. The object of doing that was that Palmers should not be able to get possession of the goods until they had paid for them. Therefore, the effect was that, notwithstanding the passing of the property, if the property had passed, the vendors were to have a lien upon the goods which they could give effect to by keeping, not possession of the goods, but possession of the bill of lading. The general result, therefore, upon those facts is that, when the oil arrived in London, Palmers were not entitled to it as between themselves and the vendors, or as between themselves and the foreign bankers who had bought their draft, until the draft was paid.

What happened was this: After Palmers got possession of the oil they went to the plaintiffs, who, as it happened, were the correspondents of the foreign bank, and were holding the bill of lading as against the draft, and holding the draft for collection, and were the bank with which Palmers had connexions. Palmers arranged with the plaintiffs that they should advance the money to take up the draft. The plaintiffs did so, and they did so on the understanding that they were to retain the bill of lading of which they already had physical possession. The plaintiffs never parted with the bill of lading, but they got Palmers to endorse it. If the bank's title had been derived solely by that endorsement there would be some difficulty about it. I was referred to *Bristol and West of England Bank* v.

Midland Railway ([1891] 2 Q.B. 653; 61 L.J. Q.B. 115), where somewhat similar circumstances had taken place, but where it is clear that the outstanding bill of lading had been endorsed, so that at the time of the delivery of the goods it had been outstanding endorsed to somebody else, and the point that was there decided was that the persons who got a title, the date of which accrued subsequently to the delivery of the goods under the bill of lading, could, nevertheless, maintain trover against the persons who had wrongfully delivered the goods, because the carrier who had wrongfully delivered the goods was not entitled to set up his own wrongful delivery. It was held that he ought still to have had the goods, and he was not allowed to say that he had parted with them, inasmuch as he had parted with them wrongfully. Obviously, if that is the reason, it could not apply if the carrier had parted with them rightfully, and, therefore, if in this case Palmers had really been the persons entitled to have the oil delivered to them the plaintiffs could not subsequently acquire a good title as against the shipowners, but inasmuch as Palmers were not entitled in fact to the possession of the bill of lading and therefore not entitled to the delivery of the oil, it seems to me that the delivery to them was wrongful. I think the substance of the transaction was that the bank took over the rights of the foreign bank upon crediting them with the amount, and they perfected them by taking Palmers' endorsement.

The general result, therefore, is that the plaintiffs are entitled to succeed in their action of trover. In an action like this between parties, each of whom has an interest in the subject matter, the plaintiffs are not necessarily entitled to the full value. In this case the amount having been reduced by payments off on other securities the plaintiffs are only entitled to the amount for which they held the bill of lading, and there will be judgment for the plaintiffs for that amount.

Judgment for plaintiffs.

In First National Bank *v.* Henderson Cotton Oil Co., 157 La. 394 (Supreme Court, 1925), four cars of cotton seed were shipped by a seller in Texas to a buyer in Louisiana under bills of lading to the order of the buyer. The seller drew drafts on the buyer for the amount, and sent them to plaintiff bank for collection with bills of lading attached. On instructions from the buyer the carrier delivered the cars to defendant, who unloaded them. The buyer arranged with plaintiff to take up the drafts drawn by the seller, and in return indorsed the bills of lading over to plaintiff and gave plaintiff his own drafts on defendant. These drafts, with bills of lading attached, were dishonored. Plaintiff brought this suit as holder of the bills of lading to recover from defendant the value of the cotton seed taken and converted. Judgment for plaintiff affirmed. Defendant was not entitled to the cotton seed, as the carrier had no right to make delivery without surrender of the bills of lading, and the cotton seed was the property of plaintiff as holder of the bill of lading.

In Babbitt *v.* The Grand Trunk Western Railway Company, 285 Ill. 267 (Supreme Court, 1918), a seller shipped a carload of beans to a buyer to be paid for on arrival and took out a bill of lading to the order of the buyer. The bill of lading, with sight draft attached, was deposited by the seller in a bank. The bank forwarded the documents for collection. The draft was dishonored, and the documents were returned to the seller. On written instructions from the buyer, the goods on arrival were delivered to a third party without surrender of the bill of lading. In an action by the seller against the carrier for loss of the goods, judgment for plaintiff affirmed. Plaintiff was the lawful holder of the bill of lading and entitled to the possession of the goods.

Compare PERE MARQUETTE RAILWAY COMPANY *v.* J. F. FRENCH & COMPANY, 254 U. S. 538 (Supreme Court, 1921). A carload of potatoes was shipped to a buyer under a consignor's order bill of lading, which was attached to a draft on the buyer. The documents, duly indorsed in blank, were sold and delivered to a bank and transmitted to another bank for collection. The bank wrongfully delivered the bill of lading to the buyer without requiring payment of the draft. The buyer having arranged to resell the potatoes, and having the bill of lading in his possession, instructed the carrier by telephone to deliver the car to the subpurchasers. This was done without surrender of the bill of lading. The subpurchasers refused to accept the potatoes, the buyer refused to pay the draft, and the documents were returned to the purchasing bank, which surrendered them to the seller on repayment of the amount for which they were originally discounted. The seller then took possession of the car, sold the potatoes at a loss, and brought the present action against the carrier to recover the amount of the loss. A judgment of the Supreme Court of Michigan for plaintiff was reversed. Plaintiff was not a *bona fide* purchaser of the bill of lading, but took it back after the events in question, with full knowledge of them, and because of them. Plaintiff was not buying commercial paper, but a lawsuit. "Having assumed the loss of their own volition they should not be permitted to pass it on to the carrier merely because of its technical failure to take up the bill of lading. The delivery was made to one in possession of the bill of lading who could, and doubtless would, have surrendered it, had he not been prevented by distance from doing so. To hold a carrier liable under such circumstances would seriously interfere with the convenience and the practice of business."

Note further BANIK *v.* CHICAGO, MILWAUKEE & ST. PAUL RAILWAY COMPANY, 147 Minn. 175 (Supreme Court, 1920). Hoop steel was shipped by plaintiff to a buyer under such circumstances that title to the steel passed to the buyer on shipment. The shipment was made under a bill of lading to the order of plaintiff. The bill of lading was attached to a draft on the buyer, and put through a bank which sent both documents through another bank for presentation. Before presentation was made, and on arrival of the shipment at destination, the buyer directed the carrier to deliver the steel to a third person. This was done. The buyer refused to honor the draft. Plaintiff having taken back the documents then made a demand on the carrier for delivery of the steel and brought this action for their value when delivery was refused. Judgment for defendant affirmed. A delivery to the true owner is a complete defense to an action by a shipper who holds an order bill of lading.

C. E. WHITE & CO. *v.* CENTURY SAVINGS BANK

CIRCUIT COURT OF APPEALS, SEVENTH CIRCUIT, 1916

[229 *Federal Reporter*, 975]

BAKER, Circuit Judge. This is an action in trover, instituted by defendant in error, a bank at Des Moines, Iowa, against White & Co., a commission house at East St. Louis, Ill. Judgment for the bank was entered upon a directed verdict.

To sustain the charge of a tortious appropriation of the bank's chattels, the following proofs were made: On June 22, 1908, Hough was a stock buyer at Des Moines and was the owner and in possession of 319 hogs. He took them that day to the Wabash Railroad, which loaded them into cars and issued to him a bill of lading for their transportation from "Shipper L. R. Hough," at Des Moines, to "Consignee C. E. White & Co.," at East St. Louis. Hough on the same day took the bill of lading to the bank, indorsed it in blank, and signed a demand draft on White & Co. in favor of the bank for $3,900. On delivery of this draft and bill of lading the bank paid Hough the face value less lawful discount. From prior similar, but separate and independent, transactions the bank knew that Hough was a stock buyer who was accustomed to retain ownership of his shipments and to place them in the hands of White & Co. and other factors to be sold on commission. In taking the draft and bill of lading now in question the bank relied on the facts being, as they were, that Hough was the owner of the 319 hogs, and that White & Co. had no title to them, and no interest except to sell them on commission. In the evening of the same day the bank deposited the draft with the bill of lading attached in the mail; but, instead of forwarding them directly to a bank at East St. Louis, it sent them to its correspondent bank at Kansas City, with which it had an arrangement for avoiding collection charges. So the draft and bill of lading did not reach East St. Louis and were not presented to White & Co. until June 25th. In the meantime, on the morning of June 23d, the hogs arrived in East St. Louis and were delivered by the railroad to White & Co. Prior to this time White & Co. had continuing authority and instructions from Hough to receive his hogs and sell them promptly on commission. During the day of June 23d White & Co. sold the hogs. Hough never directly revoked his instructions. If his transfer of the bill of lading to the bank was an indirect revocation, White & Co. had no knowledge thereof until two days after they had parted with possession of the hogs.

Do these facts sustain the judgment in tort?

Ordinarily a factor must rely upon his principal's honesty or financial responsibility to protect him in dealing with chattels placed in his hands by the principal. No matter what innocence and good faith may characterize the factor's acts, he is liable in tort to the true owner or lienor against whom the principal's act of placing the chattels with the factor is a tort. This liability, however, is limited to cases in which there were defects in the principal's right of possession when he turned the chattels over to the factor.

If the principal has in fact good title and right of possession when he delivers the chattels to the factor to sell, the factor's possession is lawful, and his authority to sell continues until he has notice of revocation. In *Jones* v. *Hodgkins*, 61 Me. 480, for example, McLaine, principal, owner of logs, put them in possession of Hodgkins, factor, with authority to sell. McLaine in March sold the logs to Jones, but neither McLaine nor Jones did anything towards transference of possession. In April Hodgkins, without knowledge of his principal's sale to Jones, sold and delivered the logs to an innocent purchaser. Held, that Jones' action in trover against Hodgkins was not sustainable on these facts. But the principle there declared does not solve the present problem. There no bill of lading as representative of the chattels was involved, and the factor was in actual possession under perfect authority before and at the time his principal transferred title to a third party. Here the hogs were in the actual possession of the carrier under a bill of lading hereinbefore described, Hough had transferred his interest as owner to the bank as collateral security, and the indorsed bill of lading was in the hands of the bank, before White & Co. came into actual possession.

Nor is an answer found in any of the following classes of cases:

1. Where, as in *Reed* v. *Racine Boat Co.*, 156 Iowa, 12, 137 N. W. 458, there is an "order" or "bearer" bill of lading, requiring production and surrender of the bill before the carrier can lawfully surrender possession, in which cases the carrier and the innocent factor may severally be liable. For here the bill of lading is not of that kind.

2. Where, as in *Taylor* v. *Turner*, 87 Ill. 296, there is a "straight" bill of lading to a named consignee other than the shipper, under which the carrier may lawfully deliver possession to the consignee without the production and surrender of the bill of lading, and where the indorsee or holder of the bill of lading has in fact consented to the sale by the factor consignee. For here the bank did not in fact consent to the sale by White & Co. If the bank's consent is found, it must be as a matter of law, contrary to the bank's actual intent.

3. Where, as in *Means* v. *Bank of Randall*, 146 U. S. 620, 13 Sup. Ct. 186, 36 L. Ed. 1107, there is a "straight" bill of lading to a factor as consignee, and the factor, while still in possession and control of the chattels, has actual notice of his principal's prior sale of the chattels and transference of the bill of lading to a third party. For here there is in fact no question of White & Co.'s ignorance of the bank's interest and of their good faith in making the sale.

In our judgment the difficulties in the present case arising from an apparent conflict between principles concerning factors and principles concerning the rights of indorsees or holders of bills of lading are solvable by reference to the different aspects in which a transference of a bill of lading may be considered.

These are three: 1. As evidence of an intended sale, pledge, or mortgage of the chattels described in the bill of lading, the same as a separate document would be evidence. 2. As an assignment of the shipper's rights against the carrier. 3. As a symbolic delivery of the chattels, equivalent in law to manual delivery. It would seem that there could be no doubt that all these elements characterize the transference of an "order" bill of lading.

But is the third element present as against the factor consignee of a "straight" bill of lading? In our judgment, No. We believe that a "straight" bill of lading is not a true document of title, possession of which is symbolic of actual possession, and that the carrier's possession, though not for all purposes the actual possession of the consignee, nevertheless is on his behalf. Williston on Sales, par. 413. If the consignor be in truth the owner and the consignee merely his factor, the consignor may transfer his interest as owner to a third person. But for that purpose his assignment on and delivery of the bill of lading are of no greater force than would be a separate bill of sale while the chattels were in the actual possession of the carrier for the factor consignee. For, "strictly speaking, no person but such consignee can, by an indorsement of the bill of lading, pass the legal title to the goods." *Conard* v. *Atlantic Inc. Co.*, 1 Pet. 386, 445, 7 L. Ed. 189. In other words, though the owner consignor may deal with his interest as owner by separate documents (and they are separate even if written upon the bill of lading), he is powerless to disturb the effect of the "straight" bill of lading as against the carrier or the factor consignee without notice. And this we believe is just, because the owner is the one who creates the bill and selects its form. Necessarily the transferee of such a bill is bound to take notice of its form and acquires no greater rights than the transferrer had. And so the bank, succeeding only to Hough's interest as owner of the consigned hogs, and failing to prove notice to White & Co. of its interest before sale by White & Co., has not sustained its declaration in trover.

In addition to the authorities hereinabove mentioned, we have examined, among others, the cases noted in the margin.

The judgment is reversed, with the direction to grant a new trial.

Compare George F. Hinrichs, Inc. *v.* Standard Trust & Savings Bank, 279 Fed. 382 (Circuit Court of Appeals, Second Circuit, 1922). Eggs were shipped to a factor consignee under a straight bill of lading. The shipper attached the bill of lading to a sight draft which was discounted by plaintiff bank, the amount being credited to the shipper's account. The draft, presented through another bank, was refused payment. The consignee later sold the eggs on arrival, retained from the proceeds the amount of a debt due from the shipper, and remitted the balance to the shipper. Plaintiff brought this action against the consignee on the theory that it acquired title to the eggs by taking the bill of lading from the shipper. Judgment for plaintiff affirmed. Transfer by the shipper of a straight bill of lading passes only such rights as he had, subject to existing equities; but "if before the goods reach the factor's hands, or thereafter while they remain in his hands he is presented with a straight bill of lading and a sight draft attached thereto, which have been transferred by his principal, this is notice to him of what amounts to a revocation of his authority to deal with the goods under the prior instructions given by his principal, unless he makes payment of the draft."

In QUALITY SHINGLE COMPANY *v.* OLD OREGON LUMBER & SHINGLE COMPANY, 110 Wash. 60 (Supreme Court, 1920), a carload of shingles was shipped from a point in Washington to a point in Montana under a straight bill of lading naming the shipper as consignor and consignee. While the shingles were in transit a contract was made for their sale, the price to be paid on delivery of the bill of lading. Thereupon the bill of lading was delivered to the buyer indorsed in blank in return for a check for the price. The check was refused payment because of insufficient funds. In the meantime the buyer had resold the shingles to defendant and had delivered the bill of lading to defendant. Defendant also had resold the shingles. The purpose of the present action brought by the original shipper was to determine the right to the proceeds of the sale in the hands of the defendant, it having been agreed that the proceeds should be substituted for the shingles in the litigation. Judgment for plaintiff affirmed. Plaintiff had the same right to the shingles against defendant as against the original buyer.

Note also C. P. HENDERSON & CO. *v.* THE COMPTOIR D'ESCOMPTE DE PARIS, L. R. 5 P. C. 253 (Privy Council, 1873), where a bill of lading called for delivery "unto Messrs. Lyall, Still & Co." In discussing the effect of such wording, it was said: "It appears that a bill of lading was made out, which is in the usual form, with this difference, that the words 'or order or assigns' are omitted. It has been argued that notwithstanding the omission of these words, this bill of lading was a negotiable instrument; and there is some authority at *Nisi Prius* for that proposition; but undoubtedly the general view of the mercantile world has been for some time that in order to make bills of lading negotiable, some such words as 'or order or assigns' ought to be in them. For the purposes of this case, in the view their Lordships take, it may be assumed that this bill of lading was not a negotiable instrument."

FT. WORTH ELEVATOR CO. *v.* STATE GUARANTY BANK

OKLAHOMA SUPREME COURT, 1923

[93 *Oklahoma Reports*, 191]

Opinion by MAXEY, C. The parties appear in this court as they did in the court below, and will be referred to as plaintiff and defendant. This is a suit by the plaintiff against the defendant for the payment of an amount paid on a draft with bill of lading attached for $2,440 drawn by H. L. Tankersley and deposited in the defendant bank at Blackwell, Okla., which sent it through its usual course to the plaintiff at Ft. Worth, Tex., which paid the draft. The bill of lading attached to the draft proved to be a forgery. It was on the regular form of bills of lading issued by the Atchison, Topeka & Santa Fe Railway Company at Hunnewell, Kan., and purported to be for a carload of wheat shipped to Galveston, Tex. As before stated, the draft with the bill of lading was deposited in the State Guaranty Bank at Blackwell, Okla., being the defendant bank, and Tankersley was given credit for same on his account. This draft was dated January 26, 1917, and on December 30, 1916, Tankersley had drawn another draft with bill of lading attached, which was identical with the draft and bill of lading involved in this case, except date and amount. That draft was proved to be a forgery and a suit involving that draft was instituted in Texas and reached the Civil Court of Appeals and was decided by that court in May, 1919, and reported in 214 S. W. 656. The court in that case held the bank not liable. It is insisted that that case is not a precedent for the case at bar, for the reason that the act of Congress approved August 29, 1916, relating to bills of lading in interstate and foreign commerce, by the last section of this act, which is as follows: That "this act shall take effect and be in force on and after the first day of January next after its passage." It will be seen that this act was not in force at the time the draft with bill of lading attached was given on December 30, 1916, but was in force on the 26th day of January, 1917, when the draft and bill of lading involved in this case was dated. . . .

This act was intended to protect interstate commerce, and we think it does, and when you apply the provisions of the section above quoted to this transaction, it will be seen that all of the reasoning of the case decided by the civil court of appeals in Texas, *supra*, has no application to the transaction involved in this case. In that case, it was governed largely by custom and what banks and shippers understood the law to be, but in this case a person who negotiates or transfers for value a bill by indorsement or delivery, unless the contrary intention appears, warrants: (1) That the bill of lading is genuine; (2) that he has a legal right to transfer it; (3) that he has knowledge of no fact which would impair the validity or worth of the bill of lading; (4) that he has a right to transfer the title to the goods, and that the goods are merchantable or fit for a particular purpose whenever such warranties would have been implied if the contract of the parties had been to transfer without a bill the goods represented thereby. This puts the indorser or transferer in quite a different position to what a transferer was in prior to the first day of January, 1917. This act has been held constitutional in an opinion by Chief Justice White in the case of *United States* v. *Ferger et al.*, 250 U. S. 199. Counsel for defendant in error has filed a strong brief, but has cited no case where the Federal Bill of Lading Act was in force. The draft was for $2,440, for which plaintiff asked judgment, with six per cent. interest from January 29, 1917, and for costs of suit. We think that under the terms imposed upon the defendant bank by the Federal Bill of Lading Act, *supra*, the bank is liable to the plaintiff for the amount sued for. We, therefore, recommend that the case be reversed and remanded, with directions to the lower court to enter judgment for the plaintiff, Ft. Worth Elevator Company, for the amount sued for and interest.

By the Court: It is so ordered.

Compare ARCHIBALD & LEWIS COMPANY *v.* BANQUE INTERNATIONALE DE COMMERCE, 216 App. Div. 322 (New York Supreme Court, Appellate Division, 1926), where it was held that a bank taking for collection a draft with bill of lading attached is not liable to the drawee for the return of the amount paid on the draft in the event that the bill of lading proves to be a forgery, notwithstanding the indorsement of the bank on the bill of lading.

Refer again also to SPRINGE *v.* THE HANOVER NATIONAL BANK and other cases, *supra*, p. 699.

NEW IBERIA NAT. BANK *v.* TECHE CANNING & SYRUP CO.

LOUISIANA SUPREME COURT, 1925

[159 *Louisiana Reports*, 946]

OVERTON, J. This suit was instituted to recover judgment on a draft and a negotiable bill of lading against the Teche Canning & Syrup Co., Inc., hereinafter referred to as the canning company, and S. O. Nuckolls, in solido, for the sum of $5,312.05 with legal interest thereon from January 3, 1919.

The suit is based on allegations showing that Nuckolls represented to plaintiff that he was the agent of the canning company and had sold to H. H. Watson of Longview, Tex., for the account of his principal, a carload of pure Louisiana cane syrup, consisting of 970 cases, for the price and sum of $5.85 per case, or a total price of $5,312.05; that Nuckolls, upon making these representations, requested plaintiff to advance the purchase price of the syrup pending the delivery thereof to the purchaser; that on or about January 3, 1919, pursuant to the foregoing request, plaintiff paid to Nuckolls the sum of $5,312.05, all of which he immediately paid to the canning company except the sum of about $500, which he retained as his commission; that, at the time said payment was made, Nuckolls delivered to plaintiff a draft for the aforesaid sum, payable on arrival of the car of syrup, to plaintiff's order, and delivered to plaintiff a negotiable bill of lading, dated January 3, 1919, reciting that the railway company had received at Enterprise, La., from the canning company, 970 cases of cane syrup, consigned to the order of S. O. Nuckolls, Longview, Tex.; that in due course the syrup was transported by rail to Longview; that, when the syrup arrived at its destination, it was in a state of fermentation, was not salable, and could not be made into a salable product without being reprocessed; that Watson refused to pay the draft on the ground that the syrup was not merchantable; that plaintiff immediately reported the condition of the syrup, and the fact that Watson refused to pay the draft, to Nuckolls and to the canning company, and called upon them to take steps immediately to prevent the absolute loss of the syrup, and to repay it the amount advanced, but that Nuckolls and the canning company refused to comply with said demand; that there was no refinery or other place at Longview, Tex., at which the syrup could be reprocessed, and none nearer than the refinery of the canning company; that, under the Uniform Bill of Lading Act of this state (Act No. 94 of 1912), and under the Bill of Lading Act of the United States (U. S. Comp. St. §§ 8604aaa–8604w), one who transfers or negotiates for value a bill of lading by indorsement or delivery, including one who assigns for value a claim secured by a bill, warrants that the goods are merchantable or fit for a particular purpose; that plaintiff advanced the aforesaid sum of money on the faith of the representations of the canning company and of its agent Nuckolls, and of the warranty implied by law that the goods were merchantable. The petition concludes with a prayer for judgment against Nuckolls and the canning company in solido for the aforesaid sum of $5,312.05, with legal interest as stated above.

Against the foregoing demand, Nuckolls filed an exception of no cause of action, based upon the theory that, as plaintiff alleged that he (Nuckolls) was acting, in conducting said transaction, as the agent of the canning company, the transaction was not his, and therefore that he is not liable under the allegations of fact contained in the petition. The trial court sustained this exception. No appeal was taken from the judgment sustaining it. In fact, the case as against Nuckolls has been abandoned; hence the suit, at present, is one only against the canning company.

The canning company also appeared and filed an exception of no cause of action. The theory upon which the exception filed by it is based is that the suit is one upon a draft only; that the draft upon which the suit is based is a foreign bill; that no allegation is made that the bill was protested for nonpayment; and that, in the absence of such an allegation, the petition discloses no cause of action.

In our view, the suit is not merely upon a draft, but is also upon the bill of lading delivered by Nuckolls to the bank. When plaintiff cashed the draft with the bill of lading attached, it became, to all intents and purposes, the owner of the bill and of the merchandise which it represented. *First National Bank* v. *Henderson Cotton Co.*, 157 La. 394, 102 So. 501; *Aleman Planting & Mfg. Co.* v. *Hines*, 157 La. 625, 102 So. 815. Such being the case, plaintiff, as holder of the bill of lading, has the right to sue the canning company, which signed it as shipper, under that company's warranty that the merchandise represented by the bill was merchantable and fit for the purpose for which it was manufactured. In order for plaintiff to sue the canning company on the bill of lading, under its warranty, it is immaterial whether it appears that the draft was protested or not. In so far as the canning company is concerned, the allegations in plaintiff's petition concerning the draft may be considered as merely serving to show how and under what circumstances plaintiff acquired the bill of lading.

As plaintiff has the right to sue on the bill of lading without reference to the draft, our conclusion is that the exception was properly overruled.

[Over three pages of the opinion, concluding that fermentation was due to the fact that the syrup was not properly prepared and canned, are here omitted.]

When the canning company sold to Nuckolls, it impliedly warranted, in the absence of anything to the contrary, and there is nothing to the contrary, that the syrup, which was intended to be put upon the market as an article of food, was properly prepared and canned, for, if it was not properly prepared and canned, it would fail to serve its purpose.

The shipment was an interstate shipment, and was therefore governed by the acts of Congress. Section 34 of the Act of Congress of date August 29, 1916, c. 415, 39 Stat. L. 538 (Fed. Stat. Ann., 1918 Supp. p. 73 [U. S. Comp. St. § 8604qq]), provides, among other things:

"That a person who negotiates or transfers for value a bill by indorsement or delivery, unless a contrary intention appears, warrants —

* * * * * * * * * *

"(d) That he has a right to transfer the title to the goods, and that the goods are merchantable or fit for a particular purpose whenever such warranties would have been implied if the contract of the parties had been to transfer without a bill the goods represented thereby."

In our opinion, not only did Nuckolls, by transferring the negotiable bill of lading herein to plaintiff, by indorsement and delivery, warrant that the syrup was properly prepared and canned, so as to be merchantable, but the effect of the transfer was also to convey to plaintiff his rights of warranty against the canning company, and hence to convey his right to sue that company. . . .

For the foregoing reasons our conclusion is that plaintiff is entitled to recover against the canning company, though not the full amount for which it sues, but the amount which Nuckolls might have recovered had he not negotiated the bill of lading, which, in this instance, is the value of the goods, at the time and place the warranty arose in favor of Nuckolls; that is, when he made the purchase from the canning company. See *Peterkin* v. *Martin*, 30 La. Ann. 894. That value, as appears from the price paid by Nuckolls for the syrup, is $4,850.

For the reasons assigned, it is ordered, adjudged, and decreed that the judgment appealed from, which is in favor of said Teche Canning & Syrup Company, Inc., be annulled and set aside, and that there now be judgment in favor of plaintiff and against said Teche Canning & Syrup Company, Inc., for said sum of $4,850, with legal interest thereon from January 3, 1919; said Teche Canning & Syrup Company, Inc., to pay the costs of this appeal, and the costs of this suit, as against it, in the lower court.

Note also BISHOP & CO., INC. *v.* MIDLAND BANK, 84 Fed. (2nd) 585 (Circuit Court of Appeals, Ninth Circuit, 1936), where the complaint in an action by a buyer for the refund of money paid to a bank on a draft alleged that the draft with bill of lading attached had been sold by the seller to the bank, and that the bank was aware when it discounted the draft and took the bill of lading that the goods shipped were not sound and marketable, and were not suitable for food and for making wine. There was a further allegation that the bank received the draft with bill of lading attached with full knowledge of the circumstances. It was held that a demurrer to the complaint was wrongly sustained.

Compare Bank of Italy *v.* Colla, 118 Ohio St. 459 (Supreme Court, 1928), where the court said:

"It is the contention of the plaintiff in error that a bank, by undertaking to pay drafts with bills of lading attached pursuant to the terms of a letter of credit received by it, does not assume the legal liabilities of the shipper or seller with respect to the kind, quality, and condition of the goods actually shipped, but its responsibility is limited to assuring itself that the bills of lading and invoices attached to the drafts comply with the requirements of the letter of credit, and that such bank, by negotiating and transferring drafts with bills of lading attached, pursuant to such letter of credit, does not thereby become subject to and governed by the provisions of Section 8993–34, General Code, as to the implied warranty of the merchantability of goods covered by the bills of lading, nor by the similar provisions of the Uniform Sales Act of Ohio, Section 8416, General Code, and Title 49, Section 114, U. S. Code, Section 8011, Barnes' Federal Code, U. S. Comp. Stats., Section 8604qq.

"It is the contention of the defendants in error that the Bank of Italy, by reason of discounting the drafts with bills of lading attached, became the owner of the specific grapes that were to be delivered in Youngstown; that the Bank of Italy had knowledge that the plaintiffs had purchased a food product, and that the money to be paid by the drafts was for such purchase price, and that hence the Bank of Italy, by purchasing the drafts with bills of lading attached, assumed the obligation of making such delivery in Youngstown, and, when it demanded payment, impliedly represented that it was delivering a food product in merchantable condition."

[After quoting the charge of the lower court, which upheld the latter contention, the opinion continued:]

"In other words, the court in his charge and by his refusal to charge held that the California bank, by the negotiation of the bills of lading, had substituted itself for the seller of the goods so far as the liability of the seller for the merchantable condition of the goods upon arrival was concerned.

"In this the court was in error. Neither the section of the bills of lading statute above quoted, nor of the Sales Act, nor of the Federal Code, applies to the transaction between the Bank of Italy and the plaintiffs. The contract between them was set forth in the letter of credit, and it was not a contract of sale. The contract between the Bank of Italy and the plaintiffs was not and never would have been 'to transfer without a bill the goods represented thereby.' The Bank of Italy was not in the business of selling grapes, or any commodity of that kind. Its contract related only to the manner in which payment should be made for the grapes which were shipped under an entirely independent contract of sale, and the transfer of the bill of lading by the bank was a mere incident of the transaction. It is true that the bill of lading attached to the draft was assigned to the Bank of Italy as security, but the bank had an interest in the goods only to an extent sufficient to protect its claim. The record is entirely silent as to any knowledge of the bank with regard to the contract between the seller and purchaser excepting that stated in the letter of credit, and the bank being holder of the draft in due course, was not liable upon a breach of the warranty of the contract between the original parties."

Refer again to HAWKINS *v.* ALFALFA PRODUCTS CO., *supra*, p. 460.

MERCHANTS TRANSFER & STORAGE CO. *v.* FIRST FEDERAL FOREIGN BANKING CORP.

UNITED STATES CIRCUIT COURT OF APPEALS, SECOND CIRCUIT, 1935

[79 *Federal Reporter* (*Second Series*), 243]

CHASE, Circuit Judge. The decree from which this appeal was taken awarded to the defendant a fund which the plaintiff and it both claimed. The essential facts are undisputed and are as follows:

In June, 1931, Berry Bros., of Detroit, Mich., ordered 100 bags of shellac of an importer in New York City named Price. Price in turn procured a like amount of shellac to be shipped to him from India with which to fill the Berry Bros.' order. On June 11, 1931, this shellac was shipped to Price from India under a bill of lading issued by the ocean carrier in a set of three originals. On July 7th Price billed Berry Bros. for the shellac at $2,255.50 on credit net 90 days. The next day Price assigned to the plaintiff-appellant this account against Berry Bros. as partial security for a loan of $6,000 then made to him by the appellant. Some time after that Price received the three originals of the bill of lading issued by the ocean carrier which were indorsed in blank by the shipper. On August 7th the ship carrying the shellac arrived in New York. On August 8th, and while the shellac was still aboard ship, Price delivered two of the originals of the bill of lading to the defendant-appellee in substitution for other collateral which appellee then held as security for a loan it had made to Price and which it then returned to him. At this time the appellee was unaware of the assignment of the account against Berry Bros. by Price to the appellant. Nor did it know that Price was retaining, as he in fact was, the third original bill of lading for the shellac, except what was to be inferred from the statement contained in each original it received that it was one of a set of three like documents. On August 11th Price presented to the ocean carrier the one original bill of lading he had retained and directed shipment of the shellac to Berry Bros., who received it in due course and paid for it by check sent to Price. Meanwhile Price absconded. The check was received by one Rankin as trustee, and Rankin cashed it. The fund so created is now being held subject to whatever decree should be entered in this action. Another fund created in a similar way is involved, but the facts relating to it need not be stated, for the legal principles applicable to one are equally so to the other, and it has been stipulated that the party entitled to one fund is entitled to both.

Regardless of the danger which lurks in the use of a bill of lading issued in sets of originals and the legal limitations in this country upon their use, it is unquestioned that this bill of lading issued in India was valid. Up to the time Price delivered the two originals to the appellee, he had done nothing to transfer the title to the shellac. He had sold a like amount of shellac to Berry Bros., had billed them for it, and had assigned his bill against them to the appellant. Yet that had no effect upon the title to the shellac en route from India. He was free to deliver any shellac of the quantity and quality ordered by Berry Bros. in fulfillment of that order. When, however, he delivered the two originals of the bill of lading to the appellee, that party acquired the title to the shellac he had ordered from India. The particular 100 bags of shellac became the defendant's property. It made no difference that Price retained one original so far as title to the shellac was concerned. His negotiation of one or two of such originals for value transferred to the defendant his title to the shellac quite as effectively, so far as validity of title is concerned, as though he had delivered all three originals to it. *Barber* v. *Meyerstein*, L. R. 4 H. L. 317; *First National Bank* v. *Ege*, 109 N. Y. 120, 16 N. E. 317, 4 Am. St. Rep. 431; Williston on Sales (2d Ed.) § 441. The retention of the one original merely permitted Price to indulge in the fraudulent conduct of which he was subsequently guilty. Doubtless his delivery of that original to the ocean carrier was sufficient justification for its relinquishing its possession of the shellac, though that question is not an issue here. It is enough for present purposes that the shellac which Price used to fill the Berry Bros. order was shellac owned by the defendant. It was this shellac for which Berry Bros. paid. That it held the title only as security for a loan which has never been paid is of no consequence upon the issue in this action.

This being so, the result is that, when Rankin received the proceeds of the Berry Bros.' check, she received the proceeds of the sale of the defendant's property. Rankin's possession of the proceeds was in law the same as that of Price. The proceeds are to be charged with a constructive trust for the benefit of the owner of the property fraudulently used to create them. . . .

Decree affirmed.

In BARBER *v.* MEYERSTEIN, L. R. 4 H. L. 317 (House of Lords, 1870), cotton was consigned for sale on commission to a firm in London under a set of three bills of lading, each bearing a notation by the master of the ship "In witness whereof I . . . have affirmed to three bills of lading . . . one of which being accomplished, the others to stand void." Two parts of the bill of lading were indorsed to plaintiff against an advance, but by retaining the third part the consignee obtained other advances from defendant in exchange for its indorsement. Defendant sold the cotton to various purchasers who took delivery by means of delivery orders issued by defendant. In an action for money had and received, with a count for wrongful conversion, judgment for plaintiff was affirmed. The person who first gets the bill of lading acquires the property which it represents, and need not do any act to assert his title, as it already has been made complete by transfer of the bill of lading.

Compare Glyn Mills Currie & Co. *v.* The East and West India Dock Company, 7 A. C. 591 (House of Lords, 1882), where it was held under similar circumstances that the first indorsee could not maintain an action for conversion against the dock company holding the goods, although the dock company had delivered the goods to the consignee who continued to hold the second bill of lading, since the delivery was made in good faith and without knowledge of the prior indorsement.

PART FOUR

THE EXECUTION OF THE CONTRACT: TRANSFER OF TITLE

COMMENT

We already have had occasion to distinguish between contracts to sell and sales, and to note that the essential difference between the two lies in the transfer of title to the goods sold from the seller to the buyer. In the one case it is common to speak of the contract as executory and in the other as executed; a phraseology which at once suggests a transaction whose aim is to bring about a change of ownership.

The answer to the question whether title has passed to the buyer is thus also a determination of whether the primary purpose of the bargain has been fulfilled. There are moreover cogent practical considerations in the ascertainment of how and at what time the transition is effected. We have seen that title is often, although not necessarily, the guide to risk. If title has passed to the buyer, an action will lie for the price of the goods; if not, the seller's remedy for a breach is limited to an action for damages. Questions of taxation may hinge on ownership. In many prize cases the incidence of title has been conclusive as to the right to seize goods afloat in times of war. It often happens too that goods which are the subject matter of a contract of sale are resold, and here again title is likely to be the deciding factor in arriving at the consequences.

Since the contract of sale always has been regarded as a consensual contract, based fundamentally on a meeting of minds in regard to its details, it might be expected that the intention of the parties would have here a controlling influence. Surely, in arranging for a sale of goods, none are better qualified than the immediate parties themselves to say when the goods are to belong to the buyer. Even those systems of law which make no distinction between sales and contracts to sell recognize this in principle by permitting buyer and seller to impose conditions which have the effect of accelerating or retarding the transfer of title.

The difficulty is that the parties are not always precise in defining their intention; and the complexities of commerce coupled with reciprocal efforts to protect conflicting interests unite too often to produce confusion. It is one thing to read the minds of horse traders presently engaged in bargaining for an animal that is ready for immediate delivery; it is something else again to guess the mental processes of men dealing at a distance in goods yet to be manufactured and surrounded with all the paraphernalia of special clauses, collateral contracts, financing agencies, and documentation. The law may lay down certain rules by way of presumption, but they can be indicative merely, without being conclusive. Like so many others previously encountered, the real problem is one of construction.

CHAPTER I

Ascertained Goods Generally

TARLING *v.* BAXTER

King's Bench, 1827

[6 *Barnewall & Cresswell's Reports*, 360]

Assumpsit to recover back 145*l.* paid by the plaintiff to the defendant's use. The declaration contained counts for money had and received, and the other common counts. Plea, general issue, with a notice of set-off for goods sold and delivered and bargained and sold. At the trial before Abbott C. J., at the London sittings after Hilary term, 1826, a verdict was found for the plaintiff for 145*l.*, subject to the opinion of this Court on the following case.

On the 4th of January 1825, the plaintiff bought of the defendant a stack of hay belonging to the defendant, and then standing in a field belonging to the defendant's brother. The note signed by the defendant, and delivered to the plaintiff was in these words: "I have this day agreed to sell James Tarling a stack of hay, standing in Canonbury Field, Islington, at the sum of one hundred and forty-five pounds, the same to be paid on the 4th day of February next, and to be allowed to stand on the premises until the first day of May next." And the following note was signed by the plaintiff, and delivered to the defendant. "I have this day agreed to buy of Mr. John Baxter, a stack of hay, standing in Canonbury Field, Islington, at the sum of 145*l.*, the same to be paid on the 4th day of February next, and to be allowed to stand on the premises until the first day of May next, the same hay not to be cut until paid for. January 4th, 1825." At the meeting at which the notes were signed, but after the signature thereof, the defendant said to the plaintiff, "You will particularly oblige me by giving me a bill for the amount of the hay." The plaintiff rather objected. The defendant's brother, S. Baxter, on the 8th of the same month of January, took a bill of exchange for 145*l.* to the plaintiff, drawn upon him by the defendant, dated the 4th of January 1825, payable one month after date, which the plaintiff accepted. The defendant afterwards indorsed it to George Baxter, and the plaintiff paid it to one Taylor, the holder, when it became due. The stack of hay remained on the same field entire until the 20th of January 1825, when it was accidentally wholly consumed by fire, without any fault or neglect of either party.

A few days after the fire, the plaintiff applied to the defendant to know what he meant to do when the bill became due; the defendant said, "I have paid it away, and you must take it up to be sure: I have nothing to do with it, why did you not remove the hay." The plaintiff said, "he could not, because there was a memorandum 'that it should not be removed until the bill was paid'; would you have suffered it to be removed?" and the defendant said, "certainly not." The defendant's set-off was for the price of the hay agreed to be sold as aforesaid. The question for the opinion of the Court was, whether the plaintiff under the circumstances was entitled to recover the sum of 145*l.* or any part thereof.

Bayley J. It is quite clear that the loss must fall upon him in whom the property was vested at the time when it was destroyed by fire. And the question is, in whom the property in this hay was vested at that time? By the note of the contract delivered to the plaintiff, the defendant agreed to sell the plaintiff a stack of hay standing in Canonbury Field at the sum of 145*l.*, the same to be paid for on the 4th day of February next, and to be allowed to stand on the premises until the first day of May next. Now this was a contract for an immediate, not a prospective sale. Then the question is, in whom did the property vest by virtue of this contract? The right of property and the right of possession are distinct from each other; the right of possession may be in one person, the right of property in another. A vendor may have a qualified right to retain the goods unless payment is duly made, and yet the property in these goods may be in the vendee. The fact in this case, that the hay was not to be paid for until a future period, and that it was not to be cut until it was paid for, makes no difference, provided it was the intention of the parties that the vendee should, by the contract, immediately acquire a right of property in the goods, and the vendor a right of property in the price. The rule of law is, that where there is an immediate sale, and nothing remains to be done by the vendor as between him and the vendee, the property in the thing sold vests in the vendee, and then all the consequences resulting from the vesting of the property follow, one of which is, that if it be destroyed, the loss falls upon the vendee. The note of the buyer imports also an immediate, perfect, absolute agreement of sale. It seems to me that the true construction of the contract is, that the parties intended an immediate sale, and if that be so, the property vested in the vendee, and the loss must fall upon him. The rule for entering a nonsuit must therefore be made absolute.

Holroyd J. I think that in this case there was an immediate sale of the hay, accompanied with a stipulation on the part of the vendee, that he would not cut it till a given period. Now, in the case of a sale of goods, if nothing remains to be done on the part of the seller, as between him and the buyer, before the thing purchased is to be delivered, the property in the goods immediately passes to the buyer, and that in the price to the seller; but if any act remains to be done on the part of the seller, then the property does not pass until that act has been done. I am of opinion, therefore, in this case, not only that the property immediately passed to the buyer by the contract, but that the seller thereby immediately acquired a right in the price stipulated to be paid for the goods, although that was not to be paid until a future day. The property having passed to the vendee, and having been accidentally destroyed before the day of payment, the loss must fall upon him.

LITTLEDALE J. The parties on the 4th of January stipulated for the sale and purchase of a stack of hay, to be paid for in a month. Thus the case would have stood, but for the note of the contract delivered to the buyer, and in that there was a stipulation, that the purchaser should not cut until the money was paid, but the property in the hay had already passed by the contract of sale to the purchaser, and the latter afterwards merely waived his right to the immediate possession. Then the property having passed to the buyer, the loss must fall upon him, and, consequently, this rule for entering a nonsuit must be made absolute.

Rule absolute.

TERRY *v.* WHEELER

NEW YORK COURT OF APPEALS, 1862

[25 *New York Reports,* 520]

Appeal from the Supreme Court. Action by the assignee of Lewis Elmore, to recover the price paid for a quantity of lumber, purchased by Elmore of the defendant, at his lumber yard in Troy, which the defendant agreed, but failed, to deliver at the railroad in Troy. The defendant denied his liability, on the ground that the title to the property vested in Elmore at the time of the sale, and that the property was destroyed by fire immediately after the sale, without fault on his part. The cause was tried before the court, which found the following facts:

1. That on the 24th of August, 1854, the defendant sold to Lewis Elmore, by a written bill of sale, a quantity of lumber of the character, at the price, and upon the terms set forth in the bill of sale, and that payment therefor was made as stated in said bill. . . .

2. That after such sale and payment, and after delivery of said bill of sale, and in the afternoon of the same day, the memorandum thereupon, as follows — "to be delivered to the cars free of charge" — was indorsed and signed by the clerk of the defendant. Whether this was done by the authority of the defendant, or whether the defendant then recognized its purport as a part of the original agreement, the court held it not necessary to decide, the parol evidence being held competent and sufficient on that point.

3. That the lumber so sold was, at the time of sale upon the defendant's yard, at the city of Troy, and had been inspected and measured; that the three first items named in the bill constituted one separate pile designated as the lumber sold to Elmore; and as to the remaining item, viz.: 600 pieces, these were to be taken from the top of another pile containing more than that number, and a mark was made, showing how far the 600 pieces came on that pile.

4. That the note mentioned in the bill of sale was transferred by the defendant before maturity, and paid by Elmore before his assignment to the plaintiff.

5. That the lumber so sold was on the same day of the sale, and within

a few hours thereafter, and before the removal of any part thereof, and without any fault or delay on the part of the defendant, accidentally consumed by fire.

6. That at the time of the written contract of sale, and as a part of the agreement for sale, the defendant stipulated by parol to deliver said lumber at the railroad free of charge, no time for such delivery being specified.

7. That Elmore, on March 1st, 1855, assigned to the plaintiff the cause of action for which this suit was brought.

The court also decided, that upon the question of an agreement to deliver the lumber, there was no conflict of evidence; that the testimony of the defendant and his witnesses upon that point was substantially to the same effect as the testimony of Elmore. And although requested, the court declined to consider the evidence upon that point as conflicting, or to pass upon the credibility of any, or either of the witnesses.

And the court decided that, as the lumber sold was to be delivered by the defendant and was not delivered by him, he was liable to the plaintiff, and on that ground judgment was rendered in favor of the plaintiff for the amount claimed.

The defendant's counsel excepted to each and every of the findings of fact and conclusions of law by the court, and to the refusal to examine and decide upon the credibility of witnesses.

After the introduction of the bill of sale, by the plaintiff, on the trial, the defendant's counsel moved that the parol evidence in regard to the sale should be stricken out, on the ground that the bill of sale was the contract, and parol evidence was not admissible to contradict it. The motion was denied, on the ground that the agreement to deliver need not be put in the bill, and that parol evidence on that subject was competent and did not disagree with it. To this decision an exception was taken.

The Supreme Court at general term affirmed the judgment, and the defendant brought this appeal.

SELDEN, J. There may be some doubt whether the parol evidence in regard to the agreement to deliver the lumber was admissible, but if it were necessary to decide that question, I should regard it as admissible, on the ground that what is called the bill of sale was in substance a mere receipt for the purchase money, and did not purport to be a contract. (*Dunn* v. *Hewitt*, 2 Denio, 637; *Blood* v. *Harrington*, 8 Pick., 552; *Filkins* v. *Whyland*, 24 N. Y., 338.) If the lumber had not been paid for, and the instrument, omitting the receipt, had been signed by the defendant and delivered, as a note or memorandum of the sale, it would then have been the evidence of a contract, executory on one part at least, and not open to explanation by parol. But looking at the whole instrument, I think it is to be regarded as a receipt, and not a contract, within the cases above cited. Of course, in this view, the memorandum at the foot of the bill is not regarded as a part of it; if it were, its character would be changed from a receipt to an executory contract, conclusive upon the parties, except so far as it was still a receipt. (*Eggleston* v. *Knickerbocker*, 6 Barb., 458.)

The point which is made upon the contradictory character of the evidence in relation to the contract to deliver the lumber on the cars, and its sufficiency to establish such contract, presents only a question of fact which this court cannot review. . . .

But in the view which I take of the remaining question, it becomes immaterial whether there was a contract to deliver at the cars or not. The lumber had not been actually delivered, but remained in the possession of the vendor. In the absence of any express contract to deliver, there was an implied one to deliver at the yard of the vendor, when called for. In either case the lumber did not remain at the risk of the vendor, if the title did not remain in him. The risk attends upon the title, not upon the possession, where there is no special agreement upon the subject. (*Tarling* v. *Baxter*, 6 B. & C., 360; *Willis* v. *Willis*, 6 Dana, 49; *Hinde* v. *Whitehouse*, 7 East, 558; *Joyce* v. *Adams*, 4 Seld., 296; 2 Kent's Com., 492, 496; Noy's Maxims, 88.) I entertain no doubt that upon the facts found in this case, the title was in the vendee. The lumber was selected by both parties and designated as the lumber sold to Elmore, except the 600 pieces, which were selected by the parties, and the precise pieces sold designated with as much precision as if the purchaser had marked every piece with his name; that which was sold by measurement was inspected and measured, and the quantity ascertained; the price for the whole was agreed upon and paid, and a bill of parcels receipted and delivered to the purchaser. These facts, I think, vested the title in the purchaser, notwithstanding the agreement of the seller to deliver the lumber free of charge, at the cars. "The sale of a specific chattel passes the property therein to the vendee, without delivery." (Chitty on Contr., 8 Am. ed., p. 332.) "It is a general rule of the common law that a mere contract for the sale of goods, where nothing remains to be done by the seller before making delivery, transfers the right of property, although the price has not been paid, nor the thing sold delivered to the purchaser." (*Olyphant* v. *Baker*, 5 Denio, 382.) The authorities are numerous, where the expression is used that if anything remains to be done by the seller, the title does not pass; but the cases which are referred to to sustain that position, only go the length of showing that where something is to be done by the seller to ascertain the identity, quantity or quality of the article sold, or to put it in the condition which the terms of the contract require, the title does not pass. (2 Kent's Com., 496; *Hanson* v. *Myer*, 6 East, 614; *Simmons* v. *Swift*, 5 B. & C., 857; *Joyce* v. *Adams*, 4 Seld., 291; *Field* v. *Moore*, Lalor's Sup., 418.) The list of cases to this effect might be indefinitely increased; but no case has been referred to by counsel, nor have I discovered any, in which, where the article sold was perfectly identified and paid for, it was held that a stipulation of the seller to deliver at a particular place prevented the title from passing. If the payment was to be made on or after delivery, at a particular place, it might fairly be inferred that the contract was executory, until such delivery; but where the sale appears to be absolute, the identity of the thing fixed, and the price for it paid, I see no room for an inference that the property remains the seller's, merely because he has engaged to transport it to a given point. I think in such case the property passes at the time of the contract, and that in carrying it, the seller acts as bailee and not as owner. The questions which arise in such cases, as to sales, are questions of intention, such as arise in all other cases of the interpretation of contracts; and when the facts are ascertained, either by the written agreement of the parties or by the findings of a court, as they are here, they are questions of law. That the parties to the contract in this case intended to pass the title to the lumber immediately, appears very clear; nor do I suppose that any one would question it, were it not for the apparent hardship of the case to the purchaser. If the property, instead of being lumber, had been sheep or cows, capable of increase, (which follows the ownership), and there had been a sudden and large increase to the flock, or drove, before they could be delivered at the point agreed upon, I think no one would have said that the defendant could have discharged his obligation to deliver, and yet retained the increase. Such, however, must be the conclusion, if the plaintiff's position is maintained. The judgment should be reversed and a new trial granted.

All the judges concurring,

Judgment reversed, and new trial ordered.

In IRON CITY GRAIN CO. *v.* ARNOLD, 215 Ala. 543 (Supreme Court, 1927), plaintiff had a car of hay standing on the tracks of a railroad. Defendant there examined the hay and found it satisfactory. Defendant testified: "I looked at the hay, and Mr. Bigsby [plaintiff's agent] made me a price on it delivered at my plant at $29. . . . The shipper paid the shipping and freight charges on those cars. . . . I told Mr. Bigsby to send it out to our warehouse; I mean to the tracks opposite our warehouse. . . . I told Mr. Bigsby I would give him $29 f. o. b. our plant for this car." The car was delivered to a spur track opposite one of the two doors in the rear of defendant's warehouse, and was there destroyed by fire. In an action for the purchase price judgment for plaintiff was affirmed. Without reference to the question of delivery, title passed to defendant at the time the contract was made.

In CITY OF BOSCOBEL *v.* MUSCODA MFG. CO., 175 Wis. 62 (Supreme Court, 1921), a contract read as follows: "Sold to Muscoda Mfg. Co., Muscoda, Wis., the power plant formerly used by the city of Boscobel as an electric light plant, consisting of 2 boilers, 2 engines, 2 steam pumps, water heaters, and all other equipment and fittings that go with outfit. Muscoda Mfg. Co. agrees to pay the sum of $1,800 for the outfit, to be paid $200 cash, which is hereby paid, and the balance, $1,600, to be paid before taking out the plant, and plant is to be taken out before June 1, 1920." This contract was made on December 23, 1919, and was signed by both parties. The plant in question was lying in a frame building covered with sheet iron. On March 12, 1920, this building was burned, and the plant rendered worthless except for junk. In an action to recover the balance of the purchase price, judgment for plaintiff affirmed. The goods were ascertained and were in a deliverable state. The buyer had the right to take them at any time on payment of the remainder of the price.

In FARMERS' RICE MILLING CO. *v.* STANDARD RICE CO., 276 S. W. 904 (Texas Commission of Appeals, 1925), there was a contract in the following terms: "Farmers' Rice Milling Company, Inc., hereby sells and agrees to deliver, and the undersigned buyer hereby purchases and agrees to pay for the following merchandise: 819 pockets Blue Rose rice, No. 62 doubles for Standard Rice Milling Company, New York City. Draft dated April 15, 1920, less 1% if paid within 10 days. Sellers to allow buyers thirty days free storage and insurance. For the price and sum of 10 cents per pound. Shipment: soon as embargo is lifted. Delivery: F. o. b. cars at Bellevue, Calcasieu Parish, La. This written agreement is the complete agreement of the parties. . . ." The rice in question was a specific lot of Blue Rose rice, which was distinctly segregated in the warehouse. The buyer refused payment of the draft, and refused to accept the rice. The seller sold the rice for the account of the buyer, and brought the present action to recover the difference between the amount realized and the agreed purchase price. Judgment for defendant reversed. The terms of the contract show a clear intention to pass title to the buyer at once.

Compare THE GRANGE COMPANY *v.* MCCABE, 26 Calif. App. (2nd) 597 (California District Court of Appeal, Third Appellate District, 1938). A contract read as follows: "In consideration of the price hereinafter named, Julia A. McCabe, the seller, has sold and The Grange Company, the buyer, has bought about 2400 sacks of grain, which said seller agrees to deliver, properly threshed, cleaned and sacked in new grain sacks, F. O. B. cars Simon Newman warehouse in Ingomar, Calif., by not later than the 30th of December, 1936. No. of Sax sold: Abt. 2500. Quality: Equal to sample. Kind of grain: Bly. Price per cwt.: $1.00 plus salvage value of the bags. Payment to be made when crop is delivered as above, on net weight, sacks to become property of the buyer. . . . 60% of purchase price to be paid on or before July 1, 1936. Balance to be paid at time of shipment on destination weights. Purchase sample furnished by buyer." Part payment was not made as agreed, and the seller refused to accept a check sent later, stating that the sale was cancelled. The seller then sold the grain to another person, and the buyer brought this action against the seller for conversion. It was held that the transaction amounted to a present sale, as "the language of the agreement seemed to indicate the parties themselves considered the transaction as a sale"; but judgment for plaintiff was reversed on other grounds.

RUGG *v.* MINETT

KING'S BENCH, 1809

[11 *East's Reports*, 210]

In an action for money had and received by the defendants to the use of the plaintiffs, a verdict was found for the plaintiffs for 1415*l.*, subject to the opinion of the Court upon the following case.

On the 28th of April 1808 the defendants, as prize agents to the commissioners for the care and disposal of Danish property, put up to public sale by auction, at Dover, the cargo of a Danish ship in lots, and the lots No. 28. to 54. inclusive consisted of turpentine in casks. The quantity contained in each lot being marked on the catalogue thus — 10 cwt. 3 qrs. 26 lbs., the mode of bidding was this; each lot (except the two last, which were sold at uncertain quantities), was to be taken at the weight at which it was marked, and the bidding was to be at so much per hundred weight on that quantity. The plaintiffs employed one Acres, the warehouseman of the defendants, to bid for them, and all the lots of turpentine (with the exception of 3 lots, which were sold to other bidders) were knocked down to Acres so acting for the plaintiffs. No conditions of sale were distributed prior to the sale; but the auctioneer, before the bidding commenced, read aloud the following conditions: 1st. The highest bidder to be the buyer; but if any dispute should arise, the lot to be put up again. 2d, 25*l*. per cent. is to be paid to the auctioneer as a deposit immediately after the sale, and the remainder in 30 days. The remainder of the purchase-money is to be paid on the goods being delivered. Should the goods remain after the limited time, the warehouse-rent from that time to be paid at the rate of 2*s*. per ton per month, by the purchaser. 3d, The goods to be taken at the neat weight printed in the catalogue. 4th, The goods to be taken away in 12 months, or resold to pay the warehouse-rent. Upon failure of complying with these conditions, the deposit-money is to be forfeited, and the commissioners to be at liberty to resell any lots belonging to defaulters, by whom all charges attending the same shall be made good. 1*s*. per lot under 10*l*. — 1*s*. 6*d*. from 10*l*. to 25*l*. — and 2*s*. above 25*l*. lot-money to be paid by the buyer to the auctioneer. Tare allowed for turpentine 1*s*. 5*d*. Upon the turpentine being put up to sale, the auctioneer, by the direction of one of the defendants present, announced to the bidders that the casks of turpentine were to be filled up before they were delivered to the purchasers: and that in order to effect this, the two last lots would be sold at uncertain quantities, and the preceding lots would be filled from them. The whole of the turpentine, with the exception of the 3 lots before mentioned, were sold to the plaintiffs; and they also were the purchasers of the two last lots, from which all the lots without exception were to be filled up; and those two last lots were accordingly marked by the auctioneer in his catalogue with the words "more or less." Immediately after the sale 200*l*. was paid by the plaintiffs to the auctioneer, as their deposit: and on the 9th of May 1808 the plaintiffs paid to the defendants 1715*l*. upon account of the turpentine, and the duties payable thereon. The turpentine remained in the warehouses of the defendants as before the sale, but was entered at the custom-house at Dover, in the name of the plaintiffs, on the morning of the 10th of May 1808, before the fire, by Acres, who paid on behalf of the plaintiffs 450*l*. as a deposit for the duties. On the same morning the cooper, who had been employed by the defendants to make up all the casks previous to the sale of the 28th of April, was sent for by Acres, who was warehouseman to the defendants, and who acted as agent for the plaintiffs, to fill up the casks of turpentine, and he had filled all of them except 8 or 10; leaving them with the bungs out to enable the custom-house officer, who was expected every minute, to take his guage in order to ascertain the duties. The two last lots, which were sold at uncertain quantities, and marked "more or less," contained more turpentine than was sufficient to fill up all those bought by the plaintiffs, and also those bought by the buyers of the three lots. In filling the casks sold to the plaintiffs one of the two last lots was used, and instead of the other of the two last lots, a preceding cask in point of number, which had been found to be an ullage cask, was substituted by the cooper, and from one of the two last lost the lots sold to the other buyers had been previously filled up. All the lots sold to the other buyers had been taken away before the cooper came on the 10th; and while the cooper was employed in filling up the plaintiffs' lots, and placing them ready, with the bungs of the casks out for the custom-house officer to guage, but before he had filled up all the casks, or bunged any of them, a fire took place in the defendant's warehouse, which consumed the whole of the turpentine knocked down to the plaintiffs; the casks not having been weighed again by the plaintiffs, or guaged by the custom-house officer. While the money paid by the plaintiffs to the defendants on account of the turpentine remained in their hands, they received notice from the plaintiffs not to pay it over; and the present verdict is composed of that sum, deducting the 450*l.* paid on account of the duty, which has been restored to the plaintiffs by the commissioners of customs. The question for the opinion of the Court was, Whether the plaintiffs were entitled to recover back the money so paid to the defendants? If they were, the verdict was to stand: if not, a nonsuit was to be entered.

Lord Ellenborough C. J. The court have already intimated their opinion, as to those casks in the first lots which were filled up, and on which nothing remained to be done on the part of the sellers, but only the casks were left to remain for 30 days at the option of the purchasers in the warehouse at the charge of the sellers: the payment of the warehouse-rent however is not material in this case: and when the casks were filled up, every thing was done which remained to be done by the sellers. It was necessary however that they should be guaged before they were removed, and the bungs were left out for the purpose of the guager's doing his office, which it was the buyer's business to have performed; and therefore according to the case of *Hanson* v. *Meyer*, and the other cases, every thing having been done by the sellers, which lay upon them to perform, in order to put the goods in a deliverable state in the place from whence they were to be taken by the buyers, the goods remained there at the risk of the latter. But with respect to the other ten casks, as the filling them up according to the contract remained to be done by the sellers, the property did not pass to the buyers, and therefore they are not bound to pay for them.

[Concurring opinions of Le Blanc and Bayley, JJ., are here omitted.]

Upon this it was agreed that the proportion to be allowed to the plaintiffs on the ten casks should be settled out of court; and that the verdict should be entered accordingly.

F. D. BARTON & CO. *v.* TURNBULL

MICHIGAN SUPREME COURT, 1924

[226 *Michigan Reports*, 685]

McDONALD, J. This is an action of replevin for the possession of 10,530 Norway and white pine logs. When replevined the logs were in possession of defendant, as sheriff, under a writ of attachment issued out of the circuit court for Luce county, in a cause wherein Erwin Yuill was defendant and one A. L. Sayles was plaintiff. In that cause judgment was rendered against Yuill in the sum of $4,710.28. The plaintiff claims title by purchase from Yuill. John C. Ross, trustee for the Bay City Bank, was the owner of the logs and land from which they were cut. He sold the premises, including the timber, to Erwin Yuill on contract for $67,500 with the privilege of lumbering and cutting the timber and selling it to the plaintiff on condition that all payments for the same should be made to the Bay City Bank, Ross to retain the title until such payments were made. Pursuant to this authority to sell, Yuill sold the logs on contract to the plaintiff herein. This contract provided that the logs should be decked on skids at banking places on the Two Hearted river where they were to be scaled and inspected and then delivered to the plaintiff in its booms at the mouth of the river. It also provided that the plaintiff should advance $10,000 to Yuill, and that when banked the logs should be insured by Yuill with loss payable to the Bay City Bank to the extent of its loan, then to the plaintiff to the extent of its advances, and thereafter to Yuill. Subsequently, another agreement between the parties was made modifying the prices on the logs under the preceding contract and extending the time of payment. It is by virtue of these contracts that the plaintiff claims title to the logs and the right to their possession. The case was tried before the circuit judge without a jury on a stipulated statement of facts. He found that the plaintiff did not have title to the logs, was not entitled to possession, and entered a judgment for the defendant for $5,008.68. The plaintiff brings error.

The principal question involved is whether the plaintiff had title to the logs in question when the suit was instituted.

"To entitle a plaintiff to recover in an action of replevin, he must establish his right to the possession of the property replevined. This he may do by proving that he was in actual and undisputed possession when defendant took the property. If he had no such possession, he must prove title. If he bases his right to recover upon proof of title, defendant may defeat his recovery by proving title in a third person." *Sanford* v. *Millikin*, 144 Mich. 312.

As the plaintiff was not in actual possession of the logs when they were taken on attachment by the defendant, its right to recover must rest on a showing of title in itself. The contract does not expressly state when the title shall pass to the plaintiff. We must therefore examine the contract and the circumstances of the case in order to determine the intention of the parties in respect to that question. In *Richardson Lumber Co.* v. *Hoey*, 219 Mich. 643, after citing various cases in which definite rules for determining intention were announced, this court said:

"These cases adhere to the rule that where nothing remains to be done by the vendor to ascertain the identity, quantity or quality of the goods sold, where nothing further is necessary to put them in the condition provided by the terms of the contract, the title passes when the contract is made."

Section 19, rule 2, of the uniform sales act (3 Comp. Laws 1915, § 11850) also states the following rule for determining the intention of the parties as to the passing of title:

"Where there is a contract to sell specific goods and the seller is bound to do something to the goods, for the purpose of putting them in a deliverable state, the property does not pass until such thing be done."

Applying these rules to the instant case, it will readily appear that the title did not pass at the time when the contract was made. When the plaintiff bought the logs they were in the standing timber, and something further was to be done by the vendor to put them in a deliverable state. He must put them in the condition provided by the terms of the contract. He must cut them, deck them on skids at banking places on the river where they could be scaled and inspected. Until he had done this, title would not vest in the buyer. It is clear, therefore, that title did not pass when the contract was made. Nor can it be said to have passed when the logs were banked, for there the quantity and quality must be determined by inspection. Then the vendor must water them, drive them to the mouth of the river and place them in the plaintiff's booms. This was a part of the consideration of the contract. The cost of watering, driving and booming the logs was to be borne by the vendor. It was something further which the contract required the vendor to do before the buyer was bound to accept delivery of the logs. The intention to be drawn from this latter provision of the contract is stated in section 19, rule 5, of the uniform sales act (3 Comp. Laws 1915, § 11850), as follows:

"If the contract to sell requires the seller to deliver the goods to the buyer at a particular place or to pay the freight or cost of transportation to the buyer or to a particular place, the property does not pass until the goods have been delivered to the buyer or reached the place agreed upon."

The uniform sales act states certain definite rules for determining the intention of the parties as to the vesting of title. These rules are controlling unless a different intention is indicated somewhere in the contract and the attendant circumstances. Our examination of the contract fails to disclose a different intention. We are therefore of the opinion that the circuit judge was right in his conclusion that the title to the logs in question was not to vest in the plaintiff until they were delivered in its booms at the mouth of the river. As they were attached by the defendant while they were decked on skids on the bank of the river, it follows that the plaintiff did not have the title and right to possession at the time the suit was instituted.

[The balance of the opinion is here omitted.]

We find no error in the record. The judgment is affirmed, with costs to the defendant.

CLARK, C. J., and BIRD, SHARPE, MOORE, STEERE, FELLOWS, and WIEST, JJ., concurred.

Note also J. B. BRADFORD PIANO COMPANY *v.* HACKER, 162 Wis. 335 (Supreme Court, 1916), where a contract for the sale of a specific player piano provided that the case was to be stained a darker color and the tone made more brilliant. Before this was done the buyer repudiated the contract. In an action for the purchase price, judgment for defendant was affirmed. "It is obvious that the piano was not in a deliverable state until the covering of the case had been altered to comply with the conditions of the sale, . . . and hence the property had not passed when defendant repudiated the sale."

In KAHN *v.* ROSENSTIEL, 298 Fed. 656 (District Court, S. D. N. Y., 1924), a contract was made by which plaintiff bought and defendant sold 2000 cases of whisky, bottled in bond, at $26 per case f. o. b. the defendant's distillery, where the whisky was lying in wood. The buyer agreed to get a withdrawal permit, and the seller was to bottle the goods and ship them within 30 days after arrival of the permit. The buyer paid down $10,000 on the price. It subsequently appeared that the buying and selling permits held by the parties were void, and the buyer brought the present action to recover the amount paid. It was held that the contract was not executed, as by its terms the seller had to bottle and ship.

In STACK *v.* BAIRD, 171 Wash. 651 (Supreme Court, 1933), defendant for $775 which was paid sold to plaintiff all the steel and iron in a building which defendant was about to raze. Under the contract plaintiff agreed to remove the material purchased "as and when it is exposed in the walls and floors of the building by the seller in the course of his wrecking operations." After eight tons had been removed by the buyer, the seller entered into a contract with a third person to complete the wrecking, and this person did not expose the steel in the walls and floors in the course of his operations. The result was that 116 tons of steel and iron were left in the building. The buyer brought the present action to recover the $775 paid plus $853 representing profit which would reasonably have been earned. Judgment for defendant reversed. Although not entitled to speculative profits, plaintiff should have been awarded the amount of the purchase price less the value of the eight tons removed. Title to 116 tons did not pass because the steel was never put in deliverable state by exposure.

Note further UNDERWOOD LIMITED *v.* BURGH CASTLE BRICK AND CEMENT SYNDICATE, [1922] 1 K. B. 123 (King's Bench Division, 1921). The plaintiffs agreed to sell to the defendants a horizontal tandem condensing engine to be delivered free on rail in London. At the time of making the contract the engine was on the sellers' premises as a trade fixture, and would have to be detached before it could be sent to the buyers. While being loaded on to a railway truck the bedplate of the engine was broken, and the defendants refused to accept it. In an action on the contract Rowlatt, J., gave judgment for defendants, saying in part:

"This case raises an important point under the Sale of Goods Act, 1893. This turns on the question whether the property in the engine had passed to the defendants at the time when the accident happened when the engine was being loaded. This engine weighed some thirty tons and was at the time when it was inspected by the defendants affixed to a bed of concrete by means of Lewis bolts and screwed down. By reason of its weight it had sunk into the concrete and become closely united with it, so that the operation of removing it not only involved unfastening it but taking it to pieces.

"The sale was that of a specific chattel to be delivered by the plaintiffs, but the fact that it was to be delivered by them is not the test whether the property passed. The test is whether anything remained to be done to the engine by the sellers to put it into a deliverable state; and by that I understand a state in which the thing will be the article contracted for by the buyer; I do not mean deliverable in the sense that it is properly packed or anything of that kind. It must have everything done to it that the sellers had to do to it as an article. I do not think therefore that the fact by itself that the sellers had to take the engine to pieces would postpone the time when the property passed. Many chattels have to be taken to pieces before they can be delivered — e.g. a sideboard or a billiard table; nevertheless the property in these passes on the sale and is not postponed until the article is actually taken to pieces and delivered. I do not, therefore, lay any stress on the fact of the engine having to be taken to pieces. I think the important point is that the parties were dealing with an article which was a fixture to the premises, and that is different from the case of a loose chattel. The buyers' intention was to buy an article which would be a loose chattel when the processes of detaching and dismantling it were completed, and to convert it into a loose chattel these processes had first to be performed. The case of a tenant's fixtures seems an analogous case. It seems a safe rule to adopt that if a fixture has to be detached so as to make it a chattel again, the act of detaching has to be done before the chattel can be deliverable."

Compare Young *v.* Matthews, L. R. 2 C. P. 127 (Court of Common Pleas, 1866). An agreement was entered into for the sale of 1,300,000 bricks in settlement of certain bills of exchange which the seller was unable to pay. An invoice was made out for the bricks, and the buyer visited the seller's brick field where the seller pointed out to him three clamps, one of finished bricks, one still burning, and the third consisting of bricks moulded but not yet burned. The buyer said: "Do I clearly understand that you are prepared and will hold and deliver this said quantity of bricks?" The seller replied "Yes." It was held that the property in the bricks thereupon passed to the buyer, as the circumstances showed a clear intention to pass title without reference to whether the bricks were finished.

Refer also to WHITTLE *v.* PHELPS, *supra*, p. 209.

HANSON *v.* MEYER

KING'S BENCH, 1805

[6 *East's Reports*, 614]

This was an action of trover, brought to recover the value of 33 cwt. 1 qr. 21 lb. of starch, which was tried before Lord Ellenborough, C. J. at the sittings at Guildhall, after Trinity Term, 1803, when there was a verdict for the Defendant; and a motion being made for a new trial, which was argued in last Michaelmas Term, the Court by consent in Hilary Term last, ordered a case to be made of the facts that were proved at the trial; which are as follows:

The Plaintiffs are assignees of J. Wallace and W. Hawes, under a commission of bankrupt issued against them. The defendant is a merchant in London. In January, 1801, the bankrupts employed Wright, their broker, to purchase, of the defendant a quantity of starch, about four tons, belonging to the defendant, and which was then lying in the Bull Porters' warehouse in Seething-lane; and Wright accordingly purchased the starch of the defendant, at 6*l.* per cwt. and sent to the bankrupts, his principals, the following note: "Dear Sirs, I have bought that small parcel of starch, which you saw, of Mr. James Meyer for your account 6*l.* per cwt. by bill at two months; 14 days for delivery from the 14th instant." "Jan. 15th, 1801. Yours, &c. T. Wright." The starch lay at the Bull Porters'. The broker purchased for the bankrupts all Meyer's starch that lay there, more or less whatever it was, at 6*l.* per hundred weight: it was in papers: the weight was to be afterwards ascertained at the price aforesaid. The mode of delivery is as follows; the seller gives the buyer a note addressed to the warehouse-keeper, to weigh and deliver the goods to the buyer. This note is taken to the warehouse-keeper, and is his authority to weigh and deliver the goods to the vendee. The following note was given by the defendant: "To the Bull Porters, Seething Lane." "Please to weigh and deliver to Messrs. Wallace and Hawes all my starch." "Jan. 17th, 1801. Per James Meyer, William Elliott." This order was lodged by the bankrupts, at the Bull Porters' warehouse on the 21st of January, 1801, on which day the bankrupts required the Bull Porters to weigh and deliver to them 450 papers of the starch, which weighed

		Cwt.	qrs.	lb.
		21	1	6
And on the 31st Jan.	250	9	1	20
And on the 2d Feb.	400	15	1	4
	1100	46	0	12

At which respective times the Bull Porters, in consequence of their order, weighed and delivered the same to the bankrupts, who immediately removed the same: the residue thereof, being 33 cwt. 1 qr. 21 lb. remained at the Bull Porters' warehouse till the failure of Wallace and Hawes. The above quantities of starch continued at the Bull Porters' warehouse, in the name and at the expence of the defendant, till they were weighed and delivered; and the residue also afterwards continued there in like manner unweighed, in his name, and charged to his expence. On the 8th of Feb. 1801, Wallace and Hawes became bankrupts. It was admitted that the defendant, after the bankruptcy, took away the remainder of the starch that had not been so weighed. The question for the opinion of the Court was, Whether the defendant were entitled to the above verdict? If the Court should be of opinion that he was, then the verdict was to stand: if not, then a new trial was to be granted upon such terms as the Court should direct.

Lord ELLENBOROUGH, C. J. now delivered judgment.

By the terms of the bargain, formed by the broker of the bankrupts on their behalf, two things, in the nature of conditions or preliminary acts on their part, necessarily preceded the absolute vesting in them of the property contracted for; the first of them is one which does so according to the generally received rule of law in contracts of sale, viz. the payment of the agreed price or consideration for the sale. The second, which is the act of weighing, does so in consequence of the particular terms of this contract, by which the price is made to depend upon the weight. The weight, therefore, must be ascertained, in order that the price may be known and paid; and unless the weighing precede the delivery, it can never for these purposes effectually take place at all. In this case a partial weighing and delivery of several quantities of the starch contracted for had taken place; the remainder of it was unweighed and undelivered; and of course no such bill of two months for the price so depending on the weight could yet be given. The question is, What is the legal effect of such part-delivery of the starch on the right of property in the undelivered residue thereof? On the part of the plaintiffs, it is contended, That a delivery of part of an entire quantity of goods contracted for, is a virtual delivery of the whole, so as to vest in the vendee the entire property in the whole; although the price for the same should not have been paid. This proposition was denied on the part of the defendant; and many authorities have been cited on both sides: but, without deciding at present what might be the legal effect of such part-delivery in a case where the payment of price was the only act necessary to be performed in order to vest the property; in this case another act, it will be remembered, was necessary to precede both payment of price and delivery of the goods bargained for, viz. weighing. This preliminary act of weighing, it certainly never was in the contemplation of the sellers to waive in respect of any part of the commodity contracted for. The order stated in the case from the defendant to the Bull Porters, his agents, is to weigh and deliver all his starch. Till it was weighed, they as his agents were not authorized to deliver it; still less were the buyers themselves, or the present plaintiffs, their assignees, authorized to take it by their own act from the Bull Porter's warehouse; and if they could not so take it, neither can they maintain this action of trover, founded on such a supposed right to take; or, in other words, founded on such a supposed right of property in the subject-matter of this action. If any thing remain to be done on the part of the seller, as between him and the buyer, before the commodity purchased is to be delivered, a complete present right of property has not attached in the buyer; and of course this action, which is accommodated to and depends on such supposed perfect right of property, is not maintainable. . . .

Without, therefore, touching the question which has been the main subject of argument in this case, and upon which my opinion at *nisi prius* principally turned, and without in any degree questioning the authority of the above mentioned two cases from the Common Pleas, this verdict may be sustained, on the ground that the weighing which was indispensably necessary to precede the delivery of the goods, inasmuch as it was necessary to ascertain the price to be paid for them, had not been performed at the time when the action was brought. The verdict therefore must stand, and judgment be entered for the defendant.

Compare Turley *v.* Bates, 2 Hurl. & C. 200 (Exchequer, 1863). A bargain was concluded for the sale of the whole of a heap of fire clay, estimated at 1500 tons, to be carted and weighed at the expense of the buyer, and to be paid for at the rate of two shillings per ton. The buyer failed to take away the entire quantity, but paid for what was removed. In an action to recover for the balance, as for goods bargained and sold, the buyer contended that the weighing was a condition precedent to the passing of title. Following a verdict for plaintiff, a rule *nisi* was granted. Rule discharged. The weighing was to be done by the buyer, and did not affect the apparent intention of the parties that title to the whole heap was to pass.

CASSINELLI *v.* HUMPHREY SUPPLY COMPANY

Nevada Supreme Court, 1919

[43 *Nevada Reports*, 208]

By the Court, Ducker, J.:

The appellant, who was plaintiff in the court below, brought his action against the Humphrey Supply Company to recover the unpaid purchase price of 296⅚ tons of hay. The complaint alleges that at the time of the sale the hay was in a deliverable condition, and was agreed to be delivered and was delivered in the stack at and where the same was then stacked, and nothing remained to be done with reference thereto to pass the title to defendant, and it was the intention of plaintiff and defendant to pass the title to the hay by agreement, and that the title did thereby pass from plaintiff to defendant. It is also alleged that no part of the purchase price of said hay has been paid except the sum of $500, and the remainder of the purchase price of the hay, the sum of $2,468.33 is due, owing, and unpaid. All of these allegations are denied in the answer except the payment of the sum of $500, and in the counter-claim the return of this sum is demanded.

The answer also alleged the following agreement in writing.

No. 964.

Humphrey Supply Company.

Dec. 1st, 1916.

Bought of Peter Cassinelli the following. I have sold all of my hay to Humphrey Supply Co., except about thirty tons at Ten Dollars per ton to be measured by same rule as sold to Nevada Packing one year ago, to be fed by P. Cassinelli free or we can feed ourselves, Cassinelli to furnish team and wagons.

The above hay to be delivered at once when measured and I hereby acknowledge receipt of $500.

His mark X Peter Cassinelli,
Seller.
H. L. Nichols,
Buyer.
W. E. Fuhrman.

On the issues thus made the trial court found that on December 2, 1916, all the hay referred to in this action was consumed by fire and destroyed; that at the time the hay was so burned and destroyed all of said hay was owned and in the possession of the plaintiff herein; that the hay in the stacks was not in a deliverable condition at the time it was burned, and had not been delivered to, or accepted by, the defendant; that the terms of said written agreement had not been complied with at the time the hay was burned; that the title to the hay or any of the hay referred to did not pass from the plaintiff to the defendant.

From the judgment rendered in favor of defendant and an order denying a motion for a new trial this appeal is taken.

A number of errors are assigned by appellant, and the principal one is that the court erred in finding that the hay in the stacks was not in a deliverable condition at the time it was sold, and had not been accepted by the defendant, and that the title had not passed from the plaintiff to defendant. It is insisted that such finding is not sustained by the evidence. On the other hand, respondent contends that the facts found are not reviewable here because they were found on a conflict of the evidence; and the only question we can consider in reference thereto is whether the conclusion that the title to the hay did not pass is a correct conclusion of law to be drawn from the facts found by the trial court. . . .

The inquiry arises, therefore, as to how far the finding of the court is based upon conflicting evidence, and necessitates a brief summary thereof.

On November 30, 1916, appellant was the owner of and in possession of two stacks of hay, situated upon his ranch near Reno, and on that day Mr. Small, representing the Humphrey Supply Company, went to appellant's ranch and entered into negotiations with him for the purchase of the hay for the company. The next day, Friday, December 1, appellant went to the office of respondent in Reno, and the agreement set out in the answer was executed by appellant and respondent. At the time of the execution of the agreement respondent gave appellant its check for $500. Mr. Small was present, and it was agreed between appellant and Mr. Small that they would measure the hay on the following Monday. At some time between the day the agreement was executed and the Monday following all the hay was burned through no fault of either party. This summary comprises all of the uncontradicted evidence that has any bearing upon the intention of the parties. There is also in the record the undisputed testimony of the two sons of the appellant that on December 1, at their father's instance, they measured the hay claimed to have been sold to respondent; but this evidence was retained in the record, by the ruling of the court, only for the purpose of showing the quantity of the hay, in case the court found that there had been a completed sale. The only evidence in which there is a conflict of a substantial nature is as to whether Mr. Small and appellant, when negotiating at the latter's ranch on November 30, segregated or identified the hay which respondent desired to purchase from the thirty tons which the appellant wished to retain. Appellant testified that on this occasion Small drove a stick in the stack on the east side to indicate the amount of hay he desired and the quantity reserved by appellant. Mr. Small testified that he did not put any stick in the stack and did nothing to designate the portion of the hay appellant was to keep for himself.

From the aforesaid ruling of the lower court on the evidence of appellant's sons, and its judgment in favor of respondent, it is apparent that the court did not consider their testimony that they found a stick in the stack and measured from it when they measured the hay on December 1.

There is no intimation of a finding on this conflicting evidence in the findings of the trial court, nor is it mentioned in the brief oral opinion of the court incorporated in the record. Even if the stick was placed in the stack by respondents' agent, the act was, at the most, a mere estimation of the amount of hay desired, and was superseded by the written agreement which fixed the amount of hay to be taken by respondent and the amount to be retained by appellant to a definite number of tons, to be ascertained by actual measurement. The testimony of appellant and Mr. Small on this question was therefore immaterial, and a finding upon it, if made, would have been ineffective.

A consideration of the provisions of the sales act (Stats. 1915, c. 159) is necessary to a determination of the principal question involved.

[Two pages of the opinion quoting from the Sales Act and holding that the hay in question was specific goods (see *supra*, p. 59), are here omitted.]

The uniform sales act, in section 19, prescribes several rules for ascertaining the intention of parties, and counsel for respondent contend that if the goods were specific rule 5 applies.

Of course these rules are mere rules of presumption, and by the terms of the act must give way if a contrary intention appears. Rule 5 reads:

"If the contract * * * requires the seller to deliver the goods to the buyer, or at a particular place, or to pay the freight or cost of transportation to the buyer, or to a particular place, the property does not pass until the goods have been delivered to the buyer or reached the place agreed upon."

This rule is declaratory of the common law. It is based upon a theory analogous to that supporting rule 2 of section 19 — something further remains to be done, not, indeed, to put the goods in a deliverable state, but in order to carry out the bargain. Williston on Sales, par. 280.

Counsel base their contention in this respect upon the theory that the agreement obligates the appellant to deliver the goods as a condition precedent to the transfer of the property, and there was no delivery.

But it is not clear that the agreement effects such an obligation. The agreement contemplates delivery after measurement. This is plain from the language, "The above hay to be delivered at once when measured." . . . We think the intention of the parties as to delivery was merely to postpone it until immediately after measurement, and therefore that rule 5 has no application.

Counsel for appellant insist that the true rule for ascertaining the intention in this case is formulated by rule 1, which provides:

"Where there is an unconditional contract to sell specific goods, in a deliverable state, the property in the goods passes to the buyer when the contract is made, and it is immaterial whether the time of payment, or the time of delivery, or both, be postponed."

This rule is also declaratory of a common-law rule, that if the buyer or seller makes a proposition of purchase or sale, and either accepts, and the goods are in possession of the seller, and nothing remains to be done to identify them, or in any way prepare them for delivery, the sale is completed, and the property in the goods passes at once. Time of payment or delivery is immaterial. This rule establishes a presumption that the title passes when the contract is made if the goods are identified, and nothing remains to be done other than delivery of the goods and payment of the price. Williston on Sales, sec. 264.

We think that this rule is also inapplicable.

The private matter in the transaction is the condition as to measurement, and, on the whole, it is fairly collectible that the parties intended this requirement as essential to consummate the sale. In the written contract it is stipulated that the hay should be measured prior to delivery and by an agreed standard of measurement, "by same rule as sold to Nevada Packing one year ago."

The written contract is silent as to the time and by whom the measurement was to be made, but these factors are supplied by the understanding between Mr. Small and appellant at the time of the execution of the contract. Mr. Small testified, and it was uncontradicted by appellant, and corroborated by Mr. Nichols, that at that time appellant agreed that the hay should be measured the following Monday. It appears that Mr. Small and appellant were to participate in the measurement. Neither of the parties had waived the stipulations concerning measurement when the hay was burned. Both had the right to participate in the measurement of the hay. Delivery had been postponed by the express terms of the contract until after measurement. There was something more to be accomplished by the measurement than the mere ascertainment of the price to be paid for the hay.

It was a necessary act under the contract to separate appellant's thirty tons from the larger mass which respondent proposed to purchase, so that the latter could be fed from the stacks to its stock without incurring the danger of feeding any portion of the hay reserved by appellant.

If respondent had contracted for all of appellant's hay in the two stacks, then it would be certain that measurement could serve no purpose except to ascertain the price to be paid.

If such was the case here, then the rule contended for by appellant, and to sustain which he has cited numerous authorities, that property in goods will pass to the buyer though the goods sold are afterwards to be weighed, measured, or counted, might apply. This rule, however, has its most frequent application when there has been a delivery, and the quantity of goods sold is yet to be ascertained to fix the price. Benjamin on Sales, secs. 418–423. In this case, however, delivery having been specially postponed until after measurement, and the former being necessary, not only to ascertain the price, but to distinguish into severalty the subject-matter of the contract so that the acts of possession and ownership mentioned in the contract might be properly exercised over it, the circumstances strongly indicate that the parties regarded measurement as essential to complete the sale. The effect of the agreement and understanding concerning measurement was to make it impossible for the buyer to take possession of the property until that had been done. The measurement was "something further to be done," as stated in Williston on Sales, *supra*, "not, indeed, to put the goods in a deliverable state, but in order to carry out the bargain," and to put the buyer in possession of the property.

Considerable stress is laid by counsel for appellant upon the words "bought" and "sold," used in the contract, as indicating a present sale. These terms are frequently used in executory contracts, consequently their literal meaning is not necessarily evidence of a present sale. . . .

We hold that, under the particular facts of this case, measurement was a condition precedent in the contract to the transfer of property in the hay, and that the title had not passed to the buyer when the hay was burned. . . .

The judgment of the district court is affirmed.

SANDERS, J.: I concur.

COLEMAN, C. J.: I concur in the order.

In RICHARDSON LUMBER CO. *v.* HOEY, *supra*, p. 77, the first defense to the action was based on the contention that the contract did not pass title to the ties. In upholding this contention the Court said: "In the instant case, we have a contract where the identity, amount, quality, price and time of payment were definitely fixed and nothing remained to be done except to count the ties to see if they checked up with the number stated in the contract."

Note also NANKA-BRUCE *v.* COMMONWEALTH TRUST, LIMITED, [1926] A. C. 77 (Privy Council, 1925). Plaintiff arranged to consign cocoa to one Laing by rail at 59 shillings per load of 60 pounds. Laing was to resell the cocoa to merchants and to transfer to them the railway consignment notes; the merchants were to check the weights, and Laing was to pay according to the weights so checked. Plaintiff consigned 160 bags of cocoa to Laing, and Laing sold this lot to defendant, turning over the consignment note. Defendant bought the cocoa in good faith without notice of the arrangement between plaintiff and Laing, and credited Laing with the amount on a large debt due from him. Plaintiff brought the present action for the value of the cocoa or alternatively for damages for conversion. In answering the contention that no property in the cocoa had passed to Laing, Lord Shaw said: "The provision as to the weight of the goods being tested was not a condition precedent to a sale. . . . In this case there was no contract whatever to carry into effect the weighing, which was simply a means to satisfy the purchaser that he had what he had bargained for and that the full price claimed per the contract was therefore due."

In ROE *v.* THE WINTER HAVEN COMPANY, 104 Fla. 317 (Supreme Court, 1932), there was a contract for the sale of citrus fruit on the trees. The contract stated that "it is agreed and understood that first party by these presents becomes the owner and second party sells to first party all the fruit at this date upon" certain described land. Other terms provided for a down payment of $1000.00 and for a price of $2.25 per field box, $2.00 to be paid for each box as taken from the grove, and the remaining twenty-five cents to be credited against the down payment; with a proviso that an accounting and final adjustment was to be made when the buyer took the last fruit from the grove. In holding that title to the fruit passed when the contract was made, the Court said:

"If it is a part of a contract of sale of personal property, that the vendor shall deliver the property at some fixed time and place and receive payment on delivery, or the agreement is one where anything remains to be done by the vendor to the goods, as by weighing, measuring or testing the goods, or where the price is to depend on the quantity or quality of the goods later to be delivered, the performance of these things is ordinarily a condition precedent to the transfer of the title to them, although the individual goods are ascertained and they are in a state in which they ought to be accepted.

"But there is abundant authority to the effect that, although personal property of large and unknown quantity may be sold by the pound, foot, yard or other measure, yet if the seller is not bound to measure, weigh or identify it before delivery, but delivers the whole to the buyer *in praesenti*, with the intention of making a present sale to him in bulk, the mere fact that the precise quantity is not known, nor the whole price ascertained, does not prevent the title from passing at the time of the making of the agreement to sell."

COLUMBIA WEIGHING MACHINE CO., INC. *v.* KLECKNER

NEW YORK SUPREME COURT, 1927

[130 *New York Miscellaneous Reports*, 861]

HATTING, J. The defendant purchased of the plaintiff a penny slot personal weighing machine under a contract, dated June 6, 1927, in the following form:

"Date, June 6, 1927. Price, $180. Freight paid. The Columbia Weighing Machine Company, Inc., 634–644 Whitlock Avenue, New York City. Payable $15 monthly. You may ship us one Columbia weighing machine, freight paid. It is sold to us with the understanding that we may return it to you with or without reason at any time within 30 days from date of arrival of the machine, instead of paying the purchase price. Return shipment to be made to above address, by freight only; freight charges collect. Should we not ship it back to you within 30 days from date of its arrival, we will pay you the purchase price thereof, namely, $180, as follows: Fifteen dollars per month, until paid; first payment to be made within 40 days from date of arrival of the machine. Should any of our payments be in arrears at any time, the entire unpaid balance of the purchase price shall then become due, together with attorney fees amounting to 20 per cent of the sum in default, if collection is made by law. It is understood you are to supply us with any mechanical parts required for the machine for a period of five years, without charge. Whenever we may want a part, we are to inform you by registered mail. Firm name, ———. Signed by George M. Kleckner (member of firm or officer). Town and state, New City, N. Y. Mail address, Main St. Bank reference, ———. Six per cent. may be deducted if the entire purchase price is paid within 40 days from date of arrival. No verbal agreement will be recognized. All orders are subject to acceptance by the company, at its home office at New York City."

Delivery of the machine was made to the defendant on June 14, 1927. Upon arrival machine was uncrated by defendant, examined and found defective in the following particulars: The coin cup was broken and the machine was otherwise inherently defective, so that the coin, when inserted in the slot, fell through the coin cup and did not register weight. The machine was thereupon recrated, and on June 20, 1927, a letter was written to the plaintiff, advising plaintiff of the defects, and advising further that the machine was being held subject to plaintiff's order, unless plaintiff repaired the same. Under this notice defendant had permitted the machine to remain in his possession. Meanwhile, on July 24, 1927, an installment of the purchase price became due and was unpaid. The plaintiff thereupon elected to declare the unpaid balance of the purchase price due, and brought this action upon the agreement of purchase.

The plaintiff pleads the usual complaint in goods sold and delivered. The defendant, by not denying, admits the agreement; the delivery on

June 14, 1927; that the goods were not shipped back within thirty days; that they were accepted by the defendant; that an installment of fifteen dollars became due and payable on July 24, 1927; that no part has been paid; that the plaintiff has elected to declare the entire purchase price of $180 due and payable; and that there also became due and payable from the defendant the additional sum of $36 as attorney's fees. The defendant by his answer denies only the legal conclusions that there is due and owing from the defendant $216 and interest, and that the plaintiff has performed all the terms of the agreement on its part to be performed. The defendant then interposes by way of an affirmative defense: "That the plaintiff warranted and represented that the machine mentioned in plaintiff's complaint would weigh accurately and serve the purpose for which defendant intended to use it; that the defendant relied upon the said warranty and representations, and upon the plaintiff's skill and judgment, and entered into and signed and delivered said contract as the same is set forth in the complaint, relying upon said warranty and representations; that the machine as delivered was not as the plaintiff had warranted and represented that it would be; that the said machine was broken and did not weigh correctly, and in general did not function and was inherently defective, and would not serve the purpose for which the plaintiff knew the defendant intended to use it; and that the defendant notified the plaintiff of said condition of the machine and wrote the plaintiff that the said machine was being held subject to plaintiff's order."

Plaintiff thereupon brings this motion under rule 113 of the Rules of Civil Practice, to strike out the answer and for summary judgment. The problem presented is the construction and legal effect of that portion of the agreement which provides: "It is sold to us with the understanding that we may return it to you with or without reason at any time within 30 days from the date of arrival of the machine, instead of paying the purchase price. Return shipment to be made to the above address by freight only; freight charges collect," etc.

The contract is one "on sale or return" and the property passed to the buyer on delivery. Section 100, rule 3, of the Personal Property Law, applies to this situation. It provides:

"Rules for Ascertaining Intention. Unless a different intention appears, the following are rules for ascertaining the intention of the parties as to the time at which the property in the goods is to pass to the buyer. * * *

"Rule 3. 1. When goods are delivered to the buyer 'on sale or return,' or on other terms indicating an intention to make a present sale, but to give the buyer an option to return the goods instead of paying the price, the property passes to the buyer on delivery, but he may revest the property in the seller, by returning or tendering the goods within the time fixed in the contract, or, if no time has been fixed, within a reasonable time."

It became the duty of the buyer upon the discovery of the defects and within the period of thirty days after its receipt to return the machine to the plaintiff if he desired to avail himself of the option. Here, although the goods were found defective upon the delivery, and notwithstanding the option, the defendant failed to return the goods during the period of option. It cannot be said that any implied warranty, if such in fact existed, survived the acceptance of the machine. The defendant admits the acceptance and it seems that his retention of the machine after the thirty-day option and with knowledge of its defects constitutes an acceptance in law independent of the admission. Professor Williston, in section 271, page 546, of the second edition of his Law on Sales, states: "Frequently the bargain of the parties will fix the time within which the buyer must return the goods. If he fails to exercise the right thus given him, his title cannot thereafter be avoided."

Here, the property in the machine having passed to the defendant upon its delivery, it remained in the defendant until the return thereof, and not having been returned, is presumed to remain there still. Performance of the agreement by the plaintiff was completed upon the delivery of the machine and the warranty, if any, relied upon by the defendant, did not survive the period of option. A somewhat similar situation is treated with in *Cronk & Carrier Mfg. Co.* v. *Galbraith Milling Co.* (197 App. Div. 568), which cites with approval *Greacen* v. *Poehlman* (191 N. Y. 493, 497): "The contract in this case belongs to a class of contracts often called 'contracts of sale or return,' being upon a condition that the buyer may return the goods within a fixed or reasonable time at his option. It has been held that goods so sold pass to the purchaser, subject to the option in him to return them, and that if he fails to exercise the option within the proper time the price of the goods may be recovered as upon an absolute sale."

It must be apparent, therefore, that the defense of the breach of an implied warranty is not available to the defendant in this action. The motion for summary judgment under rule 113 will be granted in favor of the plaintiff. Settle order on notice.

Note also COLUMBIA WEIGHING MACHINE CO. *v.* SMITH, 26 Ohio App. 321 (Ohio Court of Appeals, 1927), where under a contract in the same form the buyer wrote the seller within the thirty-day period stating that he did not wish to keep the machine and asking for shipping instructions. It was held that "the writing of the letter was not equivalent to a tender, if a tender could be a compliance with the contract."

In BERNADETTE, JOSEPH & CO. *v.* VAN BUREN, 212 App. Div. 702 (New York Supreme Court, Appellate Division, Third Department, 1925), Cochrane, P. J., said:

"This is an action to recover the purchase price of certain watches delivered by the plaintiff, doing business in Chicago, to the defendant, a merchant in the village of Schaghticoke, N. Y. The watches were stolen from the defendant without fault on his part. Plaintiff claims a sale of the watches to the defendant. The latter claims a consignment. The determination of this question will also determine which party must bear the loss occasioned by the larceny.

"The contract consists entirely of written communications between the parties. On November 18, 1922, defendant wrote plaintiff as follows:

" 'Please ship by express a small stock of watches, Elgin, Waltham, Hampden, South Bend &c. Bill them on memorandum at the net wholesale price. We will put them on sale and handle them with care. Will remit for watches sold. All not sold are to be returned when you notify us, or sooner if we desire.'

"November 23, 1922, plaintiff wrote defendant as follows:

" 'Your assortment of watches goes forward to-day by express via East Schaghticoke.

" 'The stock is billed on memorandum until after Christmas. Between January 1 and January 5, 1923, we will expect you to send us a remittance for all of the watches sold. This does not mean that you must return the unsold watches; simply send us a remittance for those disposed of, and, if you have met with reasonably good success, we will be glad to extend the time on the watches sixty days longer.

" 'Please sign the inclosed postal card and return it to us as soon as the shipment reaches you.

" 'BERNADETTE, JOSEPH & CO.

" 'Nov. 23, 1922.

" 'P. S. All watches returned must be in exactly as good condition as when received. We will not take back for credit any watches that have been worn.'

"The postal card mentioned and inclosed in the last-mentioned letter was signed by defendant and returned to plaintiff and contained this statement, '13 watches shipped Nov. 23, 1922, received. All of these that are not sold are to be sent back to you. Payment is to be made only for those not returned.'

"Defendant received the thirteen watches in a package which also contained an invoice containing an itemized statement of the watches with the prices to be paid therefor by defendant if he did not return them. This invoice contained the words: 'Sold to E. N. Van Buren.' It was evidently the memorandum asked for by defendant in his first communication to plaintiff where he said: 'Bill them on memorandum at the net wholesale price.' The invoice also contained at the bottom of each sheet thereof a statement which the defendant insists should be disregarded and which for the purposes of this action may be disregarded without affecting the result of the action. There was a subsequent delivery of watches under a precisely similar arrangement. Some of them were sold by defendant and the agreed price for those so sold was remitted to plaintiff. This action is to recover the price of those unsold and stolen. . . .

"The intention of the parties as indicated in their correspondence could not have been made much clearer. The intent was that of an accomplished sale. The invoice accompanying the property used the verb in the past tense; sold to E. N. Van Buren. The price of the watches as between the parties was fixed. Defendant could sell them at any price he wished or give them away and was only answerable to plaintiff for the price established as between themselves. He might sell or return at his option any or all of them. The contract was clearly within the statute above quoted.

There was no doubt or ambiguity as to the intention of the parties and, therefore, nothing for a jury to determine on that point. According to the statute, title to the property was in the defendant while the property was in his possession and the loss by larceny must, therefore, fall on him."

Compare KIRKHAM *v.* ATTENBOROUGH, [1897] 1 Q. B. 201 (Court of Appeal, 1896). A quantity of jewelry was delivered to a dealer on sale or return. The dealer pledged some of it with defendant. Plaintiff, the original seller claimed the value of this jewelry or its return. An appeal by defendant from a judgment for plaintiff was allowed, Lopes, L. J., saying:

"The position of a person who has received goods on sale or return is that he has the option of becoming the purchaser of them, and may become so in three different ways. He may pay the price, or he may retain the goods beyond a reasonable time for their return, or he may do an act inconsistent with his being other than a purchaser. The words of the Act are difficult to construe; but it seems to me that if the recipient of the goods retains them for an unreasonable time he does something inconsistent with the exercise of his option to return them, and thereby adopts the transaction. So if he does any other act inconsistent with their return, as if he sells them or pledges them, because if he pledges them he no longer has the free control over them so as to be in a position to return them. In all these cases he brings himself within the words of the section by adopting the transaction, and the property in the goods passes to him. If that is the state of the law, applying it to this case, it is clear that the plaintiff is not entitled to recover from the defendant either the goods or their price, and the judgment in favour of the plaintiff cannot be supported."

In DAVID W. BIOW CO. *v.* COHEN, 99 Vt. 78 (Supreme Court, 1923), the defendant, having goods in his possession under a sale or return contract, elected to return them, and delivered them to an express company in a package addressed to plaintiff, the seller. The package was delivered to another firm at the same address, and never was received by plaintiff. In an action on the contract, judgment for the plaintiff affirmed. When the buyer under a sale or return contract attempts to return the goods the title does not revest in the seller until they are delivered back to him or at the place agreed on.

KELLEY *v.* THOMAS G. PLANT CORPORATION

MASSACHUSETTS SUPREME JUDICIAL COURT, 1934

[274 *Massachusetts Report*, 102]

CARROLL, J. This action is in tort for the conversion of two lots of leather. The first count in the declaration alleges that one hundred eighty dozen black kid skins were delivered to the defendant on March 11, 1918; the second count states that one hundred ten dozen black kid skins were delivered to the defendant on May 6, 1918. The writ is dated October 15,

1927. The answer was a general denial and the statute of limitations. G. L. c. 260. The case is before us on the plaintiff's exceptions.

The plaintiff, a tanner of kid skins, from 1915 to 1924 sold to the defendant, a shoe manufacturer, each year an average of $250,000 worth of leather through the plaintiff's selling agents, Rousmanier, Williams & Company. In the year 1918 the defendant "was purchasing mostly brown or colored skins." The plaintiff testified that Brown, the defendant's purchasing agent, talked with him about "getting some black kid skins" which the plaintiff "wanted to sell the defendant"; that "he wanted some samples to submit to the defendant"; that on March 11, 1918, he shipped to the defendant one hundred eighty dozen black kid skins and on May 6, 1918, one hundred ten dozen skins of the same quality "to order from"; that the skins "were just like all other kid skins handled by the plaintiff and which he was selling to his customers in the regular course of business"; that the goods "were sent to the defendant in the hope that . . . their buyer would find them satisfactory and order that type of goods."

The defendant admitted receiving the March shipment, but denied that it received the second lot. The trial judge excluded several offers of evidence tending to show the receipt of the second shipment; the plaintiff excepted. The only evidence tending to show what became of the skins after shipment was the statement of the defendant's purchasing agent that "he believed the first lot of leather was cut up shortly after it was received." The plaintiff offered to show by oral testimony the contents of a letter indicating that on December 9, 1926, a demand was made on the defendant for the return of the goods. There was evidence that in September, 1928, the plaintiff gave the defendant notice "of the present claim . . . as to the second lot." It was agreed that on October 13, 1927, a written demand was made on the defendant for the return of the goods.

Assuming that all the goods were received by the defendant in March and May, 1918, that written demands for the return were made in December, 1926, and September, 1928, the plaintiff cannot recover in this action of tort. He desired to sell the leather to the defendant; it was similar to the material sold to his customers in the regular course of business. The defendant was not restricted to an inspection and return, it received them as a prospective buyer and it was "the hope" of the plaintiff that the defendant "would find them satisfactory and order that type of goods." The transaction is governed by the sales act, G. L. c. 106, § 21, Rule 3 (2), which is in these words: "When goods are delivered to the buyer on approval or on trial or on satisfaction, or other similar terms, the property therein passes to the buyer — (a) When he signifies his approval or acceptance to the seller or does any other act adopting the transaction. (b) If he does not signify his approval or acceptance to the seller, but retains the goods without giving notice of rejection, then, if a time has been fixed for the return of the goods, on the expiration of such time, or, if no time has been fixed, on the expiration of a reasonable time. What is a reasonable time is a question of fact." Title to the leather passed to the defendant either when it was cut up and used, if in fact it was used, or when retained beyond a reasonable time, and the plaintiff's right against the defendant was in contract for the price of the goods. Assuming in favor of the plaintiff that the merchandise was received in 1918, a reasonable time had elapsed before demand was made or action was brought; there was no evidence to the contrary and no evidence to support a finding that a reasonable time had not elapsed before the plaintiff made demand for the return or brought the action for conversion. More than six years had passed after the goods were received before demand was made, a reasonable time had elapsed and the title had passed to the defendant. As a question of fact no other result was reasonably possible. In our opinion, therefore, a verdict was directed for the defendant properly. . . .

Exceptions overruled.

In BELLEFLEUR *v.* UNITED STATES FINISHING CO., 111 Conn. 558 (Supreme Court of Errors, 1930), there was a contract for a vertical boring mill to be taken on a 30-day trial and to be returned if not satisfactory. The contract was made on December 21, 1927; the trial of the mill was begun on January 10, 1928, and was continued until January 24. On request of the buyer, the makers of the mill then sent a representative to inspect it, but owing to the absence of the buyer's superintendent the inspection could not be made until February 7. As a result of the inspection the buyer notified the makers in a letter received February 8 that the mill was unsatisfactory and asked for shipping instructions. No instructions were given, and the makers having demanded payment brought this action to recover the price named in the contract. Judgment for defendant affirmed. The buyer had 30 days from January 10 for trial, and a reasonable time thereafter in which to inform plaintiff of its acceptance or rejection.

In DINSMORE *v.* RICE, 128 Md. 209 (Supreme Court, 1916), a horse was delivered on the understanding that the buyer should indicate his acceptance or rejection by the following Monday noon. The buyer did nothing on Monday, and the horse died on Wednesday. In an action against the seller for feed, the seller set off the agreed price of the horse. Judgment for defendant affirmed. Title to the horse passed to the buyer at noon on Monday.

In BROWN *v.* POTOLSKI, 221 App. Div. 299 (New York Supreme Court, Appellate Division, 1927), a road machine was delivered under a contract which provided that it was to be kept if satisfactory, otherwise to be returned. The buyer used the machine for sixteen months, and failed to return it on demand. In an action for the purchase price it was held as a matter of law that title had passed to the buyer.

CHAPTER II

UNASCERTAINED GOODS GENERALLY: APPROPRIATION

MITCHELL *v.* WEINER

CONNECTICUT SUPREME COURT OF ERRORS, 1920

[94 *Connecticut Reports*, 446]

Action to recover the balance of the purchase-price of a crop of potatoes alleged to have been sold to the defendant, brought to the Superior Court in Hartford County and tried to the jury before Burpee, J.; verdict and judgment for the plaintiff for $2,032, and appeal by the defendant. Error and new trial ordered.

In 1917 the plaintiff, a farmer, raised a crop of potatoes which, consisting of all grades, amounted to about 3,000 bushels. On October 16th of that year he was visited by one Shindel, the duly-authorized agent of the defendant, a wholesale dealer. A bargain was then concluded for the defendant's purchase of the No. 1 potatoes, and thereupon the agreement of the parties was reduced to writing and signed by them as follows: —

Hartford, October 16, 1917.

I, Andrew Mitchell, of Buckland, Conn., have after due consideration sold my entire crop of potatoes to consist of about two thousand bushels of number one potatoes, to be well graded for two dollars per bu., to Weiner Bros. of Hartford. The grade of these potatoes shall consist of sound potatoes of similar varietal characteristics, which are to be free from dirt or other foreign substance or matter, absolutely free from frost injury, sunburn, second growth, cuts, scab, blight, dry rot, and damage caused by disease, insects, or mechanical means. The minimum diameter of the round varieties shall be two inches, and the minimum diameter of the long varieties shall be one and seven-eighths inches.

I furthermore agree to deliver the potatoes when Weiner Bros. desires to have me do so. Weiner Bros. agrees to furnish me the bags, I also agree not to sell these potatoes to any person or persons, unless instructed in writing by Weiner Bros.

A check of fifty dollars is hereby given to bind contract and to apply on account of potatoes.

Andrew Mitchell — Weiner Bros. per T. S. Shindel.

The plaintiff offered evidence to prove the following additional facts: At the time the bargain was made and the writing signed, his entire crop remained as the potatoes were dug — unsorted, ungraded and in a commingled mass made up of various grades, — and in that condition it was seen and examined by Shindel before the writing was executed. Subsequently the plaintiff sorted and graded them, obtaining therefrom about 2,000 bushels of No. 1. These latter were thereafter kept and stored by him separately and apart from those of lower grades, and for the defendant. No request for their delivery was made by the defendant until February 19th, 1918. Thereupon, on the 20th of that month, the plaintiff delivered, as requested, the first load, containing 145 bushels. A day or two later he delivered a second load, and on the 26th, the third. These three loads were accepted and paid for by the defendant at the contract price of $2 per bushel. March 8th he delivered a fourth load which, and all undelivered potatoes, the defendant refused to receive. The plaintiff thereupon sold those not delivered and accepted, at the best available market price. That price having declined, he was able to obtain only $1 a bushel. All the potatoes offered to the defendant were number one.

The defendant offered evidence to prove that the potatoes delivered on February 25th were scabby, frost-bitten and in bad condition, and not number one grade; that he requested the plaintiff to take back the inferior ones, which the latter refused to do; that the defendant thereupon told the plaintiff that he would not accept any more — that he wouldn't have anything more to do with the plaintiff; that no further attempts at delivery were made until about the 8th or 10th of March, when he refused acceptance; that he intended to use the potatoes purchased of the plaintiff as seed potatoes, the market price of which was $7 per eleven peck sack, and that scabby, frost-bitten, or No. 2 potatoes were not suitable for such use.

PRENTICE, C. J. The court instructed the jury that upon the execution of the writing of October 16th, 1917, the property in the No. 1 potatoes contained in the plaintiff's crop passed from the plaintiff to the defendant. This fundamental instruction, followed as it was by others touching the responsibility thereafter for the care and condition of the potatoes which logically flowed from it, was one which approached very nearly to a direction of a verdict for the plaintiff for some amount. The defendant complains of it as erroneous. The instruction given necessarily implies that the court interpreted the writing as evidencing the intent of the parties to conclude a present, executed sale, as distinguished from a contract to sell. Conceding, for present purposes, that its by no means unambiguous language should have that construction, there remains another factor in the situation whose significance the court evidently overlooked. The plaintiff offered evidence to prove, and the defendant, as far as appears, none to disprove, that at the time the writing was signed the plaintiff's crop of potatoes, amounting to about 3,000 bushels, had not been sorted or graded, and that those of No. 1 grade, being about two thirds of the whole, were commingled with those of different grades in an indiscriminate mass. Both selection and separation were, therefore, necessary before the identity of the particular potatoes in which the property was to pass to the defendant under the writing could be established. Until that selection and separation should be made, the potatoes coming under the contract were unascertained, and the general property in them could not pass until they were ascertained and their identity determined. That involved a selection in accordance with the specifications and requirements of the contract, and a separation of those selected from those of other grades with which they were commingled. Section 4683 of the General Statutes is specific as to this requirement of a consummated present sale passing property in the goods. It is there expressly provided that "where there is a contract to sell unascertained goods, no property in the goods is transferred to the buyer unless and until the goods are ascertained." While this section had its origin in the Sales Act, it does not lead us to a result different from that which our law antedating it would have reached.

The record states that the plaintiff offered evidence to prove that subsequent to the transaction of October 16th the plaintiff selected and separated the No. 1 potatoes from the others, and that those so selected were thereafter kept apart from the balance of the crop, and for the defendant.

It is certain that the property in specific potatoes did not pass to the defendant until such selection and separation was made, if it should be found that they ever were made. . . .

The court's instructions, that the property in the potatoes passed on October 16th, 1917, and that, therefore, the defendant was thereafter responsible for their care and assumed all risk of their deterioration, took all possible questions of fact thus indicated away from the jury and restricted the field of the defendant's defense to exceedingly narrow limits. They, in effect, closed the door to all inquiries by the jury save only as to the amount of No. 1 potatoes the plaintiff had ready for delivery, and the loss he sustained by reason of their nonacceptance.

There is error, the verdict is set aside and a new trial ordered.

In this opinion the other judges concurred.

In Busk *v.* Davis, 2 Maule & Selwyn 397 (King's Bench, 1814), a sold note read as follows: "Sold on account of Busk and Co. 10 tons of Riga flax, marked P. D. R. at Davis's wharf, sound and of a merchantable quality 'ex' The Vrow Maria, at £118 per ton, the amount to be paid by the buyer's acceptance at three months from to-day." At the time this note was given the seller had 18 tons of Riga flax at the wharf in question. The flax had been imported in mats, and the sale of 10 tons meant that the mats would have to be broken up and rearranged before the specific quantity could be determined. In holding that in such circumstances a delivery order accepted by the wharfinger could not operate as a complete delivery, Lord Ellenborough, C. J., said: "If then some further acts were to be done in order to regulate the identity, and (if I may use such a phrase) the individuality of the thing to be delivered, I cannot say that it was in a state fit for immediate delivery."

In California Animal Products Co. *v.* Lappin, 54 R. I. 75 (Supreme Court, 1934), plaintiff accepted from defendant an order for 110 cases of dog food, mailing an invoice and an order on a warehouse where a larger quantity was stored for which a warehouse receipt had been issued to plaintiff. The warehouse had no notice of this transaction. Fire damaged the entire lot before the order was presented, and before any separation was made. In an action for the purchase price, the trial court gave judgment for plaintiff. Exceptions sustained. "To constitute a sale the parties must intend to transfer immediate ownership in some specific article or articles."

PROCTER & GAMBLE COMPANY *v.* PETERS, WHITE & COMPANY

NEW YORK COURT OF APPEALS, 1922

[233 *New York Reports*, 97]

CRANE, J. On the 29th day of January, 1914, the Atlantic Phosphate and Oil Corporation, a New York company, entered into a contract with the plaintiff in this case, the Procter & Gamble Company of Ohio, wherein the Atlantic Phosphate and Oil Corporation agreed to sell to the plaintiff all the menhaden oil, grade "A" to be produced by the seller at its plant at Promised Land, Long Island, New York, during the period from the date of the contract to December 31st, 1914. The contract contained the following provision:

> The Purchaser shall receive the oil in Purchaser's tank cars, to be supplied by the Purchaser at the Seller's said factory at Promised Land, or at the Purchaser's option, from time to time, in Purchaser's barrels, to be furnished by the Purchaser at the said factory at Promised Land. * * * The Purchaser shall provide enough tanks or barrels at the factory as aforesaid to take and receive all said oil as and when produced by the Seller, except as hereinafter provided. * * * If at any time there shall not be at the factory sufficient tank cars or barrels furnished by the Purchaser to receive all the oil as fast as produced, the Seller shall store the said oil in its own tanks at its factory, and Marden, Orth & Hastings Company shall invoice the oil so soon as stored in said tanks to the Purchaser, and shall be entitled to draw on the Purchaser at sight, at the same rate of 25 cents a gallon for the said oil so stored in storage tanks, as well as for the oil placed in said tank cars or barrels; provided, however, that if at any time the oil so stored in the Seller's storage tanks shall reach the amount of fifteen thousand barrels, and there shall not be enough tank cars or barrels provided by the Purchaser to take care of all excess as fast as produced, the Seller may ship such excess oil to the Purchaser or store the same in any way that may be possible, and the Purchaser in that event shall pay to the seller any extra expenses thus incurred by the Seller.

The contract further provides for an advanced payment of $25,000 by the purchaser and the terms of subsequent payments which need not here be referred to.

Although the purchaser was to take all the menhaden oil manufactured by the seller during the period specified, there was excepted from this amount 6,000 barrels or such part thereof as Marden, Orth & Hastings Company might take under an agreement between it and the Atlantic Phosphate and Oil Corporation, dated the 15th day of October, 1913.

Marden, Orth & Hastings Company, by an agreement of said date, appeared to have been appointed the factors or agents of the Atlantic

Phosphate and Oil Corporation and to have procured the Procter & Gamble Company contract above referred to.

By another contract, dated May 1st, 1913, the defendant in this case, Peters, White & Company, a New York corporation, was appointed factor for the Atlantic Phosphate and Oil Corporation, and given the exclusive right and authority to make agreements for the sale of the oil product, to invoice for the same, and make all collections.

During August and September of 1914 seven carloads of this oil were taken from the storage tank of the Atlantic Phosphate and Oil Corporation and shipped to Swift & Company of Chicago, Illinois, pursuant to the directions of the defendant. For six of the carloads the defendant was paid by Swift & Company. Two of the tank cars thus loaded and shipped had been sent to the seller's plant at Promised Land by the plaintiff. The order for the bill of lading for these two cars was drawn to the order of Peters, White & Company, with instructions to notify Swift & Company, the destination being Union Stock Yards, Chicago, state of Illinois. The other five cars were not furnished by the plaintiff and were consigned by orders for bill of lading in the same way to the order of Peters, White & Company with directions to notify Swift & Company at the Union Stock Yards, Chicago, Illinois.

There is no question about the direction and control of the defendant over this oil and the shipments made by the Atlantic Phosphate and Oil Corporation.

This action has been brought by the plaintiff against the defendant, the factor, to recover for a conversion of this oil, the plaintiff contending that having purchased all the oil to be manufactured by the Atlantic Phosphate and Oil Corporation, title had passed to it when the oil entered the storage tanks and that the subsequent shipment and delivery by the defendant to Swift & Company amounted to a conversion of the oil. The plaintiff thus far has been successful in this contention and has recovered the full value of the seven cars thus shipped to Swift & Company. The opinion of the Appellate Division on a previous trial of this case will be found in 187 Appellate Division, 376. The point in the case is the question whether or not title was in the plaintiff, whether there had been such an appropriation of this oil to the contract by the Atlantic Phosphate and Oil Corporation as to pass title.

As the passage of title depends in each case upon the circumstances and the intention of the parties (*Hatch* v. *Oil Co.*, 100 U. S. 124) we must first ascertain the exact facts and from these gather the intention of the parties, aided by our Personal Property Law. The oil which the plaintiffs purchased was made from fish by a process described as follows: "The oil, after it was pressed from the fish, after the cooking process, the oil came out cloudy and more or less solid matter mixed through it. It had to be cooked after the pressing and permitted to stand for several days before it was clean and in condition to ship. There are a number of tanks in Promised Land, cooking tanks, in which the preliminary cooking takes place and settling tanks in which solid matter is permitted to settle out, and then storage tanks in which the oil is stored after it is settled. * * * The oil that was accumulated after settling in the storage tanks was drawn from the storage tanks into tank cars and the tank cars were weighed by the railroads and shipped to destination."

The oil, therefore, went into the storage tank as part of the process of manufacture in any and at all events. When the agreement made with Procter & Gamble Company provided, as above quoted, that in case of the plaintiff's failure to have the tank cars or barrels at the seller's plant at Promised Land the seller should store the said oil in his own tanks at the factory, it did not contemplate a setting apart and separation of the manufactured oil for the plaintiff. The oil would have gone into the storage tank whether intended for the plaintiff or any other purchaser or any number of purchasers. It was the place for keeping it after manufacture, in the same way that a bin may be a receptacle for keeping grain or a warehouse for storing merchandise. There was nothing in the nature of the act in sending the oil into the storage tank which indicated in itself that it was set apart for the plaintiff. Marden, Orth & Hastings Company had an option mentioned in the plaintiff's contract to take 6,000 barrels of this oil. They did not exercise the option and it was testified upon the trial that they consented that the plaintiff should have all the oil contracted for. There is, however, no evidence that this so-called waiver or consent was definitely or specifically communicated to the seller. If, therefore, Marden, Orth & Hastings Company had exercised the option, the 6,000 barrels or the portion thereof taken, would have run into the storage tank in the process of manufacture, together with the oil intended for, and to be delivered to, the plaintiff.

[Quotation of the pertinent sections of the Personal Property Law (Uniform Sales Act, Secs. 5 (1) and (3), 76 (4), and 18, Rule 4 (1)), is here omitted.]

It may be that upon the completion of manufactured goods, ready for delivery, title will pass to the purchaser by the intention of the parties, without any further act. In other words, that intention alone may pass title without delivery, setting apart, or appropriation of the article to or for the purchaser. (*Clarkson* v. *Stevens*, 106 U. S. 505.)

In this case, however, we think it is in harmony with the contract, with our statute, and with the decisions, to hold that there must have been some act upon the part of the seller setting apart and appropriating the oil to the purchaser before title passed. (*Haynes* v. *Quay*, 134 Mich. 229.)

When in the process of manufacture the oil passed into the storage tanks there must have been "a subsequent appropriation" to the plaintiff's contract (*Cooke* v. *Millard*, 65 N. Y. 352, 366), or after the oil was in a deliverable state, it must have been "unconditionally appropriated to the contract" (Rule 4, *supra*) before the plaintiff in this case took title to the oil. (Williston on Sales, § 274; *Cooke* v. *Millard*, *supra; Andrews* v. *Durant*, 11 N. Y. 35; *Aldridge* v. *Johnson*, 7 E. & B. 885; *Low* v. *Pew*, 108 Mass. 347; *Mucklow* v. *Mangles*, 1 Taunt. 318.)

We cannot find in this case any evidence of this appropriation or setting apart of the oil for the purpose of the purchaser's contract, with the exception of two carloads. As to the two cars belonging to the plaintiff into which the oil was put there can be no question in my mind but that the oil was not only appropriated and set apart to the contract, but that there was an actual delivery of the oil to the plaintiff as specified in the contract. . . .

As to the other five cars there was no appropriation of the oil so far as we can discover from the evidence. It went into the storage tank as part of the process of manufacture to await appropriation and delivery on contracts or to customers. It was shipped to Swift & Company, and in our judgment never became the property of the plaintiff. In so far as the plaintiff has recovered for the conversion of this oil by the defendant, there must be a reversal or a modification of the judgments below.

[The balance of the opinion is here omitted.]

For the reasons here stated, the judgments appealed from must be reversed and a new trial granted, costs to abide the event.

HISCOCK, Ch. J., HOGAN, CARDOZO, POUND, MCLAUGHLIN and ANDREWS, JJ., concur.

Judgments reversed, etc.

In STATE *ex rel.* PULVERIZING CO. *v.* FITTS, 166 Tenn. 156 (Supreme Court, 1932), there was a contract for the sale of six limestone pulverizing machines of standard design. The seller manufactured six machines as a result of this contract and for the purpose of filling the order, writing letters to the buyer to ask for shipping instructions, and sending invoices covering the machines. In an action for the purchase price based on the refusal of the buyer to take the machines, it was held that title did not pass to the buyer on completion of the machines, and that the sending of invoices could not be considered as an appropriation in the absence of assent from the buyer.

Compare HOGUE-KELLOGG CO. *v.* BAKER, *supra*, p. 48, where a contract for a sale of a crop to be grown was construed to mean that title would pass to the buyer as soon as the crop came into existence.

ANDREWS *v.* CHENEY

NEW HAMPSHIRE SUPREME COURT, 1882

[62 *New Hampshire Reports*, 404]

Assumpsit, to recover money paid for goods. Facts found by a referee. October 28, 1879, the plaintiff bought goods of the defendant and paid for them. The defendant did not have in stock the goods wanted, and the plaintiff selected the kind and quality desired from samples. The defendant agreed to have the goods at his store within two weeks, at which time the plaintiff was to call for them; if they were ready before that time the defendant agreed to notify him. Within the stipulated time the defendant got the goods into his store, set them apart by themselves, and marked them with the plaintiff's name. The goods, together with the store, were destroyed by fire November 21, 1879, the plaintiff not having called for them. The court ordered judgment for the defendant, and the plaintiff excepted.

CARPENTER, J. The property in the goods did not pass to the plaintiff by virtue of the contract, for they were not then ascertained, and may not have been in existence. The agreement on the part of the defendant was executory. He agreed to furnish goods corresponding to the samples selected by the plaintiff. If the goods, subsequently procured and set apart by the defendant, did not conform to the samples, the plaintiff had a right to reject them. It does not appear that he waived that right. The defendant was not concluded by his selection; he might have sold or otherwise disposed of the particular articles set apart by him, and substituted others in their place. A contract of sale is not complete until the specific goods upon which it is to operate are agreed upon. Until that is done the contract is not a sale, but an agreement to sell goods of a particular description. It is performed on the part of the vendor by furnishing goods which answer the description. If, as in the case of a sale by sample, the specific goods are not ascertained by the agreement, the property does not pass until an appropriation of specific goods to the contract is made with the assent of both parties. *Bog Lead Mining Co.* v. *Montague,* 10 C. B. N. S. 489; *Jenner* v. *Smith,* L. R. 4 C. P. 270; *Heilbutt* v. *Hickson,* L. R. 7 C. P. 438; *Merchants' N. Bank* v. *Bangs,* 102 Mass. 291; Black. Sales 122, 127; Benj. Sales, s. 358. If the plaintiff authorized the defendant to make the selection, the property immediately on the selection vested in the plaintiff. *Aldridge* v. *Johnson,* 7 E. & B. 885. It not appearing that the plaintiff gave such authority, the goods at the time of the fire were the property of the defendant, and their destruction was his loss.

By the terms of the contract the defendant was to have the goods at his store within two weeks, at the end of which time, or sooner if notified that they were ready, the plaintiff was to call for them, and the defendant was to deliver them. Within the stipulated time the defendant procured the goods and had them ready for delivery. This was all the agreement required him to do, and all that he could do until the plaintiff came for them. The plaintiff's call being a condition precedent to the defendant's obligation to deliver, must be shown in order to entitle the plaintiff to treat the contract as rescinded and recover back the purchase-money.

It may be that the trial before the referee proceeded upon the mistaken theory that the rights of the parties were concluded by the destruction by fire of the particular goods selected by the defendant, and that the only question was upon whom the loss of those goods should fall. The plaintiff did not call for the goods before the fire; but whether he did after the fire does not appear, and may have been considered immaterial. The rights of the parties under the agreement were not affected by the destruction of the goods. If they were set apart without authority from the plaintiff, he still had the right to call for the goods he bargained for, and the defendant was bound to deliver them. Upon the defendant's neglect or refusal to deliver them upon request as well after as before the fire, the plaintiff might at his election rescind the contract and recover the purchase-money, or affirm it and recover for the breach. *Drew* v. *Claggett*, 39 N. H. 431; *Weeks* v. *Robie*, 42 N. H. 316; *Swazey* v. *Company*, 48 N. H. 200.

The case may be recommitted to the referee, if the plaintiff desires it, for the purpose of showing a call for the goods after the fire. If recommitted, it will be open to the defendant to show that he was authorized by the plaintiff to select the goods. As the case stands the exceptions are overruled.

Exceptions overruled.

In Frank Pure Food Co. *v.* Dodson, 281 Penn. 125 (Supreme Court, 1924), there was a contract for the sale of 2000 cases of sauerkraut, the buyer to supply labels for the cans. One thousand cases were delivered and paid for, but prior to such delivery the buyer notified the seller that it would not take the second thousand, which were completed but not labelled. The seller then placed the thousand cases in a warehouse and tendered the buyer the receipt, which was refused. It was held that no title vested in the buyer.

Note also American Factors, Limited *v.* Goss, 72 Calif. App. 742 (District Court of Appeal, 1925). A contract was entered into for 800 tons of double-compressed hay for which full payment was made. Five hundred tons were taken by the buyers. Part of the balance had been double-compressed and set aside for the buyer, being so entered in the seller's books. The rest also had been compressed and was in the seller's warehouse, but had not been set aside for the buyer. The warehouse was destroyed by fire. In an action for the return of the purchase price, judgment for plaintiff was affirmed. The segregation shown was not sufficient to pass title, as it was without the assent of the buyers.

PIGNATORO *v.* GILROY

King's Bench Division, 1918

[*Law Reports*, [1919] 1 *King's Bench*, 459]

Appeal from the Middlesex County Court.

On February 12, 1918, the defendants sold to the plaintiff "140 bags of rice (130 Butterfly 10 T.Y.C.) to be taken delivery in 14 days free from date." The sale was by sample, and the particular bags that were to satisfy the contract were not then ascertained, but the plaintiff was told that 125 bags would be delivered at a wharf called Chambers' Wharf, and the remaining 15 bags at the defendants' place of business, 50 Long Acre. On February 27 the plaintiff sent a cheque for the price, and asked for a delivery order as arranged. On the following day the defendants wrote to the plaintiff enclosing a delivery order for 125 bags from Chambers' Wharf, and stating that the 15 bags were ready for delivery at 50 Long Acre. The plaintiff neglected to send for the 15 bags until March 25, when it was found that they had been stolen at some time shortly before that date.

The action was brought to recover the sum of 61*l.* 10*s.*, the value of the missing rice. The county court judge found the bags in question had been stolen without any negligence on the part of the defendants, but he gave judgment for the plaintiff upon the ground that the subject-matter of the sale being unascertained goods there was no evidence of appropriation by either party with the assent of the other, and consequently the property had not passed to the plaintiff at the time of the loss.

The defendants appealed.

ROWLATT J. This was an action for damages for non-delivery of 15 bags of rice sold by the defendants to the plaintiff. The defence was that the goods had been stolen without default of the defendants after the property had passed to the plaintiff. The county court judge held that the theft was not due to any negligence of the defendants, but he gave judgment against them on the ground that the property had not passed. The contract was held by the judge upon the evidence to be for 140 bags of rice, unascertained at the time of the sale, of which delivery was to be taken by the plaintiff in 14 days, the contract having been made on or about February 12, 1918. The contract being silent as to the time of payment, it is to be taken that this was to be against delivery. On February 20 the defendants wrote to the plaintiff stating that the 14 days were up on the following day. The plaintiff replied on February 27, sending a cheque, and asking for a delivery order as arranged. On February 28 the defendants sent a delivery order for 125 bags which were lying at the wharf of a third party, and a receipt for the cheque. With regard to the remaining 15 bags the letter reads as follows: "The bags at the above place" — meaning 50 Long Acre, from which the letter was written — "are ready for delivery, and shall be pleased if you can send for them at once as we are very short of room." The evidence was that there were only 15 bags at Long Acre, though the plaintiff did not admit this. The plaintiff did not send for the 15 bags in response to this letter, and two other letters — namely, on March 6 and March 12 — asking them to do so were found by the judge to have been written and posted by the defendants, but he said it was not proved that they were received. Matters still remaining in this position, the 15 bags were stolen towards the end of March. Under the above contract it would be the duty of the sellers to appropriate the goods to the contract; and if such appropriation were assented to, expressly or impliedly, by the buyer the property would have passed. When they received the cheque for the goods and were asked for a delivery order it was right and proper for them to appropriate and place at the disposal of the buyer the goods for which he thus paid in order to effectuate a delivery or its equivalent concurrently with the receipt of the money. They did send a delivery order for the goods at Chambers' Wharf, and as to the 15 bags, told the plaintiff that they were ready, and asked that they should be taken away. It might well be contended that not only as regards the goods covered by the delivery order, but also as regards the goods at the defendants' own premises which they thus told the plaintiff were ready to be taken away in response to the plaintiff's request for a delivery order, there was an appropriation to which by asking for the delivery order the plaintiff had assented in advance. We do not think it necessary to decide this, because we think there was what amounted to an assent subsequent. If the plaintiff had replied saying that he would remove the goods the case would be precisely the same as *Rohde* v. *Thwaites* (6 B. & C. 388). The plaintiff, however, did nothing for a month, and the question is what is the effect of that? If the goods were of the required quality it is difficult to see how the plaintiff could have dissented from the appropriation. He could not object to the place from which he was required to fetch them, because he had inspected rice lying at those premises at the time and for the purposes of this very contract. For the same reason it is not easy to see how he could have objected to their quality unless there happened to be some bags inferior to those which he had inspected. At any rate, he made no objection at all. Now it is obvious that if he made any objection he ought to do so promptly, because he could not place upon the vendors the risk involved in the continued possession of these goods, nor prolong the encumbrance of the vendors' premises. As he chose merely to say nothing for a whole month in response to an appropriation made in consequence of his own letter, we think that comes to precisely the same thing as if he had written saying he would remove them and did not. The learned judge said that there was no evidence of an appropriation with the assent of the buyer. He could only say this if he was looking for an express assent. As the assent may be implied we think that there was not only evidence of it but that it is the only inference possible upon the facts. For these reasons the appeal must be allowed, and judgment entered for the defendants. We express no opinion as to whether the proviso to s. 20 of the Sale of Goods Act would protect the defendants in this case.

Appeal allowed.

Note also COOK & LAURIE CONTRACTING CO. *v.* BELL, 177 Ala. 618 (Supreme Court, 1912). A contract was made for the sale of 2000 barrels of cement, with no provision as to time or place of delivery. At the time of making the contract the seller also was contemplating the sale of his plant and had on hand in bulk about 5000 barrels of cement. The buyer of the 2000 barrels agreed to pay the purchase price before the plant was transferred, and it was agreed further that in the meantime 2000 barrels were to be sacked and stacked in the seller's bins at the plant. In pursuance of this agreement the seller sacked 2000 barrels of cement, stored the sacks in several bins, nailed up the doors, and marked them with the name of the buyer. The seller then sent a bill for the cement to the buyer, enclosing a letter and a sketch indicating the storage of the cement. Receipt was acknowledged by the buyer, who again promised to pay as agreed. In an action for the purchase price, judgment for plaintiff affirmed. Title *prima facie* passed to the buyer when the cement was stored and the bill sent according to agreement; and even had there been no prearrangement in this respect, a subsequent assent might be inferred from the buyer's acknowledgment.

In GEORGE BOIKO & CO., INC. *v.* ATLANTIC WOOLEN MILLS, INC., 195 App. Div. 407 (New York Supreme Court, Appellate Division, 1921), a shoddy manufacturer quoted a price of 75 cents a pound for one bale of grade 55 worsted clippings to a buyer who confirmed the purchase in writing. The worsted clippings were mixed with others of different grades and colors at the time of the acceptance, but were sorted by the seller and made into a bale which was set aside and tagged with the name of the buyer. The buyer thereafter sent a truck for the bale, but was unable to get it as the truck driver called during the lunch hour and declined to wait. The seller later repeatedly telephoned the buyer to send for the bale. The buyer refused, stating that the goods no longer were required. In an action for the purchase price, judgment for plaintiff affirmed. There was an unconditional appropriation when the bale was set aside and tagged. The consent of the buyer might be implied from the sending of the truck; and by not claiming the right to make the selection or to inspect the goods after selection the buyer vested the seller with implied authority to make the selection and to pass title to the buyer. Two judges dissented on the ground that where the goods in question are unascertained there can be no implied assent to an appropriation, such assent being possible only where the selection is to be made from goods of the same kind.

In FLOODWOOD MERCANTILE CO. *v.* MAGIE, 152 Minn. 554 (Supreme Court, 1922), the contract provided for the sale of 50 cords of spruce pulpwood to be cut from live, sound timber and delivered at a certain landing, where it was to be inspected and sorted by the buyer, and then loaded on cars by the seller. It was held that the wood was appropriated to the contract by the seller when piled at the landing, and that title passed to the buyer at that time.

In CRAIG BROKERAGE CO. *v.* JOSEPH A. GODDARD CO., 92 Ind. App. 234 (Appellate Court, 1930), there was a contract for the sale of 1000 cases of canned tomatoes to be packed during the current season. The seller packed 950 cases, labelled the cans with the buyer's labels, and stacked the completed cases apart from other merchandise, notifying the buyer that the cases had been packed and labelled and were ready for shipment. The seller then resold the tomatoes to another buyer. The original buyer brought this action in replevin. Judgment for plaintiff affirmed. Title passed to the original buyer when the cans were labelled, set aside, and the buyer notified.

SMITH *v.* EDWARDS

MASSACHUSETTS SUPREME JUDICIAL COURT, 1892

[156 *Massachusetts Reports*, 221]

HOLMES, J. This case comes before us on the exception of the Old Colony Railroad Company to a ruling of the court below, that it should be charged as trustee of the defendants. The defendants have been defaulted. The bill of exceptions purports to state the evidence introduced on the motion to charge the trustee, but does not disclose the findings of the judge. We assume them to have been the most favorable for the ruling which the bill of exceptions warrants. The defendants in Ohio ordered of the plaintiffs, who are manufacturers of boots and shoes in Massachusetts, through the plaintiffs' travelling salesman, certain calf and buff shoes, to be made according to a sample shown to the defendants. It was assumed at the argument, and we assume, that the contract bound the defendants, that there is no question under the statute of frauds, and that the shoes were made according to sample. They were forwarded over the Old Colony Railroad, we must assume, if it be material, at the defendants' expense, and were delivered to the defendants. This mode of forwarding undoubtedly was authorized by the contract. The defendants accepted the buff shoes, but refused to accept the calf shoes, and shipped the latter back to the plaintiffs by the same railroad. The plaintiffs refused to accept them, sued the defendants for the price of the shoes, and trusteed the railroad company. The calf shoes mentioned are the goods for which the railroad company was charged.

It is argued for the trustees, that, although the defendants were guilty of a breach of contract in refusing to accept the calf shoes, yet, as the shoes were not in existence at the date of the contract, they did not become the defendants' property until tendered to and accepted by the defendants after they were made.

Of course the title to the shoes could not be vested in the defendants without their consent. But in the present state of the law it does not need argument to show that a contract can be made in such a way as subsequently to pass the title, as between the parties, to goods unascertained at the time when the contract is made, without a subsequent acceptance by the buyer, if the contract commits the buyer in advance to the acceptance of goods determined by other marks. *Middlesex Co.* v. *Osgood*, 4 Gray, 447, 449. *Nichols* v. *Morse*, 100 Mass. 523. *Brewer* v. *Housatonic Railroad*, 104 Mass. 593, 595. *Rodman* v. *Guilford*, 112 Mass. 405, 407. *Goddard* v. *Binney*, 115 Mass. 450. *Blanchard* v. *Cooke*, 144 Mass. 207, 227. *Aldridge* v. *Johnson*, 7 El. & Bl. 885, 899.

In the case of goods to be manufactured, the seller, as he has to tender them, generally has the right to appropriate goods to the contract so far that, if he tenders goods conformable to it, the buyer's refusal to accept them is a breach. The buyer cannot say that he would have accepted some other goods had they been tendered. When goods are to be manufactured and forwarded by a carrier to a buyer at a distance, the seller's delivery of such goods to the carrier as bailee for the purchaser passes the title. The seller cannot forward them until they are specified. The delivery is an overt dealing with the goods as those to which the contract applies, and puts them into a possession adverse to the seller. Although not strictly a delivery, it is an act having the legal effect of a true delivery, which in common legal language it is said to be. *Orcutt* v. *Nelson*, 1 Gray, 536, 543. *Merchant* v. *Chapman*, 4 Allen, 362, 364. *Kline* v. *Baker*, 99

Mass. 253, 254. *Hallgarten* v. *Oldham*, 135 Mass. 1, 9. The act is required of the seller by the terms of the contract, and thus is assented to in advance by the buyer, on the condition that, as supposed, the goods answer the requirements of the contract. Therefore it is a binding appropriation of the goods to the contract, and passes the title as we have said. *Putnam* v. *Tillotson*, 13 Met. 517, 520. *Merchant* v. *Chapman*, 4 Allen, 362, 364. *Odell* v. *Boston & Maine Railroad*, 109 Mass. 50. *Wigton* v. *Bowley*, 130 Mass. 252, 254. *Fragano* v. *Long*, 4 B. & C. 219. *Wait* v. *Baker*, 2 Exch. 1, 7.

The present case could be disposed of upon a narrower ground. It would be enough to say that, so far as we can see, the judge who heard the motion to charge the trustee was warranted in finding as a fact that the defendants authorized the plaintiffs to appropriate the shoes to the contract, even if the inference was not necessary as matter of law. The question always is what intent the parties have expressed, either in terms or by reasonable implication. *Anderson* v. *Morice*, 1 App. Cas. 713. *Calcutta & Burmah Steam Navigation Co.* v. *De Mattos*, 32 L. J. Q. B. 322, 328; S. C. 33 L. J. Q. B. 214.

Exceptions overruled.

Thus in Popper *v.* Rosen, 292 Penn. 122 (Supreme Court, 1928), there was a written order for 100 cases 45 Cathedral glass, 10 cases to be shipped at once and the balance after January 1. The buyer refused to accept the balance, and the seller sued for the price. To the contention of the buyer that the proper action was for damages for breach of contract, the Court replied: "The contract provided that the glass should be delivered through a carrier; therefore delivery to the carrier was a constructive delivery to the defendant and vested the title in him."

Similarly in Middleton *v.* Evans, 86 Utah 396 (Supreme Court, 1935), where there was a contract for the sale of 300 books, 250 copies to be sent by freight and 50 by express, it was held that delivery of the books to the carriers as requested amounted to an unconditional appropriation which passed title to the buyer.

Refer again to the cases on pages 210–221, *supra*.

THE LOWRY COFFEE COMPANY *v.* ANDRESEN–RYAN COFFEE COMPANY

Minnesota Supreme Court, 1922

[153 *Minnesota Reports*, 498]

Taylor, C. Plaintiff is an importer and dealer in coffee at Philadelphia, Pennsylvania. Defendant is a dealer in coffee at Duluth, Minnesota. In March, 1920, a broker at Duluth submitted samples of coffee to defendant and obtained an order for specified quantities of four different kinds of coffee, aggregating 430 bags, at specified prices, f. o. b. Philadelphia. The broker transmitted the order to plaintiff. To make a carload plaintiff shipped 500 bags instead of the 430 bags ordered. The shipment was 37 bags short in one of the kinds ordered, and contained 107 bags of a kind not ordered.

Before the coffee arrived, defendant received an invoice and bill of lading from plaintiff which stated the kinds of coffee shipped and the quantity and price of each kind. When the coffee arrived at Duluth and while it was still in the car, defendant discovered that a white powder on the floor of the car had sifted through the bags and damaged the coffee in 124 bags to a substantial extent, and promptly notified plaintiff thereof. Defendant had the clear right to reject the coffee, but instead of doing so accepted the entire shipment with full knowledge of all the facts, and thereafter paid $7,048.61 on the purchase price, but refused to pay the remainder. Plaintiff brought suit. The complaint alleged the sale and delivery of 500 bags of coffee to defendant, f. o. b. Philadelphia, for the agreed price of $7,386.63 of which $7,048.61 had been paid, and demanded judgment for the balance of $338.02. Defendant's answer contained a general denial, admitted the payments stated in the complaint and asserted a counterclaim. The court struck out the general denial as sham and sustained a demurrer to the counterclaim, but with leave to interpose an amended answer. Defendant interposed an amended answer and the case was tried on the merits and resulted in a judgment for plaintiff. Defendant appeals.

Defendant complains of the ruling striking the general denial from the original answer and sustaining the demurrer to the counterclaim therein, but, as defendant amended its answer and the case has since been tried on the merits, this ruling has become immaterial.

The amended answer admitted and alleged the purchase by sample of 500 bags of coffee for the sum of $7,386.63 and the payment of $7,048.61 of the purchase price, and further alleged that 124 bags of the coffee were delivered in a damaged condition and interposed a counterclaim for the amount of such damage.

The facts are not in dispute. That the coffee in 124 bags had been damaged to the extent of 3¾ cents per pound while in transit is practically admitted. The real question is whether this loss falls on the plaintiff or the defendant. Defendant concedes that, if plaintiff had complied strictly with the terms of the order, the delivery to the carrier at Philadelphia would have operated as a delivery to defendant, but contends that as plaintiff shipped 70 bags more than was ordered and 107 bags of a kind not ordered, there was no delivery until defendant received the coffee at Duluth. We think defendant is correct in this contention. Defendant's order was an offer to buy the specified kinds and quantities at the specified prices. The shipment made cannot be deemed an acceptance of this offer. It amounted in legal effect to a rejection of this offer and the making of a counter offer. *Lewis* v. *Johnson*, 123 Minn. 409, 143 N. W. 1127, L. R. A. 1915D, 150. The minds of the parties did not meet, and no sale was made and no title passed until the coffee tendered was actually accepted by defendant.

[The balance of the opinion, holding that the loss nevertheless fell on defendant because of its deliberate acceptance of the coffee at destination, is here omitted.]

In SHAPIRO *v.* GOODMAN, 236 Mich. 412 (Supreme Court, 1926), the defendant ordered of the plaintiffs from sample 34 dresses which were to be manufactured and shipped as ready. Against this order 19 dresses were shipped. Defendant accepted four and returned the rest, claiming that they were not according to sample. Plaintiffs declined to receive the dresses rejected, and brought the present action for the purchase price. The trial judge excluded evidence that the goods were not according to sample, and charged the jury that title passed to the defendant when plaintiffs delivered the dresses to the carrier on shipment. Judgment for plaintiffs reversed. The evidence should have been admitted; and title did not pass to defendant if the goods were not of the kind and quality ordered.

Note also SUTHERLAND MEDICINE COMPANY *v.* BALTIMORE, 81 Ark. 229 (Supreme Court, 1906), where it was held, in the case of a contract for the sale of goods which contained an agreement to include advertising matter, that the seller could not recover the price of the goods if they were shipped without the advertising matter in question.

In SMITH, FITZMAURICE CO. *v.* HARRIS, 126 Maine 308 (Supreme Judicial Court, 1927), defendant gave an order to plaintiffs' salesman for 12 dozen union suits to be shipped from the factory of the manufacturer. Later the salesman wrote to defendant that the mill was packing the goods that season in 16 dozen cases, adding "if for any reason you do not want these goods advise us by wire as we cannot afford to take back any goods once they are shipped." Defendant received the letter on September 18, and on the same day wrote to plaintiffs that he had that day wired "Cannot accept now. Will let you hear from me later." Plaintiffs received this letter on September 24, but did not receive the telegram, and the goods were shipped on September 20. In an action for goods sold and delivered it was held to be immaterial whether defendant actually wired as requested. Title did not pass on shipment, as the goods shipped were too many.

In COMMONWEALTH TITLE INSURANCE AND TRUST COMPANY *v.* GREGSON, 303 Ill. 458 (Supreme Court, 1922), where the seller shipped goods on a domestic bill of lading although shipping instructions already accepted called for shipment on a through bill of lading, it was held that there was no appropriation of the goods on shipment.

Refer again to the cases on pages 215–221 *supra*, dealing with exceptions to the general proposition that delivery to a carrier is tantamount to delivery to the buyer.

STATE *v.* ROSENBERGER

MISSOURI SUPREME COURT, 1908

[212 *Missouri Reports*, 648]

BURGESS, J. At the September term, 1907, of the circuit court of Webster county, under an information filed by the prosecuting attorney of said county, charging the defendant with selling one gallon of whiskey in said county, on the 2d day of February, 1907, to one Ira Morton, in violation of the Local Option Law in full force and effect in said county at that time, the defendant was found guilty and his punishment assessed at a fine of three hundred dollars. Defendant appealed in due course, after filing unsuccessful motion for new trial and in arrest of judgment.

The evidence tended to prove that the defendant was a wholesale and retail liquor dealer, with office and place of business in Kansas City, Jackson county, Missouri, and did business under the trade name of "Penwood Company." Ira Morton, a resident of Marshfield, in Webster county, Missouri, some time in January, 1907, ordered a gallon of whiskey from said Penwood Company, and on February 2, 1907, the whiskey was received by him from the agent of the Wells-Fargo Express Company, at the office of said company in Marshfield. The whiskey was sent in a package marked C. O. D., and Morton paid said express agent the price thereof, $3.50, at the time of delivery, and the express agent sent the money to defendant's office at Kansas City, where it was received. Morton testified that he mailed the order to defendant of his own motion, without any solicitation on the part of defendant, or any one on his behalf, and solely because he wanted the liquor for his own use. The express company received the package containing the whiskey from one of the defendant's employees at Kansas City, and shipped the same to Morton, at Marshfield. The evidence further tended to prove that the transaction was carried out by defendant's clerks, without his knowledge, while he was at Hot Springs, Arkansas; that while he had been making similar sales and shipments, on C. O. D. terms, to parties in other States, he had no knowledge that his clerks were making for him any such shipments to any local-option county in Missouri; that he had never solicited any business of that kind in Missouri either by agent or through the mails, and that up until the time of his arrest he was unaware that any such shipments had been made, nor had he authorized any.

The State introduced evidence tending to prove that at the time of the alleged sale of liquor, and prior thereto, the Local Option Law was in force in Webster county.

The important question presented by this appeal is whether the place of sale of the liquor which the defendant is charged with selling unlawfully was in Webster county or Jackson county, Missouri. Defendant insists that the sale was at Kansas City, Jackson county, where he was authorized by law to sell liquor, and that he was guilty of no offense in accepting and filling an order from a party in a local-option county requesting the shipment to him, C. O. D., of a specified amount of liquor, to a point in said local-option county of Webster.

As a general rule the delivery of goods by the vendor to the carrier, when the goods are to be sent that way, is equivalent to delivery to the purchaser, subject only to the right of stoppage *in transitu.* [2 Kent's Com., 490; *State* v. *Wingfield,* 115 Mo. 428; *Kerwin & Co.* v. *Doran,* 29 Mo. App. 397; *Garbracht* v. *Commonwealth,* 96 Pa. St. 449; *Dunn* v. *State,* 8 S. E. 806.] And this is true although the purchase money is afterwards collected by the vendor or agent at the place from which the goods are shipped. [*State* v. *Hughes,* 22 W. Va. 743.]

But when the goods are shipped upon order C. O. D., as in the case at bar, there is much conflict in the authorities as to where and when the title passes, that is, whether at the point of shipment or at the point of destination, upon payment of the purchase price.

[Two pages of the opinion, reviewing the cases and concluding that the weight of authority is to the effect that title passes on shipment, are here omitted.]

The great mercantile interests of the country seem to demand that the law by which such interests are governed should be uniform, and we are of opinion that, so far as concerns the title to goods delivered to a carrier for shipment, the same rule applies to C. O. D. shipments as to those in ordinary cases, in the absence of any express contract to the contrary between the shipper and the consignee.

There is no question that Morton ordered the liquor in question for his own use, C. O. D., and when it was so shipped, the sale became complete at the place of shipment. . . .

Our conclusion is that the sale of the liquor was completed when shipped at Kansas City, Jackson county, Missouri, and not at Webster county, Missouri, as charged in the information.

The judgment should be reversed and the defendant discharged. It is so ordered. All concur, except Woodson J., who concurs in what is said with respect to the place of sale of the liquor, but dissents from the view expressed on the last proposition, and Valliant, J., who is absent.

Compare LANE *v.* CHADWICK, 146 Mass. 68 (Supreme Judicial Court, 1888), where it was held that the consignee of goods ordered to be sent C. O. D. could not maintain replevin against the carrier, Morton, C. J., saying: "The delivery to the carrier was not a delivery to the plaintiff. He was not her agent, but the agent of the consignor. Until he delivered the goods to her, no title or right of possession would pass to her, and it is immaterial whether he rightfully or wrongfully refused to make the delivery."

In AMERICAN RAILWAY EXPRESS CO. *v.* READY, 232 Mich. 624 (Supreme Court, 1925), defendant used large quantities of glue purchased from Armour & Co. Many shipments were made C. O. D. through plaintiff. Armour & Co., claiming that some of these shipments had not been paid for, presented claims against plaintiff which were paid. Plaintiff then took an assignment from Armour & Co., and brought the present action to recover the amounts involved. A majority of the court held that the burden was on plaintiff to prove want of payment; but all agreed that "Plaintiff is a common carrier. A delivery to it by the consignor of goods is a delivery to the consignee. By the weight of authority this was the rule as to C. O. D. shipments before the adoption of the uniform sales act. By delivery of the goods to the carrier for shipment the right of property in the goods passed to the consignee although the right of possession did not pass until payment and the consignor retained a lien for the purchase price. The carrier was the agent of the consignee to transport the goods and the agent of the consignor to transport the money received on their delivery."

ZANK *v.* JONES

WISCONSIN SUPREME COURT, 1922

[178 *Wisconsin Reports*, 573]

This is an appeal by the plaintiff from a judgment dismissing plaintiff's complaint, and for costs in favor of the defendants.

On November 5, 1920, the defendants agreed to purchase from the plaintiff 179 sacks of potatoes, containing 150 pounds each, for the sum of $1.50 per hundredweight. It was agreed that the potatoes were to be sorted, placed in sacks and weighed, and were to be delivered by the plaintiff at the cars to be furnished by the defendants at Augusta, Wisconsin.

On November 7th the defendants furnished a sorting machine and several men, and both the plaintiff and his men and the defendants' help proceeded to sort the potatoes. The process of sorting, sacking, and weighing the potatoes continued from Monday, the 8th day of November, until Tuesday afternoon at about 5 o'clock, of the same week. On Tuesday afternoon there was a sudden drop in the temperature and it was thought that the potatoes might freeze that night, and all of the potatoes were thereupon removed to a machine shed belonging to the plaintiff. Thereafter the potatoes in the machine shed were covered with blankets and other material, but the cold was so severe that on Tuesday night they froze. Thereafter sixty-four sacks of these potatoes were removed by the plaintiff into his cellar. On Friday morning of the same week the plaintiff loaded two wagonloads of the potatoes preparatory to delivery of the same to the cars at Augusta, and at that time the employees of the defendants appeared at plaintiff's farm, under instructions from the defendants to examine the potatoes and to refuse acceptance if they were frozen. Defendants' employees, upon discovering the condition of the potatoes, refused to accept them, and on their recommendation the potatoes in the machine shed were removed to a neighbor's farm, where they were permitted to remain until the following spring. The plaintiff sold a portion of the potatoes stored in the cellar and realized therefrom the sum of $66. The balance of the potatoes were so badly damaged as to make them unsalable. The evidence in the case is practically undisputed.

The case was submitted to the jury on the following special verdict:

"(1) On November 5, 1920, when the contract was made for the purchase of the potatoes, was it the intention of the parties that the title and ownership of the potatoes should pass from the plaintiff to the defendants as soon as the potatoes were assorted and sacked, before the payment of the purchase price and before their delivery to the defendants at Augusta? *A.* Yes.

"(2) After the potatoes were sorted, sacked, what was it reasonably worth to haul them to Augusta and deliver them to the defendants, according to the terms of the contract? *A.* $24.

"(3) What was the reasonable value of the portion of the potatoes which the plaintiff afterward retained and disposed of for his own benefit? *A.* $66."

Plaintiff thereupon moved for judgment in his favor for the total amount of the contract price; and the defendants thereupon moved to change the answer of question number 1 of the special verdict from "Yes" to "No," and for judgment in their favor dismissing the plaintiff's complaint with costs. The motion of the defendants was granted by the court, and judgment was accordingly entered.

DOERFLER, J. The only material question in the case, as stated by the trial court in its opinion, involves the sufficiency of the evidence to sustain the finding of the jury as to the passing of the title.

[Pertinent sections of the Uniform Sales Act were here cited.]

On the part of the plaintiff it is contended that sub. 4 of sec. 1684*t*–19 is applicable to this case, and that when the goods were sorted, sacked, and weighed there was an unconditional appropriation of the potatoes, and that the title therein at that time passed to the buyer. On the other hand, it is contended by the defendants that sub. 5 of sec. 1684*t*–19 is applicable for the reason that the contract required the seller to deliver the goods to the buyer at a particular place, and that the goods were to be paid for by the buyer at the time they were delivered at Augusta, ready to be loaded there on board of the cars.

Had the parties not included as a part of the contract of sale a provision that the goods were to be delivered by the seller to the buyer at Augusta, there can be no question but that sub. 4 (1) of sec. 1684*t*–19 would be clearly applicable. The paragraph referred to clearly embraces all such contracts of sale which provide for the ascertainment and setting aside of goods by description so as to place them in a deliverable state, and does not involve goods so ascertained and set aside, which under the terms of the contract are to be delivered to a certain person at a certain place. In order to reach the latter situation the legislature has seen fit to enact a special provision, which is known as sub. 5 of sec. 1684*t*–19, and this provision is clearly applicable to the facts in a case like the instant one.

Sub. 4 (2) of sec. 1684*t*–19 sheds considerable light upon the intention of the legislature. That paragraph also evidently contemplates a situation where no express provision is made in the contract with respect to delivery, and so this paragraph provides that where, in pursuance of a contract to sell, the seller delivers the goods to the buyer, or to a carrier or other bailee (whether named by the buyer or not), for the purpose of transmission to or holding for the buyer, he is presumed to have unconditionally appropriated the goods to the contract; but this paragraph contains this exception: "except in the cases provided for in the next rule and in section 1684*t*–20." The provisions of sec. 1684*t*–20 are not applicable to this case, but sub. 5 of sec. 1684*t*–19, being the next rule referred to, is clearly applicable to the case, and fully covers the situation presented here.

It would therefore appear that the title to these potatoes, as a matter of law, would not pass until the plaintiff had fully complied with the terms of his contract, and such contract provided, first, for the sorting of the potatoes; second, the sacking of the same; third, the weighing process; and fourth, the delivery of the potatoes at Augusta. The plaintiff complied with all the terms of his contract with the exception of the delivery of the goods, and as the result whatever loss was sustained by reason of the damage to the potatoes must be borne by him.

It is claimed on the part of the plaintiff that inasmuch as it appears from the evidence that the defendants sorted, weighed, and sacked the potatoes, and that it was suggested by the defendants' agents that they be placed in the machine shed until they could be delivered, such evidence amounted to an absolute appropriation of the potatoes on the defendants' part, and that the title to the potatoes immediately thereafter passed. In whatever was done to the potatoes up to the time they were damaged both of the parties participated. The plaintiff's acts were directed toward preventing damage to the potatoes, and the suggestions of the defendants' employees were made in the interests of their employers so that the potatoes when delivered would be in good marketable condition. There is nothing unusual or extraordinary about the transaction. Each party intended to protect his own interests. . . .

We therefore hold that the decision of this case is governed by sub. 5 of sec. 1684*t*–19, and that the trial court properly changed the answer of the jury to the first question of the special verdict from "Yes" to "No" and ordered judgment in defendants' favor dismissing plaintiff's complaint with costs.

By the Court. — Judgment affirmed.

Note also Vogt *v.* Chase Bros. Co., 235 N. Y. 206 (Court of Appeals, 1923), where there was a contract for the sale of a quantity of apple trees with stated requirements of size and quality, delivery to be made on board cars at Dansville. After the trees were dug up, but before they were graded and sorted, the seller placed them in storage at Dansville in a warehouse selected by the buyer, where the grading and sorting were completed. While in the warehouse the trees were damaged by the cold. The seller sued for the agreed price. Judgment for plaintiff reversed. The seller was under a continuing obligation to load the trees on cars, and hence title did not pass. Two judges dissented.

Compare Louis F. Dow Co. *v.* Bitther, 187 Minn. 143 (Supreme Court, 1932). Defendants contracted with plaintiff for the purchase of 400 calendars upon which certain advertising was to be printed. After the printing was done but before delivery f. o. b. cars St. Paul, as required by the contract, defendants attempted to repudiate. In an action for the purchase price, judgment for plaintiff affirmed. Delivery is not the essential thing in the passing of title; what is essential is an unconditional appropriation of the goods to the contract by one party with the assent of the other. Here the calendars were printed with defendants' name and their special advertising matter. That, and their setting aside for shipment certainly made their appropriation to the contract irrevocable.

GULF VEGETABLE & FRUIT CO. *v.* LANE

Michigan Supreme Court, 1932

[258 *Michigan Reports*, 634]

McDonald, J. The plaintiff sold a car lot of carrots to defendant at Detroit, f. o. b. Houston, Texas. When they arrived at Detroit, acceptance was refused by defendant on the ground that they were not of the kind and quality ordered. He notified the plaintiff to make its own disposition of the shipment. Plaintiff accepted the suggestion, and, after notice to the defendant that they would be disposed of on his account, sold them for the amount of the freight charges, which it claims was the best price obtainable. This suit was then brought to recover the contract price less the proceeds received on the resale. The issue was tried by the court without a jury, and judgment was entered in favor of the plaintiff. The defendant has appealed.

On the theory that the measure of damages is the difference between the contract price and market value, the defendant claims that there is no evidence to support the judgment. No other question is discussed in his brief or included in his cause for appeal.

The defendant has correctly stated the general rule as to the measure of damages where the suit is based on the breach of an executory contract. This is not such a suit. It is an action for goods sold and delivered, and is founded on the theory that title to the goods passed to the defendant when they were delivered to the public carrier at the point specified in the contract. Under the facts in this case, the plaintiff has adopted the correct theory. The contract called for delivery, f. o. b. Houston, Texas. The plaintiff delivered the carrots to a public carrier at that point. Such a delivery constituted delivery to the defendant, and title to the property then passed to him. His right to inspect and reject if the goods were not of the kind and quality ordered did not prevent title from passing, because the trial court found that they conformed to the contract, and no complaint is made of his finding. Williston on Sales (1st Ed.), § 473, p. 830; *Dow Chemical Co.* v. *Detroit Chemical Co.*, 208 Mich. 157 (14 A. L. R. 1200); uniform sales act (2 Comp. Laws 1929, § 9485).

After wrongfully refusing to accept the shipment, the defendant notified the plaintiff to make its own disposition of it. The plaintiff responded that it would be resold on defendant's account. The plaintiff was under no legal obligation to resell, but, having undertaken to do so, it was its duty to use its best judgment and sell at the best obtainable price. We think the evidence shows the plaintiff fulfilled its duty in this respect.

In this action the plaintiff is entitled to recover the contract price less the amount received from a resale of the carrots.

The judgment is affirmed, with costs to the plaintiff.

Note also HUNTER BROS. MILLING CO. *v.* KRAMER BROS., 71 Kans. 468 (Supreme Court, 1905), where there was a contract for the sale of four carloads of bran to be shipped from Wellington, Kansas, at an agreed price f. o. b. East St. Louis. The buyer paid the entire price on receipt of the bills of lading. Two cars were caught in a flood and destroyed en route, and the buyer brought an action for damages for failure to deliver. Judgment for defendant reversed. Title to the bran did not pass until it reached East St. Louis.

Compare J. R. DENT STEVEDORING CO. *v.* LANE, 167 Miss. 99 (Supreme Court, 1933). A contract for the sale of steel rails and angle bars called for an f. a. s. delivery. The seller arranged to have the goods loaded on railroad cars so that they could be switched f. a. s., and while they were so loaded an inspection was made by the buyer, and the material was accepted. Subsequently, while the switching was in progress and while the cars were still from 600 to 1000 feet from the steamer and not within reach of the tackle, the goods were attached as property of the seller. The buyer claimed title, and in affirming a judgment of the trial court upholding this contention, the Court said: "The loading on the cars of this iron by the agents of [the seller] was equivalent to a tender of same as complying with the terms of the contract so far as quality, quantity, and the like were concerned, and the inspection and acceptance by the claimant . . . of the iron thus loaded rendered the transfer specifically irrevocable. There was a segregation and identification of the property under the written contract which up to that time was executory, but which upon the inspection and acceptance closed the transaction so far as the actual sale and the passing of title was concerned."

Compare also COMMONWEALTH *v.* WILOIL CORPORATION, 316 Penn. 33 (Supreme Court, 1934). A Pennsylvania company, with its principal office and place of business in Pennsylvania, entered into a contract to sell gasoline to a Philadelphia buyer. In performance of the contract the company obtained gasoline in Wilmington, Delaware, and shipped it to the buyer under bills of lading naming the buyer as consignee. Freight was paid by the buyer, and the invoices, which included the tax on the gasoline, stated that shipments were made f. o. b. Wilmington. In response to a tax claim the seller contended that it was not liable as title passed to the buyer at Wilmington, and stated further that the tax had been added to the invoices in ignorance of the legal position. It appeared, however, that the tax also was added in subsequent invoices. The seller never had collected the tax because of the insolvency of the buyer. It was held that the seller must pay the tax. The intention of the parties is controlling, and the inference from the facts is that the intention was to have title pass at destination, the f. o. b. provision being merely for the purpose of fixing the price.

Refer again to the cases on pages 243–253 *supra*, on the place of delivery in f. o. b. and f. a. s. contracts.

SMITH CO. LTD. *v.* MARANO

PENNSYLVANIA SUPREME COURT, 1920

[267 *Pennsylvania Reports*, 107]

Opinion by Mr. Chief Justice BROWN, April 12, 1920:

The facts in this controversy are agreed upon in a case stated. Smith Company, Limited, is a corporation, with its place of business in the City of St. Johns, Newfoundland. The defendant is a resident of the City of Philadelphia, this State, and is engaged in business there. In September, 1916, the plaintiff and defendant, by letters and telegrams, endeavored to complete a contract for the sale of codfish to the latter. As a result of preliminary negotiations, on September 26, 1916, plaintiff made the following offer to the defendant, by telegram: "Will give you first quality at nine dollars, second quality at eight dollars per drum of one hundred pounds C. I. F. Philadelphia." On the following day the defendant wired his acceptance of one thousand drums of the fish, first quality, and by letter of the same date directed the plaintiff to send with the first shipment of that quality twenty-five drums of the second quality. On or about October 4, 1916, the plaintiff shipped three hundred drums of the fish of first quality and twenty-five of second quality, in accordance with the terms of the contract. The goods were shipped by a steamer from the City of St. Johns, consigned to the plaintiff's agent at New York, for trans-shipment to Philadelphia, to be delivered to the order of plaintiff, the bill of lading being endorsed by the plaintiff in blank. Under the terms of the contract, the plaintiff paid for the customary marine insurance on the goods shipped and the freight charges on them to Philadelphia. It immediately forwarded to the Girard National Bank of Philadelphia, through a bank in New York, the insurance policy, endorsed in blank, the invoice and a through bill of lading, also endorsed in blank, all attached to a sight draft on the defendant, in accordance with the contract between them, the draft being for $2,900, covering the value of the fish shipped. About two days later the ship carrying the fish shipped by the plaintiff to the defendant was sunk by a submarine of the Imperial German Government, on the high seas, while en route to the port of destination, and the goods in question were totally destroyed. The bill of lading and the sight draft were duly tendered to the defendant after the cargo had been destroyed. He refused to accept the draft, and subsequently refused to pay any part thereof. The parties agree that the expression "C. I. F." means that the price quoted by the plaintiff to the defendant, and accepted by him, included the cost of the goods, the cost of obtaining customary insurance thereon and the freight charges to the City of Philadelphia. On the foregoing state of facts the court below entered judgment in favor of the plaintiff for the full amount of its claim.

The letters "C. I. F." are abbreviations of the words "cost, insurance and freight," and, when used in connection with commercial quotations, signify that the price to be paid for goods will include all charges to the port of destination: 11 C. J. 765. The case now under consideration calls upon us for the first time to construe what may be termed a "C. I. F." contract for the purchase of goods, and to determine when, under such contract, there is delivery to the buyer. As just stated, plaintiff and defendant agree that the term "C. I. F." means that the price quoted to the latter and accepted by him included "the cost of said goods, the cost of obtaining the customary insurance thereon and freight charges to the City of Philadelphia." In recognizing that such is the true meaning of the abbreviations, the English courts hold that property purchased under a contract in which they are used passes to the buyer upon the seller's delivery of it to a carrier: *Ireland* v. *Livingston*, L. R., 5 H. L. 395; *Arnhold Karberg & Company* v. *Blythe, Green, Joudain & Company* (1916), 1 K. B. 495.

[The Court here quoted from the opinion of Bankes, J., in the last named case, and referred also to *Mee* v. *McNider*, 109 N. Y. 500, and to *Thames & Mersey Marine Insurance Company, Limited* v. *U. S.*, 237 U. S. 19.]

Counsel for appellant admit that the judgment of the court below is in accord with the English decisions, followed in this country by the two cases cited, but their contention is that, under the Pennsylvania Sales Act of May 19, 1915, P. L. 543, the property purchased by the defendant was never delivered to him, and the plaintiff is, therefore, not entitled to recover.

[Section 18 and Section 19, Rule 5, of the Uniform Sales Act were here quoted.]

The appellant agreed to pay to the appellee a fixed price for the goods to be shipped to him. The price quoted to him, and which he agreed to pay, included not only the actual value of the fish to the seller, but insurance and freight charges to Philadelphia. If the price had not included insurance, it might be well urged that, under rule 5 of section 19 of our Sales Act, the goods were never delivered to the appellant; but, reading the contract as a whole — as it must be read — with the item for insurance included in it, "a different intention" on the part of the buyer is disclosed, and the learned court below correctly so held. If it was the intention of the parties to the contract that the property in the goods sold should not pass to the buyer until delivery to him at Philadelphia, what concern had he about their safe transportation to that port? By his acceptance of the offer made by the appellee, he admittedly agreed that he would pay a sum to the latter which would cover marine insurance on the shipment to him. Under the contention which he now makes, he had no interest in it until it reached him at Philadelphia. That he did not so intend, and that he must now be held to have understood that the delivery of the goods to the common carrier was a delivery to him, are clearly demonstrated by the court below in the following from its opinion directing judgment to be entered against him: "It is difficult to understand why the buyer should be concerned in any stipulation regarding payment of insurance, either by himself or by the seller, if he had no property in the goods during transit, and consequently no interest in the subject of their insurance. On the other hand, if he intended that they should pass to him as soon as they were delivered to the steamship the subject of insurance in transit would be vital to him. We think this reference to insurance in the contract of sales is controlling and significant of the intention of the parties. If delivery was intended to take place at the end of the voyage the reference to insurance in any communication between the parties was as superfluous as a reference to their insurance before the sale while in the seller's warehouse. No matter what is to be inferred from the reference to freight, the inference from that to insurance must also have weight. The contract must be interpreted as a whole. Both provisions must be explained, interpreted and given their due force. A provision for the payment of freight by the seller or its inclusion in the price might indicate an intention to deliver at the end of the voyage, or it might be a consideration affecting the price merely, and the cost and uncertainty of the freight charge might be a burden accepted by the seller to expedite the sale. On the other hand, the provision with regard to insurance was either fully intended, and reasonable because of the risk the buyer intended to assume, or if he did not so intend it was entirely meaningless and mere surplusage."

But a word need be added to the foregoing. Among the provisions of the Sales Act are the following:

[Sections 20 (2) and 22 (a) were here quoted.]

The bill of lading, made out to the appellee or its order, was endorsed immediately by it in blank and attached to the draft drawn upon the appellant. This merely meant that the appellee intended to retain property in the goods to secure performance by the defendant of his promise to pay for them, and did not, by the express words of the Sales Act, relieve him from the risk that was upon him from the time the goods were delivered to the carrier.

Judgment affirmed.

In ADAMS *v.* GRUNDY AND COMPANY, INCORPORATED, 252 Mass. 135 (Supreme Judicial Court, 1925), there was a contract for the sale of 500 bales of wool to be shipped from Argentina at 51½¢ c.i.f. Boston. It appeared on arrival that the wool was not of proper quality, and it was agreed that the wool should be sent to the seller's mill where the seller was to sort it carefully, allowing the buyer credit for the off-sorts, and that the seller then should comb the wool for the buyer at the buyer's expense. Subsequently the buyer repudiated the transaction on the ground that not enough off-sorts were being removed, and brought an action to recover the purchase price. In upholding a verdict directed for defendant, the court held that title passed to plaintiff when the wool was loaded on the steamer in Argentina.

In 1 THALLER ET PERCERON, TRAITÉ ÉLÉMENTAIRE DE DROIT COMMERCIAL 648 (8th ed., Paris, 1931), the author says: "It is a temptation to interpret this contract [*i.e.*, a c.i.f. contract] as a sale calling for delivery at destination; if the buyer had become owner on shipment, should he not pay the cost of transport? The contrary interpretation is more generally admitted. The transfer of title is effected on shipment. . . . The language used by the contracting parties proves that such was their intention. If the seller had wished to delay the transfer of title until arrival, he would not have included in his invoice the amount of the freight and the insurance premium, for he naturally should pay them. The fact that he has included them shows on the contrary that these incidents have been deemed to be debts of the buyer; but the seller has agreed as a favor not only to arrange for them in advance but to charge them on the principal price in such a way as to reduce that price accordingly."

Compare WARNER BROS. & CO., LIMITED *v.* ISRAEL, 101 Fed.(2nd) 59 (Circuit Court of Appeals, Second Circuit, 1939). Sugar was shipped from the Philippines to New York under a c.i.f. contract, payment of 95 per cent of the purchase price being effected under an irrevocable credit against a draft with documents attached. The sugar was in all respects of the quality and condition called for by the contract, but before the carrying vessel arrived at New York the Philippine sugar quota for the year was filled so that the sugar had to be placed in a bonded warehouse. In an action by the seller to recover the unpaid remainder of the purchase, a judgment for plaintiff was affirmed. "It has been said that a c. i. f. contract is one for the sale of documents relating to goods rather than a sale of the goods. This, though perhaps an unduly broad generalization, serves to emphasize the distinctive character of such a contract. As the goods which constitute the subject matter are really the substantial part of the transaction it seems more realistic to treat such a contract as one under which the title to the goods passes to the buyer upon the delivery of documents alone; and that is so because the requisite antecedent acts of the seller are, when followed by delivery of the documents, a complete performance of the contract by the seller."

Note also Jean Renard, *La Vente Caf en Droit français*, 9 REVUE DE DROIT MARITIME COMPARÉ 69, 75 (1924): "It must be recognized that in a c. i. f. sale title does not pass by mere agreement of the parties, as contemplated by Art. 1138 of the Civil Code. A twofold material element is necessary, corresponding to the twofold aspect of the dispossession of the seller: physical dispossession, which results from shipment; legal dispossession, which is accomplished by delivery of the documents. This symbolic surrender of possession is indispensable to the perfection of the contract."

C. GROOM, LIMITED *v.* BARBER

KING'S BENCH DIVISION, 1914

[*Law Reports,* [1915] 1 *King's Bench,* 316]

By a contract in writing dated June 8, 1914, J. F. Barber, of Mincing Lane, London (hereinafter called "the seller"), sold to C. Groom, Limited, of Gracechurch Street, London (hereinafter called "the buyers"), on the terms of the rules and regulations for the time being in force of the United Kingdom Jute Goods Association, and subject to the conditions indorsed upon the contract, 100 bales of Hessian cloth at 18*s.* 6*d.* per 100 yards for shipment from Calcutta, one half between June 1 and 30, and the other half between July 1 and 15, 1914, by steamer and/or steamers to London upon c.i.f. terms, the latter to be with particular average for gross invoice amount plus 10 per cent. for payment by cash against documents less any usual rebate. . . .

The goods in question in the arbitration proceedings were twenty-five bales which were to be shipped between July 1 and 15.

On July 15 Becker, Gray & Co. duly shipped the said goods at Calcutta in the steamship *City of Winchester,* and on July 16 took out an insurance policy upon the goods which did not cover war risk, or, in other words, contained the customary free from capture and seizure clause. . . .

On August 20 the seller received information regarding the name of the steamer carrying the goods, the information being contained in an invoice received by him from Becker, Gray & Co. Within about an hour of the receipt of this invoice the seller despatched a similar invoice to the buyers.

On August 21 at 2.27 P.M. the loss of the *City of Winchester* was posted at Lloyd's, she having been captured on August 6 by a German cruiser and subsequently sunk. It was not contended that any earlier information was received in London regarding the loss.

The invoice was the only document which the buyers received from the seller. The parties admitted that it was to be presumed from the delivery of an invoice that the seller was in a position to deliver the documents under the contract.

On August 22 the buyers wrote to the seller returning the invoices because the *City of Winchester* had been captured on August 6, and stated that although the buyers had asked previously for the name of the steamer the seller's invoice received on August 21 gave the first advice, and under the circumstances the buyers refused to accept any responsibility in the matter.

The policy which the seller was in a position to tender to the buyers was the usual form of Lloyd's policy containing the free from capture and seizure clause.

The matter was referred to arbitration under the contract, the seller claiming that he was entitled to be paid at the maturity of the shippers' draft, namely, November 23, 1914, the sum of 441*l.* 2*s.*, or such sum at an earlier date less the usual rebate, whilst the buyers contended that they were entitled to refuse the documents and regard the contract as unfulfilled.

The umpire upheld the seller's contention and made an award in his favour.

On appeal to the appeal committee it was contended on behalf of the buyers: —

[The first contention, that the seller should have insured against war risks, is here omitted.]

2. (*a*) that no property in the goods passed to the buyers because no goods in a deliverable state were unconditionally appropriated to the contract by the seller with the consent of the buyers;

(*b*) that when the seller invoiced the goods to the buyers and tendered, or was in a position to tender, the documents and purported to appropriate the goods to the contract they had ceased to exist; and as a consequence,

(*c*) that unless the seller tendered, or was in a position to tender, documents which entitled the buyers to receive the goods or to obtain a complete indemnity for their loss the buyers were not bound to pay the price.

[The committee upheld the seller on both points, and decided that the buyer should pay £441 2*s.* on November 23, 1914. Atkin, J., approved the award on the first point.]

Atkin, J. . . . The next point raises a question of general interest in reference to contracts of sale on c.i.f. terms. It is said that the seller cannot tender documents representing goods which were lost at the time of tender because at the time of the loss no goods had been appropriated to the contract so as to pass the property to the buyer. It is said, therefore, that the goods tendered were non-existent and consequently that the documents were not in order. The appeal committee deal, or appear to deal, with the point by saying "As regards the second contention the committee were of opinion that the seller fulfilled his obligation under the contract by intimating to the buyers that he was in a position to deliver the documents deliverable under the contract and that it was the buyers' obligation to take up such documents, and that the fact that the goods had been lost by a war peril and were in consequence not in a deliverable state was not a sufficient ground to relieve the buyers from their obligation under the contract"; but I am not sure that that fully deals with the question of the property not being in the buyers at the time of the loss. It was contended by the buyers that in a c.i.f. contract the seller's duty was so to act as to pass the property to the buyer, either on shipment or at any rate in case of loss at some time before the loss, and that if this were not done the seller could not make a valid delivery under the contract inasmuch as there were no goods in existence that could be said to be the buyer's goods or would be so appropriated as to become his goods.

The committee have not dealt with the question of fact as to whether there had been any appropriation of goods to this contract by or on behalf of the seller. In the view that I hold the question is immaterial, but if it became material I think I should, in the absence of any admission, have to refer the case back to the committee for a finding. Upon the evidence as disclosed in the case there does not appear to have been any appropriation, and I shall assume there was none. What is the meaning of a contract on c.i.f. terms? I think the answer has been given authoritatively in the judgment of Hamilton J. in *Biddell Brothers* v. *E. Clemens Horst Co.* ([1911] 1 K. B. 214, at p. 220) where he said this: "The meaning of a contract of sale upon cost, freight, and insurance terms is so well settled that it is unnecessary to refer to authorities upon the subject. A seller under a contract of sale containing such terms has firstly to ship at the port of shipment goods of the description contained in the contract; secondly to procure a contract of affreightment, under which the goods will be delivered at the destination contemplated by the contract; thirdly to arrange for an insurance upon the terms current in the trade which will be available for the benefit of the buyer; fourthly to make out an invoice as described by Blackburn J. in *Ireland* v. *Livingston* ((1872) L. R. 5 H. L. at p. 406) or in some similar form; and finally to tender these documents to the buyer so that he may know what freight he has to pay and obtain delivery of the goods, if they arrive, or recover for their loss if they are lost on the voyage."

In my opinion the result is that the contract of the seller is performed by delivering to the buyer within a reasonable time from the agreed date of shipment the documents, ordinarily the bill of lading, the invoice, and the policy of insurance, which will entitle the buyer to obtain on arrival of the ship delivery of goods shipped in accordance with the contract, or in case of loss will entitle him to recover on the policy the value of the goods if lost by a peril agreed in the contract to be covered, and in any case will give him any rightful claim against the ship in respect of any misdelivery or wrongful treatment of the goods. It therefore becomes immaterial whether before the date of the tender of the documents the property in the goods was the seller's or buyer's or some third person's. The seller must be in a position to pass the property in the goods by the bill of lading if the goods are in existence, but he need not have appropriated the particular goods in the particular bill of lading to the particular buyer until the moment of tender, nor need he have obtained any right to deal with the bill of lading until the moment of tender. If it were otherwise the shipper of goods in bulk, or of goods intended for several contracts, or the intermediate seller who may be the last of a chain of purchasers from an original shipper, might find it impossible to enforce a contract on c.i.f. terms. The seller's obligation cannot depend upon whether the goods are lost or not, and if when there is no loss the property has to pass to the buyer before delivery of the documents, at what stage of the transaction must it pass? Unless it be at the time of shipment I can see no reason for fixing upon any other time than on delivery of the documents, and if it be the law that a tender of documents is ineffectual unless in fact at the moment of shipment the property actually passed to the ultimate buyer, it appears to me that business operations would be very seriously embarrassed.

I do not think that the above is inconsistent with the judgment of Kennedy L.J. in *Biddell Brothers* v. *E. Clemens Horst Co.* ([1911] 1 K. B. at p. 956) in the Court of Appeal. Difficult questions arise as to the time when in performance of a contract on c.i.f. terms the property passes to the buyer. But the question when in fact the property passes is distinct from the question whether the seller undertakes as a term of the contract that the property shall pass at a given time, and the Lord Justice in the passage cited, in my view, is only dealing with the former question. After the decision of the House of Lords in the same case I do not think it necessary to consider former cases. The object of the Courts in construing commercial contracts is to try to give effect to the intention of both the contracting parties and not to impose upon business men terms which they never contemplated. If old forms are now used to express different meanings from those read into them in earlier days the Courts should be prompt to recognize the altered use if they are satisfied that there is in fact a change. I do not say that a contract on c.i.f. terms means to-day anything different to what it ever meant, but if the Courts at other times have rightly imputed to the contract a different meaning to what has been suggested, in my judgment the true meaning of the words is now altered. . . .

The result is that the award in favour of the seller stands and that the buyers must pay the costs.

Judgment for seller.

Compare MAISON HAUSER *c.* RENAULT ET CIE., [1928] Havre 1.208 (Commercial Court), where there was a contract for the sale of 22 tons of cotton at an agreed price c. i. f. Havre. On April 10 the seller tendered documents informing the buyer that certain bales of cotton by the S. S. Caracoli were appropriated to the contract. The buyer refused to accept the tender on the ground that the Caracoli had been lost a sea on April 4. The seller was aware of the loss at the time of making the appropriation by means of the tender. In upholding the buyer's position the Court said: "However numerous might be the presumptions accumulated by a c. i. f. seller to establish with respect to his buyer that unappropriated goods which have perished were intended for him, the bundle thus formed never will constitute proof, for up to the very instant when appropriation is made the seller is completely free to dispose of the goods otherwise. . . . An appropriation made after a loss would permit the seller to escape from a contract that had become burdensome."

Contrast DERODE *c.* BERRIZBEITIA ET CANDON, [1918–19] Havre 1.72 (Commercial Court, 1917). A contract for the sale of 5 tons of coffee at an agreed price c. i. f. Havre, shipment January–May, contained a provision that the contract was to be null and void in the event of a total loss. On May 26 the seller wrote the buyer that 62 bags of coffee marked B & C constituting the 5 tons in question, had been shipped by a certain vessel within the contract period, but that as the ship had been torpedoed and sunk on May 12, the contract was thereby voided. The buyer claimed that there had been no sufficient appropriation of the 5 tons to the contract, and brought an action for damages. In referring the case to an arbitrator the Court said: "Although the law does not permit a seller to appropriate goods on a ship of whose loss he has knowledge, the only reason for such a rule is to prevent the seller from taking advantage of the situation to force the buyer to pay for damaged or defective goods, or even to avoid his obligation altogether by applying to the contract goods which he knows no longer exist. . . . If therefore [the seller] established that the 62 bags marked B & C on this steamer were intended to fill the particular contract, if it is demonstrated that he has not appropriated them with a view to escaping his obligation to make delivery, and if no fault or negligence on his part appears, then the appropriation which he has made should be considered regular despite its lateness."

Refer again to the cases on pages 237–239, 253–254, and 264–266, *supra*, dealing with manner, place, and time of delivery in c. i. f. contracts.

CHAPTER III

Reservations by the Seller

1. CASH SALES

CALCARA *v.* UNITED STATES

United States Circuit Court of Appeals, Eighth Circuit, 1931

[53 *Federal Reporter* (2nd), 767]

Stone, Circuit Judge. Appellant was charged in an indictment in four counts of violating the National Prohibition Law (27 USCA). The first count was not submitted, and the jury found defendant not guilty on the fourth count. The jury found the defendant guilty on the second count for selling a pint of whisky on January 17, 1930, and on the third count for possessing a pint of whisky, upon the same date and place. There was a sentence of two years' imprisonment on the sale count and of a fine on the possession count. From such judgment this appeal is brought.

Appellant argues here three matters. The first is as to the sufficiency of the evidence to support the conviction on the two counts. There can be no sort of question that there is ample evidence to support the conviction on the possession count, and the appellant devotes very little attention to that matter. The real question on the evidence is whether there is sufficient to sustain the conviction on the sale, and the point involved therein is whether a sale was completed, since the whisky never came into actual physical possession of the buyer.

Here the evidence favorable to the prosecution and found true by the jury was that the agent Han and the appellant were total strangers. Han stopped his automobile in front of appellant's store and motioned to him. He came out to the car and asked, "What do you want?" Either Han or his companion said, "We want some whiskey." Also Han said, "Bring us some of that dollar kind, I don't want any of that seventy-five cent kind." Appellant said, "All right," and left, returning in a short time with a pint of whisky "and reached into the car door with the pint of whisky. Witness [Han] held up the dollar bill in his left hand and the defendant reached his left hand just inside of the car door. Witness [Han] put the dollar bill in the defendant's hand and then reached out the car door and caught defendant around the neck and said, 'you are under arrest, I am a Federal agent.' He struggled for a moment and then said, 'All right.' When the Italian [defendant] said 'All right,' witness started to get out of the car and that was the time the Italian threw the whisky with his right hand over the top and to the rear of the car; that occurred after witness had handed defendant the money and had told defendant that he was a Federal officer."

It is clear from this evidence that the article was definitely identified and was present for the one purpose of this sale (it was even tendered for that purpose — the whisky being offered in the right hand as the money was taken with the left hand), and that the purchase price passed.

We are dealing here with the elements of a sale as between the parties thereto. A sale always involves the passage of title to the thing bought and the payment therefor. The parties may make any agreement they desire either as to when title shall pass or as to when payment shall be made. But, whatever that agreement may be, there is no completed sale until the title to the thing sold passes to the buyer in accordance with the agreement. Possession is an attribute of title, but is separable and is often separate therefrom. Hence delivery may precede, be coincident with, or follow the passing of title. *Norfolk & West. Ry. Co.* v. *Sims*, 191 U. S. 441, 447, 24 S. Ct. 151, 48 L. Ed. 254. Whether delivery is necessary to pass title is a matter purely of the intention of the parties. *Hatch* v. *Oil Co.*, 100 U. S. 124, 131, 25 L. Ed. 554. Where no specific intention appears from the contract of the parties the court must take all of the circumstances surrounding the transaction and therefrom declare the intention. In the absence of a specifically appearing intention in what is commonly understood as a "cash" transaction, both parties contemplate the passage of title, and the payment therefor shall be simultaneous. They contemplate also that the possession shall pass at the same time. Under such a transaction the receipt of payment carries the title and the right to immediate possession. The withholding of the possession does not affect either the right thereto or the passage of the title. Here the title passed with the acceptance of the price, and the sale was completed even though attempted delivery was never fully accomplished.

[The balance of the opinion is here omitted.]

In PAUL *v.* REED, 52 N. H. 136 (Supreme Court, 1872), defendant examined certain articles belonging to the seller, and a price was agreed on for each. Some of the articles were delivered. After defendant had taken out his wallet for the purpose of making payment, but before the money was handed over, a sheriff served him with a garnishment writ in behalf of a creditor of the seller. It was held that defendant must be discharged as trustee. "If the goods are put into the possession of the buyer in the expectation that he will immediately pay the price, and he does not do it, the seller is at liberty to regard the delivery as conditional, and may at once reclaim the goods. In such a case the contract of sale is not consummated, and the title does not vest in the buyer."

BURNS BROS. *v.* BIGELOW

New York Supreme Court, Appellate Term, 1910

[122 *New York Supplement*, 253]

Lehman, J. The plaintiffs have replevined coal, which they sold and delivered to defendant, and which defendant has not paid for. The sole questions in the case are whether the sale of the coal was upon the condition that the bill should be paid upon delivery, and whether the delivery without payment waived this condition and vested title in the defendant.

While the defendant claims that the sale to her was upon credit, it seems to me that the plaintiffs have established beyond any question that this is not true.

[A page of the opinion setting forth the evidence and holding that the sale was for cash is here omitted.]

The more serious question in the case, however, is whether, upon the delivery of the coal, the condition of payment was waived. There is no contradiction of the testimony as to the circumstances of the delivery. The plaintiff's driver says that before delivering the last load of the order he presented the bill, and a ticket for the coal, saying, "Here is the bill for $118"; that he then completed the delivery, and waited for 15 minutes, but defendant did not come down again, and the gate was locked. He rang the bell, and a boy came to the door, and said Mrs. Bigelow was upstairs, and he then told the boy he had presented the bill and did not get the money. After that he drove off and reported to the office. The plaintiff's bill collector said he called a few days after the delivery, and asked to see Mrs. Bigelow. He heard a woman's voice say that Mrs. Bigelow was out, and would not be back till 6 o'clock, and he told the boy who opened the door that if they did not get the money they would be compelled to take out the coal.

Under these circumstances I think the court erred in finding that the condition was waived by the delivery. It is quite true that, where goods to be paid for in cash upon delivery are delivered to the purchaser without the cash being given or demanded at the time, the presumption is that the condition is waived and that a complete title vests in the purchaser; but this presumption may be rebutted by proof of such declarations or acts of the parties connected with the circumstances of the case as show an intention that the delivery should not be considered complete until the performance of the condition, and the question with what intention the delivery is made, where any doubt arises, is one of fact. It is also true, however, that where the testimony of such declarations and acts is undisputed, and, connected with the surrounding circumstances, allows the inference only that the condition was not waived, this testimony is controlling, and requires the trial justice to find that the delivery was conditional, and renders his finding to the contrary erroneous as a matter of law. *Parker* v. *Baxter*, 86 N. Y. 586, at pages 593, 594.

In this case the sale was for cash; the coal was delivered, and the bill presented at the same time; an attempt to demand payment was made at the completion of the delivery, and a further demand for the money or the goods was made thereafter. In spite of the fact that the bill presented was not indorsed with the words "Received payment," as is customary where the driver is to receive the payment, it is impossible to find from the circumstances any basis for the inference that the plaintiff intended an absolute delivery. *Leven* v. *Smith,* 1 Denio, 571, cited in *Empire State Type Founding Co.* v. *Grant,* 114 N. Y. 40, at page 44, 21 N. E. 40; *Fleeman* v. *McKean,* 25 Barb. 474.

Judgment should be reversed, and a new trial granted, with costs to the appellant to abide the event. All concur.

Compare FRECH *v.* LEWIS, 218 Penn. 141 (Supreme Court, 1907), where there was a contract for the sale of two carriages to be paid for on delivery. The carriages were delivered, but the buyer did not pay. For more than two months the seller vainly attempted to obtain payment, although he made no effort to take back the carriages. The seller then brought an action in replevin. In reversing a judgment for plaintiff, Stewart, J., said: "The settled doctrine of our cases is to the effect, that where the contract of sale provides for payment of the purchase price on delivery of the articles sold, and the seller delivers the goods but the buyer fails to pay, the right of property does not pass to the buyer with the possession, but remains with the seller, who may at his option reclaim the goods. In some jurisdictions the right of property is held to pass with the delivery, unless at the time the right to retake is expressly declared by the seller. We have not gone so far. Our cases proceed on the theory that until payment has been made, or waived, the contract remains executory, and that delivery in such case is not a completion of the contract, except as an intention to so regard it is expressly declared or can fairly be inferred from the circumstances attending. Possession, however, having passed, and the buyer by the act of the seller having been invested with the indicia of ownership, the policy of our law requires that this situation — the possession in one and the right of property in another — shall continue no longer than is necessary to enable the seller to recover the goods with which he has parted. The law gives the seller the right in such case to reclaim his goods, but he must do so promptly, otherwise he will be held to have waived his right, and can only thereafter look to the buyer for the price."

TURNER *v.* BENZ BROTHERS & COMPANY

WASHINGTON SUPREME COURT, 1929

[153 *Washington Reports,* 123]

MILLARD, J. — On December 16, 1927, H. M. Asbury, a hay buyer, called at the farm of W. W. Turner, with whom he orally agreed to purchase all of the hay of the latter when baled and loaded on cars at Ashue railroad siding. To Asbury's inquiry at that time, "You want a check on this?" Turner replied, "No, it isn't necessary. I will have it loaded, but anyhow I am safe because the hay is mine until it is paid for." It is clear Asbury understood that the hay would not be shipped until Turner had been paid for the same. Asbury testified: "It was Mr. Turner's hay until I paid him for it."

No one requested the railroad company to place cars at Ashue, at which point the company does not maintain an agent. Empty cars are switched onto the siding for the convenience of shippers, and it was the custom for the company to hold the cars until orders for release and instructions as to billing were given to the company's agent at Toppenish by the consignor or by the one who loaded the cars. Turner's employees hauled the hay to the siding and loaded it on two cars, the loading being concluded on Saturday, December 17. Turner went immediately to Asbury's office in Toppenish, a few miles distant, to obtain payment for the hay, but the buyer could not be found. On Monday, December 19, Asbury who had been authorized by no one so to do, gave written instructions to the railroad company to bill the two cars of hay on order of Benz Brothers, who in turn sold the hay to a customer in Seattle to whom it was shipped. Nothing was paid to Asbury by Benz Brothers for the hay. The price due was applied on Asbury's indebtedness to the defendant, for whom Asbury had previously purchased hay. Plaintiff, learning of the disposition of the hay and being unable to obtain payment therefor, commenced this action against the defendant to recover for its conversion. The cause was tried to the court. From the judgment entered upon findings and conclusion in favor of the plaintiff, the defendant appealed.

The contract herein was for a cash sale.

"The term 'cash sale,' as applied to the sale of specific goods, is sometimes used to denote a sale where title is not to pass until the cash price is paid, and sometimes to denote a sale where title has passed but possession is not to be delivered until payment is made. Tiffany, Sales, 123, 268. In either case payment and delivery are concurrent and mutually dependent acts, and if the seller gives up possession in expectation of immediate payment, and payment is not forthcoming, he may repossess himself of the goods or sue in conversion one who refuses his demand for repossession." *Welch Co.* v. *Lahart Elevator Co.*, 122 Minn. 432, 142 N. W. 828.

Under the contract, the title to the hay passed to the buyer as soon as the hay was baled.

"Where there is an unconditional contract to sell specific goods, in a deliverable state, the property in the goods passes to the buyer when the contract is made, and it is immaterial whether the time of payment, or time of delivery, or both, be postponed." Rem. 1927 Sup., § 5836–19.

It was an implied condition of the contract that possession would be surrendered and delivery made of the hay upon payment of the purchase price.

"Unless otherwise agreed, delivery of the goods and payment of the price are concurrent conditions; that is to say, the seller must be ready and willing to give possession of the goods to the buyer in exchange for the price and the buyer must be ready and willing to pay the price in exchange for possession of goods." Rem. 1927 Sup., § 5836–42.

Turner, under this contract, could retain possession of the hay until payment had been made.

"The unpaid seller of goods who is in possession of them is entitled to retain possession of them until payment or tender of the price. . . . (a) Where the goods have been sold without any stipulation as to credit. . . ." Rem. 1927 Sup., § 5836–54, subd. 1.

Did Turner surrender possession of the hay to Asbury? The evidence is clear that the right of possession of the hay was never surrendered by Turner to Asbury, for the reason that there was no valid delivery thereof, and the respondent never waived the condition of the contract of sale that the goods should be paid for in cash. Credit was never extended by Turner to Asbury. The bargain between the parties is plain. Under it, Asbury was to pay Turner when the hay was loaded on the cars at the railroad siding. The price was due and payable the moment that the task of loading was completed. There was no delivery to Asbury.

"As already suggested, the wheat is not shown to have been delivered at all. It was placed in the car ready to be turned over to the control of Smith, or to be 'delivered' when payment was made. Delivery and payment were to be contemporaneous acts. Depositing the wheat in the car, under that contract, was simply putting the wheat in a position ready for delivery." *Toledo, Wabash & Western R. Co.* v. *Gilvin*, 81 Ill. 511.

It was impossible for Turner to keep one hand upon the hay until, with the other hand, he could grasp the money or check tendered in payment. There was no intention of surrendering possession to Asbury until payment had been made. It was intended to be a cash transaction. Asbury evaded Turner to avoid paying for the hay. Following the loading of the hay on Saturday, the 17th, Asbury on Monday, the 19th, without authority, instructed the railroad company to release the cars to the appellant. The respondent never parted with legal possession of the hay. He has not been guilty of aught that would estop him from asserting his right of possession. Asbury's unlawful exercise of dominion over the property was a conversion, and did not divest the respondent of his right to the hay. Legal possession of the hay was never surrendered to Asbury, and appellant did not by its purchase acquire title superior to that held by Asbury.

The judgment should be, and it is, affirmed.

MITCHELL, C. J., FRENCH, PARKER, and MAIN, JJ., concur.

Compare MAXHERMAN Co. *v.* ALPER, 210 App. Div. 389 (New York Supreme Court, Appellate Division, 1924), where plaintiff agreed to sell the buyer a number of specific dresses, the price to be paid in cash or by certified check on delivery. The dresses were delivered and the buyer gave an uncertified check which was refused certification because of insufficient funds. The buyer assured plaintiff that payment would be made during the day, but it was not, and plaintiff, declining to wait until the next morning and attempting to remove the dresses, was forcibly prevented by the buyer. The following day the buyer continued to give assurances which did not materialize, and in the meantime sold the dresses to defendant who took them with knowledge of the circumstances. In an action to recover the value of the dresses, judgment for defendant was reversed. Title did not pass to the original buyer because there was no valid delivery, and plaintiff did not waive the condition of payment by cash or certified check.

In ISLAND TRADING CO. *v.* BERG BROTHERS, 239 N. Y. 229 (Court of Appeals, 1924), one Murat Bey of New York contracted to sell goods to plaintiff, a company in Manila. Murat Bey then bought goods of the proper description from defendants with the understanding that the sale was for cash. Defendants shipped the goods direct to plaintiff by parcel post, and gave the parcel post receipts to Murat Bey on his assertion that he would go and get the cash and pay them. Murat Bey used the receipts to collect the purchase price under a letter of credit arranged by plaintiff, but did not pay defendants. After waiting three weeks defendants secured a stop order on the Manila post office and had the goods returned. Plaintiff brought the present action for conversion. Judgment for plaintiff affirmed "Defendant put it into Murat Bey's power to obtain plaintiff's money to pay for the goods. It assented to the resale by shipping the goods to the subpurchaser and allowing Murat Bey to take the postal receipts to obtain the money from the subpurchaser which paid for them. As between two innocent victims of the fraud, the one who made possible the fraud on the other should suffer."

In MORRIS & COMPANY *v.* WALKER BROTHERS COMPANY, 29 Ga. App. 476 (Court of Appeals, 1922), plaintiffs sold certain cheeses under terms which, according to some evidence, were silent as to time of payment, and according to other evidence provided for payment on delivery. The goods were delivered at the buyer's place of business by plaintiffs' driver without obtaining payment. On the following morning plaintiffs demanded the goods or the money, but were informed that the goods had been resold to defendant. It was admitted that defendant bought in the regular course of trade and without notice of plaintiffs' rights. Judgment for defendant affirmed. Where "the purchase price is to be paid upon delivery of the goods, and the vendor, without collecting the purchase price, nevertheless proceeds to make delivery in pursuance of his contract, and the vendee, after such delivery, proceeds to resell the goods to a *bona fide* purchaser for value, the rights of such innocent third person are governed by the provisions of . . . the Civil Code relative to conditional sales, and the vendor cannot recover the goods from such innocent purchaser. . . . The justness of the rule is based upon the equitable principles that, where one of two innocent persons must suffer loss by reason of the wrong of another, the loss should fall on him by whose act or omission the wrongdoer has been enabled to commit the wrong."

SOUTH SAN FRANCISCO PACKING AND PROVISION COMPANY *v.* JACOBSEN

CALIFORNIA SUPREME COURT, 1920

[183 *California Reports*, 131]

The COURT. — This is an appeal from a judgment in favor of the defendant, Western Meat Company, and against the defendants, Taylor & Rosecrans, in an action in interpleader.

Briefly, the facts of the case are these: Taylor & Rosecrans, at the time the transaction here involved took place, were copartners engaged in the livestock business in the state of Idaho, as also was the defendant Jacobsen, their respective places of business, however, not being in the same locality. Shortly before the tenth day of June, 1915, Jacobsen, by telephone, purchased from Taylor & Rosecrans three carloads of hogs at an agreed price, the hogs to be delivered at a certain place in Idaho, where Jacobsen or his agent was to receive them and make payment therefor by check. Accordingly the hogs were delivered and a check for $3,490.98 was given in payment by Jacobsen's agent, the delivery of the check taking place at midnight on said June 10th. Before noon of the following day it was deposited for collection with the firm's bank at Burley, Idaho. It reached the bank in Idaho Falls on which it was drawn three days later, i. e., Monday, June 14th, when payment was refused for lack of funds. As is apparent, Saturday afternoon and Sunday falling within these three days, the actual business time comprehended within said period of three days was but a day and a half. There being no evidence in the record to the contrary, we will presume that the check was presented for payment in the ordinary course of business. On the tenth day of June, when the check was delivered, Jacobsen's bank balance was $1,733.37; on the next day, June 11th, Friday, said balance was increased to about five thousand dollars; on Saturday, June 12th, it had been reduced to about four thousand dollars, and on Monday, when the check was presented for payment, said balance was $1,341.57. Jacobsen had no arrangement with the bank for credit or overdraft.

Shortly after the purchase of the hogs by Jacobsen he disappeared. Commencing with June 14th many checks drawn by him were, when presented at the bank, dishonored. In the meantime, Jacobsen had shipped the hogs to the plaintiff, which in turn disposed of them in San Francisco, and the fund involved in this litigation is part of the sum realized by the plaintiff from their sale. While there is some dispute on the subject, nevertheless it fairly appears from the record not only that defendants Taylor & Rosecrans, upon learning of the dishonor of the check, demanded the fund from the plaintiff under a claim of ownership, but also that the respondent, Western Meat Company, a creditor of Jacobsen, at about the same time commenced an action against him and levied an attachment on this fund. The plaintiff, being thus confronted with two conflicting claims, commenced this action in interpleader against the partnership, Jacobsen and the Western Meat Company. Jacobsen defaulted, and judgment went for the Western Meat Company as against Taylor & Rosecrans, who have appealed.

The appellants contend that Jacobsen, having obtained delivery of the hogs by means of a worthless check, was guilty of fraud, and that therefore the sale was void, both as to Jacobsen and his attaching creditor. It is true, as contended by the appellants, that the issuance by Jacobsen of this check, payment of which was refused for lack of funds, coupled with his unexplained disappearance, is some evidence of fraud. It appears, however, that after the issuance of the check, and before its presentation for payment three business days later, Jacobsen, on two of those days, had more than sufficient money on deposit to meet the check. This circumstance, with the presumption of innocence and fair dealing, furnish some foundation for the finding of the trial court against fraud; so that in view of what may thus be regarded as a conflict of evidence we are not at liberty to disturb this finding.

There are several technical points made by the appellants in support of their appeal, but as we have concluded that the judgment must be reversed upon the main ground urged it will be unnecessary to discuss these. We are thus brought to the consideration of the principal question involved, viz., whether or not title to the hogs passed at the time of the delivery by Jacobsen's agent of the check.

We are of the opinion that this question must be answered in the negative, and, consequently, that the appellants are entitled to the fund as against Jacobsen's attaching creditor, the Western Meat Company.

Whether or not title to personal property passes through a sale thereof at the time of its delivery depends upon the intention of the parties as shown by all the facts and circumstances of the case, so that the question is ordinarily one of fact for the jury, or for the court when sitting without a jury. Where, however, the facts bearing upon the question of intent are undisputed only a question of law is presented. Here the evidence shows without conflict that Jacobsen was to pay for the hogs upon delivery by check; and it is argued by the respondent that accordingly, a check having been given and received in payment for the hogs, title to the animals passed to the buyer notwithstanding that upon due presentation the check was dishonored. This argument is supported by reference to cases holding that parties may agree to accept a check or bill or note as absolute payment for goods sold, in which case title to the goods will pass upon such acceptance irrespective of whether the paper is honored upon due presentation or not. We think, however, that the facts of this case do not bring it within the principle referred to, for it is quite apparent that the requirement of the vendor that a check should be given by the buyer upon the delivery of the hogs was intended as the equivalent of an insistence upon payment on delivery; in other words, that it was not a sale on credit, nor for the check as such, but that delivery of the animals and payment for them, though such payment might be made by check, were to be simultaneous, and the transaction was understood by the vendee in this sense. The legal situation thus arising can logically be no different from one where the terms of the sale are cash on delivery and a check is accepted by the vendor. In such case it is held that the acceptance of the check is no waiver of immediate payment, and although delivery is made of the goods upon receipt of the check, title thereto does not pass as between the parties unless, upon due presentation, the check is paid. . . .

In effect, this sale was for cash as distinguished from a sale on credit, payment to be made, as is customary in similar commercial transactions, by check, and as it was not agreed that the check was to be received as absolute payment, and the delivery of the goods also was conditional, and the check, upon due presentation, was dishonored, title to the hogs remained in the seller. . . .

There is nothing in this record indicating that the original sellers intended to accept Jacobsen's check as absolute payment. True, they were to accept a check in payment for the hogs, but this is the usual method in cash transactions of any magnitude, and it is employed as a matter of convenience and to obviate the necessity of handling and transporting large sums of money with its attendant risks. In the case of *Comptoir d'Escompte* v. *Bresbach*, 78 Cal. 15, [20 Pac. 28], it is said that the language of the manager of the plaintiff bank in stating that a check which was subsequently dishonored, was accepted in payment of the debt sued upon should not be construed as signifying anything more the provisional or conditional payment presumed by law, and is no evidence of absolute payment.

The title to the hogs, therefore, as between the parties to the sale having remained in the original sellers, it follows, we have no doubt, that the fund in the hands of the plaintiff, the purchaser from Jacobsen, constituting part of the purchase price, belongs to the original sellers, Taylor & Rosecrans; and we also entertain no doubt that so far as the attaching creditor is concerned it has no better right to the fund than Jacobsen himself. (*Ward* v. *Waterman*, 85 Cal. 491, 508, [24 Pac. 930].)

It follows that the judgment should be reversed, and it is so ordered.

Williston, in 34 HARV. L. R. 749 (1920), comments on the above cases as follows: "In two recent decisions courts have repeated what has been said many times before, though it is impossible to accept it as accurate, that where a check is given for property and the check is not paid on presentation, the title to the property never passes to the buyer. The argument in support of this conclusion is that the sale was intended to be a cash sale, and that title therefore does not pass until cash has been received. The argument is fallacious, however; the seller in fact intends to exchange the ownership of the goods for the check which he receives. He is induced to do so by the belief that the check is good. If the buyer has no funds he is committing a fraud, but this will result only in title being voidable, not in an entire failure of title to pass. If it were true, as is often stated, that no title passes until the check is paid, the buyer is a *tort feasor* if he uses the goods until the check is paid, even though there are ample funds in the bank to make the payment. If it were true, as it is also often stated, that the fact that the check is given merely in conditional payment proves that no title passes until the condition is satisfied, the same consequence would follow if a time draft were given instead of a check. Such a result would obviously be absurd. The decision in most of the cases here criticised for asserting that title did not pass to the buyer was indeed correct, because the controversy was either between the original parties or at least did not involve an innocent purchaser, and the buyer's conduct justified the conclusion that he was fraudulent; but the reasoning of the courts would warrant the inference that the seller might reclaim the goods from an innocent purchaser; for one who fraudulently acquires merely possession, without even a voidable title, cannot transfer any right even to an innocent purchaser."

In MOREHOUSE *v.* KEYPORT AUTO SALES COMPANY, 118 N. J. Eq. 368 (Court of Chancery, 1935), there was a sale and delivery of an automobile, for which the seller simultaneously received from the buyer his check in the full amount of the purchase price. The car was sold two weeks later by the buyer's receiver pursuant to a court order. The proceeds of this sale were claimed by the seller, by the receiver, and by a financing company which had advanced money to the buyer for the purpose of buying the car and had taken a chattel mortgage in return. In awarding the proceeds to the seller, Berry, V. C., said: "The transaction between the seller and the dealer being a sale of a specific chattel, the question as to when title passed is to be determined by the intention of the parties as manifested by their conduct and all the attendant circumstances. That no conditional sales agreement was entered into, that no other security for deferred payment was taken and that the dealer gave to the seller a check for the full amount of the purchase price at the same time the car was delivered all indicate beyond question that the transaction was intended by the parties to be a sale for cash. A sale for cash is a conditional sale and as between the parties no title vests thereunder by delivery without payment unless the delivery be made under such circumstances as to evince a waiver of the condition. *Central Union Trust Co.* v. *Willat Film Corp.*, 99 N. J. Eq. 748, is to the effect that payment by check is not complete until the check is honored. By analogy, delivery is no delivery (at least for the purpose of passing title), unless the check is paid. Pending payment the delivery is conditional only."

2. CONDITIONAL SALES

HELBY *v.* MATTHEWS

House of Lords, 1895

[*Law Reports*, [1895] *Appeal Cases*, 471]

The appellant was the owner of a piano, of which he had given possession to one Brewster, under an agreement in writing of the 23rd of December, 1892. On the 22nd of April 1893 Brewster, improperly and without the consent of the appellant, pledged the piano with the respondents, who are pawnbrokers, as security for an advance. The appellant, upon discovering this, demanded the piano from the respondents, and on their refusing to deliver it, brought an action of trover. The defence set up by the respondents was that they had received the piano from Brewster in good faith, and without notice of any claim on the part of the appellant, and that Brewster having "bought or agreed to buy" it from him they were protected by sect. 9 of the Factors Act 1889.

The county court judge held that the defence was not proved, and his judgment was upheld by the Divisional Court (Lord Coleridge C.J. and Day J.). The Court of Appeal (Lord Esher M.R., A. L. Smith, and Davey L.JJ.) came to the conclusion that the defence had been established, and reversed the judgment of the Divisional Court upon the ground that Brewster had agreed to buy the piano within the meaning of the Factors Act. The only question was whether the respondents had made out that Brewster had bought or agreed to buy the piano. This depended upon the true effect of the agreement under which he obtained it.

[The agreement provided for monthly payments of 10*s.* 6*d.*, and also contained the following clauses:

"A. That the hirer may terminate the hiring by delivering up to the owner the said instrument.

"B. If the hirer shall punctually pay the full sum of £18 18*s.* by 10*s.* 6*d.* at date of signing, and by 36 monthly instalments of 10*s.* 6*d.* in advance as aforesaid, the said instrument shall become the sole and absolute property of the hirer.

"C. Unless and until the full sum of £18 18*s.* be paid, the said instrument shall be and continue to be the sole property of the owner."]

Lord Herschell L.C. (after stating the facts given above): —

My Lords, it is said that the substance of the transaction evidenced by the agreement must be looked at, and not its mere words. I quite agree. But the substance must, of course, be ascertained by a consideration of the rights and obligations of the parties, to be derived from a consideration of the whole of the agreement. If Brewster agreed to buy the piano, the parties cannot, by calling it a hiring, or by any mere juggling with words, escape from the consequences of the contract into which they entered. What, then, was the real nature of the transaction? The answer to this question is not, I think, involved in any difficulty. Brewster was to obtain possession of the piano, and to be entitled to its use so long as he paid the plaintiff the stipulated sum of 10*s.* 6*d.* a month, and he was bound to make these monthly payments so long as he retained possession of the piano. If he continued to make them at the appointed times for the period of three years, the piano was to become his property, but he might at any time return it, and, upon doing so, would no longer be liable to make any further payment beyond the monthly sum then due.

My Lords, I cannot, with all respect, concur in the view of the Court of Appeal, that upon the true construction of the agreement Brewster had "agreed to buy" the piano. An agreement to buy imports a legal obligation to buy. If there was no such legal obligation, there cannot, in my opinion, properly be said to have been an agreement to buy. Where is any such legal obligation to be found? Brewster might buy or not just as he pleased. He did not agree to make thirty-six or any number of monthly payments. All that he undertook was to make the monthly payment of 10*s.* 6*d.* so long as he kept the piano. He had an option no doubt to buy it by continuing the stipulated payments for a sufficient length of time. If he had exercised that option he would have become the purchaser. I cannot see under these circumstances how he can be said either to have bought or agreed to buy the piano. The terms of the contract did not upon its execution bind him to buy, but left him free to do so or not as he pleased, and nothing happened after the contract was made to impose that obligation.

The Master of the Rolls said: "It is a contract by the seller to sell, and a contract by the purchaser, if he does not change his mind, to buy; and if this agreement goes on to its end, it ends in a purchase. Therefore, it seems to me that the true and proper construction of this instrument, after all, is this: it is an agreement by the one to sell, and an agreement by the other to buy, but with an option on the part of the buyer if he changes his mind to put an end to the contract." I cannot think that an agreement to buy, "if he does not change his mind," is any agreement to buy at all in the eye of the law. If it rests with me to do or not to do a certain thing at a future time, according to the then state of my mind, I cannot be said to have contracted to do it. It appears to me that the contract in question was in reality a contract of hiring, and not in name or pretence only. But for the provision that if the hirer punctually paid the 10*s.* 6*d.* a month for thirty-six months, the piano should be his property, it could not be doubted that it was a mere agreement for its hire, and I cannot see how the fact that this provision was added made it any the less a contract of hiring until that condition had been fulfilled.

I think it very likely that both parties thought it would probably end in a purchase, but this is far from shewing that it was an agreement to buy. The monthly payments were no doubt somewhat higher than they would have been if the agreement had contained no such provision. One can well conceive cases, however, in which a person who had not made up his mind to continue the payments for three years would nevertheless enter into such an agreement. It might be worth his while to make somewhat larger monthly payments for the use of the piano in order that he might enjoy that option if he chose to exercise it. In such a case how could it be said that he had agreed to buy when he had not only come under no obligation to buy, but had not even made up his mind to do so? The agreement is, in its terms, just as applicable to such a case as to one where the hirer had resolved to continue the payments for the three years, and it must be construed upon a consideration of the obligations which its terms create, and not upon a mere speculation as to what was contemplated, or what would probably be done under it.

It was said in the Court of Appeal that there was an agreement by the appellant to sell, and that an agreement to sell connotes an agreement to buy. This is undoubtedly true if the words "agreement to sell" be used in their strict legal sense; but when a person has, for valuable consideration, bound himself to sell to another on certain terms, if the other chooses to avail himself of the binding offer, he may, in popular language, be said to have agreed to sell, though an agreement to sell in this sense, which is in truth merely an offer which cannot be withdrawn, certainly does not connote an agreement to buy, and it is only in this sense that there can be said to have been an agreement to sell in the present case.

It was argued for the respondents that the case came within the mischief intended to be provided against by sect. 9 of the Factors Act 1889, and that the enactment ought, therefore, to be so construed as to cover it. I can see no reason for thus straining the language of the enactment. A person who is in possession of a piano under such an agreement as that which existed in the present case is no more its apparent owner than if he had merely hired it, and in the latter case any one taking it as security would have no claim to hold it as against the owner.

Reliance was placed on the decision in *Lee* v. *Butler* ([1893] 2 Q. B. 318), and it was said that the present case was not, in principle, distinguishable from it. There seems to me to be the broadest distinction between the two cases. There was there an agreement to buy. The purchase-money was to be paid in two instalments, but as soon as the agreement was entered into there was an absolute obligation to pay both of them, which might have been enforced by action. The person who obtained the goods could not insist upon returning them and so absolve himself from any obligation to make further payment. Unless there were a breach of contract by the party who engaged to make the payments the transaction necessarily resulted in a sale. That there was in that case an agreement to buy appears to me, as it did to the Court of Appeal, to be beyond question.

It was further urged for the respondents that when Brewster pledged the piano with them it became impossible for him to return it to the appellant, and he became, therefore, from that time bound to make the stipulated payments and to become the purchaser. I cannot accede to this argument. In my opinion, it is impossible to hold that Brewster, having only a right under the contract to buy, provided he complied with the prescribed conditions, could convert himself into a purchaser as against the owner by violating the conditions of the contract.

I think the judgment appealed from must be reversed. The respondents must pay the costs of this appeal, and in the Court below.

[Concurring opinions of Lords Watson, Macnaghten, Morris, and Shand, are here omitted.]

Note also MODERN LIGHT CARS, LTD. *v.* SEALS, [1933] W. N. 127 (King's Bench Division).

Compare MCENTIRE *v.* CROSSLEY BROTHERS, [1895] A. C. 457 (House of Lords), where there was a contract under which "lessors" agreed to let to a "lessee," and the latter agreed to hire a gas engine, rent to be paid by a payment of £60 cash before delivery and eight equal quarterly payments aggregating £240, the engine to become the property of the "lessee" on completion of the final payment but until that time to remain the property of the "lessor," "it being hereby expressly declared and agreed that the said gas-engine is only let on hire to the lessee until all sums of money due under this agreement are paid." While the engine was in the possession of the "lessee" under this agreement, and before all the instalments had been paid, the "lessee" became bankrupt. In affirming an order that the engine be delivered to the "lessors," Lord Herschell said: "Upon an agreement to sell it depends upon the intention of the parties whether the property passes or does not pass. Here the parties have in terms expressed their intention, and said that the property shall not pass till the full purchase-money is paid. I know of no reason to prevent that being a perfectly lawful agreement."

Note further TAYLOR *v.* THOMPSON, [1930] W. N. 16 (King's Bench Division). A written agreement was made whereby defendant agreed to hire a traction engine of plaintiff, £50 to be paid on taking the engine over, and £50 on each quarter day until a total of £400 was paid, when the engine was to become the property of defendant. Defendant made no payments beyond £150, and plaintiff claimed the return of the engine. It was held that the contract was an agreement to buy at a price payable in instalments, and that plaintiff could not recover the engine but only the unpaid balance of the price. "It was true that in this document the term 'hire' was used, but it must be borne in mind that if an agreement was really an agreement to buy, the parties could not escape liability by calling it a hire-purchase agreement."

AIR EQUIPMENT CORPORATION *v.* RUBBERCRAFT CORPORATION

CIRCUIT COURT OF APPEALS, SECOND CIRCUIT, 1935

[79 *Federal Reporter* (*Second Series*), 521]

L. HAND, Circuit Judge. This is an appeal from a decree dismissing the petition of a conditional seller, filed in a sequestration suit to reclaim the goods sold from the receiver. The seller's right is based upon an agreement between itself and the buyer, the insolvent company, for the "lease" of a sewing machine upon payment of $757.50; the record does not describe the machine further, and we do not know what was its prospective life. The seller professed to "let" the machine for $750 (with interest of $7.50); the buyer agreed to pay "as rent and compensation" for its use $257.50 on delivery and $100 a month for the five following months. If the "lessee" defaulted in any of its payments or pledged or removed the property, or became bankrupt or insolvent, and in various other contingencies, it was to return the property to the "lessor," which was authorized to enter the premises and retake it. The "lessee" was to keep it insured and might at any time "during the rental term * * * purchase the said property by paying to the company the above valuation therefor, in which event the rents theretofore paid, shall be deducted from the purchase price." The agreement was not to "constitute a sale of the property hereinabove described and no agreement of sale shall be implied herefrom."

The machine was delivered on July 5th. The "lease" was signed on the 14th; the seller's salesman in New Haven forwarded it to the seller's office. On the 19th it was mailed to the town clerk of New Haven to be filed. On the 22d the clerk returned it to the seller because it was not acknowledged, and after acknowledging it the seller sent it back to the salesman in New Haven on the 25th. He got the buyer's acknowledgment on August 4th, and filed it on the 8th. The seller asserted, first, that the agreement was in fact a lease and need not have been filed; and, second, that it was filed in season. The judge found that the transaction was a conditional sale and that the agreement was not filed in season. Following his former ruling in *Re Guild, Bloomfield & Jensen* (D. C.) 51 F.(2d) 818, he thought it relevant whether all creditors had become such after filing, but as he placed the burden of proof on this issue upon the seller, he dismissed the petition.

If the transaction was a sale, the decisions of the courts of Connecticut as to the meaning of the local conditional sales statute control; whether they should also be authoritative as to its character as sale or lease we need not say, for they do not differ from the "general law" in this regard. The attempted disguise of the transaction as a lease is so transparent as to deceive nobody and deserves little discussion. While, as we have said, the length of life of the sewing machine does not appear, we are entitled to assume merely because it was a sewing machine that it would last longer than six months; the circumstance then becomes important that the sum of the supposed "rents" was the same as the purchase price. "Rents" of such an article, which will be accepted as full payment for title, cannot really be intended as a return for its temporary use. This conclusion is confirmed by the initial payment of one-third of the whole price, with one per cent. interest on the whole sum — an unheard of provision in a real lease. The Connecticut decisions give short shrift to the contention that such transactions are not sales. In *re Wilcox & Howe Co.*, 70 Conn. 220, 39 A. 163; *Craig & Co.* v. *Uncas Paperboard Co.*, 104 Conn. 559, 133 A. 673. *Lambert Hoisting Engine Co.* v. *Carmody*, 79 Conn. 419, 65 A. 141, was entirely different; the sum of the rentals did not make up the purchase price; if the lessee chose to buy during the term, it had to pay several times their amount. Finally that stipulation was a nullity which declared that the agreement shall not be treated as a sale. The purpose of the statute being to protect the buyer's creditors, no court will pay the slightest attention to such efforts to circumvent it.

[The balance of the opinion is here omitted.]

Order affirmed.

In IN RE RAINEY, 31 Fed. (2nd) 197 (District Court, Maryland, 1929), there was an agreement to lease certain machinery valued at $812 for a term of three months. The lessee agreed to pay $325 as partial security for the fulfillment of the agreement. Rent totalling $487 was to be paid in two monthly payments of $243.50 each, secured by two promissory notes. At the expiration of the term the lessee agreed to surrender the machinery, receiving in return the amount deposited as partial security. The lessee then was to have the option of purchasing the machinery for this same amount. In holding the transaction to be a conditional sale, and hence void as against the lessee's trustee in bankruptcy because unrecorded, the Court said:

"In order to determine the true character of the agreement, it is necessary to look through form to substance. In the present case the rental of the machinery for three months, the full term of the lease, amounted to 60 per cent. of its entire value. A charge so disproportionate to the term of user in relation to the value of the articles, all of which were second-hand, in and of itself certainly suggests a sale.

"Furthermore, the so-called rental payments, plus the original deposit, equal the total value of the machinery, nothing being required to be paid at the expiration of the term, at which time the bankrupt had the option of becoming the owner. There is nothing to indicate that the machinery would deteriorate to such an extent in so short a time, and when we consider that it was purchasable at the end of the three months for $325, namely, the sum deposited as partial security in the first instance, its purchase became virtually compulsory. True, the bankrupt had the option of returning the machinery at the end of the term, and of getting back the deposit; but as a practical matter it is difficult to imagine this being done, or that it was ever in fact contemplated. It seems to the court that these considerations outweigh any language to the contrary contained in the agreement.

"The distinction between an ordinary lease and a conditional sale is obvious. A lease contemplates only the use of the property for a limited time and the return of it to the lessor at the expiration of that time; whereas, a conditional sale contemplates the ultimate ownership of the property by the buyer, together with the use of it in the meantime. In the present case, the bankrupt could not terminate the transaction by returning the property at any time prior to the end of the term, and then, as just explained, the loss in so doing, made it virtually prohibitive."

Compare GENERAL MOTORS ACCEPTANCE CORPORATION *v.* HORTON, 85 Fed. (2nd) 452 (Circuit Court of Appeals, Third Circuit, 1936), where Davis, Circuit Judge, said:

"The appellant contends that the contract in question is a bailment lease, but the appellee says it is a conditional sale. If the transaction was a conditional sale, title to the automobile was in the lessee and passed to its trustee in bankruptcy as of the date of the filing of the petition; but if the contract was a lease, title did not pass and the property belongs to the appellant.

"The contract is in the form of a lease and provides for a definite term, a fixed rental, and an agreement for the return of the automobile at the end of the term. It is true that the so-called rentals amount to more than the regular purchase price of the automobile, which was $827, while the total rentals amount to $952. The first installment or rental due upon delivery was $268, and the following rentals were $38 per month. When the total rentals were paid, the 'lessee' either had to surrender the automobile, or he could purchase it for the nominal sum of $1. The contract further provided that the appellant might repossess or 'resell' the automobile upon noncompliance by the lessee with the terms of the contract. The term 'resell' indicates that the first transaction was a sale and not a bailment lease, but that term stands alone and is not in harmony with the other provisions of the contract, and so is not decisive of the issue.

"It is evident that the parties to the contract intended by it to accomplish two results: First to retain, in the lessor, title to the automobile as against the bankruptcy or other unfortunate circumstances of the lessee; and, secondly, to provide that the lessee might, after payment of all the rentals, purchase the automobile for a nominal sum. It must be admitted that this transaction in fact, though not in form, amounted to a conditional sale. But to construe such contracts as bailment leases is a policy, regardless of what may be thought of it as a principle of law or business, which has long been pursued in Pennsylvania, and her courts have uniformly sustained them as bailment leases. This court has felt constrained to follow the decisions of the Pennsylvania courts in construing such contracts."

In AUTOMATIC VOTING MACHINE CORPORATION *v.* COUNTY OF MARICOPA, 50 Ariz. 211 (Supreme Court, 1937), there was a contract providing that in consideration of $11,068.20, receipt of which was acknowledged, the plaintiff rented to the defendant 45 voting machines for use in the 1934 elections. It was agreed that defendant at its option should have the right to rent the machines for the 1936 elections at the same price or to purchase them at any time for $1118 each, the amount paid as rent to be applied on the purchase price. If defendant decided neither to rent nor to purchase, the machines were to be returned to plaintiff in good condition. At the time this agreement was made the parties did not contemplate merely a temporary use of the machines at the 1934 and 1936 elections, but it was the intention and expectation of both parties that they would continue to be used at all succeeding elections until the payments denominated as rental, together with such other funds as defendant might have available, should be sufficient to pay the purchase price fixed in the agreement, whereupon title would pass to defendant. While the machines were thus in use the question arose as to the payment of taxes assessed on the machines, plaintiff claiming not to be liable on the ground that the transaction was a conditional sale. In holding that under the Uniform Act the contract was an option of purchase rather than a conditional sale, the Court said: "[These sections of the Act] state specifically that under a true conditional sale there is an absolute liability on the part of the buyer for the purchase price in case the seller elects to hold him therefor. . . . On examining the contract between plaintiff and defendant, it will be seen that nowhere therein is there any agreement by the defendant that it will pay the full purchase price of the machines, either as rental or otherwise, nor can the seller compel such payment."

THE SHERER–GILLETT COMPANY *v.* LONG

ILLINOIS SUPREME COURT, 1925

[318 *Illinois Reports*, 432]

Mr. Justice THOMPSON delivered the opinion of the court:

The sole question presented for decision in this case is whether under the law of this State in effect April 5, 1924, a reservation of title by the seller is good against a *bona fide* purchaser from a buyer in possession under a contract of conditional sale. The question arises out of the following transactions: April 3, 1924, appellee, the Sherer-Gillett Company, entered into a contract of conditional sale with H. C. Taylor for the sale of a display counter to be used by Taylor in his grocery store, by which Taylor agreed to pay $10 in cash and $10 each month until the full purchase price was paid, the title to remain in appellee until full payment of the purchase price had been made. Two days later Taylor sold the counter to appellant, J. W. Long, for $100, Long then having no notice of the reservation of title under the contract of conditional sale and no notice of any rights of appellee. The Appellate Court for the First District reversed a judgment of the municipal court entered in favor of appellant in an action of replevin brought by appellee and granted a certificate of importance allowing this appeal.

Before sales became a subject of uniform legislation it was settled by an overwhelming weight of authority that the seller is not estopped by his conduct in delivering the possession of goods to the buyer upon a contract of conditional sale from asserting his title against one who purchases from the buyer, relying upon the apparent title of the latter, (1 Williston on Sales,—2d ed.—sec. 324; *Harkness* v. *Russell & Co.* 118 U. S. 663, 7 Sup. Ct. 51; *Arnold* v. *Chandler Motors*, (R. I.) 123 Atl. 85); but in this State we had held that a delivery of personal property to the purchaser upon a contract of conditional sale, with a retention of title in the seller, amounts to constructive fraud, which postpones the right of the real owner in favor of those who have dealt without notice with the conditional vendee, who has been given the indicia of ownership. (*Gilbert* v. *National Cash Register Co.* 176 Ill. 288; *Brundage* v. *Camp*, 21 id. 329.) Uniformity in the law of the several States pertaining to sales being deemed essential to the commercial welfare of the country, leaders of the American bar prepared and submitted to the legislatures of the several States a uniform sales act and a uniform conditional sales act. The former was adopted in this State in 1915 and is the law to-day. By section 20 of the act the validity of a contract of conditional sale is recognized. Section 23 declares the law of this State respecting the transfer of title to be that theretofore declared by the great majority of the courts of this country. It provides: "Subject to the provisions of this act, where goods are sold by a person who is not the owner thereof, and who does not sell them under the authority or with the consent of the owner, the buyer acquires no better title to the goods than the seller had, unless the owner of the goods is by his conduct precluded from denying the seller's authority to sell."

It is a general, well-established principle that no one can transfer a better title than he has. (*Drain* v. *LaGrange State Bank*, 303 Ill. 330; *Williams* v. *Merle*, 11 Wend. 80, 25 Am. Dec. 604.) *Nemo plus juris ad alium transferre potest quam ipse habet.* Section 23 declares, in harmony with the settled law of estoppel, that the owner of the goods may by his conduct be precluded from denying the seller's authority to sell. In order to give rise to an estoppel, however, it is essential that the party estopped shall have made by act or word a representation, and that the person setting up the estoppel shall have acted on the faith of this representation in such a way that he cannot without damage withdraw from the transaction. (1 Williston on Sales,—2d ed.—sec. 312.) What representation has appellee made upon which appellant has relied to his damage? What conduct of appellee precludes it from denying the seller's authority to sell? It did not clothe Taylor with indicia of title. Clothing another person with indicia of ownership does not mean simply giving him possession of a chattel. Possession is one of the indications of title, but possession may be delivered by the owner to a lessee, a bailee, an agent or a servant. Owners of chattels must frequently entrust others with their possession, and the affairs of men could not be conducted unless they could do so with safety, so long as the possession of the chattel is not accompanied by some indicium of ownership or the right to sell. (*Drain* v. *LaGrange State Bank*, *supra.*) Whether the legislature should adopt the companion act, which provides for the recording of contracts of conditional sale, is not for this court to decide. The Uniform Sales act recognizes the validity of such contracts and specifically provides that no title can be passed by the purchaser of goods under such a contract "unless the owner of the goods is by his conduct precluded from denying the seller's authority to sell." There is no basis for the operation of an estoppel in this record.

In *National City Bank* v. *National Bank*, 300 Ill. 103, after discussing the purpose of uniform legislation, the court, in laying down a rule of construction to be followed in the consideration of a uniform law, said: "The court must take the act as it is written and should give to the words used their natural and common meaning. The law was enacted for the purpose of furnishing in itself a certain guide for the determination of all questions covered thereby, * * * and, so far as it speaks without ambiguity as to any such question, reference to case law as it existed prior to the enactment is more likely to be misleading than beneficial. If the provisions of the act harmonize with the general principles of commercial law in force before its enactment those principles should be followed, but if the language of the act conflicts with statutes or decisions in force before its enactment the courts should not give the act a strained construction in order to make it harmonize with earlier statutes or decisions. If this is done the very purpose of the act is defeated. In order to keep the law as nearly as may be uniform, the courts of all the States should keep in mind the spirit and object of the law and should give to the language of the act a natural and common construction, so that all might be more likely to come to the same conclusion." To the same effect is the statement of the Supreme Court of the United States in *Commercial Nat. Bank* v. *Canal-Louisiana Bank and Trust Co.* 239 U. S. 520, 36 Sup. Ct. 194.

The judgment of the Appellate Court is affirmed.

Judgment affirmed.

In BANCROFT STEEL CO. *v.* KUNIHOLM MFG. CO., 16 N.E. (2nd) 78, (Massachusetts Supreme Judicial Court, 1938), plaintiff entered into a written contract of conditional sale covering a quantity of steel. The buyer gave to defendant a chattel mortgage, and in a foreclosure sale under this mortgage defendant had agreed to pay plaintiff the fair value of any personal property on the premises belonging to plaintiff. In an action based on this agreement it was held that title to the steel remained in plaintiff, Donahue, J., saying: "By the terms of the conditional sale contract the plaintiff did not part with the title to the steel delivered. The vendee under the contract of sale could not give title thereto, good as against the plaintiff, either to a *bona fide* purchaser for value without notice of the plaintiff's title or to a mortgagee. Although the vendee named in the conditional sale contract had a special interest in the steel which it could mortgage or sell, a vendee or mortgagee under such a transfer would thus acquire no greater or other interest than the original vendee had, that is, the right to acquire the full title to the property by performing the conditions of the conditional sale contract."

Contrast ANCHOR CONCRETE MACHINERY CO. *v.* PENNSYLVANIA BRICK & TILE CO., 292 Penn. 86 (Supreme Court, 1928), where there was a conditional sale contract covering a number of machines. The buyer resold the machines to defendant who took and paid for them in good faith without notice. In an action of replevin by the original seller, judgment for defendant was affirmed. Sadler, J., after pointing out that Pennsylvania decisions have uniformly been to the effect that an innocent purchaser for value from a conditional vendee acquires the title as against the vendor, and after referring to the Uniform Sales Act, continued:

"It is urged that, by this legislation, the rule recognized in this State, that the delivery of personal property to the purchaser under a contract of conditional sale, with a retention of title in the seller, amounts to a constructive fraud, which postpones the right of the real owner in favor of those who have dealt without notice with the conditional vendee, who had been given the indicia of ownership, has been abolished, and our law made to conform with the contrary principle recognized in some other jurisdictions. Notwithstanding the able argument of appellant, whose conclusion finds support in Illinois (*Sherer-Gillett Co.* v. *Long*, 318 Ill. 432, 149 N. E. 225), we are not convinced that the language employed in the act indicates a legislative intention to alter our long established rule of law. Section 23 provides that the ownership of the conditional vendor may be asserted 'unless the owner of the goods is by his conduct precluded from denying the seller's authority to sell.' The decisions in Pennsylvania, — differing from those of many states (1 Williston on Sales 753), — have always been to the effect that the transfer of possession in itself constituted such conduct, and the clause relied on does not require that further acts must be established to defeat the rights of the unpaid vendor.

"It will be further noted that the Sales Act did not purport to deal with conditional sales, which were made the subject of a separate uniform law, adopted by the commissioners the same year, though not enacted as a statute in this State until 1925 (May 12th, P. L. 603). An examination of the two acts shows it was not the purpose to define the rights of the purchasers from conditional vendees by the former legislation. In the later statute, prepared also in 1915, the interests of such parties are protected, as they always have been in Pennsylvania, with the modification that the unpaid vendor could, by proper filing, conserve his title until paid. By section 5, such transactions are expressly made void as to innocent purchasers, unless the contract is made a matter of record within ten days, negativing the construction appellant would place on the effect of section 23 of the Uniform Sales Act, which evidently was not intended to cover cases such as now before us."

In FLYNN *v.* COLONIAL DISCOUNT CO., 149 Misc. 607 (New York City Court, 1933), an automobile was sold by defendant to a dealer under a conditional sale contract, and was resold to plaintiff. The dealer became bankrupt, and the car was seized under a writ of replevin in behalf of defendant. In an action for conversion judgment was given for plaintiff, the court holding that since the evidence was abundant and clear that the car was delivered to the dealer for resale, Sec. 9 of the Uniform Conditional Sale Act, in force in New Jersey where the transaction took place, was applicable.

Compare LEE *v.* BUTLER, referred to in *Helby* v. *Matthews, supra.* Having construed the contract in question as an agreement to purchase the Court of Appeal held that the seller could not recover the goods from a person to whom they had been sold by the conditional buyer, as the case came within the provision of Sec. 9 of the Factors Act.

TRUITT *v.* PATTEN

UTAH SUPREME COURT, 1930

[75 *Utah Reports*, 567]

FOLLAND, J. This is an action in conversion to recover the value of an automobile which the defendant sheriff attached and sold as the property of K. L. Carlson. Respondent sold the automobile to Carlson in March, 1927, upon condition that he would pay for the car in monthly installments, and that the car should be the property of respondent until fully paid for. The automobile was registered in the office of the secretary of state in the name of respondent. At the time of the attachment, March 24, 1928, Carlson was in arrears with his payments. Respondent had exercised forbearance, but had not extended time for payment to any definite or fixed date, and had not taken the car into his possession as he had a right to do under the contract. Carlson was an employee of respondent, and on the date of the attachment had driven the car to his place of employment and had parked it on the lot of respondent. Immediately upon learning of the attachment respondent called at the office of the sheriff and claimed the car as his own. The sheriff asked him the amount remaining unpaid and was informed the amount was between $27 and $28. No tender of this or any other sum was made, but instead respondent was told to file his claim with the sheriff, and that he (the sheriff) would request that it be paid. Later conversation was had by respondent with the attaching creditor and with the attorney for the attaching creditor, but at no time was any lawful tender made respondent of the full amount due him. The sheriff sold the automobile to satisfy judgment in the action of *Rasmussen* v. *Carlson.* Thereafter this action was commenced to recover the value of the car. The sum of $27 was tendered into court in this action to satisfy the claim of respondent, but such sum was refused. The case was tried to a jury. At the close of the evidence appellant and respondent each requested the court to direct a verdict in his favor. The court directed a verdict in favor of respondent for the market value of the car at the time it was taken on attachment.

It was and is the contention of respondent that the sheriff was a wrongdoer in taking manual possession of the car under the writ of attachment; that Carlson's interest or equity in the car should have been reached, under our statute, by serving respondent with the writ as in the nature of garnishment. This theory was adopted by the trial court. Appellant insists that he followed the statute in levying the attachment since the property was capable of manual delivery, and was, in contemplation of law, in possession of Carlson. He further alleges that respondent was, on April 3, 1928, tendered $27, the amount alleged to be his interest in the car.

We cannot approve the theory of respondent that Carlson's interest could be reached by serving respondent with the writ as in garnishment. The car was in possession of Carlson under his contract to purchase. The fact that the auto was parked on vendor's lot is immaterial. Notwithstanding this, respondent must prevail. It is well settled in this state that a conditional contract is valid between the parties, and, in the absence of fraud, as to third parties, and, when so provided therein, gives to the vendor the right to immediate possession of the property on default of any of its conditions. *Russell* v. *Harkness*, 4 Utah 197, 7 P. 865; *Lima Machine Works* v. *Parsons*, 10 Utah 105, 37 P. 244; *Lippincott* v. *Rich*, 19 Utah 140, 56 P. 806; Id., 22 Utah, 196, 61 P. 526; *Freed Furniture & Carpet Co.* v. *Sorensen*, 28 Utah 419, 79 P. 564, 107 Am. St. Rep. 731, 3 Ann. Cas. 634. Creditors of the vendee can obtain no interest in the property by attachment adverse to the rights of the vendor. *Passow* v. *Emery*, 37 Utah 49, 106 P. 935. In the last-cited case the question under what circumstances an attaching creditor may satisfy the vendor and thereby subject the vendee's interest to attachment was reserved and not decided.

At the time plaintiff demanded possession of the property from the sheriff he was entitled to its possession, not only because of delinquency in payment, but because of the attachment, one of the conditions of the contract of sale being that the vendee should not permit the car to be removed from his possession nor to be attached. *King* v. *Cline*, 49 Cal. App. 696, 194 P. 290; *McArthur* v. *Beals*, 243 Mass. 449, 137 N. E. 697; *Starr* v. *Govatos* (Del. Super.) 130 A. 392. The vendor, upon demand, was entitled to the possession of the automobile after condition of the contract of sale was broken. *Lippincott* v. *Rich*, *supra*; *Passow* v. *Emery*, *supra*.

Title to the auto was in respondent at the time it was taken on attachment by the sheriff. Appellant was charged with notice of this fact because the car was registered in respondent's name as owner in the office of the secretary of state. The amount due had neither been paid nor tendered.

The majority rule seems to be that the buyer under a conditional sale contract has no such interest in the property before the purchase price is paid as is subject to levy and sale at the instance of his creditors. Especially is this true where the buyer is in arrears with his payments. Estrich, Installment Sales, § 480, p. 902; 61 A. L. R. 782, note: *Franklin Motor Co.* v. *Hamilton*, 113 Me. 63, 92 A. 1001; *Buckmaster* v. *Smith*, 22 Vt. 203. However, in some jurisdictions it is regarded that the interests of the buyer should be subject to his debts. The levying creditor has the right to pay the balance due on the contract to the vendor, thus terminating the seller's rights and rendering the property subject to attachment or execution. 61 A. L. R. 792. We think this the better rule. It applies when attachment is levied before the buyer is in default, and in some instances where the buyer is delinquent, when payment is promptly tendered to the vendor. *Nevada Motor Co.* v. *Bream* (Nev.) 269 P. 602, 61 A. L. R. 776; 1 Williston, Sales (2d Ed.) § 326; *Newhall* v. *Kingsbury*, 131 Mass. 445; *Frank* v. *Batten*, 49 Hun, 91, 1 N. Y. S. 705; *Hervey* v. *Dimond*, 67 N. H. 342, 39 A. 331, 68 Am. St. Rep. 673; *King* v. *Cline, supra.*

The evidence fails to show seasonable or adequate compliance with these requirements. The vendor has not been paid either the balance due on the contract or the money expended by him in placing a battery in the car and replacing the top. While both the sheriff and the attaching creditor told the vendor that payment would be made, no lawful tender was ever made of the whole amount due. The vendor at no time said he would not accept the amount due if tendered. It could not necessarily be implied from his conduct that he would refuse had tender been promptly made. He, however, insisted at all times that he was the owner of the car and entitled to its possession. The sum of $27 was tendered into court in the present case, but it is clear from the evidence that this sum was not all that was owing including the battery and top. Nor was the tender timely made. The wrongful seizure and sale of the property by the sheriff amounted to a conversion thereof.

[The last page of the opinion is here omitted. Dissenting opinion of Hansen, J., is also omitted.]

Judgment affirmed, with costs to respondent.

CHERRY, C. J., and EPHRAIM HANSON, J., concur.

In HERVEY *v.* DIMOND, 67 N. H. 342 (Supreme Court, 1892), goods were attached as the property of a conditional buyer. The attaching creditor inquired as to the amount still due, and tendered the seller that amount, refusing a demand for the goods themselves. The seller rejected the tender, and brought an action in replevin against the attaching sheriff. The Court said in part: "Although by the contract it was stipulated that the plaintiffs should remain absolute owners of the goods until the full price should be paid, it does not follow that Story had no interest in the property. He had the right to pay the balance due and become the owner of the property. While the plaintiffs remained the general owners until the full price should be paid, Story's interest was that of a special owner, which the law recognizes and protects. It was an assignable and attachable interest, his assignee or attaching creditor acquiring the same rights as he had. If Story failed to make the monthly payments according to the contract and the plaintiffs might for that cause have asserted a forfeiture, they waived the default by accepting an instalment August 14.

"Although the attachment was nominally of the property, yet it plainly appears that Whitaker did not intend to attach in disregard of the plaintiffs' rights, and he fully recognized them by tendering the amount due.

If necessary, the officer's return can be amended to conform to the fact. By the tender of the amount due the plaintiffs, their title to the goods became vested in Story, subject to Whitaker's attachment. As Whitaker seasonably tendered the amount of their claim, the defendant is entitled to judgment for the value of the property and for his costs."

In MALDEN CENTER GARAGE *v.* BERKOWITZ, 269 Mass. 304 (Supreme Judicial Court, 1929), a conditional contract for the sale of an automobile provided that in case of failure to pay any instalments when due the seller should be entitled to immediate possession. The contract also provided that the buyer would not suffer or permit any attachment or levy upon the automobile, and that in case of such attachment or levy the seller might take possession. After breach of condition by the buyer, the automobile was seized under an execution in an action brought by defendant against the buyer, and was put in storage in a place not disclosed to the seller. In a bill for equitable replevin by the seller, a decree enjoining defendant to deliver the car was affirmed. "An attaching creditor would gain no greater rights . . . than those possessed by the conditional vendee. . . . By the attachment the officer attempted to hold the property by a title and to exercise a control inconsistent with and adverse to the right of the plaintiff as the true owner."

In BAKER *v.* HULL, 250 N. Y. 484 (Court of Appeals, 1929), a judgment was obtained against a conditional buyer, and execution was issued against his property on July 23. On August 11 the seller filed in the office of the clerk of the city where the buyer lived the contract evidencing the sale. Later on the same day defendant levied upon the automobile under the execution and took possession of it. The seller brought an action of replevin. Judgment for defendant reversed. Under Sec. 5 of the Uniform Conditional Sales Act defendant had not acquired a lien by levy or attachment before the contract was filed.

In CASHMAN *v.* LEWIS, 26 Ariz. 95 (Supreme Court, 1924), it was held that, the Uniform Conditional Sales Act being in force in Arizona, the rights of an attaching creditor of the buyer prevailed over the claim of a conditional seller under an unrecorded contract.

Compare JOHNSON-STEPHENS ETC. CO. *v.* MARLATT & MILLER, 181 Wash. 621 (Supreme Court, 1935), where it was held under a conditional sales statute that an unrecorded conditional sale contract was valid against the receiver of the buyer in the absence of a showing that he represented subsequent creditors.

LYNN MORRIS PLAN COMPANY *v.* GORDON

MASSACHUSETTS SUPREME JUDICIAL COURT, 1924

[251 *Massachusetts Reports,* 323]

RUGG, C.J. This is an action of tort for the conversion of an automobile. On April 1, 1920, the owner of the automobile entered into a written agreement with one Therrien for its conditional sale. By the terms of that agreement the title remained in the seller and would not pass to Therrien until the entire purchase price had been paid. At the same time Therrien paid $800 in cash and executed and delivered to the seller a promissory note to the order of the seller, payable in monthly instalments, for $1,470, the balance due on the purchase price. Thereupon Therrien was entitled to and took possession of the automobile. Shortly after, the seller, for the sum of $1,352.40, transferred the note by indorsement, waiving demand and notice, and all rights under the agreement to the plaintiff. This transfer of the agreement was not recorded. Subsequently, Therrien returned the automobile to the seller, who sold it to the defendant. The question is whether the plaintiff, default having been made in the payments due on the note and under the agreement, can maintain this action.

When and after the seller transferred his agreement for sale and indorsed the note to the plaintiff, he had no title or interest whatsoever in the automobile. He possessed no evidence of title or interest. If the question arose between the plaintiff and a creditor or one standing in the shoes of a creditor of the seller, the plaintiff would have been unable to maintain its rights without giving notice to Therrien, so that he would become bailee of the automobile for the plaintiff instead of the seller. *Mann* v. *Huston,* 1 Gray, 250. *Hallgarten* v. *Oldham,* 135 Mass. 1, 9, 10. *Clark* v. *Williams,* 190 Mass. 219. *Duffy* v. *Charak,* 236 U. S. 97. But that is not the situation. The seller retained no title or interest. Therrien had no title or interest superior to that of the plaintiff. Whatever rights he had were subject to the plaintiff's title. His wrongful conduct in conjunction with the wrongful conduct of the original seller cannot defeat the title of the plaintiff. The seller stood no better than a stranger to the transaction. The defendant acquired no greater title than his vendor was able to convey. He was in no position to dispute the title of the plaintiff. *Royle* v. *Worcester Buick Co.* 243 Mass. 143.

The transfer of the automobile by the seller to the plaintiff was not by way of security or mortgage. It was an absolute sale. It was not requisite that the instrument of transfer, which was in effect a bill of sale, be recorded under St. 1915, c. 226, in force at the time of this transaction. See now St. 1921, c. 233, amending G. L. c. 255, § 1. The case at bar is in this particular distinguishable from *Worcester Morris Plan Co.* v. *Mader,* 236 Mass. 435.

Order for judgment affirmed.

In C. I. T. Corporation *v.* The First National Bank of Winslow, 33 Ariz. 483 (Supreme Court, 1928), an automobile was sold under a conditional sale contract which was assigned to defendant. Subsequently the seller again sold the car to another buyer, who resold it under a conditional sale contract which was assigned to plaintiff. The original buyer having defaulted on his payments defendant took possession of the car and the present action of replevin followed. Judgment for plaintiff reversed. The provisions of the Uniform Conditional Sales Act are for the protection of the conditional seller against purchasers and creditors of the buyer.

Note also Anglo-California National Bank of San Francisco *v.* Rasmussen, 6 Calif. App. (2nd) 337 (District Court of Appeal, First Appellate District, 1935), where it was held that a creditor of the conditional seller could not attach as his property the car sold, after the seller had assigned the conditional sale contract to a bank.

3. DOCUMENTARY TRANSACTIONS

EASTWOOD AND HOLT *v.* STUDER

KING'S BENCH DIVISION, 1926

[31 *Commercial Cases*, 251]

Award in the form of a special case by W. N. Raeburn, K.C., in an arbitration between the buyer and the sellers of hen's albumen from China. The buyer bought from the sellers two tons of albumen out of a quantity of five tons which the sellers had bought from other sellers. When the two tons were tendered to the buyer the albumen was found to be verminous and unfit for human consumption. The buyer refused to accept, and the dispute was referred to arbitration. Various arbitration proceedings followed; and Mr. Raeburn, K.C., to whom the matter was finally referred, awarded, subject to the opinion of the Court, that the property in the albumen had passed to the buyer, and that the buyer was estopped by an award in an earlier arbitration from contending that the tender of albumen made to him by the sellers was not a valid tender under the contract. The buyer now appealed.

ROCHE, J. [The first two pages of the opinion, reviewing details of the arbitration proceedings, are here omitted.]

I hold that even assuming that the tender made must be deemed to be a good tender, nevertheless the goods were not unconditionally appropriated to the contract and the property did not pass to the buyer. That depends on the terms of the contract. There are no facts found in the case which would alter or affect the conclusions to be drawn from the contract itself. In its general nature the contract is a c.i.f. contract; it is described as a contract for cost insurance and freight. The provision for payment is cash against certain documents. Ordinarily, although as Lord Parker said in *The Parchim* ([1918] A.C. 157), which has been cited to me by Mr. Somervell in the course of his able argument, the presumption of the reservation of a right of disposal that is derived from the retention of documents until payment is made is a presumption which may be rebutted, yet the general and natural conclusion from the retention of documents is that the right of disposal of the goods is thereby retained. That depends now upon Statute. Rule 5 of section 18 of the Sale of Goods Act provides that where the contract is for the sale of unascertained goods the property passes upon unconditional appropriation to the contract. Section 19 says that where there is a contract for the sale of specific goods or where goods are subsequently appropriated to the contract, the seller may by the terms of the contract or appropriation reserve the right of disposal of the goods until certain conditions are fulfilled. That is a description of what is not an unconditional appropriation to the contract but a conditional appropriation; and ordinarily — and in my view this case falls within the ordinary rule — when documents are only to be handed over when payment is made that imports that a right of disposal is reserved. Here the particular circumstances of the case would seem to point to the same conclusion. It is contended that all that was intended to be reserved was a lien and not a right of disposal. Apart from special circumstances a lien carries with it no right of sale. Having regard to the finding as to what happened to this hen's albumen and the finding of the arbitrator as to the general nature of hen's albumen from native factories in China, I should be slow to conclude that people retain over it, not the right of disposal and getting rid of it as soon as possible if it began to go wrong, but only a lien which would give them the right of holding it. There is no circumstance such as the additional protection of a bank guarantee or a bill of exchange accepted by the buyer to even begin to rebut the assumption which, as I have said, arises from the fact that the documents are retained under the contract until payment is made. Accordingly I hold that there was no unconditional appropriation to the contract, that therefore the property never passed, and the sellers cannot recover the price. That decision in itself would, on the findings of the arbitrator — if the question of estoppel is decided in favour of the sellers — result in a judgment in favour of the sellers for damages, and, as the arbitrator finds, nominal damages of 40*s*. and no costs. That, in my judgment, is the best result to which the sellers are entitled. That conclusion as to the amount of damages was no doubt reached by this process; that inasmuch as by the estoppel the buyer cannot say that the insect ridden albumen was bad, neither can the sellers, and, in consequence, the damages are nominal. That is my decision on that part of the case.

[The balance of the opinion, holding that the buyer was not estopped from disputing that the tender was a good tender, is here omitted.]

Appeal of buyer allowed.

In Nippon Yusen Kaisha *v.* Ramjiban Serowgee, [1938] A.C. 429 (Privy Council), there was a contract for the sale of 250 bales of gunnies free alongside export vessel at Calcutta. Clause 3 provided that payment was to be made in cash in exchange for mate's receipts, and Clause 4 stipulated that the sellers were to retain a lien as unpaid vendors so long as such receipts remained in their possession. Bills of lading covering the goods were issued by the carrier to a subpurchaser from the buyer without production of the mate's receipts, and the question arose whether title had passed to the buyer. Lord Wright said: "The first issue to be determined is when under the contract the property passed. The sale was of unascertained goods. *Prima facie* on such a sale the property in the goods passes when goods answering to the contract description are unconditionally appropriated to the contract with the assent of the buyer, which, in this connection, does not mean expressed assent, but simply that the appropriation has been made in the manner contemplated by the parties. This *prima facie* rule may, however, be varied by the terms of the contract, or even by a reservation made by the seller in the act of appropriation. The general rule is that the property passes when the parties intend it to pass. In the present case, the sale being free alongside, the property *prima facie* passes when the goods are appropriated by delivery alongside in implement of the contracts. It is, however, said that cl. 3 of the contract precludes the passing of the property until the price is paid against the mate's receipts or the other documents specified. That would no doubt be so if cl. 3 were not followed by cl. 4. The contract must, however, be read as a whole. Clause 4 provides for a lien of the sellers as unpaid vendors on the mate's receipts or other documents so long as they remain in the sellers' possession, and on the goods, until payment in full. Can this be reconciled with the reservation of the *jus disponendi* which cl. 3 would import if it stood alone? That depends on the meaning to be attributed to the word 'lien' as used in regard to the goods. A common law lien is possessory and depends on possession, but it also presupposes that the property in the goods has passed. A person cannot have a lien on his own goods. Thus cl. 4 imports that notwithstanding cl. 3 the property has passed when the goods were delivered alongside, that is, placed in possession of the shipowners. The result is that the sellers have parted with both property and possession."

In CUNDILL *v.* A. W. MILLHAUSER CORPORATION, 257 N. Y. 416 (Court of Appeals, 1931), a contract for 25 tons of antimony at an agreed price c. i. f. New York contained a provision for payment "net cash against shipping documents payable on arrival of steamer." The seller did not forward the documents to the buyer, but retained them and tendered them to the buyer after the goods had arrived. The buyer refused the tender. It was held that an action for the purchase price could not be maintained, as the contract was not a straight c. i. f. contract in which title would pass to the buyer on delivering the goods to the carrier and forwarding the documents to the buyer.

In THE FRED E. HASLER, 66 Fed. (2nd) 609 (Circuit Court of Appeals, Second Circuit, 1933), there was a contract for the purchase of the entire production of a whale oil factory ship, the oil to be delivered on c. i. f. terms, and 75% of the price to be paid against documents. After such payment had been made the oil was discharged into a tank barge chartered by the buyer and the barge sank. In passing on the question whether the buyer had any cause of action against the owners of the barge for the loss of the oil, Chase, Circuit Judge, stated that the right to maintain the action could not be disputed if the buyer held title to the oil when it was lost, and then continued:

"The provision for delivery of the oil 'on c. i. f. terms' was so general that it throws little light on the passing of title. So far as this clause is concerned, it may or may not have passed before the Hasler sank. It does, however, assume considerable significance in connection with the fact that payment was actually made against documents to the extent of 75 per cent. of the estimated net value of the cargo and to the full extent called for before the cargo was weighed. The symbolical delivery of a cargo of goods by the delivery of such documents as were here delivered is well understood and recognized. When such delivery by a seller is followed, as here, by the receipt of the payment agreed to be made then by the buyer of the goods, the intention of the parties to have the title then pass to the buyer is manifested, unless the contract negatives such an intention, and as a matter of law, title does then pass because the parties intended it should."

WAIT *v.* BAKER

COURT OF EXCHEQUER, 1848

[2 *Exchequer Reports*, 1]

Trover for 500 quarters of barley. Pleas, not guilty, and not possessed; upon which issue was joined.

At the trial, before Williams, J., at the last Spring Assizes for Somersetshire, the following facts appeared: — The defendant, a corn-factor at Bristol, had occasional dealings with a person of the name of Lethbridge, who was also a corn-factor at Plymouth, and on the 5th of December, 1846, wrote to him the following letter: —

I hear that the crop of barley in the south of Hampshire is good this year, and that at Kingsbridge the price is low, compared with the markets further eastward. If you are doing anything in the article this season, and can make me an offer of a cargo, I have no doubt but we may have a transaction. Let me hear from you in due course. Send me sample in letter, describing weight, &c.

To which Lethbridge wrote the following answer on the 9th of that month: —

I beg to inform you that I have not yet commenced buying barley in Kingsbridge market, farmers there standing out for 10*s.* a bag. After Saturday's market I will send you a sample and an offer, if possible.

On the 14th, Lethbridge wrote the following letter to the defendant: —

I herewith hand you samples of common and chevalier barley of the neighbourhood of Kingsbridge, and will engage to sell you from 400 to 500 quarters f. o. b. barley at Kingsbridge, or neighbouring port, at 40*s.* per quarter common, and 42*s.* per quarter chevalier, in equal quantities, for cash, on handing bills of lading, or acceptance at two months' date, adding interest at the rate of £5 per cent. per annum, subject to your reply by course of post.

On the 16th, the defendant returned the following reply: —

I beg to accept your offer of 250 quarters of chevalier barley, at 42*s.* per quarter, and 250 quarters common, at 40*s.* per quarter f. o. b., for cash payments, on receipt of bill of lading and invoice, or acceptance at two months' date, adding interest at the rate of £5 per cent. per annum, subject to your reply by course of post.

On the 18th, Lethbridge wrote the defendant as follows: —

Your favor of the 16th came duly to hand, and note by it your acceptance of my offer of barley. I suppose I am to take up a vessel at the best possible freight I can get her for. Please instruct me in this, and say if for Bristol or any other port.

On the 19th, the defendant wrote in answer: —

I took it for granted that you would get a vessel for the barley I have bought of you f. o. b., and therefore did not instruct you to seek one. I trust that you will be particular to select a good ship, and at the lowest possible freight, for this port; and, above all, take care that the quality of the barley is fully equal to sample. A party, who will take part of it, is extremely particular in these matters; and the samples are sealed and held in the custody of a third party. Please to advise when you have taken up a vessel, with particulars of the port she loads in, so that I may get insurance done correctly.

After some further correspondence respecting the amount of the freight, Lethbridge wrote on the 23rd to the defendant: —

I now send you copy of charter-party of the "Emerald," which vessel will sail for the port of loading to-day or to-morrow, and I will lose no time in getting her loaded.

The defendant, by letter dated the 24th, acknowledged the receipt of the charter-party (not under seal), which was dated on the 22nd, and was in the name of Lethbridge, to load at Dartmouth, a portion to be filled up at Salcombe, to proceed to Bristol, or any other port.

On the 28th, Lethbridge wrote to the defendant: —

The "Emerald" will commence loading to-day. I hope to hand you bill of lading in the course of the week.

And again on the 1st of January, 1847: —

I hope to be able to send you invoice and bill of lading of "Emerald" on Tuesday or Wednesday.

And on the 6th of January he wrote to the defendant as follows: —

The "Emerald" is nearly loaded; expect the bill of lading to-day or to-morrow. I expect to be in Exeter on Friday, when it is very likely I shall run down and see you.

The vessel was loaded with common and chevalier barley; and on the 7th of January, Lethbridge received from the master the bill of lading of the cargo, which was therein expressed to be deliverable at Bristol to the order of Lethbridge or assigns, paying the freight as per charter. On the 8th, Lethbridge called upon the defendant at Bristol early in the morning, and left at his counting-house the invoice and an unindorsed bill of lading. At a subsequent part of the day, Lethbridge called again upon the defendant, when the defendant raised some objections to the quality of the cargo, and asserted that it was inferior to the samples: he also threatened he would take the cargo, but sue Lethbridge for eight shillings a quarter difference. After some further dispute upon the matter, the defendant offered Lethbridge the amount of the cargo in money, and said that he accepted the cargo. Lethbridge, however, refused to accept the money and to indorse the bill of lading to the defendant; but took the bill of lading from the counter and immediately proceeded to the plaintiffs', who were corn-factors, and had a house of business in the neighbourhood and indorsed the bill of lading to them, and received an advance upon it. The market at that time had risen considerably. The "Emerald" arrived on the 16th, and on the 18th the defendant proceeded on board and claimed the cargo as the owner, and unshipped 1240 bushels of the barley, worth 422*l.* 14*s.*; but the plaintiffs coming on board during the time the cargo was being unshipped, presented the bill of lading and obtained the rest of the cargo, and paid the captain the freight.

The jury found that the defendant did not refuse to accept the barley from Lethbridge; that the tender was unconditional; and that Lethbridge was not an agent intrusted with the bill of lading by the defendant. His Lordship thereupon directed a verdict to be entered for the plaintiffs for 422*l.* 14*s.*, reserving leave to the defendant to enter a verdict for him.

A rule to shew cause having been obtained,

Parke, B. I am of opinion that the rule in the present case ought to be discharged. It is perfectly clear that the original contract between the parties was not for a specific chattel. That contract would be satisfied by the delivery of any 500 quarters of corn, provided the corn answered the character of that which was agreed to be delivered. By the original contract, therefore, no property passed; and that matter admits of no doubt whatever. In order, therefore, to deprive the original owner of the property, it must be shewn in this form of action — the action being for the recovery of the property — that, at some subsequent time, the property passed. It may be admitted, that if goods are ordered by a person, although they are to be selected by the vendor, and to be delivered to a common carrier to be sent to the person by whom they have been ordered, the moment the goods, which have been selected in pursuance of the contract, are delivered to the carrier, the carrier becomes the agent of the vendee, and such a delivery amounts to a delivery to the vendee; and if there is a binding contract between the vendor and vendee, either by note in writing, or by part payment, or subsequently by part acceptance, then there is no doubt that the property passes by such delivery to the carrier. It is necessary, of course, that the goods should agree with the contract. In this case, it is said that the delivery of the goods on ship-board is equivalent to the delivery I have mentioned, because the ship was engaged on the part of Lethbridge as agent for the defendant. But assuming that it was so, the delivery of the goods on board the ship was not a delivery of them to the defendant, but a delivery to the captain of the vessel, to be carried under a bill of lading, and that bill of lading indicated the person for whom they were to be carried. By that bill of lading the goods were to be carried by the master of the vessel for and on account of Lethbridge, to be delivered to him in case the bill of lading should not be assigned, and if it should, then to the assignee. The goods, therefore, still continued in the possession of the master of the vessel, not as in the case of a common carrier, but as a person carrying them on behalf of Lethbridge. There is no breach of duty on the part of Lethbridge, as he stipulates under the original contract that the price is to be paid on the delivery of the bill of lading. It is clearly contemplated by the original contract, that, by the bill of lading, Lethbridge should retain control over the property. It seems to me to follow that the delivery of the 500 quarters to the captain, to be delivered to Lethbridge, is not the same as a delivery of 500 quarters to a common carrier by order of the consignee. The act of delivery, therefore, in the present case, did not pass the property. Then, what subsequent act do we find which had that effect? It is admitted by the learned counsel for the defendant, that the property does not pass, unless there is a subsequent appropriation of the goods. The word appropriation may be understood in different senses. It may mean a selection on the part of the vendor, where he has the right to choose the article which he has to supply in performance of his contract; and the contract will shew when the word is used in that sense. Or the word may mean, that both parties have agreed that a certain article shall be delivered in pursuance of the contract, and yet the property may not pass in either case. For the purpose of illustrating this position, suppose a carriage is ordered to be built at a coachmaker's, he may make any one he pleases, and, if it agree with the order, the party is bound to accept it. Now suppose that, at some period subsequent to the order, a further bargain is entered into between this party and the coachbuilder, by which it is agreed that a particular carriage shall be delivered. It would depend upon circumstances whether the property passes, or whether merely the original contract is altered from one which would have been satisfied by the delivery of any carriage answering the terms of the contract, into another contract to supply the particular carriage, — which, in the Roman law, was called *obligatio certi corporis,* where a person is bound to deliver a particular chattel, but where the property does not pass, as it never did by the Roman law, until actual delivery; although the property, after the contract, remained at the risk of the vendee, and if lost without any fault in the vendor, the vendee, and not the vendor, was the sufferer. The law of England is different: here, property does not pass until there is a bargain with respect to a specific article, and everything is done which, according to the intention of the parties to the bargain, was necessary to transfer the property in it. "Appropriation" may also be used in another sense, and is the one in which Mr. Butt uses it on the present occasion; viz. where both parties agree upon the specific article in which the property is to pass, and nothing remains to be done in order to pass it. It is contended in this case that something of that sort subsequently took place. I must own that I think the delivery on board the vessel could not be an appropriation in that sense of the word. It is an appropriation in the first sense of the word only; the vendor has made his election to deliver those 500 quarters of corn. The next question is, whether the circumstances which occurred at Bristol afterwards amount to an agreement by both parties that the property in those 500 quarters should pass. I think it is perfectly clear that there is no pretence for saying that Lethbridge agreed that the property in that corn should pass. It is clear that his object was to have the contract repudiated, and thereby to free himself from all obligation to deliver the cargo. On the other hand, as has been observed, the defendant wished to obtain the cargo, and also to have the power of bringing an action if the corn did not agree with the sample. It seems evident to me that, at the time when the unindorsed bill of lading was left, there was no agreement between the two parties that that specific cargo should become the property of the defendant. If that is so, the case remains, as to the question of property, exactly as it did after the original contract. There is a contract to deliver a cargo on board, and probably for an assignment of that cargo by indorsing the bill of lading to the defendant; but there was nothing which amounted to an appropriation, in the sense of that term which alone would pass the property. The result is, that, in this action of trover, the plaintiffs, claiming under Lethbridge by the indorsement of the bill of lading, are entitled to the property; and then Mr. Baker has his remedy against him for the non-fulfilment of his contract, which he certainly has not fulfilled.

[Alderson, B., Rolfe, B., and Platt, B., concurred.]

THE PRINZ ADALBERT

Privy Council, 1917

[*Law Reports,* [1917] *Appeal Cases,* 586]

Lord Sumner. When the German steamship *Prinz Adalbert,* bound from Philadelphia to Hamburg, was seized as prize at Falmouth on August 5, 1914, she had on board the two parcels of lubricating oil, respectively 290 and 86 barrels, which are now in question. The writ was issued on August 18, 1914.

The appellants, the Crew Levick Company, of Philadelphia, neutral shippers, filed a claim, dated April 1, 1916, alleging the oil to be their own and saying that they had shipped and consigned it to the Maschinenoel Import Actien-Gesellschaft, of Hamburg, as their agents for sale on the Continent of Europe, and that, as it had never passed to any purchaser, it had always continued to belong to them. The learned President decided that the oil had ceased to belong to the appellants on shipment. Neither the actual shipping documents nor the dates of the acceptances to the accompanying drafts appear to have been brought to his attention. At their Lordships' bar the appellants' argument made these dates crucial. The learned President was strongly and justly impressed by the absence of proper evidence of the prior course of dealing between the shippers and the consignees. The appellants petitioned their Lordships for leave to remedy this defect, but their Lordships refused to grant it for reasons of principle already given.

Both parcels were covered by bills of lading, which made the oil deliverable to the shippers' order at Hamburg and were indorsed in blank by an officer of the claimant company. The bills of lading and certificates of insurance were attached to drafts, drawn by the claimants on the Maschinenoel Import Gesellschaft and discounted in the United States, namely, a sixty days' draft for 75 per cent. of the invoice value of the 290 barrels, and a draft at three days' sight for the full value of the 86 barrels. The discounting bank forwarded the documents to Germany. The draft drawn against the 86 barrels reached Hamburg on or before August 1, 1914, on which date it was accepted by the Maschinenoel Import Gesellschaft against surrender of the bill of lading. The other draft was accompanied by a bill of lading of the same date, namely, July 20, and the evidence does not show any sufficient reason to suppose that it was not forwarded by the same mail. The appellants contended that it was not accepted till August 10, though no reason for this difference could be given. This bill of lading also was handed over to the Maschinenoel Import Gesellschaft against acceptance of the corresponding draft, and ultimately that company returned both bills of lading to the claimants at Philadelphia. Presumably they also met both bills of exchange when they fell due, for the amounts are debited against the appellants in a quarterly account current, brought down to September 30, which they rendered to the claimants on November 28. It does not appear that the claimants have either paid or otherwise settled the debit balance shown on this account, and, as the evidence leaves the matter, they have received the proceeds of the two bills of exchange, less discount, in Philadelphia, have neither paid nor agreed to pay to the acceptors the amounts of those bills, and have got back the bills of lading from the acceptors, without conditions or explanation, and so, presumably, for the acceptors' account.

By general mercantile understanding, which has the force of law where transactions originate, like the present, in time of peace without prospect of war, the delivery of an indorsed bill of lading, made out to the shipper's order while the goods are afloat, is equivalent to delivery of the goods themselves, and is effectual to transfer ownership if made with that intention. The bill of lading is the symbol of the goods. Apart from specific formalities or similar prescriptions of municipal law, which are not now material, such intention is a question of fact. The usual course of dealing in the export of merchandise and the interest of the parties concerned in it suffice for the necessary inference in the absence of evidence to the contrary. When a shipper takes his draft, not as yet accepted, but accompanied by a bill of lading, indorsed in this way, and discounts it with a banker, he makes himself liable on the instrument as drawer, and he further makes the goods, which the bill of lading represents, security for its payment. If, in turn, the discounting banker surrenders the bill of lading to the acceptor against his acceptance, the inference is that he is satisfied to part with his security in consideration of getting this further party's liability on the bill, and that in so doing he acts with the permission and by the mandate of the shipper and drawer. Possession of the indorsed bill of lading enables the acceptor to get possession of the goods on the ship's arrival. If the shipper, being then owner of the goods, authorizes and directs the banker, to whom he is himself liable and whose interest it is to continue to hold the bill of lading till the draft is accepted, to surrender the bill of lading against acceptance of the draft, it is natural to infer that he intends to transfer the ownership when this is done, but intends also to remain the owner until this has been done. Particular arrangements made between shipper and consignee may modify or rebut these inferences, but in the absence of evidence to the contrary, and apart from rules which arise only out of a state of war existing or imminent at the beginning of the transaction, the general law infers under these circumstances that the ownership in the goods is transferred when the draft drawn against them is accepted.

Their Lordships are unable to agree with the learned President's view that the property in the oil in question passed on shipment. In their opinion the claimants were owners until the Maschinenoel Import Gesellschaft accepted the drafts, drawn against the two parcels respectively, but no longer. Such is the true inference from the mercantile transactions themselves.

Sundry communications were produced, either requesting that the shipment should be made or advising that it had been made, but they are neutral in their effect; nor is it material to consider how the transaction might be worked out after the drafts had been accepted. This depends on arrangements between the parties, which are not properly proved, and the transfer of the ownership in the oil on the acceptance of the drafts is consistent either with a sale to the German company and a resale by them to German customers, or with some agency arrangement, under which they might debit the amount of the drafts paid and credit the proceeds of their sales to the claimants and obtain their own remuneration by charging an agreed commission.

It follows that the 86 barrels had ceased to belong to the claimants, and had become the property of the Maschinenoel Import Gesellschaft on August 1. How stands the other parcel? The date when the draft drawn against it was accepted depends upon an entry in the quarterly account above mentioned. That account was prepared for the purpose of showing a general balance on September 30, 1914. The acceptance transactions are only incidents in it. The dates of the acceptances are immaterial to the account, which, of course, reckons interest from the dates of payment, and are of small value even for the purpose of identifying the acceptance, which are sufficiently described by their amounts. The document is not proved, nor is it sufficient to discharge the onus, which is on the claimants. Even if the larger parcel of oil differs in its circumstances from the smaller one, at any rate it ceased to belong to the claimants before they came into Court to prove a claim as owners, and so their title fails. The probability is that there is no difference between the two parcels, and that the date of acceptance to the larger draft ought to be August 1 and not August 10. That both drafts should have been accepted together is natural, but that one, and that the larger of the two, should have been refused acceptance for over a week and then have received it is a very difficult supposition. If nothing else was known of the *Prinz Adalbert*, on August 10, at least, it was known that she was considerably overdue. Capture was, at any rate, a reasonable explanation of her non-arrival. It may well have been that having, as the appellants' case says, "called at Falmouth after her master heard of the outbreak of war between France and Germany," she was already known in Hamburg, before August 10, "to have been seized as prize by the officer of Customs of Falmouth." If so, acceptance of the draft on August 10 is most improbable. Their Lordships, however, cannot act upon conjecture, and as the original exhibit bears the date of August 10 they have accepted it, and are content to say that, as the claimants failed to prove their right to the goods, when they came before the Court as owners, their appeal must also fail.

Accordingly their Lordships, being of opinion that the claimants were not owners of either parcel at or at any time after the commencement of the proceedings in prize in this case, will humbly advise His Majesty that this appeal should be dismissed with costs.

In THE MOTCH & MERRYWEATHER MACHINERY CO. *v.* THE SIDNEY MACHINE TOOL CO., 12 Ohio App. 266 (Court of Appeals for Shelby County, 1919), there was a contract for the sale of machinery "f. o. b. Oakley [Cincinnati] delivery October, terms draft attached to B/L." The machinery was shipped at Oakley under a bill of lading to the order of the seller, and the bill of lading was forwarded with draft attached to a collecting bank. The buyer refused to accept unless credit was extended. In an action for the purchase price, judgment for defendant was affirmed. The Court referred to Sec. 20 (2) of the Uniform Sales Act, and said:

"We think, however, that provision does not apply for the reason that the transaction here does not have the effect of passing title. The seller did not surrender control of the bill of lading at the time of the shipment. The bill of lading was evidently sent from Cincinnati to the seller at Cleveland and was in the possession and control of the seller on November 4. On that date the bill of lading with sight draft was mailed to a collecting bank at Sidney. This bank was the agent of the plaintiff. The bill of lading and sight draft arrived at Sidney on November 7. Up to that date the bill of lading was in the control of the seller. In order that the transaction itself should pass the title to the buyer it should appear that the seller had surrendered control of the property.

"By paragraph 2 above quoted the retention of the bill of lading even where the shipment is to the order of the buyer is a reservation of the right of possession. For a stronger reason the retention of the bill of lading would be a reservation of the right of possession where the seller also makes the shipment to his own order. We are, therefore, of opinion that the second sentence of paragraph 2 above quoted does not apply to the case at bar and that under the first sentence of paragraph 2 the seller reserved title to the property shipped."

In THE PARCHIM, [1918] A. C. 157 (Privy Council, 1917), a German seller having a branch at Valparaiso sold to a Dutch buyer "the whole cargo of ordinary Chile saltpetre . . . per Parchim . . . at the price of 9*s.* 1*d.* per cwt. cost and freight Channel for orders to the United Kingdom or Continent. . . . The invoice price is due ninety days after receipt of the first bill of lading and to be paid by the buyer three days before maturity, or in case of an earlier arrival already then against acceptance of the documents plus ¼ per cent accept commission. The buyer provides at once first-class bank guarantee for £5000." The contract also made separate provision for insurance including a margin of profit to be covered by the seller, the policy to be accepted by the buyer against payment of the premium and costs. The carrying vessel was under charter to the seller, and at the time the contract was made was at the port named for loading. By the terms of the contract the buyer was to take over the charter, so that the sum included for freight in the price became a mere matter of calculation, to be paid separately by the buyer and deducted from the price. Bills of lading were taken out by the seller's branch at Valparaiso to the order of the seller, and were sent by the branch, apparently indorsed in blank, to the seller in Europe, the bills then being deposited with the seller's bank in Amsterdam. The seller then invoiced the buyer for the goods, the invoice being payable at a later date under the contract provisions, and the invoice was accepted by the buyer without objection. Under these circumstances the carrying vessel was detained at Plymouth and the cargo seized as prize. Unaware of the seizure, the buyer duly paid the price in to the bank and received the bills of lading. In holding that the cargo was not subject to seizure Lord Parker of Waddington said:

"Their Lordships have come to the conclusion, after carefully considering all the facts, that it was the intention of the parties to the contract that the property in the cargo should pass to the buyer upon shipment, but that the buyer was not intended to have possession of the cargo, or of the bills of lading which represented the cargo, until actual payment at due date of the purchase price. With the exception of the form of the bills of lading, everything points to this conclusion. The contract is for the sale of the whole cargo of a named ship. On shipment, or at any rate on notification of shipment, the cargo is at the risk of the buyer, who has to pay for it whether it arrives or not. The cargo is to be insured for buyer's account and benefit and insured at its arrived value, including profit, which the buyer alone could make. The buyer takes over the charterparty and names the port of discharge. The only matter which seems to point to an intention not to pass the property on shipment is the form in which the bills of lading were taken. But this form was determined by the seller's agent without knowledge of the contract, and though it may have been determined on general instructions from his principal, without particular instructions given in view of the particular contract. The way in which the seller subsequently deals with the bills of lading points rather to a desire to support his lien than to a desire to retain the property or any *jus disponendi* incident to the property. As soon as the bills of lading arrive in Europe he places them at the buyer's disposal, subject only to payment of the purchase price at due date. As soon as this is done he loses the possibility of withdrawing them from the contract, even if otherwise he could have done so. Under these circumstances the form of the bills of lading is, in their Lordships' opinion, quite insufficient to displace the strong inference of an intention to pass the property on shipment arising from the terms of the contract and the other facts."

Compare Rosenberg Bros. & Co. *v.* F. S. Buffum Co., 234 N. Y. 338 (Court of Appeals, 1922). A contract was made for the sale of two carloads of dried prunes, f. o. b. Pacific Coast rail shipping point. The seller placed the goods upon the cars in California for shipment to New York, and received bills of lading drawn to seller or order. The bills of lading indorsed in blank were forwarded to a bank in New York with drafts for the price attached and were presented to the buyer who refused to accept them. In an action by the seller for the purchase price a judgment of the Appellate Division for defendant was reversed. Said Pound, J.: "We held in *Standard Casing Co., Inc.* v. *California Casing Co., Inc.* (233 N. Y. 413) that upon a sale f. o. b., title passes to the [buyer] from the moment of delivery to the carrier; that the rule is subordinate to intention but that the fact that the bill of lading is made out to the seller or order does not indicate an inconsistent intention."

ROBINSON & LEDYARD *v.* POGUE & SON

Alabama Supreme Court, 1888

[86 *Alabama Reports*, 257]

This action was brought by E. H. Pogue & Son, merchants and partners, doing business in North Carolina, against the appellants, a partnership doing business in Montgomery, to recover several boxes of tobacco; and was commenced on the 18th December, 1885. The tobacco, which was 340 lbs. in weight, was the third and last installment of a lot of 1,000 lbs. sold by plaintiffs, or contracted to be sold, to Rushton & Co., merchants in Montgomery, in July, 1885; the other installments not being involved in the suit. The contract was made by plaintiffs' agents in Montgomery, J. Simon & Brother. Said Simon testified, on the part of the plaintiffs, that before making the contract, on the 25th July, he went to the "R. G. Dun Commercial Agency" in Montgomery, to ascertain the standing and financial condition of Rushton & Co., "and made the sale of the tobacco relying on the statement" shown by the books of said agency; that in the fall of 1885, before the last installment of the tobacco was forwarded by plaintiffs, Rushton "told him that he did not want any more tobacco, and not to ship the last installment." The defendants objected to this statement as evidence, and excepted to its admission. The witness testified, also, that he received the bill of lading for the tobacco from plaintiffs, by mail, about the 7th or 8th December, and immediately informed Rushton of the fact, "who answered, that he did not want the tobacco"; and this evidence was admitted by the court, against the objection and exception of the defendants. The tobacco was forwarded by railroad by plaintiffs, consigned to Rushton & Co.; and Simon testified, that the words, "Shipped to Rushton & Co., Montgomery," were written on the bill of lading which he received. The bill of lading was never delivered to Rushton & Co., but was retained by Simon & Bro.; the witness testifying that, "at the time of the negotiations between him and Rushton touching the sale of the tobacco, it was agreed that Simon & Bro. were to retain the bill of lading until each installment was paid." The tobacco "was delivered by the railroad company, without the production of the bill of lading, nor was the bill of sale shown"; but it was not shown when, or to whom, the tobacco was delivered. On the 16th December, 1885, the defendants bought out the entire stock of goods of Rushton & Co., with outstanding notes and accounts, in payment of a debt for moneys previously loaned and advanced, amounting to $9,000; and the validity of this purchase was not impeached. They immediately took an inventory of the goods, and removed them to their own warehouse, the tobacco here sued for being a part; and the writ in this suit was levied on the tobacco on the next day. "Said Rushton testified, that in the sale to defendants he did not sell, nor intend to sell, any goods which did not belong to Rushton & Co."

The court charged the jury, among other things, as follows: "If the jury believe from all the evidence that the plaintiffs, by sending the bill of lading to Simon & Bro. with the bill for the goods, intended that the title should not pass until Simon delivered the bill of lading to Rushton & Co., then the plaintiffs would be entitled to recover."

The defendants excepted to this charge, and also to the refusal of several charges asked by them in writing, among which were the following: (3.) "The delivery of the tobacco to the carrier, consigned to Rushton & Co., would pass the title to the tobacco to Rushton & Co., even though the bill of lading was sent to Simon & Bro., in the absence of proof that the bill of lading was not to be delivered to Rushton & Co., except upon payment, or performance of some other act or duty on their part." (4.) "If the jury believe from the evidence that the tobacco was delivered to the railroad company, and the bill of lading was made consigning the goods to Rushton & Co.; then the title to the goods passed by this delivery to Rushton & Co., although the bill of lading was sent to Simon & Bro., in the absence of proof that the contract of sale required the performance of something on the part of Rushton & Co., before the goods were delivered."

The charge given, the refusal of each of the charges asked, and several rulings on evidence to which exceptions were reserved, are now assigned as error.

SOMERVILLE, J. . . . The main contention here insisted on, and raised by the rulings of the Circuit Court, relates to the title acquired to the goods in controversy by Rushton & Co., the consignees of the plaintiffs. If the sale of the tobacco to them was completed by an actual or constructive delivery, and the intention of the vendors was that the title should unconditionally pass, then the appellants, Robinson & Ledyard, acquired a good title; otherwise not.

The contract for the sale of the goods was made by Simon & Bro., of Montgomery, Alabama, as agents of the plaintiffs. The shipment was made by railroad, and a bill of lading was taken in which Rushton & Co. were named as the consignees. This bill of lading was mailed to Simon Bros., with a bill for the goods, on which were written the words, "Shipped to Rushton & Co., Montgomery, Ala." It was agreed between Rushton & Co.

and Simon & Bro. that the latter were to "retain the bill of lading" until the goods were paid for; but there is no evidence that the goods themselves were to be retained until the price was paid. The evidence, on the contrary, tends to prove that the sale was made on credit, after closely inquiring into the financial status of the consignees. The tobacco was delivered by the railroad to the consignees, without the presentation of the bill of lading.

Where goods have been sold, and are delivered by the vendor to a common carrier, consigned without reservation to the vendee, the question as to whether the title, *eo instanti*, passes to such consignee, depends upon the intention of the vendor, to be gathered from all the circumstances of the case. There is no doubt as to the correctness of the general rule, that where the bill of lading shows a consignment by the vendor to the vendee, in ordinary form, and no other circumstance appears as to the intention, the *prima facie* legal presumption is that an unconditional delivery to the consignee is contemplated. But this presumption of fact may be rebutted by evidence showing a contrary intention. The title of the goods is commonly retained in the consignor by taking the bill of lading to his own order, or in blank, or by drawing on the consignees with the bill of lading attached to the draft, or other like procedure, indicating an intention to retain in himself a *jus disponendi* over the goods until the price is paid, or until the happening of some other contingency.

The delivery to the common carrier, in cases of the former class, is deemed *prima facie* a delivery to the consignee, not only when the consignment is made to a carrier named by the consignee, but also when made to some carrier in the usual course of trade, who thus becomes, impliedly, the agent of the consignee to receive and transport the goods at his risk; the sale thus becoming presumptively complete at the point of shipment, although the price is not to be paid until the goods reach their destination.—*Garbracht* v. *Com.*, 96 Penn. St. 449; s. c., 42 Amer. Rep. 550; *Pilgreen* v. *State*, 71 Ala. 368; *Sarbecker* v. *State*, 65 Wis. 171; s. c., 56 Amer. Rep. 624; *Hauseman* v. *Nye*, 62 Ind. 485; s. c., 30 Amer. Rep. 199. Hence it is commonly held, that the consignee in a bill of lading, where there is no reservation of title by the consignor, has vested in him such a property in the goods as to authorize him to sue the carrier, in his own name, for their injury, loss or recovery, in trover, detinue, or other appropriate action.—*Chandler* v. *Sprague*, 38 Amer. Dec. 423, note; *Potter* v. *Lansing*, 3 *Ib*. 310, 318, note; Angell on Common Carriers, § 497; *Griffith* v. *Ingleden*, 9 Amer. Dec. 444; *So. Ex. Co.* v. *Armistead*, 50 Ala. 351; *M. & G. R. R. Co.* v. *Williams*, 54 Ala. 168.

Under these principles of law, the refusal of the fourth charge requested by the appellants was error. If the facts, hypothesised in this charge, were believed by the jury, the consignees could have recovered the goods from the railroad company. Hence their delivery, without presentation of the bill of lading, did not presumptively prejudice the rights of the consignees. The case presents no question whatever involving the rights of a transferee of the consignor, claiming an interest by purchase in the property as holder of the bill of lading. If the sale was on credit, and the goods were not to be retained until the price was paid, the mere retention of the bill of lading by the agent of the consignor would not prevent the sale from becoming complete.

We can not perceive that the case is affected by Rushton & Co.'s declaration made to Simon, before delivery of the goods by the railroad, that they did not want the goods; in as much as there was no evidence tending to show the assent of Simon & Bro., or their principals, the consignors, to release the consignees from the purchase, or to rescind the trade. It required the concurring assent of both contracting parties to rescind the trade, just as fully as it did originally to make it. Neither alone could do so. The evidence on this point was irrelevant, and should have been excluded.

The judgment is reversed, and the cause remanded.

In BROWNE *v.* GIGER, 221 Ala. 176 (Supreme Court, 1930), it was held that "where draft is drawn on the purchaser for the price, and the draft with bill of lading attached is forwarded, though the bill of lading is taken in the name of the purchaser, the title does not pass until the draft is honored and the bill of lading delivered."

In THE KRONPRINSESSAN MARGARETA, THE PARANA, ETC., [1921] 1 A. C. 486 (Privy Council, 1920), Lord Sumner said:

"In the case of the *Parana* the terms stipulated on behalf of Urban & Co., the neutral sellers and shippers, were 'cost and freight Gothenburg . . . reimbursement A/S on Malareprovinsernas Bank, Stockholm.' The buyers applied to this bank to open a credit available to the sellers and to confirm to the latter the fact of their having done so, and they deposited a sum of money to make the credit effective. The bank did cable confirmation of this credit in the following terms: 'Confirmed credit opened Kroners 100,000 account Lundgren Rollven against 2,000 bags coffee shipment *Parana*.' The shippers thereupon took bills of lading making the coffee deliverable to the consignees' order and sent them with an invoice and a sight draft for its amount, through collecting agents of their own, to be presented together to the bank in Sweden. The appellants contend that the effect of this transaction was that the property in the coffee passed from the sellers to the consignees before the commencement of the voyage and that infection has accordingly no application to their case.

"The passing of property being a question of intention is ultimately a question of fact. There is no evidence of the intention of these parties beyond the inferences to be drawn from their situation and interests and from the mercantile operations which they conducted. What law they supposed would govern their transaction is not shown nor is any evidence given of the provisions of any foreign law and, for the reasons given in *The Parchim* ([1918] A. C. 157), the law to be applied must under these circumstances be that of England so far as the matter is one of law at all. That law has attached definite presumptions as to intention to definite courses of procedure and modes of expressing and dealing with common mercantile instruments.

"If the shippers had insured the goods and had attached the policy to the draft, and if they had taken the bills of lading to their own order, no question could have arisen. Again, if in pursuance of the contract the consignees had insured for the benefit, as between buyer and seller, of whom it might concern, there would have been little doubt possible. Their Lordships will assume, because the argument appeared to assume on all hands, that the insurance effected in Europe was for the consignees' benefit only, though they are by no means satisfied that it was so, and that none was effected by or for the consignor. The importance which always attaches to the incidence of insurance in international commerce makes this a significant point.

"Again, importance attaches to the fact that the shippers, having loaded the coffee on a general ship — a bailment to the carrier — took the bills of lading to the consignees' order. Without the consignees' indorsement they could not thereafter demand delivery ex ship as a matter of course, though without delivery of the bills of lading to the consignees they in their turn would not obtain delivery in the ordinary way of business."

[After deciding that under the form of credit used there was no obligation on the bank to meet the draft, which the drawers of it could have enforced, his Lordship continued:]

"Now two things are quite plain. The consignors did not propose at any time to rely for payment on the mere personal credit of the consignees, and they carefully kept the bills of lading in their own agents' hands until the draft was met: see *Moakes* v. *Nicolson* (19 C. B. (N. S.) 290). But for the absence of a policy of insurance they strictly pursued the same course of dealing with the documents, as if there had been a c.f. and i. sale.

"In these circumstances what can be inferred as to the passing of the general property? What is there to show an intention to pass that property for anything less than payment, and what motive is there for such an intention? The appellants, Messrs. Lundgren & Rollven, have to show that it passed to them and passed, too, before the beginning of the voyage. If it did, then the consignors no longer owned the goods and had nothing to show against them except a draft of their own, which could not be enforced, and a bill of lading, which would not entitle them to delivery of the goods, though its retention might seriously inconvenience the new owners, the consignees. Rights to stop *in transitu* or to exercise an unpaid vendors' lien need hardly be discussed, for, on a question of intention in fact as to which there is a good deal of evidence, it would be artificial to assume that the consignors' minds were actually determined to the contrary by consideration of legal remedies, of which it is not shown that they had any knowledge, let the legal presumption be what it will. It is said that, as a matter of business, the confirmed credit relieved the consignors of all further concern in the goods, for they could have no doubt that they would be paid by the bank in any event and that the failure to insure is proof positive of this. It may be so, though their Lordships do not desire to express any opinion as to the rights of the parties if the coffee were known to be already lost at the time of the presentation of the draft, but it seems clear that the consignors desired to retain an interest in the goods, otherwise why should they retain the bills of lading in their agents' hands? It is said that this only points to an intention to reserve a special property as security, but the omission to insure would be equally significant in this case, and there is no reason why, as a matter of actual intent, a special and not the general property should have been reserved. The case might be very different if the bills of lading had been forwarded to Lundgren & Rollven direct: *Ex parte Banner* (2 Ch. D. 278). As it is, *Shepherd* v. *Harrison* (L. R. 5 H. L. 116) would surely apply, if on presentation of the bills of lading with the draft there had been a retention of the first without payment of the second. There may be explanations of the shipper's election to be his own insurer of the coffee till the sight draft should be met, but, however this may be, there is nothing to outweigh the significance of a dealing with the documents so nearly identical with that in an ordinary transaction c.f. and i.

"No authority was forthcoming which proved to be completely in point. Cases, in which it has been held that taking the bill of lading in the shipper's own name negatives any unconditional appropriation to the buyer by the delivery of the goods on shipboard and indicates one conditional on the documents being taken up, can throw only an indirect light on the question here involved. Certainly no case was found, in which it was held that taking the bill of lading in the buyer's name, while withholding delivery of it until presentation and taking up of the documents, would not be, as an appropriation, equally conditional. . . .

"In the present case it appears to their Lordships that the retention by the seller of the bill of lading was inconsistent with an intention to pass the property. They think that it was 'clearly intended by the consignor to preserve his title to the goods until he did a further act by transferring the bill of lading.' The special circumstance of the existence of a confirmed banker's credit in this case is only indirectly relevant. It no doubt enhances the likelihood that the bills of lading will eventually be taken up and the goods be paid for, and so diminishes the importance to the seller of being still able to say that the goods are his, but it is not direct evidence of intention; it is only a reason why a particular intention is more likely to have been formed in such a case than in others. The intention has still to be inferred, principally from what was done and from the communications made with reference to it, and these point to an intention not to pass the property till the drafts were paid, and it is really rather a reason for intending to get the documents presented and taken up as soon as possible, than for an intention not to retain the ownership even until that could be effected. If the seller was paid or was holder of an enforcible contract from a bank for payment, the sooner he passed the property the better, for he was uninsured, but if he was neither he gained nothing by passing the property away. It was not onerous property."

STEIN FORBES AND CO. *v.* COUNTY TAILORING CO.

KING'S BENCH DIVISION, 1916

[115 *Law Times Reports*, 215]

[After stating the case as printed on p. 253 *supra*, and after disposing of other incidental points, Atkin, J., continued:]

But it was further said by Mr. Wright that the property in fact had passed to the defendants and that upon the plaintiffs being willing to transfer possession they were entitled to the price as in the case of goods bargained and sold. I think that there are many objections to this view. At what time property passes under a contract of sale depends upon the intention of the parties. Sect. 16 of the Sale of Goods Act 1893 says:

"Where there is a contract for the sale of unascertained goods no property in the goods is transferred to the buyer unless and until the goods are ascertained."

Then sect. 17 (1) says:

"When there is a contract for the sale of specific or ascertained goods, the property in them is transferred to the buyer at such time as the parties to the contract intend it to be transferred. (2) For the purpose of ascertaining the intention of the parties regard shall be had to the terms of the contract, the conduct of the parties, and the circumstances of the case."

The Act provides certain rules for ascertaining the intention of the parties unless a different intention appears. Many cases have dealt with the problem as to when property passes in contracts of sale on c.i.f. terms. Mr. Wright contends that as soon as the goods are unconditionally appropriated to the contract and the seller holds the documents at the disposal of the buyer the property passes. The value of that proposition depends on the meaning of unconditionally.

I doubt whether goods are appropriated unconditionally if the seller does not mean the buyer to have them unless he pays for them. But it seems to me impossible to lay down a general rule applicable to all c.i.f. contracts. The overruling question is: Does the intention of the parties appear in the course of the making and the fulfilment of the contract? By sect. 19 of the Sale of Goods Act 1893, sub-ss. 1, 2, and 3, it is provided as follows:

[The section in question was here quoted in full.]

In the present case, the goods were shipped at New York on behalf of the plaintiffs, and the bill of lading was taken to the order of the banking firm who financed the transaction for the plaintiffs. On arrival of the ship the plaintiffs had to take up the bill of lading from the bankers; and, inasmuch as the defendants would not take up the documents, the plaintiffs had to take delivery of the goods from the ship. It seems quite plain that the seller or his banker reserved the *jus disponendi.*

It was said that the property passed to the buyer on shipment, but the seller only reserved his unpaid vendor's lien. That view seems to me inconsistent with the section I have read and with every business probability. In the majority of cases where the seller takes the bill of lading to his order the goods come forward through a banker, and it seems to me very improbable that the seller means to give to the banker or the banker to take a document representing goods the property in which is in some third person, the only security given being a right to retain possession till the fine is paid. I think the intention is to keep the property in the seller till payment.

Then it is said, whatever the original intention may be, at any rate the property passes when there is an appropriation of specific goods, as by the invoice in this case, and a tender or a willingness to tender. It would be a remarkable intention in a commercial man to keep the property on shipment in order to secure payment, but yet in taking the necessary steps to procure payment by appropriation and tender to part with the property before payment is in fact made. I think that in such cases the ordinary inference to be drawn is that the seller does not intend to part with the property, except against payment. It seems to me that this view is confirmed by the statutory provisions in sect. 19, sub-sect. 3, which I have read.

Unless the property has passed I do not think that in this case the plaintiffs can sue for the price; and in my opinion it has not passed. The plaintiffs' claim, therefore, is for damages. The case will be adjourned to enable the defendants to deal with the question of damages in case the parties cannot agree. There will be liberty to apply, and I shall reserve all questions of costs.

Case adjourned.

In Ruttonjee *v.* Frame, 205 App. Div. 354 (New York Supreme Court, Appellate Division, 1923), there was a contract for the sale of 600 bales of cloves at an agreed price c. i. f. New York, buyers to pay on presentation of documents. The cloves were already on board ship at the time the contract was made, and the seller had taken out a bill of lading in the name of a New York bank. The buyer refused to accept the documents, and in an action by the seller to recover damages it was held that the taking of the bill of lading in the form indicated did not show an intention to prevent title from passing to the buyer in accordance with the usual rules of c. i. f. contracts.

In The Orteric, [1920] A. C. 724 (Privy Council), a seller in the United States sold a quantity of wheat to a buyer in Germany under a contract calling for payment by net cash in Hamburg against documents. The seller took out bills of lading to his own order, indorsed them in blank, and attached them to drafts on the buyer which he discounted with an American bank. An appeal from a judgment condemning the wheat as enemy goods was allowed. The seller manifested no intention of passing title either to the German buyer or to the bank discounting the draft.

BARTON THOMPSON AND CO. *v.* VIGERS BROTHERS

KING'S BENCH DIVISION, 1906

[19 *Commercial Cases*, 175]

KENNEDY, J. In this case the parties have come before me on the writ of summons, and there has been an agreement between them to treat my judgment on the point of law raised as the trial of the action. I am pronouncing judgment in open Court, with the agreement of the parties, so as to enable the case to be taken to the Court of Appeal if the parties desire to do so. There are really no facts in dispute, and this is a very economical way to settle the question.

The action has been brought by Barton Thompson and Co., against Vigers Brothers, claiming on the writ, the return of a bill of lading for so many pieces of timber shipped by the *Katie*, the return of the insurance certificate on the same goods, and the plaintiffs' draft for £83 11*s*. 9*d*.; and alternatively for the return of the goods or damages. The real question in the case is whether or not the present plaintiffs have a right to sue. The facts as they were explained to me by the solicitors who appeared on the two sides, and as they appeared upon the documents with which I was furnished, appear to be as follows. The defendants Messrs. Vigers Brothers, on November 9, 1905, bought certain pieces of timber from a Mr. A. E. Grube of Riga through the plaintiffs, who were in fact agents, and it would also seem were *del credere* agents of the foreign seller. The contract is a very full one, and the only material portion to which I need refer is as follows: — "Freight to be paid by the buyers as per charterparty, and the balance of invoice by approved acceptance to sellers or sellers' agent's draft, payable in London at three months from date of bill of lading, or in cash less 1½ per cent. discount at buyer's option, on receipt of, and in exchange for, shipping documents. Property in goods to be deemed for all purposes, except retention of vendor's lien for unpaid price, to have passed to buyer when goods put on board." In conformity with that contract a portion of the goods in question were shipped by a particular vessel, but not the whole consignment. The remainder followed by another ship. When the goods and the shipping documents arrived the plaintiffs, Barton Thompson and Co., appear to have accepted and paid the seller, the shipping principal at Riga, for these goods by a draft of £80 4*s*. 11*d*., dated December 11, 1905. Barton Thompson and Co., then presented the shipping documents to the defendants, the buyers of the goods, together with a draft for their acceptance, the draft itself being dated November 30, 1905, and being drawn by Barton Thompson and Co. upon Vigers Brothers of London. They sent that draft with a letter dated December 7, 1905, in which they said: — "Herewith we beg to hand you original bill of lading and insurance certificate covering 2,835 pieces 3 by 6, 7, and 8, white ends, shipped by Mr. Grube per steamship *Katie*. We also enclose our draft for £83 11*s*. 9*d*. which kindly accept and return in due course, or pay cash less 1½ per cent.

under terms of contract. Kindly note the above documents are handed to you subject to prompt acceptance of draft or payment of cash according to terms of contract dated November 9 last." The buyers, who raised some point in the correspondence as to the place of delivery, and also a question as to possible loss from a division of the total contract quantity, took the shipping documents, but did not accept, and in fact refused to accept, the draft which the plaintiffs had sent with those documents, and the acceptance of which by the defendants had been made by the plaintiffs expressly a term and condition of their keeping the shipping documents and dealing with them. The action is brought in the alternative form in consequence of that breach of contract. The only other fact to be taken into consideration, as far as I can see, is this, that not only was the purchase by the terms of the contract to be by approved acceptance to sellers or sellers' agent's draft, but also the invoice, which was furnished by Mr. Grube to the buyer, which is headed: — "Invoice of whitewood batten ends shipped by A. E. Grube on board steamship *Katie,* at Riga, for Surrey Commercial Dock, by order and for account of Messrs. Vigers Brothers, London, contract 9th November, 1905," contained this express direction: — "Payable to the order of Messrs. Barton Thompson and Co., London, in exchange for bill of lading and insurance policy." I do not think on the law there is any doubt that the plaintiffs are right in the contention which they have put forward. I think the plaintiffs had the right to say, quite apart from the fact that they were *del credere* agents, and in fact paid for these goods to the seller, the foreign principal, that they gave these goods to the defendants, the buyers, upon the terms of their accepting the draft, and that the acceptance of that draft was the condition upon which the defendants were entitled to keep or deal with the shipping documents. It has been the law since the decision of the House of Lords in *Shepherd* v. *Harrison* ([1871] L.R. 5 H.L. 116; 40 L.J.Q.B. 148) that a buyer has no right, where the delivery of the shipping documents is made conditional with the acceptance of the draft, to obtain the goods and use the documents and not accept the draft; and that is now enunciated as the general law of the country by section 19 (3) of the Sale of Goods Act, 1893. In this particular case it seems to me that even if the plaintiffs had not had the pecuniary interest which they in fact have, they would still by the terms of the contract have a right which would entitle them to maintain this action, because the purchaser bought on the terms of giving an approved acceptance to the seller or the sellers' agent's draft. By the terms of the invoice the seller directed that the sale should be carried out and completed by the payment by the defendants to the order of Barton Thompson and Co., of the debt which was due when the goods were taken by the defendants by the delivery and acceptance of the shipping documents. The fact that there may be — as, in fact, I gather from the correspondence there is — a sum claimed from the sellers abroad by the buyer here for breach of contract, does not seem to me to affect the question, which is, after all, a simple one of good faith, and also settled law, that a person who takes shipping documents which are offered to him upon the condition of his fulfilling that which was, in this case, a contractual obligation — namely, to pay for them by accepting a bill drawn upon him by the agents here for the foreign principal, cannot keep the goods with one hand and also refuse the terms upon which they are put in his possession with the other. I must therefore give judgment for the plaintiffs.

Judgment accordingly.

In T. P. Jordeson and Co. *v.* London Hardwood Company (Limited), 19 Comm. Cas. 161 (King's Bench Division, 1913), on substantially similar facts except that the agent was not referred to as a *del credere* agent, it was held that although the shipping principal was entitled to judgment against the buyer for the price of the goods, the agent had no action against the buyer for non-acceptance of the draft since there was no contract between the agent and the buyer.

In Pennsylvania Railroad Company *v.* The Bank of United States, 214 App. Div. 410 (New York Supreme Court, Appellate Division, 1925), a seller shipped 211 boxes of fish to a buyer under a contract calling for shipment f. o. b. Beach Haven, N. J., payment by draft, bill of lading attached. Through an error on the part of the carrier the goods were sent forward on a straight bill of lading. The buyer refused to take up the documents when presented with draft attached, but on learning that the bill of lading was straight, paid the freight charges and took delivery of the fish. The buyer then stored the fish in a warehouse and obtained a loan from a bank on the receipts. The present action was in replevin by the carrier to recover the fish from the bank. Judgment for plaintiff reversed. The buyer had both title and possession, and could convey a good title to third persons.

In Quigley *v.* Wiley, 107 Vt. 253 (Supreme Court, 1935), goods were shipped under a shipper's order bill of lading, which was indorsed in blank and forwarded with sight draft on the buyer attached. After the arrival of the documents the buyer executed and delivered to plaintiff a bill of sale of the goods, and plaintiff arranged with the collecting bank to take up the draft and get the bill of lading. After plaintiff had paid the draft in part, but before plaintiff received the bill of lading on completing the payment, the goods were attached by defendant as the property of the original buyer. In an action of replevin, judgment for plaintiff affirmed. The original buyer had acquired no title or right to the goods, and plaintiff acquired all the rights the bank had and consequently was entitled to possession of the lumber, at least as against defendant.

In Cahn and Meyer *v.* Pockett's Bristol Channel Steam Packet Company, Limited [1899] 1 Q. B. 643 (Court of Appeal), in fulfilment of a contract for a certain quantity of copper the sellers forwarded to the buyer a bill of lading indorsed in blank for copper shipped on defendant's ship, together with a draft for the price of the copper for acceptance. The buyer, who was insolvent, did not accept the draft, and delivered the bill of lading to plaintiffs against a contract previously made for the sale of copper. Plaintiffs took the bill of lading and paid the price of the copper in good faith. The sellers stopped the copper in transit. In an action for non-delivery a judgment for defendant was reversed. Although it was the sellers' intention that the buyer should not use the bill of lading unless he accepted the draft, he nevertheless obtained possession of the bill of lading with their consent and could pass a good title to plaintiffs.

4. THE BUYER'S RIGHT OF INSPECTION

JOHN B. FREY COMPANY, INC. *v.* S. SILK, INC.

MASSACHUSETTS SUPREME JUDICIAL COURT, 1923

[245 *Massachusetts Reports*, 534]

RUGG, C. J. . . . The plaintiff seeks to recover the purchase price of a carload of beets sold by it to the defendant. There was evidence tending to show that the order of the defendant to one Pratt then in the State of New York was a telegram dated January 10, 1920: "Buy three or more beets for me and get as late delivery as possible." The carload here in question was bought by Pratt of one McKuen, who was an agent for the plaintiff. It was an entire lot of beets stored in Sodus Cold Storage at Sodus, New York. The terms were $3 per sack f.o.b. Sodus. The beets were sold for prompt shipment, but the plaintiff held them at the request of Pratt, first until the next week, Pratt promising to send check for the beets, and then until February 18, 1920, when they were shipped. Pratt said in the meantime that McKuen need not worry as the beets belonged to the defendant. The car arrived in Boston on February 29, 1920, when it is agreed that the beets were not merchantable. The invoice to the defendant contained the words, "Car No. A. R. T. 25292. Loaded at Sodus, New York, via. B. & A. Dely. . . . Allow inspection." At the time of shipment the plaintiff drew on the defendant by draft, which read in part: "At sight, hold for arrival of car A. R. T. 25292 pay to the order of. . . ." There was also a freight bill on which were the words, "inspection allowed." There was evidence from a qualified expert in the trade in Boston to the effect that it was a custom known throughout the vegetable trade to allow inspection "at the delivery end . . . to see if the goods are as contracted for both as to quantity and quality."

Issues at the trial were whether the beets were merchantable at the time of sale and whether they were or became unmerchantable while they were at the risk of the plaintiff, or after that risk had passed to the defendant. The settlement of these issues depended in part upon the question when title passed, or was to pass, under the contract of sale from seller to buyer.

In various forms of words the plaintiff asked for a binding instruction to the jury that title to the beets passed to the defendant at the time of the contract of sale. These requests were denied. Instructions were given in substance that the question was whether it was the agreement of the parties that title should pass when the beets were put on the car for shipment by rail to the defendant, or after the defendant had inspected them on arrival in Boston with the right to reject them if "not up to standard." The jury thus were not permitted to find that the title passed at the time of contract.

The meaning, force and effect of this contract would ordinarily be ascertained according to the law of the State of New York, where it was made. *Kline* v. *Baker*, 99 Mass. 253. That law is a fact and must be proved like any other fact. The court cannot take cognizance of the law of a foreign State in the absence of evidence. No evidence was introduced as to the law upon this subject in the State of New York. Therefore the case must be decided in accordance with the common law of this Commonwealth because the common law of a sister State is presumed in the absence of evidence to be the same as that of this Commonwealth. *Royle* v. *Worcester Buick Co.* 243 Mass. 143, 146. There is no presumption that the law of another State corresponds with a statute of this Commonwealth. *Murphy* v. *Collins*, 121 Mass. 6.

The common law of this Commonwealth is, as was said by Chief Justice Gray in *Sherwin* v. *Mudge*, 127 Mass. 547, 549, "By a contract for the sale of specific goods, the title doubtless passes as between the parties, without any actual or constructive delivery, or payment of the price, unless it can be shown that their intention is different." *Parsons* v. *Dickinson*, 11 Pick. 352, 354. *Folsom* v. *Cornell*, 150 Mass. 115. *Mitchell* v. *LeClair*, 165 Mass. 308. *Wesoloski* v. *Wysoski*, 186 Mass. 495. *Bristol Manuf. Corp.* v. *Arkwright Mills*, 213 Mass. 172. This rule of the common law is embodied in the sales act. G. L. c. 106, § 21, Rule 1, where it is phrased in these words: "If there is an unconditional contract to sell specific goods, in a deliverable state, the property in the goods passes to the buyer when the contract is made, and it is immaterial whether the time of payment, or the time of delivery, or both, be delayed."

The evidence in the case at bar appears to have been undisputed that the negotiations between these parties related to an entire lot of beets on storage. They were thus specific, defined and separated goods, ready for delivery. Their shipment might have been found to have been delayed solely for the convenience of the defendant. In this connection it might also have have been found that Pratt was the agent of the defendant in the transaction, although that was for the jury in view of conflicting evidence.

It follows that the jury ought to have been permitted to find on all the evidence that the title passed at the time the contract was made. An unqualified instruction to the effect that it did so pass could not have been given. There was the evidence of custom as to inspection, and the words of the draft, of the invoice and of the freight bill as to inspection.

It would have been permissible for the jury to have found that, in view of all the circumstances, it was the intention of the parties that the right of inspection was either "a condition precedent qualifying the buyer's obligation either to take title or to pay the price, or a condition subsequent authorizing the return of the goods and the recovery of the price if title to the goods has passed, or the price been paid." Williston on Sales, § 471. *Paddleford* v. *Lane & Co. Inc.* 223 Mass. 113, 117. In the case at bar, whether the right of inspection was a condition precedent or a condition subsequent was or might be a question of importance, because on its decision might turn the determinaiton of the further question whether in the meantime risk of loss or deterioration rested upon the vendor or the vendee. If the right of inspection be a condition precedent, the risk of loss is upon the seller, but, if subsequent, this risk is upon the buyer under ordinary conditions in the absence of evidence showing a contrary purpose.

There is nothing on the record to show that this contract was in writing. The persons by whom it was made testified concerning the contract. It may have been found to have been made in view of the custom of the vegetable trade as to inspection. The words of the invoice, draft, and freight bill as to inspection were permissible sources of information as to its terms. The terms of the contract, including the time of transfer of title, and the nature and purpose of the inspection, all were questions of fact to be ascertained from the entire evidence and the most rational inferences to be drawn therefrom. No hard and fast rule of law could have been laid down. *Fechteler* v. *Whittemore*, 205 Mass. 6, 10. It was the duty of the jury to determine what was the intention of the parties in the light of correct principles of the controlling law. The jury ought to have been instructed in general terms that it was their duty to decide what contract the parties intended to make, giving due weight to what was said, written and done by each of them bearing upon the terms of the agreement and to all material circumstances. Instructions as to the general rule of law concerning the time of the transfer of title ought to have been given conformably to the decisions already quoted in part and cited.

Instructions also should have been given as to the effect of delivery to the common carrier by the seller for transportation to the buyer. A possible inference from all the evidence was that the vendor was to deliver the beets to the common carrier for transportation to the defendant as vendee, and that the freight was to be paid by the latter. If that was found to have been the agreement of the parties, then delivery to the carrier might have been found to have been the time of passage of title. *Edelstone* v. *Schimmel*, 233 Mass. 45, 49, and cases cited. *St. John Brothers Co.* v. *Falkson*, 237 Mass. 399, 401. If this were found to be the fact, then also loss would have been upon the defendant, provided the beets were at the time of such delivery in merchantable condition. *Levy* v. *Radkay*, 233 Mass. 29.

Further instructions should have been given as to the purpose and bearing of the right of inspection by the defendant, if that right was found to exist. The jury should have been directed to find whether that right of inspection by the defendant was intended by the parties to have been a condition precedent to the passing of title or a condition subsequent to the passing of title. If it was a condition precedent, then the beets must have been merchantable on arrival at destination in order to conform to the contract. In such case the risk of deterioration and loss would be wholly upon the seller, and the buyer would have the right to reject on inspection if the beets were not merchantable and otherwise did not conform to the terms of the contract. If, however, the intention of the parties, in view of the general rule as to time of passage of title, was that the right of inspection was a condition subsequent, then the risk of deterioration and loss would rest upon the defendant. His right of inspection would be for the purpose of determining whether at the time the title passed (that is to say, at the time the contract of sale was made or at the time delivery was made to the railroad for transportation to the defendant, whichever the jury might find), the beets conformed to the contract and were merchantable. *Lord* v. *Edwards,* 148 Mass. 476. *Sims* v. *Miller,* 151 Ark. 377, 389. See *Alden* v. *Hart,* 161 Mass. 576.

The testimony as to the custom of allowing inspection at place of destination was admissible. *Roach* v. *Lowe,* 226 Mass. 598, 604. But it was not decisive upon this point. The terms of that custom in respect of the precise point whether the inspection was a condition precedent or a condition subsequent was not clear, but indefinite and obscure. Perhaps it does not reach this point at all. Moreover, in view of express testimony of McKuen as to conversation between him and Pratt, to the effect that title passed at the time of the contract of sale, and of other evidence, it would in any event have been a question of fact for the jury to settle when the title and consequent risk passed to the defendant.

What has been said of course is not intended to cover every branch of a possible contract as to the effect of the right of inspection. It seems to us to cover the practical aspects of the case at bar as presented on the record.

It follows that, while the requests of the plaintiff for instructions could not rightly have been given in the form presented, yet they called attention to a principle of law which ought to have been dealt with in the charge. There was error in confining the attention of the jury solely to the time of shipment and the time of inspection as the times when title might pass by the terms of the contract, and in denying them opportunity to find that it was the intention of the parties that the title might pass at time of the contract of sale.

Exceptions sustained.

STRUTHERS-ZIEGLER COOPERAGE CO. *v.* FARMERS MANFG. CO.

MICHIGAN SUPREME COURT, 1925

[233 *Michigan Reports,* 298]

McDONALD, C. J. This action was brought to recover damages for breach of contract. The plaintiff is a wholesale dealer in cooperage stock. It is a Michigan corporation with offices in Detroit. The defendant is a Virginia corporation engaged in the business of manufacturing cooperage stock at Norfolk, Virginia, and elsewhere. Between January 2, 1923, and February 3, 1923, the parties entered into four separate contracts for the sale to the plaintiff of a quantity of staves and heading, aggregating 21 car loads. Five cars were shipped, two of which the plaintiff accepted and three of which it rejected on the claim that in quality they did not conform to the contract. The cars rejected were shipped on the plaintiff's order to customers in Maryland and West Virginia. When they reached their destination they were inspected, the defendant was notified of their rejection and requested to replace them with such material as was called for by the contract. The defendant refused to replace them or to make any other shipments unless the plaintiff would accept delivery at Norfolk, Virginia, and make inspection there. The plaintiff insisted on its right to inspection at the point of destination. No further shipments were made, and the rejected goods were not replaced. The plaintiff bought elsewhere and then began this suit to recover its damages. At the close of the plaintiff's case and again at the close of all the proofs, the defendant moved for a directed verdict on the ground that there was no liability on its part as a matter of law. Disposition of these motions was reserved under the statute and the case was submitted to the jury, which returned a verdict for the plaintiff in the sum of $4,617.23. A judgment notwithstanding the verdict was denied. The defendant moved for a new trial, to the denial of which it duly excepted. Defendant brings error.

It is first contended that the circuit judge erred in the construction which he placed upon the contracts. The defendant claimed that the goods were sold f. o. b. Norfolk, that Norfolk was the place of delivery, of inspection, and acceptance by the plaintiff, and that when it made or tendered delivery at Norfolk it had fully performed its duty under the contract. It was the plaintiff's claim that it had a right to inspect the goods at the point of destination and to reject them there if they were of inferior quality; that f. o. b. Norfolk was used merely to designate the party by whom the freight was to be paid and not the place of delivery and acceptance. The court ruled in accordance with the plaintiff's contention and this ruling presents the first question for our consideration.

The goods specified in the contract were to be shipped by the defendant as plaintiff ordered to its customers in various parts of the country. They were goods which the defendant was to manufacture. The contracts required them to be of a certain quality, but did not specify as to the time or place or right of inspection. Under such circumstances the defendant contends that the contract being for shipment f. o. b. Norfolk, acceptance and inspection must be made at Norfolk and not at the point of destination. Of the cases cited in support of this contention, the one most in point is *Lawder & Sons Co.* v. *Mackie Grocery Co.*, 97 Md. 1 (54 Atl. 634, 62 L. R. A. 795). In that case the buyer, who resided in New Orleans, sued the seller in Baltimore for breach of contract in the sale of 700 cases of canned tomatoes. The contract provided that the tomatoes be delivered f. o. b. Baltimore, and that the terms should be cash. It was the claim of the buyer that he had a right under the contract to inspect the goods and pay for them when received at the point of destination. Of this the court said:

"If it be conceded that it had such right, as it may be, the further question arises as to where, under this contract, it could be exercised. The mere fact that the buyer has the right to inspect the goods before acceptance does not necessarily mean that the inspection is to be made at the residence or place of business of the buyer. He might inspect at the seller's place of business, but, if the contract provides for delivery at a particular place, he must accept or reject at that place, unless otherwise provided for in the contract." * * *

The controlling fact in that case as to the place of inspection was that the terms were cash. It was expressly provided in the contract that delivery should be made f. o. b. Baltimore, terms cash. This meant that the goods were to be paid for when delivered to the common carrier at Baltimore. That he should pay cash when delivered at Baltimore was inconsistent with the buyer's claim that he had a right to inspect at any other time or place. The reasoning of the court in that case would not apply to a case where the terms were not cash. So that the rule there enunciated, which we have quoted above, was evidently not intended as a general rule, but was to apply only to cases where it could be inferred from some provision in the contract that the parties intended that inspection should be at the place of delivery. In that case the court further said:

"If they determine that by their contract it must control, and if it is silent as to inspection, but is as clear as this is as to delivery, any inspection that is desired before payment must be made before or at the time of delivery, when the terms are cash."

In the instant case the goods were not sold for cash, but the plaintiff had 30 days' time on each shipment.

Many other cases are cited in support of the general rule that if the sale is made for delivery f. o. b. at a designated place, and the seller there delivers the goods free of expense to the buyer, the title at once passes to him. No one will question this rule. It is conclusive on the question of delivery. But delivery and the passing of title at the point of shipment do not preclude the buyer from inspecting and rejecting at the point of destination, if the goods when delivered are not such as are stipulated in the contract. It has uniformly been held that, under such circumstances, as between the seller and the buyer, the title which passes is a conditional title subject to the right of inspection and rejection at the point of destination.

"It is the general rule that where goods are ordered of a specific quality, which the seller undertakes to deliver to a carrier to be forwarded to the buyer at a distant place, the right of inspection, in the absence of any specific provision in the contract, continues until the goods are received and accepted at their ultimate destination; in such a case the carrier is not the agent of the buyer to accept the goods as corresponding with the contract, although he may be his agent to receive and transport them." 23 R. C. L. p. 1433, and cases cited.

In *Kuppenheimer* v. *Wertheimer*, 107 Mich. 77 (61 Am. St. Rep. 317), it was said:

"The right to inspect before acceptance always exists, and a purchaser cannot be required to inspect at the shipping point, but is entitled to a reasonable opportunity after the arrival of the goods. *Fogel* v. *Brubaker*, 122 Pa. St. 7 (15 Atl. 692); 2 Benj. Sales (Corbin's Ed.), §§ 910, 966; *Erwin* v. *Harris*, 87 Ga. 333 (13 S. E. 513). If the goods are not up to the sample, the right to refuse them exists, which is, in effect, a rescission.

The title passes upon delivery to the carrier, subject to this right, of which the purchaser may avail himself or not."

General rules as to the time and place of inspection, where the stipulations of the contract do not provide for it, are not invariable because they are always subordinate to the intention of the parties. But there is nothing in the contracts in this case indicating an intention inconsistent with the buyer's right of inspection at the point of destination. In this view of the facts and the law, we hold that it was the plaintiff's right under these contracts to inspect the goods at the point of destination and to reject them if they were of inferior quality.

[The last two pages of the opinion are here omitted. Judgment for plaintiff was affirmed.]

In BOKS AND CO. *v.* J. H. RAYNER AND CO., 37 T. L. R. 800 (Court of Appeal, 1921), there was a contract to sell a quantity of palm oil f. o. b. Antwerp. In pursuance of the contract the sellers shipped 79 casks of oil from Antwerp to Liverpool, but although both parties had representatives at Antwerp the buyers did not inspect the oil until arrival at Liverpool when they found that 58 casks were not of contract quality. Arbitrators found that by the usage of trade as applied to f. o. b. contracts it was the regular custom for the buyers to inspect the goods before they were put on board. It was held notwithstanding this finding, that the buyers had not lost their right to reject the goods at Liverpool. The finding was so vague that it appeared that the arbitrators were attempting to annex an incident of law to f. o. b. contracts; but even assuming they meant to find a custom, it was not sufficiently found, and if found would be unreasonable.

Note also JARRETT *v.* J. STAUM & SONS COMPANY, 138 Md. 217 (Supreme Court, 1921), where a contract for the sale of onions f. o. b. Texas read in part "subject to inspection" at destination. Evidence was to the effect that the onions were shipped in good condition, but when inspected by the buyer after arrival at destination they were rejected because badly decayed. In an action for the purchase price the seller attempted to introduce evidence of a custom or usage in the trade as to the time within which perishable goods must be inspected after arrival. It was held that the evidence was not admissible, as the terms of the contract were clear.

In IMPERIAL PRODUCTS COMPANY, INC. *v.* CAPITOL CHEMICAL COMPANY, 187 App. Div. 599 (New York Supreme Court, Appellate Division, 1919), there was a contract for the sale of a quantity of naphthalene flakes at an agreed price f. o. b. destination, prompt shipment from seller's factory. The contract contained no provision as to terms of payment. The seller shipped the goods under bill of lading with sight draft attached, and the buyer refused to take up the draft unless given an opportunity to inspect the goods. This the seller declined to allow. In an action by the buyer for breach of contract, judgment for defendant reversed. "Inasmuch as there was no provision in the agreement between the parties inconsistent with the right of inspection before acceptance and payment, the seller could not deprive the buyer of that right by adopting a method of collection not provided in the agreement." Dowling, J., dissented on the ground that the case came within the provisions of Sec. 47 (3) of the Uniform Sales Act.

BIDDELL BROTHERS *v.* E. CLEMENS HORST COMPANY

COURT OF APPEAL, 1911

[*Law Reports,* [1911] 1 *King's Bench,* 934]

[Only the dissenting opinion of Kennedy, L. J., later adopted unanimously by the House of Lords in [1912] A. C. 18 is given.]

KENNEDY L.J. This is an appeal of the plaintiffs in the action against the judgment of Hamilton J. sitting as a judge without a jury for the trial of commercial cases in the King's Bench Division. The action before him comprised a claim of the plaintiffs for damages for breaches of two contracts, partly typewritten and partly printed, and a counter-claim of the defendants for breaches of the same contracts.

So far as regards the claim of the plaintiffs, which Hamilton J. has dismissed, his judgment was in my opinion right, and but for the contrary opinion of the other members of this Court, from whom I have the misfortune to differ, I should have ventured to think the case a reasonably simple one.

The material terms of the two contracts, with the conflicting contentions of the litigants thereon, are carefully stated by Hamilton J. in the opening portion of his judgment ([1911] 1 K. B. 214; 16 Com. Cas. 12, 13), and it is needless for me to repeat them here at length. It is sufficient, in order to make clear the reasoning of my judgment, to summarize the statement of the learned judge. Each of the contracts in question is a contract for the sale of foreign hops of specified quality, to be shipped by the defendants, the sellers, from the Pacific Coast to Sunderland, and to be paid by for by the plaintiffs, the purchasers, at the rate of 90*s.* sterling per 112 lbs., c. i. f. to London, Liverpool, or Hull, terms net cash. No point arises, as the learned judge states, upon the question of the calculation of freight being to London, Liverpool, or Hull, while the shipment was to Sunderland. Possibly the explanation of this arrangement is that Messrs. C. Vaux & Sons, Limited, the original purchasers, who assigned their interest under the contracts to the plaintiffs, carried on business at Sunderland. Anyhow, the fact is, as it has been treated throughout the argument, immaterial. The dispute between the parties is as to the conditions under which, according to the true interpretation of these contracts, the price is to be paid. The plaintiffs' case is that the price was not to be paid until they had been given an opportunity of inspecting the shipment, which could not be given until after its arrival in this country. The defendants contend that the plaintiffs' obligation was to pay for the hops, whether they arrived or not, against tender of the shipping documents. I agree with Hamilton J., and indeed it was not disputed on the argument before us, that the plaintiffs in the correspondence clearly expressed their intention not to take delivery of the 1909 shipment (which is that to which this litigation is confined) except upon the terms of payment for which they now contend; and, therefore, if they are wrong in that contention, they relieved the defendants from the obligation to tender, and they have themselves broken these contracts so far as regards this particular shipment. Before litigation began, the defendants, for the sake of peace, offered, as a matter of grace, to make the plaintiffs the reasonable and businesslike concession of attaching to the shipping documents certificates of quality of the Merchants' Exchange at San Francisco, or other competent authority. But this offer was rejected by the plaintiffs, and the parties, respectively, are now standing upon their rights, as they allege, under the documents which contain the contracts. The Court, therefore, has in the present case to decide what are the true conditions of the right of the seller to payment under a c. i. f. contract, if that commercial contract is to be performed strictly according to its tenor.

Hamilton J. has unhesitatingly decided in favour of the defendants. In his opinion it was unnecessary to refer to authorities as to the meaning of the terms "cost freight and insurance," because those terms are now well settled and, as he hoped he might add, well understood. But he has given a reasoned judgment to which I can discover no answer in the argument of the appellants' counsel, which was for all practical purposes the same as that which appears from the *Law Reports* to have been put forward by them unsuccessfully in the Court below. But for the differing opinion of Vaughan Williams L.J. and Farwell L.J., which, of course, raises in my mind a doubt of the correctness of my own, I should have been content to adopt that judgment as it stands. But, in the circumstances, and believing as I do that this appeal affects a large and important branch of import business, it is, I think, right that I should deal with the case in my own way, although this will involve a much longer judgment than I should otherwise have thought necessary or justifiable.

The plaintiffs' — that is the appellants' — argument, apart from a reference to certain subordinate and subsidiary printed clauses to which I shall advert after dealing with the main question, hangs upon considerations arising from (*a*) the absence, after the words "net cash," of such words as "against documents," or "in exchange for documents"; (*b*) the provisions of s. 28 and s. 34 of the Sale of Goods Act, 1893, in respect of the buyer's right to have delivery in exchange for the price and to have an opportunity to examine goods tendered for acceptance.

In regard to the wording of the contract, I do not think that the comment that the terms might have been more fully expressed helps one way or the other as to the interpretation of the contract as it stands. All that can be said is that, the condition of payment not being expressly stated except in so far as the words "net cash" negative payment by acceptance and the allowance of deduction or discount, it must be settled by the interpretation of the document according to established principles of mercantile law. If any implication is necessary, the law, as stated by Bowen L.J. in his judgment in *The Moorcock* (14 P. D. 64, 68), desires to give such business efficacy to the transaction as must have been intended at all events by both parties, who are business men. This is not a case, as it seems to me, of a contract the terms of which present ambiguity or conflict. There is no contrariety between "cost freight and insurance, net cash" and "cost freight and insurance, net cash against documents." Both the fuller and the shorter form are, I believe, in everyday use: examples of both can be found within the covers of modern law reports (see, for example, *Parker* v. *Schuller* (17 Times L. R. 299) and *Sanders* v. *Maclean* (11 Q. B. D. 327)); and, although it is probable, I should think, — and the present litigation certainly vindicates its expediency — that the fuller form is the more common, it has, so far as I am aware, never before this case been suggested that a contract "cost freight and insurance, net cash" or a contract "cost freight and insurance, payment by acceptance" may not imply "against documents" in each case. The well-known passage in the opinion of Lord Blackburn (then Blackburn J.) in *Ireland* v. *Livingston* (L. R. 5 H. L. 395), referred to by Hamilton J., in which a great master of the commercial law stated the course of business in the performance of a cost freight and insurance contract as very usual and well understood, plainly cannot be relied on for the respondents as an actual decision in their favour; for the statement itself is obiter, and the particular contract in that case contained the words "payment by acceptance on receiving shipping documents." But Lord Blackburn's opinion was delivered in the House of Lords forty years ago, and, speaking for myself, I do not recollect hearing it suggested until I listened to the argument of the plaintiffs' counsel in this case that the value of that opinion, as setting forth the relative rights and duties of seller and buyer in the ordinary course of procedure under a c. i. f. contract, wholly depended upon the insertion of "against (or "in exchange for") shipping documents" after the statement of the mode of payment by cash or by acceptance, as the case may be.

Let us, however, leave out of sight altogether for the present all question of usage or judicial recognition of usage. The application of the principles and rules of the common law, now embodied in the Sale of Goods Act, 1893, to the business transaction embodied in the c. i. f. contract appears to me to be decisive of the issue between these parties. Let us see, step by step, how according to those principles and rules the transaction specified in such a c. i. f. contract as that before us is and, I think, must be carried out in order to fulfil its terms.

At the port of shipment — in this case San Francisco — the vendor ships the goods intended for the purchaser under the contract. Under the Sale of Goods Act, 1893, s. 18, by such shipment the goods are appropriated by the vendor to the fulfilment of the contract, and by virtue of s. 32 the delivery of the goods to the carrier — whether named by the purchaser or not — for the purpose of transmission to the purchaser is *prima facie* to be deemed to be a delivery of the goods to the purchaser. Two further legal results arise out of the shipment. The goods are at the risk of the purchaser, against which he has protected himself by the stipulation in his c. i. f. contract that the vendor shall, at his own cost, provide him with a proper policy of marine insurance intended to protect the buyer's interest, and available for his use, if the goods should be lost in transit; and the property in the goods has passed to the purchaser, either conditionally or unconditionally. It passes conditionally where the bill of lading for the goods, for the purpose of better securing payment of the price, is made out in favour of the vendor or his agent or representative: see the judgments of Bramwell L.J. and Cotton L.J. in *Mirabita* v. *Imperial Ottoman Bank* ((1878) 3 Ex. D. 164). It passes unconditionally where the bill of lading is made out in favour of the purchaser or his agent or representative, as consignee. But the vendor, in the absence of special agreement, is not yet in a position to demand payment from the purchaser; his delivery of the goods to the carrier is, according to the express terms of s. 32, only "*prima facie* deemed to be a delivery of the goods to the buyer"; and under s. 28 of the Sale of Goods Act, as under the common law (an exposition of which will be found in the judgments of the members of the Exchequer Chamber in the old case of *Startup* v. *Macdonald* (6 Man. & G. 593)), a tender of delivery entitling the vendor to payment of the price must, in the absence of contractual stipulation to the contrary, be a tender of possession. How is such a tender to be made of goods afloat under a c. i. f. contract? By tender of the bill of lading, accompanied in case the goods have been lost in transit by the policy of insurance. The bill of lading in law and in fact represents the goods. Possession of the bill of lading places the goods at the disposal of the purchaser. "A cargo at sea," says Bowen L.J. in *Sanders* v. *Maclean* (11 Q. B. D. 327, 341), "while in the hands of the carrier, is necessarily incapable of physical delivery. During this period of transit and voyage, the bill of lading by the law merchant is universally recognized as its symbol, and the indorsement and delivery of the bill of lading operates as a symbolical delivery of the cargo. Property in the goods passes by such indorsement and delivery of the bill of lading, whenever it is the intention of the parties that the property should pass, just as under similar circumstances the property would pass by an actual delivery of the goods. And for the purpose of passing such property in the goods and completing the title of the indorsee to full possession thereof, the bill of lading, until complete delivery of the cargo has been made on shore to some one rightfully claiming under it, remains in force as a symbol, and carries with it not only the full ownership of the goods but also all rights created by the contract of carriage between the shipper and the shipowner. It is a key which in the hands of a rightful owner is intended to unlock the door of the warehouse, floating or fixed, in which the goods may chance to be." The meaning of "delivery" under the Sale of Goods Act is defined by s. 62 to be "voluntary transfer of possession from one person to another." Such delivery, as the learned draftsman of the Act and its editor remarks in his note to this section, may be either actual or constructive: see Chalmers' Sale of Goods Act, 1893, 7th ed. p. 140; and, as Bowen L.J. has pronounced, in the case of seaborne goods, the delivery of the bill of lading operates as a symbolical delivery of goods. But then I understand it to be objected on behalf of the plaintiffs: "Granted that the purchaser might, if he pleased, take this constructive delivery and pay against it the price of the goods; what is there in the 'cost freight and insurance' contract which compels him to do so? Why may he not insist on an option of waiting for a tender of delivery of the goods themselves after having had an opportunity of examining them after their arrival?"

There are, I think, several sufficient answers to such a proposition. In the first place, an option of a time of payment is not a term which can be inferred, where the contract itself is silent. So far as I am aware, there is no authority for the inference of an option as to times of payment to be found either in the law books or in the Sale of Goods Act. Secondly, if there is a duty on the vendor to tender the bill of lading, there must, it seems to me, be a corresponding duty on the part of the purchaser to pay when such tender is made. Very relevant on this point is the language of Brett L.J. in his judgment in *Sanders* v. *Maclean* (11 Q. B. D. 327, 337), which applies to this class of contract the same principle as was expounded by Bowen L.J. in *The Moorcock* (14 P. D. 64). He said: "The stipulations which are inferred in mercantile contracts are always that the party will do what is mercantilely reasonable"; and, if it be the duty implied in the c. i. f. contract, as held by Brett L.J. in that case, that the vendor shall make every reasonable exertion to send forward and tender the bill of lading as soon as possible after he has destined the cargo to the particular vendee, it is, I venture to think, "mercantilely reasonable" that the purchaser should be held bound to make the agreed payment when delivery of the goods is constructively tendered to him by the tender of the bill of lading, either drawn originally in his favour or indorsed to him, and accompanied in case of loss by the policy of insurance. For thereunder, as the bill of lading with its accompanying documents comes forward by mail, the purchaser obtains the privilege and absolute power of profitably dealing with the goods days or weeks, or, perhaps, in the case of shipments from a distant port, months, before the arrival of the goods themselves. This is, indeed, the essential and peculiar advantage which the buyer of imported goods intends to gain under the c. i. f. contract according to the construction which I put upon it.

But, in truth, the duty of the purchasers to pay against the shipping documents, under such a contract as the present, does not need the application of that doctrine of the inference in mercantile contracts that each party will do what is "mercantilely reasonable," for which we have the great authority of Lord Esher. The plaintiffs' assertion of the right under a cost freight and insurance contract to withhold payment until delivery of the goods themselves, and until after an opportunity of examining them, cannot possibly be effectuated except in one of two ways. Landing and delivery can rightfully be given by the shipowner only to the holder of the bill of lading. Therefore, if the plaintiffs' contention is right, one of two things must happen. Either the seller must surrender to the purchaser the bill of lading, whereunder the delivery can be obtained, without receiving payment, which, as the bill of lading carries with it an absolute power of disposition, is, in the absence of a special agreement in the contract of sale, so unreasonable as to be absurd; or, alternatively, the vendor must himself retain the bill of lading, himself land and take delivery of the goods, and himself store the goods on quay (if the rules of the port permit), or warehouse the goods, for such time as may elapse before the purchaser has an opportunity of examining them. But this involves a manifest violation of the express terms of the contract "90*s*. per 112 lbs. cost freight and insurance." The parties have in terms agreed that for the buyer's benefit the price shall include freight and insurance, and for his benefit nothing beyond freight and insurance. But, if the plaintiffs' contention were to prevail, the vendor must be saddled with the further payment of those charges at the port of discharge which *ex necessitate rei* would be added to the freight and insurance premium which alone he has by the terms of the contract undertaken to defray.

Finally, let me test the soundness of the plaintiffs' contention that according to the true meaning of this contract their obligation to pay arises only when delivery of the goods has been tendered to them after they have had an opportunity of examination, in this way. Suppose the goods to have been shipped, the bill of lading taken, and the insurance for the benefit of the buyer duly effected by the seller, as expressly stipulated in the contract. Suppose the goods then during the ocean transit to have been lost by the perils of the sea. The vendor tenders the bill of lading, with the insurance policy and the other shipping documents (if any) to the purchaser, to whom from the moment of shipment the property has passed, and at whose risk, covered by the insurance, the goods were at the time of loss. Is it, I ask myself, arguable that the purchaser could be heard to say, "I will not pay because I cannot have delivery of and an examination of the goods"? But it is just this which is necessarily involved in the contention of these plaintiffs. The seller's answer, and I think conclusive answer, is, "You have the bill of lading and the policy of insurance." It is noticeable that in the course of the argument in *Tregelles* v. *Sewell* ((1862) 7 H. & N. 574, 579) Martin B. observes, "The purchaser was to have a policy of insurance, which is usually considered as equivalent to the goods," and earlier in the same argument Wilde B. (7 H. & N. 578) asked, "If the meaning is 'to be delivered at Harburgh,' what necessity is there for insurance?" The contract in that case was a contract in the fuller form, namely, against documents, but it does not seem to me that that affects the value of those observations as to the relative rights of the buyer and seller.

I have only to add as to this, the main question in the present case, a few words in regard to ss. 28 and 34 of the Sale of Goods Act. As I have already said, my own view as to s. 28 is that the section is satisfied by the readiness and willingness of the seller to give possession of the bill of lading. I am, however, far from saying that the view which is suggested in the course of the judgment of Hamilton J., namely, that when the parties have entered into a c. i. f. contract they have "otherwise agreed," is not one which could be supported, as I hold that a similar view is the true view also in regard to s. 34, sub-s. 2. As to s. 34, sub-s. 1, there is no difficulty. No one suggests that the plaintiffs, if they pay against documents, become thereby precluded from rejecting the goods if, on examination after their arrival, they are found to be not goods in accordance with the contract, or from recovering damages for breach of contract if they prefer that course.

[The balance of the opinion, pointing out that a contrary conclusion would be inconsistent with the judgment of the Court of Appeal in *Parker* v. *Schuler*, 17 T. L. R. 299, is here omitted.]

Compare AMERICAN STEEL EXPÔRT Co. *c.* BORZONE & MARENGO, Gaceta del Foro, 6 March 1924, 20 (Commercial Court of Appeals, Buenos Aires), where it was held that in a case where the goods arrive in advance of the documents the c. i. f. buyer, on discovering the goods not to be in conformity with the contract, may reject the subsequent tender of the documents.

Note also HENRY W. PEABODY *c.* BARGUENO BROTHERS, Gaceta del Foro, 26 March 1924, 162 (Commercial Court of Appeals, Buenos Aires), where it was stated that a c. i. f. buyer who has agreed to pay against shipping documents has a right to inspect the goods before payment only if there is grave reason to believe that the goods shipped are not those which he has agreed to buy.

In COMPAGNIE BELGE SANSINEMA *c.* PILLER, [1924] Anvers 569 (Commercial Court of Antwerp), the court noted the general rule that a c. i. f. buyer has no right of inspection before taking up the documents, but added: "In order however to avoid possible abuses the law holds that the buyer need not take up the documents . . . when it is established that the goods are of a quality so inferior às to be denatured, unfit for the use for which intended, and so different from the goods contracted for as to make it possible to say that the seller has supplied *aliud pro alio*."

Refer again to MAURICE O'MEARA COMPANY *v.* THE NATIONAL PARK BANK, *supra*, p. 549, and particularly to the dissenting opinion of Cardozo, J.

HENRY GLASS & CO. *v.* MISROCH

NEW YORK COURT OF APPEALS, 1925

[239 *New York Reports*, 475]

CARDOZO, J. In October, 1918, plaintiffs agreed to sell and defendant to buy 6,000 yards of material, described as Palm Beach suitings, to be delivered at defendant's place of business on January 15, 1919, and to be paid for seventy days thereafter. Tender of delivery was made at the prescribed time, and rejected by the buyer's agent. The sellers thereupon gave notice to the buyer that the goods would be resold for his account and that he would be charged with the deficiency. Thus warned, the buyer telegraphed the sellers: "Had instructed receiving clerk to accept invoice of January fifteenth." At the same time his attorneys wrote that their client had need of the goods, and had not intended to reject them. "You will please send them in and if they are in accordance with the contract they will be paid for." Obeying these directions, the plaintiffs, on January twentieth, sent the goods again by their truck to the defendant's place of business and tendered them to the defendant, who received them without reservation or condition. The following day, January twenty-first, he wrote that the goods were defective, and that payment would be refused. He reiterated this position later. This action followed for the recovery of the price.

The jury found the goods to be of merchantable quality and in accordance with the contract. Upon their verdict to that effect there was a judgment for the plaintiffs. The Appellate Division reversed and dismissed the complaint upon the ground that the contract was executory and that the remedy was by action for the damages resulting from the breach.

"Where, under a contract to sell or a sale, the property in the goods has passed to the buyer, and the buyer wrongfully neglects or refuses to pay for the goods according to the terms of the contract or the sale, the seller may maintain an action against him for the price of the goods" (Pers. Prop. Law [Cons. Laws, ch. 41], § 144, subd. 1).

There has been wrongful refusal by this defendant to pay for the goods in accordance with the contract. The question is whether the property had passed to him at the time of the refusal. Up to the time of the Sales Act, the answer to that question would have been unimportant in New York. Till then, the seller, upon tender of goods in conformity with the contract, might have maintained an action for the price, if the tender was wrongfully rejected, though there had been no transfer of the title (*Dustan* v. *McAndrew*, 44 N. Y. 72, 78; *Hayden* v. *DeMets*, 53 N. Y. 426; *Mason* v. *Decker*, 72 N. Y. 595; *Van Brocklen* v. *Smeallie*, 140 N. Y. 70). All this has now been changed. With exceptions not now important (Pers. Prop. Law, § 144, subds. 2 and 3), the right of action is dependent upon a transfer of the property. To determine whether the property has passed, we look to the intention of the parties; and for the ascertainment of their intention, the statute has its rules (Pers. Prop. Law, § 100). Rules 4 and 5 are the ones applicable here. Subdivision 1 of rule 4 is to the effect that "where there is a contract to sell unascertained or future goods by description and goods of that description and in a deliverable state are unconditionally appropriated to the contract, either by the seller with the assent of the buyer, or by the buyer with the assent of the seller, the property in the goods thereupon passes to the buyer. Such assent may be expressed or implied, and may be given either before or after the appropriation is made." Subdivision 2 of the same rule is to the effect that "where, in pursuance of a contract to sell, the seller delivers the goods to the buyer, or to a carrier or other bailee (whether named by the buyer or not) for the purpose of transmission to or holding for the buyer, he is presumed to have unconditionally appropriated the goods to the contract, except in the cases provided for in the next rule and in section 101." Rule 5 provides that "if the contract to sell requires the seller to deliver the goods to the buyer, or at a particular place, or to pay the freight or cost of transportation to the buyer, or to a particular place, the property does not pass until the goods have been delivered to the buyer or reached the place agreed upon." The goods in controversy were delivered by the sellers to the buyer and in a deliverable state (§156, subds. 1 and 4). The sellers by that act are presumed to have unconditionally appropriated to the contract the goods so delivered. If the buyer by his conduct assented to the appropriation, the property has passed.

The defendant insists that the goods are not appropriated to a contract with the assent of the buyer until the buyer has so manifested his approval of their quality as to preclude him thereafter from giving notice of rescission (Pers. Prop. Law, § 128, subd. 1; § 129). In that view, the passage of title may be indefinitely postponed, for the reasonable time within which a buyer is privileged to return goods found to be defective will vary with many circumstances, as, for instance, the nature of the defects, whether patent or concealed (*Schnitzer* v. *Lang*, 239 N. Y. 1; *Bierman* v. *City Mills Co.*, 151 N. Y. 482). We think assent to appropriation is something more immediate and certain. It does not signify an acceptance so definitive and deliberate as to bar rescission for defects (Williston, Sales, § 482). It signifies the buyer's willingness to take as his own the goods appropriated by the seller, subject to rescission and return if defects are afterwards discovered. The cases are many in which goods are shipped by carriers who receive them for the buyers. An order for such shipment is an assent that the goods be appropriated by the seller, and title passes when they are delivered to the carrier "in a deliverable state" (*Standard Casing Co., Inc.* v. *California Casing Co., Inc.*, 233 N. Y. 413; *Rosenberg Bros. & Co.* v. *Buffum Co., Inc.*, 234 N. Y. 338, 343; *Kinney* v. *Horwitz*, 93 Conn. 211, 219; *Levy* v. *Radkay*, 233 Mass. 29). This does not mean that a buyer is helpless if the goods when they reach their destination are found to be defective. His assent to the appropriation of goods in a deliverable state is not assent to the appropriation of any goods, though of a kind or a quality at variance with the contract. On the other hand, his assent will stand, and may not be retracted, if the variance is pretended. There is no distinction in this respect between delivery to the buyer through a carrier or other intermediary and delivery to the buyer personally. The question in each case is whether delivery is made in such circumstances as to indicate assent to the appropriation by the seller. *Delaware, Lackawanna & Western R. R. Co.* v. *U. S.* (231 U. S. 363) was a case where hay was delivered to a railroad company not as carrier but as buyer, under a contract that delivery should be made at Buffalo, with privilege to the buyer to transport to other places on its route and there inspect (p. 371). The ruling was that title passed upon delivery, subject to the right of rescission if defects were afterwards discovered (p. 372). Acceptance, as it is there shown (p. 372), means different things in different contexts, and the shifting shades of meaning are a fruitful source of error (cf. *Rodgers* v. *Phillips*, 40 N. Y. 519; *Stone* v. *Browning*, 68 N. Y. 598, 600; Williston, Sales, § 482). The courts of Massachusetts, long before the adoption of the Uniform Sales

Act, upheld the rule, which prevailed in England also, that an action for the price would not lie until there had been a transfer of the property. They held, however, that where delivery had been made at the place of business of the buyer in accordance with the contract, the action would not fail because the buyer gave notice of rejection for defects that were unreal (*Nichols* v. *Morse*, 100 Mass. 523; *Roach* v. *Lane*, 226 Mass. 598, 604; cf. *Katz* v. *Delohery Hat Co.*, 97 Conn. 665, 673; *Pacific Iron Works* v. *L. I. R. R. Co.*, 62 N. Y. 272, 274; *Burrowes* v. *Whitaker*, 71 N. Y. 291; *Rosenberg Bros. & Co.* v. *Buffum Co., Inc.*, *supra*, at p. 343). Numberless also are the cases where without previous inspection or opportunity for inspection the buyer has received delivery at the place of business of the seller, with ensuing liability to make payment of the price (*Rohde* v. *Thwaites*, 6 B. & C. 388; *Leonard* v. *Carleton & Hovey Co.*, 230 Mass. 262, 264; Williston, Sales, § 274; Benjamin on Sales [6th ed.], p. 384, *et seq.*). It is not the locality that governs, but the character of the act and the implications that attach to it.

When we speak of delivery, we must be on our guard, none the less, against misleading ambiguities. Delivery to be operative as a transfer of the property must be assented to by the buyer (Williston, Sales, § 472; cf. § 280, p. 592). The seller may not force the goods upon a buyer unwilling to receive them. The buyer, when delivery is tendered, may refuse to assent to it at all (taking, of course, the risk of liability for damages), or may assent subject to the condition that he be allowed to see the goods before delivery or appropriation shall be deemed to be complete. "Unless otherwise agreed, when the seller tenders delivery of goods to the buyer, he is bound, on request, to afford the buyer a reasonable opportunity of examining the goods for the purpose of ascertaining whether they are in conformity with the contract" (Pers. Prop. Law, § 128, subd. 2). The law was the same before the statute was enacted. "The rule is that a tender of bulky articles in the performance of an agreement must be seasonably made, so that the person may have an opportunity to examine the articles tendered, and see that they are such as they purport to be, and such as he is entitled to demand, before the close of the day on which the delivery is to be made" (*Croninger* v. *Crocker*, 62 N. Y. 151, 158; cf. *McNeal* v. *Braun*, 53 N. J. L. 617; *Lummis* v. *Millville Mfg. Co.*, 72 N. J. L. 25, 26; Williston, Sales, §§ 455, 478, 479). There is a difference in other words between inspection following delivery, and inspection to determine whether delivery shall be permitted. Until that determination is made, the transaction is *in fieri*. Delivery remains inchoate while the buyer refuses to treat it as perfected. Even taking the goods in, may be so qualified by notice or agreement that possession will not operate as an expression of assent. "The buyer is entitled to examine the goods to decide whether he will become owner, and until the examination is completed or waived, he is under no obligation to accept the goods" (Williston, Sales, § 472). The examination is waived, however, in so far as it is a condition precedent to the transfer of the property, when there is an assent to delivery without reservation or condition accompanying the receipt and qualifying or postponing or neutralizing its effect. Examination prior to such acceptance is indeed, as we have seen, to be permitted "on request" (Pers. Prop. Law, § 128, subd. 2), yet even when requested, it is immediate and summary, closing, at least in ordinary conditions, with the close of the day, for which reason tender must be made at a seasonable hour (*Croninger* v. *Crocker, supra*). Undoubtedly, a right survives to examine and reject thereafter, but it survives as a condition subsequent, and its exercise does not bar an action for the price if the goods rejected were in truth in a deliverable state. When we speak of the condition as subsequent, we mean that assent to the appropriation stands unless revoked for a sufficient cause. It is a different question whether in the event of revocation, the seller is relieved of the burden of proving as a condition precedent to recovery that the goods, though appropriated with assent, conform in kind and quality to those called for by the contract (Williston, Sales, §§ 473, 278; Benjamin, Sales [6th ed.], p. 400; Pers. Prop. Law, § 100, rule 4, subd. 1). Enough for present purpose that the effect of receipt without reservation or disclaimer is to defer the examination indefinitely for the convenience of the buyer (Williston, Sales, § 474). True, dissent must be announced within a reasonable time (Pers. Prop. Law, § 128, subd. 1; § 129), but a reasonable time is without determinate limits and varies with the facts. If title does not pass when there is assent to a consummated delivery, the seller will have to bear the risk of the destruction of the goods during a period of indeterminate duration, though he has complied with his contract and the grounds of rejection are capricious or pretended. There can be little doubt that the announcement of such a rule will be a shock to the average merchant who believes that he is through with the transaction upon delivery accepted by the buyer, unless indeed he has made delivery of goods that are defective. If conflicting interpretations of the statute are reasonably possible, our preference should be for the one that keeps it in accord with mercantile practice. There is some suggestion, it is true, of a rule that may be said to occupy a middle ground. Acceptance after inspection survives, we are told, as a condition precedent even though delivery is perfected, yet at some intermediate point, before a reasonable time for rejection has expired, it fades into a condition subsequent. We find no basis in the statute for a distinction that would complicate by the introduction of new refinements an already complicated subject. Assent to delivery, unless otherwise qualified, is assent to appropriation, and thus, subject to rescission, an acceptance of the title.

The defendant argues that his telegram to the plaintiffs and the letter written by his attorneys do qualify the delivery, and in qualifying it rebut the inference of ownership. We do not so construe them. The telegram is in effect a notice to the plaintiffs that the buyer will assent to a delivery, if the tender, rejected by mistake, is made to him again. The letter is merely a reminder by his lawyers that payment will not be due if the goods are not as ordered. To state this is to state the obvious. Nothing in the telegram or in the letter is notice to the plaintiffs that delivery, when accepted, is to be subject to consequences or conditions other than those that by legal implication are inherent in the act. . . .

An error in the admission of evidence necessitates another trial. The plaintiffs' letter of January 28, 1919, contains a scathing arraignment of the defendant's conduct. It was erroneously received as evidence in favor of its authors.

The judgment of the Appellate Division should be modified by granting a new trial, and as so modified affirmed, with costs to abide the event.

HISCOCK, Ch. J., POUND, CRANE, ANDREWS and LEHMAN, JJ., concur; McLAUGHLIN, J., absent.

Judgment accordingly.

In HARDY AND COMPANY *v.* HILLERNS AND FOWLER, [1923] 2 K. B. 490 (Court of Appeal), wheat was sold under a c. i. f. contract to be shipped from the Argentine to England. The ship arrived and the buyers took over the documents on March 20. On March 21 the ship began to discharge and the buyers took delivery of the wheat. On the same day the buyers resold and dispatched to subpurchasers a portion of the wheat so delivered. They subsequently discovered that the wheat was not in accordance with the contract and on March 23 gave the sellers notice of rejection. In a special case under the Arbitration Act the buyers contended that before the date of the subsales the property in the wheat had passed to them so that the sellers had no ownership with which the subsales could be inconsistent. Atkin, L. J., after quoting Secs. 34 and 35 of the Sale of Goods Act, continued:

"A possible view of those two sections is that s. 34 limits the provisions of s. 35, and that under the latter section the buyer is not, even in the events there specified, to be deemed to have accepted the goods unless he has had reasonable time and opportunity for examining them. That seems to have been the view taken by the editors of the two last editions of Benjamin on Sale. It is there said (6th ed., p. 857) that: 'Section 35 contemplates a later stage of the transaction than s. 34 (1.). Under s. 34 (1.) where the buyer has not previously examined the goods, he is not deemed to have accepted them until he has been able to examine them. By s. 35 it is necessary to prove some further fact in order to show that the buyer has accepted them.' Those words 'some further fact' would seem to presume that it was necessary to prove that he had a reasonable opportunity of examination as well as that he did the act mentioned in s. 35. That is no doubt a possible view, but it seems to me to be incorrect. Indeed it was not so argued by Mr. LeQuesne. And I think the reason is obvious. It is that given by the learned judge. One of the acts upon the doing of which the buyer is deemed to have accepted the goods is that 'he intimates to the seller that he has accepted them.' I think it is plain that such an intimation may be made before he has had a reasonable opportunity of examination, and if such an intimation is made then it appears to me that without more s. 35 operates, and he is to be deemed to have accepted them. In the same way when he does an act in relation to the goods which is inconsistent with the ownership of the seller the section must be treated as coming into operation notwithstanding that the reasonable opportunity of examining them has not expired; as for instance where a man having had goods delivered to him turns them or part of them at once into his mill and uses them in the manufacture. In the present case the tribunal of appeal have found that the buyer had not had a reasonable opportunity of examination until March 23, a date which is subsequent to the act relied on by the sellers as being inconsistent with their ownership; but that finding is, in my opinion, immaterial. Therefore we have here to face the problem whether the act of the buyers in reselling and despatching the goods was inconsistent with the ownership of the sellers. If it was, they must be deemed to have accepted them. I should like to point out, in reference to that provision, that all the words of the section must have effect given to them. The words are: 'When the goods have been delivered to him' — that is to the buyer — 'and he does any act' of the kind specified. That means that the buyer must have got delivery before he does the act. Here the arbitrators have found the buyers did obtain delivery of 1877 qrs. on March 21, and that it was out of the wheat so delivered to them that they on the same day forwarded the various parcels to their sub-purchasers. It was however said on behalf of the buyers that before they did so the property in the cargo had already passed to them, and that therefore the sub-sales by them could not be inconsistent with the ownership of the sellers. What is the precise position with regard to the passing of the property under a c.i.f. contract it is perhaps not necessary here to determine. My own view is that if the goods are not in accordance with the contract the property does not pass to the purchaser upon his taking up the documents if he has not had at that time an opportunity of ascertaining whether the goods are in conformity with the contract. Though it may be that the property passes subject to its being revested when the buyer exercises his right of rejection. But it does not seem to me to matter much for the purposes of this case which of those two views is correct. In either view what happened here was enough to take away the buyers' right of rejection. If the possession was transferred by the buyers to third persons in circumstances which were inconsistent either with the goods being the property of the sellers at the time of such transfer, or inconsistent with their being restored to the sellers upon the notice of rejection being given, it appears to me that the transfer was an act which was inconsistent with the ownership of the sellers; and under those circumstances I think that it is quite immaterial that the sub-purchasers may afterwards, by agreement or otherwise, have returned the goods to the buyers. Such return cannot avail to restore a right of rejection which has been lost. That being so I think that the buyers must be content with their claim in damages."

Compare Descalzi Fruit Company *v.* William S. Sweet & Son, Inc., 30 R. I. 320 (Supreme Court, 1910), where the buyer examined a car of peaches on arrival at destination and, finding that they were not as ordered, wired the seller of his rejection and suggested diversion to Boston. The seller replied: "Car yours care not what you do with it . . . hold you responsible amount draft." The buyer again wired: "Will not accept using best judgment for you forwarded Boston." The car, thus sent to Boston to commission merchants, was sold for the account of the seller, but the seller refused to accept the proceeds and brought an action against the buyer for the price. It was held that the buyer had a right to act as agent for the seller *ex necessitate rei* and that in forwarding the fruit to be sold for the benefit of the seller the buyer did not accept the goods.

5. THE EFFECTS OF FRAUD

CUNDY *v.* LINDSAY

House of Lords, 1878

[*Law Reports*, 3 *Appeal Cases*, 459]

Appeal from a decision of the Court of Appeal, which had reversed a previous decision of the Queen's Bench.

In 1873, one Alfred Blenkarn hired a room at a corner house in Wood Street, Cheapside — it had two side windows opening into Wood Street, but though the entrance was from Little Love Lane it was by him constantly described as 37, Wood Street, Cheapside. His agreement for this room was signed "Alfred Blenkarn." The now Respondents, Messrs. Lindsay & Co., were linen manufacturers, carrying on business at Belfast. In the latter part of 1873, Blenkarn wrote to the Plaintiffs on the subject of a purchase from them of goods of their manufacture — chiefly cambric handkerchiefs. His letters were written as from "37, Wood Street, Cheapside," where he pretended to have a warehouse, but in fact occupied only a room on the top floor, and that room, though looking into Wood Street on one side, could only be reached from the entrance in 5, Little Love Lane. The name signed to these letters was always signed without any initial as representing a Christian name, and was, besides, so written as to appear "Blenkiron & Co." There was a highly respectable firm of W. Blenkiron & Son, carrying on business in Wood Street — but at number 123, Wood Street, and not at 37. Messrs. Lindsay, who knew the respectability of Blenkiron & Son, though not the number of the house where they carried on business, answered the letters, and sent the goods addressed to "Messrs. Blenkiron & Co., 37, Wood Street, Cheapside," where they were taken in at once. The invoices sent with the goods were always addressed in the same way. Blenkarn sold the goods, thus fraudulently obtained from Messrs. Lindsay, to different persons, and among the rest he sold 250 dozen of cambric handkerchiefs to the Messrs. Cundy, who were *bona fide* purchasers, and who resold them in the ordinary way of their trade. Payment not being made, an action was commenced in the Mayor's Court of London by Messrs. Lindsay, the junior partner of which firm, Mr. Thompson, made the ordinary affidavit of debt, as against Alfred Blenkarn, and therein named Alfred Blenkarn as the debtor. Blenkarn's fraud was soon discovered, and he was prosecuted at the Central Criminal Court, and convicted and sentenced. Messrs. Lindsay then brought an action against Messrs. Cundy as for unlawful conversion of the handkerchiefs. The cause was tried before Mr. Justice Blackburn, who left it to the jury to consider whether Alfred Blenkarn, with a fraudulent intent to induce the Plaintiffs to give him the credit belonging to the good character of Blenkiron & Co., wrote the letters, and by fraud induced the Plaintiffs to send the goods to 37, Wood Street — were they the same goods as those bought by the Defendants — and did the Plaintiffs by the affidavit of debt intend, as a matter of fact, to adopt Alfred Blenkarn as their debtor. The first and second questions were answered in the affirmative, and the third in the negative. A verdict was taken for the Defendants, with leave reserved to move to enter the verdict for the Plaintiffs. On motion accordingly, the Court, after argument, ordered the rule for entering judgment for the Plaintiffs to be discharged, and directed judgment to be entered for the Defendants (1 Q. B. D. 348). On appeal, this decision was reversed and judgment ordered to be entered for the Plaintiffs, Messrs. Lindsay (2 Q. B. D. 96). This appeal was then brought.

The LORD CHANCELLOR (Lord Cairns): —

My Lords, you have in this case to discharge a duty which is always a disagreeable one for any Court, namely, to determine as between two parties, both of whom are perfectly innocent, upon which of the two the consequences of a fraud practised upon both of them must fall. My Lords, in discharging that duty your Lordships can do more than apply, rigorously, the settled and well known rules of law. Now, with regard to the title to personal property, the settled and well known rules of law may, I take it, be thus expressed: by the law of our country the purchaser of a chattel takes the chattel as a general rule subject to what may turn out to be certain infirmities in the title. If he purchases the chattel in market overt, he obtains a title which is good against all the world; but if he does not purchase the chattel in market overt, and if it turns out that the chattel has been found by the person who professed to sell it, the purchaser will not obtain a title good as against the real owner. If it turns out that the chattel has been stolen by the person who has professed to sell it, the purchaser will not obtain a title. If it turns out that the chattel has come into the hands of the person who professed to sell it, by a *de facto* contract, that is to say, a contract which has purported to pass the property to him from the owner of the property, there the purchaser will obtain a good title, even although afterwards it should appear that there were circumstances connected with that contract, which would enable the original owner of the goods to reduce it, and to set it aside, because these circumstances so enabling the original owner of the goods, or of the chattel, to reduce the contract and to set it aside, will not be allowed to interfere with a title for valuable consideration obtained by some third party during the interval while the contract remained unreduced.

My Lords, the question, therefore, in the present case, as your Lordships will observe, really becomes the very short and simple one which I am about to state. Was there any contract which, with regard to the goods in question in this case, had passed the property in the goods from the Messrs. Lindsay to Alfred Blenkarn? If there was any contract passing that property, even although, as I have said, that contract might afterwards be open to a process of reduction, upon the ground of fraud, still, in the meantime, Blenkarn might have conveyed a good title for valuable consideration to the present Appellants.

Now, my Lords, there are two observations bearing upon the solution of that question which I desire to make. In the first place, if the property in the goods in question passed, it could only pass by way of contract; there is nothing else which could have passed the property. The second observation is this, your Lordships are not here embarrassed by any conflict of evidence, or any evidence whatever as to conversations or as to acts done, the whole history of the whole transaction lies upon paper. The principal parties concerned, the Respondents and Blenkarn, never came in contact personally — everything that was done was done by writing. What has to be judged of, and what the jury in the present case had to judge of, was merely the conclusion to be derived from that writing, as applied to the admitted facts of the case.

Now, my Lords, discharging that duty and answering that inquiry, what the jurors have found is in substance this: it is not necessary to spell out the words, because the substance of it is beyond all doubt. They have found that by the form of the signatures to the letters which were written by Blenkarn, by the mode in which his letters and his applications to the Respondents were made out, and by the way in which he left uncorrected the mode and form in which, in turn, he was addressed by the Respondents; that by all those means he led, and intended to lead, the Respondents to believe, and they did believe, that the person with whom they were communicating was not Blenkarn, the dishonest and irresponsible man, but was a well known and solvent house of Blenkiron & Co., doing business in the same street. My Lords, those things are found as matters of fact, and they are placed beyond the range of dispute and controversy in the case.

If that is so, what is the consequence? It is that Blenkarn — the dishonest man, as I call him — was acting here just in the same way as if he had forged the signature of Blenkiron & Co., the respectable firm, to the applications for goods, and as if, when, in return, the goods were forwarded and letters were sent, accompaying them, he had intercepted the goods and intercepted the letters, and had taken possession of the goods, and of the letters which were addressed to, and intended for, not himself but, the firm of Blenkiron & Co. Now, my Lords, stating the matter shortly in that way, I ask the question, how is it possible to imagine that in that state of things any contract could have arisen between the Respondents and Blenkarn, the dishonest man? Of him they knew nothing, and of him they never thought. With him they never intended to deal. Their minds never, even for an instant of time rested upon him, and as between him and them there was no consensus of mind which could lead to any agreement of any contract whatever. As between him and them there was merely the one side to a contract, where, in order to produce a contract, two sides would be required. With the firm of Blenkiron & Co. of course there was no contract, for as to them the matter was entirely unknown, and therefore the pretence of a contract was a failure.

The result, therefore, my Lords, is this, that your Lordships have not here to deal with one of those cases in which there is *de facto* a contract made which may afterwards be impeached and set aside, on the ground of fraud; but you have to deal with a case which ranges itself under a completely different chapter of law, the case namely in which the contract never comes into existence. My Lords, that being so, it is idle to talk of the property passing. The property remained, as it originally had been, the property of the Respondents, and the title which was attempted to be given to the Appellants was a title which could not be given to them.

My Lords, I therefore move your Lordships that this appeal be dismissed with costs, and the judgment of the Court of Appeal affirmed.

[Concurring opinions of Lord Hatherley and Lord Penzance are here omitted. Lord Gordon also concurred.]

Compare AMOLS *v.* BERNSTEIN, 214 App. Div. 469 (New York Supreme Court, Appellate Division, 1925), where a man went to plaintiff's shop and representing himself to be one Gorey bought a diamond ring for which he gave in exchange another ring and a check for $550 signed in the name of Gorey as president of an automobile company. The check was a forgery, and the purchaser of the ring, actually a man named Mitchell, pledged the ring with defendant for a loan of $450. In an action of replevin a judgment for defendant was reversed. Mitchell obtained possession of the ring by common law larceny, and under such circumstances no title passed.

See to the same effect FRYE & COMPANY *v.* BOLTMAN, 182 Wash. 447 (Supreme Court, 1935), where it was held that a team of horses parted with by the owner under similar circumstances could be recovered by the owner in an action of replevin from a subsequent innocent purchaser for value.

Compare PHELPS *v.* MCQUADE, 220 N. Y. 232 (Court of Appeals, 1917). One Walter J. Gwynne falsely represented to plaintiff that he was Baldwin J. Gwynne, a man of financial responsibility. Relying upon the truth of this statement plaintiff delivered to him a quantity of jewelry on credit. Gwynne sold the jewelry to defendant, who took it for value and in good faith. In an action of replevin, judgment for defendant affirmed. Andrews, J., said:

"The learned Appellate Division rested their decision upon the definition of common-law larceny, holding that where such larceny had been committed the thief acquired no title by his crime; where it had not, at least a voidable title passed.

"We agree with that statement of the law. But we should prefer to define the rule in another form. Where the vendor of personal property intends to sell his goods to the person with whom he deals, then title passes, even though he be deceived as to that person's identity or responsibility. Otherwise it does not. It is purely a question of the vendor's intention.

"The fact that the vendor deals with the person personally rather than by letter is immaterial, except in so far as it bears upon the question of intent.

"Where the transaction is a personal one the seller intends to transfer title to a person of credit, and he supposes the one standing before him to be that person. He is deceived. But in spite of that fact his primary intention is to sell his goods to the person with whom he negotiates.

"Where the transaction is by letter the vendor intends to deal with the person whose name is signed to the letter. He knows no one else. He supposes he is dealing with no one else. And while in both cases other facts may be shown that would alter the rule, yet in their absence, in the first title passes; in the second it does not."

See to the same effect PHILLIPS *v.* BROOKS, LIMITED, [1919] 2 K. B. 243 (King's Bench Division), where Horridge, J., quoted with approval the statement of Morton, C. J., in *Edmunds* v. *Merchants' Despatch Transportation Co.*, 135 Mass. 283, that "The minds of the parties met and agreed upon all the terms of the sale, the thing sold, the price and time of payment, the person selling and the person buying. The fact that the seller was induced to sell by fraud of the buyer made the sale voidable but not void. He could not have supposed that he was selling to any other person; his intention was to sell to the person present, and identified by sight and hearing; it does not defeat the sale because the buyer assumed a false name or practiced any other deceit to induce the vendor to sell."

CALIFORNIA CONSERVING CO. *v.* D'AVANZO

CIRCUIT COURT OF APPEALS, SECOND CIRCUIT, 1933

[62 *Federal Reporter* (*Second Series*), 528]

L. HAND, Circuit Judge. D'Avanzo, the bankrupt, owned a wholesale grocery business in New Haven and on July twenty-seventh, 1929, bought of the petitioner six hundred cases of tomato paste at ten dollars a case. The sale was f. o. b., dock at San Francisco; the terms, "90 days trade acceptance from date of shipment from California against regular 2% sight drafts with documents attached." On November sixth, the petitioner shipped three hundred and ten cases, and on November twenty-first D'Avanzo accepted a draft (trade acceptance), for $3,100, the price, and presumably then got the bills of lading, though the record does not show it. The cases reached New York on the thirtieth and D'Avanzo got possession of one hundred and twenty-five of them on December third. On the fourth, a petition was filed against him and a receiver appointed, who later took delivery of the remaining hundred and eighty-five. On December eighteenth the petitioner, learning of the bankruptcy, demanded the paste of the receiver and later filed a petition to reclaim it, which merely alleged that "the contract was entered into and the shipment made * * * as a result of untrue and fraudulent statements made by the bankrupt and his agents." In January D'Avanzo offered a composition to his creditors which was later confirmed, and his property returned to him. Although no answer was filed, the judge referred the petition of reclamation to the referee as special master, before whom the parties appeared and agreed upon the facts, incorporating earlier testimony of the bankrupt, and an accountant's report. The referee reported generally in favor of the petition, and the judge confirmed his report two days later, apparently *ex parte.* The bankrupt then moved that the report should be "reviewed and reversed," and another judge of the same court upon reconsideration on the merits, confirmed the report anew, and passed an order against the bankrupt for the amount of the draft. . . .

The petition was vague to the last degree; it is impossible to learn more from it than that the bankrupt procured the contract by fraud, and that the petitioner made the shipment in reliance upon it. As pleading, however, it served loosely to apprise the bankrupt of the claim, and apparently he was satisfied. From the evidence it did not indeed definitely appear that on July twenty-seventh, when the contract was made, the bankrupt was so far insolvent that he could not then have intended to pay, but we may by permissible latitude construe the word "shipment" to include the surrender by the seller of the documents of title on November twenty-first, when the bankrupt accepted the draft; and under the actual contract of sale the buyer was bound to return the bill of lading, if he did not honor the bill of exchange. Sales of Goods Act, § 20, subd. 4 (N. Y. Personal Property Law [Consol. Laws, c. 41] § 101, subd. 4). Therefore, if the surrender was procured by fraud, the transaction may be avoided and the lien restored to the petitioner.

On November twenty-first, D'Avanzo was within two weeks of bankruptcy, upon which his assets were found to have a book value of $83,000 and his liabilities $140,000. On February fifth a financial statement had shown net assets of $38,000; he had lost in ten months about $95,000. His books contained disbursements of nearly $20,000, not accounted for; he had long been selling below cost; he withdrew $1,500 in cash after November twenty-first; some $11,600 of his payments were not supported by his books; in November he bought over $80,000 of goods — far beyond his custom, though it is only fair to say that for this he offered a dubious explanation. As he paid his bills promptly and by this means had kept up a fictitious credit theretofore, there is some reason to suppose that, had he kept afloat until February fourth, when it fell due, he would have paid the draft. We could not say therefore that the petitioner affirmatively showed that on November twenty-first he intended not to pay; he may well have meant to do so, if he could go so long. But he must have known that his ability to keep going for ten weeks more was at best a forlorn hope, and his general conduct justifies the conclusion that he thought his end to be not far off.

Starting with *Donaldson* v. *Farwell,* 93 U. S. 631, 23 L. Ed. 993, it has been settled by a number of decisions in federal courts that it is a fraud for an insolvent, concealing his condition, to buy goods, for which he does not mean to pay. We have so held in four cases [*In re Sol Aarons & Co.,* 193 F. 646; *In re K. Marks & Co.,* 218 F. 453; *In re Sherman,* 13 F.(2d) 121; *In re Independent Coal Corp.,* 18 F.(2d) 1]. So has the Eighth Circuit [*Gillespie* v. *Piles,* 178 F. 886, 44 L. R. A. (N. S.) 1]; the Third (*Halsey* v.

Diamond Distilleries Co., 191 F. 498); and the Fourth [*Manly* v. *Ohio Shoe Co.*, 25 F.(2d) 384, 59 A. L. R. 413]. No difficulty in the application of this doctrine arises when it is proved that the buyer positively intends not to pay; but that is often not the case. He may mean to pay if he survives, though he knows that he is extremely unlikely to do so. If his promise declares only that he intends to pay, it would be hard in such a case to say that he has deceived the seller; and the doctrine presupposes some deceit. But promises, like other utterances, must be read with their usual implications. True, they are predictions and no one can foretell the future; the seller knows this as well as the buyer. However, a man's affairs may reach such a pass that ordinarily honest persons would no longer buy, if they had no greater chance to pay; and the seller is entitled to rely upon that implication. He may assume that the buyer would not promise if the odds were so heavy against him. He may read the promise as more than the declaration of a conditional intent, as affirming that the intent had reasonable hope of fruition. In that event, if the buyer knows that it has no such hope, he deceives the seller, as much as though he intended not to pay at all. This duty does not indeed depend upon what reasonable persons would think of his chances; or of how they would interpret the implication of his promise. But if he himself believes his position to be desperate, and if he understands his promise to mean what it normally would, the seller may rescind. *Manly* v. *Ohio Shoe Co.*, 25 F.(2d) 384, 385, 59 A. L. R. 413 (C. C. A. 4); *In re Krauss* (D. C.) 2 F.(2d) 999; *In re Gurvitz* (D. C.) 276 F. 931.

In the case at bar D'Avanzo's affairs by November twenty-first had become so precarious that the petitioner was justified in understanding his acceptance of the draft as a declaration that his ability to pay was not so far compromised as in fact it was. We do not believe that he thought his position brighter than it would have seemed to any one else; or that he supposed his acceptance of the draft to imply less than it did to the petitioner.

Order affirmed.

In WATSON *v.* SILSBY, 166 Mass. 57 (Supreme Judicial Court, 1895), Knowlton, J., said:

"The property which the plaintiff seeks to recover in these actions was sold by him to Phelps and Lombard, whose title the defendant represents. The question presented at the trial was whether Phelps and Lombard bought the goods with an intention not to pay for them. The court ruled that there was no evidence in favor of the plaintiff to be submitted to the jury on this question, and directed a verdict for the defendant. The exception to this ruling presents the only question before us.

"It is a general rule of law both in England and in this country, and it is well settled in this Commonwealth, that one who buys goods with a preconceived intention not to pay for them is guilty of a fraud upon the vendor, which makes the contract voidable at the vendor's election. . . . On the other hand, it is generally held that mere insolvency of the buyer, with a probability that he will not be able to pay for the property, although known to him and not disclosed to the seller, will not defeat the contract, if the purchase is made with a hope to be able to pay and with an intention to pay if possible. The ability of purchasers to pay for goods bought on credit is often a matter of great uncertainty, and in the absence of any other fraudulent conduct it would be too strict a rule to hold one guilty of fraud for buying without the present means to pay, if he has a hope and a purpose to pay if possible in the future. But one is presumed to intend the ordinary and natural consequences of his act, and a purchase of property without any reasonable expectation of paying for it may be evidence of an intention to obtain it without paying for it at any time. A purchase with such a preconceived intention is a fraudulent act.

"The precise question before us is whether the bill of exceptions shows any evidence of a fraudulent purchase. An important part of the testimony introduced by the plaintiff came from Phelps, of the firm of Phelps and Lombard, who bought the goods; and it may be assumed that, if the jury believed all of his testimony, they would be obliged to find that when his firm obtained the goods they had no intention to avoid paying for them, but expected to pay if they were able to go on with their business and expected to go on with the business long enough at least to enable them to pay the plaintiff's notes as they became due. But the jury might believe a part of the testimony of the witness and disbelieve other parts of it. The evidence tended to show that Phelps and Lombard had been deeply insolvent for a long time. Nearly a year before the last purchase from the plaintiff they had told their creditors, Richardson and Dennie, that they must fail, and that they owed about $125,000, and had assets amounting to only about $30,000 or $40,000. They then owed Richardson and Dennie about $40,000. Under some arrangement with Richardson and Dennie they continued business without disclosing their condition to their other creditors. Richardson and Dennie helped them to carry on the business by buying goods for them and helping them to credit. Before their failure Richardson and Dennie held their accommodation paper to the amount of between $80,000 and $90,000, a very large increase over the amount held when the arrangement was made. They gave bills of sale to Richardson and Dennie of the property in their factory, including the machinery and the goods which they bought from time to time, so that when they failed nearly all of their assets were claimed by the assignee of Richardson and Dennie. Richardson and Dennie were insolvent, and their failure occurred just before that of Phelps and Lombard. The goods for which these suits are brought were bought at short intervals at four different times, on four months' credit, and they amount to nearly $7,200 in value. All these matters might have been believed by the jury to be established, while they might have disbelieved many of the other statements made by Phelps in his testimony. If one buys goods in his business under circumstances which indicate that he can have no reasonable expectation of ever paying for them, when he holds himself out by his manner of doing business as a man of ample property, this is evidence from which a jury may infer that he buys with an intention not to pay for them.

"The difference between a purchase of property with an intention not to pay for it, and a purchase with knowledge that one has not the means of paying for it, nor any reasonable expectation of ever being able to pay, and with no definite intention in regard to paying, is slight, and in reference to the probability of payment is practically of but little importance. An intention is ordinarily to be inferred from conduct and circumstances. But to constitute a fraud which will avoid the contract, there must be a definite conscious intent not to pay.

"If it were held that there are no facts testified to in the present case which furnish any evidence of a fraudulent purpose, there would be very few cases in which such a purpose could ever be shown. We are of opinion that the case should have been submitted to the jury."

FOLKES *v.* KING

COURT OF APPEAL, 1922

[*Law Reports,* [1923] 1 *King's Bench,* 282]

EVE J. The question involved in this action is which of two innocent persons is to suffer for the fraudulent conduct of a third. The facts lie in a narrow compass. On March 14, 1921, the plaintiff delivered his Austin touring motor car to a partnership firm of which Thomas A. Hudson was a member and the only member with whom the plaintiff had any correspondence or dealing. The firm carried on an extensive business as dealers in motor cars and the plaintiff's car was so delivered to them with instructions to sell it for not less than 575*l.* Their practice was to charge a fixed commission of 10*l.* on the sale of a car irrespective of the price realized. The receipt of the car and the limitation of the authority are acknowledged in Hudson's letter to the plaintiff of the date already mentioned.

On the day he received the car Hudson, without the knowledge of the plaintiff, sold it and another Austin car to Benjamin Alvarez, a motor-car dealer in the Euston Road, he in turn resold it on the same day to a Mr. Simons for 390*l.* and on April 13 the defendant purchased it for 500*l.* from one Harris. No reflection is made on the *bona fides* of Alvarez — who was well acquainted with Hudson and had bought a number of cars from him before March 14 — or of the defendant or the intermediate purchasers, and if the matter rested there it cannot be doubted that the defendant's title would be unassailable and this action brought to recover the car must fail. Sect. 2 of the Factors Act, 1889, would be a complete answer to any claim by the plaintiff to impeach the transaction between Hudson and Alvarez and his remedy for breach of his instructions not to sell for less than 575*l.* would be restricted to the recovery of damages from his agents, Hudson's firm.

But the matter does not rest there, and it is argued on behalf of the plaintiff that the circumstances in which Hudson became possessed of the car establish larceny by a trick on his part, and that a person who has so obtained possession of goods cannot be held to be in possession of them with the consent of the owner. The circumstances relied on are that in March, 1921, Hudson had ceased to carry on any genuine business as a motor-car dealer and had embarked on a criminal career, getting possession of cars on the representation that he could readily dispose of them, but selling them at once for what he could obtain for them and pocketing the proceeds in fraud not only of the owner of the car but also of his own partner or partners. It appears from the evidence that at the time when the plaintiff's car was delivered to him or his firm these tactics had been resorted to in some fifty cases and that Hudson was in desperate straits for money wherewith to meet cheques drawn to satisfy the demands of owners of cars previously disposed of by him.

Assuming the proper inference to be drawn from the evidence is that Hudson was obtaining possession of the car with the deliberate and preconceived intent to steal it, was the transaction larceny by a trick? I think not, in a civil proceeding. I do not presume to offer an opinion whether it might not be so in criminal proceedings wherein the intent of the recipient may be a relevant factor. But here the plaintiff's own evidence is that he took the car to Hudson for the purpose of his selling it as soon as possible; in other words he voluntarily parted with the possession of it intending to confer a power on Hudson to pass the property to any one willing to give 575*l.* for it. It may well be that he was induced to do this in the belief engendered by the letters of March 7 that Hudson and his firm were carrying on a legitimate business, and in that sense possession of the car may be said to have been obtained by a trick, but not by larceny by a trick, possibly by false pretences if anything.

I think the facts of the case bring it entirely within the decision of this Court in *Whitehorn* v. *Davison* ([1911] 1 K. B. 463), and the extracts from the judgment of Kennedy L.J. in that case which I am about to read appear to me to apply exactly to the present one. The Lord Justice says ([1911] 1 K. B. 485): "I do not think that a case such as this, where, even on the plaintiff's view, there was a bailment and delivery, and not that alone, but a bailment and delivery for the purpose of the person to whom the article was delivered himself exercising a disposing power over the property, can be properly described . . . as larceny by a trick, resulting in a void, and not a merely voidable, contract"; and at the top of the next page he adds: "Not only was the possession parted with, but a right was also given to the bailee to confer the property in the article on a third person." I think the appeal should be allowed and the action be dismissed.

Appeal allowed.

[Bankes, L. J., and Scrutton, L. J., who delivered concurring opinions, were further of the opinion that as the plaintiff in fact consented to the mercantile agent having possession of the car, it was immaterial whether the latter committed larceny by a trick. Scrutton, L. J., said on the point: "I can understand that where by a trick there is error in the person there is no true consent and the Factors Act is excluded. But where there is agreement on the person and the true owner intends to give him possession, it does not seem to me that the fact the person apparently agreeing to accept an agency really means to disregard the agency, and act for his own benefit, destroys the consent of the true owner under the Factors Act. That Act intended to protect a purchaser in good faith carrying out an ordinary mercantile transaction with a person in the position of a mercantile agent. It does not do so completely, for it requires the purchaser to prove that the goods were in possession of the mercantile agent 'with the consent of the owner.' But it does not require the purchaser in addition to prove that the mercantile agent agreed both openly and secretly, ostensibly and really, to the terms on which the owner transferred possession to the mercantile agent. It appears to me to be enough to show that the true owner did intentionally deposit in the hands of the mercantile agent the goods in question. It is admitted that if he was induced to deposit the goods by a fraudulent misrepresentation as to external facts, he has yet consented to give possession, and the Factors Act applies, but it is argued that if he deposits the goods in the possession of an agent who secretly intends to break his contract of agency the Factors Act does not apply. I do not think Parliament had any intention of applying the artificial distinctions of the criminal law to a commercial transaction, defeating it if there were larceny by a trick, but not if there were only larceny by a bailee, or possession obtained by false pretences. I do not quite understand the view that there must be 'consent in law,' and if there is no contract there is no consent. There may be consent to a state of facts without any contract at all. The history of the Factors Acts is restriction of their language by the Courts in favour of the true owner, followed by reversal of the Courts' decisions by the Legislature. Willes J.'s discussion in *Fuentes* v. *Montis* (L. R. 3 C. P. 268), that where the owner had revoked his consent to the agency, the earlier Factors Acts did not apply, was nullified by legislation introduced in s. 2, sub-s. 2, of the Act of 1889; and there are numerous other instances of the same tendency. The purport of the Act seems to be that an ostensible mercantile agent, ostensibly in possession of goods, can give a good title in the ordinary course of business to a *bona fide* purchaser, provided that he proves that the owner intended the agent to have possession of the goods. For these reasons I think the question of larceny by a trick of the sort suggested in this case was immaterial, and did not prevent the operation of the Factors Act."]

Compare SWARTZ *v.* WHITE, 80 Utah 150 (Supreme Court, 1932), where one Stewart, hearing that defendant wished to sell her car, called on her and represented that he could and would sell the automobile, asking a commission of $25 in the event of sale. He took the car out several times for this purpose with defendant's permission, always returning it.

On one occasion he requested a certificate of ownership but defendant declined to give it to him, although she signed and took it with her when going with Stewart to investigate a prospective deal. Stewart later went to defendant's house, procured the key to the car and the certificate from defendant's husband by stating he had a sale of the car, and sold the car to plaintiff, a *bona fide* purchaser, for $125 with which he absconded. Possession of the car having been regained by defendant, plaintiff brought an action in claim and delivery. Judgment for plaintiff reversed. Title could not pass to plaintiff because Stewart obtained the car by "larceny by trick," and no estoppel could be raised against defendant.

In London Jewellers, Limited *v.* Attenborough, [1934] 2 K. B. 206 (Court of Appeal), it was held that where the owner of goods was induced by the false representation of another made with fraudulent intent that he could sell them to deliver the goods to the other on approval for that purpose, the case was not one of larceny by trick but of obtaining by false pretences; so that a *bona fide* pledgee from the fraudulent person obtained a good title.

BALDWIN *v.* CHILDS

New York Court of Appeals, 1928

[249 *New York Reports*, 212]

Cardozo, Ch. J. Plaintiffs, manufacturers, made contracts in October, 1921, for the sale to Childs & Joseph of 574 bales of cotton goods, to be marked and numbered in a stated way, payment to be made within seventy days following delivery. The buyers were then hopelessly insolvent, their liabilities being $2,518,000 in excess of their assets.

The goods were not delivered till December 20, 23 and 26. Before that date, however, negotiable bills of lading, identifying the goods by marks and numbers and calling for their transportation to a foreign country, had been issued to the buyers by the defendants Norton, Lilly & Co., agents for a steamship company. These bills of lading, dated November 29 and December 5, were issued in violation of law (U. S. Code, title 49, § 121; Penal Law, § 360; Pers. Prop. Law [Cons. Laws, ch. 41], § 230), since the goods they represented were not aboard the vessel and were not even in existence. The bills were at once negotiated to banks, who took them in good faith and in return for present value.

Upon the delivery of the bales in the latter part of December, the buyers promptly sent them to the defendants Norton, Lilly & Co., the agents for the steamship line, who held them as bailees for the account of the holders of the outstanding bills of lading. By this time the financial condition of Childs & Joseph had become more desperate than ever. A few days later, on December 29, a committee of creditors began an examination of their books. The plaintiffs gave notice of rescission on January 5, 1922, and demanded back the goods, then in the possession of Norton,

Lilly & Co., as bailees for the banks, the holders of the bills of lading. This action of replevin followed. A judgment in favor of the plaintiffs was reversed by the Appellate Division and the complaint dismissed upon two grounds, first, that the evidence was insufficient to justify a finding that the goods were bought and accepted with fraudulent intent; and, second, that even though fraud had been made out, the holders of the bills of lading had gained the better title.

We think a jury might fairly find, not merely that Childs & Joseph were insolvent, but that they bought the goods and accepted delivery with the preconceived intent to refuse payment when due (*Whitten* v. *Fitzwater*, 129 N. Y. 626; *Hotchkin* v. *T. N. Bank*, 127 N. Y. 329; *Hennequin* v. *Naylor*, 24 N. Y. 139; *Matter of Hunter, Rand Co.*, 241 Fed. Rep. 175; Williston, Sales, pp. 1585, 1586, 1608). As to this we content ourselves with stating our conclusion. No useful end would be promoted by an analysis of the evidence, for we agree with the Appellate Division that the effect of the delivery of the goods to the agents of the steamship company before notice of rescission was to validate the bills of lading and confirm the title of the banks as purchasers for value.

The bills of lading, when issued, did not pass the title to the goods, for the goods, as we have seen, were not aboard the vessel nor even manufactured (*Armour* v. *M. C. R. R. Co.*, 65 N. Y. 111; *Bank of Batavia* v. *N. Y., L. E. & W. R. R. Co.*, 106 N. Y. 195; *Pollard* v. *Vinton*, 105 U. S. 7). Even so, the effect of delivery when subsequently made was to give vitality to the bills by relation and estoppel, and confirm the title of the holders (*The Idaho*, 93 U. S. 575, 582; *Pyle* v. *Texas, etc., Co.*, 238 U. S. 90; *Halliday* v. *Hamilton*, 11 Wall. [U. S.] 560, 565; *The Capitaine Faure*, 10 Fed. Rep. [2d] 950). The case would be different if between the making of the bills and the delivery at the steamship, another lien or title had intervened (*Cook* v. *Tullis*, 18 Wall. [U. S.] 332; *Halliday* v. *Hamilton, supra*). The sale by the plaintiffs to Childs & Joseph was voidable, not void, and delivery was made upon the vessel, to feed the bills of lading, before notice of rescission had given birth to hostile rights (*Wise* v. *Grant*, 140 N. Y. 593).

We think the banks did not cease to be purchasers for present value because, when value was thus given, the bills that they bought and paid for were not yet united to the goods. Their standing as such purchasers may have added nothing to their title until the union was effected. Once it was effected, title to the goods was theirs perforce of title to the bills, and for the bills they had paid cash. Their rights would be no less, however, if the bills of lading were to be taken as coming into being when the goods were on the vessel, and till then as empty simulacra. The cash paid by the banks was then an antecedent debt, but the continuing duty rested on the carrier to validate the existing documents or to issue new ones as a substitute. The transportation was to a foreign country, with the result that the bills of lading were subject to the Federal statute (U. S. Code, title 49, §§ 81, 111; Federal Uniform Bills of Lading Act of August 29, 1916, ch. 415; 39 Stat. 538). An antecedent debt is value within the ruling of the

Federal courts (*Pere Marquette Ry. Co.* v. *French & Co.*, 254 U. S. 538, 542, 543; *Swift* v. *Tyson*, 16 Pet. [U. S.] 1; *Brooklyn City & N. R. R. Co.* v. *Nat. Bank of Republic*, 102 U. S. 14).

Nothing to the contrary was held in *Barnard* v. *Campbell* (55 N. Y. 456; 58 N. Y. 73). No bill of lading or other document of title had been issued in that case. The situation was the same as it would be here if the banks had paid their money, not in the purchase of bills of lading, but in return for a promise by a manufacturer or a customer to deliver goods thereafter when manufacture was completed. How far the rule in this State as to the meaning of "value" has been changed by the revision of the statutes in cases not affected by the Federal rule, we do not now consider. If it survives, it has been subjected to many inroads (*Turnbull* v. *Longacre Bank*, 249 N. Y. 159; *Kelso & Co.* v. *Ellis*, 224 N. Y. 528; Neg. Inst. Law [Cons. Laws, ch. 38], § 51; Pers. Prop. Law, §§ 156, 166, 183, 239; Gen. Bus. Law [Cons. Laws, ch. 20], § 142). We are not ready to extend it to a case where bills of lading issued without the goods, but bought for present value, are thereafter made effective by union with the goods described.

The judgment should be affirmed with costs.

POUND, CRANE, ANDREWS and O'BRIEN, JJ., concur; LEHMAN and KELLOGG, JJ., dissent.

Judgment affirmed.

In MERCANTILE BANK OF INDIA, LIMITED *v.* CENTRAL BANK OF INDIA, LIMITED, [1938] A. C. 287 (Privy Council, 1937), railway receipts that had been delivered to plaintiff by a mercantile firm by way of pledge were handed back to the firm for the specific purpose of clearing the goods and storing them in plaintiff's godown. The firm however fraudulently used the receipts to obtain an advance from defendant, who was unaware of the first transaction. On a claim for damages for conversion, Lord Wright said:

"It has, however, been strenuously contended on behalf of the appellants that the circumstances here raise what is called an estoppel, and that the respondents are precluded by their conduct from denying as against the appellants that the merchants had the right, which they pretended to have, of pledging the goods as owners, the *bona fides* of the appellants not being in question. The estoppel is relied on as giving to the appellants the substantive right of claiming a valid pledge of the goods, taking priority over the pledge to the respondents, since though estoppel has been described as a mere rule of evidence, it may have the effect of creating substantive rights as against the person estopped. Of the many forms which estoppel may take, it is here only necessary to refer to that type of estoppel which enables a party as against another party to claim a right of property which in fact he does not possess. Such estoppel is described as estoppel by negligence, or by conduct, or by representation, or by a holding out of ostensible authority. The argument has been variously put on behalf of the appellants. They have claimed to succeed upon the broad rule stated by Ashhurst J. in *Lickbarrow* v. *Mason* ((1787) 2 T. R. 63, 70) that 'wherever one of two innocent persons must suffer by the acts of a third, he who has enabled such third person to occasion the loss must sustain it.' The decision of the Board in *Commonwealth Trust* v. *Akotey* ([1926] A. C. 72) was cited as one in which it was said that the case was a plain one for the application of that principle. . . .

[See this case stated *supra*, p. 32.]

"What is there stated, it may be, would cover this case if it is applied without qualification. But, in their Lordships' judgment, it is impossible to accept without qualification as a true statement of law the principles there broadly laid down. It may well be that there were facts in that case not fully elucidated in the report which would justify the decision; but on the face of it their Lordships do not think that the case is one which it would be safe to follow. This was, it seems, the opinion of Lord Sumner, who, in a striking instance of a case where estoppel by conduct or representation was negatived, the case of *R. E. Jones, Ld.* v. *Waring & Gillow, Ld.* ([1926] A. C. 670), said (*ibid.* 693): 'There was no duty between Jones, Ld., and Waring & Gillow, Ld., and, without that, the wide proposition of Ashhurst J. in *Lickbarrow* v. *Mason* (2 T. R. 63) would not apply (see observations of Lord Macnaghten and Lord Lindley in *Farquharson Bros. & Co.* v. *King & Co.* ([1902] A. C. 325, 335, 342) and of Lord Parmoor in *London Joint Stock Bank* v. *Macmillan* ([1918] A. C. 777, 836), which were apparently overlooked in *Commonwealth Trust* v. *Akotey* ([1926] A. C. 72)).' Lord Sumner thus puts the principle of estoppel as depending upon a duty. . . .

"Mr. Miller, however, argued that the necessity of a duty to constitute an estoppel only applied to an estoppel based on conduct or negligence, whereas an estoppel based on representation was different. He contended that the mere form of the railway receipts contained a representation by the respondents to any person to whom the merchants might produce them that the merchants had the power to obtain a pledge on the security of the goods. There was, he contended, in this way a representation of authority which bound the respondents because it enabled the merchants to mislead the appellants. No question of duty or negligence arose on this view of the position, so he submitted. The document on its face conveyed a representation when presented by the merchants to the respondents that the merchants were invested with full disposing power. No authority was cited which in their Lordships' judgment would justify any such wide proposition. It is not, indeed, true to say without qualification that people are not bound to contemplate the possibility of, or take precautions against, forgery or fraud being committed. *London Joint Stock Bank* v. *Macmillan and Arthur* ([1918] A. C. 777) is a case in which the bank's customer was held liable because he had facilitated the fraudulent alteration of a cheque by so drawing the cheque as to leave a space which the forger could fill up, and thus alter the amount of the cheque. But that decision was expressly based on the existence of a duty arising from the contract between banker and customer, and was distinguished on that ground from *Scholfield* v. *Earl of Londesborough* ([1896] A. C. 514), where any duty was negatived.

Even if there is a duty as between the banker and the customer in drawing a cheque, it must be shown that there was a breach of the duty by the neglect of some usual and proper precaution. It was by the absence of such proof that *Slingsby* v. *District Bank, Ld.* ([1932] 1 K. B. 544), was distinguished from the *Macmillan* case ([1918] A. C. 777). In the present case not only was there an absence both of any duty or of anything amounting to a neglect of usual precautions, but there was, in their Lordships' judgment, no ground for finding any representation. There was no reason for the respondents to think that they were representing to anybody that the merchants had any title to dispose of the goods. The railway receipts were not dangerous things; there was no question of arming the merchants with them. It is only in special conditions of fact that an estoppel by representation can be established. . . .

"The railway receipt, though a document of title, was in form merely an authority to take delivery of the goods, and the possession of such a document contained no representation that the holder had any implied authority or right to dispose of the goods. It was, at the best, an ambiguous document. Its possession no more conveyed a representation that the merchants were entitled to dispose of the property than the actual possession of the goods themselves would have conveyed any such representation. It is not like a negotiable instrument; the possession of the railway receipt is no more significant for this purpose than the possession of the goods would have been. It is clear that no plea of estoppel could be raised in the cases where the merchants pledged the goods themselves after having obtained delivery under the railway receipt. It is not necessary to refer to cases where an agent entrusted with documents with a specific authority to deal with them for his principal, has fraudulently used them for his own purposes. Such cases are quite different."

Refer again to ISLAND TRADING CO., INC. *v.* BERG BROTHERS, INC., *supra*, p. 865.

In NASHVILLE GRAIN & FEED COMPANY *v.* COOPERATIVE ASSOCIATION, 203 Ky. 458 (Court of Appeals, 1924), a buyer contracted to buy goods without any intention of paying for them, and having obtained possession of the bill of lading indorsed it to defendant in settlement of a long overdue obligation to supply similar goods. Defendant had reason to suspect the buyer's honesty. In an action by the seller in claim and delivery it was held that defendant was not an innocent purchaser for value and obtained no title as against the seller.

PART FIVE

THE FAILURE OF THE CONTRACT: RIGHTS AND REMEDIES OF THE PARTIES

COMMENT

It would be a difficult task to attempt an enumeration of all the causes that in one way or another might result in thwarting the fulfillment of the sale contract. The parties themselves, we have seen, too often contribute heavily to their own undoing by failing to clarify their intentions. An honest misunderstanding in regard to the terms and conditions of the contract lies at the root of many disagreements. External circumstances also may exercise a potent influence on the course of the contract. The complicated operations of modern commerce, the handicaps of time and distance, the necessary intervention of other parties between buyer and seller, all combine to make up a background that is constantly shifting during the life of the bargain; and changing conditions lead sometimes to changing minds.

Whatever the immediate reason, however, a situation may arise where one of the parties to the contract feels that the other either has not performed or is not going to perform in the agreed manner. Under such circumstances the natural desire of the aggrieved party is to be put in the position in which he would have been had there been due performance. Neither party is wittingly buying a lawsuit. The seller wishes to get the contract price of the goods or, if that is out of the question, to look in some way to the security of the goods themselves. If he is obliged to dispose of the goods elsewhere he expects compensation for any loss. The buyer wants the kind of goods that he ordered and in the way that he ordered them. If he takes the goods in spite of deficiencies he would like a proportionate adjustment of values. If he does not get the goods at all he feels that he should be entitled to claim what the non-delivery has cost him. The task of the law is to respond so far as possible to these commercial equities.

For this purpose a good deal of machinery has been accumulated. Some of it, such as actions in trover or in replevin, was not designed with the transaction of sale specifically in mind, but has an obvious application under certain conditions of title or possession. In other cases, as in a claim for non-delivery or for goods sold and delivered, the very name employed is clear indication of adaptation to a particular use. In still further instances the working of the mercantile mind, ever alert to devise new means to meet new situations, is plainly apparent. The seller's right to stop the goods in transit, for example, marks an extension through commercial usage of the common law lien to cover the case of goods in process of despatch to the buyer.

Even with the tools available, however, the results achieved by the law will not always be completely satisfying. The tests that must be applied are more likely to be objective than subjective, and decisions as a rule must be based on generalities rather than on particularities. Individual peculiarities can receive little attention. This is perhaps inevitable. In the nature of things the parties have contracted with a view to performance. Non-performance is abnormal and cannot be expected to produce normal results.

CHAPTER I

Rights and Remedies of the Seller

1. THE UNPAID SELLER AND THE GOODS

A. Lien

BLOXAM *v.* SANDERS

King's Bench, 1825

[4 *Barnewall & Cresswell's Reports*, 941]

Bayley J. now delivered the judgment of the Court. This was an action of trover for certain quantities of hops sold by the defendants to Saxby before his bankruptcy, and for certain other hops which Saxby had placed in defendants' warehouses that defendants in their character of factors might sell them for his use, and the question as to this latter parcel stands upon perfectly distinct grounds from the question as to the others. This parcel consisted of nineteen pockets; defendants sold none of them until after Saxby's bankruptcy, and then they sold fifteen pockets, not for the use of the assignees, but to apply the proceeds, not for any debt due to them in their character of factors, but to discharge a claim they considered themselves as having upon Saxby in regard to the other hops; and the other four pockets they refused to deliver to the assignees. It was candidly admitted upon the argument, and was clear beyond all doubt, that the defendants were not warranted in applying the proceeds of the fifteen pockets to the purpose to which they attempted to apply them, and that they had no legal ground for withholding the four pockets; and, therefore, to the extent of these nineteen pockets, the value of which is 91*l.* 19*s.* 5*d.*, we think it clear that the plaintiffs are entitled to recover. The other quantities were hops Saxby had bargained to buy of the defendants on different days in August 1823, and for which defendants had delivered bought notes to Saxby. The bought notes were in this form: "Mr. J. R. Saxby, of Sanders, Parkes, and Co., T. M. Simmonds, eight pockets at 155*s.*, 8th August 1823." Part of the hops were weighed, and an account delivered to Saxby of the weights, and samples were given to Saxby, and invoices delivered. The bought notes were silent as to the time for delivering the hops, and also as to the time for paying for them, but the usual time for paying for hops was proved to be the second Saturday after the purchase. It was also proved that Saxby had said that the hops were to remain with the defendants till they were paid for; but as the admissibility of such evidence was questioned, and in our view of the case it is unnecessary to decide that point, I only mention it to dismiss it. (The learned Judge then stated the other facts set out in the special case, and then proceeded as follows.) Under these circumstances the question is, whether in respect of these hops the plaintiffs are entitled to recover. It was urged, on the part of the plaintiffs, that the sale of these hops vested the property in them in Saxby; that the hops were to be considered as sold upon credit, and that defendants had no lien therefore upon any of them for the price; that if they ever had any lien, it was destroyed as to those they sold by the act of sale, and that the plaintiffs were entitled to recover the full value of what were sold, without making any deduction for the price which was unpaid. It is, therefore, material to consider whether the property vested in Saxby to any and to what extent; and what were the respective rights of Saxby and of the defendants. Where goods are sold and nothing is said as to the time of the delivery, or the time of payment, and every thing the seller has to do with them is complete, the property vests in the buyer, so as to subject him to the risk of any accident which may happen to the goods, and the seller is liable to deliver them whenever they are demanded upon payment of the price; but the buyer has no right to have possession of the goods till he pays the price. The seller's right in respect of the price is not a mere lien which he will forfeit if he parts with the possession, but grows out of his original ownership and dominion, and payment or a tender of the price is a condition precedent on the buyer's part, and until he makes such payment or tender he has no right to the possession. If goods are sold upon credit, and nothing is agreed upon as to the time of delivering the goods, the vendee is immediately entitled to the possession, and the right of possession and the right of property vest at once in him; but his right of possession is not absolute, it is liable to be defeated if he becomes insolvent before he obtains possession, *Tooke* v. *Hollingworth* (5 T. R. 215). Whether default in payment when the credit expires will destroy his right of possession, if he has not before that time obtained actual possession, and put him in the same situation as if there had been no bargain for credit, it is not now necessary to enquire, because this is a case of insolvency, and in case of insolvency the point seems to be perfectly clear, *Hanson* v. *Meyer* (6 East, 614). If the seller has dispatched the goods to the buyer, and insolvency occurs, he has a right in virtue of his original ownership to stop them *in transitu*, *Mason* v. *Lickbarrow* (1 H. Bl. 357), *Ellis* v. *Hunt* (3 T. R. 464), *Hodgson* v. *Loy* (7 T. R. 440), *Inglis and others* v. *Usherwood* (1 East, 515), *Bohtlingk* v. *Inglis* (3 East, 381). Why? Because the property is vested in the buyer, so as to subject him to the risk of any accident; but he has not an indefeasible right to the possession, and his insolvency, without payment of the price, defeats that right. And if this be the case after he has dispatched the goods, and whilst they are *in transitu, a fortiori,* is it when he has never parted with the goods, and when no *transitus* has begun. The buyer, or those who stand in his place, may still obtain the right of possession if they will pay or tender the price, or they may still act upon their right of property if any thing unwarrantable is done to that right. If, for instance, the original vendor sell when he ought not, they may bring a special action against him for the injury they sustain by such wrongful sale, and recover damages to the extent of that injury; but they can maintain no action in which right of property and right of possession are both requisite, unless they have both those rights, *Gordon* v. *Harper* (7 T. R. 9). Trover is an action of that description, it requires right of property and right of possession to support it. And this is an answer to the argument upon the charge of warehouse rent, and the non-rescinding of the sale. If the defendants were forced to keep the hops in their warehouse longer than Saxby had a right to require them, they were entitled to charge him with that expense, but that charge gave him no better right of possession than he would have had if that charge had not been made. Indeed that charge was not made until after the bankruptcy, and until the defendants insisted that the right of possession was transferred to their second vendee. Then as to the non-rescinding of the sale, what can be its effect? It is nothing more than insisting that the defendants will not release Saxby from the obligation of his purchase, but it will give him no right beyond the right his purchase gave, and that is a right to have the possession on payment of the price. As that price has not been paid or tendered, we are of opinion that this action, which is not an action for special damage by a wrongful sale, but an action of trover cannot, as to those hops, be maintained. The verdict must, therefore, be for the plaintiffs for the sum of 91*l.* 19*s.* 5*d.* only.

Judgment for the plaintiff.

In MILES *v.* GORTON, 2 C. & M. 504 (Exchequer of Pleas, 1834), Bayley, B., said: "The general rule of law is, that where there is a sale of goods, and nothing is specified as to delivery or payment, although everything may have been done so as to devest the property out of the vendor, and so as to throw upon the vendee all risk attendant upon the goods, still there results to the vendor out of the original contract a right to retain the goods until payment of the price."

POOR *v.* AMERICAN LOCOMOTIVE CO.

CIRCUIT COURT OF APPEALS, SEVENTH CIRCUIT, 1933

[67 *Federal Reporter* (*Second Series*), 626]

This appeal is from a decree which gave appellee a purchase money lien on goods manufactured by it for the Bradford Corporation for which a receiver was appointed on June 2, 1932. In such receivership proceedings, appellee filed a claim for $37,419.84 and sought a lien on goods by it manufactured and not disposed of when the receivership proceedings were instituted. By agreement of the parties, the property was sold with an understanding that the lien, if any, should attach to the proceeds of the sale instead of to the property.

The contractual relations of the parties began in 1922, when appellee undertook for a year to manufacture all the throttle valves and parts which the Bradford Corporation would require. This latter company owned dies, jigs, templates, and patterns pertaining to the manufacture of valves or parts thereof, some of which were covered by patents. It sold the manufactured product to the trade, and the contract with appellee was one for the manufacture of the valves, etc., which the Bradford Corporation sold.

By this contract, appellee, the manufacturer, was to furnish free of charge adequate storage space for the contractor's stock of completed valves, as well as for its dies, jigs, etc., and to maintain a stock of manufactured parts "equal to a thirty (30) days' supply" based upon the sales of the preceding year. It also agreed to furnish desk room for the contractor's representative, who, as Bradford's authorized representative, was to give advice and assistance in the manufacture, assembling, and shipment of valves and who was to inspect the valves and parts as soon as manufactured and to accept or reject the same.

The manufacturer was to box and ship out the valves, etc., upon orders from the contractor, for which it was to receive no compensation "except for boxing and packing on the following basis," etc. After the lapse of one year, the contract was to remain in force "from month to month thereafter until receipt of thirty (30) days' written notice" by either party. The contract was never terminated. During its life, the manufacturer produced goods, aggregating $1,171,215.78. All were accepted and all were paid for, save the balance of $37,366.37, the correctness of which is not disputed.

Controversy arises over appellee's asserted possession of manufactured goods in the stock room (a possession which appellee asserts and appellant denies), the solution of which issue is determined by three or four provisions of the contract: to-wit, the provision which necessitated the maintenance of a stock of manufactured parts equal to thirty days' supply; the provision which called for immediate inspection and acceptance of the goods manufactured and for payment in thirty days; the provision which provided for the furnishing by appellee of adequate storage space for stock on hand; and the provision which obligated appellee to pack the goods and transport them to the depot when orders came in.

The room allocated to the Bradford Corporation for storage of its dies, jigs, etc., and its accumulated stock of throttle valves was continuously and exclusively used by it for such purpose. Its representative had desk room in appellee's factory, had the keys to the storage room, and used the same for entrance to the room in filling orders and in helping to remove the goods therefrom. Appellee's local plant superintendent also had a key to said room, but it was the understanding of the parties that such key should not be used except for limited purposes. Some very heavy parts were stored on the floor of the plant and outside the storage room, because there was not sufficient space in the latter. Appellee, at all times, had possession of the key to the front office or gate of the plant, and the Bradford representative had no key which would admit him into the plant.

The parties entered into an agreed statement of facts. The part dealing with possession is set forth verbatim:

"The said plant (American Locomotive Company) at Richmond consists of a main building, several smaller buildings and adjacent land, all surrounded by a fence with a gate to permit entrance, except for short distances where the wall of the building is on the property line. The front of the office is not surrounded by a fence but is entered by a door leading to the property. The room in which the goods of The Bradford Corporation were stored was in the main building. Said room was on a corridor of the main building. The representative of The Bradford Corporation had possession of a key to said room, but did not have keys to the front office or to the gate; and said representative used said key for entrance to said room for placing finished goods therein and for removing goods therefrom when filling orders. It was impossible for the representative of The Bradford Corporation to reach said room, unless by the use of force, without entering upon the premises through a door or gate to which the American Locomotive Company alone had keys. Mr. Bliss, Local Plant Superintendent of the American Locomotive Company, at all times had keys to said room; but it was understood between the parties that such keys should be used for purpose of maintaining and repairing the building and in case of emergency, such as fire, and should not in the usual course of business be used to take property out of the room and they were not so used prior to appointment of Receiver herein. The entire plant was continually patrolled by watchmen in the employ of the Locomotive Company. When the gate and front door were open, watchmen in the employ of the Locomotive Company were always present. * * *

"American Locomotive Company at all times had the physical power to physically exclude The Bradford Corporation from any access to such goods or such room, particularly by virtue of its control over the outer enclosure and over the entire premises upon which its plant was situated, in which plant was enclosed such room."

Orders were filled from the stock on hand without regard to the date of manufacture. As a result, part of the stock on hand at the time the receiver was appointed was fully paid for. The parties agreed that "on account of this provision and the placing and filling of stock orders from time to time, part of the goods remaining in storage when the Receiver was appointed had been there for several years and had been paid for in the usual course of business as The Bradford Corporation made payments on its open account with American Locomotive Company. The rest of the goods were not paid for. The paid for goods and the unpaid for goods were mingled without distinction. As the goods were standard, it is now impossible to distinguish between the paid for and unpaid for goods."

EVANS, Circuit Judge (after stating the facts as above).

One of the sharply controverted and determinative issues on this appeal is that of possession.

In the instant case it is clear that title to the goods upon which appellee claims a lien had passed to the Bradford Corporation. It is equally clear that the passing of title from vendor does not preclude the existence of a vendor's lien. In fact there is no need for a lien, and none exists, save when title has passed. See sections 53–56, of the Uniform Sales Act (Smith-Hurd Rev. St. Ill. 1933, c. 121½, §§ 53–56).

But in order to successfully assert a lien, there must be possession of some sort in the vendor. *Bowman* v. *Adams,* 45 Idaho 217, 261 P. 679; *Centola* v. *Italian Discount, etc., Co.,* 135 Misc. 697, 238 N. Y. S. 245; In re Jarnol (D. C.) 283 F. 547.

The two questions are, then: What possession must the vendor have to successfully maintain a vendor's lien? Do the facts in the instant case disclose such possession in appellee, the vendor?

Appellant's counsel asserts that he has no quarrel with the rule announced by text writers and the courts. He contends, however, that judicial precedents are of little value to either party fo reach case must rest on its own fact basis. With the latter postulate, we agree. The issue turns upon the question of possession which is one of fact — of physical facts, supplemented by the understanding and intention of the parties whose acts are under review.

Apparently, we have a borderline case.

Appellant relies strongly and with much justification upon the clause in the agreement:

"* * * As parts are completed by the Manufacturer, they shall be promptly inspected and accepted by the Contractor's representative, and shall be delivered to the Contractor at the Manufacturer's Works at Richmond, Virginia. The Manufacturer shall furnish desk room to the Contractor's representative, who shall, when requested by the Manufacturer, aid by his advice and assistance in the manufacture, assembling and shipment hereunder of valves and parts thereof."

Meeting this evidence squarely, what is the meaning of the words "shall be delivered to the Contractor at the Manufacturer's Works at Richmond, Virginia"? If the word "delivered" be given the meaning sometimes attributed to it, namely, a complete transfer of possession, the discussion may well come to an end, and the issue settled in favor of appellant. But the same agreement provided:

"The Manufacturer shall deliver all parts ordered to railroad freight houses located in Richmond, Virginia, without additional charges, except for boxing and packing on the following basis: * * *."

. . . Both words "delivered" and "possession" may be used by contracting parties, not anticipating financial trouble, in a somewhat colloquial sense, which the courts must interpret in the light of the surrounding facts. The parties may be their own lexicographers, and the courts must interpret their contracts accordingly. However, they must give us their definition of the words and terms by them used; otherwise we will give them the meaning which the contracted action of the parties justifies and necessitates. Where the parties use one word, such as "delivered" in two places in their contract, and the legal consequences of the act in the two instances are at direct variance, we must look to the entire agreement to ascertain whether the word divested the acting party of physical possession of the chattels and passed the same into the uncontrolled possession of the deliveree. . . .

Our conclusion is that the parties in the section above quoted and relied upon by appellant referred to the act which transferred the legal title and that the other above-quoted provision of this agreement showed that the manufacturer retained such physical possession and control of the goods as to permit it to fill its written obligation to "deliver all parts ordered to the railroad freight houses located at Richmond, Virginia, without additional charges."

Appellant's counsel earnestly argue that the manufacturer, in making these deliveries, acted as agent for the Bradford Company and therefore this proviso did not defeat his contention that possession passed under the previous proviso. We are unable to accept this view. The contract required the vendor to (a) manufacture the goods, (b) furnish a room free of charge for storage of goods manufactured and accepted, and (c) pack, box, and deliver the goods to the depot upon orders from the vendee. We can not say that in performing any part of its agreement, it was acting as the agent of the vendee. Rather must we conclude that it was carrying out its written agreement to manufacture and deliver the goods covered by the contract. Until the goods reached the freight depot, there was still some lawful possession in the vendor.

It is not necessary that the vendor's possession be complete or exclusive. Vendor's possession is sufficient to support a lien if the goods have not passed into the uncontrolled possession of the vendee.

We may approach this question of possession and vendor's lien from another angle. The property in question was without doubt at one time in the vendor's possession. If there be such a thing as a genesis of possession, it is in the maker — the manufacturer of the chattel — who in this case was also the vendor. Title and possession were both in it at one time. It could and did divest itself of title by sale and yet retain a lien — a lien for unpaid purchase price. This was done unless it parted with possession or "sold on credit." As it is conceded that the lien was not lost by sale on credit, its defeat must be traceable to a loss of possession.

Possession then was originally in the vendor. The goods thereafter never passed from under its roof. The key to the building was always exclusively in the vendor's pocket. By their agreement, the vendor was to deliver the goods when orders were received. It was holding such goods awaiting such orders when the vendee became insolvent and a receiver was appointed.

The most that can be said in favor of the transfer of complete possession is that the contract speaks of "delivery" twice. In one instance, it is consistent with uncontrolled possession in the vendee; while in the other instance, it presupposes possession in the vendor. Possession will be presumed to continue until it has changed, and in this case the physical facts, coupled with the conflicting use of the word "delivered," support the presumption of continuity of possession.

There are two other provisions of the contract which have some bearing on this question. They bear on the parties' intention, which can not be ignored. Likewise, the character of the possession and the significance of the physical facts may be somewhat clarified by such understandings or intentions.

In the instant case the parties agreed that the goods should be manufactured in advance of order and that a thirty day requirement of stock should be carried. Another provision required that payment be made within thirty days from the date of the invoice. Is there any significance in the fact that the time limit in both cases is thirty days? Does it not signify that the parties contemplated that the goods be paid for prior to their going out of appellee's factory?

Little need be said on the second point which is based on the facts set forth in the stipulation as follows:

"* * * The Bradford Corporation from time to time gave to American Locomotive Company what was known as 'stock orders' whereby a larger number of valves or parts were manufactured than were needed for immediate sale * * *; and this placing of stock orders was to further carry out the contract provision that The Bradford Corporation should maintain a stock of manufactured parts equal to a thirty days supply based upon the consumption for the next preceding year; and on account of this provision and the placing and filling of stock orders from time to time, part of the goods remaining in storage when the Receiver was appointed had been there for several years and had been paid for in the usual course of business. * * * The rest of the goods were not paid for. The paid for goods and the unpaid for goods were mingled without distinction. As the goods were standard, it is now impossible to distinguish between the paid for and unpaid for goods."

Appellant's argument is that appellee "permitted and actually aided and assisted in intermingling valves furnished under the contract and fully paid for with the same kind of valves not paid for, in the same room, so that their identities could not be ascertained," and it thereby waived and lost its claim for a vendor's lien.

In disposing of this contention the significant fact is that the vendor's lien, if it exist at all, is traceable to a single contract. All goods were made under this original and only contract of the parties. Although it covered but one year, it was self-perpetuating and remained in force until one of the parties gave written notice of its election to terminate. Such written notice was never given.

Upon such a fact situation, the vendor's lien for the unpaid balance extended to all goods in its possession. It is immaterial that some of the goods were paid for and some were not. *McElwee* v. *Metropolitan Lumber Co.* (C. C. A.) 69 F. 302; *Lane* v. *Old Colony & Fall River R. Co.*, 14 Gray (80 Mass.) 143; *Bunney* v. *Poyntz*, 4 B. & Ad. 568.

Appellee's unpaid balance was $37,366. The goods upon which it claimed a lien were not worth this amount. The sum of $25,000 was realized from their sale, to which sale the parties agreed. Appellee's inability to distinguish between the goods on hand which had been paid for and the goods recently manufactured and unpaid for, is of no consequence. Its lien, if any existed at all, was for the unpaid balance and extended to any goods in its possession, whether paid for or not.

As far as the lien was concerned, there could be no intermingling of property upon which a lien existed with property upon which no lien existed, for the reason that there was here no property involved which was free from the lien. It is unnecessary, therefore, to study or analyze the facts upon which appellant relies to sustain the statement that the vendor "intermingled" the lien goods with those unburdened by a lien.

The decree is affirmed.

Note also GREAT EASTERN RAILWAY COMPANY *v.* LORD'S TRUSTEE, [1909] A. C. 109 (House of Lords, 1908), where it was held that a railroad preserved its right of detainer over coal carried even after the coal had been unloaded from the cars and stacked in spaces in the station yard adjoining the tracks that had been definitely allocated to the owner of the coal for that purpose by the railroad in return for a fixed rental. In the Court of Appeal ([1908] 2 K. B. 54, 63), Fletcher Moulton, L. J., had said: "A lien under English law is a very peculiar right, but its precise nature has been conclusively settled by a long line of decisions. In contrast to the operations of pledging or pawning the creation of the lien does not, strictly speaking, give to the holder any property in the goods subject to it: per Lord Esher in *Yungmann* v. *Briesemann* ((1892) 67 L. T. 642). It is merely a right to retain the goods until the amount of the lien has been paid. During the period that the goods are so retained the true owner may be in very complete possession of the goods and have and exercise over them most of the ordinary powers of an owner; and indeed in my opinion it is correct to say that there is nothing in English law which prevents his possessing and exercising any and every right of an owner in possession which is not inconsistent with the maintenance by the holder of the lien of his right to retain."

CRUMMEY *v.* RAUDENBUSH

MINNESOTA SUPREME COURT, 1893

[55 *Minnesota Reports*, 426]

MITCHELL, J. Stated according to its legal effect, the contract, upon which this action was brought, was an executory one for the sale of a piano by defendant to plaintiff, a part of the price being paid at the date of the contract, and the balance to be paid in quarterly installments from and after the date of the delivery of the piano. The action is for damages for a refusal to supply the piano according to the contract. It is not alleged that the balance of the price has ever been paid or tendered, the plaintiff standing on the terms of the contract that it was to be furnished on credit. Much of the answer consists of entirely irrelevant matters, the only defense alleged being that since the making of the contract the plaintiff had become, and still is, insolvent, and the only important question in the case is whether the defendant has established a defense justifying his refusal to deliver the piano on that ground.

Where a vendor contracts to sell personal property on credit, he thereby agrees to waive his lien for the purchase money; but he does so on the implied condition that the vendee shall keep his credit good. If, therefore, before payment, and while the vendor still retains possession of the property, he discovers that the vendee is insolvent, he may hold the goods as security for the price. The insolvency of the vendee does not rescind the contract, and is not of itself a ground for rescission. It merely entitles the vendor to demand payment in cash before parting with possession of the property. Courts have differed as to the name to be given to this right, but they all recognize its existence. Like the analogous right of stoppage *in transitu,* it grows out of the vendor's original ownership and dominion, and is founded on the equitable principle that one man's property ought not to go to pay another man's debt. The right is not limited to cases where the insolvency of the vendee occurred after the date of the contract, but exists also even where the insolvency existed at that time, but was not discovered by the vendor until afterwards; and, as the presumption of both reason and law is that, where a vendor sold goods on credit, he believed that the purchaser was solvent and able to pay, the burden is on the vendee to prove that the vendor had knowledge of the insolvency at the time, and entered into the contract with that knowledge. The right is not affected by the fact that part of the price has been paid; and it makes no difference whether the sale was of a specific article appropriated to the contract, or, as in this case, a contract to supply an article of a certain description. The term "insolvent" is not used in any technical sense. It is not necessary that the vendee should have been adjudged a bankrupt or insolvent, or have made an assignment of his property. Insolvency, as applied to this branch of law, means a general inability to pay one's debts or to meet one's financial engagements. Passing to the facts of this case, an examination of the evidence satisfies us that it amply justified the trial court in finding that the plaintiff was insolvent in the fullest sense of the term. It follows that defendant had a right to refuse to deliver the property without payment in full of the price, provided he properly asserted that right, and had not in some way waived it.

The contract was made in April, 1889. The evidence is practically undisputed that for some two years afterwards the defendant was not only able and ready to furnish the piano, but repeatedly urged the plaintiff to come and select an instrument, but that he failed to do so, giving as a reason his inability to meet the payments. Finally, in the winter or early spring of 1893, after defendant had ceased to represent that make of piano in the trade, and hence no longer kept it in stock, the plaintiff for the first time formally demanded the delivery of the instrument within a specified time. Failing in some efforts to induce plaintiff to accept a piano of another kind, the defendant required some assurance that, if he procured a piano of the kind called for by the contract, the plaintiff would be ready to pay for it in cash, or give a mortgage on the instrument to secure the purchase price. The plaintiff positively refused to agree to do either, and insisted on the terms of the original contract for the delivery of the property on credit, which defendant as positively refused to do.

The evidence would fully justify the conclusion that the defendant was always willing to furnish the piano if plaintiff would pay the price in cash, or secure it by mortgage on the property, and that his refusal merely went to the extent of refusing to furnish it on credit without security.

But at no time during the negotiations did defendant assign the insolvency of the plaintiff as his reason for demanding cash or security, or give any special reason for doing so, except that when demanding the mortgage he said it was the custom of the trade. On this ground plaintiff's counsel invoke the doctrine that if a person, when called upon to deliver, places his right to retain the goods upon a ground inconsistent with a claim by virtue of a specific lien, this is a waiver of the lien; and that on the trial he will not be permitted to rest his refusal on a different and distinct ground from that on which he claimed to retain the property at the time of the demand. An examination of the authorities on the subject, from the early case of *Boardman* v. *Sill*, 1 Camp. 410, down, satisfies us that they all proceed upon principles essentially of equitable estoppel, and limit the application of the doctrine invoked by counsel to cases where the refusal to deliver the property was put on grounds inconsistent with the existence of a lien, or on grounds entirely independent of it, without mentioning a lien. Thus it has been repeatedly held that a lien is not waived by mere omission to assert it as the ground of refusal, or by a general refusal to surrender the goods, without specifying the ground of it, except in certain cases, where the lien was unknown to the person making the demand, and that fact was known to the person on whom the demand was made. In such cases, if the ground of the refusal is one that can be removed, the other party ought in fairness to have an opportunity to do so. But no such state of facts exists in this case. While defendant did not specify his vendor's lien by reason of plaintiff's insolvency as the ground of his refusal, yet he never placed his refusal on any ground inconsistent with or independent of it. On the contrary, from first to last, what he insisted on was payment of, or security for, the price of the property; and the ground of his refusal was the refusal of plaintiff to give either. True, at the last, he announced his positive refusal to furnish the piano unless plaintiff would agree to give a chattel mortgage on it, — a thing which he had no legal right to insist on; but it is very evident that this demand on defendant's part was merely an alternative for payment in cash, which he had a right to demand, but which plaintiff had refused. The plaintiff probably had a right to be informed, as he was, that the property was held for the purchase money, for that was a matter which he could remedy by payment, but it would have availed him nothing to be informed that defendant's right to retain the property for the price was based on his insolvency, for that was a fact which he could not have changed. We can see nothing in defendant's acts of omission or commission that amounted to a waiver of his title, or which should estop him from now asserting it.

The rulings of the trial court on the admissibility of evidence as to plaintiff's insolvency were not always correct, or even consistent; but the only error of which plaintiff could complain is that, in one instance, the defendant was allowed to give his opinion that plaintiff was insolvent.

We think, however, that this was error without prejudice, for the reason that the other evidence, such as plaintiff's own admission of inability to pay; the inability of others, after search and inquiry, to find any property belonging to him; and that he was not in any business in this state, of which he had practically ceased to be a resident, — was such as, in the absence of any rebutting evidence, to require a finding that he was insolvent.

Order affirmed.

Refer again to BLOXAM *v.* SANDERS, *supra*, p. 953, and to H. MUEHLSTEIN & CO. *v.* HICKMAN, *supra*, p. 524.

In MCELWEE *v.* METROPOLITAN LUMBER CO., 69 Fed. 302 (Circuit Court of Appeals, Sixth Circuit, 1895), there was a sale of lumber. Title passed to the buyer, who gave the seller ninety-day notes for the purchase price, but the lumber remained in the possession of the seller under an agreement that deliveries were to be made as required. While the notes were outstanding, many of them having been indorsed and discounted by the seller, the buyer failed. Plaintiff, claiming to have purchased the lumber from the buyer, demanded possession from the seller, and on refusal brought an action of replevin. Judgment for defendant affirmed. A lien was originally inconsistent with the terms of payment, but was revived by the insolvency of the buyer, and this revival was not affected by the fact that the purchase notes had not matured and had been negotiated, nor by the resale of the lumber to a subpurchaser.

Note also GUNN *v.* BOLCKOW, VAUGHAN & CO., 10 Ch. App. 491 (Court of Appeal in Chancery, 1875), where there was a contract for the sale of iron rails, payment to be by acceptance of drafts against inspector's certificate of approval and wharfinger's certificates. The buyer duly accepted the drafts and secured an advance from plaintiff on the strength of the wharf certificates. The buyer becoming insolvent, the acceptances were not paid, and plaintiff claimed a lien on the rails in priority to the seller's lien. It was held that the seller's lien was revived by the insolvency of the buyer and that the wharf certificates were not documents of title and passed no rights to the goods.

DUNN *v.* BARISH

OHIO COURT OF APPEALS FOR CUYAHOGA COUNTY, 1928

[32 *Ohio Appellate Reports*, 310]

VICKERY, J. This cause comes into this court on a petition in error to the municipal court of the city of Cleveland. In the court below the plaintiff in error, Ben Dunn, was plaintiff, and the defendant in error, Chana Barish, was defendant. The record shows that the plaintiff was a dealer in furniture and household supplies and at one time prior to the beginning of this lawsuit had sold to the plaintiff certain household furniture, including a stove, on which purchase plaintiff was to pay $100 down, and then $3 weekly. One hundred dollars was paid down and $3 a week was paid for some time. It does not appear that a mortgage was given upon this property, nor was a conditional contract of sale entered into, but the title to the goods at the time they were purchased vested absolutely in the defendant. The record shows that the defendant, desiring to move out of town, found it necessary to store her goods, and so she entered into a relation with the plaintiff whereby he was to receive and store these goods, and, inasmuch as they had been for a long time friends, he agreed to do it for nothing. She subsequently appeared, and upon her return wanted her goods, and I believe paid him or tendered him $25. He refused to deliver them until the whole balance of the bill had been paid, and she, not having the money, wanted him to take part of the goods and cancel the debt, giving her the remainder of the goods. He refused to do this and insisted upon keeping them until the entire account was paid. He later brought an action to recover the balance that he claims was due upon this contract.

The defendant filed a statement of defense and counter statement of claim in which she asked for a return of the money that she had paid for these goods, less a reasonable amount for their use, plaintiff having appropriated and converted the goods to his own use. Upon the trial of the action the court found against the plaintiff upon his claim, and for the defendant upon her cross-claim, and ordered a return of $100, and allowed plaintiff for the use of the goods $33 of the amount that had been paid, finding that to be a reasonable sum. Error is now prosecuted to this court.

We have gone over this record, heard the arguments of counsel, and can see no reason for disturbing the judgment. There was a clear conversion of the goods by the plaintiff. He had them in his possession and kept them without any warrant in law. Inasmuch as he was to have nothing for storing the goods, he had no lien upon them whatever, because he had given up possession, and the lien that he might have had in the first instance was lost. Consequently his retaining the goods under the circumstances was a conversion of them, and he was seeking to keep the goods and recover for their price as well

It is argued by counsel for plaintiff in error that there is no evidence of this situation. We cannot agree with him. The record is full of evidence to sustain the position, as we have outlined it. Inasmuch as the defendant below treated the actions of the plaintiff as a rescission of the contract, he having taken back the goods and converted them to his own use, she had the right to recover back what money she had paid on them, less a reasonable amount for the rental thereof. The court having found this amount to be $33, and she having paid him in all $133, a rendition of the judgment of $100 in her favor was in perfect accord with the evidence in the action.

There being no error in the proceedings, we can do nothing else but affirm the judgment.

Judgment affirmed.

Sullivan, P. J., and Levine, J., concur.

In RUMMELL *v.* BLANCHARD, *supra*, p. 234, plaintiffs sold goods stored in a warehouse for which they held warehouse receipts issued in their name and negotiable in form. These receipts plaintiffs indorsed and transferred to buyers of the goods. The buyers becoming insolvent without having paid for the goods, plaintiffs demanded the goods from the warehouse where they had remained. It was held that the seller's lien was ended by transfer of the warehouse receipts, since that was tantamount to a transfer of possession.

Note also CENTOLA v. ITALIAN DISCOUNT & TRUST Co., 135 N. Y. Misc. 697 (N. Y. City Court, 1929), where a seller operating under an irrevocable letter of credit took out a bill of lading covering the goods to the order of the bank issuing the credit. The goods were refused by the buyer, and the seller demanded them from the bank, offering to return the amount advanced under the credit. The bank refused. It was held that the seller had lost his lien by parting with the possession of the goods.

Compare THE PARCHIM, *supra*, p. 897, where it was stated that the method adopted by the seller in dealing with the bills of lading was indicative of a desire to support his lien.

B. STOPPAGE IN TRANSIT

BOOTH STEAMSHIP COMPANY, LIMITED v. CARGO FLEET IRON COMPANY, LIMITED

COURT OF APPEAL, 1916

[*Law Reports* [1916] *2 King's Bench*, 570]

Lord READING, C.J. . . . The right of stoppage *in transitu* was introduced into English law in the seventeenth century, and the first reported case on the subject is in the year 1690 — *Wiseman* v. *Vandeputt* ((1690) 2 Vern. 203). As the right arises only in the case of insolvency, it came to be recognized in our Courts in the first instance through the medium of the bankruptcy jurisdiction of the Lord Chancellor, which was of statutory creation. The right is not peculiar to the law of England; it was part of the law merchant existing in most of the commercial States of Europe before it was recognized as part of our law. In 1743 Lord Hardwicke received evidence of the custom of merchants as to stoppage *in transitu* and then applied the rule. He based his decree both upon the custom proved before him and upon the justice of the case: *Snee* v. *Prescot* ((1743) 1 Atk. 245). In 1841 Lord Abinger in *Gibson* v. *Carruthers* ((1841) 8 M. & W. 321, 338) gave a full and interesting account of the history of the introduction of stoppage *in transitu* into our law and reviewed the authorities. He referred to the opinions expressed by Courts of Equity that the right was founded upon some principle of the common law and of the practice in Courts of Law to call the right a principle of equity which the common law had adopted. He pointed out the difficulty, owing perhaps to its foreign parentage, of reducing this right to some analogy with the principles which govern the law of contract as it prevails in this country between vendor and purchaser. This difficulty, in spite of decisions and legislation, has not been entirely solved. Lord Abinger came to the conclusion that the right had been adopted as part of the law merchant and formed part of the common law of England.

What is the right? It is the right of the unpaid vendor, on discovery of the insolvency of the buyer, and notwithstanding that he has made constructive delivery of the goods to the buyer, to retake them if he can before they reach the buyer's possession. It is a right founded upon the plain reason that one man's goods shall not be applied to the payment of another man's debt: *D'Aquila* v. *Lambert* ((1761) 2 Eden, 75); Benjamin on Sale, 5th ed., p. 870. It is the right not only to countermand delivery to the purchaser but to order delivery to the vendor: *The Tigress* (32 L. J. (P. M. & A.) 97, 102); *United States Steel Products Co.* v. *Great Western Ry. Co.* ([1916] 1 A. C. 189, 202), per Lord Atkinson. Dr. Lushington adds, in *The Tigress* (32 L. J. (P. M. & A.) 97, 102), "Were it otherwise, the right to stop would be useless, and trade would be impeded." That the vendor has the right to order delivery to himself cannot be disputed, but does the notice to the carrier place the vendor under obligation to the carrier to take delivery or to give directions for delivery of the goods? I think it does. The goods have been received by the carrier to be delivered to the purchaser. When the vendor has placed the goods in the actual possession of the carrier he has performed his contract of sale and has made delivery to the purchaser. The property in the goods and the right to possession have passed to the purchaser, but the notice of stoppage operates to defeat the purchaser's right to the possession of the goods and transfers it to the vendor. Although doubts existed in the past as to whether or not the contract of sale was rescinded by the exercise of the vendor's right of stoppage *in transitu*, they have long since been dispelled: *Kemp* v. *Falk* ((1882) 7 App. Cas. 573, 581), per Lord Blackburn; and the law is now to be found in the Sale of Goods Act, 1893 (56 & 57 Vict. c. 71). Stoppage *in transitu* is dealt with in the statute by ss. 44 to 48. By s. 61, sub-s. 2, the rules of the common law, including the law merchant, save in so far as they are inconsistent with the express provisions of the Act, continue to be applicable to contracts for the sale of goods. By s. 48, sub-s. 1, it is provided that the mere exercise by an unpaid vendor of his right to stop *in transitu* does not rescind the contract of sale: see also *United States Steel Products Co.* v. *Great Western Ry. Co.* ([1916] 1 A. C. 189, 203), per Lord Atkinson. The vendor may resell the goods, provided he has complied with certain conditions, and recover damages from his original buyer for loss occasioned by the breach of the contract: s. 48, sub-s. 3. But after the notice is given by the vendor to the carrier the right to possession of the goods is resumed by the vendor; that is the effect of the notice, and the carrier is under obligation to give actual possession to the vendor only or according to his directions. To use the words of the codifying statute, the carrier "must deliver the goods to or according to the directions of the seller": s. 46, sub-s. 2. The carrier cannot be under obligation to deliver the goods upon arrival to the purchaser, his consignee, and also to the vendor who has given notice of stoppage. From the giving of the notice, and so long as the notice is operative, his obligation is to deliver, not to the consignee, but to the vendor.

IN RE ARCTIC STORES

District Court, D. New Jersey, 1919

[258 *Federal Reporter*, 688]

Rellstab, District Judge. William Silver & Co., a corporation (hereinafter called the petitioner), has brought here for review the referee's order denying its petition to recover the value of a car of tomato pulp sold by the receiver of the Arctic Stores, bankrupt. The pulp was originally sold by the petitioner to the Arctic Stores on credit. From the bill of lading it appears that the car of pulp was consigned to the "Arctic Stores, Cussen's Siding, Marion, New Jersey, f. o. b. Salem, New Jersey." The car arrived at Marion, and was placed on the siding referred to, before 7 o'clock a. m. on October 18, 1917, at which hour it was seen by the consignee's chief clerk on his arrival at the consignee's warehouse. This siding bore the name of the president (Cussen) of the Arctic Stores, and was alongside the latter's warehouse.

About noon of that day, upon the filing of an involuntary petition in bankruptcy against it, and its written admission of inability to pay its debts and willingness to be adjudged a bankrupt, the Arctic Stores was so adjudged. Later in the day a receiver was appointed to take charge of the assets of said bankrupt. On October 19th the receiver had the pulp removed from the car to the bankrupt's warehouse, and later on that day the carrier removed the empty car from the siding. On the following day (October 20th) the petitioner ordered the carrier not to make delivery of the pulp.

The referee found that both actual and constructive delivery of the pulp had been made to the receiver "before the shipper gave the railroad company notice to stop the goods in transit, and that therefore the petitioner's notice to the carrier came too late," and he thereupon made the order here under review. The petitioner seeks a reversal of this order on the ground that the possession of the receiver was not that of either the bankrupt, who, by the adjudication, was bereft of all interest in that property, or of the trustee, who had not yet been appointed, but of the persons who would be ultimately found entitled to the property, and that, as the right of stoppage *in transitu* was exercised before the appointment of the trustee, it was in time to reinvest the petitioner with the title to, and the right of possession of, the property in question.

The pulp so shipped was sold to the Arctic Stores on credit, and when it was delivered to the carrier for transportaion to the purchaser the title passed to the latter.

While the right to stop delivery of goods sold on credit is predicated on the insolvency of the buyer, yet neither insolvency nor bankruptcy of the buyer works a rescission of the contract of sale, and an effective stoppage *in transitu* does not in itself annul the sale or divest the purchaser of the title to the goods, which passed on delivery to the carrier. *Sheppard* v. *Newhall* (C. C. A. 9) 54 Fed. 306, 4 C. C. A. 352; Benj. on Sales (5th Ed.) pp. 808, 809, 816; N. J. Uniform Sale of Goods Act, *supra*, §§ 57, 61. It has been said that "the right of stoppage *in transitu* is merely an extension of the lien for the price which the vendor has after contract of sale and before delivery of goods sold on credit." *Johnson* v. *Eveleth*, 93 Me. 306, 45 Atl. 35, 48 L. R. A. 50. A more nearly accurate statement seemingly is that the insolvency of the buyer gives the vendor a right to reobtain possession of the goods from the carrier, while they are on their way to the vendee, and that upon giving notice not to deliver before the carriage is at an end he may retake and retain the goods as security for the price. See *Arnold* v. *Delano*, 4 Cush. (Mass.) 33, 50 Am. Dec. 754; N. J. Uniform Sale of Goods Act, *supra*, § 57.

However, this right to retake only continues while the goods are in transit. When the goods reach their destination, the vendor's right to repossession is gone, his potential security is lost, and his status in relation to such goods is no different from that of a general creditor of the vendee.

In the instant case, when the carrier placed the car containing the pulp on the siding designated in the bill of lading, it had reached its destination and the transit was at an end.

When the carrier placed the car on the designated siding, its duty as a carrier was ended. If that were not a delivery, what would be one on such a shipment? Certainly the carrier would not have to unload the car. It would not be liable to the vendor for failing to stop delivery, for delivery had been made at the very place designated in the bill of lading. If the carrier's placing the car on the siding was a delivery, so as to exonerate it from liability to the vendor, it is none the less so when the vendor invokes a remedy against the vendee necessarily solely predicated on the giving of a notice to stop delivery while the goods are yet in transit, i. e. before delivery made.

The bankruptcy receiver's taking the pulp out of the car the day following its delivery on the designated siding (an adjudication in bankruptcy having taken place in the meantime) was not a necessary act in order to bring the transportation to an end. Such removal was to release the car for further use and to safeguard the property of the bankrupt, which by the delivery of the day before had become absolute.

The referee could have properly denied the petitioner's claim on the ground that delivery had been made to the Arctic Stores before bankruptcy had intervened. However, as noted, he based his denial not upon that ground, but upon the ground that delivery had been made to the receiver before the stop notice had been given to the carrier.

The receiver in thus removing the pulp was acting in the line of his duty. He did nothing more than what the Arctic Stores could have done between the time the car was placed on the siding and the time of the filing of the petition in bankruptcy. In thus dealing with the pulp the receiver was not, as petitioner's counsel claims, taking goods belonging to the petitioner, but property the title to which had vested in the Arctic Stores from the time it was delivered to the carrier f. o. b. the place whence the shipment came, and which had become absolute upon its being placed on the siding referred to.

[The balance of the opinion is omitted. The referee's order was affirmed.]

In IN RE CHARLES T. STORK & CO., 271 Fed. 279 (Circuit Court of Appeals, Second Circuit, 1921), an exporter contracted with a seller for the purchase of a quantity of shoes to be delivered f. o. b. New York packed for export shipment. The goods were shipped, freight paid by the seller, and were received by a forwarding company under instructions from the exporter to forward them to order to a company at a port in the Virgin Islands. The exporter became bankrupt while the shoes were in the possession of the forwarding company. It was held that the seller's right of stoppage had been terminated as the forwarding company had received the shoes as agent for the bankrupt exporter.

Note also JOHANN PLISCHKE & SOHNE *v.* ALLISON BROTHERS, LTD., 55 Ll. L. R. 262 (King's Bench Division, 1936), where plaintiffs, merchants in Czechoslovakia, accepted an order for a quantity of linen goods, free house London, excluding duty, delivery to be made through named forwarding agents. Plaintiffs shipped the goods from Hamburg through agents acting for the London forwarding agents and under a bill of lading in favor of the latter. On arrival of the goods at London the defendant forwarding agents were instructed by the buyers to warehouse them before clearing or paying the duty and to hold them for further instructions. Under these circumstances the buyers became insolvent, and plaintiffs ordered defendants to hold the goods. In a claim for the return of the goods it was argued by plaintiffs that since the contract called for delivery at the buyers' place of business, the transit was not at an end when the stop order was issued. Judgment for defendants. Defendants, acting originally as agents for plaintiffs to deliver the goods, were acting for the buyers in warehousing them, and the transit accordingly had ended. The terms of the contract did not exclude the ordinary right of a buyer to indicate that the goods should be delivered at some other place than his own private premises. Sec. 45 (2) of the Sale of Goods Act was mentioned.

NORTHERN GRAIN COMPANY *v.* WIFFLER

NEW YORK COURT OF APPEALS, 1918

[223 *New York Reports*, 169]

HISCOCK, Ch. J. This appeal involves a consideration of the right of stoppage *in transitu* of goods sold on credit and shipped by a common carrier. The question of the existence of the right is to be determined upon an agreed statement of facts.

Plaintiff sold to one Wiffler on credit a carload of oats which were shipped to the latter over the line of the defendant railroad company. A bill of lading covering the shipment was forwarded with a draft for the purchase price of the oats and upon acceptance by the vendee of the draft the bill of lading was delivered to him. He presented the same at the office of the defendant railroad company where it was received and marked "cancelled by delivery." "Thereupon" the vendee examined and was dissatisfied with the condition of the oats and "thereupon" withdrew the bill of lading from the railroad company, caused the words "cancelled by delivery" to be stricken from the face of the bill and "thereupon" returned it to the plaintiff with the statement that he refused to accept the oats or take delivery thereof by reason of their condition and that he rejected the same.

Nothing more was done by which there is claimed to have been accomplished a delivery to or acceptance by the vendee of the oats. These, after remaining in a car in the possession of the railroad company for six months, were sold at public auction to satisfy its lien for transportation charges and the surplus of the proceeds over such charges was held by the railroad company and is the subject of the present controversy.

The draft which had been accepted by the vendee was not paid at maturity and an action was commenced against him thereon by the vendor and a judgment recovered which has never been satisfied. In such action the vendee alleged that "the draft was given by defendant in payment of a certain carload of oats which plaintiff sold to the defendant and that the same were good, marketable and useable (thus written in the agreed statement), and that when defendant received said carload the same were old and musty, and could not be sold and used, and were of no value whatsoever, and for that reason the note was given without consideration." Intermediate the commencement of this action and entry of judgment the vendee made an assignment for the benefit of creditors to the defendant Dana and thereafter plaintiff surrendered to the defendant railroad company for cancellation the bill of lading before mentioned and served upon it notice asserting the exercise of its right of stoppage *in transitu* of said oats, claiming that the latter had never been delivered to the vendee.

In the arguments addressed to us there is of course no dispute about the general principles applicable to the exercise of the right of stoppage *in transitu* and no serious question is presented but that under these principles plaintiff had the right to stop delivery of the oats to its non-paying insolvent vendee provided they still remained in the possession of the carrier under its original contract of transportation and had not been delivered either actually or constructively. It is true that some little attempt is made by respondents' counsel to argue the proposition that the surplus proceeds of the oats do not stand in the place of the latter, but we do not regard this as worth discussion. Some attention also has been paid to the fact that plaintiff recovered a judgment against its vendee for the purchase price of the oats, but this circumstance does not seem to be of importance. It may be conceded that by recovery of such judgment the title to the oats passed to the vendee and that under ordinary conditions the latter would have been entitled to take possession of them. This, however, does not defeat the right which plaintiff is now seeking to exercise. There has been at times debate whether the exercise of a right of stoppage *in transitu* was the assertion of a right in the nature of a lien against property whereof another held title or amounted to a rescission of a contract. The preponderance of authority, we think, sustains the former theory. (*Babcock* v. *Bonnell*, 80 N. Y. 244; *Coleman* v. *N. Y., N. H. & H. R. R. Co.*, 215 Mass. 45, 49.) But however this may have been, it is now provided by section 134 of article 5 of the Personal Property Law (Cons. Laws, ch. 41, amd. L. 1911, ch. 571), relating to sales of goods, that "Subject to the provisions of this article, notwithstanding that the property in the goods may have passed to the buyer, the unpaid seller of goods, as such has * * * (b) In case of the insolvency of the buyer, a right of stopping the goods *in transitu* after he has parted with the possession of them."

Thus we come to the question, stripped of accidental conditions, whether plaintiff could and did successfully exercise the right asserted by it. The tests by which to decide this question are especially found in two sections of the statute already referred to. Section 138 provides: "Subject to the provisions of this article, when the buyer of goods is or becomes insolvent, the unpaid seller who has parted with the possession of the goods has the right of stopping them *in transitu*, that is to say, he may resume possession of the goods at any time while they are in transit, * * *." Section 139 then tells when goods are to be considered in transit within the meaning of the prior section. It says that they are thus in transit —

"(a) From the time when they are delivered to a carrier by land or water, * * * until the buyer, * * * takes delivery of them from such carrier * * *;

"(b) If the goods are rejected by the buyer, and the carrier * * * continues in possession of them, even if the seller has refused to receive them back."

And throwing some light on the interpretation of the clauses stating when goods are in transit it likewise states when they are to be regarded as not in transit. The same section already quoted from enacts that they are not in transit "If, after the arrival of the goods at the appointed destination, the carrier * * * acknowledges to the buyer * * * that he holds the goods on his behalf and continues in possession of them as bailee for the buyer * * *.".

The only debatable question under the tests thus prescribed is the one whether the goods had been delivered by the carrier to the vendee. It seems to us that they had not been. The facts determinative of that question have already been stated and need not be repeated. Referring back to them, it may be conceded that if the vendee after taking his bill of lading to the carrier and permitting it to be marked "cancelled by delivery" had stopped, there would have been a constructive delivery. Also, if he had allowed the matter to rest in that situation for a substantial time before doing anything to recall this act it might be necessary to submit to the jury the question whether a delivery had not been so consummated that it could not thereafter be avoided. But he pursued neither of these courses. After the stamping of the bill of lading he "thereupon," that is, immediately, examined the oats and made what, if then permissible, was a clear and decisive refusal of acceptance of them from the vendor and of delivery from the carrier. It is only by separating these steps and regarding them as divisible and distinct transactions that a delivery can be made out. We do not think they ought to be thus separated, but that they were so closely connected in point of time and otherwise that they should be given the effect of one connected transaction. This being done it is clear that there was no delivery.

We think that the subsequent history of the shipment confirms this view. It remained in the physical possession of the carrier for months. There is no suggestion of any agreement under which it was thus held by the latter as agent or bailee for the vendee. On the other hand that which was done by the carrier, and so far as appears without objection or question by the parties, shows that the former was holding the oats under its original contract of shipment. As has been stated, it sold the oats for the purpose of satisfying its lien for freight charges and this it could not have done if by delivery it had surrendered its possession as carrier. (*Bigelow* v. *Heaton*, 4 Den. 496; *Penn. Steel Co.* v. *Ga. R. R. & Banking Co.*, 94 Ga. 636.) While in our opinion the facts which we have discussed lead necessarily and under simple principles to the conclusion which we have adopted, general support for that conclusion may be found if necessary in the discussion of the subject of stoppage *in transitu* contained in *Brewer Lumber Co.* v. *B. & A. R. R. Co.* (179 Mass. 228); *Coleman* v. *N. Y., N. H. & H. R. R. Co.* (215 Mass. 45); *Bolton* v. *L. & Y. Ry. Co.* (L. R. 1 C. P. 431); *Matter of McLaren* (L. R. 11 Ch. D. 68).

In accordance with these views the judgment should be reversed and judgment directed in favor of plaintiff against the defendant, New York Central and Hudson River Railroad Company, for the sum of $287.85, with any interest received thereon by said railroad company, together with further judgment against the defendant Dana as trustee for its disbursements incurred in this court and in the Appellate Division.

Chase, Hogan and Crane, JJ., concur; Collin and Cuddeback, JJ., concur in result; McLaughlin, J., not sitting.

Judgment accordingly.

In Rocco Perretta & Co. *v.* Ventrone & Co., Inc., 117 Atl. 534 (Rhode Island Supreme Court, 1922), a quantity of cheese was sold by plaintiff to defendant on an f. o. b. basis, the f. o. b. point apparently being the point of shipment. On arrival at destination the buyer refused to take the goods from the carrier, whereupon the seller ordered them returned, sold them to the best advantage, and brought the present action for the balance of the purchase price. Judgment for plaintiff. The buyer did not take possession and the right of stoppage remained.

In In re Nesto, 270 Fed. 503 (Circuit Court of Appeals, Third Circuit, 1921), the seller sold to the buyer a carload of macaroni on credit, and consigned it to him at Pittsburgh. The car arrived at Pittsburgh on November 12, and the buyer immediately reconsigned it to himself in New York under a fictitious name. On November 20 the buyer became bankrupt, and his receiver on the next day obtained a court order directing the carrier to deliver the car to the receiver. On November 24 the seller served notice on the carrier, claiming a right of stoppage, the car having arrived at New York on November 20 but being still in possession of the carrier. It was held that the right of stoppage had not been lost, as there had been no delivery to the buyer, either actual or constructive.

In CASHMERE FRUIT GROWERS UNION *v.* GREAT NORTHERN RAILWAY COMPANY, 149 Wash. 319 (Supreme Court, 1928), the sellers sold seven carloads of apples to the buyer. These were shipped under straight bills of lading, five of them in the name of the buyer and two in the name of one Dingfelder, an agent of the buyer who was to resell the apples and turn the proceeds over to the buyer less advances. The bills of lading were surrendered to the buyer in exchange for a draft for the price. The buyer immediately exchanged four of the bills of lading in his own name for others in the name of Dingfelder but still naming the sellers as consignors. The draft was dishonored due to insolvency, and the sellers gave notice to stop. The carrier however disregarded the order and delivered the cars to Dingfelder. The present action was brought against the carrier for conversion. Judgment for plaintiffs affirmed. The taking out of the exchange bills of lading did not initiate a new carriage.

KASDEN *v.* THE N. Y., N. H. AND H. RAILROAD COMPANY

CONNECTICUT SUPREME COURT OF ERRORS, 1926

[104 *Connecticut Reports*, 479]

Action to recover damages for the alleged wrongful refusal of the defendant railroad company to deliver a carload of composition turnings to the plaintiff, in which the defendants Louis H. and Samuel Resnick were joined as codefendants and filed a counterclaim, brought to the Superior Court in New Haven County and tried to the court, Wolfe, J.; judgment rendered for the defendants Resnick upon the complaint, and upon their counterclaim to recover $3,988, from which the plaintiffs appealed. No error.

The complaint claimed ownership and possession of 40,000 pounds of brass borings contained in a freight-car in the possession of the defendant railroad and located in the freight-yard at Bridgeport. Louis H. Resnick and Samuel Resnick, doing business as the American Steel & Iron Company, of Boston, Massachusetts, were cited in as codefendants, and filed an answer and counterclaim alleging, in substance, that the shipment involved was their property and consigned to them at Bridgeport, and that, on or about September 15th, 1924, they exercised their right of stoppage *in transitu* over the shipment, in possession of the defendant railroad company, and claiming a judgment declaring title to be vested in them or, in lieu thereof, the value of the shipment as damages. The case was tried on the issues raised by this counterclaim and the plaintiffs' reply thereto. The plaintiffs, having taken possession of the property by replevin, subsequently disposed of it, and the damages awarded were the agreed value of the shipment.

The facts, material to the present inquiry, found by the trial court, may be summarized as follows: On September 9th, 1924, the defendant the American Steel & Iron Company, shipped the carload of borings from Billerica, Massachusetts, to themselves at Bridgeport, and the carrier, the Boston and Maine Railroad Company, issued to this defendant a straight bill of lading, naming it as both consignor and consignee, and plainly marked "nonnegotiable." On September 13th the defendant arranged, by telephone, to sell the metal to the Bridgeport Iron & Metal Company provided that company would pay for another carload of metal previously purchased and not paid for, placed the following indorsement on the bill of lading: "Deliver to Bridgeport Iron & Metal Company or order, the American Steel & Iron Company, by Louis H. Resnick," and forwarded it to the Bridgeport company. On September 14th, Sunday, the defendant learned that the Bridgeport company was insolvent, and on Monday morning notified agents of the New York, New Haven & Hartford Railroad Company, in whose possession, as connecting carrier, the car then was, that the car was not to be delivered to anyone but the defendant. At the time the stop order was given no demand had been made by or for the Bridgeport company for delivery of the car. On September 15th, but subsequent to the receipt by the railroad company of the stop order, the plaintiffs, who were engaged in the metal business in New Haven, purchased the carload of borings from the Bridgeport company, paid $2,775 toward the purchase price, and received the bill of lading, with the added indorsement, "Bridgeport Iron & Metal Company, Edward Goldberg, Treasurer." Thereafter, on the same day, the plaintiffs presented the bill of lading to the railroad company and demanded the shipment, but the railroad company, because of receipt of the stop order, refused delivery. It did not appear that the plaintiffs, at the time of their purchase of the shipment from the Bridgeport Iron & Metal Company, knew that the latter was insolvent or that delivery of the goods had been stopped by the defendant.

HINMAN, J. The reasons of appeal present the propositions that the indorsement of the bill of lading by the defendant American Company in the form above stated, rendered the same negotiable; that the defendant, by such indorsement, is estopped from denying that the bill was negotiable; and that the defendant had no right of stoppage *in transitu* as against the plaintiffs as purchasers in good faith. The status and effect of the bill of lading, to be determined upon the facts found, is decisive of the appeal.

The Act of Congress of August 29th, 1916, relating to bills of lading (39 U. S. Stat. at Large, 538 *et seq.* Fed. Stat. Anno., 1918 Supp. [2d Ed.] p. 72 *et seq.*; 8 U. S. Comp. Stat., § 8604 aaa-w) provides, in § 1, that "bills of lading issued by any common carrier for the transportation of goods . . . from a place in one State to a place in another State, . . .

shall be governed by this Act." Since the shipment here under consideration was interstate, questions as to the construction and effect of the bill of lading are controlled by this Act, so far as it applies. In § 2 a "straight bill" is defined as one "in which it is stated that the goods are consigned or destined to a specified person," and in § 6 it is provided that "a straight bill shall have placed plainly upon its face by the carrier issuing it 'non-negotiable' or 'not negotiable.'" The trial court finds that the present bill of lading was a straight bill, and plainly marked nonnegotiable. Section 29 is as follows: "A bill may be transferred by the holder by delivery, accompanied with an agreement, express or implied, to transfer the title to the bill or to the goods represented thereby. A straight bill can not be negotiated free from existing equities, and the indorsement of such a bill gives the transferee no additional right." Other relevant sections of the Act are set forth in the footnote.

The very evident intention and accomplishment of the Act is to make straight bills nonnegotiable, and if the form of indorsement by defendant to the Bridgeport Iron & Metal Company might, standing by itself, be regarded as an attempt to convert the bill into an order bill, such would be an alteration after issue, without authority from the carrier, and void under § 13 as well as futile under § 29. It is clear, then, that the form of the indorsement worked no change in the nature or effect of the bill, that it continued to be nonnegotiable, and both as to the original and subsequent transferees, it is to be treated as subject to such limitations as are imposed by law upon such bills.

As between the defendant American Company as the seller and the Bridgeport Iron & Metal Company as the original buyer and transferee, the rights and remedies of an unpaid seller, including the right of stoppage *in transitu* in case of the buyer's insolvency, manifestly would obtain. General Statutes, §§ 4719, 4723, 4725, 4728; *Interstate Window Glass Co.* v. *New York, N. H. & H. R. Co.*, 104 Conn. 342, 133 Atl. 102. "Where a bill of lading is outstanding for the goods, the seller is not driven to rely upon the doctrine of stoppage *in transitu* unless the bill is either a straight bill of lading to the buyer, or unless, if negotiable in form, it has come into the hands of the buyer, either by delivery, if it originally ran to the buyer's order, or by indorsement and delivery, if it ran to the seller's order. Where the bill is a straight or nonnegotiable bill to the buyer, there can be no doubt of the applicability of the doctrine of stoppage *in transitu*. This is the typical case where the doctrine should be permitted." 2 Williston on Sales (2d Ed.) § 542.

And the sale of the goods by the buyer while they are in transit does not deprive the seller of his right to stop the goods. Unless a negotiable document of title is negotiated for value, or the seller has consented to the subsale, the right of stoppage *in transitu* still remains. General Statutes, § 4728; 2 Williston on Sales (2d Ed.) § 538. Since the bill of lading here was not a "negotiable document of title," this established principle of the law of sales would seem to be, of itself, sufficient to sustain the defendant's right of stoppage *in transitu* as against these plaintiffs as well as against the original buyer. The existence of such right is, however, further confirmed by provisions of the Federal Bills of Lading Act, especially § 29, hereinbefore quoted.

[A page of the opinion is here omitted.]

Under provisions of State bills of lading statutes which are similar to § 29 of the Federal Act (as is § 4642 of the General Statutes) it is held that indorsement of a nonnegotiable bill of lading is ineffectual to confer any additional right and the transferee obtains only such interest as the transferor had. *Ward-Lewis Lumber Co.* v. *Mahony* (Cal.) 234 Pac. 417; *Brown* v. *Floersheim Mercantile Co.*, 206 Mass. 373, 375, 92 N. E. 494; *Dewberry-Hargett Co.* v. *Arkansas State Bank*, 164 Ark. 223, 261 S. W. 301.

Again, the limited and conditional character of the title contemplated by the Federal Act as passing by the transfer of a straight bill is manifested by the provisions in § 32 as to rights of creditors of, or subsequent purchasers from, the transferor, prior to notification, to the carrier, of the transfer.

The trial court was correct in concluding that the nonnegotiable bill of lading issued to the defendant American Company, remained such notwithstanding the indorsement of it; that the plaintiffs were chargeable with knowledge of the nature of the bill and the title they obtained thereby (which conclusion eliminates any question of estoppel); and that the defendant retained the right to stop the goods *in transitu* and effectively exercised that right, and hence was entitled to recover their agreed value.

There is no error.

In this opinion the other judges concurred.

See also NORIEGA & ALVAREZ *v.* NEW YORK & PORTO RICO STEAMSHIP COMPANY, 32 Porto Rico 316 (Supreme Court, 1923), where it was held that the transfer of a non-negotiable bill of lading by the buyer to a sub-purchaser could not defeat the seller's right of stoppage.

In GASS *v.* SOUTHERN PACIFIC COMPANY, 152 App. Div. 412 (New York Supreme Court, Appellate Division, 1912), a mahogany company which had agreed to sell plaintiff a quantity of lumber delivered at New York entered into a contract with another seller to ship such lumber to New York. This seller shipped the lumber by defendant carrier taking out a straight bill of lading naming the original company as consignee. The bill of lading was indorsed and delivered to plaintiff. Plaintiff presented the bill of lading and a check for the freight charges, but defendant refused delivery unless the freight charges were paid in cash. Before the cash was forthcoming the mahogany company was adjudged a bankrupt, whereupon the seller issued a stop order to defendant. Defendant then refused to deliver the lumber to plaintiff, and the present action was brought for conversion. Judgment for plaintiff reversed.

KEMP *v.* FALK

HOUSE OF LORDS, 1882

[*Law Reports*, 7 *Appeal Cases*, 573]

In March 1878 Kiell bought on credit from Falk a cargo of salt, chartered the *Carpathian* and consigned the salt (which had been put on board by Falk) to Wiseman Mitchell & Co. of Calcutta. Through T. Wiseman & Co. of Glasgow, the agents of Wiseman Mitchell & Co., Kiell obtained an advance from the Bank of Scotland upon the security of the bills of lading which Kiell indorsed. In July Wiseman Mitchell & Co. sold the cargo "to arrive." On the 20th of July Kiell went into liquidation, and Falk on the 27th served on the shipowners in Liverpool notice to stop *in transitu.* The ship arrived at Calcutta on the 29th of July; part of the cargo was delivered to sub-purchasers on the 3rd of August, and the remainder, after notice to stop *in transitu* had been served on the captain, on the 5th of August. Wiseman Mitchell & Co. remitted the proceeds of the subsales to the Bank of Scotland, who deducted the amount of their advance and paid the balance to the appellant, Kiell's trustee in bankruptcy. Falk having applied to the Court of Bankruptcy to order the trustee to pay over the balance, which was less than the amount for which Falk sold to Kiell, the Registrar sitting as Chief Judge refused the application. On appeal the Court of Appeal (James, Baggallay and Bramwell L.JJ.) granted it.

Lord SELBORNE L.C. My Lords, you have heard the argument of the two learned counsel for the appellant, and I believe that your Lordships are all of opinion that it is unnecessary to hear any further argument in the case. To me it seems a case of very great simplicity.

It is admitted that but for the indorsement, or if there were more than one, the indorsements, of the bill of lading of the cargo in the *Carpathian*, the right of stoppage *in transitu* would have been well exercised as against everybody on the 5th of August, after which the greater part of the cargo was delivered to an amount which makes it immaterial between the parties to consider any question as to the few and small parcels which had been delivered before. Then the question is, What is the effect of the indorsement of the bill of lading? It was an indorsement to the Bank of Scotland, who had advanced money upon it; and the cases of *In re Westzinthus* (5 B. & Ad. 817) and *Spalding* v. *Ruding* (6 Beav. 376; 12 L. J. (Ch.) 503) clearly establish that the right of stoppage *in transitu* is not discharged absolutely by an indorsement of a bill of lading by way of security or pledge, but that it remains, in Equity at all events (and that is quite enough for the present purpose), as it was before, subject to a charge in favour of the indorsee of the bill of lading, which must be paid off, and which being paid off, the person entitled to, and exercising, the right of stoppage *in transitu* stands in exactly the same position as to everybody else as if there had been no security, and no pledge, and no indorsement of the bill of lading. And against what is that right of stoppage *in transitu*? Not against some imaginary interest of the purchaser, but against the goods themselves. It is a right to stop the goods; and I have no notion of any right of stoppage *in transitu* which is not a right to stop the goods when they are still *in transitu* in contemplation of law. It is a qualified right in the circumstances which I have mentioned; because it cannot be asserted as against the holder of the bill of lading without paying him off; but the instant his claim is discharged it is exactly the same right as if there had been no security, as against the original purchaser and as against, in my opinion, every one claiming under him.

It was contended that when, after an indorsement by way of security, such as was here made to the Bank of Scotland, there has been a sale of the goods "to arrive" by the original purchaser, without any document of title, (a sale which passes to the sub-purchaser such equitable interest as his immediate vendor could convey), that displaces the right of stoppage *in transitu* established by the cases of *In re Westzinthus* (5 B. & Ad. 817) and *Spalding* v. *Ruding* (6 Beav. 376; 12 L. J. (Ch.) 503). From the beginning of the argument I was totally unable to understand how that could possibly be. The indorsement of the bill of lading to the Bank of Scotland can confer no title whatever upon the other persons to whom the original purchaser transfers such rights as he has. He can transfer no greater or better right than he has; and the right which he has is a right subject to a stoppage *in transitu* in all cases in which the right of stoppage *in transitu* remains in favour of the original seller of the goods. I put, therefore, aside the whole argument founded upon the existence of sub-purchasers. I assent entirely to the proposition that where the sub-purchasers get a good title as against the right of stoppage *in transitu* there can be no stoppage *in transitu* as against the purchase-money payable by them to their vendor; at all events, until I hear authority for that proposition, I am bound to say that it is not consistent with my idea of the right of stoppage *in transitu* that it should apply to anything except to the goods which are *in transitu*. But when the right exists as against the goods which are *in transitu*, it is manifest that all other persons who have, subject to that right, any equitable interest in those goods by way of contract with the original purchaser or otherwise, may come in, and if they satisfy the claim of the seller who has stopped the goods *in transitu*, they can of course have effect given to their rights; and I apprehend that a Court of justice, in administering the rights which arise in actions of this description, would very often find that the rights of all parties were properly given effect to, if so much of the purchase-money payable by the sub-purchasers were paid to the original vendor as might be sufficient to discharge his claim; and, subject, of course, to that, the other contracts would take effect in their order and in their priorities. I observe an illustration of that in the letter of the 5th of August 1878, written by Messrs. Orr & Harris, the respondent's solicitors, in which they say that they have been told that Messrs. Wiseman Mitchell & Co. have contracted for the sale of the salt upon certain terms; that they do not want to put them to inconvenience, and that therefore they will be quite ready, upon being paid what is due to them, to let that contract receive proper effect. That is merely a way of working out the right of stoppage *in transitu*, which is a right against the goods, and which, as I said before, could be in no way whatever affected or prejudiced by any dealings between the original insolvent purchaser and persons purchasing under him without any title founded upon an indorsement of the bill of lading for value received.

I put that argument entirely aside; and I then come to the question which has been argued by Mr. Bompas upon the special circumstances of this case. I assume that there was no stoppage *in transitu* effectually made until the 5th of August. I put, therefore, entirely out of the question whatever had been *bona fide* done before that time; and the question is whether there was not, as against the cargo then remaining undelivered, an effectual stoppage *in transitu*. Now the facts stated in the second paragraph of the supplemental statement appear to me absolutely to exclude the notion of a constructive delivery of the whole cargo having taken place before the 5th of August; because it appears there that the sub-purchasers, to some of whom some small portions of the cargo had been delivered before the 5th of August, were all dealing separately from each other; each of them contracted to buy a certain quantity of salt, for which they paid Messrs. Wiseman Mitchell & Co.; they took receipts from them for their own portions; they "took those receipts to the vessel, and the quantities of salt for which they had respectively thus paid were then weighed out and delivered to them respectively in the presence and under the supervision of the master or other officer of the ship and the sircar or clerk of the consignees," without any arrangement as to the freight; from which it is apparent, that nothing could be more separate and distinct than the delivery of each parcel in that case; and if there were no more than those facts, the delivery of one parcel could not possibly operate as a delivery of the whole.

Then it was said, that it ought to be considered, on account of the terms of the letter of the 2nd of August 1878, that there was some constructive delivery of the whole cargo to the sircar or clerk of the consignees. That also appears to me to be a suggestion for which there is no warrant in the natural construction of the letter itself; a suggestion entirely unsupported by anything else, and really inconsistent with the fact that the delivery was not made by the sircar, but "in the presence and under the supervision of the master or other officer of the ship and the sircar or clerk." The sircar or clerk might be present too and might concur, but his concurrence could not mean that he had already become the possessor of the cargo, as if it had been taken out of the ship and delivered to himself.

The only other argument advanced by Mr. Bompas was founded upon the fact, stated in the first paragraph of the supplementary statement of facts, that the consignees indorsed the bill of lading (whatever that may be worth, I really will not stop to inquire), and delivered it to the captain. It was not indorsed to the captain for value, and there is nothing whatever to shew that your Lordships ought to infer that it had been indorsed to somebody else for value. We know that it had been indorsed for value to the bank, and we know the extent of their claim under it; and the bank have been satisfied or must be satisfied. The suggestion that it was indorsed, either to Messrs. Wiseman Mitchell Reid & Co. as persons who were under contract or who might be liable, or to any of the various subpurchasers through them, is entirely without foundation; and neither in the original agreed statement of facts, nor in this supplementary agreed statement of facts, is any indorsement mentioned at all except the indorsement to the Bank of Scotland. It seems to me evident, that the Bank of Scotland sent the bill indorsed to them in order that their own security might be realized, and it then came into the hands of Messrs. Wiseman Mitchell & Co. (whether directly or through some intermediate agency is really not important) for that purpose; and it is not said, in this supplementary agreed statement of facts, that the indorsement which preceded the delivery of the bill of lading to the captain by those gentlemen was for any special purpose whatever which could give any new title, legal or equitable, to anybody who had it not before.

The result is that, under these circumstances, the case seems to me to be altogether within the ruling in the cases of *In re Westzinthus* (5 B. & Ad. 817) and *Spalding* v. *Ruding* (6 Beav. 376; 12 L. J. (Ch.) 503), and therefore that the present appeal must be dismissed with costs.

[Concurring opinions of Lords Blackburn, Watson, and Fitzgerald are here omitted.]

Compare Golding, Davis & Co., Limited. In re Knight, 13 Ch. Div. 628 (Court of Appeal, 1880). A contract was entered into by buyers in London for the purchase from sellers in Widnes of 1200 drums of caustic soda f. o. b. Liverpool. On the same day the buyers contracted to sell 1200 drums of caustic soda to subpurchasers f. o. b. Liverpool. On instructions from the subpurchasers the buyers directed the sellers to ship the goods from Liverpool to New York. This was done, bills of lading being taken in the name of the subpurchasers and handed to the buyers. With matters in this state the buyers suspended and the sellers issued a stop order. The subpurchasers claimed that as the bills of lading were in their name the property in the goods had passed to them and the transit was at an end as between the sellers and buyers. It was held that the transit had not ended.

Refer again to Cahn and Mayer *v.* Pockett's Bristol Channel Steam Packet Company, Limited, *supra*, p. 909, where, in denying the seller's right to stop the goods in transit, it was held that the bill of lading, which had been indorsed in blank, was "lawfully transferred" to the original buyer within the meaning of Sec. 47 of the Sale of Goods Act.

C. Resale and Rescission

LANGFORT *v.* ADMINISTRATRIX OF TILER

At Nisi Prius

[1 *Salkeld's Reports*, 113]

The defendant, who was administratrix to her late husband, used to deal in tea in his lifetime, and bought four tubs of the plaintiff at so much per tub, one of which she paid for and took away, leaving 50*l.* in earnest for the other three; and Holt Chief Justice ruled, 1st, That the husband was liable upon the wife's contract, because they cohabited. 2dly, That notwithstanding the earnest, the money must be paid upon fetching away the goods, because no other time for payment is appointed. 3dly, That earnest only binds the bargain, and gives the party a right to demand; but then a demand without the payment of the money is void. 4thly, That after earnest given, the vendor cannot sell the goods to another, without a default in the vendee; and therefore if the vendee does not come and pay and take the goods, the vendor ought to go and request him; and then if he does not come and pay, and take away the goods in convenient time, the agreement is dissolved, and he is at liberty to sell them to any other person.

In Maclean *v.* Dunn, 4 Bing. 722 (Court of Common Pleas, 1828), there was a contract for the sale of a quantity of wool. The buyer refused to receive the wool when tendered. The seller thereupon sold the wool at a loss and brought a special action of *assumpsit* for non-acceptance and non-payment. It was objected that the resale rescinded the contract and deprived the seller of any right to sue. Best, C. J., said on this point:

"Then, with regard to the resale, it seems clear to me, that it did not rescind the contract. It is admitted that perishable articles may be resold. It is difficult to say what may be esteemed perishable articles, and what not: but if articles are not perishable, price is, and may alter in a few days, or a few hours. In that respect there is no difference between one commodity and another. It is a practice, therefore, founded on good sense, to make a resale of a disputed article, and to hold the original contractor responsible for the difference. The practice itself affords some evidence of the law, and we ought not to oppose it, except on the authority of decided cases. Those which have been cited do not apply. Where a man, in an action for goods sold and delivered, insists on having from the vendee the price at which he contracted to dispose of his goods, he cannot, perhaps, consistently with such a demand, dispose of them to another; but if he sues for damages in consequence of the vendee's refusing to complete his contract, it is not necessary that he should retain dominion over the goods: he merely alleges that a contract was entered into for the purchase of certain articles, that it has not been fulfilled, and that he has sustained damage in consequence. There is nothing in this which requires that the property should be in his hands when he commences the suit; and it is required neither by justice, nor by the practice of the mercantile world.

"In actions on the warranty of a horse, it is the constant practice to sell the horse, and to sue to recover the difference. The usage in every branch of trade is equally against the objection which has been raised on the part of the Defendants. It is urged, indeed, that in contracts entered into by the East India Company, the power of resale is expressly provided for, in case the vendee should refuse to perform his contract. That is only *ex abundanti cautelâ*, and it has never been decided that a resale of the goods is a bar to an action for damages for non-performance of a contract to purchase them: the contrary has been held at *Nisi Prius*. But, without referring to a *Nisi Prius* case as authority, we are anxious to confirm a rule consistent with convenience and law. It is most convenient that when a party refuses to take goods he has purchased, they should be resold, and that he should be liable to the loss, if any, upon the resale. The goods may become worse the longer they are kept; and, at all events, there is the risk of the price becoming lower."

In LAMOND *v.* DAVALL, 9 Q. B. 1030 (Queen's Bench, 1847), goods were sold at auction under an express condition that they might be resold if the price was not paid on the following day. The goods were resold at a loss accordingly, and the seller brought an action against the buyer in *assumpsit*. The defendant contended for a nonsuit because the power of resale was in effect a condition for making the sale void and hence inconsistent with the action. In upholding a nonsuit Lord Denman, C. J., said: "It appears to us that a power of resale implies a power of annulling the first sale, and that, therefore, the first sale is on a condition, and not absolute. There might be inconvenience to the vendor if the resale was held to be by him as agent for the defaulter; and there is injustice to the purchaser in holding him liable for the full price of the goods sold, though he cannot have the goods, and though the vendor may have received the full price from another purchaser. This inconvenience and injustice would be avoided by holding that the sale is conditioned to be void in case of default, and that the defaulter in case of resale is liable for the difference and expenses."

D'APRILE *v.* THE TURNER-LOOKER COMPANY

NEW YORK COURT OF APPEALS, 1925

[239 *New York Reports*, 427]

CARDOZO, J. The action is in tort for the conversion of the plaintiff's property.

A sale of ten barrels of whisky was made by the defendant to the plaintiff in May, 1918. The seller brought action for the price, and the buyer resisted on the ground that title had not passed. The courts held to the contrary (*Turner-Looker Co.* v. *Aprile*, 234 N. Y. 517), and judgment for the price was entered. In the meantime, however, the whisky had been sold. The bonded warehouse receipts, retained by the seller when the action was begun, were delivered to a new buyer while the case was in the courts. This fact came out upon the trial, and the seller consented to an amendment of the answer by which the first buyer would have been given a credit for the proceeds. The buyer refused to take advantage of the offer, very likely in the belief that the acceptance of the credit would shatter his defense. This, indeed, would have been its effect, for the price upon resale was only a small fraction of the price under the contract. At all events, the seller had judgment for the sum claimed without deduction. No part of that judgment has ever been collected.

The buyer, worsted in the action for the recovery of the price, has retaliated with this action for the conversion of the subject of the sale. He was unsuccessful at the Trial Term, but the Appellate Division reversed and gave judgment in his favor. The theory of the judgment is that an action for the price is inconsistent with a resale for the enforcement of a lien. The choice of the one remedy was held to bar the seller thereafter from the adoption of the other. We read the statute otherwise. Though the property in the goods may have passed to the buyer, the unpaid seller has a lien for the price (Pers. Prop. Law [Cons. Laws, ch. 41], § 135), which he may enforce by resale if default in payment has continued an unreasonable time (§ 141; *Van Brocklen* v. *Smeallie*, 140 N. Y. 70, 76). The right though denominated a lien, is in truth greater than a lien (*Tuthill* v. *Skidmore*, 124 N. Y. 148, 153; *Dunstan* v. *McAndrew*, 44 N. Y. 72; *Van Brocklen* v. *Smeallie, supra;* Williston, Sales, § 545). The lienor's position "is very nearly that of a pledgee, with power to sell at private sale in case of default" (*Tuthill* v. *Skidmore, supra*, at p. 143). The power survives till payment of the price is made (*Urbansky* v. *Kutinsky*, 86 Conn. 22, 30; *Dunstan* v. *McAndrew, supra*). An action for the price is no more inconsistent with a later enforcement of the lien than it is with the foreclosure of a mortgage or the sale by a pledgee of securities held in pledge (*Mason* v. *Decker*, 72 N. Y. 595, 599; Jones on Collateral Securities & Pledges, § 590). True, the buyer should be credited with the proceeds in reduction of the debt. As we have seen, he did not press the credit when he had an opportunity to receive it. We have little doubt that upon proper application, he may get it even now by allowance upon the execution in reduction of the judgment. Such considerations, however, are not decisive of the controversy before us. If the buyer by silence or inaction has thrown the credit away, he has not thus transformed a rightful act into a tort. The seller in disposing of these certificates was in the exercise of a lawful power. It was turning its collateral into money while suing for its debt. Blunders of procedure there may subsequently have been in respect of the time and manner of giving credit for the proceeds. The sale was rightful in the making. It did not become tortious by relation when the debt was turned into a judgment.

We are told that a resale is inconsistent with an action for the price because the surplus, if any, may be retained by the seller as his own

(Pers. Prop. Law, § 141). Exemption from the duty to account for the excess is a curious anomaly in the statutory scheme (cf. Williston, Sales, § 553). We think it does not serve to make the enforcement of the lien a resumption of the title or a rescission of the sale. The seller does not act as owner, but by virtue of a power, and like an agent or fiduciary, he must act prudently and fairly. In most instances, as here, the resale, when made, results in a deficiency (Williston, Sales, § 553), which is charged against the buyer. The exceptional contingency of a surplus and a profit does not change the basis of the power, and transmute into a plenary title what was a lien in its inception. If the unpaid seller is willing to resume the ownership, the law defines his remedy. By section 142 he is at liberty to rescind the sale and reclaim the title for himself. "An unpaid seller having a right of lien or having stopped the goods *in transitu,* may rescind the transfer of title and resume the property in the goods, where he expressly reserved the right to do so in case the buyer should make default, or where the buyer had been in default in the payment of the price an unreasonable time" (§ 142). When a sale is thus rescinded, the seller who resells thereafter, is acting for his own account. He may sacrifice the goods or waste them, for what he does, he does as owner, and not as lienor. We see no basis for a holding that an unpaid seller who resells under section 141 for the enforcement of his lien resumes title in himself to the same extent as if he had acted under section 142 and had given notice of rescission. The remedies are not one. They are several and alternative.

We are told, however, that the resale as made was not under the lien at all, but under an assumed, though unreal, authority to dispose of the certificates at pleasure and thereafter substitute equivalents. What the seller might have done as lienor is said to be more or less irrelevant. What it did, in the plaintiff's view, was not as a lienor, in subordination to the plaintiff's title, but in repudiation of that title, and hence as a wrongdoer. The record does not sustain this interpretation of its conduct. Neither word nor overt act evinces a repudiation of a duty to make allowance to the buyer for whatever was collected. On the contrary, a letter written by the buyer's counsel almost on the eve of the resale has in it a strong suggestion that the object of the transaction to the understanding of both parties was to liquidate the loss. Against this, there is nothing but the fact that the defendant, charged with a conversion of particular certificates, has stated in its answer that it is willing even now to give the plaintiff others. There was no duty to make the offer. It has neither helped nor hindered. The uncalled-for concession did not change by retroaction the quality of the act. Finally, if inferences are possible that there was repudiation by the seller of the title of the buyer, they are at most inferences of fact. The Appellate Division has made no attempt to draw them. It has placed its ruling upon the ground that there was no power to resell.

We are reminded of complications that may arise if a resale is unfairly or improvidently conducted after action begun or judgment rendered for the price. The same difficulties are possible where there is an unfair or irregular disposition of property held in pledge. The buyer or the pledgor may have his action for damages for any abuse of power by seller or pledgee.

In this case the judgment for the price was for $1,799.45. The proceeds of the resale were only $418.81. The buyer, treating the resale as a conversion, has recovered damages on the basis of market values as they stood more than a year thereafter when notice of the conversion reached him. On that basis, the credit due him was $1,846.36. By the application of that credit, the judgment against him has been wiped out, and a balance left in his favor. He may not pay his debt so easily.

The judgment of the Appellate Division should be reversed, and that of the Trial Term affirmed, with costs in the Appellate Division and in this court.

LEHMAN, J. (dissenting) . . . Whatever may have been the rule in this state prior to the Sales Act (*Westfall* v. *Peacock*, 63 Barb. 209), I agree with the views expressed in the prevailing opinion that under the Sales Act the bringing of the action for the price did not constitute a choice of one remedy which would bar the seller from the subsequent adoption of the other remedy afforded by the statute, through enforcement of his lien by resale, for both remedies are based upon the theory that title to the property had become vested in the buyer. (*Mason* v. *Decker*, *supra*.) After that sale, however, the seller was no longer entitled to recover the price of the goods, but might "recover from the buyer damages for any loss occasioned by the resale." (Personal Property Law, section 141.) In spite of the resale during the pendency of the action for the price, the seller has recovered judgment for the full price. In the case of *Urbansky* v. *Kutinsky* (86 Conn. 22), and other cases that might be cited, the buyer recovered only the balance of the purchase price after crediting the amount received upon the resale. He was entitled under the statute to that. Here the seller has recovered judgment for the full price. It was not entitled under the statute to such judgment after a resale, but only to damages for any loss. Conceding, as I do, that at the time the defendant resold the goods, it still had the right to make such sale by virtue of its lien, it seems to me that the subsequent judgment for the price precludes the defendant from urging that it resold the goods in the exercise of that right; for such a resale would, I think, be inconsistent with a judgment for the price obtained thereafter. The question is not whether the seller had the right under its lien to resell after the bringing of the action for the price, but whether it did sell as lienor. If the judgment for the price is based upon implied findings which are inconsistent with an assertion of previous sale as lienor, that judgment does not render unlawful a sale which was previously lawful; it merely conclusively adjudicates that there was no lawful sale.

I recognize that at the time of the trial of the action for the price, the seller consented to an amendment of the answer by which the first buyer would have been permitted to plead the amount received upon the resale as an offset, but as the prevailing opinion has pointed out, that would have shattered his defense, and I think it would also have constituted an admission that the resale was lawful and properly conducted. The seller may not compel the buyer to plead the resale as an offset or partial defense, if after such resale the seller is entitled to recover a judgment, not for the price, but only for damages. The decisive consideration in this case, in my opinion, is whether the judgment for the price establishes conclusively not only that title to the goods passed to the buyer, but that such title was still in the buyer at the time of the judgment. The answer to this question depends upon the nature of the seller's right of action for the price, as well as upon the nature of his right to resell.

The price is the consideration paid for a transfer of title, and under the Sales Act only under exceptional circumstances may there be a recovery of the price without transfer of title. A judgment for the price constitutes an adjudication not merely that title had passed to the buyer, but that the seller had not rescinded such transfer of title. If the resale results in a rescission of the original transfer of title and a resumption of title in the seller, then it can hardly be doubted that an action for the price, which constitutes the consideration for the transfer of title to the buyer, will not lie thereafter. It is urged that a resale made under section 141 of the statute should not be confused with a rescission of the transfer of title as provided in section 142. I find no essential difference in the nature of the rights accorded by these two sections. The rights accorded under both sections arise under the same circumstances, viz., "where the buyer has been in default in the payment of the price an unreasonable time." The result is the same: "The seller shall not thereafter be liable to the buyer upon the contract to sell or the sale, but may recover from the buyer damages for any loss occasioned by the breach of the contract or the sale." True, section 141 contains additional provisions which could be applicable only to a resale, viz., that the seller shall not be liable to the original buyer "for any profit made by such resale," and that the "seller is bound to exercise reasonable care and judgment in making a resale, and subject to this requirement may make a resale either by public or private sale." The meaning of these additional provisions is hardly open to doubt. By virtue of them the seller may on the one hand retain any profit made by a resale, and on the other hand may fix the amount of any loss through a resale, fairly and judiciously made. I find nothing in these provisions which is logically inconsistent with the view that the exercise of the seller's right to resell provided by section 141 is founded upon a total rescission of the transfer of title. That section merely provides an additional right to fix the amount of loss suffered by the seller. The right of a buyer, with title to the property, to have the profit made upon a resale seems clear "unless the seller has the right totally to rescind the sale, revest himself with the ownership of the goods, resell them as his own, and take the proceeds for his own account. That the seller has this alternative right will be seen from the following sections, but here it may be said that on whatever reasoning the doctrine is based, the law seems to recognize the seller's right to keep any profit from the resale. This is expressly so provided in the Sales Act." (Williston on Sales [2d ed.], section 553.)

Discussion of the classification into which the right of an unpaid seller to resell logically should be placed, or the philosophical basis of that right, if such basis there be, may not assist materially in the determination of the concrete question before us. We are concerned with the substance of the rights given by the statute. It is said that under section 142 a seller who rescinds the sale may resell thereafter for his own account, while the seller who proceeds under section 141 "does not act as owner, but by virtue of a power, and like an agent or fiduciary, he must act prudently and fairly." If such an obligation rests upon the seller he should be accountable, as other agents or fiduciaries are, for failure to carry out his obligation. Even though the conceded anomaly that the "fiduciary" need not account to the owner for any profits made be regarded as without decisive significance, the fact that even where the seller does not act prudently and fairly in making the resale he is not guilty of conversion, nor at least before judgment for the price, accountable for any loss suffered by his misconduct, should not be overlooked. The resale, if not fairly made, becomes a rescission under section 142 of the act, and the only effect of the seller's misconduct is that the price realized no longer serves to fix the loss, as would be the case under a resale made in accordance with section 141. In both cases the seller retains the profits, in both cases he may still hold the buyer for damages for his loss, and nothing else, and if he obtains a judgment for the price after he has disposed of the goods he has obtained more than he is entitled to.

While this court has in many early cases referred to resales made by an unpaid seller as if made by him as an agent of the buyer, in the case of *Moore* v. *Potter* (155 N. Y. 481, 487) it has noted the inaccuracy of such language. "The use of the words 'as agent of the vendee' was not intended as a determination that the relation between the parties was that which ordinarily exists between a principal who owns property and an agent who may be authorized to manage or sell it. But it is a general expression which has been somewhat inaccurately used to define the right of a vendor to make a resale and hold the vendee responsible for his loss. It is quite manifest that a resale made under such circumstances is not made by the vendor strictly as agent of the vendee, but he acts for himself in disposing of the property for the purpose of ascertaining the actual damages he may sustain." (See, also, *Ackerman* v. *Rubens*, 167 N. Y. 405.) In considering the earlier decisions in the light of these cases we may also properly give some weight to the fact that at the time they were written the right of the seller to retain any profit upon a resale was not clearly established; in fact the contrary rule was sometimes assumed. (See *Westfall* v. *Peacock*, *supra.*)

If we hold that a seller may after resale still obtain a judgment for the price, subject to an offset for the price realized, we place the buyer in an unfortunate position. He may not even know that the resale has been made, and it seems unreasonable to hold that the buyer's remedy is by an offset which he may not know exists. It may be urged that even in such case the plaintiff could obtain a satisfaction of judgment upon proof that the seller had realized upon the security and upon payment of the difference between the judgment and the amount realized, but it is somewhat anomalous to hold that a judgment may be reduced by proof of facts which might have constituted an offset at the trial. If we place our decision upon the narrow ground that in this case the buyer was informed of the resale, and he refused an offer to permit him to plead an offset, our difficulties seem no less. He could plead an offset only by admitting the fairness of the sale, yet he may desire to litigate that very question. The statute gives the seller the right to recover only for his loss, and not for the price. He must establish his loss by proof of a resale made with reasonable care and judgment. It can hardly be incumbent upon the buyer to plead as an offset the amount obtained by the seller upon a resale, for such a plea would preclude him from litigating the propriety of the resale.

If the result in this case is that the buyer pays less than the seller could have compelled him to pay if he had proceeded properly, the result is due to the attitude of the seller. It has chosen to resell the buyer's property and yet to hold the buyer for the price, instead of the loss occasioned to it by the buyer's breach. It has not attempted to account to the buyer for the proceeds of the property. It still offers as a defense to the action for conversion, to deliver to the plaintiff goods similar to the goods which belonged to the buyer. It claims the benefit of the resale but it does not assume its burden. It has itself caused any loss which it may have suffered.

The judgment should be affirmed, with costs.

POUND, MCLAUGHLIN and ANDREWS, JJ., concur with CARDOZO, J.; LEHMAN, J., reads dissenting opinion in which CRANE, J., concurs; HISCOCK, Ch. J., absent.

Judgment reversed, etc.

In ELLIS *v.* GREENBAUM SONS INVESTMENT CO., 307 Penn. 77 (Supreme Court, 1932), there was a contract for the sale of bonds with an agreement to repurchase. On refusal by the seller to repurchase as agreed the buyer brought an action in *assumpsit* against the seller on the repurchase agreement, but before bringing such action had sold some of the bonds elsewhere at a lower price. The original seller contended that the consequent inability of the buyer to return all the bonds was a bar to recovery. Judgment for plaintiff affirmed. Plaintiff had a right to sell any of the bonds without releasing defendant from liability for breach of contract.

In L. P. COURSHON COMPANY *v.* BREWER, 215 Iowa 885 (Supreme Court, 1932), there was a contract for the sale of the good will of a business and also at separate prices of the merchandise, furniture and fixtures. The buyer subsequently abandoned the last three without payment, whereupon the seller after due notice took them into possession as agent for the buyer and resold the property for the buyer's account. The present action was brought to recover the difference between the contract and the resale price. Judgment for plaintiff affirmed. The Sales Act does not cover the circumstances here presented, and plaintiff was confronted with an anomalous situation. In such a case the law merchant is to be applied, and would permit the seller to retake possession and resell the goods on abandonment by the buyer.

In JNO. DUNLOP'S SONS, INC. *v.* ALPREN, 214 N. Y. App. Div. 339 (Third Department, 1925), plaintiff sold goods to defendant and shipped them by express. On refusal of defendant to accept the goods plaintiff took them back from the express company and mixed them with other stock, in which situation it was impossible to say whether the particular goods were or were not resold. It was held that this conduct of the plaintiff amounted to a rescission of the sale and barred an action for the purchase price.

SLOSS–SHEFFIELD STEEL & IRON CO. *v.* STOVER MFG. & ENGINE CO.

UNITED STATES CIRCUIT COURT OF APPEALS, SEVENTH CIRCUIT, 1929

[37 *Federal Reporter* (*Second Series*), 876]

WOODWARD, District Judge. This is an action brought by appellant against appellee to recover damages for refusal to accept 656 tons of "Sloss Pig Iron" and 201 tons of "No-Ala Pig Iron" at the contract price.

After issue joined, a jury was waived in writing, and the cause was tried to the court. After hearing all the evidence the court made special findings of fact, finding the issue for the defendant, to which a general exception was interposed by appellant. Judgment on the findings was entered in favor of appellee.

This being the state of the record, review, on appeal, is limited to the sufficiency of the facts specially found to support the judgment, and to the rulings excepted to and presented by the bill of exceptions.

The question then is: Do the findings of fact support the judgment?

The material portions of the findings of fact may be summarized as follows:

On August 16, 1918, appellee gave appellant two orders for pig iron, both of which were accepted on September 6, 1918. One order was for 1,000 tons of "Sloss Pig Iron" at a price of $34.50 per ton f. o. b. cars at Birmingham, Ala., and the other was for 500 tons of "No-Ala Pig Iron" at a price of $33 per ton f. o. b. Florence or Sheffield, Ala., in approximately equal monthly quantities during the first half of the year 1919.

At the time the contracts were entered into, the United States was at war with Germany. The price agreed upon for the respective brands of pig iron was not in excess of the price fixed by the regulations of the government of the United States. Under this contract and during January and February, 1919, 344 tons of "Sloss Pig Iron" and 209 tons of "No-Ala Pig Iron" were delivered and paid for.

Early in 1919 a committee consisting of representatives of the American Iron & Steel Institute and the Department of Commerce of the United States, in attempting to stabilize postwar conditions, recommended to those engaged in buying and selling pig iron that contracts calling for delivery of pig iron in 1919 be reduced $6 per ton, which recommendation was purely advisory. After the promulgation of these recommendations, appellee asked appellant to reduce the price of the respective brands of pig iron $6 per ton. Appellant refused to make the reduction and insisted that deliveries be made at the contract price. Appellee refused to accept any further deliveries under the contract unless the respective contract prices were reduced $6 per ton. At that time the market was considerably below the contract price.

During the months of March, April, May, and June, 1919, appellant manufactured for defendant 656 tons of "Sloss Pig Iron" and 291 tons of "No-Ala Pig Iron" and stored the respective amounts in its yards at Birmingham and Sheffield, respectively, of which fact it notified appellee. Each brand of pig iron thus stored in the respective yards was placed in separate piles, apart from all other pig iron, was identified by particular paint markings, and a record was made upon the books of appellant that these particular piles of pig iron were the property of appellee and were being held by appellant for appellee. The pig iron so stored was afterwards, and when prices had materially advanced, sold by appellant for the account of appellee at prices in excess of the contract price of the respective brands.

The trial court, therefore, found that appellant had not sustained any damage by appellee's refusal to accept the pig iron at the contract prices.

Upon the refusal of appellee to accept the pig iron, appellant had three remedies. In the case of *Osgood* v. *Skinner*, 211 Ill. 229, 71 N. E. 869, 873, referring to the case of *Ames* v. *Moir*, 130 Ill. 582, 22 N. E. 535, these remedies are stated to be: "First, to store the goods for the vendee, give notice that he has done so, and recover the full contract price; second, to keep the goods, and recover the excess of the contract price over and above the market price of the goods at the time and place of delivery; and third, to sell the goods at a fair price, and recover from the vendee the loss if the goods fail to bring the contract price."

Appellant elected to resell the goods for the account of appellee. Having made the election, appellant is bound by it and cannot now pursue an inconsistent remedy.

The pig iron was sold upon the market at a price in excess of the contract price. Appellant is bound by the result. Its recovery is limited to the difference between the contract price and the amount received upon the resale. Having so elected, it cannot now recover the excess of the contract price over the market price at the time of the alleged breach by appellee, and, having thereafter received more on the resale of the pig iron than the contract price, there is no loss or damage to compensate.

We find no error in the admission or exclusion of evidence which was harmful to appellant.

The judgment is affirmed.

In Humphrey *v.* Sagouspe, 50 Nev. 157 (Supreme Court, 1927), there was a contract for the sale of 1200 head of sheep for a total price of $9,000 of which the buyer paid $1,000 at the time the contract was made. The balance of the price was payable on delivery, which was to be on or before October 1. The buyer refused to accept delivery, and repudiated the contract. After repeated unsuccessful efforts to deliver the sheep the seller resold them on October 20 for $8,947.50. In an action by the buyer for damages for failure to deliver, the seller established the above facts and by way of counterclaim asked general damages of $1000 and special damages of $807.78. In the lower court judgment was rendered for the seller for $390.94 plus $146.20 for costs and disbursements, the amount to be deducted from the $1000 originally paid and the balance returned to the buyer. On appeal defendant contended that the damages awarded should be without reference to the original $1000, which the defendant should be permitted to keep in any event. Judgment affirmed. "By the express terms of the uniform sales act, sec. 60, the seller who has exercised his right of resale is not liable for any profit made thereon, but we find nothing to indicate that it was intended that he should also, after fully reimbursing himself, retain all moneys paid on the contract."

W. H. PRIDE AND COMPANY *v.* W. R. MARSHALL AND COMPANY, INCORPORATED

Massachusetts Supreme Judicial Court, 1921

[239 *Massachusetts Reports,* 53]

Carroll, J. On October 7, 1918, the plaintiff sold to the defendant two thousand cases of raspberry jam packed in tins, f. o. b. Bellingham, Washington. The merchandise was shipped on October 19, 1918, and an indorsed bill of lading with ten days' draft for $16,575 was sent forward and duly presented on October 30, 1918. The jam arrived in Boston on December 14. The defendant did not accept it nor pay the draft. In January following, after the defendant had failed to sell the goods, it placed them in storage. On July 8, 1919, the plaintiff brought suit for the price of the jam together with the expenses of storage and shipment. The plaintiff on August 14 advertised the goods for resale at twelve o'clock noon, August 19, 1919, at the office of its attorney; and on the same day sent to the defendant a copy of the page of the Boston Transcript of August 14 enclosed in a letter calling attention to the column in which the advertisement appeared, and stating that the sale was to be conducted for the defendant's account and the plaintiff would look to the defendant to pay the difference between the price at which the jam was sold and the contract price, with interest and expenses. On August 15 the defendant's attorney acknowledged the receipt of the copy of the notice of sale, and in their letter stated that they neither objected nor consented to the plaintiff's proceedings, and, whatever course was pursued, "we on our part shall take advantage of any available defense at the proper time." The goods were sold as advertised to the highest of three bidders for $10,200, and the plaintiff claimed the difference between this amount and the contract price, with interest and expenses, $9,598.50.

It was undisputed that in New England there was little demand for jam packed in tins, the demand being for jam packed in glass. In the middle west there was a greater demand for jam in tins than in New England.

At the close of the evidence the plaintiff moved for a directed verdict for $9,598.50. The case was sent to the jury under instructions that if they adopted the plaintiff's theory that the resale of the goods was held at a proper time and place and manner they should find for this amount. If, on the other hand, the theory was adopted that the plaintiff did not conduct the resale as early as it should have done, nor in a place or manner calculated to acquire the best price obtainable, they were to take from the plaintiff's claim that sum in which they found the defendant was injured. They found for the plaintiff in the sum of $4,444.93, and the case was reported.

It was not questioned that the title to the goods passed to the defendant when delivered to the carrier; and that the unpaid sellers retained their lien for the price, and had the right of resale.

If the plaintiff conducted the sale under its lien with reasonable care and judgment, we see no reason why it is not entitled to the full amount of its claim. The defendant, however, contends that the sale was not properly held, for the reason that the jam was sold in Boston when there was a better market in the middle west, that the sale was not sufficiently advertised, and did not take place within a reasonable time after the arrival of the goods in Boston.

The defendant had ample notice of the time and place of the sale. From its experience in the trade it must have known the condition of the market. It did not object to selling the goods in Boston and made no suggestion indicating that a more profitable market could be found elsewhere. It had full opportunity to protect itself, and it cannot now be heard to complain that by selling the goods in Boston the plaintiff failed to use reasonable judgment and care in the conduct of the sale. *Guinzburg* v. *H. W. Downs Co.* 165 Mass. 467. *Winchester Rock & Brick Co.* v. *Murdough*, 233 Mass. 50, 54.

Even if it were essential that notice should be given by the plaintiff to the defendant of the time and place of sale, it cannot complain that the sale was not fully advertised, or, by demanding that a certified check should accompany all bids, that sufficient effort was not made to secure customers or that the sale was unfairly made. As we have said, the defendant was notified, and instead of suggesting that the request for a certified check would prevent bidders from attending the sale or that the advertisement was not adequate and that further publicity should be given, it neither consented nor objected to the course pursued by the plaintiff and claimed the right to take advantage of any available defence. It had already broken the contract by failing to pay the draft and accept the goods, and it was for its interest to see that an advantageous sale was made. It could not stand by, knowing that the sale was not properly advertised, with full opportunity to assist, and then take advantage of what it now claims was an insufficient notice or advertisement. *Guinzburg* v.

H. W. Downs Co., supra. Winchester Rock & Brick Co. v. *Murdough, supra.*

The jam arrived in Boston on December 14, 1918, and was resold on August 19, 1919. The defendant expected to sell it to the depot quartermaster of the United States Army, and in March, 1919, urged the plaintiff to let the matter rest, as it still had hopes of so disposing of it; and as late as July, 1919, assured the plaintiff it was "working to clean up that block here now," and hoped "any day to be in a position to lift the draft that is here." The merchandise was not of such a nature as to require unusual expense in keeping it, see *Putnam* v. *Glidden,* 159 Mass. 47, and even if the defendant could show that a loss was suffered by the delay in making the resale, for this delay it was itself responsible and it is not to be attributed to the plaintiff. The sale was fully executed, and the defendant had title to the property. The correspondence shows that the defendant was asking for further time in which to dispose of the goods and requesting the forbearance of the seller. As none of the material facts were in dispute it should have been ruled that as matter of law the resale, under all the circumstances, was held within a reasonable time. See *Loring* v. *Boston,* 7 Met. 409, 413.

We find nothing in the evidence to show that the sale was not fairly conducted or that the plaintiffs did not use reasonable care and judgment. The plaintiff's motion for a directed verdict should have been allowed. Judgment is to be entered for the plaintiff in the sum of $9,598.50.

So ordered.

In KATZ *v.* THE DELOHERY HAT COMPANY, 97 Conn. 665 (Supreme Court of Errors, 1922), the plaintiff sold and delivered to the defendant five cases of fur of a given quality which was shipped September 27. On October 31 the defendant wrote that the fur was unsatisfactory and five days later sent it back to the plaintiff who insisted that it conformed to the contract and at once reshipped it by rail to the defendant. The latter refused to take it from the carrier, whereupon the plaintiff on December 5 notified the defendant in writing that plaintiff was about to take possession of the fur as agent for defendant and as such to sell it upon a favorable opportunity and apply the proceeds upon the purchase price. The plaintiff took possession on December 20, and after some delay due to market conditions the fur was sold and the proceeds credited to defendant. In an action to recover the balance of the price defendant contended that the duty of plaintiff to sell arose in November, and had due diligence been exercised the fur could have been sold for a much higher price. Judgment for plaintiff affirmed. The duty of the plaintiff to use due diligence in selling the fur at the best price obtainable did not arise until after a reasonable time for defendant to act on the notice of December 5. The jury could have reasonably found that plaintiff had exercised such duty and obtained the best price available.

In MAURICE O'MEARA COMPANY *v.* THE NATIONAL PARK BANK OF NEW YORK, *supra*, p. 549, McLaughlin, J., said in part: "Finally, it is claimed that the plaintiff was not entitled to a summary judgment since there was an issue raised as to the amount of damages. It appears from the affidavits in support of the motion that after the defendant had refused to pay the drafts, due notice was given to it by the plaintiff of its intention to sell the paper for the best price possible, although no notice of such resale was necessary. (Personal Property Law [Cons. Laws, ch. 41], sec. 141, subd. 4.) No attention was paid to the notice and the paper was sold as soon as practicable thereafter and for the best price obtainable, which represented the fair market value at the time of the sale. The plaintiff's damages were, primarily, the face amount of the drafts. Plaintiff, of course, was bound to minimize such damage so far as it reasonably could. This, it undertook to do by reselling the paper, and for the amount received, less expenses connected with the sale, it was bound to give the defendant credit. There was absolutely no statement in defendant's affidavits to the effect that the plaintiff did not act in the utmost good faith or with reasonable care and diligence in making the resale. The only reference thereto is that defendant did not get the best price possible. The defendant gave no evidence, however, of a market value at the time and the plaintiff submitted the affidavits of three dealers in paper that the paper was sold at the fair market value at the time of the sale. Plaintiff's damages were, therefore, liquidated by a resale on notice. (*Second National Bank* v. *Columbia Trust Co.*, 288 Fed. Rep. 17, 26.) This is the rule which has long prevailed between seller and buyer. The only requirement is that the resale must be a fair one."

2. RECOVERY OF THE PRICE

AGAR *v.* ORDA

NEW YORK COURT OF APPEALS, 1934

[264 *New York Reports*, 248]

LEHMAN, J. An action to recover the purchase price of 200 shares of stock has been dismissed. The contract of purchase and sale was executory. The buyer refused to accept delivery of the certificates when tendered.

The Sales Act (Article V of the Personal Property Law [Cons. Laws, ch. 41]) provides: "Where, under a contract to sell or a sale, the property in the goods has passed to the buyer, and the buyer wrongfully neglects or refuses to pay for the goods according to the terms of the contract or the sale, the seller may maintain an action against him for the price of the goods." (§ 144.) Even before the Sales Act was enacted, the same rule was applied in this jurisdiction to contracts to sell or sales of personal property of all kinds.

The same rule was also applied in this jurisdiction prior to the enactment of the Sales Act, to executory contracts for the sale of personal property, where payment of the price and delivery of the personal property were to be simultaneous, if the seller made proper tender of the property he had agreed to sell. (*Hayden* v. *Demets*, 53 N. Y. 426.) Here the Sales Act changed the common-law rule as formulated by the courts of this jurisdiction. In such case the seller of goods is now relegated to an action for damages and no action for the price will lie. "Where the buyer wrongfully neglects or refuses to accept and pay for the goods, the seller may maintain an action against him for damages * * *." (§ 145.) The question now presented is whether, since the enactment of the Sales Act, an action for the price may still be maintained upon the refusal of a buyer of stock certificates to accept delivery of the certificates, though title to the certificates had not passed to the buyer.

Concededly, if certificates of stock are "goods" within the definition of the Sales Act, the complaint was properly dismissed. It does not follow that the action for the price will lie, though certificates of stock do not fall within that definition. Prior to the enactment of the Sales Act the courts held that a seller of personal property had the same remedies, regardless of the nature of the personal property. The same rule was applied to a contract to sell the shares of stock of a construction company struggling to obtain from its friends the means to live, as well as to such personal property as is the subject of general traffic and has a market value. (*Mason* v. *Decker*, 72 N. Y. 595.) It was applied alike "where the property is grain or hops, or a horse" and "where it is an interest in a partnership." (*Van Brocklen* v. *Smeallie*, 140 N. Y. 70, 76.) The logical outcome of disintegrating exception would inevitably be, the court there said, "to confuse the rule with narrow and arbitrary distinctions; to open it to attack in numerous directions; to make its operation fickle and uncertain; to breed needless litigation; and in the end to shatter the rule itself." The rule has been shattered by the Legislature. It no longer can be applied to contracts for the sale of "goods," and goods, as defined by the statute, include "all chattels personal other than things in action and money." (§ 156.) The problem is whether a fragment of the shattered rule still persists and is applicable to sales of certificates of stock.

Shares of stock are intangible property and, at least, for many purposes, must be regarded only as things in action; yet for practical purposes they are merged in stock certificates which are instrumentalities of trade and commerce. (*Hutchison* v. *Ross,* 262 N. Y. 381.) Such certificates "are treated by business men as property for all practical purposes." (*Lockwood* v. *United States Steel Corp.*, 209 N. Y. 375, 382.) Indeed, this court has held that the shares of stock are so completely merged in the certificate that conversion of the certificate may be treated as a conversion of the shares of stock represented by the certificate, even though the certificate was not indorsed by the owner, and after the conversion the original owner remained the record owner of the stock and entitled to all the benefit which flows from such ownership. (*Pierpont* v. *Hoyt,* 260 N. Y. 26.) Even so, a strong argument may be made that the Legislature did not intend to include certificates of stock in its definition of "goods." Assuming that to be true, yet the fact remains that certificates of stock, like other "goods," are freely bought and sold in the market place and pass from hand to hand, and analogy so complete may dictate that the rules governing sales be applied alike to "goods" and other personal property freely bought and sold and passing from hand to hand.

It is significant that this court so applied the same rules to sales of all personal property without distinction long before the Legislature adopted the Sales Act. Since the Sales Act was adopted, we have by analogy applied the provisions of the Personal Property Law, sections 82 and 100, governing the transfer of property in goods, to the transfer of property in certificates of stock. (*Wills* v. *Investors Bankstocks Corp.*, 257 N. Y. 451.) The common-law rules governing the sale of goods were applied without distinction to all personal property, so far as the nature of the property permitted, in order to avoid confusion with its attendant train of evils. (*Van Brocklen* v. *Smeallie,* 140 N. Y. 70.) The Legislature has changed some of these rules by the adoption of the Uniform Sales Act. It did so primarily for the purpose of promoting uniformity of rules throughout the country. By placing the rules governing the sale of "goods" in a statutory code, it shattered or destroyed general common-law rules inconsistent with the statutory code. By limiting the application of the statutory code to the sale of "goods" the Legislature gave no indication of what rule the courts should apply to the sale of other personal property. That problem it left to the courts.

The courts must formulate the rules applicable in cases not covered by the statute. The field is narrow. Inherent differences between "goods" and things in action may require at times the formulation of different rules. Perhaps that is why the Legislature excluded things in action from the scope of the statutory rules. No such differences exist here. Indeed, before the Sales Act was adopted, the courts applied the rule governing actions for the price of goods to actions for the price of other personal property because they found that logic and policy alike dictated that here no distinction should be drawn. The same considerations still apply now that the court is called upon to formulate the rule which shall be applied in cases not covered by the Sales Act. The formulation of the old general rule that "when the vendee of personal property, under an executory contract of sale, refuses to complete his purchase, the vendor may keep the article for him and sue for the entire purchase price" (*Ackerman* v. *Rubens*, 167 N. Y. 405, 408), will no longer suffice. A formulation of the rule to confine it to contracts for the sale of choses in action creates a narrower rule which is supported by none of the considerations which induced the courts originally to adopt the original general rule. It is in effect a new rule. The fragments of the rule shattered by the Legislature are essentially different from the old common-law rule.

Even the old general common law as formulated in this State differed from the common-law rule as formulated in England and many jurisdictions in this country. (See 2 Williston on Sales [2nd ed.], § 560 *et seq.*) "It seems anomalous that the seller should be able to force title upon the buyer by simply electing to do so." (§ 566.) Every reason that might be urged against the old rule as applied to all personal property has at least equal force when urged against a narrower rule to be applied only to certificates of stock. The same reasons that make uniformity in all jurisdictions desirable in regard to sale of goods apply with like force to sale of certificates of stock. After the Legislature in the Sales Act shattered and mutilated beyond recognition the general common-law rule of this State and enacted its preference for the general common-law rule as applied in England and other jurisdictions to all personal property, the courts of this State should apply the same rule not only to the sale of goods, but to the sale of all personal property. Otherwise the courts without reason introduce distinctions that are harmful and retard uniformity of rules in a field where uniformity should be sought.

The judgment should be affirmed, with costs.

[Crane, J., dissented, holding that the Uniform Sales Act does not apply to shares of capital stock of a corporation.]

In TUFTS *v.* GREWER, 83 Me. 407 (Supreme Judicial Court, 1891), Peters, C. J. said:

"The defendant ordered a soda fountain of the plaintiff, which was manufactured and tendered to him and the price demanded. It is admitted that the plaintiff performed all the requirements of the contract resting on him, and that the defendant without legal excuse failed to perform his part of the obligation, utterly refusing to pay for or accept the property. The action is special, reciting that, although the plaintiff has performed his promise, the defendant refuses to perform his, the plaintiff claiming to recover for the breach the full contract price of the article sold.

"The general rule is familiar, that for the vendee's failure to receive and pay for the goods he has contracted for, the vendor may recover the difference between the market value at the time and place stipulated for delivery and the contract price, together with the expenses of reselling the property. The general rule is not questioned, but the plaintiff contends that a special and more equitable rule governs when a vendor has manufactured the article after a particular pattern upon the order of the vendee, who refuses without excuse to accept the same. The plaintiff says, I have done all I bargained to do and now the defendant should be compelled to do what he bargained to do, namely, to pay the contract price.

"We feel that there is force in the plaintiff's position, supported as it is by considerable authority, but we are inclined to believe that there should be but one rule of damages in cases where a vendee refuses to accept goods which he has agreed to purchase, whether the article to be delivered to the vendee is already in existence or is to be manufactured on his account. Wherein does the general rule fail to furnish an efficacious remedy? The vendor was to receive in this case money and notes. While the law fully recognizes the obligation of the vendee, and cannot require specific performance, it undertakes to make full reparation by allowing recovery for all the damages sustained. What difference, practically, can there be between a seller receiving the consideration wholly from the vendee or partly from him and the balance from some one else? The law in its own way obtains for the vendor an equivalent for a full execution of the contract.

"There are courts which have held that, in all cases where a vendee refuses to accept the goods contracted for by him, the vendor may recover the contract price as damages. There is a stronger leaning among judges towards the distinction, set up in the present case, in favor of applying such a principle only when the contract calls for an article to be manufactured especially for the vendee. The ground upon which this doctrine is defended by its advocates is that the peculiarly manufactured article is of little value to any one besides the vendee, if of any marketable value whatever. The answer to this position is, of course, that the less the goods are worth to sell in the market the more the plaintiff recovers, and if they are worth nothing at all, then he recovers the full contract price. But such a result is just as logically attainable under the application of the general as by any special rule. The great ground of objection to the rule invoked by the plaintiff is that where there has been no acceptance of the property, the title still remains in the vendor, liable to be taken for his debts, or pass to his assignee in bankruptcy, or be sold by him to another purchaser. A tender does not in our law transfer the title to the vendee. The facts show that the plaintiff was to retain title to the fountain until the price should be paid. But the defendant refused to make the partial cash payment called for by the terms of sale, or to accept any possession or control of the property, so that even an equitable title to the property did not pass to him.

"The rule invoked here has not been much noticed in the English law, but finds its principal support in this country, and, still, even here it will be found, we think, to be in contradiction of most of the authorities."

SHELL-MEX LIMITED *v.* ELTON COP DYEING COMPANY, LIMITED

KING'S BENCH DIVISION, 1928

[34 *Commercial Cases*, 39]

WRIGHT J. This is a claim by plaintiffs, who are a distributing and selling agency for the well-known and large oil companies whose names shortly are indicated in the plaintiffs' title. The plaintiffs, who have oil-storage tanks at various installations throughout the country, have, amongst other installations, an installation at Barton which serves the Manchester area. The defendants, as their name indicates, are a company carrying on the business of dyeing at Bury. In June, 1926, during the coal strike, they were anxious to work their factory with the aid of oil instead of coal, or partly instead of coal; and accordingly they entered into the contract on which the present action is brought. I must refer to the terms of that contract in a little detail. It is a contract, dated June 23, 1926, for the purchase of 1,000 tons of Mex Fuel Oil at £4 per ton net, delivery to be taken at the buyers' works at Bury, Lancashire. Clause 3 says: "Delivery in sellers' road tank wagons as reasonably required by buyers in about equal monthly quantities from 23rd June, 1926, to 22nd June, 1927. Sellers shall not be called upon to deliver more than 100 tons in any one calendar month. Any departure from this stipulation shall not be considered as establishing a precedent." Clause 4: "Sellers shall not in any case be bound to offer or tender to the buyers oil under this contract, it being the intention that buyers shall give instructions to sellers for the deliveries required." Clause 5: "Each delivery shall constitute a separate contract." Clause 9: "Payment to be made in net cash within fourteen days from the date of despatch of each consignment, or net cash before delivery, if required by sellers. All payments to be made on due date whether under this or any other contracts between sellers and buyers as a condition precedent to future deliveries." Clause 12: "It is a condition of this contract that the oil is for buyers' own use, and not for resale." Then clause 15, which is the most important clause for the purpose of this action, says: "Sellers have the right at any time to invoice to buyers the due quantities of oil not taken up, and to demand payment of the invoice amounts, and such quantities (or a proportionate quantity of the bulk) shall be at buyers' risk and expense, or the sellers may, at their option, instead of invoicing, cancel such undelivered balance."

Deliveries were commenced and in due course proceeded, but towards the end of the year 1926 the defendants were not desirous of taking the balance of the contract quantity because coal was then available, and eventually, after some correspondence, in February, 1927, they wrote letters which in effect amounted to a repudiation of the contract entirely. They pointed out in those letters to the plaintiffs that the price of oil had risen above the contract price, and that they had no use for the oil as they were able to use coal; they said they had spent a lot of money on equipment with the intention of keeping on oil fuel indefinitely and expecting that after the settlement of the coal strike prices of oil fuel would come into line with the coal prices, but they found that that was not so; and they asked the plaintiffs to relieve them of the balance of the contract as the market price had risen above the contract price. The plaintiffs, however, refused to agree to that course. No further deliveries were made under the contract, and eventually the contract period expired on June 22, 1927, there being then an undelivered balance of the total 1,000 tons of 466 tons. Thereupon, after one or two letters, the plaintiffs wrote on June 27, 1927, to the defendants in these terms: "We beg to remind you that the period of delivery of Fuel Oil Contract No. 5175" — that is the contract in question — "expired on the 22nd instant and there is an undelivered balance of 466 tons remaining. We enclose invoice for this quantity and shall be glad to receive your cheque in settlement. The oil lies at our Barton Installation at your risk and expense, and we shall be obliged if you will arrange to take delivery promptly." The invoice which was enclosed was an ordinary invoice for goods sold and to be delivered, or actually delivered, and it gave the various particulars under the contract stating the amount, 466 tons, the price, 80*s.* per ton, the total, £1,864, "delivered ex Barton." The defendants in reply wrote that the contract was definitely cancelled, and they regretted that they could not do anything further in the matter. Nothing further does seem to have been done until the writ was issued on April 12, 1928, claiming the sum of £1,864 as money due under the contract. The material allegation in the Points of Claim is this: "In pursuance of clause 15 of the said contract the plaintiffs on the 27th June, 1927, invoiced to the defendants the balance of 466 tons and demanded payment thereof, but the defendants have failed, and by letters dated the 28th June, 1927, and 18th July, 1927, refused to pay the invoice amount, viz. £1,864. The plaintiffs have been at all material times and are now ready and willing to deliver the said 466 tons against payment of the price thereof."

The question is whether the plaintiffs are right in that claim, whether they are entitled to claim the money, as they do, as a debt due under the contract. The case is a somewhat difficult one to decide. The defendants contend that only damages can be claimed, and that these damages, having regard to the rise in the market price, can only be nominal.

The question depends on the true construction of clause 15 of the contract read with the other clauses, and in the light of the provisions of the Sale of Goods Act, 1893. Mr. Le Quesne's contention is that the plaintiffs, as sellers, derive from clause 15 the right to invoice the oil in respect of which the defendants, as buyers, have not given delivery instructions in due course, and thereupon to recover payment of the invoice price as a debt; and that irrespective of whether the defendants want the oil or not, or whether they have refused the oil altogether and repudiate the contract, or ever take or are even actually offered delivery; all the sellers need show is that they were ready and willing to give delivery, I presume within a reasonable time.

As a rule, the price of goods sold is only payable in respect of delivery, or in a case where the property has passed, so that the seller or other bailee of the goods holds for the buyer; or where, irrespective of delivery, there is a specific term of the contract that the price is payable at a time certain (which means at a time specified in the contract not depending on a future or contingent event, *The Merchant Shipping Company* v. *Armitage* ([1873] L. R. 9 Q. B. 99)), irrespective of the passing of the property or delivery. In the present case it is clear no property passed, because such is the rule where there is no specific appropriation of the bulk; this established rule has recently been again enunciated in *Re Wait* ([1927] 1 Ch. 606). No time certain is specified for payment in clause 15, and no delivery has been made or is contemplated, because the defendants have repudiated the contract, and the contract period has long expired. It has been held in the case of ordinary c.i.f. and f.o.b. contracts that section 49 (2) of the Sale of Goods Act, 1893, applies, and that where buyers refuse goods the sellers cannot claim the price, but only damages for non-acceptance, under section 50 of the Sale of Goods Act (*Stein Forbes and Co.* v. *County Tailoring Company* ([1916] 115 L. T. 215), *Colley* v. *Overseas Exporters* ([1921] 3 K. B. 302; 26 Com. Cas. 325)). Mr. Le Quesne distinguishes these cases on the ground that in them there was no special clause. He contends, relying on clause 55 of the Sale of Goods Act, that the parties to a contract for the sale of goods may make any lawful bargain they like so long as they do so in clear words; he refers to the case of *Lancaster* v. *Turner* ([1924] 2 K. B. 222; 29 Com. Cas. 207), where the Court of Appeal by a majority (Scrutton L.J. dissenting) held the defaulting sellers entitled to "invoice back" goods which they had sold but never tendered or delivered because they made default, and to recover from the innocent buyers a sum of money representing the difference between the contract price and the market price, which had fallen; the sellers thereby profited by their default though no goods were ever tendered under the contract, still less delivered back under the invoicing back.

No doubt parties may bind themselves by any lawful promise so long as the words are clear enough, but I have to consider if they have here used words so clear as to justify Mr. Le Quesne's contention. I do not think they have. I think clause 15 remains a term in a contract for the sale of goods, and the price invoiced under it still remains the price as of goods sold and delivered. Clause 15 is primarily, I think, intended to meet the sellers' difficulty when the buyer fails in due time to give the delivery instructions under clause 4, so that the sellers can fulfil their obligation under clause 3 to deliver by tank road wagons at the buyers' works; clause 15 may, I think, be brought into operation whenever instalment deliveries are in arrear; when the invoice is then delivered, the sellers can demand payment, just as under clause 9 payment may be required by the sellers in cash before delivery. Under clause 9 it is admitted that if the buyers refuse to pay and then refuse delivery the sellers cannot claim the price but only damages for non-acceptance. I think, likewise under clause 15, if the buyers say they will neither pay nor take the goods and thus repudiate the contract, the sellers can still only claim damages for non-acceptance of the goods, or for repudiation of the contract. Clause 15 does not in terms say that the buyers have to pay the invoice price as a debt at any specified time, or on delivery of the invoice, or at any specified time after delivery. What is invoiced under clause 15 is still the price payable under the contract, which includes the sellers' services in actually delivering the goods to the buyers' works. The sellers have never earned the price as such, and can only claim damages because they have been prevented from fulfilling their contract. It may be that clear words giving the effect claimed by the sellers can be framed; for instance, there might be an express provision for payment on a date certain, as in the *nisi prius* case of *Dunlop* v. *Grote* ([1845] 2 Car. and Kir. 153), where it was held that the whole sum was recoverable as a debt as it was agreed to be paid on a day certain, which indeed is now provided in section 49 (2) of the Sale of Goods Act. Nor are these conclusions at which I have arrived affected, in my opinion, by the remaining part of clause 15, namely that the quantities invoiced, or a proportionate quantity of the bulk, should be at buyers' risk and expense; these words mean primarily that if after delay the buyers take and pay for the contract goods, the sellers can debit them with storage and insurance charges; the words also, I am disposed to think, mean that if the contract remains alive and the bulk of oil is destroyed, say by fire, during the period of delay, the sellers may claim the price of such quantity as being at the sellers' risk when destroyed, though no property had passed, or could have passed, in the absence of appropriation. On that point, however, I have considerable doubt, because it is difficult to say in such a case that any specific goods were at the buyers' risk. *Sterns* v. *Vickers* ([1923] 1 K. B. 78) does not cover this point, because the goods in question there, though unsevered from the bulk, were in the hands of a storage company, and that company's delivery warrant for the contract quantity had been handed to and accepted by the buyers. In *Martineau* v. *Kitching* ([1872] L. R. 7 Q. B. 436) the goods were specified and had been paid for subject to an adjustment on final weighing, and were held by the Court to be at buyers' risk when destroyed in the sellers' warehouse; indeed the property seems to have passed. But even assuming that clause 15 puts a proportionate quantity of the oil at the buyers' risk, I do not think the clause entitles the sellers to recover the price as a debt in the facts of this case, namely, that the goods have not been destroyed, but the buyers refuse to give delivery instructions or accept the goods, and have entirely repudiated the contract, the contract period having long since elapsed. I think the sellers' only remedy in this case is in damages. . . .

I think the plaintiffs fail in their claim for the invoice price; no claim is made on the basis of damages because they are nominal. There will accordingly be judgment for the defendants with costs.

Judgment for the defendants.

In MULLER, MACLEAN & CO. v. LESLIE & ANDERSON, [1921] W. N. 235 (King's Bench Division), there was a contract to sell 14 gross padlocks at an agreed price f. o. b. New York to Bombay, shipment to be as soon as possible but no time fixed, terms cash against documents in London, goods to be delivered C. & F. Bombay. The sellers were to take out marine insurance. The buyers refused to accept the documents tendered, and the present action was brought for the price of goods sold and delivered and alternatively for damages. It was held that the sellers could not recover the price as the price was not payable "irrespective of delivery," but were entitled to damages.

In LIPSCHITZ v. NAPA FRUIT CO., 223 Fed. 698 (Circuit Court of Appeals, Second Circuit, 1915), plaintiff contracted to sell to defendant 1500 boxes of prunes to be shipped by water from California to New York. Payment was to be made on presentation of draft with bill of lading attached within ten days from date of shipment. The parties knew that the prunes could not arrive inside of three weeks. Defendant refused to pay the draft. In an action for the purchase price, judgment for plaintiff affirmed.

Note also GOURD v. HEALY, 176 N. Y. App. Div. 464 (First Department, 1917), where there was a contract for the sale of 50 cases of Chateau Yquem wine to be billed November 1, payable in four months. It was held that an action to recover the purchase price was properly brought and that it was not incumbent on the seller to make a tender of the goods before commencement of the suit.

ILLUSTRATED POSTAL CARD AND NOVELTY COMPANY v. HOLT

CONNECTICUT SUPREME COURT OF ERRORS, 1912

[85 *Connecticut Reports*, 140]

WHEELER, J. The plaintiff is a manufacturer of post-cards in New York City. The defendant is a wholesale dealer in post-cards in New Haven. A salesman of plaintiff procured from defendant in New Haven a verbal order for Christmas post-cards, subject to change. Subsequently, the defendant called at plaintiff's place of business in New York, and, after examinaing plaintiff's catalogue, gave it a written order for one hundred thousand Christmas post-cards No. 438, for the price of $275, and for other Christmas cards, the price for the whole order amounting to $321, the same to be shipped (by what method did not appear) on August 1st, and paid for December 1st, 1910. The plaintiff in its business manufactured post-cards of this character on special order and did not keep them in stock.

On July 16th, 1910, defendant wrote plaintiff that he was obliged to cancel the order for the one hundred thousand post-cards. After securing this order, the plaintiff began the manufacture of the cards, and all of the cards so ordered were finished and packed for shipment at the date of receipt of this letter. The plaintiff replied that it could not accept the attempted cancellation as the cards would be left on its hands. Wholesale dealers in Christmas post-cards place their orders by April 1st, the retail trade continues usually until the fall, and after July 1st there is no available market for these cards with jobbers and wholesale dealers.

The defendant twice again requested plaintiff to cancel the order for card No. 438, which plaintiff declined to do, replying to defendant's last letter of July 29th, on July 30th, and on August 4th shipped defendant's entire order by common carrier, not separating cards No. 438 from the rest of the order. Upon arrival of the goods in New Haven, defendant refused to receive them, and notified plaintiff he would receive balance of order exclusive of No. 438. Thereupon plaintiff notified him the goods were in the hands of the New England Navigation Company subject to his order, where they have since remained.

The law of the place of the contract determines the validity and construction of the contract; in short, the substantial rights under it, unless the contract is to be performed or to have its beneficial operation and effect elsewhere, or it is made with reference to the law of another place. *Chillingworth* v. *Eastern Tinware Co.*, 66 Conn. 306, 317, 33 Atl. 1009; *Beggs & Co.* v. *Bartels*, 73 Conn. 132, 133, 46 Atl. 874.

The form of remedy to be pursued and the judicial proceedings thereunder are prescribed and regulated by the law of the place of the action, while the merits and rights involved in the action are controlled by the law of the place of the contract, unless the place of performance is elsewhere, or it is made with reference to another law. *Wood* v. *Watkinson*, 17 Conn. 500, 510; *Atwater* v. *Townsend*, 4 Conn. 47, 48; *Scudder* v. *Union National Bank*, 91 U. S. 406, 412.

Though it were held upon these facts that the place of this contract and of its performance was New York, the form of the remedy would be governed by our law.

This action was begun to recover for the price of goods sold and delivered. Prior to the passage of the Sales Act (Public Acts of 1907, p. 764, Chap. 212), our law permitted an action for damages by the seller against the buyer for breach of his contract to buy goods to be manufactured for him, and it sought in such action to put the injured party in the place the contract would have placed him in had it been performed. The actual damage suffered was the recovery upheld. That was, as a rule, measured by the difference between the price of the contract of sale and the value of the goods made. When there was no market, or they were worthless, the actual damages might even be the entire value of the goods. *Allen* v. *Jarvis*, 20 Conn. 38, 48; *Jordan, Marsh & Co.* v. *Patterson*, 67 Conn. 473 480, 35 Atl. 521.

So far as we are aware, no case has ever reached this court where, upon breach of contract for the sale of goods, an action for the price of the goods was begun.

The English law denied such a remedy, and many of our State courts have followed the English law, while a number, under the lead of the New York court, have given the seller, upon breach of a contract of sale, a remedy permitting him to store or retain the goods for the buyer, and sue the buyer for the entire purchase price.

The theory of this law is that when the seller deposits the goods with a third person for the buyer, or segregates the goods and notifies the buyer that he holds them for him, the title passes, or the rights of the parties will subsequently be adjusted as if it had passed at that time. Williston on Sales, p. 945, § 563. Our law was in this condition when the Sales Act was passed.

The remedies provided by the Sales Act for the recovery of damages for nonacceptance of goods (§ 64), and for the recovery of the price (§ 63(1, 2)) when the property in the goods has passed, do not substantially differ from the remedies provided by our law at the time of its enactment.

The remedy (§ 63(3)) is an addition to the remedies up to that time known to our law, "although the property in the goods has not passed, if they cannot readily be resold for a reasonable price, and if the provisions of § 64(4) are not applicable, the seller may offer to deliver the goods to the buyer, and, if the buyer refuses to receive them, may notify the buyer that the goods are thereafter held by the seller as bailee for the buyer; and thereafter the seller may treat the goods as the buyer's and may maintain an action for the price."

Professor Williston, who wrote the Sales Act, says in a note (42 Amer. Law Rev. 900): "The rights of the seller are also enlarged as compared with his rights under the English Act both by the greater freedom in rescission allowed an unpaid seller with a lien (Section 61), and by the allowance of an action for the full price, even though the property in the goods has not passed, if they cannot readily be resold for a reasonable price (Section 63(3))."

The elements of an action under this section are: (1) A breach of the contract to sell goods; (2) that the property in the goods at the time of the breach has not passed; (3) that they cannot be sold for a reasonable price; (4) that the seller has offered to deliver them to the buyer; (5) that the buyer has refused to receive them; (6) that the seller has notified the buyer that he thereafter holds the goods as bailee for the buyer.

The notification of cancellation by this defendant and his persistence in this course constituted a breach of the contract of sale. At this time the goods had not been segregated, nor marked for the buyer, nor delivered to a carrier for the buyer, and, in the absence of provision in the contract to the contrary, the property had not passed to the buyer. 35 Cyc. 296; *Kost* v. *Reilly*, 62 Conn. 57, 60, 24 Atl. 519.

The finding that there was no available market for the goods after the breach, and that jobbers and wholesalers place no orders after April for such goods, and that these goods are not goods kept in stock, but are manufactured on special order, fully shows that the goods could not be sold for a reasonable price. There was no obligation upon the manufacturer to sell these cards at retail or to the retail trade — that would have involved the undertaking on its part of a new business.

The further finding, that the defendant refused to receive the goods, and that the seller declined to permit him to cancel the order, but shipped the goods by carrier to him, and notified him that they were in the carrier's hands subject to the defendant's order, is full compliance with the statutory requirements and ample notice to the buyer that the seller holds the goods as bailee for the buyer. Upon the plaintiff's delivery to the carrier and notice to the defendant that the carrier held the goods subject to his order, the property in these goods passed to the defendant. The carrier stands in place of the seller as bailee for the buyer to whom the goods now belong.

The fact that the plaintiff shipped the goods to the defendant after notice of cancellation, instead of retaining them, did not change the nature of the bailment. The carrier's possession was the plaintiff's possession — holding the goods for the defendant by the direction of the plaintiff.

The court properly overruled the defendant's claims of law, that title to the goods never passed to the defendant, and that because of notice of cancellation of the contract of sale the plaintiff was not justified in shipping the goods nor in shipping the whole order together and in not attempting to dispose of the cards.

The plaintiff was under no obligation to separate the order, nor to attempt to sell goods for which it knew it could not obtain a reasonable price.

It is quite probable that the retention of the goods in the hands of the seller may avoid questions in relation to the carrier's storage charges and as to the manner in which the goods have been kept; but the storage of the goods with an agent of the seller, or their delivery to a shipper for the buyer, does not add to the responsibility of the seller; he continues to be the bailee for the buyer of the goods for which no reasonable price can be obtained.

There is no error.

In this opinion the other judges concurred.

In CLAVAN *v.* HERMAN, 285 Penn. 120 (Supreme Court, 1926), there was a contract for the sale of 1000 dozen hose, deliveries to be made at the buyer's place of business. After part of the hose had been delivered the buyer asked the seller to cancel the balance of the order, but the seller declined, whereupon the buyer wrote asking for immediate shipment and promising to accept if the goods were up to sample. The seller refused to deliver, although offering to permit inspection on his own property and then to deliver on prepayment. The buyer declined to accede. In an action to recover the price of the undelivered hose, a judgment for defendant n. o. v.

was affirmed. Since plaintiff did not comply with the terms of the agreement it was immaterial whether the goods could be readily resold at a reasonable price.

In Barber-Greene Company, Inc. *v.* M. F. Dollard, Jr., Inc., 239 N. Y. App. Div. 655 (Third Department, 1934), there was a contract for the sale of a machine for excavating ditches. The buyer refused delivery, and the seller instructed its salesman to reship the machine and billed the buyer for freight and charges. Later the seller notified the buyer that the machine was being held subject to the buyer's orders. In an action for the purchase price judgment for plaintiff reversed. The conduct of the seller indicated that it elected to rescind and rely upon a claim for damages; and in any event "the fact that the goods cannot be readily resold must be affirmatively alleged and proved as a condition precedent in an action for the purchase price, and the burden of establishing this fact rests upon the plaintiff." In the present case there was no evidence that the machine could not be resold readily for a reasonable price.

Note also Rice-Macrae Motor Truck Company *v.* Wurst, 100 N. J. L. 113 (Court of Errors and Appeals, 1924), where it was held that the question whether certain goods could be resold readily at a reasonable price was one of fact.

3. DAMAGES FOR NON-ACCEPTANCE

SLOSS-SHEFFIELD STEEL & IRON CO. *v.* WISCONSIN FOUNDRY & MACHINE CO.

WISCONSIN SUPREME COURT, 1925

[187 *Wisconsin Reports*, 34]

OWEN, J. This is an appeal from a judgment of the superior court of Dane county awarding plaintiff and respondent damages against the defendant and appellant for defendant's breach of two contracts of purchase of certain pig iron from the plaintiff. The only question presented is whether the court applied the proper measure of damages.

On August 5, 1920, the parties entered into a contract whereby plaintiff agreed to sell and deliver to the defendant 150 tons of pig iron at $46.25 per ton, delivery to be made f. o. b. cars at Birmingham, Alabama, and shipments to be made during the last quarter of 1920. The defendant agreed to pay therefor $46.25 a ton "cash thirty days from average date of monthly deliveries." The contract also provided that "each month's deliveries shall be treated as a separate contract, independent of deliveries for other months."

Another contract of exact tenor was entered into between the same parties the same day for the sale and delivery of 150 tons of pig iron during the first quarter of 1921. The plaintiff delivered fifty tons under this contract in the month of October. On October 11, 1920, the defendant notified plaintiff not to make any further shipments on these contracts until defendant notified plaintiff, as defendant then had all the iron on hand it could handle at that time. Plaintiff acknowledged receipt of this letter and expressed the hope that it would be advised by the 1st of November as to what time in November defendant would be prepared to take care of the November quota. On November 9th plaintiff, having heard nothing from the defendant, wrote defendant that "we will appreciate your advice by return mail as to just what time during the month of November it will be satisfactory to you to have us make shipment of this tonnage." Plaintiff heard nothing from defendant until November 22d, when it received this telegram: "Car Santa Fe 29432 arrived today. Cannot accept it. This shipment made without order from us. We refuse to accept any further shipment on two contracts. Wire Northwestern Railroad disposition of car on track to save demurrage." It appears that this car had not been shipped by the plaintiff and it had nothing to do with it. Plaintiff so wrote defendant, and from time to time during the month of December made frequent demands upon the defendant to authorize further shipments under the contract. Plaintiff heard nothing further from defendant until January 14, 1921, when it received a communication from defendant's attorneys in which they said: "On behalf of our clients we desire to inform you that they will not accept any further shipments of iron under their contracts with you. You were wired to the same effect on November 28, 1920." The attitude of the defendant, as indicated by this letter, continued up to the 31st day of March, 1921. At no time did the defendant authorize any further shipments under the contracts.

The court held that under the first contract the date of delivery was December 31st and that under the second contract the date of delivery was March 31st, and awarded plaintiff as damages the difference between the contract price and the market price of pig iron at Birmingham on those dates. As already stated, the only question presented is whether this was the proper measure of damages.

It is a general proposition that where the buyer of goods under an executory agreement breaks the contract by refusing to accept the goods, the measure of damages is the difference between the contract price and the market price of the goods at the time when and the place where the contract should have been performed. 2 Williston, Sales (2d ed.) § 582; *Schuenemann* v. *John G. Wollaeger Co.* 170 Wis. 616, 176 N. W. 59; *Gwin* v. *Hopkinsville M. Co.* 190 Ala. 346, 67 South. 382; *Crandall-Pettee Co.* v. *Jebeles & Colias C. Co.* 195 Ala. 152, 69 South. 964; sec. 121.64, Stats. The only serious question presented by the facts of this case is when were the goods deliverable. The contracts merely provide for 150 tons of pig iron during the last quarter of 1920 and 150 tons during the first quarter of 1921. The contracts plainly contemplate that delivery shall take place from time to time during such periods. The contracts do not expressly provide, however, that any particular amount shall be delivered at any particular time, nor that any number of tons shall be delivered during any particular month. The correspondence indicates that the parties themselves contemplated that the pig iron should be delivered as called for by the defendant. That is indicated by the fact that the defendant wrote to the plaintiff not to deliver any more iron until notified. The defendant thus claimed the right to indicate when the iron should be delivered. That the plaintiff also placed a similar construction upon the contracts is indicated by the fact that it did not assume to make any shipments in the absence of directions from the defendant and that it continually appealed to defendant for shipping directions. There was no time during either three-months period when plaintiff had a right to deliver any amount of pig iron and compel the acceptance thereof by the defendant. It could not have delivered any of the pig iron prior to the last day of the period and caused a breach of the contract on the part of the defendant by its refusal to accept the shipment. We construe these contracts as calling for shipments from time to time pursuant to directions of defendant, and that the plaintiff had no absolute right to deliver the iron until the last day of each quarter. Until the last day of each quarter, therefore, there was no right on the part of the plaintiff to compel acceptance, and there could have been no breach on the part of the defendant until the last day of each quarter.

Appellant also contends that the breaches occurred on November 22d when the defendant telegraphed the plaintiff that it would not accept any further shipments under the two contracts, and if the breaches did not occur at that time the second contract was certainly breached on January 14th when defendant's attorneys wrote plaintiff that the defendant would not accept any further shipments of iron under the contracts. These notifications were repudiations rather than breaches of the contracts. They authorized the plaintiff to treat the contracts as terminated, but it was not bound to do so. One party to a contract cannot terminate it without the consent of the other. In discussing this subject Mr. Williston, in his work on Sales (2d ed.), § 584, says:

"The rule has been broadly laid down in England that in case of notice to a promisee of a promisor's intention not to perform his contract, 'the promisee, if he pleases, may treat the notice of intention as inoperative, and await the time when the contract is to be executed, and then hold the other party responsible for all the consequences of nonperformance.'" See, also, *Washburn-Crosby Co.* v. *Kubiak*, 175 Wis. 291, 185 N. W. 162.

This rule is supported by well-nigh universal authority in this country and, we think, is recognized in the Alabama cases already cited. Even though the communications of November 22d and January 14th constituted repudiations of the contracts on the part of defendant, plaintiff chose to keep the contracts alive, and the measure of damages applicable to the situation is not at all affected by the repudiations of the defendant. The plaintiff is entitled to the difference between the contract price and the market price of the goods at the time and place of delivery. The trial court correctly applied this rule, and the judgment cannot be disturbed.

By the Court. — Judgment affirmed.

In GARNER *v.* CHARLES A. KRAUSE MILLING COMPANY, 193 Wis. 80 (Supreme Court, 1927), a seller in Texas contracted for the sale of oil meal f. o. b. cars Milwaukee. The buyer notified the seller before shipment that it refused to perform the contract. The seller thereupon notified the buyer that he was taking in the oil meal at the present market price, and drew on the buyer for the difference between the current Texas price and the price fixed by the contract. The draft was dishonored. In an action by the seller for damages for breach of contract the trial court entered judgment for the full amount claimed as the difference, although it appeared that the market price in Milwaukee at the time of the breach was from $1.50 to $3.00 per ton in excess of the contract price. Judgment reversed.

In FROST *v.* KNIGHT, L. R. 7 Exch. 111 (Exchequer Chamber, 1872), Cockburn, C. J., said:

"The law with reference to a contract to be performed at a future time, where the party bound to performance announces prior to the time his intention not to perform it, as established by the cases of *Hochster* v *De la Tour* (2 E. & B. 678; 22 L. J. (Q.B.) 455) and *The Danube and Black Sea Co.* v. *Xenos* (13 C. B. (N.S.) 825; 31 L. J. (C.P.) 284) on the one hand, and *Avery* v. *Bowden* (5 E. & B. 714; 26 L. J. (Q.B.) 3), *Reid* v.

Hoskins (6 E. & B. 953; 26 L. J. (Q.B.) 5), and *Barwick* v. *Buba* (2 C. B. (N.S.) 563; 26 L. J. (C.P.) 280) on the other, may be thus stated. The promisee, if he pleases, may treat the notice of intention as inoperative, and await the time when the contract is to be executed, and then hold the other party responsible for all the consequences of non-performance: but in that case he keeps the contract alive for the benefit of the other party as well as his own; he remains subject to all his own obligations and liabilities under it, and enables the other party not only to complete the contract, if so advised, notwithstanding his previous repudiation of it, but also to take advantage of any supervening circumstance which would justify him in declining to complete it.

"On the other hand, the promisee may, if he thinks proper, treat the repudiation of the other party as a wrongful putting an end to the contract, and may at once bring his action as on a breach of it; and in such action he will be entitled to such damages as would have arisen from the non-performance of the contract at the appointed time, subject, however, to abatement in respect of any circumstances which may have afforded him the means of mitigating his loss."

WILLIAM M. ROYLANCE COMPANY *v.* JEWETT & SHERMAN COMPANY

WISCONSIN SUPREME COURT, 1927

[191 *Wisconsin Reports*, 490]

CROWNHART, J. The appellant claims that it is entitled to damages by reason of the defendant refusing to receive and pay for the carload of honey ordered through the defendant's broker from the plaintiff. The evidence before this court is substantially all in writing and consists of letters and telegrams passing between the defendant, its broker, and the plaintiff. A careful examination of these documents makes it very clear what the actual contract was and how the dispute occurred. The defendant gave its order to the broker to purchase 450 cases of honey. The defendant wanted 450 cases and the broker so understood, but through an error of the stenographer the order was for 450 tins, or half of the defendant's requirement. The plaintiff filled the order for 450 tins, and then the broker discovered the mistake and ordered the balance of the honey required by the defendant. The plaintiff filled this order in a second car and sent it on. When this second car arrived at Milwaukee, the defendant, for the first time, refused to accept the shipment or pay the draft. The whole correspondence shows absolute good faith on the part of the plaintiff and good faith on the part of the broker. The testimony of the broker at the trial plainly indicates that there was no misunderstanding as to the amount of honey wanted by the defendant at any time, until after the second car had been shipped. The testimony offered in behalf of the defendant is equally conclusive that the defendant wanted 450 cases of honey, and that it directed its broker to procure that amount. Mr. Horter, in behalf of the defendant, testified:

"I ordered 450 cases — that is what I wanted, but the confirmation was very confusing to me. . . . That is where the mistake was made, ordering 450 60-pound tins at 18c — that is one half of our order. Somebody made a mistake. That is undoubtedly where the misunderstanding arose. We had instructed the broker that we would take 450 cases and instead of that he ordered 450 tins. . . . The one point which I did not understand in this letter is this — I received an invoice calling for 225 cases, which constituted one car, together with this letter thanking me for the order. This constituted only one half of the order. I naturally wondered what happened to the other part of the order, so I advised Hilfer and he tried to straighten it up."

The fact is that the broker did straighten it out by explaining to the plaintiff that the order should have been for 450 cases, and that the defendant wanted 450 cases. The broker was the agent for the defendant in ordering the honey, and it was no fault of the plaintiff that there was a mistake in the broker's original order. The defendant was in no wise damaged because the honey was shipped in two cars instead of one. The price was the same. It is clear that the defendant breached its contract in refusing to accept and pay for the second car of honey.

Upon the refusal of the defendant to accept the second car, the plaintiff ordered the broker to dispose of the car elsewhere, but received word from the broker that he could not make the sale. In order to save the demurrage charges the plaintiff ordered the honey stored in a warehouse, and tried to sell the same through another broker, but was unsuccessful. The plaintiff, not being able to dispose of the honey through a broker, sent its agent on from Utah to dispose of the honey. He was successful in selling the honey at the same price at which the defendant had contracted, but he had to give sixty days' time and had to pay the storage and demurrage charges, together with his expense for the trip. The interest charge by reason of refusal to accept the honey, and consequent delay in final disposition thereof, amounts to $90.56. Also, there was a necessary allowance to the purchasers for shortage and damage in transit. These items, after giving credit for the amount received for the honey, leave a balance of $568.66, loss to the plaintiff.

The defendant contends that the plaintiff sold the honey for the same price that defendant was to pay, and hence there is no damage. The rule of damage is given in the Uniform Sales Act, ch. 121, Stats., as follows:

"Section 121.64 (1) . . .

"(2) The measure of damages is the estimated loss directly and naturally resulting, in the ordinary course of events, from the buyer's breach of contract.

"(3) Where there is an available market for the goods in question, the measure of damages is, in the absence of special circumstances, showing proximate damage of a greater amount, the difference between the contract price and market or current price at the time or times when the goods ought to have been accepted, or, if no time was fixed for acceptance, then at the time of the refusal to accept."

The testimony disclosed that there was no available market for the honey at the time in question. The plaintiff tried to secure a sale of the honey through the defendant's own broker and failed, and then tried to secure a sale through another broker and failed. This created a special circumstance, which takes the case out of sub. (3) and leaves the damages to be fixed under sub. (2). The plaintiff was required to use its best judgment in disposing of the honey. There is no question but it did so. The loss and expense were the result of defendant's breach of contract. It seems that the actual damages of the plaintiff, as stated, directly and naturally resulted, in the ordinary course of events, from the buyer's breach of contract, and the buyer is bound to respond accordingly.

The defendant asks for a review of the judgment of the circuit court, and contends that it is entitled to a judgment for $45.10 overpayment. Defendant contends that it should be required to pay only the actual freight, which was less than the freight rate from Provo. We think there is no dispute as to the custom of the trade, and we think the defendant fully understood it. Certainly if the shipment had been from a point where the freight rate was greater than that from Provo, it would have refused to pay the additional charge. We think the judgment of the circuit court on the first count was correct.

There is no substantial dispute as to the facts, and no good purpose will be subserved by ordering a new trial.

By the Court.—The cause is remanded, with directions to affirm the judgment of the circuit court on the first count in the complaint, and to grant judgment in favor of the plaintiff on the second count, in the sum of $568.66, with interest and costs.

A motion for a rehearing was denied, with $25 costs, on January 11, 1927.

In Brunswick-Balke-Collender Co. *v.* Wisconsin Mat Co., 24 Fed. (2nd) 78 (Circuit Court of Appeals, Seventh Circuit, 1928), there was a contract by which defendant was to purchase within a period of two years not less than 15,000 nor more than 30,000 pit mats. Defendant ordered, received, and paid for 10,325 mats within the contract period. After the expiration of the period enough more were ordered to make the total 11,030. Nearly five months after the end of the period defendant notified plaintiff that it would neither specify nor receive any more mats. In an action for damages for the breach it appeared that no other available market for the mats was open to plaintiff. A judgment awarding as damages the difference between the cost of manufacture and the contract price was affirmed.

In Gussman *v.* Byrd Cattle Co., 11 Fed. (2nd) 136 (Circuit Court of Appeals, Fifth Circuit, 1926), a contract for the sale of 43 carloads of onions to be delivered at the rate of 3 carloads per day was repudiated by the buyer after accepting and paying for 6 carloads. At that time the remaining onions were ready for delivery, although 9 carloads were still in the field only partly crated. The seller sold 24 carloads during the next

16 days, at the end of which time there was no further market for onions, and 4 fully crated carloads were thrown away. The balance in the field were left there, as they could not be sold at any price. In an action for damages the buyer contended that the amount should be restricted to the difference between the purchase price and the market price of each installment of 3 carloads at the time it was required by the contract to be delivered. In upholding a charge of the trial court that the measure of damages was the difference between the contract price of 37 carloads and the amount received from the sales of 24 carloads, the Court said: "In this case the goods were ready for delivery, and passage of title was prevented by defendant's repudiation of his contract. One of the rights which the vendor has under such circumstances is to resell the goods and measure his loss by the difference between the contract price and the price received on resale. *Gilbert Grocery Co.* v. *Howell* (C. C. A.) 289 F. 474. See, also, note 42 L. R. A. (N. S.) 670. Plaintiff was not bound to make resales in installments as large and as often as called for by the contract, but was within its rights if it acted in good faith, and did not delay sales for an unreasonable length of time. 24 R. C. L. 112. It is reasonable to suppose that defendant's sudden repudiation of the contract made it necessary for plaintiff to seek other purchasers and caused some delay."

CRANE IRON WORKS *v.* COX & SONS CO.

CIRCUIT COURT OF APPEALS, THIRD CIRCUIT, 1928

[28 *Federal Reporter* (*Second Series*), 328]

DAVIS, Circuit Judge. This case was brought here on writ of error by plaintiff on the ground of the inadequacy of the verdict, resulting from the erroneous admission of evidence and charge to the jury.

The Crane Iron Works, plaintiff, a manufacturer of pig iron, entered into a contract with the defendant on September 3, 1920, to sell 200 tons of pig iron at $51.25 per ton. Deliveries were to be made "about equally over the first half of 1921." On November 16, 1920, defendant wrote to Rogers, Brown & Co., factors of the plaintiff, that, "owing to unforeseen business conditions, we wish to cancel this contract, which as we take it injures no one, inasmuch as it is not in effect until the first of 1921." Rogers, Brown & Co. submitted the letter to plaintiff, and on November 22, 1920, wrote defendant that:

"The Crane furnaces state that this contract was entered into in good faith by them at the time it was taken, and their practice is to live up to all their deals, regardless of price or condition, and, further, in order to do this, they are compelled, when entering orders for pig iron, to protect themselves on raw material, and, inasmuch as they have covered themselves in this respect to take care of your contract, it is out of the question for them to consider cancellation."

The defendant replied on December 3, 1920, stating its intention to cancel the contract, and in conclusion said: "Please consider this and our letter of November 16th as a formal notice of the cancellation of contract dated September 3d." In reply on December 7, 1920, the plaintiff said that the contract "was entered into in good faith and is expected to be shipped by the furnace company, whether prices went up or down, and they maintain that contracts should always be respected, and they, therefore, intend to ship the iron in accordance with the agreement made." On December 15, 1920, defendant wrote: "We can only state that, if they want to start something, let them begin shipping."

The plaintiff referred the matter to its attorneys, who on December 28, 1920, wrote to defendant, asking it to refer them to its attorney, with instructions to him to accept service of a writ. This ended the negotiations between the parties, and plaintiff brought this suit against defendant on March 15, 1921, for cancellation of the contract, and demanded as damages "the difference between the contract price for the 200 tons at $51.25 per ton, and the average market price for the same grade and quantity of iron in shipments about equally over the first half of 1921."

The case was tried to the court and jury, which rendered a verdict for $1,200 damages, with interest from July, 1921. The judgment entered on the verdict was brought here on plaintiff's writ of error because of the inadequacy of the verdict. This resulted, plaintiff contends, from the admission of irrelevant evidence and the erroneous charge of the court.

This was the second trial of this case. The judgment was reversed in the first trial, because the court refused to admit testimony showing the price of ore at the time the defendant sought to cancel the contract on November 16, 1920, and on the subsequent dates when it reiterated its determination to cancel. *Cox & Sons Co.* v. *Crane Iron Works* (C. C. A.) 5 F.(2d) 314. On the retrial the court admitted evidence showing the prices on November 16 and December 3, 1920, the dates of the two letters which defendant said constituted "formal notice of the cancellation of the contract."

Plaintiff says that it was error to admit this testimony over objection, because the measure of damages is fixed by section 64 (3) of the Uniform Sales of Goods Act, which provides that:

"Where there is an available market for the goods in question, the measure of damages is, in the absence of special circumstances, showing proximate damage of a greater amount, the difference between the contract price and the market or current price at the time or times when the goods ought to have been accepted, or, if no time was fixed for acceptance, then at the time of the refusal to accept." 4 Comp. St. N. J. 1910, p. 4662.

It further says "that the only relevant testimony with respect to market prices was the market prices for the months of January, February, March, April, May, and June of 1927, being the dates on which the iron in question was to have been delivered and should have been accepted."

Counsel relies upon the case of *United States* v. *Burton Coal Co.*, 273 U. S. 337, 47 S. Ct. 351, 71 L. Ed. 670, and says that it "sets at rest any question as to the measure of damage." In administering New Jersey Law, the federal court, with exceptions not here applicable, follows the statutes and rules of law of New Jersey as declared by her highest courts. *Jackson* v. *Chew*, 12 Wheat. 153, 167, 6 L. Ed. 583; *Bucher* v. *Cheshire R. R. Co.*, 125 U. S. 555, 8 S. Ct. 974, 31 L. Ed. 795; *De Vaughn* v. *Hutchinson*, 165 U. S. 566, 17 S. Ct. 461, 41 L. Ed. 827; *Madisonville Traction Co.* v. *St. Bernard Mining Co.*, 196 U. S. 239, 25 S. Ct. 251, 49 L. Ed. 462; *Kuhn* v. *Fairmont Coal Co.*, 215 U. S. 349, 360, 30 S. Ct. 140, 54 L. Ed. 228. But the question here is whether or not the statute and cases cited are applicable, and so controlling. Defendant says that they are not, because, when it canceled the contract on a falling market, it was the duty of the plaintiff to use reasonable diligence to mitigate its damages, and, if it had done so, the damages it suffered would not have been in excess of those found by the jury. When this case was here before [*Cox & Sons Co.* v. *Crane Iron Works*, 5 F.(2d) 314] we said:

"Indeed, the court rightly announced the law when it told the jury: 'You have heard the evidence as to what the market price was during the first half of 1921, and from that you would determine what was the value of this iron which Cox & Sons would not take, and you would also from the contract figure out what was the contract price for this iron, and the difference would be the measure of damages, unless you should find that there was something that the Crane Iron Works might have done to lessen or minimize the damages.' Its error consisted in having previously ruled out the offer of the defendant's evidence of the element of the price at the time of the breach as proof 'that there was something the Crane Iron Works might have done to lessen or minimize the damages.' Its refusal to receive evidence of the market price at the time the anticipatory breach was accepted by the seller, and what the seller could have done to minimize the loss, was therefore error."

The ultimate question before us, therefore, is whether or not the Uniform Sales of Goods Act of New Jersey abrogates the rule of law requiring the injured party on breach of a contract to use reasonable diligence in mitigating his damages, and, if it does not, is the instant case one in which that rule should have been applied? The act does not expressly repeal the rule of law as to the mitigation of damages, nor is the act inconsistent with it, and so it is not repealed by implication. At the argument, counsel for plaintiff admitted that the Uniform Sales of Goods Act does not repeal this rule of law. It is still the duty of an injured party to use due diligence to mitigate his damages on the breach of a contract.

Was the plaintiff required to use due diligence to mitigate its damages in this case? The price of pig iron was constantly falling, with no prospect or indication of a rising market. The plaintiff knew, from the contents of the defendant's letters, that it persisted in its determination not to perform the contract and had definitely canceled it. In our former opinion, we said of the plaintiff: "It accepted the tendered cancellation of the defendant as a breach, anticipatory in theory, but final in fact." The testimony shows that plaintiff was constantly manufacturing and selling pig iron of the kind and quality covered by the contract. On November 16 it sold and delivered 90.04 tons, and on December 15, 234.14 tons, two of the dates defendant wrote, stating that it would not carry out the contract. For the 30 days from November 16 to December 15, plaintiff manufactured a daily average of 214.13 tons. The evidence does not show that plaintiff appropriated any particular iron to this contract.

The learned trial judge charged the jury that the measure of damages was the difference between the contract price and the market price at the time when and the place where deliveries should have been made, unless it should find that there was something that the plaintiff might have done to lessen or minimize the damages, such as making forward contracts or disposing of the goods. The defendant submitted testimony showing that, if the plaintiff had resold the iron to others on November 16, it would have lost $600, and, if it had sold on December 3, 1920, it would have lost approximately $1,800.

The price of pig iron began to drop soon after the contract was made, from the contract price of $51.25 per ton to $23.96 per ton in June, the end of the delivery period. The jury evidently found that, in view of the cancellation of the contract by the defendant, the plaintiff should have resold the iron when its damages were $1,200, some time between November 16 and December 3, 1920. We think that the question of the mitigation of damages, under the facts in this case, was for the jury, and there was evidence to justify its conclusion. The question of the mitigation of damages was not raised, and so was not before the court in the case of *United States* v. *Burton Coal Co., supra.* It has no bearing upon the question upon which this case depends. It merely restates the law as declared in the New Jersey Sales of Goods Act.

We do not find that the learned District Judge erred in the admission of evidence or in his charge to the jury, and the judgment is affirmed.

In Roth and Co. *v.* Taysen, Townsend and Co., 73 L. T. 628 (Queen's Bench Division, 1895), a contract was made on May 24 for the sale of a cargo of maize to be shipped from a port in the Argentine about July 15. The market was then falling, and on May 28 the buyers repudiated the contract. On July 24 the sellers brought an action for damages. At that time prices were still falling with no prospect of recovery. The sellers made no attempt to resell until the vessel and cargo arrived on September 5, when the loss was £3807. If a resale had been made on July 24, the loss would have been £1557. Judgment was given for plaintiffs for the latter figure.

In Jamal *v.* Moola Dawood, Sons & Co., [1916] 1 A. C. 175 (Privy Council, 1915), there was a contract for the sale of shares to be delivered and paid for by December 30. A clause in the contract gave the seller an option to resell in default of payment. The shares were tendered on December 30, but the buyers refused to take delivery. At the market price for sales on that day the shares would have realized Rs. 109,000 less than the contract price. The sellers gave notice of intention to sell against the buyers, but did not resell until February 28, and sold at various times from then until August, realizing in that way more than if resale had been made on December 30, a sum of only Rs. 79,000 less than the contract price. In an action for damages the sellers claimed to recover Rs. 109,000. Reversing the trial judge and the Chief Court of Calcutta, it was held that the sellers were entitled to recover Rs. 109,000. "If the seller retains the shares after the breach, the speculation as to the way the market will subsquently go is the speculation of the seller, not of the buyer; the seller cannot recover from the buyer the loss below the market price at the date of the breach if the market falls, nor is he liable to the purchaser for the profit if the market rises."

CHAPTER II

Rights and Remedies of the Buyer

1. WHEN TITLE TO THE GOODS HAS PASSED TO THE BUYER

ARONSON *v.* MOLOGA HOLZINDUSTRIE A/G LENINGRAD

Court of Appeal, 1927

[32 *Commercial Cases*, 276]

[This was an appeal from a decision of Roche, J., upon an award stated in the form of a Special Case.]

Scrutton L.J. I think we cannot interfere with this award, and I should like to say what I have said a good many times without anybody paying attention to it, that I wish commercial people, when they put arbitration clauses in their contracts, would be content with the arbitration that they have chosen, instead of trying to upset the arbitrator that they have chosen as soon as he decides against them.

In quality arbitrations I can quite understand that an arbitration is a much better way of dealing with the matter than proceedings in a Court; but when any questions of law are involved, first of all to go to an arbitrator who is not a legal man, and then, when he decides against you, to try and upset him in the Court, although the Court will not have a free hand to deal with the facts, seems to me to be a thoroughly unsatisfactory way of dealing with these things. As nobody has paid any attention to what I have said in the past, no doubt nobody will pay any attention to what I say now.

The contract in this case is made in December for the purchase of pulpwood lying at Leningrad, and of course it is obvious that a contract made in December for shipment at Leningrad runs the risk of the shipment being prevented by ice. The contract recognizes that and provides for what is to happen if, on the closing of navigation, the goods have not been shipped. The contract was for 1,000 Russian cubic fathoms of pulpwood, and it was provided that if the shipment was prevented by ice in certain circumstances payment should be made at once; and payment was accordingly made for the contract quantity of pulpwood, which then became what is known in the trade as "overlying" pulpwood, because it was cut in one season, overlay through the winter, and was shipped in the next season, when, in the next season, the buyer sent a ship. The sellers in this case contracted to put free alongside the ship and load into the same according to the custom of the port; but they only brought 500 fathoms of overlying pulpwood, and when asked where the other 500 fathoms were, they said: "Oh, we have sold them, but we tender you 500 fathoms of this season's pulpwood," which, according to the arbitrator, was then of the same value as overlying pulpwood was. The buyer was not satisfied with that, and he said that he had bought overlying pulpwood and he was entitled to have it; but, inasmuch as the result of his refusing the 500 fathoms tendered him of the new season's pulpwood would have been that the ship would be half empty and would make a heavy claim against him for dead freight, he, under what the arbitrator finds to be a proper protest, took the 500 fathoms of new pulpwood, thereby relieving anybody of the possibility of a claim by the ship for £1,500 worth of dead freight.

Now what is to happen? The seller says: "Oh, you have taken goods of equal value, at the time when you took them, with the goods which you ought to have had, and consequently there are no damages." It seems to me that there are two ways, on the award, of answering that: First of all, I think it is pretty clear that the goods being specified goods, and having been paid for, the property has passed, and that when the seller sold them to somebody else he converted the goods. The measure of damages for conversion is the price of the goods at the time when the conversion took place. If without accord and satisfaction, to minimize damages, other goods are accepted to mitigate the damages at a later period, the measure of damages is the difference between the value of the goods at the time of conversion and the value of the substituted goods taken to minimize damages, at the time when they were taken; and if prices have fallen in the interval, the fall of price between those two dates is the proper measure of damages, and that is the measure which was taken in *Smith* v. *Tregarthen* ([1887] 56 L. J. Q. B. 437), to which I referred during the argument. The arbitrator says, in language which in the ordinary reading I can only read as properly interpreting the damages, that "In the event of the Court deciding that the sellers were liable to the buyer in damages on account of their having disposed of part of the goods contracted for" — that they did — "and substituting other goods" — that they did — "the price of such goods having in the meantime fallen" — in the ordinary meaning of English "in the meantime" is between their disposing of and substituting — "I find that the applicant is entitled to £1,000 damages from the respondents."

In the ordinary meaning of English that is a correct measure of damages, and a finding of fact of an amount, with which we cannot interfere.

That is one way of putting it; but it is said by Mr. Le Quesne for the sellers: "Whatever the arbitrator may have said, he did not really mean that. What he meant was, in the meantime, between the contract date and the substitution." Well, he has not said so, but I will assume that in commercial language this language means that, because sometimes commercial language is not the same as ordinary English. It does not seem to me that that makes it any better, because the seller has contracted in December to sell and deliver to the ship at a later date. Mr. Le Quesne says he has fulfilled that contract by selling so that the property passes and receiving a price; but he has not, because he has not delivered to the ship at the later date, and consequently he is in breach of the contract for not having delivered to the ship the second 500 fathoms; and if so, there seems to me to be a clear cause of action for non-delivery, with, accepted as mitigation of damages, goods at a later date which were worth less than the goods that the sellers ought to have delivered. Consequently, while the buyer might have said: "I have not got 500 fathoms of the goods you purported to sell me. Give me back the money paid for them," he takes, in mitigation of that claim, goods at a later date worth less than the sum he would have received for the failure of consideration. Putting it in that way, which is the way that the learned Judge below puts it, and which does not seem to me to be subject to any difficulty as to interpretation of the award, also the same result follows.

On those two grounds I think we cannot interfere with the award of the arbitrator.

[Concurring opinions of Bankes and Atkin, L. JJ., are omitted.]

In KENNEDY *v.* WHITWELL, 4 Pick. 466 (Massachusetts Supreme Judicial Court, 1827), there was a sale of 40 barrels of gin. The buyer paid the price and demanded the gin, but the seller refused to deliver it, and the buyer brought an action in trover. Before the trial and nearly eight months after the refusal to deliver, the seller had resold the gin for 16¢ a gallon more than the contract price. It was held that damages should be assessed on the basis of the value of the gin at the time of the conversion by refusal to deliver.

In CHINERY *v.* VIALL, 5 H. & N. 288 (Court of Exchequer, 1860), sheep sold to a buyer on credit were left in the possession of the seller for the convenience of the buyer. Without any default on the part of the buyer, the seller resold the sheep to a third person. In an action of trover by the buyer against the seller it was held that he was entitled to recover as damages the value of the sheep less the price agreed to be paid.

Note also POWERS *v.* DODGSON, 194 Mich. 133 (Supreme Court, 1916), where there was a present sale of a lot of wool at a price conditioned on a maximum quantity of fine wool. On sacking it appeared that the actual quantity of fine wool was greatly in excess of that stated, whereupon the buyer claimed to adjust the price accordingly. The seller refused, and resold the wool. The buyer brought an action of *assumpsit* for breach of contract. The trial judge was upheld in charging that on such facts the measure of damages should be the difference between the contract price and the value of the wool at the time of the resale.

In FRANCE *v.* GAUDET, L. R. 6 Q. B. 199 (Exchequer Chamber, 1871), the plaintiff purchased champagne lying at the defendant's wharf at 14*s.* per dozen, and resold it at 24*s.* to the captain of a ship about to leave England. The defendant refused to deliver the wine so that the plaintiff was unable to fulfill his contract, champagne of similar quality not being procurable in the market. The defendant had no knowledge of the sale or of the purpose of which the plaintiff required the champagne. In an action for the conversion it was held that the plaintiff was entitled as damages to the price at which he had sold the champagne.

2. FOR NON-DELIVERY

THE MORRIS JOSELOFF COMPANY *v.* SPIRT

CONNECTICUT SUPREME COURT OF ERRORS, 1922

[97 *Connecticut Reports,* 447]

Action by an alleged purchaser of eight hundred bags of sugar, to recover damages for its nondelivery, brought to and tried by the Superior Court in New Haven County, Avery, J.; judgment for the plaintiff for nominal damages only ($25), from which it appealed. No error.

The plaintiff operated a chain of grocery stores in Waterbury, and on March 22d, 1920, requested defendant, a retired wholesale grocer, to purchase sugar for it. Defendant contracted to purchase of the Paragon Sales Corporation one thousand bags of sugar. Defendant on March 25th, 1920, notified plaintiff that he had purchased one thousand bags of sugar, and offered to sell and did sell plaintiff five hundred bags, with the right upon the part of the plaintiff to increase the purchase to eight hundred bags. Thereupon plaintiff and defendant entered into a contract by which defendant agreed to sell plaintiff five hundred bags, 100 pounds each, fine granulated sugar, ground by the American Sugar Refining Company, to be delivered upon a car in New York not later than March 27th, for the price of 18 cents per pound net, f. o. b. Waterbury. The defendant further agreed to give plaintiff the privilege of increasing the quantity of sugar purchased from 500 to 800 bags, and plaintiff contracted to purchase this sugar upon these terms. The plaintiff did not exercise his right to increase his purchase to 800 bags.

Defendant, on March 27th, notified plaintiff that the firm from which he had purchased the sugar had refused to deliver the same to him, and that he would be unable to deliver the sugar as agreed, and he did not, on March 27th or at any time, deliver any part of said sugar to plaintiff. Defendant broke his contract on March 27th.

The market value of said sugar from March 27th to April 1st, 1920, was 14 cents per pound, and the market value of such sugar did not reach 18 cents per pound until after May 1st, 1921. There was an available wholesale market for such sugar on March 27th and April 1st. Plaintiff purchased of the American Sugar Refining Company on April 1st, 1920, 350 bags of sugar at 14 cents per pound, and made its next attempt to purchase such sugar at the nearest wholesale market, New York City, on April 13th, 1920. The cost of transporting such sugar from New York to Waterbury was one-quarter of a cent per pound, and the market value of such sugar on March 27th and until April 1st, 1920, including the freight thereon, was 14¼ cents per pound.

The plaintiff did not introduce any evidence whatsoever to establish the market value of such sugar on March 27th, 1920, or any evidence whatsoever as to the market value of such sugar prior to April 9th, 1920. The market for such sugar was rising during March and April, 1920.

The trial court concluded that the contract was broken on March 27th, and that the measure of damages was the difference between the contract price and the wholesale market price on the date of breach, and that as such market price had not been shown to be more than the contract price, the plaintiff was entitled only to nominal damages.

WHEELER, C. J. Unless the finding be corrected in such way as to affect the judgment rendered, the appeal must fail. Plaintiff's claim to recover loss of profits, loss to its business, and loss in the purchase of Porto Rican sugar in place of the sugar which defendant did not deliver, set forth elements of special damage, each one of which must have been alleged in order to support a recovery therefor. *Tomlinson* v. *Derby,* 43 Conn. 562; *Coast Central Mill Co.* v. *Russell Lumber Co.*, 88 Conn. 109, 112, 89 Atl. 898. The complaint in this case sets forth a breach of contract for failure to deliver the sugar contracted for, and claims general damages, but does not allege any special damage suffered in consequence of the breach.

Plaintiff's exception to the court's finding that the plaintiff did not avail itself of its privilege to increase the quantity of sugar purchased from 500 to 800 bags, is not well taken. Equally without merit is the exception to the court's finding that the breach of this contract occurred on March 27th, 1920.

The measure of damages in this case, under General Statutes, § 4733, is "the difference between the contract price and the market or current price of the goods at the time or times when they ought to have been delivered." This section was declaratory of our common law. The market price was to be ascertained in the nearest wholesale market, New York City, on the date of breach, March 27th, 1920, if there was a market at this time. The trial court finds the price of said sugar on March 27th, 1920, and on April 1st, 1920, was 14 cents per pound in New York City. This was the quoted price, and the sugar could be bought in limited quantity, not to exceed 100 bags, at the quoted price. But the salesman of the American Sugar Company candidly testified that 500 bags could not then be purchased at one time. So that we do not think the court was authorized in finding that plaintiff could have purchased 500 bags of American Sugar Refining Company sugar such as this contract called for, at 14 cents on either of these dates. Nor do we think that in view of the testimony of the representative of the Sugar Company, that the court was justified in finding that there was an available wholesale market for the purchase of 500 bags of such sugar in March 27th and April 1st, 1920. But we think the court was entirely right in its conclusion that it had not been shown that the wholesale market price was more than the contract price on or about March 27th, 1920. The finding that plaintiff made no effort after April 1st, 1920, to purchase sugar in New York until the 13th of the same month, is fully supported by the evidence.

The only evidence before the court of the price of sugar between

March 27th and April 9th, 1920, was the quotation of the price of the American Sugar Refining Company of 14 cents per pound, and the sale by that Company on April 1st, 1920, of 350 bags of sugar at 14 cents per pound to plaintiff. This evidence, in view of the salesman's testimony that 500 bags could not then have been bought, was insufficient to warrant a finding that the 500 bags could have been purchased for immediate delivery at 14 cents per pound. But it was practically all the evidence before the court of the price of this sugar between these dates. The plaintiff failed to prove any damage on the date of breach, or on any day within a reasonable time therefrom, and the judgment for nominal damages was the only judgment which, upon the facts, could have been rendered.

Three weeks after the trial, plaintiff presented an amendment of its complaint, setting up certain items of special damage as within the "special circumstances showing proximate damages of a greater amount," allowed under General Statutes, § 4733. The court's ruling disallowing the amendment is assigned as error. Upon the facts of record, the matter was within the discretion of the trial court. . . .

Other assignments of error are without merit.

There is no error.

In this opinion the other judges concurred, except GAGER, J., who concurred in the result, but died before the opinion was written.

In WERTHEIM *v.* CHICOUTIMI PULP COMPANY, [1911] A. C. 301 (Privy Council, 1910), there was an action for damages for breach of contract to deliver 3000 tons of wood pulp between September 1 and November 1. The seller did not deliver until the following June, and the buyer claimed to be entitled to damages of 27*s.* 6*d.* per ton, the difference between 70*s.*, the market price at the port of delivery on the due date, and 42*s.* 6*d.*, the market price at the same place on the date of actual delivery. It appeared that the buyer sold the pulp at 65*s.* per ton. In holding that the proper measure of damages was 5*s.* per ton, Lord Atkinson said: "The rate per ton so fixed is, in their Lordships' opinion, the highest rate at which it could properly be fixed, since it covers the loss actually sustained. And it is the general intention of the law that, in giving damages for breach of contract, the party complaining should, so far as it can be done by money, be placed in the same position as he would have been in if the contract had been performed: *Irvine* v. *Midland Ry Co.* (*Ireland*) ((1880) 6 L. R. Ir. at p. 63), approved of by Palles C.B. in *Hamilton* v. *Magill* ((1883) 12 L. R. Ir. at p. 202). That is a ruling principle. It is a just principle. The rule which prescribes as a measure of damages the difference in market prices at the respective times above mentioned is merely designed to apply this principle and, as stated in one of the American cases cited, it generally secures a complete indemnity to the purchaser. But it is intended to secure only an indemnity. The market value is taken because it is presumed to be the true value of the goods to the purchaser. In the case of non-delivery, where the purchaser does not get the goods he purchased, it is assumed that these would be worth to him, if he had them, what they would fetch in the open market; and that, if he wanted to get others in their stead, he could obtain them in that market at that price. In such a case, the price at which the purchaser might in anticipation of delivery have resold the goods is properly treated, where no question of loss of profit arises, as an entirely irrelevant matter: *Rodocanachi* v. *Milburn* (18 Q. B. D. 67). The purchaser not having got his goods should receive by way of damages enough to enable him to buy similar goods in the open market. Similarly, when the delivery of goods purchased is delayed, the goods are presumed to have been at the time they should have been delivered worth to the purchaser what he could then sell them for, or buy others like them for, in the open market, and when they are in fact delivered they are similarly presumed to be, for the same reason, worth to the purchaser what he could then sell for in that market, but if in fact the purchaser, when he obtains possession of the goods, sells them at a price greatly in advance of the then market value, that presumption is rebutted and the real value of the goods to him is proved by the very fact of this sale to be more than market value, and the loss he sustains must be measured by that price, unless he is, against all justice, to be permitted to make a profit by the breach of contract, be compensated for a loss he never suffered, and be put, as far as money can do it, not in the same position in which he would have been if the contract had been performed, but in a much better position."

In DELMONT GAS COAL CO. *v.* DIAMOND ALKALI CO., 275 Penn. 535 (Supreme Court, 1923), in an action for the purchase price of coal defendant counterclaimed for damages due to short deliveries. It was held that in the absence of any evidence that defendant had supplied its wants elsewhere damages could be claimed amounting to the difference between the contract price and the market price at the time and place of delivery.

Compare CLARK *v.* PINNEY, 7 Cowen 681 (New York Court of Appeals, 1827), where there was a contract for the sale of a quantity of salt, for which the buyer paid in advance. The seller failed to deliver and the buyer immediately brought an action for the breach. It was held that the buyer was not limited in damages to the difference between the contract price and the market price at the time and place set for delivery, but was entitled to recover the highest price at any time between the delivery date and the day of trial.

SEAVER *v.* LINDSAY LIGHT COMPANY

NEW YORK COURT OF APPEALS, 1922

[233 *New York Reports*, 273]

MCLAUGHLIN, J. The defendant, in October, 1915, was located and doing business at Chicago, Ill., and plaintiff's assignor was located and doing business in London, England. About the time named they entered into a written contract, consisting of letters and cablegrams passing between their respective brokers, by which defendant agreed to sell and deliver to plaintiff's assignor 5,544 pounds of thorium in six monthly shipments at the price of $4 per pound, c. i. f. London dock. Each shipment was to be paid for in Chicago in advance. Three shipments were made and paid for according to the contract, but defendant refused to ship the balance, 2,772 pounds. This action was thereupon brought to recover the damages alleged to have been sustained. At the trial the sole issue was the proper measure of damages, the plaintiff contending it was the difference between the contract and market price at London dock at the time of the breach, and defendant contending it was the difference between the contract and market price at Chicago at that time.

If the former contention were correct, then plaintiff was entitled to recover $8,316, besides interest; if the latter contention were correct, then he was entitled to recover only $868.50, besides interest, the different amounts being the difference between the market price at London dock and Chicago at the time of the breach.

The trial court held that defendant's contention was correct, and thereupon gave judgment for the plaintiff in accordance therewith. Plaintiff appealed to the Appellate Division, which reversed the judgment and ordered a new trial, holding that the measure of damage was as contended by plaintiff. Defendant now appeals to this court.

The meaning of the letters c. i. f. in an executory contract is, and at the time the contract in question was made were, well understood in the commercial world. They mean the cost of the merchandise, insurance thereon, and freight charges to point of destination. (*Thames & Mersey Ins. Co., Ltd.* v. *U. S.*, 237 U. S. 19.) Unless there is something in a c. i. f. contract to indicate to the contrary, the seller completes his contract when he delivers the merchandise called for to the shipper, pays the freight thereon to point of destination, and forwards to the buyer bill of lading, invoice, insurance policy and receipt showing payment of freight. (*Mee* v. *McNider*, 109 N. Y. 500; *Smith Co., Ltd.* v. *Marano*, 267 Penn. St. 107; *Ireland* v. *Livingston*, L. R. 5 H. L. 395; *Klipstein* v. *Dilsizian*, 273 Fed. Rep. 473; Williston on Sales, secs. 407, 408; Mechem on Sales, vol. 2, sec. 1736.)

Where was the delivery of the thorium in the present case to be made? Was it at Chicago or at London dock? If delivery were to be made at the former place, then the measure of damage was as found by the trial court. If at London dock, then it was as found by the Appellate Division.

I am of the opinion that the trial court was right. When the correspondence and cablegrams are all construed together, as they must be, then it seems to me they clearly indicate an intention on the part of both parties that the delivery was to be made at Chicago and when defendant delivered to a carrier at that point, paid the freight to point of destination, and forwarded the other necessary documents, he had fully completed his part of the contract. Failure to make delivery at that place obligated it to respond in damages in an amount corresponding to the difference there between the contract and market price of thorium at the time of the breach plus the cost of insurance and freight. There certainly is nothing in this contract to indicate that a delivery was to be made only at point of destination. Concededly if the merchandise had been lost intermediate the delivery to the carrier and point of destination, the loss would have fallen upon the buyer and not upon the seller. That Chicago was to be the place of delivery seems to me not only to follow from the contract itself, but especially from that provision of it which required each shipment to be paid for in advance at Chicago. The trial court found as a fact that was the meaning and intention of the agreement. This finding is sustained by the evidence and a finding to the contrary would be against the evidence.

In reaching the above conclusion, *Staackman, Horschitz & Co.* v. *Cary* (197 Ill. App. 601), upon which the respondent principally relies, has not escaped my attention. I do not think that authority correctly states the law. It certainly is not binding upon this court and ought not to be followed.

The judgment appealed from should be reversed and the judgment of the trial court reinstated, with costs in this court and in the Appellate Division.

HISCOCK, Ch. J., HOGAN, CARDOZO, POUND, CRANE and ANDREWS, JJ., concur.

Judgment reversed, etc.

Compare C. SHARPE & CO., LTD. *v.* NOSAWA & CO., *supra*, p. 264.

Note further SCARAMELLI & COMPANY *v.* COURTEEN SEED COMPANY, 194 Wis. 520 (Supreme Court, 1928), where there was a contract between an Italian seller and a Wisconsin buyer for a quantity of red clover seed at an agreed price c. i. f. New York. The buyer refused the goods because of breaches by the seller in connection with shipment, and in an action for the purchase price counterclaimed for damages. It was held that damages should be calculated on the basis of the American market price on the ground that "it is perfectly apparent and must have been in contemplation of the parties that in the event of the failure of the seller to perform, the buyer would be compelled to resort to the markets of this country to supply the goods."

Refer again to STANDARD CASING COMPANY, INC. *v.* CALIFORNIA CASING COMPANY, INC., *supra*, p. 245, where it was held in an action by the buyer for non-delivery under the contract that damages should be measured by the market price at San Francisco.

In MILLETT *v.* VAN HEEK AND COMPANY, [1921] 2 K. B. 369 (Court of Appeal), there were six contracts for the sale of cotton waste for export to Holland to be delivered f. o. b. Manchester Docks. The contracts provided that shipment should be subject to government permission to export, i. e., within a reasonable time after an existing embargo was lifted. The sellers repudiated the contracts before government prohibition of the export of cotton waste was removed. The Divisional Court held that a contract for delivery within a reasonable time was not a contract for delivery at a fixed time; but that the rule of sec. 51 (3) as to the measure of damages did not apply to a case of anticipatory breach; and that damages should be the difference in price between the contract price and the price when the goods should have been delivered.

CLARK *v.* HENSHAW MOTOR COMPANY

MASSACHUSETTS SUPREME JUDICIAL COURT, 1923

[246 *Massachusetts Reports*, 386]

RUGG, C.J. This is an action to recover compensation for breach of a contract to deliver to the plaintiff in February, 1920, an automobile of designated make. The plaintiff offered to show that, having in his employ several salesmen using that make of automobile, he was deprived of the services of one of them and thereby lost substantial profits from his business by reason of not having the automobile delivered according to the contract. This offer of proof was excluded rightly.

It is matter of common knowledge that an automobile is a chattel commonly bought and sold in the market. The measure of damages for failure to deliver according to the contract was the difference between the contract price and the market value at the time stipulated for delivery. G. L. c. 106, § 56(3). *F. W. Stock & Sons* v. *Snell,* 240 Mass. 427, 431. *Hall* v. *Paine,* 224 Mass. 62, 65. No exceptional circumstances are shown which render applicable any other rule of damages.

Loss of profits on an independent business, in a subsidiary connection with which the automobile was intended by the plaintiff to have been used, is too remote to have any relation to refusal to deliver the automobile according to contract. Such loss does not directly and naturally in the ordinary course of events result from the breach of such a contract. It cannot be thought that any such element of damages was included in the nature or terms of the contract. There is nothing to indicate that the special use to which the plaintiff intended to put the automobile was made known to the defendant. *Bartlett* v. *Blanchard,* 13 Gray, 429. *National Coal Tar Co.* v. *Malden & Melrose Gas Light Co.* 189 Mass. 234, 237. *Curtis* v. *Boston Ice Co.* 237 Mass. 343, and cases collected at page 350. *McLaren* v. *Marmon-Oldsmobile Co.* 95 N. J. L. 520. Cases like *Randall* v. *Peerless Motor Car Co.* 212 Mass. 352, 380, 381, and *Orbach* v. *Paramount Pictures Corp.* 233 Mass. 281, where loss of prospective profits in business have been held recoverable, are too clearly distinguishable to require discussion.

The offer to show the rental value of an automobile during the period of nondelivery was rightly excluded for the same reasons. Moreover, it did not appear that the plaintiff hired any automobile.

The plaintiff deposited with the defendant $50 at the time of making the contract. The jury were instructed that, if the defendant had made a breach of the contract, the plaintiff was entitled to recover at least $50.

Other appropriate instructions as to damages were given. A verdict for $1 was returned. The plaintiff thereupon filed a motion for a new trial on the grounds that the verdict was contrary to the law and to the instructions of the court, and inadequate. The defendant then filed a stipulation to the effect that judgment might be entered for the plaintiff for $51 and costs. The court thereafter overruled the motion. To this the plaintiff excepted.

The trial judge has no authority after the separation of the jury to add any sum to the verdict of the jury. *Shanahan* v. *Boston & Northern Street Railway*, 193 Mass. 412. *Minot* v. *Boston*, 201 Mass. 10. *Kennon* v. *Gilmer*, 131 U. S. 22, 29. That was not what was done in the case at bar. After the filing of the stipulation as to judgment by the defendant, it became plain that the amount to be recovered by the plaintiff would be that which the jury had determined to be due him together with the deposit originally made by him. The amount in dispute between the parties then became infinitesimal provided force were given both to the verdict of the jury and to the instruction given by the court. The judge was not required as matter of law under such circumstances to grant a new trial. *Boyden* v. *Moore*, 5 Mass. 365, 371. *Abbott* v. *Walker*, 204 Mass. 71, 74. *Fallon* v. *Clifton Manuf. Co.* 207 Mass. 491, 496. *Sears* v. *Worcester*, 180 Mass. 288. *Lufkin* v. *Hitchcock*, 194 Mass. 231. The granting of a motion for a new trial commonly rests in sound judicial discretion. *Ryan* v. *Hickey*, 240 Mass. 46. *Berggren* v. *Mutual Life Ins. Co. of New York*, 231 Mass. 173, 176. The refusal to grant the motion in the case at bar shows no abuse of discretion. G. L. c. 231, § 132.

Exceptions overruled.

In HADLEY *v.* BAXENDALE, 9 Exch. 341 (Court of Exchequer, 1854), Alderson, B., said: "Where two parties have made a contract which one of them has broken, the damages which the other party ought to receive in respect of such breach of contract should be such as may fairly and reasonably be considered either arising naturally, i.e., according to the usual course of things, from such breach of contract itself, or such as may reasonably be supposed to have been in the contemplation of both parties, at the time they made the contract, as the probable result of the breach of it. Now, if the special circumstances under which the contract was actually made were communicated by the plaintiffs to the defendants, and thus known to both parties, the damages resulting from the breach of such a contract, which they would reasonably contemplate, would be the amount of injury which would ordinarily follow from a breach of contract under these special circumstances so known and communicated. But, on the other hand, if these special circumstances were wholly unknown to the party breaking the contract, he, at the most, could only be supposed to have had in his contemplation the amount of injury which would arise generally, and in the great multitude of cases not affected by any special circumstances, from such a breach of contract. For, had the special circumstances been known, the parties might have specially provided for the breach of contract by special terms as to the damages in that case; and of this advantage it would be very unjust to deprive them."

In FLORES *v.* BASSO, 229 Mich. 577 (Supreme Court, 1925), there was a contract for the sale of fifteen carloads of grapes. Only eight carloads were delivered. In an action brought by the buyer for non-delivery of the balance it appeared that there was no available market in which the buyer could buy similar grapes. The buyer testified that such grapes were in great demand, that he could readily have sold all those covered by the contract, and gave evidence of the profits made on each car received. The trial court ordered judgment for defendant on the ground that there was no evidence of damage to go to the jury. Judgment reversed. Under the circumstances damages were such as naturally and directly flowed from the failure to deliver, and plaintiff's testimony was sufficient basis for an estimate.

In PERKINS *v.* MINFORD, 235 N. Y. 301 (Court of Appeals, 1923), there was a contract for the sale of 3,200,000 pounds of sugar f. o. b. a Cuban port, payment on receipt of shipping documents in New York. Only 3,000,000 pounds were shipped. The buyer brought an action against the seller for damages. In affirming a judgment for plaintiff, Andrews, J., said:

"The buyer's measure of damages is the loss directly and naturally resulting to him in the usual course of events because of the seller's breach of contract. Generally that is fixed by the difference between the contract and the market price at the time and place when and where the delivery should have been made (sec. 148). Such was the rule we applied in the case cited above and under somewhat similar circumstances in *Seaver* v. *Lindsay Light Co.* (233 N. Y. 273), in both of which cases there was a total failure to deliver any part of the goods sold. The reason is clear. Usually, knowing of the breach of contract, the buyer may protect himself against the consequences of a rising market by buying from others. But what if he does not know? What if the delivery being made at a distance the buyer neither knows nor has means of knowledge that the contract has not been completed until he actually receives the goods or a bill of lading stating the amount shipped to him? What is the loss then directly and naturally resulting from the breach of the contract? This situation is one of those as to which an exception is made by section 148. 'Special circumstances' are present, showing 'proximate damages of a greater amount' than those provided for by the general rule. The time as to when the damages are measured is shifted. It is now the date when the buyer knew or should have known of the default.

"In the case before us the market price of sugar rose rapidly from March until April 18. This price was the same at New Orleans and at north Cuban ports. Then during all the times important here it remained stationary. The sugar was finally shipped and the bill of lading obtained on April 20th. Until the latter was received there is no claim that the buyer knew of the shortage. Measured by the price of sugar in Cuba at this time, the damages found by the Appellate Division are concededly correct."

Note also WILSON *v.* LONDON AND GLOBE FINANCE CORPORATION, 14 T. L. R. 15 (Court of Appeal, 1897), where there was a contract to allot shares "concurrently with the first issue." The first issue of shares took place on June 2. They were not delivered to the plaintiff however, and he did not become aware until August 11 that any shares had been issued. In an action for damages, it was held that damages should be measured by the difference between the contract price and the market price on August 11.

3. FOR BREACH OF WARRANTY

BERMAN *v.* HENRY N. CLARK COMPANY

MASSACHUSETTS SUPREME JUDICIAL COURT, 1907

[194 *Massachusetts Reports*, 248]

KNOWLTON, C. J. The defendant made a contract in writing to furnish and put in place specific apparatus for heating three houses belonging to the plaintiff. The contract contained a guaranty as follows: "We guarantee this apparatus to be complete in every way and when finished to be capable of warming all rooms in which radiators are placed to 70° in zero weather. We guarantee this apparatus against all imperfections in material and workmanship for one year." This action is brought to recover upon this guaranty.

An earlier action was brought by defendant company against the plaintiff, to recover the price of this apparatus, and for extra work in connection with the contract. As a defence to this former action, the present plaintiff answered, denying that the plaintiff in that action had fulfilled its contract, and averring that it failed to provide apparatus which complied with the guaranty contained in the contract, in that the apparatus furnished has been and was unable to heat the apartments to seventy degrees in zero weather, etc., and claiming a recoupment of damages. After a trial upon these pleadings, the plaintiff in that action recovered from the present plaintiff the full amount claimed in its declaration. The only question now before us is whether the judgment in the former action is a bar to the present one.

We think it plain that it is. The principles applicable to the case were considered in *Gilmore* v. *Williams*, 162 Mass. 351, in *Bradley* v. *Bradley*, 160 Mass. 258, and in *Watts* v. *Watts*, 160 Mass. 464. See also *Morse* v. *Elms*, 131 Mass. 151. In *Gilmore* v. *Williams* it was said of the plaintiff, seeking to recover on a breach of warranty, he having previously set up this breach as a defence to an action upon the note given in consideration of the warranty, "if he chose to plead the breach of warranty in answer to the claim on the note, and if a judgment was entered against him for the whole amount due on the note, or a part of it, on the issue thus raised, the judgment would be a bar to any further claim under the warranty. This would be so whether the judgment was entered by consent of parties, or upon a default after answer, or upon a verdict after trial on the facts. His election to claim his damages by way of recoupment in that suit would be conclusive on him." This doctrine is conclusive against the right of the plaintiff to recover in the present case. There is a well recognized distinction, referred to in the cases above cited, between the effect of a judgment pleaded as an estoppel as to facts arising collaterally in another action, and its effect as a final determination of the matters declared on as the cause of action, or set up in the answer as a ground for an allowance in defence.

It is immaterial that there had been no zero weather before the trial of the first action. The capacity of the apparatus was put in issue, and could be shown otherwise than by actual experiment. Evidence was introduced on the subject, and it would have been in the power of the court, upon motion, to continue the case for trial until there was an opportunity for an experiment, if it had been thought advisable to do so.

Judgment on the verdict.

In MONDEL *v.* STEEL, 8 M. & W. 858 (Exchequer of Pleas, 1841), Parke, B., said:

"In this case, the declaration is in special *assumpsit* on a contract to build a ship for the plaintiff, at a certain rate per ton, and according to a certain specification: and the breach assigned is for not building a vessel with scantlings, fastenings, and planking, according to such specification; by reason whereof the ship, on a voyage from London to New South Wales and back, was so much strained that it became necessary to re-fasten and repair her.

"To this declaration there was one plea, to which it is unnecessary to allude, as it was admitted to be bad on special demurrer, and is to be amended; and a second plea, on which the question, which we have taken time to consider, arises.

"This plea states in substance, that the defendant had sued the plaintiff for the balance of the agreed price of the vessel, after payment of £3500, and also for a sum of £134 odd for extra work, in the form of an action for work and labour, and for goods sold and delivered; that issue was joined, and, on the trial of the cause, the plaintiff gave evidence in his defence of the same breach of contract alleged in the declaration; and insisted, that if the amount of compensation to which he was entitled, exceeded or equalled the balance of the price and the value of the extra work, the now plaintiff was entitled to a verdict; if it was less, that he was entitled to a deduction from the amount of both, of such amount of compensation. The plea proceeds to state, (and, we must assume, correctly, for the purposes of this argument, though the statement has arisen from mistake), that the learned judge before whom the cause was tried, my brother Rolfe, so directed the jury; and that the jury found that the now defendant had committed a breach of contract, and was entitled to some compensation, which they deducted from the price of the vessel and value of the extra work; and the now defendant had judgment for the amount, after such deduction had been made, since the commencement of this suit.

"The plaintiff demurred to this plea, assigning several causes of special demurrer, which it is not necessary to notice, as we are all of opinion that it is bad in substance.

"The ground on which it was endeavoured to support the plea, in a very ingenious argument, was this: that a defendant in an action for the stipulated price of a chattel, which the plaintiff had contracted to make for the defendant of a particular quality, or of a specific chattel sold with a warranty, and delivered, had the option of setting up a counter claim for breach of the contract in the one instance, or the warranty in the other, in the nature of a cross action; and that if he exercised that option, he was in the same situation as if he had brought such an action; and consequently, could not, after judgment in one action, bring another; and the case was likened to a set-off under the statutes. This argument was founded on no other authority than an expression of Lord Tenterden in giving the judgment of the Court in the case of *Street* v. *Blay* (2 B. & Ad. 462), his lordship having said that a breach of warranty might be given in evidence in an action for the price of a specific article sold, in mitigation of damages, 'on the principle, it should seem, of avoiding circuity of action.' But we are all of opinion that no such inference is to be drawn from that expression; what was meant was, that the sum to be recovered for the price of the article might be reduced by so much as the article was diminished in value, by reason of the non-compliance with the warranty; and that this abatement was allowed in order to save the necessity of a cross action. Formerly, it was the practice, where an action was brought for an agreed price of a specific chattel, sold with a warranty, or of work which was to be performed according to contract, to allow the plaintiff to recover the stipulated sum, leaving the defendant to a cross action for breach of the warranty or contract; in which action, as well the difference between the price contracted for and the real value of the articles or of the work done, as any consequential damage, might have been recovered; and this course was simple and consistent. In the one case, the performance of the warranty not being a condition precedent to the payment of the price, the defendant, who received the chattel warranted, has thereby the property vested in him indefeasibly, and is incapable of returning it back; he has all that he stipulated for as the condition of paying the price, and therefore it was held that he ought to pay it, and seek his remedy on the plaintiff's contract of warranty. In the other case, the law appears to have construed the contract as not importing that the performance of every portion of the work should be a condition precedent to the payment of the stipulated price, otherwise the least deviation would have deprived the plaintiff of the whole price; and therefore the defendant was obliged to pay it, and recover for any breach of contract on the other side. But after the case of *Basten* v. *Butter* (7 East, 479), a different practice, which had been partially adopted before in the case of *King* v. *Boston* (7 East, 481, n.), began to prevail, and being attended with much practical convenience, has been since generally followed; and the defendant is now permitted to shew that the chattel by reason of the non-compliance with the warranty in the one case, and the work in consequence of the non-performance of the contract in the other, were diminished in value; *Kist* v. *Atkinson* (2 Camp. 64), *Thornton* v. *Place* (1 M. & Rob. 218), &c. The same practice has not, however, extended to all cases of work and labour, as for instance, that of an attorney, *Templer* v. *M'Lachlan* (2 T. R. 136), unless no benefit whatever has been derived from it; nor in an action for freight; *Shiels* v.

Davies (4 Camp. 119). It is not so easy to reconcile these deviations from the ancient practice with principle, in those particular cases above-mentioned, as it is in those where an executory contract, such as this, is made for a chattel, to be manufactured in a particular manner, or goods to be delivered according to a sample; *Germaine* v. *Burton* (3 Stark. 32); where the party may refuse to receive, or may return in a reasonable time, if the article is not such as bargained for; for in these cases the acceptance or non-return affords evidence of a new contract on a *quantum valebat*; whereas, in a case of a delivery with a warranty of a specific chattel, there is no power of returning, and consequently no ground to imply a new contract; and in some cases of work performed, there is difficulty in finding a reason for such presumption. It must however be considered, that in all these cases of goods sold and delivered with a warranty, and work and labour, as well as the case of goods agreed to be supplied according to a contract, the rule which has been found so convenient is established; and that it is competent for the defendant, in all of those, not to set-off, by a proceeding in the nature of a cross action, the amount of damages which he has sustained by breach of the contract, but simply to defend himself by shewing how much less the subject-matter of the action was worth, by reason of the breach of contract; and to the extent that he obtains, or is capable of obtaining, an abatement of price on that account, he must be considered as having received satisfaction for the breach of contract, and is precluded from recovering in another action to that extent; but no more.

"The opinion, therefore, attributed on this record to the learned Judge is, we think, incorrect, and not warranted by law; and all the plaintiff could by law be allowed in diminution of damages, on the former trial, was a deduction from the agreed price, according to the difference, at the time of the delivery, between the ship as she was, and what she ought to have been according to the contract: but all claim for damages beyond that, on account of the subsequent necessity for more extensive repairs, could not have been allowed in the former action, and may now be recovered."

In GENERAL MOTORS TRUCK COMPANY *v.* THE SHEPARD COMPANY, 47 R. I. 88 (Supreme Court, 1925), fourteen trucks were sold to a buyer, and the seller guaranteed the life of the trucks for a period of six years. The seller brought an action against the buyer for the price of the trucks, and the buyer brought an action against the seller to recover damages for breach of the above warranty. The actions were tried together. To the first action the buyer pleaded the breach of warranty in recoupment, but at the close of the testimony the trial judge required the buyer to elect whether it would rely on the plea in recoupment or on the cross action. The buyer elected to rely on the latter, and judgment was given for plaintiff for the purchase price. The buyer excepted on the ground that the plea should have been allowed in diminution of the price. Exception overruled. The buyer may set up the breach of warranty by way of recoupment, or may maintain an action against the seller for the breach, but may not do both.

In The Impervious Products Company *v.* Gray, 127 Md. 64 (Court of Appeals, 1915), a contract was made for the sale of binder for use in road construction with a warranty that it would meet the State's specifications. Some of the binder supplied was condemned by the State Inspector so that a portion of the road was required to be rebuilt. In an action of *assumpsit* for goods sold and delivered to recover the price of the binder, the buyer pleaded the general issue and also damages due to the breach of warranty by way of set-off, and recovered a verdict. The following year the buyer brought the present action against the seller on a bill of particulars identical with his plea in the former suit. The buyer claimed that inasmuch as a plea in set-off was improper in the first suit, that suit was not a bar to the second. Judgment for plaintiff reversed. The evidence given in the first suit was entirely proper under the general issue plea filed because it tended to show a right to recoup.

HENRY *v.* RUDGE & GUENZEL COMPANY

Nebraska Supreme Court, 1929

[118 *Nebraska Reports*, 260]

Raper, District Judge. Action by plaintiff and appellant against the defendants and appellees, who were alleged retail dealers in shoes in Lincoln. Plaintiff in her petition alleges that on May 8, 1926, she purchased a pair of shoes which, she informed defendant's salesman, she wanted for street wear, and the salesman exhibited shoes which the salesman orally warranted to be in all respects fit and proper for such use, and, relying upon such representation, she bought the shoes, and thereafter, about July 10, 1926, without fault or negligence on her part, the heel on one of the shoes came off as plaintiff was descending a flight of stairs, thereby causing her to fall and receive severe injuries. Plaintiff alleges that the shoes were inferior and defective, in that the heels were not securely nailed or fastened on the shoes, but were insecurely glued on, which defect could not be discovered by an examination prior to the time the heel came off, and that said shoes were not reasonably fit for the purpose for which the plaintiff had purchased them.

The defendants in their separate answers, in so far as pertinent to the decision in this appeal, admit the purchase of the shoes, deny generally the allegations of the petition, and allege that in July, 1926, the plaintiff returned said shoes, claiming one of the heels had come off, and the defendant Kohler Shoe Company, offered to repair the shoe and replace the detached heel, but plaintiff refused to accept said offer, and thereupon elected to return and deliver, and did at said time return and deliver, said shoes to the defendant Kohler Shoe Company, which company then and there received and accepted said shoes, and said defendants, at plaintiff's demand, then made reimbursement to plaintiff for said shoes.

Trial was had to a jury, and at the close of plaintiff's testimony, at request of defendants, the court gave peremptory instructions to the jury to return verdict for defendants, which was done, and judgment entered dismissing the action, from which judgment plaintiff appeals.

Plaintiff's evidence discloses that about May 8, 1926, she went to the store and told a clerk that she wanted a pair of shoes for street and every-day wear. The clerk showed her some shoes which she tried on, and they looked and felt all right, and she told the clerk that she had been buying her shoes at Mayer Brothers and Magee's, and that she relied on what the clerks told her, and the clerk responded that neither Mayer Brothers nor Magee had any better shoes than these she had on and that, in fact, there were no better shoes in town. She asked the price, and, on being told the price, she said, "Well, I will take your word for it and take the shoes"; and she relied on the clerk's statement, took the shoes and paid for them. She wore them five or six times, and on July 10, while visiting at a relative's home, as she started to descend a flight of stairs, the heel of one of the shoes dropped off, causing her to fall down the stairs, the fall resulting in severe injuries to her; there were no tacks in the heel of the shoe, the heel being fastened insecurely by some kind of glue.

About five days later she went to the store with her shoes and told the clerk that the heel had come off, and he said he would have the heel put on, but she told him she did not care to have them fixed, and asked the clerk for his superior. She was taken to the office of the manager, or one over the clerk, who told her they would fasten the heels on for her and the shoe would be as good as new; but she said she did not care to have them fixed that way. She told him that when the heel came off she had fallen down stairs and was hurt, and had not seen her doctor yet and did not know how badly she was injured, but would see him later about her personal injuries. The manager then told the clerk to give her a pair of new shoes. She was given another pair, which she accepted. She was then offered the old shoes for a small price, which she agreed to pay, and the old shoes were left at the store to have the heels nailed on. In four or five days she went back to the store to get the old shoes. She paid $1 that she was yet owing on them and took the old shoes. She at that time told the clerk that she had been injured by the fall down a flight of stairs and "in regard to my personal injuries I will see you folks later." This is a résumé of her testimony covering the purchase, the alleged warranty she relies on, and the alleged rescission.

There are several phases of the case treated at considerable length in the able briefs of the parties — as to whether there is a warranty, whether the retail dealer is liable for such defects in merchandise, whether, if liable at all, the dealer can be held for consequential damages, and some other questions; but it will be unnecessary to consider such questions and they are not determined.

But, assuming there was a warranty, the plaintiff's testimony shows clearly that the sale was rescinded. She returned the shoes and was fully repaid the purchase price and it was done at her request and voluntarily. Counsel urge that she did not intend to rescind, and that her statement that she would see the defendants later about her injuries indicated that she was not consenting to a rescission. There can be no such thing as a partial rescission, except in certain cases where the contract is divisible. Where the sale is for a particular article, there can be no partial rescission. After the return of the shoes and repayment to her of the purchase price, the rescission was complete. In *Apex Chemical Co.* v. *Compson,* 171 N. Y. Supp. 60, the court held that rescission seems to follow as a matter of law the return of the property, and that the return itself operates as a conclusive presumption of law that the plaintiff intended to rescind. When plaintiff returned the shoes and received payment for the purchase price, it was an irrevocable election to rescind, and her statement to the effect that she would see the defendants later about her injuries was ineffectual to modify or disaffirm her election to rescind.

Having rescinded the contract, plaintiff has no right of action for damages for breach of the warranty. She cannot rescind and claim damages for breach of the warranty.

The uniform sales act provides: "1. Where there is a breach of warranty by the seller, the buyer may, at his election, * * * (b) accept or keep the goods and maintain an action against the seller for damages for the breach of warranty; * * * (d) rescind the contract to sell or the sale and refuse to receive the goods, or, if the goods have already been received, return them or offer to return them to the seller and recover the price or any part thereof which has been paid.

"2. When the buyer has claimed and been granted a remedy in any one of these ways, no other remedy can thereafter be granted." Comp. St. 1922, sec. 2538.

This court has in several cases held that, where a party rescinds a sale and receives or demands or recovers the purchase price therefor, he cannot also demand damages for a breach of the warranty. *McCormick Harvesting Machine Co.* v. *Brown,* 5 Neb. (Unof.) 356; *Phelps* v. *Shuck,* 107 Neb. 490; *Alfree Mfg. Co.* v. *Grape,* 59 Neb. 777; *First Nat. Bank of Chadron* v. *Tootle,* 59 Neb. 44; *First Nat. Bank of Chadron* v. *McKinney,* 47 Neb. 149.

The trial court was right in directing a verdict for the defendants, because of plaintiff's rescission of the sale.

The judgment of the district court is affirmed.

In STREET *v.* BLAY, 2 B. & Ad. 456 (King's Bench, 1831), Lord Tenterden, C. J., said:

"It is to be observed, that although the vendee of a specific chattel, delivered with a warranty, may not have a right to return it, the same reason does not apply to cases of executory contracts, where an article, for instance, is ordered from a manufacturer, who contracts that it shall be of a certain quality, or fit for a certain purpose, and the article sent as such is never completely accepted by the party ordering it. In this and similar cases the latter may return it as soon as he discover the defect, provided he has done nothing more in the meantime than was necessary to give it a fair trial, *Okell* v. *Smith* (1 Stark, N. P. C. 107); nor would the purchaser of a commodity, to be afterwards delivered according to sample, be bound to receive the bulk, which may not agree with it; nor after having received what was tendered and delivered as being in accordance with the sample, will he be precluded by the simple receipt from returning the article within a reasonable time for the purpose of examination and comparison. The observations above stated are intended to apply to the purchase of a certain specific chattel, accepted and received by the vendee, and the property in which is completely and entirely vested in him.

"But whatever may be the right of the purchaser to return such a warranted article in an ordinary case, there is no authority to shew that he may return it where the purchaser has done more than was consistent with the purpose of trial; where he has exercised the dominion of an owner over it, by selling and parting with the property to another, and where he has derived a pecuniary benefit from it. These circumstances concur in the present case; and even supposing it might have been competent for the defendant to return this horse, after having accepted it, and taken it into his possession, if he had never parted with it to another, it appears to us that he cannot do so after the re-sale at a profit.

"These are acts of ownership wholly inconsistent with the purpose of trial, and which are conclusive against the defendant, that the particular chattel was his own; and it may be added, that the parties cannot be placed in the same situation by the return of it, as if the contract had not been made, for the defendant has derived an intermediate benefit in consequence of the bargain, which he would still retain."

In THE PETERSEN OVEN COMPANY *v.* GUARINO, 221 N. Y. App. Div. 146 (Fourth Department, 1927), there was an action to recover the purchase price of a baking oven. The buyer pleaded breach of warranty and a rescission of the sale. The oven, which weighed eighty or ninety tons, had been set into a concrete foundation in a building belonging to the buyer. It did not operate properly and the buyer served notice of rescission on the seller. It appeared however that the buyer subsequently leased the building containing the oven to a third person. It was held that the leasing of the building waived the former notice of rescission, and that the buyer was thereafter precluded from rescinding.

In UNITED ENGINE COMPANY *v.* JUNIS, 196 Iowa 914 (Supreme Court, 1923), in an action for the purchase price of an engine defendant pleaded rescission and a counterclaim for part payment and the expenses of installation. Plaintiff claimed there had been a waiver of the right to rescind. It appeared that defendant had told plaintiff that it could not remove the engine unless it paid damages. Defendant testified that in so speaking he had meant that plaintiff should reimburse him for the cost of installation. The trial judge charged the jury that on such facts defendant had made an election and could not afterward claim to rescind and return the engine. Judgment for plaintiff reversed. The conduct shown did not amount to a waiver of the right to rescind.

In WILSON & CO. *v.* THE M. WERK CO., 104 Ohio St. 507 (Supreme Court, 1922), there was a contract for the sale of a tank car of choice white grease stearine to be delivered to the buyer at a price of $10,915, sight draft with bill of lading attached. The buyer paid the draft and took delivery of the stearine, which proved to be of inferior quality. The buyer thereupon notified the seller that it refused to keep the stearine, asked for shipping instructions, and demanded repayment of the price. The seller refused. The buyer, after giving further notice of its intentions, made diligent efforts to dispose of the stearine elsewhere, but having received no bid in excess of 9½ cents per lb. bought the stearine itself for 10¢ per lb., at a total of $6,064. The present action was brought by the buyer against the seller claiming as damages the difference between this amount and the amount paid on the draft. Judgment for plaintiff affirmed.

DONOVAN *v.* THE AEOLIAN COMPANY

NEW YORK COURT OF APPEALS, 1936

[270 *New York Reports*, 267]

LEHMAN, J. The plaintiff, in December, 1925, purchased from the defendant a piano for which she paid the sum of $3,475. In this action, brought on August 30, 1928, she has recovered the purchase price with interest. The complaint alleges that "at the time of the said sale, and as a part thereof, and as an inducement to the plaintiff to agree to purchase said piano and equipment, the defendant warranted and represented to the plaintiff that the said piano was a new instrument of recent manufacture and had never been used."

It is undisputed that the piano was, at the time of the sale, five years old. It had been used and partially rebuilt prior to the sale. The plaintiff gave no notice of any breach of the alleged warranty, or of any election to rescind the contract, until December 2, 1927, approximately two years after the delivery to her of the piano. Upon this appeal the defendant contends that there was no warranty that the piano was new and unused and that even if such warranty had been given, the notice of election to rescind was not given within a reasonable time.

There is a conflict of evidence as to what was said to the plaintiff by the defendant's salesman at the time of the sale. The jury has resolved that conflict in favor of the plaintiff.

The evidence shows that the defendant manufactures and sells "Steinway Duo Art" pianos. The plaintiff went to the defendant's salesrooms to purchase such a piano. After hearing the tone of several pianos she selected one. She assumed that it was a new piano. Nothing was said by her that might have suggested to the salesman that she desired to purchase a used piano, and, according to her story, nothing was said by the salesman which might have suggested to her that she was buying a used piano at a small discount from the list price for new pianos of the same quality.

The question then arises whether from the silence of the salesman a warranty can be inferred or implied that the piano offered for sale was new and unused.

Certain warranties of quality are implied under the statute in every sale or contract of sale, without evidence that the seller either promised or represented that the goods supplied would possess such quality. Unless there is agreement to the contrary, the intention to include such warranty must be presumed. No warranty that goods, supplied under a contract to sell or a sale, are new or unused, is included in such implied warranties. (Pers. Prop. Law, § 96; Cons. Laws, ch. 41.) A recovery in this action, in accordance with the allegations of the complaint, must be predicated upon a finding that the defendant agreed to give such warranty. "Any affirmation of fact or any promise by the seller relating to the goods is an express warranty if the natural tendency of such affirmation or promise is to induce the buyer to purchase the goods, and if the buyer purchases the goods relying thereon." (Pers. Prop. Law, § 93.) In determining whether such an affirmation of fact or promise has been made by the seller we must apply the same tests as we would apply in determining the terms of any oral contract. If the evidence does not show such affirmation or promise in direct and express language it must, at least, show acts or words from which an intention to make such affirmation or promise can be inferred.

Here there has not been a direct affirmation by the seller that the goods were new and unused. None the less, the evidence is sufficient to sustain a finding that the plaintiff in purchasing a piano from the manufacturer believed that she was buying a new and unused piano and was induced to make the purchase by that belief. Ordinarily a buyer from a manufacturer or a dealer in new articles does not inquire whether the article supplied is new and unused. In some cases that may be due to the fact that previous use does not affect either the market value or usefulness of the article. In other cases it may be due to the fact that the buyer assumes, even without affirmation by the seller, that the article is new and unused. If the seller does not know that the buyer is acting under the belief that the article is new and unused, and has done nothing to induce that belief, the buyer cannot complain. There is no duty upon the seller to speak where silence does not constitute deception. Silence may, however, constitute fraud and deception where the seller has notice that the buyer is acting upon a mistaken belief as to a material fact. It depends upon the circumstances of each case whether failure to disclose is consistent with honest dealing. Where failure to disclose a material fact is calculated to induce a false belief, the distinction between concealment and affirmative misrepresentation is tenuous. Both are fraudulent. In this case it is clear that the defendant's salesman was under a duty to inform the plaintiff that the piano she had selected was not a new piano. Indeed, the defendant does not seriously contend otherwise. Its primary contention is that the salesman did make the required disclosure; but the jury has rejected that contention. The question remains whether the plaintiff has been awarded the proper remedy for the wrong she has suffered.

Mere failure to disclose a fact, though fraudulent, may not be equivalent to affirmation of the contrary fact. Here the jury might find that there was more than a failure to disclose. It might find that the defendant implicitly agreed that the piano it sold was an unused piano. When a manufacture offers a piano for sale in the ordinary course of business without disclosure of the fact that the piano had been used and then repaired, the acts of the manufacturer, coupled with the words of the salesman, may be regarded as an affirmation that the piano was taken out of stock and unused. Then there is a warranty that the piano is new. (Cf. *Grieb* v. *Cole*, 60 Mich. 397; *Fox* v. *Boldt*, 172 Wis. 333.)

The plaintiff did not discover the breach of such warranty until November, 1927. Then the plaintiff gave notice of the breach and of her election to rescind. For almost two years the plaintiff had the use of the piano and so far as appears she was satisfied with its quality. Then for personal reasons she decided to sell the piano and she was informed by an expert who examined it that the piano was seven years old and had previously been used and "remade." The statute provides that "if, after acceptance of the goods, the buyer fails to give notice to the seller of the breach of any promise or warranty within a reasonable time after the buyer knows, or ought to know, of such breach, the seller shall not be liable therefor." (Pers. Prop. Law, § 130.) It cannot be said that the buyer should have made such an examination of the piano as would have revealed that the piano had been previously used. That would have required the skill of an expert. The plaintiff had no reason to suspect that the piano might be old or to hire an expert to examine it to ascertain its age. Thus the notice of breach of warranty was given within the time permitted by the statute, and the defendant may be held liable for breach of its warranty. It does not follow that the plaintiff may rescind the contract of sale and recover the purchase price.

The remedies of a buyer for breach of warranty are defined by section 150 of the Personal Property Law. They include the right to accept or keep the goods and maintain an action against the seller for damages for the breach of warranty (subd. 1-b) or to "rescind the contract to sell or the sale and refuse to receive the goods, or if the goods have already been received, return them or offer to return them to the seller and recover the price or any part thereof which has been paid" (subd. 1-d). The first of these alternative remedies would have given the plaintiff complete compensation for the wrong suffered. She had selected the particular piano which she liked best. Its previous use affected its market value. It did not affect its tone. The plaintiff used it as long as she wished. She was damaged only because she paid for an old piano the price of a piano which was warranted as new. For these damages she is entitled to compensation.

By choosing the alternative remedy of rescission, the plaintiff has obtained more than the damages she has suffered and more than she is entitled to receive. That remedy is provided because it would be unjust to compel a buyer to retain goods which do not comply with the stipulated warranties or conditions. He might not desire to use the goods actually supplied and damages or recoupment in diminution of price might prove an incomplete remedy for failure to obtain goods of the stipulated quality. Then the loss should rest wholly upon the person who caused the loss. In this case, however, the plaintiff has had the use for almost two years of the piano she selected, yet she has been awarded the purchase price without diminution for the value of such use or for the inevitable loss of value of the piano through such use. The statute does not permit a rescission under such circumstances.

It provides that "where the goods have been delivered to the buyer, he cannot rescind the sale * * * if he fails to notify the seller within a reasonable time of the election to rescind, or if he fails to return or to offer to return the goods to the seller in substantially as good condition as they were in at the time the property was transferred to the buyer." (Pers. Prop. Law, § 150, subd. 3.) Here there is a distinction between the notice of breach of warranty required by section 130 to fasten liability upon the seller for its breach and the notice of election to rescind required by section 150 as a condition annexed to the remedy of rescission for such breach. The notice of breach of warranty, to fasten liability upon the seller, must be given within a reasonable time "after the buyer knows, or ought to know, of such breach." Even then the buyer may not avail himself of the remedy of rescission if he fails to notify the seller within a "reasonable time" of his election to rescind. In this additional requirement there is no indication that a "reasonable time" begins only "after the buyer knows, or ought to know, of such breach." If the Legislature had so intended it would have said so. The words here used are open only to the construction that a reasonable time must be determined by all the circumstances of the particular case, not exclusively by the time when the breach should reasonably have been discovered.

Long-continued failure to discover the defect in the goods, if the buyer is without fault, should not absolve the seller from liability for his breach of contract. So the Legislature has decreed, but it has not decreed that the buyer may rescind the contract and return the goods when such failure, though without the buyer's fault, prevents the buyer from giving notice of election to rescind until after a reasonable time for rescission of the contract has elapsed. In such case the buyer should be relegated to the remedy of recovery or recoupment of damages. It cannot be said that a notice of election to rescind is given within a reasonable time when it is postponed for almost two years and during that time the buyer has obtained substantially the benefit which he expected to derive from his contract. The buyer may not profit at the expense of the seller from such a long delay in the discovery of the breach of contract. A buyer who has received and retained substantial benefit from the contract may then recover compensation only for that which he has failed to receive. (Cf. *Ketterer* v. *Bay View Nash Co.*, 192 Wis. 343.)

The judgment of the Appellate Division and that of the Trial Term should be reversed and a new trial granted, with costs to abide the event.

CRANE, Ch. J., O'BRIEN, HUBBS, CROUCH, LOUGHRAN and FINCH, JJ., concur.

Judgments reversed, etc.

In CONNER v. THE BORLAND-GRANNIS COMPANY, 294 Ill. 58 (Supreme Court, 1920), plaintiff bought an electric brougham from defendant under a conditional sale contract, making a down payment and signing a number of notes maturing at monthly intervals. The car was defective in several particulars, but plaintiff used it for several months, paying each note as it fell due, and complaining from time to time about the defects. In giving a check for the fourth note plaintiff indorsed it as a payment under protest and on condition that defendant supply her with a car as contracted. Defendant returned the check, seized the car under a chattel mortgage given at the time of the sale, and resold it. Plaintiff then brought this action to recover the amount paid on the purchase price. The Superior Court gave judgment for plaintiff, which was reversed by the Appellate Court, holding as a matter of law that plaintiff had waived her right to rescind. Judgment of Superior Court affirmed.

In EDISON FIXTURE CO. INC. v. MACCAFERRI, 250 Mass. 460 (Supreme Judicial Court, 1924), there was an action for the purchase price of seven electrical fixtures, sold and delivered to defendant. Defendant claimed the right to rescind the sale because of alleged false representations by plaintiff in procuring the contract. The undisputed evidence showed that defendant used the goods continuously after the sale was made without any offer to return them. Judgment for plaintiff and exceptions by defendant overruled.

In HOLCOMB & HOKE MANUFACTURING COMPANY v. OSTERBERG, 181 Minn. 547 (Supreme Court, 1930), the buyer of a popcorn and peanut machine gave oral notice of rescission, but later wrote the seller stating his position as one of unwillingness to pay "unless you can make this machine fulfil its guarantee and work satisfactorily as your contract provides." In a subsequent action by the seller to recover the purchase price, the buyer interposed an answer setting up rescission and asking for damages. Judgment for defendant reversed. The oral rescission was superseded by the later inconsistent letter, and the attempt to set up rescission in the answer was too late, being eleven months after discovery of the defects.

PERMUTIT CO. v. MASSASOIT MFG. CO.

CIRCUIT COURT OF APPEALS, THIRD CIRCUIT, 1932

[61 *Federal Reporter* (*Second Series*), 529]

THOMPSON, Circuit Judge. This is an appeal from a judgment of the District Court of Delaware entered on a verdict for $32,784.79 in favor of the Massasoit Manufacturing Company, hereinafter referred to as the vendee, and against the Permutit Company, hereinafter referred to as the vendor. The vendee is engaged in manufacturing cotton yarns, commonly called cotton linters. The vendor manufactures and sells apparatus for the filtration, purification, and softening of water. The parties entered into a written contract for the purchase and installation of a water filtering plant. It appeared that, following the use of the Permutit filtration system, thousands of pounds of cotton manufactured by the vendee were off color. The vendee brought suit for damages for an alleged breach of an express warranty contained in the written contract. Shortly thereafter the vendor brought suit to recover the part of the purchase price of the filtration plant still unpaid, as well as additional sums expended by it in making changes in the filtration plant after it had been installed. These suits were consolidated on trial by agreement. The jury returned a verdict in favor of the vendee.

The main question involved in this case is: Where the guaranty in a contract expressly provides what liability the guarantor assumes thereunder, is the remedy thus provided for binding on the parties and exclusive? A second and possibly subordinate question is: Where the evidence shows that the vendor had no knowledge of the vendee's manufacturing processes, may the vendee recover, as special damages, losses sustained by it in the use of the machinery it purchased under a warranty not including fitness for the manufacturing in question?

The contract provided as follows:

We guarantee that the Permutit Filtering Plant herein offered, when connected up and operated in accordance with our instructions and under the conditions set forth in this proposal, will be capable of filtering its specified amount of water at the specified rate of flow.

We further guarantee that the water thus filtered will be clear, bright and practically free from turbidity and suspended matter.

We agree to make good at our expense, within a period of one year after date of delivery, any defects due to faulty design, workmanship or material, in such a manner as we may deem necessary to the satisfactory operation of the plant.

We guarantee that the Permutit Water Clarifying plant herein offered, when operated in accordance with our instructions and under the conditions set forth in this proposal, will deliver a water that will not have a color in excess of 2 measured in accordance with the Standards as set forth by the American Public Health Association.

That the filtered water will contain no iron.

It is the intent of this proposal that the Permutit Company will furnish to the Massasoit Manufacturing Company a complete water purification plant erected on the grounds of the Massasoit Manufacturing Company at Oakdale, Conn.

The Permutit Company supplies all equipment foundations and building including construction of pipe line from flume, near present intake, to clarification plant and to make connections into existing service lines in present mill.

It is the intent of this contract for the Permutit Company to furnish to the Massasoit Manufacturing Company a completed filtration plant in operation.

For the fulfillment of the guarantee herein, a weeks test will be made at the time set by the Permutit Company.

The vendor objected, at the trial, to the admission of evidence of special damages sustained by the vendee, on the ground that the written contract defined and limited the vendor's liability for any breach by it so as to exclude such special damages. No mention is made in the guaranty that the filtration plant was designed with any knowledge of the requirements of the manufacturing processes of the vendee, and no such information was conveyed to the vendor. To the extent that the warranty may be said to have been a warranty of fitness to deliver water of a certain color, such warranty would exclude any implied warranty of fitness; for example, that the water so purified was to be fit for the purpose of processing and purifying raw cotton. There is nothing in the express warranty to the effect that the water to be delivered by the plant would be fit for such a purpose. The trial court instructed the jury that the clause in the guaranty specifying the vendor's obligations in the event of nonperformance of the contract did not limit or define its liability under the contract and did not provide a remedy in case of breach and was not exclusive of other warranties express or implied. We think the court erred in allowing the jury to consider warranties that were not expressed in the contract. In fact, it is conceded by counsel for the vendee that no warranty could be implied. Their contention is that their cause of action may be founded on the express warranty.

It follows from what has already been said that the trial court erred in admitting evidence of special damages, consisting of damages to the manufactured cotton and of increase in production, manufacturing, and overhead costs and expenses. The authorities overwhelmingly establish the doctrine that, where the parties have set out in the written contract the warranties agreed upon and have provided for a remedy in case of a breach of warranty, the remedy thus provided is exclusive. *Sloan* v. *Wolf Co.*, 124 F. 196 (C. C. A. 8), *Hickman* v. *Sawyer*, 216 F. 281 (C. C. A. 4), and *Morris & Co.* v. *Power Mfg. Co.*, 17 F.(2d) 689 (C. C. A. 6), are but a few of the many cases so holding.

We are of the opinion that the trial judge was in error in allowing special damages to be proved and recovered by the vendee.

Judgment reversed, with directions for a new trial in the consolidated suits.

In J. I. CASE THRESHING MACHINE CO. *v.* ROSE, 191 Ky. 433 (Court of Appeals, 1921), a contract for the sale of a threshing machine contained an express warranty as to material, durability, and capacity, and provided the the seller was to have an opportunity to remedy any defects, the machine to be returned if the seller could not make it comply with the warranty.

It was held that the remedy thus provided was exclusive, and barred the buyer from any claim to damages.

Note also CRANDALL ENGINEERING COMPANY *v.* WINSLOW MARINE RAILWAY & SHIPBUILDING COMPANY, 188 Wash. 1 (Supreme Court, 1936), where a contract for the sale of a semisteel gear and equipment warranted the goods to be free from defects in material and workmanship, and limited the obligation of the seller under the warranty to the replacement of defective parts. The gear supplied proved to be cast iron, and was replaced by a semisteel gear. In a later action for the purchase price it was held that the buyer could not counterclaim for damages for the reasonable value of labor and materials expended in dismantling the broken gear and installing the new gear.

Compare AUSTIN CO. *v.* TILLMAN CO., 104 Ore. 541 (Supreme Court, 1922), where a contract for the sale of an asphalt mixing plant contained a warranty that the outfit was to be well made, of good material, free from defects, and capable of laying a certain number of square yards in ten hours. The seller also agreed under the contract to furnish new parts free in place of any that proved defective, and was to have a reasonable time to remedy defects. In the event of inability to remedy defects the machine was to be returned. On delivery it appeared that the machine supplied did not conform to the contract description. The seller was unable to furnish another machine and made repeated efforts to bring the machine in line with the contract requirements, but without success. The buyer joined in these efforts, expending more than $3000 on parts and replacements. The buyer at all times claimed that the machine did not conform to the contract, and at no time expressed an intention of accepting it, protesting that such use as was made of the machine was necessary in order to complete contracts and keep down damages. In an action by the seller to recover an unpaid balance of the purchase price, the buyer alleged general and special damages by reason of the failure of the machine to conform to the contract. Judgment for defendant affirmed.

"Defendant agreed that if plaintiff delivered to it a machine as specified and described in the contract and which required a test to disclose that it was not what it appeared to be, defendant would, when the required test developed incurable defects, return the machine and terminate the contract. The conditions upon which the obligation of defendant under that agreement were to become active were not present until the plaintiff delivered to defendant a machine corresponding to the description in the contract, and until that time the obligation of the defendant did not arise or accrue.

"For defects that developed in a machine that answered the description in the contract, while the same was being tested and which plaintiff was unable to remedy, and make the machine produce the quantity of material warranted, the return of the machine was the only remedy available to defendant; but for failure of plaintiff to perform its contract in other respects, there was open to defendant the ordinary remedies afforded by law in like cases for the breach of contracts for the sale of personal property. The provision limiting the remedy of defendant to a return of the machine was for the benefit of the plaintiff in respect to the sale of a machine manufactured by it, and should not be extended to embrace situations not clearly comprehended by its language."

4. SPECIFIC PERFORMANCE

BEHNKE *v.* BEDE SHIPPING COMPANY, LIMITED

KING'S BENCH DIVISION, 1927

[*Law Reports*, [1927] 1 *King's Bench*, 649]

Action tried before Wright J.

The plaintiff, a German shipowner, brought an action against the defendants, the owners of the British steamship *City*, claiming a declaration that he purchased the *City* by contract from the defendants, and an order for specific performance of that contract, an injunction restraining the defendants from parting with the steamship to any one but himself, and, in the alternative, damages for breach of contract.

The defendants denied the contract, and in the alternative said that if they entered into the contract it was not enforceable by reason of s. 4 of the Sale of Goods Act, 1893. They also said that in any event it was not a case in which specific performance ought to be decreed.

The facts are fully stated in the judgment and are summarized below.

The negotiations between the plaintiff and defendants were conducted through the intermediation of Mr. Sloan, of Sloan & Jackson, Ld., a firm of brokers at Glasgow. The plaintiff, who was at Rostock, communicated by letter and telegram with Mr. Sloan, who in turn communicated with the plaintiff in the same manner. Mr. Frew, on behalf of the defendants, whose office was at Newcastle-upon-Tyne, spoke on the telephone with Mr. Sloan, and letters and telegrams passed between them.

On November 17, 1926, the plaintiff wrote to the brokers with a firm offer of 7650*l.* for the *City*, but he made it a condition that the design of the boilers should be such as to satisfy the German boiler authorities. The *City* was an old vessel, having been built in 1892, but her engines and boilers were practically new and such as to satisfy the German regulations, and the plaintiff could, as a German shipowner, have her at once put on the German register. This vessel was of peculiar value to the plaintiff having regard to these facts and to her price. There was evidence that only one steamer was on the market which would suit the plaintiff's requirements, and that vessel might now be sold. On November 19 the brokers, after a long conversation with the defendants, wrote in reply that the business might be considered as a fixed sale subject to the boilers being in accordance with the German requirements. The German authorities, having been satisfied with the design and plan of the boilers submitted to them, the plaintiff telegraphed to the brokers on November 26 to send the contract of sale.

On November 19, 1926, the brokers drew up and sent a *pro forma* contract to the defendants for them to amend. The defendants replied with various suggestions which the brokers embodied in the contract. They then sent the altered contract to the defendants again for their approval. On November 24 the defendants, having made various amendments in the contract, returned it to the brokers. The contract was headed with the defendants' name as sellers. It provided that a deposit of 1500*l.* should be paid, and also contained clauses which provided that before completion and payment of the balance of the purchase price the buyer was to have the option of inspecting the vessel afloat and of requiring the sellers to place her in dry dock for inspection and of requiring the sellers to repair certain damage, if any were found. On Thursday, November 25, the defendants telegraphed to the brokers that they could not allow later than noon Saturday for definite acceptance of steamer on terms of contract, and they confirmed this by letter. Mr. Frew eventually said he would do nothing till Monday. Mr. Sloan on November 25 sent a copy of the contract to the plaintiff with a letter that he was only allowed till Saturday to say whether he accepted the steamer on the enclosed form of contract. At this time the defendants were in negotiation with other buyers for the sale of the *City*. On Monday, November 29, Mr. Sloan had a telephone conversation with Mr. Frew, and immediately afterwards sent a telegram to the plaintiff that the owners must have telegraphic acceptance of the contract before 4 P.M. on that day. His Lordship held that that telegram was sent by Mr. Sloan with the authority of Mr. Frew. The plaintiff, immediately on receipt of the telegram, wired accepting the contract, and on the same day sent by post the contract duly signed and a cheque for the deposit of 1500*l.* Mr. Sloan passed on to Mr. Frew by telephone about 2.50 P.M.. the contents of the telegram. Mr. Frew had in the meantime arranged to sell the steamer to other buyers, and he sought to revoke his offer to the plaintiff, but the revocation did not reach the plaintiff before the plaintiff sent off his acceptance. The defendants refused to give any instructions as regards the deposit, and repudiated any contract with the plaintiff, who thereupon commenced this action.

[After holding that the parties had entered into an enforceable contract, Wright, J., continued:]

It remains to consider what is the proper remedy. The plaintiff claims a decree of specific performance. This claim is strongly contested on behalf of the defendants. It is curious how little guidance there is on the question whether specific performance should be granted of a contract for the sale of a ship. Sect. 52 of the Sale of Goods Act gives the Court a discretion, if it think fit, in any action for breach of contract to deliver specific or ascertained goods, to direct that the contract shall be performed specifically. I think a ship is a specific chattel within the Act. In Fry on Specific Performance, 6th ed., p. 37, note 4, it is said a ship is probably within the general principle and reference is made to *Claringbould* v. *Curtis* (21 L. J. (Ch.) 541), which, however, is the case of a barge and contains no discussion of principle. *Hart* v. *Herwig* (L. R. 8 Ch. 860) seems to imply that a man who has contracted to purchase a ship is *prima facie* entitled to have it — that is, by an order for specific performance.

In the present case there is evidence that the *City* was of peculiar and practically unique value to the plaintiff. She was a cheap vessel, being old, having been built in 1892, but her engines and boilers were practically new and such as to satisfy the German regulations, and hence the plaintiff could, as a German shipowner, have her at once put on the German register. A very experienced ship valuer has said that he knew of only one other comparable ship, but that may now have been sold. The plaintiff wants the ship for immediate use, and I do not think damages would be an adequate compensation. I think he is entitled to the ship and a decree of specific performance in order that justice may be done. What is the position between the defendants and the other buyers, whose contract was later in time than that of the plaintiff, is irrelevant in this action.

I have not overlooked the argument of Mr. Miller, based on the clauses in the contract which provide that before completion and payment of the balance of the purchase price the buyer was to have the option of inspecting the vessel afloat and of requiring the sellers to place her in dry dock for inspection, and of requiring the sellers to repair certain damage if any were found. Mr. Miller contended that as the Court will not decree specific performance of a contract to do work or perform services, these clauses constitute a bar to a decree here. But I think this contention is not sound. The defendants are neither dry dockowners nor ship repairers. All they could be required to do would be to give the appropriate orders to a dry dockowner or ship repairer if necessary. But the plaintiff may not require inspection or dry-docking (which, if no damage be found, will be at his own expense), and no damage requiring repairs may be discovered. Thinking, as I do, that justice can only be satisfied by an order for specific performance, I do not find in the clauses referred to, the only ones relied on by Mr. Miller, any ground why I should not make the decree. There will be judgment, therefore, for the plaintiff, with a declaration that he purchased the *City* from the defendants — I do not make the declaration exactly in the terms stated — and a decree that the contract shall be specifically performed, and that an injunction be granted as prayed, and costs.

Judgment for plaintiff.
Decree for specific performance.

Refer again to In re Wait, *supra*, p. 49, where it was held that "as the goods were neither specific nor ascertained the remedy of specific performance was not open to the creditors."

In Bowman v. Adams, 45 Idaho 217 (Supreme Court, 1927), sheep were sold by plaintiff to defendant under an agreement by which plaintiff contracted to repurchase strictly fat sheep at an increased price. It was held that plaintiff was not entitled to specific performance of the repurchase agreement. In the sale of ordinary chattels having a market value the legal remedy of damages is adequate.

Compare TOBACCO GROWERS CO-OPERATIVE ASSOCIATION *v.* BATTLE, 187 N. C. 260 (Supreme Court, 1924), where the members of an association contracted to sell all their tobacco to the association. The association was held to be entitled to specific performance of the contract by one of its members. The award of damages would be inadequate, for failure to perform would frustrate the essential purpose of the contract.

STATUTORY AND CODE MATERIAL

SALE OF GOODS ACT

An Act for Codifying the Law Relating to the Sale of Goods.[1]

(Chapter 71 of 56 & 57 Victoria, February 20, 1894)

PART I

FORMATION OF THE CONTRACT

Contract of Sale

1. — (1.) A contract of sale of goods is a contract whereby the seller transfers or agrees to transfer the property in goods to the buyer for a money consideration, called the price. There may be a contract of sale between one part-owner and another.

(2.) A contract of sale may be absolute or conditional.

(3.) Where under a contract of sale the property in the goods is transferred from the seller to the buyer the contract is called a sale; but where the transfer of the property in the goods is to take place at a future time or subject to some condition thereafter to be fullfilled the contract is called an agreement to sell.

(4.) An agreement to sell becomes a sale when the time elapses or the conditions are fulfilled subject to which the property in the goods is to be transferred.

2. Capacity to buy and sell is regulated by the general law concerning capacity to contract, and to transfer and acquire property.

Provided that where necessaries are sold and delivered to an infant, or minor, or to a person who by reason of mental incapacity or drunkenness is incompetent to contract, he must pay a reasonable price therefor.

Necessaries in this section mean goods suitable to the condition in life of such infant or minor or other person, and to his actual requirements at the time of the sale and delivery.

Formalities of the Contract

3. Subject to the provisions of this Act and of any statute in that behalf, a contract of sale may be made in writing (either with or without seal), or by word or mouth, or partly in writing and partly by word of mouth, or may be implied from the conduct of the parties.

Provided that nothing in this section shall affect the law relating to corporations.

4. — (1.) A contract for the sale of any goods of the value of ten pounds or upwards shall not be enforceable by action unless the buyer shall accept part of the goods so sold, and actually receive the same, or give something in earnest to bind the contract, or in part payment, or unless some note or memorandum in writing of the contract be made and signed by the party to be charged or his agent in that behalf.

(2.) The provisions of this section apply to every such contract, notwith-

[1] Enactments in the main identical with the Sale of Goods Act have been adopted throughout the British Empire.

standing that the goods may be intended to be delivered at some future time, or may not at the time of such contract be actually made, procured, or provided, or fit or ready for delivery, or some act may be requisite for the making or completing thereof, or rendering the same fit for delivery.

(3.) There is an acceptance of goods within the meaning of this section when the buyer does any act in relation to the goods, which recognizes a pre-existing contract of sale whether there be an acceptance in performance of the contract or not.

(4.) The provisions of this section do not apply to Scotland.

Subject Matter of Contract

5. — (1.) The goods which form the subject of a contract of sale may be either existing goods, owned or possessed by the seller, or goods to be manufactured or acquired by the seller after the making of the contract of sale, in this Act called "future goods."

(2.) There may be a contract for the sale of goods, the acquisition of which by the seller depends upon a contingency which may or may not happen.

(3.) Where by a contract of sale the seller purports to effect a present sale of future goods, the contract operates as an agreement to sell the goods.

6. Where there is a contract for the sale of specific goods, and the goods without the knowledge of the seller have perished at the time when the contract is made, the contract is void.

7. Where there is an agreement to sell specific goods, and subsequently the goods, without any fault on the part of the seller or buyer, perish before the risk passes to the buyer, the agreement is thereby avoided.

The Price

8. — (1.) The price in a contract of sale may be fixed by the contract, or may be left to be fixed in manner thereby agreed, or may be determined by the course of dealing between the parties.

(2.) Where the price is not determined in acordance with the foregoing provisions the buyer must pay a reasonable price. What is a reasonable price is a question of fact dependent on the circumstances of each particular case.

9. — (1.) Where there is an agreement to sell goods on the terms that the price is to be fixed by the valuation of a third party, and such third party cannot or does not make such valuation, the agreement is avoided; provided that if the goods or any part thereof have been delivered to and appropriated by the buyer he must pay a reasonable price therefor.

(2.) Where such third party is prevented from making the valuation by the fault of the seller or buyer, the party not in fault may maintain an action for damages against the party in fault.

Conditions and Warranties

10. — (1.) Unless a different intention appears from the terms of the contract, stipulations as to time of payment are not deemed to be of the essence of a contract of sale. Whether any other stipulation as to time is of the essence of the contract or not depends on the terms of the contract.

(2.) In a contract of sale "month" means *prima facie* calendar month.

11. — (1.) In England or Ireland — (a.) Where a contract of sale is subject to any condition to be fulfilled by the seller the buyer may waive the condition,

or may elect to treat the breach of such condition as a breach of warranty, and not as a ground for treating the contract as repudiated.

(b.) Whether a stipulation in a contract of sale is a condition, the breach of which may give rise to a right to treat the contract as repudiated, or a warranty, the breach of which may give rise to a claim for damages but not to a right to reject the goods and treat the contract as repudiated, depends in each case on the construction of the contract. A stipulation may be a condition, though called a warranty in the contract.

(c.) Where a contract of sale is not severable, and the buyer has accepted the goods, or part thereof, or where the contract is for specific goods, the property in which has passed to the buyer, the breach of any condition to be fulfilled by the seller can only be treated as a breach of warranty, and not as a ground for rejecting the goods and treating the contract as repudiated, unless there be a term of the contract, express or implied, to that effect.

(2.) In Scotland, failure by the seller to perform any material part of a contract of sale is a breach of contract, which entitles the buyer either within a reasonable time after delivery to reject the goods and treat the contract as repudiated, or to retain the goods and treat the failure to perform such material part as a breach which may give rise to a claim for compensation or damages.

(3.) Nothing in this section shall affect the case of any condition or warranty, fulfilment of which is excused by law by reason of impossibility or otherwise.

12. In a contract of sale, unless the circumstances of the contract are such as to show a different intention, there is —

(1.) An implied condition on the part of the seller that in the case of a sale he has a right to sell the goods, and that in the case of an agreement to sell he will have a right to sell the goods at the time when the property is to pass:

(2.) An implied warranty that the buyer shall have and enjoy quiet possession of the goods:

(3.) An implied warranty that the goods shall be free from any charge or encumbrance in favor of any third party, not declared or known to the buyer before or at the time when the contract is made.

13. Where there is a contract for the sale of goods by description, there is an implied condition that the goods shall correspond with the description; and if the sale be by sample, as well as by description, it is not sufficient that the bulk of the goods corresponds with the sample if the goods do not also correspond with the description.

14. Subject to the provisions of this Act and of any statute in that behalf, there is no implied warranty or condition as to the quality or fitness for any particular purpose of goods supplied under a contract of sale, except as follows: —

(1.) Where the buyer, expressly or by implication, makes known to the seller the particular purpose for which the goods are required, so as to show that the buyer relies on the seller's skill or judgment, and the goods are of a description which it is in the course of the seller's business to supply (whether he be the manufacturer or not), there is an implied condition that the goods shall be reasonably fit for such purpose, provided that in the case of a contract for the sale of a specified article under its patent or other trade name, there is no implied condition as to its fitness for any particular purpose:

(2.) Where goods are bought by description from a seller who deals in goods of that description (whether he be the manufacturer or not), there is an implied condition that the goods shall be of merchantable quality; provided that if the buyer has examined the goods, there shall be no implied condition as regards defects which such examination ought to have revealed:

(3.) An implied warranty or condition as to quality or fitness for a particular purpose may be annexed by the usage of trade:

(4.) An express warranty or condition does not negative a warranty or condition implied by this Act unless inconsistent therewith.

Sale by Sample

15.—(1.) A contract of sale is a contract for sale by sample where there is a term in the contract, express or implied, to that effect.

(2.) In the case of a contract for sale by sample—

(a.) There is an implied condition that the bulk shall correspond with the sample in quality:

(b.) There is an implied condition that the buyer shall have a reasonable opportunity of comparing the bulk with the sample:

(c.) There is an implied condition that the goods shall be free from any defect, rendering them unmerchantable, which would not be apparent on reasonable examination of the sample.

PART II

EFFECTS OF THE CONTRACT

Transfer of Property as Between Seller and Buyer

16. Where there is a contract for the sale of unascertained goods no property in the goods is transferred to the buyer unless and until the goods are ascertained.

17.—(1.) Where there is a contract for the sale of specific or ascertained goods the property in them is transferred to the buyer at such time as the parties to the contract intend it to be transferred.

(2.) For the purpose of ascertaining the intention of the parties regard shall be had to the terms of the contract, the conduct of the parties, and the circumstances of the case.

18. Unless a different intention appears, the following are rules for ascertaining the intention of the parties as to the time at which the property in the goods is to pass to the buyer.

Rule 1.—Where there is an unconditional contract for the sale of specific goods, in a deliverable state, the property in the goods passes to the buyer when the contract is made, and it is immaterial whether the time of payment or the time of delivery, or both, be postponed.

Rule 2.—Where there is a contract for the sale of specific goods and the seller is bound to do something to the goods, for the purpose of putting them into a deliverable state, the property does not pass until such thing be done, and the buyer has notice thereof.

Rule 3.—Where there is a contract for the sale of specific goods in a deliverable state, but the seller is bound to weigh, measure, test, or do some other act or thing with reference to the goods for the purpose of ascertaining the price, the property does not pass until such act or thing be done, and the buyer has notice thereof.

Rule 4.—When goods are delivered to the buyer on approval or "on sale or return" or other similar terms the property therein passes to the buyer:—

(a.) When he signifies his approval or acceptance to the seller or does any other act adopting the transaction:

(b.) If he does not signify his approval or acceptance to the seller but retains the goods without giving notice of rejection, then, if a time has been fixed for the return of the goods, on the expiration of such time, and, if no time has been fixed, on the expiration of a reasonable time. What is a reasonable time is a question of fact.

Rule 5. — (1.) Where there is a contract for the sale of unascertained or future goods by description, and goods of that description and in a deliverable state are unconditionally appropriated to the contract, either by the seller with the assent of the buyer, or by the buyer with the assent of the seller, the property in the goods thereupon passes to the buyer. Such assent may be express or implied, and may be given either before or after the appropriation is made:

(2.) Where, in pursuance of the contract, the seller delivers the goods to the buyer or to a carrier or other bailee or custodier (whether named by the buyer or not) for the purpose of transmission to the buyer, and does not reserve the right of disposal, he is deemed to have unconditionally appropriated the goods to the contract.

19. — (1.) Where there is a contract for the sale of specific goods or where goods are subsequently appropriated to the contract, the seller may, by the terms of the contract or appropriation, reserve the right of disposal of the goods until certain conditions are fulfilled. In such case, notwithstanding the delivery of the goods to the buyer, or to a carrier or other bailee or custodier for the purpose of transmission to the buyer, the property in the goods does not pass to the buyer until the conditions imposed by the seller are fulfilled.

(2.) Where goods are shipped, and by the bill of lading the goods are deliverable to the order of the seller or his agent, the seller is *prima facie* deemed to reserve the right of disposal.

(3.) Where the seller of goods draws on the buyer for the price, and transmits the bill of exchange and bill of lading to the buyer together to secure acceptance or payment of the bill of exchange, the buyer is bound to return the bill of lading if he does not honor the bill of exchange, and if he wrongfully retains the bill of lading the property in the goods does not pass to him.

20. Unless otherwise agreed, the goods remain at the seller's risk until the property therein is transferred to the buyer, but when the property therein is transferred to the buyer, the goods are at the buyer's risk whether delivery has been made or not.

Provided that where delivery has been delayed through the fault of either buyer or seller the goods are at the risk of the party in fault as regards any loss which might not have occurred but for such fault.

Provided also that nothing in this section shall affect the duties or liabilities of either seller or buyer as a bailee or custodier of the goods of the other party.

Transfer of Title

21. — (1.) Subject to the provisions of this Act, where goods are sold by a person who is not the owner thereof, and who does not sell them under the authority or with the consent of the owner, the buyer acquires no better title to the goods than the seller had, unless the owner of the goods is by his conduct precluded from denying the seller's authority to sell.

(2.) Provided also that nothing in this Act shall affect —

(a.) The provisions of the Factors Acts, or any enactment enabling the apparent owner of goods to dispose of them as if he were the true owner thereof;

(b.) The validity of any contract of sale under any special common law or statutory power of sale or under the order of a court of competent jurisdiction.

22. — (1.) Where goods are sold in market overt, according to the usage of

the market, the buyer acquires a good title to the goods, provided he buys them in good faith and without notice of any defect or want of title on the part of the seller.

(2.) Nothing in this section shall affect the law relating to the sale of horses.

(3.) The provisions of this section do not apply to Scotland.

23. When the seller of goods has a voidable title thereto, but his title has not been avoided at the time of the sale, the buyer acquires a good title to the goods, provided he buys them in good faith and without notice of the seller's defect of title.

24. — (1.) Where goods have been stolen and the offender is prosecuted to conviction, the property in the goods so stolen revests in the person who was the owner of the goods, or his personal representative, notwithstanding any intermediate dealing with them, whether by sale in market overt or otherwise.

(2.) Notwithstanding any enactment to the contrary, where goods have been obtained by fraud or other wrongful means not amounting to larceny, the property in such goods shall not revest in the person who was the owner of the goods, or his personal representative, by reason only of the conviction of the offender.

(3.) The provisions of this section do not apply to Scotland.

25. — (1.) Where a person having sold goods continue or is in possession of the goods, or of the documents of title to the goods, the delivery or transfer by that person, or by a mercantile agent acting for him, of the goods or documents of title under any sale, pledge, or other disposition thereof, to any person receiving the same in good faith and without notice of the previous sale, shall have the same effect as if the person making the delivery or transfer were expressly authorized by the owner of the goods to make the same.

(2.) Where a person having bought or agreed to buy goods obtains, with the consent of the seller, possession of the goods or the documents of title to the goods, the delivery or transfer by that person, or by a mercantile agent acting for him, of the goods or documents of title, under any sale, pledge, or other disposition thereof, to any person receiving the same in good faith and without notice of any lien or other right of the original seller in respect of the goods, shall have the same effect as if the person making the delivery or transfer were a mercantile agent in possession of the goods or documents of title with the consent of the owner.

(3.) In this section the term "mercantile agent" has the same meaning as in the Factors Acts.

26. — (1.) A writ of *fieri facias* or other writ of execution against goods shall bind the property in the goods of the execution debtor as from the time when the writ is delivered to the sheriff to be executed; and, for the better manifestation of such time, it shall be the duty of the sheriff, without fee, upon the receipt of any such writ to indorse upon the back thereof the hour, day, month, and year when he received the same.

Provided that no such writ shall prejudice the title to such goods acquired by any person in good faith and for valuable consideration, unless such person had at the time when he acquired his title notice that such writ or any other writ by virtue of which the goods of the execution debtor might be seized or attached had been delivered to and remained unexecuted in the hands of the sheriff.

(2.) In this section the term "sheriff" includes any officer charged with the enforcement of a writ of execution.

(3.) The provisions of this section do not apply to Scotland.

PART III

PERFORMANCE OF THE CONTRACT

27. It is the duty of the seller to deliver the goods, and of the buyer to accept and pay for them, in accordance with the terms of the contract of sale.

28. Unless otherwise agreed, delivery of the goods and payment of the price are concurrent conditions, that is to say, the seller must be ready and willing to give possession of the goods to the buyer in exchange for the price, and the buyer must be ready and willing to pay the price in exchange for possession of the goods.

29. — (1.) Whether it is for the buyer to take possession of the goods or for the seller to send them to the buyer is a question depending in each case on the contract, express or implied, between the parties. Apart from any such contract, express or implied, the place of delivery is the seller's place of business, if he have one, and if not, his residence: Provided that, if the contract be for the sale of specific goods, which to the knowledge of the parties when the contract is made are in some other place, then that place is the place of delivery.

(2.) Where under the contract of sale the seller is bound to send the goods to the buyer, but no time for sending them is fixed, the seller is bound to send them within a reasonable time.

(3.) Where the goods at the time of sale are in the possession of a third person, there is no delivery by seller to buyer unless and until such third person acknowledges to the buyer that he holds the goods on his behalf; provided that nothing in this section shall affect the operation of the issue or transfer of any document of title to goods.

(4.) Demand or tender of delivery may be treated as ineffectual unless made at a reasonable hour. What is a reasonable hour is a question of fact.

(5.) Unless otherwise agreed, the expenses of and incidental to putting the goods into a deliverable state must be borne by the seller.

30. — (1.) Where the seller delivers to the buyer a quantity of goods less than he contracted to sell, the buyer may reject them, but if the buyer accepts the goods so delivered he must pay for them at the contract rate.

(2.) Where the seller delivers to the buyer a quantity of goods larger than he contracted to sell, the buyer may accept the goods included in the contract and reject the rest, or he may reject the whole. If the buyer accepts the whole of the goods so delivered he must pay for them at the contract rate.

(3.) Where the seller delivers to the buyer the goods he contracted to sell mixed with goods of a different description not included in the contract, the buyer may accept the goods which are in accordance with the contract and reject the rest, or he may reject the whole.

(4.) The provisions of this section are subject to any usage of trade, special agreement, or course of dealing between the parties.

31. — (1.) Unless otherwise agreed, the buyer of goods is not bound to accept delivery thereof by instalments.

(2.) Where there is a contract for the sale of goods to be delivered by stated instalments, which are to be separately paid for, and the seller makes defective deliveries in respect of one or more instalments, or the buyer neglects or refuses to take delivery of or pay for one or more instalments, it is a question in each case depending on the terms of the contract and the circumstances of the case, whether the breach of contract is a repudiation of the whole contract or whether it is a severable breach giving rise to a claim for compensation but not to a right to treat the whole contract as repudiated.

32. — (1.) Where, in pursuance of a contract of sale, the seller is authorised or required to send the goods to the buyer, delivery of the goods to a carrier, whether named by the buyer or not, for the purpose of transmission to the buyer is *prima facie* deemed to be a delivery of the goods ot the buyer.

(2.) Unless otherwise authorised by the buyer, the seller must make such contract with the carrier on behalf of the buyer as may be reasonable having regard to the nature of the goods and the other circumstances of the case. If the seller omit so to do, and the goods are lost or damaged in course of transit, the buyer may decline to treat the delivery to the carrier as a delivery to himself, or may hold the seller responsible in damages.

(3.) Unless otherwise agreed, where goods are sent by the seller to the buyer by a route involving sea transit, under circumstances in which it is usual to insure, the seller must give such notice to the buyer as may enable him to insure them during their sea transit, and, if the seller fails to do so, the goods shall be deemed to be at his risk during such sea transit.

33. Where the seller of goods agrees to deliver them at his own risk at a place other than that where they are when sold, the buyer must, nevertheless, unless otherwise agreed, take any risk of deterioration in the goods necessarily incident to the course of transit.

34. — (1.) Where goods are delivered to the buyer, which he has not previously examined, he is not deemed to have accepted them unless and until he has had a reasonable opportunity of examining them for the purpose of ascertaining whether they are in conformity with the contract.

(2.) Unless otherwise agreed, when the seller tenders delivery of goods to the buyer, he is bound, on request, to afford the buyer a reasonable opportunity of examining the goods for the purpose of ascertaining whether they are in conformity with the contract.

35. The buyer is deemed to have accepted the goods when he intimates to the seller that he has accepted them, or when the goods have been delivered to him, and he does any act in relation to them which is inconsistent with the ownership of the seller, or when after the lapse of a reasonable time, he retains the goods without intimating to the seller that he has rejected them.

36. Unless otherwise agreed, where goods are delivered to the buyer, and he refuses to accept them, having the right so to do, he is not bound to return them to the seller, but it is sufficient if he intimates to the seller that he refuses to accept them.

37. When the seller is ready and willing to deliver the goods, and requests the buyer to take delivery, and the buyer does not within a reasonable time after such request take delivery of the goods, he is liable to the seller for any loss occasioned by his neglect or refusal to take delivery, and also for a reasonable charge for the care and custody of the goods. Provided that nothing in this section shall affect the rights of the seller where the neglect or refusal of the buyer to take delivery amounts to a repudiation of the contract.

PART IV

RIGHTS OF UNPAID SELLER AGAINST THE GOODS

38. — (1.) The seller of goods is deemed to be an "unpaid seller" within the meaning of this Act —

(a.) When the whole of the price has not been paid or tendered;

(b.) When a bill of exchange or other negotiable instrument has been received as conditional payment, and the condition on which it was received has not been fulfilled by reason of the dishonor of the instrument or otherwise.

(2.) In this part of this Act the term "seller" includes any person who is in the position of a seller, as, for instance, an agent of the seller to whom the bill of lading has been indorsed, or a consignor or agent who has himself paid, or is directly responsible for, the price.

39. — (1.) Subject to the provisions of this Act, and of any statute in that behalf, notwithstanding that the property in the goods may have passed to the buyer, the unpaid seller of goods, as such, has by implication of law —

(a.) A lien on the goods or right to retain them for the price while he is in possession of them;

(b.) In case of the insolvency of the buyer, a right of stopping the goods *in transitu* after he has parted with the possession of them;

(c.) A right of re-sale as limited by this Act.

(2.) Where the property in goods has not passed to the buyer, the unpaid seller has, in addition to his other remedies, a right of withholding delivery similar to and co-extensive with his rights of lien and stoppage *in transitu* where the property has passed to the buyer.

40. In Scotland a seller of goods may attach the same while in his own hands or possession by arrestment or poinding; and such arrestment or poinding shall have the same operation and effect in a competition or otherwise as an arrestment or poinding by a third party.

Unpaid Seller's Lien

41. — (1.) Subject to the provisions of this Act, the unpaid seller of goods who is in possession of them is entitled to retain possession of them until payment or tender of the price in the following cases, namely: —

(a.) Where the goods have been sold without any stipulation as to credit;

(b.) Where the goods have been sold on credit, but the term of credit has expired;

(c.) Where the buyer becomes insolvent.

(2.) The seller may exercise his right of lien notwithstanding that he is in possession of the goods as agent or bailee or custodier for the buyer.

42. Where an unpaid seller has made part delivery of the goods, he may exercise his right of lien or retention on the remainder, unless such part delivery has been made under such circumstances as to show an agreement to waive the lien or right of retention.

43. — (1.) The unpaid seller of goods loses his lien or right of retention thereon —

(a.) When he delivers the goods to a carrier or other bailee or custodier for the purpose of transmission to the buyer without reserving the right of disposal of the goods;

(b.) When the buyer or his agent lawfully obtains possession of the goods;

(c.) By waiver thereof.

(2.) The unpaid seller of goods, having a lien or right of retention thereon, does not lose his lien or right of retention by reason only that he has obtained judgment or decree for the price of the goods.

Stoppage in Transitu

44. Subject to the provisions of this Act, when the buyer of goods becomes insolvent, the unpaid seller who has parted with the possession of the goods

has the right of stopping them *in transitu*, that is to say, he may resume possession of the goods as long as they are in course of transit, and may retain them until payment or tender of the price.

45. — (1.) Goods are deemed to be in course of transit from the time when they are delivered to a carrier by land or water, or other bailee or custodier for the purpose of transmission to the buyer, until the buyer, or his agent in that behalf, takes delivery of them from such carrier or other bailee or custodier.

(2.) If the buyer or his agent in that behalf obtains delivery of the goods before their arrival at the appointed destination, the transit is at an end.

(3.) If, after the arrival of the goods at the appointed destination, the carrier or other bailee or custodier acknowledges to the buyer, or his agent, that he holds the goods on his behalf and continues in possession of them as bailee or custodier for the buyer, or his agent, the transit is at an end, and it is immaterial that a further destination for the goods may have been indicated by the buyer.

(4.) If the goods are rejected by the buyer, and the carrier or other bailee or custodier continues in possession of them, the transit is not deemed to be at an end, even if the seller has refused to receive them back.

(5.) When goods are delivered to a ship chartered by the buyer it is a question depending on the circumstances of the particular case, whether they are in the possession of the master as a carrier, or as agent to the buyer.

(6.) Where the carrier or other bailee or custodier wrongfully refuses to deliver the goods to the buyer, or his agent in that behalf, the transit is deemed to be at an end.

(7.) Where part delivery of the goods has been made to the buyer, or his agent in that behalf, the remainder of the goods may be stopped *in transitu*, unless such part delivery has been made under such circumstances as to show an agreement to give up possession of the whole of the goods.

46. — (1.) The unpaid seller may exercise his right of stoppage *in transitu* either by taking actual possession of the goods, or by giving notice of his claim to the carrier or other bailee or custodier in whose possession the goods are. Such notice may be given either to the person in actual possession of the goods or to his principal. In the latter case the notice, to be effectual, must be given at such time and under such circumstances that the principal, by the exercise of reasonable diligence, may communicate it to his servant or agent in time to prevent a delivery to the buyer.

(2.) When notice of stoppage *in transitu* is given by the seller to the carrier, or other bailee or custodier in possession of the goods, he must redeliver the goods to, or according to the directions of, the seller. The expenses of such re-delivery must be borne by the seller.

Re-sale by Buyer or Seller

47. Subject to the provisions of this Act, the unpaid seller's right of lien or retention or stoppage *in transitu* is not affected by any sale, or other disposition of the goods which the buyer may have made, unless the seller has assented thereto.

Provided that where a document of title to goods has been lawfully transferred to any person as buyer or owner of the goods, and that person transfers the document to a person who takes the document in good faith and for valuable consideration, then, if such last-mentioned transfer was by way of sale the unpaid seller's right of lien or retention or stoppage *in transitu* is defeated, and if such last-mentioned transfer was by way of pledge or other disposition for value, the unpaid seller's right of lien or retention or stoppage *in transitu* can only be exercised subject to the rights of the transferee.

48. — (1.) Subject to the provisions of this section, a contract of sale is not rescinded by the mere exercise by an unpaid seller of his right of lien or retention or stoppage *in transitu.*

(2.) Where an unpaid seller who has exercised his right of lien or retention or stoppage *in transitu* re-sells the goods, the buyer acquires a good title thereto as against the original buyer.

(3.) Where the goods are of a perishable nature, or where the unpaid seller gives notice to the buyer of his intention to resell, and the buyer does not within a reasonable time pay or tender the price, the unpaid seller may re-sell the goods and recover from the original buyer damages for any loss occasioned by his breach of contract.

(4.) Where the seller expressly reserves a right of re-sale in case the buyer should make default, and on the buyer making default, re-sells the goods, the original contract of sale is thereby rescinded, but without prejudice to any claim the seller may have for damages.

PART V

ACTIONS FOR BREACH OF THE CONTRACT

Remedies of the Seller

49. — (1.) Where, under a contract of sale, the property in the goods has passed to the buyer, and the buyer wrongfully neglects or refuses to pay for the goods according to the terms of the contract, the seller may maintain an action against him for the price of the goods.

(2.) Where, under a contract of sale, the price is payable on a day certain irrespective of delivery, and the buyer wrongfully neglects or refuses to pay such price, the seller may maintain an action for the price, although the property in the goods has not passed, and the goods have not been appropriated to the contract.

(3.) Nothing in this section shall prejudice the right of the seller in Scotland to recover interest on the price from the date of tender of the goods, or from the date on which the price was payable, as the case may be.

50. — (1.) Where the buyer wrongfully neglects or refuses to accept and pay for the goods, the seller may maintain an action against him for damages for non-acceptance.

(2.) The measure of damages is the estimated loss directly and naturally resulting, in the ordinary course of events, from the buyer's breach of contract.

(3.) Where there is an available market for the goods in question the measure of damages is *prima facie* to be ascertained by the difference between the contract price and the market or current price at the time or times when the goods ought to have been accepted, or, if no time was fixed for acceptance, then at the time of the refusal to accept.

Remedies of the Buyer

51. — (1.) Where the seller wrongfully neglects or refuses to deliver the goods to the buyer, the buyer may maintain an action against the seller for damages for non-delivery.

(2.) The measure of damages is the estimated loss directly and naturally resulting, in the ordinary course of events, from the seller's breach of contract.

(3.) Where there is an available market for the goods in question the measure of damages is *prima facie* to be ascertained by the difference between the contract price and the market or current price of the goods at the time or times when they ought to have been delivered, or, if no time was fixed, then at the time of the refusal to deliver.

52. In any action for breach of contract to deliver specific or ascertained goods the court may, if it thinks fit, on the application of the plaintiff, by its judgment or decree direct that the contract shall be performed specifically, without giving the defendant the option of retaining the goods on payment of damages. The judgment or decree may be unconditional, or upon such terms and conditions as to damages, payment of the price, and otherwise, as to the court may seem just, and the application by the plaintiff may be made at any time before judgment or decree.

The provisions of this section shall be deemed to be supplementary to, and not in derogation of, the right of specific implement in Scotland.

53. — (1.) Where there is a breach of warranty by the seller, or where the buyer elects, or is compelled, to treat any breach of a condition on the part of the seller as a breach of warranty, the buyer is not by reason only of such breach of warranty entitled to reject the goods; but he may

(a) set up against the seller the breach of warranty in diminution or extinction of the price; or

(b) maintain an action against the seller for damages for the breach of warranty.

(2.) The measure of damages for breach of warranty is the estimated loss directly and naturally resulting, in the ordinary course of events, from the breach of warranty.

(3.) In the case of breach of warranty of quality such loss is *prima facie* the difference between the value of the goods at the time of delivery to the buyer and the value they would have had if they had answered to the warranty.

(4.) The fact that the buyer has set up the breach of warranty in diminution or extinction of the price does not prevent him from maintaining an action for the same breach of warranty if he has suffered further damage.

(5.) Nothing in this section shall prejudice or affect the buyer's right of rejection in Scotland as declared by this Act.

54. Nothing in this Act shall affect the right of the buyer or the seller to recover interest or special damages in any case where by law interest or special damages may be recoverable, or to recover money paid where the consideration for the payment of it has failed.

PART VI

SUPPLEMENTARY

55. Where any right, duty, or liability would arise under a contract of sale by implication of law, it may be negatived or varied by express agreement or by the course of dealing between the parties, or by usage, if the usage be such as to bind both parties to the contract.

56. Where, by this Act, any reference is made to a reasonable time the question what is a reasonable time is a question of fact.

57. Where any right, duty, or liability is declared by this Act, it may, unless otherwise by this Act provided, be enforced by action.

58. In the case of a sale by auction —

(1.) Where goods are put up for sale by auction in lots, each lot is *prima facie* deemed to be the subject of a separate contract of sale:

(2.) A sale by auction is complete when the auctioneer announces its completion by the fall of the hammer, or in other customary manner. Until such announcement is made any bidder may retract his bid:

(3.) Where a sale by auction is not notified to be subject to a right to bid on behalf of the seller, it shall not be lawful for the seller to bid himself or to employ any person to bid at such sale, or for the auctioneer knowingly to take any bid from the seller or any such person: Any sale contravening this rule may be treated as fraudulent by the buyer:

(4.) A sale by auction may be notified to be subject to a reserved or upset price, and a right to bid may also be reserved expressly by or on behalf of the seller.

Where a right to bid is expressly reserved, but not otherwise, the seller, or any one person on his behalf, may bid at the auction.

59. In Scotland where a buyer has elected to accept goods which he might have rejected, and to treat a breach of contract as only giving rise to a claim for damages, he may, in an action by the seller for the price, be required, in the discretion of the court before which the action depends, to consign or pay into court the price of the goods, or part thereof, or to give other reasonable security for the due payment thereof.

60. The enactments mentioned in the schedule to this Act are hereby repealed as from the commencement of this Act to the extent in that schedule mentioned.

Provided that such repeal shall not affect anything done or suffered, or any right, title, or interest acquired or accrued before the commencement of this Act, or any legal proceeding or remedy in respect of any such thing, right, title, or interest.

61. — (1.) The rules in bankruptcy relating to contracts of sale shall continue to apply thereto, notwithstanding anything in this Act contained.

(2.) The rules of the common law, including the law merchant, save in so far as they are inconsistent with the express provisions of this Act, and in particular the rules relating to the law of principal and agent and the effect of fraud, misrepresentation, duress or coercion, mistake, or other invalidating cause, shall continue to apply to contracts for the sale of goods.

(3.) Nothing in this Act or in any repeal effected thereby shall affect the enactments relating to bills of sale, or any enactment relating to the sale of goods which is not expressly repealed by this Act.

(4.) The provisions of this Act relating to contracts of sale do not apply to any transaction in the form of a contract of sale which is intended to operate by way of mortgage, pledge, charge, or other security.

(5.) Nothing in this Act shall prejudice or affect the landlord's right of hypothec or sequestration for rent in Scotland.

62. — (1.) In this Act, unless the context or subject matter otherwise requires, —

"Action" includes counterclaim and set off, and in Scotland condescendence and claim and compensation:

"Bailee" in Scotland includes custodier:

"Buyer" means a person who buys or agrees to buy goods:

"Contract of sale" includes an agreement to sell as well as a sale:

"Defendant" includes in Scotland defender, respondent, and claimant in a multiple poinding:

"Delivery" means voluntary transfer of possession from one person to another:

"Document of title to goods" has the same meaning as it has in the Factors Acts:

"Factors Acts" means the Factors Act, 1889, the Factors (Scotland) Act, 1890, and any enactment amending or substituted for the same:

"Fault" means wrongful act or default:

"Future goods" means goods to be manufactured or acquired by the seller after the making of the contract of sale:

"Goods" include all chattels personal other than things in action and money, and in Scotland all corporeal movables except money. The term includes emblements, industrial growing crops, and things attached to or forming part of the land which are agreed to be severed before sale or under the contract of sale:

"Lien" in Scotland includes right of retention:

"Plaintiff" includes pursuer, complainer, claimant in a multiple poinding and defendant or defender counterclaiming:

"Property" means the general property in goods, and not merely a special property:

"Quality of goods" includes their state or condition:

"Sale" includes a bargain and sale as well as a sale and delivery:

"Seller" means a person who sells or agrees to sell goods:

"Specific goods" mean goods identified and agreed upon at the time a contract of sale is made:

"Warranty" as regards England and Ireland means an agreement with reference to goods which are the subject of a contract of sale, but collateral to the main purpose of such contract, the breach of which gives rise to a claim for damages, but not to a right to reject the goods and treat the contract as repudiated.

As regards Scotland a breach of warranty shall be deemed to be a failure to perform a material part of the contract.

(2.) A thing is deemed to be done "in good faith" within the meaning of this Act when it is in fact done honestly, whether it be done negligently or not.

(3.) A person is deemed to be insolvent within the meaning of this Act who either has ceased to pay his debts in the ordinary course of business, or cannot pay his debts as they become due, whether he has committed an act of bankruptcy or not, and whether he has become a notour bankrupt or not.

(4.) Goods are in a "deliverable state" within the meaning of this Act when they are in such a state that the buyer would under the contract be bound to take delivery of them.

63. This Act shall come into operation on the first day of January one thousand eight hundred and ninety-four.

64. This Act may be cited as the Sale of Goods Act, 1893.

UNIFORM SALES ACT

An Act to Make Uniform the Law of Sales of Goods.[1]

PART I

FORMATION OF THE CONTRACT

Sec. 1. (Contracts to Sell and Sales.) (1) A contract to sell goods is a contract whereby the seller agrees to transfer the property in goods to the buyer for a consideration called the price.

(2) A sale of goods is an agreement whereby the seller transfers the property in goods to the buyer for a consideration called the price.

(3) A contract to sell or a sale may be absolute or conditional.

(4) There may be a contract to sell or a sale between one part owner and another.

Sec. 2. (Capacity — Liabilities for Necessaries.) Capacity to buy and sell is regulated by the general law concerning capacity to contract, and to transfer and acquire property.

Where necessaries are sold and delivered to an infant, or to a person who by reason of mental incapacity or drunkenness is incompetent to contract, he must pay a reasonable price therefor.

Necessaries in this section means goods suitable to the condition in life of such infant or other person, and to his actual requirements at the time of delivery.

Sec. 3. (Form of Contract or Sale.) Subject to the provisions of this act and of any statute in that behalf, a contract to sell or a sale may be made in writing (either with or without seal), or by word of mouth, or partly in writing and partly by word of mouth or may be inferred from the conduct of the parties.

Sec. 4. (Statute of Frauds.) (1) A contract to sell or a sale of any goods or choses in action of the value of five hundred dollars or upwards shall not be enforceable by action unless the buyer shall accept part of the goods or choses in action so contracted to be sold or sold, and actually receive the same, or give something in earnest to bind the contract, or in part payment, or unless some note or memorandum in writing of the contract or sale be signed by the party to be charged or his agent in that behalf.

(2) The provisions of this section apply to every such contract or sale, notwithstanding that the goods may be intended to be delivered at some future time or may not at the time of such contract or sale be actually made, procured, or provided, or fit or ready for delivery, or some act may be requisite for the making or completing thereof, or rendering the same fit for delivery; but if the

[1] States which have adopted the Uniform Sales Act and the dates of adoption are as follows: Alabama (1931); Alaska (1913); Arizona (1913); California (1931); Connecticut (1907); Delaware (1933); Hawaii (1929); Idaho (1919); Illinois (1915); Indiana (1929); Iowa (1919); Kentucky (1928); Maine (1923); Maryland (1910); Massachusetts (1908); Michigan (1913); Minnesota (1917); Nebraska (1921); Nevada (1915); New Hampshire (1923); New Jersey (1907); New York (1911); North Dakota (1917); Ohio (1908); Oregon (1919); Pennsylvania (1915); Rhode Island (1908); South Dakota (1921); Tennessee (1919); Utah (1917); Vermont (1921); Washington (1926); Wisconsin (1911); Wyoming (1917).

goods are to be manufactured by the seller especially for the buyer and are not suitable for sale to others in the ordinary course of the seller's business, the provisions of this section shall not apply.

(3) There is an acceptance of goods within the meaning of this section when the buyer, either before or after delivery of the goods, expresses by words or conduct his assent to becoming the owner of those specific goods.

SUBJECT MATTER OF CONTRACT

Sec. 5. (Existing and Future Goods.) (1) The goods which form the subject of a contract to sell may be either existing goods, owned or possessed by the seller, or goods to be manufactured or acquired by the seller after the making of the contract to sell, in this act called "future goods."

(2) There may be a contract to sell goods, the acquisition of which by the seller depends upon a contingency which may or may not happen.

(3) Where the parties purport to effect a present sale of future goods, the agreement operates as a contract to sell the goods.

Sec. 6. (Undivided Shares.) (1) There may be a contract to sell or a sale of an undivided share of goods. If the parties intend to effect a present sale, the buyer, by force of the agreement, becomes an owner in common with the owner or owners of the remaining shares.

(2) In the case of fungible goods, there may be a sale of an undivided share of a specific mass, though the seller purports to sell and the buyer to buy a definite number, weight or measure of the goods in the mass, and though the number, weight or measure of the goods in the mass is undetermined. By such a sale the buyer becomes owner in common of such a share of the mass as the number, weight or measure bought bears to the number, weight or measure of the mass. If the mass contains less than the number, weight or measure bought, the buyer becomes the owner of the whole mass and the seller is bound to make good the deficiency from similar goods unless a contrary intent appears.

Sec. 7. (Destruction of Goods Sold.) (1) Where the parties purport to sell specific goods, and the goods without the knowledge of the seller have wholly perished at the time when the agreement is made, the agreement is void.

(2) Where the parties purport to sell specific goods, and the goods without the knowledge of the seller have perished in part or have wholly or in a material part so deteriorated in quality as to be substantially changed in character, the buyer may at his option treat the sale:

(a) As avoided, or

(b) As transferring the property in all of the existing goods or in so much thereof as have not deteriorated, and as binding the buyer to pay the full agreed price if the sale was indivisible, or to pay the agreed price for the goods in which the property passes if the sale was divisible.

Sec. 8. (Destruction of Goods Contracted to be Sold.) (1) Where there is a contract to sell specific goods, and subsequently, but before the risk passes to the buyer, without any fault on the part of the seller or the buyer, the goods wholly perish, the contract is thereby avoided.

(2) Where there is a contract to sell specific goods, and subsequently, but before the risk passes to the buyer, without any fault of the seller or the buyer, part of the goods perish or the whole or a material part of the goods so deteriorate in quality as to be substantially changed in character, the buyer may at his option treat the contract:

(a) As avoided, or

(b) As binding the seller to transfer the property in all of the existing goods or in so much thereof as have not deteriorated, and as binding the buyer to pay the full agreed price if the contract was indivisible, or to pay the agreed price for so much of the goods as the seller, by the buyer's option, is bound to transfer if the contract was divisible.

The Price

Sec. 9. (Definition and Ascertainment of Price.) (1) The price may be fixed by the contract, or may be left to be fixed in such manner as may be agreed, or it may be determined by the course of dealing between the parties.

(2) The price may be made payable in any personal property.

(3) Where transferring or promising to transfer any interest in real estate constitutes the whole or part of the consideration for transferring or for promising to transfer the property in goods, this act shall not apply.

(4) Where the price is not determined in accordance with the foregoing provisions the buyer must pay a reasonable price. What is a reasonable price is a question of fact dependent on the circumstances of each particular case.

Sec. 10. (Sale at a Valuation.) (1) Where there is a contract to sell or a sale of goods at a price or on terms to be fixed by a third person, and such third person without fault of the seller or the buyer, cannot or does not fix the price or terms, the contract or the sale is thereby avoided; but if the goods or any part thereof have been delivered to and appropriated by the buyer he must pay a reasonable price therefor.

(2) Where such third person is prevented from fixing the price or terms by fault of the seller or the buyer, the party not in fault may have such remedies against the party in fault as are allowed by Parts IV and V of this act.

Conditions and Warranties

Sec. 11. (Effect of Conditions.) (1) Where the obligation of either party to a contract to sell or a sale is subject to any condition which is not performed, such party may refuse to proceed with the contract or sale or he may waive performance of the condition. If the other party has promised that the condition should happen or be performed, such first mentioned party may also treat the non-performance of the condition as a breach of warranty.

(2) Where the property in the goods has not passed, the buyer may treat the fulfillment by the seller of his obligations to furnish goods as described and as warranted expressly or by implication in the contract to sell as a condition of the obligation of the buyer to perform his promise to accept and pay for the goods.

Sec. 12. (Definition of Express Warranty.) Any affirmation of fact or any promise by the seller relating to the goods is an express warranty if the natural tendency of such affirmation or promise is to induce the buyer to purchase the goods, and if the buyer purchases the goods relying thereon. No affirmation of the value of the goods, nor any statement purporting to be a statement of the seller's opinion only shall be construed as a warranty.

Sec. 13. (Implied Warranties of Title.) In a contract to sell or a sale, unless a contrary intention appears, there is —

(1) An implied warranty on the part of the seller that in case of a sale he has a right to sell the goods, and that in case of a contract to sell he will have a right to sell the goods at the time when the property is to pass;

(2) An implied warranty that the buyer shall have and enjoy quiet possession of the goods as against any lawful claims existing at the time of the sale;

(3) An implied warranty that the goods shall be free at the time of the sale

from any charge of encumbrance in favor of any third person, not declared or known to the buyer before or at the time when the contract or sale is made.

(4) This section shall not, however, be held to render liable a sheriff, auctioneer, mortgagee, or other person professing to sell by virtue of authority in fact or law, goods in which a third person has a legal or equitable interest.

Sec. 14. (Implied Warranty in Sale by Description.) Where there is a contract to sell or a sale of goods by description, there is an implied warranty that the goods shall correspond with the description and if the contract or sale be by sample, as well as by description, it is not sufficient that the bulk of the goods corresponds with the sample if the goods do not also correspond with the description.

Sec. 15. (Implied Warranties of Quality.) Subject to the provisions of this act and of any statute in that behalf, there is no implied warranty or condition as to the quality or fitness for any particular purpose of goods supplied under a contract to sell or a sale, except as follows:

(1) Where the buyer, expressly or by implication, makes known to the seller the particular purpose for which the goods are required, and it appears that the buyer relies on the seller's skill or judgment (whether he be the grower or manufacturer or not), there is an implied warranty that the goods shall be reasonably fit for such purpose.

(2) Where the goods are bought by description from a seller who deals in goods of that description (whether he be the grower or manufacturer or not), there is an implied warranty that the goods shall be of merchantable quality.

(3) If the buyer has examined the goods, there is no implied warranty as regards defects which such examination ought to have revealed.

(4) In the case of a contract to sell or a sale of a specified article under its patent or other trade name, there is no implied warranty as to its fitness for any particular purpose.

(5) An implied warranty or condition as to the quality or fitness for a particular purpose may be annexed by the usage of trade.

(6) An express warranty or condition does not negative a warranty or condition implied under this act unless inconsistent therewith.

Sale by Sample

Sec. 16. (Implied Warranties in Sale by Sample.) In the case of a contract to sell or a sale by sample:

(a) There is an implied warranty that the bulk shall correspond with the sample in quality.

(b) There is an implied warranty that the buyer shall have a reasonable opportunity of comparing the bulk with the sample, except so far as otherwise provided in section 47 (3).

(c) If the seller is a dealer in goods of that kind, there is an implied warranty that the goods shall be free from any defect rendering them unmerchantable which would not be apparent on reasonable examination of the sample.

PART II

Transfer of Property as Between Seller and Buyer

Sec. 17. (No Property Passes Until Goods are Ascertained.) Where there is a contract to sell unascertained goods no property in the goods is transferred to the buyer unless and until the goods are ascertained, but property in a [sic] undivided share of ascertained goods may be transferred as provided in section 6.

Sec. 18. (Property in Specific Goods Passes When Parties so Intend.) (1) Where there is a contract to sell specific or ascertained goods, the property in them is transferred to the buyer at such time as the parties to the contract intend it to be transferred.

(2) For the purpose of ascertaining the intention of the parties, regard shall be had to the terms of the contract, the conduct of the parties, usages of trade and the circumstances of the case.

Sec. 19. (Rules for Ascertaining Intention.) Unless a different intention appears, the following are rules for ascertaining the intention of the parties as to the time at which the property in the goods is to pass to the buyer.

Rule 1. Where there is an unconditional contract to sell specific goods, in a deliverable state, the property in the goods passes to the buyer when the contract is made and it is immaterial whether the time of payment, or the time of delivery, or both, be postponed.

Rule 2. Where there is a contract to sell specific goods and the seller is bound to do something to the goods, for the purpose of putting them into a deliverable state, the property does not pass until such thing be done.

Rule 3. (1) When goods are delivered to the buyer "on sale or return," or on other terms indicating an intention to make a present sale, but to give the buyer an option to return the goods instead of paying the price, the property passes to the buyer on delivery, but he may revest the property in the seller by returning or tendering the goods within the time fixed in the contract, or, if no time has been fixed, within a reasonable time.

(2) When goods are delivered to the buyer on approval or on trial or on satisfaction, or other similar terms, the property therein passes to the buyer —

(a) When he signifies his approval or acceptance to the seller or does any other act adopting the transaction;

(b) If he does not signify his approval or acceptance to the seller, but retains the goods without giving notice of rejection, then if a time has been fixed for the return of the goods, on the expiration of such time, and, if no time has been fixed, on the expiration of a reasonable time. What is a reasonable time is a question of fact.

Rule 4. (1) Where there is a contract to sell unascertained or future goods by description, and goods of that description and in a deliverable state are unconditionally appropriated to the contract, either by the seller with the assent of the buyer, or by the buyer with the assent of the seller, and property in the goods thereupon passes to the buyer. Such assent may be expressed or implied, and may be given either before or after the appropriation is made.

(2) Where, in pursuance of a contract to sell, the seller delivers the goods to the buyer, or to a carrier or other bailee (whether named by the buyer or not) for the purpose of transmission to or holding for the buyer, he is presumed to have unconditionally appropriated the goods to the contract except in the cases provided for in the next rule and in section 20. This presumption is applicable, although by the terms of the contract, the buyer is to pay the price before receiving delivery of the goods, and the goods are marked with the words "collect on delivery" or their equivalents.

Rule 5. If the contract to sell requires the seller to deliver the goods to the buyer, or at a particular place, or to pay the freight or cost of transportation to the buyer, or to a particular place, the property does not pass until the goods have been delivered to the buyer or reached the place agreed upon.

Sec. 20. (Reservation of right of Possession or Property When Goods are

Shipped.) (1) Where there is a contract to sell specific goods, or where goods are subsequently appropriated to the contract, the seller may, by the terms of the contract or appropriation, reserve the right of possession or property in the goods until certain conditions have been fulfilled. The right of possession or property may be thus reserved notwithstanding the delivery of the goods to the buyer or to a carrier or other bailee for the purpose of transmission to the buyer.

(2) Where goods are shipped, and by the bill of lading the goods are deliverable to the seller or his agent, or to the order of the seller or of his agent, the seller thereby reserves the property in the goods. But if, except for the form of the bill of lading, the property would have passed to the buyer on shipment of the goods, the seller's property in the goods shall be deemed to be only for the purpose of securing performance by the buyer of his obligations under the contract.

(3) Where goods are shipped, and by the bill of lading the goods are deliverable to the order of the buyer or of his agent, but possession of the bill of lading is retained by the seller or his agent, the seller thereby reserves a right to the possession of the goods as against the buyer.

(4) Where the seller of goods draws on the buyer for the price and transmits the bill of exchange and bill of lading together to the buyer to secure acceptance or payment of the bill of exchange, the buyer is bound to return the bill of lading if he does not honor the bill of exchange, and if he wrongfully retains the bill of lading he acquires no added right thereby. If, however, the bill of lading provides that the goods are deliverable to the buyer or to the order of the buyer, or is indorsed in blank, or to the buyer by the consignee named therein, one who purchases in good faith, for value, the bill of lading, or goods from the buyer will obtain the property in the goods, although the bill of exchange has not been honored, provided that such purchaser has received delivery of the bill of lading indorsed by the consignee named therein, or of the goods, without notice of the facts, making the transfer wrongful.

Sec. 21. (Sale by Auction.) In the case of a sale by auction —

(1) Where goods are put up for sale by auction in lots, each lot is the subject of a separate contract of sale.

(2) A sale by auction is complete when the auctioneer announces its completion by the fall of the hammer, or in other customary manner. Until such announcement is made, any bidder may retract his bid; and the auctioneer may withdraw the goods from sale unless the auction has been announced to be without reserve.

(3) A right to bid may be reserved expressly by or on behalf of the seller.

(4) Where notice has not been given that a sale by auction is subject to a right to bid on behalf of the seller, it shall not be lawful for the seller to bid himself or to employ or induce any person to bid at such sale on his behalf, or for the auctioneer to employ or induce any person to bid at such sale on behalf of the seller or knowingly to take any bid from the seller or any person employed by him. Any sale contravening this rule may be treated as fraudulent by the buyer.

Sec. 22. (Risk of Loss.) Unless otherwise agreed, the goods remain at the seller's risk until the property therein is transferred to the buyer, but when the property therein is transferred to the buyer the goods are at the buyer's risk whether delivery has been made or not, except that —

(a) Where delivery of the goods has been made to the buyer or to a bailee for the buyer, in pursuance of the contract and the property in the goods has been retained by the seller merely to secure performance by the buyer of his obligations under the contract, the goods are at the buyer's risk from the time of such delivery.

(b) Where delivery has been delayed through the fault of either the buyer or seller the goods are at the risk of the party in fault as regards any loss which might not have occurred but for such fault.

Transfer of Title

Sec. 23. (Sale by a Person not the Owner.) (1) Subject to the provisions of this act, where goods are sold by a person who is not the owner thereof, and who does not sell them under the authority or with the consent of the owner, the buyer acquires no better title to the goods than the seller had, unless the owner of the goods is by his conduct precluded from denying the seller's authority to sell.

(2) Nothing in this act, however, shall affect:

(a) The provisions of any factors' act, recording acts, or any enactment enabling the apparent owner of goods to dispose of them as if he were the true owner thereof.

(b) The validity of any contract to sell or sale under any special common law or statutory power of sale or under the order of a court of competent jurisdiction.

Sec. 24. (Sale by One having a Voidable Title.) Where the seller of goods has a voidable title thereto, but his title has not been avoided at the time of the sale, the buyer acquires a good title to the goods, provided he buys them in good faith, for value, and without notice of the seller's defect of title.

Sec. 25. (Sale by Seller in Possession of Goods Already Sold.) Where a person having sold goods continues in possession of the goods, or of negotiable documents of title to the goods, the delivery or transfer by that person, or by an agent acting for him, of the goods or documents of title under any sale, pledge, or other disposition thereof, to any person receiving and paying value for the same in good faith and without notice of the previous sale, shall have the same effect as if the person making the delivery or transfer were expressly authorized by the owner of the goods to make the same.

Sec. 26. (Creditors' Rights Against Sold Goods in Seller's Possession.) Where a person having sold goods continues in possession of the goods, or of negotiable documents of title to the goods and such retention of possession is fraudulent in fact or is deemed fraudulent under any rule of law, a creditor or creditors of the seller may treat the sale as void.

Sec. 27. (Definition of Negotiable Documents of Title.) A document of title in which it is stated that the goods referred to therein will be delivered to the bearer, or to the order of any person named in such document is a negotiable document of title.

Sec. 28. (Negotiation of Negotiable Documents by Delivery.) A negotiable document of title may be negotiated by delivery—

(a) Where by the terms of the document the carrier, warehouseman or other bailee issuing the same undertakes to deliver the goods to the bearer, or

(b) Where by the terms of the document the carrier, warehouseman or other bailee issuing the same undertakes to deliver the goods to the order of a specified person, and such person or a subsequent indorsee of the document has indorsed it in blank or to the bearer.

Where by the terms of a negotiable document of title the goods are deliverable to bearer or where a negotiable document of title has been indorsed in blank or to bearer, any holder may indorse the same to himself or to any specified person, and in such case the document shall thereafter be negotiated only by the indorsement of such indorsee.

Sec. 29. (Negotiation of Negotiable Documents by Indorsement.) A negotiable document of title may be negotiated by the indorsement of the person to whose order the goods are by the terms of the document deliverable. Such indorsement may be in blank, to bearer or to a specified person. If indorsed to a specified person, it may be again negotiated by the indorsement of such person in blank, to bearer or to another specified person. Subsequent negotiations may be made in like manner.

Sec. 30. (Negotiable Documents of Title Marked "Not Negotiable.") If a document of title which contains an undertaking by a carrier, warehouseman or other bailee to deliver the goods to the bearer, to a specified person or order, or to the order of a specified person, or which contains words of like import, has placed upon it the words "not negotiable," "non-negotiable" or the like, such a document may nevertheless be negotiated by the holder and is a negotiable document of title within the meaning of this act. But nothing in this act contained shall be construed as limiting or defining the effect upon the obligations of the carrier, warehouseman, or other bailee issuing a document of title or placing thereon the words "not negotiable" "non-negotiable," or the like.

Sec. 31. (Transfer of Non-Negotiable Documents.) A document of title which is not in such form that it can be negotiated by delivery may be transferred by the holder by delivery to a purchaser or donee. A non-negotiable document cannot be negotiated and the indorsement of such a document gives the transferee no additional right.

Sec. 32. (Who May Negotiate a Document.) A negotiable document of title may be negotiated —

(a) By the owner thereof, or

(b) By any person to whom the possession or custody of the document has been entrusted by the owner, if, by the terms of the document the bailee issuing the documents undertakes to deliver the goods to the order of the person to whom the possession or custody of the document has been entrusted, or if at the time of such entrusting the document is in such form that it may be negotiated by delivery.

Sec. 33. (Rights of Person to Whom Document has Been Negotiated.) A person to whom a negotiable document of title has been duly negotiated acquires thereby:

(a) Such title to the goods as the person negotiating the document to him had or had ability to convey to a purchaser in good faith for value and also such title to the goods as the person to whose order the goods were to be delivered by the terms of the document had or had ability to convey to a purchaser in good faith for value, and

(b) The direct obligation of the bailee issuing the document to hold possession of the goods for him according to the terms of the document as fully as if such bailee had contracted directly with him.

Sec. 34. (Rights of Person to Whom Document has Been Transferred.) A person to whom a document of title has been transferred, but not negotiated, acquires thereby, as against the transferor, the title to the goods, subject to the terms of any agreement with the transferor.

If the document is non-negotiable, such person also acquires the right to notify the bailee who issued the document of the transfer thereof, and thereby to acquire the direct obligation of such bailee to hold possession of the goods for him according to the terms of the document.

Prior to the notification of such bailee by the transferor or transferee of a non-negotiable document of title, the title of the transferee to the goods and the right to acquire the obligation of such bailee may be defeated by the levy of an attachment or execution upon the goods by a creditor of the transferor, or by a notification to such bailee by the transferor or a subsequent purchaser from the transferor of a subsequent sale of the goods by the transferor.

Sec. 35. (Transfer of Negotiable Document Without Indorsement.) Where a negotiable document of title is transferred for value by delivery, and the indorsement of the transferor is essential for negotiation, the transferee acquires a right against the transferor to compel him to indorse the document unless a contrary intention appears. The negotiation shall take effect as of the time when the indorsement is actually made.

Sec. 36. (Warranties on Sale of Document.) A person who for value negotiates or transfers a document of title by indorsement or delivery, including one who assigns for value a claim secured by a document of title unless a contrary intention appears, warrants:

(a) That the document is genuine;

(b) That he has a legal right to negotiate or transfer it;

(c) That he has knowledge of no fact which would impair the validity or worth of the document, and

(d) That he has a right to transfer the title to the goods and that the goods are merchantable or fit for a particular purpose, whenever such warranties would have been implied if the conrtact of the parties had been to transfer without a document of title the goods represented thereby.

Sec. 37. (Indorser not a Guarantor.) The indorsement of a document of title shall not make the indorser liable for any failure on the part of the bailee who issued the document or previous indorsers thereof to fulfill their respective obligations.

Sec. 38. (When Negotiation not Impaired by Fraud, Mistake or Duress.) The validity of the negotiation of a negotiable document of title is not impaired by the fact that the negotiation was a breach of duty on the part of the person making the negotiation, or by the fact that the owner of the document was induced by fraud, mistake or duress to entrust the possession or custody thereof to such person, if the person to whom the document was negotiated or a person to whom the document was subsequently negotiated paid value therefor, without notice of the breach of duty, or fraud, mistake, or duress.

Sec. 39. (Attachment or Levy Upon Goods for Which a Negotiable Document has been Issued.) If goods are delivered to a bailee by the owner or by a person whose act in conveying the title to them to a purchaser in good faith for value would bind the owner and a negotiable document of title is issued for them, they cannot thereafter, while in the possession of such bailee, be attached by garnishment or otherwise or be levied under an execution unless the document be first surrendered to the bailee or its negotiation enjoined. The bailee shall in no case be compelled to deliver up the actual possession of the goods until the document is surrendered to him or impounded by the court.

Sec. 40. (Creditors' Remedies to Reach Negotiable Documents.) A creditor whose debtor is the owner of a negotiable document of title shall be entitled to such aid from courts of appropriate jurisdiction by injunction and otherwise in attaching such document or in satisfying the claim by means thereof as is allowed at law or in equity in regard to property which cannot readily be attached or levied upon by ordinary legal process.

PART III

Performance of the Contract

Sec. 41. (Seller Must Deliver and Buyer Accept Goods.) It is the duty of the seller to deliver the goods, and of the buyer to accept and pay for them, in accordance with the terms of the contract to sell or sale.

Sec. 42. (Delivery and Payment are Concurrent Conditions.) Unless otherwise agreed, delivery of the goods and payment of the price are concurrent conditions; that is to say, the seller must be ready and willing to give possession of the goods to the buyer in exchange for the price and the buyer must be ready and willing to pay the price in exchange for possession of the goods.

Sec. 43. (Place, Time and Manner of Delivery.) (1) Whether it is for the buyer to take possession of the goods or for the seller to send them to the buyer is a question depending in each case on the contract, express or implied, between the parties. Apart from any such contract, express or implied, or usage of trade to the contrary, the place of delivery is the seller's place of business if he have one, and if not his residence; but in case of a contract to sell or a sale of specific goods, which to the knowledge of the parties when the contract or the sale was made were in some other place, then that place is the place of delivery.

(2) Where by a contract to sell or a sale the seller is bound to send the goods to the buyer, but no time for sending them is fixed, the seller is bound to send them within a reasonable time.

(3) Where the goods at the time of sale are in the possession of a third person, the seller has not fulfilled his obligation to deliver to the buyer unless and until such third person acknowledges to the buyer that he holds the goods on the buyer's behalf; but as against all others than the seller the buyer shall be regarded as having received delivery from the time when such third person first has notice of the sale. Nothing in this section, however, shall affect the operation of the issue or transfer of any document of title to goods.

(4) Demand or tender of delivery may be treated as ineffectual unless made at a reasonable hour. What is a reasonable hour is a question of fact.

(5) Unless otherwise agreed, the expenses of and incidental to putting the goods into a deliverable state much be borne by the seller.

Sec. 44. (Delivery of Wrong Quantity.) (1) Where the seller delivers to the buyer a quantity of goods less than he contracted to sell, the buyer may reject them, but if the buyer accepts or retains the goods so delivered, knowing that the seller is not going to perform the contract in full, he must pay for them at the contract rate. If, however, the buyer has used or disposed of the goods delivered before he knows that the seller is not going to perform his contract in full, the buyer shall not be liable for more than the fair value to him of the goods so received.

(2) Where the seller delivers to the buyer a quantity of goods larger than he contracted to sell, the buyer may accept the goods included in the contract and reject the rest, or he may reject the whole. If the buyer accepts the whole of the goods so delivered he must pay for them at the contract rate.

(3) Where the seller delivers to the buyer the goods he contracted to sell mixed with goods of a different description not included in the contract, the buyer may accept the goods which are in accordance with the contract and reject the rest, or he may reject the whole.

(4) The provisions of this section are subject to any usage of trade, special agreement, or course of dealing between the parties.

Sec. 45. (Delivery in Instalments.) (1) Unless otherwise agreed, the buyer of goods is not bound to accept delivery thereof by instalments.

(2) Where there is a contract to sell goods to be delivered by stated instalments, which are to be separately paid for, and the seller makes defective deliveries in respect of one or more instalments, or the buyer neglects or refuses to take delivery of or pay for one or more instalments, it depends in each case on the terms of the contract and the circumstances of the case, whether the breach of contract is so material as to justify the injured party in refusing to proceed further and suing for damages for breach of the entire contract, or whether the breach is severable, giving rise to a claim for compensation but not to a right to treat the whole contract as broken.

Sec. 46. (Delivery to a Carrier on Behalf of the Buyer.) (1) Where, in pursuance of a contract to sell or a sale, the seller is authorized or required to send the goods to the buyer, delivery of the goods to a carrier, whether named by the buyer or not, for the purpose of transmission to the buyer is deemed to be a delivery of the goods to the buyer, except in the cases provided for in section 19, Rule 5, or unless a contrary intent appears.

(2) Unless otherwise authorized by the buyer, the seller must make such contract with the carrier on behalf of the buyer as may be reasonable, having regard to the nature of the goods and the other circumstances of the case. If the seller omit so to do, and the goods are lost or damaged in course of transit, the buyer may decline to treat the delivery to the carrier as a delivery to himself, or may hold the seller responsible in damages.

(3) Unless otherwise agreed, where goods are sent by the seller to the buyer under circumstances in which the seller knows or ought to know that it is usual to insure, the seller must give such notice to the buyer as may enable him to insure them during their transit, and, if the seller fails to do so, the goods shall be deemed to be at his risk during such transit.

Sec. 47. (Right to Examine the Goods.) (1) Where goods are delivered to the buyer which he has not previously examined, he is not deemed to have accepted them unless and until he has had a reasonable opportunity of examining them for the purpose of ascertaining whether they are in conformity with the contract.

(2) Unless otherwise agreed, when the seller tenders delivery of goods to the buyer, he is bound, on request, to afford the buyer a reasonable opportunity of examining the goods for the purpose of ascertaining whether they are in conformity with the contract.

(3) Where goods are delivered to a carrier by the seller, in accordance with an order from or agreement with the buyer, upon the terms that the goods shall not be delivered by the carrier to the buyer until he has paid the price, whether such terms are indicated by marking the goods with words "collect on delivery," or otherwise, the buyer is not entitled to examine the goods before payment of the price in the absence of agreement permitting such examination.

Sec. 48. (What Constitutes Acceptance.) The buyer is deemed to have accepted the goods when he intimates to the seller that he has accepted them, or when the goods have been delivered to him, and he does any act in relation to them which is inconsistent with the ownership of the seller, or when, after the lapse of a reasonable time, he retains the goods without intimating to the seller that he has rejected them.

Sec. 49. (Acceptance does not Bar Action for Damages.) In the absence of express or implied agreement of the parties, acceptance of the goods by the buyer shall not discharge the seller from liability in damages or other legal remedy for breach of any promise or warranty in the contract to sell or the sale. But, if, after acceptance of the goods, the buyer fail to give notice to the seller of the breach of any promise or warranty within a reasonable time after the buyer knows, or ought to know of such breach, the seller shall not be liable therefor.

Sec. 50. (Buyer is not Bound to Return Goods Wrongly Delivered.) Unless otherwise agreed, where goods are delivered to the buyer, and he refuses to accept them, having the right so to do, he is not bound to return them to the seller, but it is sufficient if he notifies the seller that he refuses to accept them.

Sec. 51. (Buyer's Liability for Failing to Accept Delivery.) When the seller is ready and willing to deliver the goods, and requests the buyer to take delivery, and the buyer does not within a reasonable time after such request take delivery of the goods, he is liable to the seller for any loss occasioned by his neglect or refusal to take delivery, and also for a reasonable charge for the care and custody of the goods. If the neglect or refusal of the buyer to take delivery amounts to a repudiation or breach of the entire contract, the seller shall have the right against the goods and on the contract hereinafter provided in favor of the seller when the buyer is in default.

PART IV

Rights of Unpaid Seller Against the Goods

Sec. 52. (Definition of Unpaid Seller.) (1) The seller of goods is deemed to be an unpaid seller within the meaning of this act —

(a) When the whole of the price has not been paid or tendered.

(b) When a bill of exchange or other negotiable instrument has been received as conditional payment, and the condition on which it was received has been broken by reason of the dishonor of the instrument, the insolvency of the buyer, or otherwise.

(2) In this part of this act the term "seller" includes an agent of the seller to whom the bill of lading has been indorsed, or a consignor or agent who has himself paid, or is directly responsible for, the price, or any other person who is in the position of a seller.

Sec. 53. (Remedies of an Unpaid Seller.) (1) Subject to the provisions of this act, notwithstanding that the property in the goods may have passed to the buyer, the unpaid seller of goods, as such, has —

(a) A lien on the goods or right to retain them for the price while he is in possession of them;

(b) In case of the insolvency of the buyer, a right of stopping the goods *in transitu* after he has parted with the possession of them;

(c) A right of resale as limited by this act;

(d) A right to rescind the sale as limited by this act.

(2) Where the property in goods has not passed to the buyer, the unpaid seller has, in addition to his other remedies, a right of withholding delivery similar to and coextensive with his rights of lien and stoppage *in transitu* where the property has passed to the buyer.

Unpaid Seller's Lien

Sec. 54. (When Right of Lien May be Exercised.) (1) Subject to the provisions of this act, the unpaid seller of goods who is in possession of them is entitled to retain possession of them until payment or tender of the price in the following cases, namely:

(a) Where the goods have been sold without any stipulation as to credit;

(b) Where the goods have been sold on credit, but the term of credit has expired;

(c) Where the buyer becomes insolvent.

(2) The seller may exercise his right of lien notwithstanding that he is in possession of the goods as agent or bailee for the buyer.

Sec. 55. (Lien After Part Delivery.) Where an unpaid seller has made part delivery of the goods, he may exercise his right of lien on the remainder, unless such part delivery has been made under such circumstances as to show an intent to waive the lien or right of retention.

Sec. 56. (When Lien is Lost.) (1) The unpaid seller of goods loses his lien thereon —

(a) When he delivers the goods to a carrier or other bailee for the purpose of transmission to the buyer without reserving the property in the goods or the right to the possession thereof;

(b) When the buyer or his agent lawfully obtains possession of the goods;

(c) By waiver thereof.

(2) The unpaid seller of goods, having a lien thereon, does not lose his lien by reason only that he has obtained judgment or decree for the price of the goods.

Stoppage in Transitu

Sec. 57. (Seller May Stop Goods on Buyer's Insolvency.) Subject to the provisions of this act, when the buyer of goods is or becomes insolvent, the unpaid seller who has parted with the possession of the goods has the right of stopping them *in transitu,* that is to say, he may resume possession of the goods at any time while they are in transit, and he will then become entitled to the same rights in regard to the goods as he would have had if he had never parted with the possession.

Sec. 58. (When Goods are in Transit.) (1) Goods are in transit within the meaning of section 57 —

(a) From the time when they are delivered to a carrier by land or water, or other bailee for the purpose of transmission to the buyer, until the buyer, or his agent in that behalf, takes delivery of them from such carrier or other bailee;

(b) If the goods are rejected by the buyer, and the carrier or other bailee continues in possession of them, even if the seller has refused to receive them back.

(2) Goods are no longer in transit within the meaning of section 57,

(a) If the buyer, or his agent in that behalf, obtains delivery of the goods before their arrival at the appointed destination;

(b) If, after the arrival of the goods at the appointed destination, the carrier or other bailee acknowledges to the buyer or his agent that he holds the goods on his behalf and continues in possession of them as bailee for the buyer or his agent; and it is immaterial that a further destination for the goods may have been indicated by the buyer;

(c) If the carrier or other bailee wrongfully refuses to deliver the goods to the buyer or his agent in that behalf.

(3) If goods are delivered to a ship chartered by the buyer, it is a question depending on the circumstances of the particular case, whether they are in the possession of the master as a carrier or as agent of the buyer.

(4) If part delivery of the goods has been made to the buyer, or his agent in that behalf, the remainder of the goods may be stopped *in transitu,* unless such part delivery has been made under such circumstances as to show an agreement with the buyer to give up possession of the whole of the goods.

Sec. 59. (Ways of Exercising the Right to Stop.) (1) The unpaid seller may exercise his right of stoppage *in transitu* either by obtaining actual possession of the goods or by giving notice of his claim to the carrier or other bailee in whose possession the goods are. Such notice may be given either to the person in actual possession of the goods or to his principal. In the latter case the notice, to be effectual, must be given at such time and under such circumstances that the principal, by the exercise of reasonable diligence, may prevent a delivery to the buyer.

(2) When notice of stoppage *in transitu* is given by the seller to the carrier, or other bailee in possession of the goods, he must redeliver the goods to, or according to the directions of, the seller. The expenses of such delivery must be borne by the seller. If, however, a negotiable document of title representing the goods has been issued by the carrier or other bailee, he shall not be obliged to deliver or justified in delivering the goods to the seller unless such document is first surrendered for cancellation.

Resale by the Seller

Sec. 60. (When and How Resale May be Made.) (1) Where the goods are of perishable nature, or where the seller expressly reserves the right of resale in case the buyer should make default, or where the buyer has been in default in the payment of the price an unreasonable time, an unpaid seller having a right of lien or having stopped the goods *in transitu* may resell the goods. He shall not thereafter be liable to the original buyer upon the contract to sell or the sale or for any profit made by such resale, but may recover from the buyer damages for any loss occasioned by the breach of the contract or the sale.

(2) Where a resale is made, as authorized in this section, the buyer acquires a good title as against the original buyer.

(3) It is not essential to the validity of a resale that notice of an intention to resell the goods be given by the seller to the original buyer. But where the right to resell is not based on the perishable nature of the goods or upon an express provision of the contract or the sale, the giving or failure to give such notice shall be relevant in any issue involving the question whether the buyer had been in default an unreasonable time before the resale was made.

(4) It is not essential to the validity of a resale that notice of the time and place of such resale should be given by the seller to the original buyer.

(5) The seller is bound to exercise reasonable care and judgment in making a resale, and subject to this requirement may make a resale either by public or private sale.

Rescission by the Seller

Sec. 61. (When and How the Seller May Rescind the Sale.) (1) An unpaid seller having the right of lien or having stopped the goods *in transitu,* may rescind the transfer of title and resume the property in the goods, where he expressly reserved the right to do so in case the buyer should make default, or where the buyer has been in default in the payment of the price an unreasonable time. The seller shall not thereafter be liable to the buyer upon the contract to sell or the sale, but may recover from the buyer damages for any loss occasioned by the breach of the contract or the sale.

(2) The transfer of title shall not be held to have been rescinded by an unpaid seller until he has manifested by notice to the buyer or by some other overt act an intention to rescind. It is not necessary that such overt act should be communicated to the buyer, but the giving or failure to give notice to the buyer of the intention to rescind shall be relevant in any issue involving the question whether the buyer had been in default an unreasonable time before the right of rescission was asserted.

Sec. 62. (Effect of Sale of Goods Subject to Lien or Stoppage *in Transitu.*) Subject to the provisions of this act, the unpaid seller's right of lien or stoppage *in transitu* is not affected by any sale, or other disposition of the goods which the buyer may have made, unless the seller has assented thereto.

If, however, a negotiable document of title has been issued for goods, no seller's lien or right of stoppage *in transitu* shall defeat the right of any purchaser for value in good faith to whom such document has been negotiated, whether such negotiations be prior or subsequent to the notification to the carrier, or other bailee who issued such document, of the seller's claim to a lien or right of stoppage *in transitu.*

PART V

Action for Breach of the Contract

Remedies of the Seller

Sec. 63. (Action for the Price.) (1) Where, under a contract to sell or a sale, the property in the goods has passed to the buyer, and the buyer wrongfully neglects or refuses to pay for the goods according to the terms of the contract or the sale, the seller may maintain an action against him for the price of the goods.

(2) Where, under a contract to sell or a sale, the price is payable on a day certain, irrespective of delivery or of transfer of title, and the buyer wrongfully neglects or refuses to pay such price, the seller may maintain an action for the price, although the property in the goods has not passed, and the goods have not been appropriated to the contract. But it shall be a defense to such an action that the seller at any time before judgment in such action has manifested an inability to perform the contract or the sale on his part or an intention not to perform it.

(3) Although the property in the goods has not passed, if they cannot readily be resold for a reasonable price, and if the provisions of section 64 (4) are not applicable, the seller may offer to deliver the goods to the buyer, and, if the buyer refuses to receive them, may notify the buyer that the goods are thereafter held by the seller as bailee for the buyer. Thereafter the seller may treat the goods as the buyer's and may maintain an action for the price.

Sec. 64. (Action for Damages for Non-Acceptance of the Goods.) (1) Where the buyer wrongfully neglects or refuses to accept and pay for the goods, the seller may maintain an action against him for damages for non-acceptance.

(2) The measure of damages is the estimated loss directly and naturally resulting, in the ordinary course of events, from the buyer's breach of contract.

(3) Where there is an available market for the goods in question, the measure of damages is, in the absence of special circumstances, showing proximate damage of a greater amount, the difference between the contract price and the market or current price at the time or times when the goods ought to have been accepted, or, if no time was fixed for acceptance, then at the time of the refusal to accept.

(4) If, while labor or expense of material amount are necessary on the part of the seller to enable him to fulfill his obligations under the contract to sell or the sale, the buyer repudiates the contract or the sale, or notifies the seller to proceed no further therewith, the buyer shall be liable to the seller for no greater damages than the seller would have suffered if he did nothing towards carrying out the contract or the sale after receiving notice of the buyer's repudiation or countermand. The profit the seller would have made if the contract or the sale had been fully performed shall be considered in estimating such damages.

Sec. 65. (When Seller May Rescind Contract or Sale.) Where the goods have not been delivered to the buyer, and the buyer has repudiated the contract to sell or sale, or has manifested his inability to perform his obligations thereunder, or has committed a material breach thereof, the seller may totally rescind the contract or the sale by giving notice of his election so to do to the buyer.

Remedies of the Buyer

Sec. 66. (Action for Converting or Detaining Goods.) Where the property in the goods has passed to the buyer and the seller wrongfully neglects or refuses to deliver the goods, the buyer may maintain any action allowed by law to the owner of goods of similar kind when wrongfully converted or withheld.

Sec. 67. (Action for Failing to Deliver Goods.) (1) Where the property in the goods has not passed to the buyer, and the seller wrongfully neglects or refuses to deliver the goods, the buyer may maintain an action against the seller for damages for non-delivery.

(2) The measure of damages is the loss directly and naturally resulting in the ordinary course of events, from the seller's breach of contract.

(3) Where there is an available market for the goods in question, the measure of damages, in the absence of special circumstances showing proximate damages of a greater amount, is the difference between the contract price and the market or current price of the goods at the time or times when they ought to have been delivered or if no time was fixed, then at the time of the refusal to deliver.

Sec. 68. (Specific Performance.) Where the seller has broken a contract to deliver specific or ascertained goods, a court having the powers of a court of equity may, if it thinks fit, on the application of the buyer, by its judgment or decree direct that the contract shall be performed specifically, without giving the seller the option of retaining the goods on payment of damages. The judgment or decree may be unconditional, or upon such terms and conditions as to damages, payment of the price and otherwise, as to the court may seem just.

Sec. 69. (Remedies for Breach of Warranty.) (1) Where there is a breach of warranty by the seller, the buyer may, at his election —

(a) Accept or keep the goods and set up against the seller, the breach of warranty by way of recoupment in diminution or extinction of the price;

(b) Accept or keep the goods and maintain an action against the seller for damages for the breach of warranty.

(c) Refuse to accept the goods, if the property therein has not passed, and maintain an action against the seller for damages for the breach of warranty;

(d) Rescind the contract to sell or the sale and refuse to receive the goods, or if the goods have already been received, return them or offer to return them to the seller and recover the price or any part thereof which has been paid.

(2) When the buyer has claimed and been granted a remedy in any one of these ways, no other remedy can thereafter be granted.

(3) Where the goods have been delivered to the buyer, he cannot rescind the sale if he knew of the breach of warranty when he accepted the goods, or if he fails to notify the seller within a reasonable time of the election to rescind, or if he fails to return or to offer to return the goods to the seller in substantially as good condition as they were in at the time the property was transferred to the buyer. But if deterioration or injury of the goods is due to the breach of warranty, such deterioration or injury shall not prevent the buyer from returning or offering to return the goods to the seller and rescinding the sale.

(4) Where the buyer is entitled to rescind the sale and elects to do so, the buyer shall cease to be liable for the price upon returning or offering to return the goods. If the price or any part thereof has already been paid, the seller shall be liable to repay so much thereof as has been paid, concurrently with the return of the goods, or immediately after an offer to return the goods in exchange for repayment of the price.

(5) Where the buyer is entitled to rescind the sale and elects to do so, if the seller refuses to accept an offer of the buyer to return the goods, the buyer shall thereafter be deemed to hold the goods as bailee for the seller, but subject to a lien to secure the repayment of any portion of the price which has been paid, and with the remedies for the enforcement of such lien allowed to an unpaid seller by section 53.

(6) The measure of damages for breach of warranty is the loss directly and naturally resulting, in the ordinary course of events, from the breach of warranty.

(7) In the case of breach of warranty of quality, such loss, in the absence of special circumstances showing proximate damage of a greater amount, is the difference between the value of the goods at the time of delivery to the buyer and the value they would have had if they had answered to the warranty.

Sec. 70. (Interest and Special Damages.) Nothing in this act shall affect the right of the buyer or the seller to recover interest or special damages in any case where by law interest or special damages may be recoverable, or to recover money paid where the consideration for the payment of it has failed.

PART VI

Interpretation

Sec. 71. (Variation of Implied Obligations.) Where any right, duty or liability would arise under a contract to sell or a sale by implication of law, it may be negatived or varied by express agreement or by the course of dealing between the parties, or by custom, if the custom be such as to bind both parties to the contract or the sale.

Sec. 72. (Rights May be Enforced by Action.) Where any right, duty or liability is declared by this act, it may, unless otherwise by this act provided, be enforced by action.

Sec. 73. (Rule for Cases not Provided for by this Act.) In any case not provided for in this act, the rules of law and equity, including the law merchant, and in particular the rules relating to the law of principal and agent and to the effect of fraud, misrepresentation, duress or coercion, mistake, bankruptcy, or other invalidating cause, shall continue to apply to contracts to sell and to sales of goods.

Sec. 74. (Interpretation Shall Give Effect to Purpose of Uniformity.) This act shall be so interpreted and construed as to effectuate its general purpose to make uniform the laws of those states which enact it.

Sec. 75. (Provisions not Applicable to Mortgages.) The provisions of this act relating to contracts to sell and to sales do not apply, unless so stated, to any transaction in the form of a contract to sell or a sale which is intended to operate by way of mortgage, pledge, charge, or other security.

Sec. 76. (Definitions.) (1) In this act, unless the context or subject matter otherwise requires —

"Action" includes counterclaim, set-off and suit in equity.

"Buyer" means a person who buys or agrees to buy goods or any legal successor in interest of such person.

"Defendant" includes a plaintiff against whom a right of set-off or counterclaim is asserted.

"Delivery" means voluntary transfer of possession from one person to another.

"Divisible contract to sell or sale" means a contract to sell or a sale in which by its terms the price for a portion or portions of the goods less than the whole is fixed or ascertainable by computation.

"Document of title to goods" includes any bill of lading, dock warrant, warehouse receipt or order for the delivery of goods, or any other document used in the ordinary course of business in the sale or transfer of goods, as proof of the possession or control of the goods, or authorizing or purporting to authorize the possessor of the document to transfer or recieve, either by indorsement or by delivery, goods represented by such document.

"Fault" means wrongful act or default.

"Fungible goods" means goods of which any unit is from its nature or by mercantile usage treated as the equivalent of any other unit.

"Future goods" means goods to be manufactured or acquired by the seller after the making of the contract of sale.

"Goods" include all chattels personal other than things in action and money. The term includes emblements, industrial growing crops, and things attached to or forming part of the land which are agreed to be severed before sale or under the contract of sale.

"Order" in sections of this act relating to documents of title means an order by indorsement on the documents.

"Person" includes a corporation or partnership or two or more persons having a joint or common interest.

"Plaintiff" includes defendant asserting a right of set-off or counterclaim.

"Property" means the general property in goods, and not merely a special property.

"Purchaser" includes mortgagee and pledgee.

"Purchases" includes taking as a mortgagee or as a pledgee.

"Quality of goods" includes their state or condition.

"Sale" includes a bargain and sale as well as a sale and delivery.

"Seller" means a person who sells or agrees to sell goods, or any legal successor in the interest of such person.

"Specific goods" means goods identified and agreed upon at the time a contract to sell or a sale is made.

"Value" is any consideration sufficient to support a simple contract. An antecedent or pre-existing claim, whether for money or not, constitutes value where goods or documents of titles are taken either in satisfaction thereof or as security therefor.

(2) A thing is done "in good faith" within the meaning of this act when it is in fact done honestly, whether it be done negligently or not.

(3) A person is insolvent within the meaning of this act who either has ceased to pay his debts in the ordinary course of business or cannot pay his debts as they become due, whether he has committed an act of bankruptcy or not, and whether he is insolvent within the meaning of the federal bankruptcy law or not.

(4) Goods are in a "deliverable state" within the meaning of this act when they are in such a state that the buyer would, under the contract, be bound to take delivery of them.

Sec. 76a. (Act does not Apply to the Existing Sales or Contracts to Sell.) None of the provisions of this act shall apply to any sale, or to any contract to sell, made prior to the taking effect of this act.

Sec. 76b. (No Repeal of Uniform Warehouse Receipts Act or Uniform Bills of Lading Act.) Nothing in this act or in any repealing clause thereof shall be construed to repeal or limit any of the provisions of the Act to Make Uniform the Law of Warehouse Receipts, or of the Act to Make Uniform the Law of Bills of Lading.

Sec. 77. (Inconsistent Legislation Repealed.) All acts or parts of acts inconsistent with this act are hereby repealed except as provided in section 76b.

Sec. 78. (Time When the Act Takes Effect.) This act shall take effect on the ...... day of .... one thousand nine hundred and ....

Sec. 79. (Name of Act.) This act may be cited as the Uniform Sales Act.

AMENDMENTS TO UNIFORM SALES ACT [1]

1. Section 32 of the Uniform Sales Act is hereby amended by striking out all of the section which follows the word "negotiated" and by substituting therefor the following:

> "by any person in possession of the same, however such possession may have been acquired if, by the terms of the document, the bailee issuing it undertakes to deliver the goods to the order of such person, or if at the time of negotiation the document is in such form that it may be negotiated by delivery."

so that the section shall read:

> "Section 32. (Who May Negotiate a Document.) A negotiable document of title may be negotiated by any person in possession of the same, however such possession may have been acquired if, by the terms of the document, the bailee issuing it undertakes to deliver the goods to the order of such person, or if at the time of negotiation the document is in such form that it may be negotiated by delivery."

[1] These amendments were approved and recommended for enactment by the Commissioners on Uniform State Laws in 1922 in order to harmonize certain provisions of the Uniform Sales Act with the Uniform Bills of Lading Act and with the Uniform Stock Transfer Act. States which have adopted the amendments and the dates of adoption are as follows:

Alabama (1931); California (1931); Michigan (1933); New York (1935); Ohio (1925); Tennessee (1923); Utah (1929); Vermont (1923); Wisconsin (1925).

2. Section 38 of the Uniform Sales Act is hereby amended by striking out the words "induced by fraud, mistake, or duress, to intrust the possession or custody thereof to such person," and substituting instead therefor the words "deprived of the possession of the same by loss, theft, fraud, accident, mistake, duress, or conversion"; and also by striking out the words "without notice of the breach of duty, or fraud, mistake or duress," and by substituting therefor the words "in good faith, without notice of the loss, theft, breach of duty, or fraud, accident, mistake, duress or conversion," so that the section shall read:

> "Section 38. (When Negotiation Not Impaired by Fraud, Mistake or Duress.) The validity of the negotiation of a negotiable document of title is not impaired by the fact that the negotiation was a breach of duty on the part of the person making the negotiation, or by the fact that the owner of the document was deprived of the possession of the same by loss, theft, fraud, accident, mistake, duress, or conversion, if the person to whom the document was negotiated or a person to whom the document was subsequently negotiated paid value therefor, in good faith without notice of the breach of duty, or loss, theft, fraud, accident, mistake, duress or conversion."

FRENCH CIVIL CODE [1]

TITLE SIXTH: OF SALES

Chapter I

Of the Nature and Form of Sales

Art. 1582. A sale is an agreement by which one person binds himself to deliver a thing and another to pay for it.

It can be made by a public instrument or by an instrument under private signature. Civ. C. 1317 *et seq.*, 1322, 1354 *et seq.*

Art. 1583. A sale is complete between the parties and the ownership passes as a matter of right to the purchaser from the vendor as soon as the thing and the price have been agreed upon, although the thing has not yet been delivered or the price paid. Civ. C. 711, 1108 *et seq.*, 1138, 1585 *et seq.*

Art. 1584. A sale can be made out and out or subject to a condition which may suspend or annul it.

It can also apply to two or more things, in the alternative.

In all cases its effect is regulated by the general principles relating to contracts. Civ. C. 1168 *et seq.*, 1181 *et seq.*, 1221.

Art. 1585. When goods are not sold in bulk but by weight, number or measure, the sale is not complete in this respect that the goods sold remain at the risk of the vendor until they have been weighed, counted or measured; but the purchaser may claim the delivery thereof, or damages, if there is cause therefor, in case the contract is not carried out. Civ. C. 1136 *et seq.*, 1142 *et seq.*, 1147 *et seq.*, 1182, 1586 *et seq.*, 1610 *et seq.*

Art. 1586. If, on the contrary, the goods have been sold in bulk, the sale is complete although the goods have not yet been weighed, counted or measured. Civ. C. 1585, 1587.

Art. 1587. As regards wine, oil and other goods which it is customary to taste

[1] The translation adopted is that by Cachard. 1930.

before buying, there is no sale so long as the purchaser has not tasted and accepted them. Civ. C. 1585 *et seq.*

Art. 1588. A sale made upon trial is always supposed to be made under a suspensive condition. Civ. C. 1181 *et seq.*, 1584.

Art. 1589. A promise of sale is equivalent to a sale when there is mutual consent of both parties as to the thing and the price. Civ. C. 1583, 1590 *et seq.*

Art. 1590. If a promise of sale has been made with payment of earnest money, each of the contracting parties is at liberty to withdraw,

The one who has given the earnest money, by losing it,

And the one who has received it, by returning twice the amount. Civ. C. 1589, 1715.

Art. 1591. The price of the sale must be fixed and stated by the parties. Civ. C. 1129, 1592.

Art. 1592. It can, nevertheless, be left to the arbitration of a third person: if such person is unwilling or unable to make an estimate, there is no sale. Civ. C. 1854.

Art. 1593. The expense for drawing the contract and the other charges relating to the sale shall be paid by the purchaser. Civ. C. 1248, 1608, 1630–3°–4°, 1646.

Chapter II

Of Those who may Buy or Sell

Art. 1594. All those not forbidden to do so by law can buy or sell. Civ. C. 128, 450, 537, 1123 *et seq.*, 1507 *et seq.*, 1554 *et seq.*, 1576, 1595 *et seq.*, 1860.

Art. 1595. A contract of sale can only take place between husband and wife in the three following cases:

1° In case either the husband or the wife, when judicially separated as to property, assigns to the other some property in payment of his or her rights;

2° When the assignment made by the husband to the wife even when not separated as to property, has a legitimate cause, such as the reinvestment of proceeds of her real estate sold, or of funds belonging to her, if such real estate or funds do not form part of the community;

3° When the wife assigns property to her husband in payment of an amount which she has promised to give him as dowry and when there is no community.

Subject in these three cases to the rights of the heirs of the contracting parties, if indirect advantages have been given. Civ. C. 913 *et seq.*, 1094 *et seq.*, 1098 *et seq.*, 1433 *et seq.*, 1441, 1443 *et seq.*, 1496, 1527.

Art. 1596. The following persons cannot, either personally or through intermediaries, become purchasers, under penalty of avoidance of the sale;

Guardians, with respect to the property of those under their guardianship;

Attorneys-in-fact, with respect to property which they have charge of selling;

Administrators, with respect to property belonging to districts or public establishments intrusted to their care;

Public officials, with respect to national property of which the sale is conducted through their instrumentality. Civ. C. 450, 911, 1991 *et seq.*

Art. 1597. Judges, their assistants, magistrates acting as Public Prosecutors, clerks of the Court, bailiffs, solicitors, counsellors and notaries cannot purchase the actions, contested rights and causes of action which come under the jurisdiction of the Tribunal in the district before which they practice, under penalty of avoidance of the sale and of costs and damages. Civ. C. 1699.

Chapter III

Of Things which can be Sold

Art. 1598. Everything which is in trade[1] can be sold when special laws do not prohibit the sale thereof. Civ. C. 538, 540, 544, 1128, 1554, 1600, 2226.

Art. 1599. The sale of a thing belonging to another person is void: it can give rise to damages when the purchaser is not aware that the thing belonged to another person. Civ. C. 1021, 1141, 1304, 1603, 1635, 1653, 1704, 2265, *et seq.*

Art. 1600. The succession of a person who is alive cannot be sold, even with his consent. Civ. C. 791, 1130, 1389.

Art. 1601. If, at the time of the sale, the thing sold had been totally destroyed, the sale shall be void.

If only a part of the thing has been destroyed, the purchaser has the choice between rescinding the purchase or claiming the part saved by having the price fixed by appraisal. Civ. C. 1193 *et seq.*, 1302 *et seq.*, 1636.

Chapter IV

Of the Vendor's Obligations

Section I

General Provisions

Art. 1602. The vendor is obliged to explain distinctly what he binds himself to.

Any obscure or ambiguous contract shall be interpreted against the vendor. Civ. C. 1156 *et seq.*, 1162 *et seq.*, 1190.

Art. 1603. He has two principal obligations, one to make delivery, and the other to warrant the thing sold. Civ. C. 1136 *et seq.*, 1604 *et seq.*, 1625 *et seq.*

Section II

Of Delivery

Art. 1604. Delivery is the transfer of the thing sold into the power and possession of the purchaser. Civ. C. 1136 *et seq.*, 1582 *et seq.*, 1605 *et seq.*

Art. 1605. The obligation to deliver real estate is fulfilled on the part of the vendor when he has handed over the keys in case of a building, or when he has handed over the title deeds. Civ. C. 1606 *et seq.*

Art. 1606. The delivery of personal property takes places:

Either by actual transfer,

Or by handing over the keys of the buildings in which it is contained,

Or even by the mere consent of the parties, if the transfer cannot take place at the time of the sale, or if the purchaser already had the property in his possession in another manner. Civ. C. 727 *et seq.*, 1138 *et seq.*

Art. 1607. The transfer of incorporeal rights is made either by handing over the title deeds or by the use which the purchaser makes of such rights with the consent of the vendor. Civ. C. 1689 *et seq.*, 2075.

Art. 1608. The expenses of delivery are paid by the vendor and those of re-

[1] These words must be taken in a broad sense and apply to property belonging to private individuals in contradiction to public property.

moval by the purchaser, unless there is a stipulation to the contrary. Civ. C. 1248.

Art. 1609. Delivery must be made at the place where the thing sold was at the time of the sale, unless otherwise agreed upon. Civ. C. 1247, 1264, 1651.

Art. 1610. If the vendor fails to make delivery at the time agreed upon between the parties, the purchaser has the choice of either applying for the cancellation of the sale or asking to be given possession, if the delay has been caused solely by the vendor. Civ. C. 1142, 1184, 1621, 1654 *et seq.*

Art. 1611. In all cases the Court must order the vendor to pay damages if the purchaser has suffered a loss, because the delivery was not made at the time agreed upon. Civ. C. 1142, 1146 *et seq.*, 1184, 1610.

Art. 1612. A vendor is not obliged to deliver the thing if the purchaser does not pay the price thereof, unless the vendor has given him time to pay. Civ. C. 1186, 1650 *et seq.*, 2102–4°.

Art. 1613. Neither shall he be obliged to make delivery, even if he has allowed him time to pay, if, since the sale, the purchaser has become a bankrupt or is in a state of insolvency, so that the vendor finds himself in imminent danger of losing his money, unless the purchaser furnishes security to pay at the time agreed upon. Civ. C. 1188, 1653, 2011 *et seq.*

Art. 1614. The thing must be delivered in the state in which it was at the time of the sale.

From that day the entire revenue belongs to the purchaser. Civ. C. 547 *et seq.*, 583 *et seq.*, 604, 1137 *et seq.*, 1182, 1583, 1682.

Art. 1615. The obligation to deliver the thing includes its accessories and everything that was intended for its perpetual use. Civ. C. 522 *et seq.*, 546 *et seq.*, 551 *et seq.*, 1018 *et seq.*, 1692.

Art. 1616. A vendor is obliged to deliver the quantity as it is specified in the contract, subject to the modifications hereinafter expressed. Civ. C. 1617 *et seq.*, 1765.

Section III

Of Warranty

Art. 1625. The warranty which the vendor owes to the purchaser has a double object: first, the peaceful possession of the property sold; second, the hidden defects of such property or the defects rendering the sale void. Civ. C. 1603, 1626 *et seq.*, 1641 *et seq.*

. . . .

Art. 1641. A vendor is bound to warrant against the hidden defects of the thing sold which render it unfit for the use for which it was intended, or which impair its use to such an extent that the purchaser would not have acquired it, or would only have given a smaller price if he had known of them. Civ. C. 1110, 1625, 1638 *et seq.*, 1642 *et seq.*, 1891.

Art. 1642. A vendor is not responsible for the apparent defects which the purchaser has been able to ascertain for himself. Civ. C. 1629, 1644.

Art. 1643. He is responsible for the hidden defects, even if he did not know of them, unless it has been stipulated that he would not be bound to any warranty in such case. Civ. C. 1627 *et seq.*, 1644 *et seq.*

Art. 1644. In the cases specified in articles 1641 and 1643 the purchaser may elect either to return the thing and have the price repaid to him or to keep the thing and have such part of the price repaid as shall be decided by experts. Civ. C. 1617, 1638.

Art. 1645. If the vendor knew of the defects of the thing, he is bound not only to return the price which he has received, but he is also liable to the purchaser for all damages. Civ. C. 1149, 1151, 1382, 1630 *et seq.*, 1635, 1891.

Art. 1646. If the vendor was ignorant of the defects of the thing, he shall only be bound to return the price and to reimburse to the purchaser the expenses occasioned by the sale. Civ. C. 1150, 1593, 1630.

Art. 1647. If the thing which had defects perishes owing to its bad condition, the loss falls upon the vendor and he is bound towards the purchaser to return the price and to make the other amends specified in the two foregoing articles.

But if the loss happens by accident, it falls upon the purchaser. Civ. C. 1148 *et seq.*, 1302 *et seq.*, 1631.

Art. 1648. The action resulting from defects which render the sale void must be brought by the purchaser within a short time, according to the nature of such defects and the customs of the place where the sale was made. Civ. C. 1159.

Art. 1649. It cannot be maintained in case of sales made by order of the Court. Civ. C. 1684.

Chapter V

Of the Purchaser's Obligations

Art. 1650. The principal obligation of the purchaser is to pay the price upon the day and at the place fixed by the sale. Civ. C. 1235 *et seq.*, 1247, 1582 *et seq.*, 1591 *et seq.*, 1612 *et seq.*, 1651 *et seq.*, 2102–4°, 2103–1°.

Art. 1651. If nothing has been arranged in that respect at the time of the sale, the purchaser must pay at the time and at the place where the delivery is to take place. Civ. C. 1247, 1264, 1609, 1612.

Art. 1652. The purchaser owes interest on the purchase price up to the time of the payment of the capital in the three following cases:

If it has been so agreed at the time of the sale;

If the thing sold and delivered bears fruit or produces any other revenue;

If the purchaser has been summoned to pay.

In the last case the interest only runs from the time of the summons.[1] Civ. C. 520, 583 *et seq.*, 1139, 1153, 1614, 1682, 1905, 1907.

Art. 1653. If the purchaser is threatened or has a just cause for fearing that he will be troubled by an action upon a mortgage or for recovery, he may suspend the payment of the price until the vendor has caused the trouble to cease, unless the latter prefers to give security or unless it has been stipulated that the purchaser will pay notwithstanding the disturbance. Civ. C. 1612 *et seq.*, 1704, 1725 *et seq.*, 2040.

Art. 1654. If the purchaser does not pay the price, the vendor may ask for the cancellation of the sale. Civ. C. 1184, 1234, 1610, 1655 *et seq.*, 1978, 2102–4°, 2103–1°.

. . . .

Art. 1657. In case of sale of goods and personal effects, the cancellation of the sale shall take place as a matter of right for the benefit of the vendor, and without a summons[1] after the expiration of the time agreed upon for the removal of the thing. Civ. C. 1184, 1585 *et seq.*, 1905, 2102–4°.

[1] A summons here means a legal demand made by a bailiff.

Chapter VI

Of Avoidance and Rescission of Sales

Art. 1658. Independently of the causes of avoidance and rescission above explained in this title or of those which apply to all contracts, a contract of sale can be rescinded by means of a power of redemption and on account of insufficiency of the price. Civ. C. 1183 *et seq.*, 1234, 1304 *et seq.*, 1610, 1618 *et seq.*, 1626, 1644 *et seq.*, 1654 *et seq.*, 1674 *et seq.*

Section I

Of Right of Redemption

Art. 1659. The right of redemption or repurchase is an agreement by which the vendor retains the power of taking back the thing sold, by returning the purchase price and reimbursing what is specified in article 1673. Civ. C. 1582, 1660 *et seq.*, 1751, 2085 *et seq.*

Art. 1660. The right of redemption cannot be stipulated for a period exceeding five years.

If it has been stipulated for a longer time, it is reduced to that period. Civ. C. 6, 1662.

Art. 1661. The time fixed is imperative and cannot be extended by the Court. Civ. C. 1655 *et seq.*

Art. 1662. If the vendor has not brought his action for redemption within the time fixed, the purchaser remains the irrevocable owner. Civ. C. 1751, 2088.

Art. 1663. The time runs against all persons, even against a minor, subject to the remedy against whomsoever is concerned, if there is occasion therefor. Civ. C. 1304, 1676, 2252, 2278.

Art. 1664. The vendor holding a covenant of redemption may bring his action against a second purchaser, even if the power of redemption is not mentioned in the second contract. Civ. C. 1165, 1183, 1599.

Art. 1665. The purchaser subject to a covenant of redemption may exercise all the rights of his vendor: he takes advantage of prescription as well against the real owner as against those who might claim to have rights or mortgages over the thing sold. Civ. C. 1583, 1659, 1673, 1751, 2229, 2235, 2262 *et seq.*, 2265 *et seq.*

Art. 1666. He can oppose the benefit of seizure[1] against the creditors of the vendor. Civ. C. 1166, 2021 *et seq.*, 2170 *et seq.*

GERMAN CIVIL CODE[2]

SEVENTH DIVISION: VARIOUS RELATIONS OF INDEBTEDNESS

First Title: Purchase and Sale: Exchange

I. GENERAL PROVISIONS

433. By the contract of purchase, the seller of a thing is obliged to deliver it and to obtain the ownership in the thing. The seller of a right is obliged to obtain the right for the purchaser, and if the right includes the possession of a thing to deliver the thing.

[1] See article 2021.

[2] The translation adopted is that of Loewy in the edition by the University of Pennsylvania, 1909.

The purchaser is obliged to pay to the seller the agreed purchase price and to take the purchased thing.

434. The seller is obliged to obtain for the purchaser the sold thing free of rights, which can be enforced by third parties against the purchaser.

. . . .

440. If the seller does not fulfill the obligations due from him under §§ 433–437, 439, the rights of the buyer are determined according to the provisions of §§ *320–327*.

If a movable thing has been sold and has been delivered to the buyer for the purpose of transferring the ownership, the buyer may by reason of the rights of a third party, entitled to the possession of the thing, demand damages for non-fulfillment only, when he has delivered the thing to the third party with respect to the right of the latter or if he has re-transferred it to the seller, or if the thing has perished.

If the third party is the heir of the buyer or the latter is the heir of the third party, or if the buyer otherwise acquires the right of the third party, or satisfies the latter, the effect is the same as upon the delivery of the thing to a third party.

If the buyer has a claim against another for delivery, the re-transfer is sufficient in place of the return.

441. The provisions of § 440, par. 2–4, shall also apply, when a right to a movable thing is sold, which entitles to the possession of the thing.

442. If the seller denies the defect in the right, asserted by the buyer, the buyer has to prove the defect.

443. An agreement, by which the obligation of security, due according to §§ 433–437, 439–442 from the seller by reason of a defective right, is remitted or limited, is void if the seller deceitfully conceals the defect.

444. The seller is obliged to give to the purchaser the necessary information as to the legal conditions relating to the thing sold, and in the case of the sale of a lot of land as to the boundaries, rights and burdens and to deliver to him the instruments in his possession constituting the proof of the right. If the contents of such instrument extend also to other matters, the vendor is only obliged to deliver a publicly authenticated extract.

445. The provisions of §§ 433–444 correspondingly apply to other contracts, which have in view the sale or the encumbering of a thing for a consideration.

446. With the transfer of the sold thing, the risk of accidental ruin and of an accidental depreciation passes to the buyer. From the time of the transfer, the emoluments belong to the buyer, who also bears the burdens of the thing.

If the buyer of a piece of land, before the delivery, is entered as owner in the Land Register, these results take effect upon the entry.

447. If the seller on demand of the buyer sends the sold thing to a place other than the place of fulfillment, the risk is transferred to the buyer from the time when the seller delivers the thing to the forwarding agent, the freighter or to the party or business designated for the transportation.

If the buyer gives special instruction as to the mode of sending and if the seller deviates without urgent cause from the instruction, the seller is responsible to the buyer for the resulting damages.

448. The cost of the delivery of the thing sold, in particular the cost of measuring and weighing are to be borne by the seller, the cost of the receiving and of the transportation to a place other than the place of fulfillment are to be borne by the buyer.

If a right is sold, the expense of the proof or transfer of the right is to be borne by the seller.

. . . .

450. If before the delivery of the thing, the risk has shifted to the vendee, and if the vendor before delivery incurs expenditures upon the thing, which after the shifting of the risk became necessary, he may demand compensation from the vendee as if the latter had charged him with the keeping of the thing.

The obligation of the buyer to make compensation for other outlays is determined according to the provisions as to transacting business without authority.

451. If a right to a thing is sold, which entitled to the possession of the thing, the provisions of §§ 446–450 correspondingly apply.

452. The buyer is obliged to pay interest upon the purchase price from the time, from which the income of the purchased things belong to him, unless time of payment is extended.

453. If the market price is fixed as purchase price, in case of doubt, the market price ruling at the place and at the time of fulfillment is regarded as agreed upon.

454. If the vendor has fulfilled the contract and has given time for payment, he is not entitled to the right of withdrawal provided in § 325, par. 2, and in § 326.

455. If the seller of a movable thing has reserved the ownership up to the payment of the purchase price, in case of doubt, it is to be assumed, that the transfer of the ownership takes place under the precedent condition of the entire payment of the purchase price, and that the seller is entitled to withdraw from the contract, if the buyer is in default as to payment.

456. At a sale under execution, the person, who is charged with the making or the conducting of the sale and the assistants employed by him including the recording clerk are not permitted to buy the thing on sale neither for themselves, nor through another nor as agent for another.

457. The provision of § 456 is also applicable to a sale aside from execution sale, if the instruction for the sale has been given in pursuance of a legal order, which authorizes the party giving the instruction to have the thing sold for account of another, especially in cases of sales of pledges and of the sales authorized by §§ 383, 385, and also in case of a sale by a Receiver in Insolvency. (*Konkursverwalter.*)

458. The effect of a purchase and of the transfer of the thing sold in violation of the provisions of §§ 456, 457, depends on the consent of the parties interested in the sale as debtors, owners or creditors. If the buyer calls upon an interested party to declare whether he consents, the provisions of § 177, par. 2, are correspondingly applicable.

If in case of refusal of the consent, a new sale is made, the former buyer is responsible for the costs of a new sale as well as for deficiency of the purchase price.

II. WARRANTY AGAINST DEFECTS OF THE THING

459. The seller of a thing warrants to the buyer, that at the time, at which the risk is transferred to the buyer, it is not subject to defects, which destroy or diminish the value or fitness for the ordinary use or for the use assumed by the contract. An unessential diminution of the value or of aptness is not to be regarded.

The seller also guarantees, that the thing has the warranted qualities at the time of the transfer of the risk.

460. The seller is not responsible for a defect of the thing sold, if the buyer knows the defect at the conclusion of the sale. If the buyer, owing to gross carelessness remains in ignorance of a defect of the kind designated in § 459, par. 1, the seller, unless he has asserted the absence of the defect is responsible only if he has craftily concealed the defect.

461. The seller is not responsible for the defect of a thing sold, if the thing is sold at public auction by reason of a pledge and is designated as a pledge.

462. On account of a defect, for which the seller is responsible, according to §§ 459, 460, the buyer may claim rescission of the purchase (*Wandelung*) or reduction of the purchase price (*Minderung*).

463. If at the time of sale, the thing sold is deficient in a warranted quality, the buyer may, instead of rescission, or reduction of price, claim indemnity for non-fulfillment. The same applies, if the seller has craftily concealed a defect.

464. If the buyer accepts a defective thing, he is entitled to the rights designated in §§ 462, 463, only if he, at the time of acceptance, reserves his rights as to the defect.

465. The rescission or the reduction takes place, if the seller on request of the buyer consents to it.

466. If the buyer asserts a defect of the thing towards the seller, the latter may by offering rescission and limiting a suitable time, ask the buyer to declare, whether he demands rescission. The rescission can in this case be demanded only up to the expiration of the time limited.

467. As to the rescission, the provisions of §§ 346 to 348, 350 to 354, 356 in force in relation to the contractual right of withdrawal, are correspondingly applicable; in the case of § 352, the rescission is not excluded, if the defect has not been apparent until the transformation of the thing. The seller must also repay to the purchaser the costs of the contract.

468. If the seller assures the buyer of the certain extent of a piece of land, he is liable for that extent as for a warranted quality. The buyer may, however, demand rescission by reason of insufficiency of the warranted extent only, if the insufficiency is so considerable, that the fulfillment of the contract is of no interest to the buyer.

469. If of several things sold only a few are defective, rescission can only be claimed as to these, though a total price has been fixed for all. If, however, the things are sold as belonging together, each party may claim, that the rescission extends to all things, if the defective things cannot, without disadvantage to him, be separated from the others.

470. The rescission on account of a defect of the principal thing extends also to the secondary thing. If the secondary thing is defective, rescission can be claimed as to that only.

471. If in case of sale of several things for a total price, there is a rescission only in regard to single things, the total price is to be reduced in the proportion, in which at the time of the sale, the total value of the things in perfect condition would have borne to the value of the things not affected by the rescission.

472. As to a reduction, the purchase price is to be reduced in the proportion, which, at the time of sale, the value of the thing in perfect condition would have borne to the actual value.

If in the case of sale of several things for an aggregate price, the reduction is made only as to single things, the aggregate value of all things is to be the basis in the reduction of the price.

473. If besides the fixed purchase price in money, performances are agreed upon, which relate to things, that cannot be measured (*nicht vertretbar*), these

performances in the cases of §§ 471, 472 are to be estimated in money according to the value at the time of sale. The reduction of the counter-performance of the buyer is made in the price fixed in money; if the latter is less than the amount to be deducted, the seller has to make up to the buyer the excess of the amount.

474. If several persons are interested on one side or the other, reduction may be demanded by and from each of them.

With the making of the reduction demanded by the purchaser, the right of rescission is excluded.

475. By the reduction by reason of a defect, the right of the buyer to demand rescission or further reduction by reason of another defect is not affected.

476. An agreement, by which the buyer's obligation of warranty for defects of the thing is released, or limited, is void, if the seller craftily conceals the defect.

477. The claim for rescission or for reduction, as well as the claim for indemnity on account of a warranted quality, is barred by limitation, unless the seller has craftily concealed the defect, in the case of movable things in six months from delivery, in case of real property in one year from the transfer. The limitation can be prolonged only by agreement.

The limitation is interrupted, when the purchaser makes a motion to have evidence taken judicially in order to preserve that evidence. The interruption continues to the end of the proceedings. The provisions of § 211, paragraph 2 and of § 212 are correspondingly applicable.

The stop or interruption of the limitation of one of the claims designated in paragraph 1 effects also the stop or interruption of the limitation of the other claims.

478. If the buyer has informed the seller of the defect, or has sent notice to him before the claim for rescission or reduction was barred, he may also, after the barring, refuse payment of the purchase price, in so far as he would be entitled thereto by reason of the rescission or reduction. The same is the case, if the buyer, before the completion of the limitation, makes a motion to have evidence taken judicially in order to preserve it, or if, in a lawsuit between him and the later acquirer of the thing, has informed the seller of the controversy.

If the seller has craftily concealed the defect, notice or an act equivalent to it, as stated in paragraph 1, is not necessary.

479. The claim for indemnity can, after completion of the limitation, be charged only, if the buyer has done one of the acts mentioned in § 478. This restriction does not apply, if the seller has craftily concealed the defect.

480. The buyer of a thing, designated only according to a species, may claim instead of rescission or reduction, that in place of the defective thing, a perfect one be delivered.

To this claim the provisions of §§ 464 to 466, of § 467, paragraph 1, and §§ 469, 470, 474 to 479 have corresponding application. If the thing, at the time when the risk is transferred to the buyer, is wanting in a warranted quality, or if the seller has craftily concealed a defect, the buyer may instead of rescission, reduction or delivery of a perfect thing, demand indemnity on account of nonfulfillment.

481. For the sale of horses, asses, mules, (*Mauleseln und Maultieren*) cattle, sheep and hogs, the provisions of §§ 459 to 467, 469 to 480 are applicable only in so far, as it is not otherwise provided in §§ 482 to 492.

482. The seller has to be responsible only for certain defects (principal de-

fects) and these only then when they become apparent within a certain time (warranty time (*Gewaehrsfrist*)).

The principal defects and the warranty time are determined by imperial ordinance to be issued with consent of the Federal Council. The determination can be supplemented or altered in the same way.

483. The warranty time commences with the expiration of the day on which the risk is transferred to the buyer.

484. If a principal defect becomes apparent within the warranty time, it is presumed that the defect has already existed at the time, when the risk was transferred to the buyer.

485. The buyer loses the rights to which he is entitled on account of the defect, if he does not, at least two days after the expiration of the warranty limitation, or in case the animal has been killed before the expiration of the time, or has died in some other manner, after the death of the animal, give notice to the seller of the defect or send notice to him or bring suit against the seller on account of the defect or give notice to him of the controversy, or move to have judicial proof taken to preserve the evidence. The buyer's rights are not barred, however, if the seller has maliciously concealed the defect (*den Mangel arglistig verschwiegen hat*).

486. The warranty limitation may be extended or shortened by agreement. The agreed limitation takes the place of the legal limitation.

487. The buyer may only demand rescission not reduction.

Rescission can also be demanded in the cases of §§ 351 to 353, especially if the animal has been slaughtered; in place of return-warranty the buyer has to render the value of the animal. The same is applicable in other cases in which the buyer in consequence of a circumstance, for which he is responsible, especially a disposition made of the animal, is unable to return the animal.

If before the rescission, non-essential depreciation of the animal has taken place owing to a circumstance for which the buyer is responsible, the buyer has to make good the deficiency in value.

The buyer has to render indemnity for profits only in so far as he has drawn them.

488. The seller in case of rescission has to indemnify the buyer also for the expense of feed and care-taking, the cost of veterinary examinations and treatment, as well as the expenses of the necessary killing and removal of the animal.

489. If an action is pending as to the claim to rescission, on application of the one or the other party, the public sale of the animal and the temporary deposit of the proceeds is to be ordered, when the inspection of the animal is not further required.

490. The claim for rescission as well as the claim for indemnity on account of a principal deficiency, the absence of which the seller has warranted, is barred in six weeks from the expiration of the warranty time, otherwise the provisions of § 477 remain unchanged.

A limitation of six weeks takes the place of the limitation designated in §§ 210, 212, 215.

The buyer can also, after limitation of the claim for rescission, refuse payment of the purchase price. The charging up of the claim for indemnity is not subject to the restrictions provided in § 479.

491. The purchaser of an animal designated only by species may demand instead of rescission, that in place of the defective animal, a faultless one be delivered to him. As to this claim the provisions of §§ 488 to 490 are correspondingly applicable.

492. If the seller assumes the warranty for a defect not belonging to the principal defects, or if he warrants a quality of the animal, the provisions of §§ 487 to 491 apply, and if a warranty-time is agreed upon, the provisions of §§ 483 to 485 are also correspondingly applicable. The limitation provided in § 490 commences, if a warranty-time is not agreed upon, with the delivery of the animal.

493. The provisions as to the obligation of the seller for warranty on account of defects of the thing are correspondingly applicable to other agreements having in view the depositing or burdening of a thing for a consideration.

III. PARTICULAR KINDS OF SALE

1. Purchase According to Test. Purchase on Approval.

494. At a sale by test or according to sample the qualities of the specimen or of the sample are to be regarded as warranted.

495. At a sale on probation or inspection, the approval of the thing bought is in the discretion of the purchaser. In case of doubt, the purchase is made under the postponing condition precedent of approval.

The seller is obliged to permit the buyer to examine the thing.

496. The approval of a thing bought on probation or on inspection can be declared only within the time agreed upon, and if none agreed upon, only up to the expiration of a suitable time, given by the seller to the buyer; if the thing was delivered to the buyer for the purpose of trial or inspection, his silence is equivalent to approval.

2. Re-purchase.

497. If the seller has in the agreement of purchase reserved the right of re-purchase, the re-purchase takes place, when the seller declares towards the buyer, that he avails himself of his right of re-purchase. The declaration does not require the form provided for the agreement of purchase.

The selling price is, in case of doubt, also the price for the re-purchase.

498. The re-seller is obliged to deliver to the re-purchaser the thing sold together with belongings.

If the re-seller before the exercise of the right of re-purchase has caused the depreciation, the loss or an impossibility brought about in another way, to deliver the thing bought, or if he has altered the thing materially, he is responsible for the injury caused thereby. If the thing is depreciated without the fault of the re-seller, or if the alteration is not essential, the re-purchaser may not demand reduction of the purchase price.

499. If the re-seller before exercising the right of re-purchase has disposed of the thing bought, he is obliged to remove the rights of third parties thereby created. A disposal in course of an execution or of attachment or through the Receiver in Insolvency is of the same effect as a disposal by the re-seller.

500. The re-seller may, in so far, claim indemnity for expenditures made before the re-sale upon the thing bought, as the value of the thing has been increased by the expenditures. An arrangement, which he has added to the thing to be delivered, may be removed by him.

501. If the appraised valuation of the thing purchased at the time of the re-purchase is agreed upon as the price of the re-purchase, the re-seller is not responsible for a depreciation, the loss, or the impossibility of the delivery of the thing due to any other cause, neither is the re-purchaser liable to compensation for expenditures.

502. If the right of re-purchase pertains to several parties in common, it can be exercised only as an entirety. If it has expired as to one of the parties entitled, or, if one of them does not avail himself of his right, the others are entitled to exercise the right of re-purchase as an entirety.

. . . .

3. Pre-emption.

504. One, who has the right of pre-emption to a thing, can exercise the right of pre-emption as soon as the obligee has concluded with a third party a contract of purchase.

505. The right of pre-emption is exercised by notice (declaration) to the obligee. The notice does not require the form provided for the contract of purchase.

With the exercise of the right of pre-emption, the purchase between the party having the right and the obligee takes effect under the conditions agreed upon between the obligee and the third party.

506. An agreement of the obligee with the third party, by which the purchase is made subject to the non-user of the pre-emption right, is of no effect as to the party having the right of pre-emption.

507. If the third party has bound himself in the agreement to an additional performance, which the party entitled to the pre-emption right is unable to effect, the party entitled to the pre-emption right has in place of the additional performance to render its value. If the additional performance cannot be valued in money, the exercise of the pre-emption right is excluded; the agreement of the additional performance is not to be considered, if the agreement with the third party would have been made without it.

508. If the third party has bought the things to which the pre-emption right relates, with other things at an aggregate price, the pre-emptioner has to render a proportionate part of the aggregate price. The obligee may demand, that the pre-emption be extended to all things, which cannot be separated without injury to him.

509. If in the agreement, the purchase price is credited to the third party, the pre-emptor can claim the credit only, if he gives security for the credited amount.

If a piece of ground is the subject of the pre-emption, security is not required, in so far as a mortgage on the lot for the credited purchase price is agreed upon, or if on account of the purchase price a debt is assumed for which a mortgage on the lot exists.

510. The obligee has to notify the pre-emptor immediately of the existence of the agreement entered into with the third party. Notice by the third party is of equal effect as that by the obligee.

The pre-emption right can be exercised, as to land, only up to the expiration of two months; as to other things only up to the expiration of a week after the receipt of the notice. If a limitation is fixed for the exercise, the same takes the place of the legal limitation.

511. The pre-emption right does not, in case of doubt, extend to a sale, which is made to a lawful heir with respect to a future right of inheritance.

512. The pre-emption right is excluded, if the sale takes place through execution or by a receiver in bankruptcy.

513. If the pre-emption right belongs to several parties, it can be exercised only as an entirety. If it has expired as to one of the parties entitled or if one of them does not exercise his right, the others are entitled to exercise the pre-emption right as an entirety.

514. The pre-emption right is not transferable and does not go to the heirs of the party entitled, unless it is otherwise provided. If the right is limited to a certain time, it is in case of doubt, inheritable.

DRAFT OF AN INTERNATIONAL LAW OF THE SALE OF GOODS[1]

CHAPTER I

THE SCOPE OF THE LAW

Article 1. The present law applies to sales of goods (corporeal movables). It does not apply to sales of:

(*a*) stocks or shares, negotiable instruments or money;

(*b*) ships, or vessels used in inland navigation or aircraft.

Article 2. For the purposes of the present law, contracts for the delivery of goods (corporeal movables) to be manufactured or produced are deemed to be sales, if the party undertaking delivery is required to supply the raw materials necessary for such manufacture or production.

Article 3. The present law shall apply regardless of the commercial or civil character of the parties or of the contract.

Article 4. The provisions of this law concerning defects in goods shall not apply to sales of living animals.

Article 5. The present law does not deal with the effects of the conclusion of the contract on the ownership of the goods.

Article 6. The present law shall apply where the parties have their business establishment or, in default thereof, their habitual residence in the territory of countries in which sales of goods are not governed by the same rules of law, and the goods are destined by virtue of the contract to become or are at the time of the conclusion of the contract the subject matter of international transport. International transport means transport from the territory of one State to the territory of another.

Article 7. Where a corporation or an association or a person having several business establishments becomes a party to the contract the business establishment to be taken into consideration shall be that from which the first communication is despatched.

Where a contract is concluded through an agent the business establishment or residence to be taken into consideration shall be that of his principal.

Article 8. The nationality of the parties is immaterial.

CHAPTER II

GENERAL PROVISIONS

Article 9. The parties may entirely exclude the application of the present law provided that they expressly mention the law of the country, which is to govern their contract.

[1] This preliminary draft of an International Law on the Sale of Goods was presented in 1935 to the Council of the International Institute in Rome for the Unification of Private Law by a special committee appointed in 1930. The draft then was submitted to the governments of member states of the League of Nations for comment, and a second draft is now in process of formulation.

The parties may derogate in part from the provisions of the present law provided that they agree on alternative provisions, either by expressly mentioning them or by referring to specific rules.

Article 10. The parties shall be bound by usages the existence of which is or ought to be known to them. The Court may disregard a usage which is unreasonable if its purport was unknown to one of the parties when he entered into the contract.

Where clauses or regulations used in a trade are employed the Court shall interpret them in accordance with the usage of the trade.

In case of any conflict between the present law and usage of the trade the usage shall override the present law.

Article 11. If a question arises which is not expressly covered by the provisions of the present law, and the present law does not expressly refer such question to the provisions of the national law, the Court shall apply the general principles by which the present law is inspired.

Article 12. The expression "communication without undue delay" means a communication which is made as soon as possible having regard to the usual means of communication employed in similar circumstances.

Article 13. A current price is the price on the market to which the buyer would resort in the ordinary course of business to satisfy his requirements in that class of goods which is the subject matter of the contract.

Article 14. National law, within the meaning of the present law, is the law of the country which is applicable according to the rules of private international law.

Article 15. No particular form is required for a contract of sale; oral evidence shall be admissible.

CHAPTER III

THE OBLIGATIONS OF THE SELLER

Section I. — Delivery

Article 16. The seller undertakes to deliver the goods to the buyer. The seller is bound to consign to the buyer, simultaneously with the goods, their accessories and any documents concerning the goods which must be annexed to them by the usage of the trade.

Article 17. By delivery is meant the doing of any act or acts which must be done by the seller in order to make it possible for the goods to be consigned to the buyer. The acts which are necessary for this purpose shall be determined in accordance with the nature of the contract.

In the case of a sale with obligation to dispatch the goods from the place where the goods are to be delivered, delivery shall be effected by consigning the goods to the first carrier or forwarding agent, or, if the first part of the journey is by sea, by placing them on board ship and sending to the buyer such documents as will enable him to obtain the goods on arrival. Where, under the contract or by usage of the trade, the seller is entitled to present a received for shipment bill of lading to the buyer it shall be sufficient to deliver the goods to the shipowner.

A. PLACE OF DELIVERY

Article 18. The seller is bound to deliver the goods at the place where, at the time of the conclusion of the contract, he has his business establishment or, in default thereof, at his ordinary residence.

If the contract be for the sale of specific goods which, to the knowledge of the parties at the time of the conclusion of the contract, are in some other place, such place is the place of delivery. The same rule applies where the contract is for the sale of unascertained goods which are to be taken from a given stock or bulk, or which the seller undertakes to produce or manufacture in a certain place.

Article 19. Where there is a doubt as to whether goods are to be delivered at the place of dispatch or at their destination, it shall be presumed that the parties intended delivery to be made at the place from which the goods are to be dispatched.

B. DATE OF DELIVERY

Article 20. Where the parties have agreed on a date for delivery, or where such date is fixed by usage of the trade, such agreement or usage shall conclusively and without any other formality fix the date at which the seller is bound to deliver the goods, provided that the date thus fixed is determined or determinable by the calendar or is related to a definite event the exact date of which can be ascertained by the parties (*e. g.* first open water).

Article 21. Where a period of time within which delivery must take place is agreed upon (*e. g.* a particular month or a certain season of the year) the seller may fix the precise date of delivery unless the circumstances indicate that such choice was reserved to the buyer.

Article 22. Where the date of delivery has not been fixed in accordance with the provisions of Articles 20 and 21 the seller is bound to deliver the goods within a reasonable time after the conclusion of the contract, regard being had to the nature of the goods and the circumstances.

C. SANCTIONS IN THE EVENT OF NON-DELIVERY OR DELAY IN DELIVERY

Article 23. In the event of total or partial failure to deliver or of delay in delivery the buyer may, subject to the provisions of Articles 24 and 25, require specific performance of the contract, provided that specific performance is possible and is recognised by the national law of the Court in which the action is brought.

The buyer may, subject to the provisions of Articles 26 to 32, avoid the contract by a simple statement to that effect.

He may also sue for damages as provided by Articles 33 to 40.

In no event is the seller entitled to obtain a period of grace from the Court.

(a) Specific Performance of the Contract

Article 24. Notwithstanding that the national law of the Court recognises his right to require delivery of the goods, the buyer shall not be entitled ot require such delivery where it is in accordance with the usage of the trade to repurchase the goods or where he can repurchase them without appreciable inconvenience or expense.

Article 25. If, in circumstances other than those contemplated by Article 27, the buyer elects to demand specific performance of the contract, he must notify the seller to this effect without undue delay; otherwise he will only be entitled to avoid the contract, as provided by the present law, without prejudice to his claim to damages.

(*b*) *Avoidance of the Contract*

Article 26. Where delivery has not been made on the date or during the period agreed upon or fixed by usage of the trade or at the expiration of the reasonable time provided for in Article 22, the buyer can only avoid the contract:

1. if he proves that by reason of the circumstances of the case or the terms of the contract the date of delivery was an essential condition of the contract, or
2. of the date of delivery has been fixed by the seller or by the buyer in the case contemplated by Article 21.

Article 27. Where the date of delivery is not an essential condition of the contract and where it has not been determined as provided by Article 21, the buyer may allow the seller a further period of time for delivery of reasonable duration, stating that on the expiration of that period he will refuse to accept the goods. If the period thus fixed by the buyer is not of reasonable duration, the seller must, without undue delay, notify the buyer that he will only deliver at the expiration of a reasonable period. Failing such notification the seller shall be deemed to accept the period fixed by the buyer.

Should the seller not deliver the goods at the expiration of the further period the contract shall *ipso facto* be avoided.

Article 28. Where the goods are delivered by the seller on a date later than that fixed by the contract, or by usage of the trade, or by the present law, a buyer who is entitled by the provisions of the present law to avoid the contract must give notice of avoidance without undue delay.

Article 29. Terms in a contract relating to the date of delivery of goods for which there is a market available where the seller may procure them shall be deemed to be of the essence for the purposes indicated in the three preceding articles.

Article 30. In contracts for delivery by instalments, the buyer shall be entitled to avoid the contract, as regards future instalments, if by reason of default in delivery of an instalment already due, he has good reason to fear that future instalments will not be delivered; but he shall not be entitled to avoid the contract in respect of deliveries already received, unless he proves that by reason of the interdependence of all the deliveries stipulated for in the contract, the absence of certain deliveries deprives the deliveries already received of all value to him.

Article 31. In the event of partial default in delivery or of delay in delivery of part of the goods the buyer shall not be entitled to avoid the contract as a whole unless he can prove that such partial delivery or partial delay constitutes a breach which goes to the root of the contract.

Article 32. Where the buyer is not entitled to avoid the whole of the contract he may avoid it in part, and only pay so much of the price as is proportionate to the value of the part which has been delivered to him, without prejudice to his right to claim damages in respect of the part which has not been delivered to him, calculated in accordance with the provisions of Articles 36 to 40.

(*c*) *Damages*

1. The case of delay in delivery without avoidance of the contract

Article 33. Where delivery of the goods, or part of the goods, has been delayed, the seller shall, notwithstanding that the time for delivery has been extended in accordance with Article 27, be liable in damages equal to the actual loss suffered by the buyer, including any profit of which he has been deprived, provided that such damages shall not be greater than those which result from circumstances which could reasonably have been foreseen at the time of the conclusion of the contract.

Article 34. The seller shall not be liable for the damages contemplated in the preceding article if he proves that the delay was due to an event which constituted an insurmountable obstacle which he was not bound to foresee at the time of the conclusion of the contract.

Whether and how far events other than those specified in the preceding paragraph may relieve the seller from liability for damages shall be determined by the national law.

Article 35. In the case referred to in the preceding article, it shall be the duty of the seller, as soon as he can foresee the delay, to notify the buyer that it will be impossible to deliver on the fixed date and to state the probable duration of the delay. The seller will be responsible for any damage caused to the buyer by any breach of this duty.

Where the seller in notifying the buyer of the impossibility to deliver on the fixed date, is unable on reasonable grounds to indicate the probable duration of the delay, the impossibility shall be deemed to be final, and either the seller or the buyer may avoid the contract. In that event the seller may claim exception from damages as provided by Article 36.

2. The case of avoidance on the ground of delay or failure to deliver

Article 36. Where the contract is avoided on account of delay or default in delivery of the goods the seller shall make good any loss caused to the buyer by non-delivery, unless he proves that such non-delivery was due to an event which constituted an insurmountable obstacle which he was not bound to foresee at the time of the conclusion of the contract.

Whether and how far events other than those specified in the preceding paragraph may relieve the seller from liability for damages shall be determined by the national law.

Article 37. Where the contract is avoided on account of delay or default in the delivery of goods for which there is a current price, the damages payable by the seller shall equal the difference between the price fixed by the contract and the current price which prevails immediately after the date upon which the buyer was entitled to avoid the contract, or upon which the contract was *ipso facto* avoided. Regard shall further be had to the normal cost of a repurchase.

If the buyer has repurchased the goods with due diligence and as a prudent man of business, the price of such repurchase shall be taken into account in the calculation of the damages.

Article 38. The damages fixed in accordance with the preceding Article may be increased so as to cover the loss actually suffered by the buyer if the buyer can prove that at the time of the conclusion of the contract the seller foresaw or could reasonably have foreseen the events to which such loss is due.

The buyer shall, nevertheless, not be entitled to claim the above-mentioned increase if he has failed to make a repurchase without delay in any case in which repurchase is required by the usage of the trade or could be effected without appreciable inconvenience or cost.

Article 39. Where there is no current price for the goods the damages shall be equal to the loss actually suffered by the buyer inclusive of any profit which he has lost owing to non-performance of the contract, provided that such damages shall not be greater than those which are the result of circumstances which could reasonably have been foreseen at the time of the conclusion of the contract.

Article 40. Where a epriod of time is fixed by the contract or by usage of the trade for the delivery of goods for which there is a current price, and where, before the expiration of such period, the seller has notified the buyer that he will not deliver the goods or has acted in such a way as to show that he does not intend to perform the contract, the damages shall be calculated on the basis of the current price of the goods on the last day of such period.

Where no period of time has been fixed by the contract or by the usage of the trade, the damages shall be calculated on the basis of the current price on the day on which the buyer has given notice of avoidance of the contract.

Section II. — The Seller's Undertaking against Defects in the Goods

Article 41. The seller undertakes that the goods shall be free from defects.

A. Definition of Defects

Article 42. The undertaking shall apply:

1. Where the goods do not possess the qualities necessary for their ordinary or commercial use;
2. where the goods do not possess the qualities necessary for a particular purpose expressly or impliedly contemplated by the contract;
3. where the goods do not possess the qualities and characteristics described in the contract including any express undertaking contained therein.

The absence of any immaterial quality or characteristic shall not be taken into account.

Article 43. In sales by sample or by model the undertaking shall extend to all want of correspondence between the goods and the sample or model.

Strict correspondence is not necessary, however, unless the parties have made a clear stipulation to that effect.

Where the sample is inconsistent with the description of the goods in the contract, the sample shall prevail; where the two are different but not inconsistent, the goods must combine the qualities of both.

Article 44. There is no sale by sample or model where the seller proves that such sample or model was merely submitted to the buyer by way of information without any undertaking that the goods would correspond thereto.

Article 45. Whether the goods are defective, or whether they correspond to the sample or model, is to be determined by their condition at the time when risk passes. Nevertheless, where defects which occur thereafter are due to the act or omission of the seller or a person for whose acts he is responsible the seller shall be liable for such defects.

Article 46. The seller shall not be liable for defects which he proves to have been within the knowledge of the buyer at the time of the conclusion of the contract. The same rule shall apply where the buyer has been grossly negligent in not being aware of such defects. In the latter case, however, the seller shall nevertheless be bound by his undertaking if he has promised qualities which do not exist, or if he has in bad faith concealed the existence of defects; the burden of proof shall be on the buyer.

B. Ascertainment and Notification of Defects

Article 47. On receipt of the goods the buyer is bound to examine them or to cause them to be examined without undue delay.

Where the goods have been transported, the buyer is bound to examine them, without undue delay, at their destination. Where the goods are re-dispatched by the buyer they must be examined at the first place where such examination is reasonably possible. The form of the examination shall be determined by agreement between the parties or, in default of such agreement, by the laws or usage of the place of examination.

Where the buyer intends to rely on such examination, he must give reasonable notice to the seller or his representative to be present thereat, unless the goods are in danger of perishing.

Article 48. Where the examination reveals a defect in the goods, the buyer is bound to notify the seller of the defect without undue delay.

Where the buyer fails to give such notice he shall not be entitled to rely on any defects. Nevertheless, where a defect subsequently appears which could not have been discovered by a mere examination, the buyer may rely thereon, provided he notifies the seller thereof without undue delay after its discovery. In notifying the defect the buyer must state its exact nature in accordance with the usage of the trade and good faith.

Article 49. The seller may deliver other goods in place of those which have been notified by the buyer as being defective, provided that delivery takes place within the time fixed by the contract.

Article 50. The seller shall not be entitled to rely on the provisions of Articles 47 to 49 if he has fraudulently concealed any defect.

C. SANCTIONS IN CASE OF DEFECTS

Article 51. A buyer who has duly notified the existence of defects may elect:

(1) either to avoid the contract, or

(2) to claim a reduction of price, or

(3) where in a sale of unascertained goods he would be entitled to specific performance if the goods had not been delivered, to claim the delivery of other goods or the repair of the defective goods.

He may also claim damages.

Article 52. The buyer must bring his action within two years from the date at which the goods were tendered to him, except where he is prevented from doing so by the fraud of the seller. After the expiration of this period the buyer cannot rely on a defect even by way of defence to an action.

Article 53. When only part of the goods are defective the buyer may treat the delivery as a partial delivery in accordance with Articles 31 and 32.

Article 54. In the case of contracts for delivery by instalments the buyer may avoid the contract as regards future instalments, on the ground of defects ascertained in one or more of the previous deliveries, whenever he has good reason to fear that future deliveries will also be defective; but he shall not be entitled to avoid the contract in respect of previous deliveries already received which are not defective, except where he proves that, by reason of the interdependence of all the deliveries stipulated for in the contract, the defects in certain deliveries deprive the deliveries which were not defective of all their value.

Article 55. Where the buyer elects not to avoid the contract he may claim a reduction in price corresponding to the diminution in value caused to the goods by the defect having regard to the value of the goods at the time of the conclusion of the contract.

Article 56. Where under the contract the seller is bound to produce or manufacture goods in accordance with the special orders of the buyer, he shall be bound to make good within a reasonable time any defect of which he has been notified. He also has the right to make good within a reasonable time any such defect, provided that no appreciable inconvenience or expense is caused thereby to the buyer.

The buyer may thereupon exercise the rights respecting defects in goods which are given to him by Article 51 hereof but only after the expiration of the reasonable time referred to in the preceding paragraph. He may also claim any damages to which he may be entitled by reason of the loss which he has suffered through the first defective delivery.

Article 57. The buyer is entitled to damages:

(1) where he avoids the contract;

(2) where in a sale of unascertained goods he demands delivery by the seller of other goods free from defects and this further delivery is not effected within the time prescribed for delivery;

(3) where the defect is repaired but the defective delivery has involved him in loss;

(4) where without avoiding the contract or claiming a reduction of price he desires to obtain compensation for loss which the defect has caused to him.

Article 58. Where the contract is avoided damages shall be assessed in accordance with the provisions of Articles 37 to 39. Where the buyer, without avoiding the contract, claims compensation for loss sustained by delay resulting from a further delivery or for loss arising from the defect itself the damages shall be assessed in accordance with Article 33.

Article 59. The buyer shall not be entitled to damages where the seller proves that the defective delivery of the goods was due to circumstances which constituted an insurmountable obstacle which he was not bound to foresee at the time of the conclusion of the contract.

Whether and how far circumstances other than those specified in the preceding paragraph may exempt the seller from liability for damages shall be determined by the national law.

Section III. — Other Obligations of the Seller

Article 60. Where the seller should be aware from the circumstances that it is usual to insure the goods and is not bound to effect such insurance himself, he shall furnish the buyer with the information requisite to effect insurance of the goods during transit.

Article 61. The non-performance of the obligations of the seller other than those of delivery and of the undertaking against defects in the goods, whether they are imposed on the seller by the present law or by usage of the trade or by the contract shall confer on the buyer a right to damages, unless performance has been prevented by an event constituting an insurmountable obstacle which the seller was not bound to foresee at the time of the conclusion of the contract.

Whether and how far circumstances other than those specified in the preceding paragraph may exempt the seller from liability for damages shall be determined by the national law.

These damages shall be equal to the actual loss sustained but may never exceed the amount of damages resulting from events which have been or could reasonably have been foreseen at the time of the conclusion of the contract.

If the obligation which is not performed is an essential one, the buyer may avoid the contract, without losing his right to damages in accordance with Articles 36 to 39.

An obligation is essential where it appears that the buyer would not have concluded the contract without such an undertaking.

CHAPTER IV

OBLIGATIONS OF THE BUYER

Article 62. The buyer is bound to take delivery of the goods and to pay the price.

Section I. — Payment of the Price

Article 63. The obligation to pay the price includes an obligation to take all steps required by the contract or usage of the trade for the purpose of providing for or guaranteeing payment, such as the acceptance of a bill of exchange, the opening of a documentary credit, the giving of a banker's guarantee or the like.

A. FIXING OF THE PRICE

Article 64. Where a sale is concluded but no price is fixed the buyer is bound to pay the price demanded by the seller. Where, however, the buyer shows that such price is excessive, he is bound to pay the price usually demanded by the seller or, if the seller fails to prove the existence of such a price, a reasonable price estimated, if possible, by the prices generally charged for such goods.

Article 65. Where the price is payable according to weight, then the price shall be payable on the net weight.

Article 66. Where import duties are payable by the seller, and where, after the conclusion of the contract, such duties are increased, the amount of such increase shall be added to the price.

Nevertheless if the delivery of the goods on which the duties are payable has been delayed by an act or omission on the part of the seller or of some person for whom he is responsible, the increase in the duties shall be payable by the seller whenever the buyer can prove that the increase would not have been payable if delivery had been made punctually in accordance with Articles 20 to 22.

Reductions in customs duties payable by the seller shall be deducted from the price.

B. PLACE AND DATE OF PAYMENT

Article 67. The buyer is bound to pay the price at the place of business or residence of the seller, except where payment is not due until tender of the goods or the documents, and the parties have agreed to fulfill their mutual obligations elsewhere.

If, in consequence of a change in the business establishment or habitual residence of the seller subsequent to the conclusion of the contract the cost of consignment is increased, such increase shall be borne by the seller.

Article 68. Where the parties have agreed on a date for payment, or where such date is fixed by the usage of the trade, such agreement or usage shall itself conclusively fix the date of payment without the need for any further formality.

Article 69. Where in a sale on credit, the date of payment has not been fixed in accordance with the preceding article, the buyer is bound to pay the price without undue delay after receipt of the goods or of the documents enabling him to obtain delivery thereof.

C. SANCTIONS IN THE EVENT OF NON-PAYMENT OR DELAY

Article 70. Where the buyer fails to pay the price in accordance with the terms of the contract, the seller shall be entitled to sue for the price if his right to do so is recognised by the national law of the Court to which he applies.

Instead of demanding payment of the price, the seller may avoid the contract in accordance with the provisions of Articles 72 and 73.

In either event the seller shall be entitled to damages in accordance with Articles 74 to 79.

In no event may the buyer obtain a period of grace from the Court.

(a) Specific Performance of the Contract

Article 71. The seller is only entitled to claim payment of the price if the sale is of goods which are such that there is no usage of the trade to effect a resale.

(b) Avoidance of the Contract

Article 72. Where the buyer has failed to pay the purchase price the contract may be avoided by a mere declaration to that effect by the seller. Where, however, the goods have been delivered unconditionally to the buyer the seller cannot avoid the contract.

Article 73. Where the contract provides for delivery by instalments the seller is entitled to avoid the contract as regards future instalments on the ground of failure to pay for instalments already delivered if he has good reason to fear that future payments will not be made.

(c) Damages

Article 74. Whenever the buyer is liable in damages under the following Articles he shall, nevertheless, be relieved of such liability if he proves that the delay in payment or failure to pay the price is due to an event which constituted an insurmountable obstacle which he was not bound to foresee at the time of the conclusion of the contract.

Whether and how far events other than those specified in the preceding paragraph may relieve the buyer from liability to damages shall be determined by the national law.

1. Delay in payment of the price without avoidance of the contract

Article 75. In case of delay in payment the seller is entitled to interest on the arrears of the price. If the seller, by reason of the delay, has suffered damage (including loss of profit) in excess of interest on the arrears, the buyer shall compensate the seller in so far as the buyer foresaw or at the time of the conclusion of the contract could reasonably have foreseen the events causing the damage.

The rate of interest shall be equal to the official discount rate of the country of the buyer plus 1%. Compound interest shall not be allowed except where there is a current account between the buyer and the seller.

2. Avoidance for delay in or default of payment

Article 76. Where the contract is avoided on account of delay in or default of payment the buyer is liable for the damage thereby resulting to the seller.

Article 77. Where there is a current price for the goods the damages payable by the buyer shall equal the difference between the price fixed by the contract and the current price prevailing immediately after the date upon which the seller was entitled to avoid the contract or upon which the contract was *ipso facto* avoided.

If the seller has resold the goods with due diligence and as a prudent man of business the price realised by such resale shall be taken into account in the calculation of the damages.

Article 78. The damages fixed in accordance with the preceding Article may be increased so as to cover the loss actually suffered by the seller if the seller can prove that the buyer at the time of the conclusion of the contract foresaw or could reasonably have foreseen the events to which such loss is due.

The seller shall, nevertheless, not be entitled to claim the above mentioned increase if he has failed to resell the goods in any case in which a resale is required by the usage of the trade or could be effected without appreciable inconvenience or cost.

Article 79. Where there is no current price for the goods the damages shall be equal to the loss actually suffered by the seller inclusive of any profit which he has lost owing to non-performance of the contract, provided always that such damages shall not exceed those due to events which were or could reasonably have been foreseen at the time of the conclusion of the contract.

Section II. — Other Obligations of the Buyer

Article 80. Where the buyer fails to take delivery of the goods in accordance with the terms of the contract, the seller shall be entitled to avoid the contract if the default on the part of the buyer is ground for thinking that he will not pay the price, or if it appears from the circumstances that acceptance of the goods was an essential condition of the contract.

Article 81. In the event of delay in acceptance of the goods the seller may, without avoidance of the contract, claim damages equal to the loss he has suffered owing to the delay.

Article 82. Where the seller has avoided the contract on the ground of delay in or default of acceptance of the goods the buyer is liable to make good the damage which is caused to the seller by the avoidance of the contract. The amount of such damage shall be assessed in accordance with the provisions of Articles 76 to 79.

Article 83. In the circumstances contemplated by the two preceding Articles, the buyer shall not be liable to damages, if he can prove that the delay in or default of acceptance is due to an event which constituted an insurmountable obstacle which he was not bound to foresee at the time of the conclusion of the contract.

Whether and how far events other than those specified in the preceding paragraph may relieve the buyer from liability for damages shall be determined by the national law.

Article 84. Where the buyer is guilty of delay in accepting the goods and requests the seller to state whether he is still ready and willing to deliver, the contract shall be determined *ipso facto* if the seller does not reply without undue delay.

Article 85. Where the contract reserves to the buyer a right subsequently to determine the form, measurement or other feature of the goods (sale by specification) but he fails to make such specification, either on the date expressly or impliedly agreed upon, or after receipt of a communication from the seller made after the lapse of a reasonable time, the seller may avoid the contract and claim damages in accordance with Articles 76 to 79 without making any specification himself.

Where the national law administered by the Court allows specific performance of the contract, the seller may also make the specification himself in accordance with the requirements of the buyer as known to himself.

The seller shall in this event inform the buyer of the contents of the specification which he has made and shall afford the buyer a reasonable opportunity to submit a different specification. Should the buyer not avail himself of such opportunity, the specification made by the seller shall be binding.

CHAPTER V

PROVISIONS COMMON TO THE OBLIGATIONS BOTH OF THE SELLER AND THE BUYER

Section I. — Coincidence between Delivery and Payment of the Price

Article 86. Unless otherwise provided by the contract or by the usage of the trade, delivery of the goods and payment of the price are concurrent conditions.

Article 87. Where delivery of the goods is required to be concurrent with payment of the price, the seller shall be entitled to withhold the goods until payment of the price, and the buyer shall be entitled to withhold the price until delivery of the goods.

Where the goods are to be dispatched from the place of delivery, the seller shall not be entitled to postpone dispatch on the ground that the price has not been paid. Nevertheless, if under the law which governs the contract of carriage or under the provisions of the contract of carriage itself, the seller retains the right of disposal over the goods during transit he shall not be bound to tender the goods to the buyer at destination until the price is paid.

Article 88. The seller, notwithstanding that the buyer is entitled to time for payment of the price, may postpone delivery of the goods until the buyer shall give him adequate security for payment whenever the financial position of the buyer has, subsequent to the conclusion of the contract, become so difficult that the seller has good reason to fear that payment will not be made on the agreed date.

Article 89. If, in the circumstances detailed in the preceding Article, the seller has undertaken to send the goods to the buyer and has already sent them, the seller upon learning the change in the buyer's position, may stop the goods from being tendered to the buyer notwithstanding that the buyer already holds a bill of lading or other document of title to the goods.

Nevertheless, the seller shall not be entitled to withhold the goods if they are claimed by a third party who is the lawful holder of the bill of lading or other document of title, unless the said bill of lading or document of title contains reservations concerning the effects of its negotiation or transfer, or unless the seller can establish that there has been collusion between the buyer and the holder of the said bill of lading or document of title.

Article 90. Where the buyer is bound under the contract to pay the price before receipt of the goods or documents, he may postpone payment until the seller shall give him adequate security for due delivery, whenever the financial position of the seller has, subsequent to the conclusion of the contract, become so difficult that the buyer has good reason to fear that delivery will not be made on the agreed date.

Article 91. The buyer is not bound to pay the price until he has had an opportunity of examining the goods, notwithstanding that payment and delivery are to be concurrent.

Where the seller must dispatch the goods from the place where delivery is to be made and a bill of lading or any other document of title is issued which gives the holder the right to obtain the goods and precludes the seller from disposing of the goods, the contract shall be deemed to be one providing for payment against documents; in this event the buyer shall not be entitled to withhold payment on the ground he has not had an opportunity of examining the goods.

Section II. — Supplementary Rules Regarding Delay and Avoidance of the Contract

Article 92. Where the buyer is guilty of delay in acceptance of the goods or in payment of the price, it shall be the duty of the seller to preserve the goods on behalf of the buyer. He has the right to retain them until he shall have recovered from the buyer the cost of preserving them.

Article 93. Where the goods have been received by the buyer it shall be his duty, if he intends to reject them, to preserve them on behalf of the seller. He has the right to retain them until he shall have recovered from the seller the cost of preserving them.

Where goods dispatched to the buyer have been placed at his disposal at their destination, the buyer, should he refuse to accept them, is bound to take possession of them on behalf of the seller, provided that this may be done without payment of the price and without appreciable inconvenience or cost. This provision does not apply where the seller or a person authorised to take charge of the goods on his behalf is present at such destination.

Article 94. The party who is under a duty to preserve the goods may deposit them in the warehouse of a third party at the expense of the party in default.

Article 95. Where there is a current price for the goods, the party who, in the circumstances contemplated by Articles 92 and 93, is under a duty to preserve them, may, after giving notice, sell them at the current price on behalf of the other party either through a broker officially authorised to conduct such sales or through a duly qualified public auctioneer.

Where there is no current price for the goods the party who, in the circumstances contemplated by Articles 92 and 93, is under a duty to preserve them may, after giving notice, sell them by private treaty. Should the other party prove that the party under a duty to preserve the goods could have sold them at a higher price, he shall be entitled to recover such price.

Article 96. Where, in the circumstances contemplated by Articles 92 and 93, the goods are subject to rapid loss or deterioration, or where their preservation would involve unreasonable expense, the party under the duty to preserve them is bound to sell them in accordance with the preceding Article.

Article 97. The avoidance of the contract releases both parties from their obligations thereunder, subject to any damages which may be due.

Where either party has performed his part of the contract either wholly or partially, such party may claim restitution.

Where there has been performance by both parties each may withhold restitution until the other shall make restitution.

Article 98. The purchase price shall carry interest, to be calculated from the day of payment, in all cases where the seller is bound to refund it.

Article 99. Although he may not be in a position to return the goods in the condition in which he received them the buyer retains his right to avoid the contract:

(1) where the goods or part of the goods have perished or deteriorated without any fault on his part or on the part of any person for whom he is responsible;

(2) where the goods or part of the goods have been transformed by him before he was able to discover the defect upon which he relies for avoidance of the contract;

(3) where the change which the goods have undergone is immaterial.

Section III. — Miscellaneous Provisions

Article 100. The party who sets up a breach of the contract is under a duty to adopt all reasonable measures in order to mitigate the loss which has occurred, provided that he can do so without appreciable inconvenience or cost. Should he fail to do so, the party guilty of the breach may claim a reduction in the damages.

Article 101. Where prior to the date agreed upon for performance of the contract either party so conducts himself as to disclose an intention to repudiate the contract, the other party may avoid the contract provided that he makes his intention known without undue delay.

Article 102. The expenses of delivery, such as measuring or weighing, shall be borne by the seller. All expenses incurred after delivery shall be borne by the buyer.

CHAPTER VI

THE PASSING OF THE RISK

Article 103. Once the goods are delivered the risk passes to the buyer, who, accordingly, notwithstanding that any of the goods perish, deteriorate or are otherwise diminished in value, is bound to pay the purchase price.

Article 104. The mere fact that the parties have inserted terms in their contract concerning expenses, and in particular the fact that they shall have agreed that such expenses shall be borne by the seller, shall not of itself suffice to pass the risk.

Article 105. Where the failure of the seller to do all that is requisite to comply with his obligation to deliver is due to the act or omission of the buyer the risk shall pass to the buyer as from the date at which delivery should have taken place.

This provision shall not apply to unascertained goods unless goods clearly appropriated to the contract have been set aside on behalf of the buyer, and the seller has notified the buyer accordingly. Where the goods are unascertained and form part of an undivided whole and are of such a nature that the seller cannot set part of them aside until delivery is taken by the buyer, it shall be sufficient if the seller has done all the acts which are required in order to enable the buyer to take delivery.

Article 106. Notwithstanding the provisions of Article 103 where goods are sold free on board, the risk does not pass to the buyer until they are placed on board the vessel, even if the seller is obliged to dispatch them to the port of loading from the place where delivery is due.

Where under the terms of the contract or by virtue of a trade usage, the seller is entitled to tender a received for shipment bill of lading to the buyer, the risk shall pass when the goods are handed over to the shipowner.

Article 107. Where the goods are sold on cost and freight or cost, insurance and freight terms the risk shall pass to the buyer as detailed in the preceding Article.

In the case of a through transit commencing by land, where, under the contract or by a usage of the trade the seller is entitled to tender to the buyer a through bill of lading or other document of title covering the transit, the risk shall pass to the buyer as soon as the goods are in the hands of a forwarding agent or carrier in the manner mentioned in Article 17 second paragraph.

Article 108. Where goods are shipped in bulk the risk shall pass to each of the buyers, in proportion to his share of the bulk, as soon as the seller has sent to him the bill of lading or given notice of shipment in some other way.

ANNEXES

Annexe I

CONTRACTS OF SALE WITH A RESERVATION OF THE PROPERTY IN GOODS

Article 1. This Annexe shall only apply to cases which are governed by the international law of the sale of goods.

Article 2. The following Articles shall apply to sales of machines, including automobiles, provided always that the thing sold has not become an immovable according to the law of the country of importation. As regards all other goods the law of the country of importation shall apply.

Article 3. The parties may agree in writing that the buyer shall not acquire any right of property in the thing sold until the whole of the price has been paid (agreement of reservation of property).

Article 4. Any provisions of the law of the country of importation, which require registration of an agreement of reservation of property or other measures of publicity in order to give validity to it, or to enable it to be set up against third parties, must be complied with.

Article 5. Where the seller knows that the goods are purchased for resale, the property shall remain vested in him by virtue of an agreement of reservation of property until the sub-purchaser has received either the goods themselves or a document enabling him to dispose of them.

Article 6. An agreement reserving property to the seller as aforesaid shall take effect notwithstanding the bankruptcy of the buyer or the seizure of the goods in execution by creditors of the buyer.

The term "bankruptcy" includes all forms of procedure which contemplate an organised distribution of assets amongst creditors.

Article 7. Apart from the cases mentioned in Articles 5 and 6 the competent national law shall determine whether and in what circumstances third parties can acquire rights over the goods in priority to the property reserved to the seller.

Article 8. In default of payment of the price or of payment on account the seller may only retake the goods in pursuance of agreement of reservation of property if he is entitled to avoid the contract of sale and has already done so.

Article 9. Any right of lien or charge created in favour of the seller by the national law shall remain in being, together with the rights, given by an agreement of reservation of property.

ANNEXE II

THE LETTERS OF TRUST

The letter of trust is an expedient which is in common use in Great Britain and the United States in connection with agreements by which the price of imported goods is to be paid by a banker, who issues a letter of credit in favour of the seller for that purpose. In such cases the documents of title to the goods are retained by the banker as security for the reimbursement of the monies which he advances to the importer, and a situation frequently arises in which it would be advantageous both to the financing banker and the importer that the importer should warehouse the goods on arrival and should sell them and deliver them in his own name to the ultimate buyer. The difficulty is that if this is done and the documents of title are surrendered to the importer by the banker for that purpose, the security of the banker, which is dependent on possession of the documents, ceases to be effective in law.

The procedure by way of letter of trust has been adopted in order to meet this difficulty, and to enable the banker to give possession of the goods or of the documents of title to his customer, the importer, for the purpose of facilitating the warehousing or sale of the goods, and at the same time to retain his security unimpaired.

The procedure adopted is broadly speaking as follows. On arrival of the goods the banker hands the documents to the importer in exchange for the letter of trust. This is a letter signed by the importer and addressed to the banker which is usually expressed in the following terms:

"I undertake to hold the documents of title and the goods when received and the proceeds thereof when sold as trustee for the bank.[1]

"*A*. As I require the said documents in order to obtain delivery of the goods[2] I undertake to warehouse them in the name of the bank and to hand the warrants to the bank forthwith; also to insure the goods against fire to their full insurable value and to hold the policies on behalf of the bank and in case of loss to pay the insurance monies to the bank.

"*B*. As I require the said documents in order to deliver the goods[2] to the buyer I undertake to pay the proceeds of sale to the bank without deduction immediately on receipt thereof within ...... days from this date and to furnish the bank on request with full authority to receive the purchase price from any person or persons. In the meantime I undertake to hold the goods on trust for the bank.[3] The bank may at any time cancel this letter and take possession of the goods until they have been delivered to the purchasers and the price has been received from them and may collect the price if the same has not been paid by the purchasers."

Letters of trust in this form have been treated as valid by the Courts of law in Great Britain and the United States though the juridical basis of such recognition is still a matter of some uncertainty.[4] An importer who has signed a letter of trust and deals fraudulently with the goods also commits a crime for which he can be punished. It is believed that letters of trust in a modified form are in use at Le Havre in connection with the importation of grain, sugar and tobacco, though only to a limited extent because their validity is doubtful according to French law. We have also been informed that documents of this nature are employed in Germany, but have no information before us as to their exact nature or as to their validity in German law. In Great Britain and the United States they operate not merely to keep the banker's security in existence, notwithstand-

[1] Although the word "trust" is used in this connection this is technically inaccurate as the transaction is not the creation of a trust. See GUTTERIDGE, *Banker's Commercial Credits*, p. 75; also FREDERICK, *The Trust Receipt as Security*, a brochure published by the American Acceptance Council.

[2] *A* and *B* are alternative and one or other will apply according as it is desired either that the importer should merely warehouse the goods or that he should deliver them to the ultimate buyer.

[3] The importer is sometimes required to declare that he is not indebted to the seller of the goods.

[4] See GUTTERIDGE, *op. cit.*; FREDERICK, *op. cit.*

The Committee were also informed that they have been recognised as valid by the Brazilian Courts.

ing the fact that he has parted with the documents, but to enable the banker to enforce such security as against the other creditors of the importer in the event of his insolvency. They are ineffective, however, against the claims of a purchaser who has received the goods and paid the price without notice of the existence of a letter of trust.

Although they are chiefly used in connection with the importation of goods from abroad they are sometimes used in the United States, but not in Great Britain, in connection with domestic transactions, *e.g.*, the sale of automobiles.

That letters of trust serve a valuable purpose in international commerce cannot be doubted. They relieve bankers of the trouble and expense of warehousing the goods on arrival and they enable the goods to be marketed by the person who is, as a rule, best able to sell them to advantage, *i.e.*, the importer, without causing the loss of commercial prestige which might result if it were apparent that he was trading with borrowed funds. It seems that they would be utilised to a wide extent if their validity was admitted by all systems of law. The question of the legal recognition of letters of trust is one which, in our opinion, calls for serious and immediate consideration from an international point of view. It would be a misfortune if the matter were left to be dealt with by isolated action on the part of the countries concerned. This would lead to a regrettable diversity of laws which we think can be avoided if an effort is made now to secure the co-ordination of legislation on the question.

We do not, however, consider that the international code of the law of sale should deal with this transaction, which is of a somewhat special character. In any event any attempt on our part to frame international rules governing letters of trust would, in our opinion, be premature, as the legal problems involved call for careful study in their relation to the rules of the different systems of law which are concerned. So far as it is possible, at present, to envisage the nature of these problems the difficulties which will be encountered are the following:

(1) The banker must be vested with property in the documents which will be adequate in order to enable him to control the sale of the goods until such time as his claims are satisfied by the importer;

(2) His right of property must not be destroyed by the surrender of the documents to the importer;

(3) He must be protected, in the event of the importer's insolvency, against claims by the general body of creditors.

The matter is also one which must be explored in its relation to the business practice of bankers throughout the world and regard must no doubt also be had to other economic aspects of the question.

We, therefore, confine ourselves to addressing an invitation to the Council to take such steps as they may consider to be advisable for the purpose.

UNIFORM CONDITIONAL SALES ACT

An Act Concerning Conditional Sales and to Make Uniform the Law Relating Thereto [1]

Section 1. (Definition of Terms.) In this Act "Conditional sale" means (1) any contract for the sale of goods under which possession is delivered to the buyer and the property in the goods is to vest in the buyer at a subsequent time upon the payment of part or all of the price, or upon the performance of any other condition or the happening of any contingency; or (2) any contract for the bailment or leasing of goods by which the bailee or lessee contracts to pay as compensation a sum substantially equivalent to the value of the goods, and by which it is agreed that the bailee or lessee is bound to become, or has the option of becoming the owner of such goods upon full compliance with the terms of the contract.

"Buyer" means the person who buys or hires the goods covered by the conditional sale, or any legal successor in interest of such person.

"Filing district" means the sub-division of the state in which conditional sale contracts, or copies thereof, are required by this act to be filed.

"Goods" means all chattels personal other than things in action and money, and includes emblements, industrial growing crops, and things attached to or forming a part of land which are agreed to be severed before sale or under the conditional sale.

"Performance of the condition" means the occurrence of the event upon which the property in the goods is to vest in the buyer, whether such event is the performance of an act by the buyer or the happening of a contingency.

"Person" includes an individual, partnership, corporation, and any other association.

"Purchase" includes mortgage and pledge.

"Purchaser" includes mortgagee and pledgee.

"Seller" means the person who sells or leases the goods covered by the conditional sale, or any legal successor in interest of such person.

Section 2. (Primary Rights of Buyer.) The buyer shall have the right when not in default to retain possession of the goods, and he shall also have the right to acquire the property in the goods on the performance of the conditions of the contract. The seller shall be liable to the buyer for the breach of all promises and warranties, express or implied, made in the conditional sale contract, whether or not the property in the goods has passed to the buyer.

Section 3. (Primary Rights of Seller.) The buyer shall be liable to the seller for the purchase price, or for installments thereof, as the same shall become due, and for breach of all promises made by him in the conditional sale contract, whether or not the property in the goods has passed to the buyer.

Section 4. (Conditional Sales Valid Except as Otherwise Provided.) Every provision in a conditional sale reserving property in the seller after possession

[1] Approved and recommended for enactment by the Commissioners on Uniform State Laws in 1918. States which have adopted the Act and dates of adoption are as follows:

Alaska (1919); Arizona (1919); Delaware (1919); Indiana (1935); New Jersey (1919); New York (1922); Pennsylvania (1925); South Dakota (1919); West Virginia (1921); Wisconsin (1919).

of the goods is delivered to the buyer, shall be valid as to all persons, except as hereinafter otherwise provided.

Section 5. (Conditional Sales Void as to Certain Persons.) Every provision in a conditional sale reserving property in the seller shall be void as to any purchaser from or creditor of the buyer, who, without notice of such provision, purchases the goods or acquires by attachment or levy a lien upon them, before the contract or a copy thereof shall be filed as hereinafter provided, unless such contract or copy is so filed within ten days after the making of the conditional sale.

Section 6. (Place of Filing.) The conditional sale contract or copy shall be filed in the office .... in [the city] [county] [registration district] in which the goods are first kept for use by the buyer after the sale. It shall not be necessary to the validity of such conditional sale contract, or in order to entitle it to be filed, that it be acknowledged or attested. This section shall not apply to the contracts described in Section 8.

Section 7. (Fixtures.) If the goods are so affixed to realty, at the time of a conditional sale or subsequently as to become a part thereof and not to be severable wholly or in any portion without material injury to the freehold, the reservation of property as to any portion not so severable shall be void after the goods are so affixed, as against any person who has not expressly assented to the reservation. If the goods are so affixed to realty at the time of a conditional sale or subsequently as to become part thereof but to be severable without material injury to the freehold, the reservation of property shall be void after the goods are so affixed as against subsequent purchasers of the realty for value and without notice of the conditional seller's title, unless the conditional sale contract, or a copy thereof, together with a statement signed by the seller briefly describing the realty and stating that the goods are or are to be affixed thereto, shall be filed before such purchase in the office where a deed of the realty would be recorded or registered to affect such realty. As against the owner of realty the reservation of the property in goods by a conditional seller shall be void when such goods are to be so affixed to the realty as to become part thereof but to be severable without material injury to the freehold, unless the conditional sale contract, or a copy thereof, together with a statement signed by the seller briefly describing the realty and stating that the goods are to be affixed thereto, shall be filed before they are affixed, in the office where a deed would be recorded or registered to affect such realty.

Section 8. (Railroad Equipment or Rolling Stock.) No conditional sale of railroad, or street or interurban railway equipment or rolling stock shall be valid as against the purchasers and creditors described in Section 5, unless the contract shall be acknowledged by the buyer or attested in like manner as a deed of real property, and the contract, or a copy thereof, shall be filed or recorded in the office of ....; and unless when any engine or car so sold is delivered there shall then be plainly and conspicuously marked upon each side thereof the name of the seller, followed by the word "owner."

Section 9. (Conditional Sale of Goods for Resale.) When goods are delivered under a conditional sale contract and the seller expressly or impliedly consents that the buyer may resell them prior to performance of the condition, the reservation of property shall be void against purchasers from the buyer for value in the ordinary course of business, and as to them the buyer shall be deemed the owner of the goods, even though the contract or a copy thereof shall be filed according to the provisions of this act.

Section 10. (Filing.) The filing officer shall mark upon the contract or copy filed with him the day and hour of filing and shall file the contract or copy in his office for public inspection. He shall keep a separate book in which he shall enter the names of the seller and buyer, the date of the contract, the day and hour of filing, a brief description of goods, the price named in the contract and the date of cancellation thereof; except that in entering the contracts mentioned in Section 8 the .... shall record either the sum remaining to be paid upon the contract or the price of the goods. Such book shall be indexed under the names of both seller and buyer. For filing and entering such contract or copy the filing officer shall be entitled to a fee of [ten cents], except that for filing and entering a contract described in Section 8 the .... shall be entitled to a fee of [one dollar].

Section 11. (Refiling.) The filing of conditional sale contracts provided for in Sections 5, 6 and 7 shall be valid for a period of three years only. The filing of the contract provided for by Section 8 shall be valid for a period of fifteen years only. The validity of the filing may in each case be extended for successive additional periods of one year from the date of refiling by filing in the proper filing district a copy of the original contract within thirty days next preceding the expiration of each period, with a statement attached signed by the seller, showing that the contract is in force and the amount remaining to be paid thereon. Such copy, with statement attached, shall be filed and entered in the same manner as a contract or copy filed and entered for the first time, and the filing officer shall be entitled to a like fee as upon the original filing.

Section 12. (Cancellation of Contract.) After the performance of the condition, upon written demand delivered personally or by registered mail by the buyer or any other person having an interest in the goods, the seller shall execute, acknowledge and deliver to the demandant a statement that the condition in the contract has been performed. If for ten days after such demand the seller fails to mail or deliver such a statement of satisfaction, he shall forfeit to the demandant five dollars [$5.00] and be liable for all damages suffered. Upon presentation of such statement of satisfaction the filing officer shall file the same and note the cancellation of the contract and the date thereof on the margin of the page where the contract has been entered. For filing and entering the statement of satisfaction the filing officer shall be entitled to a fee of [ten cents], except that the .... shall be entitled to a fee of [fifty cents] for filing and entering a statement of the satisfaction of a contract described in Section 8.

Section 13. (Prohibition of Removal or Sale Without Notice.) Unless the contract otherwise provides, the buyer may, without the consent of the seller, remove the goods from any filing district and sell, mortgage or otherwise dispose of his interest in them; but prior to the performance of the condition, no such buyer shall remove the goods from a filing district in which the contract or a copy thereof is filed, except for temporary uses for a period of not more than thirty days, unless the buyer not less than ten days before such removal shall give the seller personally or by registered mail written notice of the place to which the goods are to be removed and the approximate time of such intended removal; not prior to the performance of the condition shall the buyer sell, mortgage or otherwise dispose of his interest in the goods, unless he, or the person to whom he is about to sell, mortgage or otherwise dispose of the same, shall notify the seller in writing personally or by registered mail of the name and address of the person to whom his interest in the goods is about to be sold, mortgaged or otherwise transferred, not less than ten days before such sale, mortgage or other disposal. If any buyer does so remove the goods, or does so sell, mortgage or otherwise dispose of his interest in them without such notice or in violation of the contract, the seller may retake possession of the goods and deal with them as in case of default in payment of part or all of the purchase price. The provisions of this section regarding the removal of goods shall not apply, however, to the goods described in Section 8.

Section 14. (Refiling on Removal.) When, prior to the performance of the condition, the goods are removed by the buyer from a filing district in this state to another filing district in this state in which such contract or a copy thereof is not filed, or are removed from another state into a filing district in this state where such contract or copy is not filed, the reservation of the property in the seller shall be void as to the purchasers and creditors described in Section 5, unless the conditional sale contract or a copy thereof shall be filed in the filing district to which the goods are removed, within ten days after the seller has received notice of the filing district to which the goods have been removed. The provisions of this section shall not apply, however, to the goods described in Section 8. The provisions of Sections 11 regarding the duration of the validity of the filing and the necessity for refiling shall apply to contracts or copies which are filed in a filing district other than that where the goods are originally kept for use by the buyer after the sale.

Section 15. (Fraudulent Injury, Concealment, Removal or Sale.) When, prior to the performance of the condition, the buyer maliciously or with intent to defraud, shall injure, destroy or conceal the goods, or remove them to a filing district where the contract or a copy thereof is not filed, without having given the notice required by Section 13, or shall sell, mortgage, or otherwise dispose of such goods under claim of full ownership, he shall be guilty of a crime and upon conviction thereof shall be imprisoned [in the county jail] for not more than [one year] or be fined not more than [$500] or both.

Section 16. (Retaking Possession.) When the buyer shall be in default in the payment of any sum due under the contract, or in the performance of any other condition which the contract requires him to perform in order to obtain the property in the goods, or in the performance of any promise the breach of which is by the contract expressly made a ground for the retaking of the goods, the seller may retake possession thereof. Unless the goods can be retaken without breach of the peace, they shall be retaken by legal process, but nothing herein shall be construed to authorize a violation of the criminal law.

Section 17. (Notice of Intention to Retake.) Not more than forty nor less than twenty days prior to the retaking, the seller, if he so desires, may serve upon the buyer personally or by registered mail a notice of intention to retake the goods on account of the buyer's default. The notice shall state the default and the period at the end of which the goods will be retaken, and shall briefly and clearly state what the buyer's rights under this act will be in case they are retaken. If the notice is so served and the buyer does not perform the obligations in which he has made default before the day set for retaking, the seller may retake the goods and hold them subject to the provisions of Sections 19, 20, 21, 22 and 23 regarding resale, but without any right of redemption.

Section 18. (Redemption.) If the seller does not give the notice of intention to retake described in Section 17, he shall retain the goods for ten days after the retaking within the state in which they were located when retaken, during which period the buyer, upon payment or tender of the amount due under the contract at the time of retaking and interest, or upon performance or tender of performance of such other condition as may be named in the contract as precedent to the passage of the property in the goods, or upon performance or tender of performance of any other promise for the breach of which the goods were retaken, and upon payment of the expenses of retaking, keeping and storage, may redeem the goods and become entitled to take possession of them and to continue in the performance of the contract as if no default had occurred. Upon written demand delivered personally or by registered mail by the buyer, the seller shall furnish to the buyer a written statement of the sum due under the contract and the expense of retaking, keeping and storage. For failure to furnish such statement within a reasonable time after demand, the seller shall forfeit to the buyer [$10] and also be liable to him for all damages suffered because of such failure. If the goods are perishable so that retention for ten days as herein prescribed would result in their destruction or substantial injury, the provisions of this section shall not apply, and the seller may resell the goods immediately upon their retaking. The provision of this section requiring the retention of the goods within the state during the period allowed for redemption shall not apply to the goods described in Section 8.

Section 19. (Compulsory Resale by Seller.) If the buyer does not redeem the goods within ten days after the seller has retaken possession, and the buyer has paid at least fifty per cent of the purchase price at the time of the retaking, the seller shall sell them at public auction in the state where they were at the time of the retaking, such sale to be held not more than thirty days after the retaking. The seller shall give to the buyer not less than ten days' written notice of the sale, either personally or by registered mail, directed to the buyer at his last known place of business or residence. The seller shall also give notice of the sale by at least three notices posted in different public places within the filing district where the goods are to be sold, at least five days before the sale. If at the time of the retaking $500 or more has been paid on the purchase price, the seller shall also give notice of the sale at least five days before the sale by publication in a newspaper published or having a general circulation within the filing district where the goods are to be sold. The seller may bid for the goods at the resale. If the goods are of the kind described in Section 8, the parties may fix in the conditional sale contract the place where the goods shall be resold.

Section 20. (Resale at Option of Parties.) If the buyer has not paid at least fifty per cent of the purchase price at the time of the retaking, the seller shall not be under a duty to resell the goods as prescribed in Section 19, unless the buyer serves upon the seller, within ten days after the retaking, a written notice demanding a resale, delivered personally or by registered mail. If such notice is served, the resale shall take place within thirty days after the service, in the manner, at the place and upon the notice prescribed in Section 19. The seller may voluntarily resell the goods for account of the buyer on compliance with the same requirements.

Section 21. (Proceeds of Resale.) The proceeds of the resale shall be applied (1) to the payment of the expenses thereof, (2) to the payment of the expenses of retaking, keeping and storing the goods, (3) to the satisfaction of the balance due under the contract. Any sum remaining after the satisfaction of such claims shall be paid to the buyer.

Section 22. (Deficiency on Resale.) If the proceeds of the resale are not sufficient to defray the expenses thereof, and also the expenses of retaking, keeping and storing the goods and the balance due upon the purchase price, the seller may recover the deficiency from the buyer, or from anyone who has succeeded to the obligations of the buyer.

Section 23. (Rights of Parties Where There Is No Resale.) Where there is no resale, the seller may retain the goods as his own property without obligation to account to the buyer except as provided in Section 25, and the buyer shall be discharged of all obligation.

Section 24. (Election of Remedies.) After the retaking of possession as provided in Section 16 the buyer shall be liable for the price only after a resale and only to the extent provided in Section 22. Neither the bringing of an action by the seller for the recovery of the whole or any part of the price, nor the recovery of judgment in such action nor the collection of a portion of the price, shall be deemed inconsistent with a later retaking of the goods as provided in Section 16. But such right of retaking shall not be exercised by the seller after he has collected the entire price, or after he has claimed a lien upon the goods, or attracted them, or levied upon them as the goods of the buyer.

Section 25. (Recovery of Part Payments.) If the seller fails to comply with the provisions of Sections 18, 19, 20, 21 and 23 after retaking the goods, the buyer may recover from the seller his actual damages, if any, and in no event less than one-fourth of the sum of all payments which have been made under the contract, with interest.

Section 26. (Waiver of Statutory Protection.) No act or agreement of the buyer before or at the time of the making of the contract nor any agreement or statement by the buyer in such contract, shall constitute a valid waiver of the provisions of Sections 18, 19, 20, 21 and 25; except that the contract may stipulate that on such default of the buyer as is provided for in Section 16, the seller may rescind the conditional sale, either as to all the goods or as to any part thereof for which a specific price was fixed in the contract. If the contract thus provides for rescission, the seller at his option may retake such goods without complying with or being bound by the provisions of Sections 17 to 25 inclusive, as to the goods retaken, upon crediting the buyer with the full purchase price of those goods. So much of this credit as is necessary to cancel any indebtedness of the buyer to the seller shall be so applied, and the seller shall repay to the buyer on demand any surplus not so required.

Section 27. (Loss and Increase.) After the delivery of the goods to the buyer and prior to the retaking of them by the seller, the risk of injury and loss shall rest upon the buyer. The increase of the goods shall be subject to the same conditions as the original goods.

Section 28. (Act Prospective Only.) This act shall not apply to conditional sales made prior to the time when it takes effect.

Section 29. (Rules for Cases Not Provided For.) In any case not provided for in this act the rules of law and equity, including the law merchant, and in particular those relating to principal and agent and to the effect of fraud, misrepresentation, duress or coercion, mistake, bankruptcy, or other invalidating cause, shall continue to apply to conditional sales.

Section 30. (Uniformity of Interpretation.) This act shall be so interpreted and construed as to effectuate its general purpose to make uniform the law of those states which enact it.

Section 31. (Short Title.) This act may be cited as the Uniform Conditional Sales Act.

Section 32. (Inconsistent Laws Repealed.) Except so far as they are applicable to conditional sales made prior to the time when this act takes effect, the following acts shall be and hereby are repealed. (Here repeal all existing acts in the field of conditional sales.)

Section 33. (Time of Taking Effect.) This act shall take effect............

HIRE–PURCHASE ACT, 1938

(1 & 2 Geo. 6, Chap. 53)

Be it enacted by the King's most Excellent Majesty, by and with the advice and consent of the Lords Spiritual and Temporal, and Commons, in this present Parliament assembled, and by the authority of the same, as follows: —

1. This Act shall apply in relation to all hire-purchase agreements and credit-sale agreements under which the hire-purchase price or total purchase price, as the case may be, does not exceed —

(*a*) where the agreement relates to a motor vehicle or railway wagon or other railway rolling stock, the sum of fifty pounds,

(*b*) where the agreement relates to livestock, the sum of five hundred pounds, and

(*c*) in any other case, the sum of one hundred pounds,

and the expressions "hire-purchase agreement" and "credit-sale agreement" shall be construed accordingly.

2. — (1) Before any hire-purchase agreement is entered into in respect of any goods, the owner shall state in writing to the prospective hirer, otherwise than in the note or memorandum of the agreement, a price at which the goods may be purchased by him for cash (in this section referred to as the "cash price"):

Provided that this subsection shall be deemed to have been sufficiently complied with —

(*a*) if the hirer has inspected the goods or like goods and at the time of his inspection tickets or labels were attached to or displayed with the goods clearly stating the cash price, either of the goods as a whole or of all the different articles or sets of articles comprised therein, or

(*b*) if the hirer has selected the goods by reference to a catalogue, price list, or advertisement, which clearly stated the cash price either of the goods as a whole or of all the different articles or sets of articles comprised therein.

(2) An owner shall not be entitled to enforce a hire-purchase agreement or any contract of guarantee relating thereto or any right to recover the goods from the hirer, and no security given by the hirer in respect of money payable under the hire-purchase agreement or given by a guarantor in respect of money payable under such a contract of guarantee as aforesaid shall be enforceable against the hirer or guarantor by any holder thereof, unless the requirement specified in the foregoing subsection has been complied with, and —

(*a*) a note or memorandum of the agreement is made and signed by the hirer and by or on behalf of all other parties to the agreement, and

(*b*) the note or memorandum contains a statement of the hire-purchase price and of the cash price of the goods to which the agreement relates and of the amount of each of the instalments by which the hire-purchase price is to be paid and of the date, or the mode of determining the date, upon which each instalment is payable, and contains a list of the goods to which the agreement relates sufficiently to identify them, and

(*c*) The note or memorandum contains a notice, which is at least as prominent as the rest of the contents of the note or memorandum, in the terms prescribed in the Schedule to this Act, and

(*d*) a copy of the note or memorandum is delivered or sent to the hirer within seven days of the making of the agreement:

Provided that, if the court is satisfied in any action that a failure to comply with the requirement specified in the foregoing subsection or any requirement specified in paragraph (*b*), (*c*), or (*d*) of this subsection has not prejudiced the hirer, and that it would be just and equitable to dispense with the requirement, the court may, subject to any conditions that it thinks fit to impose, dispense with that requirement for the purposes of the action.

3. — (1) Before making any credit-sale agreement under which the total purchase price exceeds five pounds, the seller shall state in writing to the prospective buyer, otherwise than in the note or memorandum of the agreement, a price at which the goods may be purchased by him for cash (in this section referred to as the "cash price"):

Provided that this subsection shall be deemed to have been sufficiently complied with —

(*a*) if the buyer has inspected the goods or like goods and at the time of his inspection tickets or labels were attached to or displayed with the goods clearly stating the cash price, either of the goods as a whole or of all the different articles or sets of articles comprised therein, or

(*b*) if the buyer has selected the goods by reference to a catalogue, price list, or advertisement which clearly stated the cash price either of the goods as a whole or of all the different articles or sets of articles comprised therein.

(2) A person who has sold goods by a credit-sale agreement under which the total purchase price exceeds five pounds shall not be entitled to enforce the agreement or any contract of guarantee relating thereto, and no security given by the buyer in respect of money payable under the credit-sale agreement or given by a guarantor in respect of money payable under such a contract of guarantee as aforesaid shall be enforceable against the buyer or guarantor by any holder thereof, unless the requirement specified in the foregoing subsection has been complied with, and —

(*a*) a note or memorandum of the agreement is made and signed by the buyer and by or on behalf of all other parties to the agreement, and

(*b*) the note or memorandum contains a statement of the total purchase price and of the cash price of the goods to which the agreement relates and of the amount of each of the instalments by which the total purchase price is to be paid and of the date, or the mode of determining the date, upon which each instalment is payable, and contains a list of the goods to which the agreement relates sufficient to identify them, and

(*c*) a copy of the note or memorandum is delivered or sent to the buyer within seven days of the making of the agreement:

Provided that, if the court is satisfied in any action that a failure to comply with the requirement specified in the foregoing subsection or any requirement specified in paragraph (*b*) or (*c*) of this subsection has not prejudiced the buyer, and that it would be just and equitable to dispense with the requirement, the court may, subject to any conditions that it thinks fit to impose, dispense with that requirement for the purposes of the action.

4. — (1) A hirer shall, at any time before the final payment under a hire-purchase agreement falls due, be entitled to determine the agreement by giving notice of termination in writing to any person entitled or authorised to receive the sums payable under the agreement, and shall, on determining the agreement under this section, be liable, without prejudice to any liability which has accrued before the termination, to pay the amount, if any, by which one-half of the hire-purchase price exceeds the total of the sums paid and the sums due in respect

of the hire-purchase price immediately before the termination, or such less amount as may be specified in the agreement.

(2) Where a hire-purchase agreement has been determined under this section, the hirer shall, if he has failed to take reasonable care of the goods, be liable to pay damages for the failure.

(3) Where a hirer, having determined a hire-purchase agreement under this section, wrongfully retains possession of the goods, then, in any action brought by the owner to recover possession of the goods from the hirer, the court shall, unless it is satisfied that having regard to the circumstances it would not be just and equitable so to do, order the goods to be delivered to the owner, without giving the hirer an option to pay the value of the goods.

(4) Nothing in this section shall prejudice any right of a hirer to determine a hire-purchase agreement otherwise than by virtue of this section.

5. Any provision in any agreement —

(*a*) whereby an owner or any person acting on his behalf is authorised to enter upon any premises for the purpose of taking possession of goods which have been let under a hire-purchase agreement, or is relieved from liability for any such entry, or

(*b*) whereby the right conferred on a hirer by this Act to determine the hire-purchase agreement is excluded or restricted, or whereby any liability in addition to the liability imposed by this Act is imposed on a hirer by reason of the termination of the hire-purchase agreement by him under this Act, or

(*c*) whereby a hirer, after the determination of the hire-purchase agreement or the bailment in any manner whatsoever, is subject to a liability which exceeds the liability to which he would have been subject if the agreement had been determined by him under this Act, or

(*d*) whereby any person acting on behalf of an owner or seller in connection with the formation or conclusion of a hire-purchase or credit-sale agreement is treated as or deemed to be the agent of the hirer or the buyer, or

(*e*) whereby an owner or seller is relieved from liability for the acts or defaults of any person acting on his behalf in connection with the formation or conclusion of a hire-purchase agreement or credit-sale agreement,

shall be void.

6. — (1) At any time before the final payment has been made under a hire-purchase agreement or credit-sale agreement, any person entitled to enforce the agreement against the hirer or buyer shall, within four days after he has received a request in writing from the hirer or buyer and the hirer or buyer has tendered to him the sum of one shilling for expenses, supply to the hirer or buyer a copy of any memorandum or note of the agreement, together with a statement signed by the said person or his agent showing —

(*a*) the amount paid by or on behalf of the hirer or buyer,

(*b*) the amount which has become due under the agreement but remains unpaid, and the date upon which each unpaid instalment became due, and the amount of each such instalment, and

(*c*) the amount which is to become payable under the agreement, and the date or the mode of determining the date upon which each future instalment is to become payable, and the amount of each such instalment.

(2) In the event of a failure without reasonable cause to comply with the last foregoing subsection, then, while the default continues —

(*a*) no person shall be entitled to enforce the agreement against the hirer or buyer or to enforce any contract of guarantee relating to the agreement, and, in the case of a hire-purchase agreement, the owner shall not be entitled to enforce any right to recover the goods from the hirer, and

(*b*) no security given by the hirer or buyer in respect of money payable under the agreement or given by a guarantor in respect of money payable under such a contract of guarantee as aforesaid shall be enforceable against the hirer or buyer or the guarantor by any holder thereof,

and, if the default continues for a period of one month, the defaulter shall be liable on summary conviction to a fine not exceeding ten pounds.

7.—(1) Where by virtue of a hire-purchase agreement a hirer is under a duty to keep the goods comprised in the agreement in his possession or control, the hirer shall, on receipt of a request in writing from the owner, inform the owner where the goods are at the time when the information is given or, if it is sent by post, at the time of posting.

(2) If a hirer fails without reasonable cause to give the said information within fourteeen days of the receipt of the notice, he shall be liable on summary conviction to a fine not exceeding ten pounds.

8.—(1) In every hire-purchase agreement there shall be—

(*a*) an implied warranty that the hirer shall have and enjoy quiet possession of the goods;

(*b*) an implied condition on the part of the owner that he shall have a right to sell the goods at the time when the property is to pass;

(*c*) an implied warranty that the goods shall be free from any charge or encumbrance in favour of any third party at the time when the property is to pass;

(*d*) except where the goods are let as second hand goods, and the note or memorandum of the agreement made in pursuance of section two of this Act contains a statement to that effect, an implied condition that the goods shall be of merchantable quality, so, however, that no such condition shall be implied by virtue of this paragraph as regards defects of which the owner could not reasonably have been aware at the time when the agreement was made, or, if the hirer has examined the goods or a sample thereof, as regards defects which the examination ought to have revealed.

(2) Where the hirer expressly or by implication makes known the particular purpose for which the goods are required, there shall be an implied condition that the goods shall be reasonably fit for such purpose.

(3) The warranties and conditions set out in subsection (1) of this section shall be implied notwithstanding any agreement to the contrary, and the owner shall not be entitled to rely on any provision in the agreement excluding or modifying the condition set out in subsection (2) of this section unless he proves that before the agreement was made the provision was brought to the notice of the hirer and its effect made clear to him.

(4) Nothing in this section shall prejudice the operation of any other enactment or rule of law whereby any condition or warranty is to be implied in any hire-purchase agreement.

9. A hirer who is liable to make payments in respect to two or more hire-purchase agreements to the same owner shall, notwithstanding any agreement to the contrary, be entitled, on making any payment in respect of the agreements which is not sufficient to discharge the total amount then due under all the agreements, to appropriate the sum so paid by him in or towards the satisfaction of the sum due under any one of the agreements, or in or towards the satisfaction of the sums due under any two or more of the agreements in such proportions

as he thinks fit, and, if he fails to make any such appropriation as aforesaid, the payment shall by virtue of this section be appropriated towards the satisfaction of the sums due under the respective hire-purchase agreements in the proportions which those sums bear to one another.

10. Where, in an action by an owner of goods which have been let under a hire-purchase agreement to enforce a right to recover possession of the goods from the hirer, the owner proves that, before the commencement of the action and after the right to recover possession of the goods accrued, the owner made a request in writing to the hirer to surrender the goods, the hirer's possession of the goods shall, for the purpose of the owner's claim to recover possession thereof, be deemed to be adverse to the owner.

Nothing in this section shall affect a claim for damages for conversion.

11. — (1) Where goods have been let under a hire-purchase agreement and one-third of the hire-purchase price has been paid, whether in pursuance of a judgment or otherwise, or tendered by or on behalf of the hirer or any guarantor, the owner shall not enforce any right to recover possession of the goods from the hirer otherwise than by action.

(2) If an owner recovers possession of goods in contravention of the foregoing subsection, the hire-purchase agreement, if not previously determined, shall determine, and —

(*a*) the hirer shall be released from all liability under the agreement and shall be entitled to recover from the owner in an action for money had and received all sums paid by the hirer under the agreement or under any security given by him in respect thereof, and

(*b*) any guarantor shall be entitled to recover from the owner in an action for money had and received all sums paid by him under the contract of guarantee or under any security given by him in respect thereof.

(3) The provisions of this section shall not apply in any case in which the hirer has determined the agreement or the bailment by virtue of any right vested in him.

12. — (1) Where, in any case to which the last foregoing section applies, an owner commences an action to enforce a right to recover possession of goods from a hirer after one-third of the hire-purchase price has been paid or tendered as aforesaid, the action shall be commenced in the county court for the district in which the hirer resides or carries on business or resided or carried on business at the date on which he last made a payment under the hire-purchase agreement, and after the action has been commenced the owner shall not take any step to enforce payment of any sum due under the hire-purchase agreement or under any contract of guarantee relating thereto, except by claiming the sum in the said action.

(2) Subject to such exceptions as may be provided for by county court rules, all the parties to the agreement and any guarantor shall be made parties to the action.

(3) Pending the hearing of the action the court shall, in addition to any other powers, have power, upon the application of the owner, to make such orders as the court thinks just for the purpose of protecting the goods from damage or depreciation, including orders restricting or prohibiting the user of the goods or giving directions as to their custody.

(4) On the hearing of the action the court may, without prejudice to any other power, —

(*a*) make an order for the specific delivery of all the goods to the owner, or

(*b*) make an order for the specific delivery of all the goods to the owner and postpone the operation of the order on condition that the hirer or any guarantor pays the unpaid balance of the hire-purchase price at such times and in such amounts as the court, having regard to the means of the hirer and of any guarantor, thinks just, and subject to the fulfilment of such other conditions by the hirer or a guarantor as the court thinks just, or

(*c*) make an order for the specific delivery of a part of the goods to the owner and for the transfer to the hirer of the owner's title to the remainder of the goods.

(5) No order shall be made under paragraph (*b*) of the last foregoing subsection unless the hirer satisfies the court that the goods are in his possession or control at the time when the order is made.

(6) The court shall not make an order transferring to the hirer the owner's title to a part of the goods unless it is satisfied that the amount which the hirer has paid in respect of the hire-purchase price exceeds the price of that part of the goods by at least one-third of the unpaid balance of the hire-purchase price.

(7) Where damages have been awarded against the owner in the proceedings, the court may treat the hirer as having paid in respect of the hire-purchase price, in addition to the actual amount paid, the amount of the damages, or such part thereof as the court thinks fit, and thereupon the damages shall accordingly be remitted either in whole or in part.

(8) In this section the expression "order for the specific delivery of the goods" means an order for the delivery of the goods to the owner without giving the hirer an option to pay their value, and the expression "price" in relation to any goods means such part of the hire-purchase price as is assigned to those goods by the note or memorandum of the hire-purchase agreement, or, if no such assignment is made, such part of the hire-purchase price as the court may determine.

(9) If at any time before the hearing of an action to which this section applies the owner has recovered possession of a part of the goods, the references in subsection (4) hereof to all the goods shall be construed as references to all the goods which the owner has not recovered, and, if the parties have not agreed upon an adjustment of the hire-purchase price in respect of the goods so recovered, the court may for the purposes of paragraphs (*b*) and (*c*) of subsection (4) hereof make such reduction of the hire-purchase price and of the unpaid balance thereof as the court thinks just.

(10) Where an owner has recovered a part of the goods let under a hire-purchase agreement, and the recovery was effected in contravention of the last foregoing section, the provisions of this section shall not apply in relation to any action by the owner to recover the remainder of the goods.

13.—(1) While the operation of an order for the specific delivery of goods to the owner is postponed under the last foregoing section, the hirer shall be deemed to be a bailee of the goods under and on the terms of the hire-purchase agreement:

Provided that—

(*a*) no further sum shall be or become payable by the hirer or a guarantor on account of the unpaid balance of the hire-purchase price, except in accordance with the terms of the order, and

(*b*) the court may make such further modification of the terms of the hire-purchase agreement and of any contract of guarantee relating thereto as the court considers necessary having regard to the variation of the terms of payment.

(2) If while the operation of an order for the specific delivery of the goods

to the owner is so postponed the hirer or a guarantor fails to comply with any condition of the postponement, or with any term of the agreement as varied by the court, or wrongfully disposes of the goods, the owner shall not take any civil proceedings against the hirer or guarantor otherwise than by making an application to the court by which the order was made:

Provided that, in the case of a breach of any condition relating to the payment of the unpaid balance of the hire-purchase price, it shall not be necessary for the owner to apply to the court for leave to execute the order unless the court has so directed.

(3) When the unpaid balance of the hire-purchase price has been paid in accordance with the terms of the order, the owner's title to the goods shall vest in the hirer.

(4) The court may at any time during the postponement of the operation of such an order as aforesaid —

(*a*) vary the conditions of the postponement, and make such further modification of the hire-purchase agreement and of any contract of guarantee relating thereto as the court considers necessary having regard to the variation of the conditions of the postponement;

(*b*) revoke the postponement;

(*c*) make an order, in accordance with the provisions of the last foregoing section, for the specific delivery of a part of the goods to the owner and for the transfer to the hirer of the owner's title to the remainder of the goods.

14. — (1) Where a hire-purchase agreement validly provides for the payment by the hirer on or after the determination of the agreement or the bailment of such sum as, when added to the sums paid and the sums due in respect of the hire-purchase price before the determination, is equal to a fixed amount, and a claim is made in respect of any such sum in an action to which section twelve of this Act applies, then —

(*a*) if the court makes an order for the specific delivery of a part of the goods to the owner and the transfer to the hirer of the owner's title to the remainder of the goods, the claim shall be disallowed,

(*b*) if the court postpones the operation of an order for the specific delivery of the goods to the owner, it shall not entertain the claim unless and until the postponement is revoked, and shall then deal with the claim as if the agreement had just been determined.

(2) Where the hirer or a guarantor has paid or has been ordered to pay any such sum as aforesaid, and the owner subsequently seeks to recover the goods in an action to which section twelve of this Act applies, the court may treat the said sum as a sum paid or payable, as the case may be, in respect of the hire-purchase price.

15. Where goods have been let under a hire-purchase agreement and at any time after one-third of the hire-purchase price has been paid or tendered the owner makes a further hire-purchase agreement with the hirer comprising those goods, the provisions of sections eleven and twelve of this Act shall have effect in relation to that further agreement as from the commencement thereof.

16. — (1) Where, under the powers conferred by this Act, the court has postponed the operation of an order for the specific delivery of goods to any person, the goods shall not, during the postponement, be treated as goods which are by the consent or permission of that person in the possession, order, or disposition of the hirer for the purposes of section four of the Law of Distress Amendment Act, 1908, or of section thirty-eight of the Bankruptcy Act, 1914.

(2) After the determination of a hire-purchase agreement, or after an owner, having a right to recover from a hirer goods which have been let under a hire-purchase agreement, has commenced an action to enforce that right, the goods which have been let under the agreement, or the goods claimed in the action, as the case may be, shall not (notwithstanding that the court in any such action postpones the operation of an order for the specific delivery of the goods to the owner) be treated as goods comprised in the hire-purchase agreement for the purposes of section four of the Law of Distress Amendment Act, 1908.

17. If, whilst by virtue of this Act the enforcement by an owner of a right to recover possession of goods from a hirer subject to any restriction, the hirer refuses to give up possession of the goods to the owner, the hirer shall not, by reason only of the refusal, be liable to the owner for conversion of the goods.

18. — (1) His Majesty may by Order in Council direct that the jurisdiction conferred upon county courts by this Act may be exercised by any inferior court specified in the Order, and whilst any such Order is in force with respect to any inferior court, an action to which section twelve of this Act applies may, where the hirer resides or carries on business within the jurisdiction of that inferior court or resided or carried on business within the jurisdiction of that court at the date on which he last made a payment under the hire-purchase agreement, be commenced either in a county court in accordance with the provisions of the said section or in that inferior court.

(2) The Order may contain such provisions as appear to His Majesty to be expedient with respect to the rules of court for regulating the procedure to be followed in any such action, and may also, where it appears to His Majesty to be necessary, contain provisions authorising the making of such rules.

(3) Any Order made under this section may be revoked or varied by a subsequent Order in Council made in like manner.

19. — (1) Where under any hire-purchase agreement made after the commencement of this Act the owner is required to carry out any installation, and the note or memorandum of the agreement specifies as part of the hire-purchase price the amount to be paid in respect of the installation, the references in section four of this Act to one-half of the hire-purchase price and in sections eleven, twelve and fifteen of this Act to one-third of the hire-purchase price shall be construed as references to the aggregate of the said amount and either one-half of the remainder of the hire-purchase price or one-third of the remainder of the hire-purchase price as the case may be.

(2) For the purpose of this section the expression "installation" means —

(*a*) the installing of any electric line as defined by the Electric Lighting Act, 1882, or any gas or water pipe,

(*b*) the fixing of goods to which the agreement relates to the premises where they are to be used, and the alteration of premises to enable any such goods to be used thereon, and

(*c*) where it is reasonably necessary that any such goods should be constructed or erected on the premises where they are to be used, any work carried out for the purpose of such construction or erection.

20. — (1) The following sections of this Act shall, to the extent hereinafter specified, apply in relation to all hire-purchase agreements whether made before or after the commencement of this Act, that is to say: —

(*a*) section nine of this Act, so far as it relates to payments made after the commencement of this Act,

(*b*) sections eleven and fifteen of this Act, so far as they relate to the recovery of possession of goods after the commencement of this Act, (*c*) sections ten, twelve, thirteen, fourteen and fifteen of this Act, so far as they relate to actions commenced after the commencement of this Act,

(*d*) subsection (1) of section sixteen of this Act, so far as it relates to orders made after the commencement of this Act, and subsection (2) of the said section so far as it relates to agreements determined or actions commenced, as the case may be, after the commencement of this Act, and

(*e*) section seventeen of this Act, so far as it relates to a refusal to give up possession of goods after the commencement of this Act.

(2) Where goods have been let under a hire-purchase agreement made before the commencement of this Act, and the owner has, as part of the consideration for the hire-purchase price, carried out in relation to those goods any installation within the meaning of the last foregoing section, then, if the owner has served upon the hirer a notice specifying a sum not exceeding the expense actually incurred by the owner in respect of the installation, sections eleven, twelve and fifteen of this Act, so far as by virtue of the last foregoing subsection they apply in relation to that agreement, shall, as respects the recovery of possession of goods after the expiration of twenty-eight days from the service of the notice, and as respects actions commenced after the expiration of the said period, have effect as if for the references in the said sections to one-third of the hire-purchase price there were substituted references to the aggregate of the said sum and one-third of the amount which remains after deducting that sum from the hire-purchase price.

(3) Save as aforesaid this Act shall not apply in relation to any hire-purchase agreement or credit-sale agreement made before the commencement of this Act.

21. — (1) In this Act, unless the context otherwise requires, the following expressions have the meanings hereby assigned to them, that is to say: —

"Action," "buyer," "delivery," "goods," "property," "sale," "seller," "warranty" have the meanings respectively assigned to them by the Sale of Goods Act, 1893;

"Hire-purchase agreement" means an agreement for the bailment of goods under which the bailee may buy the goods or under which the property in the goods will or may pass to the bailee, and where by virtue of two or more agreements, none of which by itself constitutes a hire-purchase agreement, there is a bailment of goods and either the bailee may buy the goods, or the property therein will or may pass to the bailee, the agreements shall be treated for the purposes of this Act as a single agreement made at the time when the last of the agreements was made;

"Credit-sale agreement" means an agreement for the sale of goods under which the purchase price is payable by five or more instalments;

"Hire-purchase price" means the total sum payable by the hirer under a hire-purchase agreement in order to complete the purchase of goods to which the agreement relates, exclusive of any sum payable as a penalty or as compensation or damages for a breach of the agreement;

"Owner" means the person who lets or has let goods to a hirer under a hire-purchase agreement and includes a person to whom the owner's property in the goods or any of the owner's rights or liabilities under the agreement has passed by assignment or by operation of law;

"Hirer" means the person who takes or has taken goods from an owner under a hire-purchase agreement and includes a person to whom the hirer's rights or liabilities under the agreement have passed by assignment or by operation of law;

"Contract of guarantee" means, in relation to any hire-purchase agreement or credit-sale agreement, a contract, made at the request express or implied of the hirer or buyer, to guarantee the performance of the hirer's or buyer's obligations under the hire-purchase agreement or credit-sale agreement, and the expression "guarantor" shall be construed accordingly;

"Total purchase price" means the total sum payable by the buyer under a credit-sale agreement, exclusive of any sum payable as a penalty or as compensation or damages for a breach of the agreement;

"Motor vehicle" has the same meaning as in the Road Traffic Act, 1930;

"Livestock" means horses, cattle, sheep, goats, pigs, or poultry.

(2) Where an owner has agreed that any part of the hire-purchase price may be discharged otherwise than by the payment of money, any such discharge shall, for the purposes of sections four, six, eleven, twelve, thirteen, fourteen and fifteen of this Act, be deemed to be a payment of that part of the hire-purchase price.

22. — (1) This Act may be cited as the Hire-Purchase Act, 1938.

(2) This Act shall come into force on the first day of January nineteen hundren and thirty-nine.

(3) This Act shall not extend to Scotland or Northern Ireland.

FACTORS ACT, 1889

(52 & 53 Vict., Chap. 45)

Be it enacted by the Queen's most Excellent Majesty, by and with the advice and consent of the Lords Spiritual and Temporal and Commons, in this present Parliament assembled, and by the authority of the same, as follows:

Preliminary

1. For the purposes of this Act —

(1) The expression "mercantile agent" shall mean a mercantile agent having in the customary course of his business as such agent authority either to sell goods, or to consign goods for the purpose of sale, or to buy goods, or to raise money on the security of goods:

(2) A person shall be deemed to be in possession of goods or of the documents of title to goods, where the goods or documents are in his actual custody or are held by any other person subject to his control or for him or on his behalf:

(3) The expression "goods" shall include wares and merchandise:

(4) The expression "document of title" shall include any bill of lading, dock warrant, warehouse-keeper's certificate, and warrant or order for the delivery of goods, and any other document used in the ordinary course of business as proof of the possession or control of goods, or authorising or purporting to authorise, either by endorsement or by delivery, the possessor of the document to transfer or receive goods thereby represented:

(5) The expression "pledge" shall include any contract pledging, or giving a lien or security on, goods, whether in consideration of an original advance or of any further or continuing advance or of any pecuniary liability:

(6) The expression "person" shall include any body of persons corporate or unincorporate.

Dispositions by Mercantile Agents

2.—(1) Where a mercantile agent is, with the consent of the owner, in possession of goods or of the documents of title to goods, any sale, pledge, or other disposition of the goods, made by him when acting in the ordinary course of business of a mercantile agent, shall, subject to the provisions of this Act, be as valid as if he were expressly authorised by the owner of the goods to make the same; provided that the person taking under the disposition acts in good faith, and has not at the time of the disposition notice that the person making the disposition has not authority to make the same.

(2) Where a mercantile agent has, with the consent of the owner, been in possession of goods or of the documents of title to goods, any sale, pledge, or other disposition, which would have been valid if the consent had continued, shall be valid notwithstanding the determination of the consent: provided that the person taking under the disposition has not at the time thereof notice that the consent has been determined.

(3) Where a mercantile agent has obtained possession of any documents of title to goods by reason of his being or having been, with the consent of the owner, in possession of the goods represented thereby, or of any other documents of title to the goods, his possession of the first-mentioned documents shall, for the purposes of this Act, be deemed to be with the consent of the owner.

(4) For the purposes of this Act the consent of the owner shall be presumed in the absence of evidence to the contrary.

3. A pledge of the documents of title to goods shall be deemed to be a pledge of the goods.

4. Where a mercantile agent pledges goods as security for a debt or liability due from the pledgor to the pledgee before the time of the pledge, the pledgee shall acquire no further right to the goods than could have been enforced by the pledgor at the time of the pledge.

5. The consideration necessary for the validity of a sale, pledge, or other disposition, of goods, in pursuance of this Act, may be either a payment in cash, or the delivery or transfer of other goods, or of a document of title to goods, or of a negotiable security, or any other valuable consideration; but where goods are pledged by a mercantile agent in consideration of the delivery or transfer of other goods, or of a document of title to goods, or of a negotiable security, the pledgee shall acquire no right or interest in the goods so pledged in excess of the value of the goods, documents, or security when so delivered or transferred in exchange.

6. For the purposes of this Act an agreement made with a mercantile agent through a clerk or other person authorised in the ordinary course of business to make contracts of sale or pledge on his behalf shall be deemed to be an agreement with the agent.

7.—(1) Where the owner of goods has given possession of the goods to another person for the purpose of consignment or sale, or has shipped the goods in the name of another person, and the consignee of the goods has not had notice that such person is not the owner of the goods, the consignee shall, in respect of advances made to or for the use of such person, have the same lien on the goods as if such person were the owner of the goods, and may transfer any such lien to another person.

(2.) Nothing in this section shall limit or affect the validity of any sale, pledge, or disposition, by a mercantile agent.

Dispositions by Sellers and Buyers of Goods

8. Where a person, having sold goods, continues, or is, in possession of the goods or of the documents of title to the goods, the delivery or transfer by that person, or by a mercantile agent acting for him, of the goods or documents of title under any sale, pledge, or other disposition thereof, or under any agreement for sale, pledge, or other disposition thereof, to any person receiving the same in good faith and without notice of the previous sale, shall have the same effect as if the person making the delivery or transfer were expressly authorised by the owner of the goods to make the same.

9. Where a person, having bought or agreed to buy goods, obtains with the consent of the seller possession of the goods or the documents of title to the goods, the delivery or transfer, by that person or by a mercantile agent acting for him, of the goods or documents of title, under any sale, pledge, or other disposition thereof, or under any agreement for sale, pledge, or other disposition thereof, to any person receiving the same in good faith and without notice of any lien or other right of the original seller in respect of the goods, shall have the same effect as if the person making the delivery or transfer were a mercantile agent in possession of the goods or documents of title with the consent of the owner.

10. Where a document of title to goods has been lawfully transferred to a person as a buyer or owner of the goods, and that person transfers the document to a person who takes the document in good faith and for valuable consideration, the last-mentioned transfer shall have the same effect for defeating any vendor's lien or right of stoppage in transitu as the transfer of a bill of lading has for defeating the right of stoppage in transitu.

Supplemental

11. For the purposes of this Act, the transfer of a document may be by endorsement, or, where the document is by custom or by its express terms transferable by delivery, or makes the goods deliverable to the bearer, then by delivery.

12.—(1) Nothing in this Act shall authorise an agent to exceed or depart from his authority as between himself and his principal, or exempt him from any liability, civil or criminal, for so doing.

(2) Nothing in this Act shall prevent the owner of goods from recovering the goods from an agent or his trustee in bankruptcy at any time before the sale or pledge thereof, or shall prevent the owner of goods pledged by an agent from having the right to redeem the goods at any time before the sale thereof, on satisfying the claim for which the goods were pledged, and paying to the agent, if by him required, any money in respect of which the agent would by law be entitled to retain the goods or the documents of title thereto, or any of them, by way of lien as against the owner, or from recovering from any person with whom the goods have been pledged any balance of money remaining in his hands as the produce of the sale of the goods after deducting the amount of his lien.

(3) Nothing in this Act shall prevent the owner of goods sold by an agent from recovering from the buyer the price agreed to be paid for the same, or any part of that price, subject to any right of set off on the part of the buyer against the agent.

13. The provisions of this Act shall be construed in amplification and not in derogation of the powers exerciseable by an agent independently of this Act.

14. The enactments mentioned in the schedule to this Act are hereby repealed

as from the commencement of this Act, but this repeal shall not affect any right acquired or liability incurred before the commencement of this Act under any enactment hereby repealed.

15. This Act shall commence and come into operation on the first day of January one thousand eight hundred and ninety.

16. This Act shall not extend to Scotland.

17. This Act may be cited as the Factors Act, 1889.

NEW YORK FACTORS ACT [1]

1. Every factor or other agent, entrusted with the possession of any bill of lading, custom-house permit, or warehouseman's receipt for the delivery of any merchandise, and every such factor or agent not having the documentary evidence of title, who shall be intrusted with the possession of any merchandise for the purpose of sale, or as a security for any advances to be made or obtained thereon, shall be deemed to be the true owner thereof, so far as to give validity to any contract made by such agent with any other person, for the sale or disposition of the account receivable or other chose in action created by sale or other disposition of such merchandise, for any money advanced, or negotiable instrument or other obligation in writing given by such other person upon the faith thereof.

2. Every person who shall hereafter accept or take any such merchandise and any account receivable or other chose in action created by sale or other disposition of such merchandise in deposit from any such agent, as a security for any antecedent debt or demand, shall not acquire thereby, or enforce any right or interest in or to such merchandise or document, other than was possessed or might have been enforced by such agent at the time of such deposit.

3. Nothing contained in the preceding subdivisions of this section shall be construed to prevent the true owner of any merchandise and any account receivable or other chose in action created by sale or other disposition of such merchandise so deposited, from demanding or receiving the same, upon prepayment of the money advanced, or on restoration of the security given, on the deposit of such merchandise and any account receivable or other chose in action created by sale or other disposition of such merchandise, and upon satisfying such lien as may exist thereon in favor of the agent who may have deposited the same; nor from recovering any balance which may remain in the hands of the person with whom such merchandise and any account receivable or other chose in action created by sale or other disposition of such merchandise shall have been deposited, as the produce of the sale thereof, after satisfying the amount justly due to such person by reason of such deposit.

4. Nothing contained in this section shall authorize a common carrier, warehouseman, or other person to whom merchandise or other property may be committed for transportation or storage only, to sell or hypothecate the same.

[1] Chap. 42, sec. 43 Cahill's Consolidated Laws of New York, 1923. Substantially similar acts have been given effect in other states as follows: California, Civ. Code, sec. 2369 (1931); Maine, R.S., c. 44, secs. 1–3 (1930); Maryland, Art. 2, secs. 1–20, Ann. Code (1924); Massachusetts, c. 104, Ann. Laws (1933); Montana, c. 152, sec. 7976, Rev. Code (1935); New York, Pers. Prop. Law, sec. 43, Cahill's Cons. Laws of New York (1923); North Dakota, sec. 6145, Comp. Laws (1913); Ohio Gen. Code, secs. 8358–8364, Ann. Code (1934); Pennsylvania, Title 6, c. 2, Purdon's Pa. Statutes (1930); Rhode Island, Title xxxix, sec. 6078, Gen. Laws (1923); and South Dakota, Art. 8, secs. 1288–1294, Comp. Laws (1929).

UNIFORM WAREHOUSE RECEIPTS ACTS

An Act
To Make Uniform the Law of Warehouse Receipts [1]

PART I

THE ISSUE OF WAREHOUSE RECEIPTS

Section 1. (Persons Who May Issue Receipts.) Warehouse receipts may be issued by any warehouseman.

Sec. 2. (Form of Receipts. Essential Terms.) Warehouse receipts need not be in any particular form, but every such receipt must embody within its written or printed terms —

(a) The location of the warehouse where the goods are stored,

(b) The date of issue of the receipt,

(c) The consecutive number of the receipt,

(d) A statement whether the goods received will be delivered to the bearer, to a specified person, or to a specified person or his order,

(e) The rate of storage charges,

(f) A description of the goods or of the packages containing them,

(g) The signature of the warehouseman, which may be made by his authorized agent,

(h) If the receipt is issued for goods of which the warehouseman is owner, either solely or jointly or in common with others, the fact of such ownership, and

(i) A statement of the amount of advances made and of liabilities incurred for which the warehouseman claims a lien. If the precise amount of such advances made or of such liabilities incurred is, at the time of the issue of the receipt, unknown to the warehouseman or to his agent who issues it, a statement of the fact that advances have been made or liabilities incurred and the purpose thereof is sufficient.

A warehouseman shall be liable to any person injured thereby, for all damage caused by the omission from a negotiable receipt of any of the terms herein required.

Sec. 3. (Form of Receipts. What Terms May be Inserted.) A warehouseman may insert in a receipt, issued by him, any other terms and conditions, provided that such terms and conditions shall not:

(a) Be contrary to the provisions of this act.

[1] Approved and recommended for adoption by the Commissioners on Uniform State Laws in 1906. The Act has been adopted as follows: Alabama (1915); Alaska (1913); Arizona (1921); Arkansas (1915); California (1909); Colorado (1911); Connecticut (1907); Delaware (1917); District of Columbia (1910); Florida (1917); Idaho (1915); Illinois (1907); Indiana (1921); Iowa (1907); Kansas (1909); Louisiana (1908); Maine (1917); Maryland (1910); Massachusetts (1907); Michigan (1909); Minnesota (1913); Mississippi (1920); Missouri (1911); Montana (1917); Nebraska (1909); Nevada (1913); New Jersey (1907); New Mexico (1909); New York (1907); North Carolina (1917); North Dakota (1917); Ohio (1908); Oklahoma (1915); Oregon (1913); Pennsylvania (1909); Philippine Islands (1912); Porto Rico (1919); Rhode Island (1908); South Dakota (1913); Tennessee (1909); Texas (1919); Utah (1911); Vermont (1912); Virginia (1908); Washington (1913); West Virginia (1917); Wisconsin (1909); Wyoming (1917).

(b) In any wise impair his obligation to exercise that degree of care in the safe-keeping of the goods entrusted to him which a reasonably careful man would exercise in regard to similar goods of his own.

Sec. 4. (Definition of Non-Negotiable Receipt.) A receipt in which it is stated that the goods received will be delivered to the depositor, or to any other specified person, is a non-negotiable receipt.

Sec. 5. (Definition of Negotiable Receipt.) A receipt in which it is stated that the goods received will be delivered to the bearer, or to the order of any person named in such a receipt is a negotiable receipt.

No provision shall be inserted in a negotiable receipt that it is non-negotiable. Such provision, if inserted, shall be void.

Sec. 6. (Duplicate Receipts Must be so Marked.) When more than one negotiable receipt is issued for the same goods, the word "duplicate" shall be plainly placed upon the face of every such receipt, except the one first issued. A warehouseman shall be liable for all damage caused by his failure so to do to any one who purchased the subsequent receipt for value supposing it to be an original, even though the purchase be after the delivery of the goods by the warehouseman to the holder of the original receipt.

Sec. 7. (Failure to Mark "Not Negotiable.") A non-negotiable receipt shall have plainly placed upon its face by the warehouseman issuing it "non-negotiable," or "not negotiable." In case of the warehouseman's failure so to do, a holder of the receipt who purchased it for value supposing it to be negotiable, may, at his option, treat such receipt as imposing upon the warehouseman the same liabilities he would have incurred had the receipt been negotiable.

This section shall not apply, however, to letters, memoranda, or written acknowledgments of an informal character.

PART II

OBLIGATIONS AND RIGHTS OF WAREHOUSEMEN UPON THEIR RECEIPTS

Sec. 8. (Obligation of Warehouseman to Deliver.) A warehouseman, in the absence of some lawful excuse provided by this act, is bound to deliver the goods upon a demand made either by the holder of a receipt for the goods or by the depositor, if such demand is accompanied with:

(a) An offer to satisfy the warehouseman's lien,

(b) An offer to surrender the receipt if negotiable, with such indorsements as would be necessary for the negotiation of the receipt, and

(c) A readiness and willingness to sign, when the goods are delivered, an acknowledgment that they have been delivered, if such signature is requested by the warehouseman.

In case the warehouseman refuses or fails to deliver the goods in compliance with a demand by the holder or depositor so accompanied, the burden shall be upon the warehouseman to establish the existence of a lawful excuse for such refusal.

Sec. 9. (Justification of Warehouseman in Delivering.) A warehouseman is justified in delivering the goods, subject to the provisions of the three following sections, to one who is:

(a) The person lawfully entitled to the possession of the goods, or his agent,

(b) A person who is either himself entitled to delivery by the terms of a non-negotiable receipt issued for the goods, or who has written authority from the person so entitled either indorsed upon the receipt or written upon another paper, or

(c) A person in possession of a negotiable receipt by the terms of which the goods are deliverable to him or order or to bearer, or which has been endorsed to him or in blank by the person to whom delivery was promised by the terms of the receipt or by his mediate or immediate indorsee.

Sec. 10. (Warehouseman's Liability for Misdelivery.) Where a warehouseman delivers the goods to one who is not in fact lawfully entitled to the possession of them, the warehouseman shall be liable as for conversion to all having a right of property or possession in the goods if he delivered the goods otherwise than as authorized by subdivisions (b) and (c) of the preceding section and though he delivered the goods as authorized by said subdivisions he shall be so liable, if prior to such delivery he had either:

(a) Been requested, by or on behalf of the person lawfully entitled to a right of property or possession in the goods, not to make such delivery, or

(b) Had information that the delivery about to be made was to one not lawfully entitled to the possession of the goods.

Sec. 11. (Negotiable Receipts Must be Canceled When Goods Delivered.) Except as provided in Section 36, where a warehouseman delivers goods for which he has issued a negotiable receipt, the negotiation of which would transfer the right to the possession of the goods, and fails to take up and cancel the receipt, he shall be liable to any one who purchases for value in good faith such receipt, for failure to deliver the goods to him, whether such purchaser acquired title to the receipt before or after the delivery of the goods by the warehouseman.

Sec. 12. (Negotiable Receipts Must be Canceled or Marked When Part of Goods Delivered.) Except as provided in section 36, where a warehouseman delivers part of the goods for which he had issued a negotiable receipt and fails either to take up and cancel such receipt, or to place plainly upon it a statement of what goods or packages have been delivered he shall be liable, to any one who purchases for value in good faith such receipt, for failure to deliver all the goods specified in the receipt, whether such purchaser acquired title to the receipt before or after the delivery of any portion of the goods by the warehouseman.

Sec. 13. (Altered Receipts.) The alteration of a receipt shall not excuse the warehouseman who issued it from any liability if such alteration was:

(a) Immaterial,

(b) Authorized, or

(c) Made without fraudulent intent.

If the alteration was authorized, the warehouseman shall be liable according to the terms of the receipt as altered. If the alteration was unauthorized, but made without fraudulent intent, the warehouseman shall be liable according to the terms of the receipt, as they were before alteration.

Material and fraudulent alteration of a receipt shall not excuse the warehouseman who issued it from liability to deliver, according to the terms of the receipt as originally issued, the goods for which it was issued, but shall excuse him from any other liability to the person who made the alteration and to any person who took with notice of the alteration. Any purchaser of the receipt for value without notice of the alteration shall acquire the same rights against the warehouseman which such purchaser would have acquired if the receipt had not been altered at the time of the purchase.

Sec. 14. (Lost or Destroyed Receipts.) Where a negotiable receipt has been lost or destroyed, a court of competent jurisdiction may order the delivery of the goods upon satisfactory proof of such loss or destruction and upon the giving of a bond with sufficient sureties to be approved by the court to protect the warehouseman from any liability or expense, which he or any person injured by such delivery may incur by reason of the original receipt remaining outstanding. The court may also in its discretion order the payment of a warehouseman's reasonable costs and counsel fees.

The delivery of the goods under an order of the court as provided in this section, shall not relieve the warehouseman from liability to a person to whom the negotiable receipt has been or shall be negotiated for value without notice of the proceedings or of the delivery of the goods.

Sec. 15. (Effect of Duplicate Receipts.) A receipt upon the face of which the word "duplicate" is plainly placed is a representation and warranty by the warehouseman that such receipt is an accurate copy of an original receipt properly issued and uncanceled at the date of the issue of the duplicate, but shall impose upon him no other liability.

Sec. 16. (Warehouseman Cannot Set up Title in Himself.) No title or right to the possession of the goods, on the part of the warehouseman, unless such title or right is derived directly or indirectly from a transfer made by the depositor at the time of or subsequent to the deposit for storage, or from the warehouseman's lien, shall excuse the warehouseman from liability for refusing to deliver the goods according to the terms of the receipt.

Sec. 17. (Interpleader of Adverse Claimants.) If more than one person claims the title or possession of the goods, the warehouseman may, either as a defense to an action brought against him for non-delivery of the goods, or as an original suit, whichever is appropriate, require all known claimants to interplead.

Sec. 18. (Warehouseman has Reasonable Time to Determine Validity of Claims.) If some one other than the depositor or person claiming under him has a claim to the title or possession of the goods, and the warehouseman has information of such claim, the warehouseman shall be excused from liability for refusing to deliver the goods, either to the depositor or person claiming under him or to the adverse claimant, until the warehouseman has had a reasonable time to ascertain the validity of the adverse claim or to bring legal proceedings to compel all claimants to interplead.

Sec. 19. (Adverse Title is no Defense Except as Above Provided.) Except as provided in the two preceding sections and in sections 9 and 36, no right or title of a third person shall be a defense to an action brought by the depositor or person claiming under him against the warehouseman for failure to deliver the goods according to the terms of the receipt.

Sec. 20. (Liability for Non-Existence or Misdescription of Goods.) A warehouseman shall be liable to the holder of a receipt for damages caused by the non-existence of the goods or by the failure of the goods to correspond with the description thereof in the receipt at the time of its issue. If, however, the goods are described in a receipt merely by a statement of marks or labels upon them, or upon packages containing them, or by a statement that the goods are said to be goods of a certain kind, or that the packages containing the goods are said to contain goods of a certain kind, or by words of like purport, such statements, if true, shall not make liable the warehouseman issuing the receipt, although the goods are not of the kind which the marks or labels upon them indicate, or of the kind they were said to be by the depositor.

Sec. 21. (Liability for Care of Goods.) A warehouseman shall be liable for any loss or injury to the goods caused by his failure to exercise such care in regard to them as a reasonably careful owner of similar goods would exercise, but he shall not be liable, in the absence of an agreement to the contrary, for any loss or injury to the goods which could not have been avoided by the exercise of such care.

Sec. 22. (Goods Must be Kept Separate.) Except as provided in the following section, a warehouseman shall keep the goods so far separate from goods of other depositors, and from other goods of the same depositor for which a separate receipt has been issued, as to permit at all times the identification and re-delivery of the goods deposited.

Sec. 23. (Fungible Goods May be Commingled, if Warehouseman Authorized.) If authorized by agreement or by custom, a warehouseman may mingle fungible goods with other goods of the same kind and grade. In such case the various depositors of the mingled goods shall own the entire mass in common and each depositor shall be entitled to such portion thereof as the amount deposited by him bears to the whole.

Sec. 24. (Liability of Warehouseman to Depositors of Commingled Goods.) The warehouseman shall be severally liable to each depositor for the care and re-delivery of his share of such mass to the same extent and under the same circumstances as if the goods had been kept separate.

Sec. 25. (Attachment or Levy Upon Goods for Which Negotiable Receipt Has Been Issued.) If goods are delivered to a warehouseman by the owner or by a person whose act in conveying the title to them to a purchaser in good faith for value would bind the owner, and a negotiable receipt is issued for them, they can not thereafter, while in the possession of the warehouseman, be attached by garnishment or otherwise, or be levied upon under an execution, unless the receipt be first surrendered to the warehouseman, or its negotiation enjoined. The warehouseman shall in no case be compelled to deliver up the actual possession of the goods until the receipt is surrendered to him or impounded by the court.

Sec. 26. (Creditors' Remedies to Reach Negotiable Receipts.) A creditor whose debtor is the owner of a negotiable receipt shall be entitled to such aid from courts of appropriate jurisdiction, by injunction and otherwise, in attaching such receipt or in satisfying the claim by means thereof as is allowed at law or in equity, in regard to property which cannot readily be attached or levied upon by ordinary legal process.

Sec. 27. (What Claims are Included in the Warehouseman's Lien.) Subject to the provisions of Section 30, a warehouseman shall have a lien on goods deposited or on the proceeds thereof in his hands, for all lawful charges for storage and preservation of the goods; also for all lawful claims for money advanced, interest, insurance, transportation, labor, weighing, coopering and other charges and expenses in relation to such goods; also for all reasonable charges and expenses for notice, and advertisements of sale, and for sale of the goods where default has been made in satisfying the warehouseman's lien.

Sec. 28. (Against What Property the Lien May be Enforced.) Subject to the provisions of Section 30 a warehouseman's lien may be enforced:

(a) Against all goods, whenever deposited, belonging to the person who is liable as debtor for the claims in regard to which the lien is asserted, and

(b) Against all goods belonging to others which have been deposited at any time by the person who is liable as debtor for the claims in regard to which the lien is asserted if such person had been so entrusted with the possession of the goods that a pledge of the same by him at the time of the deposit to one who took the goods in good faith for value would have been valid.

Sec. 29. (How the Lien May be Lost.) A warehouseman loses his lien upon goods:

(a) By surrendering possession thereof, or

(b) By refusing to deliver the goods when a demand is made with which he is bound to comply under the provisions of this act.

Sec. 30. (Negotiable Receipt Must State Charges for Which Lien is Claimed.) If a negotiable receipt is issued for goods, the warehouseman shall have no lien thereon, except for charges for storage of those goods subsequent to the date of the receipt, unless the receipt expressly enumerates other charges for which a lien is claimed. In such case there shall be a lien for the charges enumerated so far as they are within the terms of Section 27, although the amount of the charges so enumerated is not stated in the receipt.

Sec. 31. (Warehouseman Need Not Deliver Until Lien is Satisfied.) A warehouseman having a lien valid against the person demanding the goods may refuse to deliver the goods to him until the lien is satisfied.

Sec. 32. (Warehouseman's Lien Does Not Preclude Other Remedies.) Whether a warehouseman has or has not a lien upon the goods, he is entitled to all remedies allowed by law to a creditor against his debtor, for the collection from the depositor of all charges and advances which the depositor has expressly or impliedly contracted with the warehouseman to pay.

Sec. 33. (Satisfaction of Lien by Sale.) A warehouseman's lien for a claim which has become due may be satisfied as follows:

The warehouseman shall give a written notice to the person on whose account the goods are held, and to any other person known by the warehouseman to claim an interest in the goods. Such notice shall be given by delivery in person or by registered letter addressed to the last known place of business or abode of the person to be notified. The notice shall contain:

(a) An itemized statement of the warehouseman's claim, showing the sum due at the time of the notice and the date or dates when it became due,

(b) A brief description of the goods against which the lien exists,

(c) A demand that the amount of the claim as stated in the notice, and of such further claim as shall accrue, shall be paid on or before a day mentioned, not less than ten days from the delivery of the notice if it is personally delivered, or from the time when the notice should reach its destination, according to the due course of post, if the notice is sent by mail, and

(d) A statement that unless the claim is paid within the time specified the goods will be advertised for sale and sold by auction at a specified time and place.

In accordance with the terms of a notice so given, a sale of the goods by auction may be had to satisfy any valid claim of the warehouseman for which he has a lien on the goods. The sale shall be had in the place where the lien was acquired, or, if such place is manifestly unsuitable for the purpose, at the nearest suitable place. After the time for the payment of the claim specified in the notice to the depositor has elapsed, an advertisement of the sale, describing the goods to be sold, and stating the name of the owner or person on whose account the goods are held, and the time and place of the sale, shall be published once a week for two consecutive weeks in a newspaper published in the place where such sale is to be held. The sale shall not be held less than fifteen days from the time of the first publication. If there is no newspaper published in such place, the advertisement shall be posted at least ten days before such sale in not less than six conspicuous places therein.

From the proceeds of such sale the warehouseman shall satisfy his lien, including the reasonable charges of notice, advertisement, and sale. The balance, if any, of such proceeds shall be held by the warehouseman, and delivered on demand to the person to whom he would have been bound to deliver or justified in delivering the goods.

At any time before the goods are so sold any person claiming a right of property or possession therein may pay the warehouseman the amount necessary to satisfy his lien and to pay the reasonable expenses and liabilities incurred in serving notices and advertising and preparing for the sale up to the time of such payment. The warehouseman shall deliver the goods to the person making such payment if he is a person entitled, under the provisions of this act, to the possession of the goods on payment of charges thereon. Otherwise the warehouseman shall retain possession of the goods according to the terms of the original contract of deposit.

Sec. 34. (Perishable and Hazardous Goods.) If goods are of a perishable nature, or by keeping will deteriorate greatly in value, or by their odor, leakage, inflammability, or explosive nature, will be liable to injure other property, the warehouseman may give such notice to the owner, or to the person in whose name the goods are stored, as is reasonable and possible under the circumstances, to satisfy the lien upon such goods, and to remove them from the warehouse, and in the event of the failure of such person to satisfy the lien and to remove the goods within the time so specified, the warehouseman may sell the goods at public or private sale without advertising. If the warehouseman after a reasonable effort is unable to sell such goods, he may dispose of them in any lawful manner, and shall incur no liability by reason thereof.

The proceeds of any sale made under the term of this section shall be disposed of in the same way as the proceeds of sales made under the terms of the preceding section.

Sec. 35. (Other Methods of Enforcing Liens.) The remedy for enforcing a lien herein provided does not preclude any other remedies allowed by law for the enforcement of a lien against personal property nor bar the right to recover so much of the warehouseman's claim as shall not be paid by the proceeds of the sale of the property.

Sec. 36. (Effect of Sale.) After goods have been lawfully sold to satisfy a warehouseman's lien, or have been lawfully sold or disposed of because of their perishable or hazardous nature, the warehouseman shall not thereafter be liable for failure to deliver the goods to the depositor, or owner of the goods, or to a holder of the receipt given for the goods when they were deposited, even if such receipt be negotiable.

PART III

NEGOTIATION AND TRANSFER OF RECEIPTS

Sec. 37. (Negotiation of Negotiable Receipts by Delivery.) A negotiable receipt may be negotiated by delivery:

(a) Where, by the terms of the receipt, the warehouseman undertakes to deliver the goods to the bearer, or

(b) Where, by the terms of the receipt, the warehouseman undertakes to deliver the goods to the order of a specified person, and such person or a subsequent indorsee of the receipt has indorsed it in blank or to bearer.

Where, by the terms of a negotiable receipt, the goods are deliverable to bearer or where a negotiable receipt has been indorsed in blank or to bearer, any holder may indorse the same to himself or to any other specified person, and in such case the receipt shall thereafter be negotiated only by the indorsement of such indorsee.

Sec. 38. (Negotiation of Negotiable Receipts by Indorsement.) A negotiable receipt may be negotiated by the indorsement of the person to whose order the goods are, by the terms of the receipt, deliverable. Such indorsement may be in blank, to bearer or to a specified person. If indorsed to a specified person, it may be again negotiated by the indorsement of such person in blank, to bearer or to another specified person. Subsequent negotiation may be made in like manner.

Sec. 39. (Transfer of Receipts.) A receipt which is not in such form that it can be negotiated by delivery may be transferred by the holder by delivery to a purchaser or donee.

A non-negotiable receipt cannot be negotiated, and the indorsement of such a receipt gives the transferee no additional right.

Sec. 40. (Who May Negotiate a Receipt.) (A negotiable receipt may be negotiated:

(a) By the owner thereof, or

(b) By any person to whom the possession or custody of the receipt has been entrusted by the owner, if, by the terms of the receipt, the warehouseman undertakes to deliver the goods to the order of the person to whom the possession or custody of the receipt has been entrusted, or if at the time of such entrusting the receipt is in such form that it may be negotiated by delivery.

Sec. 41. (Rights of Person to Whom a Receipt Has Been Negotiated.) A person to whom a negotiable receipt has been duly negotiated acquires thereby:

(a) Such title to the goods as the person negotiating the receipt to him had or had ability to convey to a purchaser in good faith for value, and also such title to the goods as the depositor or person to whose order the goods were to be delivered by the terms of the receipt had or had ability to convey to a purchaser in good faith for value, and

(b) The direct obligation of the warehouseman to hold possession of the goods for him according to the terms of the receipt as fully as if the warehouseman had contracted directly with him.

Sec. 42. (Rights of Person to Whom a Receipt has Been Transferred.) A person to whom a receipt has been transferred but not negotiated, acquires thereby, as against the transferor, the title of the goods, subject to the terms of any agreement with the transferor.

If the receipt is non-negotiable such person also acquires the right to notify the warehouseman of the transfer to him of such receipt, and thereby to acquire the direct obligation of the warehouseman to hold possession of the goods for him according to the terms of the receipt.

Prior to the notification of the warehouseman by the transferor or transferee of a non-negotiable receipt, the title of the transferee to the goods and the right to acquire the obligation of the warehouseman may be defeated by the levy of an attachment or execution upon the goods by a creditor of the transferor, or by a notification to the warehouseman by the transferor or a subsequent purchaser from the transferor of a subsequent sale of the goods by the transferor.

Sec. 43. (Transfer of Negotiable Receipt Without Indorsement.) Where a negotiable receipt is transferred for value by delivery, and the indorsement of the transferor is essential for negotiation, the transferee acquires a right against the transferor to compel him to indorse the receipt, unless a contrary intention appears. The negotiation shall take effect as of the time when the indorsement is actually made.

Sec. 44. (Warranties on Sale of Receipt.) A person who for value negotiates or transfers a receipt by indorsement or delivery, including one who assigns for value a claim secured by a receipt, unless a contrary intention appears, warrants:

(a) That the receipt is genuine,

(b) That he has a legal right to negotiate or transfer it,

(c) That he has knowledge of no fact which would impair the validity or worth of the receipt, and

(d) That he has a right to transfer the title to the goods and that the goods are merchantable or fit for a particular purpose whenever such warranties would have been implied, if the contract of the parties had been to transfer without a receipt the goods represented thereby.

Sec. 45. (Indorser not a Guarantor.) The indorsement of a receipt shall not make the indorser liable for any failure on the part of the warehouseman or previous indorsers of the receipt to fulfil their respective obligations.

Sec. 46. (No Warranty Implied From Accepting Payment of a Debt.) A mortgagee, pledgee or holder for security of a receipt who in good faith demands or receives payment of the debt for which such receipt is security, whether from a party to a draft drawn for such debt or from any other person, shall not by so doing be deemed to represent or to warrant the genuineness of such receipt or the quantity or quality of the goods therein described.

Sec. 47. (When Negotiations Not Impaired by Fraud, Mistake, or Duress.) The validity of the negotiation of a receipt is not impaired by the fact that such negotiation was a breach of duty on the part of the person making the negotiation, or by the fact that the owner of the receipt was induced by fraud, mistake, or duress to entrust the possession or custody of the receipt to such person, if the person to whom the receipt was negotiated, or a person to whom the receipt was subsequently negotiated, paid value therefor, without notice of the breach of duty, or fraud, mistake of duress.

Sec. 48. (Subsequent Negotiation.) Where a person having sold, mortgaged, or pledged goods which are in a warehouse and for which a negotiable receipt has been issued, or having sold, mortgaged, or pledged the negotiable receipt representing such goods, continues in possession of the negotiable receipt, the subsequent negotiation thereof by that person under any sale, or other disposition thereof to any person receiving the same in good faith, for value and without notice of the previous sale, mortgage or pledge, shall have the same effect as if the first purchaser of the goods or receipt had expressly authorized the subsequent negotiation.

Sec. 49. (Negotiation Defeats Vendor's Lien.) Where a negotiable receipt has been issued for goods, no seller's lien or right of stoppage *in transitu* shall defeat the rights of any purchaser for value in good faith to whom such receipt has been negotiated, whether such negotiation be prior or subsequent to the notification to the warehouseman who issued such receipt of the seller's claim to a lien or right of stoppage *in transitu*. Nor shall the warehouseman be obliged to deliver or justified in delivering the goods to an unpaid seller unless the receipt is first surrendered for cancellation.

PART IV

CRIMINAL OFFENSES

Sec. 50. (Issue of Receipt for Goods Not Received.) A warehouseman, or any officer, agent, or servant of a warehouseman, who issues or aids in issuing a receipt knowing that the goods for which such receipt is issued have not been actually received by such warehouseman, or are not under his actual control at the time of issuing such receipt, shall be guilty of a crime, and upon conviction shall be punished for each offense by imprisonment not exceeding five years, or by a fine not exceeding five thousand dollars, or by both.

Sec. 51. (Issue of Receipt Containing False Statement.) A warehouseman, or any officer, agent or servant of a warehouseman, who fraudulently issues or aids in fraudulently issuing a receipt for goods knowing that it contains any false statement, shall be guilty of a crime, and upon conviction shall be punished for each offense by imprisonment not exceeding one year, or by a fine not exceeding one thousand dollars, or by both.

Sec. 52. (Issue of Duplicate Receipts Not so Marked.) A warehouseman, or any officer, agent, or servant of a warehouseman, who issues or aids in issuing a duplicate or additional negotiable receipt for goods knowing that a former negotiable receipt for the same goods or any part of them is outstanding and uncanceled, without plainly placing upon the face thereof the word "Duplicate" except in the case of a lost or destroyed receipt after proceedings as provided for in Section 14, shall be guilty of a crime, and upon conviction shall be punished for each offense by imprisonment not exceeding five years, or by a fine not exceeding five thousand dollars, or by both.

Sec. 53. (Issue for Warehouseman's Goods of Receipts Which do Not State That Fact.) Where there are deposited with or held by a warehouseman goods of which he is owner, either solely or jointly or in common with others, such warehouseman, or any of his officers, agents, or servants who, knowing this ownership, issues or aids in issuing a negotiable receipt for such goods which does not state such ownership, shall be guilty of a crime, and upon conviction shall be punished for each offense by imprisonment not exceeding one year, or by a fine not exceeding one thousand dollars, or by both.

Sec. 54. (Delivery of Goods Without Obtaining Negotiable Receipt.) A warehouseman, or any officer, agent, or servant of a warehouseman who delivers goods out of the possession of such warehouseman, knowing that a negotiable receipt the negotiation of which would transfer the right to the possession of such goods is outstanding and uncanceled, without obtaining the possession of such receipt at or before the time of such delivery, shall, except in the cases provided for in Sections 14 and 36, be found guilty of a crime, and upon conviction shall be punished for each offense by imprisonment not exceeding one year, or by a fine not exceeding one thousand dollars, or by both.

Sec. 55. (Negotiation of Receipt for Mortgaged Goods.) Any person who deposits goods to which he has not title, or upon which there is a lien or mortgage, and who takes for such goods a negotiable receipt which he afterwards negotiates for value with intent to deceive and without disclosing his want of title or the existence of the lien or mortgage shall be guilty of a crime, and upon conviction shall be punished for each offense by imprisonment not exceeding one year, or by a fine not exceeding one thousand dollars, or by both.

PART V

INTERPRETATION

Sec. 56. (Cases Not Provided for in Act.) In any case not provided for in this act, the rules of law and equity, including the law merchant, and in particular the rules relating to the law of principal and agent and to the effect of fraud, misrepresentation, duress or coercion, mistake, bankruptcy, or other invalidating cause, shall govern.

Sec. 57. (Interpretation shall give Effect to Purpose of Uniformity.) This act shall be so interpreted and construed as to effectuate its general purpose to make uniform the law of those states which enact it.

Sec. 58. (Definitions.) (1) In this act, unless the context or subject matter otherwise requires:

"Action" includes counter claim, set-off, and suit in equity.

"Delivery" means voluntary transfer of possession from one person to another.

"Fungible goods" means goods of which any unit is, from its nature or by mercantile custom, treated as the equivalent of any other unit.

"Goods" means chattels or merchandise in storage, or which has been or is about to be stored.

"Holder" of a receipt means a person who has both actual possession of such receipt and a right of property therein.

"Order" means an order by indorsement on the receipt.

"Owner" does not include mortgagee or pledgee.

"Person" includes a corporation or partnership or two or more persons having a joint or common interest.

To "purchase" includes to take as mortgagee or as pledgee.

"Purchaser" includes mortgagee and pledgee.

"Receipt" means a warehouse receipt.

"Value" is any consideration sufficient to support a simple contract. An antecedent or pre-existing obligation, whether for money or not, constitutes value where a receipt is taken either in satisfaction thereof or as security therefor.

"Warehouseman" means a person lawfully engaged in the business of storing goods for profit.

(2) A thing is done "in good faith" within the meaning of this act, when it is in fact done honestly, whether it be done negligently or not.

Sec. 59. (Act Does Not Apply to Existing Receipts.) The provisions of this act do not apply to receipts made and delivered prior to the taking effect of this act.

Sec. 60. (Inconsistent Legislation Repealed.) All acts or parts of acts inconsistent with this act are hereby repealed.

Sec. 61. (Time when the Act Takes Effect.) This act shall take effect on the .... day of ...., one thousand nine hundred and ....

Sec. 62. (Name of Act.) This act may be cited as the Uniform Warehouse Receipts Act.

AMENDMENTS TO THE UNIFORM WAREHOUSE RECEIPTS ACT[1]

1. Section 40 of the Uniform Warehouse Receipts Act is hereby amended by striking out all of the section which follows the word "negotiated" and by substituting therefor the following:

> "by any person in possession of the same, however such possession may have been acquired if, by the terms of the receipt, the warehouseman undertakes

[1] These amendments were recommended in order to harmonize certain provisions of the original Act with the Uniform Bills of Lading Act and with the Uniform Stock Transfer Act. States which have adopted the amendments and the dates of adoption are as follows: Alabama (1923); California (1923); Colorado (1923); Idaho (1925); Louisiana (1932); Michigan (1933); Nevada (1927); New York (1924); North Carolina (1931); Ohio (1925); Utah (1929); Vermont (1923); Wisconsin (1925).

to deliver the goods to the order of such person, or if at the time of negotiation the receipt is in such form that it may be negotiated by delivery."

so that the section shall read:

"Section 40. (Who May Negotiate a Receipt.) A negotiable receipt may be negotiated by any person in possession of the same, however such possession may have been acquired if, by the terms of the receipt, the warehouseman undertakes to deliver the goods to the order of such person, or if at the time of negotiation the receipt is in such form that it may be negotiated by delivery."

2. Section 47 of the Uniform Warehouse Receipts Act is hereby amended by striking out the words "induced by fraud, mistake or duress, to intrust the possession or custody of the receipt to such person," and by substituting therefor the words "deprived of the possession of the same by loss, theft, fraud, accident, mistake, duress, or conversion"; and also by striking out the words "without notice of the breach of duty, or fraud, mistake or duress," and substituting therefor the words "in good faith, without notice of the breach of duty, or loss, theft, fraud, accident, mistake, duress, or conversion," so that the section shall read:

"Section 47. (When Negotiation Not Impaired by Fraud, Mistake, or Duress.) The validity of the negotiation of a receipt is not impaired by the fact that such negotiation was a breach of duty on the part of the person making the negotiation, or by the fact that the owner of the receipt was deprived of the possession of the same by loss, theft, fraud, accident, mistake, duress, or conversion, if the person to whom the receipt was negotiated, or the person to whom the receipt was subsequently negotiated, paid value therefor, in good faith, without notice of the breach of duty, or loss, theft, fraud, accident, mistake, duress, or conversion."

UNIFORM TRUST RECEIPTS ACT

An Act With Reference to Trust Receipts and Pledges of Personal Property Unaccompanied by Possession in the Pledgee and to Make Uniform the Law With Reference Thereto [1]

Section 1. (Definitions.) In this act, unless the context or subject matter otherwise requires:

"Buyer in the ordinary course of trade" means a person to whom goods are sold and delivered for new value and who acts in good faith and without actual knowledge of any limitation on the trustee's liberty of sale, including one who takes by conditional sale or under a preexisting mercantile contract with the trustee to buy the goods delivered, or like goods, for cash or on credit. "Buyer in the ordinary course of trade" does not include a pledgee, a mortgagee, a lienor, or a transferee in bulk.

"Document" means any document of title to goods.

"Entruster" means the person who has or directly or by agent takes a security interest in goods, documents or instruments under a trust receipt transaction,

[1] Approved and recommended for enactment by the Commissioners on Uniform State Laws in 1933. States which have adopted the Act and dates of adoption are as follows: California (1935); Illinois (1935); Indiana (1935); New York (1934); Oregon (1935).

and any successor in interest of such person. A person in the business of selling goods or instruments for profit, who at the outset of the transaction has, as against the buyer, general property in such goods or instruments, and who sells the same to the buyer on credit, retaining title or other security interest under a purchase money mortgage or conditional sales contract or otherwise, is excluded.

"Goods" means any chattels personal other than: money, things in action, or things so affixed to land as to become a part thereof.

"Instrument" means

(a) any negotiable instrument as defined in the Uniform Negotiable Instruments Law and amendments thereto, or

(b) any certificate of stock, or bond or debenture for the payment of money issued by a public or private corporation as part of a series, or

(c) any interim, deposit, or participation certificate or receipt, or other credit or investment instrument of a sort marketed in the ordinary course of business or finance, of which the trustee, after the trust receipt transaction, appears by virtue of possession and the face of the instrument to be the owner. "Instrument" does not include any document of title to goods.

"Lien creditor" means any creditor who has acquired a specific lien on the goods, documents or instruments by attachment, levy, or by any other similar operation of law of judicial process, including a destraining landlord.

"New value" includes new advances or loans made, or new obligation incurred, or the release or surrender of a valid and existing security interest, or the release of a claim to proceeds under Section 10; but "new value" shall not be construed to include extensions or renewals of existing obligations of the trustee, nor obligations substituted for such existing obligations.

"Person" means, as the case may be, an individual, trustee, receiver or other fiduciary, partnership, corporation, business trust, or other association, and two or more persons having a joint or common interest.

"Possession," as used in this act with reference to possession taken or retained by the entruster, means actual possession of goods, documents or intruments, or, in the case of goods, such constructive possession as, by means of tags or signs or other outward marks placed and remaining in conspicuous places, may reasonably be expected in fact to indicate to the third party in question that the entruster has control over or interest in the goods.

"Purchase" means taking by sale, conditional sale, lease, mortgage, or pledge, legal or equitable.

"Purchaser" means any person taking by purchase. A pledgee, mortgagee or other claimant of a security interest created by contract is, insofar as concerns his specific security, a purchaser and not a creditor.

"Security interest" means a property interest in goods, documents or instruments, limited in extent to securing performance of some obligation of the trustee or of some third person to the entruster, and includes the interest of a pledgee, and title, whether or not expressed to be absolute, whenever such title is in substance taken or retained for security only.

"Transferee in bulk" means a mortgagee or a pledgee or a buyer of the trustee's business substantially as a whole.

"Trustee" means the person having or taking possession of goods, documents or instruments under a trust receipt transaction, and any successor in interest of such person. The use of the word "Trustee" herein shall not be interpreted or construed to imply the existence of a trust or any right or duty of a trustee in the sense of equity jurisprudence other than as provided by this act.

"Value" means any consideration sufficient to support a simple contract. An antecedent or preexisting claim, whether for money or not, and whether against the transferor or against another person, constitutes value where goods, documents or instruments are taken either in satisfaction thereof or as security therefor.

Section 2. (What Constitutes Trust Receipt Transaction and Trust Receipt.)

1. (A trust receipt transaction within the meaning of this act is any transaction to which an entruster and a trustee are parties, for one of the purposes set forth in Subsection 3, whereby

(a) the entruster or any third person delivers to the trustee goods, documents or instruments in which the entruster (i) prior to the transaction has, or for new value (ii) by the transaction acquires or (iii) as the result thereof is to acquire promptly, a security interest; or

(b) the entruster gives new value in reliance upon the transfer by the trustee to such entruster of a security interest in instruments[1] which are actually exhibited to such entruster, or to his agent in that behalf, at a place of business of either entruster or agent, but possession of which is retained by the trustee; provided that the delivery under paragraph (a) or the giving of new value under paragraph (b) either

(i) be against the signing and delivery by the trustee of a writing designating the goods, documents or instruments concerned, and reciting that a security interest therein remains in or will remain in, or has passed to or will pass to, the entruster, or

(ii) be pursuant to a prior or concurrent written and signed agreement of the trustee to give such a writing.

The security interest of the entruster may be derived from the trustee or from any other person, and by pledge or by transfer of title or otherwise.

If the trustee's rights in the goods, documents or instruments are subject to a prior trust receipt transaction, or to a prior equitable pledge, Section 9 and Section 3, respectively, of this act, determine the priorities.

2. A writing such as is described in Subsection 1, paragraph (i), signed by the trustee, and given in or pursuant to such a transaction, is designated in this act as a "trust receipt." No further formality of execution or authentication shall be necessary to the validity of a trust receipt.

3. A transaction shall not be deemed a trust receipt transaction unless the possession of the trustee thereunder is for a purpose substantially equivalent to any one of the following:

(a) in the case of goods, documents or instruments, for the purpose of selling or exchanging them, or of procuring their sale or exchange; or

(b) in the case of goods or documents, for the purpose of manufacturing or processing the goods delivered or covered by the documents, with the purpose of ultimate sale, or for the purpose of loading, unloading, storing, shipping, transshipping or otherwise dealing with them in a manner preliminary to or necessary to their sale; or

(c) in the case of instruments, for the purpose of delivering them to a principal, under whom the trustee is holding them, or for consummation of some transaction involving delivery to a depositary or registrar, or for their presentation, collection, or renewal.

Section 3. (Attempted Creation or Continuance of Pledge Without Delivery or Retention of Possession.)

[1] The words "or documents" were inadvertently omitted here in the draft, as approved.

1. An attempted pledge or agreement to pledge not accompanied by delivery of possession, which does not fulfill the requirements of a trust receipt transaction, shall be valid as against creditors of the pledgor only as follows:

(a) to the extent that new value is given by the pledgee in reliance thereon, such pledge or agreement to pledge shall be valid as against all creditors with or without notice, for ten days from the time the new value is given;

(b) to the extent that the value given by the pledgee is not new value, and in the case of new value after the lapse of ten days from the giving thereof, the pledge shall have validity as against lien creditors without notice, who become such as prescribed in Section 8, only as of the time the pledgee takes possession, and without relation back.

2. Purchasers (including entrusters) for value and without notice of the pledgee's interest shall take free of any such pledge or agreement to pledge unless, prior to the purchase, it has been perfected by possession taken.

3. Where, under circumstances not constituting a trust receipt transaction, a person, for a temporary and limited purpose, delivers goods, documents, or instruments, in which he holds a pledgee's or other security interest, to the person holding the beneficial interest therein, the transaction has like effect with a purported pledge for new value under this section.

Section 4. (Contract to Give Trust Receipt.)

1. A contract to give a trust receipt, if in writing and signed by the trustee, shall, with reference to goods, documents or instruments thereafter delivered by the entruster to the trustee in reliance on such contract, be equivalent in all respects to a trust receipt.

2. Such a contract shall as to such goods, documents, or instruments be specifically enforceable against the trustee; but this subsection shall not enlarge the scope of the entruster's rights against creditors of the trustee as limited by this act.

Section 5. (Validity Between the Parties.) Between the entruster and the trustee the terms of the trust receipt shall, save as otherwise provided by this act, be valid and enforceable. But no provision for forfeiture of the trustee's interest shall be valid except as provided in Subsection 5 of Section 6.

Section 6. (Repossession, and Entruster's Rights on Default.)

1. The entruster shall be entitled as against the trustee to possession of the goods, documents or instruments on default, and as may be otherwise specified in the trust receipt.

2. An entruster entitled to possession under the terms of the trust receipt or of Subsection 1 may take such possession without legal process, whenever that is possible without breach of the peace.

3. (a) After possession taken, the entruster shall, subject to subdivision (b) and Subsection 5, hold such goods, documents or instruments with the rights and duties of a pledgee.

(b) An entruster in possession may, on or after default, give notice to the trustee of intention to sell, and may, not less than five days after the serving or sending of such notice, sell the goods, documents or instruments for the trustee's account, at public or private sale, and may at a public sale himself become a purchaser. The proceeds of any such sale, whether public or private, shall be applied (i) to the payment of the expenses thereof, (ii) to the payment of the expenses of re-taking, keeping and storing the goods, documents, or instruments, (iii) to the satisfaction of the trustee's indebtedness. The trustee shall receive any surplus and shall be liable to the entruster for any deficiency. Notice of sale shall be deemed sufficiently given if in writing, and either (i) personally served on the trustee, or (ii) sent by postpaid ordinary mail to the trustee's last known business address.

(c) A purchaser in good faith and for value from an entruster in possession takes free of the trustee's interest, even in a case in which the entruster is liable to the trustee for conversion.

4. Surrender of the trustee's interest to the entruster shall be valid, on any terms upon which the trustee and the entruster may, after default, agree.

5. As to articles manufactured by style or model, the terms of the trust receipt may provide for forfeiture of the trustee's interest, at the election of the entruster, in the event of the trustee's default, against cancellation of the trustee's then remaining indebtedness; provided that in the case of the original maturity of such an indebtedness there must be cancelled not less than 80 per cent of the purchase price to the trustee, or of the original indebtedness, whichever is greater; or, in the case of a first renewal, not less than 70 per cent, or, in the case of a second or further renewal, not less than 60 per cent.

Section 7. (General Effect of Entruster's Filing or Taking Possession.)

1. (a) If the entruster within the period of thirty days specified in subsection 1 of Section 8 files as in this act provided, such filing shall be effective to preserve his security interest in documents or goods against all persons, save as otherwise provided by Sections 8, 9, 10, 11, 14 and 15 of this act.

(b) Filing after the lapse of the said period shall be valid; but in such event, save as provided in subdivision 2(b) of Section 9, the entruster's security interest shall be deemed to be created by the trustee as of the time of such filing, without relation back, as against all persons not having notice of such interest.

2. The taking of possession by the entruster shall, so long as such possession is retained, have the effect of filing, in the case of goods or documents; and of notice of the entruster's security interest to all persons, in the case of instruments.

Section 8. (Validity Against Creditors.)

1. The entruster's security interest in goods, documents or instruments under the written terms of a trust receipt transaction, shall without any filing be valid as against all creditors of the trustee, with or without notice, for thirty days after delivery of the goods, documents or instruments to the trustee, and thereafter except as in this act otherwise provided.

But where the trustee at the time of the trust receipt transaction has and retains instruments,[1] the thirty days shall be reckoned from the time such instruments are actually shown to the entruster, or from the time that the entruster gives new value under the transaction, whichever is prior.

2. Save as provided in Subsection 1, the entruster's security interest shall be void as against lien creditors who become such after such thirty day period and without notice of such interest and before filing.

(a) Where a creditor secures the issuance of process which within a reasonable time after such issuance results in attachment of or levy on the goods, he is deemed to have become a lien creditor as of the date of the issuance of the process.

(b) Unless prior to the acquisition of notice by all creditors filing has occurred or possession has been taken by the entruster, (i) an assignee for the benefit of creditors, from the time of assignment, or (ii) a receiver in equity from the time of his appointment, or (iii) a trustee in bankruptcy or judicial insolvency proceedings from the time of filing of the petition in bankruptcy or

[1] The words "or documents" were inadvertently omitted here in the draft, as approved.

judicial insolvency by or against the trustee, shall, on behalf of all creditors, stand in the position of a lien creditor without notice, without reference to whether he personally has or has not, in fact, notice of the entruster's interest.

Section 9. (Limitations on Entruster's Protection Against Purchasers.)

1. (Purchasers of Negotiable Documents or Instruments.)

(a) Nothing in this act shall limit the rights of purchasers in good faith and for value from the trustee of negotiable instruments or negotiable documents, and purchasers taking from the trustee for value, in good faith, and by transfer in the customary manner instruments in such form as are by common practice purchased and sold as if negotiable, shall hold such instruments free of the entruster's interest; and filing under this act shall not be deemed to constitute notice of the entruster's interest to purchasers in good faith and for value of such documents or instruments, other than transferees in bulk.

(b) The entrusting (directly, by agent, or through the intervention of a third person) of goods, documents or instruments by an entruster to a trustee, under a trust receipt transaction or a transaction falling within Section 3 of this act, shall be equivalent to the like entrusting of any documents or instruments which the trustee may procure in substitution, or which represent the same goods or instruments or the proceeds thereof, and which the trustee negotiates to a purchaser in good faith and for value.

2. Where a purchaser from the trustee is not protected under Subsection 1 hereof, the following rules shall govern:

(a) (Sales by trustee in the ordinary course of trade.)

(i) Where the trustee, under the trust receipt transaction, has liberty of sale and sells to a buyer in the ordinary course of trade, whether before or after the expiration of the thirty day period specified in Subsection 1 of Section 8 of this act, and whether or not filing has taken place, such buyer takes free of the entruster's security interest in the goods so sold, and no filing shall constitute notice of the entruster's security interest to such a buyer.

(ii) No limitation placed by the entruster on the liberty of sale granted to the trustee shall affect a buyer in the ordinary course of trade, unless the limitation is actually known to the latter.

(b) (Purchasers other than buyers in the ordinary course of trade.)

In the absence of filing, the entruster's security interest in goods shall be valid, as against purchasers, save as provided in this Section; but any purchaser, not a buyer in the ordinary course of trade, who, in good faith and without notice of the entruster's security interest and before filing, either (i) gives new value before the expiration of the thirty day period specified in Subsection 1 of Section 8, or (ii) gives value after said period, and who in either event before filing also obtains delivery of goods from a trustee shall hold the subject matter of his purchase free of the entruster's security interest; but a transferee in bulk can take only under (ii) of this subdivision (b).

(c) (Liberty of Sale.) If the entruster consents to the placing of goods subject to a trust receipt transaction in the trustee's stock in trade or in his sales or exhibition rooms, or allows such goods to be so placed or kept, such consent or allowance shall have like effect as granting the trustee liberty of sale.

3. As to all cases covered by this section the purchase of goods, documents or instruments on credit shall constitute a purchase for new value, but the entruster shall be entitled to any debt owing to the trustee and any security therefor, by reason of such purchase; except that the entruster's right shall be subject to any set-off or defense valid against the trustee and accruing before the purchaser has actual notice of the entruster's interest.

Section 10. (Entruster's Right to Proceeds.) Where, under the terms of the trust receipt transaction, the trustee has no liberty of sale or other disposition, or, having liberty of sale or other disposition, is to account to the entruster for the proceeds of any disposition of the goods, documents or instruments, the entruster shall be entitled, to the extent to which and as against all classes of persons as to whom his security interest was valid at the time of disposition by the trustee, as follows:

(a) to the debts described in Section 9 (3); and also

(b) to any proceeds or the value of any proceeds (whether such proceeds are identifiable or not) of the goods, documents or instruments, if said proceeds were received by the trustee within ten days prior to either application for appointment of a receiver of the trustee, or the filing of a petition in bankruptcy or judicial insolvency proceedings by or against the trustee, or demand made by the entruster for prompt accounting; and to a priority to the amount of such proceeds or value; and also

(c) to any other proceeds of the goods, documents or instruments which are identifiable, unless the provision for accounting has been waived by the entruster by words or conduct; and knowledge by the entruster of the existence of proceeds, without demand for accounting made within ten days from such knowledge, shall be deemed such a waiver.

Section 11. (Liens in Course of Business Good Against Entruster.) Specific liens arising out of contractual acts of the trustee with reference to the processing, warehousing, shipping or otherwise dealing with specific goods in the usual course of the trustee's business preparatory to their sale shall attach against the interest of the entruster in said goods as well as against the interest of the trustee, whether or not filing has occurred under this act; but this section shall not obligate the entruster personally for any debt secured by such lien; nor shall it be construed to include the lien of a landlord.

Section 12. (Entruster not Responsible on Sale by Trustee.) An entruster holding a security interest shall not, merely by virtue of such interest or of his having given the trustee liberty of sale or other disposition, be responsible as principal or as vendor under any sale or contract to sell made by the trustee.

Section 13. (Filing and Refiling Concerning Trust Receipt Transactions Covering Documents or Goods.)

1. Any entruster undertaking or contemplating trust receipt transactions with reference to documents or goods is entitled to file with the [Secretary of State] a statement, signed by the entruster and the trustee, containing:

(a) a designation of the entruster and the trustee, and of the chief place of business of each within this state, if any; and if the entruster has no place of business within the state, a designation of his chief place of business outside the state; and

(b) a statement that the entruster is engaged, or expects to be engaged, in financing under trust receipt transactions the acquistion of goods by the trustee; and

(c) a description of the kind or kinds of goods covered or to be covered by such financing.

2. The following form of statement (or any other form of statement containing substantially the same information) shall suffice for the purposes of this act:

"*Statement of Trust Receipt Financing*

"The entruster, ... whose chief place of business within this state is at ...., [or who has no place of business within this state and whose chief place of business outside this state is at ....,] is or expects to be engaged in financing under trust receipt transactions the acquisition by the trustee, ... whose chief place of business within this state is at .... of goods of the following description: [coffee, silk, automobiles, or the like.]

(Signed) .... Entruster
(Signed) Trustee."

3. It shall be the duty of the filing officer to mark each statement filed with a consecutive file number, and with the date and hour of filing, and to keep such statement in a separate file; and to note and index the filing in a suitable index, indexed according to the name of the trustee and containing a notation of the trustee's chief place of business as given in the statement. The fee for such filing shall be one dollar.

4. Presentation for filing of the statement described in subsection 1, and payment of the filing fee, shall constitute filing under this act, in favor of the entruster, as to any documents or goods falling within the description in the statement which are within one year from the date of such filing, or have been, within thirty days previous to such filing, the subject-matter of a trust receipt transaction between the entruster and the trustee.

5. At any time before expiration of the validity of the filing, as specified in subsection 4, a like statement, or an affidavit by the entruster alone, setting out the information required by subsection 1, may be filed in like manner as the original filing. Any filing of such further statement or affidavit shall be valid in like manner and for like period as an original filing, and shall also continue the rank of the entruster's existing security interest as against all junior interests. It shall be the duty of the filing officer to mark, file and index the further statement or affidavit in like manner as the original.

Section 14. (Limitations on Extent of Obligation Secured.) As against purchasers and creditors, the entruster's security interest may extend to any obligation for which the goods, documents or instruments were security before the trust receipt transaction, and to any new value given or agreed to be given as a part of such transaction; but not, otherwise, to secure past indebtedness of the trustee; nor shall the obligation secured under any trust receipt transaction extend to obligations of the trustee to be subsequently created.

Section 15. (Act Not Applicable to Certain Transactions.)

This act shall not apply to single transactions of legal or equitable pledge, not constituting a course of business, whether such transactions be unaccompanied by delivery of possession, or involve constructive delivery, or delivery and redelivery, actual or constructive, so far as such transactions involve only an entruster who is an individual natural person, and a trustee entrusted as a fiduciary with handling investments or finances of the entruster; nor shall it apply to transactions of bailment or consignment in which the title of the bailor or consignor is not retained to secure an indebtedness to him of the bailee or consignee.

Section 16. (Election Among Filing Statutes.) As to any transaction falling within the provisions both of this act and of any other act requiring filing or recording, the entruster shall not be required to comply with both, but by complying with the provisions of either at his election may have the protection given by the act complied with; except that buyers in the ordinary course of trade as described in subsection 2 of Section 9, and lienors as described in Section 11, shall be protected as therein provided, although the compliance of the entruster be with the filing or recording requirements of another act.

Section 17. (Cases Not Provided For.) In any case not provided for in this act the rules of law and equity, including the law merchant, shall continue to apply to trust receipt transactions and purported pledge transactions not accompanied by delivery of possession.

Section 18. (Uniformity of Interpretation.) This act shall be so interpreted and construed as to effectuate its general purpose to make uniform the law of the states which enact it.

Section 19. (Constitutionality.) If any provision of this act or the application thereof to any person or circumstances is held invalid, such invalidity shall not affect other provisions or applications of the act which can be given effect without the invalid provision or application, and to this end the provisions of this act are declared to be severable.

Section 20. (Short Title.) This act may be cited as the Uniform Trust Receipts Act.

Section 21. (Inconsistent Laws Repealed.) [Except so far as they are applicable to trust receipt and pledge transactions entered into before this act takes effect, the following acts shall be and hereby are repealed . . . ; and] all acts or parts of acts inconsistent with this act are hereby repealed.

Section 22. (Time and Manner of Taking Effect.) This act shall take effect . . .

UNIFORM CUSTOMS AND PRACTICES FOR COMMERCIAL DOCUMENTARY CREDITS [1]

A. General Provisions

(*a*) The provisions, definitions, interpretations, *et cetera*, contained in the following Articles are to be understood as uniform directions in regard to Commercial Documentary Credits, applicable exclusively when other express and previously agreed arrangements between the parties do not intervene, and when such contrary agreements are not expressed in the conditions of credits or of Commercial Letters of Credit.

(*b*) It is essential that instructions regarding papers or documents required be complete and precise. If, however, this should not be the case and Banks find themselves obliged to pay against documents without these being particularly specified, they will refer to Section C of the present text. It is also necessary that the use of technical terms should not give rise to confusion owing to different interpretation.

(*c*) The beneficiary of a credit can in no case avail himself of the legal relations existing between banks, or between the Bank of the principal (purchaser) and the latter.

Article 1. Commercial Documentary Credits are essentially distinct transactions from sales contracts, on which they may be based, with which Banks are not concerned.

[1] The rules, regulations, and definitions here set forth were agreed upon at the Vienna Congress of the International Chamber of Commerce in 1933. They have been adopted as standard practice by voluntary agreement of the banks of Belgium, France, Germany, Italy, the Netherlands, Rumania, Switzerland, and the United States, becoming effective in this country from October 1, 1938.

Article 2. Commercial Documentary Credits may be either: (*a*) revocable, or (*b*) irrevocable.

Article 3. All credits, unless clearly stipulated as irrevocable, are considered revocable, even though an expiry date is specified.

Article 4. Revocable credits are not legally binding undertakings between Banks and beneficiaries. Such credits may be modified or cancelled at any moment without the Bank being obliged to notify the beneficiary. When a credit of this nature has been transmitted to a correspondent or to a branch, its modifications or cancellation can take effect only upon receipt of notification by the said correspondent or branch with which the credit has been made available.

Article 5. Irrevocable credits are definite undertakings by an opening Bank in favor of the beneficiary. Such undertakings can neither be modified nor cancelled without the agreement of all concerned.

Article 6. Irrevocable credits may be notified to the beneficiary through an advising Bank without responsibility on the latter's part when it has merely been asked to notify the beneficiary.

Article 7. An advising Bank may be called upon by the opening Bank to confirm an irrevocable credit. In this case, the advising Bank makes itself responsible to the beneficiary as from the date on which it gives confirmation.

Article 8. In the event of the period of validity of the credit not being stipulated in an order to open, to notify or to confirm an irrevocable credit, the beneficiary will be advised of the credit for information only, and this implies no responsibility on the part of the correspondent or advising Bank. The credit will only be irrevocably opened or notified or confirmed later when the correspondent or the advising Bank have received supplementary details on the duration of validity.

Article 9. When an irrevocable credit is opened in the form of a Commercial Letter of Credit, the Letter of Credit itself must include notification of the opening of an irrevocable credit and constitute the definite engagement by the issuing Bank towards the beneficiary and holder in good faith to honor all drafts issued by virtue of and in conformity with the clauses and conditions contained in the document. This document may be transmitted and/or notified by another Bank without engagement for the latter.

When a correspondent is instructed by cable or telegram to notify such Letter of Credit, the issuing Bank must send the original of the said Letter of Credit to the said correspondent, if it is intended to put the document itself into circulation; if any other procedure were followed, the issuing Bank would be responsible for all consequences which may result therefrom.

All the other provisions applicable to Commercial Documentary Credits are also applicable to the Commercial Letter of Credit.

B. Liability

Article 10. Banks must examine all documents and papers with care so as to ascertain that on their face they appear to be in order.

Payment against documents in accordance with the terms and conditions of a credit by a Bank instructed to do so binds its principal to take them up.

Article 11. Banks assume no liability or responsibility for the form, sufficiency, correctness, genuineness, falsification or legal effect of any documents or papers, or for the description, quantity, weight, quality, condition, packing delivery or value of goods represented thereby, or for the general and/or particular conditions stipulated in the documents, or for the good faith or acts of the consigner or any other person whomsoever, or for the solvency, standing, etc., of the carriers or insurers of the goods.

Article 12. Banks assume no liability or responsibility for the consequences arising out of delay and/or loss in transit of cables or telegrams, letters and/or documents, or for delay, mutilation or other errors in the transmission of cables or telegrams, or for errors in translation or interpretation of technical terms, and Banks reserve the right to transmit credit terms without translating them.

Article 13. Banks assume no liability or responsibility for consequences arising out of the interruption of their business either by a decision of a public authority, or by strikes, lockouts, riots, wars, acts of God or other causes beyond their control. On credits expiring during such interruption of business, Banks will be able to make no settlement after expiration, except on specific instructions from their principal.

Article 14. Banks utilizing the services of another Bank assume no liability or responsibility towards their principal (unless they themselves are at fault) should the instructions they transmit not be carried out exactly even if they have themselves taken the initiative in the choice of their correspondent. Banks consider themselves authorized to make provision for credits with the Banks whose services they utilize, for the account and at the risk of the principal, and without any responsibility.

The principal (purchaser) is responsible to the Banks for all obligations imposed upon the latter by foreign laws and customs.

C. Documents

Article 15. Unless otherwise instructed, Banks consider themselves authorized to honor the documents which they judge necessary, if presented in a suitable form, viz.:

(*a*) In maritime traffic: Full set of Sea or Ocean Bills of Lading in negotiable and transferable form; Transferable Policy or Certificate of Insurance; Invoice.

(*b*) In inland traffic: Complete set of negotiable and transferable Inland Waterway Bills of Lading, or Inland Waterway Consignment Note, or Railway Consignment Note, or Counterfoil Waybill; Transferable Policy or Certificate of Insurance; Invoice.

(*c*) In postal traffic: Postal Receipt; Transferable Policy or Certificate of Insurance; Invoice.

Banks have the right to waive insurance papers, if the beneficiary furnishes proof satisfactory to them that the insurance is covered by the principal or the consignee of the goods.

Article 16. The date of the bill of lading, or date indicated on the reception stamp of the Railway or Inland Waterway Consignment Notes, Counterfoil Waybills, Postal Receipts or other shipping documents will be taken in each case to be the date of shipment of the goods.

Article 17. Proof of payment of the freight will be considered by the Banks sufficient if the mention "freight paid" or other similar expression is affixed by stamp or in handwriting on the shipping documents.

Article 18. Shipping documents bearing reservations as to the apparent good order and conditions of the goods may be refused.

Unless otherwise implied by the conditions of credit or documents presented, Banks may honor documents stating that the goods are subject to C.O.D. ("Cash on Delivery"), insofar as such C.O.D. represents freight or transportation charges.

BILLS OF LADING

Article 19. When Sea or Ocean Bills of Lading are required, the following may be accepted:

(*a*) "Received for Shipment" or "Alongside" Bills of Lading;

(*b*) "Port" or "Custody" Bills of Lading for shipments of cotton from the United States of America, drawn under the "Liverpool Cotton Bill of Lading Conference" of 1907;

(*c*) Transshipment Bills of Lading which, apart from printed clauses, permit transshipment on the way, on condition however that the entire voyage be effected under one and the same Bill of Lading.

Should it, for technical reasons be impossible that the entire voyage be covered by the same document, transshipment Bills of Lading may nevertheless be accepted without any responsibility for the Banks;

(*d*) "Through Bills of Lading" issued by steamship companies or their agents.

Article 20. Bills of Lading issued by forwarding agents will be refused, as also Bills of Lading for shipment by sailing vessels.

Article 21. Banks have the right to accept Bills of Lading mentioning the stowage on deck of goods of a special nature, on condition that the insurance covers the risks arising therefrom.

Article 22. When shipment by steamship is required, Banks may consider themselves authorized to accept Bills of Lading for shipment by motor vessels.

Article 23. When "On Board" shipment is required and is evidenced by a "Shipped" or "On Board" Bill of Lading, the Bill of Lading date will be taken as evidence that the goods have been shipped on or before that date at the place of shipment indicated on the Bill of Lading.

When loading on board is evidenced by means of a notation, and if the documents are presented for payment or for negotiation after the date of shipment stipulated in the credit, this notation must give the date of the loading on board in the port of shipment indicated on the Bill of Lading. If the date of the loading on board is not given, the date of the notation will be considered as that of the loading on board.

Article 24. Banks have the right to require that the name of the beneficiary of the credit appear on the Bill of Lading as shipper or endorser.

RAILWAY OR INLAND WATERWAY CONSIGNMENT NOTES, COUNTERFOIL WAYBILLS, POSTAL RECEIPTS

Article 25. Banks will consider these documents as regular when they bear the reception stamp of the railway or postal authorities, or, in the case of Inland Waterways Consignment Notes, when signed by the master. The documents must indicate as consignee either the principal (purchaser) or the opening Bank.

Article 26. When an attestation or certificate of weight is required in the case of railway transport, Banks may refer to the indications contained in the shipping documents on condition that weighing has been duly witnessed by means of a weight stamp or other official means. A weight attestation will only be required on special request.

Article 27. If, in the case of shipment by rail, by inland waterway or by post, the name of the beneficiary does not appear on the transport documents Banks may require them to be countersigned by him.

INSURANCE

Article 28. Banks may accept either Policies or Certificates of Insurance issued by companies or their agents, by underwriters or eventually by brokers.

Article 29. The minimum value insured must be the C.I.F. value of the goods insofar as it is possible to check it by means of the documents tendered, but in no case should it be less than the amount of the settlement, or than that of the invoice if the latter is higher.

Article 30. Failing instructions as to the risks to be covered, Banks will accept insurance documents as tendered providing that these cover the goods against transport risks.

Article 31. When a credit stipulates "Insurance against all Risks" Banks can in no way be held responsible if any particular risk is not covered.

INVOICES

Article 32. Invoices must be made out in the name of the principal (purchaser) or in the name of any other person designated by him.

Article 33. In order to determine the quality of the goods, Banks may refer to the indications given in the Invoices, which should correspond with those stipulated in the credit. Banks will accept shipping or insurance documents bearing the generic description of the goods.

OTHER DOCUMENTS

Article 34. When other documents are required, such as: Warehouse Receipts, Delivery Orders, Consular Invoices, Certificates of Origin, Certificates of Weight, of quality or of Analysis, without further definition, Banks may accept such documents as tendered without responsibility on their part.

In special cases to be determined by Banks, the latter will require all other documents which they may consider necessary.

D. Interpretation of Terms

"ABOUT," "CIRCA" OR SIMILAR TERMS

Article 35. These terms to be construed as allowing a difference not to exceed 10 per cent more or less applicable, according to their place in the instructions or letters of credit, to the amount of the credit, or to the quantity or unit price of the goods. (*Note:* Swedish Law only admits for these terms a difference not exceeding 5 per cent more or less.)

When the goods, by their nature, do not allow the delivery of the exact quantity indicated — as, for instance, oil in barrels, ore in bulk, chemicals in bulk or in cylinders, etc. — a difference of 3 per cent more or less will be allowed, even if the terms of the credit call for a fixed weight or measurement.

PARTIAL SHIPMENTS

Article 36. Banks may refuse to pay for partial shipments if they think it advisable.

Article 37. If shipment by instalments within given periods is specified each instalment shall be treated as a separate transaction. The instalment not shipped within a given period cannot be added to subsequent shipments and is considered as *ipso facto* cancelled. Banks may however pay against documents for subsequent shipments provided they are made within the given periods.

MATURITY OR VALIDITY

Article 38. The period for which all irrevocable credits are to remain in force must be stipulated. The period may be either a time for payment or a time for shipment. If the credit does not specify which, the Bank shall consider the date to be the date for payment and after its expiration shall refuse payment, even if the documents bear a date within the time for payment.

Article 39. The word "to," "until," "till" and words of similar import applying to dates of maturity for payment or negotiation are understood to include the date mentioned.

Article 40. When the stipulated expiry date falls on a Sunday or legal or local holiday, or upon any holiday recognized as such by the Banks, the last day of the period of validity will be extended until the first following business day. This does not apply to the last day for shipment which must be respected whatever the day.

Article 41. The validity of a revocable credit, if no date is specified, will be considered to have expired six months from the date of the notification sent to the beneficiary by the Bank with which the credit is available and this Bank may refuse any payment after said period, unless its principal gives special instructions to the contrary.

SHIPMENT, LOADING OR DISPATCH

Article 42. "Prompt," "immediately," "as soon as possible," etc., these terms, and others of similar import, are to be interpreted as a request for shipment within thirty days from the notification to the beneficiary, unless a date has been stipulated.

When the words "departure," "dispatch," or "loading" are used in Commercial Documentary Credits, and unless specific evidence in respect thereto is required, the Banks will consider these words as synonymous to "shipment," and they may be guided by the date appearing upon the Bills of Lading or other shipping documents.

PRESENTATION

Article 43. Documents must be presented without delay. Banks may refuse the documents if presented to them too late, in other words at a date not justified by the usual time taken to cover the distance between the place of dispatch and the place where payment is made.

Article 44. Banks are under no obligation to accept documents outside their banking hours.

EXTENSION

Article 45. Any extension of the period for shipment shall extend for an equal period the time fixed for presentation or negotiation of documents or drafts.

DATE TERMS

Article 46. The terms "first half," "second half" of a month shall be construed respectively as from the 1st to the 15th and the 16th to the last day of each month, inclusive.

Article 47. The terms "beginning," "middle," or "end" of a month shall be construed respectively as from the 1st to the 10th, the 11th to the 20th, and the 21st to the last day of each month, inclusive.

Article 48. When a credit is opened as good "for one month," "for six months," and the principal has not specified the date from which the time is to run, the time shall run from the date on which the beneficiary is advised by the Bank which notified the opening of the credit, and at which the credit is to be payable.

E. TRANSFER

Article 49. A credit can only be transferred on the express authority of the principal. In this case the credit can be transferred once only, and on the terms and conditions specified in the original credit, with the exception of the amount of the credit and of the time of validity, which both may be reduced.

If a Commercial Documentary Credit is transferred by fractions, such fractional transfers shall be considered as constituting one single transfer only.

Authority to transfer a credit covers authority to transfer it to another place. Bank charges entailed by such transfers are payable by the original beneficiary unless otherwise specified. During the validity of the original credit, payment may be made at the place to which the credit has been transferred.

BILLS OF EXCHANGE ACT, 1882 [1]

(45 and 46 Vict., Chap. 61)

Be it enacted by the Queen's most Excellent Majesty, by and with the advice and consent of the Lords Spiritual and Temporal, and Commons, in this present Parliament assembled, and by the authority of the same, as follows:

PART I

PRELIMINARY

1. This Act may be cited as the Bills of Exchange Act, 1882.
2. In this Act, unless the context otherwise requires, —

"Acceptance" means an acceptance completed by delivery or notification.

"Action" includes counter claim and set off.

"Banker" includes a body of persons whether incorporated or not who carry on the business of banking.

"Bankrupt" includes any person whose estate is vested in a trustee or assignee under the law for the time being in force relating to bankruptcy.

"Bearer" means the person in possession of a bill or note which is payable to bearer.

"Bill" means bill of exchange, and "note" means promissory note.

"Delivery" means transfer of possession, actual or constructive, from one person to another.

"Holder" means the payee or indorsee of a bill or note who is in possession of it, or the bearer thereof.

"Indorsement" means an indorsement completed by delivery.

"Issue" means the first delivery of a bill or note, complete in form to a person who takes it as a holder.

"Person" includes a body of persons whether incorporated or not.

"Value" means valuable consideration.

"Written" includes printed, and "writing" includes print.

[1] Acts in substantially similar terms have been adopted throughout the British Empire.

PART II

BILLS OF EXCHANGE

Form and Interpretation

3. (1.) A bill of exchange is an unconditional order in writing, addressed by one person to another, signed by the person giving it, requiring the person to whom it is addressed to pay on demand or at a fixed or determinable future time a sum certain in money to or to the order of a specified person, or to bearer.

(2.) An instrument which does not comply with these conditions, or which orders any act to be done in addition to the payment of money, is not a bill of exchange.

(3.) An order to pay out of a particular fund is not unconditional within the meaning of this section; but an unqualified order to pay, coupled with (*a*) an indication of a particular fund out of which the drawee is to re-imburse himself or a particular account to be debited with the amount, or (*b*) a statement of the transaction which gives rise to the bill, is unconditional.

(4.) A bill is not invalid by reason —

(*a*) That it is not dated;

(*b*) That it does not specify the value given, or that any value has been given therefor;

(*c*) That it does not specify the place where it is drawn or the place where it is payable.

4. (1.) An inland bill is a bill which is or on the face of it purports to be (*a*) both drawn and payable within the British Islands, or (*b*) drawn within the British Islands upon some person resident therein. Any other bill is a foreign bill.

For the purposes of this Act "British Islands" mean any part of the United Kingdom of Great Britain and Ireland, the islands of Man, Guernsey, Jersey, Alderney, and Sark, and the islands adjacent to any of them being part of the dominions of Her Majesty.

(2.) Unless the contrary appear on the face of the bill the holder may treat it as an inland bill.

5. (1.) A bill may be drawn payable to, or to the order of, the drawer; or it may be drawn payable to, or to the order of, the drawee.

(2.) Where in a bill drawer and drawee are the same person, or where the drawee is a fictitious person or a person not having capacity to contract, the holder may treat the instrument, at his option, either as a bill of exchange or as a promissory note.

6. (1.) The drawee must be named or otherwise indicated in a bill with reasonable certainty.

(2.) A bill may be addressed to two or more drawees whether they are partners or not, but an order addressed to two drawees in the alternative or to two or more drawees in succession is not a bill of exchange.

7. (1.) Where a bill is not payable to bearer, the payee must be named or otherwise indicated therein with reasonable certainty.

(2.) A bill may be made payable to two or more payees jointly, or it may be made payable in the alternative to one of two, or one or some of several payees. A bill may also be made payable to the holder of an office for the time being.

(3.) Where the payee is a fictitious or non-existing person the bill may be treated as payable to bearer.

8. (1.) When a bill contains words prohibiting transfer, or indicating an intention that it should not be transferable, it is valid as between the parties thereto, but it not negotiable.

(2.) A negotiable bill may be payable either to order or to bearer.

(3.) A bill is payable to bearer which is expressed to be so payable, or on which the only or last indorsement is an indorsement in blank.

(4.) A bill is payable to order which is expressed to be so payable, or which is expressed to be payable to a particular person, and does not contain words prohibiting transfer or indicating an intention that it should not be transferable.

(5.) Where a bill, either originally or by indorsement, is expressed to be payable to the order of a specified person, and not to him or his order, it is nevertheless payable to him or his order at his option.

9. (1.) The sum payable by a bill is a sum certain within the meaning of this Act, although it is required to be paid —

(*a*) With interest.

(*b*) By stated instalments.

(*c*) By stated instalments, with a provision that upon default in payment of any instalment the whole shall become due.

(*d*) According to an indicated rate of exchange or according to a rate of exchange to be ascertained as directed by the bill.

(2.) Where the sum payable is expressed in words and also in figures, and there is a discrepancy between the two, the sum denoted by the words is the amount payable.

(3.) Where a bill is expressed to be payable with interest, unless the instrument otherwise provides, interest runs from the date of the bill, and if the bill is undated from the issue thereof.

10. (1.) A bill is payable on demand —

(*a*) Which is expressed to be payable on demand, or at sight, or on presentation; or

(*b*) In which no time for payment is expressed.

(2.) Where a bill is accepted or indorsed when it is overdue, it shall, as regards the acceptor who so accepts, or any indorser who so indorses it, be deemed a bill payable on demand.

11. A bill is payable at a determinable future time within the meaning of this Act which is expressed to be payable —

(1.) At a fixed period after date or sight.

(2.) On or at a fixed period after the occurrence of a specified event which is certain to happen, though the time of happening may be uncertain.

An instrument expressed to be payable on a contingency is not a bill, and the happening of the event does not cure the defect.

12. Where a bill expressed to be payable at a fixed period after date is issued undated, or where the acceptance of a bill payable at a fixed period after sight is undated, any holder may insert therein the true date of issue or acceptance, and the bill shall be payable accordingly.

Provided that (1) where the holder in good faith and by mistake inserts a wrong date, and (2) in every case where a wrong date is inserted, if the bill subsequently comes into the hands of a holder in due course the bill shall not be avoided thereby, but shall operate and be payable as if the date so inserted had been the true date.

13. (1.) Where a bill or an acceptance or any indorsement on a bill is dated, the date shall, unless the contrary be proved, be deemed to be the true date of the drawing, acceptance, or indorsement, as the case may be.

(2.) A bill is not invalid by reason only that it is ante-dated or post-dated, or that it bears date on a Sunday.

14. Where a bill is not payable on demand the day on which it falls due is determined as follows:

(1.) Three days, called days of grace, are, in every case where the bill itself does not otherwise provide, added to the time of payment as fixed by the bill, and the bill is due and payable on the last day of grace: Provided that —

(*a*) When the last day of grace falls on Sunday, Christmas Day, Good Friday, or a day appointed by Royal proclamation as a public fast or thanksgiving day, the bill is, except in the case herein-after provided for, due and payable on the preceding business day;

(*b*) When the last day of grace is a bank holiday (other than Christmas Day or Good Friday) under the Bank Holidays Act, 1871, and Acts amending or extending it, or when the last day of grace is a Sunday and the second day of grace is a Bank Holiday, the bill is due and payable on the succeeding business day.

(2.) Where a bill is payable at a fixed period after date, after sight, or after the happening of a specified event, the time of payment is determined by excluding the day from which the time is to begin to run and by including the day of payment.

(3.) Where a bill is payable at a fixed period after sight, the time begins to run from the date of the acceptance if the bill be accepted, and from the date of noting or protest if the bill be noted or protested for non-acceptance, or for non-delivery.

(4.) The term "month" in a bill means calendar month.

15. The drawer of a bill and any indorser may insert therein the name of a person to whom the holder may resort in case of need, that is to say, in case the bill is dishonoured by non-acceptance or nonpayment. Such person is called the referee in case of need. It is in the option of the holder to resort to the referee in case of need or not as he may think fit.

16. The drawer of a bill, and any indorser, may insert therein an express stipulation —

(1.) Negativing or limiting his own liability to the holder:

(2.) Waiving as regards himself some or all of the holder's duties.

17. (1.) The acceptance of a bill is the signification by the drawee of his assent to the order of the drawer.

(2.) An acceptance is invalid unless it complies with the following conditions, namely:

(*a*) It must be written on the bill and be signed by the drawee. The mere signature of the drawee without additional words is sufficient.

(*b*) It must not express that the drawee will perform his promise by any other means than the payment of money.

18. A bill may be accepted —

(1.) before it has been signed by the drawer, or while otherwise incomplete:

(2.) When it is overdue, or after it has been dishonoured by a previous refusal to accept, or by non-payment:

(3.) When a bill payable after sight is dishonoured by non-acceptance, and the drawee subsequently accepts it, the holder, in the absence of any different agreement, is entitled to have the bill accepted as of the date of first presentment to the drawee for acceptance.

19. (1.) An acceptance is either (*a*) general or (*b*) qualified.

(2.) A general acceptance assents without qualification to the order of the drawer. A qualified acceptance in express terms varies the effect of the bill as drawn.

In particular an acceptance is qualified which is —

(*a*) conditional, that is to say, which makes payment by the acceptor dependent on the fulfilment of a condition therein stated:

(*b*) partial, that is to say, an acceptance to pay part only of the amount for which the bill is drawn:

(*c*) local, that is to say, an acceptance to pay only at a particular specified place:

An acceptance to pay at a particular place is a general acceptance, unless it expressly states that the bill is to be paid there only and not elsewhere:

(*d*) qualified as to time:

(*e*) the acceptance of some one or more of the drawees, but not of all.

20. (1.) Where a simple signature on a blank stamped paper is delivered by the signer in order that it may be converted into a bill, it operates as a *prima facie* authority to fill it up as a complete bill for any amount the stamp will cover, using the signature for that of the drawer, or the acceptor, or an indorser; and, in like manner, when a bill is wanting in any material particular, the person in possession of it has a *prima facie* authority to fill up the omission in any way he thinks fit.

(2.) In order that any such instrument when completed may be enforceable against any person who became a party thereto prior to its completion, it must be filled up within a reasonable time, and strictly in accordance with the authority given. Reasonable time for this purpose is a question of fact.

Provided that if any such instrument after completion is negotiated to a holder in due course it shall be valid and effectual for all purposes in his hands, and he may enforce it as if it had been filled up within a reasonable time and strictly in accordance with the authority given.

21. (1.) Every contract on a bill, whether it be the drawer's, the acceptor's, or an indorser's, is incomplete and revocable, until delivery of the instrument in order to give effect thereto.

Provided that where an acceptance is written on a bill, and the drawee gives notice to or according to the directions of the person entitled to the bill that he has accepted it, the acceptance then becomes complete and irrevocable.

(2.) As between immediate parties, and as regards a remote party other than a holder in due course, the delivery —

(*a*) in order to be effectual must be made either by or under the authority of the party drawing, accepting, or indorsing, as the case may be:

(*b*) may be shown to have been conditional or for a special purpose only, and not for the purpose of transferring the property in the bill.

But if the bill be in the hands of a holder in due course a valid delivery of the bill by all parties prior to him so as to make them liable to him is conclusively presumed.

(3.) Where a bill is no longer in the possession of a party who has signed it as drawer, acceptor, or indorser, a valid and unconditional delivery by him is presumed until the contrary is proved.

CAPACITY AND AUTHORITY OF PARTIES

22. (1.) Capacity to incur liability as a party to a bill is co-extensive with capacity to contract.

Provided that nothing in this section shall enable a corporation to make itself liable as drawer, acceptor, or indorser of a bill unless it is competent to it so to do under the law for the time being in force relating to corporations.

(2.) Where a bill is drawn or indorsed by an infant, minor, or corporation having no capacity or power to incur liability on a bill, the drawing or indorsement entitles the holder to receive payment of the bill, and to enforce it against any other party thereto.

23. No person is liable as drawer, indorser, or acceptor of a bill who has not signed it as such: Provided that

(1.) Where a person signs a bill in a trade or assumed name, he is liable thereon as if he had signed it in his own name:

(2.) The signature of the name of a firm is equivalent to the signature by the person so signing of the names of all persons liable as partners in that firm.

24. Subject to the provisions of this Act, where a signature on a bill is forged or placed thereon without the authority of the person whose signature it purports to be, the forged or unauthorised signature is wholly inoperative, and no right to retain the bill or to give a discharge therefor or to enforce payment thereof against any party thereto can be acquired through or under that signature, unless the party against whom it is sought to retain or enforce payment of the bill is precluded from setting up the forgery or want of authority.

Provided that nothing in this section shall affect the ratification of an unauthorised signature not amounting to a forgery.

25. A signature by procuration operates as notice that the agent has but a limited authority to sign, and the principal is only bound by such signature if the agent in so signing was acting within the actual limits of his authority.

26. (1.) Where a person signs a bill as drawer indorser, or acceptor, and adds words to his signature, indicating that he signs for or on behalf of a principal, or in a representative character, he is not personally liable thereon; but the mere addition to his signature of words describing him as an agent, or as filling a representative character, does not exempt him from personal liability.

(2.) In determining whether a signature on a bill is that of the principal or that of the agent by whose hand it is written, the construction most favourable to the validity of the instrument shall be adopted.

THE CONSIDERATION FOR A BILL

27. (1.) Valuable consideration for a bill may be constituted by,—

(*a*) Any consideration sufficient to support a simple contract;

(*b*) An antecedent debt or liability. Such a debt or liability is deemed valuable consideration whether the bill is payable on demand or at a future time.

(2.) Where value has at any time been given for a bill the holder is deemed to be a holder for value as regards the acceptor and all parties to the bill who became parties prior to such time.

(3.) Where the holder of a bill has a lien on it arising either from contract or by implication of law, he is deemed to be a holder for value to the extent of the sum for which he has a lien.

28. (1.) An accommodation party to a bill is a person who has signed a bill as drawer, acceptor, or indorser, without receiving value therefor, and for the purpose of lending his name to some other person.

(2.) An accommodation party is liable on the bill to a holder for value; and it is immaterial whether, when such holder took the bill, he knew such party to be an accommodation party or not.

29. (1.) A holder in due course is a holder who has taken a bill, complete and regular on the face of it, under the following conditions; namely,

(*a*) That he became the holder of it before it was overdue, and without notice that it had been previously dishonoured, if such was the fact:

(*b*) That he took the bill in good faith and for value, and that at the time the bill was negotiated to him he had no notice of any defect in the title of the person who negotiated it.

(2.) In particular the title of a person who negotiates a bill is defective within the meaning of this Act when he obtained the bill, or the acceptance thereof, by fraud, duress, or force and fear, or other unlawful means, or for an illegal consideration, or when he negotiates it in breach of faith, or under such circumstances as amount to a fraud.

(3.) A holder (whether for value or not), who derives his title to a bill through a holder in due course, and who is not himself a party to any fraud or illegality affecting it, has all the rights of that holder in due course as regards the acceptor and all parties to the bill prior to that holder.

30. (1.) Every party whose signature appears on a bill is *prima facie* deemed to have become a party thereto for value.

(2.) Every holder of a bill is *prima facie* deemed to be a holder in due course; but if in an action on a bill it is admitted or proved that the acceptance, issue, or subsequent negotiation of the bill is affected with fraud, duress, or force and fear, or illegality, the burden of proof is shifted, unless and until the holder proves that, subsequent to the alleged fraud or illegality, value has in good faith been given for the bill.

NEGOTIATION OF BILLS

31. (1.) A bill is negotiated when it is transferred from one person to another in such a manner as to constitute the transferee the holder of the bill.

(2.) A bill payable to bearer is negotiated by delivery.

(3.) A bill payable to order is negotiated by the indorsement of the holder completed by delivery.

(4.) Where the holder of a bill payable to his order transfers it for value without indorsing it, the transfer gives the transferee such title as the transferor had in the bill, and the transferee in addition acquires the right to have the indorsement of the transferor.

(5.) Where any person is under obligation to indorse a bill in a representative capacity, he may indorse the bill in such terms as to negative personal liability.

32. An indorsement in order to operate as a negotiation must comply with the following conditions, namely, —

(1.) It must be written on the bill itself and be signed by the indorser. The simple signature of the indorser on the bill, without additional words, is sufficient.

An indorsement written on an allonge, or on a "copy" of a bill issued or negotiated in a country where "copies" are recognised, is deemed to be written on the bill itself.

(2.) It must be an indorsement of the entire bill. A partial indorsement, that is to say, an indorsement which purports to transfer to the indorsee a part only of the amount payable, or which purports to transfer the bill to two or more indorsees severally does not operate as a negotiation of the bill.

(3.) Where a bill is payable to the order of two or more payees or indorsees who are not partners all must indorse, unless the one indorsing has authority to indorse for the others.

(4.) Where, in a bill payable to order, the payee or indorsee is wrongly designated, or his name is mis-spelt, he may indorse the bill as therein described, adding, if he think fit, his proper signature.

(5.) Where there are two or more indorsements on a bill, each indorsement is deemed to have been made in the order in which it appears on the bill, until the contrary is proved.

(6.) An indorsement may be made in blank or special. It may also contain terms making it restrictive.

33. Where a bill purports to be indorsed conditionally the condition may be disregarded by the payer, and payment to the indorsee is valid whether the condition has been fulfilled or not.

34. (1.) An indorsement in blank specifies no indorsee, and a bill so indorsed becomes payable to bearer.

(2.) A special indorsement specifies the person to whom, or to whose order, the bill is to be payable.

(3.) The provisions of this Act relating to a payee apply with the necessary modifications to an indorsee under a special indorsement.

(4.) When a bill has been indorsed in blank, any holder may convert the blank indorsement into a special indorsement by writing above the indorser's signature a direction to pay the bill to or to the order of himself or some other person.

35. (1.) An indorsement is restrictive which prohibits the further negotiation of the bill or which expresses that it is a mere authority to deal with the bill as thereby directed and not a transfer of the ownership thereof, as, for example, if a bill be indorsed "Pay D. only," or "Pay D. for the account of X," or "Pay D. or order for collection."

(2.) A restrictive indorsement gives the indorsee the right to receive payment of the bill and to sue any party thereto that his indorser could have sued, but gives him no power to transfer his rights as indorsee unless it expressly authorise him to do so.

(3.) Where a restrictive indorsement authorises further transfer, all subsequent indorsees take the bill with the same rights and subject to the same liabilities as the first indorsee under the restrictive indorsement.

36. (1.) Where a bill is negotiable in its origin it continues to be negotiable until it has been (*a*) restrictively indorsed or (*b*) discharged by payment or otherwise.

(2.) Where an overdue bill is negotiated, it can only be negotiated subject to any defect of title affecting it at its maturity, and thenceforward no person who takes it can acquire or give a better title than that which the person from whom he took it had.

(3.) A bill payable on demand is deemed to be overdue within the meaning and for the purposes, of this section, when it appears on the face of it to have been in circulation for an unreasonable length of time. What is an unreasonable length of time for this purpose is a question of fact.

(4.) Except where an indorsement bears date after the maturity of the bill, every negotiation is *prima facie* deemed to have been effected before the bill was overdue.

(5.) Where a bill which is not overdue has been dishonoured any person who takes it with notice of the dishonour takes it subject to any defect of title attaching thereto at the time of dishonour, but nothing in this sub-section shall affect the rights of a holder in due course.

37. Where a bill is negotiated back to the drawer, or to a prior indorser or to the acceptor, such party may, subject to the provisions of this Act, re-issue and

further negotiate the bill, but he is not entitled to enforce payment of the bill against any intervening party to whom he was previously liable.

38. The rights and powers of the holder of a bill are as follows:

(1.) He may sue on the bill in his own name:

(2.) Where he is a holder in due course, he holds the bill free from any defect of title of prior parties, as well as from mere personal defences available to prior parties among themselves, and may enforce payment against all parties liable on the bill:

(3.) Where his title is defective (*a*) if he negotiates the bill to a holder in due course, that holder obtains a good and complete title to the bill, and (*b*) if he obtains payment of the bill the person who pays him in due course gets a valid discharge for the bill.

GENERAL DUTIES OF THE HOLDER

39. (1.) Where a bill is payable after sight, presentment for acceptance is necessary in order to fix the maturity of the instrument.

(2.) Where a bill expressly stipulates that it shall be presented for acceptance, or where a bill is drawn payable elsewhere than at the residence or place of business of the drawee, it must be presented for acceptance before it can be presented for payment.

(3.) In no other case is presentment for acceptance necessary in order to render liable any party to the bill.

(4.) Where the holder of a bill, drawn payable elsewhere than at the place of business or residence of the drawee, has not time, with the exercise of reasonable diligence, to present the bill for acceptance before presenting it for payment on the day that it falls due, the delay caused by presenting the bill for acceptance before presenting it for payment is excused, and does not discharge the drawer and indorsers.

40. (1.) Subject to the provisions of this Act, when a bill payable after sight is negotiated, the holder must either present it for acceptance or negotiate it within a reasonable time.

(2.) If he do not do so, the drawer and all indorsers prior to that holder are discharged.

(3.) In determining what is a reasonable time within the meaning of this section, regard shall be had to the nature of the bill, the usage of trade with respect to similar bills, and the facts of the particular case.

41. (1.) A bill is duly presented for acceptance which is presented in accordance with the following rules:

(*a*) The presentment must be made by or on behalf of the holder to the drawee or to some person authorised to accept or refuse acceptance on his behalf at a reasonable hour on a business day and before the bill is overdue:

(*b*) Where a bill is addressed to two or more drawees, who are not partners, presentment must be made to them all, unless one has authority to accept for all, then presentment may be made to him only:

(*c*) Where the drawee is dead presentment may be made to his personal representative:

(*d*) Where the drawee is bankrupt, presentment may be made to him or to his trustee:

(*e*) Where authorised by agreement or usage, a presentment through the post office is sufficient.

(2.) Presentment in accordance with these rules is excused, and a bill may be treated as dishonoured by non-acceptance —

(*a*) Where the drawee is dead or bankrupt, or is a fictitious person or a person not having capacity to contract by bill:

(*b*) Where, after the exercise of reasonable diligence, such presentment cannot be effected:

(*c*) Where although the presentment has been irregular, acceptance has been refused on some other ground.

(3.) The fact that the holder has reason to believe that the bill, on presentment, will be dishonoured does not excuse presentment.

42. (1.) When a bill is duly presented for acceptance and is not accepted within the customary time, the person presenting it must treat it as dishonoured by non-acceptance. If he do not, the holder shall lose his right of recourse against the drawer and indorsers.

43. (1.) A bill is dishonoured by non-acceptance —

(*a*) when it is duly presented for acceptance, and such an acceptance as is prescribed by this Act is refused or cannot be obtained; or

(*b*) when presentment for acceptance is excused and the bill is not accepted.

(2.) Subject to the provisions of this Act when a bill is dishonoured by non-acceptance, an immediate right of recourse against the drawer and indorsers accrues to the holder, and no presentment for payment is necessary.

44. (1.) The holder of a bill may refuse to take a qualified acceptance, and if he does not obtain an unqualified acceptance may treat the bill as dishonoured by non-acceptance.

(2.) Where a qualified acceptance is taken, and the drawer or an indorser has not expressly or impliedly authorised the holder to take a qualified acceptance, or does not subsequently assent thereto, such drawer or indorser is discharged from his liability on the bill.

The provisions of this sub-section do not apply to a partial acceptance, whereof due notice has been given. Where a foreign bill has been accepted as to part, it must be protested as to the balance.

(3.) When the drawer or indorser of a bill receives notice of a qualified acceptance, and does not within a reasonable time express his dissent to the holder he shall be deemed to have assented thereto.

45. Subject to the provisions of this Act a bill must be duly presented for payment. If it be not so presented the drawer and indorsers shall be discharged.

A bill is duly presented for payment which is presented in accordance with the following rules: —

(1.) Where the bill is not payable on demand, presentment must be made on the day it falls due.

(2.) Where the bill is payable on demand, then, subject to the provisions of this Act, presentment must be made within a reasonable time after its issue in order to render the drawer liable, and within a reasonable time after its indorsement, in order to render the indorser liable.

In determining what is a reasonable time, regard shall be had to the nature of the bill, the usage of trade with regard to similar bills, and the facts of the particular case.

(3.) Presentment must be made by the holder or by some person authorised to receive payment on his behalf at a reasonable hour on a business day, at the proper place as herein-after defined, either to the person designated by the bill as payer, or to some person authorised to pay or refuse payment on his behalf if with the exercise of reasonable diligence such person can there be found.

(4.) A bill is presented at the proper place: —

(*a*) Where a place of payment is specified in the bill and the bill is there presented.

(*b*) Where no place of payment is specified, but the address of the drawee or acceptor is given in the bill, and the bill is there presented.

(*c*) Where no place of payment is specified and no address given, and the bill is presented at the drawee's or acceptor's place of business if known, and if not, at his ordinary residence if known.

(*d*) In any other case if presented to the drawee or acceptor wherever he can be found, or if presented at his last known place of business or residence.

(5.) Where a bill is presented at the proper place, and after the exercise of reasonable diligence no person authorised to pay or refuse payment can be found there, no further presentment to the drawee or acceptor is required.

(6.) Where a bill is drawn upon, or accepted by two or more persons who are not partners, and no place of payment is specified, presentment must be made to them all.

(7.) Where the drawee or acceptor of a bill is dead, and no place of payment is specified, presentment must be made to a personal representative, if such there be, and with the exercise of reasonable diligence he can be found.

(8.) Where authorised by agreement or usage a presentment through the post office is sufficient.

46. (1.) Delay in making presentment for payment is excused when the delay is caused by circumstances beyond the control of the holder, and not imputable to his default, misconduct, or negligence. When the cause of delay ceases to operate presentment must be made with reasonable diligence.

(2.) Presentment for payment is dispensed with, —

(*a*) Where, after the exercise of reasonable diligence presentment, as required by this Act, cannot be effected.

The fact that the holder has reason to believe that the bill will, on presentment, be dishonoured, does not dispense with the necessity for presentment.

(*b*) Where the drawee is a fictitious person.

(*c*) As regards the drawer where the drawee or acceptor is not bound, as between himself and the drawer, to accept or pay the bill, and the drawer has no reason to believe that the bill would be paid if presented.

(*d*) As regards an indorser, where the bill was accepted or made for the accommodation of that indorser, and he has no reason to expect that the bill would be paid if presented.

(*e*) By waiver of presentment, express or implied.

47. — (1.) A bill is dishonoured by nonpayment (*a*) when it is duly presented for payment and payment is refused or cannot be obtained, or (*b*) when presentment is excused and the bill is overdue and unpaid.

(2.) Subject to the provisions of this Act, when a bill is dishonoured by nonpayment, an immediate right of recourse against the drawer and indorsers accrues to the holder.

48. Subject to the provisions of this Act, when a bill has been dishonoured by non-acceptance or by nonpayment, notice of dishonour must be given to the drawer and each indorser, and any drawer or indorser to whom such notice is not given is discharged; Provided that —

(1.) Where a bill is dishonoured by non-acceptance, and notice of dishonour is not given, the rights of a holder in due course subsequent to the omission, shall not be prejudiced by the omission.

(2.) Where a bill is dishonoured by non-acceptance, and due notice of dishonour is given, it shall not be necessary to give notice of a subsequent dishonour by nonpayment unless the bill shall in the meantime have been accepted.

49. Notice of dishonour in order to be valid and effectual must be given in accordance with the following rules: —

(1.) The notice must be given by or on behalf of the holder, or by or on behalf of an indorser who, at the time of giving it, is himself liable on the bill.

(2.) Notice of dishonour may be given by an agent either in his own name, or in the name of any party entitled to give notice whether that party be his principal or not.

(3.) Where the notice is given by or on behalf of the holder, it enures for the benefit of all subsequent holders and all prior indorsers who have a right of recourse against the party to whom it is given.

(4.) Where notice is given by or on behalf of an indorser entitled to give notice as herein-before provided, it enures for the benefit of the holder and all indorsers subsequent to the party to whom notice is given.

(5.) The notice may be given in writing or by personal communication, and may be given in any terms which sufficiently identify the bill, and intimate that the bill has been dishonoured by non-acceptance or nonpayment.

(6.) The return of a dishonoured bill to the drawer or an indorser is, in point of form, deemed a sufficient notice of dishonour.

(7.) A written notice need not be signed, and an insufficient written notice may be supplemented and validated by verbal communication. A misdescription of the bill shall not vitiate the notice unless the party to whom the notice is given is in fact misled thereby.

(8.) Where notice of dishonour is required to be given to any person, it may be given either to the party himself, or to his agent in that behalf.

(9.) Where the drawer or indorser is dead, and the party giving notice knows it, the notice must be given to a personal representative if such there be, and with the exercise of reasonable diligence he can be found.

(10.) Where the drawer or indorser is bankrupt, notice may be given either to the party himself or to the trustee.

(11.) Where there are two or more drawers or indorsers who are not partners, notice must be given to each of them, unless one of them has authority to receive such notice for the others.

(12.) The notice may be given as soon as the bill is dishonoured and must be given within a reasonable time thereafter.

In the absence of special circumstances notice is not deemed to have been given within a reasonable time, unless —

(*a*) where the person giving and the person to receive notice reside in the same place, the notice is given or sent off in time to reach the latter on the day after the dishonour of the bill.

(*b*) where the person giving and the person to receive notice reside in different places, the notice is sent off on the day after the dishonour of the bill, if there be a post at a convenient hour on that day, and if there be no such post on that day then by the next post thereafter.

(13.) Where a bill when dishonoured is in the hands of an agent, he may either himself give notice to the parties liable on the bill, or he may give notice to his principal. If he give notice to his principal, he must do so within the same time as if he were the holder, and the principal upon receipt of such notice has himself the same time for giving notice as if the agent had been an independent holder.

(14.) Where a party to a bill receives due notice of dishonour, he has after the receipt of such notice the same period of time for giving notice to antecedent parties that the holder has after the dishonour.

(15.) Where a notice of dishonour is duly addressed and posted, the sender is deemed to have given due notice of dishonour, notwithstanding any miscarriage by the post office.

50. — (1.) Delay in giving notice of dishonour is excused where the delay is caused by circumstances beyond the control of the party giving notice, and not imputable to his default, misconduct, or negligence. When the cause of delay ceases to operate the notice must be given with reasonable diligence.

(2.) Notice of dishonour is dispensed with —

(*a*) When, after the exercise of reasonable diligence, notice as required by this Act cannot be given to or does not reach the drawer or indorser sought to be charged:

(*b*) By waiver express or implied. Notice of dishonour may be waived before the time of giving notice has arrived, or after the omission to give due notice:

(*c*) As regards the drawer in the following cases, namely, (1) where drawer and drawee are the same person, (2) where the drawee is a fictitious person or a person not having capacity to contract, (3) where the drawer is the person to whom the bill is presented for payment, (4) where the drawee or acceptor is as between himself and the drawer under no obligation to accept or pay the bill, (5) where the drawer has countermanded payment:

(*d*) As regards the indorser in the following cases, namely, (1) where the drawee is a fictitious person or a person not having capacity to contract and the indorser was aware of the fact at the time he indorsed the bill, (2) where the indorser is the person to whom the bill is presented for payment, (3) where the bill was accepted or made for his accommodation.

51. — (1.) Where an inland bill has been dishonoured it may, if the holder think fit, be noted for non-acceptance or nonpayment, as the case may be; but it shall not be necessary to note or protest any such bill in order to preserve the recourse against the drawer or indorser.

(2.) Where a foreign bill, appearing on the face of it to be such, has been dishonoured by non-acceptance it must be duly protested for non-acceptance, and where such a bill, which has not been previously dishonoured by non-acceptance, is dishonoured by nonpayment it must be duly protested for nonpayment. If it be not so protested the drawer and indorsers are discharged. Where a bill does not appear on the face of it to be a foreign bill, protest thereof in case of dishonour is unnecessary.

(3.) A bill which has been protested for non-acceptance may be subsequently protested for nonpayment.

(4.) Subject to the provisions of this Act, when a bill is noted or protested, it must be noted on the day of its dishonour. When a bill has been duly noted, the protest may be subsequently extended as of the date of the noting.

(5.) Where the acceptor of a bill becomes bankrupt or insolvent or suspends payment before it matures, the holder may cause the bill to be protested for better security against the drawer and indorsers.

(6.) A bill must be protested at the place where it is dishonoured: Provided that —

(*a*) When a bill is presented through the post office, and returned by post dishonoured, it may be protested at the place to which it is returned and on the day of its return if received during business hours, and if not received during business hours, then not later than the next business day:

(*b*) When a bill drawn payable at the place of business or residence of some person other than the drawee, has been dishonoured by non-acceptance, it must be protested for nonpayment at the place where it is expressed to be payable, and no further presentment for payment to, or demand on, the drawee is necessary.

(7.) A protest must contain a copy of the bill, and must be signed by the notary making it, and must specify —

(*a*) The person at whose request the bill is protested:

(*b*) The place and date of protest, the cause or reason for protesting the bill, the demand made, and the answer given, if any, or the fact that the drawee or acceptor could not be found.

(8.) Where a bill is lost or destroyed, or is wrongly detained from the person entitled to hold it, protest may be made on a copy or written particulars thereof.

(9.) Protest is dispensed with by any circumstance which would dispense with notice of dishonour. Delay in noting or protesting is excused when the delay is caused by circumstances beyond the control of the holder, and not imputable to his default, misconduct, or negligence. When the cause of delay ceases to operate the bill must be noted or protested with reasonable diligence.

52. — (1.) When a bill is accepted generally presentment for payment is not necessary in order to render the acceptor liable.

(2.) When by the terms of a qualified acceptance presentment for payment is required, the acceptor, in the absence of an express stipulation to that effect, is not discharged by the omission to present the bill for payment on the day that it matures.

(3.) In order to render the acceptor of a bill liable it is not necessary to protest it, or that notice of dishonour should be given to him.

(4.) Where the holder of a bill presents it for payment, he shall exhibit the bill to the person from whom he demands payment, and when a bill is paid the holder shall forthwith deliver it up to the party paying it.

LIABILITIES OF PARTIES

53. — (1.) A bill, of itself, does not operate as an assignment of funds in the hands of the drawee available for the payment thereof, and the drawee of a bill who does not accept as required by this Act is not liable on the instrument. This sub-section shall not extend to Scotland.

(2.) In Scotland, where the drawee of a bill has in his hands funds available for the payment thereof, the bill operates as an assignment of the sum for which it is drawn in favour of the holder, from the time when the bill is presented to the drawee.

54. The acceptor of a bill, by accepting it —

(1.) Engages that he will pay it according to the tenor of his acceptance:

(2.) Is precluded from denying to a holder in due course:

(*a*) The existence of the drawer, the genuineness of his signature, and his capacity and authority to draw the bill;

(*b*) In the case of a bill payable to drawer's order, the then capacity of the drawer to indorse, but not the genuineness or validity of his indorsement;

(*c*) In the case of a bill payable to the order of a third person, the existence of the payee and his then capacity to indorse, but not the genuineness or validity of his indorsement.

55.—(1.) The drawer of a bill by drawing it—

(*a*) Engages that on due presentment it shall be accepted and paid according to its tenor, and that if it be dishonoured he will compensate the holder or any indorser who is compelled to pay it, provided that the requisite proceedings on dishonour be duly taken;

(*b*) Is precluded from denying to a holder in due course the existence of the payee and his then capacity to indorse.

(2.) The indorser of a bill by indorsing it—

(*a*) Engages that on due presentment it shall be accepted and paid according to its tenor, and that if it be dishonoured he will compensate the holder or a subsequent indorser who is compelled to pay it, provided that the requisite proceedings on dishonour be duly taken;

(*b*) Is precluded from denying to a holder in due course the genuineness and regularity in all respects of the drawer's signature and all previous indorsements;

(*c*) Is precluded from denying to his immediate or a subsequent indorsee that the bill was at the time of his indorsement a valid and subsisting bill, and that he had then a good title thereto.

56. Where a person signs a bill otherwise than as drawer or acceptor, he thereby incurs the liabilities of an indorser to a holder in due course.

57. Where a bill is dishonoured, the measure of damages, which shall be deemed to be liquidated damages, shall be as follows:

(1.) The holder may recover from any party liable on the bill, and the drawer who has been compelled to pay the bill may recover from the acceptor, and an indorser who has been compelled to pay the bill may recover from the acceptor or from the drawer, or from a prior indorser—

(*a*) The amount of the bill:

(*b*) Interest thereon from the time of presentment for payment if the bill is payable on demand, and from the maturity of the bill in any other case:

(*c*) The expenses of noting, or, when protest is necessary, and the protest has been extended, the expenses of protest.

(2.) In the case of a bill which has been dishonoured abroad, in lieu of the above damages, the holder may recover from the drawer or an indorser, and the drawer or an indorser who has been compelled to pay the bill may recover from any party liable to him, the amount of the re-exchange with interest thereon until the time of payment.

(3.) Where by this Act interest may be recovered as damages, such interest may, if justice require it, be withheld wholly or in part, and where a bill is expressed to be payable with interest at a given rate, interest as damages may or may not be given at the same rate as interest proper.

58.—(1.) Where the holder of a bill payable to bearer negotiates it by delivery without indorsing it, he is called a "transferor by delivery."

(2.) A transferor by delivery is not liable on the instrument.

(3.) A transferor by delivery who negotiates a bill thereby warrants to his immediate transferee being a holder for value that the bill is what it purports to be, that he has a right to transfer it, and that at the time of transfer he is not aware of any fact which renders it valueless.

DISCHARGE OF BILL

59.—(1.) A bill is discharged by payment in due course by or on behalf of the drawee or acceptor.

"Payment in due course" means payment made at or after the maturity of the bill to the holder thereof in good faith and without notice that his title to the bill is defective.

(2.) Subject to the provisions herein-after contained, when a bill is paid by the drawer or an indorser it is not discharged; but

(*a*) Where a bill payable to, or to the order of, a third party is paid by the drawer, the drawer may enforce payment thereof against the acceptor, but may not re-issue the bill.

(*b*) Where a bill is paid by an indorser, or where a bill payable to drawer's order is paid by the drawer, the party paying it is remitted to his former rights as regards the acceptor or antecedent parties, and he may, if he thinks fit, strike out his own and subsequent indorsements, and again negotiate the bill.

(3.) Where an accommodation bill is paid in due course by the party accommodated the bill is discharged.

60. When a bill payable to order on demand is drawn on a banker, and the banker on whom it is drawn pays the bill in good faith and in the ordinary course of business, it is not incumbent on the banker to show that the indorsement of the payee or any subsequent indorsement was made by or under the authority of the person whose indorsement it purports to be, and the banker is deemed to have paid the bill in due course, although such indorsement has been forged or made without authority.

61. When the acceptor of a bill is or becomes the holder of it at or after its maturity, in his own right, the bill is discharged.

62. (1.) When the holder of a bill at or after its maturity absolutely and unconditionally renounces his rights against the acceptor the bill is discharged.

The renunciation must be in writing, unless the bill is delivered up to the acceptor.

(2.) The liabilities of any party to a bill may in like manner be renounced by the holder before, at, or after its maturity; but nothing in this section shall affect the rights of a holder in due course without notice of the renunciation.

63. (1.) Where a bill is intentionally cancelled by the holder or his agent, and the cancellation is apparent thereon, the bill is discharged.

(2.) In like manner any party liable on a bill may be discharged by the intentional cancellation of his signature by the holder or his agent. In such case any indorser who would have had a right of recourse against the party whose signature is cancelled, is also discharged.

(3.) A cancellation made unintentionally, or under a mistake, or without the authority of the holder is inoperative; but where a bill or any signature thereon appears to have been cancelled the burden of proof lies on the party who alleges that the cancellation was made unintentionally, or under a mistake, or without authority.

64. (1.) Where a bill or acceptance is materially altered without the assent of all parties liable on the bill, the bill is avoided except as against a party who has himself made, authorised, or assented to the alteration, and subsequent indorsers.

Provided that,

Where a bill has been materially altered, but the alteration is not apparent, and the bill is in the hands of a holder in due course, such holder may avail himself of the bill as if it had not been altered, and may enforce payment of it according to its original tenour.

(2.) In particular the following alterations are material, namely, any alteration of the date, the sum payable, the time of payment, the place of payment, and, where a bill has been accepted generally, the addition of a place of payment without the acceptor's assent.

ACCEPTANCE AND PAYMENT FOR HONOUR

65. (1.) Where a bill of exchange has been protested for dishonour by non-acceptance, or protested for better security, and is not overdue, any person, not being a party already liable thereon, may, with the consent of the holder, intervene and accept the bill *supra* protest, for the honour of any party liable thereon, or for the honour of the person for whose account the bill is drawn.

(2.) A bill may be accepted for honour for part only of the sum for which it is drawn.

(3.) An acceptance for honour *supra* protest in order to be valid must —

(*a*) be written on the bill, and indicate that it is an acceptance for honour:

(*b*) be signed by the acceptor for honour.

(4.) Where an acceptance for honour does not expressly state for whose honour it is made, it is deemed to be an acceptance for the honour of the drawer.

(5.) Where a bill payable after sight is accepted for honour, its maturity is calculated from the date of the noting for non-acceptance, and not from the date of the acceptance for honour.

66. (1.) The acceptor for honour of a bill by accepting it engages that he will, on due presentment, pay the bill according to the tenor of his acceptance, if it is not paid by the drawee, provided it has been duly presented for payment, and protested for nonpayment, and that he receives notice of these facts.

(2.) The acceptor for honour is liable to the holder and to all parties to the bill subsequent to the party for whose honour he has accepted.

67. (1.) Where a dishonoured bill has been accepted for honour *supra* protest, or contains a reference in case of need, it must be protested for nonpayment before it is presented for payment to the acceptor for honour, or referee in case of need.

(2.) Where the address of the acceptor for honour is in the same place where the bill is protested for nonpayment, the bill must be presented to him not later than the day following its maturity; and where the address of the acceptor for honour is in some place other than the place where it was protested for nonpayment, the bill must be forwarded not later than the day following its maturity for presentment to him.

(3.) Delay in presentment or non-presentment is excused by any circumstance which would excuse delay in presentment for payment or non-presentment for payment.

(4.) When a bill of exchange is dishonoured by the acceptor for honour it must be protested for nonpayment by him.

68. (1.) Where a bill has been protested for nonpayment, any person may intervene and pay it *supra* protest for the honour of any party liable thereon, or for the honour of the person for whose account the bill is drawn.

(2.) Where two or more persons offer to pay a bill for the honour of different parties, the person whose payment will discharge most parties to the bill shall have the preference.

(3.) Payment for honour *supra* protest, in order to operate as such and not as a mere voluntary payment, must be attested by a notarial act of honour which may be appended to the protest or form an extension of it.

(4.) The notarial act of honour must be founded on a declaration made by the payer for honour, or his agent in that behalf, declaring his intention to pay the bill for honour, and for whose honour he pays.

(5.) Where a bill has been paid for honour, all parties subsequent to the party for whose honour it is paid are discharged, but the payer for honour is subrogated for, and succeeds to both the rights and duties of, the holder as regards the party for whose honour he pays, and all parties liable to that party.

(6.) The payer for honour on paying to the holder the amount of the bill and the notarial expenses incidental to its dishonour is entitled to receive both the bill itself and the protest. If the holder do not on demand deliver them up he shall be liable to the payer for honour in damages.

(7.) Where the holder of a bill refuses to receive payment *supra* protest he shall lose his right of recourse against any party who would have been discharged by such payment.

LOST INSTRUMENTS

69. Where a bill has been lost before it is overdue, the person who was the holder of it may apply to the drawer to give him another bill of the same tenor, giving security to the drawer if required to indemnify him against all persons whatever in case the bill alleged to have been lost shall be found again.

If the drawer on request as aforesaid refuses to give such duplicate bill he may be compelled to do so.

70. In any action or proceeding upon a bill, the court or a judge may order that the loss of the instrument shall not be set up, provided an indemnity be given to the satisfaction of the court or judge against the claims of any other person upon the instrument in question.

BILL IN A SET

71. (1.) Where a bill is drawn in a set, each part of the set being numbered, and containing a reference to the other parts, the whole of the parts constitute one bill.

(2.) Where the holder of a set indorses two or more parts to different persons, he is liable on every such part, and every indorser subsequent to him is liable on the part he has himself indorsed as if the said parts were separate bills.

(3.) Where two or more parts of a set are negotiated to different holders in due course, the holder whose title first accrues is as between such holders deemed the true owner of the bill; but nothing in this sub-section shall affect the rights of a person who in due course accepts or pays the part first presented to him.

(4.) The acceptance may be written on any part, and it must be written on one part only.

If the drawee accepts more than one part, and such accepted parts get into the hands of different holders in due course, he is liable on every such part as if it were a separate bill.

(5.) When the acceptor of a bill drawn in a set pays it without requiring the part bearing his acceptance to be delivered up to him, and that part at maturity is outstanding in the hands of a holder in due course, he is liable to the holder thereof.

(6.) Subject to the preceding rules, where any one part of a bill drawn in a set is discharged by payment or otherwise, the whole bill is discharged.

CONFLICT OF LAWS

72. Where a bill drawn in one country is negotiated, accepted, or payable in another, the rights, duties, and liabilities of the parties thereto are determined as follows: —

(1.) The validity of a bill as regards requisites in form is determined by the law of the place of issue, and the validity as regards requisites in form of the supervening contracts, such as acceptance, or indorsement, or acceptance *supra* protest, is determined by the law of the place where such contract was made.

Provided that —

(*a*) Where a bill is issued out of the United Kingdom it is not invalid by reason only that it is not stamped in accordance with the law of the place of issue:

(*b*) Where a bill, issued out of the United Kingdom, conforms, as regards requisites in form, to the law of the United Kingdom, it may, for the purpose of enforcing payment thereof, be treated as valid as between all persons who negotiate, hold, or become parties to it in the United Kingdom.

(2.) Subject to the provisions of this Act, the interpretation of the drawing, indorsement, acceptance, or acceptance *supra* protest of a bill, is determined by the law of the place where such contract is made.

Provided that where an inland bill is indorsed in a foreign country the indorsement shall as regards the payer be interpreted according to the law of the United Kingdom.

(3.) The duties of the holder with respect to presentment for acceptance or payment and the necessity for or sufficiency of a protest or notice of dishonour, or otherwise, are determined by the law of the place where the act is done or the bill is dishonoured.

(4.) Where a bill is drawn out of but payable in the United Kingdom and the sum payable is not expressed in the currency of the United Kingdom, the amount shall, in the absence of some express stipulation, be calculated according to the rate of exchange for sight drafts at the place of payment on the day the bill is payable.

(5.) Where a bill is drawn in one country and is payable in another, the due date thereof is determined according to the law of the place where it is payable.

PART III

CHEQUES ON A BANKER

73. A cheque is a bill of exchange drawn on a banker payable on demand.

Except as otherwise provided in this Part, the provisions of this Act applicable to a bill of exchange payable on demand apply to a cheque.

74. Subject to the provisions of this Act —

(1.) Where a cheque is not presented for payment within a reasonable time of its issue, and the drawer or the person on whose account it is drawn had the right at the time of such presentment as between him and the banker to have the cheque paid and suffers actual damage through the delay, he is discharged to the extent of such damage, that is to say, to the extent to which such drawer or person is a creditor of such banker to a larger amount than he would have been had such cheque been paid.

(2.) In determining what is a reasonable time regard shall be had to the nature of the instrument, the usage of trade and of bankers, and the facts of the particular case.

(3.) The holder of such cheque as to which such drawer or person is discharged shall be a creditor, in lieu of such drawer or person, of such banker to the extent of such discharge, and entitled to recover the amount from him.

75. The duty and authority of a banker to pay a cheque drawn on him by his customer are determined by —

(1.) Countermand of payment:

(2.) Notice of the customer's death.

CROSSED CHEQUES

76. (1.) Where a cheque bears across its face an addition of —

(*a*) The words "and company" or any abbreviation thereof between two parallel transverse lines, either with or without the words "not negotiable"; or

(*b*) Two parallel transverse lines simply, either with or without the words "not negotiable";

that addition constitutes a crossing, and the cheque is crossed generally.

(2.) Where a cheque bears across its face an addition of the name of the banker, either with or without the words "not negotiable," that addition constitutes a crossing, and the cheque is crossed specially and to that banker.

77. (1.) A cheque may be crossed generally or specially by the drawer.

(2.) Where a cheque is uncrossed, the holder may cross it generally or specially.

(3.) Where a cheque is crossed generally the holder may cross it specially.

(4.) Where a cheque is crossed generally or specially, the holder may add the words "not negotiable."

(5.) Where a cheque is crossed specially, the banker to whom it is crossed may again cross it specially to another banker for collection.

(6.) Where an uncrossed cheque, or a cheque crossed generally, is sent to a banker for collection, he may cross it specially to himself.

78. A crossing authorised by this Act is a material part of the cheque; it shall not be lawful for any person to obliterate or, except as authorised by this Act, to add to or alter the crossing.

79. (1.) Where a cheque is crossed specially to more than one banker except when crossed to an agent for collection being a banker, the banker on whom it is drawn shall refuse payment thereof.

(2.) Where the banker on whom a cheque is drawn which is so crossed nevertheless pays the same, or pays a cheque crossed generally otherwise than to a banker, or if crossed specially otherwise than to the banker to whom it is crossed, or his agent for collection being a banker, he is liable to the true owner of the cheque for any loss he may sustain owing to the cheque having been so paid.

Provided that where a cheque is presented for payment which does not at the time of presentment appear to be crossed, or to have had a crossing which has been obliterated, or to have been added to or altered otherwise than as authorised by this Act, the banker paying the cheque in good faith and without negligence shall not be responsible or incur any liability, nor shall the payment be questioned by reason of the cheque having been crossed, or of the crossing having been obliterated or having been added to or altered otherwise than as authorised by this Act, and of payment having been made otherwise than to a banker or to the banker to whom the cheque is or was crossed, or to his agent for collection being a banker, as the case may be.

80. Where the banker, on whom a crossed cheque is drawn, in good faith and without negligence pays it, if crossed generally, to a banker, and if crossed specially, to the banker to whom it is crossed, or his agent for collection being a banker, the banker paying the cheque, and, if the cheque has come into the hands of the payee, the drawer, shall respectively be entitled to the same rights and be placed in the same position as if payment of the cheque had been made to the true owner thereof.

81. Where a person takes a crossed cheque which bears on it the words "not negotiable," he shall not have and shall not be capable of giving a better title to the cheque than that which the person from whom he took it had.

82. Where a banker in good faith and without negligence receives payment for a customer of a cheque crossed generally or specially to himself, and the customer has no title or a defective title thereto, the banker shall not incur any liability to the true owner of the cheque by reason only of having received such payment.

PART IV

PROMISSORY NOTES

83. (1.) A promissory note is an unconditional promise in writing made by one person to another signed by the maker, engaging to pay, on demand or at a fixed or determinable future time, a sum certain in money, to, or to the order of, a specified person or to bearer.

(2.) An instrument in the form of a note payable to maker's order is not a note within the meaning of this section unless and until it is indorsed by the maker.

(3.) A note is not invalid by reason only that it contains also a pledge of collateral security with authority to sell or dispose thereof.

(4.) A note which is, or on the face of it purports to be, both made and payable within the British Islands is an inland note. Any other note is a foreign note.

84. A promissory note is inchoate and incomplete until delivery thereof to the payee or bearer.

85. (1.) A promissory note may be made by two or more makers, and they may be liable thereon jointly, or jointly and severally according to its tenour.

(2.) Where a note runs "I promise to pay" and is signed by two or more persons it is deemed to be their joint and several note.

86. (1.) Where a note payable on demand has been indorsed, it must be presented for payment within a reasonable time of the indorsement. If it be not so presented the indorser is discharged.

(2.) In determining what is a reasonable time, regard shall be had to the nature of the instrument, the usage of trade, and the facts of the particular case.

(3.) Where a note payable on demand is negotiated, it is not deemed to be overdue, for the purpose of affecting the holder with defects of title of which he had no notice, by reason that it appears that a reasonable time for presenting it for payment has elapsed since its issue.

87. (1.) Where a promissory note is in the body of it made payable at a particular place, it must be presented for payment at that place in order to render the maker liable. In any other case, presentment for payment is not necessary in order to render the maker liable.

(2.) Presentment for payment is necessary in order to render the indorser of a note liable.

(3.) Where a note is in the body of it made payable at a particular place, presentment at that place is necessary in order to render an indorser liable; but when a place of payment is indicated by way of memorandum only, presentment at that place is sufficient to render the indorser liable, but a presentment to the maker elsewhere, if sufficient in other respects, shall also suffice.

88. The maker of a promissory note by making it —

(1.) Engages that he will pay it according to its tenour;

(2.) Is precluded from denying to a holder in due course the existence of the payee and his then capacity to indorse.

89. (1.) Subject to the provisions in this part, and except as by this section provided, the provisions of this Act relating to bills of exchange apply, with the necessary modifications, to promissory notes.

(2.) In applying those provisions the maker of a note shall be deemed to correspond with the acceptor of a bill, and the first indorser of a note shall be deemed to correspond with the drawer of an accepted bill payable to drawer's order.

(3.) The following provisions as to bills do not apply to notes; namely, provisions relating to —

(*a*) Presentment for acceptance;

(*b*) Acceptance;

(*c*) Acceptance *supra* protest;

(*d*) Bills in a set.

(4.) Where a foreign note is dishonoured, protest thereof is unnecessary.

PART V

SUPPLEMENTARY

90. A thing is deemed to be done in good faith, within the meaning of this Act, where it is in fact done honestly, whether it is done negligently or not.

91. (1.) Where, by this Act, any instrument or writing is required to be signed by any person, it is not necessary that he should sign it with his own hand, but it is sufficient if his signature is written thereon by some other person by or under his authority.

(2.) In the case of a corporation, where, by this Act, any instrument or writing is required to be signed, it is sufficient if the instrument or writing be sealed with the corporate seal.

But nothing in this section shall be construed as requiring the bill or note of a corporation to be under seal.

92. Where, by this Act, the time limited for doing any act or thing is less than three days, in reckoning time, non-business days are excluded.

"Non-business days" for the purposes of this Act mean —

(*a*) Sunday, Good Friday, Christmas Day:

(*b*) A bank holiday under the Bank Holidays Act, 1871, or Acts amending it:

(*c*) A day appointed by Royal proclamation as a public fast or thanksgiving day.

Any other day is a business day.

93. For the purposes of this Act, where a bill or note is required to be protested within a specified time or before some further proceeding is taken, it is sufficient that the bill has been noted for protest before the expiration of the specified time or the taking of the proceeding; and the formal protest may be extended at any time thereafter as of the date of the noting.

94. Where a dishonoured bill or note is authorised or required to be protested, and the services of a notary cannot be obtained at the place where the bill is dishonoured, any householder or substantial resident of the place may, in the presence of two witnesses, give a certificate, signed by them, attesting the dishonour of the bill, and the certificate shall in all respects operate as if it were a formal protest of the bill.

The form given in Schedule 1 to this Act may be used with necessary modifications, and if used shall be sufficient.

95. The provisions of this Act as to crossed cheques shall apply to a warrant for payment of dividend.

96. The enactments mentioned in the second schedule to this Act are hereby repealed as from the commencement of this Act to the extent in that schedule mentioned.

Provided that such repeal shall not affect anything done or suffered, or any right, title, or interest acquired or accrued before the commencement of this Act, or any legal proceeding or remedy in respect of any such thing, right, title, or interest.

97. (1.) The rules in bankruptcy relating to bills of exchange, promissory notes, and cheques, shall continue to apply thereto notwithstanding anything in this Act contained.

(2.) The rules of common law including the law merchant, save in so far as they are inconsistent with the express provisions of this Act, shall continue to apply to bills of exchange, promissory notes, and cheques.

(3.) Nothing in this Act or in any repeal effected thereby shall affect —

(*a*) The provisions of the Stamp Act, 1870, or Acts amending it, or any law or enactment for the time being in force relating to the revenue:

(*b*) The provisions of the Companies Act, 1862, or Acts amending it, or any Act relating to joint stock banks or companies:

(*c*) The provisions of any Act relating to or confirming the privileges of the Bank of England or the Bank of Ireland respectively:

(*d*) The validity of any usage relating to dividend warrants, or the indorsements thereof.

98. Nothing in this Act or in any repeal effected thereby shall extend or restrict, or in any way alter or affect the law and practice in Scotland in regard to summary diligence.

99. Where any Act or document refers to any enactment repealed by this Act, the Act or document shall be construed, and shall operate, as if it referred to the corresponding provisions of this Act.

100. In any judicial proceeding in Scotland, any fact relating to a bill of exchange, bank cheque, or promissory note, which is relevant to any question of liability thereon, may be proved by parole evidence: Provided that this enactment shall not in any way affect the existing law and practice whereby the party who is, according to the tenour of any bill of exchange, bank cheque, or promissory note, debtor to the holder in the amount thereof, may be required, as a condition of obtaining a sist of diligence, or suspension of a charge, or threatened charge, to make such consignation, or to find such caution as the court or judge before whom the cause is depending may require.

This section shall not apply to any case where the bill of exchange, bank cheque, or promissory note has undergone the sesennial prescription.

UNIFORM NEGOTIABLE INSTRUMENTS LAW [1]

TITLE I.—NEGOTIABLE INSTRUMENTS IN GENERAL

ARTICLE I. — FORM AND INTERPRETATION

Section 1. Be it enacted, etc., An instrument to be negotiable must conform to the following requirements:

1. It must be in writing and signed by the maker or drawer;
2. Must contain an unconditional promise or order to pay a sum certain in money;
3. Must be payable on demand, or at a fixed or determinable future time;
4. Must be payable to order or to bearer; and,
5. Where the instrument is addressed to a drawee, he must be named or otherwise indicated therein with reasonable certainty.

Sec. 2. The sum payable is a sum certain within the meaning of this act, although it is to be paid —

1. With interest; or
2. By stated instalments; or
3. By stated instalments, with a provision that upon default in payment of any instalment or of interest the whole shall become due; or
4. With exchange, whether at a fixed rate or at the current rate; or
5. With costs of collection or an attorney's fee, in case payment shall not be made at maturity.

Sec. 3. An unqualified order or promise to pay is unconditional within the meaning of this act, though coupled with —

1. An indication of a particular fund out of which reimbursement is to be made, or a particular account to be debited with the amount; or
2. A statement of the transaction which gives rise to the instrument.

But an order or promise to pay out of a particular fund is not unconditional.

Sec. 4. An instrument is payable at a determinable future time, within the meaning of this act, which is expressed to be payable —

1. At a fixed period after date or sight; or
2. On or before a fixed or determinable future time specified therein; or
3. On or at a fixed period after the occurrence of a specified event, which is certain to happen, though the time of happening be uncertain.

An instrument payable upon a contingency is not negotiable, and the happening of the event does not cure the defect.

Sec. 5. An instrument which contains an order or promise to do any act in addition to the payment of money is not negotiable. But the negotiable character of an instrument otherwise negotiable is not affected by a provision which —

1. Authorizes the sale of collateral securities in case the instrument be not paid at maturity; or
2. Authorizes a confession of judgment if the instrument be not paid at maturity; or
3. Waives the benefit of any law intended for the advantage or protection of the obligor; or

[1] The Act has been adopted with occasional local variations by all the States in the United States, in Alaska, in Hawaii, and in Porto Rico. For dates of adoption and for comparative tables of differences see Brannan, Uniform Negotiable Instruments Law (6th ed., Beutel, 1938).

4. Gives the holder an election to require something to be done in lieu of payment of money.

But nothing in this section shall validate any provision or stipulation otherwise illegal.

Sec. 6. The validity and negotiable character of an instrument are not affected by the fact that —

1. It is not dated; or
2. Does not specify the value given, or that any value has been given therefor; or
3. Does not specify the place where it is drawn or the place where it is payable; or
4. Bears a seal; or
5. Designates a particular kind of current money in which payment is to be made.

But nothing in this section shall alter or repeal any statute requiring in certain cases the nature of the consideration to be stated in the instrument.

Sec. 7. An instrument is payable on demand:

1. Where it is expressed to be payable on demand, or at sight, or on presentation; or
2. In which no time for payment is expressed.

Where an instrument is issued, accepted, or indorsed when overdue, it is, as regards the person so issuing, accepting, or indorsing it, payable on demand.

Sec. 8. The instrument is payable to order where it is drawn payable to the order of a specified person or to him or his order. It may be drawn payable to the order of —

1. A payee who is not maker, drawer, or drawee; or
2. The drawer or maker; or
3. The drawee; or
4. Two or more payees jointly; or
5. One or some of several payees; or
6. The holder of an office for the time being.

Where the instrument is payable to order the payee must be named or otherwise indicated therein with reasonable certainty.

Sec. 9. The instrument is payable to bearer —

1. When it is expressed to be so payable; or
2. When it is payable to a person named therein or bearer; or
3. When it is payable to the order of a fictitious or non-existing person, and such fact was known to the person making it so payable; or
4. When the name of the payee does not purport to be the name of any person; or
5. When the only or last indorsement is an indorsement in blank.

Sec. 10. The instrument need not follow the language of this act, but any terms are sufficient which clearly indicate an intention to conform to the requirements hereof.

Sec. 11. Where the instrument or an acceptance or any indorsement thereon is dated, such date is deemed *prima facie* to be the true date of the making, drawing, acceptance, or indorsement as the case may be.

Sec. 12. The instrument is not invalid for the reason only that it is antedated or post-dated, provided this is not done for an illegal or fraudulent purpose. The person to whom an instrument so dated is delivered acquires the title thereto as of the date of delivery.

Sec. 13. Where an instrument expressed to be payable at a fixed period after date is issued undated, or where the acceptance of an instrument payable at a fixed period after sight is undated, any holder may insert therein the true date of issue or acceptance, and the instrument shall be payable accordingly. The insertion of a wrong date does not avoid the instrument in the hands of a subsequent holder in due course; but as to him, the date so inserted is to be regarded as the true date.

Sec. 14. Where the instrument is wanting in any material particular, the person in possession thereof has a *prima facie* authority to complete it by filling up the blanks therein. And a signature on a blank paper delivered by the person making the signature in order that the paper may be converted into a negotiable instrument operates as a *prima facie* authority to fill it up as such for any amount. In order, however, that any such instrument when completed may be enforced against any person who became a party thereto prior to its completion, it must be filled up strictly in accordance with the authority given and within a reasonable time. But if any such instrument, after completion, is negotiated to a holder in due course, it is valid and effectual for all purposes in his hands, and he may enforce it as if it had been filled up strictly in accordance with the authority given and within a reasonable time.

Sec. 15. Where an incomplete instrument has not been delivered it will not, if completed and negotiated, without authority, be a valid contract in the hands of any holder, as against any person whose signature was placed thereon before delivery.

Sec. 16. Every contract on a negotiable instrument is incomplete and revocable until delivery of the instrument for the purpose of giving effect thereto. As between immediate parties, and as regards a remote party other than a holder in due course, the delivery, in order to be effectual, must be made either by or under the authority of the party making, drawing, accepting, or indorsing, as the case may be; and in such case the delivery may be shown to have been conditional, or for a special purpose only, and not for the purpose of transferring the property in the instrument. But where the instrument is in the hands of a holder in due course, a valid delivery thereof by all parties prior to him so as to make them liable to him is conclusively presumed. And where the instrument is no longer in the possession of a party whose signature appears thereon, a valid and intentional delivery by him is presumed until the contrary is proved.

Sec. 17. Where the language of the instrument is ambiguous or there are omissions therein, the following rules of construction apply:

1. Where the sum payable is expressed in words and also in figures and there is a discrepancy between the two, the sum denoted by the words is the sum payable; but if the words are ambiguous or uncertain, reference may be had to the figures to fix the amount;

2. Where the instrument provides for the payment of interest, without specifying the date from which interest is to run, the interest runs from the date of the instrument, and if the instrument is undated, from the issue thereof;

3. Where the instrument is not dated, it will be considered to be dated as of the time it was issued;

4. Where there is a conflict between the written and printed provisions of the instrument, the written provisions prevail;

5. Where the instrument is so ambiguous that there is doubt whether it is a bill or note, the holder may treat it as either at his election;

6. Where a signature is so placed upon the instrument that it is not clear in what capacity the person making the same intended to sign, he is to be deemed an indorser;

7. Where an instrument containing the words, "I promise to pay," is signed by two or more persons, they are deemed to be jointly and severally liable thereon.

Sec. 18. No person is liable on the instrument whose signature does not appear thereon, except as herein otherwise expressly provided. But one who signs in a trade or assumed name will be liable to the same extent as if he had signed in his own name.

Sec. 19. The signature of any party may be made by a duly authorized agent. No particular form of appointment is necessary for this purpose; and the authority of the agent may be established as in other cases of agency.

Sec. 20. Where the instrument contains or a person adds to his signature words indicating that he signs for or on behalf of a principal, or in a representative capacity, he is not liable on the instrument if he was duly authorized; but the mere addition of words describing him as an agent, or as filling a representative character, without disclosing his principal, does not exempt him from personal liability.

Sec. 21. A signature by "procuration" operates as notice that the agent has but a limited authority to sign, and the principal is bound only in case the agent in so signing acted within the actual limits of his authority.

Sec. 22. The indorsement or assignment of the instrument by a corporation or by an infant passes the property therein, notwithstanding that from want of capacity the corporation or infant may incur no liability thereon.

Sec. 23. When a signature is forged or made without the authority of the person whose signature it purports to be, it is wholly inoperative, and no right to retain the instrument, or to give a discharge therefor, or to enforce payment thereof against any party thereto, can be acquired through or under such signature, unless the party, against whom it is sought to enforce such right, is precluded from setting up the forgery or want of authority.

Article II. — Consideration

Sec. 24. Every negotiable instrument is deemed *prima facie* to have been issued for a valuable consideration; and every person whose signature appears thereon to have become a party thereto for value.

Sec. 25. Value is any consideration sufficient to support a simple contract. An antecedent or pre-existing debt constitutes value; and is deemed such whether the instrument is payable on demand or at a future time.

Sec. 26. Where value has at any time been given for the instrument, the holder is deemed a holder for value in respect to all parties who became such prior to that time.

Sec. 27. Where the holder has a lien on the instrument, arising either from contract or by implication of law, he is deemed a holder for value to the extent of his lien.

Sec. 28. Absence or failure of consideration is matter of defence as against any person not a holder in due course; and partial failure of consideration is a defence *pro tanto*, whether the failure is an ascertained and liquidated amount or otherwise.

Sec. 29. An accommodation party is one who has signed the instrument as maker, drawer, acceptor, or indorser, without receiving value therefor, and for the purpose of lending his name to some other person. Such a person is liable on the instrument to a holder for value, notwithstanding such holder at the time of taking the instrument knew him to be only an accommodation party.

Article III. — Negotiation

Sec. 30. An instrument is negotiated when it is transferred from one person to another in such manner as to constitute the transferee the holder thereof. If payable to bearer it is negotiated by delivery; if payable to order it is negotiated by the indorsement of the holder completed by delivery.

Sec. 31. The indorsement must be written on the instrument itself or upon a paper attached thereto. The signature of the indorser, without additional words, is a sufficient indorsement.

Sec. 32. The indorsement must be an indorsement of the entire instrument. An indorsement, which purports to transfer to the indorsee a part only of the amount payable, or which purports to transfer the instrument to two or more indorsees severally, does not operate as a negotiation of the instrument. But where the instrument has been paid in part, it may be indorsed as to the residue.

Sec. 33. An indorsement may be either special or in blank; and it may also be either restrictive or qualified, or conditional.

Sec. 34. A special indorsement specifies the person to whom, or to whose order, the instrument is to be payable; and the indorsement of such indorsee is necessary to the further negotiation of the instrument. An indorsement in blank specifies no indorsee, and an instrument so indorsed is payable to bearer, and may be negotiated by delivery.

Sec. 35. The holder may convert a blank indorsement into a special indorsement by writing over the signature of the indorser in blank any contract consistent with the character of the indorsement.

Sec. 36. An indorsement is restrictive, which either —

1. Prohibits the further negotiation of the instrument; or
2. Constitutes the indorsee the agent of the indorser; or
3. Vests the title in the indorsee in trust for or to the use of some other person.

But the mere absence of words implying power to negotiate does not make an indorsement restrictive.

Sec. 37. A restrictive indorsement confers upon the indorsee the right —

1. To receive payment of the instrument;
2. To bring any action thereon that the indorser could bring;
3. To transfer his rights as such indorsee, where the form of the indorsement authorizes him to do so.

But all subsequent indorsees acquire only the title of the first indorsee under the restrictive indorsement.

Sec. 38. A qualified indorsement constitutes the indorser a mere assignor of the title to the instrument. It may be made by adding to the indorser's signature the words "without recourse," or any words of similar import. Such an indorsement does not impair the negotiable character of the instrument.

Sec. 39. Where an indorsement is conditional, a party required to pay the instrument may disregard the condition, and make payment to the indorsee or his transferee, whether the condition has been fulfilled or not. But any person to whom an instrument so indorsed is negotiated, will hold the same, or the proceeds thereof, subject to the rights of the person indorsing conditionally.

Sec. 40. Where an instrument, payable to bearer, is indorsed specially, it may nevertheless be further negotiated by delivery; but the person indorsing specially is liable as indorser to only such holders as make title through his indorsement.

Sec. 41. Where an instrument is payable to the order of two or more payees or indorsees who are not partners, all must indorse, unless the one indorsing has authority to indorse for the others.

Sec. 42. Where an instrument is drawn or indorsed to a person as "Cashier" or other fiscal officer of a bank or corporation, it is deemed *prima facie* to be payable to the bank or corporation of which he is such officer, and may be negotiated by either the indorsement of the bank or corporation, or the indorsement of the officer.

Sec. 43. Where the name of a payee or indorsee is wrongly designated or misspelled, he may indorse the instrument as therein described, adding, if he think fit, his proper signature.

Sec. 44. Where any person is under obligation to indorse in a representative capacity, he may indorse in such terms as to negative personal liability.

Sec. 45. Except where an indorsement bears date after the maturity of the instrument, every negotiation is deemed *prima facie* to have been effected before the instrument was overdue.

Sec. 46. Except where the contrary appears, every indorsement is presumed *prima facie* to have been made at the place where the instrument is dated.

Sec. 47. An instrument negotiable in its origin continues to be negotiable until it has been restrictively indorsed or discharged by payment or otherwise.

Sec. 48. The holder may at any time strike out any indorsement which is not necessary to his title. The indorser whose indorsement is struck out, and all indorsers subsequent to him, are thereby relieved from liability on the instrument.

Sec. 49. Where the holder of an instrument payable to his order transfers it for value without indorsing it, the transfer vests in the transferee such title as the transferor had therein, and the transferee acquires, in addition, the right to have the indorsement of the transferor. But for the purpose of determining whether the transferee is a holder in due course, the negotiation takes effect as of the time when the indorsement is actually made.

Sec. 50. Where an instrument is negotiated back to a prior party, such party may, subject to the provisions of this act, reissue and further negotiate the same. But he is not entitled to enforce payment thereof against any intervening party to whom he was personally liable.

Article IV. — Rights of the Holder

Sec. 51. The holder of a negotiable instrument may sue thereon in his own name; and payment to him in due course discharges the instrument.

Sec. 52. A holder in due course is a holder who has taken the instrument under the following conditions:

1. That it is complete and regular upon its face;
2. That he became the holder of it before it was overdue, and without notice that it had been previously dishonored, if such was the fact;
3. That he took it in good faith and for value;
4. That at the time it was negotiated to him he had no notice of any infirmity in the instrument or defect in the title of the person negotiating it.

Sec. 53. Where an instrument payable on demand is negotiated an unreasonable length of time after its issue, the holder is not deemed a holder in due course.

Sec. 54. Where the transferee receives notice of any infirmity in the instrument or defect in the title of the person negotiating the same before he has paid the full amount agreed to be paid therefor, he will be deemed a holder in due course only to the extent of the amount theretofore paid by him.

Sec. 55. The title of a person who negotiates an instrument is defective within the meaning of this act when he obtained the instrument, or any signature thereto, by fraud, duress, or force and fear, or other unlawful means, or for an illegal consideration, or when he negotiates it in breach of faith, or under such circumstances as amount to a fraud.

Sec. 56. To constitute notice of an infirmity in the instrument or defect in the title of the person negotiating the same, the person to whom it is negotiated must have had actual knowledge of the infirmity or defect, or knowledge of such facts that his action in taking the instrument amounted to bad faith.

Sec. 57. A holder in due course holds the instrument free from any defect of title of prior parties, and free from defences available to prior parties among themselves, and may enforce payment of the instrument for the full amount thereto against all parties liable thereon.

Sec. 58. In the hands of any holder other than a holder in due course, a negotiable instrument is subject to the same defences as if it were non-negotiable. But a holder who derives his title through a holder in due course, and who is not himself a party to any fraud or illegality affecting the instrument, has all the rights of such former holder in respect of all parties prior to the latter.

Sec. 59. Every holder is deemed *prima facie* to be a holder in due course; but when it is shown that the title of any person who has negotiated the instrument was defective, the burden is on the holder to prove that he or some person under whom he claims acquired the title as holder in due course. But the last-mentioned rule does not apply in favor of a party who became bound on the instrument prior to the acquisition of such defective title.

Article V. — Liabilities of Parties

Sec. 60. The maker of a negotiable instrument by making it engages that he will pay it according to its tenor, and admits the existence of the payee and his then capacity to indorse.

Sec. 61. The drawer by drawing the instrument admits the existence of the payee and his then capacity to indorse; and engages that on due presentment the instrument will be accepted or paid, or both, according to its tenor, and that if it be dishonored, and the necessary proceedings on dishonor be duly taken, he will pay the amount thereof to the holder, or to any subsequent indorser who may be compelled to pay it. But the drawer may insert in the instrument an express stipulation negativing or limiting his own liability to the holder.

Sec. 62. The acceptor by accepting the instrument engages that he will pay it according to the tenor of his acceptance; and admits —

1. The existence of the drawer, the genuineness of his signature, and his capacity and authority to draw the instrument; and

2. The existence of the payee and his then capacity to indorse.

Sec. 63. A person placing his signature upon an instrument otherwise than as maker, drawer or acceptor, is deemed to be an indorser, unless he clearly indicates by appropriate words his intention to be bound in some other capacity.

Sec. 64. Where a person, not otherwise a party to an instrument, places thereon his signature in blank before delivery, he is liable as indorser, in accordance with the following rules:

1. If the instrument is payable to the order of a third person, he is liable to the payee and to all subsequent parties.

2. If the instrument is payable to the order of the maker or drawer, or is payable to bearer, he is liable to all parties subsequent to the maker or drawer.

3. If he signs for the accommodation of the payee, he is liable to all parties subsequent to the payee.

Sec. 65. Every person negotiating an instrument by delivery or by a qualified indorsement, warrants —

1. That the instrument is genuine and in all respects what it purports to be;
2. That he has a good title to it;
3. That all prior parties had capacity to contract;
4. That he has no knowledge of any fact which would impair the validity of the instrument or render it valueless.

But when the negotiation is by delivery only, the warranty extends in favor of no holder other than the immediate transferee.

The provisions of subdivision three of this section do not apply to persons negotiating public or corporation securities, other than bills and notes.

Sec. 66. Every indorser who indorses without qualification, warrants to all subsequent holders in due course:

1. The matters and things mentioned in subdivisions one, two, and three of the next preceding section; and
2. That the instrument is at the time of his indorsement valid and subsisting.

And, in addition, he engages that on due presentment, it shall be accepted or paid, or both, as the case may be, according to its tenor, and that if it be dishonored, and the necessary proceedings on dishonor be duly taken, he will pay the amount thereof to the holder, or to any subsequent indorser who may be compelled to pay it.

Sec. 67. Where a person places his indorsement on an instrument negotiable by delivery he incurs all the liabilities of an indorser.

Sec. 68. As respects one another, indorsers are liable *prima facie* in the order in which they indorse; but evidence is admissible to show that as between or among themselves they have agreed otherwise. Joint payees or joint indorsees who indorse are deemed to indorse jointly and severally.

Sec. 69. Where a broker or other agent negotiates an instrument without indorsement, he incurs all the liabilities prescribed by section sixty-five of this act, unless he discloses the name of his principal, and the fact that he is acting only as agent.

Article VI. — Presentment for Payment

Sec. 70. Presentment for payment is not necessary in order to charge the person primarily liable on the instrument; but if the instrument is, by its terms, payable at a special place, and he is able and willing to pay it there at maturity, such ability and willingness are equivalent to a tender of payment upon his part. But except as herein otherwise provided, presentment for payment is necessary in order to charge the drawer and indorsers.

Sec. 71. Where the instrument is not payable on demand, presentment must be made on the day it falls due. Where it is payable on demand, presentment must be made within a reasonable time after its issue, except that in the case of a bill of exchange, presentment for payment will be sufficient if made within a reasonable time after the last negotiation thereof.

Sec. 72. Presentment for payment, to be sufficient, must be made —

1. By the holder, or by some person authorized to receive payment on his behalf;
2. At a reasonable hour on a business day;
3. At a proper place as herein defined;
4. To the person primarily liable on the instrument, or if he is absent or inaccessible, to any person found at the place where the presentment is made.

Sec. 73. Presentment for payment is made at the proper place —

1. Where a place of payment is specified in the instrument and it is there presented;

2. Where no place of payment is specified, but the address of the person to make payment is given in the instrument and it is there presented;

3. Where no place of payment is specified and no address is given and the instrument is presented at the usual place of business or residence of the person to make payment;

4. In any other case if presented to the person to make payment wherever he can be found, or if presented at his last known place of business or residence.

Sec. 74. The instrument must be exhibited to the person from whom payment is demanded, and when it is paid must be delivered up to the party paying it.

Sec. 75. Where the instrument is payable at a bank, presentment for payment must be made during banking hours, unless the person to make payment has no funds there to meet it at any time during the day, in which case presentment at any hour before the bank is closed on that day is sufficient.

Sec. 76. Where the person primarily liable on the instrument is dead, and no place of payment is specified, presentment for payment must be made to his personal representative if such there be, and if, with the exercise of reasonable diligence, he can be found.

Sec. 77. Where the persons primarily liable on the instrument are liable as partners, and no place of payment is specified, presentment for payment may be made to any one of them, even though there has been a dissolution of the firm.

Sec. 78. Where there are several persons, not partners, primarily liable on the instrument, and no place of payment is specified, presentment must be made to them all.

Sec. 79. Presentment for payment is not required in order to charge the drawer where he has no right to expect or require that the drawee or acceptor will pay the instrument.

Sec. 80. Presentment for payment is not required in order to charge an indorser where the instrument was made or accepted for his accommodation and he has no reason to expect that the instrument will be paid if presented.

Sec. 81. Delay in making presentment for payment is excused when the delay is caused by circumstances beyond the control of the holder, and not imputable to his default, misconduct, or negligence. When the cause of delay ceases to operate, presentment must be made with reasonable diligence.

Sec. 82. Presentment for payment is dispensed with:

1. Where after the exercise of reasonable diligence presentment as required by this act cannot be made;

2. Where the drawee is a fictitious person;

3. By waiver of presentment, express or implied.

Sec. 83. The instrument is dishonored by non-payment when,—

1. It is duly presented for payment and payment is refused or cannot be obtained; or

2. Presentment is excused and the instrument is overdue and unpaid.

Sec. 84. Subject to the provisions of this act, when the instrument is dishonored by non-payment, an immediate right of recourse to all parties secondarily liable thereon accrues to the holder.

Sec. 85. Every negotiable instrument is payable at the time fixed therein without grace. When the day of maturity falls upon Sunday, or a holiday, the instrument is payable on the next succeeding business day. Instruments falling due on Saturday are to be presented for payment on the next succeeding business day, except that instruments payable on demand may, at the option of the holder, be presented for payment before twelve o'clock noon on Saturday when that entire day is not a holiday.

Sec. 86. Where the instrument is payable at a fixed period after date, after sight, or after the happening of a specified event, the time of payment is determined by excluding the day from which the time is to begin to run, and by including the date of payment.

Sec. 87. Where the instrument is made payable at a bank it is equivalent to an order to the bank to pay the same for the account of the principal debtor thereon.

Sec. 88. Payment is made in due course when it is made at or after the maturity of the instrument to the holder thereof in good faith and without notice that his title is defective.

Article VII. — Notice of Dishonor

Sec. 89. Except as herein otherwise provided, when a negotiable instrument has been dishonored by non-acceptance or non-payment, notice of dishonor must be given to the drawer and to each indorser, and any drawer or indorser to whom such notice is not given is discharged.

Sec. 90. The notice may be given by or on behalf of the holder, or by or on behalf of any party to the instrument who might be compelled to pay it to the holder, and who, upon taking it up would have a right to reimbursement from the party to whom the notice is given.

Sec. 91. Notice of dishonor may be given by an agent either in his own name or in the name of any party entitled to give notice, whether that party be his principal or not.

Sec. 92. Where notice is given by or on behalf of the holder, it enures for the benefit of all subsequent holders and all prior parties who have a right of recourse against the party to whom it is given.

Sec. 93. Where notice is given by or on behalf of a party entitled to give notice, it enures for the benefit of the holder and all parties subsequent to the party to whom notice is given.

Sec. 94. Where the instrument has been dishonored in the hands of an agent, he may either himself give notice to the parties liable thereon, or he may give notice to his principal. If he give notice to his principal, he must do so within the same time as if he were the holder, and the principal upon the receipt of such notice has himself the same time for giving notice as if the agent had been an independent holder.

Sec. 95. A written notice need not be signed, and an insufficient written notice may be supplemented and validated by verbal communication. A misdescription of the instrument does not vitiate the notice unless the party to whom the notice is given is in fact misled thereby.

Sec. 96. The notice may be in writing or merely oral and may be given in any terms which sufficiently identify the instrument, and indicate that it had been dishonored by non-acceptance or non-payment. It may in all cases be given by delivering it personally or through the mails.

Sec. 97. Notice of dishonor may be given either to the party himself or to his agent in that behalf.

Sec. 98. When any party is dead, and his death is known to the party giving notice, the notice must be given to a personal representative, if there be one, and if with reasonable diligence he can be found. If there be no personal representative, notice may be sent to the last residence or last place of business of the deceased.

Sec. 99. Where the parties to be notified are partners, notice to any one partner is notice to the firm even though there has been a dissolution.

Sec. 100. Notice to joint parties who are not partners must be given to each of them, unless one of them has authority to receive such notice for the others.

Sec. 101. Where a party has been adjudged a bankrupt or an insolvent, or has made an assignment for the benefit of creditors, notice may be given either to the party himself or to his trustee or assignee.

Sec. 102. Notice may be given as soon as the instrument is dishonored; and unless delay is excused as hereinafter provided, must be given within the times fixed by this act.

Sec. 103. Where the person giving and the person to receive notice reside in the same place, notice must be given within the following times:

1. If given at the place of business of the person to receive notice, it must be given before the close of business hours on the day following.

2. If given at his residence, it must be given before the usual hours of rest on the day following.

3. If sent by mail, it must be deposited in the post-office in time to reach him in usual course on the day following.

Sec. 104. Where the person giving and the person to receive notice reside in different places, the notice must be given within the following times:

1. If sent by mail, it must be deposited in the post-office in time to go by mail the day following the day of dishonor, or if there be no mail at a convenient hour on that day, by the next mail thereafter.

2. If given otherwise than through the post-office, then within the time that notice would have been received in due course of mail, if it had been deposited in the post-office within the time specified in the last subdivision.

Sec. 105. Where notice of dishonor is duly addressed and deposited in the post-office, the sender is deemed to have given due notice, notwithstanding any miscarriage in the mails.

Sec. 106. Notice is deemed to have been deposited in the post-office when deposited in any branch post-office or in any letter box under the control of the post-office department.

Sec. 107. Where a party receives notice of dishonor, he has, after the receipt of such notice, the same time for giving notice to antecedent parties that the holder has after the dishonor.

Sec. 108. Where a party has added an address to his signature, notice of dishonor must be sent to that address; but if he has not given such address, then the notice must be sent as follows:

1. Either to the post-office nearest to his place of residence, or to the post-office where he is accustomed to receive his letters; or

2. If he live in one place, and have his place of business in another, notice may be sent to either place; or

3. If he is sojourning in another place, notice may be sent to the place where he is so sojourning.

But where the notice is actually received by the party within the time specified in this act, it will be sufficient, though not sent in accordance with the requirements of this section.

Sec. 109. Notice of dishonor may be waived, either before the time of giving notice has arrived, or after the omission to give due notice, and the waiver may be express or implied.

Sec. 110. Where the waiver is embodied in the instrument itself, it is binding upon all parties; but where it is written above the signature of an indorser, it binds him only.

Sec. 111. A waiver of protest, whether in the case of a foreign bill of exchange or other negotiable instrument, is deemed to be a waiver not only of a formal protest, but also of presentment and notice of dishonor.

Sec. 112. Notice of dishonor is dispensed with when, after the exercise of reasonable diligence, it cannot be given to or does not reach the parties sought to be charged.

Sec. 113. Delay in giving notice of dishonor is excused when the delay is caused by circumstances beyond the control of the holder, and not imputable to his default, misconduct, or negligence. When the cause of delay ceases to operate, notice must be given with reasonable diligence.

Sec. 114. Notice of dishonor is not required to be given to the drawer in either of the following cases:

1. Where the drawer and drawee are the same person;
2. When the drawee is a fictitious person or a person not having capacity to contract;
3. When the drawer is the person to whom the instrument is presented for payment;
4. Where the drawer has no right to expect or require that the drawee or acceptor will honor the instrument;
5. Where the drawer has countermanded payment.

Sec. 115. Notice of dishonor is not required to be given to an indorser in either of the following cases:

1. Where the drawee is a fictitious person or a person not having capacity to contract, and the indorser was aware of the fact at the time he indorsed the instrument;
2. Where the indorser is the person to whom the instrument is presented for payment;
3. Where the instrument was made or accepted for his accommodation.

Sec. 116. Where due notice of dishonor by non-acceptance has been given, notice of a subsequent dishonor by non-payment is not necessary, unless in the meantime the instrument has been accepted.

Sec. 117. An omission to give notice of dishonor by non-acceptance does not prejudice the rights of a holder in due course subsequent to the omission.

Sec. 118. Where any negotiable instrument has been dishonored it may be protested for non-acceptance or non-payment, as the case may be; but protest is not required except in the case of foreign bills of exchange.

Article VIII. — Discharge of Negotiable Instruments

Sec. 119. A negotiable instrument is discharged:

1. By payment in due course by or on behalf of the principal debtor;
2. By payment in due course by the party accommodated, where the instrument is made or accepted for accommodation;
3. By the intentional cancellation thereof by the holder;
4. By any other act which will discharge a simple contract for the payment of money;
5. When the principal debtor becomes the holder of the instrument at or after maturity in his own right.

Sec. 120. A person secondarily liable on the instrument is discharged:

1. By any act which discharges the instrument;
2. By the intentional cancellation of his signature by the holder;

3. By the discharge of a prior party;

4. By a valid tender of payment made by a prior party;

5. By a release of the principal debtor, unless the holder's right of recourse against the party secondarily liable is expressly reserved;

6. By any agreement binding upon the holder to extend the time of payment, or to postpone the holder's right to enforce the instrument, unless made with the assent of the party secondarily liable, or unless the right of recourse against such party is expressly reserved.

Sec. 121. Where the instrument is paid by a party secondarily liable thereon, it is not discharged; but the party so paying it is remitted to his former rights as regards all prior parties, and he may strike out his own and all subsequent indorsements, and again negotiate the instrument, except:

1. Where it is payable to the order of a third person, and has been paid by the drawer; and

2. Where it was made or accepted for accommodation, and has been paid by the party accommodated.

Sec. 122. The holder may expressly renounce his rights against any party to the instrument, before, at or after its maturity. An absolute and unconditional renunciation of his rights against the principal debtor made at or after the maturity of the instrument discharges the instrument. But a renunciation does not affect the rights of a holder in due course without notice. A renunciation must be in writing, unless the instrument is delivered up to the person primarily liable thereon.

Sec. 123. A cancellation made unintentionally, or under a mistake or without the authority of the holder, is inoperative; but where an instrument or any signature thereon appears to have been cancelled the burden of proof lies on the party who alleges that the cancellation was made unintentionally, or under a mistake or without authority.

Sec. 124. Where a negotiable instrument is materially altered without the assent of all parties liable thereon, it is avoided, except as against a party who has himself made, authorized or assented to the alteration, and subsequent indorsers.

But when an instrument has been materially altered and is in the hands of a holder in due course, not a party to the alteration, he may enforce payment thereof according to its original tenor.

Sec. 125. Any alteration which changes:

1. The date;

2. The sum payable, either for principal or interest:

3. The time or place of payment;

4. The number or the relations of the parties;

5. The medium or currency in which payment is to be made;

Or which adds a place of payment where no place of payment is specified, or any other change or addition which alters the effect of the instrument in any respect, is a material alteration.

TITLE II. — BILLS OF EXCHANGE

Article I. — Form and Interpretation

Sec. 126. A bill of exchange is an unconditional order in writing addressed by one person to another, signed by the person giving it, requiring the person to whom it is addressed to pay on demand or at a fixed or determinable future time a sum certain in money to order or to bearer.

Sec. 127. A bill of itself does not operate as an assignment of the funds in the hands of the drawee available for the payment thereof, and the drawee is not liable on the bill unless and until he accepts the same.

Sec. 128. A bill may be addressed to two or more drawees jointly, whether they are partners or not; but not to two or more drawees in the alternative or in succession.

Sec. 129. An inland bill of exchange is a bill which is, or on its face purports to be, both drawn and payable within this state. Any other bill is a foreign bill. Unless the contrary appears on the face of the bill, the holder may treat it as an inland bill.

Sec. 130. Where in a bill drawer and drawee are the same person, or where the drawee is a fictitious person, or a person not having capacity to contract, the holder may treat the instrument, at his option, either as a bill of exchange or a promissory note.

Sec. 131. The drawer of a bill and any indorser may insert thereon the name of a person to whom the holder may resort in case of need, that is to say, in case the bill is dishonored by non-acceptance or non-payment. Such person is called the referee in case of need. It is in the option of the holder to resort to the referee in case of need or not as he may see fit.

Article II. — Acceptance

Sec. 132. The acceptance of a bill is the signification by the drawee of his assent to the order of the drawer. The acceptance must be in writing and signed by the drawee. It must not express that the drawee will perform his promise by any other means than the payment of money.

Sec. 133. The holder of a bill presenting the same for acceptance may require that the acceptance be written on the bill, and, if such request is refused, may treat the bill as dishonored.

Sec. 134. Where an acceptance is written on a paper other than the bill itself, it does not bind the acceptor except in favor of a person to whom it is shown and who, on the faith thereof, receives the bill for value.

Sec. 135. An unconditional promise in writing to accept a bill before it is drawn is deemed an actual acceptance in favor of every person who, upon the faith thereof, receives the bill for value.

Sec. 136. The drawee is allowed twenty-four hours after presentment, in which to decide whether or not he will accept the bill; but the acceptance, if given, dates as of the day of presentation.

Sec. 137. Where a drawee to whom a bill is delivered for acceptance destroys the same, or refuses within twenty-four hours after such delivery, or within such other period as the holder may allow, to return the bill accepted or non-accepted to the holder, he will be deemed to have accepted the same.

Sec. 138. A bill may be accepted before it has been signed by the drawer, or while otherwise incomplete, or when it is overdue, or after it has been dishonored by a previous refusal to accept, or by non-payment. But when a bill payable after sight is dishonored by non-acceptance and the drawee subsequently accepts it, the holder, in the absence of any different agreement, is entitled to have the bill accepted as of the date of the first presentment.

Sec. 139. An acceptance is either general or qualified. A general acceptance assents without qualification to the order of the drawer. A qualified acceptance in express terms varies the effect of the bill as drawn.

Sec. 140. An acceptance to pay at a particular place is a general acceptance, unless it expressly states that the bill is to be paid there only and not elsewhere.

Sec. 141. An acceptance is qualified, which is:

1. Conditional, that is to say, which makes payment by the acceptor dependent on the fulfilment of a condition therein stated;

2. Partial, that is to say, an acceptance to pay part only of the amount for which the bill is drawn;

3. Local, that is to say, an acceptance to pay only at a particular place;

4. Qualified as to time;

5. The acceptance of some one or more of the drawees, but not of all.

Sec. 142. The holder may refuse to take a qualified acceptance, and if he does not obtain an unqualified acceptance, he may treat the bill as dishonored by non-acceptance. Where a qualified acceptance is taken, the drawer and indorsers are discharged from liability on the bill, unless they have expressly or impliedly authorized the holder to take a qualified acceptance, or subsequently assent thereto. When the drawer or an indorser receives notice of a qualified acceptance, he must, within a reasonable time, express his dissent to the holder, or he will be deemed to have assented thereto.

Article III. — Presentment for Acceptance

Sec. 143. Presentment for acceptance must be made:

1. Where the bill is payable after sight, or in any other case, where presentment for acceptance is necessary in order to fix the maturity of the instrument; or

2. Where the bill expressly stipulates that it shall be presented for acceptance; or

3. Where the bill is drawn payable elsewhere than at the residence or place of business of the drawee.

In no other case is presentment for acceptance necessary in order to render any party to the bill liable.

Sec. 144. Except as herein otherwise provided, the holder of a bill which is required by the next preceding section to be presented for acceptance must either present it for acceptance or negotiate it within a reasonable time. If he fails to do so, the drawer and all indorsers are discharged.

Sec. 145. Presentment for acceptance must be made by or on behalf of the holder at a reasonable hour, on a business day and before the bill is overdue, to the drawee or some person authorized to accept or refuse acceptance on his behalf; and:

1. Where a bill is addressed to two or more drawees who are not partners, presentment must be made to them all, unless one has authority to accept or refuse acceptance for all, in which case presentment may be made to him only;

2. Where the drawee is dead, presentment may be made to his personal representative;

3. Where the drawee has been adjudged a bankrupt or an insolvent or has made an assignment for the benefit of creditors, presentment may be made to him or to his trustee or assignee.

Sec. 146. A bill may be presented for acceptance on any day on which negotiable instruments may be presented for payment under the provisions of sections seventy-two and eighty-five of this act. When Saturday is not otherwise a holiday, presentment for acceptance may be made before twelve o'clock, noon, on that day.

Sec. 147. Where the holder of a bill drawn payable elsewhere than at the place of business or the residence of the drawee has not time with the exercise of reasonable diligence to present the bill for acceptance before presenting it for payment on the day that it falls due, the delay caused by presenting the bill for acceptance before presenting it for payment is excused, and does not discharge the drawers and indorsers.

Sec. 148. Presentment for acceptance is excused, and a bill may be treated as dishonored by non-acceptance, in either of the following cases:

1. Where the drawee is dead, or has absconded, or is a fictitious person or a person not having capacity to contract by bill.

2. Where, after the exercise of reasonable diligence, presentment cannot be made.

3. Where, although presentment has been irregular, acceptance has been refused on some other ground.

Sec. 149. A bill is dishonored by non-acceptance:

1. When it is duly presented for acceptance, and such an acceptance as is prescribed by this act is refused or cannot be obtained; or

2. When presentment for acceptance is excused, and the bill is not accepted.

Sec. 150. Where a bill is duly presented for acceptance and is not accepted within the prescribed time, the person presenting it must treat the bill as dishonored by non-acceptance or he loses the right of recourse against the drawer and indorsers.

Sec. 151. When a bill is dishonored by non-acceptance, an immediate right of recourse against the drawers and indorsers accrues to the holder and no presentment for payment is necessary.

Article IV. — Protest

Sec. 152. Where a foreign bill, appearing on its face to be such is dishonored by non-acceptance, it must be duly protested for non-acceptance, and where such a bill which has not previously been dishonored by non-acceptance is dishonored by non-payment, it must be duly protested for non-payment. If it is not so protested, the drawer and indorsers are discharged. Where a bill does not appear on its face to be a foreign bill, protest thereof in case of dishonor is unnecessary.

Sec. 153. The protest must be annexed to the bill, or must contain a copy thereof, and must be under the hand and seal of the notary making it, and must specify: —

1. The time and place of presentment;

2. The fact that presentment was made and the manner thereof;

3. The cause or reason for protesting the bill;

4. The demand made and the answer given, if any, or the fact that the drawee or acceptor could not be found.

Sec. 154. Protest may be made by: —

1. A notary public; or

2. By any respectable resident of the place where the bill is dishonored, in the presence of two or more credible witnesses.

Sec. 155. When a bill is protested, such protest must be made on the day of its dishonor, unless delay is excused as herein provided. When a bill has been duly noted, the protest may be subsequently extended as of the date of the noting.

Sec. 156. A bill must be protested at the place where it is dishonored, except that when a bill drawn payable at the place of business or residence of some person other than the drawee, has been dishonored by non-acceptance, it must be protested for non-payment at the place where it is expressed to be payable, and no further presentment for payment to, or demand on, the drawee is necessary.

Sec. 157. A bill which has been protested for non-acceptance may be subsequently protested for non-payment.

Sec. 158. Where the acceptor has been adjudged a bankrupt or an insolvent or has made an assignment for the benefit of creditors, before the bill matures, the holder may cause the bill to be protested for better security against the drawer and indorsers.

Sec. 159. Protest is dispensed with by any circumstances which would dispense with notice of dishonor. Delay in noting or protesting is excused when delay is caused by circumstances beyond the control of the holder and not imputable to his default, misconduct, or negligence. When the cause of delay ceases to operate, the bill must be noted or protested with reasonable diligence.

Sec. 160. When a bill is lost or destroyed or is wrongly detained from the person entitled to hold it, protest may be made on a copy or written particulars thereof.

Article V. — Acceptance for Honor

Sec. 161. Where a bill of exchange has been protested for dishonor by non-acceptance or protested for better security and is not overdue, any person not being a party already liable thereon, may, with the consent of the holder, intervene and accept the bill *supra protest* for the honor of any party liable thereon or for the honor of the person for whose account the bill is drawn. The acceptance for honor may be for part only of the sum for which the bill is drawn; and where there has been an acceptance for honor for one party, there may be a further acceptance by a different person for the honor of another party.

Sec. 162. An acceptance for honor *supra protest* must be in writing and indicate that it is an acceptance for honor, and must be signed by the acceptor for honor.

Sec. 163. Where an acceptance for honor does not expressly state for whose honor it is made, it is deemed to be an acceptance for the honor of the drawer.

Sec. 164. The acceptor for honor is liable to the holder and to all parties to the bill subsequent to the party for whose honor he has accepted.

Sec. 165. The acceptor for honor by such acceptance engages that he will on due presentment pay the bill according to the terms of his acceptance, provided it shall not have been paid by the drawee, and provided also, that it shall have been duly presented for payment and protested for non-payment and notice of dishonor given him.

Sec. 166. Where a bill payable after sight is accepted for honor, its maturity is calculated from the date of the noting for non-acceptance and not from the date of the acceptance for honor.

Sec. 167. Where a dishonored bill has been accepted for honor *supra protest* or contains a reference in case of need, it must be protested for non-payment before it is presented for payment to the acceptor for honor or referee in case of need.

Sec. 168. Presentment for payment to the acceptor for honor must be made as follows: —

1. If it is to be presented in the place where the protest for non-payment was made, it must be presented not later than the day following its maturity;

2. If it is to be presented in some other place than the place where it was protested, then it must be forwarded within the time specified in section one hundred and four.

Sec. 169. The provisions of section eighty-one apply where there is delay in making presentment to the acceptor for honor or referee in case of need.

Sec. 170. When the bill is dishonored by the acceptor for honor it must be protested for non-payment by him.

Article VI. — Payment for Honor

Sec. 171. Where a bill has been protested for non-payment, any person may intervene and pay it *supra protest* for the honor of any person liable thereon or for the honor of the person for whose account it was drawn.

Sec. 172. The payment for honor *supra protest* in order to operate as such and not as a mere voluntary payment must be attested by a notarial act of honor which may be appended to the protest or form an extension to it.

Sec. 173. The notarial act of honor must be founded on a declaration made by the payer for honor or by his agent in that behalf declaring his intention to pay the bill for honor and for whose honor he pays.

Sec. 174. Where two or more persons offer to pay a bill for the honor of different parties, the person whose payment will discharge most parties to the bill is to be given the preference.

Sec. 175. Where a bill has been paid for honor, all parties subsequent to the party for whose honor it is paid are discharged, but the payer for honor is subrogated for, and succeeds to, both the rights and duties of the holder as regards the party for whose honor he pays and all parties liable to the latter.

Sec. 176. Where the holder of a bill refuses to receive payment *supra protest*, he loses his right of recourse against any party who would have been discharged by such payment.

Sec. 177. The payer for honor, on paying to the holder the amount of the bill and the notarial expenses incidental to its dishonor, is entitled to receive both the bill itself and the protest.

Article VII. — Bills in a Set

Sec. 178. Where a bill is drawn in a set, each part of the set being numbered and containing a reference to the other parts, the whole of the parts constitutes one bill.

Sec. 179. Where two or more parts of a set are negotiated to different holders in due course, the holder whose title first accrues is as between such holders the true owner of the bill. But nothing in this section affects the rights of a person who in due course accepts or pays the part first presented to him.

Sec. 180. Where the holder of a set indorses two or more parts to different persons he is liable on every such part, and every indorser subsequent to him is liable on the part he has himself indorsed, as if such parts were separate bills.

Sec. 181. The acceptance may be written on any part and it must be written on one part only. If the drawee accepts more than one part, and such accepted parts are negotiated to different holders in due course, he is liable on every such part as if it were a separate bill.

Sec. 182. When the acceptor of a bill drawn in a set pays it without requiring the part bearing his acceptance to be delivered up to him, and that part at maturity is outstanding in the hands of a holder in due course, he is liable to the holder thereon.

Sec. 183. Except as herein otherwise provided where any one part of a bill drawn in a set is discharged by payment or otherwise the whole bill is discharged.

TITLE III. — PROMISSORY NOTES AND CHECKS

Article I

Sec. 184. A negotiable promissory note within the meaning of this act is an unconditional promise in writing made by one person to another signed by the maker engaging to pay on demand, or at a fixed or determinable future time, a sum certain in money to order or to bearer. Where a note is drawn to the maker's own order, it is not complete until indorsed by him.

Sec. 185. A check is a bill of exchange drawn on a bank payable on demand. Except as herein otherwise provided, the provisions of this act applicable to a bill of exchange payable on demand apply to a check.

Sec. 186. A check must be presented for payment within a reasonable time after its issue or the drawer will be discharged from liability thereon to the extent of the loss caused by the delay.

Sec. 187. Where a check is certified by the bank on which it is drawn, the certification is equivalent to an acceptance.

Sec. 188. Where the holder of a check procures it to be accepted or certified the drawer and all indorsers are discharged from liability thereon.

Sec. 189. A check of itself does not operate as an assignment of any part of the funds to the credit of the drawer with the bank, and the bank is not liable to the holder, unless and until it accepts or certifies the check.

TITLE IV. — GENERAL PROVISIONS

Article I

Sec. 190. This act may be cited as the Uniform Negotiable Instruments Act.

Sec. 191. In this act, unless the context otherwise requires —

"Acceptance" means an acceptance completed by delivery or notification.

"Action" includes counterclaim and set-off.

"Bank" includes any person or association of persons carrying on the business of banking, whether incorporated or not.

"Bearer" means the person in possession of a bill or note which is payable to bearer.

"Bill" means bill of exchange, and "note" means negotiable promissory note.

"Delivery" means transfer of possession, actual or constructive, from one person to another.

"Holder" means the payee or indorsee of a bill or note, who is in possession of it, or the bearer thereof.

"Indorsement" means an indorsement completed by delivery.

"Instrument" means negotiable instrument.

"Issue" means the first delivery of the instrument, complete in form, to a person who takes it as a holder.

"Person" includes a body of persons, whether incorporated or not.

"Value" means valuable consideration.

"Written" includes printed, and "writing" includes print.

Sec. 192. The person "primarily" liable on an instrument is the person who by the terms of the instrument is absolutely required to pay the same. All other parties are "secondarily" liable.

Sec. 193. In determining what is a "reasonable time" or an "unreasonable time," regard is to be had to the nature of the instrument, the usage of trade or business (if any) with respect to such instruments, and the facts of the particular case.

Sec. 194. Where the day, or the last day, for doing any act herein required or permitted to be done falls on Sunday or on a holiday, the act may be done on the next succeeding secular or business day.

Sec. 195. The provisions of this act do not apply to negotiable instruments made and delivered prior to the taking effect hereof.

Sec. 196. In any case not provided for in this act the rules of the law merchant shall govern.

Sec. 197. Of the laws enumerated in the schedules hereto annexed that portion specified in the last column is repealed.

Sec. 198. This chapter shall take effect on

THE GENEVA LAW [1]

Uniform Law on Bills of Exchange and Promissory Notes

TITLE I

BILLS OF EXCHANGE

Chapter I. — Issue and Form of a Bill of Exchange

Article 1

A bill of exchange contains:

1. The term "bill of exchange" inserted in the body of the instrument and expressed in the language employed in drawing up the instrument;
2. An unconditional order to pay a determinate sum of money;
3. The name of the person who is to pay (drawee);
4. A statement of the time of payment;
5. A statement of the place where payment is to be made;
6. The name of the person to whom or to whose order payment is to be made;
7. A statement of the date and of the place where the bill is issued;
8. The signature of the person who issues the bill (drawer).

Article 2

An instrument in which any of the requirements mentioned in the preceding article is wanting is invalid as a bill of exchange, except in the cases specified in the following paragraphs:

A bill of exchange which does not mention the place of its issue is deemed to be payable at sight.

In default of special mention, the place specified beside the name of the drawee is deemed to be the place of payment, and at the same time the place of the domicile of the drawee.

A bill of exchange which does not mention the place of its issue is deemed to have been drawn in the place mentioned beside the name of the drawer.

[1] The so-called Geneva Law was formulated at an international conference sponsored by the League of Nations at Geneva in 1930. It has been enacted into legislation in most of the important commercial countries of continental Europe, including Belgium, Denmark, France, Germany, Italy, the Netherlands, Norway, and Sweden. The law also has been adopted in Japan.

Article 3

A bill of exchange may be drawn payable to drawer's order.
It may be drawn on the drawer himself.
It may be drawn for account of a third person.

Article 4

A bill of exchange may be payable at the domicile of a third person either in the locality where the drawee has his domicile or in another locality.

Article 5

When a bill of exchange is payable at sight, or at a fixed period after sight, the drawer may stipulate that the sum payable shall bear interest. In the case of any other bill of exchange, this stipulation is deemed not to be written (*non écrite*).

The rate of interest must be specified in the bill; in default of such specification, the stipulation shall be deemed not to be written (*non écrite*).

Interest runs from the date of the bill of exchange, unless some other date is specified.

Article 6

When the sum payable by a bill of exchange is expressed in words and also in figures, and there is a descrepancy between the two, the sum denoted by the words is the amount payable.

Where the sum payable by a bill of exchange is expressed more than once in words or more than once in figures, and there is a discrepancy, the smaller sum is the sum payable.

Article 7

If a bill of exchange bears signatures of persons incapable of binding themselves by a bill of exchange, or forged signatures, or signatures of fictitious persons, or signatures which for any other reason cannot bind the persons who signed the bill of exchange or on whose behalf it was signed, the obligations of the other persons who have signed it are none the less valid.

Article 8

Whosoever puts his signature on a bill of exchange as representing a person for whom he had no power to act is bound himself as a party to the bill and, if he pays, has the same rights as the person for whom he purported to act. The same rule applies to a representative who has exceeded his powers.

Article 9

The drawer guarantees both acceptance and payment.

He may release himself from guaranteeing acceptance; every stipulation by which he releases himself from the guarantee of payment is deemed not to be written (*non écrite*).

Article 10

If a bill of exchange, which was incomplete when issued, has been completed otherwise than in accordance with the agreements entered into, the non-observance of such agreements may not be set up against the holder unless he has acquired the bill of exchange in bad faith or, in acquiring it, has been guilty of gross negligence.

Chapter II. — Endorsement

Article 11

Every bill of exchange, even if not expressly drawn to order, may be transferred by means of endorsement.

When the drawer has inserted in a bill of exchange the words "not to order" or an equivalent expression, the instrument can only be transferred according to the form, and with the effects, of an ordinary assignment.

The bill may be endorsed even in favour of the drawee, whether he has accepted or not, or of the drawer, or of any other party to the bill. These persons may re-endorse the bill.

Article 12

An endorsement must be unconditional. Any condition to which it is made subject is deemed not to be written (*non écrite*).

A partial endorsement is null and void.

An endorsement "to bearer" is equivalent to an endorsement in blank.

Article 13

An endorsement must be written on the bill of exchange or on a slip affixed thereto (*allonge*). It must be signed by the endorser.

The endorsement may leave the beneficiary unspecified or may consist simply of the signature of the endorser (endorsement in blank). In the latter case, the endorsement, to be valid, must be written on the back of the bill of exchange or on the slip attached thereto (*allonge*).

Article 14

An endorsement transfers all the rights arising out of a bill of exchange.

If the endorsement is in blank, the holder may:

1. Fill up the blank either with his own name or with the name of some other person;
2. Re-endorse the bill in blank, or to some other person;
3. Transfer the bill to a third person without filling up the blank, and without endorsing it.

Article 15

In the absence of any contrary stipulation, the endorser guarantees acceptance and payment.

He may prohibit any further endorsement; in this case, he gives no guarantee to the persons to whom the bill is subsequently endorsed.

Article 16

The possessor of a bill of exchange is deemed to be the lawful holder if he establishes his title to the bill through an uninterrupted series of endorsements, even if the last endorsement is in blank. In this connection, cancelled endorsements are deemed not to be written (*non écrits*). When an endorsement in blank is followed by another endorsement, the person who signed this last endorsement is deemed to have acquired the bill by the endorsement in blank.

Where a person has been dispossessed of a bill of exchange, in any manner whatsoever, the holder who establishes his right thereto in the manner mentioned in the preceding paragraph is not bound to give up the bill unless he has acquired it in bad faith, or unless in acquiring it he has been guilty of gross negligence.

Article 17

Persons sued on a bill of exchange cannot set up against the holder defences founded on their personal relations with the drawer or with previous holders, unless the holder, in acquiring the bill, has knowingly acted to the detriment of the debtor.

Article 18

When an endorsement contains the statements "value in collection" ("*valeur en recouvrement*"), "for collection" ("*pour encaissement*"), "by procuration" ("*par procuration*") or any other phrase implying a simple mandate, the holder may exercise all rights arising out of the bill of exchange, but he can only endorse it in his capacity as agent.

In this case, the parties liable can only set up against the holder defences which could be set up against the endorser.

The mandate contained in an endorsement by procuration does not terminate by reason of the death of the party giving the mandate or by reason of his becoming legally incapable.

Article 19

When an endorsement contains the statements "value in security" ("*valeur en garantie*"), "value in pledge" ("*valeur en gage*"), or any other statement implying a pledge, the holder may exercise all the rights arising out of the bill of exchange, but an endorsement by him has the effects only of an endorsement by an agent.

The parties liable cannot set up against the holder defences founded on their personal relations with the endorser, unless the holder, in receiving the bill, has knowingly acted to the detriment of the debtor.

Article 20

An endorsement after maturity has the same effects as an endorsement before maturity. Nevertheless, an endorsement after protest for non-payment, or after the expiration of the limit of time fixed for drawing up the protest, operates only as an ordinary assignment.

Failing proof to the contrary, an endorsement without date is deemed to have been placed on the bill before the expiration of the limit of time fixed for drawing up the protest.

Chapter III. — Acceptance

Article 21

Until maturity, a bill of exchange may be presented to the drawee for acceptance at his domicile, either by the holder or by a person who is merely in possession of the bill.

Article 22

In any bill of exchange, the drawer may stipulate that it shall be presented for acceptance, with or without fixing a limit of time for presentment.

Except in the case of a bill payable at the address of a third party or in a locality other than that of the domicile of the drawee, or, except in the case of a bill drawn payable at a fixed period after sight, the drawer may prohibit presentment for acceptance.

He may also stipulate that presentment for acceptance shall not take place before a named date.

Unless the drawer has prohibited acceptance, every endorser may stipulate that the bill shall be presented for acceptance, with or without fixing a limit of time for presentment.

Article 23

Bills of exchange payable at a fixed period after sight must be presented for acceptance within one year of their date.

The drawer may abridge or extend this period.

These periods may be abridged by the endorsers.

Article 24

The drawee may demand that a bill shall be presented to him a second time on the day after the first presentment. Parties interested are not allowed to set up that this demand has not been complied with unless this request is mentioned in the protest.

The holder is not obliged to surrender to the drawee a bill presented for acceptance.

Article 25

An acceptance is written on the bill of exchange. It is expressed by the word "accepted" or any other equivalent term. It is signed by the drawee. The simple signature of the drawee on the face of the bill constitutes an acceptance.

When the bill is payable at a certain time after sight, or when it must be presented for acceptance within a certain limit of time in accordance with a special stipulation, the acceptance must be dated as of the day when the acceptance is given, unless the holder requires that it shall be dated as of the day of presentment. If it is undated, the holder, in order to preserve his right of recourse against the endorsers and the drawer, must authenticate the omission by a protest drawn up within the proper time.

Article 26

An acceptance is unconditional, but the drawee may restrict it to part of the sum payable.

Every other modification introduced by an acceptance into the tenor of the bill of exchange operates as a refusal to accept. Nevertheless, the acceptor is bound according to the terms of his acceptance.

Article 27

When the drawer of a bill has indicated a place of payment other than the domicile of the drawee without specifying a third party at whose address payment must be made, the drawee may name such third party at the time of acceptance. In default of this indication, the acceptor is deemed to have undertaken to pay the bill himself at the place of payment.

If a bill is payable at the domicile of the drawee, the latter may in his acceptance indicate an address in the same place where payment is to be made.

Article 28

By accepting, the drawee undertakes to pay the bill of exchange at its maturity.

In default of payment, the holder, even if he is the drawer, has a direct action on the bill of exchange against the acceptor for all that can be demanded in accordance with Articles 48 and 49.

Article 29

Where the drawee who has put his acceptance on a bill has cancelled it before restoring the bill, acceptance is deemed to be refused. Failing proof to the contrary, the cancellation is deemed to have taken place before the bill was restored.

Nevertheless, if the drawee has notified his acceptance in writing to the holder or to any party who has signed the bill, he is liable to such parties according to the terms of his acceptance.

Chapter IV. — "Avals"

Article 30

Payment of a bill of exchange may be guaranteed by an "aval" as to the whole or part of its amount.

This guarantee may be given by a third person or even by a person who has signed as a party to the bill.

Article 31

The "aval" is given either on the bill itself or on an "allonge."

It is expressed by the words "good as aval" ("*bon pour aval*") or by any other equivalent formula. It is signed by the giver of the "aval."

It is deemed to be constituted by the mere signature of the giver of the "aval" placed on the face of the bill, expect in the case of the signature of the drawee or of the drawer.

An "aval" must specify for whose account it is given. In default of this, it is deemed to be given for the drawer.

Article 32

The giver of an "aval" is bound in the same manner as the person for whom he has become guarantor.

His undertaking is valid even when the liability which he has guaranteed is inoperative for any reason other than defect of form.

He has, when he pays a bill of exchange, the rights arising out of the bill of exchange against the person guaranteed and against those who are liable to the latter on the bill of exchange.

Chapter V. — Maturity

Article 33

A bill of exchange may be drawn payable:

At sight;

At a fixed period after sight;

At a fixed period after date;

At a fixed date.

Bills of exchange at other maturities or payable by instalments are null and void.

Article 34

A bill of exchange at sight is payable on presentment. It must be presented for payment within a year of its date. The drawer may abridge or extend this period. These periods may be abriged by the endorsers.

The drawer may prescribe that a bill of exchange payable at sight must not be presented for payment before a named date. In this case, the period for presentment begins from the said date.

Article 35

The maturity of a bill of exchange payable at a fixed period after sight is determined either by the date of the acceptance or by the date of the protest.

In the absence of the protest, an undated acceptance is deemed, so far as regards the acceptor, to have been given on the last day of the limit of time for presentment for acceptance.

Article 36

Where a bill of exchange is drawn at one or more months after date or after sight the bill matures on the corresponding date of the month when payment must be made. If there be no corresponding date, the bill matures on the last day of this month.

When a bill of exchange is drawn at one or more months and a-half after date or sight, entire months must first be calculated.

If the maturity is fixed at the commencement, in the middle (mid-January or mid-February, etc.) or at the end of the month, the first, fifteenth or last day of the month is to be understood.

The expressions "eight days" or "fifteen days" indicate not one or two weeks, but a period of eight or fifteen actual days.

The expression "half-month" means a period of fifteen days.

Article 37

When a bill of exchange is payable on a fixed day in a place where the calendar is different from the calendar in the place of issue, the day of maturity is deemed to be fixed according to the calendar of the place of payment.

When a bill of exchange drawn between two places having different calendars is payable at a fixed period after date, the day of issue is referred to the corresponding day of the calendar in the place of payment, and the maturity is fixed accordingly.

The time for presenting bills of exchange is calculated in accordance with the rules of the preceding paragraph.

These rules do not apply if a stipulation in the bill or even the simple terms of the instrument indicate an intention to adopt some different rule.

Chapter VI. — Payment

Article 38

The holder of a bill of exchange payable on a fixed day or at a fixed period after date or after sight must present the bill for payment either on the day on which it is payable or on one of the two business days which follow.

The presentment of a bill of exchange at a clearing-house is equivalent to a presentment for payment.

Article 39

The drawee who pays a bill of exchange may require that it shall be given up to him receipted by the holder.

The holder may not refuse partial payment.

In case of partial payment the drawee may require that mention of this payment shall be made on the bill, and that a receipt therefor shall be given to him.

Article 40

The holder of a bill of exchange cannot be compelled to receive payment thereof before maturity.

The drawee who pays before maturity does so at his own risk and peril.

He who pays at maturity is validly discharged, unless he has been guilty of fraud or gross negligence. He is bound to verify the regularity of the series of endorsements, but not the signature of the endorsers.

Article 41

When a bill of exchange is drawn payable in a currency which is not that of the place of payment, the sum payable may be paid in the currency of the country, according to its value on the date of maturity. If the debtor is in default, the holder may at his option demand that the amount of the bill be paid in the currency of the country according to the rate on the day of maturity or the day of payment.

The usages of the place of payment determine the value of foreign currency. Nevertheless, the drawer may stipulate that the sum payable shall be calculated according to a rate expressed in the bill.

The foregoing rules shall not apply to the case in which the drawer has stipulated that payment must be made in a certain specified currency (stipulation for effective payment in foreign currency).

If the amount of the bill of exchange is specified in a currency having the same denomination, but a different value in the country of issue and the country of payment, reference is deemed to be made to the currency of the place of payment.

Article 42

When a bill of exchange is not presented for payment within the limit of time fixed by Article 38, every debtor is authorised to deposit the amount with the competent authority at the charge, risk and peril of the holder.

Chapter VII. — Recourse for Non-Acceptance or Non-Payment

Article 43

The holder may exercise his right of recourse against the endorsers, the drawer and the other parties liable:

At maturity:

If payment has not been made;

Even before maturity:

(1) If there has been total or partial refusal to accept;

(2) In the event of the bankruptcy (*faillite*) of the drawee, whether he has accepted or not, or in the event of a stoppage of payment on his part, even when not declared by a judgment, or where execution has been levied against his goods without result;

(3) In the event of the bankruptcy (*faillite*) of the drawer of a non-acceptable bill.

Article 44

Default of acceptance or of payment must be evidenced by an authentic act (protest for non-acceptance or non-payment).

Protest for non-acceptance must be made within the limit of time fixed for presentment for acceptance. If, in the case contemplated by Article 24, paragraph 1, the first presentment takes place on the last day of that time, the protest may nevertheless be drawn up on the next day.

Protest for non-payment of a bill of exchange payable on a fixed day or at a fixed period after date or sight must be made on one of the two business days following the day on which the bill is payable. In the case of a bill payable at sight, the protest must be drawn up under the conditions specified in the foregoing paragraph for the drawing up of a protest for non-acceptance.

Protest for non-acceptance dispenses with presentment for payment and protest for non-payment.

If there is a stoppage of payment on the part of the drawee, whether he has accepted or not, or if execution has been levied against his goods without result, the holder cannot exercise his right of recourse until after presentment of the bill to the drawee for payment and after the protest has been drawn up.

If the drawee, whether he has accepted or not, is declared bankrupt (*faillite déclarée*), or in the event of the declared bankruptcy of the drawer of a non-acceptable bill, the production of the judgment declaring the bankruptcy suffices to enable the holder to exercise his right of recourse.

Article 45

The holder must give notice of non-acceptance or non-payment to his endorser and to the drawer within the four business days which follow the day for protest or, in case of a stipulation "*retour sans frais*," the day for presentment. Every endorser must, within the two business days following the day on which he receives notice, notify his endorser of the notice he has received, mentioning the names and addresses of those who have given the previous notices, and so on through the series until the drawer is reached. The periods mentioned above run from the receipt of the preceding notice.

When, in conformity with the preceding paragraph, notice is given to a person who has signed a bill of exchange, the same notice must be given within the same limit of time to his *avaliseur*.

Where an endorser either has not specified his address or has specified it in an illegible manner, it is sufficient that notice should be given to the preceding endorser.

A person who must give notice may give it in any form whatever, even by simply returning the bill of exchange.

He must prove that he has given notice within the time allowed. This time-limit shall be regarded as having been observed if a letter giving the notice has been posted within the prescribed time.

A person who does not give notice within the limit of time mentioned above does not forfeit his rights. He is responsible for the injury, if any, caused by his negligence, but the damages shall not exceed the amount of the bill of exchange.

Article 46

The drawer, an endorser, or a person guaranteeing payment by *aval* (*avaliseur*) may, by the stipulation "*retour sans frais*," "*sans protêt*," or any other equivalent expression written on the instrument and signed, release the holder from having a protest of non-acceptance or non-payment drawn up in order to exercise his right of recourse.

This stipulation does not release the holder from presenting the bill within the prescribed time, nor from the notices he has to give. The burden of proving the non-observance of the limits of time lies on the person who seeks to set it up against the holder.

If the stipulation is written by the drawer, it is operative in respect of all persons who have signed the bill; if it is written by an endorser or an *avaliseur*, it is operative only in respect of such endorser or *avaliseur*. If, in spite of the stipulation written by the drawer, the holder has the protest drawn up, he must bear the expenses thereof. When the stipulation emanates from an endorser or *avaliseur*, the costs of the protest, if one is drawn up, may be recovered from all the persons who have signed the bill.

Article 47

All drawers, acceptors, endorsers or guarantors by *aval* of a bill of exchange are jointly and severally liable to the holder.

The holder has the right of proceeding against all these persons individually or collectively without being required to observe the order in which they have become bound.

The same right is possessed by any person signing the bill who has taken it up and paid it.

Proceedings against one of the parties liable do not prevent proceedings against the others, even though they may be subsequent to the party first proceeded against.

Article 48

The holder may recover from the person against whom he exercises his right of recourse:

(1) The amount of the unaccepted or unpaid bill of exchange with interest, if interest has been stipulated for;

(2) Interest at the rate of 6 per cent from the date of maturity;

(3) The expenses of protest and of the notices given as well as other expenses.

If the right of recourse is exercised before maturity, the amount of the bill shall be subject to a discount. This discount shall be calculated according to the official rate of discount (bank-rate) ruling on the date when recourse is exercised at the place of domicile of the holder.

Article 49

A party who takes up and pays a bill of exchange can recover from the parties liable to him:

(1) The entire sum which he has paid;

(2) Interest on the said sum calculated at the rate of 6 per cent, starting from the day when he made payment;

(3) Any expenses which he has incurred.

Article 50

Every party liable against whom a right of recourse is or may be exercised, can require, against payment, that the bill shall be given up to him with the protest and a receipted account.

Every endorser who has taken up and paid a bill of exchange may cancel his own endorsement and those of subsequent endorsers.

Article 51

In the case of the exercise of the right of recourse after a partial acceptance, the party who pays the sum in respect of which the bill has not been accepted can require that this payment shall be specified on the bill and that he shall be given a receipt therefor. The holder must also give him a certified copy of the bill, together with the protest, in order to enable subsequent recourse to be exercised.

Article 52

Every person having the right of recourse may, in the absence of agreement to the contrary, reimburse himself by means of a fresh bill (redraft) to be drawn at sight on one of the parties liable to him and payable at the domicile of that party.

The redraft includes, in addition to the sums mentioned in Articles 48 and 49, brokerage and the cost of stamping the redraft.

If the redraft is drawn by the holder, the sum payable is fixed according to the rate for a sight bill drawn at the place where the original bill was payable upon the party liable at the place of his domicile. If the redraft is drawn by an endorser, the sum payable is fixed according to the rate for a sight bill drawn at the place where the drawer of the redraft is domiciled upon the place of domicile of the party liable.

Article 53

After the expiration of the limits of time fixed:

For the presentment of a bill of exchange drawn at sight or at a fixed period after sight;

For drawing up the protest for non-acceptance or non-payment;

For presentment for payment in the case of a stipulation *retour sans frais*,

the holder loses his rights of recourse against the endorsers, against the drawer and against the other parties liable, with the exception of the acceptor.

In default of presentment for acceptance within the limit of time stipulated by the drawer, the holder loses his right of recourse for non-payment, as well as for non-acceptance, unless it appears from the terms of the stipulation that the drawer only meant to release himself from the guarantee of acceptance.

If the stipulation for a limit of time for presentment is contained in an endorsement, the endorser alone can avail himself of it.

Article 54

Should the presentment of the bill of exchange or the drawing up of the protest within the prescribed limits of time be prevented by an insurmountable obstacle (legal prohibition (*prescription légale*) by any State or other case of *vis major*), these limits of time shall be extended.

The holder is bound to give notice without delay of the case of *vis major* to his endorser and to specify this notice, which he must date and sign, on the bill or on an *allonge*; in other respects the provisions of Article 45 shall apply.

When *vis major* has terminated, the holder must without delay present the bill of exchange for acceptance or payment and, if need be, draw up the protest.

If *vis major* continues to operate beyond thirty days after maturity, recourse may be exercised, and neither presentment nor the drawing up of a protest shall be necessary.

In the case of bills of exchange drawn at sight or at a fixed period after sight, the time-limit of thirty days shall run from the date on which the holder, even before the expiration of the time for presentment, has given notice of *vis major* to his endorser. In the case of bills of exchange drawn at a certain time after sight, the above time-limit of thirty days shall be added to the period after sight specified in the bill of exchange.

Facts which are purely personal to the holder or to the person whom he has entrusted with the presentment of the bill or drawing up of the protest are not deemed to constitute cases of *vis major*.

Chapter VIII. — Intervention for Honour

1. General Provisions

Article 55

The drawer, an endorser, or a person giving an *aval* may specify a person who is to accept or pay in case of need.

A bill of exchange may, subject as hereinafter mentioned, be accepted or paid by a person who intervenes for the honour of any debtor against whom a right of recourse exists.

The person intervening may be a third party, even the drawee, or, save the acceptor, a party already liable on the bill of exchange.

The person intervening is bound to give, within two business days, notice of his intervention to the party for whose honour he has intervened. In default, he is responsible for the injury, if any, due to his negligence, but the damages shall not exceed the amount of the bill of exchange.

2. Acceptance by Intervention (for Honour)

Article 56

There may be acceptance by intervention in all cases where the holder has a right of recourse before maturity on a bill which is capable of acceptance.

When the bill of exchange indicates a person who is designated to accept or pay it in case of need at the place of payment, the holder may not exercise his rights of recourse before maturity against the person naming such referee in case of need and against subsequent signatories, unless he has presented the bill of exchange to the referee in case of need and until, if acceptance is refused by the latter, this refusal has been authenticated by a protest.

In other cases of intervention the holder may refuse an acceptance by intervention. Nevertheless, if he allows it, he loses his right of recourse before maturity against the person on whose behalf such acceptance was given and against subsequent signatories.

Article 57

Acceptance by intervention is specified on the bill of exchange. It is signed by the person intervening. It mentions the person for whose honour it has been given and, in default of such mention, the acceptance is deemed to have been given for the honour of the drawer.

Article 58

The acceptor by intervention is liable to the holder and to the endorsers, subsequent to the party for whose honour he intervened, in the same manner as such party.

Notwithstanding an acceptance by intervention, the party for whose honour it has been given and the parties liable to him may require the holder, in exchange for payment of the sum mentioned in Article 48, to deliver the bill, the protest, and a receipted account, if any.

3. PAYMENT BY INTERVENTION

Article 59

Payment by intervention may take place in all cases where, either at maturity or before maturity, the holder has a right of recourse on the bill.

Payment must include the whole amount payable by the party for whose honour it is made.

It must be made at the latest on the day following the last day allowed for drawing up the protest for non-payment.

Article 60

If a bill of exchange has been accepted by persons intervening who are domiciled in the place of payment, or if persons domiciled there have been named as referees in case of need, the holder must present the bill to all these persons and, if necessary, have a protest for non-payment drawn up at the latest on the day following the last day allowed for drawing up the protest.

In default of protest within this limit of time, the party who has named the referee in case of need, or for whose account the bill has been accepted, and the subsequent endorsers, are discharged.

Article 61

The holder who refuses payment by intervention loses his right of recourse against any persons who would have been discharged thereby.

Article 62

Payment by intervention must be authenticated by a receipt given on the bill of exchange mentioning the person for whose honour payment has been made. In default of such mention, payment is deemed to have been made for the honour of the drawer.

The bill of exchange and the protest, if any, must be given up to the person paying by intervention.

Article 63

The person paying by intervention acquires the rights arising out of the bill of exchange against the party for whose honour he has paid and against persons who are liable to the latter on the bill of exchange. Nevertheless, he cannot re-endorse the bill of exchange.

Endorsers subsequent to the party for whose honour payment has been made are discharged.

In case of competition for payment by intervention, the payment which effects the greater number of releases has the preference. Any person who, with a knowledge of the facts, intervenes in a manner contrary to this rule, loses his right of recourse against those who would have been discharged.

CHAPTER IX. — PARTS OF A SET, AND COPIES

I. PARTS OF A SET

Article 64

A bill of exchange can be drawn in a set of two or more identical parts.

These parts must be numbered in the body of the instrument itself; in default, each part is considered as a separate bill of exchange.

Every holder of a bill which does not specify that it has been drawn as a sola bill may, at his own expense, require the delivery of two or more parts. For this purpose he must apply to his immediate endorser, who is bound to assist him in proceeding against his own endorser, and so on in the series until the drawer is reached. The endorsers are bound to reproduce their endorsements on the new parts of the set.

Article 65

Payment made on one part of a set operates as a discharge, even though there is no stipulation that this payment annuls the effect of the other parts. Nevertheless, the drawee is liable on each accepted part which he has not recovered.

An endorser who has transferred parts of a set to different persons, as well as subsequent endorsers, are liable on all the parts bearing their signature which have not been restored.

Article 66

A party who has sent one part for acceptance must indicate on the other parts the name of the person in whose hands this part is to be found. That person is bound to give it up to the lawful holder of another part.

If he refuses, the holder cannot exercise his right of recourse until he has had a protest drawn up specifying:

(1) That the part sent for acceptance has not been given up to him on his demand;

(2) That acceptance or payment could not be obtained on another of the parts.

2. COPIES

Article 67

Every holder of a bill of exchange has the right to make copies of it.

A copy must reproduce the original exactly, with the endorsements and all other statements to be found therein. It must specify where the copy ends.

It may be endorsed and guaranteed by *aval* in the same manner and with the same effects as the original.

Article 68

A copy must specify the person in possession of the original instument. The latter is bound to hand over the said instrument to the lawful holder of the copy.

If he refuses, the holder may not exercise his right of recourse against the persons who have endorsed the copy or guaranteed it by *aval* until he has had a protest drawn up specifying that the original has not been given up to him on his demand.

Where the original instrument, after the last endorsement before the making of the copy, contains a clause "commencing from here an endorsement is only valid if made on the copy" or some equivalent formula, a subsequent endorsement on the original is null and void.

Chapter X. — Alterations

Article 69

In case of alteration of the text of a bill of exchange, parties who have signed subsequent to the alteration are bound according to the terms of the altered text; parties who have signed before the alteration are bound according to the terms of the original text.

Chapter XI. — Limitation of Actions

Article 70

All actions arising out of a bill of exchange against the acceptor are barred after three years, reckoned from the date of maturity.

Actions by the holder against the endorsers and against the drawer are barred after one year from the date of a protest drawn up within proper time, or from the date of maturity where there is a stipulation *retour sans frais*.

Actions by endorsers against each other and against the drawer are barred after six months, reckoned from the day when the endorser took up and paid the bill or from the day when he himself was sued.

Article 71

Interruption of the period of limitation is only effective against the person in respect of whom the period has been interrupted.

Chapter XII. — General Provisions

Article 72

Payment of a bill of exchange which falls due on a legal holiday (*jour férié légal*) cannot be demanded until the next business day. So, too, all other proceedings relating to a bill of exchange, in particular, presentment for acceptance and protest, can only be taken on a business day.

Where any of these proceedings must be taken within a certain limit of time the last day of which is a legal holiday (*jour férié légal*), the limit of time is extended until the first business day which follows the expiration of that time. Intermediate holidays (*jours fériés*) are included in computing limits of time.

Article 73

Legal or contractual limits of time do not include the day on which the period commences.

Article 74

No days of grace, whether legal or judicial, are permitted.

TITLE II

Promissory Notes

Article 75

A promissory note contains:

(1) The term "promissory note" inserted in the body of the instrument and expressed in the language employed in drawing up the instrument;

(2) An unconditional promise to pay a determinate sum of money;

(3) A statement of the time of payment;

(4) A statement of the place where payment is to be made;

(5) The name of the person to whom or to whose order payment is to be made;

(6) A statement of the date and of the place where the promissory note is issued;

(7) The signature of the person who issues the instrument (maker).

Article 76

An instrument in which any of the requirements mentioned in the preceding article are wanting is invalid as a promissory note except in the cases specified in the following paragraphs.

A promissory note in which the time of payment is not specified is deemed to be payable at sight.

In default of special mention, the place where the instrument is made is deemed to be the place of payment and at the same time the place of the domicile of the maker.

A promissory note which does not mention the place of its issue is deemed to have been made in the place mentioned beside the name of the maker.

Article 77

The following provisions relating to bills of exchange apply to promissory notes so far as they are not inconsistent with the nature of these instruments, viz.:

Endorsement (Articles 11 to 20);
Time of payment (Articles 33 to 37);
Payment (Articles 38 to 42);
Recourse in case of non-payment (Articles 43 to 50, 52 to 54);
Payment by intervention (Articles 55, 59 to 63);
Copies (Articles 67 to 68);
Alterations (Article 69);
Limitation of actions (Articles 70 and 71);
Holidays, computation of limits of time and prohibition of days of grace (Articles 72, 73 and 74).

The following provisions are also applicable to a promissory note: The provisions concerning a bill of exchange payable at the address of a third party or in a locality other than that of the domicile of the drawee (Articles 4 and 27); stipulation for interest (Article 5); discrepancies as regards the sum payable (Article 6); the consequences of signature under the conditions mentioned in Article 7, the consequences of signature by a person who acts without authority or who exceeds his authority (Article 8); and provisions concerning a bill of exchange in blank (Article 10).

The following provisions are also applicable to a promissory note: Provisions relating to guarantee by *aval* (Articles 30–32); in the case provided for in Article 31, last paragraph, if the *aval* does not specify on whose behalf it has been given, it is deemed to have been given on behalf of the maker of the promissory note.

Article 78

The maker of a promissory note is bound in the same manner as an acceptor of a bill of exchange.

Promissory notes payable at a certain time after sight must be presented for the visa of the maker within the limits of time fixed by Article 23. The limit of time runs from the date of the visa signed by the maker on the note. The refusal of the maker to give his visa with the date thereon must be authenticated by a protest (Article 25), the date of which marks the commencement of the period of time after sight.

BILLS OF LADING ACT, 1855

(18 and 19 Vict., Chap. 111)

"Whereas by the Custom of Merchants a Bill of Lading of Goods being transferable by Endorsement the Property in the Goods may thereby pass to the Endorsee, but nevertheless all Rights in respect of the Contract contained in the Bill of Lading continue in the original Shipper or Owner, and it is expedient that such Rights should pass with the Property: And whereas it frequently happens that the Goods in respect of which Bills of Lading purport to be signed have not been laden on board, and it is proper that such Bills of Lading in the Hands of a *bonâ fide* Holder for Value should not be questioned by the Master or other Person signing the same on the Ground of the Goods not having been laden as aforesaid:" Be it therefore enacted by the Queen's most Excellent Majesty, by and with the Advice and Consent of the Lords Spiritual and Temporal, and Commons, in this present Parliament assembled, and by the Authority of the same, as follows:

I. Every Consignee of Goods named in a Bill of Lading, and every Endorsee of a Bill of Lading to whom the Property in the Goods therein mentioned shall pass, upon or by reason of such Consignment or Endorsement, shall have transferred to and vested in him all Rights of Suit, and be subject to the same Liabilities in respect of such Goods as if the Contract contained in the Bill of Lading had been made with himself.

II. Nothing herein contained shall prejudice or affect any Right of Stoppage *in transitu*, or any Right to claim Freight against the original Shipper or Owner, or any Liability of the Consignee or Endorsee by reason or in consequence of his being such Consignee or Endorsee, or of his Receipt of the Goods by reason or in consequence of such Consignment or Endorsement.

III. Every Bill of Lading in the Hands of a Consignee or Endorsee for valuable Consideration representing Goods to have been shipped on board a Vessel shall be conclusive Evidence of such Shipment as against the Master or other Person signing the same, notwithstanding that such Goods or some Part thereof may not have been so shipped, unless such Holder of the Bill of Lading shall have had actual Notice at the Time of receiving the same that the Goods had not been in fact laden on board: Provided, that the Master or other Person so signing may exonerate himself in respect of such Misrepresentation by showing that it was caused without any Default on his Part, and wholly by the Fraud of the Shipper, or of the Holder, or some Person under whom the Holder claims.

UNIFORM BILLS OF LADING ACT[1]

An Act to Make Uniform the Law of Bills of Lading

PART I

THE ISSUE OF BILLS OF LADING

Section 1. (Bills Governed by this Act.) Bills of Lading issued by any common carrier shall be governed by this act.

[1] Approved and recommended for adoption by the Commissioners on Uniform State Laws in 1909. States which have adopted the Act and dates of adoption are as follows: Alabama (1931); Alaska (1913); Arizona (1921); California (1915); Con-

Sec. 2. (Form of Bills. Essential Terms.) Every bill must embody within its written or printed terms:

(a) The date of its issue.

(b) The name of the person from whom the goods have been received.

(c) The place where the goods have been received.

(d) The place to which the goods are to be transported.

(e) A statement whether the goods received will be delivered to a specified person, or to the order of a specified person.

(f) A description of the goods or of the packages containing them which may, however, be in such general terms as are referred to in Section 23, and

(g) The signature of the carrier.

A negotiable bill shall have the words "order of" printed thereon immediately before the name of the person upon whose order the goods received are deliverable.

A carrier shall be liable to any person injured thereby for the damage caused by the omission from a negotiable bill of any of the provisions required in this section.

Sec. 3. (Form of Bills. What Terms May be Inserted.) A carrier may insert in a bill, issued by him, any other terms and conditions, provided that such terms and conditions shall not:

(a) Be contrary to law or public policy, or

(b) In anywise impair his obligation to exercise at least that degree of care in the transportation and safe-keeping of the goods entrusted to him which a reasonably careful man would exercise in regard to similar goods of his own.

Sec. 4. (Definition of Non-Negotiable or Straight Bill.) A bill in which it is stated that the goods are consigned or destined to a specified person, is a non-negotiable or straight bill.

Sec. 5. (Definition of Negotiable or Order Bill.) A bill in which it is stated that the goods are consigned or destined to the order of any person named in such bill, is a negotiable or order bill.

Any provision in such a bill that it is non-negotiable shall not affect its negotiability within the meaning of this act.

Sec. 6. (Negotiable Bills Must Not be Issued in Sets.) Negotiable bills issued in this state for the transportation of goods to any place in the United States on the continent of North America, except Alaska, shall not be issued in parts or sets.

If so issued the carrier issuing them shall be liable for failure to deliver the goods described therein to any one who purchases a part for value in good faith, even though the purchase be after the delivery of the goods by the carrier to a holder of one of the other parts.

Sec. 7. (Duplicate Negotiable Bills Must be so Marked.) When more than one negotiable bill is issued in this state for the same goods to be transported to any place in the United States on the continent of South America, except Alaska, the word "duplicate" or some other word or words indicating

---

necticut (1911); Delaware (1927); District of Columbia (1916); Idaho (1915); Illinois (1911); Iowa (1911); Louisiana (1912); Maine (1917); Maryland (1910); Massachusetts (1910); Michigan (1911); Minnesota (1917); Missouri (1923); Nevada (1923); New Hampshire (1917); New Jersey (1913); New York (1911); North Carolina (1919); Ohio (1911); Pennsylvania (1911); Rhode Island (1914); South Carolina (1930); Vermont (1915); Washington (1915); Wisconsin (1917).

The Federal Bills of Lading Act of August 19, 1916, 39 Statutes at Large 538, is in substantially the same language as that of the Uniform Bills of Lading Act.

that the document is not an original bill shall be placed plainly upon the face of every such bill, except the one first issued. A carrier shall be liable for the damage caused by his failure so to do to any one who has purchased the bill for value in good faith as an original, even though the purchase be after the delivery of the goods by the carrier to the holder of the original bill.

Sec. 8. (Non-Negotiable Bills Shall be so Marked.) A non-negotiable bill shall have placed plainly upon its face by the carrier issuing it "non-negotiable" or "not negotiable."

This section shall not apply, however, to memoranda or acknowledgments of an informal character.

Sec. 9. (Insertion of Name of Person to be Notified.) The insertion in a negotiable bill of the name of a person to be notified of the arrival of the goods shall not limit the negotiability of the bill, or constitute notice to a purchaser thereof of any rights or equities of such person in the goods.

Sec. 10. (Acceptance of Bill Indicates Assent to its Terms.) Except as otherwise provided in this act, where a consignor receives a bill and makes no objection to its terms or conditions at the time he receives it, neither the consignor nor any person who accepts delivery of the goods, nor any person who seeks to enforce any provision of the bill, shall be allowed to deny that he is bound by such terms and conditions, so far as they are not contrary to law or public policy.

PART II

OBLIGATIONS AND RIGHTS OF CARRIERS UPON THEIR BILLS OF LADING

Sec. 11. (Obligation of Carrier to Deliver.) A carrier, in the absence of some lawful excuse, is bound to deliver goods upon a demand made either by the consignee named in the bill for the goods, or if the bill is negotiable, by the holder thereof, if such demand is accompanied by:

(a) An offer in good faith to satisfy the carrier's lawful lien upon the goods,

(b) An offer in good faith to surrender, properly indorsed, the bill which was issued for the goods, if the bill is negotiable, and

(c) A readiness and willingness to sign, when the goods are delivered, an acknowledgment that they have been delivered, if such signature is requested by the carrier.

In case the carrier refuses or fails to deliver the goods in compliance with a demand by the consignee or holder so accompanied, the burden shall be upon the carrier to establish the existence of a lawful excuse for such refusal or failure.

Sec. 12. (Justification of Carrier in Delivering.) A carrier is justified, subject to the provisions of the three following sections, in delivering goods to one who is:

(a) A person lawfully entitled to the possession of the goods, or

(b) The consignee named in a non-negotiable bill for the goods, or

(c) A person in possession of a negotiable bill for the goods by the terms of which the goods are deliverable to his order, or which has been indorsed to him or in blank by the consignee or by the mediate or immediate indorsee of the consignee.

Sec. 13. (Carrier's Liability for Misdelivery.) Where a carrier delivers goods to one who is not lawfully entitled to the possession of them, the carrier shall be liable to any one having a right of property or possession in the goods if he delivered the goods otherwise than as authorized by subdivisions (b) and (c) of the preceding section; and, though he delivered the goods as authorized by either of said subdivisions, he shall be so liable if prior to such delivery he:

(a) Had been requested, by or on behalf of a person having a right of property or possession in the goods, not to make such delivery, or

(b) Had information at the time of the delivery that it was to a person not lawfully entitled to the possession of the goods.

A request or information to be effective within the meaning of this section must be given to an officer or agent of the carrier, the actual or apparent scope of whose duties includes action upon such a request or information, and must be given in time to enable the officer or agent to whom it is given, acting with reasonable diligence, to stop delivery of the goods.

Sec. 14. (Negotiable Bills Must be Canceled When Goods Delivered.) Except as provided in Section 27, and except when compelled by legal process, if a carrier delivers goods for which a negotiable bill had been issued, the negotiation of which would transfer the right to the possession of the goods, and fails to take up and cancel the bill, such carrier shall be liable for failure to deliver the goods to any one who for value and in good faith purchases such bill, whether such purchaser acquired title to the bill before or after the delivery of the goods by the carrier, and notwithstanding delivery was made to the person entitled thereto.

Sec. 15. (Negotiable Bills Must be Canceled or Marked When Parts of Goods Delivered.) Except as provided in Section 27, and except when compelled by legal process, if a carrier delivers part of the goods for which a negotiable bill had been issued and fails either:

(a) To take up and cancel the bill, or

(b) To place plainly upon it a statement that a portion of the goods has been delivered, with a description, which may be in general terms, either of the goods or packages that have been so delivered or of the goods or packages which still remain in the carrier's possession, he shall be liable for failure to deliver all the goods specified in the bill, to any one who for value and in good faith purchases it, whether such purchaser acquired title to it before or after the delivery of any portion of the goods by the carrier, and notwithstanding such delivery was made to the person entitled thereto.

Sec. 16. (Altered Bills.) Any alteration, addition or erasure in a bill after its issue without authority from the carrier issuing the same either in writing or noted on the bill shall be void, whatever be the nature and purpose of the change, and the bill shall be enforceable according to its original tenor.

Sec. 17. (Lost or Destroyed Bills.) Where a negotiable bill has been lost or destroyed, a court of competent jurisdiction may order the delivery of the goods upon satisfactory proof of such loss or destruction and upon the giving of a bond with sufficient surety to be approved by the court to protect the carrier or any person injured by such delivery from any liability or loss, incurred by reason of the original bill remaining outstanding. The court may also in its discretion order the payment of the carrier's reasonable costs and counsel fees.

The delivery of the goods under an order of the court as provided in this section, shall not relieve the carrier from liability to a person to whom the negotiable bill has been or shall be negotiated for value without notice of the proceedings or of the delivery of the goods.

Sec. 18. (Effect of Duplicate Bills.) A bill upon the face of which the word "duplicate" or some other word or words indicating that the document is not an original bill is placed plainly shall impose upon the carrier issuing the same the liability of one who represents and warrants that such bill is an accurate copy of an original bill properly issued, but no other liability.

Sec. 19. (Carrier Cannot set up Title in Himself.) No title to goods or right to their possession, asserted by a carrier for his own benefit, shall excuse him from liability for refusing to deliver the goods according to the terms of a bill issued for them, unless such title or right is derived directly or indirectly from a transfer made by the consignor or consignee after the shipment, or from the carrier's lien.

Sec. 20. (Interpleader of Adverse Claimants.) If more than one person claims the title or possession of goods, the carrier may require all known claimants to interplead, either as a defence to an action brought against him for non-delivery of the goods, or as an original suit, whichever is appropriate.

Sec. 21. (Carrier has Reasonable Time to Determine Validity of Claims.) If some one other than the consignee or person in possession of the bill, has a claim to the title or possession of the goods, and the carrier has information of such claim, the carrier shall be excused from liability for refusing to deliver the goods either to the consignee or person in possession of the bill, or to the adverse claimant, until the carrier has had a reasonable time to ascertain the validity of the adverse claim or to bring legal proceedings to compel all claimants to interplead.

Sec. 22. (Adverse Title is no Defence, Except as Above Provided.) Except as provided in the two preceding sections and in section 12, no right or title of a third person unless enforced by legal process shall be a defence to an action brought by the consignee of a non-negotiable bill or by the holder of a negotiable bill against the carrier for failure to deliver the goods on demand.

Sec. 23. (Liability for Non-Receipt or Misdescription of Goods.) If a bill of lading has been issued by a carrier or on his behalf by an agent or employee the scope of whose actual or apparent authority includes the issuing of bills of lading, the carrier shall be liable to:

(a) The consignee named in a non-negotiable bill, or

(b) The holder of a negotiable bill,

Who has given value in good faith relying upon the description therein of the goods, for damages caused by the non-receipt by the carrier or a connecting carrier of all or part of the goods or their failure to correspond with the description thereof in the bill at the time of its issue.

If, however, the goods are described in a bill merely by a statement of marks or labels upon them or upon packages containing them, or by a statement that the goods are said to be goods of a certain kind or quantity, or in a certain condition, or it is stated in the bill that packages are said to contain goods of a certain kind or quantity or in a certain condition, or that the contents or condition of the contents of packages are unknown, or words of like purport are contained in the bill, such statements, if true, shall not make liable the carrier issuing the bill, although the goods are not of the kind or quantity or in the condition which the marks or labels upon them indicate, or of the kind or quantity or in the condition they were said to be by the consignor. The carrier may, also by inserting in the bill the words "shipper's load and count" or other words of like purport indicate that the goods were loaded by the shipper and the description of them made by him; and if such statement be true, the carrier shall not be liable for damages caused by the improper loading or by the non-receipt or by the misdescription of the goods described in the bill.

Sec. 24. (Attachment or Levy Upon Goods for Which a Negotiable Bill has Been Issued.) If goods are delivered to a carrier by the owner or by a person whose act in conveying the title to them to a purchaser for value in good faith would bind the owner and a negotiable bill is issued for them, they cannot thereafter, while in the possession of the carrier, be attached by garnishment or otherwise, or be levied upon under an execution, unless the bill be first surrendered to the carrier or its negotiation enjoined. The carrier shall in no such case be compelled to deliver the actual possession of the goods until the bill is surrendered to him or impounded by the court.

Sec. 25. (Creditor's Remedies to Reach Negotiable Bills.) A creditor whose debtor is the owner of a negotiable bill shall be entitled to such aid from courts of appropriate jurisdiction by injunction and otherwise in attaching such bill, or in satisfying the claim by means thereof as is allowed at law or in equity in regard to property which cannot readily be attached or levied upon by ordinary legal process.

Sec. 26. (Negotiable Bill Must State Charges for Which Lien is Claimed.) If a negotiable bill is issued the carrier shall have no lien on the goods therein mentioned, except for charges on those goods for freight, storage, demurrage and terminal charges, and expenses necessary for the preservation of the goods or incident to their transportation subsequent to the date of the bill, unless the bill expressly enumerates other charges for which a lien is claimed. In such case there shall also be a lien for the charges enumerated so far as they are allowed by law and the contract between the consignor and the carrier.

Sec. 27. (Effect of Sale.) After goods have been lawfully said to satisfy a carrier's lien, or because they have not been claimed, or because they are perishable or hazardous, the carrier shall not thereafter be liable for failure to deliver the goods to the consignee or owner of the goods, or to a holder of the bill given for the goods when they were shipped, even if such bill be negotiable.

PART III

NEGOTIATION AND TRANSFER OF BILLS

Sec. 28. (Negotiation of Negotiable Bills by Delivery.) A negotiable bill may be negotiated by delivery where, by the terms of the bill, the carrier undertakes to deliver the goods to the order of a specified person, and such person or a subsequent indorsee of the bill has indorsed it in blank.

Sec. 29. (Negotiation of Negotiable Bills by Indorsement.) A negotiable bill may be negotiated by the indorsement of the person to whose order the goods are deliverable by the tenor of the bill. Such indorsement may be in blank or to a specified person. If indorsed to a specified person, it may be negotiated again by the indorsement of such person in blank or to another specified person. Subsequent negotiation may be made in like manner.

Sec. 30. (Transfer of Bills.) A bill may be transferred by the holder by delivery, accompanied with an agreement, express or implied, to transfer the title to the bill or to the goods represented thereby.

A non-negotiable bill cannot be negotiated, and the indorsement of such a bill gives the transferee no additional right.

Sec. 31. (Who May Negotiate a Bill.) A negotiable bill may be negotiated by any person in possession of the same, however such possession may have been acquired if, by the terms of the bill, the carrier undertakes to deliver the goods to the order of such person, or if at the time of negotiation the bill is in such form that it may be negotiated by delivery.

Sec. 32. (Rights of Person to Whom a Bill has Been Negotiated.) A person to whom a negotiable bill has been duly negotiated acquires thereby:

(a) Such title to the goods as the person negotiating the bill to him had or had ability to convey to a purchaser in good faith for value, and also such title to the goods as the consignee and consignor had or had power to convey to a purchaser in good faith for value, and

(b) The direct obligation of the carrier to hold possession of the goods for him according to the terms of the bill as fully as if the carrier had contracted directly with him.

Sec. 33. (Rights of Person to Whom a Bill has Been Transferred.) A person to whom a bill has been transferred but not negotiated acquires thereby as against the transferor, the title to the goods, subject to the terms of any agreement with the transferor. If the bill is non-negotiable, such person also acquires the right to notify the carrier of the transfer to him of such bill, and thereby to become the direct obligee of whatever obligations the carrier owed to the transferor of the bill immediately before the notification.

Prior to the notification of the carrier by the transferor or transferee of a non-negotiable bill, the title of the transferee to the goods and the right to acquire the obligation of the carrier may be defeated by garnishment or by attachment or execution upon the goods by a creditor of the transferor, or by a notification to the carrier by the transferor or a subsequent purchaser from the transferor of a subsequent sale of the goods by the transferor.

A carrier has not received notification within the meaning of this section unless an officer or agent of the carrier, the actual or apparent scope of whose duties includes action upon such a notification, has been notified; and no notification shall be effective until the officer or agent to whom it is given has had time with the exercise of reasonable diligence to communicate with the agent or agents having actual possession or control of the goods.

Sec. 34. (Transfer of Negotiable Bill Without Indorsement.) Where a negotiable bill is transferred for value by delivery, and the indorsement of the transferor is essential for negotiation, the transferee acquires a right against the transferor to compel him to indorse the bill, unless a contrary intention appears. The negotiation shall take effect as of the time when the indorsement is actually made. This obligation may be specifically enforced.

Sec. 35. (Warranties on Sale of Bill.) A person who negotiates or transfers for value a bill by indorsement or delivery, including one who assigns for value a claim secured by a bill, unless a contrary intention appears, warrants:

(a) That the bill is genuine,

(b) That he has a legal right to transfer it,

(c) That he has knowledge of no fact which would impair the validity or worth of the bill, and

(d) That he has a right to transfer the title to the goods, and that the goods are merchantable or fit for a particular purpose whenever such warranties would have been implied, if the contract of the parties had been to transfer without a bill the goods represented thereby.

In the case of an assignment of a claim secured by a bill, the liability of the assignor shall not exceed the amount of the claim.

Sec. 36. (Indorser not a Guarantor.) The indorsement of a bill shall not make the indorser liable for any failure on the part of the carrier or previous indorsers of the bill to fulfill their respective obligations.

Sec. 37. (No Warranty Implied From Accepting Payment of a Debt.) A mortgagee or pledgee, or other holder of a bill for security who in good faith demands or receives payment of the debt for which such bill is security, whether from a party to a draft drawn for such debt or from any other person, shall not be deemed by so doing to represent or to warrant the genuineness of such bill or the quantity or quality of the goods therein described.

Sec. 38. (When Negotiation not Impaired by Fraud, Accident, Mistake, Duress or Conversion.) The validity of the negotiation of a bill is not impaired by the fact that such negotiation was a breach of duty on the part of the person making the negotiation, or by the fact that the owner of the bill was deprived of the possession of the same by fraud, accident, mistake, duress or conversion, if the person to whom the bill was negotiated, or a person to whom the bill was subsequently negotiated, gave value therefor, in good faith, without notice of the breach of duty, or fraud, accident, mistake, duress or conversion.

Sec. 39. (Subsequent Negotiation.) Where a person having sold, mortgaged, or pledged goods which are in a carrier's possession and for which a negotiable bill has been issued, or having sold, mortgaged, or pledged the negotiable bill representing such goods, continues in possession of the negotiable bill, the subsequent negotiation thereof by that person under any sale, pledge, or other disposition thereof to any person receiving the same in good faith, for value and without notice of the previous sale, shall have the same effect as if the first purchaser of the goods or bill had expressly authorised the subsequent negotiation.

Sec. 40. (Form of the Bill as Indicating Rights of Buyer and Seller.) Where goods are shipped by the consignor in accordance with a contract or order for their purchase, the form in which the bill is taken by the consignor shall indicate the transfer or retention of the property or right to the possession of the goods as follows:

(a) Where by the bill the goods are deliverable to the buyer or to his agent, or to the order of the buyer or of his agent, the consignor thereby transfers the property in the goods to the buyer.

(b) Where by the bill the goods are deliverable to the seller or to his agent, or to the order of the seller or of his agent, the seller thereby reserves the property in the goods. But if, except for the form of the bill, the property would have passed to the buyer on shipment of the goods, the seller's property in the goods shall be deemed to be only for the purpose of securing performance by the buyer of his obligations under the contract.

(c) Where by the bill the goods are deliverable to the order of the buyer or of his agent, but possession of the bill is retained by the seller or his agent, the seller thereby reserves a right to the possession of the goods, as against the buyer.

(d) Where the seller draws on the buyer for the price and transmits the draft and bill together to the buyer to secure acceptance or payment of the draft, the buyer is bound to return the bill if he does not honor the draft, and if he wrongfully retains the bill he acquires no added right thereby. If, however, the bill provides that the goods are deliverable to the buyer, or to the order of the buyer, or is endorsed in blank or to the buyer by the consignee named therein, one who purchases in good faith, for value, the bill or goods from the buyer, shall obtain the title to the goods, although the draft has not been honored, if such purchaser has received delivery of the bill indorsed by the consignee named therein, or of the goods, without notice of the facts making the transfer wrongful.

Sec. 41. (Demand, Presentation or Sight Draft Must be Paid, but Draft on More Than Three Days Time Merely Accepted Before Buyer is Entitled to the Accompanying Bill.) Where the seller of goods draws on the buyer for the price of the goods and transmits the draft and a bill of lading for the goods either directly to the buyer or through a bank or other agency, unless a different intention on the part of the seller appears, the buyer and all other parties interested shall be justified in assuming:

(a) If the draft is by its terms or legal effect payable on demand or presentation or at sight, or not more than three days thereafter (whether such three days be termed days of grace or not), that the seller intended to require payment of the draft before the buyer should be entitled to receive or retain the bill.

(b) If the draft is by its terms payable on time, extending beyond three days after demand, presentation or sight (whether such three days be termed days of grace or not), that the seller intended to require acceptance, but not payment of the draft before the buyer should be entitled to receive or retain the bill.

The provisions of this section are applicable whether by the terms of the bill the goods are consigned to the seller, or to his order, or to the buyer, or to his order, or to a third person, or to his order.

Sec. 42. (Negotiation Defeats Vendor's Lien.) Where a negotiable bill has been issued for goods, no seller's lien or right of stoppage in transitu shall defeat the rights of any purchaser for value in good faith to whom such bill has been negotiated, whether such negotiation be prior or subsequent to the notification to the carrier who issued such bill of the seller's claim to a lien or right of stoppage in transitu. Nor shall the carrier be obliged to deliver or justified in delivering the goods to an unpaid seller unless such bill is first surrendered for cancellation.

Sec. 43. (When Rights and Remedies Under Mortgages and Liens are not Limited.) Except as provided in Section 42, nothing in this act shall limit the rights and remedies of a mortgagee or lienholder whose mortgage or lien on goods would be valid, apart from this act, as against one who for value and in good faith purchased from the owner, immediately prior to the time of their delivery to the carrier, the goods which are subject to the mortgage or lien and obtained possession of them.

PART IV

CRIMINAL OFFENCES

Sec. 44. (Issue of Bill for Goods not Received.) Any officer, agent, or servant of a carrier, who with intent to defraud issues or aids in issuing a bill knowing that all or any part of the goods for which such bill is issued have not been received by such carrier, or by an agent or such carrier or by a connecting carrier, or are not under the carrier's control at the time of issuing such bill, shall be guilty of a crime, and upon conviction shall be punished for each offence by imprisonment not exceeding five years, or by a fine not exceeding five thousand dollars, or by both.

Sec. 45. (Issue of Bill Containing False Statement.) Any officer, agent, or servant of a carrier, who with intent to defraud issues or aids in issuing a bill for goods knowing that it contains any false statement, shall be guilty of a crime, and upon conviction shall be punished for each offense by imprisonment not exceeding one year, or by a fine not exceeding one thousand dollars, or by both.

Sec. 46. (Issue of Duplicate Bills not so Marked.) Any officer, agent, or servant of a carrier, who with intent to defraud issues or aids in issuing a duplicate or additional negotiable bill for goods in violation of the provisions of section 7, knowing that a former negotiable bill for the same goods or any part of them is outstanding and uncanceled, shall be guilty of a crime, and upon conviction shall be punished for each offence by imprisonment not exceeding five years, or by a fine not exceeding five thousand dollars, or by both.

Sec. 47. (Negotiation of Bill for Mortgaged Goods.) Any person who ships goods to which he has not title, or upon which there is a lien or mortgage, and who takes for such goods a negotiable bill which he afterwards negotiates for value with intent to deceive and without disclosing his want of title or the existence of the lien or mortgage, shall be guilty of a crime, and upon conviction shall be punished for each offence by imprisonment not exceeding one year, or by a fine not exceeding one thousand dollars, or by both.

Sec. 48. (Negotiation of Bill When Goods are not in Carrier's Possession.) Any person who with intent to deceive negotiates or transfers for value a bill knowing that any or all of the goods which by the terms of such bill appear to have been received for transportation by the carrier which issued the bill, are not in the possession or control of such carrier, or of a connecting carrier, without disclosing this fact, shall be guilty of a crime, and upon conviction shall be punished for each offense by imprisonment not exceeding five years, or by a fine not exceeding five thousand dollars, or by both.

Sec. 49. (Inducing Carrier to Issue Bill When Goods Have not Been Received.) Any person who with intent to defraud secures the issue by a carrier of a bill knowing that at the time of such issue, any or all of the goods described in such bill as received for transportation have not been received by such carrier, or an agent of such carrier or a connecting carrier, or are not under the carrier's contol, by inducing an officer, agent, or servant of such carrier falsely to believe that such goods have been received by such carrier, or are under its control, shall be guilty of a crime, and upon conviction shall be punished for each offence by imprisonment not exceeding five years, or by a fine not exceeding five thousand dollars, or by both.

Sec. 50. (Issue of Non-Negotiable Bill not so Marked.) Any person who with intent to defraud issues or aids in issuing a non-negotiable bill without the words "not negotiable" placed plainly upon the face thereof, shall be guilty of a crime, and upon conviction shall be punished for each offence by imprisonment not exceeding five years or by a fine not exceeding five thousand dollars, or by both.

PART V

INTERPRETATION

Sec. 51. (Rule for Cases Not Provided for in this Act.) In any case not provided for in this act, the rules of law and equity, including the law merchant, and in particular the rules relating to the law of principal and agent, executors, administrators and trustees, and to the effect of fraud, misrepresentation, duress or coercion, accident, mistake, bankruptcy, or other invalidating cause, shall govern.

Sec. 52. (Interpretation Shall Give Effect to Purpose of Uniformity.) This act shall be so interpreted and construed as to effectuate its general purpose to make uniform the law of those States which enact it.

Sec. 53. (Definitions.) (1) In this act, unless the context or subject matter otherwise requires:

"Action" includes counter claim, set-off, and suit in equity.

"Bill" means bill of lading.

"Consignee" means the person named in the bill as the person to whom delivery of the goods is to be made.

"Consignor" means the person named in the bill as the person from whom the goods have been received for shipment.

"Goods" means merchandise or chattels in course of transportation, or which have been or are about to be transported.

"Holder" of a bill means a person who has both actual possession of such bill and a right of property therein.

"Order" means an order by indorsement on the bill.

"Owner" does not include mortgagee or pledgee.

"Person" includes a corporation or partnership or two or more persons having a joint or common interest.

To "purchase" includes to take as mortgagee and to take as pledgee.

"Purchaser" includes mortgagee and pledgee.

"Value" is any consideration sufficient to support a simple contract. An antecedent or pre-existing obligation, whether for money or not, constitutes value where a bill is taken either in satisfaction thereof or as security therefor.

(2) A thing is done "in good faith," within the meaning of this act, when it is in fact done honestly, whether it be done negligently or not.

Sec. 54. (Act Does Not Apply to Existing Bills.) The provisions of this act do not apply to bills made and delivered prior to the taking effect thereof.

Sec. 55. (Inconsistent Legislation Repealed.) All acts or parts of acts inconsistent with this act are hereby repealed.

Sec. 56. (Time When the Act Takes Effect.) This act shall take effect on the.......... day of.............., one thousand nine hundred and.........

Sec. 57. (Name of Act.) This act may be cited as the Uniform Bills of Lading Act.

HARTER ACT

(52nd Congress, First Session, Chap. 105)

Be it enacted by the Senate and House of Representatives of the United States of America in Congress assembled, That it shall not be lawful for the manager, agent, master, or owner of any vessel transporting merchandise or property from or between ports of the United States and foreign ports to insert in any bill of lading or shipping document any clause, covenant, or agreement whereby it, he, or they shall be relieved from liability for loss or damage arising from negligence, fault, or failure in proper loading, stowage, custody, care, or proper delivery of any and all lawful merchandise or property committed to its or their charge. Any and all words or clauses of such import inserted in bills of lading or shipping receipts shall be null and void and of no effect.

Sec. 2. That it shall not be lawful for any vessel transporting merchandise or property from or between ports of the United States of America and foreign ports, her owner, master, agent, or manager, to insert in any bill of lading or shipping document any covenant or agreement whereby the obligations of the owner or owners of said vessel to exercise due diligence, properly equip, man, provision, and outfit said vessel, and to make said vessel seaworthy and capable of performing her intended voyage, or whereby the obligations of the master, officers, agents, or servants to carefully handle and stow her cargo and to care for and properly deliver same, shall in any wise be lessened, weakened, or avoided.

Sec. 3. That if the owner of any vessel transporting merchandise or property to or from any port in the United States of America shall exercise due diligence to make the said vessel in all respects seaworthy and properly manned, equipped, and supplied, neither the vessel, her owner or owners, agent, or charterers shall become or be held responsible for damage or loss resulting from faults or errors in navigation or in the management of said vessel nor shall the vessel, her owner or owners, charterers, agent, or master be held liable for losses arising from dangers of the sea or other navigable waters, acts of God, or public enemies, or the inherent defect, quality, or vice of the thing carried, or from insufficiency of package, or seizure under legal process, or for loss resulting from any act or omission of the shipper or owner of the goods, his agent or representative, or from saving or attempting to save life or property at sea, or from any deviation in rendering such service.

Sec. 4. That it shall be the duty of the owner or owners, masters, or agent of any vessel transporting merchandise or property from or between ports of the United States and foreign ports to issue to shippers of any lawful merchandise a bill of lading, or shipping document, stating, among other things, the marks necessary for identification, number of packages, or quantity, stating whether it be carrier's or shipper's weight, and apparent order or condition of such merchandise or property delivered to and received by the owner, master, or agent of the vessel for transportation, and such document shall be prima facie evidence of the receipt of the merchandise therein described.

Sec. 5. That for a violation of any of the provisions of this act the agent, owner, or master of the vessel guilty of such violation, and who refuses to issue on demand the bill of lading herein provided for, shall be liable to a fine not exceeding two thousand dollars. The amount of the fine and costs for such violation shall be a lien upon the vessel, whose agent, owner, or master is guilty of such violation, and such vessel may be libeled therefor in any district court of the United States, within whose jurisdiction the vessel may be found. One-half of such penalty shall go to the party injured by such violation and the remainder to the Government of the United States.

Sec. 6. That this act shall not be held to modify or repeal sections forty-two hundred and eighty-one, forty-two hundred and eighty-two, and forty-two hundred and eighty-three of the Revised Statutes of the United States, or any other statute defining the liability of vessels, their owners, or representatives.

Sec. 7. Sections one and four of this act shall not apply to the transportation of live animals.

Sec. 8. That this act shall take effect from and after the first day of July, eighteen hundred and ninety-three.

Approved, February 13, 1893.

CARRIAGE OF GOODS BY SEA ACT, 1936[1]

(74th Congress, Second Session, Chap. 229)

Be it enacted by the Senate and House of Representatives of the United States of America in Congress assembled, That every bill of lading or similar document of title which is evidence of a contract for the carriage of goods by sea to or from ports of the United States, in foreign trade, shall have effect subject to the provisions of this Act.

Title I

Section 1. When used in this Act—

(a) The term "carrier" includes the owner or the charterer who enters into a contract of carriage with a shipper.

(b) The term "contract of carriage" applies only to contracts of carriage covered by a bill of lading or any similar document of title, insofar as such document relates to the carriage of goods by sea, including any bill of lading or any similar document as aforesaid issued under or pursuant to a charter party from the moment at which such bill of lading or similar document of title regulates the relations between a carrier and a holder of the same.

(c) The term "goods" includes goods, wares, merchandise, and articles of every kind whatsoever, except live animals and cargo which by the contract of carriage is stated as being carried on deck and is so carried.

(d) The term "ship" means any vessel used for the carriage of goods by sea.

(e) The term "carriage of goods" covers the period from the time when the goods are loaded on to the time when they are discharged from the ship.

RISKS

Sec. 2. Subject to the provisions of section 6, under every contract of carriage of goods by sea, the carrier in relation to the loading, handling, stowage, carriage, custody, care, and discharge of such goods, shall be subject to the responsibilities and liabilities and entitled to the rights and immunities hereinafter set forth.

RESPONSIBILITIES AND LIABILITIES

Sec. 3. (1) The carrier shall be bound, before and at the beginning of the voyage, to exercise due diligence to—

(a) Make the ship seaworthy;

(b) Properly man, equip, and supply the ship;

[1] The Act is the result of an international conference held at Brussels in 1923, following recommendations of the International Law Association at a meeting at the Hague in 1922. Acts in substantially similar terms have been adopted throughout the British Empire, in Belgium, in France, in Germany, in Italy, in Japan, and in Norway.

(c) Make the holds, refrigerating and cooling chambers, and all other parts of the ship in which goods are carried, fit and safe for their reception, carriage, and preservation.

(2) The carrier shall properly and carefully load, handle, stow, carry, keep, care for, and discharge the goods carried.

(3) After receiving the goods into his charge the carrier, or the master or agent of the carrier, shall, on demand of the shipper, issue to the shipper a bill of lading showing among other things —

(a) The leading marks necessary for identification of the goods as the same are furnished in writing by the shipper before the loading of such goods starts, provided such marks are stamped or otherwise shown clearly upon the goods if uncovered, or on the cases or coverings in which such goods are contained, in such a manner as should ordinarily remain legible until the end of the voyage.

(b) Either the number of packages or pieces, or the quantity or weight, as the case may be, as furnished in writing by the shipper.

(c) The apparent order and condition of the goods: *Provided*, That no carrier, master, or agent of the carrier, shall be bound to state or show in the bill of lading any marks, number, quantity, or weight which he has reasonable ground for suspecting not accurately to represent the goods actually received, or which he has had no reasonable means of checking.

(4) Such a bill of lading shall be prima facie evidence of the receipt by the carrier of the goods as therein described in accordance with paragraphs (3) (a), (b), and (c), of this section: *Provided*, That nothing in this Act shall be construed as repealing or limiting the application of any part of the Act, as amended, entitled "An Act relating to bills of lading in interstate and foreign commerce," approved August 29, 1916 (U. S. C., title 49, secs. 81–124), commonly known as the "Pomerene Bills of Lading Act."

(5) The shipper shall be deemed to have guaranteed to the carrier the accuracy at the time of shipment of the marks, number, quantity, and weight, as furnished by him; and the shipper shall indemnify the carrier against all loss, damages, and expenses arising or resulting from inaccuracies in such particulars. The right of the carrier to such indemnity shall in no way limit his responsibility and liability under the contract of carriage to any person other than the shipper.

(6) Unless notice of loss or damage and the general nature of such loss or damage be given in writing to the carrier or his agent at the port of discharge before or at the time of the removal of the goods into the cutody of the person entitled to delivery thereof under the contract of carriage, such removal shall be prima facie evidence of the delivery by the carrier of the goods as described in the bill of lading. If the loss or damage is not apparent, the notice must be given within three days of the delivery.

Said notice of loss or damage may be endorsed upon the receipt for the goods given by the person taking delivery thereof.

The notice in writing need not be given if the state of the goods has at the time of their receipt been the subject of joint survey or inspection.

In any event the carrier and the ship shall be discharged from all liability in respect of loss or damage unless suit is brought within one year after delivery of the goods or the date when the goods should have been delivered: *Provided*, That if a notice of loss or damage, either apparent or concealed, is not given as provided for in this section, that fact shall not affect or prejudice the right of the shipper to bring suit within one year after the delivery of the goods or the date when the goods should have been delivered.

In the case of any actual or apprehended loss or damage the carrier and the receiver shall give all reasonable facilities to each other for inspecting and tallying the goods.

(7) After the goods are loaded the bill of lading to be issued by the carrier, master, or agent of the carrier to the shipper shall, if the shipper so demands, be a "shipped" bill of lading: *Provided*, That if the shipper shall have previously taken up any document of title to such goods, he shall surrender the same as against the issue of the "shipped" bill of lading, but at the option of the carrier such document of title may be noted at the port of shipment by the carrier, master, or agent with the name or names of the ship or ships upon which the goods have been shipped and the date or dates of shipment, and when so noted the same shall for the purpose of this section be deemed to constitute a "shipped" bill of lading.

(8) Any clause, covenant, or agreement in a contract of carriage relieving the carrier or the ship from liability for loss or damage to or in connection with the goods, arising from negligence, fault, or failure in the duties and obligations provided in this section, or lessening such liability otherwise than as provided in this Act, shall be null and void and of no effect. A benefit of insurance in favor of the carrier, or similar clause, shall be deemed to be a clause relieving the carrier from liability.

RIGHTS AND IMMUNITIES

Sec. 4. (1) Neither the carrier nor the ship shall be liable for loss or damage arising or resulting from unseaworthiness unless caused by want of due diligence on the part of the carrier to make the ship seaworthy, and to secure that the ship is properly manned, equipped, and supplied, and to make the holds, refrigerating and cool chambers, and all other parts of the ship in which goods are carried fit and safe for their reception, carriage, and preservation in accordance with the provisions of paragraph (1) of section 3. Whenever loss or damage has resulted from unseaworthiness, the burden of proving the exercise of due diligence shall be on the carrier or other persons claiming exemption under this section.

(2) Neither the carrier nor the ship shall be responsible for loss or damage arising or resulting from —

(a) Act, neglect, or default of the master, mariner, pilot, or the servants of the carrier in the navigation or in the management of the ship;

(b) Fire, unless caused by the actual fault or privity of the carrier;

(c) Perils, dangers, and accidents of the sea or other navigable waters;

(d) Act of God;

(e) Act of war;

(f) Act of public enemies;

(g) Arrest or restraint of princes, rulers, or people, or seizure under legal process;

(h) Quarantine restrictions;

(i) Act or omission of the shipper or owner of the goods, his agent or representative;

(j) Strikes or lockouts or stoppage or restraint of labor from whatever cause, whether partial or general: *Provided*, that nothing herein contained shall be construed to relieve a carrier from responsibility for the carrier's own acts;

(k) Riots and civil commotions;

(l) Saving or attempting to save life or property at sea;

(m) Wastage in bulk or weight or any other loss or damage arising from inherent defect, quality, or vice of the goods;

(n) Insufficiency of packing;

(o) Insufficiency or inadequacy of marks;

(p) Latent defects not discoverable by due diligence; and

(q) Any other cause arising without the actual fault and privity of the carrier and without the fault or neglect of the agents or servants of the carrier, but the burden of proof shall be on the person claiming the benefit of this exception to show that neither the actual fault or privity of the carrier nor the fault or neglect of the agents or servants of the carrier contributed to the loss or damage.

(3) The shipper shall not be responsible for loss or damage sustained by the carrier or the ship arising or resulting from any cause without the act, fault, or neglect of the shipper, his agents, or his servants.

(4) Any deviation in saving or attempting to save life or property at sea, or any reasonable deviation shall not be deemed to be an infringement or breach of this Act or of the contract of carriage, and the carrier shall not be liable for any loss or damage resulting therefrom: *Provided, however*, That if the deviation is for the purpose of loading or unloading cargo or passengers it shall, prima facie, be regarded as unreasonable.

(5) Neither the carrier nor the ship shall in any event be or become liable for any loss or damage to or in connection with the transportation of goods in an amount exceeding $500 per package lawful money of the United States, or in case of goods not shipped in packages, per customary freight unit, or the equivalent of that sum in other currency, unless the nature and value of such goods have been declared by the shipper before shipment and inserted in the bill of lading. This declaration, if embodied in the bill of lading, shall be prima facie evidence, but shall not be conclusive on the carrier.

By agreement between the carrier, master, or agent of the carrier, and the shipper another maximum amount than that mentioned in this paragraph may be fixed: *Provided*, That such maximum shall not be less than the figure above named. In no event shall the carrier be liable for more than the amount of damage actually sustained.

Neither the carrier nor the ship shall be responsible in any event for loss or damage to or in connection with the transportation of the goods if the nature or value thereof has been knowingly and fraudulently misstated by the shipper in the bill of lading.

(6) Goods of an inflammable, explosive, or dangerous nature to the shipment whereof the carrier, master or agent of the carrier, has not consented with knowledge of their nature and character, may at any time before discharge be landed at any place or destroyed or rendered innocuous by the carrier without compensation, and the shipper of such goods shall be liable for all damages and expenses directly or indirectly arising out of or resulting from such shipment. If any such goods shipped with such knowledge and consent shall become a danger to the ship or cargo, they may in like manner be landed at any place, or destroyed or rendered innocuous by the carrier without liability on the part of the carrier except to general average, if any.

SURRENDER OF RIGHTS AND IMMUNITIES AND INCREASE OF RESPONSIBILITIES AND LIABILITIES

Sec. 5. A carrier shall be at liberty to surrender in whole or in part all or any of his rights and immunities or to increase any of his responsibilities and liabilities under this Act, provided such surrender or increase shall be embodied in the bill of lading issued to the shipper.

The provisions of this Act shall not be applicable to charter parties; but if bills of lading are issued in the case of a ship under a charter party, they shall comply with the terms of this Act. Nothing in this Act shall be held to prevent the insertion in a bill of lading of any lawful provision regarding general average.

SPECIAL CONDITIONS

Sec. 6. Notwithstanding the provisions of the preceding sections, a carrier, master or agent of the carrier, and a shipper shall, in regard to any particular goods be at liberty to enter into any agreement in any terms as to the responsibility and liability of the carrier for such goods, and as to the rights and immunities of the carrier in respect of such goods, or his obligation as to seaworthiness (so far as the stipulation regarding seaworthiness is not contrary to public policy), or the care or diligence of his servants or agents in regard to the loading, handling, stowage, carriage, custody, care, and discharge of the goods carried by sea: *Provided,* That in this case no bill of lading has been or shall be issued and that the terms agreed shall be embodied in a receipt which shall be a nonnegotiable document and shall be marked as such.

Any agreement so entered into shall have full legal effect: *Provided,* That this section shall not apply to ordinary commercial shipments made in the ordinary course of trade but only to other shipments where the character or condition of the property to be carried or the circumstances, terms, and conditions under which the carriage is to be performed are such as reasonably to justify a special agreement.

Sec. 7. Nothing contained in this Act shall prevent a carrier or a shipper from entering into any agreement, stipulation, condition, reservation, or exemption as to the responsibility and liability of the carrier or the ship for the loss or damage to or in connection with the custody and care and handling of goods prior to the loading on and subsequent to the discharge from the ship on which the goods are carried by sea.

Sec. 8. The provisions of this Act shall not affect the rights and obligations of the carrier under the provisions of the Shipping Act, 1916, or under the provisions of sections 4281 to 4289, inclusive, of the Revised Statutes of the United States, or of any amendments thereto; or under the provisions of any other enactment for the time being in force relating to the limitation of the liability of the owners of seagoing vessels.

TITLE II

Section 9. Nothing contained in this Act shall be construed as permitting a common carrier by water to discriminate between competing shippers similarly placed in time and circumstances, either (a) with respect to their right to demand and receive bills of lading subject to the provisions of this Act; or (b) when issuing such bills of lading, either in the surrender of any of the carrier's rights and immunities or in the increase of any of the carrier's responsibilities and liabilities pursuant to section 5, title I, of this Act; or (*c*) in any other way prohibited by the Shipping Act, 1916, as amended.

Sec. 10. Section 25 of the Interstate Commerce Act is hereby amended by adding the following proviso at the end of paragraph 4 thereof: "*Provided, however,* That insofar as any bill of lading authorized hereunder relates to the carriage of goods by sea, such bill of lading shall be subject to the provisions of the Carriage of Goods by Sea Act."

Sec. 11. Where under the customs of any trade the weight of any bulk cargo inserted in the bill of lading is a weight ascertained or accepted by a third party other than the carrier or the shipper, and the fact that the weight is so ascertained or accepted is stated in the bill of lading, then, notwithstanding anything in this Act, the bill of lading shall not be deemed to be prima facie evidence against the carrier of the receipt of goods of the weight so inserted in the bill of lading, and the accuracy thereof at the time of shipment shall not be deemed to have been guaranteed by the shipper.

Sec. 12. Nothing in this Act shall be construed as superseding any part of the Act entitled "An Act relating to navigation of vessels, bills of lading, and to certain obligations, duties, and rights in connection with the carriage of property," approved February 13, 1893, or of any other law which would be applicable in the absence of this Act, insofar as they relate to the duties, responsibilities, and liabilities of the ship or carrier prior to the time when the goods are loaded on or after the time they are discharged from the ship.

Sec. 13. This Act shall apply to all contracts for carriage of goods by sea to or from ports of the United States in foreign trade. As used in this Act the term "United States" includes its districts, territories, and possessions: *Provided, however,* That the Philippine Legislature may by law exclude its application to transportation to or from ports of the Philippine Islands. The term "foreign trade" means the transportation of goods between the ports of the United States and ports of foreign countries. Nothing in this Act shall be held to apply to contracts for carriage of goods by sea between any port of the United States or its possessions, and any other port of the United States or its possessions: *Provided, however,* That any bill of lading or similar document of title which is evidence of a contract for the carriage of goods by sea between such ports, containing an express statement that it shall be subject to the provisions of this Act, shall be subjected hereto as fully as if subject hereto by the express provisions of this Act: *Provided further,* That every bill of lading or similar document of title which is evidence of a contract for the carriage of goods by sea from ports of the United States, in foreign trade, shall contain a statement that it shall have effect subject to the provisions of this Act.

Sec. 14. Upon the certification of the Secretary of Commerce that the foreign commerce of the United States in its competition with that of foreign nations is prejudiced by the provisions, or any of them, of title I of this Act, or by the laws of any foreign country or countries relating to the carriage of goods by sea, the President of the United States may, from time to time, by proclamation, suspend any or all provisions of title I of this Act for such periods of time or indefinitely as may be designated in the proclamation. The President may at any time rescind such suspension of title I hereof, and any provisions thereof which may have been suspended shall thereby be reinstated and again apply to contracts thereafter made for the carriage of goods by sea. Any proclamation of suspension or rescission of any such suspension shall take effect on a date named therein, which date shall be not less than ten days from the issue of the proclamation.

Any contract for the carriage of goods by sea, subject to the provisions of this Act, effective during any period when title I hereof, or any part thereof, is suspended, shall be subject to all provisions of law now or hereafter applicable to that part of title I which may have thus been suspended.

Sec. 15. This Act shall take effect ninety days after the date of its approval; but nothing in this Act shall apply during a period not to exceed one year following its approval to any contract for the carriage of goods by sea, made before the date on which this Act is approved, nor to any bill of lading or similar document of title issued, whether before or after such date of approval in pursuance of any such contract as aforesaid.

Sec. 16. This Act may be cited as the "Carriage of Goods by Sea Act."

Approved, April 16, 1936.

SPECIMEN FORMS

NO PROTEST TEAR THIS OFF BEFORE PRESENTING

$ __________ __________ 19__

__________ Pay to

the order of __________

__________ Dollars

Value received and charge the same to account of

To __________

No. __________ } __________

Gibsons 556 Main U.S. Bond.

DOMESTIC BILL OF EXCHANGE

First

Exch. for __________ __________

__________ after Sight pay this First of Exchange

(the Second being unpaid) to the Order of

____

Value received and charge the same to account of

To __________

____

No. __________ __________

1

Second

Exch. for __________ __________

__________ after Sight pay this Second of Exchange

(the First being unpaid) to the Order of

____

Value received and charge the same to account of

To __________

____

No. __________ __________

2

FOREIGN BILL OF EXCHANGE

APPLICATION FOR COMMERCIAL CREDIT

DATE________________________

TO THE CHASE NATIONAL BANK OF THE CITY OF NEW YORK,
FOREIGN DEPARTMENT,
PINE STREET CORNER OF NASSAU,
NEW YORK, N. Y.

PLEASE ISSUE {BY CABLE / BY MAIL} FOR OUR ACCOUNT AN **IRREVOCABLE CREDIT** AS FOLLOWS:

IN FAVOR OF________________________

UP TO THE AGGREGATE AMOUNT OF________________________

FOR ACCOUNT OF________________________

AVAILABLE BY DRAFTS AT________________________DRAWN AT YOUR OPTION

ON YOU OR YOUR CORRESPONDENTS FOR____________% OF THE INVOICE VALUE.

DOCUMENTS REQUIRED: PLEASE INDICATE BY CHECK (✓)

SPECIMEN

- ☐ COMMERCIAL INVOICE________________________
- ☐ CONSULAR INVOICE________________________
- ☐ MARINE INSURANCE CERTIFICATE________________________
  (IF INSURANCE EFFECTED OTHER THAN BY SHIPPER, GIVE NAME OF ISSUING COMPANY)
- ☐ OTHER DOCUMENTS________________________
  (IF SPECIAL DOCUMENTS ARE REQUIRED, PLEASE STATE NAME OF COMPANY TO ISSUE SAME)
- ☐ FULL SET BILLS OF LADING TO ORDER OF THE CHASE NATIONAL BANK OF THE CITY OF NEW YORK, NEW YORK, N. Y.

EVIDENCING SHIPMENT OF ________________________
(PLEASE MENTION COMMODITY ONLY, OMITTING DETAILS AS TO GRADE, QUALITY, PRICE, ETC.)

FROM____________________ TO____________________

CREDIT TO REMAIN IN FORCE UNTIL________________________

SPECIAL INSTRUCTIONS ________________________

In consideration of your opening, at our request, your Commercial Letter of Credit (herein called "The Credit") substantially in accordance with the foregoing application, we hereby agree as follows:

1. As to drafts or acceptances under or purporting to be under the Credit, which are payable in United States Currency, we agree: (a) in the case of each sight draft, to reimburse you at your office, on demand, in United States currency, the amount paid on such drafts, or, if so demanded by you, to pay to you at your office in advance in such currency, the amount required to pay such draft; and (b) in the case of each acceptance, to pay to you, at your office, in United States currency, the amount thereof, on demand but in any event not later than one business day prior to maturity, or, in case the acceptance is not payable at your office, then on demand but in any event in time to reach the place of payment in the course of the mails not later than one business day prior to maturity.

2. As to drafts or acceptances under or purporting to be under the Credit, which are payable in currency other than United States currency, we agree: (a) in the case of each sight draft, to reimburse you, at your office, on demand, the equivalent of the amount paid, in United States currency, at the rate of exchange then current in New York for cable transfers to the place of payment in the currency in which such draft is drawn; and (b) in the case of each acceptance, to furnish you, at your office, on demand, but in any event in time to reach the place of payment in the course of the mails not later than one business day prior to maturity with first class bankers' demand bills of exchange to be approved by you for the amount of acceptance, payable in the currency of the acceptance and bearing our endorsement, or, if you so request, to pay to you, at your office, on demand, the equivalent of the acceptance in United States currency at the rate of exchange current in New York for cable transfers at time of transmission to the place of payment in the currency in which the acceptance is payable.

3. We also agree to pay you, on demand, your commission and, in any event, a minimum commission, and all charges and expenses paid or incurred by you in connection therewith, and interest where chargeable.

(OVER)

F. X. 332 11-38

Application for Credit

4. We hereby recognize and admit your ownership in and unqualified right to the possession and disposal of all property shipped under or pursuant to or in connection with the Credit or in any way relative thereto or to the drafts drawn thereunder, whether or not released to us on trust or bailee receipt, and also in and to all shipping documents, warehouse receipts, policies or certificates of insurance and other documents accompanying or relative to drafts drawn under the credit, and in and to the proceeds of each and all of the foregoing, until such time as all the obligations and liabilities of us or any of us to you at any time existing under or with reference to the Credit or this agreement, or any other credit or any other obligation or liability to you, have been fully paid and discharged, all as security for such obligations and liabilities; and that all or any of such property and documents, and the proceeds of any thereof, coming into the possession of you or any of your correspondents, may be held and disposed of by you as hereinafter provided; and the receipt by you, or any of your correspondents, at any time of other security, of whatsoever nature, including cash, shall not be deemed a waiver of any of your rights or powers herein recognized.

5. In the event that you deliver to us any of the goods, wares or merchandise covered by the said credit prior to your having received reimbursement with respect to the relative drafts or acceptances as herein provided, we agree to sign and deliver to you a Trust Receipt or Trust Receipts as defined in and complying with the requirements of the Uniform Trust Receipts Law of the State of New York and a Statement of Trust Receipt Financing in the form specified in the said statute, and we further agree that your rights specified herein shall be in addition to and not in limitation of your rights under the said statute or any other applicable statute.

6. Except in so far as instructions have been heretofore given by us in writing expressly to the contrary, we agree that you and any of your correspondents may receive and accept as "Bills of lading" under the Credit, any documents issued or purporting to be issued by or on behalf of any carrier which acknowledge receipt of property for transportation, whatever the specific provisions of such documents, and that the date of each such document shall be deemed the date of shipment of the property mentioned therein; and that you may receive and accept as documents of insurance either insurance policies or insurance certificates.

7. Except in so far as instructions have been heretofore given by us in writing expressly to the contrary, we agree that part shipments may be made under the Credit and you may honor the relative drafts; and that if the Credit specifies shipments in instalments within stated periods, and the shipper fails to ship in any designated period, shipments of subsequent instalments may nevertheless be made in their respective designated periods and you may honor the relative drafts.

8. We agree that in the event of any extension of the maturity or time for presentation of drafts, acceptances or documents, or any other modification of the terms of the Credit, at the request of any of us, with or without notification to the others, or in the event, of any increase in the amount of the Credit at our request, this agreement shall be binding upon us with regard to the credit so increased or otherwise modified, to drafts, documents and property covered thereby, and to any action taken by you or any of your correspondents in accordance with such extension, increase or other modification.

9. The users of the Credit shall be deemed our agents and we assume all risks of their acts or omissions. Neither you nor your correspondents shall be responsible: for the existence, character, quality, quantity, condition, packing, value or delivery of the property purporting to be represented by documents; for any difference in character, quality, quantity, condition, or value of the property from that expressed in documents; for the validity, sufficiency, or genuineness of documents, even if such documents should in fact prove to be in any or all respects invalid, insufficient, fraudulent or forged; for the time, place, manner or order in which shipment is made; for partial or incomplete shipment or failure or omission to ship any or all of the property referred to in the Credit; for the character, adequacy, validity, or genuineness of any insurance; for the solvency or responsibility of any insurer, or for any other risk connected with insurance; for any deviation from instructions, delay, default or fraud by the shipper or anyone else in connection with the property or the shipping thereof; for the solvency, responsibility or relationship to the property of any party issuing any documents in connection with the property; for delay in arrival or failure to arrive of either the property or any of the documents relating thereto; for delay in giving or failure to give notice of arrival or any other notice; for any breach of contract between the shippers or vendors and ourselves or any of us; or for any laws, customs and regulations which may be effective in countries of negotiation and/or payment of this credit; for failure of any draft to bear any reference or adequate reference to the Credit, or failure of documents to accompany any draft at negotiation, or failure of any person to note the amount of any draft on the reverse of the Credit or to surrender or take up the Credit or to send forward documents apart from drafts as required by the terms of the Credit; each of which provisions, if contained in the Credit itself, it is agreed may be waived by you, or for errors, omissions, interruptions or delays in transmission, or delivery of any messages, by mail, cable, telegraph, wireless or otherwise, whether or not they be in cipher; nor shall you be responsible for any error, neglect, or default of any of your correspondents; and none of the above shall affect, impair, or prevent the vesting of any of your rights or powers hereunder. In furtherance and extension and not in limitation of the specific provisions hereinbefore set forth, we agree that any action taken by you or by any correspondent of yours under or in connection with the Credit or the relative drafts, documents or property, if taken in good faith, shall be binding on us and shall not put you or your correspondent under any resulting liability to us; and we make like agreement as to any inaction or omission, unless in breach of good faith.

10. We agree to procure promptly any necessary import and export or other licenses for the import or export or shipping of the property and to comply with all foreign and domestic governmental regulations in regard to the shipment of the property or the financing thereof, and to furnish such certificates in that respect as you may at any time require, and to keep the property adequately covered by insurance satisfactory to you, in companies satisfactory to you, and to assign the policies or certificates of insurance to you, or to make the loss or adjustment, if any, payable to you, at your option; and to furnish you if demanded with evidence of acceptance by the insurers of such assignment.

11. Each of us agrees at any time and from time to time, on demand, to deliver, convey, transfer, or assign to you, as security for any and all of his and/or our obligations and liabilities hereunder, and also for any and all other obligations and liabilities, absolute or contingent, due or to become due, which are now or may at any time hereafter be owing by him or us to you, additional security of a value and character satisfactory to you, or to make such payment as you may require. Each of us agrees that all property belonging to him, or us, or in which he or we may have an interest, of every name and nature whatsoever, now or at any time hereafter delivered, conveyed, transferred, assigned, or paid to you, or coming into your possession or into the possession of anyone for you in any manner whatsoever, whether expressly as security for any of the obligations or liabilities by him or us to you, or for safekeeping or otherwise, including any items received for collection or transmission and the proceeds thereof whether or not such property is in whole or in part released to us on trust or bailee receipt are hereby made security for each and all such obligations and liabilities. Each of us agrees that upon his or our failure at all times to keep a margin of security with you satisfactory to you, or upon the making by him or us of any assignments for the benefit of creditors, or upon the filing of any voluntary or involuntary petition in bankruptcy by or against him or us, or upon the application for the appointment of a receiver of any of his or our property, or upon any act of bankruptcy or state of insolvency of him or us, all of such obligations and liabilities shall become and be immediately due and payable without demand or notice, notwithstanding any credit or time allowed to him or us, or any instrument evidencing any such obligations or liabilities or otherwise; and each of us, as to property in which he may have any interest, and all of us, as to property in which we may have any interest expressly authorize you in any such event, or upon his or our failure to pay any of such obligations or liabilities when it or they shall become or be made due, to sell immediately, without demand for payment, without advertisement and without notice to us or any of us, all of which are hereby expressly waived, any and all such property, arrived or to arrive, at private sale or at public auction or at brokers' board or otherwise, at your option, in such parcel or parcels and at such time or times and at such place or places and for such price or prices and upon such terms and conditions as you may deem proper, and to apply the net proceeds of such sale or sales, together with any balance of deposits and any sums credit by or due from you to him or us in general account or otherwise, to the payment of any and all of his and/or our obligations or liabilities to you however arising. If any such sale be at brokers' board or at public auction you may yourself be a purchaser at such sale, free from any right of redemption, which we and each of us hereby expressly waive and release.

12. You shall not be deemed to have waived any of your rights hereunder, unless you or your authorized agent shall have signed such waiver in writing. No such waiver unless expressly as stated therein, shall be effective as to any transaction which occurs subsequent to the date of such waiver, nor as to any continuance of a breach after such waiver.

13. The word "property" as used in this agreement includes goods, merchandise, securities, funds, choses in action, and any and all other forms of property, whether real, personal or mixed and any right or interest therein.

14. If this agreement is signed by one individual, the terms "we," "our," "us," shall be read throughout as "I," "my," "me," as the case may be. If this agreement is signed by two or more parties, it shall be the joint and several agreement of such parties.

15. The obligations hereof shall continue in force, and apply, notwithstanding any change in the membership of any partnership undersigned, whether arising from the death or retirement of one or more partners or the accession of one or more new partners, and the obligations hereof shall bind the heirs, executors, administrators, successors and assigns of the undersigned, and all rights, benefits and privileges hereby conferred on you shall be and hereby are extended to and conferred upon and may be enforced by your successors and assigns.

16. This guaranty and all rights, obligations and liabilities arising hereunder shall be construed according to the laws of the State of New York.

____

____

PLEASE SIGN OFFICIALLY

APPLICATION FOR CREDIT (*Reverse*)

COMMERCIAL LETTER OF CREDIT AGREEMENT

____________________19____

TO THE CHASE NATIONAL BANK OF THE CITY OF NEW YORK,
FOREIGN DEPARTMENT,
PINE STREET CORNER OF NASSAU,
NEW YORK, N. Y.

We hereby appoint you to act as our agent solely to the extent of issuing your commercial letter of credit

No.____________________

for account of____________________

in favor of____________________

amounting to____________________

available by____________________sight drafts.

In consideration of your issuing or having issued as our agent the above letter of credit, we hereby agree to indemnify and save you and your correspondents harmless from any and all loss, liability or expense arising from or in connection with the said credit.

As security for the payment, performance and discharge of any and all obligations and liabilities of the undersigned to you, direct or indirect, absolute or contingent, due or not due, now existing or hereafter arising, the undersigned pledges to you, and/or gives to you a lien upon, and/or right of set-off of, all deposit balances now or hereafter existing in any accounts of the undersigned, and all property and securities of every kind and nature now or at any time hereafter given unto or left in your possession or custody for safekeeping or for any other purpose whatever, or coming into your possession or in transit to you, or anyone for you, in any way, by or for account of the undersigned, or in which the undersigned may have any interest, whether you shall accept the same for the purpose for which it is delivered or not, and any and all proceeds of said property and securities and every part thereof; with the right to you, in your discretion, to resort first to any part of said security.

We further agree that all property deposited with us by our customer as security in connection with the issuance of the above described Letter of Credit shall be held by us in trust to secure the obligation of our said customer to you thereon; and for such purpose we assign to you our rights in the said security.

All obligations and liabilities, direct or indirect, absolute or contingent, of the undersigned to you, whether now existing or hereafter arising, shall, simultaneously with the happening of any of the following events, become and be immediately due and payable, without demand or notice, notwithstanding any credit or time allowed by any instrument evidencing any such obligations or liabilities, unless you shall, at your option, the exercise of which option need not be communicated to the undersigned, elect not to treat any/or all such obligations and liabilities as immediately due and payable, to wit: (1) default in payment of any obligation or liability of the undersigned to you in whole or in part; (2) or if the undersigned shall become insolvent (however such insolvency may be evidenced), or make a general assignment for the benefit of Creditors, or file a voluntary petition in bankruptcy, or for any relief under any bankruptcy or insolvency laws, or if a petition in bankruptcy or for any relief under any bankruptcy or insolvency laws shall be filed against the undersigned, or a receiver or liquidator shall be appointed of the property or assets, or any thereof, of the undersigned, or if any governmental authority shall take possession of any substantial part of the property of the undersigned, or if the transaction of the usual business of the undersigned shall be suspended, or if a judgment be entered against, or a writ of attachment, whether valid or not, be issued against any property of the undersigned.

It is understood that neither you, nor your agents here or abroad, will be responsible for the validity, correctness and/or genuineness of the documents purporting to relate to aforesaid credit, nor for the quality, quantity, and/or arrival of the merchandise described in such documents.

We also agree to pay you, on demand, your commission and, in any event, a minimum commission, together with all expenses incurred by you in connection with arranging the credit and the execution thereof. At least one day prior to maturity of each time draft, and at or before the time of presentation to you of each sight draft, drawn under such credit, the undersigned agrees to place you in New York funds sufficient to pay each such draft, with interest, if any, and all other charges relating thereto.

____

____

F. X. 156A 10-37

Credit Agreement

The Chase National Bank

OF THE CITY OF NEW YORK

PINE STREET CORNER OF NASSAU

New York

FOREIGN DEPARTMENT

ADVICE OF AUTHORITY TO

ADVICE NO. E

GENTLEMEN:

WE ADVISE YOU THAT

HAVE AUTHORIZED US TO YOUR DRAFTS FOR ACCOUNT OF

UNDER THEIR REFERENCE NUMBER FOR A SUM OR SUMS NOT EXCEEDING A TOTAL OF

ON US AT

TO BE ACCOMPANIED BY

SPECIMEN

ALL DRAFTS SO DRAWN MUST BE MARKED "DRAWN UNDER CHASE NATIONAL BANK ADVICE NO. E

DRAFTS SO DRAWN, WITH DOCUMENTS AS SPECIFIED, MUST BE PRESENTED AT THIS OFFICE NOT LATER THAN

THE AUTHORITY GIVEN US IS SUBJECT TO REVOCATION OR MODIFICATION AT ANY TIME WITHOUT NOTICE TO YOU.

UNLESS OTHERWISE EXPRESSLY STATED, THIS ADVICE IS SUBJECT TO THE UNIFORM CUSTOMS AND PRACTICE FOR COMMERCIAL DOCUMENTARY CREDITS FIXED BY THE SEVENTH CONGRESS OF THE INTERNATIONAL CHAMBER OF COMMERCE AND CERTAIN GUIDING PROVISIONS.

THIS ADVICE CONVEYS NO ENGAGEMENT ON OUR PART OR ON THE PART OF THE ABOVE MENTIONED CORRESPONDENT AND IS SIMPLY FOR YOUR GUIDANCE IN PREPARING AND PRESENTING DRAFTS AND DOCUMENTS.

YOURS VERY TRULY,

ASSISTANT CASHIER
ASSISTANT MANAGER

AMERICAN BANK NOTE CO. LITHO.

Authority to Purchase

IRREVOCABLE COMMERCIAL LETTER OF CREDIT

The Chase National Bank

CABLE ADDRESS
CHASEBANK, NEW YORK

OF THE CITY OF NEW YORK

PINE STREET CORNER OF NASSAU

No.

New York

GENTLEMEN:

WE HEREBY AUTHORIZE YOU TO VALUE ON

BY ORDER OF

AND FOR ACCOUNT OF
UP TO AN AGGREGATE AMOUNT OF

AVAILABLE BY YOUR DRAFTS AT
ACCOMPANIED BY

SPECIMEN

DRAFTS MUST BE DRAWN AND NEGOTIATED NOT LATER THAN

EACH DRAFT MUST STATE THAT IT IS "DRAWN UNDER LETTER OF CREDIT OF THE CHASE NATIONAL BANK, NEW YORK, NO. DATED ". AND THE AMOUNT ENDORSED ON THIS LETTER OF CREDIT.

WE HEREBY AGREE WITH THE DRAWERS, ENDORSERS, AND BONA FIDE HOLDERS OF ALL DRAFTS DRAWN UNDER AND IN COMPLIANCE WITH THE TERMS OF THIS CREDIT, THAT SUCH DRAFTS WILL BE DULY HONORED UPON PRESENTATION TO THE DRAWEE.

YOURS VERY TRULY,

SECOND VICE PRESIDENT
ASSISTANT CASHIER

ASSISTANT MANAGER, FOREIGN DEPARTMENT

AMERICAN BANK NOTE CO. LITHO.

IRREVOCABLE LETTER OF CREDIT

ACKNOWLEDGMENT AND TRUST RECEIPT **RETURN TO** THE CHASE NATIONAL BANK
OF THE CITY OF NEW YORK
PINE STREET CORNER OF NASSAU

FOREIGN DEPARTMENT $
CABLE ADDRESS
CHASEBANK, NEW YORK

FROM

NEW YORK,

TRUST RECEIPT NO.

WE ENCLOSE THE FOLLOWING DESCRIBED DOCUMENTS RELATIVE TO LETTER OF CREDIT NUMBER

FOR ACCOUNT OF

COVERING SHIPMENT OF PER S/S

FROM TO

	INVOICE	INSURANCE CTF.	CONSULAR INV.	B/L	PAR. POST RECEIPT	DELIVERY ORDER	FORWARDERS RECEIPT	CTF. OF ORIGIN	SPECIF.	INSPECTION CTF.	WEIGHT CTF.
DOCUMENTS ENCLOSED											

MARKS AND NUMBERS	REMARKS
	SPECIMEN

PLEASE OFFICIALLY SIGN THE TRUST RECEIPT APPEARING ON THE REVERSE HEREOF, AND RETURN THIS FORM TO US.

THE CHASE NATIONAL BANK
OF THE CITY OF NEW YORK

Trust Receipt

TRUST RECEIPT

DATE ______________________

The undersigned (hereinafter called the "Trustee") hereby acknowledges receipt from The Chase National Bank of the City of New York, New York, N. Y., (hereinafter called the "Entruster") of the documents listed on the obverse hereof representing the goods therein specified, a security interest as defined in the Uniform Trust Receipts Law of the State of New York, in both said documents and said goods remaining in or hereby passing to the Entruster.

In consideration of such receipt and other valuable considerations, the Trustee agrees to hold said documents and goods in trust for the Entruster and subject to its security interest, to be used promptly by the Trustee without expense to the Entruster for the purpose of selling said goods or manufacturing and selling said goods, but for no other purpose and without liberty to pledge the same.

The Trustee agrees to account by delivering to the Entruster, immediately upon the receipt thereof by the Trustee, the proceeds of the sale of such goods in whatever form received, to be applied by the Entruster under the terms of its Letter of Credit of which the number is noted on the obverse hereof issued for the Trustee's account and/or to the payment of any obligations for which said goods and documents are security or [illegible] security before this transaction and of any obligations arising as part of this transaction and of any renewals of any such obligations. If such proceeds be notes, bills receivable, acceptances, or in any form other than cash, they shall not be so applied by the Entruster until paid; the Entruster, however, to have the option at any time to sell or discount such items and so apply, conditionally upon final payment of such items, the net proceeds thereof.

The Trustee agrees to pay all charges in connection with said goods, documents, and any proceeds thereof, and will at all times hold said goods, documents, and proceeds separate and apart from the property of the Trustee and will definitely show such separation in all its records and entries.

The Trustee will at all times keep said goods fully insured at the Trustee's expense in favor of, and to the satisfaction of the Entruster against loss by fire, theft, and any other risk to which said goods may be subject. The Trustee will deposit the insurance policies with the Entruster upon its demand.

The Entruster may at any time cancel this trust and bailment and take possession of said goods, manufactured or unmanufactured, and any documents representing the same (until delivery of said goods and documents to the purchaser(s) pursuant to a sale hereby authorized and the receipt by the Trustee of the proceeds of such sale) and the proceeds of any sale, wherever said goods, manufactured or unmanufactured, documents, or proceeds may then be found. As to the articles manufactured by style or model, the Trustee's interest therein may be forfeited, at the election of the Entruster, in the event of any default on the part of the Trustee, against cancellation to the extent and as provided by law of the Trustee's then remaining indebtedness with respect to such articles.

The Trustee agrees that the Entruster assumes no responsibility for the correctness, validity, or genuineness of the documents released to the Trustee hereunder or for the existence, character, quantity, quality, condition, value, or delivery of any goods purported to be represented by any of such documents.

No waiver of any rights or powers of the Entruster or consent by it shall be valid unless in writing signed by it The rights and powers herein given the Entruster are in addition to those otherwise created.

SPECIMEN

____

____
OFFICIAL SIGNATURE OF TRUSTEE

TRUST RECEIPT (*Reverse*)

NEW YORK TERMINAL WAREHOUSE CO.
INCORPORATED

№ 3767

CHICAGO OFFICE
120 South LaSalle Street
Chicago, Illinois

MAIN OFFICE, 25 SOUTH WILLIAM STREET
NEW YORK, N. Y.

ATLANTA OFFICE
Healey Building
Atlanta, Georgia

..................................19......

Issued at..................................

This is to Certify that we have received for the account of.. in Storage Warehouse.. in apparent good order, except as noted hereon, contents, condition and quality unknown, the following described property, subject to all the terms and conditions contained herein and the published standard warehouse terms and conditions of the Company in effect on the date of this receipt on file in its offices, such property to be delivered to.. upon the payment of all storage, handling and other charges.

CANCELLED

ITEM	LOT NO.	QUANTITY	UNIT	SAID TO BE OR CONTAIN
				CANCELLED NOT-NEGOTIABLE

Received Ex..

Storage and other charges as per contract with

....

dated.. the provisions of which will be disclosed to the holder hereof upon request to the Warehouseman.

The New York Terminal Warehouse Co., Incorporated, certifies that its only relationship to the depositor is that of a warehouseman and that it has no financial interest in the goods covered by this receipt, except that it claims a lien for all lawful charges for the storage, handling, and preservation of the goods.

NEW YORK TERMINAL WAREHOUSE CO.

By CANCELLED

Location of goods is not given for insurance purposes and the Warehouseman disclaims all liability for error or insufficiency of the location shown.

RECORD OF DELIVERIES AND BALANCES ON HAND

ITEM A				ITEM B				ITEM C				ITEM D			
Date	W.W.O. No.	Delivered	Balance	Date	W.W.O. No.	Delivered	Balance	Date	W.W.O. No.	Delivered	Balance	Date	W.W.O. No.	Delivered	Balance
ITEM E				ITEM F				ITEM G				ITEM H			
Date	W.W.O. No.	Delivered	Balance	Date	W.W.O. No.	Delivered	Balance	Date	W.W.O. No.	Delivered	Balance	Date	W.W.O. No.	Delivered	Balance

NON-NEGOTIABLE WAREHOUSE RECEIPT (*Two Sides*)

No. BN

New York Terminal Warehouse Co.

INCORPORATED

MAIN OFFICE 27th STREET & 11th AVENUE,

NEW YORK, N. Y.

New York..............................193....

This is to certify that we have received for the account of.. in Storage Warehouse ....in apparent good order, except as noted hereon, contents, condition and quality unknown, the following described property, subject to all the terms and conditions contained herein and the published standard warehouse terms and conditions of the Company in effect on the date of this receipt on file in its main office, 27th Street and 11th Avenue, New York, N. Y., such property to be delivered to..............................order, upon the payment of all storage, handling and other charges and the surrender of this Warehouse Receipt properly endorsed.

ITEM	LOT. NO.	QUANTITY	UNIT	SAID TO BE OR CONTAIN	
SPECIMEN COPY				NEGOTIABLE	SPECIMEN COPY

Location of goods is not given for insurance purposes and the Warehouseman disclaims all liability for error or insufficiency of the location shown.

Received Ex ....

Storage and other charges as per contract with

....

Dated ....

Storage ....per..................per month.

Handling ....per.................. in and out inclusive.

The New York Terminal Warehouse Co., Inc., certifies that its only relationship to the depositor is that of a public warehouseman, and that it has no financial interest in the goods covered by this receipt, except that it claims a lien for all lawful charges for the storage, handling, and preservation of the goods.

NEW YORK TERMINAL WAREHOUSE CO.
Incorporated

By ....VOID..................

By ....

Not valid unless signed by two officers of the Company

A/C

Negotiable Receipt No. BN

RECORD OF DELIVERIES AND BALANCES DUE ON RECEIPT

ITEM A

Date	Release No.	Delivered	Balance on Receipt	Signature

ITEM B

Date	Release No.	Delivered	Balance on Receipt	Signature

ITEM C

Date	Release No.	Delivered	Balance on Receipt	Signature

ITEM D

Date	Release No.	Delivered	Balance on Receipt	Signature

ENDORSEMENTS

Negotiable Warehouse Receipt (*Two Sides*)

PRINTED IN U. S. A.

NYCS
FTD-4-A

1

(Uniform Domestic Straight Bill of Lading, adopted by Carriers in Official, Southern, Western and Illinois Classification territories, March 15, 1922, as amended August 1, 1930.)

UNIFORM STRAIGHT BILL OF LADING
ORIGINAL—NOT NEGOTIABLE

Shipper's No.______

Agent's No.______

NEW YORK CENTRAL SYSTEM

THE NEW YORK CENTRAL RAILROAD COMPANY

RECEIVED, subject to the classifications and tariffs in effect on the date of the issue of this Bill of Lading,

*At*______ *193*___ *From*______

the property described below, in apparent good order, except as noted (contents and condition of contents of packages unknown), marked, consigned, and destined as indicated below, which said company (the word company being understood throughout this contract as meaning any person or corporation in possession of the property under the contract) agrees to carry to its usual place of delivery at said destination, if on its own road or its own water line, otherwise to deliver to another carrier on the route to said destination. It is mutually agreed, as to each carrier of all or any of said property over all or any portion of said route to destination, and as to each party at any time interested in all or any of said property, that every service to be performed hereunder shall be subject to all the conditions not prohibited by law, whether printed or written, herein contained, including the conditions on back hereof, which are hereby agreed to by the shipper and accepted for himself and his assigns.

(Mail or street address of consignee—For purposes of notification only.)

Consigned to______

Destination______ State of______ County of______

Route______

Delivering Carrier______ Car Initial______ Car No.______

No. Pkgs.	DESCRIPTION OF ARTICLES, SPECIAL MARKS, AND EXCEPTIONS	*Weight (Sub. to Cor.)	Class or Rate	Check Col.

Subject to Section 7 of conditions, if this shipment is to be delivered to the consignee without recourse on the consignor, the consignor shall sign the following statement:

The carrier shall not make delivery of this shipment without payment of freight and all other lawful charges.

______
(Signature of Consignor.)

If charges are to be prepaid, write or stamp here, "To be Prepaid."

Received $______ to apply in prepayment of the charges on the property described hereon.

______
Agent or Cashier

Per______
(The signature here acknowledges only the amount prepaid.)

Charges Advanced:

$______

*If the shipment moves between two ports by a carrier by water, the law requires that the bill of lading shall state whether it is "carrier's or shipper's weight."

NOTE—Where the rate is dependent on value, shippers are required to state specifically in writing the agreed or declared value of the property.

The agreed or declared value of the property is hereby specifically stated by the shipper to be not exceeding______ per______

______Shipper ______Agent

Per______ Per______

Permanent postoffice address of shipper______

RAILROAD STRAIGHT BILL OF LADING
(Issued in triplicate)

CONTRACT TERMS AND CONDITIONS

Sec. 1. (a) The carrier or party in possession of any of the property herein described shall be liable as at common law for any loss thereof or damage thereto, except as hereinafter provided.

(b) No carrier or party in possession of all or any of the property herein described shall be liable for any loss thereof or damage thereto or delay caused by the Act of God, the public enemy, the authority of law, or the act or default of the shipper or owner, or for natural shrinkage. The carrier's liability shall be that of warehouseman, only, for loss, damage, or delay caused by fire occurring after the expiration of the free time allowed by tariffs lawfully on file (such free time to be computed as therein provided) after notice of the arrival of the property at destination or at the port of export (if intended for export) has been duly sent or given, and after placement of the property for delivery at destination, or tender of delivery of the property to the party entitled to receive it, has been made. Except in case of negligence of the carrier or party in possession (and the burden to prove freedom from such negligence shall be on the carrier or party in possession), the carrier or party in possession shall not be liable for loss, damage, or delay occurring while the property is stopped and held in transit upon the request of the shipper, owner, or party entitled to make such request, or resulting from a defect or vice in the property, or for country damage to cotton, or from riots or strikes.

(c) In case of quarantine the property may be discharged at risk and expense of owners into quarantine depot or elsewhere, as required by quarantine regulations or authorities, or for the carrier's dispatch at nearest available point in carrier's judgment, and in any such case carrier's responsibility shall cease when property is so discharged, or property may be returned by carrier at owner's expense to shipping point, earning freight both ways. Quarantine expenses of whatever nature or kind upon or in respect to property shall be borne by the owners of the property or be a lien thereon. The carrier shall not be liable for loss or damage occasioned by fumigation or disinfection or other acts required or done by quarantine regulations or authorities even though the same may have been done by carrier's officers, agents, or employees, nor for detention, loss, or damage of any kind occasioned by quarantine or the enforcement thereof. No carrier shall be liable, except in case of negligence, for any mistake or inaccuracy in any information furnished by the carrier, its agents, or officers, as to quarantine laws or regulations. The shipper shall hold the carriers harmless from any expense they may incur, or damages they may be required to pay, by reason of the introduction of the property covered by this contract into any place against the quarantine laws or regulations in effect at such place.

Sec. 2. (a) No carrier is bound to transport said property by any particular train or vessel, or in time for any particular market or otherwise than with reasonable dispatch. Every carrier shall have the right in case of physical necessity to forward said property by any carrier or route between the point of shipment and the point of destination. In all cases not prohibited by law, where a lower value than actual value has been represented in writing by the shipper or has been agreed upon in writing as the released value of the property as determined by the classification or tariffs upon which the rate is based, such lower value plus freight charges if paid shall be the maximum amount to be recovered, whether or not such loss or damage occurs from negligence.

(b) As a condition precedent to recovery, claims must be filed in writing with the receiving or delivering carrier, or carrier issuing this bill of lading, or carrier on whose line the loss, damage, injury or delay occurred, within nine months after delivery of the property (or, in case of export traffic, within nine months after delivery at port of export) or, in case of failure to make delivery, then within nine months after a reasonable time for delivery has elapsed; and suits shall be instituted against any carrier only within two years and one day from the day when notice in writing is given by the carrier to the claimant that the carrier has disallowed the claim or any part or parts thereof specified in the notice. Where claims are not filed or suits are not instituted thereon in accordance with the foregoing provisions, no carrier hereunder shall be liable, and such claims will not be paid.

(c) Any carrier or party liable on account of loss of or damage to any of said property shall have the full benefit of any insurance that may have been effected upon or on account of said property, so far as this shall not avoid the policies or contracts of insurance: **Provided,** That the carrier reimburse the claimant for the premium paid thereon.

Sec. 3. Except where such service is required as the result of carrier's negligence, all property shall be subject to necessary cooperage and baling at owner's cost. Each carrier over whose route cotton or cotton linters is to be transported hereunder shall have the privilege, at its own cost and risk, of compressing the same for greater convenience in handling or forwarding, and shall not be held responsible for deviation or unavoidable delays in procuring such compression. Grain in bulk consigned to a point where there is a railroad, public or licensed elevator, may (unless otherwise expressly noted herein, and then if it is not promptly unloaded) be there delivered and placed with other grain of the same kind and grade without respect to ownership (and prompt notice thereof shall be given to the consignor), and if so delivered shall be subject to a lien for elevator charges in addition to all other charges hereunder.

Sec. 4. (a) Property not removed by the party entitled to receive it within the free time allowed by tariffs, lawfully on file (such free time to be computed as therein provided), after notice of the arrival of the property at destination or at the port of export (if intended for export) has been duly sent or given, and after placement of the property for delivery at destination has been made, may be kept in vessel, car, depot, warehouse or place of delivery of the carrier, subject to the tariff charge for storage and to carrier's responsibility as warehouseman, only, or at the option of the carrier, may be removed to and stored in a public or licensed warehouse at the place of delivery or other available place, at the cost of the owner, and there held without liability on the part of the carrier, and subject to a lien for all freight and other lawful charges, including a reasonable charge for storage.

(b) Where nonperishable property which has been transported to destination hereunder is refused by consignee or the party entitled to receive it, or said consignee or party entitled to receive it fails to receive it within 15 days after notice of arrival shall have been duly sent or given, the carrier may sell the same at public auction to the highest bidder, at such place as may be designated by the carrier: **Provided,** That the carrier shall have first mailed, sent, or given to the consignor notice that the property has been refused or remains unclaimed, as the case may be, and that it will be subject to sale under the terms of the bill of lading if disposition be not arranged for, and shall have published notice containing a description of the property, the name of the party to whom consigned, or, if shipped order notify, the name of the party to be notified, and the time and place of sale, once a week for two successive weeks, in a newspaper of general circulation at the place of sale or nearest place where such newspaper is published: **Provided,** That 30 days shall have elapsed before publication of notice of sale after said notice that the property was refused or remains unclaimed was mailed, sent, or given.

(c) Where perishable property which has been transported hereunder to destination is refused by consignee or party entitled to receive it, or said consignee or party entitled to receive it shall fail to receive it promptly, the carrier may, in its discretion, to prevent deterioration or further deterioration, sell the same to the best advantage at private or public sale: **Provided,** That if time serves for notification to the consignor or owner of the refusal of the property or the failure to receive it and request for disposition of the property, such notification shall be given, in such manner as the exercise of due diligence requires, before the property is sold.

(d) Where the procedure provided for in the two paragraphs last preceding is not possible, it is agreed that nothing contained in said paragraphs shall be construed to abridge the right of the carrier at its option to sell the property under such circumstances and in such manner as may be authorized by law.

(e) The proceeds of any sale made under this section shall be applied by the carrier to the payment of freight, demurrage, storage, and any other lawful charges and the expense of notice, advertisement, sale, and other necessary expense and of caring for and maintaining the property, if proper care of the same requires special expense, and should there be a balance it shall be paid to the owner of the property sold hereunder.

(f) Property destined to or taken from a station, wharf, or landing at which there is no regularly appointed freight agent shall be entirely at risk of owner after unloaded from cars or vessels or until loaded into cars or vessels, and, except in case of carrier's negligence, when received from or delivered to such stations, wharves, or landings shall be at owner's risk until the cars are attached to and after they are detached from locomotive or train or until loaded into and after unloaded from vessels.

Sec. 5. No carrier hereunder will carry or be liable in any way for any documents, specie, or for any articles of extraordinary value not specifically rated in the published classifications or tariffs unless a special agreement to do so and a stipulated value of the articles are indorsed hereon

Sec. 6. Every party, whether principal or agent, shipping explosives or dangerous goods, without previous full written disclosure to the carrier of their nature, shall be liable for and indemnify the carrier against all loss or damage caused by such goods, and such goods may be warehoused at owner's risk and expense or destroyed without compensation.

Sec. 7. The owner or consignee shall pay the freight and average, if any, and all other lawful charges accruing on said property; but, except in those instances where it may lawfully be authorized to do so, no carrier by railroad shall deliver or relinquish possession at destination of the property covered by this bill of lading until all tariff rates and charges thereon have been paid. The consignor shall be liable for the freight and all other lawful charges, except that if the consignor stipulates, by signature, in the space provided for that purpose on the face of this bill of lading that the carrier shall not make delivery without requiring payment of such charges and the carrier, contrary to such stipulation, shall make delivery without requiring such payment, the consignor (except as hereinafter provided) shall not be liable for such charges. **Provided, that,** where the carrier has been instructed by the shipper or consignor to deliver said property to a consignee other than the shipper or consignor, such consignee shall not be legally liable for transportation charges in respect of the transportation of said property (beyond those billed against him at the time of delivery for which he is otherwise liable) which may be found to be due after the property has been delivered to him, if the consignee (a) is an agent only and has no beneficial title in said property, and (b) prior to delivery of said property has notified the delivering carrier in writing of the fact of such agency and absence of beneficial title, and, in the case of a shipment reconsigned or diverted to a point other than that specified in the original bill of lading, has also notified the delivering carrier in writing of the name and address of the beneficial owner of said property; and, in such cases the shipper or consignor, or, in the case of a shipment so reconsigned or diverted, the beneficial owner, shall be liable for such additional charges. If the consignee has given to the carrier erroneous information as to who the beneficial owner is, such consignee shall himself be liable for such additional charges. Nothing herein shall limit the right of the carrier to require at time of shipment the prepayment or guarantee of the charges. If upon inspection it is ascertained that the articles shipped are not those described in this bill of lading, the freight charges must be paid upon the articles actually shipped.

Sec. 8. If this bill of lading is issued on the order of the shipper, or his agent, in exchange or in substitution for another bill of lading, the shipper's signature to the prior bill of lading as to the statement of value or otherwise, or election of common law or bill of lading liability, in or in connection with such prior bill of lading, shall be considered a part of this bill of lading as fully as if the same were written or made in or in connection with this bill of lading.

Sec. 9. (a) If all or any part of said property is carried by water over any part of said route, such water carriage shall be performed subject to all the terms and provisions of, and all the exemptions from liability contained in, the Act of the Congress of the United States, approved on February 13, 1893, and entitled "An act relating to the navigation of vessels, etc.," and of other statutes of the United States according carriers by water the protection of limited liability, and to the conditions contained in this bill of lading not inconsistent therewith or with this section.

(b) No such carrier by water shall be liable for any loss or damage resulting from any fire happening to or on board the vessel, or from explosion, bursting of boilers or breakage of shafts, unless caused by the design or neglect of such carrier.

(c) If the owner shall have exercised due diligence in making the vessel in all respects seaworthy and properly manned, equipped, and supplied, no such carrier shall be liable for any loss or damage resulting from the perils of the lakes, seas, or other waters, or from latent defects in hull, machinery, or appurtenances whether existing prior to, at the time of, or after sailing, or from collision, stranding, or other accidents of navigation, or from prolongation of the voyage. And, when for any reason it is necessary, any vessel carrying any or all of the property herein described shall be at liberty to call at any port or ports, in or out of the customary route, to tow and be towed, to transfer, trans-ship, or lighter, to load and discharge goods at any time, to assist vessels in distress, to deviate for the purpose of saving life or property, and for docking and repairs. Except in case of negligence such carrier shall not be responsible for any loss or damage to property if it be necessary or is usual to carry the same upon deck.

(d) General Average shall be payable according to the York-Antwerp Rules of 1924, Sections 1 to 15, inclusive, and Sections 17 to 22, inclusive, and as to matters not covered thereby according to the laws and usages of the Port of New York. If the owners shall have exercised due diligence to make the vessel in all respects seaworthy and properly manned, equipped and supplied, it is hereby agreed that in case of danger, damage or disaster resulting from faults or errors in navigation, or in the management of the vessel, or from any latent or other defects in the vessel, her machinery or appurtenances, or from unseaworthiness, whether existing at the time of shipment or at the beginning of the voyage (provided the latent or other defects or the unseaworthiness was not discoverable by the exercise of due diligence), the shippers, consignees and/or owners of the cargo shall nevertheless pay salvage and any special charges incurred in respect of the cargo, and shall contribute with the shipowner in general average to the payment of any sacrifices, losses or expenses of a general average nature that may be made or incurred for the common benefit or to relieve the adventure from any common peril.

(e) If the property is being carried under a tariff which provides that any carrier or carriers party thereto shall be liable for loss from perils of the sea, then as to such carrier or carriers the provisions of this section shall be modified in accordance with the tariff provisions, which shall be regarded as incorporated into the conditions of this bill of lading.

(f) The term "water carriage" in this section shall not be construed as including lighterage in or across rivers, harbors, or lakes, when performed by or on behalf of rail carriers.

Sec. 10. Any alteration, addition, or erasure in this bill of lading which shall be made without the special notation hereon of the agent of the carrier issuing this bill of lading, shall be without effect, and this bill of lading shall be enforceable according to its original tenor.

(Revised August 1, 1930)

Railroad Straight Bill of Lading
(Reverse)

Printed in U.S.A.

NYCS
FTD-6

(Uniform Domestic Order Bill of Lading, adopted by carriers in Official, Southern, Western and Illinois Classification territories March 15, 1922, as amended August 1, 1930.)

UNIFORM ORDER BILL OF LADING
ORIGINAL

Shipper's No.

Agent's No.

NEW YORK CENTRAL SYSTEM

THE NEW YORK CENTRAL RAILROAD COMPANY

RECEIVED, subject to the classifications and tariffs in effect on the date of the issue of this Bill of Lading,

at , 193

from

the property described below, in apparent good order, except as noted (contents and condition of contents of packages unknown), marked, consigned, and destined as indicated below, which said company (the word company being understood throughout this contract as meaning any person or corporation in possession of the property under the contract) agrees to carry to its usual place of delivery at said destination, if on its own road or its own water line, otherwise to deliver to another carrier on the route to said destination. It is mutually agreed, as to each carrier of all or any of said property over all or any portion of said route to destination, and as to each party at any time interested in all or any of said property, that every service to be performed hereunder shall be subject to all the conditions not prohibited by law, whether printed or written, herein contained, including the conditions on back hereof, which are hereby agreed to by the shipper and accepted for himself and his assigns.

The surrender of this Original ORDER Bill of Lading properly indorsed shall be required before the delivery of the property. Inspection of property covered by this bill of lading will not be permitted unless provided by law or unless permission is indorsed on this original bill of lading or given in writing by the shipper.

Consigned to ORDER of

Destination State of County of

Notify

At State of County of

Route

Delivering Carrier Car Initial Car No.

DUPLICATE

No. Packages	DESCRIPTION OF ARTICLES, SPECIAL MARKS AND EXCEPTIONS	*WEIGHT (Subject to Correction)	Class or Rate	Check Column

Subject to Section 7 of conditions, if this shipment is to be delivered to the consignee without recourse on the consignor, the consignor shall sign the following statement:

The carrier shall not make delivery of this shipment without payment of freight and all other lawful charges.

(Signature of consignor.)

If charges are to be prepaid, write or stamp here, "To be Prepaid."

Received $
to apply in prepayment of the charges on the property described hereon.

Agent or Cashier.

Per
(The signature here acknowledges only the amount prepaid.)

Charges Advanced:

$

* If the shipment moves between two ports by a carrier by water, the law requires that the bill of lading shall state whether it is "carrier's or shipper's weight."

Note—Where the rate is dependent on value, shippers are required to state specifically in writing the agreed or declared value of the property.

The agreed or declared value of the property is hereby specifically stated by the shipper to be not exceeding

per

Shipper. Agent.

Per Per

Permanent post-office address of shipper

(1)8420g

Railroad Order Bill of Lading
(Issued in triplicate)

ENDORSEMENTS

CONTRACT TERMS AND CONDITIONS

Sec. 1. (a) The carrier or party in possession of any of the property herein described shall be liable as at common law for any loss thereof or damage thereto, except as hereinafter provided.

(b) No carrier or party in possession of all or any of the property herein described shall be liable for any loss thereof or damage thereto or delay caused by the act of God, the public enemy, the authority of law, or the act or default of the shipper or owner, or for natural shrinkage. The carrier's liability shall be that of warehouseman, only, for loss, damage, or delay caused by fire occurring after the expiration of the free time allowed by tariffs lawfully on file (such free time to be computed as therein provided) after notice of the arrival of the property at destination or at the port of export (if intended for export) has been duly sent or given, and after placement of the property for delivery at destination, or tender of delivery of the property to the party entitled to receive it, has been made. Except in case of negligence of the carrier or party in possession (and the burden to prove freedom from such negligence shall be on the carrier or party in possession), the carrier or party in possession shall not be liable for loss, damage, or delay occurring while the property is stopped and held in transit upon the request of the shipper, owner, or party, entitled to make such request, or resulting from a defect or vice in the property, or for country damage to cotton, or from riots or strikes.

(c) In case of quarantine the property may be discharged at risk and expense of owners into quarantine depot or elsewhere, as required by quarantine regulations or authorities, or for the carrier's dispatch at nearest available point in carrier's judgment, and in any such case carrier's responsibility shall cease when property is so discharged, or property may be returned by carrier at owner's expense to shipping point, earning freight both ways. Quarantine expenses of whatever nature or kind upon or in respect to property shall be borne by the owners of the property or be a lien thereon. The carrier shall not be liable for loss or damage occasioned by fumigation or disinfection or other acts required or done by quarantine regulations or authorities even though the same may have been done by carrier's officers, agents, or employees nor for detention, loss, or damage of any kind occasioned by quarantine or the enforcement thereof. No carrier shall be liable, except in case of negligence for any mistake or inaccuracy in any information furnished by the carrier, its agents, or officers, as to quarantine laws or regulations. The shipper shall hold the carriers harmless from any expense that may incur, or damages they may be required to pay, by reason of the introduction of the property covered by this contract into any place against the quarantine laws or regulations in effect at such place.

Sec. 2. (a) No carrier is bound to transport said property by any particular train or vessel, or in time for any particular market or otherwise than with reasonable dispatch. Every carrier shall have the right in case of physical necessity to forward said property by any carrier or route between the point of shipment and the point of destination. In all cases not prohibited by law, where a lower value than actual value has been represented in writing by the shipper or has been agreed upon in writing as the released value of the property as determined by the classification or tariffs upon which the rate is based, such lower value plus freight charges if paid shall be the maximum amount to be recovered, whether or not such loss or damage occurs from negligence.

(b) As a condition precedent to recovery, claims must be filed in writing with the receiving or delivering carrier, or carrier issuing this bill of lading, or carrier on whose line the loss, damage, injury or delay occurred, within nine months after delivery of the property (or, in case of export traffic, within nine months after delivery at port of export) or, in case of failure to make delivery, then within nine months after a reasonable time for delivery has elapsed; and suits shall be instituted against any carrier only within two years and one day from the day when notice in writing is given by the carrier to the claimant that the carrier has disallowed the claim or any part or parts thereof specified in the notice. Where claims are not filed or suits are not instituted thereon in accordance with the foregoing provisions, no carrier hereunder shall be liable, and such claims will not be paid.

(c) Any carrier or party liable on account of loss of or damage to any of said property shall have the full benefit of any insurance that may have been effected upon or on account of said property, so far as this shall not avoid the policies or contracts of insurance: **Provided**, That the carrier reimburse the claimant for the premium paid thereon.

Sec. 3. Except where such service is required as the result of carrier's negligence, all property shall be subject to necessary cooperage and baling at owner's cost. Each carrier over whose route cotton or cotton linters is to be transported hereunder shall have the privilege, at its own cost and risk, of compressing the same for greater convenience in handling or forwarding, and shall not be held responsible for deviation or unavoidable delays in procuring such compression. Grain in bulk consigned to a point where there is a railroad, public or licensed elevator, may (unless otherwise expressly noted herein, and then if it is not promptly unloaded) be there delivered and placed with other grain of the same kind and grade without respect to ownership (and prompt notice thereof shall be given to the consignor), and if so delivered shall be subject to a lien for elevator charges in addition to all other charges hereunder.

Sec. 4. (a) Property not removed by the party entitled to receive it within the free time allowed by tariffs, lawfully on file (such free time to be computed as therein provided), after notice of the arrival of the property at destination or at the port of export (if intended for export) has been duly sent or given, and after placement of the property for delivery at destination has been made, may be kept in vessel, car, depot, warehouse or place of delivery of the carrier, subject to the tariff charge for storage and to carrier's responsibility as warehouseman, only, or at the option of the carrier, may be removed to and stored in a public or licensed warehouse at the place of delivery or other available place, at the cost of the owner, and there held without liability on the part of the carrier, and subject to a lien for all freight and other lawful charges, including a reasonable charge for storage.

(b) Where non-perishable property which has been transported to destination hereunder is refused by consignee or the party entitled to receive it, or said consignee or party entitled to receive it fails to receive it within 15 days after notice of arrival shall have been duly sent or given, the carrier may sell the same at public auction to the highest bidder, at such place as may be designated by the carrier: **Provided**, That the carrier shall have first mailed, sent, or given to the consignor notice that the property has been refused or remains unclaimed, as the case may be, and that it will be subject to sale under the terms of the bill of lading, if disposition be not arranged for, and shall have published notice containing a description of the property, the name of the party to whom consigned, or, if shipped order notify, the name of the party to be notified, and the time and place of sale, once a week for two successive weeks, in a newspaper of general circulation at the place of sale or nearest place where such newspaper is published: **Provided**, That 30 days shall have elapsed before publication of notice of sale after said notice that the property was refused or remains unclaimed was mailed, sent, or given.

(c) Where perishable property which has been transported hereunder to destination is refused by consignee or party entitled to receive it, or said consignee or party entitled to receive it shall fail to receive it promptly, the carrier may, in its discretion, to prevent deterioration or further deterioration, sell the same to the best advantage at private or public sale. **Provided**, That if time serves for notification to the consignor or owner of the refusal of the property or the failure to receive it and request for disposition of the property, such notification shall be given, in such manner as the exercise of due diligence requires, before the property is sold.

(d) Where the procedure provided for in the two paragraphs last preceding is not possible, it is agreed that nothing contained in said paragraphs shall be construed to abridge the right of the carrier at its option to sell the property under such circumstances and in such manner as may be authorized by law.

(e) The proceeds of any sale made under this section shall be applied by the carrier to the payment of freight, demurrage, storage, and any other lawful charges and the expense of notice, advertisement, sale and other necessary expense and of caring for and maintaining the property, if proper care of the same requires special expense, and should there be a balance it shall be paid to the owner of the property sold hereunder.

(f) Property destined to or taken from a station, wharf, or landing at which there is no regularly appointed freight agent shall be entirely at risk of owner after unloaded from cars or vessels or until loaded into cars or vessels, and, except in case of carrier's negligence when received from or delivered to such stations, wharves, or landings shall be at owner's risk until the cars are attached to and after they are detached from locomotive or train or until loaded into and after unloaded from vessels.

Sec. 5. No carrier hereunder will carry or be liable in any way for any documents, specie, or for any articles of extraordinary value not specifically rated in the published classifications or tariffs unless a special agreement to do so and a stipulated value of the articles are indorsed hereon.

Sec. 6. Every party, whether principal or agent, shipping explosives or dangerous goods, without previous full written disclosure to the carrier of their nature shall be liable for and indemnify the carrier against all loss or damage caused by such goods, and such goods may be warehoused at owner's risk and expense or destroyed without compensation.

Sec. 7. The owner or consignee shall pay the freight and average, if any, and all other lawful charges accruing on said property; but, except in those instances where it may lawfully be authorized to do so, no carrier by railroad shall deliver or relinquish possession at destination of the property covered by this bill of lading until all tariff rates and charges thereon have been paid. The consignor shall be liable for the freight and all other lawful charges, except that if the consignor stipulates, by signature in the space provided for that purpose on the face of this bill of lading that the carrier shall not make delivery without requiring payment of such charges and the carrier, contrary to such stipulation, shall make delivery without requiring such payment, the consignor (except as hereinafter provided) shall not be liable for such charges: **Provided**, that, where the carrier has been instructed by the shipper or consignor to deliver said property to a consignee other than the shipper or consignor, such consignee shall not be legally liable for transportation charges in respect of the transportation of said property (beyond those billed against him at the time of delivery for which he is otherwise liable) which may be found to be due after the property has been delivered to him, if the consignee (a) is an agent only and has no beneficial title in said property, and (b) prior to delivery of said property has notified the delivering carrier in writing of the fact of such agency and absence of beneficial title, and in the case of a shipment reconsigned or diverted to a point other than that specified in the original bill of lading, has also notified the delivering carrier in writing of the name and address of the beneficial owner of said property and, in such cases the shipper or consignor, or, in the case of a shipment so reconsigned or diverted, the beneficial owner, shall be liable for such additional charges. If the consignee has given to the carrier erroneous information as to who the beneficial owner is, such consignee shall himself be liable for such additional charges. Nothing herein shall limit the right of the carrier to require at time of shipment the prepayment or guarantee of the charges. If upon inspection it is ascertained that the articles shipped are not those described in this bill of lading, the freight charges must be paid upon the articles actually shipped.

Sec. 8. If this bill of lading is issued on the order of the shipper, or his agent, in exchange or in substitution for another bill of lading the shipper's signature to the prior bill of lading as to the statement of value or otherwise, or election of common law or bill of lading liability, in or in connection with such prior bill of lading, shall be considered a part of this bill of lading as fully as if the same were written or made in or in connection with this bill of lading.

Sec. 9. (a) If all or any part of said property is carried by water over any part of said route, such water carriage shall be performed subject to all the terms and provisions of, and all the exemptions from liability contained in, the Act of the Congress of the United States, approved on February 13, 1893, and entitled "An act relating to the navigation of vessels, etc.," and of other statutes of the United States according carriers by water the protection of limited liability, and to the conditions contained in this bill of lading not inconsistent therewith or with this section.

(b) No such carrier by water shall be liable for any loss or damage resulting from any fire happening to or on board the vessel or from explosion, bursting of boilers or breakage of shafts, unless caused by the design or neglect of such carrier.

(c) If the owner shall have exercised due diligence in making the vessel in all respects seaworthy and properly manned, equipped, and supplied, no such carrier shall be liable for any loss or damage resulting from the perils of the lakes, seas, or other waters, or from latent defects in hull, machinery, or appurtenances whether existing prior to, at the time of, or after sailing, or from collision, stranding, or other accidents of navigation, or from prolongation of the voyage. And, when for any reason it is necessary, any vessel carrying any or all of the property herein described shall be at liberty to call at any port or ports, in or out of the customary route, to tow and be towed, to transfer, trans-ship, or lighter, to load and discharge goods at any time, to assist vessels in distress, to deviate for the purpose of saving life or property, and for docking and repairs. Except in case of negligence such carrier shall not be responsible for any loss or damage to property if it be necessary or is usual to carry the same upon deck.

(d) General Average shall be payable according to the York-Antwerp Rules of 1924, Sections 1 to 15, inclusive, and Sections 17 to 22 inclusive and as to matters not covered thereby according to the laws and usages of the Port of New York. If the owners shall have exercised due diligence to make the vessel in all respects seaworthy and properly manned, equipped and supplied, it is hereby agreed that in case of danger, damage or disaster resulting from faults or errors in navigation, or in the management of the vessel, or from any latent or other defects in the vessel, her machinery or appurtenances, or from unseaworthiness, whether existing at the time of shipment or at the beginning of the voyage (provided the latent or other defects or the unseaworthiness was not discoverable by the exercise of due diligence), the shippers, consignees and/or owners of the cargo shall nevertheless pay salvage and any special charges incurred in respect of the cargo, and shall contribute with the shipowner in general average to the payment of any sacrifices, losses or expenses of a general average nature that may be made or incurred for the common benefit or to relieve the adventure from any common peril.

(e) If the property is being carried under a tariff which provides that any carrier or carriers party thereto shall be liable for loss from perils of the sea, then as to such carrier or carriers the provisions of this section shall be modified in accordance with the tariff provisions, which shall be regarded as incorporated into the conditions of this bill of lading.

(f) The term "water carriage" in this section shall not be construed as including lighterage in or across rivers, harbors, or lakes, when performed by or on behalf of rail carriers.

Sec. 10. Any alteration, addition, or erasure in this bill of lading which shall be made without the special notation hereon of the agent of the carrier issuing this bill of lading, shall be without effect, and this bill of lading shall be enforceable according to its original tenor. ① 5194

RAILROAD ORDER BILL OF LADING
(Reverse)

UNITED STATES LINES CO.

LONDON SERVICE

NEW YORK	BOSTON	LONDON, E. C. 3	LIVERPOOL, 2
1 Broadway	563 Boylston St.	38 Leadenhall St.	563, Martin's Bank Bldg., Water St.

Received by UNITED STATES LINES CO., hereinafter called the Carrier, from the Shipper hereinafter named, the goods or packages said to contain goods hereinafter mentioned in apparent good order and condition unless otherwise indicated in this bill of lading, to be transported subject to all the terms of this bill of lading with liberty to proceed via any port or ports within the scope of the voyage described herein, to the port of discharge or so near thereunto as the ship can always safely get and leave, always afloat at all stages and conditions of water and weather, and there to be delivered or transhipped on payment of the charges thereon. If the goods in whole or in part are shut out from the ship named herein for any cause, the carrier shall have liberty to forward them under the terms of this bill of lading on the next available ship of this line, or, at carrier's option, of any other line.

It is agreed that the custody and carriage of the goods are subject to the following terms which shall govern the relations, whatsoever they may be, between the shipper, consignee, and the Carrier, master and ship in every contingency, wheresoever and whensoever occurring, and also in the event of deviation, or of unseaworthiness of the ship at the time of loading or inception of the voyage or subsequently, and none of the terms of this bill of lading shall be deemed to have been waived by the Carrier unless by express waiver in writing signed by a duly authorized agent of the Carrier:

1. This bill of lading shall have effect subject to the provisions of the Carriage of Goods by Sea Act of the United States, approved April 16, 1936, which shall be deemed to be incorporated herein, and nothing herein contained shall be deemed a surrender by the Carrier of any of its rights or immunities or an increase of any of its responsibilities or liabilities under said Act. The provisions stated in said Act shall (except as may be otherwise specifically provided herein) govern before the goods are loaded on and after they are discharged from the ship and throughout the entire time the goods are in the custody of the Carrier. The Carrier shall not be liable in any capacity whatsoever for any delay, nondelivery or misdelivery, or loss of or damage to the goods occurring while the goods are not in the actual custody of the Carrier.

2. In this bill of lading, the word "ship" shall include any substituted vessel, and any craft, lighter or other means of conveyance owned, chartered or operated by the carrier; the word "carrier" shall include the ship, her owner, operator, demise charterer, time charterer, master and any substituted carrier, whether the owner, operator, charterer or master shall be acting as carrier or bailee; the word "shipper" shall include the person named as such in this bill of lading and the person for whose account the goods are shipped; the word "consignee" shall include the holder of the bill of lading, properly endorsed, and the receiver and the owner of the goods; the word "charges" shall include freight and all expenses and money obligations incurred and payable by the goods, shipper, consignee, or any of them.

3. The scope of voyage herein contracted for shall include usual or customary or advertised ports of call whether named in this contract or not, also ports in or out of the advertised, geographical, usual or ordinary route or order, even though in proceeding thereto the ship may sail beyond the port of discharge or in a direction contrary thereto, or depart from the direct or customary route. The ship may call at any port for the purposes of the current voyage or of a prior or subsequent voyage. The ship may omit calling at any port or ports whether scheduled or not, and may call at the same port more than once; may, either with or without the goods on board, and before or after proceeding toward the port of discharge, adjust compasses, dry dock, go on ways or to repair yards, shift berths, take fuel or stores, remain in port, sail without pilots, tow and be towed, and save or attempt to save life or property, and all of the foregoing are included in the contract voyage.

4. In any situation whatsoever or wheresoever occurring and whether existing or anticipated before commencement of or during the voyage, which in the judgment of the carrier or master is likely to give rise to capture, seizure, detention, damage, delay or disadvantage to or loss of the ship or any part of her cargo, or to make it unsafe, imprudent, or unlawful for any reason to proceed on or continue the voyage or to enter or discharge the goods at the port of discharge, or to give rise to delay or difficulty in arriving, discharging at or leaving the port of discharge or the usual place of discharge in such port the Master, whether or not proceeding toward or entering or attempting to enter the port of discharge or reaching or attempting to reach the usual place of discharge therein or attempting to discharge the goods there, may, without giving any prior notice, discharge the goods into depot, lazaretto, craft, or other place and the goods shall be liable for any extra expense thereby incurred; or the master may proceed or return, directly or indirectly, to or stop at such other port or place whatsoever as he or the carrier may consider safe or advisable under the circumstances, and discharge the goods or any part thereof there without giving any prior notice, and when landed as hereinabove provided, the goods shall be at their own risk and expense, the delivery thereof by the carrier shall be considered complete and the carrier shall be freed from any further responsibility in respect thereof except to mail notice of the disposition of the goods directed to the shipper or consignee named in this bill of lading at such address as may be stated herein; or the master may retain the cargo on board until the return trip or until such time as he or the carrier thinks advisable; or the master may forward the goods by any means by water or by land, or by both such means, at the risk and expense of the goods. For any services rendered to the goods as hereinabove provided, the carrier shall be entitled to a reasonable extra compensation.

5. The carrier, master and ship shall have liberty to comply with any orders or directions as to loading, departure, arrival, routes, ports of call, stoppages, discharge, destination, delivery or otherwise howsoever given by the government of any nation or department thereof or any person acting or purporting to act with the authority of such government or of any department thereof, or by any committee or person having, under the terms of the war risk insurance on the ship, the right to give such orders or directions. Delivery or other disposition of the goods in accordance with such orders or directions shall be a fulfillment of the contract voyage. The ship may carry contraband, explosives, munitions, warlike stores, hazardous cargo, and may sail armed or unarmed and with or without convoy.

6. Unless otherwise stated herein, the description of the goods and the particulars of the packages mentioned herein are those furnished in writing by the shipper and the carrier shall not be concluded as to the correctness of leading marks, number, quantity, weight, gauge, measurement, contents, nature, quality or value. Single pieces or packages exceeding 4480 lbs. in weight shall be liable to pay extra charges in accordance with tariff rates in effect at time of shipment for loading, handling, transhipping or discharging and the weight of each such piece or package shall be declared in writing by the shipper on shipment and clearly and durably marked on the outside of the piece or package. The shipper and the goods shall also be liable for, and shall indemnify the carrier in respect of any injury, loss or damage arising from shipper's failure to declare and mark the weight of any such piece or package or from the incorrect weight of any such piece or package having been declared or marked thereon.

7. Goods may be stowed in poop, forecastle, deck house, shelter deck, passenger space, or any other covered-in space commonly used in the trade for the carriage of goods, and when so stowed shall be deemed for all purposes to be stowed under deck. In respect of goods carried on deck and stated herein to be so carried, all risks of loss or damage by perils inherent in such carriage shall be borne by the consignee but in all other respects the custody and carriage of such goods shall be governed by the terms of this bill of lading and the provisions stated in said Carriage of Goods by Sea Act notwithstanding Sec. 1. (C) thereof. Specially heated or specially cooled stowage is not to be furnished unless contracted for at an increased freight rate.

8. Live animals, birds and fish are received and carried at shipper's risk of accident or mortality, and the Carrier shall not be liable for any loss or damage thereto arising or resulting from any matters mentioned in Section 4, Sub-section 2, a to p inclusive of said Carriage of Goods by Sea Act or from any other cause whatsoever not due to the fault of the Carrier, any warranty of seaworthiness in the premises being hereby waived by the shipper. Except as provided above such shipments shall be deemed goods, and shall be subject to all terms and provisions in this bill of lading relating to goods.

9. If the ship comes into collision with another ship as a result of the negligence of the other ship and any act, neglect or default of the master, mariner, pilot or the servants of the Carrier in the navigation or in the management of the ship, the owners of the goods carried hereunder will indemnify the Carrier against all loss or liability to the other or non-carrying ship or her owners in so far as such loss or liability represents loss of, or damage to, or any claim whatsoever of the owners of said goods, paid or payable by the other or non-carrying ship or her owners to the owners of said goods and set off, recouped or recovered by the other or non-carrying ship or her owners as part of their claim against the carrying ship or Carrier.

10. General Average shall be adjusted and payable at New York according to 1924 York-Antwerp Rules, F and 1 to 15 and 17 to 22, both inclusive, and, as to matters not therein provided for, according to the laws and usages at the port of New York or port of destination at shipowner's option. In such adjustment foreign currency shall be exchanged into dollars as of the last day of discharge at the last outward port (or at the time of payment, if later); and any deposit shall be converted promptly into United States dollars if requested by the holder of deposit receipt.

In the event of accident, danger, damage, or disaster, before or after commencement of the voyage resulting from any cause whatsoever, whether due to negligence or not, for which, or for the consequence of which, the carrier is not responsible, by statute, contract, or otherwise, the goods, shippers, consignees, or owners of the goods shall contribute with the carrier in general average to the payment of any sacrifices, losses, or expenses of a general average nature that may be made or incurred, and shall pay salvage and special charges incurred in respect of the goods. If a salving ship is owned or operated by the carrier, salvage shall be paid for as fully as if such salving ship or ships belonged to strangers. Such deposit as the carrier or his agents may deem sufficient to cover the estimated contribution of the goods and any salvage and special charges thereon shall, if required, be made by the goods, shippers, consignees or owners of the goods to the carrier before delivery.

11. Whenever the carrier or master may deem it advisable or in any case where the goods are consigned to a point where the ship does not expect to discharge, the carrier or master may, without notice, forward the whole or any part of the goods before or after loading at the original port of shipment, or any other place or places even though outside the scope of the voyage or the route to or beyond the port of discharge or the destination of the goods, by any vessel, vessels or other means of transportation by water or by land or by both such means, whether operated by the carrier or by others and whether departing or arriving or scheduled to depart or arrive before or after the ship expected to be used for the transportation of the goods. This carrier, in making arrangements for any transhipping or forwarding vessel or means of transportation not operated by this carrier shall be considered solely the forwarding agent of the shipper and without any other responsibility whatsoever.

The carriage by any transhipping or forwarding carrier and all transhipment or forwarding shall be subject to all the terms whatsoever in the regular form of bill of lading, freight note, contract or other shipping document used at the time by such carrier, whether issued for the goods or not, and even though such terms may be less favorable to the shipper or consignee than the terms of this bill of lading and may contain more stringent requirements as to notice of claim or commencement of suit and may exempt the on-carrier from liability for negligence. The shipper expressly authorizes the carrier to arrange with any such transhipping or forwarding carrier that the lowest valuation of the goods or limitation of liability contained in the bill of lading or shipping document of such carrier shall apply even though lower than the valuation or limitation herein. Pending or during transhipment the goods may be stored ashore or afloat at their risk and expense and the carrier shall not be liable for detention.

12. The port authorities are hereby authorized to grant a general order for discharging immediately upon arrival of the ship and the carrier without giving notice either of arrival or discharge, may discharge the goods directly they come to hand, at or onto any wharf, craft or place that the carrier may select, and continuously, Sundays and holidays included, at all such hours by day or by night as the carrier may determine no matter what the state of the weather or custom of the port may be. The carrier shall not be liable in any respect whatsoever if heat or refrigeration or special cooling facilities shall not be furnished during loading or discharge or any part of the time that the goods are upon the wharf, craft, or other loading or discharging place. All lighterage and use of craft in discharging shall be at the risk and expense of the goods. Landing and delivery charges and pier dues shall be at the expense of the goods unless included in the freight herein provided for. If the goods are not taken away by the consignee by the expiration of the next working day after the goods are at his disposal, the goods may, at carrier's option and subject to carrier's lien, be sent to store or warehouse, or be permitted to lie where landed, but always at the expense and risk of the goods. The responsibility of the carrier in any capacity shall altogether cease and the goods shall be considered to be delivered and at their own risk and expense in every respect when taken into the custody of customs or other authorities. The carrier shall not be required to give any notification of disposition of the goods.

13. The carrier shall not be liable for failure to deliver in accordance with leading marks unless such marks shall have been clearly and durably stamped or marked by the shipper before shipment upon the goods or packages, in letters and numbers not less than two inches high, together with name of the port of discharge. Goods that cannot be identified as to marks or numbers, cargo sweepings, liquid residue and any unclaimed goods not otherwise accounted for shall be allocated for completing delivery to the various consignees of goods of like character in proportion to any apparent shortage, loss of weight or damage.

When grain is stowed without separation from other grain shipped either by the same shipper or by other shippers, any loss or damage to the combined shipments shall be divided in proportion among the several shipments.

14. The goods shall be liable for all expense of mending, cooperage, baling or reconditioning of the goods or packages and gathering of loose cargo or contents of packages; also for any payment, expense, fine, dues, duty, tax, impost, loss, damage or detention sustained or incurred by or levied upon the carrier or the ship in connection with the goods, howsoever caused, including any action or requirement of any government or governmental authority or person purporting to act under the authority thereof, seizure under legal process or attempted seizure, incorrect or insufficient marking, numbering or addressing of packages or description of the contents, failure of the shipper to procure consular, Board of Health or other certificates to accompany the goods or to comply with laws or regulations of any kind imposed with respect to the goods by the authorities at any port or place or any act or omission of the shipper or consignee.

15. Freight shall be payable on actual gross intake weight or measurement or, at carrier's option, on actual gross discharged weight or measurement. Freight may be calculated on the basis of the particulars of the goods furnished by the shipper herein but the carrier may at any time open the packages and examine, weigh, measure and value the goods. In case shipper's particulars are found to be erroneous and additional freight is payable, the goods shall be liable for any expense incurred for examining, weighing, measuring and valuing the goods. Full freight shall be paid on damaged or unsound goods. Full freight hereunder to port of discharge named herein shall be considered completely earned on receipt of the goods by the carrier, whether the freight be stated or intended to be prepaid or to be collected at destination; and the carrier shall be entitled to all freight and charges due hereunder, whether actually paid or not, and to receive and retain them under all circumstances whatsoever ship and/or cargo lost or not lost. If there shall be a forced interruption or abandonment of the voyage at the port of shipment or elsewhere any forwarding of the goods or any part thereof shall be at the risk and expense of the goods. All unpaid charges shall be paid in full and without any offset, counterclaim or deduction in the currency of the country of the port of shipment, or, at carrier's option, in the currency of the port of discharge at the demand rate of New York exchange as quoted on the day of the ship's entry at the Custom House of her port of discharge. The carrier shall have a lien on the goods, which shall survive delivery, for all charges due hereunder and may enforce this lien by public or private sale and without notice. The shipper and consignee shall be jointly and severally liable to the carrier for the payment of all charges and for the performance of the obligation of each of them hereunder.

16. Neither the carrier nor any corporation owned by, subsidiary to or associated or affiliated with the carrier shall be liable to answer for or make good any loss or damage to the goods occurring at any time and even though before loading on or after discharge from the ship, by reason or by means of any fire whatsoever, unless such fire shall be caused by its design or neglect.

17. In case of any loss or damage to or in connection with goods exceeding in actual value $500. lawful money of the United States, per package, or, in case of goods not shipped in packages, per customary freight unit, the value of the goods shall be deemed to be $500. per package or per unit, on which basis the freight is adjusted and the carrier's liability, if any, shall be determined on the basis of a value of $500. per package or per customary freight unit, or pro rata in case of partial loss or damage, unless the nature of the goods and a valuation higher than $500. shall have been declared in writing by the shipper upon delivery to the carrier and inserted in this bill of lading and extra freight paid if required and in such case if the actual value of the goods per package or per customary freight unit shall exceed such declared value, the value shall nevertheless be deemed to be the declared value and the carrier's liability, if any, shall not exceed the declared value and any partial loss or damage shall be adjusted pro rata on the basis of such declared value.

18. Unless notice of loss or damage and the general nature of such loss or damage be given in writing to the carrier or his agent at the port of discharge before or at the time of the removal of the goods into the custody of the person entitled to delivery thereof under the contract of carriage, such removal shall be *prima facie* evidence of the delivery by the carrier of the goods as described in the bill of lading. If the loss or damage is not apparent the notice must be given within three days of the delivery.

In any event the carrier and the ship shall be discharged from all liability in respect of loss or damage unless suit is brought within one year after the delivery of the goods or the date when the goods should have been delivered.

L 7436—100M

(CONTINUED OVER PAGE)

B/L No.........................

(CONTINUED FROM OVERPAGE)

19. All agreements or freight engagements for the shipment of the goods are superseded by this bill of lading, and all its terms, whether written, typed, stamped, or printed, are accepted and agreed by the shipper to be binding as fully as if signed by the shipper, any local customs or privileges to the contrary notwithstanding. Nothing in this bill of lading shall operate to limit or deprive the carrier of any statutory protection or exemption from, or limitation of, liability. If required by the carrier, one signed bill of lading duly endorsed must be surrendered to the agent of the ship at the port of discharge in exchange for delivery order.

SHIP: { M.S. / S.S. .... PORT OF LOADING: **NEW YORK**

SHIPPER: ....

CONSIGNEE: ORDER OF..

ARRIVAL NOTICE TO BE ADDRESSED TO:..

PORT OF DISCHARGE FROM SHIP: **LONDON**

DESTINATION OF GOODS (If goods to be transhipped at port of discharge) :..

THE SCOPE OF THE VOYAGE INCLUDES **NEW YORK, PLYMOUTH, LONDON.**

PARTICULARS FURNISHED BY SHIPPER OF GOODS

Leading Marks	Description of Goods	Gross Weight Pounds

Attention of shippers is called to the provisions of 18 U.S.C.A. Sec. 385 (Criminal Code Sec. 235 as amended), imposing upon shippers a penalty of $2,000 or imprisonment for 18 months, or both, for delivering to a carrier packages containing explosives or other dangerous articles without having the contents plainly marked on the outside thereof, or without informing the agent of the carrier in writing of the true character thereof; and also, to the provisions of 46 U.S.C.A. Sec. 175, which provides that any person shipping oil or vitriol, inflammable matches or gun powder in a vessel which is a common carrier, without delivering a note in writing expressing the nature and character of the merchandise to the person in charge of loading the vessel, shall be liable to the United States in the penalty of $1,000.

Attention of shippers, consignors, consignees, forwarders, brokers and other persons is called to the provisions of Sec. 16 of the Shipping Act, 1916, as amended by the Act approved June 16, 1936, in relation to penalty of not more than $5,000 in relation to false billing, false classification, false weighing, false report of weight, or any other unjust or unfair device or means to obtain or attempt to obtain transportation by water of property at less than the rates or charges which would otherwise be applicable.

LONDON CLAUSE (A) The Shipowners shall, at their option, be entitled to land the goods within mentioned on the quay, or to discharge them into craft hired by them immediately on arrival at dock, quay, river wharf or other wharf or landing place selected by the shipowner, and at consignee's risk and expense; the Shipowners being entitled to collect the same charges on goods entered for landing at the docks, as on goods entered for delivery to lighters. Consignees desirous of conveying their goods elsewhere, shall, on making application to the Ship's Agents, or to the Dock or Wharf Company, within 72 hours after vessel shall have been reported, except as provided hereafter, be entitled to delivery in consignee's lighters or land conveyances at the following rates, to be paid with the freight to the Ship's Agents, against release, or to the Dock or Wharf Company, if so directed by the Ship's Agents, viz.: Following wooden goods in packages; clothes-pegs, handles, blind rollers, hubs, spokes, wheels and oars, 1/3 per ton measurement; hops, 2/9 per ton weight; lumber and logs, 2/- per ton measurement or 2/6 per ton weight at ship's option; slates, 2/- per ton weight; Wheaten flour, 1/3 per ton weight. All other general cargo 1/9 per ton weight or measurement at ship's option; minimum charge, one ton.

(B) Grain for overside delivery is to be applied for within twenty-four hours of vessel's arrival (or thereafter immediately it becomes clear) at any dock, quay, river wharf or other wharf or landing place selected by the vessel owners or agents. In the absence of sufficient consignee's craft, with responsible persons in charge, to receive as fast as vessel can discharge overside into lighters during usual working hours, the Master or Agent may land or discharge into lighters at the risk and expense of the consignee. The vessel-owners or agents may land or discharge continuously day and/or night, any grain landed or discharged for vessel's convenience during usual working hours (consignee's craft being duly in attendance) and any grain that may be landed or discharged before or after usual working hours (whether craft are then in attendance or not) is to be given up free to consignee's craft applying for same within seventy-two hours from its landing or dicharge, otherwise it will be subject to the usual dock, quay, river wharf or other wharf or landing place charges. An extra freight of 7d. per ton shall be paid to the vessel-owners or agents on each consignment of grain whether any portion be landed or not. The grain to be weighed at time of discharge, either on deck and/or dock, quay, river wharf or other wharf or landing place and/or craft at vessel's option. Working out charges (including weighing) as fixed by the Port of London Authority for grain in bulk and/or vessel's bags to be paid by the consignee with the freight to the vessel's agents or to the authorized representative of the dock, quay, river wharf or other wharf or landing place if so directed by the vessel's agents in exchange for release. Neither party shall be liable for any interference with the perfogmance of the contract herein contained, which is caused by strikes, or lockout of seamen, lightermen, stevedores or shore laborers, or railway or transport or other disturbances of any kind or in furtherance thereof, whether partial or otherwise, nor for any consequences thereof, and in such case the vessel-owner or agents shall be entitled to land or put into craft at the risk and expense of consignee. In case the grain shipped under this Bill of Lading forms part of a larger bulk, each bill of lading to bear its proportion of shortage and damage, if any.

(C) ACETONE, ASPHALT, CARBON BLACK, CELLULOID, COTTON, COTTON WASTE, HAY, HEMP, HYDROLENE, ISTLE, JUTE, LAMPBLACK, ILLUMINATING and OIL OF ALL KINDS, whether ANIMAL, VEGETABLE, or MINERAL, and the liquid products of them or any of them, PITCH, RAGS, ROSIN, STRAW, TAR, TURPENTINE, VARNISH, WOOD SPIRITS, also any other goods of a more or less hazardous nature. Consignees to have craft in attendance immediately on ship's arrival at any discharging berth selected by the shipowners, to take delivery from ship or otherwise (at ship's option), of any of the above-mentioned commodities, the ship-owners having the option of working continuously by day and/or night, and consignees to pay 1/3d. per ton weight or measurement at ship's option. If consignee's craft is not in attendance, the goods may be put into Captain's entry craft at risk and expense of consignees.

(D) REFRIGERATOR CARGO:—Goods may be discharged immediately on arrival at dock, quay, river wharf or other wharf or landing place selected by the Shipowners, who shall have the option of working continuously day and/or night and are to be removed by consignees within 24 hours after ship shall have been reported at the Custom House; consignee to pay 1/9d. per ton weight or measurement at ship's option; otherwise, the Shipowners have the right of removing or of calling upon the dock, quay or wharf authorities to receive or remove all or any part thereof for storage or realization at consignee's risk and expense.

(E) In the case of heavy timber of rafting size delivered into the water in one of the docks in the river Thames, each consignee of such timber shall pay two-thirds of the vessel's dock dues payable in respect of the space occupied by his portion of such cargo so delivered into the water.

This London Clause is in respect of goods destined to that port, to form part of this bill of lading, and any words at variance with them are hereby cancelled.

Craft which are in attendance for delivery under above clauses and stipulations shall wait free of demurrage their regular turn to receive goods or grain as required by vessel-owners, either from vessel or quay or Captain's entry craft.

All Port of London Authority charges to be paid by consignee of the goods, and the vessel owners shall have the same lien, rights, and remedies on goods or grain referred to in the above clauses or under any other clauses of the bill of lading, as they have by law in respect to freight.

FREIGHT AND CHARGES

..........@..........*per 2240 lbs.* $..........
..........@..........*per 2240 lbs.* $..........
..........@..........*per 100 lbs.* $..........
..........@..........*per 100 lbs.* $..........
..........*Ft*..........*in.* @..........*per 40 cu. ft.* $..........
..........*Ft*..........*in.* @..........*per 40 cu. ft.* $..........
..........*Ft*..........*in.* @..........*per cu. ft.* $..........
..........*Ft*..........*in.* @..........*per cu. ft.* $..........
..........@..........*per*.......... $..........
..........@..........*per*.......... $..........
..........*Items* @..........*per item* $..........

Advanced Charges $..........

Total $..........

Freight and Charges Payable

By.......................... **In**..........................

IN WITNESS WHEREOF, the master or agent of the said vessel has signed.......... **T H R E E**.......... Bills of Lading, all of this tenor and date, and if one is accomplished, the others shall be void.

Dated, **N E W Y O R K** this.................day of..........................193......

UNITED STATES LINES CO.

By..........................

For the Master.

OCEAN BILL OF LADING (*Reverse*)

Form 5138

Marks and Numbers

ORIGINAL

$ **CERTIFICATE OF INSURANCE** No.

FEDERAL INSURANCE COMPANY,

CHUBB & SON, Managers,
90 John Street, New York City, N. Y.

NEW YORK,

This is to Certify, *that on the* *this Company insured under Policy No.* **FO-68492,** *for the sum of* *Dollars,*
on
valued at *shipped on board of the*
at and from

and it is hereby understood and agreed, that in the case of loss, such loss is payable to the Order of *on surrender of this Certificate.*

This Certificate represents and takes the place of the Policy, is subject to all the terms thereof, and conveys all the rights of the Original Policy-Holder (for the purpose of collecting any loss or claims), as fully as if the property were covered by a Special Policy direct to the holder of this Certificate, and free from any liability for unpaid premiums.

Original and Duplicate issued, one of which being accomplished the other to stand null and void.

It is hereby agreed that any loss or claim under this Certificate shall be paid at the office of the Company in New York, or at the offices of the Agents of the Company, Exchange Buildings, Liverpool or at the Agency of the Company at port or place of destination, or, if the Company is not represented at port or place of destination, at the nearest Agency amongst those specified in the list on back hereof.

In case of loss or damage please follow instructions on the reverse side of this certificate.

Claims to be adjusted according to the usages of Lloyds, but subject to the conditions of the Policy and Contract of Insurance.

NOTICE.—To conform with the Revenue Laws of Great Britain, in order to collect a claim under this certificate, it must be stamped within ten days after its receipt in the United Kingdom.

Warranted free from capture, seizure, arrest, restraint, detainment, confiscation, preemption, requisition or nationalization, and the consequences thereof or of any attempt thereat, whether in time of peace or war and whether lawful or otherwise; also warranted free from all consequences of hostilities or warlike operations (whether there be a declaration of war or not), piracy, civil war, revolution, rebellion or insurrection, or civil strife arising therefrom.

Warranted free of loss or damage caused by or resulting from strikes, lockouts, labor disturbances, riots, civil commotions or the acts of any person or persons taking part in any such occurrence or disorder.

SPECIAL CONDITIONS

Cotton Piece Goods, Blankets, Fasteners, Zippers and other approved merchandise shipped UNDER DECK, INSURED:—Against all risks of physical loss or damage from any external cause excepting risks excluded by the F. C. & S. (Free of Capture & Seizure) and Strikes, Riots and Civil Commotions warranties appearing elsewhere hereon.

This insurance attaches from the moment the goods, being at the risk of the insured, leave store, warehouse or factory at initial point of shipment and covers continuously thereafter during the ordinary course of transit until safely deposited in store, warehouse or factory at final place of destination.

On shipments to the River Plate, however, notwithstanding the foregoing, the risk of fire under this certificate shall cease upon arrival at any shed (transit or otherwise), store, custom house or warehouse or upon the expiry of ten days subsequent to landing, whichever may first occur.

Provided prompt notice be given the Insurers when such facts are known to the Assured and additional premium be paid if required, it is understood and agreed that in case of short shipment in whole or in part by the vessel reported for insurance hereunder, or if the goods be transhipped by another vessel or vessels, or be carried beyond or discharged short of destination, or in the event of deviation, or change of voyage, or any interruption or other variation of the voyage or risk beyond the control of the Assured, this insurance shall nevertheless cover the goods until arrival at the final destination named in the declaration or certificate of insurance or until the subject matter insured is no longer at the risk of the Assured, whichever may first occur. No additional risk (whether of delay or of any other description) are insured under this clause, which is intended merely to continue the insurance in force against the same risks named elsewhere in this policy; and if the risks of War, Strikes, Riots or Civil Commotions, or any of these risks, are insured against, the insurance against such risks shall not be extended by this clause to cover contrary to any express provision of such insurance.

Where goods are shipped under a bill of lading containing the so-called "Both-to-Blame Collision" Clause these assurers agree, as to all losses covered by this insurance, to indemnify the assured for any amount (up to the amount insured) which the assured may be legally bound to pay to the shipowners under such clause. In the event that such liability is asserted the assured agree to notify the assurers who shall have the right, at their own cost and expense, to defend the assured against such claim.

Where the words "including War Risk" are typed in the space below at the time the Certificate is issued, the War Risk Clauses on the back of the Certificate shall attach.

Not Valid unless Countersigned by Assured

*Countersigned,*____________________

Chubb & Son *Managers*

SPECIMEN

Made in U. S. 36087

Marine Insurance Certificate
(Issued in quadruplicate)

When so provided by endorsement on this Special Policy (or Certificate) at the time the same is issued (but not otherwise) the shipment described herein shall be separately insured against war risks subject to the terms and conditions hereinafter set forth.

WAR RISK INSURANCE (Form No. 3-C)

1. This insurance is only against the risks of capture, seizure, destruction or damage by men of war, piracy, takings at sea, arrests, restraints and detainments and other warlike operations and acts of kings, princes and peoples in prosecution of hostilities or in the application of sanctions under international agreements, whether before or after declaration of war and whether by a belligerent or otherwise, including factions engaged in civil war, revolution, rebellion or insurrection, or civil strife arising therefrom, and including the risks of aerial bombardment, floating or stationary mines and stray or derelict torpedoes; but excluding claims for delay, deterioration and/or loss of market, and warranted not to abandon (on any ground other than physical damage to ship or cargo) until after condemnation of the property insured. Also warranted not to abandon in case of blockade, and free from any claims for loss or expense in consequence of blockade or of any attempt to evade blockade; but in the event of blockade, to be at liberty to proceed to an open port and there end the voyage.
2. Warranted free from any claim based upon loss of, or frustration of, the insured voyage or adventure caused by arrests, restraints or detainments.
3. This insurance does not cover any loss or damage caused by or resulting from any of the following causes:
   (a) Commandeering, preemption, requisition or nationalization by the government (de facto or otherwise) of the country to or from which the goods are insured.
   (b) Seizure or destruction under quarantine or customs regulations.
   (c) Capture, seizure, arrest, restraint, detainment or condemnation by the Government of the United States of America, or of any State therein.
4. This insurance shall not attach to the interest hereby insured or to any part thereof
   (a) prior to being on board an overseas Vessel (for the purpose of this clause 4 an overseas Vessel shall be deemed to mean a Vessel carrying the interest from one port or place to another where such voyage involves a sea passage by that Vessel),
   (b) after being discharged overside from an overseas Vessel at the final port of discharge,

   or

   after expiry of fifteen days counting from midnight of the day on which the overseas Vessel is safely anchored or moored at the final port of discharge, whichever shall first occur,
   (c) at a port or place of transhipment to another overseas Vessel after the expiry of fifteen days (counting from midnight of the day on which the overseas Vessel entering with the interest is safely anchored or moored) until the interest is on board the oncarrying overseas Vessel.

   In the event of the exercise of any liberty granted to the Shipowner or Charterer under the contract of affreightment whereby such contract is terminated at a port or place other than the destination named therein such port or place shall be deemed the final port of discharge for the purpose of this clause 4.
5. Subject to the terms of Clause 4 above and to any conditions or warranties which may be endorsed hereon, it is agreed that this insurance shall not be vitiated by deviation, over-carriage, change of voyage, or by any error or unintentional omission in the description of interest, Vessel or voyage, provided the same be communicated to this Company as soon as known to the Assured and an additional premium paid if required.
6. And in case of any loss or misfortune, it shall be lawful and necessary to and for the Assured, his or their factors, servants and assigns, to sue, labor and travel for, in and about the defense, safeguard and recovery of the said goods and merchandises, or any part thereof, without prejudice to this insurance; nor shall the acts of the Assured or Assurers, in recovering, saving and preserving the property insured, in case of disaster, be considered a waiver or an acceptance of an abandonment; and to the charges whereof, the said Assurers will contribute according to the rate and quantity of the sum hereby insured.
7. General Average and salvage charges (resulting from a peril hereby insured against) payable according to Foreign Statement or York-Antwerp Rules if in accordance with the contract of affreightment.
8. The description and valuation of the merchandise hereby insured and the ports of loading on and discharge from the overseas Vessel shall be determined by reference to the insurance against marine risks as set forth in this Certificate or special Policy, and shall be deemed incorporated herein; but it is agreed that this war risk insurance constitutes a separate contract which (excepting as expressly provided in this clause 8) is not subject to any of the other printed terms or conditions of this Certificate or special Policy or by any clause or provision stamped or endorsed thereon unless the same refers specifically to war risk insurance.

INSTRUCTIONS TO CLAIMANTS

Any loss or damage which may happen to the property insured under this certificate shall be reported as soon as the goods are landed or the loss is known or expected, to the agent of the Insurers located at the port of discharge or disaster (see list below). If there be no such agent at or near such port, such notice shall be given to an accredited representative of the Board of Underwriters of New York. *In case of loss or damage, produce this certificate for said agent's or representative's inspection and request him to hold a survey and issue a certificate stating the cause and extent of the loss or damage.* If there be no agent of the Insurers at the port of discharge or disaster, nor a representative of the Board of Underwriters of New York, certificate of survey should be obtained from Lloyds agent at destination.

After the foregoing formalities have been complied with, the complete documents (survey report, policy, invoice, bill of lading, letter to carrier and latter's reply) should be sent to the Insurer's agents (named below) to enable them to decide as to the liability of the Insurers.

IMPORTANT NOTICE

When cargo is received from the carrier in a damaged condition, in order to save for yourselves or your underwriters, any rights which you may have against the carrier, it is necessary for you to file notice of claim in writing against the carrier before taking delivery of the goods. Claim in writing must be filed with the carrier as soon as the actual loss or damage is known. Filing claim against the carrier will not affect your rights under your insurance policy.

When sending claim papers for collection of any loss under this policy, be sure to attach thereto a copy of your letter to the carrier, also the latter's reply.

AGENCIES OF THE FEDERAL INSURANCE COMPANY, WHERE CLAIMS MAY BE PRESENTED FOR PAYMENT

U. S. A. AND CANADA

NEW YORK	Chubb & Son, Managers, Head Office—90 John Street
ATLANTA	Chubb & Son, Managers, Branch Office—1028 Hurt Bldg.
CHICAGO	Chubb & Son, Mgrs., Branch Office—Insurance Exchange
JERSEY CITY	Chubb & Son, Mgrs., Branch Office—1 Newark Ave.
MONTREAL	Chubb & Son, Mgrs., Branch Office—Royal Bank Bldg.
ROCHESTER	Chubb & Son, Mgrs., Branch Office— 1410 Lincoln Alliance Bank Building
BOSTON	Boit, Dalton & Church, 89 Broad Street
LOS ANGELES	Seyler-Day Company, 724 South Spring Street
SAN FRANCISCO	Rathbone, King & Seeley, 114 Sansome Street
SEATTLE	Bowden, Gazzam & Arnold, Dexter Horton Building
VANCOUVER CITY	Chas. Gardner Johnson, Ltd., 901 Hastings St. W.
VICTORIA, B. C.	Rithet Consolidated, Ltd.

UNITED KINGDOM

BELFAST (Surveys only)	James Johnston & Son, 8 Waring Street
LIVERPOOL	Sea Insurance Co., Ltd., Exchange Buildings
LONDON (Surveys only)	E. L. Johnson's Sons & Mowat, 37, Walbrook, London, E.C. 4

EUROPE

AMSTERDAM	E. S. Orobio de Castro & Zoon
ANTWERP	Leon Van Peborgh (Fred Jamine—A. Verhaegen) 21 Rue Kipdorp
BARCELONA	F. Ferrer Romaguera, Fontanella 9
BERLIN	Willis, Faber & Hubener, Agenturen G.m.b.H., Budapester Strasse, 28
BORDEAUX	Louis Berger, 25, Rue Saint Remi
BREMEN	F. Reck & Co., Postfach 519
BUDAPEST	J. W. Thompson-V. Zoltan Utcza 8
COPENHAGEN	Hecksher & Son, Successors, Amaliegade 39
DANZIG	Bergrrans Shipping Co., Ld., 3 Langer markt, Danzig
DUNKERQUE	A. Bourbonnaud & Co., 7, Rue Van Stabel
GENOA	Amministrazione Mackenzie, Casolla Postale 434
GDYNIA	Bergenske Baltic Transports, Limited, 9/11, ul Portowa
GIBRALTAR	Smith, Imossi & Co.
GOTHENBURG	Lindahl & Collin, 9 Vestra Hamngatan
HAMBURG	Carstens & Schues, Monckebergstrasse 27
HAVRE	Paul Giblain, 8, Place Jules Ferry
ISTANBUL (Surveys only)	A. Georgiades-Galata, P. Box 1088
KLAIPEDA-MEMEL	Dr. Michael Fratkin, Prezidento Smetonos al 9
LISBON	James Rawes & Co., Rua do Corpo Santo
MALMO	Frick & Frick, Ltd., Gustaf Adolfs Torg, 4
MALTA	T. C. Smith & Co., 11a Strada Cristoforo, Valetta
MARSEILLES	Stephen Gaubert, 7, Rue Paradis
NAPLES	Holme & Co., 126/8 Via A. Depritis
OPORTO	Rawes & Co., Rua da Nova Alfandega
OSLO	William Shepherd, Bogstadveien 15
PARIS	A. Santerre, 19, Rue Vivienne
PIRAEUS	J. A. Saunders, 77, Notara Street and 6, Dragatsaniou St., Athens
REVAL	E. Sporleder Ltd., 24, Kalda Tanav
ROTTERDAM	W. Ledeboer
SALONICA	Citterich & Sons
STOCKHOLM	A. B. Matthiessen & Son, Bredgrand 2
SWITZERLAND	Dr. Carl Ott, Case Postale 1971, Neuchatel
TRIESTE	Edgar Henry Greenham, P.O. Box 428 Via Della Borsa, 3 (Tergesteo)
Sub-Agents:	
FIUME	Fratelli Gerbaz, P.O. Box 313
ZARA	Luigi Bauch
DUBROVNIK	Narciso Detoni
VOLO	Henderson & Co.
WARSAW	Bain & Sons, 16/18, Krak Przedm

ASIA

AMARAH—Kut, Khorramshahr, Ahwaz, Bahrein, Kerveit, Muscat, Dubai, Bushire, Bunderabbas, and Lingah	Gray Mackenzie & Co., Ltd.
BAGDAD	Stephen Lynch & Co., Ltd.
BANGKOK	The Manager, The Borneo Co., Ltd.
BATAVIA	Galestin & Co.
BATAVIA	Maclaine Watson & Co.
BEYROUT	J. V. Delbourgo & Son, P.O. Box 104
BOMBAY	Gillanders, Arbuthnot & Co., Patel House, Churchgate St., Fort
BUSHIRE	Gray Mackenzie & Co., Ltd.
BUSREH	Gray Mackenzie & Co., Ltd.
CALCUTTA	Bird & Co., P.O. Box 46
CANTON	G. E. Huygen, 11 Sai Hing Kai, P. O. Box 112
COCANADA	The Coromondel Co., Ltd.
COCHIN	Pierce, Leslie & Co., Ltd.
COLOMBO	Aitken, Spence & Co., Ltd., P.O. Box 5
DELHI (Surveys only)	Gillanders Arbuthnot & Co., Imperial Bank Chas.
FUSAN (Chosen)	Y. Tanaka & Co.
GENSAN (Chosen)	Bennett & Co., Nissen Kaiun Bld. No. 2, Hon Machi, 4 Chome
HAIFA	J. V. Delbourgo & Son
FOOCHOW	Dodwell & Co., Ltd.
HANKOW	American Foreign Ins. Association
HONG KONG	J. M. Da Rocha & Co., 6 Des Boeux Road, Central P.O. Box 400, Bank of Canton Bldg.
JAFFA	J. V. Delbourgo & Son
KARACHI	Forbes Forbes, Campbell & Co., Ltd., P.O. Box 10
KERMANSHAH	Stephen Lynch & Co., Ltd.
KOBE	Mackinnon, Mackenzie & Co. (Japan) Ltd. Crescent Bld., 72, Kyo Machi P.O. Box 109, Kobe
LAHORE (Surveys only)	Gillanders, Arbuthnot & Co., The Mall
MACASSAR	Michael Stephens & Co., Ltd.
MADRAS	Wilson & Co., P.O. Box 2, 5/8, Jehangir Street, George Town
MANGALORE	Pierce, Leslie & Co., Ltd.
MANILA	Warner, Barnes & Co., Ltd., P.O. Box 294
NAGASAKI	Holme, Ringer & Co.
PADANG	Van Houten, Steffan & Co.
PENANG	G. H. Slot & Co., Ltd., 2, Weld Quay
RANGOON	Geo. Gordon & Co. (Burma), Ltd., 25, Merchant Street, P.O. Box 20
SABANG	The Sabang Bay Harbour & Coal Co., Ltd.
SAIGON	Denis Freres, P.O. Box 9
SAMARANG	McNeill & Co.
SHANGHAI	American Foreign Ins. Association, No. 3 Canton Road
SINGAPORE	G. H. Slot & Co., Ltd., 3/5 Robinson Road
SOERABAYA	Fraser Eaton & Co.
SULTANABAD	Stephen Lynch & Co., Ltd.
TEHEREN	Stephen Lynch & Co., Ltd.
TEL-AVIV	J. V. Delbourgo & Son
TIENTSIN	American Foreign Insurance Association
TRIPOLI (SYRIA)	J. V. Delbourgo & Son
TUTICORIN	The Madura Co., Ltd.
YOKOHAMA	Mackinnon, Mackenzie & Co. (Japan), Ltd., 75, Yamashitacho, P.O. Box 20

SOUTH AMERICA, MEXICO, CENTRAL AMERICA & WEST INDIES

ACAJUTLA	F. A. Gutierrez, Sonsenate
ANTOFAGASTA (Surveys only)	E. Barnett, Casilla 360
BAHIA BLANCA	C. H. Richards, San Martin 88
BAHIA	Duder & Co., Ltd., Rua das Princezas, 20
BUENOS AYRES	F. B. O'Grady & Co., Soc. Resp., Ltd., Avenida R. Saenz, Pena 567
BOGOTA	The Sea Ins. Co., Ltd., Apartado de Correo 2550
CALLAO (Surveys only)	H. M. Beausire & Co.
CARTAGENA	H. L. Tyrer, Calle del Cancel
CARACAS	The British Trading Company, Apartado 1031, Caracas
CEARA	Casa Salgado, S.A., P.O. Box No. 1
CONCEPCION (Surveys only)	Gibbs & Co., Casilla 34c
COQUIMBO (Surveys only)	J. J. MacAuliffe, Casilla 6D
CORINTO	C. L. Hinckel, Ltd.
DEMERARA	Booker Bros., McConnell & Co., Ltd., Georgetown
ETEN (Surveys only)	J. M. Araujo
GUATEMALA	G. W. Franklin, Lloyd's Agent
GUAYAQUIL	Soc. Comercial Anglo Ecuatoriana Ltda., P.O. Box 410
HAVANA	Dussaq & Toral, S.A., P.O. Box 1617
IQUIQUE (Surveys only)	Gibbs, Williamson, Ltda., 344 Calle San Martin
LA GUAIRA	The British Trading Company, Apartado 1031, Caracas
LIMA (Surveys only)	H. M. Beausire & Co.
MOLLENDO (Surveys only)	Wm. J. Donnelly
MONTE VIDEO	Edward M. Cooper, Calle Piedras, 357
PANAMA	D. L. Humber, P.O. Box 11, Panama City
PERNAMBUCO	John Alfred Thom, P.O. Box 46
PORTO ALEGRE	Wilson Sons & Co., Ltd., Praca Senador Florencio
RIO DE JANEIRO	W. S. Cunningham & E. R. Zander P.O. Box 548, Av. Rio Branco, 111-1° Andar Sala 105
ROSARIO	A. P. Ferguson
SAN JOSE DE COSTA RICA	Lyon Hnos & Cia Sucs. Sociedad Anonyma
SAN PAULO	Brazilian Warrant Agency & Finance Coy., Ltd. P.O. Box 914, Rua Alvares Penteado, 23-2° Andar
SANTOS	E. Johntson & Co., Ltd., Rua do Commercio 71
ST. THOMAS, W. I.	The West Indian Co., Ltd.
TALCAHUANO (Surveys only)	Edward Hyde, Avenida Blanca Encalada 340, Cacilla 108
TOCOPILLA (Surveys only)	Charles Wesley Nicholls, Cacilla 68
VALPARAISO	Rea Hanna, P.O. Box 1910
VERA CRUZ	J. H. Drake, Morelos 7, Apartado 116

AFRICA

ALEXANDRIA	Rodocanachi & Co., P.O. Box 64, 5, Rue de L'Eglisse Debbane
ALGIERS	D. Venian, 6, Boulevard Baudin
BEIRA	Manica Trading Co., Ltd., P.O. Box 14
BLOEMFONTEIN	Parry, Leon & Hayhoe, Ltd., P. O. Box 709, Barclays Bank Bldg., 105 St. Andrew St., Bloemfontein
CAPE TOWN	Thomson, Watson & Co., 4, Adderley Street
CASABLANCA	Louis Bouchet, 6, Rue Coli
DAKAR	Cie Du Niger Francais, 5, Rue Decemet
DURBAN AND PORT NATAL	J. T. Rennie & Sons, 394, Smith Street
EAST LONDON	Parry, Leon & Hayhoe, Ltd., P.O. Box 2, Marine Chambers, 31, Cambridge Street
JOHANNESBURG	Parry, Leon & Hayhoe, Ltd., P.O. Box 1101, 30 Rissik Street
KHARTOUM	Gellatly, Hankey & Co. (Sudan), Ltd., P.O. Box 17
KILINDINI	Smith Mackenzie & Co., P.O. Box 120
LAMU	Smith Mackenzie & Co., P.O. Box 120
LOURENCO MARQUES	Parry, Leon & Hayhoe, Ltd., Box 790
MAURITIUS	Ireland, Fraser & Co., P.O. Box 58
MOMBASA	Smith, Mackenzie & Co., P.O. Box 120
PORT ELIZABETH	Parry, Leon & Hayhoe, Ltd., P.O. Box 185, 5, Jetty Street
PORT SUDAN	Gellatly, Hankey & Co. (Sudan), Ltd., P.O. Box 17
SUAKIM	Gellatly, Hankey & Co. (Sudan), Ltd., P.O. Box 17
TENERIFFE	Hamilton & Co., Apartado 102
ZANZIBAR	Smith, Mackenzie & Co., P.O. Box 92
WEST COAST	John Holt & Co. (Liverpool), Ltd. NIGERIA (Lagos, Kano, Warri, Port Harcourt, Calabar). GOLD COAST (Accra, Keta, Takoradi). TOGOLAND (Lome). DAHOMEY (Cotonou). CAMEROONS (Doala, Victoria, Kribi). FERNANAO PO. (Sta. Isabel). GABOON (Libreville, Port Gentil). SPANISH GUINEA (Bata).

AUSTRALIA AND TASMANIA

SYDNEY	Alliance Assurance Co., Ltd., 97, Pitt Street
MELBOURNE	Alliance Assurance Co., Ltd., 410, Collins Street
ADELAIDE	Alliance Assurance Co., Ltd., 20, Grenfell Street
BRISBANE	Alliance Assurance Co., Ltd., 70/2, Eagle Street
PERTH	Alliance Assurance Co., Ltd., 96, St. George's Terrace
HOBART	Alliance Assurance Co., Ltd., 131, Macquarie Street
LAUNCESTON	Alliance Assurance Co., Ltd., c/o C. H. Smith & Co., Resident Inspector, Pty., Ltd.

NEW ZEALAND

WELLINGTON	Alliance Assurance Co., Ltd., 23/25, Grey Street
AUCKLAND	Alliance Assurance Co., Ltd., 5, O'Connell Street
DUNEDIN	Alliance Assurance Co., Ltd., Bond Street
CHRISTCHURCH	Alliance Assurance Co., Ltd., 135, Hereford Street
TIMARU	Alliance Assurance Co., Ltd., Stafford Street
INVERCARGILL	Alliance Assurance Co., Ltd., Don St.
NAPIER	Alliance Assurance Co., Ltd. Hawkes Bay Farmers' Co-op. Assn., Ltd.
NEW PLYMOUTH	Alliance Assurance Co., Ltd., Duff & Wynyard
WANGANIU	Alliance Assurance Co., Ltd. Freeman R. Jackson & Co., Ltd.

MARINE INSURANCE CERTIFICATE
(Reverse)

TABLE OF CASES

TABLE OF CASES

INDEX

INDEX

Bei Fragen zur Produktsicherheit wenden Sie sich bitte an:
If you have any questions regarding product safety,
please contact:

Walter de Gruyter GmbH
Genthiner Straße 13
10785 Berlin
productsafety@degruyterbrill.com